Special Education Law and Practice

Special Education Law and Practice

Cases and Materials

Deborah N. Archer
Professor of Law
New York Law School

Richard D. Marsico
Professor of Law
New York Law School

Carolina Academic Press
Durham, North Carolina

Copyright © 2017
Carolina Academic Press, LLC
All Rights Reserved

ISBN 978-1-59460-607-6
eISBN 978-1-53100-846-8
LCCN 2017910296

Carolina Academic Press, LLC
700 Kent Street
Durham, North Carolina 27701
Telephone (919) 489-7486
Fax (919) 493-5668
www.cap-press.com

Printed in the United States of America

To my husband, Richard, and to my boys, Ellis and Ethan.

—DNA

To JMB, for dedicating three decades of her formidable legal talent to the needs of children, and to KMD, a very special educator.

—RDM

Contents

Table of Authorities

Page numbers in italics indicate principal authorities.

Code of Federal Regulations

Federal Register

Cases

Secondary Sources

Foreword

The Individuals with Disabilities Education Act (IDEA) is a unique federal law. By placing an affirmative obligation on public school districts to identify and evaluate children with disabilities, determine whether they are eligible for special education and related services, and if so, to provide each child with a disability with a free appropriate public education, the IDEA creates a positive right to an education for children with disabilities. The IDEA is a transformative law. By requiring school districts to provide educational services to children with disabilities from age three through twenty-one (and requiring local social services agencies to provide services from birth to age three), the IDEA works to ensure that all children with disabilities will have the opportunity to learn and function in society in a way that is consistent with their abilities. Finally, the IDEA is complex. It creates a multi-step process, with a significant role for parents, to implement its goals. It creates an administrative process to allow parents of children with disabilities to challenge any aspect of their child's education program, and establishes a unique system of judicial review.

We hope this casebook will play a modest role in helping attorneys, parents, and school administrators navigate their way through the IDEA. The casebook covers the IDEA's substantive education rights, including the right to a free appropriate public education (FAPE), related services, and to be free of racially discriminatory practices. It covers placement rights including the right to learn in the least restrictive environment and the right of parents to remove their child from a public school that is not providing a FAPE to their child and be reimbursed for the cost of their child's tuition at a private school that is providing an appropriate education. The book covers the IDEA's procedural protections, including a school district's obligation to identify and evaluate children with disabilities, to prepare and implement an IEP for each child with a disability who needs special education and related services, to provide an impartial hearing to parents who disagree with any aspect of their child's education, and to maintain the child in her current educational setting pending the outcome of the hearing and any subsequent appeals. Finally, the book has several chapters on enforcing the IDEA in federal court, including chapters on constitutional and statutory requirements, remedies available for IDEA violations, and the availability of attorneys fees for prevailing parties in IDEA cases.

Each chapter begins with a problem rich in facts and law that places the student in the position of an attorney trying to resolve a problem for a client using that chapter's materials. Comprehensive notes expand the areas covered by featured cases. We hope that the book's combination of an experiential focus and comprehensive coverage will appeal both to clinical faculty who can use it as a clinical teaching tool and traditional faculty who seek to take a problem-oriented approach in teaching special education law. We also hope that the book will be useful as a reference to attorneys and other special education practitioners, school administrators, and parents and others who are interested in learning more about special education law.

We offer a few notes about the text. In the problems that begin each chapter, we use initials to identify the children and parents. This is a conventional part of special education law practice to ensure confidentiality. It is never too soon to internalize special education practice norms. We have edited the cases in the text to demonstrate as clearly as possible the legal points the case represents. We use ellipses to indicate when we have excluded text, but for the most part, we do not use ellipses to indicate the exclusion of case citations or citations to the record. Finally, different states use different names for administrative officers who decide impartial hearings in special education cases at the local level and for administrative officers at the state level who decide appeals from decisions of these local officers. For convenience, we will generally refer to local administrative officers as impartial hearing officers (IHOs) and state level administrative officers as state review officers (SROs).

The IDEA is an extensive statute, covering more than one hundred pages in the United States Code. In addition, the United States Department of Education has issued regulations implementing the IDEA that occupy an entire volume of the Code of Federal Regulations. We reproduce specific provisions of the IDEA and the regulations as relevant throughout the casebook. In addition, Appendix A contains relevant excerpts from the IDEA. Finally, the full text of the IDEA and its implementing regulations are available on the website of the Government Printing Office, https://www.gpo.gov/fdsys/browse/collectionUScode.action?collectionCode=USCODE and https://www.gpo.gov/fdsys/browse/collectionCfr.action?collectionCode=CFR .

As with many specialized areas of practice, special education practice uses a number of acronyms. We have listed and defined some of these in Appendix B.

Many people have offered their help and support to us as we have prepared this book. At the risk of leaving some of them out unintentionally, we offer our gratitude as follows.

From Deborah: Thank you to Richard Buery, Ellis Buery, and Ethan Buery for their constant support and encouragement. Thank you to Felicia Reid, Charlene Barker, and Christopher O'Donnell for their invaluable research assistance. And, thank you to New York Law School for so many forms of support it is impossible to list them all.

From Rick: Thanks to Jean Marie for her priceless advice and input and infinite patience. Thanks to Richard, Christine, and David for never complaining about how a chapter or case file or the Bluebook seemed to follow me around at nights, on weekends, on holidays, and during family vacations. Thanks to my parents, Rosalie and Richard, for their support and for Mom's sharp-eyed proofreading as Dad read along. Thanks to Quinn Rapp-Ellis, Felicia Reid, Eugene Schlesinger, Jennifer Lo, and

Sean Campbell for their excellent research assistance. Thanks to the participants of three New York Law School Faculty Workshop seminars whose valuable feedback confirmed my approach to one chapter and helped me re-think my approach to two other chapters. Finally, thanks to New York Law School for its summer research support and more importantly for making it possible for me to pursue my research interests in an environment of support and encouragement.

Part I

Introduction

Chapter 1

The Evolution of the Right to a Free Appropriate Public Education for Children With Disabilities

Introduction

Public schools in the United States have not always been open to all children. Using the "separate but equal" doctrine, public schools excluded Black children from schools for white children until 1954, when the Supreme Court ruled in *Brown v. Board of Education* that this violated the Equal Protection Clause of the Fourteenth Amendment to the United States Constitution. Less well-known is the discrimination that public schools practiced against children with disabilities. Until as recently as the 1970s, public school officials, backed by state statutes and judicial decisions, excluded children with disabilities from public schools, admitted them to schools but segregated them from other children, or placed them in general education classrooms without providing them educational services tailored to their needs. As a result, millions of children with disabilities received little, inadequate, or no education at all.

This began to change in the 1970s. Fueled in large part by *Brown*, a social movement that challenged the educational treatment of children with disabilities grew. The movement led to two landmark federal court cases, *Pennsylvania Association for Retarded Children v. Pennsylvania* ("*PARC*") and *Mills v. Board of Education of the District of Columbia* ("*Mills*"), which in 1972 resulted in consent decrees that granted children with disabilities the right to attend public schools and receive an appropriate education while there. Following *PARC* and *Mills*, Congress passed the Education for All Handicapped Children Act of 1975, Pub. L. No. 94-142, 89 Stat. 773 (EAHCA), which offered federal financial assistance to states that agreed to provide special education to children with disabilities consistent with the terms of the EAHCA. The EAHCA, which evolved into and is now known as the Individuals with Disabilities Education Act (IDEA), 20 U.S.C. §§ 1400–1482 (2012), established the framework for contemporary special education law.

This chapter traces the history of the law relating to the education of children with disabilities from the time public school officials had virtually unfettered discretion to exclude them from school, to today's regime that recognizes the right of a child with a disability to a free appropriate public education in the least restrictive environment. Section One contains examples of state court decisions between 1893 and 1958 that involved children whom local public school officials excluded from school because of their disabilities. Section Two highlights *Brown*, which prohibited intentional racial segregation in public schools and helped set the stage for litigation that successfully challenged the exclusion of children with disabilities from public schools. Section Three features *PARC* and *Mills*, which recognized a legal right to education for children with disabilities. Finally, Section Four describes the congressional response to discrimination against children with disabilities, culminating in the IDEA.

Problem

As you read through this chapter, consider the following:

1. You are the principal of a public elementary school in 1950. C.M. comes to your office to enroll her son, D.M. You send D.M. to the school psychologist who administers an IQ test. According to the result, D.M. has an IQ of 70. In your experience, children with an IQ of 70 cannot manage grade-level work. As a result, they fall behind, have behavior problems, and disrupt other children in the classroom. Are you required to admit D.M. into the school? If not, what factors would you take into account in making your decision? What decision would you make? If you do admit D.M., where would you place him?

2. You are now an attorney, also in 1950. J.K., D.M.'s father, comes to see you. He tells you that the local public school refused to admit D.M. because his IQ is too low. He wants you to file a lawsuit to get D.M. admitted. What would you do? What legal theories supporting D.M.'s admission would you develop?

3. Now you are a judge in 1950. J.K. has filed a lawsuit on behalf of D.M. seeking D.M.'s admission to public school. How would you rule? On what legal grounds?

4. How would your answers to questions one through three change if it were 1955? Today?

5. It is 1950 again, and you are the legislative director for the U.S. Representative representing D.M.'s Congressional district. The representative has heard about D.M.'s case, and constituents and advocacy groups are urging him to "take a stand" to protect children with disabilities. The school district is urging the representative to take a "hands-off" approach to education issues that are better left to the judgment of educators. The representative wants you to draft a statute that would help children like D.M. attend public schools while allowing educators the discretion to make decisions about the substance of D.M.'s education. What would you include in such a statute? Would your answer change if you were the legislative director for a state legislator?

Section One
The Exclusion of Children with Disabilities from Public Schools

Watson v. Cambridge

157 Mass. 561 (1893)

Knowlton, J. The records of the school committee of the defendant city set forth that the plaintiff in 1885 was excluded from the schools "because he was too weak-minded to derive profit from instruction." He was afterwards taken again on trial for two weeks, and at the end of that time again excluded. The records further recite that "it appears from the statements of teachers who observed him, and from certificates of physicians, that he is so weak in mind as not to derive any marked benefit from instruction, and, further, that he is troublesome to other children, making unusual noises, pinching others, etc. He is also found unable to take ordinary, decent, physical care of himself." The evidence at the trial tended strongly to show that the matters set out in the records were true.

The defendant requested the court to rule that if the facts are true which are set forth in the records of the committee, as the cause of the exclusion of the plaintiff from the public schools, the determination of the school committee thereon, acting in good faith, was final, and not subject to revision in the courts. The court refused so to rule, and submitted to the jury the question whether the facts stated, if proved, showed that the plaintiff's presence in school "was a serious disturbance to the good order and discipline of the school."

The exceptions present the question whether the decision of the school committee of a city or town, acting in good faith in the management of the schools, upon matters of fact directly affecting the good order and discipline of the schools, is final, so far as it relates to the rights of pupils to enjoy the privileges of the school, or is subject to revision by a court . . . .

Under the law the school committee[s] "have the general charge and superintendence of all the public schools in the town" or city. Pub. St. c. 44, § 21. The management of the schools involves many details; and it is important that a board of public officers, dealing with these details, and having jurisdiction to regulate the internal affairs of the schools, should not be interfered with or have their conduct called in question before another tribunal, so long as they act in good faith within their jurisdiction. Whether certain acts of disorder so seriously interfere with the school that one who persists in them, either voluntarily or by reason of imbecility, should not be permitted to continue in the school, is a question which the statute makes it their duty to answer; and if they answer honestly, in an effort to do their duty, a jury composed of men of no special fitness to decide educational questions should not be permitted to say that their answer is wrong. We are of the opinion that the ruling requested should have been given.

Exceptions sustained.

Beattie v. Board of Educ. of Antigo

169 Wis. 231 (1919)

This is an action of mandamus brought in the municipal court of Langlade county to compel the Board of Education of the City of Antigo to reinstate and admit petitioner's son to the public schools of said city. From a judgment in favor of the petitioner the defendant Board of Education appealed.

Merritt Beattie, thirteen years of age on March 27, 1918, son of petitioner, has been a resident of the city of Antigo since he was two years of age. Merritt has been a crippled and defective child since his birth, being afflicted with a form of paralysis which affects his whole physical and nervous make-up. He has not the normal use and control of his voice, hands, feet, and body. By reason of said paralysis his vocal cords are afflicted. He is slow and hesitating in speech and has a peculiarly high, rasping, and disturbing tone of voice, accompanied with uncontrollable facial contortions, making it difficult for him to make himself understood. He also has an uncontrollable flow of saliva which drools from his mouth on to his clothing and books, causing him to present an unclean appearance. He has a nervous and excitable nature. It is claimed on the part of the school board that his physical condition and ailment produces a depressing and nauseating effect upon the teachers and school children; that by reason of his physical condition he takes up an undue portion of the teacher's time and attention, distracts the attention of other pupils, and interferes generally with the discipline and progress of the school. He did not walk until he was six or seven years of age and did not attend school until he was eight years old. He then entered the first grade of the Antigo public school and continued therein until he was through the fifth grade in 1917. It appears that he is normal mentally and that he kept pace with the other pupils in the respective grades, although the teachers had difficulty in understanding him, and he was not called upon to recite as frequently as the others for the reason that he was slow in speech, requiring more time for him to recite than the other pupils. The city of Antigo maintains a day school . . . "for the instruction of deaf persons or persons with defective speech." In the fall of 1916 he was placed by the school authorities in this department. He remained there five weeks, when he was transferred to the Fourth Ward public school. During the school year of 1916 and 1917 a representative of the state department of public instruction visited the Antigo schools. The boy Merritt came under her observation and she protested against his being in the public schools and suggested that he be placed in the department for instruction of deaf persons or persons with defective speech. Merritt refused to attend this department, in which he was upheld by his parents and family. At the beginning of the school year in 1917 Merritt presented himself to the Second Ward public school, but on the second day those in charge refused to accept him as a pupil. The matter was taken by the parents to the superintendent of schools and finally laid before the Board of Education. On September 13, 1917, the Board of Education had a regular meeting to consider the demand of the petitioner that his son be reinstated and admitted to the public schools. The matter was considered for an hour, during which time one member of the board moved that the boy be reinstated in the schools. This motion did not receive a second .... [T]he petitioner brought this action to compel his reinstatement. The case was tried before a jury. A general verdict in favor of the petitioner was returned.

Owen, J. The right of a child of school age to attend the public schools of this state cannot be insisted upon when its presence therein is harmful to the best interests of the school. This, like other individual rights, must be subordinated to the general welfare. It will be conceded, we think, that the foregoing statement of facts presents a fair question as to the effect of the boy's presence upon the school and the individual pupils attending the same. The question then arises as to what body or tribunal is vested with the authority of determining the question. The trial court seemed to be of the opinion that, while such authority rested with the school board in the first instance, its action in that behalf was reviewable by a jury and subordinate to the jury's opinion thereon, as indicated by its charge to the jury to the effect that "It is incumbent upon the defendant to prove to you the needfulness of the rule in denying Merritt Beattie the privileges of the graded school by a fair preponderance of the evidence." The power of the school board ... is set forth in sub. 5, sec. 101, ch. 197 (vol. II), Laws 1889, as follows:

> "To have in all respects the supervision and management of the common schools of said city, and from time to time, to make, alter, modify and repeal as they may deem expedient, rules and regulations for their organization, government or instruction, ... and the transfer of pupils from one department to another, and generally for their good order and advancement."

The situation here presented aroused the power of the board under that provision of law. Having acted, its determination should not be interfered with by the courts unless it acted illegally or unreasonably. That it acted legally is without question. That it acted unreasonably cannot be said. The duty confronting the school board was a delicate one. It was charged with the responsibility of saying whether this boy should be denied a constitutional right because the exercise of that right would be harmful to the school and to the pupils attending the same. He should not be excluded from the schools except for considerations affecting the general welfare. But if his presence in school was detrimental to the best interests of the school, then the board could not, with due regard to their official oaths, refrain from excluding him, even though such action be displeasing and painful to them. The record convinces us that the board took this view of the situation and considered the question with the highest motives and with a full appreciation of its responsibility. There is no suggestion that any of the members were prompted by bad faith or considerations of ill will. The action of the board in refusing to reinstate the boy seems to have been the result of its best judgment exercised in good faith and the record discloses no grounds for the interference of courts with its action.

....

The action of the school board, unless illegal or unreasonable, is not subject to the interference of the courts, from which it follows that the complaint of the petitioner should be dismissed.

Eschweiler, J. (*dissenting*). I cannot agree with the result arrived at in the majority opinion in this case for two reasons:

First, because, even under the rule of law adopted by the majority as to the power vested in the school board, it was still a question for the jury as to whether or not there was an unreasonable interference with plaintiff's rights, there being no evidence that as a fact this boy's presence did have any harmful influence on the other children.

Second, because I believe there is no such exclusive power intended to be vested in such school board.

Those who drafted the constitution of this state evidently intended to secure to every child a substantial and fundamental right to attend the common schools. Sec. 3, art. X, Const., reads as follows:

> "The legislature shall provide by law for the establishment of district schools, which shall be as nearly uniform as practicable; *and such schools shall be free and without charge for tuition to all children between the ages of four and twenty years;* and no sectarian instruction shall be allowed therein."

Unquestionably the right of the individual child under such constitutional provision is subject to the equal rights of all other children to the same, and when the attendance of any one child in the public school is a material infringement upon the rights of other children to also enjoy the benefits of free schooling his right must yield.

The majority opinion finds the warrant for the construction it gives to the power of the school board in this case upon the statute giving such school boards the supervision, management, and control of the common schools. I cannot agree that a statutory power can be exalted above a guaranty of the constitution. Even were the statute to say, as it does not, that the decision of such a school board is to be exclusive and controlling save and except the one complaining of the exercise thereof is able to show that the exercise of such power by the school board was arbitrary and unreasonable, it would be subject to the substantial objection that it placed an unwarranted burden of proof upon one deprived of a constitutional right.

I think the burden was properly laid, by the instruction given by the trial court to the jury in this case, upon the defendants to show that their action was a reasonable exercise of their statutory duty. If they were unable to convince a jury to that effect their order should be set aside.

. . . .

Department of Pub. Welfare v. Haas

15 Ill. 2d 204 (1958)

Davis, Justice.

The Department of Public Welfare of the State of Illinois . . . brought an action in the county court of Cook County against the defendant, Edward C. Haas, to enforce payment of maintenance charges for defendant's son, Richard, an inmate of the Lincoln State School. . . . The court allowed the Department's motion for summary judgment and entered judgment against defendant in the sum of $2,040 and costs. Defendant appealed . . . .

The complaint . . . prayed for the recovery of maintenance charges for defendant's son for the months of January, 1952, through October, 1954, at the rate of $60 per month. Plaintiff alleged . . . that Richard Haas had been adjudicated an incompetent person and since August 28, 1949, had been confined in Lincoln State Hospital under the control of the Department, that the incompetent was unable to pay maintenance and had no estate sufficient to defray them. . . .

. . . .

Defendant's lengthy and argumentative counteraffidavit . . . stated that . . . his son Richard, is . . . mentally deficient, or feeble minded; that he was committed to the Lincoln State School because the State and city failed to provide "educational and training facilities for children of the type and who develop at the rate of development" of his son; and that the latter was committed to "receive training and education suited to his needs and for his development" to the end that "he may become partially self-sufficient and a limited asset to the community." . . . .

. . . .

Defendant argues that the provisions of the code imposing maintenance charges have the effect of charging him individually with the responsibility of providing for his son's common school education and thereby violate section 1 of article VIII of the Illinois constitution which provides: "The general assembly shall provide a thorough and efficient system of free schools, whereby all children of this state may receive a good common school education." In support of his position, defendant contends, first, that the constitutional mandate embraces mentally deficient children as well as those of normal intelligence, and, second, that the institution at Lincoln is not a hospital but a school and, as such, is part of the common school system. Defendant cites *People ex rel. Leighty v. Young,* 309 Ill. 27 . . . , and *People v. Moore,* 240 Ill. 408 . . . . These cases hold that the constitution requires that the school system and schools provided thereunder shall be free to all children of the State for the purpose of providing a good common school education, and that the legislature has the power to determine what shall constitute such education. While this constitutional guarantee applies to all children in the State, it cannot assure that all children are educable. The term "common school education" implies the capacity, as well as the right, to receive the common training, otherwise the educational process cannot function. Defendant has admitted that his son was properly adjudicated incompetent and that the boy is described as "mentally deficient or feeble minded." Existing legislation does not require the State to provide a free educational program, as a part of the common school system, for the feeble minded or mentally deficient children who, because of limited intelligence, are unable to receive a good common school education. Under the circumstances, this constitutional mandate has no application.

. . . .

The judgment of the county court of Cook County is affirmed.

Notes, Comments, and Questions

1. In *Beattie*, Judge Owen, in denying Merritt Beattie's request to be reinstated to school, stated:

> The right of a child of school age to attend the public schools of this state cannot be insisted upon when its presence therein is harmful to the best interests of the school. This, like other individual rights, must be subordinated to the general welfare.

169 Wis. at 233–34. Did excluding Merritt Beattie from the public school serve the general welfare? How was Merritt's presence "harmful" to the best interests of the school? Did the allegedly "depressing" and "nauseating" effect he had on other students and teachers justify his exclusion? Should the facts that he was "normal mentally" and "kept pace" with the other students have mattered? Even if Merritt's presence did have a harmful impact on other students, was this worse than the harm to him from depriving him of an education? The IDEA requires school districts to educate children with disabilities in the "least restrictive environment." 20 U.S.C. § 1412(a)(5) (2012). Do you think that Merritt would be required to be educated in the regular education classroom under the IDEA?

2. In both *Watson* and *Beattie*, the courts invoked the authority of a school board to govern the schools and make judgments about student admission. In both cases, jurors had reversed the school boards' decisions. The courts, however, were unwilling to subordinate a school board's judgment to a jury's decision. As long as the Board did not act illegally or unreasonably, the courts would not intervene. What are the costs and benefits of this standard? Would you impose a different standard? Did the boards in these cases act reasonably? Did the boards have any options for dealing with the children other than excluding them?

3. Not only did school boards have discretion to exclude children from the public schools, parents had few or no procedural protections to challenge a board's decision. "Two federal-court decisions . . . demonstrated that many disabled children were excluded pursuant to state statutes or local rules and policies, typically without any consultation with, or even notice to, their parents." Honig v. Doe, 484 U.S. 305, 309–10 (1988). The IDEA currently offers parents significant procedural protections, including the right to request a hearing to challenge a school district's decision regarding the identification, evaluation, or educational program or placement of a child with a disability.

4. In both *Beattie* and *Haas*, plaintiffs argued that their particular state constitutions provided the children with the right to an education. Do you agree with the judge in *Haas* that implicit in a right to education clause is that the child must be educable? How would you define educable? Who should decide who is educable? The IDEA answers these questions relatively simply. The IDEA mandates that all children with disabilities, "educable" or not, are entitled to a free appropriate public education. This obligation to educate a child includes the obligation to pay for a child like

Richard Haas, whom the public school cannot successfully educate, to attend a private school that will provide him with an appropriate education.

5. What was the fate of children who were excluded from the public schools? The student in *Haas* was in a state institution. It is unclear whether the children in *Watson* and *Beattie* received any education at all. According to a report by the Office of Education, more than four million children with disabilities were not receiving an appropriate education and two million children with disabilities were not receiving any education. *See* Timothy W. v. Rochester, N.H., Sch. Dist., 875 F.2d 954, 963 (1st Cir. 1989). One commentator cited statistics different in magnitude but not in significance. *See* Richard C. Handel, *The Role of the Advocate in Securing the Handicapped Child's Right to an Effective Minimal Education*, 36 OHIO ST. L.J. 349, 350–51 (1975) (stating that one million children with disabilities received no education and slightly more than 3.5 million did not receive special education). This treatment of children with disabilities was prevalent through the 1960s and into the 1970s. *See* Rebecca W. Goldman, *A Free Appropriate Education in the Least Restrictive Environment: Promises Made, Promises Broken by the Individuals with Disabilities Education Act*, 20 U. DAYTON L. REV. 243, 246–47 (1994).

Section Two
Segregation of Black Children in Public Schools

The Supreme Court's decision in *Brown v. Board of Education* set the stage for legal challenges to discrimination against children with disabilities by public schools. As you read *Brown*, consider the similarities and differences between public school discrimination against Black children and children with disabilities.

Brown v. Bd. of Educ. of Topeka, Kan.

347 U.S. 483 (1954)

Mr. Chief Justice WARREN delivered the opinion of the Court.

These cases come to us from the States of Kansas, South Carolina, Virginia, and Delaware. They are premised on different facts and different local conditions, but a common legal question justifies their consideration together in this consolidated opinion.

In each of the cases, minors of the Negro race . . . seek the aid of the courts in obtaining admission to the public schools of their community on a nonsegregated basis. In each instance, they have been denied admission to schools attended by white children under laws requiring or permitting segregation according to race. This segregation was alleged to deprive the plaintiffs of the equal protection of the laws under the Fourteenth Amendment. In each of the cases other than the Delaware case, a three-judge federal district court denied relief to the plaintiffs on the so-called "separate but equal" doctrine announced by this Court in *Plessy v. Ferguson*, 163 U.S. 537 . . . . Under that doctrine, equality of treatment is accorded when the races are provided substantially equal facilities, even though these facilities be separate. In the Delaware case, the Supreme Court of Delaware adhered to that doctrine, but ordered that the plaintiffs be admitted to the white schools because of their superiority to the Negro schools.

The plaintiffs contend that segregated public schools are not "equal" and cannot be made "equal,"and that hence they are deprived of the equal protection of the laws. . . .

. . . .

. . . . The doctrine of "separate but equal" did not make its appearance in this Court until 1896 in the case of Plessy v. Ferguson, supra, involving not education but transportation. American courts have since labored with the doctrine for over half a century. In this Court, there have been six cases involving the "separate but equal" doctrine in the field of public education. . . . In none of these cases was it necessary to re-examine the doctrine to grant relief to the Negro plaintiff. . . .

In the instant cases, that question is directly presented. Here . . . , there are findings below that the Negro and white schools involved have been equalized, or are being equalized, with respect to buildings, curricula, qualifications and salaries of teachers, and other "tangible" factors. Our decision, therefore, cannot turn on merely a comparison of these tangible factors in the Negro and white schools involved in each of the cases. We must look instead to the effect of segregation itself on public education.

In approaching this problem, we cannot turn the clock back to 1868 when the Amendment was adopted, or even to 1896 when *Plessy v. Ferguson* was written. We must consider public education in the light of its full development and its present place in American life throughout the Nation. Only in this way can it be determined if segregation in public schools deprives these plaintiffs of the equal protection of the laws.

Today, education is perhaps the most important function of state and local governments. Compulsory school attendance laws and the great expenditures for education both demonstrate our recognition of the importance of education to our democratic society. It is required in the performance of our most basic public responsibilities, even service in the armed forces. It is the very foundation of good citizenship. Today it is a principal instrument in awakening the child to cultural values, in preparing him for later professional training, and in helping him to adjust normally to his environment. In these days, it is doubtful that any child may reasonably be expected to succeed in life if he is denied the opportunity of an education. Such an opportunity, where the state has undertaken to provide it, is a right which must be made available to all on equal terms.

We come then to the question presented: Does segregation of children in public schools solely on the basis of race, even though the physical facilities and other "tangible" factors may be equal, deprive the children of the minority group of equal educational opportunities? We believe that it does.

In *Sweatt v. Painter, supra* [339 U.S. 629 . . .], in finding that a segregated law school for Negroes could not provide them equal educational opportunities, this Court relied in large part on "those qualities which are incapable of objective measurement but which make for greatness in a law school." In *McLaurin v. Oklahoma State Regents, supra* [339 U.S. 637 . . .] the Court, in requiring that a Negro admitted to a white graduate school be treated like all other students, again resorted to intangible considerations: " . . . his ability to study, to engage in discussions and exchange views with other students, and, in general, to learn his profession."

Such considerations apply with added force to children in grade and high schools. To separate them from others of similar age and qualifications solely because of their race generates a feeling of inferiority as to their status in the community that may affect their hearts and minds in a way unlikely ever to be undone. The effect of this separation on their educational opportunities was well stated by a finding in the Kansas case by a court which nevertheless felt compelled to rule against the Negro plaintiffs:

> "Segregation of white and colored children in public schools has a detrimental effect upon the colored children. The impact is greater when it has the sanction of the law; for the policy of separating the races is usually interpreted as denoting the inferiority of the Negro group. A sense of inferiority affects the motivation of a child to learn. Segregation with the sanction of law, therefore, has a tendency to [retard] the educational and mental development of Negro children and to deprive them of some of the benefits they would receive in a racial[ly] integrated school system."[10]

Whatever may have been the extent of psychological knowledge at the time of *Plessy v. Ferguson*, this finding is amply supported by modern authority. Any language in *Plessy v. Ferguson* contrary to this finding is rejected.

We conclude that in the field of public education the doctrine of "separate but equal" has no place. Separate educational facilities are inherently unequal. Therefore, we hold that the plaintiffs and others similarly situated for whom the actions have been brought are, by reason of the segregation complained of, deprived of the equal protection of the laws guaranteed by the Fourteenth Amendment. . . .

. . . .

---

10. A similar finding was made in the Delaware case: "I conclude from the testimony that in our Delaware society, State-imposed segregation in education itself results in the Negro children, as a class, receiving educational opportunities which are substantially inferior to those available to white children otherwise similarly situated."

Notes, Comments, and Questions

1. Based on the Supreme Court's reasoning in *Brown*, can you develop an argument that excluding children with disabilities from public schools violates the Equal Protection Clause?

2. For a compelling study of the history of the efforts to end school segregation that both culminated in and started with the *Brown* decision, including a description of the inequality of public schools for Black children under the separate but equal doctrine, see Richard Kluger, Simple Justice (1975).

3. The state-imposed stigma that segregated schools placed on Black children was a significant reason for the Court's decision in *Brown*. Does the same stigma attach to children with disabilities who are excluded from or segregated within public schools because of their disabilities?

Section Three
Legal Challenges to the Exclusion of Children With Disabilities from Public Schools

By the 1970s, a significant movement in support of the rights of children with disabilities had grown. Organizations such as The National Association for Retarded Citizens and the Council for Exceptional Children had hundreds of chapters and tens of thousands of members across the nation. Erwin L. Levine & Elizabeth M. Wexler, PL 94-142: An Act of Congress 15–16 (1981); *see also* James Siegel, Comment, *Equal Educational Opportunity: The Visually Impaired and Public Law 94-142*, 33 U.C.L.A. L. Rev. 549, 564 n. 60 (1985). Advocates filed lawsuits around the country alleging that excluding children with disabilities from public schools violated the Equal Protection Clause. Two landmark cases, known as *PARC* and *Mills*, resulted in settlements and consent decrees that established the foundation for contemporary special education law.

Pennsylvania Ass'n for Retarded Children v. Pennsylvania

343 F. Supp. 279 (E.D. Pa. 1972)

Masterson, District Judge.

This civil rights case, a class action, was brought by the Pennsylvania Association for Retarded Children and the parents of thirteen individual retarded children on behalf of all mentally retarded persons between the ages 6 and 21 whom the Commonwealth of Pennsylvania, through its local school districts and intermediate units, is presently excluding from a program of education and training in the public schools. . . .

The exclusions of retarded children complained of are based upon four State statutes: (1) 24 Purd.Stat. Sec. 13–1375 which relieves the State Board of Education from any obligation to educate a child whom a public school psychologist certifies as uneducable and untrainable . . . ; (2) 24 Purd.Stat. Sec. 13–1304 which allows an indefinite postponement of admission to public school of any child who has not attained a mental age of five years; (3) Purd.Stat. Sec. 13–1330 which appears to *excuse* any child from compulsory school attendance whom a psychologist finds unable to profit therefrom and (4) 24 Purd.Stat. Sec. 13–1326 which defines compulsory school age as 8 to 17 years but has been used in practice to postpone admissions of retarded children until age 8 or to eliminate them from public schools at age 17.

Plaintiffs allege that Sections 1375 (uneducable and untrainable) and 1304 (mental age of 5 years) are constitutionally infirm both on their faces and as applied in three broad respects. First, plaintiffs argue that these statutes offend due process because they lack any provision for notice and a hearing before a retarded person is either excluded from a public education or a change is made in his educational assignment within the public system. Secondly, they assert that the two provisions violate equal protection because the premise of the statute which necessarily assumes that certain retarded children are uneducable and untrainable lacks a rational basis in fact.[11] Finally, plaintiffs contend that because the Constitution and laws of Pennsylvania guarantee an education to all children, these two sections violate due process in that they arbitrarily and capriciously deny that given right to retarded children. Plaintiffs' third contention also raises a pendent question of state law, that is, whether the Pennsylvania Constitution as well as other laws of the Commonwealth already afford them a right to public education.

It is not alleged that Sections 1330 (excusal from compulsory attendance) or 1326 (definition of compulsory school age) are facially defective under the United States Constitution. Rather, plaintiffs contend that these provisions violate due process (lack of a prior hearing) and equal protection (no basis in fact to support exclusion) *as applied* to retarded children.

In addition, plaintiffs contend that the clear intent of Section 1330 is to forgive *parents* from any criminal penalty for what otherwise would be a violation of compulsory attendance requirements, and consequently, use of this provision to *exclude* retarded children constitutes an impermissible misinterpretation of state law. Likewise, plaintiffs assert that Section 1326 relates only to the obligation of *parents* (under penalty of criminal sanctions) to place their children in public schools, and its use to *exclude* retarded children contravenes the obvious meaning of the statute. . . .

. . . .

[T]he parties agreed upon a Stipulation which basically provides that no child who is mentally retarded or thought to be mentally retarded can be assigned initially (or re-assigned) to either a regular or special educational status, or excluded from a

---

11. Counsel for the plaintiffs asserts . . . that the right to an education, once given, constitutes a fundamental right, and therefore the defendants must show a compelling state interest in order to lawfully exclude retarded children. *Cf.* Brown v. Board of Education, 349 U.S. 294 . . . (1955) . . . .

public education without a prior recorded hearing before a special hearing officer. At that hearing, parents have the right to representation by counsel, to examine their child's records, to compel the attendance of school officials who may have relevant evidence to offer, to cross-examine witnesses testifying on behalf of school officials and to introduce evidence of their own. On June 18th, this Court entered an interim order approving the Stipulation.

....

Although no party questions the quality of plaintiffs' constitutional claims, it is basic constitutional law that federal district courts cannot acquire jurisdiction over the subject matter of a dispute by consent. Rather our jurisdiction (power) necessarily depends upon the United States Constitution and Acts of Congress. For this reason, consensus of the parties cannot interfere with our fundamental obligation to act only where the Constitution and Congress permit. Consequently, we conclude that this court has a constitutional obligation to examine the record independently and satisfy ourselves that plaintiffs' claims are not "wholly insubstantial and frivolous."

....

We begin with the contention that due process requires a hearing before retarded children may be denied a public education. It is not disputed that prior to this suit, parents of retarded children who are plaintiffs were not afforded a hearing or, in many instances, even notice of their child's exclusion from public school. For example, the parents of David Tupi, a retarded child, were never officially informed of the decision to exclude him from school. Rather they were only made aware of the situation when the school bus which regularly brought him to school failed to show up. Such crass and summary treatment of these children becomes suspect, we think, because of the stigma which our society unfortunately attaches to the label of mental retardation. Dr. Goldberg testified at length concerning the historical roots of the stigma.

Organized efforts to educate the mentally retarded began about 1848 with the establishment of residential centers which were geared toward preparing mentally retarded individuals for a greater contribution to society as well as sheltering these individuals from a hostile society. About 1900, special education classes for the mentally retarded were started in public schools. These classes were originally denominated "opportunity classes," which indicated that the child was merely waiting somewhere to join the mainstream of the school life.

But Dr. Goldberg stated that in the next decade:

> "[T]he wonderful idea of adjusting the individuals to our society became the dumping grounds for children who could not manage in other classes and started to be called classes for the feebleminded, classes for idiots, and so on ....
>
> And then the Eugenic Association in the United States started to raise quite of lot of cry that the American Society is going to pieces, mental retardation is hereditary, mentally retardeds are criminals, are prostitutes as the [I.Q.] tests proved. Therefore, something very drastic has to be done.

> And in 1912, the Eugenic Society, the Research Section of the Eugenic Society, namely, the American Breeders Association suggested that drastic measures be taken to prevent the Americans from becoming all feebleminded [such as] segregation or segregation during the reproductive period, for women, . . . organizing institutions for feebleminded women of child-bearing age in order to prevent them from having children, . . . compulsory sterilization law for women, and castration for men. . . . Another recommendation was euthanasia. This, of course, just introduced and I hope was not implemented. . . . I really want to point out that the days we are talking about are not so far removed, that the stigma attached to mental retardation is still with us, with the general public."

Empirical studies show that stigmatization is a major concern among parents of retarded children. Some parents liken it to a "sentence of death."

Experts agree that it is primarily the *school* which imposes the mentally-retarded label and concomitant stigmatization upon children, either initially or later on through a change in educational assignment. This follows from the fact that the school constitutes the first social institution with which the child comes into contact.

Not only is the school the institution which normally imposes the stigma; sometimes, and perhaps quite often, a child is incorrectly labeled. A recent study of 378 educable mentally retarded students from 36 independent school districts in the five county Greater Philadelphia Area found that "the diagnosis for 25% of the youngsters found in classes for the [educable mentally] retarded may be considered erroneous. An additional 43% may be questioned." The authors conclude: "[O]ne cannot help but be concerned about the consequences of subjecting these children to the 'retarded' curriculum . . . . The stigma of bearing the label 'retarded' is bad enough, but to bear the label when placement is questionable or outright erroneous is an intolerable situation."

In the recent case of *Wisconsin v. Constantineau*, 400 U.S. 433 . . . (1971), the United States Supreme Court considered the necessity of a due process hearing before the state stigmatizes any citizen. There the police, without notice to her or a prior hearing, had posted a notice in all retail liquor establishments forbidding sales to Mrs. Constantineau because of her "excessive drinking." The Court wrote:

> "The only issue present here is whether the label or characterization given a person by 'posting,' though a mark of serious illness to some, is to others such a stigma or badge of disgrace that procedural due process requires notice and an opportunity to be heard. We agree with the district court that the private interest is such that those requirements . . . must be met."

Considering just *Constantineau* and the evidence presented here, we are convinced that the plaintiffs have established a colorable claim under the Due Process Clause.

Our jurisdiction over plaintiffs' equal protection claims also stands on firm ground. Without exception, expert opinion indicates that:

> "[A]ll mentally retarded persons are capable of benefitting from a program of education and training; that the greatest number of retarded persons, given such education and training, are capable of achieving self-sufficiency and the remaining few, with such education and training are capable of achieving some degree of self-care; that the earlier such education and training begins, the more thoroughly and the more efficiently a mentally retarded person will benefit from it and, whether begun early or not, that a mentally retarded person can benefit at any point in his life and development from a program of education."

Despite this evidence and despite the fact that Pennsylvania provides an education to most children, the State's 1965 Pennsylvania Mental Retardation Plan estimates that while 46,000 school age retarded children were enrolled in public schools, another 70,000 to 80,000 retarded children between the ages of 5 and 21 were denied access to *any* public education services in schools, home or day care or other community facilities, or state residential institutions.

Because of an absence of adequate resources, facilities and teachers as well as the lack of a structured plan, even those whom the State serves in its institutions (i.e. residential centers, hospitals, etc.) do not always benefit. For example, Dr. Edward R. Goldman, Commissioner of the Office of Mental Retardation, Department of Welfare, testified that there are presently 4,159 children of school age in state institutions. But only 100 of these children are in a full program of education and training; 1,700 are in partial but inadequate programs, and 3,259 are in no program of any kind. Moreover, the 1965 Pennsylvania Mental Retardation Plan reports that because of a lack of space, the State housed 900 mentally retarded persons at Dallas State Correction Institution, 3,462 at State mental hospitals and 104 in Youth Development Centers. And:

> "Fewer than two percent of the residents of Pennsylvania's state schools leave the rolls each year; and half of those by death, rather than by discharge. A discharge rate of less than one percent has two implications: First, that beds are not opening up for persons in the community who need them; and second, that the state institutions continue to provide a program that barely rises above purely custodial care, if it rises at all."

Finally, the Report concludes:

> "Nowhere is there a suitable commonwealth-supported local program for children of school age who are adjudged uneducable and untrainable by the public schools. Their normal fate is a waiting list for a state school and hospital, at which services do not conform to the spirit of the school code."

With these facts in mind, we turn to plaintiffs' equal protection argument. Plaintiffs do not challenge the separation of special classes for retarded children from regular classes or the proper assignment of retarded children to special classes. Rather plaintiffs question whether the state, having undertaken to provide public education to some children (perhaps all children) may deny it to plaintiffs entirely. We are satisfied that the evidence raises serious doubts (and hence a colorable claim) as to the existence of a rational basis for such exclusions. *See, e.g.*, Brown v. Board of Education, 349 U.S. 294 . . . (1955).

. . . .

ORDER AND INJUNCTION

And now, this 5th day of May, 1972, it is ordered that the Amended Stipulation and Amended Consent Agreement are approved and adopted as fair and reasonable to all members of both the plaintiff and defendant classes.

It is further ordered that the defendants . . . are enjoined as follows:

(a) from applying Section 1304 of the Public School Code of 1949 . . . so as to postpone or in any way deny to any mentally retarded child access to a free public program of education and training;

(b) from applying Section 1326 or Section 1330(2) of the School Code of 1949 . . . so as to postpone, to terminate or in any way deny to any mentally retarded child access to a free program of education and training;

(c) applying Section 1371(1) of the School Code of 1949 . . . so to deny to any mentally retarded child access to a free public program of education and training;

. . . .

(f) from applying Section 1375 of the School Code of 1949 . . . so as to deny to any mentally retarded child access to a free public program of education and training;

(g) to provide, as soon as possible . . . , to every retarded person between the ages of six and twenty-one years as of the date of this Order and thereafter, access to a free public program of education and training appropriate to his learning capacities;

. . . .

(i) to provide notice and the opportunity for a hearing prior to a change in educational status of any child who is mentally retarded or thought to be mentally retarded.

(j) to re-evaluate the educational assignment of every mentally retarded child not less than every two years, or annually upon the parents' request, and upon such re-evaluation, to provide notice and the opportunity for a hearing.

APPENDIX A

AMENDED STIPULATION

And now, this 14th day of February, 1972, subject to the approval and Order of the Court, it is agreed by the parties that the Stipulation of June 18, 1971, be amended to provide as follows:

. . . .

2. No child of school age who is mentally retarded or who is thought by any school official, the intermediate unit, or by his parents or guardian to be mentally retarded,

shall be subjected to a change in educational status without first being accorded notice and the opportunity of a due process hearing as hereinafter prescribed. . . .

. . . .

3. [T]he State Board of Education shall adopt regulations . . . which . . . shall . . . provide as follows:

(a) Whenever any mentally retarded or allegedly mentally retarded child of school age is recommended for a change in educational status . . . , notice of the proposed action shall first be given to the parent or guardian of the child.

. . . .

(c) The notice shall describe the proposed action in detail . . . and a clear and full statement of the reasons therefor, including specification of any tests or reports upon which such action is proposed.

(d) The notice shall advise the parent or guardian of any alternative education opportunities available to his child other than that proposed.

(e) The notice shall inform the parent or guardian of his right to contest the proposed action at a full hearing before the Secretary of Education . . . , before the proposed action may be taken.

(f) The notice shall inform the parent or guardian of his right to be represented at the hearing by any person of his choosing, including legal counsel, of his right to examine before the hearing his child's school records including any tests or reports upon which the proposed action may be based, of his right to present evidence of his own, including expert medical, psychological and educational testimony, and of his right to call and question any school official, employee, or agent of a school district, intermediate unit or the department who may have evidence upon which the proposed action may be based.

. . . .

(v) There shall be no change in the child's educational status without prior notice and the opportunity to be heard as set forth herein, except that in extraordinary circumstances the Director of the Bureau of Special Education, upon written request to him by the district or intermediate unit . . . , may approve an interim change in educational assignment prior to the hearing, in which event the hearing will be held as promptly as possible after the interim change. . . .

. . . .

APPENDIX B

. . . .

AMENDED CONSENT AGREEMENT

. . . .

Now, Therefore, the parties agree this 14th day of February, 1972, subject to the approval and Order of this Court, to the following final amended Consent Agreement.

. . . .

5. The Commonwealth of Pennsylvania has undertaken to provide a free public education to all of its children between the ages of six and twenty-one years, and further, has undertaken to provide education and training for all of its mentally retarded children.

6. Having undertaken to provide a free public education to all of its children, including its mentally retarded children, the Commonwealth of Pennsylvania may not deny any mentally retarded child access to a free public program of education and training.

7. It is the Commonwealth's obligation to place each mentally retarded child in a free, public program of education and training appropriate to the child's capacity, within the context of the general educational policy that, among the alternative programs of education and training required by statute to be available, placement in a regular public school class is preferable to placement in a special public school class and placement in a special public school class is preferable to placement in any other type of program of education and training.

. . . .

Mills v. Bd. of Educ. of D.C.

348 F. Supp. 866 (D.D.C. 1972)

Waddy, District Judge.

This is a civil action brought on behalf of seven children of school age . . . in which they seek a declaration of rights and to enjoin the defendants from excluding them from the District of Columbia Public Schools and/or denying them publicly supported education and to compel the defendants to provide them with immediate and adequate education and educational facilities in the public schools or alternative placement at public expense. . . . They allege that although they can profit from an education either in regular classrooms with supportive services or in special classes adopted to their needs, they have been labeled as behavioral problems, mentally retarded, emotionally disturbed or hyperactive, and denied admission to the public schools or excluded therefrom after admission, with no provision for alternative educational placement or periodic review. . . .

. . . .

The Problem

The genesis of this case is found (1) in the failure of the District of Columbia to provide publicly supported education and training to plaintiffs and other "exceptional" children, members of their class, and (2) the excluding, suspending, expelling, reassigning and transferring of "exceptional" children from regular public school classes without affording them due process of law.

The problem of providing special education for "exceptional" children (mentally retarded, emotionally disturbed, physically handicapped, hyperactive and other children with behavioral problems) is one of major proportions in the District of Columbia. . . . Plaintiffs estimate that there are " . . . 22,000 retarded, emotionally disturbed, blind, deaf, and speech or learning disabled children, and perhaps as many as 18,000 of these children are not being furnished with programs of specialized education." According to data prepared by the Board of Education . . . , the District of Columbia provides publicly supported special education programs of various descriptions to at least 3880 school age children. However, in a 1971 report to the Department of Health, Education and Welfare, the District of Columbia Public Schools admitted that an estimated 12,340 handicapped children were not to be served in the 1971–72 school year.

. . . .

Plaintiffs allege in their complaint and defendants admit as follows:

> "PETER MILLS is twelve years old, black, and a committed dependent ward of the District of Columbia resident at Junior Village. He was excluded from the Brent Elementary School on March 23, 1971, at which time he was in the fourth grade. Peter allegedly was a 'behavior problem' and was recommended and approved for exclusion by the principal. Defendants have not provided him with a full hearing or with a timely and adequate review of his status. . . . Peter remains excluded from any publicly-supported education.
>
> "DUANE BLACKSHEARE is thirteen years old, black, resident at Saint Elizabeth's Hospital, Washington, D.C., and a dependent committed child. He was excluded from the Giddings Elementary School in October, 1967, at which time he was in the third grade. Duane allegedly was a "behavior problem." Defendants have not provided him with a full hearing or with a timely and adequate review of his status. Despite repeated efforts by his mother, Duane remained largely excluded from all publicly-supported education until February, 1971. Education experts at the Child Study Center examined Duane and found him to be capable of returning to regular class if supportive services were provided. Following several articles in the Washington Post and Washington Star, Duane was placed in a regular seventh grade classroom on a two-hour a day basis without any catch-up assistance and without an evaluation or diagnostic interview of any kind. Duane has remained on a waiting list for a tuition grant and is now excluded from all publicly-supported education.
>
> "GEORGE LIDDELL, JR., is eight years old, black, resident with his mother . . . , and an AFDC recipient. George has never attended public school because of the denial of his application to the Maury Elementary School on the ground that he required a special class. George allegedly was retarded. Defendants have not provided him with a full hearing or with a timely and adequate review of his status. George remains excluded from all publicly-supported education, despite a medical opinion that he is capable of

profiting from schooling, and despite his mother's efforts to secure a tuition grant from Defendants.

"STEVEN GASTON is eight years old, black, resident with his mother . . . , and unable to afford private instruction. He has been excluded from the Taylor Elementary School since September, 1969, at which time he was in the first grade. Steven allegedly was slightly brain-damaged and hyperactive, and was excluded because he wandered around the classroom. Defendants have not provided him with a full hearing or with a timely and adequate review of his status. Steven was accepted in the Contemporary School, a private school, provided that tuition was paid in full in advance. Despite the efforts of his parents, Steven has remained on a waiting list for the requisite tuition grant from Defendant school system and excluded from all publicly-supported education.

"MICHAEL WILLIAMS is sixteen years old, black, resident at Saint Elizabeth's Hospital . . . , and unable to afford private instruction. Michael is epileptic and allegedly slightly retarded. He has been excluded from the Sharpe Health School since October, 1969, at which time he was temporarily hospitalized. Thereafter Michael was excluded from school because of health problems and school absences. Defendants have not provided him with a full hearing or with a timely and adequate review of his status. Despite his mother's efforts, and his attending physician's medical opinion that he could attend school, Michael has remained on a waiting list for a tuition grant and excluded from all publicly-supported education.

"JANICE KING is thirteen years old, black, resident with her father . . . , and unable to afford private instruction. She has been denied access to public schools since reaching compulsory school attendance age, as a result of the rejection of her application, based on the lack of an appropriate educational program. Janice is brain-damaged and retarded, with right hemiplegia, resulting from a childhood illness. Defendants have not provided her with a full hearing or with a timely and adequate review of her status. Despite repeated efforts by her parents, Janice has been excluded from all publicly-supported education.

JEROME JAMES is twelve years old, black, resident with his mother . . . , and an AFDC recipient. Jerome is a retarded child and has been totally excluded from public school. Defendants have not given him a full hearing or a timely and adequate review of his status. Despite his mother's efforts to secure either public school placement or a tuition grant, Jerome has remained on a waiting list for a tuition grant and excluded from all publicly supported education."

Although all of the named minor plaintiffs are identified as Negroes the class they represent is not limited by their race. They sue on behalf of and represent all other District of Columbia residents of school age who are eligible for a free public education and who have been, or may be, excluded from such education or otherwise deprived by defendants of access to publicly supported education.

Minor plaintiffs are poor and without financial means to obtain private instruction. There has been no determination that they may not benefit from specialized instruction adapted to their needs. Prior to the beginning of the 1971–72 school year minor plaintiffs, through their representatives, sought to obtain publicly supported education and certain of them were assured by the school authorities that they would be placed in programs of publicly supported education and certain others would be recommended for special tuition grants at private schools. However, none of the plaintiff children were placed for the 1971 Fall term and they continued to be entirely excluded from all publicly supported education. After thus trying unsuccessfully to obtain relief from the Board of Education the plaintiffs filed this action . . . .

. . . .

THERE IS NO GENUINE ISSUE OF MATERIAL FACT

Congress has decreed a system of publicly supported education for the children of the District of Columbia. The Board of Education has the responsibility of administering that system in accordance with law and of providing such publicly supported education to all of the children of the District, including these "exceptional" children.

Defendants have admitted in these proceedings that they are under an affirmative duty to provide plaintiffs and their class with publicly supported education suited to each child's needs, including special education and tuition grants, and also, a constitutionally adequate prior hearing and periodic review. They have also admitted that they failed to supply plaintiffs with such publicly supported education and have failed to afford them adequate prior hearing and periodic review. . . .

PLAINTIFFS ARE ENTITLED TO RELIEF

Plaintiffs' entitlement to relief in this case is clear. The applicable statutes and regulations and the Constitution of the United States require it.

Statutes and Regulations

Section 31-201 of the District of Columbia Code requires that:

> "Every parent, guardian, or other person residing [permanently or temporarily] in the District of Columbia who has custody or control of a child between the ages of seven and sixteen years shall cause said child to be regularly instructed in a public school or in a private or parochial school or instructed privately during the period of each year in which the public schools of the District of Columbia are in session . . ."

Under Section 31-203, a child may be "excused" from attendance only when

> ". . . upon examination . . . [the child] is found to be unable mentally or physically to profit from attendance at school: Provided, however, that if such examination shows that such child may benefit from specialized instruction adapted to his needs, he shall attend upon such instruction."

Failure of a parent to comply with Section 31-201 constitutes a criminal offense. The Court need not belabor the fact that requiring parents to see that their children attend school under pain of criminal penalties presupposes that an educational opportunity will be made available to the children. The Board of Education is required to make such opportunity available. It has adopted rules and regulations consonant with the statutory direction. Chapter XIII of the Board Rules contains the following:

> 1.1—All children of the ages hereinafter prescribed who are bona fide residents of the District of Columbia are entitled to admission and free tuition in the Public Schools of the District of Columbia, subject to the rules, regulations, and orders of the Board of Education and the applicable statutes.
>
> 14.1—Every parent, guardian, or other person residing permanently or temporarily in the District of Columbia who has custody or control of a child residing in the District of Columbia between the ages of seven and sixteen years shall cause said child to be regularly instructed in a public school or in a private or parochial school or instructed privately during the period of each year in which the Public Schools of the District of Columbia are in session, provided that instruction given in such private or parochial school, or privately, is deemed reasonably equivalent by the Board of Education to the instruction given in the Public Schools.
>
> 14.3—The Board of Education of the District of Columbia may, upon written recommendation of the Superintendent of Schools, issue a certificate excusing from attendance at school a child who, upon examination by the Department of Pupil Appraisal, Study and Attendance or by the Department of Public Health of the District of Columbia, is found to be unable mentally or physically to profit from attendance at school: Provided, however, that if such examination shows that such child may benefit from specialized instruction adapted to his needs, he shall be required to attend such classes.

Thus the Board of Education has an obligation to provide whatever specialized instruction that will benefit the child. By failing to provide plaintiffs and their class the publicly supported specialized education to which they are entitled, the Board of Education violates the above statutes and its own regulations.

The Constitution—Equal Protection and Due Process

The Supreme Court in *Brown v. Board of Education*, 347 U.S. 483, 493 . . . (1954) stated:

> "Today, education is perhaps the most important function of state and local governments. Compulsory school attendance laws and the great expenditures for education both demonstrate our recognition of the importance of education to our democratic society. It is required in the performance of our most basic public responsibilities, even service in the armed forces. It is the very foundation of good citizenship. Today it is a principal instrument in awakening the child to cultural values, in preparing him for later professional

> training, and in helping him to adjust normally to his environment. In these days, it is doubtful that any child may reasonably be expected to succeed in life if he is denied the opportunity of an education. *Such an opportunity, where the state has undertaken to provide it, is a right which must be made available to all on equal terms.* (emphasis supplied)

Bolling v. Sharpe, 347 U.S. 497 . . . , decided the same day as *Brown*, applied the *Brown* rationale to the District of Columbia public schools by finding that:

> "Segregation in public education is not reasonably related to any proper governmental objective, and thus it imposes on Negro children of the District of Columbia a burden that constitutes an arbitrary deprivation of their liberty in violation of the Due Process Clause."

. . . .

Not only are plaintiffs and their class denied the publicly supported education to which they are entitled many are suspended or expelled from regular schooling or specialized instruction or reassigned without any prior hearing and are given no periodic review thereafter. Due process of law requires a hearing prior to exclusion, termination of classification into a special program. Goldberg v. Kelly, 397 U.S. 254 . . . (1970).

. . . .

JUDGMENT AND DECREE

Plaintiffs having filed their verified complaint seeking an injunction and declaration of rights . . . , and this court having reviewed the record of this cause . . . , it is hereby ordered, adjudged and decreed that summary judgment in favor of plaintiffs and against defendants be, and hereby is, granted, and judgment is entered in this action as follows:

1. That no child eligible for a publicly supported education in the District of Columbia public schools shall be excluded from a regular public school assignment . . . unless such child is provided (a) adequate alternative educational services suited to the child's needs, which may include special education or tuition grants, and (b) a constitutionally adequate prior hearing and periodic review of the child's status, progress, and the adequacy of any educational alternative.

2. The defendants . . . are . . . enjoined from maintaining, enforcing or otherwise continuing in effect any and all rules, policies and practices which exclude plaintiffs and the members of the class they represent from a regular public school assignment without providing them at public expense (a) adequate and immediate alternative education or tuition grants, consistent with their needs, and (b) a constitutionally adequate prior hearing and periodic review of their status, progress and the adequacy of any educational alternatives; and it is further ORDERED that:

3. The District of Columbia shall provide to each child of school age a free and suitable publicly-supported education regardless of the degree of the child's mental, physical or emotional disability or impairment. . . .

. . . .

13. Hearing Procedures.

a. Each member of the plaintiff class is to be provided with a publicly-supported educational program suited to his needs, within the context of a presumption that among the alternative programs of education, placement in a regular public school class with appropriate ancillary services is preferable to placement in a special school class.

b. Before placing a member of the class in such a program, defendants shall notify his parent or guardian of the proposed educational placement, the reasons therefor, and the right to a hearing before a hearing officer if there is an objection to the placement proposed. Any such hearing shall be held in accordance with Paragraph 13.e., below.

c. Hereinafter, children who are residents of the District of Columbia and are thought by any of the defendants, or by officials, parents or guardians, to be in need of a program of special education, shall neither be placed in, transferred from or to, nor denied placement in such a program unless defendants shall have first notified their parents or guardians of such proposed placement, transfer or denial, the reasons therefor, and of the right to a hearing before a Hearing Officer if there is an objection to the placement, transfer or denial of placement. . . .

. . . .

e. Whenever defendants take action regarding a child's placement, denial of placement, or transfer . . . , the following procedures shall be followed.

(1) Notice required hereinbefore shall be given in writing by registered mail to the parent or guardian of the child.

. . . .

(15) Pending a determination by the Hearing Officer, defendants shall take no action described in Paragraphs 13.b. or 13.c., above, if the child's parent or guardian objects to such action. Such objection must be in writing and postmarked within five (5) days of the date of receipt of notification hereinabove described.

. . . .

Notes, Comments, and Questions

1. What is your evaluation of the constitutional analyses the courts in *PARC* and *Mills* employed? Was the judge's analysis of the stigmatization of children with retardation in *PARC* analogous to the Supreme Court's analysis of the stigmatization of Black children in *Brown*?

2. The stipulations and injunctions in *PARC* and *Mills* contain significant procedural protections parents can follow if they disagree with the educational services the school district is providing to their child. Contemporary special education law also contains significant procedural protections, and adds that a child must receive

a free appropriate public education comprised of special education and related services, memorialized in an individualized education program that includes the type of instruction the child will receive and annual performance goals.

3. All of the named plaintiffs in *Mills* were Black. The court noted this, but stated that the plaintiffs did not limit the class membership in the lawsuit by race. Why do you think the plaintiffs in *Mills* did not make a race discrimination claim? Do you think race plays a role in the provision of special education? Consider the following excerpt from *United States v. Yonkers Bd. of Educ.*, 837 F.2d 1181, 1212–13 (2d Cir. 1987), in which the court found that the City of Yonkers had engaged in housing and school segregation:

> The court also found that the Board's special education program, which resulted in the placement of a disproportionate number of minority children in classes for the emotionally disturbed, was "operated in an unlawfully discriminatory manner." The evaluative process was particularly prone to unwarranted racial assumptions and was unusually discriminatory in its impact. No race-neutral factor was likely to explain the disproportionately high numbers of minority children in such classes, and the discriminatory treatment and the consequent stigmatization of the children so placed was not educationally justifiable. In addition, the assignment of these disproportionately minority-populated special classes to schools that were predominantly white, and the isolation of and refusal to mainstream the special class students increased the stigmatization.

Compare the court's analysis of stigmatization in *Yonkers* with the analyses in *PARC* and *Brown*.

4. The "over-identification" of minority children as in need of special education noted in *Yonkers* remains a significant one. In its 2004 amendments to the IDEA, Congress recognized the problem and added the following findings to the IDEA:

> (12)(A) Greater efforts are needed to prevent the intensification of problems connected with mislabeling and high dropout rates among minority children with disabilities.
>
> (B) More minority children continue to be served in special education than would be expected from the percentage of minority students in the general school population.
>
> (C) African-American children are identified as having intellectual disabilities and emotional disturbance at rates greater than their White counterparts.
>
> (D) In the 1998–1999 school year, African-American children represented just 14.8 percent of the population aged 6 through 21, but comprised 20.2 percent of all children with disabilities.
>
> (E) Studies have found that schools with predominantly White students and teachers have placed disproportionately high numbers of their minority students into special education.

Individuals with Disabilities Education Improvement Act of 2004, Pub. L. No. 108-446, § 601(C)(12)(A)-(E), 118 Stat. 2647, 2651 (codified at 20 U.S.C. § 1400(c)(12)(A)–(E) (2012).

5. In 2016, the United States Department of Education issued regulations addressing disproportionate treatment on the basis of race in connection with "the identification of children as children with disabilities," their educational placement, and discipline. Disproportionality Regulations, 81 Fed. Reg. 92,376, 92,463 (Dec. 19, 2016) (to be codified at 34 C.F.R. pt. 300). According to the regulations, whether a school district is treating children disproportionately on the basis of race is determined by dividing the likelihood that a child from one particular ethnic or racial group will experience a particular outcome with the likelihood that all other children will experience the outcome. It is up to the particular state to identify the ratio that indicates disproportionate treatment. *Id.* at 92,463–64. Thus, for example, if a Black child is twice as likely as other children to be identified as a child with a disability and the child's state has identified 1.5 as a ratio that indicates disproportionate treatment, then that school district is treating Black children disproportionately. If a school district is treating children disproportionately on the basis of race in connection with identification, placement, or discipline, it must annually review its relevant policies and amend them to prevent disproportionate treatment. *Id.* at 92,463. What do you think of this approach to addressing disproportionality? Is data analysis and policy review likely to be effective? What other analytical methods and remedies could be used?

Section Four
Congressional Action Following *Brown*, *PARC*, and *Mills*: The Road to the IDEA

1. Following *Brown*, Congress took small but important steps to assist states to educate children with disabilities. In 1958, Congress authorized the federal commissioner of education to make grants to states and institutions of higher learning to assist them in training teachers of children with mental retardation. Act of September 6, 1958, Pub. L. No. 85-926, 72 Stat. 1777. In 1961, Congress authorized a similar grant program for training teachers of students with hearing impairments. Act of September 22, 1961, Pub. L. No. 87-276, 75 Stat. 575. Then, in 1963, Congress expanded its teacher funding programs to include funding for teachers and other specialists to assist them in training teachers of "mentally retarded, hard of hearing, deaf, speech impaired, visually handicapped, seriously emotionally disturbed, crippled, or other health impaired children who by reason thereof require special education . . . ." Mental Retardation Facilities and Community Mental Health Centers Construction Act of 1963, Pub. L. No. 88-164, § 301(a)(3), 77 Stat. 282, 294. The 1963 Act is especially noteworthy because it contained two provisions that were precursors of the IDEA: a list of disabilities that are eligible

for assistance and a link between the disability and the need for special education.

2. Three years later, Congress passed another key statute, the Elementary and Secondary Education Amendments of 1966, Pub. L. No. 89-750, Title VI, 80 Stat. 1191, 1204, which was an important cornerstone for contemporary special education law. *See also* the Education of the Handicapped Act, Pub. L. No. 91-230, Title VI, 84 Stat. 121, 175 (1970) (EHA) (repealing and replacing previous federal laws relating to educating children with disabilities). The 1966 Amendments established the basic framework for the federal government's role in special education that continues today: Congress made funds available to states to educate children with disabilities provided that the states used the funds to educate children with disabilities in accord with federal requirements. § 604, 80 Stat. at 1205–07. *See Honig v. Doe*, 484 U.S. 305, 310 (1988) (noting that federal funding to states for educating children with disabilities is conditioned on "state compliance with the substantive and procedural goals of the Act.").

3. Despite making progress in providing education for children with disabilities, the 1966 amendments and the EHA were "largely hortatory.... Neither statute ... provided specific guidance as to how States were to use the funds, nor did they condition the availability of the grants on compliance with any procedural or substantive safeguards." *Honig v. Doe*, 484 U.S. 305, 310–311 n. 1 (1988). This changed in 1974, when Congress passed the Education of the Handicapped Amendments of 1974, Pub. L. No. 93–380, § 611–621, 88 Stat. 484, 579 (the "1974 Amendments"), which required states to adopt certain policies and practices in return for receiving federal funds. First, Congress required states to establish procedural protections for parents, including prior notice of a proposed change in the child's educational placement, an opportunity to request an impartial due process hearing to challenge the decision, and the right to obtain an independent educational evaluation of a child. *Id.* § 614(d), 88 Stat. 582. Second, Congress introduced the concept of "least restrictive environment," requiring school districts, to the extent appropriate, to educate children with disabilities in general education settings. *Id.* Finally, Congress introduced "child find" requirements, pursuant to which local school districts are responsible for locating, identifying, and evaluating children with disabilities who are in need of special education. *Id.* § 615(c)(1), 88 Stat. 583.

4. In 1975, Congress passed the Education for All Handicapped Children Act of 1975, Pub. L. No. 94-142, 89 Stat. 773 (EAHCA). The EAHCA was the culmination of nearly twenty years of legislative efforts to address the educational needs of children with disabilities. Congress received an assist in its efforts to address the educational needs of children with disabilities from *PARC* and *Mills*, which were "the impetus" for the passage of the EAHCA. *See* Bd. of Educ. of the Hendrick Hudson Cent. Sch. Dist. v. Rowley, 458 U.S. 176, 192–93 (1982). By the time Congress passed the EAHCA in 1975, "parents had brought legal challenges to similar exclusionary practices in 27 other States." Honig v. Doe, 484 U.S. 305, 310 (1988). In *Timothy W. v. Rochester, N.H., Sch. Dist.* 875 F.2d 954 (1st Cir. 1989), the court explained that the purpose of the EAHCA was to provide a public education for all children with disabilities:

An examination of the legislative history [of the EAHCA] reveals that Congress intended the Act to provide a public education for all handicapped children, without exception . . . .

. . . .

The Act was a response to tomes of testimony and evidence that handicapped children were being systematically excluded from education outright, or were receiving grossly inadequate education. The Office of Education provided Congress with a report documenting that there were eight million handicapped children, and that more than four million of them were not receiving an appropriate education, including almost two million who were receiving *no* education at all. There were innumerable individuals, including parents, teachers, and other professionals, who gave testimony at the congressional hearings confirming the exclusion of handicapped children from educational services.

The record is replete with statements by legislators that the Act was in response to this deplorable state of affairs:

> *Exclusion from school*, institutionalization, the lack of appropriate services to provide attention to the individual child's need—indeed, the *denial of equal rights* by a society which proclaims liberty and justice for all of its people—are echoes which the subcommittee has found throughout all of its hearings. . . .

Senate Hearings at 1155–56 (emphasis added) (remarks of Sen. Williams, Committee Chairman, principal author of bill).

> For many years handicapped children have been placed in institutions, or segregated in schools and classes, or *left to sit at home*, where they have not received the educational opportunity which is their right under the law.

Senate Hearings at 1153 (emphasis added) (remarks of Sen. Mondale, Subcommittee member).

> What we are after in this legislation is to rewrite one of the saddest chapters in American education, a chapter in which we were silent while young children were shut away and condemned to a life without hope. This legislation offers them hope, hope that *whatever their handicap*, they will be given the chance to develop their abilities as individuals and to reach out with their peers for their own personal goals and dreams.

Senate Hearings at 341 (emphasis added) (remarks of Sen. Kennedy, co-sponsor of the bill).

Moreover, the legislative history is unambiguous that the primary purpose of the Act was to remedy the then current state of affairs, and provide a public education for *all* handicapped children. As the Committee Chairman, Senator Williams stated:

> We must recognize our responsibility to provide education for *all* children which meets their unique needs. The denial of the right to education and to

> equal opportunity within this Nation for handicapped children—whether it be outright exclusion from school, the failure to provide an education which *meets the needs of a single handicapped child*, or the refusal to recognize the handicapped child's right to grow—is a travesty of justice and a denial of equal protection of the law.

120 Cong.Rec. S15271 (1974).

> Most states have legal provisions which authorize school authorities to exclude certain [handicapped] children from public school. . . . [This] act establishes a target date of 1976 for bringing *all* of the Nation's handicapped children into adequate programs.

Senate Hearings at 342 (emphasis added) (remarks of Sen. Brooke, co-sponsor of the bill).

> Recent court decisions . . . have made it clearer than ever that we have not only a moral but also a legal obligation to provide the opportunity for *every handicapped citizen* to insure his or her highest educational potential. An important provision of the bill before us today would require that every State have in effect a policy stating the *right of all handicapped children* to a "free appropriate public education" . . . . The bill would also require that each handicapped child be treated as an individual with unique strengths and weaknesses, and not as a member of a category of children all presumed to have the same needs.

Senate Hearings at 1153–54 (emphasis added) (remarks of Sen. Mondale, Subcommittee member). The Senate Committee recognized "the need for a final date in legislation by which time *all* handicapped children are to be provided a free appropriate public education," and that "the failure to provide a right to education to handicapped children cannot be allowed to continue." Senate Report at 7, 9 (1975) . . . . Senator Williams, the principal author of the statute, described the Conference Report:

> This measure fulfills the promise of the Constitution that there shall be equality of education for all people and that handicapped children no longer will be left out. . . . The conference report establishes as a matter of law . . . provisions which will assure the right to education for *all* handicapped children in the United States. It establishes a process by which the goal of educating *all* handicapped can and will be established. . . . [I]t require[s] an individualized education program tailored to the unique needs of *each* handicapped child. . . . [It] protects against handicapped children being excluded from school by requiring that *all* such children aged 3 to 18 be served. . . . [It] establishes the State educational agency as solely responsible for the provision of free appropriate education to *all* handicapped children in the State. . . . The timetable and priorities assure that the goals of this act will be met *for each and every handicapped child* within a State.

121 Cong.Rec. S37413-14 (1975) (emphasis added).

Id. at 962–64.

5. The EAHCA confirmed and expanded previous requirements and established several key definitions and principles that continue to govern special education law today. These include the federalist structure of special education law, pursuant to which states must comply with federal law in order to qualify for federal financial assistance; a free appropriate public education for all children with disabilities; related services; education in the least restrictive environment; private school placement of children with disabilities; identification and evaluation of children with disabilities; the individualized education program; parental due process rights; and the right of a child with a disability to remain in the current educational placement pending resolution of a dispute over her educational placement.

6. After 1975, Congress passed several significant amendments to the EAHCA. Three of these amendments are briefly described below. The Education of the Handicapped Act Amendments of 1990, Pub. L. No. 101–76, 104 Stat. 1103 (the "1990 Amendments"), amended the EAHCA by adding autism and traumatic brain injury to the definition of disabilities, requiring states to provide transition services no later than age sixteen to students with disabilities, and abrogating states' sovereign immunity against lawsuits for EAHCA violations. *Id.* §§ 101 and 103, 104 Stat. 1103–04, 1106. The 1990 Amendments also changed the EAHCA's name to the Individuals with Disabilities Education Act. *Id.* § 901, 104 Stat. 1141–42. They also adopted new language for referring to children with disabilities, placing "child" before "disability." *Id.* at § 101(a) 104 Stat. 1103. Thus, under the 1990 amendments, the IDEA refers to a "child with" a disability instead of a "disabled" child.

The Individuals with Disabilities Education Act Amendments of 1997, Pub. L. No. 105–17, 111 Stat. 37, amended the IDEA by clarifying and creating disciplinary rules and procedures for children with disabilities. *Id.* § 101, 111 Stat. 90, 93–95.

Finally, the Individuals with Disabilities Education Improvement Act of 2004, Pub. L. No. 108–446, 118 Stat. 2647, expanded the membership of the individualized education program (IEP) team, *id.* §§ 614(d)(1)(B), 118 Stat. 2709–10; modified the student achievement goals the IEP is required to include, *id.* § 614(d)(1)(A)(II), 118 Stat. 2647; amended procedures for disciplining students with disabilities, *id.* § 615(f)(3)(C), 118 Stat. 2722; and created a two-year statute of limitations for filing requests for impartial hearings, *id* § 615(k), 118 Stat. 2725–29. *See* MITCHELL L. YELL, THE LAW AND SPECIAL EDUCATION 6–11 (2d ed. 2006).

The IDEA is codified at 20 U.S.C. §§ 1400–1482 (2012). Selected provisions of the IDEA appear throughout the book and are reprinted in Appendix A. You can find the complete IDEA on the website of the Government Printing Office, https://www.gpo.gov/fdsys/browse/collectionUScode.action?collectionCode=USCODE.

The United States Department of Education has published regulations implementing the IDEA at Title 34, Part 300 of the Code of Federal Regulations. Selected provisions of the IDEA regulations appear throughout the book. You can also find the entire set of IDEA regulations on the website of the Government Printing Office, https://www.gpo.gov/fdsys/browse/collectionCfr.action?collectionCode=CFR.

7. In addition to the IDEA, two other federal statutes play a significant role in providing education to children with disabilities. These are Section 504 the Rehabilitation Act of 1973, 29 U.S.C. § 794 (2012), and the Americans with Disabilities Act of 1990 (ADA), 42 U.S.C. §§ 12101–12213 (2012). Section 504 prohibits discrimination on the basis of disability in federally-funded programs. The ADA prohibits discrimination against people with disabilities, including in public accommodations. It requires that school buildings be accessible to staff, parents, and students with disabilities.

Part II

Substantive Educational Rights

Chapter 2

Free Appropriate Public Education

Introduction

The Individuals with Disabilities Education Act (IDEA) requires states that receive funds pursuant to the IDEA to provide all children with disabilities, ages three to twenty-one, a free appropriate public education (FAPE). 20 U.S.C. § 1412(a)(1) (2012). The IDEA defines FAPE as:

> special education and related services that—
>
> (A) have been provided at public expense, under public supervision and direction, and without charge;
>
> (B) meet the standards of the State educational agency;
>
> (C) include an appropriate preschool, elementary school, or secondary school education in the State involved; and
>
> (D) are provided in conformity with the [child's] individualized education program . . . .

Id. § 1401(9); *see also* 34 C.F.R. § 300.17 (2015). "Special education" is:

> specially designed instruction, at no cost to parents, to meet the unique needs of a child with a disability, including—
>
> (A) instruction conducted in the classroom, in the home, in hospitals and institutions, and in other settings; and
>
> (B) instruction in physical education.

20 U.S.C. § 1401(29); *see also* 34 C.F.R. § 300.39(a)(1). Finally, "related services" are:

> transportation, and such developmental, corrective, and other supportive services (including speech-language pathology and audiology services, interpreting services, psychological services, physical and occupational therapy, recreation, including therapeutic recreation, social work services, school nurse services designed to enable a child with a disability to receive a free appropriate public education as described in the individualized education program of the child, counseling services, including rehabilitation counseling, orientation and mobility services, and medical services, except that such medical services shall be for diagnostic and evaluation purposes only) as may be required to assist a child with a disability to benefit from special

> education, and includes the early identification and assessment of disabling conditions in children.

20 U.S.C. § 1401(26)(A); *see also* 34 C.F.R. § 300.34(a).

Chapter Two has four sections. Section One covers the elements of a FAPE. Section Two considers the level of educational benefit a school must provide to a child with a disability in order to provide a FAPE. Section Three considers the contours of a FAPE for a child with severe disabilities, and Section Four addresses the FAPE standard for children with average and above-average intelligence.

Problem

K.N. is a fifth grade student in School District Nine (SDN). She has a higher than average IQ. K.N. did well in kindergarten and first grade, but starting in second grade, she fell behind in all of her classes. K.N.'s parents became concerned, and asked the school to evaluate her. The school psychologist determined that although K.N. has a relatively high IQ, she was one year behind grade level in reading and math. Following this evaluation, the school provided supplemental reading and math instruction to K.N. K.N.'s parents asked the district to conduct additional testing, but the district declined, saying that it was not unusual for children, even with above-average intelligence, to fall behind in second grade, and they usually catch up by third grade.

Despite the extra services K.N. received, she received failing grades in reading, math, science, and social studies in second grade. Nevertheless, pursuant to its social promotion policy, the school promoted K.N. to third grade. K.N.'s performance worsened during third grade. The school conducted an evaluation and determined K.N. has dyslexia. An IEP team met and prepared an IEP for K.N. The IEP provided that for the remainder of third grade and fourth grade K.N. would receive specialized reading and math instruction designed to address dyslexia for one hour per day in resource room.

By the end of third grade, K.N.'s performance had improved. Her grades in reading, math, social studies and science, although still failing grades, were somewhat higher. In addition, although K.N. was still below grade level in math and reading, she had caught up a bit, and was now eight months behind. During fourth grade, K.N. became aware that she was struggling in school and not doing as well as other kids. She developed school phobia, and missed approximately one day a week. Nevertheless, by the end of the first semester, K.N. had passed all of her classes—although with below-average grades—and had improved to six months behind in reading and math. Unsatisfied with this progress, K.N.'s parents asked the district to provide K.N. with counseling to address her school phobia and for individual reading and math instruction. The district declined, citing the progress K.N. was making. K.N.'s parents arranged for private tutoring and counseling for K.N.

In June of K.N.'s fourth grade year, the IEP team met to prepare an IEP for K.N. for fifth grade. By this time, K.N. had started to attend school regularly and her grades had improved, although they were not yet at average levels. She was also catching up in reading and math, and was only two months below grade level. K.N.'s parents arranged for a private evaluation of K.N. and presented it to district administrators at the meeting. The evaluation confirmed K.N.'s diagnosis of dyslexia and indicated that the variation between K.N.'s potential and her performance was statistically significant. The evaluation recommended that in addition to specialized reading and math instruction in resource room, K.N. should receive one hour of after-school tutoring four times per week and individual counseling one hour per week. The district considered these proposals but concluded that K.N. was receiving educational benefit under the current IEP and that K.N.'s fourth grade IEP would continue to provide no more than one hour of specialized instruction in resource room each day.

K.N.'s parents requested an impartial hearing claiming that the IEP denied K.N. a FAPE and also seeking reimbursement for the cost of the private tutoring and counseling they had provided for K.N. in fourth grade. How should the IHO rule?

Section One
The Elements of a FAPE

Board of Educ. of Hendrick Hudson Sch. Dist. v. Rowley

458 U.S. 176 (1982)

Justice Rehnquist delivered the opinion of the Court.

This case presents a question of statutory interpretation. Petitioners contend that the Court of Appeals and the District Court misconstrued the requirements imposed by Congress upon States which receive federal funds under the Education of the Handicapped Act. We agree and reverse the judgment of the Court of Appeals.

I

The Education of the Handicapped Act (Act) provides federal money to assist state and local agencies in educating handicapped children, and conditions such funding upon a State's compliance with extensive goals and procedures. The Act represents an ambitious federal effort to promote the education of handicapped children, and was passed in response to Congress' perception that a majority of handicapped children in the United States "were either totally excluded from schools or [were] sitting idly in regular classrooms awaiting the time when they were old enough to 'drop out.'" The Act's evolution and major provisions shed light on the question of statutory interpretation which is at the heart of this case.

Congress first addressed the problem of educating the handicapped in 1966 when it amended the Elementary and Secondary Education Act of 1965 to establish a grant program "for the purpose of assisting the States in the initiation, expansion, and improvement of programs and projects . . . for the education of handicapped children." That program was repealed in 1970 by the Education of the Handicapped Act, Part B of which established a grant program similar in purpose to the repealed legislation. Neither the 1966 nor the 1970 legislation contained specific guidelines for state use of the grant money; both were aimed primarily at stimulating the States to develop educational resources and to train personnel for educating the handicapped.

Dissatisfied with the progress being made under these earlier enactments, and spurred by two District Court decisions holding that handicapped children should be given access to a public education, Congress in 1974 greatly increased federal funding for education of the handicapped and for the first time required recipient States to adopt "a goal of providing full educational opportunities to all handicapped children." The 1974 statute was recognized as an interim measure only, adopted "in order to give the Congress an additional year in which to study what if any additional Federal assistance [was] required to enable the States to meet the needs of handicapped children." The ensuing year of study produced the Education for All Handicapped Children Act of 1975.

In order to qualify for federal financial assistance under the Act, a State must demonstrate that it "has in effect a policy that assures all handicapped children the right to a free appropriate public education." . . . States receiving money under the Act must provide education to the handicapped by priority, first "to handicapped children who are not receiving an education" and second "to handicapped children . . . with the most severe handicaps who are receiving an inadequate education," and "to the maximum extent appropriate" must educate handicapped children "with children who are not handicapped." The Act broadly defines "handicapped children" to include "mentally retarded, hard of hearing, deaf, speech impaired, visually handicapped, seriously emotionally disturbed, orthopedically impaired, [and] other health impaired children, [and] children with specific learning disabilities."

The "free appropriate public education" required by the Act is tailored to the unique needs of the handicapped child by means of an "individualized educational program" (IEP). The IEP, which is prepared at a meeting between a qualified representative of the local educational agency, the child's teacher, the child's parents or guardian, and, where appropriate, the child, consists of a written document containing

> "(A) a statement of the present levels of educational performance of such child,
>
> (B) a statement of annual goals, including short-term instructional objectives,
>
> (C) a statement of the specific educational services to be provided to such child, and the extent to which such child will be able to participate in regular educational programs,
>
> (D) the projected date for initiation and anticipated duration of such services, and

(E) appropriate objective criteria and evaluation procedures and schedules for determining, on at least an annual basis, whether instructional objectives are being achieved."

Local or regional educational agencies must review, and where appropriate revise, each child's IEP at least annually.

In addition to the state plan and the IEP already described, the Act imposes extensive procedural requirements upon States receiving federal funds under its provisions. Parents or guardians of handicapped children must be notified of any proposed change in "the identification, evaluation, or educational placement of the child or the provision of a free appropriate public education to such child," and must be permitted to bring a complaint about "any matter relating to" such evaluation and education. Complaints brought by parents or guardians must be resolved at "an impartial due process hearing," and appeal to the state educational agency must be provided if the initial hearing is held at the local or regional level. Thereafter, "[a]ny party aggrieved by the findings and decision" of the state administrative hearing has "the right to bring a civil action with respect to the complaint . . . in any State court of competent jurisdiction or in a district court of the United States without regard to the amount in controversy."

Thus, although the Act leaves to the States the primary responsibility for developing and executing educational programs for handicapped children, it imposes significant requirements to be followed in the discharge of that responsibility. . . .

. . . .

II

This case arose in connection with the education of Amy Rowley, a deaf student at the Furnace Woods School in the Hendrick Hudson Central School District, Peekskill, N.Y. Amy has minimal residual hearing and is an excellent lipreader. During the year before she began attending Furnace Woods, a meeting between her parents and school administrators resulted in a decision to place her in a regular kindergarten class in order to determine what supplemental services would be necessary to her education. Several members of the school administration prepared for Amy's arrival by attending a course in sign-language interpretation, and a teletype machine was installed in the principal's office to facilitate communication with her parents who are also deaf. At the end of the trial period it was determined that Amy should remain in the kindergarten class, but that she should be provided with an FM hearing aid which would amplify words spoken into a wireless receiver by the teacher or fellow students during certain classroom activities. Amy successfully completed her kindergarten year.

As required by the Act, an IEP was prepared for Amy during the fall of her first-grade year. The IEP provided that Amy should be educated in a regular classroom at Furnace Woods, should continue to use the FM hearing aid, and should receive instruction from a tutor for the deaf for one hour each day and from a speech therapist for three hours each week. The Rowleys agreed with parts of the IEP, but insisted that Amy also be provided a qualified sign-language interpreter in all her academic classes in lieu of the assistance proposed in other parts of the IEP. Such an interpreter had been placed in Amy's kindergarten class for a 2-week experimental period, but the interpreter had reported that Amy did not need his services at that time. The school administrators likewise concluded that Amy did not need such an interpreter in her first-grade classroom. They reached this conclusion after consulting the school district's Committee on the Handicapped, which had received expert evidence from Amy's parents on the importance of a sign-language interpreter, received testimony from Amy's teacher and other persons familiar with her academic and social progress, and visited a class for the deaf.

When their request for an interpreter was denied, the Rowleys demanded and received a hearing before an independent examiner. After receiving evidence from both sides, the examiner agreed with the administrators' determination that an interpreter was not necessary because "Amy was achieving educationally, academically, and socially" without such assistance. The examiner's decision was affirmed on appeal by the New York Commissioner of Education on the basis of substantial evidence in the record. Pursuant to the Act's provision for judicial review, the Rowleys then brought an action in the United States District Court for the Southern District of New York, claiming that the administrators' denial of the sign-language interpreter constituted a denial of the "free appropriate public education" guaranteed by the Act.

The District Court found that Amy "is a remarkably well-adjusted child" who interacts and communicates well with her classmates and has "developed an extraordinary rapport" with her teachers. It also found that "she performs better than the average child in her class and is advancing easily from grade to grade," but "that she understands considerably less of what goes on in class than she could if she were not deaf" and thus "is not learning as much, or performing as well academically, as she would without her handicap[.]" This disparity between Amy's achievement and her potential led the court to decide that she was not receiving a "free appropriate public education," which the court defined as "an opportunity to achieve [her] full potential commensurate with the opportunity provided to other children." According to the District Court, such a standard "requires that the potential of the handicapped child be measured and compared to his or her performance, and that the resulting differential or 'shortfall' be compared to the shortfall experienced by nonhandicapped children." The District Court's definition arose from its assumption that the responsibility for "giv[ing] content to the requirement of an 'appropriate education'" had "been left entirely to the [federal] courts and the hearing officers."

A divided panel of the United States Court of Appeals for the Second Circuit affirmed. . . .

We granted certiorari to review the lower courts' interpretation of the Act. Such review requires us to consider . . . : What is meant by the Act's requirement of a "free appropriate public education"? . . .

III

A

This is the first case in which this Court has been called upon to interpret any provision of the Act. As noted previously, the District Court and the Court of Appeals concluded that "[t]he Act itself does not define 'appropriate' education," but leaves to the courts and hearing officers the responsibility of "giv[ing] content to the requirement of an 'appropriate education.' "

We are loath to conclude that Congress failed to offer any assistance in defining the meaning of the principal substantive phrase used in the Act. It is beyond dispute that, contrary to the conclusions of the courts below, the Act does expressly define "free appropriate public education":

> "The term 'free appropriate public education' means *special education* and *related services* which (A) have been provided at public expense, under public supervision and direction, and without charge, (B) meet the standards of the State educational agency, (C) include an appropriate preschool, elementary, or secondary school education in the State involved, and (D) are provided in conformity with the individualized education program required under section 1414(a)(5) of this title."

"Special education," as referred to in this definition, means "specially designed instruction, at no cost to parents or guardians, to meet the unique needs of a handicapped child, including classroom instruction, instruction in physical education, home instruction, and instruction in hospitals and institutions." "Related services" are defined as "transportation, and such developmental, corrective, and other supportive services . . . as may be required to assist a handicapped child to benefit from special education."

Like many statutory definitions, this one tends toward the cryptic rather than the comprehensive, but that is scarcely a reason for abandoning the quest for legislative intent. Whether or not the definition is a "functional" one, as respondents contend it is not, it is the principal tool which Congress has given us for parsing the critical phrase of the Act. We think more must be made of it than either respondents or the United States seems willing to admit.

According to the definitions contained in the Act, a "free appropriate public education" consists of educational instruction specially designed to meet the unique needs of the handicapped child, supported by such services as are necessary to permit the child "to benefit" from the instruction. Almost as a checklist for adequacy under the Act, the definition also requires that such instruction and services be provided at public expense and under public supervision, meet the State's educational standards, approximate the grade levels used in the State's regular education, and comport with the child's IEP. Thus, if personalized instruction is being provided with sufficient supportive services to permit the child to benefit from the instruction, and the other items on the definitional checklist are satisfied, the child is receiving a "free appropriate public education" as defined by the Act.

Other portions of the statute also shed light upon congressional intent. Congress found that of the roughly eight million handicapped children in the United States at the time of enactment, one million were "excluded entirely from the public school system" and more than half were receiving an inappropriate education. In addition . . . , the Act requires States to extend educational services first to those children who are receiving no education and second to those children who are receiving an "inadequate education." When these express statutory findings and priorities are read together with the Act's extensive procedural requirements and its definition of "free appropriate public education," the face of the statute evinces a congressional intent to bring previously excluded handicapped children into the public education systems of the States and to require the States to adopt procedures which would result in individualized consideration of and instruction for each child.

Noticeably absent from the language of the statute is any substantive standard prescribing the level of education to be accorded handicapped children. Certainly the language of the statute contains no requirement like the one imposed by the lower courts—that States maximize the potential of handicapped children "commensurate with the opportunity provided to other children." That standard was expounded by the District Court without reference to the statutory definitions or even to the legislative history of the Act. Although we find the statutory definition of "free appropriate public education" to be helpful in our interpretation of the Act, there remains the question of whether the legislative history indicates a congressional intent that such education meet some additional substantive standard. For an answer, we turn to that history.

B

(I)

[F]ederal support for education of the handicapped is a fairly recent development. Before passage of the Act some States had passed laws to improve the educational services afforded handicapped children, but many of these children were excluded completely from any form of public education or were left to fend for themselves in classrooms designed for education of their non-handicapped peers. As previously noted, the House Report begins by emphasizing this exclusion and misplacement, noting that millions of handicapped children "were either totally excluded from schools or [were] sitting idly in regular classrooms awaiting the time when they were old enough to 'drop out.'"

This concern, stressed repeatedly throughout the legislative history, confirms the impression conveyed by the language of the statute: By passing the Act, Congress sought primarily to make public education available to handicapped children. But in seeking to provide such access to public education, Congress did not impose upon the States any greater substantive educational standard than would be necessary to make such access meaningful. Indeed, Congress expressly "recognize[d] that in many instances the process of providing special education and related services to handicapped children is not guaranteed to produce any particular outcome." Thus, the intent of the Act was more to open the door of public education to handicapped children on appropriate terms than to guarantee any particular level of education once inside.

Both the House and the Senate Reports attribute the impetus for the Act and its predecessors to two federal-court judgments rendered in 1971 and 1972. As the Senate Report states, passage of the Act "followed a series of landmark court cases establishing in law the right to education for all handicapped children." The first case, *Pennsylvania Assn. for Retarded Children* v. *Commonwealth*, 334 F.Supp. 1257 (E.D. Pa. 1971) and 343 F.Supp. 279 (1972) (*PARC*), was a suit on behalf of retarded children challenging the constitutionality of a Pennsylvania statute which acted to exclude them from public education and training. The case ended in a consent decree which enjoined the State from "deny[ing] to any mentally retarded child *access* to a free public program of education and training." (emphasis added). 334 F.Supp., at 1258.

PARC was followed by *Mills v. Board of Education of District of Columbia*, 348 F.Supp. 866 (D.C. 1972), a case in which the plaintiff handicapped children had been excluded from the District of Columbia public schools. The court's judgment provided that

> "no [handicapped] child eligible for a publicly supported education in the District of Columbia public schools shall be excluded from a regular school assignment by a Rule, policy, or practice of the Board of Education of the District of Columbia or its agents unless such child is provided (a) *adequate* alternative educational services suited to the child's needs, which may include special education or tuition grants, and (b) a constitutionally adequate prior hearing and periodic review of the child's status, progress, and the adequacy of any educational alternative." 348 F.Supp., at 878 (emphasis added).

Mills and *PARC* both held that handicapped children must be given *access* to an adequate, publicly supported education. Neither case purports to require any particular substantive level of education. Rather, like the language of the Act, the cases set forth extensive procedures to be followed in formulating personalized educational programs for handicapped children. . . .

That the Act imposes no clear obligation upon recipient States beyond the requirement that handicapped children receive some form of specialized education is perhaps best demonstrated by the fact that Congress, in explaining the need for the Act, equated an "appropriate education" to the receipt of some specialized educational services. The Senate Report states: "[T]he most recent statistics provided by the Bureau of Education for the Handicapped estimate that of the more than 8 million children . . . with handicapping conditions requiring special education and related services, only 3.9 million such children are receiving an appropriate education." This statement, which reveals Congress' view that 3.9 million handicapped children were "receiving an appropriate education" in 1975, is followed immediately in the Senate Report by a table showing that 3.9 million handicapped children were "served" in 1975 and a slightly larger number were "unserved."

It is evident from the legislative history that the characterization of handicapped children as "served" referred to children who were receiving some form of specialized educational services from the States, and that the characterization of children as "unserved" referred to those who were receiving no specialized educational services. For example, a letter sent to the United States Commissioner of Education by the House Committee on Education and Labor, signed by two key sponsors of the Act in the House, asked the Commissioner to identify the number of handicapped "children served" in each State. The letter asked for statistics on the number of children "being served" in various types of "special education program[s]" and the number of children who were not "receiving educational services." Similarly, Senator Randolph, one of the Act's principal sponsors in the Senate, noted that roughly one-half of the handicapped children in the United States "are receiving special educational services." By characterizing the 3.9 million handicapped children who were "served" as children who were "receiving an appropriate education," the Senate and House Reports unmistakably disclose Congress' perception of the type of education required by the Act: an "appropriate education" is provided when personalized educational services are provided.

(ii)

Respondents contend that "the goal of the Act is to provide each handicapped child with an equal educational opportunity." We think, however, that the requirement that a State provide specialized educational services to handicapped children generates no additional requirement that the services so provided be sufficient to maximize each child's potential "commensurate with the opportunity provided other children." Respondents and the United States correctly note that Congress sought "to provide assistance to the States in carrying out their responsibilities under . . . the Constitution of the United States to provide equal protection of the laws." But we do not think that such statements imply a congressional intent to achieve strict equality of opportunity or services.

The educational opportunities provided by our public school systems undoubtedly differ from student to student, depending upon a myriad of factors that might affect a particular student's ability to assimilate information presented in the classroom. The requirement that States provide "equal" educational opportunities would thus seem to present an entirely unworkable standard requiring impossible measurements and comparisons. Similarly, furnishing handicapped children with only such services as are available to non-handicapped children would in all probability fall short of the statutory requirement of "free appropriate public education"; to require, on the other hand, the furnishing of every special service necessary to maximize each handicapped child's potential is, we think, further than Congress intended to go. Thus to speak in terms of "equal" services in one instance gives less than what is required by the Act and in another instance more. The theme of the Act is "free appropriate public education," a phrase which is too complex to be captured by the word "equal" whether one is speaking of opportunities or services.

The legislative conception of the requirements of equal protection was undoubtedly informed by the two District Court decisions referred to above. But cases such as *Mills* and *PARC* held simply that handicapped children may not be excluded entirely from public education. In *Mills*, the District Court said:

> "If sufficient funds are not available to finance all of the services and programs that are needed and desirable in the system then the available funds must be expended equitably in such a manner that no child is entirely excluded from a publicly supported education consistent with his needs and ability to benefit therefrom." 348 F.Supp., at 876.

The *PARC* court used similar language, saying "[i]t is the commonwealth's obligation to place each mentally retarded child in a free, public program of education and training appropriate to the child's capacity...." 348 F.Supp., at 1260. The right of access to free public education enunciated by these cases is significantly different from any notion of absolute equality of opportunity regardless of capacity. To the extent that Congress might have looked further than these cases which are mentioned in the legislative history, at the time of enactment of the Act this Court had held at least twice that the Equal Protection Clause of the Fourteenth Amendment does not require States to expend equal financial resources on the education of each child. *San Antonio Independent School Dist. v. Rodriguez*, 411 U.S. 1 ... (1973); *McInnis v. Shapiro*, 293 F.Supp. 327 (N.D. Ill. 1968), aff'd *sub nom. McInnis v. Ogilvie*, 394 U.S. 322 ... (1969).

In explaining the need for federal legislation, the House Report noted that "no congressional legislation has required a precise guarantee for handicapped children, i.e. a basic floor of opportunity that would bring into compliance all school districts with the constitutional right of equal protection with respect to handicapped children." Assuming that the Act was designed to fill the need identified in the House Report—that is, to provide a "basic floor of opportunity" consistent with equal protection—neither the Act nor its history persuasively demonstrates that Congress thought that equal protection required anything more than equal access. Therefore, Congress' desire to provide specialized educational services, even in furtherance of "equality," cannot be read as imposing any particular substantive educational standard upon the States.

The District Court and the Court of Appeals thus erred when they held that the Act requires New York to maximize the potential of each handicapped child commensurate with the opportunity provided nonhandicapped children. Desirable though that goal might be, it is not the standard that Congress imposed upon States which receive funding under the Act. Rather, Congress sought primarily to identify and evaluate handicapped children, and to provide them with access to a free public education.

(iii)

Implicit in the congressional purpose of providing access to a "free appropriate public education" is the requirement that the education to which access is provided be sufficient to confer some educational benefit upon the handicapped child. It would do little good for Congress to spend millions of dollars in providing access to a public education only to have the handicapped child receive no benefit from that education. The statutory definition of "free appropriate public education," in addition to requiring that States provide each child with "specially designed instruction," expressly requires the provision of "such . . . supportive services . . . as may be required to assist a handicapped child *to benefit* from special education." § 1401(17) (emphasis added). We therefore conclude that the "basic floor of opportunity" provided by the Act consists of access to specialized instruction and related services which are individually designed to provide educational benefit to the handicapped child.

The determination of when handicapped children are receiving sufficient educational benefits to satisfy the requirements of the Act presents a more difficult problem. The Act requires participating States to educate a wide spectrum of handicapped children, from the marginally hearing-impaired to the profoundly retarded and palsied. It is clear that the benefits obtainable by children at one end of the spectrum will differ dramatically from those obtainable by children at the other end, with infinite variations in between. One child may have little difficulty competing successfully in an academic setting with non-handicapped children while another child may encounter great difficulty in acquiring even the most basic of self-maintenance skills. We do not attempt today to establish any one test for determining the adequacy of educational benefits conferred upon all children covered by the Act. Because in this case we are presented with a handicapped child who is receiving substantial specialized instruction and related services, and who is performing above average in the regular classrooms of a public school system, we confine our analysis to that situation.

The Act requires participating States to educate handicapped children with non-handicapped children whenever possible. When that "mainstreaming" preference of the Act has been met and a child is being educated in the regular classrooms of a public school system, the system itself monitors the educational progress of the child. Regular examinations are administered, grades are awarded, and yearly advancement to higher grade levels is permitted for those children who attain an adequate knowledge of the course material. The grading and advancement system thus constitutes an important factor in determining educational benefit. Children who graduate from our public school systems are considered by our society to have been "educated" at least to the grade level they have completed, and access to an "education" for handicapped children is precisely what Congress sought to provide in the Act.

C

When the language of the Act and its legislative history are considered together, the requirements imposed by Congress become tolerably clear. Insofar as a State is required to provide a handicapped child with a "free appropriate public education," we hold that it satisfies this requirement by providing personalized instruction with sufficient support services to permit the child to benefit educationally from that instruction. Such instruction and services must be provided at public expense, must meet the State's educational standards, must approximate the grade levels used in the State's regular education, and must comport with the child's IEP. In addition, the IEP, and therefore the personalized instruction, should be formulated in accordance with the requirements of the Act and, if the child is being educated in the regular classrooms of the public education system, should be reasonably calculated to enable the child to achieve passing marks and advance from grade to grade.

. . . .

VI

Applying these principles to the facts of this case, we conclude that the Court of Appeals erred in affirming the decision of the District Court. Neither the District Court nor the Court of Appeals found that petitioners had failed to comply with the procedures of the Act, and the findings of neither court would support a conclusion that Amy's educational program failed to comply with the substantive requirements of the Act. On the contrary, the District Court found that the "evidence firmly establishes that Amy is receiving an 'adequate' education, since she performs better than the average child in her class and is advancing easily from grade to grade." In light of this finding, and of the fact that Amy was receiving personalized instruction and related services calculated by the Furnace Woods school administrators to meet her educational needs, the lower courts should not have concluded that the Act requires the provision of a sign-language interpreter. Accordingly, the decision of the Court of Appeals is reversed, and the case is remanded for further proceedings consistent with this opinion.

Justice Blackmun, concurring in the judgment.

Although I reach the same result as the Court does today, I read the legislative history and goals of the Education of the Handicapped Act differently. Congress unambiguously stated that it intended to "take a more active role under its responsibility for equal protection of the laws to guarantee that handicapped children are provided *equal educational opportunity*." S. Rep. No. 94–168, p. 9 (1975), U.S. Code Cong. & Admin. News 1975, p. 1483 (emphasis added).

As I have observed before, "[i]t seems plain to me that Congress, in enacting [this statute], intended to do more than merely set out politically self-serving but essentially meaningless language about what the [handicapped] deserve at the hands of state . . . authorities." The clarity of the legislative intent convinces me that the relevant question here is not, as the Court says, whether Amy Rowley's individualized education program was "reasonably calculated to enable [her] to receive educational benefits," measured in part by whether or not she "achieve[s] passing marks and advance[s] from grade to grade . . . [.]" Rather, the question is whether Amy's program, *viewed as a whole*, offered her an opportunity to understand and participate in the classroom that was substantially equal to that given her nonhandicapped classmates. This is a standard predicated on equal educational opportunity and equal access to the educational process, rather than upon Amy's achievement of any particular educational outcome.

. . . .

. . . . By concentrating on whether Amy was "learning as much, or performing as well academically, as she would without her handicap," the District Court and the Court of Appeals paid too little attention to whether, on the entire record, respondent's individualized education program offered her an educational opportunity substantially equal to that provided her nonhandicapped classmates. Because I believe that standard has been satisfied here, I agree that the judgment of the Court of Appeals should be reversed.

Justice WHITE, with whom Justice BRENNAN and Justice MARSHALL join, dissenting.

In order to reach its result in this case, the majority opinion contradicts itself, the language of the statute, and the legislative history. . . . [T]he majority's standard for a "free appropriate education" . . . disregard[s] congressional intent.

I

The majority first turns its attention to the meaning of a "free appropriate public education.". . . . The majority reads this statutory language as establishing a congressional intent limited to bringing "previously excluded handicapped children into the public education systems of the States and [requiring] the States to adopt *procedures* which would result in individualized consideration of and instruction for each child." In its attempt to constrict the definition of "appropriate" and the thrust of the Act, the majority opinion states: "Noticeably absent from the language of the statute is any substantive standard prescribing the level of education to be accorded handicapped children. Certainly the language of the statute contains no requirement like the one imposed by the lower courts—that States maximize the potential of handicapped children 'commensurate with the opportunity provided to other children.'"

I agree that the language of the Act does not contain a substantive standard beyond requiring that the education offered must be "appropriate." However, if there are limits not evident from the face of the statute on what may be considered an "appropriate education," they must be found in the purpose of the statute or its legislative history. The Act itself announces it will provide a "*full* educational opportunity to all handicapped children." 20 U.S.C. § 1412(2)(A) (emphasis added). This goal is repeated throughout the legislative history, in statements too frequent to be "'passing references and isolated phrases.'"[1] These statements elucidate the meaning of

1. The Court's opinion relies heavily on the statement, which occurs throughout the legislative history, that, at the time of enactment, one million of the roughly eight million handicapped children in the United States were excluded entirely from the public school system and more than half were receiving an inappropriate education. But this statement was often linked to statements urging equal educational opportunity. . . . That is, Congress wanted not only to bring handicapped children into the schoolhouse, but also to benefit them once they had entered.

"appropriate." According to the Senate Report, for example, the Act does "guarantee that handicapped children are provided *equal* educational opportunity." S. Rep. No. 94-168, p. 9 (1975) (emphasis added). This promise appears throughout the legislative history. See 121 Cong. Rec. 19482–19483 (1975) (remarks of Sen. Randolph); *id.*, at 19504 (Sen. Humphrey); *id.*, at 19505 (Sen. Beall); *id.*, at 23704 (Rep. Brademas); *id.*, at 25538 (Rep. Cornell); *id.*, at 25540 (Rep. Grassley); *id.*, at 37025 (Rep. Perkins); *id.*, at 37030 (Rep. Mink); *id.*, at 37412 (Sen. Taft); *id.*, at 37413 (Sen. Williams); *id.*, at 37418–37419 (Sen. Cranston); *id.*, at 37419-37420 (Sen. Beall). Indeed, at times the purpose of the Act was described as tailoring each handicapped child's educational plan to enable the child "to achieve his or her maximum potential." H. R. Rep. No. 94–332, pp. 13, 19 (1975); see 121 Cong. Rec. 23709 (1975). Senator Stafford, one of the sponsors of the Act, declared: "We can all agree that education [given a handicapped child] should be equivalent, at least, to the one those children who are not handicapped receive." The legislative history thus directly supports the conclusion that the Act intends to give handicapped children an educational opportunity commensurate with that given other children.

The majority opinion announces a different substantive standard, that "Congress did not impose upon the States any greater substantive educational standard than would be necessary to make such access meaningful." While "meaningful" is no more enlightening than "appropriate," the Court purports to clarify itself. Because Amy was provided with *some* specialized instruction from which she obtained *some* benefit and because she passed from grade to grade, she was receiving a meaningful and therefore appropriate education.

This falls far short of what the Act intended. The Act details as specifically as possible the kind of specialized education each handicapped child must receive. It would apparently satisfy the Court's standard of "access to specialized instruction and related services which are individually designed to provide educational benefit to the handicapped child," for a deaf child such as Amy to be given a teacher with a loud voice, for she would benefit from that service. The Act requires more. It defines "special education" to mean "specifically designed instruction, at no cost to parents or guardians, to *meet the unique needs* of a handicapped child . . . ." Providing a teacher with a loud voice would not meet Amy's needs and would not satisfy the Act. The basic floor of opportunity is instead, as the courts below recognized, intended to eliminate the effects of the handicap, at least to the extent that the child will be given an equal opportunity to learn if that is reasonably possible. Amy Rowley, without a sign-language interpreter, comprehends less than half of what is said in the classroom—less than half of what normal children comprehend. This is hardly an equal opportunity to learn, even if Amy makes passing grades.

Despite its reliance on the use of "appropriate" in the definition of the Act, the majority opinion speculates that "Congress used the word as much to describe the settings in which handicapped children should be educated as to prescribe the substantive content or supportive services of their education." Of course, the word "appropriate" can be applied in many ways; at times in the Act, Congress used it to recommend mainstreaming handicapped children; at other points, it used the word to refer to the content of the individualized education. The issue before us is what standard the word "appropriate" incorporates when it is used to modify "education." The answer given by the Court is not a satisfactory one.

. . . .

Notes, Comments, and Questions

1. *Rowley* rejected the parents' argument that the state must "maximize the potential of handicapped children 'commensurate with the opportunity provided other children.' " 458 U.S. at 189–90. Instead, the court concluded that the " 'basic floor of opportunity' provided by the Act consists of access to specialized instruction and related services which are individually designed to provide educational benefit to the handicapped child." *Id.* at 201; *see also id.* at 200 ("Implicit in the congressional purpose of providing access to a 'free appropriate public education' is the requirement that the education to which access is provided be sufficient to confer some educational benefit upon the handicapped child."). Lower courts have relied on this language to reject any suggestion that a local school district must provide children with disabilities the "best" educational program. *See* C.M. v. Sch. Bd. of Miami-Dade Cnty., 437 F.3d 1085, 1103 (11th Cir. 2006) (rejecting parents' claim that the school district denied a FAPE to a child with a hearing impairment when the school district would not provide the "best" program to the child); L.E. v. Ramsey Bd. of Educ., 435 F.3d 384, 390 (3d Cir. 2006) (stating that the IDEA does not require the state to maximize the child's potential); Pace v. Bogalusa City Sch. Bd., 403 F.3d 272, 291 (5th Cir. 2005) (stating that FAPE "need not be the best possible education nor one that will maximize the child's educational potential."); Fort Zumwalt Sch. Dist. v. Clynes, 119 F.3d 607, 612 (8th Cir. 1997), *cert. denied*, 523 U.S. 1137 (1998) (stating that the "IDEA does not require that a school either maximize a student's potential or provide the best possible education at public expense."); Carlisle Area Sch. v. Scott P., 62 F.3d 520, 533–34 (3d Cir. 1995) (ruling that a school district "need not provide the optimal level of services, or even a level that would confer additional benefits, since the IEP required by the IDEA represents only a 'basic floor of opportunity.' ").

2. Courts have also rejected parents' attempts to advocate for particular programs and methodologies for their children, instead deferring to the expertise of school districts in selecting a methodology or program appropriate to meet a child's educational needs. *See* Bradley v. Ark. Dep't of Educ., 443 F.3d 965, 975 (8th Cir. 2006) (stating that the IDEA does not require a school district to implement parental preferences); C.M. v. Sch. Bd. of Miami-Dade Cnty., 437 F.3d 1085, 1103 (11th Cir. 2006) (rejecting parents' request for a specific methodology for educating their child with a hearing impairment); Lachman v. Ill. Bd. of Educ., 852 F.2d 290, 297 (7th Cir. 1988), *cert. denied*, 488 U.S. 925 (1988) ("*Rowley* and its progeny leave no doubt that parents, no matter how well-motivated, do not have a right under the . . . [Act] to compel a school district to provide a specific program or employ a specific methodology in providing for the education of their handicapped child.").

3. In *Rowley*, the court recognized Congress' inclusion of extensive procedural safeguards and meaningful input from parents into all decisions affecting their child's education and suggested that such procedural safeguards would in most cases ensure positive educational outcomes:

> When the elaborate and highly specific procedural safeguards embodied in § 1415 are contrasted with the general and somewhat imprecise substantive admonitions contained in the Act, we think that the importance Congress attached to these procedural safeguards cannot be gainsaid. It seems to us no exaggeration to say that Congress placed every bit as much emphasis upon compliance with procedures giving parents and guardians a large measure of participation at every stage of the administrative process . . . as it did upon the measurement of the resulting IEP against a substantive standard. We think that the congressional emphasis upon full participation of concerned parties throughout the development of the IEP . . . demonstrates the legislative conviction that adequate compliance with the procedures prescribed would in most cases assure much if not all of what Congress wished in the way of substantive content in an IEP.
>
> . . . .
>
> Entrusting a child's education to state and local agencies does not leave the child without protection. Congress sought to protect individual children by providing for parental involvement in the development of state plans and policies, and in the formulation of the child's individual educational program. As the Senate Report States:
>
>> "The Committee recognizes that in many instances the process of providing special education and related services to handicapped children is not guaranteed to produce any particular outcome. By changing the language [of the provision relating to individualized educational programs] to emphasize the process of parent and child involvement and to provide a written record of reasonable expectations, the Committee intends to clarify that such individualized planning conferences are a way to provide parent involvement and protection to assure that appropriate services are provided to a handicapped child."
>
> As this very case demonstrates, parents and guardians will not lack ardor in seeking to ensure that handicapped children receive all of the benefits to which they are entitled by the Act.

458 U.S. at 205–06, 208–09. Are the IDEA's procedural safeguards sufficient to ensure that each child receives an appropriate level of education? Based on the legislative history cited in both the majority and dissenting opinions, do you agree that Congress placed as much importance on procedural compliance as substantive outcomes?

4. *Rowley* established the test for IDEA compliance that courts have employed since. The first part of the test reflects the Court's emphasis on procedures:

> Therefore, a court's inquiry in suits brought under § 1415(e)(2) is twofold. First, has the State complied with the procedures set forth in the Act? And second, is the individualized educational program developed through the Act's procedures reasonably calculated to enable the child to receive educational benefits? If these requirements are met, the State has complied with the obligations imposed by Congress and the courts can require no more.

Id. at 206–07.

5. *Rowley* also established that courts must not impose their judgments about education on educators. Instead, courts must give deference:

> In assuring that the requirements of the Act have been met, courts must be careful to avoid imposing their view of preferable educational methods upon the States. The primary responsibility for formulating the education to be accorded a handicapped child, and for choosing the educational method most suitable to the child's needs, was left by the Act to state and local educational agencies in cooperation with the parents or guardian of the child. The Act expressly charges States with the responsibility of "acquiring and disseminating to teachers and administrators of programs for handicapped children significant information derived from educational research, demonstration, and similar projects, and [of] adopting, where appropriate, promising educational practices and materials." In the face of such a clear statutory directive, it seems highly unlikely that Congress intended courts to overturn a State's choice of appropriate educational theories in a proceeding conducted pursuant to § 1415(e)(2). We previously have cautioned that courts lack the "specialized knowledge and experience" necessary to resolve "persistent and difficult questions of educational policy." We think that Congress shared that view when it passed the Act. As already demonstrated, Congress' intention was not that the Act displace the primacy of States in the field of education, but that States receive funds to assist them in extending their educational systems to the handicapped. Therefore, once a court determines that the requirements of the Act have been met, questions of methodology are for resolution by the States.

Id. at 207–08.

Section Two
Level of Educational Benefit

Following *Rowley*, courts attempted to determine the level of educational benefit necessary to satisfy the IDEA. For contrasting views, *compare* Hall v. Vance Cnty. Bd. of Educ., 774 F.2d 629, 636 (4th Cir. 1985) (ruling that the school district denied a FAPE when the child remained functionally illiterate), *with* CJN v. Minneapolis Pub. Sch., 323 F.3d 630, 642 (8th Cir. 2003), *cert. denied*, 540 U.S. 984 (2003) ("IDEA does not require that schools attempt to maximize a child's potential, or . . .

guarantee that the student actually make any progress at all."). The Supreme Court addressed this issue in *Endrew F. v. Douglas County School District*, in which the Tenth Circuit ruled that the *Rowley* standard is satisfied by an education that provides "merely . . . more than *de minimis*" educational benefit. Endrew F. v. Douglas Cnty. Sch. Dist., 798 F.3d 1329,1338 (10th Cir. 2015), *vacated and remanded*, Endrew F. v Douglas Cnty. Sch. Dist., No. 15-827, 2017 WL 1066260 (U.S. March 22, 2017). As you read *Endrew F.*, consider the differences between *Endrew F.* and *Rowley* and how much of *Rowley*, if any, survives *Endrew F.*

Endrew F. v Douglas Cnty. Sch. Dist.

No. 15-827, 2017 WL 1066260 (U.S. March 22, 2017)

Chief Justice Roberts delivered the opinion of the Court

Thirty-five years ago, this Court held that the Individuals with Disabilities Education Act establishes a substantive right to a "free appropriate public education" for certain children with disabilities. *Board of Ed. of Hendrick Hudson Central School Dist., Westchester Cty. v. Rowley*, 458 U.S. 176 (1982). We declined, however, to endorse any one standard for determining "when handicapped children are receiving sufficient educational benefits to satisfy the requirements of the Act." That "more difficult problem" is before us today.

I

A

The Individuals with Disabilities Education Act (IDEA or Act) offers States federal funds to assist in educating children with disabilities. In exchange for the funds, a State pledges to comply with a number of statutory conditions. Among them, the State must provide a free appropriate public education — a FAPE, for short — to all eligible children.

A FAPE, as the Act defines it, includes both "special education" and "related services." "Special education" is "specially designed instruction . . . to meet the unique needs of a child with a disability"; "related services" are the support services "required to assist a child . . . to benefit from" that instruction. A State covered by the IDEA must provide a disabled child with such special education and related services "in conformity with the [child's] individualized education program," or IEP.

. . . .

The IDEA requires that every IEP include "a statement of the child's present levels of academic achievement and functional performance," describe "how the child's disability affects the child's involvement and progress in the general education curriculum," and set out "measurable annual goals, including academic and functional goals," along with a "description of how the child's progress toward meeting" those goals will be gauged. The IEP must also describe the "special education and related services . . . that will be provided" so that the child may "advance appropriately toward attaining the annual goals" and, when possible, "be involved in and make progress in the general education curriculum."

. . . .

B

[The Court's description of *Rowley* is excluded.]

In view of Amy Rowley's excellent progress and the "substantial" suite of specialized instruction and services offered in her IEP, we concluded that her program satisfied the FAPE requirement. But we went no further. Instead, we expressly "confine[d] our analysis" to the facts of the case before us. Observing that the Act requires States to "educate a wide spectrum" of children with disabilities and that "the benefits obtainable by children at one end of the spectrum will differ dramatically from those obtainable by children at the other end," we declined "to establish any one test for determining the adequacy of educational benefits conferred upon all children covered by the Act."

C

Petitioner Endrew F. was diagnosed with autism at age two. Autism is a neurodevelopmental disorder generally marked by impaired social and communicative skills, "engagement in repetitive activities and stereotyped movements, resistance to environmental change or change in daily routines, and unusual responses to sensory experiences." 34 C.F.R. § 300.8(c)(1)(I) (2016). A child with autism qualifies as a "[c]hild with a disability" under the IDEA, and Colorado (where Endrew resides) accepts IDEA funding. Endrew is therefore entitled to the benefits of the Act, including a FAPE provided by the State.

Endrew attended school in respondent Douglas County School District from preschool through fourth grade. Each year, his IEP Team drafted an IEP addressed to his educational and functional needs. By Endrew's fourth grade year, however, his parents had become dissatisfied with his progress. Although Endrew displayed a number of strengths—his teachers described him as a humorous child with a "sweet disposition" who "show[ed] concern[ ] for friends"—he still "exhibited multiple behaviors that inhibited his ability to access learning in the classroom." Endrew would scream in class, climb over furniture and other students, and occasionally run away from school. He was afflicted by severe fears of commonplace things like flies, spills, and public restrooms. As Endrew's parents saw it, his academic and functional progress had essentially stalled: Endrew's IEPs largely carried over the same basic goals and objectives from one year to the next, indicating that he was failing to make meaningful progress toward his aims. His parents believed that only a thorough overhaul of the school district's approach to Endrew's behavioral problems could reverse the trend. But in April 2010, the school district presented Endrew's parents with a proposed fifth grade IEP that was, in their view, pretty much the same as his past ones. So his parents removed Endrew from public school and enrolled him at Firefly Autism House, a private school that specializes in educating children with autism.

Endrew did much better at Firefly. The school developed a "behavioral intervention plan" that identified Endrew's most problematic behaviors and set out particular strategies for addressing them. Firefly also added heft to Endrew's academic goals. Within months, Endrew's behavior improved significantly, permitting him to make a degree of academic progress that had eluded him in public school.

In November 2010, some six months after Endrew started classes at Firefly, his parents again met with representatives of the Douglas County School District. The district presented a new IEP. Endrew's parents considered the IEP no more adequate than the one proposed in April, and rejected it. They were particularly concerned that the stated plan for addressing Endrew's behavior did not differ meaningfully from the plan in his fourth grade IEP, despite the fact that his experience at Firefly suggested that he would benefit from a different approach. In February 2012, Endrew's parents filed a complaint with the Colorado Department of Education seeking reimbursement for Endrew's tuition at Firefly. To qualify for such relief, they were required to show that the school district had not provided Endrew a FAPE in a timely manner prior to his enrollment at the private school. Endrew's parents contended that the final IEP proposed by the school district was not "reasonably calculated to enable [Endrew] to receive educational benefits" and that Endrew had therefore been denied a FAPE. An Administrative Law Judge (ALJ) disagreed and denied relief.

Endrew's parents sought review in Federal District Court. Giving "due weight" to the decision of the ALJ, the District Court affirmed. The court acknowledged that Endrew's performance under past IEPs "did not reveal immense educational growth." But it concluded that annual modifications to Endrew's IEP objectives were "sufficient to show a pattern of, at the least, minimal progress." Because Endrew's previous IEPs had enabled him to make this sort of progress, the court reasoned, his latest, similar IEP was reasonably calculated to do the same thing. In the court's view, that was all *Rowley* demanded. The Tenth Circuit affirmed. The Court of Appeals recited language from *Rowley* stating that the instruction and services furnished to children with disabilities must be calculated to confer "*some* educational benefit." The court noted that it had long interpreted this language to mean that a child's IEP is adequate as long as it is calculated to confer an "educational benefit [that is] merely . . . more than *de minimis*." Applying this standard, the Tenth Circuit held that Endrew's IEP had been "reasonably calculated to enable [him] to make *some* progress." Accordingly, he had not been denied a FAPE.

We granted certiorari.

II

A

The Court in *Rowley* declined "to establish any one test for determining the adequacy of educational benefits conferred upon all children covered by the Act." The school district, however, contends that *Rowley* nonetheless established that "an IEP need not promise any particular *level* of benefit," so long as it is "'reasonably calculated' to provide *some* benefit, as opposed to *none*."

The district relies on several passages from *Rowley* to make its case. It points to our observation that "any substantive standard prescribing the level of education to be accorded" children with disabilities was "[n]oticeably absent from the language of the statute." The district also emphasizes the Court's statement that the Act requires States to provide access to instruction "sufficient to confer *some* educational benefit," reasoning that any benefit, however minimal, satisfies this mandate. Finally, the district urges that the Court conclusively adopted a "some educational benefit" standard when it wrote that "the intent of the Act was more to open the door of public education to handicapped children . . . than to guarantee any particular level of education."

These statements in isolation do support the school district's argument. But the district makes too much of them. Our statement that the face of the IDEA imposed no explicit substantive standard must be evaluated alongside our statement that a substantive standard was "implicit in the Act." Similarly, we find little significance in the Court's language concerning the requirement that States provide instruction calculated to "confer some educational benefit." The Court had no need to say anything more particular, since the case before it involved a child whose progress plainly demonstrated that her IEP was designed to deliver more than adequate educational benefits. The Court's principal concern was to correct what it viewed as the surprising rulings below: that the IDEA effectively empowers judges to elaborate a federal common law of public education, and that a child performing *better* than most in her class had been denied a FAPE. The Court was not concerned with precisely articulating a governing standard for closer cases. And the statement that the Act did not "guarantee any particular level of education" simply reflects the unobjectionable proposition that the IDEA cannot and does not promise "any particular [educational] outcome." No law could do that—for any child.

More important, the school district's reading of these isolated statements runs headlong into several points on which *Rowley* is crystal clear. For instance—just after saying that the Act requires instruction that is "sufficient to confer some educational benefit"—we noted that "[t]he determination of when handicapped children are receiving *sufficient* educational benefits . . . presents a . . . difficult problem." And then we expressly declined "to establish any one test for determining the *adequacy* of educational benefits" under the Act. It would not have been "difficult" for us to say when educational benefits are sufficient if we had just said that *any* educational benefit was enough. And it would have been strange to refuse to set out a test for the adequacy of educational benefits if we had just done exactly that. We cannot accept the school district's reading of *Rowley*.

B

While *Rowley* declined to articulate an overarching standard to evaluate the adequacy of the education provided under the Act, the decision and the statutory language point to a general approach: To meet its substantive obligation under the IDEA, a school must offer an IEP reasonably calculated to enable a child to make progress appropriate in light of the child's circumstances. The "reasonably calculated" qualification reflects a recognition that crafting an appropriate program of education requires a prospective judgment by school officials. The Act contemplates that this fact-intensive exercise will be informed not only by the expertise of school officials, but also by the input of the child's parents or guardians. Any review of an IEP must appreciate that the question is whether the IEP is *reasonable,* not whether the court regards it as ideal.

The IEP must aim to enable the child to make progress. After all, the essential function of an IEP is to set out a plan for pursuing academic and functional advancement. This reflects the broad purpose of the IDEA, an "ambitious" piece of legislation enacted "in response to Congress' perception that a majority of handicapped children in the United States 'were either totally excluded from schools or [were] sitting idly in regular classrooms awaiting the time when they were old enough to "drop out."' " A substantive standard not focused on student progress would do little to remedy the pervasive and tragic academic stagnation that prompted Congress to act. That the progress contemplated by the IEP must be appropriate in light of the child's circumstances should come as no surprise. A focus on the particular child is at the core of the IDEA. The instruction offered must be "*specially* designed" to meet a child's "*unique* needs" through an "[*i*]*ndividualized* education program." An IEP is not a form document. It is constructed only after careful consideration of the child's present levels of achievement, disability, and potential for growth. As we observed in *Rowley,* the IDEA "requires participating States to educate a wide spectrum of handicapped children," and "the benefits obtainable by children at one end of the spectrum will differ dramatically from those obtainable by children at the other end, with infinite variations in between." *Rowley* sheds light on what appropriate progress will look like in many cases. There, the Court recognized that the IDEA requires that children with disabilities receive education in the regular classroom "whenever possible." When this preference is met, "the system itself monitors the educational progress of the child." "Regular examinations are administered, grades are awarded, and yearly advancement to higher grade levels is permitted for those children who attain an adequate knowledge of the course material." Progress through this system is what our society generally means by an "education." And access to an "education" is what the IDEA promises. Accordingly, for a child fully integrated in the regular classroom, an IEP typically should, as *Rowley* put it, be "reasonably calculated to enable the child to achieve passing marks and advance from grade to grade."

This guidance is grounded in the statutory definition of a FAPE. One of the components of a FAPE is "special education," defined as "specially designed instruction . . . to meet the unique needs of a child with a disability." In determining what it means to "meet the unique needs" of a child with a disability, the provisions governing the IEP development process are a natural source of guidance: It is through the IEP that "[t]he 'free appropriate public education' required by the Act is tailored to the unique needs of" a particular child. The IEP provisions reflect *Rowley* 's expectation that, for most children, a FAPE will involve integration in the regular classroom and individualized special education calculated to achieve advancement from grade to grade. Every IEP begins by describing a child's present level of achievement, including explaining "how the child's disability affects the child's involvement and progress in the general education curriculum." It then sets out "a statement of measurable annual goals . . . designed to . . . enable the child to be involved in and make progress in the general education curriculum," along with a description of specialized instruction and services that the child will receive. The instruction and services must likewise be provided with an eye toward "progress in the general education curriculum." Similar IEP requirements have been in place since the time the States began accepting funding under the IDEA. The school district protests that these provisions impose only procedural requirements—a checklist of items the IEP must address—not a substantive standard enforceable in court. But the procedures are there for a reason, and their focus provides insight into what it means, for purposes of the FAPE definition, to "meet the unique needs" of a child with a disability. When a child is fully integrated in the regular classroom, as the Act prefers, what that typically means is providing a level of instruction reasonably calculated to permit advancement through the general curriculum.[2]

Rowley had no need to provide concrete guidance with respect to a child who is not fully integrated in the regular classroom and not able to achieve on grade level. That case concerned a young girl who was progressing smoothly through the regular curriculum. If that is not a reasonable prospect for a child, his IEP need not aim for grade-level advancement. But his educational program must be appropriately ambitious in light of his circumstances, just as advancement from grade to grade is appropriately ambitious for most children in the regular classroom. The goals may differ, but every child should have the chance to meet challenging objectives.

Of course this describes a general standard, not a formula. But whatever else can be said about it, this standard is markedly more demanding than the "merely more than *de minimis*" test applied by the Tenth Circuit. It cannot be the case that the Act typically aims for grade-level advancement for children with disabilities who can be educated in the regular classroom, but is satisfied with barely more than *de minimis* progress for those who cannot.

When all is said and done, a student offered an educational program providing "merely more than *de minimis*" progress from year to year can hardly be said to have been offered an education at all. For children with disabilities, receiving instruction that aims so low would be tantamount to "sitting idly . . . awaiting the time when they were old enough to 'drop out.'" The IDEA demands more. It requires an educational program reasonably calculated to enable a child to make progress appropriate in light of the child's circumstances.

2. This guidance should not be interpreted as an inflexible rule. We declined to hold in *Rowley*, and do not hold today, that "every handicapped child who is advancing from grade to grade . . . is automatically receiving a [FAPE]."

C

Endrew's parents argue that the Act goes even further. In their view, a FAPE is "an education that aims to provide a child with a disability opportunities to achieve academic success, attain self-sufficiency, and contribute to society that are substantially equal to the opportunities afforded children without disabilities."

This standard is strikingly similar to the one the lower courts adopted in *Rowley*, and it is virtually identical to the formulation advanced by Justice Blackmun in his separate writing in that case. . . . Mindful that Congress (despite several intervening amendments to the IDEA) has not materially changed the statutory definition of a FAPE since *Rowley* was decided, we decline to interpret the FAPE provision in a manner so plainly at odds with the Court's analysis in that case.

D

We will not attempt to elaborate on what "appropriate" progress will look like from case to case. It is in the nature of the Act and the standard we adopt to resist such an effort: The adequacy of a given IEP turns on the unique circumstances of the child for whom it was created. This absence of a bright-line rule, however, should not be mistaken for "an invitation to the courts to substitute their own notions of sound educational policy for those of the school authorities which they review."

At the same time, deference is based on the application of expertise and the exercise of judgment by school authorities. The Act vests these officials with responsibility for decisions of critical importance to the life of a disabled child. The nature of the IEP process, from the initial consultation through state administrative proceedings, ensures that parents and school representatives will fully air their respective opinions on the degree of progress a child's IEP should pursue. By the time any dispute reaches court, school authorities will have had a complete opportunity to bring their expertise and judgment to bear on areas of disagreement. A reviewing court may fairly expect those authorities to be able to offer a cogent and responsive explanation for their decisions that shows the IEP is reasonably calculated to enable the child to make progress appropriate in light of his circumstances.

The judgment of the United States Court of Appeals for the Tenth Circuit is vacated, and the case is remanded for further proceedings consistent with this opinion.

Note

Endrew F. rejected the "merely . . . more than *de minimis*" educational benefit test for providing a FAPE to children with disabilities:

> When all is said and done, a student offered an educational program providing " 'merely more than *de minimis*' " progress from year to year can hardly be said to have been offered an education at all. For children with disabilities, receiving instruction that aims so low would be tantamount to " 'sitting idly . . . awaiting the time when they were old enough to "drop out." ' "

Id. at *12. However, *Endrew F.* did much more than reject the *de minimis* standard; it is a landmark decision that, like *Rowley*, will likely shape the landscape of special education law for decades to come. Understanding the full implications of *Endrew F.* will await its application in the schools by educators and its interpretation by IHOs, SROs, and the courts. The following notes are some tentative thoughts about its implications.

The test for evaluating whether a school district provided a FAPE: *Endrew F.* replaced *Rowley*'s "educational benefit" test with the following test: "To meet its substantive obligation under the IDEA, a school must offer an IEP reasonably calculated to enable a child to make progress appropriate in light of the child's circumstances." Endrew F., 2017 WL 1066260, at *10. In announcing this test, the Court elaborated on its three key parts. First, an analysis of an IEP must examine whether it is "reasonable," not ideal. Second, "The IEP must aim to enable the child to make progress. After all, the essential function of an IEP is to set out a plan for pursuing academic and functional advancement." *Id.* Finally, "That the progress contemplated by the IEP must be appropriate in light of the child's circumstances should come as no surprise. A focus on the particular child is at the core of the IDEA." *Id.* Thus, although achieving passing grades and advancing from grade to grade might be appropriate progress for children like Amy Rowley, it is not necessarily appropriate for children who are not able to participate in the general education curriculum. Instead, the IEP for such children "must be appropriately ambitious in light of his circumstances, just as advancement from grade to grade is appropriately ambitious for most children in the regular classroom. The goals may differ, but every child should have the chance to meet challenging objectives." *Id.* at *11.

The standard for measuring academic progress for children with disabilities in the regular education classroom: The Court made clear that *Rowley*'s standard of measuring benefit—achieving passing grades and advancing from grade to grade—applies to children who are participating in the general education curriculum:

> *Rowley* sheds light on what appropriate progress will look like in many cases. There, the court recognized that the IDEA requires that children with disabilities receive education in the regular classroom " 'whenever possible.' "
>
> . . . .
>
> The IEP provisions reflect *Rowley*'s expectation that, for most children, a FAPE will involve integration in the regular classroom and individualized special education calculated to achieve advancement from grade to grade.

Id. at *10–11.

Providing a FAPE to children with severe disabilities and to children with above-average abilities: Sections Three and Four examine whether *Endrew F.*'s new FAPE test and flexible standard for measuring progress have implications for the requirements for providing a FAPE to children with severe disabilities and to children with disabilities who have higher than average capabilities.

Equal educational opportunities for students with disabilities: *Rowley* ruled that the IDEA does not require school districts to provide educational opportunities to students with disabilities to maximize their potential equal to the opportunities they offer to typically developing students. The parents in *Endrew F.* argued in support of a similar standard, but the Court rejected it:

> This standard is strikingly similar to the one the lower courts adopted in *Rowley*, and it is virtually identical to the formulation advanced by Justice Blackmun in his separate writing in that case. . . . Mindful that Congress (despite several intervening amendments to the IDEA) has not materially changed the statutory definition of a FAPE since *Rowley* was decided, we decline to interpret the FAPE provision in a manner so plainly at odds with the Court's analysis in that case.

Id. at *12.

Although the Court in *Endrew F.* rejected equal educational opportunities for children with disabilties, can you make an argument that its test is, in essence, a test for equal opportunity? Is a school's obligation to "offer an IEP reasonably calculated to enable a child to make progress appropriate in light of the child's circumstances" similar to the opportunity public schools offer to typically developing children? Did the decision in *Endrew F.* vindicate the concurring and dissenting opinions in *Rowley*?

The emphasis on process: *Rowley* emphasized the importance of the IDEA process, suggesting that following the IDEA's procedures for identifying and evaluating children, preparing the IEP, and providing an impartial hearing to parents who want to challenge their child's special education would generally produce the educational results for children with disabilities that Congress intended. Adherence to process was so important that *Rowley* made it the first step of the two-step test for determining whether a school district violated the IDEA.

Endrew F. did not remove procedural compliance from the test for IDEA compliance and maintained the Court's view of the important role of process:

> The nature of the IEP process, from the initial consultation through state administrative proceedings, ensures that parents and school representatives will fully air their respective opinions on the degree of progress a child's IEP should pursue. By the time any dispute reaches court, school authorities will have had a complete opportunity to bring their expertise and judgment to bear on areas of disagreement.

Id. at *12.

However, *Endrew F.* did not prioritize process over substance as in *Rowley*, and suggested that the process exists to lead to educational standards. The Court rejected the school district's argument that the IEP provisions are simply procedural requirements: "But the procedures are there for a reason, and their focus provides insight into what it means, for purposes of the FAPE definition, to 'meet the unique needs' of a child with a disability." *Id.* at *11.

In addition, *Endrew F.* seemed to pull back from *Rowley*'s rulings that the IDEA does not contain substantive educational standards and that in passing the IDEA Congress was more concerned with opening the door to an education for children with disabilities than with guaranteeing educational outcomes. In rejecting the school district's attempt to use these rulings to support its argument in support of the *de minimis* standard, the Court stated:

> These statements in isolation do support the school district's argument. But the district makes too much of them. Our statement that the face of the IDEA imposed no explicit substantive standard must be evaluated alongside our statement that a substantive standard was "implicit in the Act." Similarly, we find little significance in the Court's language concerning the requirement that States provide instruction calculated to "confer some educational benefit." The Court had no need to say anything more particular, since the case before it involved a child whose progress plainly demonstrated that her IEP was designed to deliver more than adequate educational benefits.

Id. at 9.

Deference to local education officials: *Endrew F.* reinforced *Rowley*'s ruling that courts should give deference to local education officials:

> We will not attempt to elaborate on what "appropriate" progress will look like from case to case. It is in the nature of the Act and the standard we adopt to resist such an effort: The adequacy of a given IEP turns on the unique circumstances of the child for whom it was created. This absence of a bright-line rule, however, should not be mistaken for "an invitation to the courts to substitute their own notions of sound educational policy for those of the school authorities which they review." *Rowley,* 458 U.S., at 206.
>
> At the same time, deference is based on the application of expertise and the exercise of judgment by school authorities. The Act vests these officials with responsibility for decisions of critical importance to the life of a disabled child. The nature of the IEP process, from the initial consultation through state administrative proceedings, ensures that parents and school representatives will fully air their respective opinions on the degree of progress a child's IEP should pursue. By the time any dispute reaches court, school authorities will have had a complete opportunity to bring their expertise and judgment to bear on areas of disagreement. A reviewing court may fairly expect those authorities to be able to offer a cogent and responsive explanation for their decisions that shows the IEP is reasonably calculated to enable the child to make progress appropriate in light of his circumstances.

Id. at *12.

Section Three
Providing a FAPE to a Child with Severe Disabilities

Rowley did not address how the Court's definition of a FAPE and the requirement that special education and related services allow a disabled child to receive educational benefit should be applied to children with severe disabilities who are not participating in general education. *Endrew F.* did address this issue. In elaborating on how to apply its FAPE standard to a child who is not capable of progressing in the regular education classroom, the Court stated:

> [H]is educational program must be appropriately ambitious in light of his circumstances, just as advancement from grade to grade is appropriately ambitious for most children in the regular classroom. The goals may differ, but every child should have the chance to meet challenging objectives.

Endrew F., 2017 WL 1066260, at *11. As you read the cases below, consider whether *Endrew F.* effectively affirmed the decisions and the principles for which they stand.

Timothy W. v. Rochester, N.H., Sch. Dist.

875 F.2d 954 (1st Cir. 1989),
cert. denied, 493 U.S. 983 (1989)

Bownes, Circuit Judge.

Plaintiff-appellant Timothy W. appeals an order of the district court which held that under the Education for All Handicapped Children Act, a handicapped child is not eligible for special education if he cannot benefit from that education, and that Timothy W., a severely retarded and multiply handicapped child was not eligible under that standard. We reverse.

I. BACKGROUND

Timothy W. was born two months prematurely on December 8, 1975 with severe respiratory problems, and shortly thereafter experienced an intracranial hemorrhage, subdural effusions, seizures, hydrocephalus, and meningitis. As a result, Timothy is multiply handicapped and profoundly mentally retarded. He suffers from complex developmental disabilities, spastic quadriplegia, cerebral palsy, seizure disorder and cortical blindness. His mother attempted to obtain appropriate services for him, and while he did receive some services from the Rochester Child Development Center, he did not receive any educational program from the Rochester School District when he became of school age.

On February 19, 1980, the Rochester School District convened a meeting to decide if Timothy was considered educationally handicapped under the state and federal statutes, thereby entitling him to special education and related services. The school district heard testimony from Dr. Robert Mackey, Timothy's pediatrician and Medical Consultant for SSI (Supplemental Security Income Program), to the effect that Timothy was severely handicapped. Dr. Mackey recommended the establishment of an educational program for Timothy, which emphasized physical therapy and stimulation. Reports by Susan Curtis, M.S., and Mary Bamford, O.T.R., an occupational therapist, also recommended an educational program consisting of occupational therapy and increasing Timothy's responses to his environment. Testimony of Timothy's mother indicated that he responded to sounds. Carrie Foss, director of the Rochester Child Development Center, testified that Timothy localized sound, responded to his name, and responded to his mother. On the other hand, Dr. Alan Rozycki, a pediatrician at the Hitchcock Medical Center, reported that Timothy had no educational potential, and Dr. Patricia Andrews, a developmental pediatrician, stated that hydrocephalus had destroyed part of Timothy's brain. The school district adjourned without making a finding. In a meeting on March 7, 1980, the school district decided that Timothy was not educationally handicapped—that since his handicap was so severe he was not "capable of benefitting" from an education, and therefore was not entitled to one. During 1981 and 1982, the school district did not provide Timothy with any educational program.

. . . .

In response to a letter from Timothy's attorney, on January 17, 1984, the school district's placement team met. In addition to the previously listed reports, it had available a report from Lynn Miller, an expert in physical therapy for handicapped children, who had seen Timothy seven times, and concluded that he responded to motion and handling and enjoyed loud music. She determined that his educational needs included postural drainage, motion exercises, sensory stimulation, positioning, and stimulation of head control. The placement team recommended that Timothy be placed at the Child Development Center so that he could be provided with a special education program. The Rochester School Board, however, refused to authorize the placement team's recommendation to provide educational services for Timothy, contending that it still needed more information. The school district's request to have Timothy be given a neurological evaluation, including a CAT Scan, was refused by his mother.

. . . .

On November 17, 1984, Timothy filed a complaint in the United States District Court . . . alleging that his rights under the Education for All Handicapped Children Act, the corresponding New Hampshire state law, § 504 of the Rehabilitation Act of 1973, and the equal protection and due process clauses of the United States and New Hampshire Constitutions, had been violated by the Rochester School District. The complaint sought preliminary and permanent injunctions directing the school district to provide him with special education . . . .

. . . .

In September, 1986, Timothy again requested a special education program. In October, 1986, the school district continued to refuse to provide him with such a program, claiming it still needed more information. . . .

. . . .

On July 15, 1988, the district court rendered its opinion .... It first ruled that "under EAHCA [the Education for All Handicapped Children Act], an initial determination as to the child's ability to benefit from special education, must be made in order for a handicapped child to qualify for education under the Act." .... The court ... found that "Timothy W. is not capable of benefitting from special education.... As a result, the defendant [school district] is not obligated to provide special education .... "

....

II. THE LANGUAGE OF THE ACT

A. The Plain Meaning of the Act Mandates a Public Education for All Handicapped Children

The Education for All Handicapped Children Act, [hereinafter the Act], 20 U.S.C. §§ 1400 et seq., was enacted in 1975 to ensure that handicapped children receive an education which is appropriate to their unique needs. In assessing the plain meaning of the Act, we first look to its title: The Education for *All* Handicapped Children Act. (Emphasis added). The Congressional Findings section of the Act states that there were eight million handicapped children, that more than half of them did not receive appropriate educational services, and that one million were excluded entirely from the public school system. 20 U.S.C § 1400(b)(1), (3) and (4). Given these grim statistics, Congress concluded that "State and local educational agencies have a responsibility to provide education for *all* handicapped children...." 20 U.S.C. § 1400(b)(8) (emphasis added). In directly addressing the educability of handicapped children, Congress found that "developments in the training of teachers and in diagnostic and instructional procedures and methods have advanced to the point that, given appropriate funding, State and local educational agencies *can and will* provide effective special education and related services to meet the needs of handicapped children." 20 U.S.C. § 1400(b)(7) (emphasis added). The Act's stated purpose was "to assure that *all* handicapped children have available to them ... a free appropriate public education which emphasizes special education and related services designed to meet their unique needs, ... [and] to assist states and localities to provide for the education of *all* handicapped children ..." 20 U.S.C. § 1400(c) (emphasis added).

The Act's mandatory provisions require that for a state to qualify for financial assistance, it must have "in effect a policy that assures *all* handicapped children the right to a free appropriate education." 20 U.S.C. § 1412(1) (emphasis added). The state must "set forth in detail the policies and procedures which the State will undertake ... to assure that—there is established a goal of providing full educational opportunity to *all* handicapped children ..., [and that] a free appropriate public education will be available for *all* handicapped children between the ages of three and eighteen ... not later than September 1, 1978, and for *all* handicapped children between the ages of three and twenty-one ... not later than September 1, 1980...." 20 U.S.C. § 1412(2)(A) and (B) (emphasis added). The state must also assure that "*all* children residing in the State who are handicapped, *regardless of the severity of their handicap*, and who are in need of special education and related services are identified, located, and evaluated . . . ." 20 U.S.C. § 1412(2)(C) (emphasis added). *See also* 20 U.S.C. § 1414(a)(1)(A). The Act further requires a state to:

> *establish[ ] priorities* for providing a free appropriate public education to *all* handicapped children, . . . first with respect to handicapped children who are not receiving an education, and second *with respect to handicapped children, within each disability, with the most severe handicaps* who are receiving an inadequate education. . . .

20 U.S.C. § 1412(3) (emphasis added). *See also* 20 U.S.C. § 1414(a)(1)(C). Thus, not only are severely handicapped children not excluded from the Act, but the most severely handicapped are actually given *priority* under the Act.

In addition, the duties of the Secretary are listed as including the evaluation of "the effectiveness of State efforts to assure the free appropriate public education of *all* handicapped children" and transmitting "a report on the progress being made toward the provision of free appropriate public education to *all* handicapped children." 20 U.S.C. § 1418(a) and (c) (emphasis added). In its discussion of reallocation of funds, the Act states that "whenever a State educational agency determines that a local educational agency is adequately providing a free appropriate public education to *all* handicapped children . . . [it] may reallocate funds . . ." 20 U.S.C. § 1414(e) (emphasis added).

The language of the Act could not be more unequivocal. The statute is permeated with the words "*all* handicapped children" whenever it refers to the target population. It never speaks of any exceptions for severely handicapped children. Indeed, as indicated *supra*, the Act gives priority to the most severely handicapped. Nor is there any language whatsoever which requires as a prerequisite to being covered by the Act, that a handicapped child must demonstrate that he or she will "benefit" from the educational program. Rather, the Act speaks of the *state's* responsibility to design a special education and related services program that will meet the unique "needs" of all handicapped children. The language of the Act in its entirety makes clear that a "zero-reject" policy is at the core of the Act, and that no child, regardless of the severity of his or her handicap, is to ever again be subjected to the deplorable state of affairs which existed at the time of the Act's passage, in which millions of handicapped children received inadequate education or none at all. In summary, the Act mandates an appropriate public education for all handicapped children, regardless of the level of achievement that such children might attain.

B. Timothy W.: A Handicapped Child Entitled to An Appropriate Education

Given that the Act's language mandates that all handicapped children are entitled to a free appropriate education, we must next inquire if Timothy W. is a handicapped child, and if he is, what constitutes an appropriate education to meet his unique needs.

(1) *handicapped children*:

The implementing regulations define handicapped children as "being mentally retarded, hard of hearing, deaf, speech impaired, visually handicapped, seriously emotionally disturbed, orthopedically impaired, other health impaired, deaf-blind, multi-handicapped, or as having specific learning disabilities, who because of those impairments need special education and related services." 34 C.F.R. § 300.5. *See also* 20 U.S.C. § 1401(1). "Mentally retarded" is described as "significantly subaverage general intellectual functioning existing concurrently with deficits in adaptive behavior and manifested during the developmental period, which adversely affects a child's educational performance." 34 C.F.R. § 300.5(b)(4). "Multi-handicapped" is defined as "concomitant impairments (such as mentally retarded-blind, mentally retarded-orthopedically impaired, etc.), the combination of which causes such severe educational problems that they cannot be accommodated in special education programs solely for one of the impairments." 34 C.F.R. § 300.5(b)(5). "Orthopedically impaired" means "a severe orthopedic impairment which adversely affects a child's educational performance" and "includes impairments caused by congenital anomaly, ... disease, ... [and] from other causes (e.g. cerebral palsy, ...)." 34 C.F.R. § 300.5(b)(6). "Specific learning disability" includes such conditions as "perceptual handicaps, brain injury, minimal brain disfunction." 34 C.F.R. § 300.5(b)(9).

There is no question that Timothy W. fits within the Act's definition of a handicapped child: he is multiply handicapped and profoundly mentally retarded. He has been described as suffering from severe spasticity, cerebral palsy, brain damage, joint contractures, cortical blindness, is not ambulatory, and is quadriplegic.

(2) *appropriate public education*:

The Act and the implementing regulations define a "free appropriate public education" to mean "special education and related services which are provided at public expense ... [and] are provided in conformity with an individualized education program." 34 C.F.R. § 300.4; 20 U.S.C. § 1401(a)(18).

(a) "*Special education*" means "specially designed instruction, at no cost to the parent, to meet the unique needs of a handicapped child, including classroom instruction, instruction in *physical education*, home instruction, and instruction in hospitals and institutions." 34 C.F.R. § 300.14(a)(1); 20 U.S.C. § 1401(a)(16) (emphasis added). It is of significance that the Act explicitly provides for education of children who are so severely handicapped as to require hospitalization or institutionalization. Timothy W.'s handicaps do not require such extreme measures, as he can be educated at home. The Act goes on to define "physical education" as the "development of: physical and motor fitness; fundamental motor skills and patterns ... [and] includes special physical education, adapted physical education, movement education, and motor development." 34 C.F.R. § 300.14(b)(2). Thus, the Act's concept of special education is broad, encompassing not only traditional cognitive skills, but basic functional skills as well.

. . . .

The record shows that Timothy W. is a severely handicapped and profoundly retarded child in need of special education and related services. Much of the expert testimony was to the effect that he is aware of his surrounding environment, makes or attempts to make purposeful movements, responds to tactile stimulation, responds to his mother's voice and touch, recognizes familiar voices, responds to noises, and parts his lips when spoon fed. The record contains testimony that Timothy W.'s needs include sensory stimulation, physical therapy, improved head control, socialization, consistency in responding to sound sources, and partial participation in eating. The educational consultants who drafted Timothy's individualized education program recommended that Timothy's special education program should include goals and objectives in the areas of motor control, communication, socialization, daily living skills, and recreation. The special education and related services that have been recommended to meet Timothy W.'s needs fit well within the statutory and regulatory definitions of the Act.

We conclude that the Act's language dictates the holding that Timothy W. is a handicapped child who is in need of special education and related services because of his handicaps. He must, therefore, according to the Act, be provided with such an educational program. There is nothing in the Act's language which even remotely supports the district court's conclusion that "under [the Act], an initial determination as to a child's ability to benefit from special education, must be made in order for a handicapped child to qualify for education under the Act." The language of the Act is directly to the contrary: a school district has a duty to provide an educational program for every handicapped child in the district, regardless of the severity of the handicap.

III. LEGISLATIVE HISTORY

. . . .

B. Priority For The Most Severely Handicapped

Not only did Congress intend that all handicapped children be educated, it expressly indicated its intent that the most severely handicapped be given priority. This resolve was reiterated over and over again in the floor debates and congressional reports, as well as in the final legislation.

The principal author, Senator Williams, stated that the bill "assures that handicapped children in the greatest need will be given *priority* by requiring that services be provided first to those children not receiving an education; and second, *to those children with the most severe handicaps* receiving an inadequate education." 121 Cong. Rec. S37413 (1975) (emphasis added).

The Senate Committee's report stated:

> [T]he Committee has provided that States shall provide second priority . . . to handicapped children with the most severe handicaps . . . . It is the intent of the Committee that States follow this priority by providing services to handicapped children who, within each disability group, . . . have the most

> severe handicaps. *Priority must be given to multi-handicapped children who are the most severely disabled* . . . .

Senate Report at 22 (1975), 1975 U.S. Code Cong. & Admin. News, 1446. *See also id.* at 18, 46. The House report also included such priorities: "In conformance with the overall goal of ending exclusion . . . [the bill gives] first priority to children 'unserved' [and] second priority to severely handicapped children." House Report at 12 (1975).

This priority reflected congressional acceptance of the thesis that early educational intervention was very important for severely handicapped children.

If the order of the district court denying Timothy W. the benefits of the Act were to be implemented, he would be classified by the Act as in even greater need for receiving educational services than a severely multi-handicapped child receiving inadequate education. He would be in the *highest priority*—as a child who was not receiving any education at all.

C. Guarantees of Educational Benefit Are Not A Requirement For Child Eligibility

In mandating a public education for all handicapped children, Congress explicitly faced the issue of the possibility of the non-educability of the most severely handicapped. The Senate Report stated, "The Committee recognizes that in many instances the process of providing special education and related services to handicapped children is *not guaranteed to produce any particular outcome*." Senate Report at 11 (1975), 1975 U.S. Code Cong. & Admin. News, 1435 (emphasis added). The report continued: "The Committee has deleted the language of the bill as introduced which required objective criteria and evaluation procedures by which to assure that the short term instructional goals were met." *Id.* at 12, 1975 U.S. Code Cong. & Admin. News, 1436.

Thus, the district court's major holding, that proof of an educational benefit is a prerequisite before a handicapped child is entitled to a public education, is specifically belied, not only by the statutory language, but by the legislative history as well. We have not found in the Act's voluminous legislative history, nor has the school district directed our attention to, a single affirmative averment to support a benefit/eligibility requirement. But there is explicit evidence of a contrary congressional intent, that *no* guarantee of any particular educational outcome is required for a child to be eligible for public education.

We sum up. In the more than three years of legislative history leading to passage of the 1975 Act, covering House and Senate floor debates, hearings, and Congressional reports, the Congressional intention is unequivocal: Public education is to be provided to all handicapped children, unconditionally and without exception. It encompasses a universal right, and is not predicated upon any type of guarantees that the child will benefit from the special education and services before he or she is considered eligible to receive such education. Congress explicitly recognized the particular plight and special needs of the severely handicapped, and rather than excluding them from the Act's coverage, gave them priority status. The district court's holding is directly contradicted by the Act's legislative history, as well as the statutory language.

. . . .

IV. CASE LAW

. . . .

D. Proof of Benefit is Not Required

The district court relied heavily on . . . *Rowley* in concluding that as a matter of law a child is not entitled to a public education unless he or she can benefit from it. The district court, however, has misconstrued *Rowley*. In that case, the Supreme Court held that a deaf child, who was an above average student and was advancing from grade to grade in a regular public school classroom, and who was already receiving substantial specialized instruction and related services, was not entitled, in addition, to a full time sign-language interpreter, because she was already benefitting from the special education and services she was receiving. The Court held that the school district was not required to *maximize* her educational achievement. It stated, "if personalized instruction is being provided with sufficient supportive services to permit the child to benefit from the instruction . . . the child is receiving a 'free appropriate public education' as defined by the Act," *id.* at 189, . . . and that "certainly the language of the statute contains no requirement . . . that States maximize the potential of handicapped children." *Id.* at 189 . . . .

Rowley focused on the *level* of services and the quality of programs that a *state* must provide, not the criteria for *access* to those programs. The Court's use of "benefit" in *Rowley* was a substantive limitation placed on the state's choice of an educational program; it was not a license for the state to exclude certain handicapped children. In ruling that a state was not required to provide the maximum benefit possible, the Court was *not* saying that there must be proof that a child will benefit before the state is obligated to provide any education at all. Indeed, the Court in *Rowley* explicitly acknowledged Congress' intent to ensure public education to all handicapped children without regard to the level of achievement that they might attain.

> Congress expressly 'recognize[d] that in many instances the process of providing special education and related services to handicapped children *is not guaranteed to produce any particular outcome.*' S.Rep., at 11 [1975 U.S.Code Cong. & Admin.News at 1435]. Thus, the *intent of the Act was more to open the door of public education to handicapped children on appropriate terms than to guarantee any particular level of education once inside.*

Id. at 192 . . . (emphasis added).

Rowley simply does not lend support to the district court's finding of a benefit/eligibility standard in the Act. As the Court explained, while the Act does not require a school to maximize a child's potential for learning, it does provide a "basic floor of opportunity" for the handicapped, consisting of "*access* to specialized instruction and related services." *Id.* at 201 . . . (emphasis added). Nowhere does the Court imply that such a "floor" contains a trap door for the severely handicapped. Indeed, *Rowley* explicitly states: "[t]he Act requires special educational services for children 'regardless of the severity of their handicap,'" *id.* at 181 n. 5 . . . and "[t]he Act requires participating States to educate a wide spectrum of handicapped children, from the marginally hearing-impaired to the profoundly retarded and palsied." *Id.* at 202 . . . . This is a far cry from a requirement of proof that educational benefit *will definitely result*, before a child is entitled to receive that education.

. . . .

V. CONCLUSION

The statutory language of the Act, its legislative history, and the case law construing it, mandate that all handicapped children, regardless of the severity of their handicap, are entitled to a public education. The district court erred in requiring a benefit/eligibility test as a prerequisite to implicating the Act. School districts cannot avoid the provisions of the Act by returning to the practices that were widespread prior to the Act's passage, and which indeed were the impetus for the Act's passage, of unilaterally excluding certain handicapped children from a public education on the ground that they are uneducable.

The law explicitly recognizes that education for the severely handicapped is to be broadly defined, to include not only traditional academic skills, but also basic functional life skills, and that educational methodologies in these areas are not static, but are constantly evolving and improving. It is the school district's responsibility to avail itself of these new approaches in providing an education program geared to each child's individual needs. The only question for the school district to determine, in conjunction with the child's parents, is what constitutes an appropriate individualized education program (IEP) for the handicapped child. We emphasize that the phrase "appropriate individualized education program" cannot be interpreted, as the school district has done, to mean "no educational program."

. . . .

The judgment of the district court is reversed, judgment shall issue for Timothy W. The case is remanded to the district court which shall retain jurisdiction until a suitable individualized education program (IEP) for Timothy W. is effectuated by the school district. . . .

. . . .

Polk v. Cent. Susquehanna Intermediate Unit 16

853 F.2d 171 (3d Cir. 1988)
cert. denied, 488 U.S. 1030 (1988)

Becker, Circuit Judge.

This appeal requires that we examine the contours of the "free appropriate public education" requirement of the Education of the Handicapped Act, as amended, 20 U.S.C. §§ 1401–1461 (1982) (EHA) as it touches on the delivery of physical therapy, which is a "related service" under the EHA. Ronald and Cindy Polk are parents of Christopher Polk, a child with severe mental and physical impairments. They claim that defendants, the local school district and the larger administrative Intermediate Unit (which oversees special education for students in a five-county area) violated the EHA because they failed to provide Christopher with an adequate program of special education. Specifically, plaintiffs contend that defendants' failure to provide direct "hands-on" physical therapy from a licensed physical therapist once a week has hindered Christopher's progress in meeting his educational goals.

The district court granted summary judgment in favor of defendants. The court held that because Christopher derived "*some* educational benefit" from his educational program, the requirements of the EHA, as interpreted by the Supreme Court in . . . *Rowley* have been met.

We will reverse the district court's grant of summary judgment for two reasons. First, we discern a genuine issue of material fact as to whether the defendants, in violation of the EHA procedural requirement for *individualized* educational programs, have refused, as a blanket rule, to consider providing handicapped students with direct physical therapy from a licensed physical therapist. Second, we conclude that the district court applied the wrong standard in evaluating the appropriateness of the child's education. Although the district court relied upon language from a recent Supreme Court case, it took that language out of context and applied it beyond the narrow holding of the Supreme Court's opinion. More specifically, we believe that the district court erred in evaluating this severely handicapped child's educational program by a standard under which even trivial advancement satisfied the substantive provisions of the EHA's guarantee of a free and appropriate education. There is evidence in the record that would support a finding that the program prescribed for Christopher afforded no more than trivial progress. We will therefore reverse and remand for further proceedings consistent with this opinion.

I. STATUTORY BACKGROUND

The EHA requires that Pennsylvania, as a recipient of federal assistance thereunder, ensure that each disabled student in the state receive a "free appropriate public education." 20 U.S.C. § 1412(1) (1982). The EHA mandates that participating states provide such education for all children "regardless of the severity of their handicap." 20 U.S.C. § 1412(2)(C) (1982). In pertinent part, the Act defines a free appropriate public education as:

> special education and related services which (A) have been provided at public expense, under public supervision and direction, and without charge, ... and (D) are provided in conformity with the individualized education program required under section 1414(a)(5) of this title.

20 U.S.C. § 1401(18) (1982). The term "related services" includes "physical and occupational therapy . . . as may be required to assist a handicapped child to benefit from special education. 20 U.S.C.§ 1401(17) (1982). Such special education and related

services must be tailored to the unique needs of the handicapped child by means of an Individualized Education Program (IEP). 20 U.S.C.§ 1401(16).

. . . .

II. FACTS & PROCEDURAL HISTORY

Christopher Polk is severely developmentally disabled. At the age of seven months he contracted encephalopathy, a disease of the brain similar to cerebral palsy. He is also mentally retarded. Although Christopher is fourteen years old, he has the functional and mental capacity of a toddler. All parties agree that he requires "related services" in order to learn. He receives special education from defendants, the Central Susquehanna Intermediate Unit #16 (the IU) and Central Columbia Area School District (the school district). Placed in a class for the mentally handicapped, Christopher has a full-time personal classroom aide. His education consists of learning basic life skills such as feeding himself, dressing himself, and using the toilet. He has mastered sitting and kneeling, is learning to stand independently, and is showing some potential for ambulation. Christopher is working on basic concepts such as "behind," "in," "on," and "under," and the identification of shapes, coins, and colors. Although he is cooperative, Christopher finds such learning difficult because he has a short attention span.

Although the record is not clear on this point, until 1980, the defendants apparently provided Christopher with direct physical therapy from a licensed physical therapist. Since that time, however, under a newer, so-called consultative model, Christopher no longer receives direct physical therapy from a physical therapist. Instead, a physical therapist (one of two hired by the IU) comes once a month to train Christopher's teacher in how to integrate physical therapy with Christopher's education. Although the therapist may lay hands on Christopher in demonstrating to the teacher the correct approach, he or she does not provide any therapy to Christopher directly, but uses such interaction to teach the teacher. Plaintiffs do not object to the consultative method per se, but argue that, to meet Christopher's individual needs, the consultative method must be supplemented by direct ("hands on") physical therapy.

In support of this position, plaintiffs adduced evidence that direct physical therapy from a licensed physical therapist has significantly expanded Christopher's physical capacities. In the summer of 1985, Christopher received two weeks of intensive physical therapy from a licensed physical therapist at Shriner's Hospital in Philadelphia. According to Christopher's parents, this brief treatment produced dramatic improvements in Christopher's physical capabilities. A doctor at Shriner's prescribed that Christopher receive at least one hour a week of direct physical therapy. Because the defendants were unwilling to provide direct physical therapy as part of Christopher's special education program, the Polks hired a licensed physical therapist, Nancy Brown, to work with Christopher at home. At the time of the hearing, she was seeing Christopher twice a week.

Plaintiffs acknowledge that the school program has benefited Christopher to some degree, but argue that his educational program is not appropriate because it is not individually tailored to his specific needs, as the EHA requires. Moreover, throughout all of the administrative and judicial proceedings that we now describe, plaintiffs have maintained that to comply with the EHA the defendants must provide, as part of Christopher's "free appropriate public education," one session a week with a licensed physical therapist.

Plaintiffs first challenged Christopher's IEP before a Commonwealth of Pennsylvania Department of Education Hearing Officer. At that hearing and in later depositions, the administrator of the IU, Christopher's teachers, the IU's physical therapy consultant, Christopher's current private physical therapist, and his therapist from Shriner's all testified concerning Christopher's capabilities and educational needs. The Hearing Officer found that Christopher was benefiting from his education, and that his education was appropriate. This finding was affirmed by the Pennsylvania Secretary of Education.

After exhausting administrative remedies to their dissatisfaction, the Polks brought suit in the district court for the Middle District of Pennsylvania. . . . [T]he district court granted summary judgment for the defendants. Relying on the Supreme Court's decision in *Rowley,* the court held that the provisions of EHA had been met because Christopher had received *some* benefit from his education. This appeal followed.

Plaintiffs present two arguments on appeal. First, they submit that the defendants violated EHA's procedural requirements because Christopher's program is not truly individualized. Plaintiffs rely, in this regard, on the defendants' failure to provide direct ("hands on") physical therapy from a licensed physical therapist to *any* of the children in the intermediate unit (a fact they learned during Christopher's due process hearing before the state examiner). This failure, they contend, is evidence that the defendants have an inflexible rule prohibiting direct therapy and that such a rigid rule conflicts with the EHA's mandate of providing *individualized* education. Plaintiffs argue that genuine questions of material fact exist as to the defendants' willingness to provide direct physical therapy under any circumstances, and that such disputes preclude summary judgment.

Second, plaintiffs assert that Christopher's education is inadequate to meet his unique needs. They claim that the district court found Christopher's education appropriate only because it applied an erroneous legal standard in judging the educational benefit of Christopher's program.

III. ROLE OF PHYSICAL THERAPY IN PROVIDING A FREE APPROPRIATE PUBLIC EDUCATION UNDER THE EHA

For some handicapped children, the related services provided by the EHA serve as important facilitators of classroom learning. In *Irving Independent School District v. Tatro,* 468 U.S. 883 . . . (1984), the Supreme Court unanimously held that the EHA required the provision of in-school intermittent catheterization services to a child with spina bifida so that she could attend a regular public school class. The Court distinguished between the types of related services contemplated by the EHA and the medical care that requires a doctor. In so doing, the Court explicitly acknowledged the importance of related services to the scheme of the EHA: "Congress plainly required schools to hire various specially trained personnel to help handicapped children, such as 'trained occupational therapists.'" *Id.* at 893.

For children like Christopher with severe disabilities, related services serve a dual purpose. First, because these children have extensive physical difficulties that often interfere with development in other areas, physical therapy is an essential prerequisite to education. For example, development of motor abilities is often the first step in overall educational development. As we explained in *Battle v. Pennsylvania*, 629 F.2d 269, 275 (3d Cir. 1980), in discussing children with severe emotional disturbances:

> Where basic self-help and social skills such as toilet training, dressing, feeding and communication are lacking, formal education begins at that point. If the child masters these fundamentals, the education moves on to more difficult but still very basic language, social and arithmetic skills, such as counting, making change, and identifying simple words.

Id. at 275.

Second, the physical therapy itself may form the core of a severely disabled child's special education. This court has recognized that "[t]he educational program of a handicapped child, particularly a severely and profoundly handicapped child . . . is very different from that of a non-handicapped child. The program may consist largely of 'related services' such as physical, occupational, or speech therapy." *DeLeon v. Susquehanna Community School Dist.*, 747 F.2d 149, 153 (3d Cir.1984). In Christopher's case, physical therapy is not merely a conduit to his education, but constitutes, in and of itself, a major portion of his special education, teaching him basic skills such as toileting, feeding, ambulation, etc.

. . . .

V. PLAINTIFFS' SUBSTANTIVE CLAIM (THAT THE COURT MISAPPLIED THE LEGAL STANDARD FOR EVALUATING APPROPRIATE EDUCATION)

. . . .

B. *EHA Requires More than a De Minimis* Benefit

We hold that the EHA calls for more than a trivial educational benefit. That holding rests on the Act and its legislative history as well as interpretation of *Rowley.*

1.

The opinion of the district court, anchored to the "some benefit" language of *Rowley*, 458 U.S. at 200 . . . , explained its holding as follows:

> The fact that Christopher would advance more quickly with intensive therapy rather than the therapy he now receives does not make the School District's program for Christopher defective. Programs need only render some

> benefit; they need not maximize potential. . . . The Supreme Court has determined that the Act is primarily a procedural statute and does not impose a substantive duty on the state to provide a student with other than *some* educational benefits. Increased muscle tone may well fall outside of the scope of the requirement that Christopher receive some educational benefits from the program in which he is enrolled.

Plaintiffs argue on appeal that the district court applied the wrong standard in measuring the educational benefit of Christopher's program and that the case should be remanded for further proceedings consistent with the correct standard, one that requires more than a *de minimis* benefit. Defendants rejoin that *Rowley* 's announcement of a "some benefit" test precludes judicial inquiry into the substantive education conferred by the Act, so long as the handicapped child receives any benefit at all. Noting that Christopher's parents acknowledge that he derives some benefit from his education, defendants submit that the inquiry is over and that the district court's summary judgment must be affirmed.

. . . .

2.

Because *Rowley* is a narrow decision, our decision must perforce also be informed by the text of the EHA and the legislative history of the 1975 amendments. Accordingly, we turn to a discussion thereof. Our interpretation of "educational benefit" is informed by the text of the EHA and by the legislative history concerning the passage of the 1975 amendments. The self-defined purpose of the EHA is to provide "*full* educational opportunity to all handicapped children." 20 U.S.C. § 1412(2)(A) (emphasis added). Similarly, the Senate Report on the 1975 amendments defined related services as "transportation, developmental, corrective, and supportive services (specifically including at least speech pathology and audiology, psychological services, counseling services, physical and occupational therapy, and recreation) necessary for a handicapped child to *fully benefit* from special education." Sen. R. No. 168, 94th Cong., 1st Sess. at 42 (emphasis added). The House Report echoes this language, citing the EHA's "goal of providing each handicapped child with a free, *full*, public education." H.Rep.No. 332, 94th Cong. at 11 (1975) (emphasis added). Although the Supreme Court has instructed that Congress did not intend to provide optimal benefit, the Act's use of the phrase "full educational opportunity" and the EHA's legislative history indicate an intent to afford more than a trivial amount of educational benefit.

. . . .

Furthermore, we observe, as did the majority in *Rowley*, that a key concern of and primary justification for the EHA lay in the important goal of fostering self-sufficiency in handicapped children. *See* H.Rep.No. 332, 94th Cong., 1st Sess. at 11 (1975) ("taxpayers will spend many billions of dollars over the lifetime of these handicapped individuals simply to maintain such persons as dependents on welfare and often in institutions"); *Rowley*, 458 U.S. at 201 n. 23 . . . (quoting extensively from the legislative history of the EHA concerning self-sufficiency). The EHA's sponsors stressed the importance of teaching skills that would foster personal independence for two reasons. First, they advocated dignity for handicapped children. Second, they stressed the long-term financial savings of early education and assistance for handicapped children. A chief selling point of the Act was that although it is penny dear, it is poundwise—the expensive individualized assistance early in life, geared toward teaching basic life skills and self-sufficiency, eventually redounds to the benefit of the public fisc as these children grow to become productive citizens. 121 Cong. Rec. 19492 (1975) (remarks of Senator Williams); *id.* at 19505 (remarks of Senator Beall).

Implicit in the legislative history's emphasis on self-sufficiency is the notion that states must provide some sort of meaningful education—more than mere access to the schoolhouse door. We acknowledge that self-sufficiency cannot serve as a substantive standard by which to measure the appropriateness of a child's education under the Act. Indeed, Christopher Polk is not likely ever to attain this coveted status, no matter how excellent his educational program. Instead, we infer that the emphasis on self-sufficiency indicates in some respect the quantum of benefits the legislators anticipated: they must have envisioned that significant learning would transpire in the special education classroom—enough so that citizens who would otherwise become burdens on the state would be transformed into productive members of society. Therefore, the heavy emphasis in the legislative history on self-sufficiency as one goal of education, where possible, suggests that the "benefit" conferred by the EHA and interpreted by *Rowley* must be more than *de minimis.*

We believe that the teaching of *Rowley* is not to the contrary. As discussed above, the *Rowley* Court described the education that must be provided under the EHA as "meaningful." The use of the term "meaningful" indicates that the Court expected more than *de minimis* benefit. We note in this regard that the facts of *Rowley* clearly indicate that the "benefit" Amy was receiving from her educational program was substantial, and that "some benefit," in the case of Amy, meant a great deal more than a negligible amount.

....

4.

To summarize, in our view, the danger of the district court's formulation is that under its reading of *Rowley* the conferral of any benefit, no matter how small, could qualify as "appropriate education" under the EHA. Under the district court's approach, carried to its logical extreme, Christopher Polk would be entitled to no physical therapy because his occupational therapy offers him "some benefit." We do not believe that such a formulation reflects congressional intent in light of the importance of related services (particularly physical therapy) in the statutory and regulatory scheme. Just as Congress did not write a blank check, neither did it anticipate that states would engage in the idle gesture of providing special education designed to confer only trivial benefit. Put differently, and using *Rowley's* own terminology, we hold that Congress intended to afford children with special needs an education that would confer meaningful benefit.

We further conclude that *Rowley*, although it prescribes restraint and warns that Congress did not intend the Act to maximize a child's potential, does not militate against the standard we have announced. Because the test employed by the district court ostensibly could have allowed only a *de minimis* benefit, we must remand in light of our interpretation. Finally, we do not read the Supreme Court's salutary warnings against interference with educational methodology as an invitation to abdicate our obligation to enforce the statutory provisions that ensure a free and appropriate education to Christopher.

Obviously, this court is in no position to determine the factual question whether the treatment the defendants currently provide for Christopher is appropriate. We are, however, obligated to correct errors of law on appeal, and we hold that the district court applied the wrong standard in granting summary judgment for defendants when it allowed for the possibility of only *de minimis* benefit.

C. *Under the Correct Standard Must Summary Judgment Nevertheless be Affirmed?*

Although defendants acknowledge that direct hands-on therapy would be beneficial to Christopher, they argue it is not essential to the conferral of an appropriate education. Defendants submit that "in view of Christopher's exceptionality, . . . Christopher's progress has been outstanding." The defendants presented testimony from the licensed physical therapist who consults with Christopher's teachers that indicates that he is progressing as quickly as can be expected given his multiple handicaps, and that the consultative model serves his needs.

Plaintiffs, by virtue of the evidence they adduced concerning Christopher's remarkable improvements in a short period of time at Shriner's, have provided at least some indication that his education may be inappropriate. Furthermore, they claim that Christopher has been working on some of the same skills for years, and that even accounting for his exceptionalities, his progress has been *de minimis*. For instance, there is a factual dispute among the parties concerning Christopher's progress in self-dressing and self-feeding. Plaintiffs contend that significant improvements in these areas attributable to the program at Shriner's and the direct physical therapy Christopher receives at home contrast markedly with the trivial advancement in fine and gross motor control that Christopher experienced as a result of seven years of public education under the consultative model.

Two private therapists who worked with Christopher at the Shriner's Hospital in Philadelphia in July 1985 each testified that Christopher needs direct physical and occupational therapy in his school by licensed and trained professionals. As their attorney explained at oral argument, the plaintiffs contend that the physical therapy provided by Christopher's teacher is akin to a sophisticated gym class, where Christopher practices bouncing a ball and other physical activities. They assert that such guidance, though helpful to Christopher, cannot substitute for direct physical therapy by a licensed physical therapist, which involves professional monitoring of discrete muscle behavior and frequent adjustments in response to improvement by the student.

Most important to plaintiffs are their contentions that Christopher cannot improve [his] muscle tone without the assistance of a licensed physical therapist and that the state has ignored whole categories of need. They adduced testimony in support of their assertion that a teacher and a teacher's aide are not qualified to deliver certain essential services and that Christopher's IEP contains goals requiring the direct attention of licensed physical therapists beyond the capacity of the consultative model.

We recognize the difficulty of measuring levels of benefit in severely handicapped children. Obviously, the question whether benefit is *de minimis* must be gauged in relation to the child's potential. However, we believe that the extent of the factual dispute concerning the level of benefit Christopher received from his educational program precludes summary judgment under the standard that we announce today. The judgment of the district court will therefore be reversed and the case remanded for further proceedings consistent with this opinion.

Notes, Comments, and Questions

1. Other lower courts have agreed with *Timothy W.* and *Polk* that children with severe disabilities are entitled to a free appropriate public education. *See* Kruelle v. New Castle Cnty. Sch. Dist., 642 F.2d 687, 693 (3d Cir. 1981) (holding that the IDEA requires a school district to provide education to child with profound mental retardation); Battle v. Pennsylvania, 629 F.2d 269, 274, 280–81 (3d Cir. 1980), *cert. denied*, 452 U.S. 698 (recognizing that the IDEA protects the educational rights of children with profound mental retardation and severe emotional disturbance); Garrity v. Gallen, 522 F. Supp. 171, 215, 226–27 (D.N.H. 1981) (holding that the school district must provide educational services to children with severe disabilities); Gladys J. v. Pearland Indep. Sch. Dist., 520 F. Supp. 869, 879 (S.D. Tex. 1981) (holding that school district must provide an appropriate education to a child with a marginal chance of "acquiring the degree of self-sufficiency necessary to avoid institutionalization ....").

2. Lower courts have also made it clear that for children with severe disabilities, education is to be broadly defined. *See* DeLeon v. Susquehanna Cmty. Sch. Dist., 747 F.2d 149, 153 (3d Cir. 1984) ("The educational program of a handicapped child, particularly a severely and profoundly handicapped child such as Lorin ... may consist largely of 'related services' such as physical, occupational, or speech therapy."); Abrahamson v. Hershman, 701 F.2d 223, 228 (1st Cir. 1983) (stating that for some severely disabled children, "education will not consist of classroom training but rather training in very basic skills."); *Kruelle*, 642 F.2d at 693 (stating "the concept of education is necessarily broad" with respect to children with severe disabilities); Campbell v. Talladega Cnty. Bd. of Educ., 518 F. Supp. 47, 55 (N.D. Ala. 1981) (holding that the educational programs for children with severe disabilities should focus on teaching them "functional" skills in daily living, vocational and recreational activities, and social adjustment).

3. The cost of educating a child with a severe disability is often substantial compared with the costs of educating other children. Should this be a factor in designing an educational program for a child with a severe disability? Should the cost to the school district ever be weighed against the potential benefit to the child?

Section Four
Providing a FAPE to a Child with Average or Above-Average Intelligence

Rowley rejected the argument that the IDEA requires school districts to provide children with disabilities the opportunity to maximize their potential commensurate with the opportunity they provide to typically developing children. Thus, for children like Amy Rowley, who are of average or above-average intelligence, in the general education curriculum, and passing their classes and progressing from grade, *Rowley* did not promise much. Will *Endrew F.* change this? Does the Court's statement that "every child should have the chance to meet challenging objectives," *Endrew F.*, 2017 WL 1066260, at *11, apply to all children with disabilities, as the words suggest, or only to children with severe disabilities, as the context suggests? Consider this question as you read the cases below. How would they have been decided under *Endrew F.*?

Hall v. Vance Cnty. Bd. of Educ.

774 F.2d 629 (4th Cir. 1985)

Harrison L. Winter, Chief Judge:

Defendants . . . appeal from a decision of the district court that they had failed to provide James Hall, IV, with a free appropriate public education (FAPE) prior to January 1982 . . . . Defendants appeal from . . . the finding that they denied James a FAPE . . . .

. . . .

I.

James A. Hall, IV, is a bright sixteen year-old boy of above average intelligence. Yet at age eleven, as he prepared to enter the fifth grade in the Vance County, North Carolina, public schools, he was functionally illiterate, unable to distinguish between the words "ladies" and "gentlemen" on restroom doors, or to go to the store to make small purchases for his mother. James suffers from dyslexia, a severe learning disability that hinders his ability to decipher written symbols. Although there is no cure for dyslexia, a dyslexic child can learn methods of unscrambling words that will enable him to read.

. . . In the fall of . . . [1974, James] began kindergarten in the Vance County public schools. He progressed through kindergarten and first grade, and was promoted to second grade for the 1976–77 school year. During that year the Halls became increasingly aware of James' reading problems and requested that he be evaluated by the school psychologist. Dr. A.B. Laspina conducted this evaluation in May of 1977. His tests revealed that James had a high IQ, but that his reading level was more than a year behind his grade level. The tests did not indicate a perceptual basis for James' problems. Dr. Laspina recommended further evaluation by the school's learning disabilities teacher, reading remediation and special help, and part-time learning disability class placement. He also recommended that the parents employ a private tutor. The Vance County School Board and the school took none of the steps recommended by Dr. Laspina. Instead, the school merely endorsed his recommendation that the Halls employ, at their own expense, a tutor for James. . . .

James did not successfully complete the second grade. He received six failing grades and a "D" for the 1976–77 school year, and he repeated the second grade during the 1977–78 school year. That year his grades were improved, although they revealed continued weakness in reading.

James entered the third grade in the Fall of 1978. His third-grade teacher recognized that he had learning difficulties and recommended further evaluation, to which the Halls consented. An evaluation committee met and identified James as learning disabled. They also drafted an "individualized educational program" ("IEP") to cover the second half of the 1978–79 school year (James' third grade) and all of the 1979–80 school year. The IEP called for James' placement in a regular classroom ninety-five percent of the time, and his placement in a learning disabilities resource room with other learning disabled students the remainder of the time. Apparently the school implemented the IEP by having James attend resource room twice a week for thirty minute periods during the remainder of his third grade, and by increasing the number of sessions to four a week in fourth grade. In January 1979 the school system's placement committee approved the recommended IEP, and Mrs. Hall signed a consent form to James' placement. . . .

Despite institution of the IEP, James continued to receive poor grades, including a failing grade in reading in third grade. He was promoted to the fourth grade, apparently because of a school policy against having a child repeat two grades in succession. James did not improve much in the fourth grade. Moreover, a battery of tests administered to James in December of 1978, before institution of the IEP, and again in May of 1980, after three semesters of the IEP, indicated little overall improvement. Most notably, he still tested at the second grade level for reading, and his reading recognition score had not improved at all. . . . His test scores on other standardized tests given in 1979 and 1980 similarly indicated substantial learning problems. His performance on the California Achievement Test, taken in April of 1980, showed him scoring in the lowest two percent of the nation's fourth-grade students in reading comprehension and the lowest four percent in "total mathematics."

Despite this lack of progress, the school proposed to promote James to the fifth grade and to continue for the 1980–81 school [year] substantially the same IEP as the one that had to date not helped him. The new IEP again called for James to spend ninety-five percent of his time in a regular class and the remaining time, four thirty-minute periods a week, in a special education resource room. In desperation, the Halls decided to enroll James in a local private school, Vance Academy, for the 1980–81 school year. Because Vance Academy was not equipped to teach learning disabled children, James was unable to keep up. He left the school within two months of enrolling.

On the academy's recommendation, the Halls sought a private evaluation of James. In September 1980, the Halls had James tested by Sharon Fox White who diagnosed him as dyslexic. She later stated that in her nine years of experience with learning disabled children she had "seen very few with James' impressive ability and *extremely* poor achievement." A second private evaluation, conducted by Dr. John A. Gorman, confirmed the diagnosis. Dr. Gorman found that James was functionally illiterate and that his reading comprehension was untestable. He also found that James' repeated failure at school had resulted in emotional harm and that he had begun to develop a "school phobia." He recommended residential placement for James, and suggested a number of schools including Oakland School in Boyds Tavern, Virginia. The Halls chose Oakland because it was the closest residential school that accepted learning disabled children....

....

The [school district's] December 1981 evaluation indicated that James had made considerable progress at Oakland. His reading recognition, reading comprehension, and spelling scores had all increased at least one grade level from when he was last tested. Based on this evaluation, the school proposed placement in the Vance County Schools and a new IEP that called for most of James' time to be spent in specialized instruction classes. The Halls opposed this proposal. On January 22, 1982, the case was heard before a local hearing examiner who found the IEP inadequate and in need of modification, but who also found placement in the Vance County public schools appropriate. Upon further administrative review, the State Hearing Review Officer similarly held that the placement was appropriate though the IEP was not. He also held that the Vance County schools had not provided James a FAPE before January 1982, but he stated that he had no authority to award reimbursement for tuition and other costs. Following the decision of the State Hearing Review Officer, the Halls filed this action in the district court.

The district court ruled that the Vance County Board of Education had failed to provide James a FAPE ... at any time prior to January 1982.... Finally, the district court held that the Board of Education would not be able to give James a FAPE during the 1983–84 school year and must pay the costs of James' schooling at Oakland School for that year.

....

III.

....

... The district court ... found ... that the county schools had failed to provide James with an education reasonably calculated to enable him to receive educational benefits. Defendants contend that the district court erred by disregarding *Rowley* 's rule that the EAHCA does not require schools to provide an education that will allow a handicapped child to fulfill his maximum potential. Nowhere, however, does the district court's opinion suggest that it held the defendants to that impermissible standard. Instead, it properly considered the evidence introduced at trial, including two independent evaluations and the results of several standardized tests, in determining that James' education was not reasonably calculated to enable him to receive educational benefits, as required by the Act and *Rowley.*

Rowley recognized that no single substantive standard can describe how much educational benefit is sufficient to satisfy the Act. Instead, the Supreme Court left that matter to the courts for case-by-case determination. In approaching this question, the district court adopted the *Rowley* court's strategy. It considered James' capabilities and intellectual progress and what the school had provided him.

Defendants contend, however, that James' academic progress, as measured by his grade promotions and test scores, evinces educational benefit and requires under *Rowley* that the district court's ruling be overturned. We disagree. Although the *Rowley* Court considered Amy Rowley's promotions in determining that she had been afforded a FAPE, the Court limited its analysis to that one case and recognized that promotions were a fallible measure of educational benefit. The district court did not err in discounting James' promotions in light of the school's policy of social promotion and James' test scores and independent evaluations. Nor was the district court compelled by a showing of minimal improvement on some test results to rule that the school had given James a FAPE. *Rowley* recognized that a FAPE must be tailored to the individual child's capabilities and that while one might demand only minimal results in the case of the most severely handicapped children, such results would be insufficient in the case of other children. Clearly, Congress did not intend that a school system could discharge its duty under the EAHCA by providing a program that produces some minimal academic advancement, no matter how trivial. We do not believe that the district court committed error in determining from the tests taken as a whole and the independent evaluations pronouncing James "functionally illiterate" and "untestable" that the Vance County schools had failed to provide James with a FAPE before January 1982.

. . . .

A.B. v. Lawson

354 F.3d 315 (4th Cir. 2004)

Gregory, Circuit Judge:

Kenneth Lawson, in his capacity as Superintendent of the Anne Arundel County Public Schools ("AACPS"), and the Board of Education of Anne Arundel County appeal from a judgment of the . . . District Court . . . , entered under the Individuals with Disabilities Education Act ("IDEA"), 20 U.S.C. § 1400 *et seq.*, ordering payment of reimbursement to the parent of a learning disabled child for two years' tuition at a private school. The district court concluded that such reimbursement was necessary because AACPS denied AB a free appropriate public education ("FAPE").

... Because, as explained below, AACPS complied with IDEA and formulated an IEP reasonably calculated to provide AB with some educational benefit, we reverse the district court and direct that summary judgment be entered for Appellants. ...

I.

A.

This case involves the application of IDEA, a statute designed to provide free appropriate educational services to millions of children with learning disabilities in the United States. One of Congress' primary purposes in enacting IDEA in 1990 was "to ensure that all children with disabilities have available to them a [FAPE] that emphasizes special education and related services designed to meet their unique needs. ..." 20 U.S.C. § 1400(d)(1)(A). To receive federal funding under IDEA, the state must provide all children with disabilities a FAPE. A FAPE requires the school district to provide instruction that suits the child's needs as well as related services to ensure that the child receives some educational benefit from instruction.

Under the act, the state must provide children with "meaningful access" to public education. *Bd. of Ed. of Hendrick Hudson Cent. Sch. Dist. v. Rowley*, 458 U.S. 176, 192 ... (1982). The FAPE must only be "calculated to confer *some* educational benefit on a disabled child." *MM*, 303 F.3d at 526 (citing *Rowley*, 458 U.S. at 207 ... (emphasis added). The Supreme Court has held that under IDEA Congress intended to provide a satisfactory level of educational opportunity, not the best education that money could buy. *See Rowley*, 458 U.S. at 189. ... The Court noted that "[w]hatever Congress meant by an 'appropriate' education, it is clear that it did not mean a potential-maximizing education." *Id.* at 197 n. 21 ....

....

B.

AB is a student that all parties now agree is learning disabled in the areas of writing and reading, thus he is considered disabled under IDEA. The dispute between AACPS and DB arose because AB was not initially coded as learning disabled, and once coded, DB and her experts disagreed with the IEPs proposed by AACPS.

AB was born in 1990. He attended kindergarten through third grade at Annapolis Area Christian School ("Annapolis Christian") during the school years from 1995–1999. During 1997–1998, because of AB's difficulties with reading, DB brought her son to AACPS for educational and psychological testing. The AACPS test results showed various IQ scores between 93 and 113, and its report noted that AB's full scale IQ placed him in the 58th percentile and that he was in the average range of intellectual ability. On educational tests, AB scored below average for his grade in writing and word recognition, but he scored above his grade level in mathematics. AACPS concluded that the student should be able to "perform academically at a level consistent with same-aged peers."

During the spring of 1998, Annapolis Christian administered multiple achievement tests, finding that while AB was at an advanced level in arithmetic, he had difficulties in written language and reading. The following spring, Annapolis Christian conducted more tests, and AB scored in the average range in reading but scored below his grade level in spelling. His arithmetic performance continued to be above his grade level. At the administrative hearing, DB testified that her son was frustrated at Annapolis Christian and he was "shutting down" and "withdrawing" at the end of the third grade. At the end of the 1998–1999 school year, Annapolis Christian recommended that AB repeat the third grade.

In July 1999, DB had AB evaluated by the Kennedy Krieger Institute ("KKI"). KKI tests results revealed AB's Verbal IQ (WISC-III) was in the high average range, Performance IQ in the superior range, and Full Scale IQ in the high average range. By other testing indicia, however, KKI found that AB's "reading and writing skills [were] poor enough to qualify him as learning disabled."

Though Annapolis Christian recommended that AB repeat third grade, DB withdrew her son from that school and enrolled him in the fourth grade in AACPS at Millersville Elementary School for the 1999–2000 school year. . . . AACPS held an IEP meeting on September 27, 1999. Based on the information presented at the meeting, AACPS recommended that AB receive further evaluations to be completed by November 22, 1999.

On October 5, 1999, AACPS's school psychologist Sabbino Strippoli ("Strippoli") administered the Oral and Written Language Scales (OWLS) to AB, and he found all of AB's scores were within the average range. On October 18, 1999, the IEP Team held another meeting and determined that AB did not have a learning disability. . . .

. . . .

On January 5 and 10, 2000, Dr. Sue Antell conducted . . . [an] independent evaluation. Dr. Antell concluded that AB was "a child of superior intellectual abilities with problems in complex language formulation giving rise to a Disorder of Written Expression, Reading Disabilities with problems in both vocabulary and comprehension." . . . .

On March 22, 2000, the IEP Team reconvened and identified AB as having a "special education disability." . . . . On April 7, 2000, Strippoli prepared a report regarding the IEP Team's interpretation of the various assessment results. . . . At the rescheduled May 3 meeting, the Team presented the draft IEP . . . . The draft IEP found AB had a disability limited to the area of written expression.

On May 15, 2000, Dr. Antell sent AACPS's counsel a letter stating that the proposed IEP was unacceptable. She concluded that a mainstream public school education would not provide AB proper flexibility, but also that "[AB]'s superior intelligence render [sic] it inappropriate to place him in a public school's 'special class' for children with far more severe and pervasive disabilities. Again, the *only available option* appears to be placement in a specialized private school for intelligent children with significant learning disabilities, such as Summit School." At the May 30 IEP meeting, at DB's insistence supported by Dr. Antell and the KKI evaluation, the IEP Team agreed to further consider whether AB was also learning disabled in reading. . . .

. . . .

On August 12, 2000, AACPS administered the Lindamood Auditory Conceptualization (LAC) test to AB. The test showed that AB could read and spell at approximately the third grade level and his "phonemic ability" was not fully developed. On August 15, 2000, DB notified AACPS that she would be placing AB in the Summit School for the 2000–2001 school year at AACPS's expense. On August 23, 2000, AACPS administered the Wechsler Individual Achievement Test to AB. That test found reading difficulties; AB scored approximately two years below his grade level on each of the tests.

AB enrolled in and attended the Summit School for the 2000–01 school year. On August 30, 2000, counsel for AACPS notified DB's counsel that an IEP meeting was scheduled . . . . At the . . . meeting, the IEP Team defined AB as having a learning disability in the area of reading in addition to the already identified disability in written expression. AACPS presented an IEP plan whereby AB would attend 31.25 hours of general (integrated) education per week and various forms of special education each day, amounting to 9.0 hours of special education each week. DB requested time to review the IEP. On October 17, 2000, Dr. Antell wrote AACPS again, contesting the IEP's sufficiency and requesting that it provide AB with (among other things): books on tape, a reader, a note taker, extra time for math assignments, oral presentations of math lessons, a dictation system or similar apparatus and other accommodations.

Again, per DB's request, the IEP meeting was scheduled for November 29, 2000. At the November 29 IEP meeting, the Team considered Dr. Antell's letter as well as a speech/language pathology evaluation from April 2000, which DB presented for the first time. DB additionally requested that AB be placed in a full-day special education program. The IEP Team agreed to review the April 2000 evaluation and discuss it at a follow-up meeting.

On February 8, 2001, DB proposed that an IEP meeting be held on March 14, 2001, and she stated that Dr. Joan McCarthy of the Summit School would attend. At the March 14, 2001 meeting, the IEP Team submitted a revised IEP which called for 10.5 hours of special education. DB again declined to accept the IEP because it did not entail full-time special education. Dissatisfied with AACPS's proposal, DB left AB enrolled at the Summit School and pursued her challenge to the proposed IEP through a due process hearing.

C.

On May 23 and June 6, 2001, an ALJ conducted the due process hearing at AACPS's offices in Annapolis . . . .

. . . .

The ALJ concluded that the IEP was "reasonably calculated" to provide AB educational benefit, citing IDEA's mandate that "to the maximum extent appropriate, children with disabilities be educated with children who are not disabled." In holding that the proposed IEP offered a FAPE, the ALJ credited the testimony of AACPS's experts, finding that the child did not require all-day special education and that the proposed IEP offered the least restrictive means of conferring educational benefit to the child. The judge cited AACPS's expert testimony, which she credited, finding that the Summit School program was "overly restrictive." Thus, the ALJ rejected the views of DB and her experts, who had maintained that AB required an entire school day with special educational services. In so holding, she rejected DB's contention that the child must "be placed in a private school that serves only students with learning disabilities."

In supporting her holding that the IEP offered a FAPE, the ALJ noted her reliance on testimony from Millersville personnel as well as evidence of AB's educational progress as measured by his report card and teacher's comments. In reviewing such data, the ALJ noted that AB's reading ability increased nearly two grade levels while attending Millersville despite the fact that he was not receiving special education. On the basis of such evidence, the ALJ concluded "there is no indication that the Child's needs cannot be met at Millersville Elementary School." The ALJ concluded that under IDEA, "[t]he issue is not whether the Summit School is better, or even appropriate, but whether AACPS has offered . . . an appropriate program for the Child at Millersville Elementary." In denying DB's claim, the ALJ acknowledged that while she appreciated DB's concern that given AB's high IQ, he should have performed at a greater academic level at Millersville and in contrast was "thriving" at the Summit School, "IDEA does not require a program that would maximize a student' [s] potential, but instead simply a program that is appropriate,". . . .

D.

On January 8, 2002, DB filed a complaint in the United States District Court for the District of Maryland, appealing the ALJ's decision . . . . [T]he magistrate judge granted summary judgment for the Bs, holding that AACPS's IEPs did not offer a FAPE. . . .

. . . .

III.

A.

On appeal, AACPS argues that the district court erred in finding a violation of IDEA. AACPS contends that, as the ALJ held, the IEP for the 2000–2001 and 2001–2002 school years was . . . reasonably calculated to offer a FAPE . . . .

B.

. . . . The ALJ found the [IEP] Team crafted an IEP reasonably calculated to provide AB with some educational benefit and that AACPS officials made professional judgments in accord with federal and Maryland regulations. The ALJ correctly noted that the AACPS IEP Team considered a litany of factors concerning AB's educational background, and proposed an IEP that focused on the child's difficulties in reading and writing, providing him with individualized services to improve in those areas. Further, the ALJ found that the proposed IEPs reflected the studied determinations of AACPS's experts that the child did not require intensive special education in a segregated classroom. Finally, the ALJ correctly and explicitly held that under IDEA, the . . . IEP Team was not required to rely on the KKI report and complied with state and federal law.

C.

DB has nonetheless continuously maintained that the proposed IEPs did not offer a FAPE because AB did not make progress in the general educational setting. DB and her experts assert that AB would regress in general education, and that he required full-time special education services. Undergirding all of DB's arguments are her claims that because AB, a child of above-average IQ, was not fulfilling his potential within a general education setting—and, in contrast, allegedly was "thriving" and "getting the help he needs" at the Summit School—AACPS was not in compliance with IDEA. Although, as discussed above, nowhere does IDEA require that a school system "maximize" a student's potential, the district court ignored the findings of the ALJ and adopted DB's contrary reading of the statute.

Whereas the ALJ found that the IEP was formulated to meet AB's educational needs and a general education setting was appropriate because, in part, "the Child made educational progress during the academic year he spent at Millersville, albeit not as great as the Parent had hoped for," the district court consistently reached diametrically opposing conclusions.

Appellees contend, however, that the district court properly discarded the ALJ's factual findings in reversing the administrative body. However, we find the district court repudiated the findings of the ALJ and discarded the expertise of the IEP Team without reason or explanation. . . .

. . . .

First, the district court did not apply the proper standard in determining whether the IEP at Millersville would provide an educational benefit, rather it essentially assessed "whether the IEP would replicate the benefit to [AB] of the [Summit School program], which [the district court found] successful for him." The district court ignored the fact that the ALJ found that AB was obtaining "some educational benefit" at AACPS even when he was receiving *no special education*. Yet the district court did not even bother to refer to the ALJ's findings that AB made progress at Millersville, rather the Magistrate Judge simply accepted—contrary to the findings of fact and weight of the evidence—Dr. McCarthy's testimony that AB "would degenerate in a general educational setting."

. . . .

In "chiefly relying" on Dr. Antell's testimony, the district court adopted DB's preferred reading of what IDEA requires. DB and her experts testified before the ALJ [that] they believed the Summit School environment was "ideal;" AB was "thriving" and "getting the help he needs there;" and "given his high IQ, he should be performing at a much greater academic level than he has done in the past." However, as the ALJ recognized, but the district court ignored, this is *not* what IDEA requires. Indeed, "[t]he issue is not whether the Summit School is better, or even appropriate, but whether AACPS has offered . . . an appropriate program for the Child at Millersville Elementary." As discussed above, IDEA's FAPE standards are far more modest than to require that a child excel or thrive. The requirement is satisfied when the state provides the disabled child with "personalized instruction with sufficient support services to permit the child to benefit educationally from the instruction." *Rowley*, 458 U.S. at 203. . . . In this case, the record shows that AACPS's proposed IEPs offered AB a FAPE.

. . . .

Comments and Questions

It appears that *Hall* would have come out the same under *Endrew F.* James had higher than average intelligence, he was functionally illiterate, and he was making little or no progress. But what about *A.B.*? A.B. also possessed above-average intelligence but he was scoring in the average range and passing. The court ruled that *Rowley* required no more, even though A.B. was not achieving his potential. Would this result differ under *Endrew F*? How significant are the child's personal circumstances in determining progress under *Endrew F.*? Would *Endrew F.*'s reference to challenging objectives have applied to A.B.?

Chapter 3

Related Services

Introduction

The IDEA requires school districts to provide "a free appropriate public education" (FAPE) to children with disabilities. 20 U.S.C. § 1412(a)(1)(A) (2012). A FAPE is comprised of "special education and related services" provided to a child with a disability "in conformity with" her "individualized education program . . . ." *Id.* § 1401(9). "Special education" is "specially designed instruction . . . to meet the unique needs of a child with a disability, including—(A) instruction conducted in the classroom, in the home, in hospitals and institutions, and in other settings . . . ." *Id.* at § 1401(29). "Related services" are:

> transportation, and such developmental, corrective, and other supportive services (including speech-language pathology and audiology services, interpreting services, psychological services, physical and occupational therapy, recreation, including therapeutic recreation, social work services, school nurse services designed to enable a child with a disability to receive a free appropriate public education as described in the individualized education program of the child, counseling services, including rehabilitation counseling, orientation and mobility services, and medical services, except that such medical services shall be for diagnostic and evaluation purposes only) as may be required to assist a child with a disability to benefit from special education, and includes the early identification and assessment of disabling conditions in children.

Id. § 1401(26)(A); *see also* 34 C.F.R. § 300.34(a) (2015). The IDEA thus establishes a two-part test to determine whether a particular service is a related service. First, the service must be:

1) transportation; or
2) developmental, corrective, and other supporting services, including:
    a) speech-language pathology services;
    b) audiology services;
    c) interpreting services;
    d) psychological services;
    e) physical therapy;
    f) occupational therapy;

g) recreation;

h) social work services;

i) school nurse services;

j) counseling services;

k) orientation and mobility services; or

l) diagnostic or evaluative medical services.

Second, the service must be required to assist a child with a disability to benefit from special education.

Chapter Three explores a school district's obligation to provide related services to children with disabilities. It includes four sections. Section One explores the definition of related services, focusing on whether a service that is medical in nature is a medical service and thus not a related service. Section Two investigates eligibility for related services. Sections Three and Four examine transportation and hospitalization respectively.

Problems

As you read the cases and other materials in this chapter, consider the following problems.

1. H.S. is a seven-year old child who suffers from a disability that makes it difficult for her to breathe. In order to address this, doctors performed a tracheostomy, which involved making an incision in her throat and inserting a breathing tube into it. The tracheostomy tube requires various levels of care. The tube must be regularly suctioned to remove secretions so they do not build up and block H.S. from breathing. If the tube becomes dislodged, H.S. will not be able to breathe, so the tube must be restored immediately. Finally, if H.S. stops breathing, ventilation with an AMBU bag must be administered within a very short time or she could die. H.S.'s parents have asked her school district to provide H.S. with a full-time certified nurse during the school day to attend to her needs. Without the nurse, H.S. would be unable to attend school. Must the school district provide the nurse at no cost?

2. Eight-year old H.K. has a low IQ. H.K. will never learn to read or write, hold a job, or be able to care for himself fully. H.K.'s school district prepared an IEP for him. The IEP includes goals for H.K. that consist of learning to walk, use the bathroom, feed himself, and dress. The IEP includes consultative physical therapy, meaning that a physical therapist will train H.K.'s classroom teacher to provide him with the physical therapy he needs to reach his goals. H.K. was not making progress towards his goals under the IEP. His parents, frustrated with his slow progress, asked the school district to provide H.K. with physical therapy directly from a physical therapist. They claim that when they hired a physical therapist for him during a one-month period, his physical abilities improved. The district refused to provide a physical therapist because it claimed that a physical therapist is not likely to make it more likely that

H.K. will achieve his goals. Must the school district provide the physical therapist at no cost?

3. Following a series of emotional disturbances, sixteen-year old N.U., diagnosed with schizophrenia, was committed by her parents to a hospital in order to receive treatment. Prior to her hospitalization, N.U. had an IEP. She was classified as emotionally disturbed and her IEP provided for special education in a special class with twelve students, one teacher, and one aide; group counseling once a week for one hour; and individual counseling once a week for one hour. While in the hospital, N.U. received medication, individual counseling three times each week for one hour, group counseling once a week for one hour, and two hours of education each day provided by school district tutors. A psychiatrist designed and implemented N.U.'s treatment program and prescribed medication to N.U. The psychiatrist conducted the individual counseling sessions. A psychologist conducted the group counseling sessions. N.U.'s school district planned and paid for her educational program, which focused on math and English and was not as comprehensive as the education she received while in school. N.U.'s parents asked the school district to reimburse them for the cost of the hospitalization, including room and food charges, the medication, and the counseling. For which of the costs, if any, must the school district reimburse N.U.'s parents?

Section One
The Definition of Related Services

"Related services" include "developmental, corrective, and other supportive services" that are "required to assist a child with a disability to benefit from special education . . . ." 20 U.S.C. § 1401(26)(A) (2012). The IDEA excludes medical services, except for diagnostic and evaluation purposes, from the definition of related services. *Id.* How far does this exclusion extend? Are all services that are medical in nature medical services? If so, a child who needs such services would not receive them from the district and would have to make other arrangements to receive and pay for them. In *Irving Independent School District v. Tatro*, the Supreme Court addressed this issue in the context of an eight-year-old girl who needed clean intermittent catheterization during school hours in order to attend school.

Irving Indep. Sch. Dist. v. Tatro

468 U.S. 883 (1984)

Chief Justice Burger delivered the opinion of the Court.

We granted certiorari to determine whether the Education of the Handicapped Act [(EHA)] . . . requires a school district to provide a handicapped child with clean intermittent catheterization during school hours.

I

Amber Tatro is an 8-year-old girl born with a defect known as spina bifida. As a result, she suffers from orthopedic and speech impairments and a neurogenic bladder, which prevents her from emptying her bladder voluntarily. Consequently, she must be catheterized every three or four hours to avoid injury to her kidneys. In accordance with accepted medical practice, clean intermittent catheterization (CIC), a procedure involving the insertion of a catheter into the urethra to drain the bladder, has been prescribed. The procedure is a simple one that may be performed in a few minutes by a layperson with less than an hour's training. Amber's parents, babysitter, and teenage brother are all qualified to administer CIC, and Amber soon will be able to perform this procedure herself.

In 1979, petitioner Irving Independent School District agreed to provide special education for Amber, who was then three and one-half years old. In consultation with her parents . . . , petitioner developed an individualized education program [(IEP)] for Amber . . . . The individualized education program provided that Amber would attend early childhood development classes and receive special services such as physical and occupational therapy. That program, however, made no provision for school personnel to administer CIC.

Respondents unsuccessfully pursued administrative remedies to secure CIC services for Amber during school hours. . . . [R]espondents brought the present action in District Court . . . . They sought an injunction ordering petitioner to provide Amber with CIC . . . .

. . . .

. . . The District Court held that under Texas law a nurse or other qualified person may administer CIC without engaging in the unauthorized practice of medicine, provided that a doctor prescribes and supervises the procedure. The District Court then held that, because a doctor was not needed to administer CIC, provision of the procedure was not a "medical service" . . . . Finding CIC to be a "related service" . . . , the District Court ordered petitioner . . . to modify Amber's individualized education program to include provision of CIC during school hours. . . .

. . . .

The Court of Appeals affirmed. That court accepted the District Court's conclusion that state law permitted qualified persons to administer CIC without the physical presence of a doctor . . . .

We granted certiorari . . . and we affirm . . . .

II

. . . .

States receiving funds under the . . . [EHA] are obliged to satisfy certain conditions. A primary condition is that the state implement a policy "that assures all handicapped children the right to a free appropriate public education." 20 U.S.C.

§ 1412(1). Each educational agency applying to a state for funding must provide assurances in turn that its program aims to provide "a free appropriate public education to all handicapped children." § 1414(a)(1)(C)(ii).

A "free appropriate public education" is explicitly defined as "special education and related services." § 1401(18). The term "special education" means

> "specially designed instruction, at no cost to parents or guardians, to meet the unique needs of a handicapped child, including classroom instruction, instruction in physical education, home instruction, and instruction in hospitals and institutions." § 1401(16).

"Related services" are defined as

> "transportation, and such developmental, corrective, and other *supportive services* (*including* speech pathology and audiology, psychological services, physical and occupational therapy, recreation, and *medical* and counseling *services, except that such medical services shall be for diagnostic and evaluation purposes only) as may be required to assist a handicapped child to benefit from special education*, and includes the early identification and assessment of handicapping conditions in children." § 1401(17) (emphasis added).

The issue in this case is whether CIC is a "related service" that petitioner is obliged to provide to Amber. We must answer two questions: first, whether CIC is a "supportive servic[e] . . . required to assist a handicapped child to benefit from special education"; and second, whether CIC is excluded from this definition as a "medical [service]" serving purposes other than diagnosis or evaluation.

A

The Court of Appeals was clearly correct in holding that CIC is a "supportive [service] . . . required to assist a handicapped child to benefit from special education." It is clear on this record that, without having CIC services available during the school day, Amber cannot attend school and thereby "benefit from special education." CIC services therefore fall squarely within the definition of a "supportive service."

As we have stated before, "Congress sought primarily to make public education available to handicapped children" and "to make such access meaningful." *Board of Education of Hendrick Hudson Central School District* v. *Rowley*, 458 U.S. 176, 192 . . . (1982). A service that enables a handicapped child to remain at school during the day is an important means of providing the child with the meaningful access to education that Congress envisioned. The Act makes specific provision for services, like transportation, for example, that do no more than enable a child to be physically present in class; and the Act specifically authorizes grants for schools to alter buildings and equipment to make them accessible to the handicapped. Services like CIC that permit a child to remain at school during the day are no less related to the effort to educate than are services that enable the child to reach, enter, or exit the school.

We hold that CIC services in this case qualify as a "supportive [service] . . . required to assist a handicapped child to benefit from special education."

B

We also agree with the Court of Appeals that provision of CIC is not a "medical [service]," which a school is required to provide only for purposes of diagnosis or evaluation. We begin with the regulations of the Department of Education, which are entitled to deference. The regulations define "related services" for handicapped children to include "school health services," 34 C.F.R. § 300.13(a) (1983), which are defined in turn as "services provided by a qualified school nurse or other qualified person," § 300.13(b)(10). "Medical services" are defined as "services provided by a licensed physician." § 300.13(b)(4). Thus, the Secretary has determined that the services of a school nurse otherwise qualifying as a "related service" are not subject to exclusion as a "medical service," but that the services of a physician are excludable as such.

This definition of "medical services" is a reasonable interpretation of congressional intent. Although Congress devoted little discussion to the "medical services" exclusion, the Secretary could reasonably have concluded that it was designed to spare schools from an obligation to provide a service that might well prove unduly expensive and beyond the range of their competence. From this understanding of congressional purpose, the Secretary could reasonably have concluded that Congress intended to impose the obligation to provide school nursing services.

Congress plainly required schools to hire various specially trained personnel to help handicapped children, such as "trained occupational therapists, speech therapists, psychologists, social workers and other appropriately trained personnel." S. Rep. No. 94-168, *supra*, at 33. School nurses have long been a part of the educational system, and the Secretary could therefore reasonably conclude that school nursing services are not the sort of burden that Congress intended to exclude as a "medical service." By limiting the "medical services" exclusion to the services of a physician or hospital, both far more expensive, the Secretary has given a permissible construction to the provision.

Petitioner's contrary interpretation of the "medical services" exclusion is unconvincing. In petitioner's view, CIC is a "medical service," even though it may be provided by a nurse or trained layperson; that conclusion rests on its reading of Texas law that confines CIC to uses in accordance with a physician's prescription and under a physician's ultimate supervision. Aside from conflicting with the Secretary's reasonable interpretation of congressional intent, however, such a rule would be anomalous. Nurses in petitioner School District are authorized to dispense oral medications and administer emergency injections in accordance with a physician's prescription. This kind of service for nonhandicapped children is difficult to distinguish from the provision of CIC to the handicapped. It would be strange indeed if Congress, in attempting to extend special services to handicapped children, were unwilling to guarantee them services of a kind that are routinely provided to the nonhandicapped.

To keep in perspective the obligation to provide services that relate to both the health and educational needs of handicapped students, we note several limitations that should minimize the burden petitioner fears. First, to be entitled to related services, a child must be handicapped so as to require special education. In the absence of a handicap that requires special education, the need for what otherwise might qualify as a related service does not create an obligation under the Act.

Second, only those services necessary to aid a handicapped child to benefit from special education must be provided, regardless how easily a school nurse or layperson could furnish them. For example, if a particular medication or treatment may appropriately be administered to a handicapped child other than during the school day, a school is not required to provide nursing services to administer it.

Third, the regulations state that school nursing services must be provided only if they can be performed by a nurse or other qualified person, not if they must be performed by a physician. It bears mentioning that here not even the services of a nurse are required; as is conceded, a layperson with minimal training is qualified to provide CIC. . . .

. . . .

We conclude that provision of CIC to Amber is not subject to exclusion as a "medical service," and we affirm the Court of Appeals' holding that CIC is a "related service" under the Education of the Handicapped Act.

[The separate opinions of Justices Brennan and Stevens are omitted.]

Notes, Comments, and Questions

1. The current IDEA regulations define "related services" to include "school health services" and "school nurse services." The regulations define "school health services and school nurse services" as "health services that are designed to enable a child with a disability to receive FAPE as described in the child's IEP." 34 C.F.R. § 300.34 (c)(13) (2015). "School nurse services" are "services provided by a qualified school nurse." *Id.* "School health services" are "services that may be provided by either a qualified school nurse or other qualified person." *Id.* In contrast, the regulations define "medical services" as "services provided by a licensed physician to determine a child's medically related disability that results in the child's need for special education and related services." *Id.* at § (c)(5). Do these regulations reflect the court's decision in *Tatro*? The statutory definition of related services?

2. Various competing interests are implicated in deciding whether services that are medical in nature are related services. These include the need for clear rules consistently applied, the educational needs of children with disabilities, and managing public funds efficiently. How well did the court in *Tatro* balance these interests? Would you adopt a different rule? What would it be? Would your rule define related services based on the provider of the services? The service provided? Something else?

3. Recall from Chapter Two that in *Rowley*, the Court ruled that the IDEA does not require school districts to provide children with disabilities an opportunity to attain an education commensurate with the opportunity provided to typically

developing children. The Court in *Tatro*, however, invoked equal treatment of children with disabilities to support its conclusion about a school district's obligation to provide related services. The Court pointed out that a school nurse can dispense oral medication and emergency injections to typically developing children, and that these services are difficult to distinguish from providing CIC to children with disabilities: "It would be strange indeed if Congress, in attempting to extend special services to handicapped children, were unwilling to guarantee them services of a kind that are routinely provided to the nonhandicapped." *Tatro*, 468 U.S. at 893–94. Can you explain the Court's rejection of equal treatment in *Rowley* and its embrace of equal treatment in *Tatro*? Does *Endrew F.* embrace equal treatment?

4. After the Supreme Court's decision in *Tatro*, two lines of cases arose. One line construed *Tatro* as creating a "bright-line" test that only medical services that must be provided by a physician are not related services. *See* Skelly v. Brookfield LaGrange Park Sch. Dist. 95, 968 F. Supp. 385, 395 (N.D. Ill. 1997) (holding that caring for a tracheostomy tube is not a medical service); Macomb Cnty. Intermediate Sch. Dist. v. Joshua S., 715 F. Supp. 824, 828 (E.D. Mich. 1989) (ruling that suctioning a tracheostomy tube is not a medical service). The court in *Skelly* explained its reasons for applying this "bright-line" test:

> This court recognizes the split in the authorities on this issue across the country and acknowledges that other court decisions . . . have eschewed the bright-line test recognized in *Tatro* . . . . [T]his court declines to apply the burden test here because this court believes that a bright-line test is not only appropriate legally, but is necessary according to public policy in order to further the efficient and proper use of public funds earmarked for education.
>
> School district boards of education across this country are the elected, primary decision makers for according disabled children the proper educational opportunities under the IDEA. As long as the courts of the country allow the IDEA's application to a particular set of factual circumstances to be determined by a balancing-of-burdens test, litigation that is expensive, both for the parents of children with disabilities who seek relief under the IDEA and for the school districts from which that relief is sought, will flourish. Education funds should be spent on education not litigation. Likewise, courts by their decisions should attempt to quell, not fan, the flame of increasing litigation in this country. Litigation, such as is before this court, is disruptive to a child's education as well as to the work of the educators and support personnel who provide that education. The most educationally efficient place for educators to spend their professional time (and I am sure the place they would rather be) is the classroom not the courtroom. Yet, without a hard and fast bright-line test that is factually easy for school districts to apply, litigation will continue to be spawned, as in this case in which District 95 appears bent on spending tens of thousands of dollars on litigation to try to save a few hundred dollars on an aide to ride the school bus with Eddie.

968 F. Supp. at 394.

The majority of the lower courts that considered the issue rejected *Tatro's* bright-line test in favor of a balancing test. The test considered several criteria, including the nature, extent, and cost of the services; the consequences of failing to provide them properly; and the expertise required to provide them. *See* Neely v. Rutheford Cnty. Sch., 68 F.3d 965, 973 (6th Cir. 1995), *cert. denied*, 517 U.S. 1134 (1996) (holding that caring for a tracheostomy tube is a medical service); Fulginiti v. Roxbury Twp. Pub. Sch., 921 F. Supp. 1320, 1325–26 (D.N.J. 1996) (ruling that caring for a tracheotomy tube is a medical service); Granite Sch. Dist. v. Shannon M., 787 F. Supp. 1020, 1029–30 (D. Utah 1992) (ruling that full-time nursing care including feeding and tending to a tracheostomy tube at an annual cost of $30,000 is a medical service); Bevin H. v. Wright, 666 F. Supp. 71, 73, 75–76 (W.D. Pa. 1987) (ruling that an attending nurse who accompanies child, cleans her tracheostomy and gastrostomy tubes, provides an oxygen supply, and suctions mucous from her lungs provides medical services); Detsel v. Bd. of Educ. of the Auburn Enlarged City Sch. Dist., 637 F. Supp. 1022, 1027 (N.D.N.Y. 1986), *aff'd*, 820 F.2d 587 (2d Cir. 1987), *cert. denied*, 484 U.S. 981 (1987) (ruling that a full-time nurse who tends to a child who is on a respirator provides a medical service).

In *Cedar Rapids Community School District v. Garret F.*, the Supreme Court resolved the conflict in the lower courts over the interpretation of *Tatro.*

Cedar Rapids Cmty. Sch. Dist. v. Garret F.

526 U.S. 66 (1999)

Justice Stevens delivered the opinion of the Court.

The . . . (IDEA) . . . was enacted, in part, "to assure that all children with disabilities have available to them . . . a free appropriate public education which emphasizes special education and related services designed to meet their unique needs." 20 U.S.C. § 1400(c). Consistent with this purpose, the IDEA authorizes federal financial assistance to States that agree to provide disabled children with special education and "related services." See §§ 1401(a)(18), 1412(1). The question presented in this case is whether the definition of "related services" in § 1401(a)(17) requires a public school district in a participating State to provide a ventilator-dependent student with certain nursing services during school hours.

I

Respondent Garret F. is a friendly, creative, and intelligent young man. When Garret was four years old, his spinal column was severed in a motorcycle accident. Though paralyzed from the neck down, his mental capacities were unaffected. He is able to speak, to control his motorized wheelchair through use of a puff and suck straw, and to operate a computer with a device that responds to head movements. Garret is currently a student in the Cedar Rapids Community School District (District), he attends regular classes in a typical school program, and his academic performance has been a success. Garret is, however, ventilator dependent, and therefore requires a responsible individual nearby to attend to certain physical needs while he is in school.

During Garret's early years at school his family provided for his physical care during the schoolday. When he was in kindergarten, his 18-year-old aunt attended him; in the next four years, his family used settlement proceeds they received after the accident, their insurance, and other resources to employ a licensed practical nurse. In 1993, Garret's mother requested the District to accept financial responsibility for the health care services that Garret requires during the school day. The District denied the request, believing that it was not legally obligated to provide continuous one-on-one nursing services.

... Garret's mother requested a hearing before the Iowa Department of Education. An Administrative Law Judge (ALJ) received extensive evidence concerning Garret's special needs, the District's treatment of other disabled students, and the assistance provided to other ventilator-dependent children in other parts of the country. In his 47-page report, the ALJ found that the District has about 17,500 students, of whom approximately 2,200 need some form of special education or special services. Although Garret is the only ventilator-dependent student in the District, most of the health care services that he needs are already provided for some other students. "The primary difference between Garret's situation and that of other students is his dependency on his ventilator for life support." The ALJ noted that the parties disagreed over the training or licensure required for the care and supervision of such students, and that those providing such care in other parts of the country ranged from nonlicensed personnel to registered nurses. However, the District did not contend that only a licensed physician could provide the services in question.

.... The ALJ ... concluded that the IDEA required the District to bear financial responsibility for all of the services in dispute, including continuous nursing services.

The District challenged the ALJ's decision in Federal District Court, but that Court approved the ALJ's IDEA ruling and granted summary judgment against the District. The Court of Appeals affirmed. The Court of Appeals read our opinion in *Tatro* to provide a two-step analysis of the "related services" definition in § 1401(a)(17)—asking first, whether the requested services are included within the phrase "supportive services"; and second, whether the services are excluded as "medical services." The Court of Appeals succinctly answered both questions in Garret's favor. The Court found the first step plainly satisfied, since Garret cannot attend school unless the requested services are available during the schoolday. As to the second step, the Court reasoned that *Tatro* "established a bright-line test: the services of a physician (other than for diagnostic and evaluation purposes) are subject to the medical services exclusion, but services that can be provided in the school setting by a nurse or qualified layperson are not."

In its petition for certiorari, the District challenged only the second step of the Court of Appeals' analysis. The District pointed out that some federal courts have not asked whether the requested health services must be delivered by a physician, but instead have applied a multifactor test that considers, generally speaking, the nature and extent of the services at issue. We granted the District's petition to resolve this conflict.

II

The District contends that § 1401(a)(17) does not require it to provide Garret with "continuous one-on-one nursing services" during the schoolday, even though Garret cannot remain in school without such care. However, the IDEA's definition of "related services," our decision in *Tatro*, and the overall statutory scheme all support the decision of the Court of Appeals.

The text of the "related services" definition broadly encompasses those supportive services that "may be required to assist a child with a disability to benefit from special education." As we have already noted, the District does not challenge the Court of Appeals' conclusion that the in-school services at issue are within the covered category of "supportive services." As a general matter, services that enable a disabled child to remain in school during the day provide the student with "the meaningful access to education that Congress envisioned." *Tatro*, 468 U.S. at 891 . . . .

This general definition of "related services" is illuminated by a parenthetical phrase listing examples of particular services that are included within the statute's coverage. § 1401(a)(17). "[M]edical services" are enumerated in this list, but such services are limited to those that are "for diagnostic and evaluation purposes." The statute does not contain a more specific definition of the "medical services" that are excepted from the coverage of § 1401(a)(17).

The scope of the "medical services" exclusion is not a matter of first impression in this Court. In *Tatro* we concluded that the Secretary of Education had reasonably determined that the term "medical services" referred only to services that must be performed by a physician, and not to school health services. Accordingly, we held that a specific form of health care (clean intermittent catheterization) that is often, though not always, performed by a nurse is not an excluded medical service. We referenced the likely cost of the services and the competence of school staff as justifications for drawing a line between physician and other services, but our endorsement of that line was unmistakable. It is thus settled that the phrase "medical services" in § 1401(a)(17) does not embrace all forms of care that might loosely be described as "medical" in other contexts, such as a claim for an income tax deduction.

The District does not ask us to define the term so broadly. Indeed, the District does not argue that any of the items of care that Garret needs, considered individually, could be excluded from the scope of 20 U.S.C. § 1401(a)(17). It could not make such an argument, considering that one of the services Garret needs (catheterization) was at issue in *Tatro*, and the others may be provided competently by a school nurse or other trained personnel. . . . [M]ost of the requested services are already provided by the District to other students, and the in-school care necessitated by Garret's ventilator dependency does not demand the training, knowledge, and judgment of a licensed physician. While more extensive, the in-school services Garret needs are no more "medical" than was the care sought in *Tatro*.

Instead, the District points to the combined and continuous character of the required care, and proposes a test under which the outcome in any particular case would "depend upon a series of factors, such as [1] whether the care is continuous or intermittent, [2] whether existing school health personnel can provide the service, [3] the cost of the service, and [4] the potential consequences if the service is not properly performed."

The District's multifactor test is not supported by any recognized source of legal authority. The proposed factors can be found in neither the text of the statute nor the regulations that we upheld in *Tatro*. Moreover, the District offers no explanation why these characteristics make one service any more "medical" than another. The continuous character of certain services associated with Garret's ventilator dependency has no apparent relationship to "medical" services, much less a relationship of equivalence. Continuous services may be more costly and may require additional school personnel, but they are not thereby more "medical." Whatever its imperfections, a rule that limits the medical services exemption to physician services is unquestionably a reasonable and generally workable interpretation of the statute. Absent an elaboration of the statutory terms plainly more convincing than that which we reviewed in *Tatro*, there is no good reason to depart from settled law.

Finally, the District raises broader concerns about the financial burden that it must bear to provide the services that Garret needs to stay in school. The problem for the District in providing these services is not that its staff cannot be trained to deliver them; the problem, the District contends, is that the existing school health staff cannot meet all of their responsibilities and provide for Garret at the same time. Through its multi-factor test, the District seeks to establish a kind of undue-burden exemption primarily based on the cost of the requested services. The first two factors can be seen as examples of cost-based distinctions: intermittent care is often less expensive than continuous care, and the use of existing personnel is cheaper than hiring additional employees. The third factor—the cost of the service—would then encompass the first two. The relevance of the fourth factor is likewise related to cost because extra care may be necessary if potential consequences are especially serious.

The District may have legitimate financial concerns, but our role in this dispute is to interpret existing law. Defining "related services" in a manner that *accommodates* the cost concerns Congress may have had, is altogether different from using cost *itself* as the definition. Given that § 1401(a)(17) does not employ cost in its definition of "related services" or excluded "medical services," accepting the District's cost-based standard as the sole test for determining the scope of the provision would require us to engage in judicial lawmaking without any guidance from Congress. It would also create some tension with the purposes of the IDEA. The statute may not require public schools to maximize the potential of disabled students commensurate with the opportunities provided to other children, and the potential financial burdens imposed on participating States may be relevant to arriving at a sensible construction of the IDEA. But Congress intended "to open the door of public education" to all qualified children and "require[d] participating States to educate handicapped children with nonhandicapped children whenever possible." *Rowley*, 458 U.S., at 192, 202.

This case is about whether meaningful access to the public schools will be assured, not the level of education that a school must finance once access is attained. It is undisputed that the services at issue must be provided if Garret is to remain in school. Under the statute, our precedent, and the purposes of the IDEA, the District must fund such "related services" in order to help guarantee that students like Garret are integrated into the public schools.

The judgment of the Court of Appeals is accordingly

Affirmed.

JUSTICE THOMAS, with whom JUSTICE KENNEDY joins, dissenting.

The majority, relying heavily on our decision in . . . *Tatro*, concludes that the . . . [IDEA] requires a public school district to fund continuous, one-on-one nursing care for disabled children. Because *Tatro* cannot be squared with the text of IDEA, the Court should not adhere to it in this case. Even assuming that *Tatro* was correct in the first instance, the majority's extension of it is unwarranted and ignores the constitutionally mandated rules of construction applicable to legislation enacted pursuant to Congress' spending power.

I

. . . .

The primary problem with *Tatro*, and the majority's reliance on it today, is that the Court focused on the provider of the services rather than the services themselves. We do not typically think that automotive services are limited to those provided by a mechanic, for example. Rather, anything done to repair or service a car, no matter who does the work, is thought to fall into that category. Similarly, the term "food service" is not generally thought to be limited to work performed by a chef. The term "medical" similarly does not support *Tatro*'s provider-specific approach, but encompasses services that are "of, *relating to, or concerned with* physicians *or* the practice of medicine." See Webster's Third New International Dictionary 1402 (1986) (emphasis added); see also *id*., at 1551 (defining "nurse" as "a person skilled in caring for and waiting on the infirm, the injured, or the sick; *specif*: one esp. trained to carry out such duties under the supervision of a physician").

IDEA's structure and purpose reinforce this textual interpretation. Congress enacted IDEA to increase the *educational* opportunities available to disabled children, not to provide medical care for them. See 20 U.S.C. § 1400(c) ("It is the purpose of this chapter to assure that all children with disabilities have . . . a free appropriate public education"); see also § 1412 ("In order to qualify for assistance . . . a State shall demonstrate . . . [that it] has in effect a policy that assures all children with disabilities the right to a free appropriate public education"). As such, where Congress decided to require a supportive service—including speech pathology, occupational therapy, and audiology—that appears "medical" in nature, it took care to do so explicitly. See § 1401(a)(17). Congress specified these services precisely because it recognized that they would otherwise fall under the broad "medical services" exclusion. Indeed, when it crafted the definition of related services, Congress could have, but chose not to, include "nursing services" in this list.

. . . .

II

Assuming that *Tatro* was correctly decided in the first instance, it does not control the outcome of this case. Because IDEA was enacted pursuant to Congress' spending power, *Rowley, supra*, at 190, n.11 . . . , our analysis of the statute in this case is governed by special rules of construction. We have repeatedly emphasized that, when Congress places conditions on the receipt of federal funds, "it must do so unambiguously." *Pennhurst State School and Hospital v. Halderman*, 451 U.S. 1, 17 . . . (1981). This is because a law that "condition[s] an offer of federal funding on a promise by the recipient . . . amounts essentially to a contract between the Government and the recipient of funds." As such, "[t]he legitimacy of Congress' power to legislate under the spending power . . . rests on whether the State voluntarily and knowingly accepts the terms of the 'contract.' There can, of course, be no knowing acceptance if a State is unaware of the conditions or is unable to ascertain what is expected of it." *Pennhurst, supra*, at 17. It follows that we must interpret Spending Clause legislation narrowly, in order to avoid saddling the States with obligations that they did not anticipate.

The majority's approach in this case turns this Spending Clause presumption on its head. We have held that, in enacting IDEA, Congress wished to require "States to educate handicapped children with nonhandicapped children whenever possible," *Rowley*, 484 U.S. at 202 . . . . Congress, however, also took steps to limit the fiscal burdens that States must bear in attempting to achieve this laudable goal. These steps include requiring States to provide an education that is only "appropriate" rather than requiring them to maximize the potential of disabled students, see 20 U.S.C. § 1400(c); *Rowley, supra,* at 200 . . . , recognizing that integration into the public school environment is not always possible, see § 1412(5), and clarifying that, with a few exceptions, public schools need not provide "medical services" for disabled students, §§ 1401(a)(17) and (18).

For this reason, we have previously recognized that Congress did not intend to "impos[e] upon the States a burden of unspecified proportions and weight" in enacting IDEA. *Rowley, supra*, at 190, n. 11. These federalism concerns require us to interpret IDEA's related services provision, consistent with *Tatro*, as follows: Department of Education regulations require districts to provide disabled children with health-related services that school nurses can perform as part of their normal duties. This reading of *Tatro*, although less broad than the majority's, is equally plausible and certainly more consistent with our obligation to interpret Spending Clause legislation narrowly. Before concluding that the district was required to provide clean intermittent catheterization for Amber Tatro, we observed that school nurses in the district were authorized to perform services that were "difficult to distinguish from the provision of [clean intermittent catheterization] to the handicapped." *Tatro*, 468 U.S. at 893. We concluded that "it would be strange indeed if Congress, in attempting to extend special services to handicapped children, were unwilling to guarantee them services of a kind that are routinely provided to the nonhandicapped." *Id.* at 893–894.

Unlike clean intermittent catheterization, however, a school nurse cannot provide the services that respondent requires and continue to perform her normal duties. To the contrary, because respondent requires continuous, one-on-one care throughout the entire schoolday, all agree that the district must hire an additional employee to attend solely to respondent. This will cost a minimum of $18,000 per year. Although the majority recognizes this fact, it nonetheless concludes that the "more extensive" nature of the services that respondent needs is irrelevant to the question whether those services fall under the medical services exclusion. This approach disregards the constitutionally mandated principles of construction applicable to Spending Clause legislation and blindsides unwary States with fiscal obligations that they could not have anticipated.

. . . .

Notes, Comments, and Questions

1. In the last paragraph of his opinion, Justice Stevens stated:

> This case is about whether meaningful access to the public schools will be assured, not the level of education that a school must finance once access is attained. It is undisputed that the services at issue must be provided if Garret is to remain in school. Under the statute, our precedent, and the purposes of the IDEA, the District must fund such "related services" in order to help guarantee that students like Garret are integrated into the public schools.

Garret F., 526 U.S. at 79. What are the implications of this statement? Must a school district provide all related services necessary to assist a child to benefit from special education? If so, is this obligation greater than a school district's obligation to provide special education as articulated in *Rowley*? *Endrew F.*?

2. Justice Thomas criticized the majority's definition of medical services because it focused on the provider of the service rather than on the service itself. He argued that we do not think that car repairs are limited to repairs done by an auto mechanic or that food services are limited to food prepared by a chef. Similarly, we do not think of medical services as limited to those services that a doctor must perform. Do you agree with Justice Thomas? If so, are all services that are medical in nature excluded medical services? Is this consistent with the language and purpose of the IDEA?

3. Justice Thomas referred to *Webster's* definition of "medical services" to construe the term. What role should dictionary definitions play in statutory interpretation?

4. Justice Thomas stated that courts should construe legislation such as the IDEA, passed pursuant to the Constitution's Spending Clause, narrowly so as not to "'impos[e] upon the States a burden of unspecified proportions and weight' in enacting IDEA." *Garret F.*, 526 U.S. at 84 (quoting *Rowley*, 458 U.S. at 190 n. 11). The Spending Clause of the Constitution gives Congress the power "[T]o lay and collect

Taxes, Duties, Imposts and Excises, to pay the debts and provide for the common defence and general welfare of the United States ...." U.S. CONST. art. 1, § 8, cl. 1. Congress also has authority under Section Five of the Fourteenth Amendment to "enforce, by appropriate legislation, the provisions of this article." U.S. CONST. amend. XIV, § 5. As described in Chapter One, *PARC* suggested that school districts have obligations under the Due Process and Equal Protection Clauses of the Fourteenth Amendment to educate students with disabilities. Pa. Ass'n for Retarded Children v. Pennsylvania, 343 F.Supp. 279, 295, 297 (E.D. Pa. 1972) (ruling that children with disabilities whom the Commonwealth excluded from school had colorable Due Process and Equal Protection claims); *cf.* Mills v. Bd. of Educ. of the Dist. of Columbia, 348 F.Supp. 866, 875 (D.D.C. 1972) (ruling that excluding children with disabilities from public schools in the District of Columbia violated their Fifth Amendment Due Process rights). As we will see in subsequent chapters, several cases have suggested that Congress passed the IDEA pursuant to its Fourteenth Amendment authority. If these decisions are correct, what impact does this have on Justice Thomas' Spending Clause analysis?

5. "Psychological services" are related services under the IDEA. 20 U.S.C. § 1401(26) (A) (2012); 34 C.F.R. § 300.34(c)(2) and (10) (2015). *See* Seals v. Loftis, 614 F. Supp. 302, 305 (E.D. Tenn. 1985) (ruling that a psychological evaluation is a related service); T.G. v. Bd. of Educ. of Piscataway, 576 F. Supp. 420, 424 (D.N.J. 1983) (ruling that psychotherapy provided to a child by a hospital was a related service because it "was designed as an essential service to allow ... [the child] to simply benefit from the educational program designed for him."); Papacoda v. Connecticut, 528 F. Supp. 68, 72 (D. Conn. 1981) (ruling that psychotherapy is a related service). The plaintiff in *Darlene L. v. Ill. State Bd. of Educ.*, 568 F. Supp. 1340, 1344 (N.D. Ill. 1983), argued that psychiatric services should be considered psychological services and hence a related service. The Court ruled that in contrast to psychologists, counselors, and therapists, psychiatrists are licensed physicians and thus the services they provide are medical services. In contrast, in *Max M. v. Thompson*, 592 F. Supp. 1437, 1445 (N.D. Ill. 1984), the court ruled that psychotherapy services performed by a psychiatrist are related services because psychotherapy services are not services that must be performed by a licensed physician but could be performed by other professionals.

6. In 2006, Congress amended the IDEA's related services provision to add the following exception: "The term [related services] does not include a medical device that is surgically implanted, or the replacement of such device." 20 U.S.C. § 1401(26) (B) (2012). *See* Petit v. U.S. Dep't of Educ., 578 F.Supp. 2d 145, 149 (D.D.C. 2008). In 2006, the Secretary of Education promulgated regulations pursuant to this amendment "excluding cochlear mapping from the definition of 'related services.'" *Petit*, 578 F.Supp. 2d at 149. *See* 34 C.F.R. § 300.34 (b)(1) (2015). Cochlear mapping is the process by which a specialist "adjusts a cochlear implant to ensure that it provides the optimal amount of stimulation to the auditory nerve." *Id.* In *Petit*, the plaintiff argued that the Secretary promulgated this regulation in violation of the Administrative Procedure Act. The court ruled that the regulatory exclusion of cochlear mapping as a related service did not violate the Act. *Id.* at 159–60. The

Court stated, "Having concluded that Congress did not speak directly to the question of whether cochlear implant mapping constitutes a 'related service' under the IDEA, the Court must defer to the Department's position as long as it is reasonable and does not conflict with the statute's plain language." *Id.* at 159. The Department of Education (DOE) offered several justifications for excluding cochlear mapping: it is expensive; school audiologists do not have the skill to do it; and the mapping need not be done at school or during school hours. *Id.* at 159–60. The court held these justifications to be reasonable and upheld the regulation. *Id.* Was the court's decision in *Petit* consistent with *Tatro* and *Garret F*? Did the court create another test for defining a related service beyond the bright-line rule announced in *Tatro* and *Garret F.*? Does the procedural setting of *Petit* limit its applicability?

Section Two
Eligibility for Related Services

A child is eligible for related services if the services are "required to assist a child with a disability to benefit from special education . . . ." 20 U.S.C. § 1401(26)(2012). In *Tatro*, the Supreme Court found that CIC was required to assist Amber to benefit from special education because without it she could not remain in school. The Court in *Garret F.* made the same finding regarding the services Garret required. In contrast, recall from Chapter Two that in *Rowley*, the Court ruled that Amy Rowley did not need a sign-language interpreter to assist her to benefit from special education because she was performing better than average and advancing from grade to grade. Bd. of Educ. of Hendrick Hudson Sch. Dist. v. Rowley, 458 U.S. 176, 209–10 (1982). In light of *Tatro*, *Garret F.*, and *Rowley*, consider the decisions on eligibility for related services in the next two cases.

S.K. v. N.Y.C. Dep't of Educ.

819 F.Supp. 2d 90 (E.D.N.Y. 2011)

aff'd, 526 F. App'x 135 (2d Cir. 2013)

[The order of Senior District Judge Johnson adopting the Report and Recommendation of United States Magistrate Judge Gold is omitted.]

Gold, S., United States Magistrate Judge:

Plaintiffs P.K. and T.K. bring this action on behalf of their daughter, S.K. [diagnosed with autism], against the New York City Department of Education ("Department") under the Individual[s] with Disabilities Education Act ("IDEA"), 20 U.S.C. § 1400 *et seq.* Plaintiffs seek review of the administrative decision that denied their application to have the Department pay for S.K.'s tuition at a private special education school for the 2008–2009 school year. In their challenge to that decision, plaintiffs allege that the Department deprived S.K. of a free and appropriate public education ("FAPE") . . . .

. . . .

Facts

. . . .

On May 12, 2008, plaintiffs filed a request for a due process hearing to challenge the [Individualized Educational Program ("IEP") the district prepared for S.K.] . . . . Plaintiffs contended, among other things, that the IEP was deficient because the Department failed to conduct and develop a behavior plan, failed to identify clear goals, failed to . . . comply with New York regulations for students diagnosed with autism that require a specified amount of speech therapy and that parent training be provided, and generally failed to offer S.K. a FAPE.

. . . .

[T]he impartial hearing officer ("IHO") concluded that S.K.'s IEP . . . failed to provide sufficient speech therapy and did not offer any parent counseling and training . . . .

The Department appealed the IHO's decision to a State Review Officer ("SRO") . . . . The SRO reversed the IHO's decision . . . .

Discussion

. . . .

3. Related Services

The IDEA requires that an IEP include a statement of the "related services" to be provided to a student or on the student's behalf. 20 U.S.C. § 1414(d)(1)(A)(i)(IV). Speech therapy and parent counseling and training are among the types of related services that a student might require in order to make progress. New York regulations in effect at the time S.K.'s IEP was prepared called for students with autism to receive a minimum level of speech therapy and for their parents to receive training and counseling. . . .

The IHO found that the Department failed to provide the speech therapy and parent training required by 8 N.Y.C.R.R. § 200.13. . . . Based upon this finding, among other things, the IHO concluded that S.K.'s IEP failed to offer her a FAPE. . . .

In his decision, the SRO acknowledged that the governing state regulations provided that a student with autism should receive speech therapy for a minimum of thirty minutes each day individually or with only one other student, or for sixty minutes each day in groups of six or less. The IEP prepared for S.K., though, called for three thirty-minute sessions per week in a group of three. The SRO found this adequate based upon testimony from S.K.'s proposed special education teacher that she provides specialized language instruction in her classroom throughout the day; as described by the SRO, the teacher testified that "specialized language instruction takes place 'all throughout the day because communication is all throughout the day.'" The SRO also relied on the view expressed by the Department's supervisor of psychologists that, when students are pulled out of classroom settings for specialized services, they lose an opportunity to interact with fellow students and enhance their social and communication skills. For these reasons, the SRO concluded that, "although not specifically delineated on the student's IEP, as a whole, the hearing record reflects that the student's program, including specific speech-language therapy and in-class language instruction, were [sic] appropriate to meet the student's individual speech-language and communication needs."

With respect to parent training, the SRO relied on testimony of the defendant's psychology supervisor that S.K.'s recommended school placement "did a great deal to support parents," including offering a six-week parent training program provided by a non-profit agency, monthly meetings, and support groups. The SRO concluded that "although parent counseling and training was not specifically set forth in the March 31, 2008 IEP, in light of the evidence presented herein regarding the available services for parent counseling and training at the proposed placement, the district's failure to include these services on the IEP did not procedurally or substantively [ ] result in the denial of a FAPE to the student."

In addition to its failure to provide 1:1 speech therapy or parent counseling and training, S.K.'s IEP made no provision for 1:1 ABA therapy. Indeed, the only 1:1 service identified in the IEP consisted of three thirty-minute occupational therapy sessions each week. At the time the IEP was prepared, though, S.K. was receiving 1:1 speech therapy for thirty minutes three times per week, 1:1 occupational therapy for thirty minutes three times per week, and ten hours per week of 1:1 ABA therapy. With these support services, S.K. was making significant progress. According to her parents, S.K. had experienced a "vocabulary explosion since last July when a new therapist began doing ABA" with her. S.K.'s parents also reported that S.K. "is always smiling and making eye contact and is a happy child who is not as withdrawn as she was initially prior to all the intervention she has received." Moreover . . . , S.K.'s mother and preschool teacher had noted that S.K.'s interfering behaviors had significantly diminished.

Having reviewed the record, I conclude that the evidence demonstrates that S.K. required substantial related services and greater individualized attention in order to make meaningful progress and receive an educational benefit from her schooling. S.K.'s IEP, by calling upon her to attend a new school where she would be working under a new teaching staff and with new classmates, while at the same time eliminating her 1:1 speech therapy, terminating her 1:1 home ABA therapy and failing to provide training and counseling to her parents, was likely to lead to regression rather than produce progress. The IEP therefore deprived S.K. of her right to a FAPE.

In his decision rejecting plaintiffs' challenge to S.K.'s IEP, the SRO pointed to no evidence indicating that S.K. no longer needed individualized speech and ABA therapy. For example, other than the IEP itself, no report of any expert suggested that S.K. would continue to make meaningful progress even if her home ABA therapy and 1:1 speech therapy sessions were eliminated. Nor did the SRO cite to any studies or expert testimony in the record indicating that autistic children generally benefit from such services only for a limited period of time, or that they are able to make progress without continued one-on-one support if they show progress after a brief period.

To the contrary, the evidence in the record strongly indicates that S.K. had substantial deficits and continued to require individualized therapy to make progress. The record included several reports prepared by experts who worked with or evaluated S.K. strongly suggesting that S.K. required continued one-on-one support. For example, Annette Rhoomes, S.K.'s ABA therapist, noted that S.K. was "making rapid and consistent progress" in the few months she had been working with S.K., but required continued home ABA therapy "to generalize her skills across different settings with different providers." . . . .

A second relevant report was written by the speech therapist who worked with S.K. at her preschool. The report was prepared in January of 2008, about two months before the Department prepared S.K.'s kindergarten IEP. While noting that S.K. had made substantial progress, the speech therapist also described "significant delays in her receptive language, expressive language and speech intelligibility." The therapist concluded that S.K. continued to require one-on-one assistance: "[S.K.] would continue to benefit from speech and language intervention 3 times weekly in a 1:1 ratio with the final determination made at the review."

Finally, the record includes an evaluation prepared by the McCarton Center, a private provider retained by S.K.'s parents. The McCarton Center report was written based upon testing and observations of S.K. conducted in February 2008, the month before the IEP was prepared. The report, like the one prepared by her preschool speech therapist, describes S.K.'s verbal skills as "significantly delayed in all areas, including vocabulary, reasoning, knowledge of concepts and short-term auditory memory. Based on clinical observations and test results, the McCarton Center recommended *increased* individual speech therapy and continued home ABA therapy. . . .

The consistent recommendations of S.K.'s ABA therapist, her speech therapist, and the McCarton Center stand in sharp contrast to the lack of any expert opinion supporting the SRO's conclusion that, despite its lack of 1:1 speech therapy, ABA therapy or parent training and counseling, the IEP did not deprive S.K. of a FAPE. Even the Department's witness—Ms. Finkelstein, supervisor of psychologists for the Department's Committee on Special Education—acknowledged that S.K. was still substantially delayed at the time the IEP was prepared and that there was a strong basis for continuing S.K.'s 1:1 speech therapy.

The record similarly indicates that parent training and counseling would have been important to S.K.'s ability to progress. As noted above, the SRO reached his decision in part based upon the services available to parents at the school recommended for S.K. by the Department. It seems that these services would have focused on issues of general concern to parents of children with special needs and would not have been specifically tailored to S.K.'s needs and educational program. The evidence indicates, however, that it is important for the parents of a student with autism to reinforce the specific teaching methods used by the student's service providers. . . .

For the reasons stated above, I conclude that terminating S.K.'s 1:1 speech and ABA therapy and failing to provide training to her parents, taken in combination, deprived S.K. of a FAPE. Moreover, I find the arguments mustered by the SRO in support of his decision and those advanced by the Department in this litigation to be unpersuasive. For example, it seems that one of the reasons the SRO concluded it was appropriate not to provide S.K. with individualized speech therapy is that pulling a student out of a classroom deprives the student of the opportunity to interact with other students. However, the IEP *does* provide for S.K. to receive speech therapy outside of the classroom, but in groups of three rather than one or two. The SRO also apparently relied upon the testimony of the special education teacher at the school recommended for S.K. that specialized language instruction takes place throughout the day because communication takes place all day. This generalized approach is, simply put, not a meaningful substitute for the focused, individualized attention and instruction determined by the experts cited above to be necessary for S.K.'s continued development.

Ms. Finkelstein, the Department's witness, attempted to justify the decision to discontinue S.K.'s 1:1 speech therapy by pointing out that plaintiffs "could always get more services if necessary." This is hardly a compelling rationale for denying necessary services for two reasons. First, it is not clear what showing would suffice to secure additional services if the McCarton Center report and the recommendation of S.K.'s preschool speech therapist were insufficient. Furthermore, plaintiffs—who apparently felt they had already demonstrated that additional services were necessary—were put in the position of evaluating the IEP and recommended placement without any assurance that 1:1 speech therapy would ever be provided.

In its supplemental letter, the Department argues that it is not required to "offer a student a service one year simply because it benefitted the child in a previous year;" and that an IEP must be "based on [a student's] current educational needs." I do not base my conclusion that S.K. required individualized speech and ABA therapy on the mere fact that S.K. was receiving 1:1 speech therapy and home ABA therapy at the time her IEP was prepared. Rather, I base my decision on the significant progress S.K. was just beginning to make with those support services in place, the consistent expert opinions in the record that S.K. required continued individualized speech and ABA therapy to maintain her progress, and the absence of any evidence in the record suggesting that S.K. would receive a non-trivial educational benefit without these support services. . . . .

For all these reasons, I find that S.K.'s IEP was not "reasonably calculated to enable [S.K.] to receive educational benefits," *Rowley*, 458 U.S. at 207 . . . , and was not "tailored" to S.K.'s "unique needs," *id.* at 181 . . . . S.K. was denied a FAPE because the IEP failed to provide for "personalized instruction with sufficient support services to permit [S.K.] to benefit educationally from that instruction." *Id.* at 203. . . .

. . . .

James M. v. Haw. Dep't of Educ.

803 F. Supp. 2d 1150 (D. Haw. 2011)

Leslie E. Kobayashi, District Judge.

Before the Court is an appeal by . . . James M. . . . of a hearings officer's . . . [d]ecision . . . concluding that James M. was offered a free appropriate public education ("FAPE") . . . .

BACKGROUND

I. *Factual History*

James M. is a nineteen-year-old student who has been diagnosed with dysarthia and hypotonia. He has been eligible for special education and related services from Defendant under the category of Autism since 1999. James M.'s neurological, motor, and speech deficits affect, *inter alia*, his handwriting, gait, saliva control, attention span, visual and sensory perception, and word retrieval.

. . . .

II. *Procedural History*

On or about February 1, 2010, Plaintiffs filed a request with Defendant for an impartial due process hearing. . . .

. . . The Hearings Officer held a four-day due process hearing commencing April 6, 2010. . . . In a decision issued on May 31, 2010, the Hearings Officer concluded that Defendant offered James M. a FAPE and that Plaintiffs were not entitled to reimbursement for their private school expenditures. The instant appeal followed.

. . . Plaintiffs argue that the IEPs of April 24, 2009 and September 17, 2009 fail to sufficiently address James M.'s academic, developmental, and functional needs. Specifically, Plaintiffs claim the following deficiencies: (1) insufficient speech language therapy; (2) inadequate provision of one-on-one paraprofessional services; (3) absence of direct occupational therapy services; (4) absence of a transition plan; and (5) absence of mental health therapy.

. . . .

IV. *Substantive Compliance*

. . . .

A. *Insufficient Speech Language Therapy*

Plaintiffs claim that the School District failed to provide James M. with an adequate amount of speech language therapy. They reject the School District's offer of 120 minutes per week of such therapy and insist that James M. "need[s] at least 300 minutes per week of speech/language services[.]" . . . .

The September 17, 2009 IEP provided for 120 minutes per week of speech language therapy, including "at least 1 hour of an [i]ndividual session with a [l]icensed [s]peech [l]anguage [p]athologist per week and 1 hour [of consultative services] to be spread between . . . teachers and adult support professionals[.]" The IEP further states that James M.'s "[s]peech [l]anguage [t]herapy objectives will continue to be worked on throughout the entire school day in all classes and educational settings." As noted by the Hearings Officer, placement at Kahuku [the public school] would also have enabled James M. to "practice his speech and communication skills with typically developing peers in a variety of different settings, exactly what he will need to do when he leaves the high school setting."

In contrast, Loveland [James' private school] provided James M. with 300 minutes per week of speech language services, including one-to-one direct services, group speech services, combined speech-occupational therapy, and after-school speech activities. While James M. may have benefited from these additional services, the Hearings Officer found that the School District's therapy services "were sufficient for [James M.] to access his education and address his speech language needs."

Department of Education Speech Language Pathologist Helen-Jean Kaniho . . . testified at the administrative hearing that, from approximately January 2006 to July 2008, James M. received approximately the same amount of speech language therapy at Kahuku as the IEP Team granted him for his 2009–2010 IEPs: two hours per week. Pathologist Kaniho explained that, during the two-and-a-half-year period she assisted James M., he learned to control his drooling sufficient "to access his curriculum." In preparation for the September 2009 IEP meetings, Pathologist Kaniho observed James M. at Loveland Academy to evaluate his progress and needs. She testified at the administrative hearing that, while she noticed a slight improvement in James M.'s ability to control his saliva, he suffered from diminished eye contact and demonstrated no marked improvement in intelligibility.

Plaintiffs fail to prove that James M. requires 300 minutes per week of speech language services. They also fail to prove why the School District's offer—the same amount of services provided to James M. while previously enrolled at Kahuku—does not create a "basic floor of opportunity" or bestow James M. with a "meaningful benefit." The Court FINDS that there is no clear evidence that the IEPs were deficient in their provision of speech language services.

B. *Inadequate Provision of One-to-One Paraprofessional Services*

Plaintiffs . . . argue that the School District improperly curtailed the quantity of one-to-one services because it "did not explain whether any data were collected or reviewed to support [Defendant's] basis for the reduction." . . . .

Department of Education District Education Specialist Jennifer Luke-Payne . . . testified during the administrative hearing that James M.'s reduction in services was the result of his reduced class schedule. Rather than attending class for a full school day as well as after-school services, James M. required only a half day of classes. . . .

. . . .

For the reasons outlined above, the Court FINDS that the School District's reduction in one-to-one paraprofessional services was rationally grounded and adequately explained.

. . . .

C. *Absence of Direct Occupational Therapy Services*

Plaintiffs dismiss the School District's offer of consultative occupational therapy and argue that James M. requires direct occupational services to adequately address his needs. Noting the testimony of Certified Occupational Therapy Assistant Tenora Watt . . . , a therapy assistant employed by Loveland, Plaintiffs claim that James M. has fine motor, gross motor, motor planning, and sensory deficits. Plaintiffs further claim that James M. has low muscle tone that affects his "overall body and his hand usage," including the ability to write. The Hearings Officer recognized James M.'s writing problem in her Hearing Decision, explaining that "[a]ny type of fine motor skill or handwriting produced by [James M.] clearly takes a lot of time and effort on his part and is a very exhausting venture."

Loveland provided James M. with between 90 and 120 minutes per week of direct occupational services to address his motor control and sensory needs. Occupational Therapy Assistant Watt testified that James M. needed such services both in April 2009 and September 2009. She explained that the primary goal of the direct service program was to develop James M.'s hand strength, coordination, and dexterity.

In contrast, the School District offered James M. occupational therapy on a consultation basis three times per quarter. The Hearings Officer found that this offer was a minimum requirement and that James M. "would get as much occupational therapy consult as his needs dictated." The Hearings Officer also found that the School District was willing to modify James M.'s 2009–2010 IEP to include direct services should the need arise.

The Hearings Officer further concluded that James M. could access his education without direct occupational therapy by using computers or word processors to complete his school work. The Hearings Officer noted that James M. used computers or word processors at both Kahuku and Loveland to complete written assignments, and that sharpening his typing skills would serve him well in the future.

Based on the findings above, the Court CONCLUDES that the occupational services in James M.'s IEPs sufficiently allowed him to access his education.

. . . .

F. *James M. Was Offered a FAPE*

The Court notes that, throughout the proceedings, Plaintiff Sherry M. has sought, as all good parents do, to secure the best services for her child. James M.'s grade point average and academic successes are commendable, and a credit to his hard work, his mother's commitment and devotion, and the proficiency and excellence of his teachers and therapists. The role of the district court in IDEA appeals, however, is not to determine whether an educational agency offered the best services, but whether the services offered confer the child with a meaningful benefit. Further, while the parties appear divided by honest differences of opinion, the Court finds compelling evidence that the School District constructed an individualized program tailored to meet James M.'s educational, developmental, and functional needs. Based on the preponderance of the evidence, the Court therefore CONCLUDES that Defendant offered James M. a FAPE in substantive compliance with the IDEA.

....

Notes, Comments, and Questions

1. The courts in *S.K.* and *James M.* reached opposite conclusions on two issues: whether general speech and communication throughout the school day could take the place of individualized speech instruction and whether the possibility that the district could amend an IEP to include additional services if necessary justified reduced services. With which decision do you agree? Why?

2. What if a child has disabilities that are so severe that the child cannot benefit from special education? Is the child nevertheless eligible for related services? Recall, from Chapter Two, *Polk v. Cent. Susquehanna Intermediate Unit 16*, 853 F.2d 171 (3d Cir. 1988), in which the court ruled that the IDEA required the school district to provide related services to a child with severe disabilities who was not receiving and who might never receive special education. The court stated:

> For children like Christopher with severe disabilities, related services serve a dual purpose. First, because these children have extensive physical difficulties that often interfere with development in other areas, physical therapy is an essential prerequisite to education. For example, development of motor abilities is often the first step in overall educational development....
>
> Second, the physical therapy itself may form the core of a severely disabled child's special education. This court has recognized that "[t]he educational program of a handicapped child, particularly a severely and profoundly handicapped child ... is very different from that of a non-handicapped child. The program may consist largely of 'related services' such as physical, occupational, or speech therapy." *DeLeon v. Susquehanna Community School Dist.*, 747 F.2d 149, 153 (3d Cir. 1984). In Christopher's case, physical therapy is not merely a conduit to his education but constitutes, in and of itself, a major portion of his special education, teaching him basic skills such as toileting, feeding, ambulation, etc.

Id. at 176.

3. Recall that under the IDEA medical services are not related services unless they are for evaluative or diagnostic purposes and are required to assist a child to benefit from special education. In *Richardson Indep. Sch. Dist. v. Michael Z.*, 561 F.Supp. 2d 610 (N.D. Tex. 2008), *vacated and remanded on other grounds*, 580 F.3d 286 (5th Cir.

2009), the parents of a child sought reimbursement for several laboratory diagnostic tests their child's hospital performed. The court ruled:

> The Court now addresses Plaintiff's substantive objection—that the lab diagnostics did not confer an educational benefit to Leah. In her affidavit, Dr. Mehta identifies two categories of lab diagnostics administered: the tests were conducted "either for purpose of a neurological diagnostic workup or as diagnostic tools to monitor blood levels while various psychotropic medications and/or combinations of psychotropic medications were prescribed for Leah to control her behaviors." The first category of tests—neurological diagnostics—identified potential causes of Leah's behavioral difficulties, including thyroid problems, anemia, autoimmune disorders, and other neurological conditions presenting as psychiatric problems. By enabling more precise diagnosis of Leah's behavioral and emotional disorders, neurological tests enabled TNRC to develop an effective treatment regimen to improve Leah's function in the classroom. Because the first category of tests . . . was required to enable Leah to benefit from a special education program, Defendants' expenditures for these tests are reimbursable.
>
> The second category of tests—blood diagnostics—was administered while Leah was taking Clozaril and Lithium. The tests . . . were used to evaluate potential side effects from these drugs, including liver and kidney problems, hypothyroidism, and changes in Leah's white blood and neutrophil counts. The connection between these tests, designed to avoid harmful side effects from Leah's medications, and Leah's academic progress is too tenuous to justify their classification as "related services." Thus, Defendants' expenditures for blood diagnostics are not reimbursable.

Id. at 620. Do you think that the connection between the blood diagnostics and Leah's educational progress was too tenuous? Could Leah have benefitted from special education if Clozaril and Lithium had harmful side effects?

4. What evidence should a court use to determine whether a particular related service is required to assist a child with a disability to benefit from special education? In *Johnson v. Lancaster-Lebanon Intermediate Unit* 13, 757 F. Supp. 606 (E.D. Pa. 1991), the plaintiffs contended that their son did not make meaningful educational progress in school without the private speech therapy for which they paid. The court agreed:

> Dr. Knast, whom I found to be the most qualified expert presented by either side at trial, testified that Owen's progress during the period the . . . [private] sessions were halted was not meaningful. Specifically, Dr. Knast and Ms. Giovannitti noted that although Owen's sound production in therapy sessions showed some improvement during the break in private therapy, there was no improvement in the intelligibility of his speech, nor in his ability to make spontaneous speech. By contrast, Dr. Knast testified that Owen has made meaningful progress since the . . . [private] lessons were restarted in 1990, showing sixteen months of progress from February 1990 to December 15, 1990, versus two months of progress from February 1989 to February 1990.

> The fact that Owen regressed when his private therapy halted is sufficient evidence that the . . . [district] was not providing him with a meaningful education. . . .
>
> . . . Based on Owen's excellent potential for speech, the fact that he has not reached that potential, his regression when his private therapy stopped, and his minimal progress in spontaneous and intelligible speech from February 1989 to February 1990, I hold that the . . . [district] did not provide him with an appropriate education as required by the EHA.

Id. at 619–20. Do you agree with the court's conclusion?

Section Three
Transportation

The IDEA and its implementing regulations include transportation as a related service. 20 U.S.C. § 1401(26)(A) (2012). The courts disagree, however, about when transportation is required to assist a child with a disability to benefit from special education. Must the school district provide transportation only when the need for transportation relates to or arises from the child's disability? Or must the school district also provide transportation to a child with a disability if the only reason the child needs transportation is that she cannot get to school without it? The following cases utilize contrasting tests for determining when a school district must provide transportation, each concluding that the district was not required to provide transportation.

McNair v. Oak Hills Local Sch. Dist.

872 F.2d 153 (6th Cir. 1989)

Joiner, Senior District Judge.

On October 3, 1985, James, Mary and Kelly McNair (McNair), filed a complaint against the Oak Hills Local School District . . . under the Education of the Handicapped Act (EHA), 20 U.S.C. §§ 1400 *et seq.* The McNairs sought, among other things, a determination that Oak Hills had to provide their child, Kelly, with transportation to and from St. Rita's School for the Deaf, a private school. . . . [T]he district court . . . dismissed the McNairs' action . . . .

We affirm the decision of the district court . . . .

I.

Upon learning from Oak Hills that the school district would not provide transportation to and from St. Rita's, the McNairs obtained an impartial due process hearing on the matter. . . .

. . . .

II.

. . . .

The McNairs want Oak Hills to provide transportation for Kelly to and from St. Rita's as a related service under the EHA. They will succeed only if they establish that which § 1400(c) requires:

(1) that the child is handicapped;

(2) that transportation is a related service;

(3) that the related service is designed to meet the unique needs of the child caused by the handicap; and

(4) the school district must be responsible under the EHA and its regulations for providing the related services under the particular circumstances of the case at hand.

In the instant case, the parties have stipulated that Kelly is handicapped under the EHA because of her hearing impairment. The second requirement is also satisfied, as the service at issue in this case is transportation to and from school, and this is by statute made a related service under the EHA. The third requirement of the statute, the showing that the related services are "designed to meet . . . unique needs" of the child is not met in this case. The parties have stipulated that Kelly's handicap does not require any special transportation needs, therefore, she could utilize the same transportation service as a non-handicapped child. The need for transportation, although a related service, is no more unique to Kelly because she is deaf than it would be if she were not deaf. Since the statute specifically requires a relationship between the related service and the unique needs of the child, the third requirement under the EHA has not been satisfied, and the Act does not require Oak Hills to provide Kelly with transportation to St. Rita's.

It is argued that *Tatro* holds to the contrary. *Tatro* does not counsel against this analysis as claimed by plaintiffs at oral argument. In *Tatro*, the question was whether clean intermittent catheterization (CIC) was a related service as defined in the EHA. This involved an analysis of the EHA definition of related services, which under our analysis is step two of a four-step approach. The *Tatro* opinion did include dicta in a brief discussion of how transportation will always be a related service under the EHA, but the court went no further than that. The issue in this case is not whether transportation is a related service, but the requirement of its relationship to "unique needs." The court did not discuss the unique needs requirement of the statute which is at issue in the instant case, most likely because it was not in dispute in *Tatro* that CIC was a service designed to meet that child's unique needs. Consequently, the discussion in *Tatro* concerning transportation is not relevant to the specific issue which is central to the instant appeal.

The court is not reaching any determination as to whether a school district in a situation similar to the instant one would have to provide the related service to the child if it was designed to meet that child's unique needs. In other words, because the third requirement set out above was not satisfied, the court reaches no conclusion as to the final requirement. We leave that for another court on another day. All we hold today is that when a child is voluntarily placed in a private school, a public school district need not provide a related service to that child under the EHA if that particular service is not designed to meet the unique needs of the child.

. . . .

AFFIRMED.

Donald B. v. Bd. of Sch. Comm'rs of Mobile Cnty.

117 F.3d 1371 (11th Cir. 1997)

KRAVITCH, Senior Circuit Judge.

Donald B., by and through his mother, Christine B., appeals the district court's order granting judgment as a matter of law to the Board of School Commissioners of Mobile County, Alabama ("the Board"), its superintendent and its members on Donald B.'s claim under the Individuals with Disabilities Education Act ("the IDEA" or "the Act"), 20 U.S.C. §§ 1440–1491 . . . . Donald B. contends that the district court erred in ruling that under the IDEA the Board had no obligation either to transport him three blocks between his private school and the public school that offered the speech therapy he needed or to provide such services at his private school. We affirm.

I.

Based on the parties' stipulation of undisputed matters . . . , the district court found the following facts: (1) . . . the Board identified Donald B. as a disabled child; (2) the Board determined that Donald B. should receive special education for impaired speech; (3) at the time of the eligibility decision, Donald B. was enrolled unilaterally by his mother in a private, parochial academy, St. Paul's Episcopal School ("St. Paul's"); (4) St. Paul's stands approximately three blocks from the Mary B. Austin School ("Austin"), a public school that offers speech therapy; (5) the Board receives funds under the IDEA and thus must extend special education and related services to disabled children in its geographic area; (6) . . . the Board agreed to provide speech therapy to Donald B. at Austin as part of an individualized education plan ("IEP") developed for him pursuant to the IDEA, but it declined to transport him between St. Paul's and Austin or to send a speech therapist to St. Paul's; (7) an administrative hearing officer upheld the Board's decision; (8) Donald B. then filed the instant action; and (9) Donald B. was, at the time of the district court's order, six years old and healthy, apart from his speech impairment.

In evaluating Donald B.'s legal claim in light of the facts it found, the district court correctly observed that this court had not delineated an analytical framework for the resolution of IDEA cases involving demands for related services. After reviewing the relevant authority, the district court concluded that *McNair* prescribed the proper test in this context. It further held that Donald B. failed to satisfy *McNair*'s third prong which limits relief to cases in which the sought after "related service is designed to meet the unique needs of the child caused by the handicap. . . ." *Id.* at 156. . . .

II.

. . . .

As noted above, the district court, following the Sixth Circuit's ruling in *McNair*, determined that although transportation constituted a related service, the Board did not have to convey Donald B. to and from St. Paul's because that related service did not address the unique needs caused by his particular handicap. Specifically, it reasoned that because "Donald B. is afflicted with a speech impairment only and not a handicap affecting his ability to walk or move . . . [his] handicap does not require any special transportation, and the transportation requested by Plaintiffs is not a reasonable and necessary service for meeting Donald B.'s unique needs." Although we agree that Donald B.'s speech-related disability does not *cause* directly a unique need on his part for transportation, we find the portion of the *McNair* test which could be construed to require such a showing inconsistent with the text of the IDEA.

Some language in the IDEA facially supports the view that a disabled child's right to related services attaches only when his or her impairment directly *causes* a unique need for a particular service. Specifically, the Act's purpose subsection appears to link both "special education" and "related services" to a disabled child's "unique needs". *See* 20 U.S.C. § 1400(c) (stating that purpose of IDEA is to provide disabled children access to "free appropriate public education which emphasizes special education and related services designed to meet their unique needs"). The Supreme Court, however, has noted that the definition section of the IDEA indicates that only "special education," and not "related services," must correlate to the "unique needs" associated with a child's specific disability. *See Irving Indep. Sch. Dist.*, 468 U.S. at 889 . . . In contrast, the Court recognized that the Act defines a "related service" as an aid that " 'may be required to assist a handicapped child to benefit from special education. . . .' " *Id.* at 889–90 . . . . *See also id.* at 891 . . . (noting that the IDEA "makes specific provision for services, like transportation, for example, that do no more than enable a child to be physically present in class").

Based upon the foregoing analysis, we conclude that, read in context, the IDEA requires transportation if that service is necessary for a disabled child "to benefit from special education," 20 U.S.C. § 1401(a)(17), even if that child has no ambulatory impairment that directly *causes* a "unique need" for some form of specialized transport. This conclusion, however, does not resolve the instant case. We still must determine whether transportation is necessary for Donald B. to benefit from the special education to which he is entitled. To answer this question, we look both to the Supreme Court's construction of the IDEA and the Department of Education's regulations implementing the Act.

The Court has emphasized that "only those services necessary to aid a handicapped child to benefit from special education must be provided, regardless [of] how easily a school [official] could furnish them." *Irving Indep. Sch. Dist.*, 468 U.S. at 894 . . . . [We] must focus on the meaning of the word "necessary" in this context. We conclude that, based on the implementing regulations for the IDEA, transportation may be "necessary," under these or similar circumstances, if in its absence a disabled child in private school would be denied "a genuine opportunity for equitable participation in [a special education program]," 34 C.F.R. § 76.651(a)(1), or special education program benefits "comparable in quality, scope, and opportunity for participation . . . [to those provided for] students enrolled in public schools," 34 C.F.R. § 76.654(a).

The Board has offered Donald B. speech therapy pursuant to an IEP, just as it provides for other students at Austin. The only obstacle to Donald B.'s full participation in the special education program at Austin is literally three blocks. In our view, the factors relevant in determining whether a child in this situation needs transportation as a related service include at least: (1) his or her age; (2) the distance he or she must travel; (3) the nature of the area through which the child must pass; (4) his or her access to private assistance in making the trip; and (5) the availability of other forms of public assistance in route, such as crossing guards or public transit.

In this case, Donald B. has presented evidence of his age and the distance he must travel. Although he is young (six at the time of the district court order, and, now, seven), he must cross only a short distance. Further, Donald B. has not offered any evidence that these three blocks encompass high crime or high traffic areas that he could not traverse easily. As to the other cited factors, the only possible showing by Donald B. stems from his counsel's assertion at oral argument that Donald B.'s mother cannot leave her job to assist Donald B. This specific fact does not appear in the record, although it arguably could be inferred from the stipulated facts regarding Christine B. Even if this assertion were credited, Donald B. still has failed to present evidence regarding other means, private and public, he might have at his disposal to assist him in covering the three blocks. On balance then, Donald B. has not carried his burden of showing that he is unable to travel to Austin without the Board's help.

. . . .

Notes, Comments, and Questions

1. In *McNair*, the Court used the purpose clause of the IDEA to create a test for when a school district is required to provide a related service. The key component of the *McNair* test is whether the need for the service arises from the child's disability. In contrast, the court in *Donald B.* based its test on 20 U.S.C. § 1401(17) (currently § 1401(26)), which defines related services. The *Donald B.* test asks whether the related service is required to assist the child to benefit from special education. Was it appropriate for *McNair* to use the IDEA's general purpose clause to establish a test for eligibility for a related service?

2. At least one court has followed the *McNair* test, but in contrast to *McNair*, it found for the child. In *Felter v. Cape Girardeau Sch. Dist.*, 810 F. Supp. 1062 (E.D. Mo. 1993), the child attended a parochial school and received special education at

the local public school.... The school district refused to provide transportation for Sarah from her school to the public school. *Id.* at 1064. The court stated that the key question in determining whether a district must provide transportation "is whether or not the related service (transportation) is designed to meet the unique needs of... [the child] caused by the handicap." *Id.* at 1066–67. The court ruled that because the child's special education committee found that "'transportation is necessary for Sarah due to lack of mobility, visual impairment, and school location,'" transportation from her private school to her public school was a necessary related service. *Id.* at 1067.

3. At least one district court has followed the *Donald B.* test. In *Malehorn v. Hill City Sch. Dist.*, 987 F. Supp. 772 (D.S.D. 1997), the court applied the *Donald B.* test to find that the child was not eligible for transportation because transportation was not required for her to benefit from special education. *Id.* at 782. The court considered the distance to the child's school (13.5 miles), that the bus stop was unsafe because oncoming traffic, and that the child could follow instructions not to cross the street into traffic.

Section Four
Hospitalization

A school district must provide special education to a child with a disability who is hospitalized or placed in a residential institution. 20 U.S.C. § 1401(29) (2012). A school district is not required to pay medical expenses, except for diagnostic and evaluative purposes. *Id.* at § 1401(26)(A). However, between these two poles lie several expenses connected to hospitalization that are not clearly educational or medical. These include room, board, and other therapeutic services. Are these related services for which a school district must pay? There is not an easy answer to this question. Consider how the court in *Richardson Independent School District v. Michael Z.* handled this question and the test it developed.

Richardson Indep. Sch. Dist. v. Michael Z.

580 F.3d 286 (5th Cir. 2009)

Emilio M. Garza, Circuit Judge:

... Richardson Independent School District ("RISD" or the "District") appeals the district court's judgment in favor of... Leah Z. Specifically, the district court determined that RISD failed to provide Leah with a free appropriate public education as required under IDEA, and that RISD was therefore required to reimburse the parents for certain costs associated with Leah's placement in a private residential facility.... For the following reasons, we vacate and remand.

Leah Z.... was diagnosed with attention deficit disorder, oppositional defiant disorder, bipolar disorder, autism, separation anxiety disorder, and pervasive developmental disorder. After experiencing emotional and behavioral difficulties at numerous private schools, Leah entered RISD for fifth grade in the fall of 1999. Leah's various diagnoses qualified her for special education and related services from RISD. . . . In Texas, the committee responsible for preparing Leah's IEP was an Admission, Review, and Dismissal Committee ("ARD Committee" or "Committee").

In seventh grade, Leah entered Westwood Junior High School where she was placed in a Behavior Adjustment ("BA") class. . . . [I]n October 2002, during Leah's eighth-grade year, she was writing at a second-to third-grade level, reading at a third-grade level, and performing math at a sixth-grade level. Leah's behavioral and academic difficulties increased in eighth grade and she experienced significant regression over the summer prior to ninth grade. When Leah began ninth grade at Westwood Junior High School . . . she began leaving class without permission almost daily. Leah arrived at school late, took lengthy breaks of up to two hours at a time, and left early. In November, Leah ran away from school and was eventually caught by the school police officer. . . .

After winter break, Leah returned to Westwood and was placed in a different BA class. . . . [B]y mid-January Leah was again arriving late, leaving early, and wandering outside the classroom without permission. Numerous incidents occurred, including Leah evading school officers, overturning furniture, insulting teachers, using profane language, and disrupting testing. . . .

In February, it was discovered that during unsupervised absences from class Leah was engaging in sexual activities with other students in the bathroom. . . . In March, Leah was transferred to Richardson High School ("RHS") and placed in a BA class. . . . Leah remained at RHS for only two weeks, during which the pattern of disruptive behavior and refusal to work continued. Later in March, an incident occurred at home where Leah scratched her father and caused him to bleed. Her psychiatrist recommended Leah's admission to a psychiatric facility, and Leah's parents eventually placed her at the Texas NeuroRehab Center ("TNRC"). . . .

At TNRC, Leah attended the on-site University Charter School ("UCS"), a public charter school. UCS developed an IEP for Leah and provided her with physical therapy, occupational therapy, and counseling. Her adverse behavior continued and included numerous instances of groping staff members and other patients, attempting to remove other patients' clothing, refusing to follow directions or attend class, and engaging in self-mutilation. She was frequently physically restrained or placed in locked confinement. Leah's doctor, Dr. Mehta, considered Leah one of her most difficult patients. . . . Dr. Mehta testified that Leah's behavior did not significantly improve until shortly after Leah started taking the medication Clozaril. The doctor attributed Leah's improvement to a combination of TNRC's structured environment, the medication, and intensive counseling and therapy sessions. Leah was discharged from TNRC on November 12, 2004, with the recommendation that she attend a special education class with one-on-one supervision to prevent future behavioral problems related to lack of supervision.

Meanwhile, in June 2004 Leah's parents requested an ARD Committee meeting to request Leah's placement at TNRC. After reviewing Leah's assessments from TNRC, the ARD Committee found that RISD remained capable of providing her with a free appropriate public education and denied the request for private residential placement. The Committee developed an updated IEP (the "June 2004 IEP") that attempted to account for Leah's sexual and aggressive behavior. Leah's parents argued to the Committee that the new IEP failed to adequately account for her behavioral or academic regression. The district court found that the June 2004 IEP was substantially similar to Leah's previous IEPs.

In July 2004, Leah's parents filed a request for an administrative due process hearing alleging that RISD failed to provide Leah with a free appropriate public education and requesting reimbursement for her placement at TNRC. The Hearing Officer found in favor of the parents and awarded them $56,000. The district court agreed, and awarded the parents $54,714.40 as reimbursement for the room and board, comprehensive therapy services, nursing services, and neurological diagnostics....

....

.... IDEA authorizes reimbursement for private residential placements in certain situations. A free appropriate public education includes special education and related services that have been provided at public expense.... "Related services" are

> transportation, and such developmental, corrective, and other supportive services (including speech-language pathology and audiology services, psychological services, physical and occupational therapy, recreation, including therapeutic recreation, social work services, counseling services, including rehabilitation counseling, orientation and mobility services, and medical services, except that such medical services shall be for diagnostic and evaluation purposes only) as may be required to assist a child with a disability to benefit from special education ....

Id. § 1401(22). Department of Education regulations provide that "[i]f placement in a public or private residential program is necessary to provide special education and related services to a child with a disability, the program, including non-medical care and room and board, must be at no cost to the parents of the child." 34 C.F.R. § 300.302. Thus, it is clear that, in some situations, a public school district must reimburse a disabled child's parents for the costs of a private residential program.

The Fifth Circuit has not yet articulated a test for determining when, in the face of an inappropriate IEP, a private residential placement is proper under the Act. Among circuits that have considered the issue two apparently distinct approaches have emerged, as articulated in the Third Circuit's decision in *Kruelle v. New Castle County Sch. Dist.*, 642 F.2d 687 (3d Cir.1981), and the Seventh Circuit's decision in *Dale M. v. Bd. of Educ. of Bradley-Bourbonnais High Sch. Dist. No. 307*, 237 F.3d 813, 817 (7th Cir.2001). Though the tests adopted by each circuit contain overlapping language and arguable degrees of semantic similarity, one major characteristic separates the Third and Seventh Circuit's approaches. Specifically, the Third Circuit's test focuses on whether a child's medical, social, or emotional problems are "inextricably intertwined" with the learning process, while the Seventh Circuit's test focuses on whether the private residential placement is "primarily educational."

In *Kruelle,* the Third Circuit enunciated the following test for determining when a private residential placement is appropriate under IDEA:

> [a]nalysis must focus . . . on whether full-time placement may be considered necessary for educational purposes, or whether the residential placement is a response to medical, social or emotional problems that are segregable from the learning process.

642 F.2d at 693. Under the Third Circuit's test, if a court cannot segregate a child's medical, social, or emotional problems from the learning process, the school district must reimburse the parents for the private residential placement.

In *Dale M.,* the Seventh Circuit enunciated a different test for determining when private residential placement is required under IDEA:

> [t]he essential distinction is between services primarily oriented toward enabling a disabled child to obtain an education and services oriented more toward enabling the child to engage in noneducational activities. The former are "related services" within the meaning of the statute, the latter not.

237 F.3d at 817. Accordingly, the proper inquiry in the Seventh Circuit is whether the private residential placement is "primarily educational." Though the court cited *Kruelle* favorably, the *Dale M.* test differs markedly from the *Kruelle* test in that the focus is not on whether the child's medical, social, or emotional problems are segregable from the learning process, but rather on whether the services provided at the residential facility are geared primarily toward helping the child obtain an education. Under this standard, courts have drawn a distinction between those services that are primarily for treating a child's medical or behavioral problems and those services that are primarily for enabling educational instruction.

Undoubtedly, it is difficult to conceive of a disabled child, particularly a child with mental disabilities, whose medical, social, or emotional problems would have no effect on the child's ability to learn and would therefore be segregable from the learning process. Some courts applying the *Kruelle* test appear to have recognized the breadth of the "inextricably intertwined" inquiry and have attempted to limit its application. *See, e.g., Clovis,* 903 F.2d at 643 ("a child who must be maintained on kidney dialysis certainly cannot physically benefit from education to the extent that such services are necessary to keep him alive, but . . . it is not the responsibility of the school district to provide such maintenance care"). . . . However, if such services affected the child's ability to physically or psychologically receive an education, they were not segregable from the learning process and under *Kruelle*'s broad language would have been reimbursable.

Certainly, IDEA has a broad conception of education and seeks to ensure that all disabled children are provided, at public expense, with a meaningful opportunity to learn. However, IDEA does not require school districts to pay for private residential placements that are not essential for a disabled child to receive an education. By requiring courts to undertake the Solomonic task of determining when a child's medical, social, and emotional problems are segregable from education, *Kruelle* expands school district liability beyond that required by IDEA. Put another way, it is not difficult to imagine a case where a disabled child's various difficulties may be impossible for a court to segregate, but the child is still capable of receiving an educational benefit without private residential placement. *Kruelle* does not account for this situation.

Considering this, we adopt the following test:

> In order for a residential placement to be appropriate under IDEA, the placement must be 1) essential in order for the disabled child to receive a meaningful educational benefit, and 2) primarily oriented toward enabling the child to obtain an education.

Unlike *Kruelle,* this test does not make the reimbursement determination contingent on a court's ability to conduct the arguably impossible task of segregating a child's medical, social, emotional, and educational problems. The first prong of our test requires a court to find that the placement is *essential* for the child to receive a meaningful educational benefit. In other words, if a child is able to receive an educational benefit without the residential placement, even if the placement is helpful to a child's education, the school is not required to pay for it under IDEA. . . . .

Our second prong asks the question posed in *Dale M.*: Was the residential placement primarily oriented toward enabling the child to obtain an education? IDEA, though broad in scope, does not require school districts to bear the costs of private residential services that are primarily aimed at treating a child's medical difficulties or enabling the child to participate in non-educational activities. IDEA ensures that all disabled children receive a meaningful *education,* but it was not intended to shift the costs of treating a child's disability to the public school district. . . .

Unlike the first prong of our test, which asks whether the private placement was appropriate in general by determining whether it was essential in order for the child to obtain a meaningful educational benefit, the second prong focuses on appropriateness at a more specific level, asking whether the particular treatments that the private facility provided were primarily oriented towards enabling the child to receive a meaningful educational benefit. . . . [H]ere we would expect Leah's treatment at TNRC to have been primarily oriented towards educational improvement, if indeed her problems were primarily educational in nature.

The second prong of our test is necessarily a fact-intensive inquiry. A court should consider the extent to which the services provided by the residential placement fall within the IDEA's definition of "related services." This "related services" analysis should inform other factors a court may consider in determining whether the placement is primarily oriented toward enabling a child to obtain an education. Such factors include, but are not limited to: whether the child was placed at the facility for educational reasons and whether the child's progress at the facility is primarily judged by educational achievement. If, upon analysis of the services as a whole, the court determines that the residential placement is primarily oriented toward enabling the child to obtain an education, the court must then examine each constituent part of the placement to weed out inappropriate treatments from the appropriate (and therefore reimburseable) ones. In other words, a finding that a particular private placement is appropriate under IDEA does not mean that all treatments received there are *per se* reimburseable; rather, reimbursement is permitted only for treatments that are related services . . . .

Therefore, we hold that the district court erred by adopting the *Kruelle* inextricably intertwined test. Applying our new test, it appears that the district court made the factual finding that residential placement was essential for Leah to receive a meaningful educational benefit. Specifically, the district court concluded that "Leah could achieve no academic progress short of residential placement." The record supports the district court's conclusion, and we therefore conclude that the first prong of our test has been met. However, the district court has not made any factual findings regarding the second prong, namely whether Leah's treatment at TNRC was primarily oriented toward, i.e. primarily designed for and directed to, enabling her to receive a meaningful educational benefit. Accordingly, we find that the district court erred by not considering this issue. Our remand, therefore, is limited to the question of whether the second prong of our new test has been satisfied. Specifically, on remand the district court should review the facts and determine whether Leah's treatment at TNRC was primarily oriented toward enabling her to receive a meaningful educational benefit.

. . . .

Notes, Comments, and Questions

1. In *Richardson*, the court employed a two-step test to determine whether the school district or the parents were responsible for the payment of hospital costs; the first step focuses on whether the placement was essential for the child to receive an education and the second on whether the placement is primarily oriented toward enabling the child to obtain an education. What do you think of this test? Is it consistent with the IDEA's definition of related services? Should the court have asked the second question, or is the only relevant question under the IDEA whether the service is necessary for the child to benefit from special education?

2. Recall that in both *Tatro* and *Garret F.* the child's disability was not related to the child's ability to learn. The Supreme Court, however, required each school district to treat the disability so each child could have access to special education. Based on these rulings, should the only questions in hospitalization cases be whether the service is necessary to assist the child to benefit from special education and, if so, whether the service is medical in nature as defined in *Tatro* and *Garret F.*? Consider how the court in *Field v. Haddonfield Board of Education* addressed the issue of payment for hospitalization when it involved a child hospitalized for substance abuse.

Field v. Haddonfield Bd. of Educ.

769 F. Supp. 1313 (D.N.J. 1991)

Gerry, Chief Judge:

Plaintiffs filed a . . . petition . . . for a determination of whether the defendant Haddonfield Board of Education ("the Board") was responsible for the cost of a substance abuse treatment program that [their son] Daniel attended. . . .

. . . .

. . . During the 1988–89 school year Daniel was a tenth grade student who was classified as emotionally disturbed. In particular, Daniel has expressive and attention disorders, and has a tendency to become frustrated because of his inability to express himself and because of very low self esteem. . . .

On January 13, 1989, Daniel was suspended . . . as a result of an altercation he had with a teacher. At that time, the child study team recommended that Daniel be placed as a day student at the Yale School in Cherry Hill, a special education school for emotionally disturbed children. The Fields responded that they did not consider Yale appropriate because of the level of the program. Rather, after consulting with . . . an educational consultant, the Fields sought to have Daniel placed in a residential, twenty-four hour per day placement. . . .

. . . .

After negotiation, the parties agreed to a consent order which . . . provided that the Board would . . . place Daniel in the Mill Creek School . . . .

By February of 1990, Daniel's behavior at the Mill Creek School was deteriorating. He was inattentive in class, verbally abusive to teachers, unmotivated, and doing poor academically. One day, Daniel was discovered showing a bottle of Valium to other students. The school immediately convened a "crisis meeting" with Daniel's parents. During that meeting, Daniel admitted taking the Valium from his mother, and also admitted to smoking marijuana and occasional drinking.

The possession of drugs on campus is grounds for automatic suspension from Mill Creek. Mill Creek advised both the Board and Daniel's parents that Daniel was expelled and that he would have to attend a residential substance abuse program in order to be readmitted to Mill Creek. Mill Creek recommended the Strecker program . . . , and stated that Daniel could remain in school if he attended that program. Sandra Schoenholtz, assistant director of Mill Creek, opined that Daniel's possession of drugs may have been part of a larger problem, his emotional disturbance, and that his behavior and performance in school were linked together.

Plaintiffs asked the Board whether they would pay for the substance abuse program at Strecker, and whether it wished to look at other programs. Dr. Rell responded with approval of the Strecker program, but indicated the Board's position that drug rehabilitation is considered a medical matter and, therefore, not the responsibility of school districts.

The Fields enrolled Daniel in the Strecker program at their expense. Although Mill Creek recommended a sixty day admission, Daniel attended Strecker for twenty-eight days, which exhausted his lifetime insurance benefits for psychiatric care. As a result of the Board's refusal to pay for the substance abuse program, the plaintiffs sought a hearing before the Department of Education....

....

The core issue presented ... is whether Daniel's placement in the Strecker substance abuse program was a "related service" or rather whether the program was an excluded "medical service." ....

Where a child's education is adversely affected by substance abuse, successful completion of a substance abuse program can be expected to increase the effectiveness of the child's educational program....

However, the fact that a particular program may benefit a classified child's special education program clearly does not *ipso facto* compel the conclusion that that program is a "related service" and thus a school district responsibility under the EHA. For example, courts have held that psychiatric treatment geared to combat mental illness is an excluded medical service although the treatment may be related to education in the sense that the child cannot fully benefit from his or her education without it.

....

Although we have found no case on point dealing with a substance abuse program, we conclude under the facts of this case that the services performed at the Strecker program constitute medical services for which the plaintiffs must bear the cost under the EHA. According to the hospital brochure that describes the Strecker program, the program operates under the recognition that drug dependency is a disease, and treatment is geared with this in mind....

Moreover, although Mill Creek may have "required" Daniel to attend a substance abuse program as a condition for his continued enrollment at the school, this is not to say that a substance abuse program was "required to assist the child to benefit from special education." 20 U.S.C. § 1401(17). Although the Strecker program addressed some of Daniel's emotional problems as a "dual diagnosis" program,[15] the testimony and records reveal that the program provided intensive therapy for Daniel's underlying psychiatric disorders, which included psychiatric counselling, numerous physical evaluations as well as medication. Strecker provided medical treatment which Mill Creek could not, as an educational institution, provide.... Significantly, in developing a treatment program, each patient is assigned a treating physician, in Daniel's case Dr. Michael McCarthy. *Compare Taylor v. Honig*, 910 F.2d 627 (9th Cir. 1990) (residential program was "related service" where handicapped child's program

15. "(... [Strecker is] a dual-diagnosis program, meaning that the adolescents who come into the program are viewed as people who have a substance abuse problem, but also other psychiatric problems").

developed through IEP by the school system), *with Clovis*, 903 F.2d at 644–45 (residential program was excluded "medical service" where handicapped child's program was developed by a medical team supervised by a licensed physician).

The "[a]nalysis . . . focuses . . . on whether full-time placement may be considered necessary for educational purposes, or whether the residential placement is a response to medical, social or emotional problems that are segregable from the learning process." *Kruelle v. New Castle County School Dist.*, 642 F.2d 687, 693 (3d Cir. 1981). Here, Strecker provided treatment which was clearly "segregable" from, though beneficial to, Daniel's learning process. For instance, although Mill Creek's educational program was integrated with the Strecker program, Mill Creek personnel is not involved in the patient's daily therapy sessions conducted by the psychiatrist, nor other group sessions such as Alcoholics Anonymous and Narcotics Anonymous. . . .

Although school districts are not required to pay for non-diagnostic or non-evaluative medical services, the school must provide educational services to students who are confined to a hospital. 20 U.S.C. § 1401(16). Strecker's standard billing policy is consistent with this requirement. The patient is billed for the treatment administered at Strecker while the school district is separately billed for the educational component offered through Mill Creek (for those patients who, like Daniel, were enrolled in Mill Creek). In fact, the Board continued to pay for Daniel's enrollment at Mill Creek while he was in the Strecker program. Mill Creek's practice has always been to bill the parents for all clinical programs at the hospital that are inpatient programs, such as Strecker, and to bill the school district for the educational portion provided by Mill Creek. This practice is harmonious with the EHA's requirements.

. . . .

Finally, we note that our conclusion is not inconsistent with the Department of Education's Policy letter of April 18, 1988. In that advisory opinion, an inquiry was made as to a school district's responsibility for a child who becomes handicapped as a result of drug addiction. The Office of Special Education Programs had previously determined that addiction itself is not considered to be a handicapping condition covered by the EHA. The Secretary responded that

> if a residential program is necessary to provide FAPE . . . then it must be made available. If a child is addicted and handicapped, public agencies are only required to provide the aspects of the child's program that would enable the child to receive FAPE. If a service is required solely to treat the child's addiction and is not required to provide FAPE, then the public agency is not required to provide the service or to provide it at no cost.

The Board has fulfilled its obligation under the EHA by providing for Daniel's education through the Mill Creek program. However, the Fields must pay for Daniel's enrollment in the Strecker program since we find that that program renders medical services within the meaning of 20 U.S.C. section 1401(17). . . .

. . . .

Notes, Comments, and Questions

1. The court in *Field* emphasized that the treatment Daniel received was medical in nature. Referring to an advisory opinion from the Department of Education, the court stated that "addiction itself" is not a disability under the IDEA. *Field*, 769 F.Supp. at 1328. The court then stated, "the Fields must pay for Daniel's enrollment in the Strecker program, since that program renders medical services within the meaning of 20 U.S.C. section 1401(17)." *Id.* at 1328–29. Were all the services that David received at Strecker (other than the Mill Creek educational program) strictly medical? Was the treatment for substance abuse necessary for Daniel to benefit from special education? Would the court's decision have been different if it had been issued after *Garrett F.*?

2. The court in *Field* referred to *Clovis Unified Sch. Dist. v. Shorey*, 903 F. 2d 635 (9th Cir. 1990), and *Taylor v. Honig*, 910 F. 2d 627 (9th Cir. 1990), each of which considered whether the services the child received while institutionalized were related services. Each case focused on whether the placement was for medical or educational purposes and each case reached a different conclusion.

In *Clovis*, Michelle Shorey was placed in an acute care psychiatric hospital. The district argued it was not responsible to pay for Michelle's hospital care because her hospitalization was in response to a medical rather than an educational need. *Clovis*, 903 F.2d at 640. The district also claimed that the "intensive, extended psychological treatment" Michelle received was medical in nature and thus an excluded medical service. *Id.* at 642. Michelle's parents argued that the treatment she received was not an excluded medical service because she could not benefit from her education without it and that the medical treatment she received while at the hospital was comparable to the treatment provided in other residential placement centers or day schools. *Id.* at 642. While at the school, Michelle attended class for one to two hours per day. However, her educational program was not implemented by an IEP; rather, her medical team, supervised by a licensed physician, implemented it. The Ninth Circuit ruled that because Michelle was hospitalized primarily for medical, and not educational, reasons, the hospitalization was not a related service. *Id.* at 645.

In contrast, in *Taylor*, the court upheld a preliminary injunction that ordered reimbursement for Todd Taylor's placement in San Marcos Treatment Center, a residential facility that operated as a school and psychiatric hospital. *Taylor*, 910 F.2d at 628. The court contrasted the placement in San Marcos with the placement in *Clovis*:

> The situation in this case is thus different from that presented in *Clovis* where we recently held that a school district did not bear financial responsibility for a seriously emotionally disturbed child's placement at a psychiatric hospital. Unlike San Marcos, the facility at issue in *Clovis* did not operate a full-time school. Rather, the school district provided classroom instructors to meet the educational needs of children hospitalized there. In *Clovis*, a medical team supervised by a licensed physician determined the handicapped child's treatment program. Here, in contrast, an IEP designed by the

> school system determines Todd's program. Furthermore, the child in *Clovis*, unlike Todd Taylor, was hospitalized primarily for medical as opposed to educational reasons. Unlike Todd, the *Clovis* child was not "medically stable." In fact, she required hospitalization to treat an "acute" psychiatric crisis.

Id. at 632. Ultimately, the court found that Todd's placement at San Marcos was necessary to meet his educational as opposed to his medical needs. *Id.* at 632–33.

4. It is difficult to synthesize the judicial opinions on reimbursement for hospitalization. Perhaps the best generalization is that courts that award reimbursement emphasize the educational nature of the hospital program while courts that deny reimbursement focus on the medical nature of the services. *See* Mary Courtney T. v. Sch. Dist. of Phila., 575 F.3d 235, 239, 248 (3d Cir. 2009) (holding that services provided in a long-term residential psychiatric treatment center were not for educational purposes and were excluded medical services); McKenzie v. Jefferson, 566 F. Supp. 404, 412 (D.D.C. 1983) (holding that the purpose of the hospitalization of a child with a severe mental illness was medical and not educational). In *Butler v. Evans*, 225 F.3d 887, 894–95 (7th Cir. 2000), the court ruled that because the residential placement for the child was primarily for medical treatment and not to assist her to benefit from special education, the hospitalization was not a related service. "Niki Butler endured a series of emotional disturbances during her childhood and was diagnosed with severe schizophrenia. By her sixteenth birthday, she had suffered from auditory and visual hallucinations, attempted suicide and struggled with paranoia and psychotic episodes." *Id.* at 890. While her school district and parents were developing an IEP for Niki, "Niki's condition demanded immediate medical intervention." *Id.* Her parents voluntarily admitted her to a hospital. "During her hospital stay, Niki received medical treatment for her psychiatric needs .... The hospital retained two teachers and a teacher's aide on staff for patients from 9 to 11 a.m., and Niki received assignments from school ...." *Id.* In reaching its decision to deny reimbursement, the court stated, "Niki was admitted to Our Lady of Mercy Hospital almost exclusively for medical reasons, not educational purposes, and received almost exclusively medical services, not educational ones." *Id.* at 893. The court continued, "Niki's hospitalization was prompted by a psychiatric crisis, was not approved by her IEP and occurred at a medical facility that did not provide educational services and had not been approved by the state as her residential educational institution." *Id.* According to the court:

> The IDEA requires in certain cases that the state pay for institutionalized care or for tutors and trained specialists at residential educational placements, but only if "necessary to provide special education and related services." The IDEA does not require reimbursement of medical-care costs for psychiatric hospitalization when, as here, the hospitalization addresses the child's medical, social or emotional disabilities apart from her special education needs.

Id. at 894. Is the court correct that a child's medical, social, or economic disabilities are separate from the child's special education needs? Is it possible to compartmentalize a child with complex needs in this way? Could Nikki have received any education without the hospitalization?

5. In contrast, courts that granted reimbursement for the costs of hospitalization emphasized that the residential placement was necessary for the child to have access to a FAPE. For example, in *Vander Malle v. Ambach*, 667 F. Supp. 1015 (S.D.N.Y. 1987), the child required hospitalization for his severe emotional disturbance. The court considered both whether the residential placement was required to provide the child a FAPE and which of the services the child received were related services. The court stated, "As long as the child is properly educable only through a residential placement, when the medical, social, or emotional problems that require hospitalization create or are intertwined with the educational problem, the states remain responsible for the costs of the residential placement." *Id.* at 1039. In a hospitalization case, the question is whether the placement was "reasonably calculated to enable . . . [the child] to receive free, appropriate educational benefits." *Id.* at 1040. The issue is:

> whether full-time placement may be considered necessary for educational purposes, or whether the residential placement is a response solely to medical, social, or emotional problems that are segregable from the learning process. Should it turn out that the placement was required, the Court is empowered to order reimbursement.

Id. The court ruled that the placement was required for the child to receive an education. "[T]he extreme emotional outbursts, antisocial behavior, and tendency to assault his fellow students, teachers, and parents precluded . . . [the child] from attending regular public or private day schools." *Id.* Further, "Bruce's educational disability could not be separated and treated apart from his emotional and behavioral problems. The residential placement responded to both." *Id.* The court stated:

> Bruce's placement at the Institute intended to address both educational and medical needs. The Institute's *per diem* rate includes a bed in a psychiatric ward, board, routine hospital services, floor duty nursing, professional services from the Institute's doctors, psychologists and staff, rehabilitation services and participation in DRS vocational programs.

Id. at 1042. The court, however, did not order full reimbursement but stated that a trial was necessary to determine which costs were covered as related services and which were primarily medical. *Id.* In *Papacoda v. Connecticut*, 528 F. Supp. 68 (D. Conn. 1981), the plaintiff lived in residential placements for nearly two years due to her emotional problems. *Id.* at 69. The placement provided educational and therapeutic services to the child and the school district conceded that she could not learn without them. *Id.* at 70. The school district argued, however, that it was not required to pay the non-educational costs of the placement because the placement was for emotional treatment rather than for educational purposes. The court ruled that because the placement was necessary for educational purposes, the district was responsible for the cost of room and board. *Id.* at 71–72. *See also* Christopher T. v. San Fran. Unified Sch. Dist., 553 F. Supp. 1107, 1120 (N.D. Cal. 1982) (finding that child required "residential placement in order to benefit from special education . . . .").

6. Although psychological services are related services if they are required to assist a child to benefit from special education, several school districts have challenged their obligation to provide psychological services to students while they are hospitalized. Courts have generally ruled that psychological services provided in a hospital are related services as long as they are necessary to assist a child to benefit from special education. *See* Babb v. Knox Cnty. Sch. Sys., 965 F.2d 104, 109 (6th Cir. 1992) (ruling that child was eligible for psychological services); Doe v. Anrig, 651 F. Supp. 424, 431 (D. Mass. 1987) (holding that "psychotherapy and group therapy were required to assist Timothy to benefit from special education."); T.G. v. Bd .of Educ. of Piscataway, N.J., 576 F. Supp. 420, 421–22, 424 (D. N.J. 1983) (holding that program that included individual, group, and family therapy "was designed as an essential service to allow D.G. to benefit from the educational program that was planned for him.").

Chapter 4

Eligibility for a Free Appropriate Public Education

Introduction

Although the stated purpose of the IDEA is "to ensure that all children with disabilities have available to them a free appropriate public education," 20 U.S.C. § 1400(d)(1)(A) (2012), not every child who is diagnosed with a disability is eligible for special education and related services. The IDEA requires that to be eligible for special education services, a child must have an enumerated disability that adversely affects her educational performance, necessitating special education and related services. An eligibility determination is a critical decision, determining whether or not a child with a disability will receive special education and related services. However, the IDEA's eligibility criteria are not entirely clear. Each child is different, and the impact of a disability on each child's educational achievement is different and difficult to measure. As a result, a bright-line rule regarding eligibility is not in effect and may not be possible.

Chapter Four has two sections. Section One covers the basic statutory standards for eligibility for special education and related services. Section Two considers, in turn, each element of the showing a child must make to demonstrate eligibility for special education and related services: the child must have a disability that is enumerated in the IDEA; the disability must have an adverse effect on the child's educational performance; and, as a result, the child needs special education and related services.

Problem

K.J. was born prematurely and has had a seizure disorder since birth. She has attention deficit hyperactivity disorder (ADHD), a mild learning disability, and asthma. She has also been diagnosed as having speech and language impairments because she speaks with a lisp and stutter. K.J. completed first grade with average grades, although she occasionally required home tutoring because her seizures and asthma prevented her from attending school.

Several months into K.J.'s second grade year her parents sought special education services for her from the local school district. K.J.'s parents were concerned that her articulation difficulties and difficulty with fine motor coordination were inhibiting her educational progress and social interactions. K.J.'s parents were further concerned that K.J. was not prepared to meet the demands of the third grade curriculum and did not have the "tools" to manage her learning disability in a more rigorous academic environment. After the school's special education placement team evaluated K.J., it determined that she was not eligible for special education and related services because she was making satisfactory progress and achieving at an average level for her grade and her medical problems did not have a significant impact on her grades.

Was the school district correct? Does K.J. qualify for special education and related services? If not, should she qualify? Can a child whose academic progress is "satisfactory" and achievement is "average" demonstrate that her disability adversely affects her academic performance? Should "educational performance" mean exclusively "academic performance" in determining eligibility? What role should emotional or social development play in eligibility decisions? Should a child with a disability be eligible for special education and related services simply because she can benefit from them?

Section One
Eligibility Standards

A. IDEA Statutory and Regulatory Requirements

Despite its broad, sweeping language, not "all" children with disabilities are eligible for special education and related services under the IDEA. In order to be eligible for special education and related services, a child must be between three and twenty-one years old and meet the definition of a child with a disability. 20 U.S.C. § 1412(a)(1)(A) (2012). The IDEA defines a "child with a disability" as a child:

> (i) with intellectual disabilities, hearing impairments (including deafness), speech or language impairments, visual impairments (including blindness), serious emotional disturbance . . . , orthopedic impairments, autism, traumatic brain injury, other health impairments, or specific learning disabilities; and
>
> (ii) who, by reason thereof, needs special education and related services.

Id. § 1401(3)(A)(i)–(ii). The IDEA regulations further define each of the qualifying disabilities. 34 C.F.R. § 300.8(c)(1)–(13)(2015). The regulations require, in the definition of each qualifying disability—with the exception of specific learning disabilities—that the disability at issue "adversely affect" the student's academic performance. Therefore, based on the IDEA and its regulations, in order to qualify for special education and related services, a child must establish that: (1) she has an enumerated disability; (2) the disability adversely affects her educational performance; and (3) by reason of the disability's adverse effect on her educational performance, she needs special education and related services. What effect, if any, will *Endrew F.* have on eligibility determinations? Will the definition of "needs" special education change?

This eligibility standard has led to significant challenges for those charged with making eligibility determinations because many of the key terms in the provision do not contain clear definitions or guidance.

B. The Importance of Eligibility Requirements

The importance of eligibility determinations cannot be overestimated as they lead to serious consequences for students and school districts. Harmful results can stem from both over-identification and under-identification of eligible children. In fact, an eligibility determination may be "one of the most important, if not the most important, decision that will ever be made in . . . [a student's] life." Robert T. Stafford, *Education for the Handicapped: A Senator's Perspective*, 3 Vt. L. Rev. 71, 79 (1978). Over-identification can result in significant adverse consequences for a student, including exclusion from a school's core curriculum, limited post-secondary education and employment opportunities, and stigmatization. Moreover, over-identification can result in the misuse of limited financial resources dedicated to students with disabilities.

Conversely, under-identification can harm children by denying them the resources they need to progress educationally and participate as full, productive members of society. This is particularly true for students with emotional disabilities, as they are more likely to drop out of school and become engaged with the criminal justice system without proper educational and emotional interventions. *See* Catherine Y. Kim et al., The School-to-Prison Pipeline: Structuring Legal Reform 51–56 (2010). Indeed, students with emotional disabilities have a national high school graduation rate of 35% compared with the overall high school graduation rate of 76%. Jim Comstock-Galagan & Rhonda Brownstein, *Stopping the Schoolhouse to Jailhouse Pipeline by Enforcing the Federal Special Education Law*, Children's Rts. (A.B.A. Children's Rts. Litigation Committee), Winter 2007 at 1, 3–4. For those who do drop out of school, "73 percent are arrested within five years of leaving school." *Id.*; *see also* Martha L. Thurlow, *et al.*, *Students with Disabilities who Drop Out of School—Implications for Policy and Practice*, Issue Brief (Nat'l Center on Secondary Educ. and Transition), June 2002, at 1–2; Joseph B. Tulman & Douglas M. Weck, *Shutting off the School-to-Prison Pipeline for Status Offenders with Education-Related Disabilities*, 54 N.Y.L. Sch. L. Rev. 875 (2009–2010); Joseph B. Tulman, *Disability and Delinquency: How Failures to Identify, Accommodate, and Serve Youth with Education-Related Disabilities Lead to Their Disproportionate Representation in the Delinquency System*, 3 Whittier J. Child. & Fam. Advoc. 3 (2003).

Eligibility determinations also have important consequences for Congress and local school districts. Establishing standards for those who receive special education and related services ensures that school districts use federal funds allocated under the IDEA to serve children with disabilities. *See, e.g.*, Jeri D. Barclay, *Fiscal Accountability Under the Individuals with Disabilities Act: How Do We Ensure the Money is Spent on Handicapped Education and Related Services?*, 28 J.L. & Educ. 327, 329 (1999) (recommending accountability procedures for overseeing expenditure of special education funds). Eligibility provisions also help limit the costs of educating children with disabilities by controlling the number of children who are entitled to the provision of services under the IDEA.

C. 2004 Reauthorization of the IDEA: The Individuals With Disabilities Education Improvement Act (IDEIA)

In 2004, Congress reauthorized the IDEA and made several changes to the law that have an impact on eligibility. First, the 2004 reauthorization permits school districts to use new methods for determining the existence of specific learning disabilities. 20 U.S.C. § 1414(b)(6) (2012). Previously, school districts relied on a discrepancy between the student's academic achievement and the student's intellectual ability. Previous methods for determining the existence of a specific learning disability were criticized for reliance on IQ tests and the perception that they required students to fail before being deemed eligible. Now, a school district may use methods based on how "the child responds to scientific, research-based intervention . . . ." *Id.* § 1414(b)(6)(B); 34 C.F.R. § 300.307(a)(2) (2015).

The 2004 reauthorization also allows a school district to use up to 15% of its federal special education funding for "early intervening services" for children "who need additional academic and behavioral support to succeed in a general education environment" even if they "have not been identified as needing special education and related services . . . ." 20 U.S.C. § 1413(f).

During the reauthorization process, Congress placed significant focus on the disproportionate percentage of racial and ethnic minorities, particularly Black children, who are placed in special education and more restrictive educational settings under the categories of emotional disturbance or intellectual disabilities. The 2004 reauthorization requires states receiving federal funds under the IDEA to have "policies and procedures designed to prevent the inappropriate overidentification or disproportionate representation by race and ethnicity of children as children with disabilities . . . ." 20 U.S.C. § 1412(a)(24). It also mandates the:

> collection and examination of data to determine if significant disproportionality based on race and ethnicity is occurring" with respect to—
>
> (A) the identification of children . . . with disabilities . . . ;
>
> (B) the placement in particular educational setting of such children; and
>
> (C) the incidence, duration, and type of disciplinary actions . . . .

Id. § 1418(d)(1). If a significant disproportionate impact is identified, the school district must review and, if necessary, revise its policies and practices used during the identification and placement process. *Id.* § 1418(d)(2)(A). The Department of Education issued regulations implementing this statutory provision in 2016. These regulations are described more fully in Chapter Two.

Notes, Comments, and Questions

1. Should Congress and local educational agencies attempt to limit the number of children eligible for special education and related services under the IDEA? Are strict eligibility standards consistent with the IDEA's goal of providing education to "all children with disabilities"? What are the competing interests at stake?

2. Under the Individuals with Disabilities Education Improvement Act, local educational agencies may use some special education funds for early intervention services for children who have not been identified as having a disability. As a result, some children who do not have a disability will benefit from funds allocated under the IDEA. Is this an appropriate use of these federal education resources? Is it consistent with the purpose of the IDEA?

Section Two
The Elements of a Claim of Eligibility For Special Education

This section examines each element of the showing that a child must make to establish eligibility for special education and related services. Section Two begins its examination by looking at the enumerated disability of serious emotional disturbance.

A. Enumerated Disability: Severe Emotional Disturbance

The IDEA and its implementing federal regulations define serious emotional disturbance in relatively vague language, giving school administrators broad discretion in reaching eligibility determinations. 34 C.F.R. § 300.8(c)(4) (2015). Accordingly, there is significant conflict over whether a child with behavioral issues that affect her education has a severe emotional disturbance. Further, one of the most contested issues in eligibility determinations is whether a serious emotional disturbance or other social or family problems is the cause of a child's educational and behavioral issues. Consider how the courts in the next two cases treated these issues.

Muller v. Comm. on Special Educ. of East Islip Union Free Sch. Dist.

145 F.3d 95 (2d Cir. 1988)

Chin, District Judge.

The principal issue in this case is whether Treena Muller ("Treena"), a minor, qualified for benefits under the Individuals with Disabilities Education Act (the "IDEA"),

20 U.S.C. § 1400 *et seq.* (1994) (amended 1997), as a child with a "serious emotional disturbance." Defendants-appellants . . . determined that she did not qualify, and on administrative review, an Impartial Hearing Officer and a State Review Officer agreed. The district court, however, concluded that Treena did qualify. Accordingly, the district court vacated the administrative decision, ordered the District to classify Treena as having an emotional disability under the IDEA, and awarded compensatory damages and attorneys' fees. We affirm.

STATEMENT OF THE CASE

A. *The Facts*

The following facts are undisputed. Treena Muller was born in Thailand in 1977 and lived in an orphanage until the age of four, when she was adopted by plaintiffs-appellees Henry and Catherine Muller (the "Mullers"). At that time, Treena had virtually no verbal abilities and could speak neither English nor Thai. Treena entered the East Islip School District in kindergarten, but immediately experienced difficulties in school. She was classified as "speech impaired" by the District after having had to repeat the first grade, and received special education services into the fourth grade, when she was declassified. She received remedial reading services through the seventh grade. Despite failing multiple subjects in the seventh and eighth grades, Treena was never held back and advanced to the ninth grade on schedule. Although her grades began to improve during the first quarter of ninth grade, she began to exhibit behavior problems, such as poor attendance in school, cutting classes, failing to complete assignments, staying out late at night, and generally disobeying her parents.

On January 10, 1993, following a fight with her parents, Treena attempted suicide by ingesting between 10 and 40 aspirins. After being hospitalized for three days, she returned to school but continued to perform poorly. On February 3, 1993, Treena's parents decided to admit her to South Oaks Hospital ("South Oaks"), a private psychiatric treatment facility, for examination. Upon admission, Dr. Vera Liang conducted the initial psychiatric examination of Treena. Her report noted Treena's history of depression and behavioral problems, and her provisional diagnosis was "Conduct Disorder, Undifferent[iated]" and "Depression [Not Otherwise Specified]."

Treena remained at South Oaks for 25 days. Upon discharge, she was referred to an aftercare day treatment program to further address her "anger, depression, impulse control and family problems." She remained in the day treatment program for another three weeks before returning to East Islip High School on March 19, 1993.

Treena's emotional and behavioral problems continued, however, and on April 5, 1993, she was readmitted to South Oaks. Treena was again diagnosed as having a conduct disorder, and the examining doctor noted her continued "dysphoric" mood. Her treatment plan indicated the probable need for continued residential treatment following her stay at South Oaks. Dr. Mark Golden, a consultant at South Oaks who treated Treena and was involved in her discharge plan, testified at a 1994 administrative hearing that Treena's emotional and behavioral problems extended back several years. He further testified that, in his opinion, Treena should be placed in a residential treatment center or she would likely resume her pattern of harmful behavior. After several more weeks at South Oaks, Treena was discharged and on April 30, 1993 she was referred to the Wellspring Foundation ("Wellspring"), a private residential treatment and educational facility in Connecticut primarily for individuals with serious psychological problems.

Dr. Jeffrey Wold, the Director of Psychiatric Services at Wellspring, diagnosed Treena's condition as a "conduct disorder." Seven months later, he prepared a psychiatric evaluation that specified a "current diagnosis" of "Oppositional Defiant Disorder—in remission" and "Post Traumatic Stress Disorder—delayed and related to childhood deprivation/adoption." Treena's Wellspring records are also replete with references to her continued depression, and attending to her depression is repeatedly identified as one of Treena's treatment goals.

The professionals at Wellspring observed that Treena responded well, both emotionally and academically, to the small, highly structured environment at Wellspring and recommended that, for the future, Treena remain in small group settings in which she could receive much needed emotional support and individualized attention. Indeed, they cautioned that Treena was likely to relapse if she were readmitted to the public school system.

In early November, 1993, while Treena was still at Wellspring, the Mullers contacted East Islip's Director of Special Education, Patricia Cuccia, inquiring whether the District would begin paying for Treena's private schooling at Wellspring when the Mullers' insurance coverage ran out. Ms. Cuccia informed the Mullers that a referral to the East Islip Committee on Special Education (the "CSE") was required first, and the proper referral was made on November 8, 1993. As part of the referral process, Treena was required to undergo further educational and psychological evaluations administered by professionals employed by the District.

Dr. Phyllis Cooperman, a psychologist for the District, conducted the psychological evaluation. In her report, she concluded that, although Treena exhibited a "tendency for depression" and had difficulty dealing with emotional stress and conflict with her parents due to poor verbal skills, at that time there was "no indication of a depressive condition which would adversely affect her ability to learn." Tom Barry, the District employee who conducted Treena's educational evaluation, concluded in his report that "[a]lthough Treena's scores reveal a low average performance level, they do not indicate the need for Special Education placement."

On January 5, 1994, following Treena's evaluations by the District, the CSE held a meeting to consider whether Treena was in need of special education services. This initial meeting was adjourned because additional information on Treena's prior history was needed. The CSE reconvened on January 28, 1994, at which time it considered

Treena's educational and psychological evaluations administered by the District, the admission and treatment documentation from Treena's stays at South Oaks and Wellspring, information regarding Treena's academic progress, and a January 27, 1994 psychiatric evaluation of Treena performed by Dr. Wold. In this evaluation, Dr. Wold indicated a current diagnosis of oppositional defiant disorder in remission and post traumatic stress disorder, but stated that Treena's admission diagnosis had been "Oppositional Defiant Disorder with Depression." Dr. Wold also noted in the report that Treena had made "major improvement in treatment" while in the private facilities.

At the conclusion of the January 28, 1994 meeting, the CSE was ready to vote on whether Treena needed special education services. Before the CSE could vote, however, the Mullers' advocate, Merrilee Shannon, requested a second adjournment so that she could gather more documentation from South Oaks and Wellspring concerning Treena's condition. The CSE reconvened on February 23, 1994. Ms. Shannon presented an additional psychiatric report by Dr. Wold, dated February 21, 1994, in which he then identified Treena's clinical diagnosis as "Major Depression in an adolescent with diagnosed Learning Disabilities," and noted that post traumatic stress disorder and "the complications of a fragile personality organization" had been "working" diagnoses.

At the end of the February 23, 1994 meeting, the CSE concluded that Treena did not meet the eligibility criteria for special education services under the IDEA ....

... [I]n March 1994, the Mullers enrolled Treena in a local special education program run by the Educational Assistance Corporation (the "EAC Program"). The EAC Program was the only private special education program the Mullers could find that would accept Treena without a referral from the District. During the time Treena was in the EAC Program, she showed improvement, both behaviorally and academically.

B. *The Proceedings Below*

1. *State Administrative Proceedings*

a. *Before the Impartial Hearing Officer*

The Mullers, unhappy with the CSE's conclusions and recommendations, appealed to an Impartial Hearing Officer ("IHO"). Several of the professionals who treated Treena, including Dr. Golden and Dr. Lynne Albukerk, a psychologist at South Oaks, testified at the hearing that Treena's emotional problems were having a seriously detrimental impact on her education. They testified that Treena exhibited marked academic and social improvement while at South Oaks and Wellspring, and strongly recommended that she continue her secondary education in a private facility where her unique emotional and educational needs could be met. They further testified that aspects of the District's proposed plan would be inappropriate for Treena because returning to East Islip High School would likely cause a setback.

After four days of hearings, ... the IHO concluded that Treena's problems stemmed from "family issues" and that there was an insufficient nexus between those problems, as manifested in her "conduct disorder," and her educational performance to entitle her to special education services under the IDEA.

b. Before the State Review Officer

The Mullers next appealed to the New York State Department of Education, seeking review by a State Review Officer ("SRO"). . . . The SRO dismissed the Mullers' appeal, concluding as follows: "[T]here is no evidence that the child requires special education and/or related services to benefit from instruction. Therefore, I . . . find that the CSE correctly determined that the child would not be appropriately classified as emotionally disturbed."

2. The District Court's Decision

The Mullers then brought suit in federal district court . . . . [T]he district court vacated the findings and conclusions reached in the state administrative proceedings. . . . [T]he district court found that Treena's emotional and behavioral problems adversely affected her academic performance, and held that Treena qualified under the IDEA as "emotionally disturbed" as defined by the relevant state and federal regulations. . . .

DISCUSSION

. . . .

B. *Treena's Entitlement to Educational Services Under the IDEA*

1. *Legal Standards*

Congress passed the IDEA to "assure that all children with disabilities have available to them . . . a free appropriate public education which emphasizes special education and related services designed to meet their unique needs, [and] to assure that the rights of children with disabilities and their parents or guardians are protected." 20 U.S.C. § 1400(c). The term "children with disabilities" includes children with various physical impairments as well as children with a "serious emotional disturbance." *Id.* § 1401(a)(1)(A)(i). Whether a student has a serious emotional disturbance is determined by the individual school district in accordance with state law. Pursuant to New York State regulations, an emotionally disturbed student is defined as:

> A student with an inability to learn which cannot be explained by intellectual, sensory or health factors and who exhibits one or more of the following characteristics over a long period of time and to a marked degree:
>
> (i) an inability to build or maintain satisfactory interpersonal relationships with peers and teachers;
>
> (ii) inappropriate types of behavior or feelings under normal circumstances;
>
> (iii) a generally pervasive mood of unhappiness or depression; or
>
> (iv) a tendency to develop physical symptoms or fears associated with personal or school problems.

> The term does not include socially maladjusted students unless it is determined that they are emotionally disturbed.

N.Y. Comp.Codes R. & Regs. tit. 8, § 200.1(mm)(4) (1996).

....

2. *Analysis*

....

In our view, the district court correctly concluded that Treena suffered from a "serious emotional disturbance" within the meaning of the relevant state and federal regulations .... To qualify as having a "serious emotional disturbance" under the New York State regulations, a child must (1) demonstrate an inability to learn, and (2) exhibit at least one of the four enumerated characteristics over a long period of time and to a marked degree. Here, the record establishes that Treena demonstrated an inability to learn and exhibited *two* of the four enumerated characteristics over a long period of time and to a marked degree.

First, the record clearly establishes that Treena displayed an inability to learn that was not explained solely by intellectual, sensory, or health factors. She was required to repeat the first grade, was classified as speech and language impaired thereafter, received special education services through the fourth grade, received remedial reading services through the seventh grade, and failed multiple subjects in the seventh and eighth grades. Psychologists who examined her testified that her emotional difficulties adversely affected her educational development. This testimony, together with evidence that Treena's academic performance improved in settings in which her emotional problems were being addressed clinically, adequately supports the conclusion that Treena had an inability to learn . . . that stemmed at least in part from her emotional problems, rather than only from her early childhood speech disability or her borderline-range intellectual abilities.

Second, the record also demonstrates that Treena exhibited two of the four characteristics enumerated in the definition of emotional disturbance over a long period of time and to a marked degree. To begin with, the evidence showed that Treena exhibited the third of the four characteristics, a "generally pervasive mood of unhappiness or depression," and that she did so for a long period of time and to a marked degree. While Treena was never formally diagnosed with clinical depression, the regulation does not require that the student be clinically or medically depressed but only that she exhibit a "generally pervasive mood of unhappiness or depression." Treena displayed signs not only of unhappiness and depression but of despondency, as evidenced by her suicide attempt. Moreover, nearly every doctor and psychologist who examined Treena noted in his or her report that Treena exhibited symptoms of depression, and her treatment reports from South Oaks and Wellspring unequivocally demonstrate that Treena was treated for depression.

The record also demonstrates that Treena exhibited the second of the four characteristics, "inappropriate types of behavior or feelings under normal circumstances," for a long period of time and to a marked degree. The district court found numerous examples of Treena's inappropriate behavior, such as "suicide attempts, . . . arson attempts, . . . lies, cutting classes, failure to complete homework, stealing things, quitting the basketball team, . . . defiance, poor grades and academic performance." Many of these behaviors, of course, are not unusual or "inappropriate" by themselves. In combination, however, they provide more than an adequate basis for the district court's conclusion that Treena exhibited "inappropriate types of behavior or feelings under normal circumstances." Moreover, this behavior spanned a period of several years and existed to a marked degree.

The district court correctly concluded, from the record before it, that Treena's problems amounted to more than a mere conduct disorder. Accordingly, we affirm the district court's determination that Treena suffered from a "serious emotional disturbance" . . . and uphold its reversal of the state administrative finding to the contrary.

. . . .

Eschenasy v. N.Y.C. Dep't of Educ.

604 F. Supp. 2d 639 (S.D.N.Y. 2009)

Cedarbaum, District Judge.

Rachel and Dan Eschenasy, plaintiffs as parents of Ann Eschenasy, move for summary judgment that Ann should have been classified as a student with an emotional disturbance as defined in [the] Individuals with Disabilities Education Act (IDEA) and that they should receive tuition reimbursement for John Dewey Academy and the Elan School. The New York City Department of Education ("NYC DOE") and the City of New York, defendants, also move for summary judgment on the grounds that the State Review Officer correctly concluded that Ann was not emotionally disturbed and, therefore, properly denied plaintiffs' request for tuition reimbursement. . . . For the reasons that follow, plaintiffs' motion for summary judgment that Ann is a student with a disability who, by reason thereof, needs special education is granted. . . .

BACKGROUND

I. Ann's Educational History

Ann Eschenasy was a nineteen-year-old girl attending the Elan School when the motions for summary judgment were filed. Her educational history, based on undisputed factual findings and testimony in the administrative hearings below, began with her enrollment in P.S. 199 for kindergarten. Ann had no reported problems in kindergarten but her parents moved her to private school the following year because class sizes were too large. From first to eighth grade, Ann attended Park East Day School, where she began exhibiting social and academic problems. Ann developed a pattern of stealing at the age of eight. She also dressed inappropriately and engaged in sexual misconduct by touching boys. In addition, because Ann had difficulty learning to read and struggled to complete her homework, her parents arranged for extra tutoring.

Ann began high school at the Heschel Day School. During her time at Heschel, Ann exhibited serious behavioral problems. She stole, broke school rules, obtained a tattoo and body piercings, made inappropriate friends on the internet, began using drugs, and ran away from home. Furthermore, she failed a number of her classes.

Also while she was at Heschel, Ann began cutting herself and purging. Ann's pediatrician started her on Effexor, a mood stabilizing drug. Her pediatrician then referred her to Dr. Markus Kraebber, a child and adolescent psychiatrist. Dr. Kraebber diagnosed Ann with a mood disorder and cluster B (histrionic, borderline and antisocial) traits. He recommended that Ann continue to take the mood stabilizing drug and that she be placed in a structured educational environment to address her needs for positive feedback, containment and consistent limits.

Ann was asked to leave Heschel after the 10th grade because of stealing. After her expulsion, Ann was caught forging $3,000 worth of checks. Shortly thereafter, she overdosed on Effexor and was hospitalized. Following hospitalization, Ann began dialectical behavioral therapy (DBT) with Susan Cappi. Ann's participation in DBT was described as poor. Ann came to multiple DBT group sessions high on marijuana and discussed securing cocaine for another group member.

Ann's next school was the Beekman School, where she spent the first semester of her eleventh grade year. At Beekman, Ann used drugs heavily and repeatedly cut classes. She was suspended several times for refusal to attend class and was finally expelled in December of 2004 because of absenteeism. Ann also ran away from home for the first time in December of 2004.

For the spring semester of her eleventh grade year, Ann was sent to the Smith School. At Smith, Ann continued to use drugs and misbehave. After two months, Ann was suspended for theft and use of a classmate's credit card. Ann finished the semester at home with a tutor and was asked not to return to Smith.

Ann ran away from home for the second time in March of 2005. Around this time, Ann's DBT therapist, Susan Cappi, recommended that Ann be placed in a therapeutic boarding school. In order to facilitate boarding school admissions, plaintiffs obtained a neuropsychological evaluation to assess Ann's intellectual, cognitive and emotional function. In May and June of 2005, a private evaluation was conducted by a neuropsychologist, Dr. Barron, who reported that Ann's intellectual ability was in the average range and her academic achievement was on or above the expected level. Dr. Barron also noted that Ann experienced considerable personal stress stemming from lack of self esteem and the conflict engendered by her persistent need for nurturing and affection and her impulsive, willful and obstinate behavior. She found that Ann had a mild, but measurable anomia, a word-finding problem. She diagnosed Ann with conduct disorder, trichotillomania (pulling out hair), borderline personality features and expressive language disorder with mild amnestic features.

By letter dated June 23, 2005, Rachel Eschenasy requested an evaluation of Ann by the NYC DOE's Committee on Special Education ("CSE"). Despite their request for a CSE evaluation, plaintiffs unilaterally enrolled Ann at the John Dewey Academy ("Dewey"), a therapeutic boarding school in Great Barrington, Massachusetts, on August 17, 2005, before the CSE had convened. Ann attended Dewey for several months but was confronted by the headmaster and students about lying and breaking school rules in December of 2005. Ann then entered a wilderness crisis intervention program, anticipating that she would be allowed to return to Dewey once she completed the program. Ann was allowed to return, but was asked to leave Dewey shortly thereafter because the staff believed that Ann required a more restrictive and structured program.

Plaintiffs then enrolled her in the Elan School, another boarding school recommended by the Dewey staff as a more appropriate placement for Ann. Ann was attending the Elan School when summary judgment motions were filed.

. . . .

III. The Administrative Determinations Below

. . . The CSE determined that Ann was not emotionally disturbed and therefore not disabled under the IDEA.

Plaintiffs filed a complaint with the DOE appealing this determination. . . . . The impartial hearing officer ("IHO") found that Ann is "socially maladjusted" and also "seriously emotionally disturbed." According to the IHO, Ann's lying, stealing, truancy and drug abuse are symptomatic of social maladjustment. Ann's cutting and hair pulling are symptomatic of emotional disturbance. The IHO concluded that Elan, but not Dewey, was reasonably calculated to provide Ann an educational benefit and ordered that plaintiffs be reimbursed for Elan's tuition. . . .

On appeal . . . the State Review Officer ("SRO") reversed the IHO's opinion, holding that Ann was not properly classified as emotionally disturbed and therefore plaintiffs were not entitled to any tuition reimbursement. Although the SRO acknowledged that Ann exhibited inappropriate behaviors such as cutting and hair pulling, the SRO concluded that plaintiffs had "not shown that these behaviors affect [Ann's] educational performance to the extent that she needed special education."

Plaintiffs filed this federal suit to challenge the decision of the SRO.

DISCUSSION

I. The Statutory Scheme of the IDEA

. . . .

B) The Standard for Determining Whether Ann Has A Serious Emotional Disturbance

The IDEA defines a "child with a disability" as "a child with mental retardation, hearing impairments, . . . serious emotional disturbance (referred to in this title as 'emotional disturbance') . . . or specific learning disabilities; and who, by reason thereof, needs special education and related services." 20 U.S.C. § 1401(3)(A). Both New York State and federal regulations define an emotional disturbance in the same way, as:

> i) a condition exhibiting one or more of the following characteristics over a long period of time and to a marked degree that adversely affects a child's educational performance:
>
> (A) An inability to learn that cannot be explained by intellectual, sensory, or health factors.
>
> (B) An inability to build or maintain satisfactory interpersonal relationships with peers and teachers.
>
> (C) Inappropriate types of behavior or feelings under normal circumstances.
>
> (D) A general pervasive mood of unhappiness or depression.
>
> (E) A tendency to develop physical symptoms or fears associated with personal or school problems.
>
> ii) Emotional disturbance includes schizophrenia. The term does not apply to children who are socially maladjusted, unless it is determined that they have an emotional disturbance under paragraph (c)(4)(i) of this section.

34 CFR § 300.8(c)(4)(i)-(ii); 8 NYCRR § 200.1(zz)(4).

The regulatory definition delineates four specific conditions a student must satisfy in order to qualify as seriously emotionally disturbed: the student must demonstrate that she has (1) exhibited one of the five listed symptoms, (2) "over a long period of time," and (3) "to a marked degree," and (4) that this condition adversely affects her educational performance. Finally, the definition excludes students whose behavior is attributable to social maladjustment, unless they also suffer from emotional disturbance.

II. Whether Ann Has A Serious Emotional Disturbance

A) Ann's Symptoms

I find that Ann has exhibited two of the five symptoms of emotional disturbance over a long period of time and to a marked degree.

1) Ann Exhibits Inappropriate types of behavior or feelings under normal circumstances

Ann's trichotillomania, self-cutting and suicide attempt are inappropriate behavior under otherwise normal circumstances. According to Ann's father, the hair pulling and cutting behavior was still continuing during her time at Elan when this suit was filed.

Defendants argue that Ann's behavior is simply delinquent and is attributable to Ann's diagnosed conduct disorder rather than an emotional disturbance. In their briefing, Defendants compare Ann to the case of Edward Springer, whom the Fourth Circuit found was not disabled. *Springer v. Fairfax County Sch. Bd.*, 134 F.3d 659

(4th Cir.1998). In *Springer,* the Fourth Circuit reasoned that any adverse effects on the student's educational performance were the result of his truancy and drug use, not an emotional disturbance. The Court credited the testimony of a psychiatrist who found that the student was in control of his actions, unlike emotionally disturbed individuals who may be "in such pain and in such difficulty that they cannot get to their goals." *Id.* at 665. Distinguishing *Springer,* the IHO in this case found "Ann's behavior, her cutting and hair pulling, in particular, reveals a girl in such pain and such difficulty that she cannot get to her goals." The IHO determined that Ann's case was also distinguishable from *Springer* because her behavior has continued for a long time and to a marked degree, noting that Ann has been lying and stealing since she was eight years old, when no drugs were involved, and is now cutting herself and pulling out her hair.

Whether or not such behavior "adversely affected" Ann's "educational performance" (a question addressed below), the IHO was correct in finding that Ann exhibits inappropriate types of behavior or feelings under normal circumstances.

2) Ann Has A Generally Pervasive Mood of Unhappiness or Depression

There is not a significant amount of evidence in the record about Ann's mood. However, Ann has been diagnosed with a mood disorder, and prescribed drugs to treat it. Ann also attempted suicide in June 2004. In *Muller,* the Second Circuit found that Treena Muller exhibited a pervasive mood of depression. Although Muller was "never formally diagnosed with clinical depression, the regulation does not require that the student be clinically or medically depressed." *Muller,* 145 F.3d at 104. Because Treena displayed signs "not only of unhappiness and depression, but of despondency, as evidenced by her suicide attempt," the court held that she exhibited a pervasive mood of unhappiness as enumerated in the definition of emotional disturbance. Comparing Ann's case with that of *Muller,* Ann has also exhibited a general pervasive mood of unhappiness over a long period of time and to a marked degree, as evidenced by her hair pulling, cutting, mood disorder and her suicide attempt.

B) Impact on Ann's "Educational Performance"

To qualify as an emotional disturbance, Ann's symptoms must adversely affect her "educational performance." 34 CFR § 300.8(c)(4); 8 NYCRR § 200.1(zz)(4). The SRO concluded that Ann's emotional problems did not adversely impact her educational performance. Despite acknowledging testimony in the record that Ann failed several courses in high school, the SRO stated that there was no documentary evidence of failing grades nor was there any testimony from her teachers or any indication that she had been held back a grade. Based on this lack of evidence, the SRO found that Ann had not shown that her emotional problems adversely affected her educational performance.

In order to address the SRO's contention that there was insufficient evidence of Ann's academic problems, plaintiffs have proffered additional evidence to this court, in the form of her high school transcripts and an affidavit, that was not proffered in the administrative hearings below. The transcripts show that Ann failed many courses at Beekman and Smith, the first two high schools she attended. The affidavit is sworn to by plaintiffs and describes the problems Ann experienced in school. . . .

. . . .

2) Adverse Effects on Ann's Educational Performance

The SRO concluded that there was insufficient evidence of an adverse effect on Ann's educational performance. The SRO's finding is directly contradicted by Ann's failing grades, repeated expulsions, suspensions, need for tutors and need for summer school.

However, Defendants allege that in order for Ann to qualify as emotionally disturbed, there must be some further evidence that these negative effects on Ann's education were caused by her emotional disturbance symptoms—i.e. her inappropriate behavior under normal circumstances and her pervasive depressive state—and not simply by her bad behavior. The regulation defining emotional disturbance specifies that social maladjustment by itself is not a disability. 34 C.F.R. § 300.8(c)(4); 8 NYCRR § 200.1(zz)(4).

It is undisputed that Ann repeatedly misbehaved in school by cutting class, taking drugs, and stealing. Indeed, psychologist Susan Cappi and neuropsychologist Dr. Barron both diagnosed Ann with conduct disorder. However, Ann also engages in hair pulling and cutting herself, was diagnosed with a mood disorder, diagnosed with borderline personality features and attempted to commit suicide. Ann's neuropsychologist, Dr. Barron, testified that she had considered the criteria for the educational definition of emotional disturbance and determined that Ann met those criteria.

In *Muller*, the Second Circuit stated that the testimony of psychologists that a student's emotional difficulties adversely affected her education, together with evidence that her educational performance improved in settings where her emotional problems were being addressed clinically, adequately supported the conclusion that she was emotionally disturbed. *Muller*, 145 F.3d at 103–04. Similarly, in this case, Dr. Barron testified before the IHO that Ann meets the criteria for emotional disturbance. Ann has also shown significant progress at Elan, where she is receiving the type of structured educational program her doctors recommended. The students at Elan participate in a daytime work program which emphasizes work ethic and is designed to motivate students through promotions. In this program, Ann has been promoted from a worker to a service crew member, where her responsibilities include supervision of other children. In addition, Ann has received high grades at Elan, consisting of two A's, one B and one P.

Reviewing Ann's eligibility de novo, it is more likely than not that all of Ann's problems, not just her misconduct, underlie her erratic grades, expulsions and need for tutoring and summer school. Although Ann exhibits conduct disorder, she also meets the criteria for emotional disturbance as a student exhibiting inappropriate behavior under normal circumstances and a pervasive depressive state, which adversely affect her educational performance. She therefore qualifies as a disabled student who, by reason thereof, needs special education.

. . . .

Notes, Comments, and Questions

1. The IDEA's regulations specifically exclude students who suffer from "social maladjustment" from the definition of severe emotional disturbance, but do not define "social maladjustment." *See* 34 C.F.R. § 300.8(c)(4)(ii) (2015). Does the exclusion of "social maladjustment" from the definition of severe emotional disturbance increase the likelihood that students whose issues may be partially attributed to family issues, alcohol abuse, or drug abuse will be denied necessary special education services? Does the IDEA or its regulations provide sufficient guidance for distinguishing between social maladjustment and severe emotional disturbance? Did the opinions in *Muller* or *Eschenasy* provide guidance in making this determination? On what evidence did the courts rely?

2. Antisocial or disruptive conduct can easily be attributed to poor behavior, lack of respect for authority, adolescent rebellion, or the absence of parental control, instead of an emotional disturbance. Does the lack of guidance in distinguishing between the different types of behavior leave space for personal bias or prejudice against mental disability?

3. Should local educational agencies be responsible for providing drug and alcohol rehabilitation treatment to children with severe emotional disturbances?

4. In *Eschenasy*, the school district argued that there was insufficient evidence to prove that the negative effects on Ann's education were the result of her emotional disturbance and not her conduct disorder. Similarly, in *Muller*, the IHO concluded that there was an "insufficient nexus" between Treena's poor educational performance and her conduct disorder as opposed to her "family issues." If you represented Ann or Treena, what type of evidence would you seek to support a link between the girls' alleged conduct and their poor educational performances?

B. Adverse Effects on Educational Performance

After a child is determined to have a disabling condition, the question turns to whether the disabling condition adversely affects that child's educational performance. Courts have often encountered the questions of how broadly to interpret "educational performance," and how significant an adverse impact the child's disabling condition must have on her educational performance to meet the eligibility requirements. Should educational performance be construed so it is strictly synonymous with academic achievement?

J.D. v. Pawlet Sch. Dist.

224 F.3d 60 (2d Cir. 2000)

KATZMANN, Circuit Judge:

J.D., by his parent J.D., appeals from a final judgment of the United States District Court for the District of Vermont . . . , granting the defendants-appellees' motion for summary judgment dismissing the complaint in its entirety. The district court held that . . . J.D. failed to meet the "adverse effect" eligibility criterion of the Vermont Department of Education Special Education Regulations ("VSER"), which implement the Individuals with Disabilities Education Act ("IDEA"), 20 U.S.C. § 1400 et seq. . . . We affirm.

I. BACKGROUND

A. *Factual Background*

The following facts are undisputed except where noted. J.D., a minor of high school age at all times relevant to this action, is an academically gifted child who also has emotional and behavioral problems. . . .

J.D. attended Pawlet Elementary School through the third grade when he transferred to Poultney Elementary School outside the Pawlet School District for the fourth and fifth grades. Partly because of his academic progress, he skipped the sixth grade and was placed in Poultney High School ("PHS") for the seventh grade, where he was allowed to take ninth grade English. While in the seventh grade, J.D. took an IQ test on which he scored in the top two percent of his age group. In the eighth grade, J.D. took the Comprehensive Test of Basic Skills, a norm-based examination on which he received grade equivalency scores for reading, language, and mathematics that were predominantly in the tenth, eleventh, and twelfth grade levels. Even his lowest score, in spelling, placed him at the mid-eighth grade level. In the ninth grade, he took classes at or above his grade level in a variety of subjects and achieved grades ranging from B to A+.

1. *The IDEA Evaluation*

During the summer of 1996, between J.D.'s ninth and tenth grade years, J.D.'s parents requested that he be evaluated for special education because they were concerned that PHS was not meeting their son's intellectual or emotional needs. In response, the School District convened an Evaluation and Planning Team (the "EPT") to determine J.D.'s eligibility for special education. The EPT considered J.D.'s results on standardized academic achievement tests, his cumulative school file consisting of grades, progress reports, and teacher comments, and a psychological evaluation conducted by Dr. Roger Meisenhelder, a psychologist selected by J.D.'s parents. According to Dr. Meisenhelder, J.D. had "superior" verbal and language skills, together with good concentration and "highly developed" conceptual and abstract thinking skills. These conclusions were largely consistent with J.D.'s academic record from kindergarten through the ninth grade.

However, Dr. Meisenhelder also observed that J.D. experienced "frustration, boredom, alienation, apathy, and hopelessness" because of an absence of intellectual peers at PHS, and that these feelings persisted despite a "somewhat differentiated curriculum at school," leading to passive resistance as well as aggressive behavior at school. Dr. Meisenhelder recommended that J.D. be: (1) classified as a student with an "emotional and behavioral" disability; (2) placed in a school environment in which he has academically challenging courses and intellectual peers; and (3) given individual and family counseling.

Based on Dr. Meisenhelder's report, the EPT concluded that J.D. had an emotional-behavioral disability within the meaning of Rule 2362.1(h) of the VSER, as further explained below. When the EPT members were unable to reach consensus on whether J.D.'s disability adversely affected his educational performance, the School District, pursuant to Rule 2364.1, offered its decision that J.D. did not meet this criterion and notified J.D.'s parents of their right to challenge this decision.

. . . .

3. *The Proceedings Below*

. . . J.D.'s parents requested an administrative due process hearing . . . , seeking reimbursement for J.D.'s tuition and costs at Simon's Rock. . . .

[T]he hearing officer rendered an oral decision granting partial summary judgment for the School District on the substantive IDEA claim. The oral decision was confirmed by a thorough written opinion . . . which held that . . . J.D. was ineligible for special education under the IDEA because he was performing at or above age and grade norms in each of eight basic skill areas . . . . J.D. appealed to the United States District Court for the District of Vermont, which affirmed for substantially the reasons stated in the administrative decision.

II. DISCUSSION

. . . .

B. *The Substantive IDEA Claim*

. . . The substantive claim presents a matter of first impression: whether an academically gifted child with an emotional-behavioral disability is eligible for special education under the IDEA and the corresponding Vermont regulations. We agree with the district court that he is not.

1. *The IDEA*

The IDEA was enacted, in part, "'to assure that all children with disabilities have available to them . . . a free appropriate public education which emphasizes special education and related services designed to meet their unique needs.'" The instruction must "meet the State's educational standards, approximate the grade levels used in the State's regular education, and comport with the child's IEP [individualized education program.]" Recognizing that educational policy and practice are traditional State and local functions, in enacting the IDEA, Congress did not prescribe any substantive standard of education, instead seeking only "to open the door of public education to handicapped children on appropriate terms." . . . .

Under the IDEA, the term "children with disabilities" means, among others, children with a "serious emotional disturbance . . . who, by reason thereof, *need special education* and related services." *Id.* § 1401(a)(1)(A) (emphasis added); *see* 34 C.F.R. § 300.7(a)(1). The federal regulations promulgated under the statute further define "serious emotional disturbance" as:

> a condition exhibiting one or more of the following characteristics over a long period of time and to a marked degree that adversely affects a child's educational performance—
>
> . . . .
>
> (B) An inability to build or maintain satisfactory interpersonal relationships with peers and teachers;
>
> (C) Inappropriate types of behavior or feelings under normal circumstances;
>
> (D) A general pervasive mood of unhappiness or depression; or
>
> (E) A tendency to develop physical symptoms or fears associated with personal or school problems.

Id. 34 C.F.R. § 300.7(b)(9)(i) (emphasis added). However, neither the IDEA nor the federal regulations define the terms "need special education" or "adverse effect on educational performance," leaving it to each State to give substance to these terms.

2. The Vermont Special Education Regulations

The VSER, promulgated by the Vermont Department of Education, have been approved by the U.S. Department of Education. Rule 2362(1) establishes three eligibility criteria for special education that are consistent with the IDEA:

> To be determined eligible for special education, an elementary or secondary student must receive a comprehensive evaluation . . . under the auspices of a Basic Staffing Team . . . ; and based on the results of the comprehensive evaluation, the Basic Staffing Team must determine that the student:
>
> (a) meets one or more disability categories (Rule 2362.1);
>
> (b) *exhibits the adverse effect of the disability on educational performance;* and
>
> (c) is in need of special education.

VSER 2362(1) (emphasis added).

Rule 2362(2)(b) defines "adverse effect of the disability on educational performance" as follows:

> To establish that a disability has an adverse effect on the student's educational performance, the Basic Staffing Team shall determine and document that the student is functioning significantly below expected age or grade norms,

> *in one or more of the basic skills.* This determination of adverse effect, usually defined as 1.0 standard deviation or its equivalent, shall be documented and supported by two or more measures of school performance. These measures may include but are not limited to:
>
> —parent or teacher observation
>
> —grades
>
> —curriculum-based measures
>
> —work or language samples
>
> —other test results.

VSER 2362(2)(b) (emphasis added).

Rule 2362(3) further provides:

> [U]nless otherwise stated in an individual category of disability (Rule 2362.1), basic skill areas are defined as:
>
> (a) oral expression;
>
> (b) listening comprehension;
>
> (c) written expression;
>
> (d) basic reading skills;
>
> (e) reading comprehension;
>
> (f) mathematics calculation;
>
> (g) mathematics reasoning; and
>
> (h) motor skills.

VSER 2362(3).

3. *J.D.'s Eligibility*

a. "Adverse Effect" Measured by Effect on Basic Skills

The defendants contend that J.D. did not meet the "adverse effect" eligibility criterion under Rule 2362(1). Relying on the list of basic skills in Rule 2362(3), the defendants argue that J.D.'s emotional disability had no adverse effect on his educational performance because he consistently performed at or above the level of his age cohorts in each of the enumerated areas. J.D., on the other hand, points out that Rule 2362(3) states that the list of basic skills is used to determine eligibility for special education, "unless otherwise stated in an individual category of disability (Rule 2362.1)." J.D. interprets Rule 2362(3) to mean that the basic skills enumerated therein do not apply to a student, such as himself, who has a disability enumerated in Rule 2362.1. In lieu of the 2362(3) factors, J.D. argues that we should look to Rule 2362.1 for indicators of adverse effect. Rule 2362.1, entitled "Categories of Disability," states that "[t]he existence of one or more of the following categories of disability shall be established according to the criteria set forth below." Included among the categories is "emotional-behavioral disability":

> An emotional-behavioral disability shall be identified by the occurrence of one or more of the following conditions exhibited over a long period of time and to a marked degree:
>
> . . . .
>
> 2. An inability to build or maintain satisfactory interpersonal relationships with peers and teachers;
>
> 3. Inappropriate types of behavior or feelings under normal circumstances;
>
> 4. A general pervasive mood of unhappiness or depression[.]

VSER 2362.1(1)(h). . . .

Based on the language and structure of the VSER, we have no choice but to reject J.D.'s interpretation. First, Rule 2362.1(1)(h) provides that the criteria set forth therein shall be used to establish "the existence of" a covered disability (*i.e.*, the *first* eligibility criterion under Rule 2362(1)), not the presence of an adverse effect on educational performance (*i.e.*, the *second* eligibility criterion under Rule 2362(1)). This is confirmed by Rule 2362(1)(a) (existence of a disability), which specifically cross-references Rule 2362.1. In contrast, Rule 2362(1)(b) (adverse effect) does not cross-reference Rule 2362.1. Second, Rule 2362.1(1)(c), which defines the disability of visual impairment, expressly states: "For the purposes of this disability, mobility and orientation skills shall also be considered to be basic skills." Such modification of the 2362(3) list of basic skills is what is meant by the phrase "unless otherwise stated in an individual category of disability" in Rule 2362(3). Thus, the district court correctly evaluated the effect of J.D.'s emotional-behavioral disability on his educational performance by reference to the basic skills in Rule 2362(3).

b. *Measures of Educational Performance*

J.D. also argues that his educational performance cannot be measured by his grades and achievement test results alone, which were indisputably at or above the norm for his age group. Rule 2362(2)(b) provides that the determination of adverse effect "shall be documented and supported by two or more measures of school performance," including, among others, grades and "other test results." Conversely, if a plaintiff is unable to identify at least two school performance measures that point to an adverse effect, the plaintiff would not qualify for special education under the IDEA. In this case, the district court highlighted J.D.'s grades and norm-referenced achievement test results as well as the psychologist's comments. These measures showed that J.D. consistently performed above the mean in math and other basic skills. Although not discussed in the district court's opinion, the record also contains reports and comments from teachers and various personality evaluations. For example, four teachers commented in J.D.'s 1995–1996 academic year report card that he exhibited "excellent application." One of these teachers also characterized his academic ability as "outstanding" compared to other applicants for college preparatory schools. Based on the overwhelming evidence in the record, the district court did not err in concluding that J.D.'s basic skills, and hence his educational performance, were not adversely affected by his disability within the meaning of the Vermont Rule.

J.D., on the other hand, emphasizes his emotional condition, including his difficulty with interpersonal relationships and negative feelings. However, while these are signs of an emotional disability, under the statutory and administrative schemes, they are not measures of an adverse effect on basic skills by which educational performance must be assessed. . . .

. . . .

Mr. I. v. Me. Sch. Admin. Dist. No. 55

480 F.3d 1 (1st Cir. 2007)

Howard, Circuit Judge.

This case presents an issue of eligibility for benefits under the Individuals with Disabilities Education Act, 20 U.S.C. § 1400 *et seq.* (Supp. 2006) (the "IDEA"). . . . The appellant, Maine School Administrative District No. 55 ("the district"), appeals the district court's determination that the appellees' daughter ("LI") qualifies as a "child with a disability" eligible for special education and related services under the IDEA as a result of her Asperger's Syndrome. . . . We affirm the judgment of the district court.

. . . .

II.

A.

LI attended Cornish Elementary School in Cornish, Maine, until 2003. Though she excelled academically, by the fourth grade she began to experience sadness, anxiety, and difficulty with peer relationships. These problems persisted into the fifth grade, when LI sought to distance herself physically from most of her classmates. Her parents sought psychological counseling for LI and she started taking a prescription anti-depressant. Her grades also dropped from "high honors" to "honors." As the school year progressed, however, LI became more successful at interacting with her peers and participating in class.

During the summer recess preceding sixth grade, LI asked her mother, as she had the previous summer, to allow her to be home-schooled. LI also expressed her desire to attend The Community School ("TCS"), a private school in South Tamworth, New Hampshire, where her older sister had matriculated. Nevertheless, LI started the 2003–2004 school year at Cornish, where Mrs. I believed her daughter would benefit, in particular, from her assigned sixth grade teacher.

By mid-September, however, LI was "slacking off" in her academic work and regularly missing school, prompting a meeting between her teacher and Mrs. I. At this meeting, also attended by LI, Mrs. I noticed cuts or scratches on her daughter's arms; the teacher offered that LI might have inflicted those wounds on herself during her "lengthy bathroom breaks" from class. According to the teacher, LI was also having continued trouble relating with her peers due to a "serious lack of awareness" of their social and emotional states, which bordered on "hostility." The teacher added that she could not "reach" LI, who had refused to complete assignments and shown a "passive resistance to meeting learning goals." Yet the teacher considered LI "a very bright young girl with strong language and math skills . . . capable of powerful insights in her reading and writing . . . ."

The teacher and Mrs. I came up with a "contract" that would have entitled LI to study more advanced topics in her areas of interest in November if she satisfactorily completed her assignments for October. As October approached, however, LI refused to sign the contract and stayed home from school on both September 30 and October 1. On October 1, following an argument with Mrs. I over one of LI's academic assignments, LI deliberately ingested excessive quantities of one [of] her prescription drugs and two over-the-counter medications in a suicide attempt.

LI spent the balance of the day in the emergency room at a nearby hospital and was discharged with instructions to remain out of school for two days under high safety precautions. The hospital social worker also directed Mr. and Mrs. I to "share with [LI] something that would change in her life, and produce a positive impact on her emotional functioning." Based on LI's comments to hospital personnel that she hated school, Mr. and Mrs. I told her that she would not have to return to Cornish Elementary and discussed enrollment at TCS as an alternative.

In the wake of her attempted suicide, LI met with a new counselor, who, suspecting that LI might suffer from Asperger's Syndrome, referred her to Dr. Ellen Popenoe for neuropsychological testing. Mr. and Mrs. I conveyed this information, as well as the news of LI's suicide attempt, to the district's director of special services, Jim McDevitt. They added that LI would not return to Cornish Elementary "for the time being" and that they were looking at other options, including TCS. McDevitt explained the process for seeking reimbursement from the district for placing LI in a private school and also told the parents that the district planned to convene a pupil evaluation team for LI at the end of the month. At that meeting, the PET decided that LI should receive up to ten hours of tutoring outside of school each week pending completion of her neuropsychological testing.

The testing, finished by early November, further suggested that LI had Asperger's Syndrome, as well as adjustment disorder with depressed mood. Popeneo, the neuropsychologist, observed that LI "experiences significant limitations in many areas of adaptive skills" and executive skills, "which likely contribute[s] to her behavioral and emotional difficulties." These behavioral difficulties, particularly LI's poor pragmatic language abilities and restricted range of social interests, supported a diagnosis of Asperger's. Popeneo recommended that LI begin seeing both a social skills coach, who would help her develop social abilities and judgment, and a therapist familiar with Asperger's, who would use a cognitive-behavioral approach.

Popeneo also recommended that LI undergo a speech-language evaluation, which was completed in January 2004 by Amber Lambke, a speech-language pathologist. Lambke observed that LI suffered "significant social understanding deficits which impact her overall emotional and social well-being." Like Popeneo, Lambke recommended that LI receive direct teaching of social skills.

In the meantime, McDevitt told Mrs. I that he would attempt to find LI a tutor in accordance with the PET's decision. Mrs. I had not heard back from him by November 10, however, so she started home-schooling LI. Despite additional prodding by Mrs. I in November and December, the district never provided a tutor as ordered by the PET, nor explained its failure to do so. While LI preferred home-schooling to attending Cornish Elementary, Mrs. I was having trouble getting LI to complete her assignments, and her counselor believed that LI should resume formal schooling.

On January 5, 2004, LI began attending TCS. Although she was withdrawn and isolated at the outset, over time LI developed positive relationships with some of her peers. She also thrived academically, completing assignments at the seventh- and eighth-grade level with ease. TCS, however, provided LI with neither the direct teaching of social skills nor the cognitive behavioral therapy that had been recommended as treatment for her Asperger's.

When the PET reconvened in early March, it accepted Popenoe's conclusion that LI suffered from both Asperger's and adjustment disorder with depressed mood. The PET also agreed that LI needed social skills and pragmatic language instruction. The PET, however, could not reach consensus on whether LI qualified as a "child with a disability" under the IDEA. The district's representatives argued that LI's condition, whether denominated "autism," "emotional disturbance," or "other health impairment," 20 U.S.C. § 1401(3)(A)(i), had not affected her academic performance "to a marked degree" or "over a long period of time," which they deemed essential to IDEA eligibility. The district then issued a "prior written notice" announcing its refusal to offer special education services on the stated basis of "no significant adverse effect on education." . . . .

. . . .

. . . LI completed the 2003–2004 academic year at TCS, and stayed on for the 2004–2005 and 2005–2006 school years as well. While she has done well academically, she continues to experience "atypical" peer relationships and spent the summer of 2004 shunning her TCS classmates in favor of solitary pursuits. LI also generally refuses to go outdoors or to eat more than a severely limited variety of foods. Her current social worker believes that, without social skills coaching, LI is unlikely to master the flexible thinking, problem solving, teamwork, and communication abilities she will need for employment in the future.

B.

After the final PET decision, Mr. and Mrs. I requested a due process hearing to challenge the district's refusal to identify LI as a child with a disability under the IDEA. The hearing officer upheld the district's decision that LI was ineligible for IDEA services. The hearing officer noted the parties' agreement that LI had Asperger's and a depressive disorder, making her "a troubled young woman," but further observed that she was not entitled to IDEA benefits unless these disabilities "'adversely affect[ed]' [her] educational performance."

The hearing officer recognized that both the IDEA and Maine's implementing regulations define "educational performance" to include more than just academic proficiency, but concluded that the IDEA does not call for services "to address social and emotional needs when there are *no* academic needs." Accordingly, because LI "completes homework independently, is well behaved in class, is successful at test taking and successfully completes projects," the hearing officer determined that "neither the [IDEA] nor the Maine Special Education Regulations require a school district to provide special education services to address what is essentially a mental health issue."

In response, Mr. and Mrs. I commenced an action in the district court ....

The district court ... conclud[ed] that LI's "condition did adversely affect her educational performance as Maine defines that term and that the events of the fall of 2003 cannot be isolated from [her] underlying condition." The district court determined that LI's Asperger's had exerted an adverse effect on her educational performance as measured by state criteria, most significantly in the areas of socialization and communication. The district court also disagreed with the view that any downturn in LI's educational performance was too fleeting to constitute an "adverse effect." Reasoning that neither the Maine regulations defining the disabilities ... nor their federal counterparts used any restrictive modifier in conjunction with the term "adversely affects," the district court ruled that "*any* negative effect should be sufficient" to constitute a disability under the IDEA.

Turning to the second prong of the IDEA's eligibility standard ..., the district court concluded that LI needed special education and related services by reason of her disability. First, the district court found that the PET had agreed to provide LI with a number of accommodations that fit the definition of "special education" under both the IDEA and Maine law, including one-on-one tutoring and instruction in social pragmatics. Second, observing that "the PET, the experts, the School District and the parents all initially believed that [LI] 'needed' the identified services," the district court decided to "hold the parties to their original understandings" and therefore treated "need" as an uncontested issue. Based on its determination that LI satisfied both elements of the IDEA eligibility test, the district court ordered the district "to convene a PET meeting ... to develop an IEP for [LI] that meets her unique needs as a student with Asperger's Syndrome and a depressive disorder."

....

III.

....

A.

1.

....

As we have seen, the right to special education and related services under the IDEA extends to children "with" one or more of a variety of disabilities, 20 U.S.C. § 1401(3)

(A)(i), "who, by reason thereof, need[ ] special education and related services." *Id.* § 1401(3)(A)(ii). The IDEA does not itself define any of the qualifying disabilities listed in § 1401(3)(A)(i), though the Department of Education has issued a regulation fleshing them out. 34 C.F.R. § 300.8(c). The regulatory definitions, with one exception not relevant here, state, among other requirements, that each condition must "adversely affect[] a child's educational performance." *Id.* § 300.8(c)(1)-(c)(13). In keeping with the IDEA's respect for state policy judgments, however, the regulation does not expand upon this phrase, "leaving it to each State to give substance to these terms."

It is here that the district's argument as to the proper scope of § 1401(3)(A) begins to encounter difficulty. While Maine's Department of Education has promulgated its own regulation defining the disabilities recognized under the IDEA, those definitions simply ape their federal counterparts, including the requirement that a disability "adversely affect [] the student's educational performance." 05-071-101 Me.Code. R. §§ 3.2-3.14 (2006). The regulation, like its federal cousin, also does not further elaborate on this phrase, although Maine has adopted its own definition of "educational performance" for IDEA purposes:

> The term "educational performance" includes academic areas (reading, math, communication, etc.), non-academic areas (daily life activities, mobility, etc.), extracurricular activities, progress in meeting goals established for the general curriculum, and performance on State-wide and local assessments.

Id. § 2.7. Despite this expansive notion of educational performance, and in the absence of any regulatory guidance as to the term "adversely affects," the district asks us to hold that a child meets the first criterion of IDEA eligibility in Maine "only if the student's condition imposes a significant negative impact on the child's educational performance . . . limited to those areas of performance actually being measured and assessed by the local unit, in accordance with law." We decline to do so.

At the outset, Maine does not look only at "areas of performance actually being measured and assessed by the local unit" when determining whether a child has a disability under the IDEA. That much is clear from the regulatory definition of "educational performance" itself, which counts "performance on state-wide and local assessments" as just one of a number of different indicators embraced by the concept. As the district points out, the term "general curriculum," which also appears in the definition of educational performance, has a narrower meaning under the regulations, *i.e.*, "the school administrative unit's local curriculum for grades K-12, which incorporate the content standards and performance indicators of the Learning Results." 05-071-010 Me.Code R. § 2.11. Based on this definition, the district argues that "educational performance" encompasses only those "performance indicators" measured as part of the local curriculum. Even if the district's reading of "general curriculum" is correct, however, the fact remains that a student's progress in that regard comprises but one of the aspects of "educational performance" as defined by the regulation. More far-ranging measurements, such as "academic areas" and "non-academic areas," are also included.

As the magistrate judge and the district court observed, Maine's broad definition of "educational performance" squares with the broad purpose behind the IDEA: "to ensure that all children with disabilities have available to them a free and appropriate public education that emphasizes special education and related services designed to meet their unique needs and prepare them for further education, *employment,* and *independent living.*" 20 U.S.C. § 1400(d)(1)(A) (emphases added). We have likewise held that the IDEA entitles qualifying children to services that "target '*all* of [their] special needs,' whether they be academic, physical, emotional, or social." It is true that we have also stated that IDEA services need not address "problems truly 'distinct' from learning problems." But it does not follow, as the hearing officer wrongly concluded, that a child without "academic needs" is per se ineligible for IDEA benefits, especially when the state has conditioned eligibility on a standard that explicitly takes "non-academic areas" into account. In other words, as the district admits, "educational performance in Maine is more than just academics."

In light of Maine's broad notion of "educational performance" as the standard of IDEA eligibility, we see no basis for restricting that standard to "areas of performance actually being measured and assessed by the local unit." Indeed, "there is nothing in IDEA or its legislative history that supports the conclusion that . . . 'educational performance' is limited only to performance that is graded." To be sure, some states have adopted more circumscribed criteria for identifying children with disabilities under the IDEA, requiring, for example, that a student perform poorly in a specific area of "basic skills." Maine, however, has chosen not to do so. We therefore decline the district's invitation to reformulate state educational policy by narrowing the indicia of educational performance used as the test for IDEA eligibility under Maine law. The district court properly articulated this standard as "whether [LI's] condition adversely affected her performance in any of the educational areas Maine has identified."

The district also argues that the district court misconstrued the "adversely affects" component of the test to include disabilities with "any adverse effect on educational performance, however slight . . . ." The correct formulation, the district urges, requires "some significant impact on educational performance." In rejecting this proposal, the district court reasoned that the phrase "adversely affects," as it appears in the relevant regulations, "has no qualifier such as 'substantial,' 'significant,' or 'marked,'" and declined to infer such a limitation "from Maine's regulatory silence." We agree with this interpretation of the "adversely affects" standard.

Though the district marshals a number of arguments in support of its contrary position, they all sound a common theme: that an unlimited definition of "adversely affects" will qualify every child with one of the listed disabilities—no matter how minor—for IDEA benefits. This contention, however, overlooks the structure of the IDEA's eligibility standard, which requires not only that a child have one of the listed conditions, § 1401(3)(A)(i), but also that, "by reason thereof," the child "needs special education and related services," *id.* § 1401(3)(A)(ii). So a finding that a child meets the first criterion because his or her disability adversely affects educational performance—to whatever degree—does not itself entitle the child to special education and related services under the IDEA. The child must also need special education and related services by reason of the disability.

In fact, an adverse effect on educational performance, standing alone, does not even satisfy the first prong of the eligibility test. The child's condition must also possess the additional characteristics required by the regulatory definitions of each of the disabilities enumerated in § 1401(3)(A)(i). For example, to meet the first part of the eligibility standard on the basis of autism, a child must have "[1] a developmental disability [2] significantly affecting [3] verbal and [4] nonverbal communication and [5] social interaction, [6] generally evident before age three, [7] that adversely affects a child's educational performance." 34 C.F.R. § 300.8(c)(1)(i); 05-071-101 Me.Code. R. § 3.2. Thus, the "adversely affects educational performance" requirement serves as but one of a list of factors that must be present for a child's condition to qualify as a disability under § 1401(3)(A)(i)—and, to receive IDEA benefits, the child must also need special education and related services by reason of the disability under § 1401(3)(A)(ii). The district court's interpretation of "adversely affects," then, is unlikely to loose the torrent of IDEA claims forecast by the district and its amici.

. . . .

We reject the district's argument that such a limitation lurks in the term "adversely," which the district equates with "calamitously" or "perniciously" on the authority of an unabridged dictionary. We think it considerably more likely that federal regulators used "adverse" in its ordinary sense, namely "against." In this way, the regulation sensibly demands that a disability cannot qualify a child for IDEA benefits unless it has a negative effect on educational performance; no effect, or a positive one, will not do. The regulation does not, however, put any quantitative limit, "significant" or otherwise, on the disability.

Maine's regulation, cribbed from 34 C.F.R. § 300.8, also requires no particular degree of impact on educational performance. 05-071-101 Me.Code R. §§ 3.2–3.14. This fact alone distinguishes this case from the decisions of other courts, cited by the district, which derived a higher standard from state law. In *J.D.*, for example, the Second Circuit considered a Vermont regulation that defined "adverse effect of the disability on educational performance" to require a determination "that the student is functioning significantly below expected age or grade norms, in one or more of the basic skills." This provision further required that the "determination of adverse effect, usually defined as 1.0 standard deviation or its equivalent, shall be documented and supported by two or more measures of school performance," which were themselves specified by the regulation. Based on this standard, the Second Circuit concluded that the child did not qualify for IDEA benefits because he was "unable to identify at least two school performance measures that point to an adverse effect," despite his emotional-behavioral disability.

The Second Circuit reached its decision in *J.D.,* then, by applying the highly specific definition of "adversely affects educational performance" set forth in state law, not by imposing its own gloss on that language, as the district invites us to do here. For the reasons we have stated, we decline that invitation. States wishing to put meat on the bones of the "adversely affects" standard are free to do so—provided, of course, they do not transgress the "floor" of substantive protection set by the IDEA. On its own, however, the federal regulation does not contain the "significant impact" requirement the district desires, and we cannot put it there. The district court correctly ruled that any negative impact, regardless of degree, qualifies as an "adverse effect" under the relevant federal and state regulations defining the disabilities listed in § 1401(3)(A)(i).

2.

... As the hearing officer noted, the parties agree that LI suffers from Asperger's, manifested in her poor pragmatic language skills and social understanding difficulties, as well as from a depressive disorder brought on by the stress of managing these problems; indeed, the district has never questioned the opinions of LI's neuropsychologist and speech therapist in this regard. The parties disagree, however, on whether these conditions have adversely affected LI's educational performance in light of her strong grades, generally nondisruptive classroom behavior, and what the district court called her "undisputed intellectual ability." In a lengthy written opinion, the district court tackled this issue head on, ultimately finding that, despite LI's above-average academic performance, "many of [her] social and communication deficits, including her isolation, inflexibility, and self-mutilation during schooltime, are precisely in the content areas and skills that Maine mandates educationally." This finding, the district court reasoned, compelled the conclusion that LI's disability had exerted an adverse effect on her educational performance under the governing standard.

Much of the district's challenge to this outcome relies on its contention that the district court applied the "adversely affects educational performance" test too leniently, which we have already rejected. A few of the district's supplemental points, however, merit additional discussion. First, the district argues that the district court mistakenly gauged LI's educational performance on the basis of selected "performance indicators," *see* 05-071-131 Me.Code R. §§ 1–8, that Maine has developed to measure students' proficiency in various "content standard subject areas." Me. Rev.Stat. Ann. tit. 20–A, § 6209. This was error, the district asserts, because Maine does not mandate the actual use of the performance indicators by local school districts, but has simply instructed them to develop their own "local assessment systems." *Id.* § 6202–A. While we have our doubts about this proposition, *see* 05-071-127 Me.Code R. § 4.02 (requiring each district to "implement a local assessment system as the measure of student progress on achievement of the content standards of the system of Learning Results established in" 05-071-131 Me.Code R. §§ 1–8), the district court did not assess LI's educational performance solely by reference to the performance indicators. Our review of the record convinces us that, even if the district court erred by also using the performance indicators to measure LI's educational performance, the error did not affect the outcome of its analysis.

In particular, the district court found that LI had difficulty with "communication," an area of "educational performance" specifically incorporated in Maine's definition of that term for IDEA purposes. The district disputes this finding, emphasizing certain aspects of both her educators' observations and the results of the testing conducted by Popeneo and Lambke. The district court, however, focused on other aspects of those materials, such as the educators' reports of LI's "distancing" herself from her teachers and peers and, most significantly, the experts' express conclusions that LI had "poor pragmatic language skills" and "significant social understanding deficits." The district court was by no means required to second-guess these conclusions, especially after they had been unreservedly accepted by both the districts' representatives at the PET and the hearing officer. Though the record of the administrative hearing might permit a different view, the district court did not commit clear error in finding that LI's Asperger's has impaired her ability to communicate.

Moreover, the district court's ruling that LI had demonstrated an adverse effect on her educational performance did not rest solely on her deficits in communication, but also on other difficulties implicating "the career preparation component of the Maine general curriculum." The district does not question that "career preparation"—which comprises one of the "content standards" dictated by statute, Me.Rev.Stat. Ann. tit. 20–A, § 6209(2)(A), rather than one of the "performance indicators" established by regulation—is irrelevant to the "educational performance" inquiry for purposes of the IDEA. Indeed, the IDEA exists, in part, to ensure children with disabilities receive an education preparing them for employment. Nor does the district question the lower court's specific finding, consistent with the opinion of LI's current social worker, that a number of LI's symptoms have hindered her in this area. This finding was itself an adequate basis for the district's court's conclusion that LI's educational performance has suffered, even if, as the district argues, her condition has not impacted her communication skills.

Second, the district argues that the impact of LI's condition on her educational performance, which it sees as limited to her suicide attempt and the events immediately preceding it in the fall of 2003, was not sustained enough to constitute an adverse effect. Though the magistrate judge accepted this point of view, the district court disagreed, treating the suicide attempt as simply the darkest point in the spectrum of LI's educational difficulties. There is ample support for this approach in the record. The signs of LI's Asperger's revealed themselves in the fourth grade, when she began experiencing difficulty with peer relationships, and first translated into a measurable impact on her schoolwork in the fifth and sixth grades, when her grades declined. More importantly, there is every indication that these symptoms will persist, to one degree or another: they have not completely subsided since LI's enrollment at TCS, and both Popeneo and LI's current social worker believe that continued intervention is essential to LI's long-term success. In light of this evidence, the district's argument that LI's suicide attempt did not adversely affect her educational performance is beside the point; as Popeneo explained, the suicide attempt was but a manifestation of LI's Asperger's and associated depression. The district court properly treated these disorders, rather than the suicide attempt, as the relevant condition for assessing the impact of LI's disability upon her educational performance.

. . . .

. . . Having found that the district court's ruling as to the first prong also holds up we affirm the district court's decision that LI is eligible for services under the IDEA.

. . . .

Notes, Comments, and Questions

1. The court recognized that some of J.D.'s emotional issues stemmed from his lack of intellectual peers. However, the court ultimately concluded that J.D.'s academic gifts were not a disabling condition under the IDEA. Should it be a school district's responsibility under the IDEA either to address such emotional issues or ensure placement in an academic environment in which a child is surrounded by his intellectual peers? Does the analysis and impact of the availability of "intellectual peers" change if we are discussing a child who is struggling academically? Should being academically gifted be considered a disabling condition?

2. Both *J.D.* and *Mr. I.* provide a lens through which to view the relationship between the IDEA and the state laws that implement it. Were the definitions and standards the courts employed from the Vermont and Maine laws different enough to explain the differing outcomes in the two cases under the IDEA? Should state laws and regulations enable differing eligibility determinations under a single federal statutory scheme?

3. The court in *Mr. I.* discussed the varying tests that can be used to determine the "adversely affects" component of the IDEA eligibility analysis. The court discussed whether "any adverse effect on educational performance, however slight," is sufficient or if the disabling condition must have "some significant impact on educational performance." Both the court of appeals and the district court ultimately rejected the requirement of a significant impact, noting that the regulations contain no qualifiers. What legal or policy arguments could the school district have made in support of the argument that the IDEA requires more than a *de minimis* adverse impact on educational performance? What legal or policy arguments could the school district have made in support of the position that the IDEA requires an academic impact in addition to adverse emotional effects?

4. The court in *J.D.* concluded that the school district had accommodated J.D.'s disability in accord with Section 504 of the Rehabilitation Act of 1973. 224 F.3d at 71.

Section 504 ensures that schools that receive federal funding do not discriminate against students with disabilities . . . . 29 U.S.C. § 794(a) (2012). Unlike the IDEA and its list of specific qualifying conditions, Section 504 employs a broad definition of disability that includes any physical or mental impairment that substantially limits a major life activity. 34 C.F.R. § 104.3(j) (2015). As a result, Section 504 often affords protection to students who do not qualify for special education services under the IDEA. Why would a child who qualifies for services under Section 504 also seek coverage under the IDEA? Can you think of some services that a child is entitled to under IDEA but not under 504? *See, e.g.*, Yankton Sch. Dist. v. Schramm, 93 F.3d 1369, 1371–72, 1376 (8th Cir. 1996) (child found eligible for services under Section 504 sought eligibility under IDEA because Section 504 does not require transition services).

5. In addition to an initial evaluation for eligibility for special education services, a child with a disability must be re-evaluated by a local education agency at least every three years, but not more than once a year. 20 U.S.C. § 1414(a)(2)(B) (2012). During the eligibility reevaluation, the school district must determine whether the child continues to need special education and related services under the IDEA. *Id.* § 1414(c)(1)(B)(iii).

C. Needs Special Education and Related Services

Although the IDEA requires a link between a qualifying disabling condition and the need for special education and related services, the IDEA itself and its implementing regulations provide little guidance for how to interpret and implement this requirement.

Alvin Indep. Sch. Dist. v. A.D.

503 F.3d 378 (5th Cir. 2007)

BENAVIDES, Circuit Judge:

Appellant A.D. appeals the district court's judgment in favor of Appellee Alvin Independent School District ("AISD"), finding that the Special Education Hearing Officer ("Hearing Officer") improperly determined that A.D. meets the definition of "child with a disability" under the Individuals with Disabilities Education Act ("IDEA"), 20 U.S.C. §§ 1400–91. We AFFIRM.

I.

A.D. is a student in AISD diagnosed with Attention Deficit Hyperactivity Disorder ("ADHD"). A.D. receives medical treatment for his ADHD, including prescriptions for ADHD medications. He has attended AISD schools since he was three years old, and he participated in the district's Early Childhood and Preschool Program for Children with Disabilities on the basis of a speech impediment. Because of both the speech impediment and the ADHD, A.D. qualified for special education services through third grade, at which point his mother and school personnel agreed that he no longer qualified for those services. After his dismissal from special education, A.D. performed well throughout elementary school.

Starting in seventh grade, however, A.D. began to exhibit behavioral problems. He received numerous discipline referrals, and teachers removed him several times from the classroom and sent him to in-school suspension. A.D. was placed in the "At Risk" program at Alvin Junior High, which involved a Student Success Team consisting of several school personnel meeting regularly to discuss his performance. A.D. continued to pass all of his classes and met the statewide standards required by the Texas Assessment of Knowledge and Skills ("TAKS").

A.D.'s behavioral problems continued throughout eighth grade. Around this time, A.D. faced the tragic death of his baby brother. Additionally, A.D. began to abuse alcohol, developed a strained relationship with his stepfather, and his mother was expecting a new baby. In response to these events and A.D.'s ongoing behavioral problems, the Student Success Team met with A.D. and drafted an "Academic and Behavior Contract," which required A.D. to abide by certain standards, such as taking his medication every day, following the dress code, and completing assignments on time. A.D. signed the contract and attended all but three of the remaining days in the school year. However, the behavioral problems continued. The Student Success Team recommended, but did not implement, two interventions.

A.D.'s behavioral issues culminated in theft of property and robbery of a school-sponsored concession stand. Due to the latter incident, A.D. was sent to in-school suspension for ten days, and AISD eventually recommended A.D.'s placement in an alternative education program. Even with these issues, however, A.D. passed the eighth grade with one A, three Bs, two Cs, and one D and passed the TAKS test, receiving an evaluation of "commended" on the reading portion.

On May 11, 2005, while the disciplinary decision for A.D.'s theft was pending, A.D.'s mother requested that A.D. receive special education services. On May 25, 2005, she requested a due process hearing before an impartial hearing officer selected by the Texas Education Agency, alleging that AISD violated A.D.'s right to a "free appropriate public education" by failing to: (1) identify A.D. as a child with a disability, (2) evaluate A.D. as a child with a disability, and (3) place A.D. in special education. In response, the Admissions, Review, and Dismissal Committee ("ARD Committee") undertook a "full and independent evaluation" of A.D. that involved various psychological, behavioral, and intelligence tests; informal evaluations with a psychologist, an educational diagnostician, teachers, and A.D.'s mother; and a review of school files. . . .

In the written report, A.D.'s cognitive abilities were found to be in the average range. Dr. Peters, the evaluating psychologist, concluded that A.D.'s symptoms of ADHD did not prevent him from making age-appropriate academic and social progress. Ms. McDaniel, the educational diagnostician, concluded that A.D.'s academic performance was "high average" in basic reading skills and "average" in all remaining areas. Approximately one month later, AISD received the information requested from A.D.'s treating physicians, Dr. Kazmi and Dr. Nguyen, who recommended special education services for A.D. AISD also received a report from Dr. Rasheed, a new, privately obtained psychiatrist, who recommended special education services. On August 25, 2005, the ARD Committee met to consider the reports and concluded that A.D. was not eligible for special education services. A.D.'s mother disagreed with the result and requested an "independent educational evaluation" pursuant to 20 U.S.C. § 1415(b)(1). AISD denied the request and initiated a due process hearing.

... The Hearing Officer concluded that A.D. was a "child with a disability" entitled to special education services and that AISD failed to provide him with a "free appropriate public education." ...

AISD appealed the decision in federal district court, and both parties filed cross-motions for summary judgment. On October 6, 2006, the district court granted AISD's motion for summary judgment and denied A.D.'s motion, finding that A.D. did not need special education and related services by reason of his ADHD and was, therefore, not a "child with a disability" under the IDEA. A.D. now appeals.

....

III.

The IDEA places several conditions on the provision of federal aid to state special education programs, including that the state provide a "free appropriate public education" to children with disabilities. 20 U.S.C. § 1412(a)(1). ...

Only certain students with disabilities, however, are eligible for IDEA's benefits. Specifically, to qualify for special education services a student must both: (1) have a qualifying disability and (2) "by reason thereof, need[ ] special education and related services." 20 U.S.C. § 1401(3)(A). In making this determination, a state or local education agency (here, the ARD Committee) must conduct a "full and individual evaluation" following statutorily prescribed standards.

In this case, there is no dispute that A.D. satisfies the first prong because ADHD is considered an "other health impairment," a recognized qualifying disability. 20 U.S.C. § 1401(3)(A)(i). Thus, the central dispute pertains to the second prong: *by reason of* his ADHD, does A.D. *need* special education and related services? AISD contends that A.D. does not need special education services because his educational performance is adequate without them, and, in the alternative, any need for special education services derives from sources other than his ADHD.

....

B.

A.D. also argues that the district court applied the wrong legal standard when determining "need" under 20 U.S.C. § 1401(3)(A). Specifically, A.D. argues that the district court should have looked to whether or not his ADHD "adversely affects his educational performance" rather than whether his ADHD adversely impacts his ability to "benefit from regular education."[7]

A.D.'s argument is flawed for two reasons. First, the "adversely affects a child's educational performance" standard is a subpart of the definition of "other health impairment." 34 C.F.R. § 300.8(c)(9). Thus, establishing an adverse effect on educational performance demonstrates that A.D. has an "other health impairment." As described above, however, determining that a child has an "other health impairment" only fulfills the first prong of the "child with a disability" analysis under 20 U.S.C. § 1401(3)(A). A.D. must still fulfill the second prong by demonstrating that, by reason of his ADHD, he needs special education services. Therefore, the fact that A.D.'s ADHD adversely affects his educational performance does not necessarily mean that he is eligible for special education services under the IDEA.

Second, contrary to A.D.'s assertion, the district court did not base its holding upon the "benefit from regular education" standard. Under this standard, the district court would have focused exclusively on A.D.'s passing grades and TAKS scores. Rather, the district court also considered "a variety of sources, including aptitude and achievement tests, parent input, and teacher recommendations, as well as information about the child's physical condition, social or cultural background, and adaptive behavior . . . ." 34 C.F.R. § 300.306(c)(1)(i) (outlining procedures for determining "eligibility and educational need"). Therefore, in determining whether A.D. needs special education services by reason of his ADHD, the district court properly considered the unique facts and circumstances of this case.

C.

Finally, A.D. argues that the district court reached an incorrect conclusion in holding that he has no need for special education by reason of his disability. A.D. relies primarily on the reports and testimony of his doctors; his past behavioral issues; his failing grades on various exams and progress report cards; and AISD's attempts to assist A.D., such as the Academic and Behavior Contract and A.D.'s placement in the "At Risk" program. He argues that the district court placed undue weight on his academic performance, as determined by the TAKS test and final class grades.

AISD responds, and the district court agreed, that A.D. does not need special education services for several reasons. First, A.D.'s passing grades and success on the TAKS test demonstrate academic progress. *See Rowley*, 458 U.S. at 207 n. 28, 102 S.Ct. 3034 ("[T]he achievement of passing marks and advancement from grade to grade will be one important factor in determining educational benefit."). Second, A.D.'s teachers testified that, despite his behavioral issues, he did not need special education and was achieving social success in school. AISD argues that the district court properly determined that the testimony of A.D.'s teachers, who observed his educational progress

7. A.D. correctly asserts that this standard is used to determine what services need to be provided to a child after he is deemed eligible for special education services under the IDEA. *See Rowley*, 458 U.S. at 200. Because A.D. is not eligible for special education services, this standard is inapplicable.

first-hand, is more reliable than much of the testimony from A.D.'s physicians, who based their opinions on faulty information culled from isolated visits, select documents provided by A.D.'s mother, and statements from A.D.'s mother about what she believed was happening in school. Finally, AISD argues that much of A.D.'s behavioral problems are derived from non-ADHD related occurrences, such as alcohol abuse and the tragic death of A.D.'s brother. Thus, AISD asserts, any educational need is not by reason of A.D.'s ADHD, as required by the statute. We agree with AISD's argument and find that the district court's factual findings were not clearly erroneous.

After reviewing the record, we hold that the district court properly considered evidence of A.D.'s academic, behavioral, and social progress in determining that A.D. does not need special education services by reason of his ADHD and, therefore, is not a "child with a disability" under the IDEA. . . .

. . . .

Mr. I. v. Me. Sch. Admin. Dist. No. 55

480 F.3d 1 (1st Cir. 2007)

[Review the facts of *Mr. I.* excerpted earlier in this chapter.]

B.

The district also argues that the district court misapplied § 1401(3)(A)(ii), which requires that a child "need[ ] special education and related services" as a result of his or her disability in order to qualify for them under the IDEA. The district asserts two errors: first, the district court used the wrong definition of "special education," and, second, it found that the district had waived any argument that LI does not "need" special education based on the position it took before the PET and the hearing officer. We believe the district court correctly defined "special education" under § 1401(3)(A)(ii). We do not decide, however, whether the district court properly treated the "need" issue as waived, because the district has not adequately explained to us why LI does not need special education, even under its view of the proper standard for making that determination.

1.

The IDEA defines "special education," in relevant part, as "specially designed instruction, at no cost to parents, to meet the unique needs of a child with a disability. . . ." 20 U.S.C. § 1401(29). . . . As the district court noted, Maine law also contains its own definition of "special education": "classroom, home, hospital, institutional or other instruction; educational diagnosis and evaluation; transportation and other supportive assistance, services, activities, or programs, as defined by the commissioner [of education], required by exceptional students." Me.Rev.Stat. Ann. tit. 20–A, § 7001(5)(1993).

The district court ruled that a number of the interventions recommended by Popeneo and Lambke, and included in the services offered by the PET under the

Rehabilitation Act, were "special education" within the meaning of federal law as well as "under Maine's broader definition." In challenging this conclusion, the district principally argues that the district court misinterpreted Maine law to exceed IDEA requirements as to the definition of "special education." We have little trouble with the district court's interpretation, given the expansive language of Me.Rev.Stat. Ann. tit. 20–A, § 7001(5), but, in any event, that provision was not essential to the district court's view that LI needs special education. The district court also specifically ruled that certain of the services recommended for LI constituted "special education" as defined by *federal* law.

Most significantly, the district court reasoned that "extra instructional offerings such as social-skills and pragmatic-language instruction are 'specially designed instruction' to ensure [LI's] 'access . . . to the general curriculum.'" *Id.* quoting 34 C.F.R. § 300.39(b)(3). The district protests that its proffered "social pragmatics instruction," which "was aimed more at counseling LI at how she could better interact with others" than at traditional "speech services," qualifies as a "related service," not "special education." under the IDEA. The district has it backwards, however. While "speech-language pathology services" comprise a category of "related services," 20 U.S.C. § 1401(26)(A), directly teaching social skills and pragmatic language to LI amounts to adapting the content of the usual instruction to address her unique needs and to ensure that she meets state educational standards, *viz.,* those defining educational performance to include "communication" and requiring progress in "career preparation." The district court did not err in ruling that the services recommended for LI by her neuropsychologist and speech-language pathologist, and agreed to by the PET as part of its Rehabilitation Act plan, are "special education."

2.

The district also challenges the district court's resolution of whether LI "needs" the special education in question. The district court made no finding on this point, electing to "hold the parties to their original understandings" that "'[n]eed' is not a contested issue." In support of this course of action, the district court noted that "the factual record on need is poorly developed" because "the PET meetings proceeded on the basis that everyone agreed that LI 'needed' and should be afforded what the experts recommended for her" and because the district gave no indication that it disputed LI's need for special education in either the prior written notice heralding its denial of IDEA benefits or its brief filed in advance of the due process hearing. Accordingly, the district court reasoned that "[w]hether or not waiver is the correct term," it had no sensible option but to conclude that LI "'needed' the identified services" as the parties "all initially believed."

The district insists that it preserved the issue of LI's need for special education by presenting argument and evidence on that score at the due process hearing. We agree with the district that it adduced some evidence at the hearing, in the form of testimony from McDevitt, as to LI's need for special education. Specifically, in response to a question from counsel for the district on whether he believed that LI "requires special education, specialized instruction, take your pick, to do acceptably well in school," McDevitt replied, "No, I don't." He went on to state his view that LI was "having a successful time" at TCS, even without "special services." McDevitt then explained why the district's offer of Rehabilitation Act services should not be construed as its opinion that "these interventions are necessary interventions for [LI] to participate meaningfully in public school," *i.e.*, because they did not constitute special education, but accommodations intended to make LI and her parents feel comfortable about her return to Cornish.

We need not decide whether this presentation came too late to raise the issue of LI's need for special education, as the district court ruled, because the district does not explain why LI does not need special education under the standard it urges us to follow in making that determination. The district contends that "whether a child needs special education for IDEA eligibility should depend on whether that child requires special education to benefit in those areas of educational performance that are adversely affected," but does not argue that LI does not pass that test. Instead, the district argues, based on McDevitt's testimony and LI's performance at TCS, that she does not need special education "to benefit from school" or "to do well in school."

But whether a child requires special education "to do well in school," or even "to benefit from school," presents a different question from whether the child requires special education "to benefit in those areas of educational performance that are adversely affected by her disability." The former inquiry considers the effect of special education on the child's overall achievement in school, while the latter focuses on the effect of special education on the components of that achievement hampered by the child's disability. Indeed, a child may "do well in school" without special education, accumulating a high grade point average, but may nevertheless perform below acceptable levels in other areas, such as behavior. The questions of whether such a child "needs special education" under a proper interpretation of § 1401(3)(A)(ii)—and how to articulate that interpretation in the first instance—have generated a cacophony of different answers.

We do not attempt to compose the correct standard of "need" here. We simply note the significant variance between the standard the district urges us to adopt and the standard it argues has been satisfied. McDevitt's testimony may have supported a finding that LI does not require special education "to do well in school," had the district court not ruled that the issue had been waived. But the district does not explain how such a finding would support the conclusion that LI does not "need special education" under the IDEA and, in fact, argues that the proper inquiry incorporates a substantially different standard, *i.e.*, whether LI "requires special education to benefit in those areas of educational performance that are adversely affected." Conversely, the district does not explain how the evidence received at the due process hearing falls short of that standard. The district has therefore failed to show that the district court's treatment of the "need" issue as settled had any effect on its ultimate conclusion that LI qualified for IDEA benefits. Even if the district court erred in finding the district had waived the "need" argument, then, the error was harmless.

The district has not directed us to any error undermining the district court's determination that LI meets the second prong of the standard for IDEA eligibility, 20 U.S.C. § 1401(3)(A)(ii). Having found that the district court's ruling as to the first prong also holds up we affirm the district court's decision that LI is eligible for services under the IDEA.

....

Notes, Comments, and Questions

1. In *Alvin*, the Court found that A.D.'s ADHD adversely affected his educational performance, thereby qualifying A.D. as a child with an "other health impairment." It was under the second prong of the analysis that the court reached its conclusion that A.D. did not qualify for special education services. Why should the analysis proceed to the second prong if a court finds that the ADHD adversely affects a child's educational performance? Why must a child with a disabling condition that affects his educational performance establish an independent need for special education services?

2. If you represented A.D. and his parents, what arguments would you make to support his need for special education services? How should a school district measure A.D.'s needs? How much weight should it place on academic performance? What other factors should courts consider in determining need? Consider the "need" discussion in the eligibility analysis of *Mr. I.* In *Mr. I.*, the court stated, "whether a child requires special education 'to do well in school,' or even 'to benefit from school,' presents a different question from whether the child requires special education 'to benefit in those areas of educational performance that are adversely affected by her disability.'" Mr. I. v. Me. Sch. Admin. Dist. No. 55, 480 F.3d 1, 22 (1st Cir. 2007).

3. The court concluded that many of A.D.'s behavioral issues were the result of non-ADHD events in A.D.'s life, but did not elaborate on the basis for its conclusion. In reaching this conclusion, did the court modify the IDEA's requirement that "by reason thereof" to mean "solely by reason thereof" when evaluating the source of a child's need for special education? If you represented A.D., how could you prove that his behavioral issues were connected to his ADHD and not to his brother's death or to his abuse of alcohol? What evidence would you need to prove this?

4. Although the court initially distinguished *Rowley* as inapplicable to eligibility determinations, it went on to quote *Rowley* in finding that a child's passing grades are an important factor in determining educational benefit. Did the court's use of a case concerning the level of services a district must provide to a child with a disability to place a restrictive interpretation on the eligibility requirement inappropriately limit access to special education under the IDEA? Would the court's analysis have been different under *Endrew F.*?

5. In the absence of a clear definition of need, may courts conclude that a child capable of academic progress cannot ever establish the need for special education? Are the goals of the IDEA achieved if students are required to fail?

Part III

Placement Rights

Chapter 5

The Least Restrictive Environment

Introduction

As a corollary to the requirement that each child receive a free appropriate public education, the IDEA mandates that school districts educate children with disabilities in the least restrictive environment ("LRE") to the maximum extent appropriate. Specifically, the IDEA requires that:

> To the maximum extent appropriate, children with disabilities . . . are educated with children who are not disabled, and special classes, separate schooling, or other removal of children with disabilities from the regular educational environment occurs only when the nature or severity of the disability of a child is such that education in regular classes with the use of supplementary aids and services cannot be achieved satisfactorily.

20 U.S.C. § 1412(a)(5)(A) (2012).

The U.S. Department of Education has adopted a variety of regulations to implement this statutory provision and give guidance to school districts and courts in determining the least restrictive environment. *See* 34 C.F.R. §§ 300.114, 300.115, 300.116(b)–(e), 300.117, and § 300.320(a) (2015). The regulations require school districts to provide a continuum of services, ranging from regular education to specialized schools, to facilitate placing each child in the least restrictive environment according to his or her specific needs. *Id.* §§ 300.39 and 300.115. *See* L. E. v. Ramsey Bd. of Educ., 435 F.3d 384, 390 (3d Cir. 2006) (stating that a court must determine whether a school district offers a continuum of placements); Oberti v. Bd. of Educ., 995 F.2d 1204, 1216 (3d Cir. 1993) (stating that the continuum of services must include supplementary services to a student in a regular education classroom); Straube v. Florida Union Free Sch. Dist., 801 F. Supp. 1164, 1173 (S.D.N.Y. 1992) (stating that the continuum must include "audiology, counseling, and medical services in addition to occupational and physical therapy and recreation."). Not surprisingly, decisions in LRE cases have revealed some tensions between the IDEA's dual mandate that school districts provide children with disabilities a free appropriate public education and that the education is in the least restrictive environment.

Problem

J.A. is a ten-year-old girl with an intellectual disability. Her IQ is sixty. Pursuant to her IEP, J.A. completed first grade in a special education class. The class had twelve children, ages eight to eleven. All the children in the class have intellectual disabilities. Their IQs were from fifty to seventy. One special education teacher taught the class with the assistance of a full-time aide. Each child in the class received physical and occupational therapy. The students in the class joined the children in the regular education classes for lunch and recess.

The objectives in J.A.'s first grade IEP included speaking in short sentences, following instructions for two-step tasks, counting to twenty, developing a fifty-word vocabulary, eating lunch on her own, and playing cooperatively with at least one other child at a time. In a meeting to develop J.A.'s IEP for second grade, the school district told J.A.'s parents that she was making limited progress in meeting these objectives. J.A. could not speak in sentences, could not follow two-step instructions, had difficulty playing with other children, and needed assistance in eating. Her vocabulary was limited to twenty words and she could not count past ten.

Ever since J.A.'s kindergarten year, her parents have taken the position that the school district should educate J.A. in a general education classroom with children who do not have disabilities. They explained to the district their belief that J.A. would benefit from interacting with children in a regular education class and would be able to model her learning and social skills on the other children. During their meeting with the school district to discuss J.A.'s second grade IEP, J.A's parents expressed dissatisfaction with her progress on reaching her IEP objectives. They blamed J.A.'s lack of progress on her placement in the special education class. They repeated their request that the district place J.A. in a general education second grade classroom with a teacher trained in both special education and regular education and a full-time aide for J.A. The district representative expressed the district's position that J.A. would not learn in a general education class. However, the district was willing to meet J.A.'s parents' demands on a pilot basis and re-visit the issue of J.A.'s second-grade placement after one month.

After J.A. finished one month in the regular education second grade class, the district and her parents met to assess her progress. According to J.A's parents, J.A was more enthusiastic about going to school, had her first play-date with a classmate, and had begun to speak to them in short sentences. J.A.'s teacher, however, had a different perspective. According to the teacher, J.A. had not made any progress on her IEP objectives. In fact, according to the teacher, J.A. could no longer count to ten and the number of words in her vocabulary had decreased to fifteen. The teacher also indicated that as a result of J.A.'s frustration at being in a general education class, J.A. had an occasional temper tantrum, approximately once a week, that disrupted the class. J.A.'s parents stated that the district did not live up to its promise. J.A.'s teacher was not trained in special education and J.A.'s aide was not full-time. According to the district, there were not enough teachers trained in general and special education and there were no budget funds to hire another teacher. The district also stopped sending the aide as frequently when it became apparent that J.A. was not benefitting from the aide's assistance. At the end of the meeting, the district decided that it was going to place J.A. back in the special education class. J.A.'s parents announced that they would request a hearing challenging this decision and asking for an order to place J.A. in the regular education class with appropriate supports.

As you read the cases that follow, consider the following questions:

1) Which rules apply to J.A's case?

2) Which rules should the hearing officer apply?

3) What are the issues in J.A.'s case?

4) What are some of the key facts? What additional facts are necessary?

5) How should the hearing officer rule?

Roncker v. Walter

700 F.2d 1058 (6th Cir. 1983),
cert. denied, 464 U.S. 864 (1983)

Contie, Circuit Judge.

In this appeal, the plaintiff challenges the placement of her retarded son under the Education for All Handicapped Children Act of 1975, 20 U.S.C. § 1401 *et seq.*, (the Act). As a condition for receiving federal aid, the Act provides that a free appropriate education must be provided to all children. It further requires states to establish "procedures to assure that, to the maximum extent appropriate, handicapped children, including children in public or private institutions or other care facilities, are educated with children who are not handicapped and that special classes, separate schooling, or other removal of handicapped children from the regular educational environment occurs only when the nature or severity of the handicap is such that education in regular classes with the use of supplementary aids and services cannot be achieved satisfactorily." 20 U.S.C. § 1412(5)(B).

... In this case, we examine the Act's requirement that handicapped children be educated with non-handicapped children to the "maximum extent appropriate."

I

The plaintiff's son, Neill Roncker, is nine years old and is severely mentally retarded. He is classified as Trainable Mentally Retarded (TMR), a category of children with an IQ of below 50. Less severely retarded students are classified as Educable Mentally Retarded (EMR) and are generally educated in special classes within the regular public schools.

There is no dispute that Neill is severely retarded and has a mental age of two to three with regard to most functions. Neill also suffers from seizures but they are not convulsive and he takes medication to control them. No evidence indicates that Neill is dangerous to others but he does require almost constant supervision because of his inability to recognize dangerous situations.

In 1976, Neill was evaluated and recommended for the Arlitt Child Development Center. It was believed that he would benefit from contact with non-handicapped children. In the spring of 1979, a conference was held to evaluate Neill's Individual Education Plan (IEP) as required by the Act. Present at the conference were Neill's parents, school psychologists, and a member of the Hamilton County Board of Mental Retardation. After evaluating Neill, the school district decided to place him in a county school. Since these county schools were exclusively for mentally retarded children, Neill would have received no contact with non-handicapped children.

. . . .

The Ronckers refused to accept the placement and sought a due process hearing before an impartial hearing officer pursuant to the Act. The hearing officer found that the school district had not satisfied its burden of proving that its proposed placement afforded the maximum appropriate contact with non-handicapped children. He ordered that Neill "be placed within the appropriate special education class in the regular elementary school setting."

The school district appealed to the Ohio State Board of Education . . . . The State Board found that Neill required the educational opportunities provided by the county school. It also found, however, that he needed interaction with non-handicapped children during lunch, recess and transportation to and from school. Accordingly, the State Board held that Neill should be placed in a county school so long as some provision was made for him to receive contact with non-handicapped children. The State Board did not indicate how this split program was to be administered.

While the dispute over placement continued, Neill began attending a class for the severely mentally retarded at Pleasant Ridge Elementary School in September 1979. Pleasant Ridge is a regular public school which serves both handicapped and non-handicapped children. Neill's contact with non-handicapped children at Pleasant Ridge is limited to lunch, gym and recess. Neill has remained at Pleasant Ridge during the pendency of this action.

In January 1980, Neill's mother filed this action against . . . the school district. . . .

. . . .

The district court found in favor of the school district. The court interpreted the Act's mainstreaming requirement as allowing school districts broad discretion in the placement of handicapped children. In this case, the district court found that the school district did not abuse its discretion in placing Neill Roncker in a school where he would receive no contact with non-handicapped children. This conclusion was supported by the district court's finding that Neill had made no significant progress after 18 months at Pleasant Ridge. . . .

. . . .

III

Since the district court employed an improper standard of review, we remand this case in order to allow the district court to re-examine the mainstreaming issue in light of the proper standard of review.

The Act does not require mainstreaming in every case but its requirement that mainstreaming be provided to the *maximum* extent appropriate indicates a very strong congressional preference. The proper inquiry is whether a proposed placement is appropriate under the Act. In some cases, a placement which may be considered better for academic reasons may not be appropriate because of the failure to provide for mainstreaming. The perception that a segregated institution is academically superior for a handicapped child may reflect no more than a basic disagreement with the mainstreaming concept. Such a disagreement is not, of course, any basis for not following the Act's mandate. In a case where the segregated facility is considered superior, the court should determine whether the services which make that placement superior could be feasibly provided in a non-segregated setting. If they can, the placement in the segregated school would be inappropriate under the Act. Framing the issue in this manner accords the proper respect for the strong preference in favor of mainstreaming while still realizing the possibility that some handicapped children simply must be educated in segregated facilities either because the handicapped child would not benefit from mainstreaming, because any marginal benefits received from mainstreaming are far outweighed by the benefits gained from services which could not feasibly be provided in the non-segregated setting, or because the handicapped child is a disruptive force in the non-segregated setting. Cost is a proper factor to consider since excessive spending on one handicapped child deprives other handicapped children. Cost is no defense, however, if the school district has failed to use its funds to provide a proper continuum of alternative placements for handicapped children. The provision of such alternative placements benefits all handicapped children.

In the present case, the district court must determine whether Neill's educational, physical or emotional needs require some service which could not feasibly be provided in a class for handicapped children within a regular school or in the type of split program advocated by the State Board of Education. Although Neill's progress, or lack thereof, at Pleasant Ridge is a relevant factor in determining the maximum appropriate extent to which he can be mainstreamed, it is not dispositive since the district court must determine whether Neill could have been provided with additional services, such as those provided at the county schools, which would have improved his performance at Pleasant Ridge.

We recognize that the mainstreaming issue imposes a difficult burden on the district court. Since Congress has chosen to impose that burden, however, the courts must do their best to fulfill their duty. The district courts are not without guidance inasmuch as they have the benefit of two state administrative proceedings and may justifiably give due weight to those administrative findings.

. . . .

The judgment of the district court is VACATED and the case is REMANDED for further proceedings consistent with this opinion.

Oberti v. Bd. of Educ. of Clementon Sch. Dist.

995 F.2d 1204 (3d Cir. 1993)

Becker, Circuit Judge.

The Individuals with Disabilities Education Act (IDEA), 20 U.S.C. §§ 1400–1485 . . . , provides that states receiving funding under the Act must ensure that children with disabilities are educated in regular classrooms with nondisabled children "to the maximum extent appropriate." 20 U.S.C. § 1412(5)(B). Plaintiff-appellee Rafael Oberti is an eight year old child with Down's Syndrome who was removed from the regular classroom by defendant-appellant Clementon School District Board of Education (the "School District") and placed in a segregated special education class. In this appeal, we are asked by the School District to review the district court's decision in favor of Rafael and his co-plaintiff parents Carlos and Jeanne Oberti concerning Rafael's right under IDEA to be educated in a regular classroom with nondisabled classmates. This court has not previously had occasion to interpret or apply the "mainstreaming" requirement of IDEA.

We construe IDEA's mainstreaming requirement to prohibit a school from placing a child with disabilities outside of a regular classroom if educating the child in the regular classroom, with supplementary aids and support services, can be achieved satisfactorily. In addition, if placement outside of a regular classroom is necessary for the child to receive educational benefit, the school may still be violating IDEA if it has not made sufficient efforts to include the child in school programs with nondisabled children whenever possible. We also hold that the school bears the burden of proving compliance with the mainstreaming requirement of IDEA, regardless of which party (the child and parents or the school) brought the claim under IDEA before the district court.

Although our interpretation of IDEA's mainstreaming requirement differs somewhat from that of the district court, we will affirm the decision of the district court that the School District has failed to comply with IDEA. More precisely, we will affirm the district court's order that the School District design an appropriate education plan for Rafael Oberti in accordance with IDEA, and we will remand for further proceedings consistent with this opinion. . . .

I. FACTUAL AND PROCEDURAL BACKGROUND

A. *Rafael Oberti's educational history*

Rafael is an eight year old child with Down's syndrome, a genetic defect that severely impairs his intellectual functioning and his ability to communicate. Now and throughout the period in question, Rafael and his parents have lived within the Clementon School District, in southern New Jersey. Prior to his entry into kindergarten, Rafael was evaluated in accordance with federal and state law by the School

District's Child Study Team (the "Team"). Based on its evaluation, the Team recommended to Rafael's parents that he be placed in a segregated special education class located in another school district for the 1989–90 school year. The Obertis visited a number of special classes recommended by the School District and found them all unacceptable. Thereafter the Obertis and the School District came to an agreement that Rafael would attend a "developmental" kindergarten class (for children not fully ready for kindergarten) at the Clementon Elementary School (Rafael's neighborhood school) in the mornings, and a special education class in another school district in the afternoons.

The Individualized Education Plan (IEP) developed by the School District for Rafael for the 1989–90 school year assigned all of Rafael's academic goals to the afternoon special education class. In contrast, the only goals for Rafael in the morning kindergarten class were to observe, model and socialize with nondisabled children.

While Rafael's progress reports for the developmental kindergarten class show that he made academic and social progress in that class during the year, Rafael experienced a number of serious behavioral problems there, including repeated toileting accidents, temper tantrums, crawling and hiding under furniture, and touching, hitting and spitting on other children. On several occasions Rafael struck at and hit the teacher and the teacher's aide.

These problems disrupted the class and frustrated the teacher, who consulted the school psychologist and other members of the Child Study Team to discuss possible approaches to managing Rafael's behavior problems. The teacher made some attempts to modify the curriculum for Rafael, but Rafael's IEP provided no plan for addressing Rafael's behavior problems. Neither did the IEP provide for special education consultation for the kindergarten teacher, or for communication between the kindergarten teacher and the special education teacher. In March of 1990, the School District finally obtained the assistance of an additional aide, which had been requested by the parents much earlier in the school year, but the presence of the extra aide in the kindergarten class did little to resolve the behavior problems. According to Rafael's progress reports for the afternoon special education class, and as the district court found, Rafael did not experience similar behavior problems in that class.

At the end of the 1989–90 school year, the Child Study Team proposed to place Rafael for the following year in a segregated special education class for children classified as "educable mentally retarded." Since no such special education class existed within the Clementon School District, Rafael would have to travel to a different district. The Team's decision was based both on the behavioral problems Rafael experienced during the 1989–90 school year in the developmental kindergarten class and on the Team's belief that Rafael's disabilities precluded him from benefiting from education in a regular classroom at that time.

The Obertis objected to a segregated placement and requested that Rafael be placed in the regular kindergarten class in the Clementon Elementary School. The School District refused, and the Obertis sought relief by filing a request for a due process hearing. The parties then agreed to mediate their dispute, pursuant to New Jersey regulations, as an alternative to a due process hearing. Through mediation, the Obertis and the School District came to an agreement that for the 1990–91 school year Rafael would attend a special education class for students labeled "multiply handicapped" in a public elementary school in the Winslow Township School District ("Winslow"), approximately 45 minutes by bus from Rafael's home. As part of the agreement, the School District promised to explore mainstreaming possibilities at the Winslow school and to consider a future placement for Rafael in a regular classroom in the Clementon Elementary School.

The special education class in Winslow that Rafael attended during the 1990–91 school year was taught by an instructor and an instructional aide and included nine children. Although Rafael initially exhibited some of the same behavioral problems he had experienced in the Clementon kindergarten class, his behavior gradually improved: he became toilet trained and his disruptiveness abated. Rafael also made academic progress. However, by December of 1990, Rafael's parents found that the School District was making no plans to mainstream Rafael. The Obertis also learned that Rafael had no meaningful contact with nondisabled students at the Winslow school.

B. *The due process hearing*

In January of 1991, the Obertis brought another due process complaint, renewing their request under IDEA that Rafael be placed in a regular class in his neighborhood elementary school. A three-day due process hearing was held in February of 1991 before an Administrative Law Judge (ALJ) of the New Jersey Office of Administrative Law. On March 15, 1991, the ALJ affirmed the School District's decision that the segregated special education class in Winslow was the "least restrictive environment" for Rafael. Based on the testimony of Rafael's kindergarten teacher and other witnesses for the School District who described Rafael's disruptive behavior in the developmental kindergarten class, the ALJ found that Rafael's behavior problems in that class were extensive and that he had achieved no meaningful educational benefit in the class. The ALJ concluded that Rafael was not ready for mainstreaming.

In reaching this conclusion, the ALJ discounted the testimony of the Obertis' two expert witnesses. Dr. Gail McGregor, a professor of education at Temple University and an expert in the education of children with disabilities, testified that Rafael could be educated satisfactorily in a regular class at the Clementon Elementary School with supplementary aids and services, and that Rafael would learn important skills in a regular classroom that could not be learned in a segregated setting. The ALJ disregarded Dr. McGregor's testimony because, unlike the School District's witnesses, she did not have daily experience with Rafael. Likewise, the ALJ discounted the testimony of the Obertis' other expert witness, Thomas Nolan, a teacher and special education specialist who had taught a child with Down's syndrome in a regular classroom, because he too had not had day-to-day experience with Rafael. The ALJ thus concluded that the Winslow placement was in compliance with IDEA.

C. *The proceedings before the district court*

....

In May of 1992, the district court held a three-day bench trial, receiving new evidence from both parties to supplement the state agency record. The Obertis presented the testimony of two additional experts who had not testified in the administrative proceedings: Dr. Lou Brown, a professor of special education at the University of Wisconsin, and Amy Goldman, an expert in communication with children with developmental disabilities.

Dr. Brown, who over the past twenty years has been a consultant to hundreds of school districts throughout the country regarding the education of severely disabled children, interviewed and evaluated Rafael on two occasions, and reviewed Rafael's educational records, as well as a set of videotapes showing Rafael at age seven working with his mother, being taught by a language professional, and participating in a Sunday school class with nondisabled children. Dr. Brown testified that he saw no reason why Rafael could not be educated at that time in a regular classroom with appropriate supplementary aids and services. He told the court that if such aids and services were provided, he had no reason to believe that Rafael would be disruptive at that time (more than two years after the experience in the Clementon kindergarten class). He also stated that integrating Rafael in a regular class at his local school would enable Rafael to develop social relationships with nondisabled students and to learn by imitating appropriate role models, important benefits which could not be realized in a segregated, special education setting.

Dr. Brown outlined a number of commonly applied strategies which could be used, in combination, by the School District to integrate Rafael in a regular classroom, including: (1) modifying some of the curriculum to accommodate Rafael's different level of ability; (2) modifying only Rafael's program so that he would perform a similar activity or exercise to that performed by the whole class, but at a level appropriate to his ability; (3) "parallel instruction," i.e., having Rafael work separately within the classroom on an activity beneficial to him while the rest of the class worked on an activity that Rafael could not benefit from; and (4) removing Rafael from the classroom to receive some special instruction or services in a resource room, completely apart from the class. Dr. Brown explained that with proper training, a regular teacher would be able to apply these techniques and that, in spite of Rafael's severe intellectual disability, a regular teacher with proper training would be able to communicate effectively with Rafael. Dr. Brown also testified that many of the special educational techniques applied in the segregated Winslow class could be provided for Rafael within a regular classroom.

Based on her evaluation of Rafael and her expertise in developing communication skills for disabled children, Amy Goldman testified that the speech and language therapy Rafael needs could be most effectively provided within a regular classroom; otherwise, she explained, a child with Rafael's disabilities would have great difficulty importing the language skills taught in a separate speech therapy session into the regular class environment, where those skills are most needed. She testified that language and speech therapy could easily be provided by a therapist inside the regular class during ongoing instruction if the therapist were able to collaborate ahead of time with the instructor regarding the upcoming lesson plans.

In addition, Dr. McGregor reaffirmed her prior opinion in the administrative proceedings that placement in a regular classroom was not only feasible but preferable for Rafael. Further, she testified that, given the resources and expertise available to public schools in New Jersey, the School District should be able to design an inclusive program for Rafael with assistance from professionals who have experience integrating children with disabilities in regular classes.

....

To counter the Obertis' experts, the School District offered Dr. Stanley Urban, a professor of special education at Glassboro State College. After observing Rafael in a special class for perceptually impaired children at the St. Luke's School (a private school that Rafael attended for two months in the fall of 1991), observing Rafael for two hours in his home, reviewing the programs available at the Clementon Elementary School, reviewing Rafael's education records, and reviewing the written evaluations of the Obertis' experts, Dr. Urban testified that in his opinion Rafael could not be educated satisfactorily in a regular classroom, and that the special education program at Winslow was appropriate for Rafael.

More specifically, Dr. Urban testified that Rafael's behavior problems could not be managed in a regular class, that a regular teacher would not be able to communicate with a child of Rafael's ability level, and that it would be difficult if not impossible to adapt a first grade-level curriculum to accommodate Rafael without adversely affecting the education of the other children in the class. Dr. Urban, however, also stated that if Rafael did not have serious behavior problems, integration in a regular classroom might be feasible.

The School District presented several additional witnesses, including the teacher and teacher's aide of a non-academic summer school class for elementary school children which Rafael attended in the summer of 1991, and the teacher of the St. Luke's class, which Rafael attended for two months in the fall of 1991. These witnesses recounted examples of Rafael's disruptive behavior, including pushing and hitting other children, disobeying and running away from the instructors, and throwing books.

In August of 1992, after reviewing all of this new evidence along with the evidence that had been adduced at the administrative proceedings, the district court issued its decision, finding that the School District had failed to establish by a preponderance of the evidence that Rafael could not at that time be educated in a regular classroom with supplementary aids and services. The court therefore concluded that the School District had violated IDEA.

In particular, the court was persuaded by the Obertis' experts that many of the special education techniques used in the Winslow class could be implemented in a regular classroom. The court also found that the School District did not make reasonable efforts to include Rafael in a regular classroom with supplementary aids and services (e.g., an itinerant teacher trained in aiding students with mental retardation, a behavior management program, modification of the regular curriculum to accommodate Rafael, and special education training and consultation for the regular teacher); that Rafael's behavior problems during the 1989–90 school year in the developmental kindergarten class were largely the result of the School District's failure to provide adequate supplementary aids and services; and that the record did not support the School District's contention that Rafael would present similar behavior problems at that time (more than two years after the kindergarten class) if included in a regular classroom setting with adequate aids and services. The court declined to defer to the findings of the ALJ because it found that "they were largely and improperly based upon Rafael's behavior problems in the developmental kindergarten as well as upon his intellectual limitations, without proper consideration of the inadequate level of supplementary aids and services provided by the School District."

... Accordingly, the court ordered the School District "to develop an inclusive plan for Rafael Oberti for the 1992–93 school year consistent with the requirements" of IDEA .... This appeal followed....

II. THE MAINSTREAMING REQUIREMENT OF IDEA

....

In addition to the free public education requirement, IDEA provides that states must establish

> procedures to assure that, to the maximum extent appropriate, children with disabilities ... are educated with children who are not disabled, and that special classes, separate schooling, or other removal of children with disabilities from the regular educational environment occurs only when the nature and severity of the disability is such that education in regular classes with the use of supplementary aids and services cannot be achieved satisfactorily ....

20 U.S.C. § 1412(5)(B). As numerous courts have recognized, this provision sets forth a "strong congressional preference" for integrating children with disabilities in regular classrooms.

One of our principal tasks in this case is to provide standards for determining when a school's decision to remove a child with disabilities from the regular classroom and to place the child in a segregated environment violates IDEA's presumption in favor of mainstreaming. This issue is particularly difficult in light of the apparent tension within the Act between the strong preference for mainstreaming, and the requirement that schools provide individualized programs tailored to the specific needs of each disabled child.

The key to resolving this tension appears to lie in the school's proper use of "supplementary aids and services," 20 U.S.C. § 1412(5)(B), which may enable the school to educate a child with disabilities for a majority of the time within a regular classroom, while at the same time addressing that child's unique educational needs. We recognize, however, that "[r]egular classes . . . will not provide an education that accounts for each child's particular needs in every case."

We also recognize that "[i]n assuring that the requirements of the Act have been met, courts must be careful to avoid imposing their view of preferable educational methods upon the States." *Rowley*, 458 U.S. at 207 . . . . We are mindful that the Act leaves questions of educational policy to state and local officials. On the other hand, as the Supreme Court recognized in *Rowley*, the Act specifically "requires participating States to educate handicapped children with nonhandicapped children whenever possible." *Rowley*, 458 U.S. at 202 . . . . It is our duty to enforce that statutory requirement.

In *Daniel R.R.*, the Fifth Circuit derived from the language of 20 U.S.C. § 1412(5)(B) a two-part test for determining whether a school is in compliance with IDEA's mainstreaming requirement. First, the court must determine "whether education in the regular classroom, with the use of supplementary aids and services, can be achieved satisfactorily." 874 F.2d at 1048. Second, if the court finds that placement outside of a regular classroom is necessary for the child to benefit educationally, then the court must decide "whether the school has mainstreamed the child to the maximum extent appropriate," i.e., whether the school has made efforts to include the child in school programs with nondisabled children whenever possible. *Id.* We think this two-part test, which closely tracks the language of § 1412(5)(B), is faithful to IDEA's directive that children with disabilities be educated with nondisabled children "to the maximum extent appropriate," 20 U.S.C. § 1412(5)(B), and to the Act's requirement that schools provide individualized programs to account for each child's specific needs, 20 U.S.C. §§ 1401, 1414(a)(5).

The district court in this case adopted the somewhat different test set forth by the Sixth Circuit in *Roncker v. Walter*, 700 F.2d 1058 (6th Cir.1983), the first federal court of appeals case to interpret IDEA's mainstreaming requirement. In *Roncker*, the court stated:

> In a case where the segregated facility is considered superior [academically], the court should determine whether the services which make that placement superior could be feasibly provided in a non-segregated setting. If they can, the placement in the segregated school would be inappropriate under the Act.

700 F.2d at 1063. We believe, however, that the two-part *Daniel R.R.* test is the better standard because the *Roncker* test fails to make clear that even if placement in the regular classroom cannot be achieved satisfactorily for the major portion of a particular child's education program, the school is still required to include that child in school programs with nondisabled children (specific academic classes, other classes such as music and art, lunch, recess, etc.) whenever possible. We therefore adopt the two-part *Daniel R.R.* test rather than the standard espoused in *Roncker*.

In applying the first part of the *Daniel R.R.* test, i.e., whether the child can be educated satisfactorily in a regular classroom with supplementary aids and services, the court should consider several factors. First, the court should look at the steps that the school has taken to try to include the child in a regular classroom. As we have explained, the Act and its regulations require schools to provide supplementary aids and services to enable children with disabilities to learn whenever possible in a regular classroom. The regulations specifically require school districts to provide "a continuum of placements . . . to meet the needs of handicapped children." 34 C.F.R. §§ 300.551(a). The continuum must "[m]ake provision for supplementary services (such as resource room (footnote omitted) or itinerant instruction) to be provided in conjunction with regular class placement." 34 C.F.R. § 300.551(b).

Accordingly, the school "must consider the whole range of supplemental aids and services, including resource rooms and itinerant instruction," *Greer*, 950 F.2d at 696, speech and language therapy, special education training for the regular teacher, behavior modification programs, or any other available aids or services appropriate to the child's particular disabilities. The school must also make efforts to modify the regular education program to accommodate a disabled child. If the school has given no serious consideration to including the child in a regular class with such supplementary aids and services and to modifying the regular curriculum to accommodate the child, then it has most likely violated the Act's mainstreaming directive. "The Act does not permit states to make mere token gestures to accommodate handicapped students; its requirement for modifying and supplementing regular education is broad." *Daniel R.R.*, 874 F.2d at 1048.

A second factor courts should consider in determining whether a child with disabilities can be included in a regular classroom is the comparison between the educational benefits the child will receive in a regular classroom (with supplementary aids and services) and the benefits the child will receive in the segregated, special education classroom. The court will have to rely heavily in this regard on the testimony of educational experts. Nevertheless, in making this comparison the court must pay special attention to those unique benefits the child may obtain from integration in a regular classroom which cannot be achieved in a segregated environment, i.e., the development of social and communication skills from interaction with nondisabled peers. As IDEA's mainstreaming directive makes clear, Congress understood that a fundamental value of the right to public education for children with disabilities is the right to associate with nondisabled peers.

Thus, a determination that a child with disabilities might make greater *academic* progress in a segregated, special education class may not warrant excluding that child from a regular classroom environment. We emphasize that the Act does *not* require states to offer *the same* educational experience to a child with disabilities as is generally provided for nondisabled children. To the contrary, states must address the unique needs of a disabled child, recognizing that that child may benefit differently from education in the regular classroom than other students. In short, the fact that a child with disabilities will learn differently from his or her education within a regular classroom does not justify exclusion from that environment.

A third factor the court should consider in determining whether a child with disabilities can be educated satisfactorily in a regular classroom is the possible negative effect the child's inclusion may have on the education of the other children in the regular classroom. While inclusion of children with disabilities in regular classrooms may benefit the class as a whole, a child with disabilities may be "so disruptive in a regular classroom that the education of other students is significantly impaired." 34 C.F.R. § 300.552 *comment* (citing 34 C.F.R. part 104–Appendix, Para. 24). Moreover, if a child is causing excessive disruption of the class, the child may not be benefiting educationally in that environment. Accordingly, if the child has behavioral problems, the court should consider the degree to which these problems may disrupt the class. In addition, the court should consider whether the child's disabilities will demand so much of the teacher's attention that the teacher will be required to ignore the other students.

We emphasize, however, that in considering the possible negative effect of the child's presence on the other students, the court must keep in mind the school's obligation under the Act to provide supplementary aids and services to accommodate the child's disabilities. An adequate individualized program with such aids and services may prevent disruption that would otherwise occur. With respect to the concerns of nondisabled children in the regular classroom, we note that the comment to 34 C.F.R. § 300.552 (citing 34 C.F.R. part 104–Appendix, Para. 24) reads: "[I]t should be stressed that, where a handicapped child is so disruptive in a regular classroom that the education of other students is significantly impaired, the needs of the handicapped child cannot be met in that environment. Therefore, regular placements would not be appropriate to his or her needs. . . ." On the other hand, "a handicapped child who merely requires more teacher attention than most other children is not likely to be so disruptive as to significantly impair the education of other children." *Greer*, 950 F.2d at 697.

In sum, in determining whether a child with disabilities can be educated satisfactorily in a regular class with supplemental aids and services (the first prong of the two-part mainstreaming test we adopt today), the court should consider several factors, including: (1) whether the school district has made reasonable efforts to accommodate the child in a regular classroom; (2) the educational benefits available to the child in a regular class, with appropriate supplementary aids and services, as compared to the benefits provided in a special education class; and (3) the possible negative effects of the inclusion of the child on the education of the other students in the class.

If, after considering these factors, the court determines that the school district was justified in removing the child from the regular classroom and providing education in a segregated, special education class, the court must consider the second prong of the mainstreaming test—whether the school has included the child in school programs with nondisabled children to the maximum extent appropriate. IDEA and its regulations "do not contemplate an all-or-nothing educational system in which handicapped children attend either regular or special education." The regulations under IDEA require schools to provide a "continuum of alternative placements . . . to meet the needs of handicapped children." 34 C.F.R. § 300.551(a). As the Fifth Circuit stated:

> the school must take intermediate steps wherever appropriate, such as placing the child in regular education for some academic classes and in special education for others, mainstreaming the child for nonacademic classes only, or providing interaction with nonhandicapped children during lunch and recess. The appropriate mix will vary from child to child and, it may be hoped, from school year to school year as the child develops.

Daniel R.R., 874 F.2d at 1050. Thus, even if a child with disabilities cannot be educated satisfactorily in a regular classroom, that child must still be included in school programs with nondisabled students wherever possible.

....

IV. DID THE SCHOOL DISTRICT COMPLY WITH IDEA?

We now reach the dispositive question in this case: whether the district court erred in holding that the School District failed to comply with IDEA's mainstreaming requirement. Initially, applying the first part of the two-part test set forth above we consider whether the School District has met its burden of proving that Rafael could not be educated satisfactorily in a regular classroom with supplementary aids and services.

....

B. *Application of the Daniel R.R. Test*

In Part II of this opinion, we outlined three factors that should be considered by a court in determining whether a child with disabilities can be educated satisfactorily in a regular classroom (the first part of the *Daniel R.R.* test): (1) whether the school district has made reasonable efforts to accommodate the child in a regular classroom with supplementary aids and services; (2) a comparison of the educational benefits available in a regular class and the benefits provided in a special education class; and (3) the possible negative effects of inclusion on the other students in the class. We now consider each of these factors, looking to the relevant fact findings of the district court to determine whether those findings are clearly erroneous, and if not, whether they support the district court's ultimate legal conclusion that the School District violated the mainstreaming requirement of IDEA.

As to the first factor, the district court found that the School District made only negligible efforts to include Rafael in a regular classroom. Specifically, the court found that during the 1989–90 school year, the only period during which the School District mainstreamed Rafael in a regular classroom, the School District placed Rafael in the developmental kindergarten class "without a curriculum plan, without a behavior management plan, and without providing adequate special education support to the teacher." Further, the court found that the School District has since refused to include Rafael in a regular classroom largely based on the behavioral problems experienced by Rafael in the kindergarten class during the 1989–90 school year. For the 1990–91 year, the court found that Rafael was placed in a segregated class with "no meaningful mainstreaming opportunities," and that "[t]he School District's consideration of less restrictive alternatives for the 1990–91 school year was perfunctory."

There is very little evidence in the record that conflicts with these findings. The School District produced some evidence that the kindergarten teacher and the school psychologist attempted to modify the curriculum in that class and to come up with methods of controlling Rafael's behavior problems. However, the record reflects that the School District had access to information and expertise about specific methods and services to enable children with disabilities like Rafael to be included in a regular classroom, but that the School District did not provide such supplementary aids and services for Rafael in the kindergarten class.

Rafael's IEP for the 1989–90 school year included no provisions for supplementary aids and services in the kindergarten class aside from stating that there will be "modification of regular class expectations" to reflect Rafael's disability. The only goal provided for the regular kindergarten teacher was to "facilitate Rafael's adjustment to the kindergarten classroom." After reviewing this IEP along with the rest of Rafael's education records, Dr. McGregor testified that no supplementary aids and services were provided for Rafael in the 1989–90 kindergarten class.

Moreover, there is no evidence in the record that the School District gave any serious consideration to including Rafael in a regular classroom with supplementary aids and services *after* the 1989–90 school year; and the School District does not appear to dispute this fact. Further, Nancy Leech, the Winslow speech therapist (and one of the School District's witnesses) admitted that Rafael had not been included in any school programs with nondisabled children at Winslow, apart from attending lunch and school assemblies.

In view of the foregoing, the district court's finding that the School District has not taken meaningful steps to try to include Rafael in a regular classroom with supplementary aids and services is not clearly erroneous. We also note that the district court did not fail to give "due weight" to the agency proceedings on this issue since the ALJ did not even consider whether the School District had made efforts to include Rafael in a regular classroom with supplementary aids and services, as is required by IDEA. Accordingly, the School District's failure to give adequate consideration to including Rafael in a regular classroom with supplementary aids and services supports the district court's legal conclusion that the School District violated IDEA.

As to the second factor—a comparison of the educational benefits of the segregated placement in Winslow with the benefits Rafael could obtain from placement in a regular classroom—the district court found that "[v]arious experts who testified on Rafael's behalf have convincingly refuted the School District's assertion that such services could not be delivered within the matrix of a regular education class without disrupting the class or converting it into a special education class." The court also found that Rafael would benefit academically and socially from inclusion in a regular classroom. Moreover, the district court found, based on expert testimony, that "nondisabled children in the class will likewise benefit" from the inclusion of Rafael in a regular classroom.

The School District points to some evidence in the record that conflicts with these findings. Specifically, Dr. Urban testified for the School District that, in his opinion, a regular teacher would not be able to communicate with Rafael and that a regular curriculum would have to be modified beyond recognition to accommodate Rafael. However, the Obertis' experts, Drs. Brown and McGregor, described various commonly applied methods that could be used to educate Rafael in a regular classroom and testified that, although Rafael has severe intellectual disabilities, a regular teacher with appropriate training would be able to communicate effectively with Rafael. They testified that many of the special education techniques used in the segregated Winslow class could be imported successfully into a regular classroom and that the regular teacher could be trained to apply these techniques. Further, the Obertis' experts testified at length that inclusion in a classroom with nondisabled students would benefit Rafael substantially. In addition, Amy Goldman testified that speech and language therapy not only could be provided in a regular classroom, but would be more effective for Rafael in an integrated setting.

In short, the parties' experts disagreed on the respective benefits of a segregated versus an integrated placement for Rafael, and the district court was in a better position than we are to evaluate their testimony. We therefore defer to that court's findings, which, at all events, are not clearly erroneous. . . . Additionally, we agree with the district court's legal conclusion that, although including Rafael in a regular classroom would require the School District to modify the curriculum, the need for such modification is "not a legitimate basis upon which to justify excluding a child" from the regular classroom unless the education of other students is significantly impaired. Thus, a comparison of the educational benefits of a segregated versus an integrated placement for Rafael supports the district court's conclusion that the School District's selection of a segregated placement did not comply with IDEA.

As to the third factor—the potentially disruptive effect of Rafael's presence on the other children in a regular classroom—the record again contains conflicting evidence. The School District presented numerous witnesses before both the ALJ and the district court who testified to Rafael's extremely disruptive behavior in the 1989–90 kindergarten class and in several other teaching environments. In contrast, the Obertis' experts Drs. McGregor and Brown evaluated Rafael and testified that in their opinion he would not at that point in time (nearly two years after Rafael's experience in the kindergarten class) cause any significant disruption in a regular classroom if provided with adequate supplementary aids and services, such as the assistance of an itinerant instructor with special education training, special education training for the regular teacher, modification of some of the academic curriculum to accommodate Rafael's disabilities, parallel instruction to allow him to learn at his academic level, and use of a resource room.

After evaluating the evidence on both sides, the district court found that "[t]here is nothing in the record which would suggest that *at this point in time* Rafael would present similar behavior problems if provided with an adequate level of supplementary aids and related services within the matrix of a regular education class. In fact, the record supports the opposite conclusion." The court found that the behavioral problems Rafael experienced during the 1989–90 school year in the developmental kindergarten class "were exacerbated and remained uncontained due to the inadequate level of services provided there," that Rafael's behavioral problems were diminished in settings where an adequate level of supplementary aids and services were provided, and that both the School District and the ALJ "improperly justified Rafael's exclusion from less restrictive placements in subsequent years based upon those behavior problems."

Although the School District presented ample evidence of Rafael's disruptive behavior in the 1989–90 kindergarten class, the Obertis' evidence supports the district court's finding that Rafael would not have had such severe behavior problems had he been provided with adequate supplementary aids and services in that kindergarten class, and that Rafael (who at the time of the district court trial was two years older than when he attended the kindergarten class) would most likely not present such problems if he were included in a regular class at that time. We therefore conclude that the district court's findings on this issue are not clearly erroneous, and, accordingly, that consideration of the possible negative effects of Rafael's presence on the regular classroom environment does not support the School District's decision to exclude him from the regular classroom.

We also conclude that the district court did not abuse its discretion in deciding not to defer to the findings of the ALJ on the issue of whether Rafael would significantly disrupt a regular classroom. As the court noted, the ALJ's findings "were largely and improperly based upon Rafael's behavior problems in the developmental kindergarten, as well as upon his intellectual limitations, *without proper consideration of the inadequate level of supplementary aids and services provided by the School District.*" (emphasis added).

For all of these reasons, we agree with the district court's conclusion that the School District did not meet its burden of proving by a preponderance of the evidence that Rafael could not be educated satisfactorily in a regular classroom with supplementary aids and services. We will therefore affirm the district court's decision that the School District has violated the mainstreaming requirement of IDEA. Because we have come to this conclusion based on application of the first part of the *Daniel R.R.* two-part test, we need not apply the second part of the test (whether the child has been included in programs with nondisabled children whenever possible). We note, however, that in the event that the Child Study Team were to determine in designing an IEP for Rafael in the future that education in a regular classroom with supplementary aids and services could not be achieved satisfactorily at that time and therefore would not be required under IDEA, the Team would then have to satisfy the second part of the *Daniel R.R.* test, ensuring that Rafael is included in regular school programs with nondisabled students whenever possible.

Finally, in affirming the district court's order that the School District develop a more inclusive program for Rafael in compliance with IDEA for the upcoming school year, we emphasize that neither this court nor the district court is mandating a specific IEP for Rafael. The development of Rafael's IEP, and the specific nature of his placement, is, of course, the job of the Child Study Team.

The order of the district court will be affirmed.

P. v. Newington Bd. of Educ.

546 F.3d 111 (2d Cir. 2008)

KATZMANN, Circuit Judge.

This case calls upon us to adopt a standard by which courts in this circuit should assess whether a disabled child has been placed in the "least restrictive environment," as required by the Individuals with Disabilities Education Act (IDEA), 20 U.S.C. § 1412(a)(5). The plaintiff, P., suing by and through his parents, is a child with Down Syndrome attending public school in the Town of Newington, Connecticut. He contends that the 2005–2006 Individualized Education Plan (IEP) devised for him at his elementary school did not include enough regular-classroom time, and therefore did not place him in the least restrictive environment as mandated by the IDEA. P. challenged the IEP before an administrative hearing officer, who held that the school complied with the statute. P. appealed that decision to the United States District Court for the District of Connecticut which affirmed, granting summary judgment to the defendant Newington Board of Education. Today, we affirm the decision of the district court and join several of our sister circuits in holding that determining whether a student has been placed in the "least restrictive environment" requires a flexible, fact-specific analysis, considering whether, with the aid of appropriate supplemental aids and services, education in the regular classroom may be achieved, and, if not, whether the school has included the student in regular classes, programs, and activities to the maximum extent appropriate. Applying that analysis to the case before us, we affirm the decisions of the hearing officer and district court that the defendant fulfilled its obligations under the IDEA.

....

II. Factual Background

A. The Development of P.'s 2004–2005 and 2005–2006 IEPs

P. suffers from Down Syndrome, hearing impairment, and other significant health problems that have required several serious procedures, including surgery to repair a hole in his heart and multiple bowel operations, as a result of which he is not toilet trained. At the time relevant to this litigation, he was a student at the Anna Reynolds Elementary School in Newington, Connecticut. Among the assigned staff at the school working with P. have been the special-education teacher, two paraprofessionals, a speech pathologist, a physical therapist, and an occupational therapist. In the spring of 2004, when P. was eight, the school district's behavioral consultant, Greg Smith, informed his parents that it was becoming increasingly difficult to keep P. in a regular classroom, as the gap in ability between P. and his peers was growing and would grow larger. Moreover, at various times, P. had exhibited some behavior problems, including kicking, grabbing, and pulling hair. P's mother strongly disagreed with Smith's assessment and wanted her son to remain in a regular classroom with his non-disabled peers as much as possible.

On May 28, 2004, the group assigned to formulate P.'s IEP, the "Performance and Planning Team" (PPT), met to discuss plans for the 2004–2005 school year. At that meeting, P.'s parents stated that they wanted their son to be in a regular classroom at least 80% of the time during the upcoming school year. Instead, the IEP provided that P. be in the classroom for 60% of the school day, with "pull-out" services for occupational and speech therapy in separate classrooms, and the plan did not include any measures to deal with P.'s burgeoning behavior problems. In order to facilitate increased inclusion in the regular classroom, P.'s parents asked that a consultant specializing in such matters be hired, and in accordance with their request, the Board retained Dr. Kathleen Whitbread to evaluate P. Additionally, later in the summer of 2004, the Connecticut Children's Medical Center (CCMC) performed a psychological evaluation of P., in which he was found to have social-interaction and communication skills equivalent to those of an average two-year-old child. The report also found that P. communicated primarily through "signs, gestures, and single words" and exhibited "serious problem behaviors," including "disruptive behavior, destructiveness to property, and hurting others." The report concluded that "[P.] will need pervasive support, much more than others his age, because of very limited adaptive behaviors and because of problem behaviors." A "functional behavior assessment" (FBA) to assess behavior problems was not performed, nor was an "assistive technology evaluation" (ATE), which tests the extent to which assistive technology may facilitate inclusion into the regular-classroom environment.

Dr. Whitbread completed her evaluation on December 13, 2004. In the report, based on two hours of observation of P. at home and 4.5 hours of observation of him in the classroom, Dr. Whitbread described P.'s behavior problems as "moderately serious" and opined that the PPT had done "a commendable job of ensuring that [P.] spends the majority of the day with non-disabled peers." Nevertheless, she recommended that P.'s instruction be more closely connected to the general education curriculum. Dr. Whitbread also recommended consultation with a teacher of the hearing impaired and a program of literacy instruction.

According to the testimony of his second-grade teacher, Ms. Mazur, P.'s behavior improved during 2004–2005. He was only removed from the regular classroom three times due to behavior problems that caused or risked physical harm to another person, though timeouts were used. Ms. Mazur also explained that, although she frequently co-taught classes with the special-education teacher, Nancy Wilcock, to integrate P. into regular lessons, in at least some circumstances, "[P.] will need individualized instruction to make sure that he . . . is receiving the best instruction without distraction."

The PPT next met with Dr. Whitbread to discuss her findings and the CCMC evaluation on February 11, 2005. At the meeting, the PPT accepted her recommendations for an ATE and literacy instruction. Although Dr. Whitbread stated at the meeting that P. would benefit from additional regular-classroom time, she also contended that some of his literacy instruction might need to take place outside the classroom. The PPT did not, however, reach any conclusions and decided to reconvene in April.

Prior to the April meeting, Dr. Whitbread and Ms. Wilcock, the special-education teacher who had been working with P. for three years, exchanged e-mails regarding appropriate next steps. In one of these e-mails, Dr. Whitbread stated:

> Time out of the classroom is a concern of [P.'s] parents and it is important to them that [P.] be fully included. Their goal is 100% of the time in a gen. ed. class. I have shared with them that I feel some pullout time is beneficial. To me, a reasonable goal over the next year would be to increase his time in the general ed. environment from the current 60 or 65% to about 80%. I would not recommend that this be done suddenly. I realize this is going to be a difficult discussion since there are differences in opinion about what is best for [P.]. My hope is that we can have a productive conversation, with the understanding that compromise may be necessary.

This email is consistent with Dr. Whitbread's later testimony before the hearing officer in this case, during which she confirmed that she "recommended working up to 80 percent . . . that in [her] experience it's not productive to go in and say right now you must do this." But Dr. Whitbread also clarified her definition of "gradual": "I would have liked to see that happen over a month, two months, maybe three months, but certainly not years."

The PPT next convened on April 15, 2005, with Dr. Whitbread again in attendance. At the meeting, the special-education teacher, Ms. Wilcock, noted that P.'s behavior had improved, but that his attention span was limited. P.'s parents again emphasized their preference that their son's regular-classroom time increase from 60% to 80% in the upcoming year. Although the PPT scheduled another meeting in June to discuss the question, it indicated that at least some of P.'s speech-therapy sessions would occur in the regular classroom, and that all parties agreed that he would undergo some physical therapy instead of regular physical education (although he would still participate in some regular physical education). Dr. Whitbread again stated her recommendation that the team "gradually increase to 80% inclusion for [P.]."

The PPT next met on June 3, 2005. Notes from the meeting indicate that an FBA for P. had begun two weeks prior, and that all parties agreed that the school would hire a mutually agreeable behavioral specialist. With respect to the percentage of time P. would spend in the classroom, however, the parties were unable to reach a consensus, and P.'s parents lodged their disagreement with the plan in writing. Dr. Whitbread later testified that the PPT engaged in a "very long tedious process" while attempting to determine the appropriate amount of classroom time. Ultimately, the IEP provided that P.'s regular-classroom time would increase from 60% to 74%, with participation in "all regular class[es]," except when he needed to be educated separately to "increase his focus/attention" or when he needed to be removed from the regular classroom "due to fatigue . . . or behavior which indicates [a] need for a break from the group." The IEP also mandated the following supplemental assistance for P.: daily check of P.'s hearing aids in the health room, adult assistance in all activities in the regular classroom, assistive computer programs, extra time and directions on assignments, routines and schedules in pictures instead of words, preferential seating, and a clear work area. The IEP also provided for weekly consultation between the regular and special education teachers.

On June 9, 2005, P.'s parents requested an administrative hearing to challenge both the 2004–2005 and 2005–2006 IEPs, primarily on the ground that P. was not sufficiently integrated into the regular classroom.

Meanwhile, the PPT met again prior to the beginning of the school year, on August 18, 2005. At that meeting, the parties agreed to the hiring of a mutually agreeable behavioral and inclusion consultant, Dr. Ann Majure. Also, by that time, the school had hired a hearing-impairment consultant and another consultant to assist with implementing assistive-technology recommendations.

During a meeting on April 7, 2006, the PPT mandated that P. be placed in a regular classroom for 80% or more of the school day, pursuant in part to the recommendation of Dr. Majure. At oral argument in this case, the parties noted that since that time P. has been included in the regular classroom at least 80% of the time.

B. Litigation Before the Hearing Officer and the District Court

. . . .

The hearing officer found . . . that the 2005–2006 IEP complied with the requirements of the IDEA. Emphasizing Dr. Whitbread's statements that she thought P.'s regular-classroom time should increase gradually to 80% and that P. required some special-education services outside of the classroom, the hearing officer found that the PPT gave sufficient consideration to including P. in the classroom to the maximum extent appropriate. The hearing officer also took note of the extensive efforts the school had made on P.'s behalf, including the numerous supplemental aids, services, and additional teachers employed to assist P. throughout the day, the mutually agreed-upon behavioral consultant hired in 2005, and that the school had modified the curriculum to meet P.'s needs. Moreover, it was clear that P. was included with non-disabled students for around 73% of the time in 2005–2006, and "participate[d] in all specials, lunch, [and] recess."

P. subsequently appealed to the United States District Court for the District of Connecticut the ruling that the 2005–2006 IEP was sufficient and the sufficiency of the remedy awarded for the deficiencies in the 2004–2005 IEP. Both parties cross-moved for summary judgment, and the district court issued an opinion affirming the hearing officer's decision . . . . Applying the two-pronged test adopted by the Third Circuit in *Oberti v. Clementon School District*, 995 F.2d 1204, 1215 (3d Cir. 1993), the district court held that the evidence supported the hearing officer's ruling. P. now appeals the district court's decision.

III. Discussion

. . . .

B. Fashioning a Test for Assessing Placement in the "Least Restrictive Environment"

The IDEA mandates that "[t]o the maximum extent appropriate, children with disabilities . . . are educated with children who are not disabled, and special classes, separate schooling, or other removal of children with disabilities from the regular educational environment occurs only when the nature or severity of the disability of a child is such that education in regular classes with the use of supplementary aids and services cannot be achieved satisfactorily." 20 U.S.C. § 1412(a)(5)(A). "Educating a handicapped child in a regular education classroom . . . is familiarly known as 'mainstreaming.'" *Daniel R.R. v. State Bd. of Educ.*, 874 F.2d 1036, 1039 (5th Cir. 1989). We have underscored the IDEA's "strong preference for children with disabilities to be educated, 'to the maximum extent appropriate,' together with their non-disabled peers." Nevertheless, we have also acknowledged that, "[w]hile mainstreaming is an important objective, we are mindful that the presumption in favor of mainstreaming must be weighed against the importance of providing an appropriate education to handicapped students. Under the [IDEA], where the nature or severity of the handicap is such that education in regular classes cannot be achieved satisfactorily, mainstreaming is inappropriate." Understandably, courts have recognized some tension between the IDEA's goal of providing an education suited to a student's particular needs and its goal of educating that student with his non-disabled peers as much as circumstances allow. As such, courts have used a case-by-case analysis in reviewing whether both of those goals have been optimally accommodated under particular circumstances.

We have not yet explicitly stated a test for whether an IEP places a student in the least restrictive environment. We conclude today that the two-pronged approach adopted by the Third, Fifth, Ninth, Tenth, and Eleventh Circuits provides appropriate guidance to the district courts without "too intrusive an inquiry into the educational policy choices that Congress deliberately left to state and local school officials." Pursuant to that test, a court should consider, first, "whether education in the regular classroom, with the use of supplemental aids and services, can be achieved satisfactorily for a given child," and, if not, then "whether the school has mainstreamed the child to the maximum extent appropriate." We today explicitly endorse that two-pronged test, as elucidated and augmented by Judge Becker for the Third Circuit in *Oberti:*

> In sum, in determining whether a child with disabilities can be educated satisfactorily in a regular class with supplemental aids and services (the first prong of the two-part mainstreaming test we adopt today), the court should consider several factors, including: (1) whether the school district has made reasonable efforts to accommodate the child in a regular classroom; (2) the educational benefits available to the child in a regular class, with appropriate supplementary aids and services, as compared to the benefits provided

> in a special education class; and (3) the possible negative effects of the inclusion of the child on the education of the other students in the class.
>
> If, after considering these factors, the court determines that the school district was justified in removing the child from the regular classroom and providing education in a segregated, special education class, the court must consider the second prong of the mainstreaming test—whether the school has included the child in school programs with nondisabled children to the maximum extent appropriate.

995 F.2d at 1217–18. Both counsel for the parents and the Board in the case at hand support this framework.

Although we adopt the *Oberti* approach, we also note that this list of factors is not exhaustive; courts facing these cases must engage in an individualized and fact-specific inquiry into the nature of the student's condition and the school's particular efforts to accommodate it, ever mindful of the IDEA's purpose of educating children with disabilities, "'to the maximum extent appropriate,' together with their non-disabled peers." Moreover, courts must keep in mind our deferential position with respect to state educational authorities crafting educational policy. Nevertheless, our review must be searching, and we must recognize that even when educational authorities act with the best intentions they may sometimes fall short of their obligations under the IDEA, and courts must then act to ensure compliance with Congress's directives.

C. The *Oberti* Analysis Applied to This Case

We now turn to whether the Board's actions with respect to the 2005–2006 IEP pass muster under the test we have adopted, which both the district court and hearing officer referenced and applied. Our review is against the backdrop of the ultimate conclusion of the IEP, which resolved that P. would be in the regular classroom 74% of the time, and Dr. Whitbread's statements that P.'s regular-classroom time should be gradually ramped up to 80%. The first prong of the test asks whether a student can be satisfactorily educated in the regular classroom with the benefit of supplemental aids and services. As noted, we also consider whether the school made reasonable efforts to accommodate the student, the benefits and drawbacks to the student of full-time integration into the regular classroom, and the possible negative impact on other students of the disabled student's presence. Although, in light of the improvements in P.'s behavior, there did not appear to be a significant negative impact on other students arising from his inclusion in the regular classroom, we see no error in the district court's conclusions that P. could not be educated in the regular class room full-time and that the school had made significant efforts to integrate P. to the maximum extent possible. The school utilized a variety of supplemental aids, including several additional professionals, and modified the curriculum appropriately. Moreover, the hearing officer permissibly relied on the testimony of Dr. Whitbread that P. required pull-out services for reading, math, and speech therapy. We therefore agree with this district court's conclusion that "the evidence produced during the administrative proceeding demonstrates that education in the regular classroom, with the use of supplemental aids and services, could not be achieved satisfactorily for the 2005–2006 school year."

Turning to the second prong of the test, we must assess "whether the school has included the child in school programs with nondisabled children to the maximum extent appropriate." Continuing to keep in mind that the IEP mandated 74% inclusion in the regular classroom, as opposed to P.'s parents' proposed 80%—a difference of approximately 2–3 hours per week—we find no error in the district court's conclusion that, given P.'s need for some specialized instruction outside the regular classroom, he was mainstreamed to the maximum extent appropriate.

....

We recognize and appreciate P.'s parents' dedicated advocacy on his behalf. But the evidence before the hearing officer and the records of the several PPT meetings devoted to developing P.'s 2005–2006 IEP demonstrate that the school fulfilled its duty under the IDEA to craft a tailored educational plan that included P. in regular classes to the maximum extent appropriate. We therefore affirm the district court's conclusion that the school's actions were sufficient under the two-pronged test and that the 2005–2006 IEP placed P. in the "least restrictive environment" under the IDEA.

....

Notes, Comments, and Questions

1. The *Roncker* and *Oberti* courts took different approaches in determining the least restrictive environment. Which test do you find more faithful to the language and purpose of the IDEA? If you represented a school district, which test would you want applied to judge your client's actions? How does the court in *Newington* address the two different tests?

2. The opinions in *Oberti* and *Newington* attempted to balance the IDEA's foundational requirements: that a school district provide a child with a FAPE based on her individualized needs in the least restrictive environment. Is there a conflict between these two requirements? Have the courts been successful in developing a test for determining whether a district is educating a child in the least restrictive environment in a way that does not interfere with the child's right to an appropriate education based on the child's individual educational needs?

3. In *Roncker*, the Court discussed whether legitimate financial concerns should have an impact on a school district's obligation to educate a child in the least restrictive environment. The IDEA does not allow the denial of FAPE because of the cost of providing the necessary services. However, cost may be a factor when choosing between several alternatives that would each provide an appropriate education because it is within the school district's authority to select among appropriate programs. *See* Greer v. Rome City Sch. Dist., 950 F.2d 688, 697 (11th Cir. 1991) (stating that a "school district must balance the needs of each handicapped child against the needs of other children in the district."); *see also* Board of Educ. of the Hendrick Hudson Sch. Dist. v. Rowley, 458 U.S. 176, 200 (1982) (ruling that Congress did not

intend to require school districts to provide all services necessary to allow a child with a disability to maximize her potential).

4. In *Sacramento City Unified Sch. Dist. Bd. of Educ. v. Rachel H.*, 14 F.3d 1398 (9th Cir. 1994), *cert. denied*, 512 U.S. 1207 (1994), the Ninth Circuit adopted the test that the district court utilized for determining whether the school district was educating the child in the least restrictive environment:

> Although the district court relied principally on *Daniel R.R.* and *Greer*, it did not specifically adopt the *Daniel R.R.* test over the *Roncker* test. Rather, it employed factors found in both lines of cases in the analysis. The result was a four-factor balancing test in which the court considered (1) the educational benefits of placement full-time in a regular class; (2) the non-academic benefits of such placement; (3) the effect Rachel had on the teacher and children in the regular class; and (4) the costs of mainstreaming Rachel. This analysis directly addresses the issue of the appropriate placement for a child with disabilities under the requirements of 20 U.S.C. § 1412(5)(B). Accordingly, we approve and adopt the test employed by the district court.

Id. at 1404.

5. The cases in this chapter have involved disputes between schools that want to place children in restrictive educational environments in order to receive a FAPE and parents who want children to be in regular education classrooms. In Chapter Six, the positions switch: over the opposition of the school district, parents removed their children from their school districts and placed them in private schools because they believed the district placements were not providing a FAPE to their children.

6. Increased mainstreaming and interactions between children with disabilities and children who do not have disabilities have led to integration and significant benefits for both groups. But these benefits have not come without new challenges for children with disabilities who may struggle to integrate into the social environment of general education classrooms. Many students with disabilities are victims of harassment in their integrated environments. Although attention to incidents of bullying have increased for all children, children with disabilities are more likely to be the victims of harassment than their peers who do not have disabilities. Does this harassment impede their ability to get a FAPE?

T.K. v. N.Y.C. Dep't of Educ.

779 F. Supp. 2d 289 (E.D.N.Y. 2011)

Jack B. Weinstein, Senior District Judge:

I. Introduction

This case presents the largely unresolved issue of the extent to which bullying by other students inhibits a disabled child from being educated appropriately, and what her school must do about it. A strict legal test is developed and applied.

Plaintiff L.K., acting through her parents, challenges her public school placement by the New York City Department of Education ("DOE") under the Individuals with Disabilities Education Act. After exhausting her administrative remedies, she brings this action arguing that the placement was procedurally and substantively inappropriate, and her parents seek reimbursement for private school tuition. The DOE moves for summary judgment.

The primary complaint is that L.K. was deprived of an appropriate education because her assigned public school did nothing to prevent her from being so bullied by other students as to seriously reduce the opportunity for an appropriate education. Such a contention, under the Individuals with Disability Education Act ("IDEA") provisions that require a proper school placement and appropriate education, apparently have not yet been ruled upon by the Court of Appeals for the Second Circuit. For the reasons stated below, the issue requires a court evidentiary hearing, and, a possible remand to the state authorities for a rehearing.

Access to a free and appropriate education for all students remains one of the central issues for our time. For children with disabilities, the struggle for equal access to education at their local public schools is now decades old. Thirty-five years ago, passage of the Individuals with Disabilities Education Act required communities to provide equal access for students with special needs.

In 1970, before the IDEA's passage, United States schools provided special education to only one in five children with a disability. By 2008, 95 percent of children with disabilities received special education in their neighborhood public schools. But an effective and appropriate education may be negated by child bullying. When a school fails to take reasonable steps to prevent such objectionable harassment of a student, it has denied her an educational benefit protected by statute.

No one gains from ignoring school bullying—not even the bullies themselves. The students who are bullied may suffer lasting scars in the form of an inferior education, emotional damage, and decreased self-confidence; the bullies are left to continue on a path that may lead to future violence. Bullying and inappropriate peer harassment in its many forms provides an unacceptable toxic learning environment. For the reasons stated below, defendant's motion for summary judgment is denied....

II. Facts

A. Party's Contentions

Plaintiff presents two arguments. First, that bullying made L.K.'s educational environment hostile—a factor not properly taken into account during the administrative process.

L.K. argues that in considering bullying during the administrative review, the test for determining if a school district is liable for sexual harassment of a student developed in *Davis v. Monroe County Bd. of Educ.*, 526 U.S. 629 ... (1999) should be applied.

Plaintiff alleges that she was subjected to repeated bullying at school as a result of her disability, that the school was aware of this conduct, and that the school stonewalled her parents' attempts to address the issue, establishing its deliberate indifference.

....

As an initial matter, defendant urges this court to defer to the opinions rendered by the Independent Hearing Officer and the State Review Officer that L.K. was not denied a free, appropriate public education ("FAPE"). It asserts that bullying as a denial of a FAPE is "unsupported by any law, and is not relevant. . . ."

....

The facts set out below are based on filed documents in the case. For the purposes of this summary judgment motion, they are assumed to be true.

B. L.K.'s Academic Program

L.K. is a 12-year-old girl who was originally diagnosed as autistic, but has since been reclassified as learning disabled. During the 2007–2008 school year, the DOE placed her in a "Collaborative Team Teaching" ("CTT") classroom, which involved teaching students who are learning disabled alongside those who are not. To assist L.K. with her studies, she was provided a teacher's aide on a one-to-one basis. She received additional school services including speech therapy, occupation therapy, and physical therapy.

On June 4, 2008 a meeting was held to develop L.K.'s IEP for the 2008–2009 school year. . . .

During this CSE meeting, L.K.'s parents sought to discuss bullying of their daughter, but were rebuffed by the school's principal. The principal stated that it was not the appropriate time to discuss bullying, but the matter could be discussed later. No future meeting was scheduled or took place. L.K.'s parents contend that this failure to address their concerns is just one example of many where bullying was brought [to] the school's attention and nothing was done.

Prior to the CSE meeting, L.K.'s parents placed a deposit to secure a place for her at the Summit School, a private institution. After the IEP meeting, the parents rejected the proposed placement at P.S. 6, where L.K. had been the year before, and instead enrolled her in the Summit School. A not-for-profit organization approved by the New York State Education Department; it provides educational and therapeutic services for learning disabled students.

The instant action is brought to recover tuition and related expenses only for the 2008–2009 school year. Since that school year, the family has moved outside of the New York City Department of Education District.

L.K.'s parents appealed from the DOE administrative decision to an Impartial Hearing Officer (IHO) and then to a State Review Officer (SRO). Both appellate officers sided with the DOE.

C. Evidence of Bullying

During the 2007–2008 school year, L.K complained to her parents almost daily about being bullied at school. Her father insists that this constant bullying made her "emotionally unavailable to learn." L.K.'s parents contend that their attempts to address the bullying issue with the school principal both in person and in writing were summarily denied.

Throughout the 2007–2008 school year, L.K. had [a] one-on-one teacher's aide help in her classroom during the day. This support was supplied by two women who worked on alternate days. Both report that L.K. was ostracized in the classroom and the subject of ridicule from other students.

Shannon Maloney was L.K.'s teacher's aide on Tuesdays and Thursdays beginning in November 2007. When she arrived at the school, she described it as a "hostile environment" in which she was simply "just trying to get . . . [L.K.] by each day." Maloney reported that there was a great deal of teasing of L.K., with other children physically backing away to avoid her.

Dominique Faber was L.K.'s aide on Mondays, Wednesdays, and Fridays during the 2007–2008 school year. She testified that there was "constant negative interaction" between L.K. and other students on a daily basis. Other children would intentionally stay away from L.K. and at times physically push her away for fun. "She would be tripped, where she was walking by and they would stick out their feet just to see what would happen. And then if she fell, well, then the teachers would get upset with her for making a scene."

Testimony from a substitute aide supports these contentions. Sharifa Wiggins worked as a substitute aide for L.K. four times during the 2007–2008 school year. Her reaction was that "[L.K.] was isolated by girls and boys in her classroom. There was an incident in the classroom when there was a group of students at one table that [L.K.] was sitting at, where they had to write an assignment, and there was a pencil that [L.K.] touched. And for some reason, she put it down and no one wanted to touch the pencil." This behavior continued when L.K. tried to participate in class. "And a question was asked of the class . . . to give an opinion about a situation. And [L.K.] raised her hand and kind of people laughed at her."

Others at the school for brief periods of time noticed the same isolation. Mary Kutch, who was the director of L.K.'s school program referred to an incident where a student refused to take a paper from L.K. to grade it, requiring an aide to intervene.

Specific incidents of bullying include: a drawing in the record made by a student in L.K.'s class depicting L.K. in a disparaging light; a student chasing L.K. with what he claimed was blood but was in fact ketchup; other students refusing to touch things once L.K had; and a prank phone call made to L.K.'s home, which the school was informed about. No incident reports were generated by the school relating to these occurrences. This lack of records is significant because it raises questions about whether the school was actually on notice, or, if it was, whether it was deliberately indifferent.

The DOE has no incident reports of bullying where L.K. was the victim. It has, however, provided several reports where the school alleges she was the aggressor, including one where she is accused of hitting her teacher. These documents were furnished after repeated requests by the plaintiff, leading the State Review Office to find a procedural violation of the IDEA, but not one that rose to the level of a denial of FAPE.

L.K.'s parents maintain that bullying caused their daughter to resist attending school, hurt her academic performance, and damaged her emotional well-being. The DOE points to progress reports showing L.K.'s academic progress and portraying her as an enthusiastic classroom participant.

D. School's Knowledge of Bullying

L.K.'s parents sent several letters to her school about her being bullied, which the school principal says she responded to via telephone call. The principal recalls receiving letters from L.K.'s parents specifically reporting two acts of bullying.

During the 2007–2008 school year, L.K.'s parents brought her to the school principal's office to discuss bullying in the school. After showing them into her office, the principal asked L.K.'s parents to have the conversation outside of L.K.'s presence. When L.K.'s parents continued to try to discuss the matter, the principal asked them to leave. As the parents continued to try to discuss their daughter's problem the principal opened the door to her office and said she would call security if they did not leave.

No subsequent meeting about bullying with school personnel took place. The principal does not recall what she did to investigate any claims of bullying. ("Question: What, if anything, did you do to investigate [claims of bullying] internally? Answer: I can't recall."). When L.K.'s parents tried raising the issue of bullying during a meeting to set the educational plan at issue they were rebuffed. The school principal did not permit this discussion because she said she thought it was not appropriate for a CSE meeting.

Maloney, the school aide, testified that when she brought incidents of bullying to the attention of classroom teachers, it was ignored. When trying to discuss a particular incident with the principal, Maloney says that she was turned away and told there was no time for a meeting.

E. Bullying in America

. . . .

5. Bullying and Students With Disabilities

The United States Department of Education has defined disability harassment as "intimidation or abusive behavior based on disability that creates a hostile environment." Studies have shown that students with a disability, whether it is visible or non-visible, are subject to increased bullying that is often directed at the disability.

These students are also at more risk for bullying directed at factors other than their disability. Harassing conduct may take many forms, including verbal acts and name-calling, as well as nonverbal behavior, such as graphic written statements, or conduct that is physically threatening, harmful, or humiliating.

Overall, students with disabilities are less popular, have fewer friends, and struggle more with loneliness and peer rejection, increasing the likelihood they will become the victim of bullying. Students who suffer from learning disabilities and emotional disorders often lack social awareness, which makes them more vulnerable. Some research concludes that disabled students themselves are more likely to perpetuate bullying behavior in response to being bullied.

Despite an increased focus in recent years on instructing special education students in general education classrooms, there has not been a corresponding concern about the way these children integrate socially in the classroom. Without healthy social interaction, students with disabilities become targets of harassment.

One study found that four factors were predictive of a student being bullied: 1) receiving extra help in school; 2) being alone at playtime; 3) having fewer than two friends; and 4) being male. While disabled students often receive extra help, they sometimes struggle to make friends. In one study, learning disabled children reported that they were threatened, assaulted, or had their possessions taken away from them with greater frequency than non-learning disabled students.

Some states have recognized that students who suffer from a learning disability are at a greater risk for bullying than their non-disabled peers and that IEPs should take this into account. In passing a comprehensive law dealing with school bullying, Massachusetts recently adopted the following requirement:

> Whenever the evaluation of the Individualized Education Program team indicates that the child has a disability that affects social skills development or that *the child is vulnerable to bullying,* harassment or teasing *because of the child's disability,* the Individualized Education Program shall address the skills and proficiencies needed to avoid and *respond to bullying,* harassment or teasing.

Mass. Senate No. 2404 (2010) (emphasis added).

Massachusetts Advocates for Children sought to determine how often children along the autism spectrum are harassed at school. Eighty-eight percent of those parents who responded indicated their child was bullied while at school.

. . . .

III. Law

. . . .

B. Obligations of Schools to Remedy Bullying

1. Due Process

The central question raised by this case is what actions, if any, a school is required to take to stop bullying of disabled students. Generally, the Due Process Clause of the Constitution does not require that the state "protect the life, liberty, and property of its citizens against invasion by private actors." *DeShaney v. Winnebago County Dep't of Soc. Services*, 489 U.S. 189, 195 . . . (1989). The Due Process Clause forbids the state from itself depriving citizens of those rights, but it does not require the state to provide aid, even when it may be necessary.

Nevertheless, there are limited circumstances where the state has created a danger or has a special relationship with an individual, when it will be required to protect a person's right to personal inviolability from private or public abuse. *See Estelle v. Gamble,* 429 U.S. 97 . . . (1976) (holding that a state is required to provide medical care to incarcerated individuals); *Youngberg v. Romeo,* 457 U.S. 307 . . . (1982) (holding that the state must provide involuntarily committed mental patients with services that insure their reasonable safety).

The Court of Appeals for the Second Circuit apparently has not squarely been presented with a claim that by failing to prevent harm to a student in their care, school officials have violated substantive due process. Where such claims have been brought elsewhere, they have not been successful.

Where an elementary school student is required to attend school, and truancy laws forcing attendance are in effect, that student may be "owed *some* duty of care."

. . . .

It is uncertain whether under the Due Process Clause, a public school has the duty to protect an elementary school student from bullying where truancy laws are in effect. This question need not be answered now since students have a right to be secure in school and schools have a duty to prevent students from harassment under IDEA and Title IX.

2. Guaranteed Right to Be Protected From Abuse in School

Students can find a right to "be secure and to be let alone" in Supreme Court school First Amendment jurisprudence. *Tinker v. Des Moines Independent School District,* 393 U.S. 503 . . . (1969). *Tinker* addressed the question of when a school could discipline a student for private expression. In assessing the claim, the Supreme Court ruled that the proper test is whether the student's expression created a material or substantial disruption of school work or infringed on a student's right to be let alone.

First Amendment cases have held that "there is no constitutional right to be a bully." *Sypniewski v. Warren Hills Reg'l Bd. of Educ.,* 307 F.3d 243, 264 (3d Cir.2002). "Intimidation of one student by another, including intimidation by name calling, is the kind of behavior school authorities are expected to control or prevent." *Id.* One First Amendment case found that the right to be let alone includes the right to be free from physical intrusions as well as psychological attacks. *Harper v. Poway Unified Sch. Dist.,* 445 F.3d 1166, 1178 (9th Cir.2006), *vacated as moot,* 549 U.S. 1262 . . . (2007) ("Public school students who may be injured by verbal assaults on the basis of a core identifying characteristic such as race, religion, or sexual orientation, have a right to be free from such attacks while on school campuses. As *Tinker* clearly states, students have the right to be secure and to be let alone. Being secure involves not only freedom from physical assaults but from psychological attacks that cause young people to question their self-worth and their rightful place in society.")

3. Title IX of the Civil Rights Act and Individuals with Disability Education Act (IDEA)

Title IX, IDEA, and Section 504 of the Rehabilitation Act place upon schools the affirmative duty to address bullying and harassment. The United States Department of Education has been advising schools of their obligations, and possible liability under these statutes, for at least ten years. "Where the institution learns that disability harassment may have occurred, the institution must investigate the incident(s) promptly and respond appropriately."

Section 504 of the Rehabilitation Act is distinct from the Individuals with Disability Education Act, but both statutes require the same outcome—recipients of federal funds must provide students with a free, appropriate public education. *See* 29 U.S.C. § 701(c).

Proof of a violation of Section 504 requires a plaintiff to prove: 1) a disability; 2) that the defendant was subject to the relevant statute; and 3) that plaintiff was denied an opportunity to benefit scholastically because of the disability. Guidance provided under Section 504 is applicable to IDEA.

. . . .

D. Bullying and IDEA

While the general requirements of IDEA are well established, the question of whether bullying can be grounds for finding that a school district deprived a student of a free and appropriate education is an open question in the Second Circuit. There is, however, some indication from this circuit's court of appeals that it might be willing to extend FAPE protections to bullying. . . .

1. Court of Appeals for the Second Circuit

In *Smith v. Guilford Board of Education*, the Second Circuit Court of Appeals vacated the district court's granting of a motion for summary judgment in a FAPE case where the allegations involved a diminutive student being bullied. 226 F. Appx. 58 (2d Cir. 2007). The court reasoned that the district court had "failed to consider whether Plaintiffs sufficiently alleged a violation of the student's *statutory* right to a FAPE; instead, the court considered his right to a FAPE only to the extent that it might constitute a property interest protected by procedural due process." Though the student did suffer from attention deficit hyperactive disorder, his complaint alleged that the bullying was the result of his diminutive size, and not his learning disability. The court found that it was unable to determine whether and to what extent liability may arise out of behavior unrelated to a student's disability because the student's education plan was not before it. It suggested that liability might be founded on disability.

2. Court of Appeals for the Third Circuit

In finding that a student was denied a free and appropriate public education due to bullying, the Court of Appeals for the Third Circuit did not provide the rubric under which it analyzed the plaintiff's claims. *See Shore Regional High Sch. Bd. of Ed. v. P.S.*, 381 F.3d 194 (3d Cir. 2004). Instead it looked at the alleged conduct to find that the lack of a school environment free from harassment was grounds for finding a denial of FAPE.

P.S. was socially isolated from his classmates and the victim of relentless physical and verbal abuse. The focus of ridicule was P.S.'s perceived effeminate nature and lack of athletic prowess. A long list of derogatory words were directed to P.S. Many times the words turned into violence. When new students came to school, they were told not to associate with him. When P.S. sat down for lunch at a table, he quickly found himself sitting alone. The school administration was informed, but did nothing. Ultimately, after an IEP was developed that would have sent P.S. back to school with the same bullies who had tormented him, P.S.'s parents sent him to another school and sought reimbursement for their expenses.

The appellate court credited an administrative law judge's assessment that P.S. was deprived of a FAPE because of legitimate and real fears that harassment would continue in the future. Conclusive testimony at the administrative hearing established that the school "would not have been able to remedy the problem because, among other things, the same bullies would be present at [the school]; bullies generally do not stop on their own; even intensive interventions are often not effective when they are not begun until after a course of harassment has continued for some time. . . ." In reaching its conclusion, the court recognized, but did not consider, knowledge of the school district. It did note the improved educational performance of P.S. upon switching schools, but it did not expressly factor this into its decision. Instead, as a basis for reversing the district court, it relied on a lack of due weight given to expert testimony.

. . . .

3. Court of Appeals for the Seventh Circuit

The Seventh Circuit Court of Appeals found that "at least in principle" harassment can be a denial of a FAPE. *Charlie F.*, 98 F.3d at 993. The case involved a teacher who invited students to list their complaints about another student, which led to his loss of confidence, self-esteem, and fistfights. The court was unable to delve deeper into the merits of the claims because the parents bringing the case on behalf of the child had not exhausted their administrative remedies.

4. Court of Appeals for the Ninth Circuit

The Court of Appeals for the Ninth Circuit has developed a test, which asks whether a teacher was deliberately indifferent to bullying and the abuse so severe that a child can derive *no* educational benefit. *M.L.*, 394 F.3d at 650. The court based its reasoning on the gender discrimination case of *Davis v. Monroe County Board of Education*, 526 U.S. 629 . . . (1999), but seemingly modified *Davis* by requiring a finding that no educational benefit was received. In *Davis*, the test required a showing that harassment bars access to an educational opportunity or benefit.

The student involved in *M.L.* only remained in his elementary school for five days, which failed to give the school a chance to remedy the teasing. Additionally, the court found that the plaintiff had not demonstrated that the bullying interfered with his education.

This test is too rigid and too narrow. It fails to acknowledge that a student may have her academic success stunted as a result of harassment, but still achieve some success. A student who received some educational benefit despite bullying might have received more if not faced with the serious obstacle of peer harassment.

5. Possible Legal Standards

. . . .

d. Applicable Standard

The applicable standard should take into account administrative advice that has long been given to schools in how to apply the IDEA and other child protective legislation. By giving weight to this guidance, the expectations of the parties are not upset, and precise notice of expected conduct is provided. To that end, under IDEA the question to be asked is whether school personnel was deliberately indifferent to, or failed to take reasonable steps to prevent bullying that substantially restricted a child with learning disabilities in her educational opportunities.

This standard does not impose a new obligation on schools. For at least ten years the Department of Education has informed schools that they are legally obligated to comply with it.

> A school is responsible for addressing harassment incidents about which it knows or reasonably should have known. In some situations, harassment may be in plain sight, widespread or well-known to students and staff, such as harassment occurring in hallways, during academic or physical education classes, during extracurricular activities, at recess, on a school bus, or through graffiti in public areas. In these cases, the obvious signs of the harassment are sufficient to put the school on notice. In other situations, the school may become aware of misconduct, triggering an investigation that could lead to the discovery of additional incidents that, taken together, may constitute a hostile environment.

U.S. Dep't of Educ., Office of Civil Rights, Dear Colleague Letter: Bullying and Harassment, at 2 (Oct. 26, 2010).

Earlier, the Department of Education had advised schools that "[w]hen disability harassment limits or denies a student's ability to participate in or benefit from an educational institution's programs or activities, the institution must respond effectively. Where the institution learns that disability harassment may have occurred, the institution must investigate the incident promptly and respond appropriately."

Conduct need not be outrageous to fit within the category of harassment that rises to a level of deprivation of rights of a disabled student. The conduct must, however, be sufficiently severe, persistent, or pervasive that it creates a hostile environment. Where a student is verbally abused repeatedly and suffers other indignities, such as having his property taken or is struck by his fellow students, and a school does nothing to discipline the offending students despite its knowledge that the actions have occurred, the student has been deprived of substantial educational opportunities.

The rule to be applied is as follows: When responding to bullying incidents, which may affect the opportunities of a special education student to obtain an appropriate education, a school must take prompt and appropriate action. It must investigate if the harassment is reported to have occurred. If harassment is found to have occurred, the school must take appropriate steps to prevent it in the future. These duties of a school exist even if the misconduct is covered by its anti-bullying policy, and regardless of whether the student has complained, asked the school to take action, or identified the harassment as a form of discrimination.

It is not necessary to show that the bullying prevented all opportunity for an appropriate education, but only that it is likely to affect the opportunity of the student for an appropriate education. The bullying need not be a reaction to or related to a particular disability.

. . . .

IV. Application of Law to Facts

L.K. has provided evidence of each element of the test. First, her parents have produced witnesses who have testified that L.K., a disabled student, was isolated and the victim of harassment from her peers. The school denies these allegations. The IHO erred in finding that bullying went to placement and not to the adequacy of a program, and in making judgments about the veracity of the witnesses' accounts. A fact finder could conclude on this record that L.K. was the victim of bullying.

Second, the parents allege that they sent letters and tried to speak to the principal about the issue. There is evidence on both sides. The principal acknowledged knowing about an incident of bullying but cannot recall what she did to investigate it. She admits receiving letters that reveal incidents of bullying. She acknowledges asking L.K.'s parents to leave a meeting designed to discuss concerns about bullying. This meeting was never rescheduled. Aides who helped L.K. state that they tried to bring the bullying to the attention of their superiors but were ignored. No determination was made by the IHO about whether school personnel had notice of substantial bullying.

Third, L.K. presents evidence that could reasonably be construed as proving the school's failure to take reasonable steps to address the harassment. The school has not provided documentation that it either investigated claims of bullying or took steps to remedy the conduct. This evidence was not touched upon by the fact finder.

Fourth, L.K.'s parents state that she withdrew emotionally, did not want to go to school, and suffered social scars as a result of the bullying. The school district refutes this by pointing to academic progress for L.K. Whether the harassment rose to a level that deprived L.K. of an educational benefit was not decided in the administrative hearings. A student is not required to prove that she was denied all educational benefit. She may not be deprived of her entire educational benefit, but still may suffer adverse educational effects as a result of bullying. To be denied educational benefit, a student need not regress, but need only have her educational benefit adversely affected.

Academic growth is not an all-or-nothing proposition. There are levels of progress. A child may achieve substantial educational gains despite harassment, and yet she still may have been seriously hindered. Growth may be stunted providing an education below the level contemplated by IDEA. In New York, IEP's are required to give children more than an opportunity for just "trivial advancement." The law recognizes that a student can grow academically, but still be denied the educational benefit that is guaranteed by IDEA. Where bullying reaches a level where a student is substantially restricted in learning opportunities she has been deprived a FAPE. Whether bullying rose to this level is a question for the fact finder.

. . . .

The IHO and the SRO both touched upon the issue of bullying, but they did not apply the proper standard. The IDEA gives a court broad authority to grant appropriate relief. The motion of defendant for summary judgment dismissing the case is denied.

Notes, Comments, and Questions

1. Judge Weinstein discussed the impact that bullying has on the emotional well-being of children with disabilities. If you represented a school board, what arguments would you advance against Judge Weinstein's consideration of this factor? Is taking the emotional well-being of children with disabilities into account consistent with the language of the IDEA? Is it consistent with the definition of FAPE advanced in *Rowley*?

2. The Court in *Rowley* held that a disabled child receives a FAPE if he receives "some educational benefit" from the special education program or services. Is Judge Weinstein's test—that the bullying "is likely to affect the opportunity of the student for an appropriate education"—consistent with *Rowley*? What about his statement that the bullying need not be motivated by a child's particular disability? Do school districts owe a higher duty of care to children with disabilities than children who do not have disabilities? Why or why not?

3. As discussed in the opinion, one study found that bullying in kindergarten and first grade occurs on the playground every three to six minutes. Given the

pervasiveness of bullying, is requiring that school districts investigate and resolve all alleged incidents of bullying "regardless of whether the student has complained, asked the school to take action, or identified the harassment as a form of discrimination" too high a burden on school districts?

4. How critical is the definition of bullying to the reasonableness of the test announced in this case? Should it make a difference if a child with a disability is being bullied or harassed by another child with a disability? Should the parent of the child being bullied or the school district be given deference in determining whether a student interaction or altercation constitutes bullying?

5. Judge Weinstein remanded *T.K.* to the impartial hearing officer to render a decision consistent with his opinion. On remand, both the hearing officer and the state review officer found that, although L.K. was bullied, the bullying did not result in a denial of FAPE. Judge Weinstein disagreed and found in favor of L.K. T.K. v. N.Y.C. Dep't of Educ., 32 F. Supp. 3d 405 (E.D.N.Y. 2014), *aff'd*, 810 F.3d 869 (2d Cir. 2016). In affirming, the Second Circuit did not decide whether bullying could result in the denial of FAPE. *Id.* at 876. Instead, the court decided the case on procedural grounds:

> We conclude that the Department denied L.K. a FAPE by violating her parents' procedural right to participate in the development of her IEP. At two separate meetings, both of which were integral to the development of L.K.'s IEP, Plaintiffs sought to discuss L.K.'s bullying, but school officials refused to do so. The undisputed record evidence confirms that, in asking to speak with the officials about the bullying, L.K.'s parents had reason to believe that the bullying would interfere with L.K.'s ability to receive meaningful educational benefits and could prevent L.K.'s public education from producing progress, not regression.

Id. What do you think the standard should be for determining whether bullying violates a student's substantive right to a FAPE?

Chapter 6

Tuition Reimbursement for Unilateral Parental Placement of Children with Disabilities in Private Schools

Introduction

Every parent has the right to seek the best services for his or her own child, including a private school education. Issues arise when parents place their child in a private school because the parent believes the public school either has not or cannot provide the child with a FAPE and then seeks reimbursement for the private school tuition and other costs. Such unilateral parental placement in private school raises questions about the relative authority of parents and schools under the IDEA, the adequacy of the administrative and judicial process for resolving disputes between parents and school districts regarding the appropriateness of a private school placement, and the presumed good faith of school districts and parents in meeting the educational needs of children with disabilities. Should a parent be able unilaterally to place his or her child in a private school at public expense if the parent feels that the school district is not providing a FAPE to her child? What steps should a parent have to take before making a unilateral placement?

Section One covers the genesis of the right to reimbursement for private school tuition. Section Two covers the codification of this right in 1997 amendments to the IDEA.

Problem

Re-read the problem at the beginning of Chapter Four.

After the school district decided that K.J. was not eligible for special education, it sent K.J.'s parents a notice informing them of its decision. In response, K.J.'s parents sent the school district a letter that read in part as follows, "We disagree with your decision. As we have repeatedly told you, K.J.'s disability has had a negative effect on her ability to learn. Without special education, she will not learn and will not be on grade level or graduate from high school. We intend to take all actions within the law to ensure that K.J. receives an appropriate education." K.J.'s parents then requested an impartial hearing challenging the school district's decision and asking the hearing officer to rule that K.J. is eligible for special education. K.J.'s parents also removed K.J. from the school district. For her third grade year, they placed her in All Children Can Learn (ACCL), a private school that specializes in teaching students with ADHD and learning disabilities. The tuition at ACCL is $60,000 per year. However, K.J.'s parents could not afford to pay the tuition. They entered into an agreement with ACCL as follows:

> ACCL will not charge tuition to K.J.'s parents. However, in return, K.J.'s parents agree that they will request an impartial hearing asking the school district to pay ACCL $60,000 for K.J.'s third grade tuition.

K.J.'s parents requested a second impartial hearing, this time asking for an order requiring the school district to pay ACCL $60,000 for K.J.'s third-grade tuition. The impartial hearing officer consolidated this hearing request with the first request. The hearing officer ruled that K.J. was eligible for special education. How should the hearing officer rule on the request for tuition reimbursement?

Section One
Establishing the Right to Reimbursement for Unilateral Placement

In a pair of unanimous decisions, the Supreme Court established that the IDEA requires school districts to reimburse parents who unilaterally placed their child in a private school when the school district denied the child a FAPE and the private school provided an appropriate education.

Sch. Comm. of Burlington v. Dep't of Educ. of Mass.

471 U.S. 359 (1985)

Justice Rehnquist delivered the opinion of the unanimous Court.

The Education of the Handicapped Act (Act) requires participating state and local educational agencies "to assure that handicapped children and their parents or guardians are guaranteed procedural safeguards with respect to the provision of free appropriate public education" to such handicapped children. These procedures include the right of the parents to participate in the development of an "individualized education program" (IEP) for the child and to challenge in administrative and court proceedings a proposed IEP with which they disagree. Where as in the present case review of a contested IEP takes years to run its course—years critical to the child's development—important practical questions arise concerning interim placement of the child and financial responsibility for that placement. This case requires us to address some of those questions.

Michael Panico . . . was a first grader in the public school system of petitioner Town of Burlington, Mass., when he began experiencing serious difficulties in school. It later became evident that he had "specific learning disabilities" and thus was "handicapped" within the meaning of the Act. This entitled him to receive at public expense specially designed instruction to meet his unique needs, as well as related transportation. . . .

In the spring of 1979, Michael attended the third grade of the Memorial School, a public school in Burlington, Mass., under an IEP calling for individual tutoring by a reading specialist for one hour a day and individual and group counseling. Michael's continued poor performance and the fact that Memorial School was not equipped to handle his needs led to much discussion between his parents and Town school officials about his difficulties and his future schooling. Apparently the course of these discussions did not run smoothly; the upshot was that the Panicos and the Town agreed that Michael was generally of above average to superior intelligence, but had special educational needs calling for a placement in a school other than Memorial. They disagreed over the source and exact nature of Michael's learning difficulties, the Town believing the source to be emotional and the parents believing it to be neurological.

In late June, the Town presented the Panicos with a proposed IEP for Michael for the 1979–1980 academic year. It called for placing Michael in a highly structured class of six children with special academic and social needs, located at another Town public school, the Pine Glen School. On July 3, Michael's father rejected the proposed IEP and sought review . . . by respondent Massachusetts Department of Education's Bureau of Special Education Appeals (BSEA). . . .

Meanwhile the Panicos received the results of the latest expert evaluation of Michael by specialists at Massachusetts General Hospital, who opined that Michael's "emotional difficulties are secondary to a rather severe learning disorder characterized by perceptual difficulties" and recommended "a highly specialized setting for children with learning handicaps . . . such as the Carroll School," a state-approved private school for special education located in Lincoln, Mass. Believing that the Town's proposed placement of Michael at the Pine Glen School was inappropriate in light of Michael's needs, Mr. Panico enrolled Michael in the Carroll School in mid-August at his own expense, and Michael started there in September.

The BSEA held several hearings during the fall of 1979, and in January 1980 the hearing officer decided that the Town's proposed placement at the Pine Glen School was inappropriate and that the Carroll School was "the least restrictive adequate program within the record" for Michael's educational needs. The hearing officer ordered the Town to pay for Michael's tuition and transportation to the Carroll School for the 1979–1980 school year, including reimbursing the Panicos for their expenditures on these items for the school year to date.

The Town sought judicial review of the State's administrative decision in the United States District Court for the District of Massachusetts . . . .

. . . .

[T]he District Court in August 1982 overturned the BSEA decision, holding that the appropriate 1979–1980 placement for Michael was the one proposed by the Town in the IEP and that the parents had failed to show that this placement would not also have been appropriate for subsequent years. Accordingly, the court concluded that the Town was "not responsible for the cost of Michael's education at the Carroll School for the academic years 1979–80 through 1981–82."

. . . .

[After lengthy and complex litigation, the Town lost on several issues before the First Circuit Court of Appeals.]

The Town filed a petition for a writ of certiorari . . . challenging the decision of the Court of Appeals on numerous issues. . . . We granted certiorari, only to consider the following two issues: whether the potential relief available under § 1415(e)(2) includes reimbursement to parents for private school tuition and related expenses, and whether § 1415(e)(3) bars such reimbursement to parents who reject a proposed IEP and place a child in a private school without the consent of local school authorities. . . .

. . . .

The *modus operandi* of the Act is the already mentioned "individualized educational program." The IEP is in brief a comprehensive statement of the educational needs of a handicapped child and the specially designed instruction and related services to be employed to meet those needs. The IEP is to be developed jointly by a school official qualified in special education, the child's teacher, the parents or guardian, and, where appropriate, the child. In several places, the Act emphasizes the participation of the parents in developing the child's educational program and assessing its effectiveness.

Apparently recognizing that this cooperative approach would not always produce a consensus between the school officials and the parents, and that in any disputes the school officials would have a natural advantage, Congress incorporated an elaborate set of what it labeled "procedural safeguards" to insure the full participation of the parents and proper resolution of substantive disagreements. Section 1415(b) entitles the parents "to examine all relevant records with respect to the identification, evaluation, and educational placement of the child," to obtain an independent educational evaluation of the child, to notice of any decision to initiate or change the identification, evaluation, or educational placement of the child, and to present complaints with respect to any of the above. The parents are further entitled to "an impartial due process hearing" . . . to resolve their complaints.

The Act also provides for judicial review in state or federal court to "[a]ny party aggrieved by the findings and decision" made after the due process hearing. The Act confers on the reviewing court the following authority:

> "[T]he court shall receive the records of the administrative proceedings, shall hear additional evidence at the request of a party, and, basing its decision

> on the preponderance of the evidence, shall grant such relief as the court determines is appropriate." § 1415(e)(2).

The first question on which we granted certiorari requires us to decide whether this grant of authority includes the power to order school authorities to reimburse parents for their expenditures on private special education for a child if the court ultimately determines that such placement, rather than a proposed IEP, is proper under the Act.

We conclude that the Act authorizes such reimbursement. The statute directs the court to "grant such relief as [it] determines is appropriate." The ordinary meaning of these words confers broad discretion on the court. The type of relief is not further specified, except that it must be "appropriate." Absent other reference, the only possible interpretation is that the relief is to be "appropriate" in light of the purpose of the Act. As already noted, this is principally to provide handicapped children with "a free appropriate public education which emphasizes special education and related services designed to meet their unique needs." The Act contemplates that such education will be provided where possible in regular public schools, with the child participating as much as possible in the same activities as nonhandicapped children, but the Act also provides for placement in private schools at public expense where this is not possible. In a case where a court determines that a private placement desired by the parents was proper under the Act and that an IEP calling for placement in a public school was inappropriate, it seems clear beyond cavil that "appropriate" relief would include a prospective injunction directing the school officials to develop and implement at public expense an IEP placing the child in a private school.

If the administrative and judicial review under the Act could be completed in a matter of weeks, rather than years, it would be difficult to imagine a case in which such prospective injunctive relief would not be sufficient. As this case so vividly demonstrates, however, the review process is ponderous. A final judicial decision on the merits of an IEP will in most instances come a year or more after the school term covered by that IEP has passed. In the meantime, the parents who disagree with the proposed IEP are faced with a choice: go along with the IEP to the detriment of their child if it turns out to be inappropriate or pay for what they consider to be the appropriate placement. If they choose the latter course, which conscientious parents who have adequate means and who are reasonably confident of their assessment normally would, it would be an empty victory to have a court tell them several years later that they were right but that these expenditures could not in a proper case be reimbursed by the school officials. If that were the case, the child's right to a free appropriate public education, the parents' right to participate fully in developing a proper IEP, and all of the procedural safeguards would be less than complete. Because Congress undoubtedly did not intend this result, we are confident that by empowering the court to grant "appropriate" relief Congress meant to include retroactive reimbursement to parents as an available remedy in a proper case.

In this Court, the Town repeatedly characterizes reimbursement as "damages," but that simply is not the case. Reimbursement merely requires the Town to belatedly pay expenses that it should have paid all along and would have borne in the first instance had it developed a proper IEP. Such a *post hoc* determination of financial responsibility was contemplated in the legislative history:

> "If a parent contends that he or she has been forced, at that parent's own expense, to seek private schooling for the child because an appropriate program does not exist within the local educational agency responsible for the child's education and the local educational agency disagrees, that disagreement and *the question of who remains financially responsible* is a matter to which the due process procedures established under [the predecessor to § 1415] appl[y]." S.Rep. No. 94-168, p. 32 (1975), U.S.Code Cong. & Admin. News 1975, pp. 1425, 1456 (emphasis added).

Regardless of the availability of reimbursement as a form of relief in a proper case, the Town maintains that the Panicos have waived any right they otherwise might have to reimbursement because they violated 1415(e)(3), which provides:

> "During the pendency of any proceedings conducted pursuant to [§ 1415], unless the State or local educational agency and the parents or guardian otherwise agree, the child shall remain in the then current educational placement of such child . . . ."

We need not resolve the academic question of what Michael's "then current educational placement" was in the summer of 1979, when both the Town and the parents had agreed that a new school was in order. For the purposes of our decision, we assume that the Pine Glen School, proposed in the IEP, was Michael's current placement and, therefore, that the Panicos did "change" his placement after they had rejected the IEP and had set the administrative review in motion. In so doing, the Panicos contravened the conditional command of § 1415(e)(3) that "the child shall remain in the then current educational placement."

As an initial matter, we note that the section calls for agreement by *either* the *State or* the *local educational agency.* The BSEA's decision in favor of the Panicos and the Carroll School placement would seem to constitute agreement by the State to the change of placement. The decision was issued in January 1980, so from then on the Panicos were no longer in violation of § 1415(e)(3). This conclusion, however, does not entirely resolve the instant dispute because the Panicos are also seeking reimbursement for Michael's expenses during the fall of 1979, prior to the State's concurrence in the Carroll School placement.

We do not agree with the Town that a parental violation of § 1415(e)(3) constitutes a waiver of reimbursement. The provision says nothing about financial responsibility, waiver, or parental right to reimbursement at the conclusion of judicial proceedings. Moreover, if the provision is interpreted to cut off parental rights to reimbursement, the principal purpose of the Act will in many cases be defeated in the same way as if reimbursement were never available. As in this case, parents will often notice a child's learning difficulties while the child is in a regular public school program. If the school officials disagree with the need for special education or the adequacy of the public school's program to meet the child's needs, it is unlikely they will agree to an interim private school placement while the review process runs its course. Thus, under the Town's reading of § 1415(e)(3), the parents are forced to leave the child in what may turn out to be an inappropriate educational placement or to obtain the appropriate placement only by sacrificing any claim for reimbursement. The Act was intended to give handicapped children both an appropriate education and a free one; it should not be interpreted to defeat one or the other of those objectives.

The legislative history supports this interpretation, favoring a proper interim placement pending the resolution of disagreements over the IEP:

> "The conferees are cognizant that an impartial due process hearing may be required to assure that the rights of the child have been completely protected. We did feel, however, that the placement, or change of placement should not be unnecessarily delayed while long and tedious administrative appeals were being exhausted. Thus the conference adopted a flexible approach to try to meet the needs of both the child and the State."
>
> 121 Cong.Rec. 37412 (1975) (Sen. Stafford).

We think at least one purpose of § 1415(e)(3) was to prevent school officials from removing a child from the regular public school classroom over the parents' objection pending completion of the review proceedings. As we observed in *Rowley*, the impetus for the Act came from two federal-court decisions, *Pennsylvania Assn. for Retarded Children v. Commonwealth*, and *Mills v. Board of Education of District of Columbia*, which arose from the efforts of parents of handicapped children to prevent the exclusion or expulsion of their children from the public schools. Congress was concerned about the apparently widespread practice of relegating handicapped children to private institutions or warehousing them in special classes. We also note that § 1415(e)(3) is located in a section detailing procedural safeguards which are largely for the benefit of the parents and the child.

This is not to say that § 1415(e)(3) has no effect on parents. While we doubt that this provision would authorize a court to order parents to leave their child in a particular placement, we think it operates in such a way that parents who unilaterally change their child's placement during the pendency of review proceedings, without the consent of state or local school officials, do so at their own financial risk. If the courts ultimately determine that the IEP proposed by the school officials was appropriate, the parents would be barred from obtaining reimbursement for any interim period in which their child's placement violated § 1415(e)(3). This conclusion is supported by the agency's interpretation of the Act's application to private placements by the parents:

> "(a) If a handicapped child has available a free appropriate public education and the parents choose to place the child in a private school or facility, the public agency is not required by this part to pay for the child's education at the private school or facility. . . .

> "(b) Disagreements between a parent and a public agency regarding the availability of a program appropriate for the child, and the question of financial responsibility, are subject to the due process procedures under [§ 1415]." 34 CFR § 300.403 (1984).

We thus resolve the questions on which we granted certiorari; because this case is here in an interlocutory posture, we do not consider . . . the specific equitable factors identified by the Court of Appeals for granting relief. We do think that the court was correct in concluding that "such relief as the court determines is appropriate," within the meaning of § 1415(e)(2), means that equitable considerations are relevant in fashioning relief.

The judgment of the Court of Appeals is *Affirmed*.

Florence Cnty. Sch. Dist. v. Carter

510 U.S. 7 (1993)

Justice O'Connor delivered the opinion of the Court.

The Individuals with Disabilities Education Act (IDEA or Act), requires States to provide disabled children with a "free appropriate education." This case presents the question whether a court may order reimbursement for parents who unilaterally withdraw their child from a public school that provides an inappropriate education under IDEA and put the child in a private school that provides an education that is otherwise proper under IDEA, but does not meet all the requirements of § 1401(a)(18). We hold that the court may order such reimbursement, and therefore affirm the judgment of the Court of Appeals.

I

Respondent Shannon Carter was classified as learning disabled in 1985, while a ninth grade student in a school operated by petitioner Florence County School District Four. School officials met with Shannon's parents to formulate an individualized education program (IEP) for Shannon, as required under IDEA. The IEP provided that Shannon would stay in regular classes except for three periods of individualized instruction per week, and established specific goals in reading and mathematics of four months' progress for the entire school year. Shannon's parents were dissatisfied, and requested a hearing to challenge the appropriateness of the IEP. Both the local educational officer and the state educational agency hearing officer rejected Shannon's parents' claim and concluded that the IEP was adequate. In the meantime, Shannon's parents had placed her in Trident Academy, a private school specializing in educating children with disabilities. Shannon began at Trident in September 1985 and graduated in the spring of 1988.

Shannon's parents filed this suit in July 1986, claiming that the school district had breached its duty under IDEA to provide Shannon with a "free appropriate public education," and seeking reimbursement for tuition and other costs incurred at Trident. After a bench trial, the District Court ruled in the parents' favor. The court held that the school district's proposed educational program and the achievement goals of the IEP "were wholly inadequate" and failed to satisfy the requirements of the Act. The court further held that "[a]lthough [Trident Academy] did not comply with all of the procedures outlined in [IDEA]," the school "provided Shannon an excellent education in substantial compliance with all the substantive requirements" of the statute. The court found that Trident "evaluated Shannon quarterly, not yearly as mandated in [IDEA], it provided Shannon with low teacher-student ratios, and it developed a plan which allowed Shannon to receive passing marks and progress from grade to grade." The court also credited the findings of its own expert, who determined that Shannon had made "significant progress" at Trident and that her reading comprehension had risen three grade levels in her three years at the school. The District Court concluded that Shannon's education was "appropriate" under IDEA, and that Shannon's parents were entitled to reimbursement of tuition and other costs.

The Court of Appeals for the Fourth Circuit affirmed. The court agreed that the IEP proposed by the school district was inappropriate under IDEA. It also rejected the school district's argument that reimbursement is never proper when the parents choose a private school that is not approved by the State or that does not comply with all the terms of IDEA. According to the Court of Appeals, neither the text of the Act nor its legislative history imposes a "requirement that the private school be approved by the state in parent-placement reimbursement cases." To the contrary, the Court of Appeals concluded, IDEA's state-approval requirement applies only when a child is placed in a private school by public school officials. Accordingly, "when a public school system has defaulted on its obligations under the Act, a private school placement is 'proper under the Act' if the education provided by the private school is 'reasonably calculated to enable the child to receive educational benefits.'"

The court below recognized that its holding conflicted with *Tucker v. Bay Shore Union Free School Dist.,* in which the Court of Appeals for the Second Circuit held that parental placement in a private school cannot be proper under the Act unless the private school in question meets the standards of the state education agency. We granted certiorari, to resolve this conflict among the Courts of Appeals.

II

In . . . *Burlington*, we held that IDEA's grant of equitable authority empowers a court "to order school authorities to reimburse parents for their expenditures on private special education for a child if the court ultimately determines that such placement, rather than a proposed IEP, is proper under the Act." Congress intended that IDEA's promise of a "free appropriate public education" for disabled children would normally be met by an IEP's provision for education in the regular public schools or in private schools chosen jointly by school officials and parents. In cases where cooperation fails, however, "parents who disagree with the proposed IEP are faced with a choice: go along with the IEP to the detriment of their child if it turns out to be inappropriate or pay for what they consider to be the appropriate placement." For parents willing and able to make the latter choice, "it would be an empty victory to have a court tell them several years later that they were right but that these expenditures could not in a proper case be reimbursed by the school officials." Because such a result would be contrary to IDEA's guarantee of a "free appropriate public education," we held that "Congress meant to include retroactive reimbursement to parents as an available remedy in a proper case."

As this case comes to us, two issues are settled: (1) the school district's proposed IEP was inappropriate under IDEA, and (2) although Trident did not meet the § 1401(a)(18) requirements, it provided an education otherwise proper under IDEA. This case presents the narrow question whether Shannon's parents are barred from reimbursement because the private school in which Shannon enrolled did not meet the § 1401(a)(18) definition of a "free appropriate public education." We hold that they are not, because § 1401(a)(18)'s requirements cannot be read as applying to parental placements.

Section 1401(a)(18)(A) requires that the education be "provided at public expense, under public supervision and direction." Similarly, § 1401(a)(18)(D) requires schools to provide an IEP, which must be designed by "a representative of the local educational agency," and must be "establish[ed]," "revise[d]," and "review[ed]" by the agency. These requirements do not make sense in the context of a parental placement. In this case, as in all *Burlington* reimbursement cases, the parents' rejection of the school district's proposed IEP is the very reason for the parents' decision to put their child in a private school. In such cases, where the private placement has necessarily been made over the school district's objection, the private school education will not be under "public supervision and direction." Accordingly, to read the § 1401(a)(18) requirements as applying to parental placements would effectively eliminate the right of unilateral withdrawal recognized in *Burlington.* Moreover, IDEA was intended to ensure that children with disabilities receive an education that is both appropriate and free. To read the provisions of § 1401(a)(18) to bar reimbursement in the circumstances of this case would defeat this statutory purpose.

Nor do we believe that reimbursement is necessarily barred by a private school's failure to meet state education standards. Trident's deficiencies, according to the school district, were that it employed at least two faculty members who were not state-certified and that it did not develop IEPs. As we have noted, however, the § 1401(a)(18) requirements—including the requirement that the school meet the standards of the state educational agency, § 1401(a)(18)(B)—do not apply to private parental placements. Indeed, the school district's emphasis on state standards is somewhat ironic. As the Court of Appeals noted, "it hardly seems consistent with the Act's goals to forbid parents from educating their child at a school that provides an appropriate education simply because that school lacks the stamp of approval of the same public school system that failed to meet the child's needs in the first place." Accordingly, we disagree with the Second Circuit's theory that "a parent may not obtain reimbursement for a unilateral placement if that placement was in a school that was not on [the State's] approved list of private" schools. Parents' failure to select a program known to be approved by the State in favor of an unapproved option is not itself a bar to reimbursement.

Furthermore, although the absence of an approved list of private schools is not essential to our holding, we note that parents in the position of Shannon's have no way of knowing at the time they select a private school whether the school meets state standards. South Carolina keeps no publicly available list of approved private schools, but instead approves private school placements on a case-by-case basis. In fact, although public school officials had previously placed three children with disabilities at Trident, Trident had not received blanket approval from the State. South Carolina's case-by-case approval system meant that Shannon's parents needed the cooperation of state officials before they could know whether Trident was state-approved. As we recognized in *Burlington*, such cooperation is unlikely in cases where the school officials disagree with the need for the private placement.

III

The school district also claims that allowing reimbursement for parents such as Shannon's puts an unreasonable burden on financially strapped local educational authorities. The school district argues that requiring parents to choose a state approved private school if they want reimbursement is the only meaningful way to allow States to control costs; otherwise States will have to reimburse dissatisfied parents for any private school that provides an education that is proper under the Act, no matter how expensive it may be.

There is no doubt that Congress has imposed a significant financial burden on States and school districts that participate in IDEA. Yet public educational authorities who want to avoid reimbursing parents for the private education of a disabled child can do one of two things: give the child a free appropriate public education in a public setting, or place the child in an appropriate private setting of the State's choice. This is IDEA's mandate, and school officials who conform to it need not worry about reimbursement claims.

Moreover, parents who, like Shannon's, "unilaterally change their child's placement during the pendency of review proceedings, without the consent of state or local school officials, do so at their own financial risk." *Burlington*, at 373–374 . . . . They are entitled to reimbursement *only* if a federal court concludes both that the public placement violated IDEA and that the private school placement was proper under the Act.

Finally, we note that once a court holds that the public placement violated IDEA, it is authorized to "grant such relief as the court determines is appropriate." 20 U.S.C. § 1415(e)(2). Under this provision, "equitable considerations are relevant in fashioning relief," *Burlington*, 471 U.S. at 374 . . . , and the court enjoys "broad discretion" in so doing, *id.*, at 369. Courts fashioning discretionary equitable relief under IDEA must consider all relevant factors, including the appropriate and reasonable level of reimbursement that should be required. Total reimbursement will not be appropriate if the court determines that the cost of the private education was unreasonable.

Accordingly, we affirm the judgment of the Court of Appeals.

Notes, Comments, and Questions

1. In both *Burlington* and *Carter*, the parents alleged that the school district failed to provide their children with IEPs that satisfied the IDEA's assurance of a FAPE. In *Burlington*, the Court found that without reimbursement, "the child's right to a *free* appropriate public education, the parents' right to participate fully in developing a proper IEP, and all of the procedural safeguards would be less than complete." 471 U.S. at 370. If you represented the school district in *Burlington* or *Carter*, what arguments would you make to counter the Court's assertion?

2. One of the core issues in *Burlington* and *Carter* was Congressional intent in defining the rights and responsibilities of parents and school districts under the IDEA. Does the Court's interpretation give all of the "responsibilities" to the school district but all of the "rights" to the parents?

3. The school district in *Carter* raised the issue of its inability to control costs when a parent can unilaterally place a child in a private school, including those not approved by the state, giving the school district no control over the cost of the education. The Court responded by stating that if school districts do what is necessary to provide each child with an appropriate education, they will not have to be concerned about the cost of reimbursement. Is this a sufficient response? Is the cost a fair burden to put on school districts? Does the court overstate the level of control a district has over its budgetary realities or its ability to predict that a hearing officer or court will rule that it was not providing an appropriate education?

4. In *Carter*, the Court held that reimbursement is not barred if a private school does not meet state education standards; *see also* Ridgewood Bd. of Educ. v. N.E., 172 F.3d 238, 248–49 (3d Cir. 1999) (holding that parent need not seek the perfect private school in order to satisfy the IDEA). Courts have also allowed reimbursement even when the private school was not the least restrictive environment as long as the school provided an appropriate education to the child. Muller v. Comm. on Special Educ. of the East Islip Union Free Sch. Dist., 145 F.3d 95, 105 (2d Cir. 1998) (granting reimbursement to parents because private school was appropriate, despite not being the least restrictive environment); Cleveland Heights-Univ. Heights City Sch. Dist. v. Boss, 144 F.3d 391, 400 (6th Cir. 1998) (holding that the unilateral placement of the student at a school that did not satisfy the IDEA's least restrict environment requirement did not bar reimbursement). Although a private school need not be a perfect placement, the school must provide the child with an appropriate education in order for the parent to qualify for reimbursement. *See* Davis v. Wappingers Cent. Sch. Dist, 431 F. App'x 12, 16 (2d Cir. 2011) (denying reimbursement because private placement did not develop behavioral plans or provide multisensory teaching methods recommended for child with ADHD); Mary T. v. Sch. Dist. of Phila., 575 F.3d 235, 245 (3d Cir. 2009) (denying reimbursement because residential facility was designed to address medical rather than educational needs, did not have state educational accreditation, and had no on-site educators); Gagliardo v. Arlington Cent. Sch. Dist., 489 F.3d 105, 107, 113–14 (2d Cir. 2007)

(rejecting request for reimbursement because private placement did not provide the kind of special education services the student needed); Mr. I. v. Me. Sch. Admin. Dist. No. 55, 480 F.3d 1, 24–25 (1st Cir. 2007) (denying reimbursement because private placement did not offer specific special education services unanimously recommended by experts and school committee to child with Asperger's Syndrome).

5. Taking their lead from *Burlington* and *Carter*, federal courts have ruled that school districts must also reimburse parents for the costs they incurred to provide necessary related services to their child when the district failed to do so. *See, e.g.*, Jefferson Cnty. Bd. of Educ. v. Breen, 853 F.2d 853, 855, 857 (11th Cir. 1988) (affirming order requiring school district to reimburse parents for "therapeutic, educational, and related services"). Related services expenses for which courts have ordered districts to reimburse parents include:

ABA therapy: L.B. v. Nebo Sch. Dist., 379 F.3d 966, 979 (10th Cir. 2004) (ordering school district to pay reasonable cost of ABA therapy because it supported child's mainstream private education); Delaware Cnty. Intermediate Unit No. 25 v. Martin K., 831 F. Supp. 1206, 1227 (E.D. Pa. 1993) (ordering school district to reimburse parents for reasonable costs of ABA therapy).

Psychotherapy: Max M. v. Ill. State Bd. of Educ., 629 F. Supp. 1504, 1519–20 (N.D. Ill. 1986) (ordering school district to reimburse parents $8,855 for cost of psychotherapy).

Speech and language therapy: L.E. v. Ramsey Bd. of Educ., 435 F.3d 384, 394 (3d Cir. 2006) (ordering district to reimburse parents for the difference between the amount of speech therapy the school district offered and the amount the child should have received); Mary P. v. Ill. State Bd. of Educ., 919 F. Supp. 1173, 1181–82 (N.D. Ill. 1996) (ordering school district to reimburse the parents for the cost of speech therapy they provided for child up to thirty minutes per week for three previous years); Johnson v. Lancaster-Lebanon Intermediate Unit 13, 757 F. Supp. 606, 622 (E.D. Pa. 1991) (ordering the district to provide the child with four weekly thirty-minute sessions of speech therapy and to reimburse his parents $1,745 for paying for previous private speech therapy).

Transportation: Hurry v. Jones, 734 F.2d 879, 884–85 (1st Cir. 1984) (upholding reimbursement of $4,600 for the service parents rendered in transporting their child to school when the district failed to do so); Malehorn v. Hill City Sch. Dist., 987 F. Supp. 772, 780 (D.S.D. 1997) (ordering district to reimburse parents for transportation they provided over the course of eight months); Briere v. Fair Haven Grade Sch. Dist., 948 F. Supp. 1242, 1258 (D. Vt. 1996) (reimbursing parents $1,495 for transportation costs); Adams v. Hansen, 632 F. Supp. 858, 866–67 (N.D. Cal. 1985) (ordering district to reimburse parent for the cost of transportation to private day school).

Tutoring: W.G. v. Bd. of Trustees of Target Range Sch. Dist. No. 23, 960 F.2d 1479, 1486–87 (9th Cir. 1992) (ordering the school district to reimburse the parents for the cost of a tutor).

In contrast, parents are not eligible for reimbursement for the costs of related services if the school district provided their child with a FAPE or if equitable factors weigh against them. M.C. v. Voluntown Bd. of Educ., 226 F.3d 60, 69 (2d Cir. 2000) (refusing to order district to reimburse parents for psychological services because they did not complain to the district about counseling services until eight months after the private treatment had ended); Gregory K. v. Longview Sch. Dist., 811 F.2d 1307, 1315 (9th Cir. 1987) (denying reimbursement for tutoring because the district provided appropriate education).

Section Two
Codification of the Right to Tuition Reimbursement: The 1997 Amendments to the IDEA

In 1997, following the Supreme Court's decisions in *Burlington* and *Carter*, Congress amended the IDEA to codify the right to tuition reimbursement for parents who unilaterally place their children in private school and to impose some limits on the right. Congress further amended this provision of the IDEA in 2004. The IDEA currently provides:

> **(C) Payment for education of children enrolled in private schools without consent of or referral by the public agency**
>
> **(i) In general**
>
> Subject to subparagraph (A), this subchapter does not require a local educational agency to pay for the cost of education, including special education and related services, of a child with a disability at a private school or facility if that agency made a free appropriate public education available to the child and the parents elected to place the child in such private school or facility.
>
> **(ii) Reimbursement for private school placement**
>
> If the parents of a child with a disability, who previously received special education and related services under the authority of a public agency, enroll the child in a private elementary school or secondary school without the consent of or referral by the public agency, a court or a hearing officer may require the agency to reimburse the parents for the cost of that enrollment if the court or hearing officer finds that the agency had not made a free appropriate public education available to the child in a timely manner prior to that enrollment.
>
> **(iii) Limitation on reimbursement**
>
> The cost of reimbursement described in clause (ii) may be reduced or denied—
>
> (I) if—
>
> (aa) at the most recent IEP meeting that the parents attended prior to removal of the child from the public school, the parents did not

inform the IEP Team that they were rejecting the placement proposed by the public agency to provide a free appropriate public education to their child, including stating their concerns and their intent to enroll their child in a private school at public expense; or

(bb) 10 business days (including any holidays that occur on a business day) prior to the removal of the child from the public school, the parents did not give written notice to the public agency of the information described in item (aa);

(II) if, prior to the parents' removal of the child from the public school, the public agency informed the parents, through the notice requirements described in section 1415(b)(3) of this title, of its intent to evaluate the child (including a statement of the purpose of the evaluation that was appropriate and reasonable), but the parents did not make the child available for such evaluation; or

(III) upon a judicial finding of unreasonableness with respect to actions taken by the parents.

(iv) Exception

Notwithstanding the notice requirement in clause (iii)(I), the cost of reimbursement—

(I) shall not be reduced or denied for failure to provide such notice if—

(aa) the school prevented the parent from providing such notice;

(bb) the parents had not received notice, pursuant to section 1415 of this title, of the notice requirement in clause (iii)(I); or

(cc) compliance with clause (iii)(I) would likely result in physical harm to the child; and

(II) may, in the discretion of a court or a hearing officer, not be reduced or denied for failure to provide such notice if—

(aa) the parent is illiterate or cannot write in English; or

(bb) compliance with clause (iii)(I) would likely result in serious emotional harm to the child.

20 U.S.C. § 1412(a)(10)(C) (2012).

Notes, Comments, and Questions

1. How does the right to reimbursement as codified differ from the right as established in *Burlington* and *Carter*? What do you think motivated Congress to make these changes?

2. Do the amendments to the IDEA address all of the equitable factors the courts should consider in determining whether a parent should be entitled to reimbursement for a unilateral placement? What other factors do you think the courts should consider?

3. The IDEA amendments left several important questions regarding a parent's right to reimbursement for a unilateral placement up to the courts to resolve. These include the meaning of the requirement that the child "previously received special education and related services under the authority of a public agency," whether a school district can be required to pay tuition for a public school placement that the parents are obliged to pay but have not yet paid, and the equitable factors relevant to determining whether to reimburse the parents. Consider how the courts in the following cases have treated these issues.

A. The Meaning of "[P]reviously received special education and related services under the authority of a public agency ...."

Section 1412(a)(10)(C)(ii) of the IDEA provides that a court may order a school district to reimburse a parent for the cost of a unilateral placement in a private school if the child has "previously received special education and related services under the authority of a public agency ...." Does this provision limit the availability of reimbursement to children who have already received special education from the school district?

Forest Grove Sch. Dist. v. T.A.

557 U.S. 230 (2009)

Justice Stevens delivered the opinion of the Court.

The Individuals with Disabilities Education Act (IDEA or Act) requires States receiving federal funding to make a ... FAPE ... available to all children with disabilities residing in the State. We have previously held that when a public school fails to provide a FAPE and a child's parents place the child in an appropriate private school without the school district's consent, a court may require the district to reimburse the parents for the cost of the private education. The question presented in this case is whether the IDEA Amendments of 1997 (Amendments) categorically prohibit reimbursement for private-education costs if a child has not "previously received special education and related services under the authority of a public agency." § 1412(a)(10)(C)(ii). We hold that the Amendments impose no such categorical bar.

I

Respondent T.A. attended public schools in the Forest Grove School District (School District or District) from the time he was in kindergarten through the winter of his junior year of high school. From kindergarten through eighth grade, respondent's teachers observed that he had trouble paying attention in class and completing his assignments. When respondent entered high school, his difficulties increased.

In December 2000, during respondent's freshman year, his mother contacted the school counselor to discuss respondent's problems with his schoolwork. At the end of the school year, respondent was evaluated by a school psychologist. After interviewing him, examining his school records, and administering cognitive ability tests, the psychologist concluded that respondent did not need further testing for any learning disabilities or other health impairments, including attention deficit hyperactivity disorder (ADHD). The psychologist and two other school officials discussed the evaluation results with respondent's mother in June 2001, and all agreed that respondent did not qualify for special-education services. Respondent's parents did not seek review of that decision, although the hearing examiner later found that the School District's evaluation was legally inadequate because it failed to address all areas of suspected disability, including ADHD.

With extensive help from his family, respondent completed his sophomore year at Forest Grove High School, but his problems worsened during his junior year. In February 2003, respondent's parents discussed with the School District the possibility of respondent completing high school through a partnership program with the local community college. They also sought private professional advice, and in March 2003 respondent was diagnosed with ADHD and a number of disabilities related to learning and memory. Advised by the private specialist that respondent would do best in a structured, residential learning environment, respondent's parents enrolled him at a private academy that focuses on educating children with special needs.

Four days after enrolling him in private school, respondent's parents hired a lawyer to ascertain their rights and to give the School District written notice of respondent's private placement. A few weeks later, in April 2003, respondent's parents requested an administrative due process hearing regarding respondent's eligibility for special-education services. In June 2003, the District engaged a school psychologist to assist in determining whether respondent had a disability that significantly interfered with his educational performance. Respondent's parents cooperated with the District during the evaluation process. In July 2003, a multidisciplinary team met to discuss whether respondent satisfied IDEA's disability criteria and concluded that he did not because his ADHD did not have a sufficiently significant adverse impact on his educational performance. Because the School District maintained that respondent was not eligible for special-education services and therefore declined to provide an individualized education program (IEP), respondent's parents left him enrolled at the private academy for his senior year.

The administrative review process resumed in September 2003. After considering the parties' evidence, including the testimony of numerous experts, the hearing officer issued a decision in January 2004 finding that respondent's ADHD adversely affected his educational performance and that the School District failed to meet its obligations under IDEA in not identifying respondent as a student eligible for special-education services. Because the District did not offer respondent a FAPE and his private-school placement was appropriate under IDEA, the hearing officer ordered the District to reimburse respondent's parents for the cost of the private-school tuition.

The School District sought judicial review . . . , arguing that the hearing officer erred in granting reimbursement. The District Court accepted the hearing officer's findings of fact but set aside the reimbursement award after finding that the 1997 Amendments categorically bar reimbursement of private-school tuition for students who have not "previously received special education and related services under the authority of a public agency." The District Court further held that, "[e]ven assuming that tuition reimbursement may be ordered in an extreme case for a student not receiving special education services, under general principles of equity where the need for special education was obvious to school authorities," the facts of this case do not support equitable relief.

The Court of Appeals for the Ninth Circuit reversed and remanded for further proceedings. The court first noted that, prior to the 1997 Amendments, "IDEA was silent on the subject of private school reimbursement, but courts had granted such reimbursement as 'appropriate' relief under principles of equity pursuant to 20 U.S.C. § 1415(i)(2)(C)." It then held that the Amendments do not impose a categorical bar to reimbursement when a parent unilaterally places in private school a child who has not previously received special-education services through the public school. Rather, such students "are eligible for reimbursement, to the same extent as before the 1997 amendments, as 'appropriate' relief pursuant to § 1415(i)(2)(C)."

The Court of Appeals also rejected the District Court's analysis of the equities as resting on two legal errors. First, because it found that § 1412(a)(10)(C)(ii) generally bars relief in these circumstances, the District Court wrongly stated that relief was appropriate only if the equities were sufficient to " 'override' " that statutory limitation. The District Court also erred in asserting that reimbursement is limited to " 'extreme' " cases. The Court of Appeals therefore remanded with instructions to reexamine the equities, including the failure of respondent's parents to notify the School District before removing respondent from public school. . . .

Because the Courts of Appeals that have considered this question have reached inconsistent results, we granted certiorari to determine whether § 1412(a)(10)(C) establishes a categorical bar to tuition reimbursement for students who have not previously received special-education services under the authority of a public education agency.

II

. . . .

The dispute giving rise to the present litigation differs from those in *Burlington* and *Carter* in that it concerns not the adequacy of a proposed IEP but the School District's failure to provide an IEP at all. And, unlike respondent, the children in those cases had previously received public special-education services. These differences are insignificant, however, because our analysis in the earlier cases depended on the language and purpose of the Act and not the particular facts involved. Moreover, when a child requires special-education services, a school district's failure to propose an IEP of any kind is at least as serious a violation of its responsibilities under IDEA as a failure to provide an adequate IEP. It is thus clear that the reasoning of *Burlington* and *Carter* applies equally to this case. The only question is whether the 1997 Amendments require a different result.

III

Congress enacted IDEA in 1970 to ensure that all children with disabilities are provided "'a free appropriate public education which emphasizes special education and related services designed to meet their unique needs [and] to assure that the rights of [such] children and their parents or guardians are protected.'" *Burlington*. After examining the States' progress under IDEA, Congress found in 1997 that substantial gains had been made in the area of special education but that more needed to be done to guarantee children with disabilities adequate access to appropriate services. The 1997 Amendments were intended "to place greater emphasis on improving student performance and ensuring that children with disabilities receive a quality public education."

Consistent with that goal, the Amendments preserved the Act's purpose of providing a FAPE to all children with disabilities. And they did not change the text of the provision we considered in *Burlington*, § 1415(i)(2)(C)(iii), which gives courts broad authority to grant "appropriate" relief, including reimbursement for the cost of private special education when a school district fails to provide a FAPE. "Congress is presumed to be aware of an administrative or judicial interpretation of a statute and to adopt that interpretation when it re-enacts a statute without change." Accordingly, absent a clear expression elsewhere in the Amendments of Congress' intent to repeal some portion of that provision or to abrogate our decisions in *Burlington* and *Carter*, we will continue to read § 1415(i)(2)(C)(iii) to authorize the relief respondent seeks.

The School District and the dissent argue that one of the provisions enacted by the Amendments, § 1412(a)(10)(C), effects such a repeal. Section 1412(a)(10)(C) is entitled "Payment for education of children enrolled in private schools without consent of or referral by the public agency," and it sets forth a number of principles applicable to public reimbursement for the costs of unilateral private-school placements. Section 1412(a)(10)(C)(i) states that IDEA "does not require a local educational agency to pay for the cost of education . . . of a child with a disability at a private school or facility if that agency made a free appropriate public education available to the child" and his parents nevertheless elected to place him in a private school. Section 1412(a)(10)(C)(ii) then provides that a "court or hearing officer may require [a public] agency to reimburse the parents for the cost of [private-school] enrollment if the court or hearing officer finds that the agency had not made a free appropriate public education available" and the child has "previously received special education and related services under the authority of [the] agency." Finally, § 1412(a)(10)(C)(iii) discusses circumstances under which the "cost of reimbursement described in clause (ii) may be reduced or denied," as when a parent fails to give 10 days' notice before removing a child from public school or refuses to make a child available for evaluation, and § 1412(a)(10)(C)(iv) lists circumstances in which a parent's failure to give notice may or must be excused.

Looking primarily to clauses (i) and (ii), the School District argues that Congress intended § 1412(a)(10)(C) to provide the exclusive source of authority for courts to order reimbursement when parents unilaterally enroll a child in private school. According to the District, clause (i) provides a safe harbor for school districts that provide a FAPE by foreclosing reimbursement in those circumstances. Clause (ii) then sets forth the circumstance in which reimbursement is appropriate—namely, when a school district fails to provide a FAPE to a child who has previously received special-education services through the public school. The District contends that because § 1412(a)(10)(C) only discusses reimbursement for children who have previously received special-education services through the public school, IDEA only authorizes reimbursement in that circumstance. The dissent agrees.

For several reasons, we find this argument unpersuasive. First, the School District's reading of the Act is not supported by its text and context, as the 1997 Amendments do not expressly prohibit reimbursement under the circumstances of this case, and the District offers no evidence that Congress intended to supersede our decisions in *Burlington* and *Carter*. Clause (i)'s safe harbor explicitly bars reimbursement only when a school district makes a FAPE available by correctly identifying a child as having a disability and proposing an IEP adequate to meet the child's needs. The clause says nothing about the availability of reimbursement when a school district fails to provide a FAPE. Indeed, its statement that reimbursement *is not* authorized when a school district provides a FAPE could be read to indicate that reimbursement *is* authorized when a school district does not fulfill that obligation.

Clause (ii) likewise does not support the District's position. Because that clause is phrased permissively, stating only that courts "may require" reimbursement in those circumstances, it does not foreclose reimbursement awards in other circumstances. Together with clauses (iii) and (iv), clause (ii) is best read as elaborating on the general rule that courts may order reimbursement when a school district fails to provide a FAPE by listing factors that may affect a reimbursement award in the common situation in which a school district has provided a child with some special-education services and the child's parents believe those services are inadequate. Referring as they do to students who have previously received special-education services through a public school, clauses (ii) through (iv) are premised on a history of cooperation and together encourage school districts and parents to continue to cooperate in developing and implementing an appropriate IEP before resorting to a unilateral private placement. The clauses of § 1412(a)(10)(C) are thus best read as elucidative rather than exhaustive.

This reading of § 1412(a)(10)(C) is necessary to avoid the conclusion that Congress abrogated *sub silentio* our decisions in *Burlington* and *Carter*. In those cases, we construed § 1415(i)(2)(C)(iii) to authorize reimbursement when a school district fails to provide a FAPE and a child's private-school placement is appropriate, without regard to the child's prior receipt of services. It would take more than Congress' failure to comment on the category of cases in which a child has not previously received special-education services for us to conclude that the Amendments substantially superseded our decisions and in large part repealed § 1415(i)(2)(C)(iii).... We accordingly adopt the reading of § 1412(a)(10)(C) that is consistent with those decisions.

The School District's reading of § 1412(a)(10)(C) is also at odds with the general remedial purpose underlying IDEA and the 1997 Amendments. The express purpose of the Act is to "ensure that all children with disabilities have available to them a free appropriate public education that emphasizes special education and related services designed to meet their unique needs,"—a factor we took into account in construing the scope of § 1415(i)(2)(C)(iii). Without the remedy respondent seeks, a "child's right to a *free* appropriate education ... would be less than complete." The District's position similarly conflicts with IDEA's "child find" requirement, pursuant to which States are obligated to "identif[y], locat[e], and evaluat[e]" "[a]ll children with disabilities residing in the State" to ensure that they receive needed special-education services. § 1412(a)(3)(A). A reading of the Act that left parents without an adequate remedy when a school district unreasonably failed to identify a child with disabilities would not comport with Congress' acknowledgment of the paramount importance of properly identifying each child eligible for services.

Indeed, by immunizing a school district's refusal to find a child eligible for special-education services no matter how compelling the child's need, the School District's interpretation of § 1412(a)(10)(C) would produce a rule bordering on the irrational. It would be particularly strange for the Act to provide a remedy, as all agree it does, when a school district offers a child inadequate special-education services but to leave parents without relief in the more egregious situation in which the school district unreasonably denies a child access to such services altogether. That IDEA affords parents substantial procedural safeguards, including the right to challenge a school district's eligibility determination and obtain prospective relief is no answer. We roundly rejected that argument in *Burlington,* observing that the "review process is ponderous" and therefore inadequate to ensure that a school's failure to provide a FAPE is remedied with the speed necessary to avoid detriment to the child's education. Like *Burlington,* this case vividly demonstrates the problem of delay, as respondent's parents first sought a due process hearing in April 2003, and the District Court issued its decision in May 2005—almost a year after respondent graduated from high school. The dissent all but ignores these shortcomings of IDEA's procedural safeguards.

IV

The School District advances two additional arguments for reading the Act to foreclose reimbursement in this case. First, the District contends that because IDEA was an exercise of Congress' authority under the Spending Clause, U.S. Const., Art. I, § 8, cl. 1, any conditions attached to a State's acceptance of funds must be stated unambiguously. Applying that principle, we held in *Arlington Central School Dist. Bd. of*

Ed. v. Murphy, 548 U.S. 291 . . . (2006), that IDEA's fee-shifting provision, § 1415(i)(3)(B), does not authorize courts to award expert-services fees to prevailing parents in IDEA actions because the Act does not put States on notice of the possibility of such awards. But *Arlington* is readily distinguishable from this case. In accepting IDEA funding, States expressly agree to provide a FAPE to all children with disabilities. An order awarding reimbursement of private-education costs when a school district fails to provide a FAPE merely requires the district "to belatedly pay expenses that it should have paid all along." *Burlington.* And States have in any event been on notice at least since our decision in *Burlington* that IDEA authorizes courts to order reimbursement of the costs of private special-education services in appropriate circumstances. . . .

Finally, the District urges that respondent's reading of the Act will impose a substantial financial burden on public school districts and encourage parents to immediately enroll their children in private school without first endeavoring to cooperate with the school district. The dissent echoes this concern. For several reasons, those fears are unfounded. Parents "are entitled to reimbursement *only* if a federal court concludes both that the public placement violated IDEA and the private school placement was proper under the Act." *Carter.* And even then courts retain discretion to reduce the amount of a reimbursement award if the equities so warrant—for instance, if the parents failed to give the school district adequate notice of their intent to enroll the child in private school. In considering the equities, courts should generally presume that public-school officials are properly performing their obligations under IDEA. As a result of these criteria and the fact that parents who "'unilaterally change their child's placement during the pendency of review proceedings, without the consent of state or local school officials, do so at their own financial risk,'" *Carter,* the incidence of private-school placement at public expense is quite small.

V

The IDEA Amendments of 1997 did not modify the text of § 1415(i)(2)(C)(iii), and we do not read § 1412(a)(10)(C) to alter that provision's meaning. Consistent with our decisions in *Burlington* and *Carter,* we conclude that IDEA authorizes reimbursement for the cost of private special-education services when a school district fails to provide a FAPE and the private-school placement is appropriate, regardless of whether the child previously received special education or related services through the public school.

When a court or hearing officer concludes that a school district failed to provide a FAPE and the private placement was suitable, it must consider all relevant factors, including the notice provided by the parents and the school district's opportunities for evaluating the child, in determining whether reimbursement for some or all of the cost of the child's private education is warranted. As the Court of Appeals noted, the District Court did not properly consider the equities in this case and will need to undertake that analysis on remand. Accordingly, the judgment of the Court of Appeals is affirmed.

Justice SOUTER, with whom Justice SCALIA and Justice THOMAS join, dissenting.

I respectfully dissent.

Burlington held that the Education of the Handicapped Act, now known as the individuals with Disabilities Education Act (IDEA), authorized a district court to order reimbursement of private school tuition and expenses to parents who took their disabled child from public school because the school's special education services did not meet the child's needs. We said that, for want of any specific limitation, this remedy was within the general authorization for courts to award "such relief as [they] determin[e] is appropriate." In 1997, however, Congress amended the IDEA with a number of provisions explicitly addressing the issue of "[p]ayment for education of children enrolled in private schools without consent of or referral by the public agency." § 1412(a)(10)(C). These amendments generally prohibit reimbursement if the school district made a "free appropriate education" (FAPE) available, § 1412(a)(10)(C)(i), and if they are to have any effect, there is no exception except by agreement, § 1412(a)(10)(B), or for a student who previously received special education services that were inadequate, § 1412(a)(10)(C)(ii).

The majority says otherwise and holds that § 1412(a)(10)(C)(ii) places no limit on reimbursements for private tuition. The Court does not find the provision clear enough to affect the rule in *Burlington,* and it does not believe Congress meant to limit public reimbursement for unilaterally incurred private school tuition. But there is no authority for a heightened standard before Congress can alter a prior judicial interpretation of a statute, and the assessment of congressional policy aims falls short of trumping what seems to me to be the clear limitation imposed by § 1412(a)(10)(C)(ii).

I

. . . .

. . . We emphasized [in *Burlington*] that the Act did not speak specifically to the issue of reimbursement, and held that "[a]bsent other reference," reimbursement for private tuition and expenses would be an " 'appropriate' " remedy in light of the purposes of the Act. In short, we read the general provision for ordering equitable remedies in § 1415(i)(2)(C)(iii) as authorizing a reimbursement order, in large part because Congress had not spoken more specifically to the issue.

But Congress did speak explicitly when it amended the IDEA in 1997. It first said that whenever the State or a local educational agency refers a student to private special education, the bill is a public expense. It then included several clauses addressing "[p]ayment for education of children enrolled in private schools without consent of or referral by the public agency." § 1412(a)(10)(C). The first contrasts with the provision covering an agency referral:

> "(i) In general
>
> ". . . this subchapter does not require a local educational agency to pay for the cost of education . . . of a child with a disability at a private school or facility if that agency made a free appropriate public education available to

> the child and the parents elected to place the child in such private school or facility." § 1412(a)(10)(C).

The second clause covers the case in which the school authority failed to make a FAPE available in its schools. It does not, however, provide simply that the authority must pay in this case, no matter what. Instead it provides this:

> "(ii) Reimbursement for private school placement
>
> "If the parents of a child with a disability, who previously received special education and related services under the authority of a public agency, enroll the child in a private elementary school or secondary school without the consent of or referral by the public agency, a court or a hearing officer may require the agency to reimburse the parents for the cost of that enrollment if the court or hearing officer finds that the agency had not made a free appropriate public education available to the child in a timely manner prior to that enrollment." § 1412(a)(10)(C).
>
> . . . .

As a purely semantic matter, these provisions are ambiguous in their silence about the case with no previous special education services and no FAPE available. As the majority suggests, clause (i) could theoretically be understood to imply that reimbursement may be ordered whenever a school district fails to provide a FAPE, and clause (ii) could be read as merely taking care to mention one of a variety of circumstances in which such reimbursement is permitted. But this is overstretching. When permissive language covers a special case, the natural sense of it is taken to prohibit what it fails to authorize. When a mother tells a boy that he may go out and play after his homework is done, he knows what she means.

So does anyone who reads the authorization of a reimbursement order in the case of "a child with a disability, who previously received special education and related services under the authority of a public agency." § 1412(a)(10)(C)(ii). If the mother did not mean that the homework had to be done, why did she mention it at all, and if Congress did not mean to restrict reimbursement authority by reference to previous receipt of services, why did it even raise the subject? "[O]ne of the most basic interpretive canons [is] that [a] statute should be construed so that effect is given to all its provisions, so that no part will be inoperative or superfluous, void or insignificant. . . ." But not on the Court's reading, under which clause (ii) does nothing but describe a particular subset of cases subject to remedial authority already given to courts by § 1415(i)(2)(C)(iii) and recognized in *Burlington:* a court may order reimbursement for a child who previously received special education [and] related services, but it may do this for any other child, too. But this is just not plausible, the notion that Congress added a new provision to the IDEA entitled "Reimbursement for private school placement" that had no effect whatsoever on reimbursement for private school placement. I would read clause (i) as written on the assumption that the school authorities can be expected to honor their obligations and as stating the general rule that unilateral placement cannot be reimbursed. And I would read clause (ii) as imposing a receipt of prior services limit on any exceptions to that general rule when school officials fall short of providing a FAPE.

This reading can claim the virtue of avoiding a further anomaly. Section 1412(a)(10)(C)(iii), which limits otherwise available reimbursement, is expressly directed to "[t]he cost of reimbursement described in clause (ii)." This makes perfect sense under my reading. Since clause (ii) is now the exclusive source of authority to order reimbursement, it is natural to refer to it in the clause setting out the conditions for reducing or even denying reimbursement otherwise authorized. Yet, as T.A. and the Government concede, under the majority's reading, Congress has called for reducing reimbursement only for the most deserving (parents described in clause (ii) who consult with the school district and give public special education services a try before demanding payment for private education), but provided no mechanism to reduce reimbursement to the least deserving (parents who have not given public placement a chance).

The Court responds to this point by doubling down. According to the majority, the criteria listed in clause (iii) can justify a reduction not only of "reimbursement described in clause (ii)," § 1412(a)(10)(C)(iii), but can also do so for a reimbursement order authorized elsewhere as well. That is, the majority avoids ascribing perverse motives to Congress by concluding that in both clause (ii) and clause (iii), Congress meant to add nothing to the statutory scheme. This simply leads back to the question of why Congress in § 1412(a)(10)(C) would have been so concerned with cases in which children had not previously received special education services when, on the majority's reading, the prior receipt of services has no relevance whatsoever to the subject of that provision.

Because any other interpretation would render clause (ii) pointless and clause (iii) either pointless or perverse, § 1412(a)(10)(C)(ii) must be read to allow reimbursement only for "parents of a child with a disability, who previously received special education and related services under the authority of a public agency."

II

Neither the majority's clear statement rule nor its policy considerations prevail over the better view of the 1997 Amendments.

A

The majority says that, because of our previous interpretation of the Act as authorizing reimbursement for unilateral private placement, Congress was obliged to speak with added clarity to alter the statute as so understood. The majority refers to two distinct principles for support: first, statutes are to be read with a presumption against implied repeals, and second, congressional reenactment of statutory text without change is deemed to ratify a prior judicial interpretation of it. I think neither principle is up to the task.

Section 1412(a)(10)(C) in no way repealed the provision we considered in *Burlington*. The relief that "is appropriate" under § 1415(i)(2)(C)(iii) depends on the substantive provisions of the IDEA as surely as if the provision authorized equitable relief "consistent with the provisions of this statute." When we applied § 1415(i)(2)(C)(iii) in *Burlington,* we expressly referred to those provisions and concluded that, in the absence of a specific rule, "appropriate" relief included the reimbursement sought. By introducing new restrictions on reimbursement, the 1997 Amendments produce a different conclusion about what relief is "appropriate." But § 1415(i)(2)(C)(iii) remains in effect, just as it would remain in effect if Congress had explicitly amended the IDEA to prohibit reimbursement absent prior receipt of services.

As for the rule that reenactment incorporates prior interpretation, the Court's reliance on it to preserve *Burlington*'s reading of § 1415(i)(2)(C)(iii) faces two hurdles. First, so far as I can tell, this maxim has never been used to impose a clear statement rule. If Congress does not suggest otherwise, reenacted statutory language retains its old meaning; but when a new enactment includes language undermining the prior reading, there is no presumption favoring the old, and the only course open is simply to read the revised statute as a whole. This is so because there is no reason to distinguish between amendments that occur in a single clause (as if Congress had placed all the changes in § 1415(i)(2)(C)(iii)), and those that take the form of a separate section (here, § 1412(a)(10)(C). If Congress had added a caveat within § 1415(i)(2)(C)(iii), or in an immediately neighboring provision, I assume the majority would not approach it with skepticism on the ground that it purported to modify a prior judicial interpretation.

Second, nothing in my reading of § 1412(a)(10)(C)(ii) is inconsistent with the holdings of *Burlington* and . . . *Carter.* Our opinion in *Burlington* was expressly premised on there being no "other reference" that would govern reimbursement for private tuition, and this all but invited Congress to provide one. Congress's provision of such a reference in 1997 is, to say the very least, no reason for skepticism that Congress wished to alter the law on reimbursement. The 1997 legislation, read my way, would not, however, alter the result in either *Burlington* or *Carter.* In each case, the school district had agreed that the child was disabled, the parents had cooperated with the district and tried out an IEP, and the only question was whether parents who later resorted to a private school could be reimbursed "'if the court ultimately determines that such placement, rather than a proposed IEP, is proper under the Act.'" In ordering reimbursement, the Court in both *Burlington* and *Carter* emphasized that the parents took part in devising an IEP, and expressed concern for parents who had sought an IEP before placing their child in private school, but received one that was inadequate. The result in each case would have been the same under my reading of the amended Act, both sets of parents being "parents of a child with a disability, who previously received special education and related services under the authority of a public agency." § 1412(a)(10)(C)(ii). It is therefore too much to suggest that my reading of § 1412(a)(10)(C)(ii) would "abrogat[e] *sub silentio* our decisions in *Burlington* and *Carter.*"

The majority argues that the policy concerns vindicated in *Burlington* and *Carter* justify reading those cases to authorize a reimbursement authority going beyond their facts, and would hold reimbursement possible even for parents who, like those here, unilaterally resort to a private school without first establishing at the administrative or appellate level that the child is disabled, or engaging in a collaborative process with the school officials. But how broadly one should read *Burlington* and *Carter* is beside the point, Congress having explicitly addressed the subject with statutory language that precludes the Court's result today.

B

The Court also rejects the natural sense of § 1412(a)(10)(C) as an interpretation that would be "at odds with the general remedial purpose underlying IDEA and the 1997 Amendments." The majority thinks my reading would place the school authorities in total control of parents' eligibility for reimbursement: just refuse any request for special education or services in the public school, and the prior service condition for eligibility under clause (ii) can never be satisfied. Thus, as the majority puts it, it would "borde[r] on the irrational" to "immuniz[e] a school district's refusal to find a child eligible for special-education services no matter how compelling the child's need." I agree that any such scheme would be pretty absurd, but there is no absurdity here. The majority's suggestion overlooks the terms of the IDEA process, the substantial procedures protecting a child's substantive rights under the IDEA, and the significant costs of its rule.

To start with the costs, special education can be immensely expensive, amounting to tens of billions of dollars annually and as much as 20% of public schools' general operating budgets. The more private placement there is, the higher the special education bill, a fact that lends urgency to the IDEA's mandate of a collaborative process in which an IEP is "developed jointly by a school official qualified in special education, the child's teacher, the parents or guardian, and, where appropriate, the child." *Burlington.*

The Act's repeated emphasis on the need for cooperative joint action by school and parent does not, however, leave the school in control if officials should wish to block effective (and expensive) action for the child's benefit, for if the collaborative approach breaks down, the IDEA provides for quick review in a "due process hearing" of the parents' claim that more services are needed to provide a FAPE than the school is willing to give. See § 1415(c)(2) (district must respond to due process hearing complaint within 10 days and hearing officer must assess facial validity of complaint within 5 days); § 1415(e) (mediation is available, provided it does not delay due process hearing); § 1415(f)(1)(B) (district must convene a meeting with parents within 15 days to attempt to resolve complaint); 34 CFR § 300.510(b)(1)-(2) (2008) (if complaint is not resolved, a hearing must be held within 30 days of complaint and a decision must be issued within 75 days of complaint). Parents who remain dissatisfied after these first two levels of process may have a right of appeal to the state educational agency and in any case may bring a court action in federal district court. This scheme of administrative and judicial review is the answer to the Court's claim that reading the prior services condition as restrictive, not illustrative, immunizes a school district's intransigence, giving it an effective veto on reimbursement for private placement.

That said, the Court of course has a fair point that the prior services condition qualifies the remedial objective of the statute, and pursuing appeals to get a satisfactory IEP with special services worth accepting could be discouraging. The child who needs help does not stop needing it, or stop growing, while schools and parents argue back and forth. But we have to decide this case on the premise that most such arguments will be carried on in good faith, and even on the assumption that disagreements about the adequacy of IEPs will impose some burdens on the Act's intended beneficiaries, there is still a persuasive reason for Congress to have written the statute to mandate just what my interpretation requires. Given the burden of private school placement, it makes good sense to require parents to try to devise a satisfactory alternative within the public schools, by taking part in the collaborative process of developing an IEP that is the "*modus operandi*" of the IDEA. And if some time, and some educational opportunity, is lost in consequence, this only shows what we have realized before, that no policy is ever pursued to the ultimate, single-minded limit, and that "[t]he IDEA obviously does not seek to promote [its] goals at the expense of all considerations, including fiscal considerations." *Arlington Cent. Sch. Dist. Bd. of Educ. v. Murphy*, 584 U.S. 291 . . . (2006).

Notes, Comments, and Questions

1. The Court's two previous decisions regarding reimbursement for unilateral placements were unanimous. Why did the issue in *Forest Grove* split the court?

2. One of the most telling differences between the majority and the dissent was their views of the adequacy of the IDEA's due process protections and procedures. The majority discusses the lengthy review process as one justification for the permissive rules for reimbursement for a unilateral placement. The dissent views the due process protections as providing for a speedy resolution of all outstanding issues. Why are the procedural protections important in this context? How does the dissent's view compare with the Court's view of the adequacy of due process in *Burlington*?

3. Do you agree with the majority or the dissent in *Forest Grove*? Do you think Congress intended to limit reimbursement for private school tuition to parents of children who had already received special education from the school district? If not, how do you explain the language of Section (C)(iii)?

4. As described in the notes following *Burlington* and *Carter*, lower federal courts have ordered school districts to reimburse parents for the costs of related serviced they incurred in providing their a child a FAPE when the school district failed to do so. The Supreme Court has not ruled on this issue. How do you think the Court would rule in such a case? Would the 1997 amendments to the IDEA, discussed in *Forest Grove*, be relevant to the Court's analysis? Why didn't Congress include reimbursement for the cost of related services in the 1997 amendments?

B. Payment of Tuition Parents Have Not Paid

The right to obtain tuition reimbursement for unilateral placement of a child in a private school if the school district fails to offer a FAPE to the child provides leverage to parents with sufficient financial resources to afford private school tuition. While the courts have been clear that a parent who has financial resources and an understanding of the IDEA may unilaterally place his or her child in an appropriate private school setting and be reimbursed for it if the District did not provide a FAPE and the private school does, should this opportunity also be available to less affluent parents? Can the intent of the IDEA reimbursement scheme be effective if it is available only to parents with financial means to "front" the cost of a private school tuition and then seek reimbursement? Consider how the court in *D.A.* answered this question.

D.A. v. N.Y.C. Dep't of Educ.

769 F. Supp. 2d 403 (S.D.N.Y. 2011)

Paul G. Gardephe, District Judge.

This case presents the following question of first impression:

1. When a child with disabilities has been denied a free and appropriate public education; and

2. the child's parents have enrolled the child in an appropriate private school; and

3. the equities favor an award of the costs of private school tuition; but

4. the parents, due to a lack of financial resources, have not made tuition payments but are legally obligated to do so;

does this Court's authority under Section 1415(i)(2)(C)(iii) of the . . . IDEA . . . "to grant such relief as the court determines is appropriate," include the power to order a school district to make a retroactive tuition payment directly to the private school? The New York City Department of Education and its Chancellor, defendants herein, contend that IDEA grants courts no such authority, arguing that the private school tuition remedy is available only to parents with the financial means to pay—in the first instance—private school tuition out-of-pocket. This Court concludes that imposing such a limitation on this remedy is inconsistent with the statutory language and with Supreme Court jurisprudence interpreting IDEA, and would be entirely antithetical to Congress's clearly expressed legislative intent and purpose in enacting IDEA.

In this action, Plaintiffs seek funding under IDEA for their son D.A.'s tuition at the Rebecca School for the 2007–08 school year. In state administrative proceedings, an impartial hearing officer ("IHO") found that (1) Defendants had failed to provide D.A., who has autism, with a . . . FAPE . . . for the 2007–08 school year; (2) the Rebecca School—where his parents unilaterally enrolled him—was an appropriate placement for D.A.; and (3) equitable considerations favor an award of tuition funding. Consistent with the principles articulated by the Supreme Court in . . .

Burlington . . . and its progeny, the IHO directed the New York City Department of Education ("DOE") to pay D.A.'s tuition balance for the 2007–08 school year, upon submission of appropriate documentation.

On DOE's appeal, a state review officer ("SRO") affirmed the IHO's determinations as to all three prongs of the *Burlington* test, but "annulled" the IHO's determination as to the tuition remedy, concluding that because the parents had not been able to pay D.A.'s tuition at the Rebecca School out-of-pocket, they "are not entitled to funding of the student's tuition." Plaintiffs then filed this action seeking to overturn the SRO's determination.

The parties have cross-moved for summary judgment. Plaintiffs argue that this Court should overturn the SRO's determination that the private school tuition remedy is unavailable where parents have not paid the tuition out-of-pocket. Defendants contend that the IHO and SRO erred in determining that Plaintiffs had satisfied all three elements of the *Burlington* test, but that the SRO's determination as to the unavailability of the private school tuition remedy should be upheld. For the reasons stated below, Plaintiffs' motion for summary judgment will be GRANTED and Defendants' motion for summary judgment will be DENIED.

I. *STATUTORY BACKGROUND*

. . . .

It is well settled that parents pursuing an administrative challenge "may, at their own financial risk, enroll the child in a private school and seek retroactive reimbursement for the cost of the private school from the state." Such reimbursement covers "'expenses that [the school district] should have paid all along.'" Courts considering a reimbursement request for the cost of private special education services must consider (1) whether "the school district [has] fail[ed] to provide a FAPE"; (2) whether "the private school placement is appropriate"; and (3) whether the "equities" warrant a reimbursement award in full or in part. Parents bear the burden of persuasion as to each element of a claim for reimbursement.

Here, however, the parent-plaintiffs were unable to make more than a nominal payment towards the $84,900 annual tuition at the school in which they unilaterally enrolled D.A. Accordingly, Plaintiffs do not seek reimbursement of their out-of-pocket expenses, but rather retroactive direct payment to the Rebecca School for tuition associated with the 2007–08 school year.

. . . .

DISCUSSION

. . . .

II. SECTION 1415(i)(2)(C)(iii) OF IDEA AUTHORIZES COURTS TO ORDER RETROACTIVE DIRECT PAYMENT OF PRIVATE SCHOOL TUITION WHERE A SCHOOL DISTRICT HAS DENIED A FAPE TO A CHILD ENTITLED TO SPECIAL EDUCATION SERVICES

. . . .

B. Scope of the Remedy Under Section 1415 of IDEA

1. Statutory Language

Section 1415 of IDEA authorizes a reviewing court to "grant such relief as the court determines is appropriate." In considering whether the private school tuition remedy under § 1415(i)(2)(C)(iii) is limited only to those parents who can afford to pay the cost of private school tuition in the first instance, it is worth recalling that numerous provisions of IDEA demonstrate special Congressional solicitude for the educational needs of disabled children from low-income families.

IDEA was prompted by Congress's recognition that "there is an urgent and substantial need . . . to enhance the capacity of State and local agencies and service providers to identify, evaluate, and meet the needs of all children [with disabilities], particularly minority, low-income, inner city, and rural children." 20 U.S.C. § 1431(a)(5). This finding animates IDEA's requirement that special education services are to be provided "at no cost to parents," and numerous provisions of IDEA reflect Congress's determination that the guarantee of a FAPE should extend to all children with disabilities, regardless of their financial means. *See, e.g.*, § 1437(b)(7) (requiring that when any state seeks federal grant money for its early childhood intervention programs, its application "shall provide satisfactory assurance that policies and procedures have been adopted to ensure meaningful involvement of underserved groups, including . . . low-income . . . families"); § 1453(b)(8) (requiring states seeking grants for educational personnel development to "describe the steps that the State educational agency will take to ensure that poor . . . children are not taught at higher rates by teachers who are not highly qualified"); § 1471(a)(2)(iii) (providing for federal grants to nonprofit parent organizations only when "the parent and professional members of which are broadly representative of the population to be served, including low-income parents"); § 1481(d)(3)(C) (providing that in awarding general educational grants, the Secretary may "give priority to . . . projects that address the needs of . . . children from low income families").

The legislative history of IDEA and its reauthorizations also reflects Congress's concern with protecting the rights of low-income children and ensuring universal access to special education services. *See, e.g.*, 136 Cong. Rec. S14410–02 (daily ed. Oct. 2, 1990) (statement of Sen. Kennedy) (expressing concern over the "already pervasive condition" of "mislabeling and over-referral of minority, poor, and limited-English proficient children"); 136 Cong. Rec. H9632–01 (daily ed. Oct. 15, 1990) (statement of Rep. Miller) ("The legislation before us today clarified ambiguities in current law to ensure that all children who need special services are not excluded because of definitional barriers."); 150 Cong. Rec. S11658–01 (daily ed. Nov. 19, 2004) (statement of Sen. Bingaman) (noting that IDEA was intended to address the fact that "[t]he likelihood of exclusion was significantly greater for children with disabilities living in low-income, ethnic and racial minority, or rural communities").

The theme of concern for children from low-income families that runs through IDEA and its legislative history counsels caution in adopting an interpretation of

§ 1415(i)(2)(C)(iii) that would limit a private school tuition remedy to those who have the means to pay the tuition in the first instance.

2. Supreme Court Jurisprudence

Any discussion of judicial interpretation of the scope of remedial power set forth in § 1415(i)(2)(C)(iii) must begin with *Burlington.*

....

Burlington is instructive here in several respects. As an initial matter, it is apparent that the Court—although speaking in *dicta*—believed that the sort of direct payment to a private school sought by Plaintiffs here is available relief under the Act. Second, the decision indicates that the term "appropriate" relief should be given its "ordinary meaning," and that courts enjoy "broad discretion" in determining "appropriate" relief. Finally, the failure of the Act to make explicit mention of a particular remedy does not mean that the remedy is not, "in a proper case," "appropriate" relief.

In the years since *Burlington,* the Supreme Court has repeatedly rejected invitations to restrict the scope of remedial authority provided in Section 1415(i)(2)(C)(iii) .... [The court described *Carter* and *Forest Grove.*]

....

The Supreme Court's jurisprudence in this area reveals a consistent effort to read the remedial language of IDEA in a manner that is consistent with its statutory purpose of providing all disabled children with access to a FAPE. Efforts to limit the broad discretionary language of § 1415(i)(2)(C)(iii) have proven unsuccessful. While the cases have focused on parents' right to private school tuition reimbursement where their child has been denied a FAPE—rather than prospective or retroactive direct payment relief—that fact reflects the practical realities and limitations of the administrative and judicial review process set forth in IDEA rather than a statutory limitation on the availability of prospective or retroactive direct payment relief.

3. Lower Court Authority

While research has disclosed no federal decision holding that IDEA authorizes courts to order retroactive direct tuition payments to a private school under the circumstances here—where the parents incurred a debt for private school tuition and then chose to litigate whether their child had received a FAPE—courts have ordered prospective direct tuition payment in the context of the pendency or "stay put" provision of IDEA, 20 U.S.C. § 1415(j), and in the context of compensatory education (remedying a prior denial of FAPE where a child has or will shortly age out of the Act). In these decisions, courts have consistently refused to impose limitations on § 1415 relief that would favor wealthy parents over those of limited means, and have resisted a "price of admission"—or "front the funds"—approach to the assertion of rights under IDEA.

For example, in *Susquenita Sch. Dist. v. Raelee S.*, 96 F.3d 78 (3d Cir.1996), the Third Circuit ruled that § 1415(i)(2)(C)(iii) empowers district courts to order prospective payment of private school tuition during the pendency of placement litigation. The court noted that if such payment were not an available remedy, "[f]amilies without means will be hard pressed to pay for private education in what will almost invariably be the significant time lapse between a ruling in their favor and the ultimate close of litigation,"and that "[t]he prospect of reimbursement at the end of the litigation turnpike is of little consolation to those who cannot afford to pay the toll at the outset." The court further noted that:

> [t]he purpose of the Act, which is to ensure that every child receives a "free and appropriate public education" is not advanced by requiring parents, who have succeeded in obtaining a ruling that a proposed IEP is inadequate, to front the funds for continued private education.

Susquenita, 96 F.3d at 86; *see also Lester H. v. Gilhool,* 916 F.2d 865, 872–73 (3d Cir.1990) (compensatory education claim; "we conclude that Congress, by allowing the courts to fashion an appropriate remedy to cure the deprivation of a child's right to a free appropriate public education, did not intend to offer a remedy only to those parents able to afford an alternative private education.").

Similarly, in *Draper v. Atlanta Indep. Sch. Sys.,* 518 F.3d 1275, 1286 (11th Cir. 2008), the Eleventh Circuit concluded that the district court was authorized under § 1415 to award plaintiff placement in private school as compensatory education for the school district's past failure to provide a FAPE. The school district had argued that while IDEA provided for private school tuition reimbursement, it did not provide for an award of placement in a private school. The Circuit rejected that argument:

> We do not read the Act as requiring compensatory awards of prospective education to be inferior to awards of reimbursement. The Act does not relegate families who lack the resources to place their children unilaterally in private schools to shouldering the burden of proving that the public school cannot adequately educate a child before those parents can obtain a placement in a private school. The Act instead empowers the district court to use broad discretion to fashion appropriate equitable relief.

Draper, 518 F.3d at 1286.

Likewise in *Reid v. Dist. of Columbia,* 401 F.3d 516, 522–23 (D.C. Cir. 2005), the D.C. Circuit upheld an award of compensatory education services to a child who had been denied a FAPE over many years. Noting the availability of the tuition reimbursement remedy under *Burlington,* the court commented that if an award of compensatory education services was not an available remedy,

> children's access to appropriate education could depend on their parents' capacity to front its costs—a result manifestly incompatible with IDEA's purpose of "ensur[ing] that *all* children with disabilities have available to them a free appropriate public education," 20 U.S.C. § 1400(d)(1)(A)

Reid, 401 F.3d at 523. (emphasis in original).

Finally, in *Miener v. Missouri,* 800 F.2d 749 (8th Cir. 1986), plaintiff sought to recover educational services for a three-year period in which she was denied a FAPE.

The child's father claimed that "he did not have the money to pay [for a proper placement]," and had been forced to place his daughter in an inappropriate facility. The State argued that plaintiff's case should be dismissed, and that compensatory educational services "do not fit within the purview of *Burlington* because they do not constitute 'retroactive reimbursement.'" The court flatly rejected that argument:

> We cannot agree with the defendants that they should escape liability for these services simply because Clyde Meiner was unable to provide them in the first instance; we believe that such a result would be consistent neither with *Burlington* nor with congressional intent. Like the retroactive reimbursement in *Burlington,* imposing liability for compensatory educational services on the defendants "merely requires [them] to belatedly pay expenses that [they] should have paid all along." Here, as in *Burlington,* recovery is necessary to secure the child's right to a free appropriate public education. We are confident that Congress did not intend the child's entitlement to a *free* education to turn upon her parent's ability to "front" its costs.

Id. (emphasis in original).

Within this Circuit, a number of courts have stated or suggested in *dicta* that a direct tuition remedy is available where parents have presented a meritorious *Burlington* claim but lack the financial means to pay private school tuition out-of-pocket. For example, in *Connors v. Mills,* 34 F.Supp.2d 795 (N.D.N.Y. 1998), plaintiff sought prospective payment of tuition costs at a non-approved private school, where the school district had conceded that it could not provide a FAPE to her child. The school district contended that IDEA does not authorize prospective direct payment of private school tuition, and that plaintiff was required "to front the costs of unilateral placement and thereafter to request due process review in order to obtain reimbursement for same." The court concluded that the school district could be required, under § 1415, "to pay the tuition directly" to the private school:

> once the *Burlington* prerequisites relative to a non-approved private school are met, and a parent shows that his or her financial circumstances eliminate the opportunity for unilateral placement in the non-approved school, the public school must pay the cost of private placement immediately.

Id. at 805-06.

The court reasoned that a contrary rule would leave parents of modest means with no options, while wealthier families pursued a reimbursement remedy:

> By prohibiting prospective placement, Defendants would deny assistance to families that are not able to front the cost of a private, non-approved school, without exception. Under Defendant's reading of the IDEA, therefore, even in a situation as the one presented here where both the school and the parent agree that the child's unique needs require placement in a private non-approved school and that there are no approved schools that would be appropriate, a destitute child would be left in an inappropriate program because the

> parents would not be able to front the tuition of the private placement. Given the fragile state of many disabled children, and their dire need for constant and consistent care, even brief periods of inappropriate schooling could lead to tremendous educational, social, emotional, and psychological deterioration. Families of greater economic means would not be faced with such a grim prospect. It simply cannot be the case that an act designed to grant "all" disabled children access to needed services would undermine that very goal by making such access dependent upon a family's financial situation.

Id. at 805.

Similarly, in *S.W. v. New York City Dept. of Educ.*, 646 F.Supp.2d 346 (S.D.N.Y. 2009), the court considered a claim for retroactive direct tuition payment where the school district had denied a child a FAPE. The court noted that

> [t]he parties have cited no case in which a court has ordered direct tuition payment to a private school on a retrospective basis. In a case where the equities favor such an award, there may be good reasons why direct tuition payment should be a remedy available to a needy parent, on either a prospective or retrospective basis.

S.W., 646 F.Supp. 2d at 360.

The consistent message of the lower court decisions is that a child's access to a FAPE cannot be made to depend on his or her family's financial ability to "front" the costs of private school tuition.

C. *Application of the Law*

This Court concludes that where, as here, parents have satisfied each of the *Burlington* factors, this Court's "broad discretion" to "grant such relief as . . . is appropriate" under § 1415(i)(2)(C)(iii) includes the power, in a proper case, to award retroactive direct payment of private school tuition. This conclusion flows directly from the language of this provision, which—as the Supreme Court stated in *Burlington,* and reiterated in *Forest Grove*—means what it says.

Under *Burlington,* a district court may (1) impose "a prospective injunction directing the school officials to develop and implement at public expense an IEP placing the child in a private school," and (2) require retroactive reimbursement for private school placement. Given the well established nature of these remedies and the breadth of the language used in § 1415(i)(2)(C)(iii), there is no basis for this Court to conclude that the retroactive direct tuition payment relief sought by Plaintiffs here is unavailable. It is entirely counter-intuitive to argue, as do Defendants here, that a court may, under § 1415(i)(2)(C)(iii), require a school district to pay a private school directly and prospectively for special education, may require the district to retroactively reimburse parents for private school tuition previously paid, but may not order a school district to pay the private school directly and retroactively for expenses already incurred. Defendants offer no authority that supports such a result.

The fact that IDEA does not explicitly reference this remedy is not dispositive. Tuition reimbursement was not mentioned in IDEA when the *Burlington* court issued its ruling, yet the Supreme Court had no difficulty in finding that IDEA provides a reimbursement remedy.

Section 1415(i)(2)(C)(iii) authorizes a direct retroactive tuition remedy for the same reasons that the *Burlington* court found that the Act authorizes a tuition reimbursement remedy. Given the nature of the administrative and judicial review process, parents who request an impartial hearing will rarely, if ever, be able to obtain a ruling prior to the onset of the school year. Accordingly, denying parents the opportunity to seek retroactive relief is tantamount to denying them any relief at all under the Act. Where parents have the financial resources to enroll their child in an appropriate private school, they may do so and seek retroactive reimbursement in a due process hearing. Where, as here, parents lack the financial resources to "front" the costs of private school tuition, and in the rare instance where a private school is willing to enroll the student and take the risk that the parents will not be able to pay tuition costs—or will take years to do so—parents who satisfy the *Burlington* factors have a right to retroactive direct tuition payment relief.

A contrary ruling would be entirely inconsistent with IDEA's statutory purpose, including the goal of ensuring a FAPE to the least privileged of the disabled children in our nation. Such a ruling would also be irreconcilable with decades of case law, summarized above, holding that the exercise of rights under IDEA cannot be made to depend on the financial means of a disabled child's parents. Limiting "the right of unilateral withdrawal" only to those with the financial means to pay the costs of private school tuition in the first instance, is entirely antithetical to IDEA's universal guarantee of a "free, appropriate public education" to all children with disabilities, regardless of means. Defendants' arguments to the contrary are not persuasive.

Defendants first contend that Plaintiffs' claim should be denied because IDEA does not explicitly authorize direct payment of tuition costs to a private school. As an initial matter, and as discussed above, IDEA's failure to explicitly reference a particular remedy does not mean that courts lack the authority to grant that remedy under 1415(i)(2)(C)(iii). Defendants' related argument that Congress's 1997 amendments to IDEA—which reference reimbursement but not direct payment of tuition costs—were intended to bar any remedy other than reimbursement, is foreclosed by the Supreme Court's decision in *Forest Grove.*

As discussed above, in *Forest Grove*, the school district argued that § 1412(a)(10)(C)(ii) of IDEA—which addresses tuition reimbursement where a child has received special education services in public school—was intended to limit the reimbursement remedy under § 1415(i)(2)(C)(iii) only to such children. The Supreme Court rejected that argument, holding that § 1412(a)(10)(C)(ii) was not intended to limit the remedy provided in § 1415, and was "elucidative rather than exhaustive."

In an argument nearly identical to that rejected in *Forest Grove,* Defendants contend ... that because § 1412(a)(10)(C)(ii) refers only to "reimburse[ment]" and not to direct payment of tuition to a private school, the latter remedy is not available under § 1415(i)(2)(C)(iii). Defendants go on to argue "that although 20 U.S.C. § 1415(i)(2)(C)(iii) states that the reviewing court may 'grant such relief as the court determines is appropriate,' this provision should be viewed in light of the statute's explicit remedy of reimbursement—at the exclusion of direct tuition payment."

This argument is foreclosed by *Forest Grove.* The Supreme Court held that § 1412(a)(10)(C)(ii) does not limit the remedies available under § 1415(i)(2)(C)(iii). Use of the term "reimburse" in the former provision does not establish that reimbursement is the only available remedy under the latter provision, nor does it establish that a direct tuition payment remedy is not authorized under § 1415(i)(2)(C)(iii).

Defendants also point to *Diaz–Fonseca v. Puerto Rico,* 451 F.3d 13 (1st Cir. 2006), in which the First Circuit stated that

> [u]nder normal IDEA principles, Diaz is . . . not entitled to be reimbursed for educational expenses that she has yet to pay. She is entitled to no more than the sum of the educational expenses *she has already paid.*

451 F.3d at 32 (emphasis in original).

In that case, Diaz was seeking "prospective relief in the amount of future educational expenses until [her daughter] reaches maximum school age." Accordingly, the First Circuit's remarks about reimbursement were directed to Diaz's effort to obtain recovery for future school years. The court correctly noted that IDEA's remedial provisions are designed to guarantee each child a FAPE, and not to provide parents with " 'a tort-like mechanism for compensating personal injury.' "

Here, however, Plaintiffs do not seek a recovery for their anticipated expenditures in future school years, nor do they seek reimbursement of any sort. Instead, they seek a retroactive direct tuition payment to a private school for costs associated with the 2007–08 school year. They seek an order requiring the school district "belatedly [to] pay expenses that it . . . [sh]ould have borne in the first instance." *Burlington*, 471 U.S. at 370–71. *Diaz–Fonseca* does not address the type of relief at issue in this case.

Defendants also contend that "there is no dispute that the student D.A. was accepted to the Rebecca School for the school year in question and attended throughout the school year . . . [so] there was no elimination of the opportunity for unilateral placement." This argument ignores IDEA's requirement that school districts provide each child with disabilities with a FAPE. That obligation was not met here. The fact that Plaintiffs convinced the Rebecca School to enroll D.A. in the absence of public funding does not alter that fact.

Finally, Defendants argue that important policy interests are served by their proposed limitation on IDEA's remedial provisions. They argue that if Plaintiffs' arguments are accepted, parents and private schools will

> enter into . . . sham transaction[s] in which it is tacitly understood that, should funding from the public school district . . . not be granted, the parent will be relieved from payment. In such . . . [sham] transaction[s], the

parent has no incentive to agree to a reasonable tuition price, and the private school could inflate that price to an amount that is well above market rate.

Hearing officers and reviewing courts, however, already possess ample authority to reject or reduce tuition funding or payment requests where there is collusion between parents and private schools.... Where there is evidence that a private school has artificially inflated its tuition, hearing officers and courts are required to take this into account in determining an appropriate tuition award, whether that award constitutes prospective relief, retroactive reimbursement, or retroactive direct payment of tuition.

Here, Defendants have not alleged bad faith on the part of either the parents or the Rebecca School. There has been no suggestion that the Rebecca School's standard tuition is less than the $84,900 that the parents agreed to pay. Nor have Defendants suggested that the tuition charged was unreasonable in light of the education and related services the School provided.

The lenient payment schedule the Rebecca School entered into with Plaintiffs does not require that their claim be rejected. The payment schedule reflects the fact that tuition expenses at the Rebecca School dwarf Plaintiffs' annual income. Even assuming *arguendo* that "the Rebecca School intended to rely on the DOE to provide tuition funding," as Defendants argue this does not change the nature of DOE's obligations to D.A. and his parents under IDEA. Presumably, nearly all parents who make a unilateral placement under IDEA and then seek tuition reimbursement act at least in part out of a hope, belief, or expectation that the school district will ultimately be forced to fund their placement. The only difference in this case is that the Rebecca School absorbed some of that risk, by agreeing with a needy family to a permissive payment schedule. That agreement does not change the fact that Defendants denied D.A. a FAPE, that the Rebecca School was an appropriate placement, that the equities favor payment of tuition, and that § 1415(i)(2)(C)(iii) is sufficiently broad to encompass the retroactive direct tuition payment relief Plaintiffs seek.

CONCLUSION

For the reasons stated above, Plaintiffs' motion for summary judgment is GRANTED, and Defendants' motion for summary judgment is DENIED.

Notes, Comments, and Questions

1. The court in *D.A.* discussed portions of the IDEA that it believed provide for special consideration to children from low-income families. Is this kind of special consideration appropriate? Are there other areas of the IDEA that suggest that decisionmakers should consider the financial resources of the families involved? On balance, does the IDEA favor children of lower-income families? Affluent families? Is it income-neutral? Are the provisions the court cited related to its authority under § 1415(i)(2)(C)(iii) neutral? Could these provisions form the basis of a cause of action by parents who claim that a neutral state practice discriminates against them because of their income or wealth?

2. The defendant argued that, "parents and private schools will enter into . . . sham transaction[s] in which it is tacitly understood that, should funding from the public school district . . . not be granted, the parent will be relieved from payment." *D.A.*, 769 F. Supp. 2d at 429. Is this a legitimate concern? Does the court's answer to this fear adequately respond to the issue?

3. The defendant reiterated arguments the school district made in *Forest Grove* about the impact of the 1997 IDEA amendments. The court rejected these arguments. Is the court's reading of § 1415(i)(2)(C)(iii) in *D.A.* the sort of expansive reading the dissent in *Forest Grove* feared?

C. Equitable Factors

A.S. v. Five Town Cmty. Sch. Dist.

513 F.3d 279 (1st Cir. 2008)

Selya, Senior Circuit Judge.

This case requires us to examine the rights of a disabled child under the Individuals with Disabilities Education Act. The principal issue, scantily addressed in the case law, involves how judicial review should proceed when the last individualized education program (IEP) proposed by the school system is incomplete.

Here, the district court found that the IEP's incompleteness was due to the parents' obstruction of the developmental process. It proceeded to consider extrinsic evidence and concluded that, had the parents permitted the process to run its course, the school system would have provided the child with a satisfactory IEP. On that basis, it decreed that the parents were not entitled either to reimbursement for costs incurred in a private placement or to compensatory education benefits.

The parents now appeal. We conclude that the lower court committed no clear error in weighing the facts. While we reach the same ultimate conclusion as did the court below, that court's meticulous fact finding allows us to take a different, more direct analytic path. In the end, we affirm the judgment below.

I. BACKGROUND

The district judge . . . referred this case to a magistrate judge for a report and recommendation. The magistrate judge canvassed the record, made extensive findings of fact, and set forth various conclusions of law. The district judge, in a summary order, adopted the magistrate judge's recommended analysis in its entirety and entered judgment accordingly. . . .

. . . . C.G. and B.S. are the parents of A.S., a teenage girl who suffers from an emotional disability. . . . Five Town Community School District . . . is the school system in which A.S. is entitled to receive public education.

The parents first met formally with Five Town about A.S.'s potential to qualify for services under the IDEA on March 3, 2004. They requested that the School District pay for A.S., who was then fourteen years old, to enroll in a private residential placement. Before the School District could evaluate the bona fides of this request, A.S. hit a crisis point and her parents unilaterally transferred her into a private residential placement outside of Maine. The parents do not seek to recover the costs of that placement in this appeal ....

Notwithstanding efforts on the part of the School District to re-start the IDEA eligibility process, nothing of consequence happened for well over a year. In the interim (unbeknownst to the School District), A.S. returned to Maine, enrolled for several months as a residential student in a private school, and upon leaving spent two additional months without any scholastic affiliation.

In June of 2005, A.S.'s parents demanded a due process hearing under the IDEA. The School District sought to meet with them in order to resume the earlier eligibility discussions. The due process hearing was deferred pending the completion of this attempt to reach a consensus.

The common practice is to form a team of parents, teachers, school administrators, and others to evaluate a child with a disability and, if she is found eligible for remedial services, to develop an IEP. In Maine, this cohort is called a Peer Evaluation Team (PET). The School District assembled such a team and scheduled the initial PET meeting for September 1, 2005. During that session, the parents agreed that an independent evaluator, Dr. Frank McCabe, could assess A.S.

After the PET participants received the evaluator's report, the School District scheduled a second PET meeting for October 12, 2005. At that session, the participants discussed the evaluator's assessment, concluded that A.S. qualified for services as a disabled child, and began work to develop an IEP. . . .

During the same meeting, some placement options were discussed. The independent evaluator indicated that A.S. could receive an adequate and appropriate education in a public school day program. In response, the School District described some public school options, including Camden Hills Regional High School (CHRHS) and the Zenith program. A.S. previously had attended CHRHS, and her parents expressed concern about a placement there. They seemed willing, however, to learn more about the Zenith non-residential day program or any similar regime.

The School District indicated that it would send the parents a copy of a proposed IEP prior to the next PET meeting. On October 18, 2005, it transmitted an IEP document to the parents by facsimile. The October 18 version of the IEP included the main components of the program to which the participants previously had agreed. Consistent with the discussions at the October 12 conclave, however, the IEP left open other areas for later development. It is nose-on-the-face plain from even a cursory inspection of the October 18 submission that the IEP was not intended to constitute a completed IEP.

The next PET meeting took place on October 20, 2005. At that session, the participants discussed placement options. The meeting was "very contentious." The participants quickly reached an impasse: the parents insisted that A.S. be educated in a therapeutic residential setting, whereas the School District insisted that a non-residential public school placement could provide A.S. with an adequate and appropriate education. The meeting ended abruptly when the parents announced that they had decided to send A.S. to the F.L. Chamberlain School (an out-of-state residential institution) and would seek reimbursement for the costs incurred. The meeting never progressed to a discussion either of the IEP or of how to fill the gaps in it.

A.S.'s parents memorialized their unilateral placement decision in a letter sent the following week to the School District. Given this parting of the ways, the due process hearing moved forward. Arguing that the School District's proposed IEP and refusal to sanction a residential placement betokened a failure to provide A.S. with a free and appropriate public education (FAPE), the parents sought compensatory education and/or reimbursement for the expenses incurred in educating A.S. at Chamberlain. The School District denied any breach of its duties under the IDEA. The hearing went forward, and the hearing officer ultimately rejected the parents' entreaties.

Undaunted, the parents shifted the battleground to the federal district court. As previously noted, the district judge, on de novo review of the magistrate judge's report and recommendation, upheld the hearing officer's decision. This appeal followed.

II. ANALYSIS

. . . .

B. *Incompleteness of the IEP.*

In this case, the district court determined that the October 18 IEP was not "final" because the parents had disrupted the IEP process midstream. Having made that finding, the court proceeded to consider information outside the IEP to assure itself that the School District's partially formulated position was consistent with its responsibilities to A.S. under the IDEA. It concluded that, had the parents continued to cooperate and allowed the School District to fill in the gaps, the result would have been a satisfactory IEP that provided A.S. with a FAPE.

. . . .

C. *Obstructive Conduct.*

The district court also found, as had the hearing officer, that the parents' precipitous actions had prevented the consummation of the IEP. The court found that the parents harbored a fixed purpose: to effect a residential placement for their daughter at the School District's expense, come what may. Once the parents realized that the School District was focused on a non-residential placement, they essentially lost interest in the IEP process. That finding, which was not clearly erroneous, supported an inference of parental obstruction. In turn, the finding of obstructionism, coupled with the finding of incompleteness, underbraced the court's decision to consider extrinsic evidence.

Viewed in context, that decision makes perfect sense: while considering extrinsic information in the adequacy calculus may not be appropriate in the mine-run of cases, that course is peculiarly appropriate where, as here, the record reveals with conspicuous clarity that all the participants in the October 12 PET meeting wanted Dr. Miller's input in order to develop a proper crisis plan and positive behavior support plan for A.S. as part and parcel of a final IEP. Neither plan had been formulated when the School District transmitted the October 18 IEP to the parents. The parents cannot ignore these facts, nor expect a reviewing court to blind itself to them.

From this point forward, the court, like the hearing officer, considered whether a public school day placement was appropriate and what benefits a finalized IEP would have provided. It supportably concluded that a public school non-residential placement constituted the least restrictive environment. It also concluded that, had the parents allowed the process to run its course, the School District would have developed a sound behavioral support plan and formulated a menu of psychiatric services to be offered to A.S. (which were in line with the goals limned in the proposed IEP). And, finally, it held that because the resultant IEP would have been adequate to afford A.S. a FAPE, the parents' claim failed.

In the last analysis, we need not probe too deeply into the adequacy of the IEP. Given the district court's comprehensive factual findings, we can decide this case on a less nuanced ground. We explain briefly.

Congress deliberately fashioned an interactive process for the development of IEPs. In so doing, it expressly declared that if parents act unreasonably in the course of that process, they may be barred from reimbursement under the IDEA. *See* 20 U.S.C. § 1412(a)(10)(C)(iii)(III) (providing that "[t]he cost of reimbursement . . . may be reduced or denied . . . upon a judicial finding of unreasonableness with respect to actions taken by the parents").

Here, the School District argues persuasively that the parents' conduct was unreasonable and that this unreasonableness precludes relief. Although the district court drew no conclusions with regard to this provision of the IDEA, we are free to affirm its decision on any alternative ground that is evident from the record. Moreover, where the evidence supports a district court's findings of fact, we may realign those findings under a different legal matrix and decide the case on that basis.

This is such a case. The district court supportably found that the parents' actions disrupted the IEP process, stalling its consummation and preventing the development of a final IEP. Moreover, the court found, the parents did so despite their knowledge that the School District planned to complete the unfinished portions with the parents' help. Tellingly, the court determined that the cause of the disruption was the parents' single-minded refusal to consider any placement other than a residential one. Such Boulwarism, whether or not well-intentioned, constitutes an unreasonable approach to the collaborative process envisioned by the IDEA. Here, that attitude sufficed to undermine the process.

To sum up, the district court found that the October 18 IEP was incomplete and that the parents' unreasonable actions had frustrated the completion of the IEP process. Given these warrantable findings of fact, section 1412(a)(10)(C)(iii)(III) provides a solid ground for resolving the case against the parents. Their unreasonable obstruction of an otherwise promising IEP process fully justifies a denial of reimbursement under the IDEA.

. . . .

E. *Requests for Relief.*

This essentially ends our inquiry. Although reimbursement of parental expenses for private residential placements sometimes is available under the IDEA, such reimbursement is contingent upon a showing that the parents diligently pursued the provision of appropriate services from the public school system, yet the school system failed to provide those services; and that the private placement is a suitable alternative. When the parents make a unilateral choice, they must bear the associated risk: if the conditions for reimbursement are not met, the financial burdens are theirs.

That is precisely what transpired here. The parents made a unilateral choice to abandon the collaborative IEP process without allowing that process to run its course. Thus, the parents are precluded from obtaining reimbursement for the costs of the Chamberlain School placement, and a fortiori, they have not satisfied that prong of the reimbursement analysis.

. . . .

III. CONCLUSION

We need go no further. For the reasons elucidated above, we uphold the district court's judgment.

Note

In addressing the weight of equitable factors in reimbursement decisions, one important consideration is the adequacy of the notice parents provided to the school district prior to the withdrawal of their child. *See, e.g.*, J.W. v. Kingston City Sch. Dist., No. 1:08-CV-1371, 2010 U.S. Dist. WESTLAW 3907829 at *6-7 (N.D.N.Y. Sept. 29, 2010) (reducing reimbursement for unilateral placement when parent notified school district in 2005 of intention to remove child, but did not notify school district of removal for the 2007–2008 school year until five days before the start of school because IDEA notice requirement must be fulfilled every school year); Ashland Sch. Dist. v. Parents of Student E.H., 583 F. Supp. 2d 1220, 1228 (D. Or. 2008), *aff'd*, 587 F.3d 1175 (9th Cir. 2009) (holding that although parents' failure to notify school that they were rejecting the proposed placement prior to unilaterally placing child in private residential facility did not categorically bar reimbursement claim, parents did not demonstrate that balancing the equities warranted waiving the notice requirement); Garland Indep. Sch. Dist. v. Wilks, 657 F. Supp. 1163, 1167 (N.D. Tex. 1987) (denying reimbursement for portion of expenses incurred prior to parent challenging the IEP).

Chapter 7

Special Education and Related Services for Children with Disabilities in Private Schools When a FAPE is Not an Issue

Introduction

Chapter Six addressed the rights of parents who place their children in private schools when they believe the school district is not providing a FAPE. This chapter also involves parental placement of children with disabilities in private schools, but with a twist: the school district's provision of FAPE is not an issue; parents placed their children in private schools for other reasons. The IDEA requires school districts to provide special education and related services to children with disabilities in private schools when FAPE is not an issue, but not to the same extent as to children with disabilities in public schools.

Section One features three Supreme Court cases that established the constitutional right of parents to place their children in private schools and the rights of children in private religious schools to receive public aid, including pursuant to the IDEA: *Pierce v Society of Sisters*; *Zobrest v. California*; and *Locke v. Davey*. In *Pierce*, the Supreme Court struck down a state law that required children to attend public schools. In *Zobrest*, the Supreme Court ruled that the Establishment Clause does not prohibit a school district from using IDEA funds to pay for a sign-language interpreter for a child with a disability at his religious high school. Finally, in *Locke*, the Court upheld against a Free Exercise challenge a state law that prohibited state scholarship recipients from studying devotional theology. Section Two provides excerpts from 1997 amendments to the IDEA and subsequent regulations that placed obligations on school districts to provide special education and related services to children with disabilities who attend private school. Finally, Section Three addresses legal issues surrounding the 1997 amendments, including the location at which a school district must provide special education and related services to children with disabilities in private schools and the constitutionality of the amendments under the Establishment and Free Exercise Clauses.

Problems

1. For religious purposes, M.S.' parents sent her to a local religious school starting in kindergarten. When M.S. was in third grade, her school district identified her as having a speech and language processing disorder and in need of speech and language therapy. M.S.' parents decided to keep her in the religious school and asked the local school district to provide speech and language therapy services to M.S. at her religious school. Alternatively, they asked the district to transport M.S. by bus from her school to the district school to receive the speech and language therapy services there, and then to provide her a bus to go back to her religious school. M.S.' school is one mile from the district school. There is a sidewalk along the street leading from M.S.' school to the district school and stoplights at each of the four intersections (and a crossing guard at only one of them). M.S. is eight years old. What are M.S.' and her parents' rights under the IDEA? Must the school district provide speech and language therapy to M.S.? If the district provides speech and language therapy to M.S., where must the district provide it? What recourse do M.S. and her parents have if the district declines to provide speech and language therapy to M.S.? What recourse does the district have if they decline to provide the therapy at M.S.' school or to transport her to and from the district school?

2. You have been the general counsel for a public school district for many years. After Congress passed the 1997 amendments, the school district's board of trustees and superintendent asked for your advice about developing a policy statement to ensure compliance with the amendments. How would you counsel the district's leaders? What would the policy say?

3. After you gave your advice to the school district, the district asked for your opinion about the legality of the following policies it is considering adopting regarding provision of IDEA services to students with disabilities in private schools when FAPE is not an issue. How would you respond?

*The district will provide only speech and language therapy, occupational therapy, and physical therapy to private school students.

*The district will offer such services to private school students, including religious school students, only at public school locations.

*The district will not provide transportation to the private school students, including religious school students, to the public school to receive their services.

Section One
The Right to Attend Private School and to Receive IDEA Services at Religious Schools

The religion clauses of the First Amendment to the United States Constitution have helped foster the creation of and protect our nation's private schools, and in particular, religious schools. The clauses read as follows:

> Congress shall make no law respecting an establishment of religion, or prohibiting the free exercise thereof....

U.S. Const. amend. I.

While the Establishment Clause prohibits public schools from inculcating religious views or providing religious training, the Free Exercise Clause guarantees parents the right to excuse their children from attending public schools and instead send their children to private religious schools. The relationship between the Establishment and Free Exercise Clauses and the constitutional issues surrounding public aid to religious schools are complex and extensive legal topics beyond the scope of this book. What is important for special education law is a basic understanding of the constitutional issues regarding the right to attend private school and the provision of IDEA services in private religious schools. The trio of Supreme Court cases featured below provides a foundation for understanding these issues.

Pierce v. Soc'y of Sisters

268 U.S. 510 (1925)

MR. JUSTICE MCREYNOLDS delivered the opinion of the Court.

These appeals are from decrees ... which granted preliminary orders restraining appellants from threatening or attempting to enforce the Compulsory Education Act....

The challenged Act ... requires every parent, guardian or other person having control or charge or custody of a child between 8 and 16 years to send him "to a public school for the period of time a public school shall be held during the current year" in the district where the child resides; and failure so to do is declared a misdemeanor. There are exemptions—not specially important here—for children who are not normal, or who have completed the eighth grade, or whose parents or private teachers reside at considerable distances from any public school, or whose parents or guardians hold special permits from the county superintendent. The manifest purpose is to compel general attendance at public schools by normal children, between 8 and 16, who have not completed the eighth grade. And without doubt enforcement of the statute would seriously impair, perhaps destroy, the profitable features of appellees' business and greatly diminish the value of their property.

Appellee, the Society of Sisters is an Oregon corporation, organized in 1880, with power to care for orphans, educate and instruct the youth, establish and maintain academies or schools, and acquire necessary real and personal property. It has long devoted its property and effort to the secular and religious education and care of children, and has acquired the valuable good will of many parents and guardians. It conducts interdependent primary and high schools and junior colleges, and maintains orphanages for the custody and control of children between 8 and 16. In its primary schools many children between those ages are taught the subjects usually pursued in Oregon public schools during the first eight years. Systematic religious instruction and moral training according to the tenets of the Roman Catholic Church are also regularly provided. All courses of study, both temporal and religious, contemplate continuity of training under appellee's charge; the primary schools are essential to the system and the most profitable. It owns valuable buildings, especially constructed and equipped for school purposes. The business is remunerative—the annual income from primary schools exceeds $30,000—and the successful conduct of this requires long time contracts with teachers and parents. The Compulsory Education Act of 1922 has already caused the withdrawal from its schools of children who would otherwise continue, and their income has steadily declined. . . .

After setting out the above facts, the Society's bill alleges that the enactment conflicts with the right of parents to choose schools where their children will receive appropriate mental and religious training, the right of the child to influence the parents' choice of a school, the right of schools and teachers therein to engage in a useful business or profession, and is accordingly repugnant to the Constitution and void. . . .

. . . .

. . . The [district] court ruled that the Fourteenth Amendment guaranteed appellees against the deprivation of their property without due process of law consequent upon the unlawful interference by appellants with the free choice of patrons, present and prospective. It declared the right to conduct schools was property and that parents and guardians, as a part of their liberty, might direct the education of children by selecting reputable teachers and places. Also, that these schools were not unfit or harmful to the public, and that enforcement of the challenged statute would unlawfully deprive them of patronage and thereby destroy their owners' business and property. . . .

No question is raised concerning the power of the State reasonably to regulate all schools, to inspect, supervise and examine them, their teachers and pupils; to require that all children of proper age attend some school, that teachers shall be of good moral character and patriotic disposition, that certain studies plainly essential to good citizenship must be taught, and that nothing be taught which is manifestly inimical to the public welfare.

The inevitable practical result of enforcing the Act under consideration would be destruction of appellees' primary schools, and perhaps all other private primary schools for normal children within the state of Oregon. Appellees are engaged in a kind of undertaking not inherently harmful, but long regarded as useful and meritorious. Certainly there is nothing in the present records to indicate that they have failed to discharge their obligations to patrons, students or the state. And there are no peculiar circumstances or present emergencies which demand extraordinary measures relative to primary education.

Under the doctrine of *Meyer v. Nebraska*, 262 U.S. 390 . . . , we think it entirely plain that the Act of 1922 unreasonably interferes with the liberty of parents and guardians to direct the upbringing and education of children under their control. As often heretofore pointed out, rights guaranteed by the Constitution may not be abridged by legislation which has no reasonable relation to some purpose within the competency of the State. The fundamental theory of liberty upon which all governments in this Union repose excludes any general power of the State to standardize its children by forcing them to accept instruction from public teachers only. The child is not the mere creature of the State; those who nurture him and direct his destiny have the right, coupled with the high duty, to recognize and prepare him for additional obligations.

. . . .

The decrees below are affirmed.

Notes, Comments, and Questions

1. The Court in *Pierce* used the phrase "normal" in referring to children at least three times: 1) the compulsory school attendance laws excuse "children who are not normal"; 2) the law's purpose "is to compel general attendance at public schools by normal children"; and 3) the law will result in the "destruction of appellees' primary schools, and perhaps all other private primary schools for normal children within the state of Oregon." 268 U.S. at 531, 534. What assumptions underlie the Court's use of the term "normal" in these contexts? Recall the systematic exclusion of children with disabilities from public schools described in Chapter One. How deeply entrenched were the assumptions about children with disabilities such that the Supreme Court of the United States would accept their exclusion from compulsory education laws without questioning it? And how difficult do references like those in *Pierce* suggest that it was to overcome these assumptions?

2. The Court in *Pierce* referred to *Meyer v. Nebraska*, 262 U.S. 390 (1923), to support its decision. In *Meyer*, the Court reversed the conviction of a German language teacher under a Nebraska statute that prohibited teachers from teaching a subject in any language other than English to a student who had not completed the eighth grade. In holding that the application of the statute as applied was "arbitrary and without reasonable relation to any end within the competency of the state," *id.* at 403, the court referred to liberty interests protected by the Fourteenth Amendment, including the right of the teacher to teach German and "the right of the parents to engage him so to instruct their children . . . ." *Id.* at 399–400. Combined with *Pierce* and *Meyer*, a third Supreme Court case establishes the rights of parents to exert significant control over the education of their children. In *Wisconsin v. Yoder*, 406 U.S. 205 (1972), the Supreme Court reversed the convictions under Wisconsin's compulsory education laws of parents who were members of the Old Order Amish religion and the Conservative Amish Mennonite Church and refused to send their children to public school after they finished eighth grade. The parents had challenged the convictions

as invalid under the Free Exercise Clause of the First Amendment. In its ruling, the Court stated:

> However read, the Court's holding in *Pierce* stands as a charter of the rights of parents to direct the religious upbringing of their children. And, when the interests of parenthood are combined with a free exercise claim of the nature revealed by this record, more than merely a "reasonable relation to some purpose within the competency of the State" is required to sustain the validity of the State's requirement under the First Amendment. To be sure, the power of the parent, even when linked to a free exercise claim, may be subject to limitation . . . if it appears that parental decisions will jeopardize the health or safety of the child, or have a potential for significant social burdens. But in this case, the Amish have introduced persuasive evidence undermining the arguments the State has advanced to support its claims in terms of the welfare of the child and society as a whole. . . .

Id. at 233–34. The evidence that the parents introduced was that compelling their children to attend school past eighth grade would violate their religious beliefs and threaten their lifestyle, and that they provide sufficient education for their children at home. As a result of *Meyer*, *Pierce*, and *Yoder*, parents have the right to send their children to private school, to arrange the subject matter of the school, and to educate their children at home, as long as private and home schools comply with state educational oversight and requirements.

3. *Pierce* established the right of a child to attend a private school and in particular a private religious school. Once a child is in a private religious school, what is his right to receive services funded by public money? *Zobrest* addresses this question in connection with the IDEA.

Zobrest v. Catalina Foothills Sch. Dist.

509 U.S. 1 (1993)

Chief Justice Rehnquist delivered the opinion of the Court.

Petitioner James Zobrest, who has been deaf since birth, asked respondent school district to provide a sign-language interpreter to accompany him to classes at a Roman Catholic high school in Tucson, Arizona, pursuant to the Individuals with Disabilities Education Act (IDEA) . . . . The United States Court of Appeals for the Ninth Circuit decided, however, that provision of such a publicly employed interpreter would violate the Establishment Clause of the First Amendment. We hold that the Establishment Clause does not bar the school district from providing the requested interpreter.

James Zobrest attended grades one through five in a school for the deaf, and grades six through eight in a public school operated by respondent. While he attended public school, respondent furnished him with a sign-language interpreter. For religious reasons, James' parents . . . enrolled him for the ninth grade in Salpointe Catholic High School, a sectarian institution. When petitioners requested that respondent supply James with an interpreter at Salpointe, respondent referred the matter to the County Attorney, who concluded that providing an interpreter on the school's premises would violate the United States Constitution. . . . Respondent accordingly declined to provide the requested interpreter.

Petitioners then instituted this action in the United States District Court for the District of Arizona . . . . Petitioners asserted that the IDEA and the Free Exercise Clause of the First Amendment require respondent to provide James with an interpreter at Salpointe, and that the Establishment Clause does not bar such relief. . . . The District Court . . . granted respondent summary judgment, on the ground that "[t]he interpreter would act as a conduit for the religious inculcation of James—thereby, promoting James' religious development at government expense. . . . That kind of entanglement of church and state," the District Court concluded, "is not allowed." . . .

The Court of Appeals affirmed by a divided vote, applying the three-part test announced in *Lemon v. Kurtzman*, 403 U.S. 602, 613 . . . (1971). It first found that the IDEA has a clear secular purpose: " 'to assist States and Localities to provide for the education of all handicapped children.' " Turning to the second prong of the *Lemon* inquiry, though, the Court of Appeals determined that the IDEA, if applied as petitioners proposed, would have the primary effect of advancing religion and thus would run afoul of the Establishment Clause. "By placing its employee in the sectarian school," the Court of Appeals reasoned, "the government would create the appearance that it was a 'joint sponsor' of the school's activities." This, the court held, would create the "symbolic union of government and religion" found impermissible in *School Dist. of Grand Rapids v. Ball*, 473 U.S. 373, 392 . . . (1985). . . . We granted certiorari, and now reverse.

. . . .

We have never said that "religious institutions are disabled by the First Amendment from participating in publicly sponsored social welfare programs." *Bowen v. Kendrick*, 487 U.S. 589, 609 . . . (1988). For if the Establishment Clause did bar religious groups from receiving general government benefits, then "a church could not be protected by the police and fire departments, or have its public sidewalk kept in repair." *Widmar v. Vincent*, 454 U.S. 263, 274-275 . . . (1981). Given that a contrary rule would lead to such absurd results, we have consistently held that government programs that neutrally provide benefits to a broad class of citizens defined without reference to religion are not readily subject to an Establishment Clause challenge just because sectarian institutions may also receive an attenuated financial benefit. Nowhere have we stated this principle more clearly than in *Mueller v. Allen*, 463 U.S. 388 . . . (1983), and *Witters v. Washington Dept. of Services for Blind*, 474 U.S.

481 . . . (1986), two cases dealing specifically with government programs offering general educational assistance.

In *Mueller*, we rejected an Establishment Clause challenge to a Minnesota law allowing taxpayers to deduct certain educational expenses in computing their state income tax, even though the vast majority of those deductions (perhaps over 90%) went to parents whose children attended sectarian schools. Two factors, aside from States' traditionally broad taxing authority, informed our decision. We noted that the law "permits *all* parents—whether their children attend public school or private—to deduct their children's educational expenses." We also pointed out that under Minnesota's scheme, public funds become available to sectarian schools "only as a result of numerous private choices of individual parents of school-age children," thus distinguishing *Mueller* from our other cases involving "the direct transmission of assistance from the State to the schools themselves."

Witters was premised on virtually identical reasoning. In that case, we upheld against an Establishment Clause challenge the State of Washington's extension of vocational assistance, as part of a general state program, to a blind person studying at a private Christian college to become a pastor, missionary, or youth director. Looking at the statute as a whole, we observed that "any aid provided under Washington's program that ultimately flows to religious institutions does so only as a result of the genuinely independent and private choices of aid recipients." The program, we said, "creates no financial incentive for students to undertake sectarian education." We also remarked that, much like the law in *Mueller*, "Washington's program is 'made available generally without regard to the sectarian-nonsectarian, or public-nonpublic nature of the institution benefitted.'" In light of these factors, we held that Washington's program—even as applied to a student who sought state assistance so that he could become a pastor—would not advance religion in a manner inconsistent with the Establishment Clause.

That same reasoning applies with equal force here. The service at issue in this case is part of a general government program that distributes benefits neutrally to any child qualifying as "handicapped" under the IDEA, without regard to the "sectarian-nonsectarian, or public-nonpublic nature" of the school the child attends. By according parents freedom to select a school of their choice, the statute ensures that a government-paid interpreter will be present in a sectarian school only as a result of the private decision of individual parents. In other words, because the IDEA creates no financial incentive for parents to choose a sectarian school, an interpreter's presence there cannot be attributed to state decisionmaking. Viewed against the backdrop of *Mueller* and *Witters*, then, the Court of Appeals erred in its decision. When the government offers a neutral service on the premises of a sectarian school as part of a general program that "is in no way skewed towards religion," it follows under our prior decisions that provision of that service does not offend the Establishment Clause. Indeed, this is an even easier case than *Mueller* and *Witters* in the sense that, under the IDEA, no funds traceable to the government ever find their way into sectarian schools' coffers. The only indirect economic benefit a sectarian school might receive by dint of the IDEA is the handicapped child's tuition—and that is, of course, assuming that the school makes a profit on each student; that, without an IDEA interpreter, the child would have gone to school elsewhere; and that the school, then, would have been unable to fill that child's spot.

Respondent contends, however, that this case differs from *Mueller* and *Witters*, in that petitioners seek to have a public employee physically present in a sectarian school to assist in James' religious education. In light of this distinction, respondent argues that this case more closely resembles *Meek v. Pittenger*, 421 U.S. 349 . . . (1975), and *School Dist. of Grand Rapids v. Ball*, 473 U.S. 373 . . . (1985). In *Meek*, we struck down a statute that, *inter alia*, provided "massive aid" to private schools—more than 75% of which were church related—through a direct loan of teaching material and equipment. The material and equipment covered by the statute included maps, charts, and tape recorders. According to respondent, if the government could not place a tape recorder in a sectarian school in *Meek*, then it surely cannot place an interpreter in Salpointe. The statute in *Meek* also authorized state-paid personnel to furnish "auxiliary services"—which included remedial and accelerated instruction and guidance counseling—on the premises of religious schools. We determined that this part of the statute offended the First Amendment as well. *Ball* similarly involved two public programs that provided services on private school premises; there, public employees taught classes to students in private school classrooms. We found that those programs likewise violated the Constitution, relying largely on *Meek*. According to respondent, if the government could not provide educational services on the premises of sectarian schools in *Meek* and *Ball*, then it surely cannot provide James with an interpreter on the premises of Salpointe.

Respondent's reliance on *Meek* and *Ball* is misplaced for two reasons. First, the programs in *Meek* and *Ball*—through direct grants of government aid—relieved sectarian schools of costs they otherwise would have borne in educating their students. See *Witters*, *supra*, at 487 ("The State may not grant aid to a religious school, whether cash or in kind, where the effect of the aid is 'that of a direct subsidy to the religious school' from the State") (quoting *Ball*, *supra*, 473 U.S., at 394). For example, the religious schools in *Meek* received teaching material and equipment from the State, relieving them of an otherwise necessary cost of performing their educational function. "Substantial aid to the educational function of such schools," we explained, "necessarily results in aid to the sectarian school enterprise as a whole," and therefore brings about "the direct and substantial advancement of religious activity." So, too, was the case in *Ball*: The programs challenged there, which provided teachers in addition to instructional equipment and material, "in effect subsidized the religious functions of the parochial schools by taking over a substantial portion of their responsibility for teaching secular subjects." "This kind of direct aid," we determined, "is indistinguishable from the provision of a direct cash subsidy to the religious school." The extension of aid to petitioners, however, does not amount to "an impermissible 'direct subsidy'" of Salpointe, ... for Salpointe is not relieved of an expense that it otherwise would have assumed in educating its students. And, as we noted above, any attenuated financial benefit that parochial schools do ultimately receive from the IDEA is attributable to "the private choices of individual parents." Disabled children, not sectarian schools, are the primary beneficiaries of the IDEA; to the extent sectarian schools benefit at all from the IDEA, they are only incidental beneficiaries. Thus, the function of the IDEA is hardly "'to provide desired financial support for nonpublic, sectarian institutions.'"

Second, the task of a sign-language interpreter seems to us quite different from that of a teacher or guidance counselor. Notwithstanding the Court of Appeals' intimations to the contrary, the Establishment Clause lays down no absolute bar to the placing of a public employee in a sectarian school. Such a flat rule, smacking of antiquated notions of "taint," would indeed exalt form over substance. Nothing in this record suggests that a sign-language interpreter would do more than accurately interpret whatever material is presented to the class as a whole. In fact, ethical guidelines require interpreters to "transmit everything that is said in exactly the same way it was intended." James' parents have chosen of their own free will to place him in a pervasively sectarian environment. The sign-language interpreter they have requested will neither add to nor subtract from that environment, and hence the provision of such assistance is not barred by the Establishment Clause.

The IDEA creates a neutral government program dispensing aid not to schools but to individual handicapped children. If a handicapped child chooses to enroll in a sectarian school, we hold that the Establishment Clause does not prevent the school district from furnishing him with a sign-language interpreter there in order to facilitate his education. The judgment of the Court of Appeals is therefore

Reversed.

[The dissenting opinion of Justice Blackmun, joined by Justice Souter, and as to Part I by Justice Stevens and Justice O'Connor, is omitted. The dissenting opinion by Justice O'Connor, joined by Justice Stevens, is omitted.]

Notes, Comments, and Questions

1. *Zobrest* is one of a quartet of cases that established the proposition that the Establishment Clause does not prohibit a state from providing funds to local school districts to pay for teachers and aides in private religious schools. These cases, in turn, are part of a large and complex body of Establishment Clause law involving provision of public aid to religious institutions, which is beyond the scope of this book.

2. The quartet of cases to which *Zobrest* belongs begins with *Aguilar v. Felton*, 473 U.S. 402 (1985), *overruled*, *Agostini v. Felton*, 521 U.S. 203 (1997), which involved the federal Title I program, pursuant to which the federal government distributes funds to school districts to enhance educational programs for children from lower-income families. The Court ruled that sending teachers funded by Title I into private religious schools to teach secular subjects violated the Establishment Clause because the government's efforts to monitor the teachers to ensure they do not promote religious beliefs unconstitutionally entangled church and state. *Id.* at 412–14. The Court, however,

began to take a different direction the next year in *Witters v. Wash. Dep't of Serv. for the Blind*, 474 U.S. 481 (1986). There, the Court upheld against an Establishment Clause challenge the provision of tuition assistance pursuant to a state vocational rehabilitation assistance program to a student with a visual impairment who was attending a Christian college and intended to become a pastor, missionary, or youth director. The Court ruled that because the aid was paid directly to the student who used the funds to attend the school of his choice, the program did not support religion in violation of the Establishment Clause. *Id.* at 488–89. *Zobrest*, which relied heavily on *Witters*, was next. Finally, in turn relying heavily on *Zobrest* and *Witters*, the Court in *Agostini v. Felton*, 521 U.S. 203 (1997), overruled *Aguilar*. The Court ruled that the Title I program:

> does not run afoul of any of three primary criteria we currently use to evaluate whether government aid has the effect of advancing religion: It does not result in governmental indoctrination; define its recipients by reference to religion; or create an excessive entanglement. We therefore hold that a federally funded program providing supplemental, remedial instruction to disadvantaged children on a neutral basis is not invalid under the Establishment Clause when such instruction is given on the premises of sectarian schools by government employees pursuant to a program containing safeguards such as those present here.

Id. at 234–35. *Aguilar's* companion case was *Ball*, which the Court in *Zobrest* distinguished. What effect, if any, did the Court's decision in *Agostini*, overruling *Aguilar*, have on *Zobrest*?

3. The *Zobrest* quartet of cases stands for the proposition that the Establishment Clause does not prohibit the state from providing assistance to students who attend private religious schools. Although the parents in *Zobrest* argued that the Free Exercise Clause requires the district to provide the sign language interpreter, the Court did not reach that issue; *see also Witters*, 474 U.S. at 489–90 ("We decline petitioner's invitation to [hold] . . . that the Free Exercise Clause *requires* Washington to extend vocational rehabilitation aid to petitioner regardless of what the State Constitution commands or further factual development reveals, and we express no opinion on that matter.") (emphasis in original). The Supreme Court did consider this question in *Locke v. Davey*, which involved a scholarship program very similar to the program in *Witters* and a Free Exercise Clause challenge to the state's denial of a scholarship to a student studying devotional theology.

Locke v. Davey

540 U.S. 712 (2004)

Chief Justice Rehnquist delivered the opinion of the Court.

The State of Washington established the Promise Scholarship Program to assist academically gifted students with postsecondary education expenses. In accordance with the State Constitution, students may not use the scholarship at an institution where they are pursuing a degree in devotional theology. We hold that such an exclusion from an otherwise inclusive aid program does not violate the Free Exercise Clause of the First Amendment.

....

Respondent, Joshua Davey, was awarded a Promise Scholarship, and chose to attend Northwest College. Northwest is a private, Christian college affiliated with the Assemblies of God denomination, and is an eligible institution under the Promise Scholarship Program. Davey had "planned for many years to attend a Bible college and to prepare [himself] through that college training for a lifetime of ministry, specifically as a church pastor." To that end, when he enrolled in Northwest College, he decided to pursue a double major in pastoral ministries and business management/administration. There is no dispute that the pastoral ministries degree is devotional and therefore excluded under the Promise Scholarship Program.

At the beginning of the 1999–2000 academic year, Davey met with Northwest's director of financial aid. He learned for the first time at this meeting that he could not use his scholarship to pursue a devotional theology degree. He was informed that to receive the funds appropriated for his use, he must certify in writing that he was not pursuing such a degree at Northwest. He refused to sign the form and did not receive any scholarship funds.

Davey then brought an action under 42 USC § 1983 against various state officials . . . in the District Court for the Western District of Washington to enjoin the State from refusing to award the scholarship solely because a student is pursuing a devotional theology degree, and for damages. He argued the denial of his scholarship based on his decision to pursue a theology degree violated, *inter alia*, the Free Exercise, Establishment, and Free Speech Clauses of the First Amendment . . . . After the District Court denied Davey's request for a preliminary injunction, the parties filed cross-motions for summary judgment. The District Court rejected Davey's constitutional claims and granted summary judgment in favor of the State.

A divided panel of the United States Court of Appeals for the Ninth Circuit reversed. The court concluded that the State had singled out religion for unfavorable treatment and thus . . . the State's exclusion of theology majors must be narrowly tailored to achieve a compelling state interest. Finding that the State's own antiestablishment concerns were not compelling, the court declared Washington's Promise Scholarship Program unconstitutional. We granted certiorari and now reverse.

The Religion Clauses of the First Amendment provide: "Congress shall make no law respecting an establishment of religion, or prohibiting the free exercise thereof." These two Clauses, the Establishment Clause and the Free Exercise Clause, are frequently in tension. Yet we have long said that "there is room for play in the joints" between them. In other words, there are some state actions permitted by the Establishment Clause but not required by the Free Exercise Clause.

This case involves that "play in the joints" described above. Under our Establishment Clause precedent, the link between government funds and religious training is broken by the independent and private choice of recipients. As such, there is no doubt that the State could, consistent with the Federal Constitution, permit Promise Scholars to pursue a degree in devotional theology, and the State does not contend otherwise. The question before us, however, is whether Washington, pursuant to its own constitution, which has been authoritatively interpreted as prohibiting even indirectly funding religious instruction that will prepare students for the ministry, can deny them such funding without violating the Free Exercise Clause.

Davey urges us to answer that question in the negative. He contends that under the rule we enunciated in *Church of Lukumi*, the program is presumptively unconstitutional because it is not facially neutral with respect to religion. We reject his claim of presumptive unconstitutionality, however; to do otherwise would extend the *Lukumi* line of cases well beyond not only their facts but their reasoning. In *Lukumi*, the city of Hialeah made it a crime to engage in certain kinds of animal slaughter. We found that the law sought to suppress ritualistic animal sacrifices of the Santeria religion. In the present case, the State's disfavor of religion (if it can be called that) is of a far milder kind. It imposes neither criminal nor civil sanctions on any type of religious service or rite. It does not deny to ministers the right to participate in the political affairs of the community. And it does not require students to choose between their religious beliefs and receiving a government benefit. The State has merely chosen not to fund a distinct category of instruction.

Justice Scalia argues, however, that generally available benefits are part of the "baseline against which burdens on religion are measured." Because the Promise Scholarship Program funds training for all secular professions, Justice Scalia contends the State must also fund training for religious professions. But training for religious professions and training for secular professions are not fungible. Training someone to lead a congregation is an essentially religious endeavor. Indeed, majoring in devotional theology is akin to a religious calling as well as an academic pursuit. And the subject of religion is one in which both the United States and state constitutions embody distinct views—in favor of free exercise, but opposed to establishment—that find no counterpart with respect to other callings or professions. That a State would deal differently with religious education for the ministry than with education for other callings is a product of these views, not evidence of hostility toward religion.

Even though the differently worded Washington Constitution draws a more stringent line than that drawn by the United States Constitution, the interest it seeks to further is scarcely novel. In fact, we can think of few areas in which a State's antiestablishment interests come more into play. Since the founding of our country, there have been popular uprisings against procuring taxpayer funds to support church leaders, which was one of the hallmarks of an "established" religion.

Most States that sought to avoid an establishment of religion around the time of the founding placed in their constitutions formal prohibitions against using tax funds to support the ministry. The plain text of these constitutional provisions prohibited *any* tax dollars from supporting the clergy. We have found nothing to indicate, as Justice Scalia contends, that these provisions would not have applied so long as the

State equally supported other professions or if the amount at stake was *de minimis*. That early state constitutions saw no problem in explicitly excluding *only* the ministry from receiving state dollars reinforces our conclusion that religious instruction is of a different ilk.

Far from evincing the hostility toward religion which was manifest in *Lukumi*, we believe that the entirety of the Promise Scholarship Program goes a long way toward including religion in its benefits. The program permits students to attend pervasively religious schools, so long as they are accredited. As Northwest advertises, its "concept of education is distinctly Christian in the evangelical sense." It prepares *all* of its students, "through instruction, through modeling, [and] through [its] classes, to use . . . the Bible as their guide, as the truth," no matter their chosen profession. And under the Promise Scholarship Program's current guidelines, students are still eligible to take devotional theology courses. Davey notes all students at Northwest are required to take at least four devotional courses, "Exploring the Bible," "Principles of Spiritual Development," "Evangelism in the Christian Life," and "Christian Doctrine," and some students may have additional religious requirements as part of their majors.

In short, we find neither in the history or text of Article I, § 11 of the Washington Constitution, nor in the operation of the Promise Scholarship Program, anything that suggests animus towards religion. Given the historic and substantial state interest at issue, we therefore cannot conclude that the denial of funding for vocational religious instruction alone is inherently constitutionally suspect.

Without a presumption of unconstitutionality, Davey's claim must fail. The State's interest in not funding the pursuit of devotional degrees is substantial and the exclusion of such funding places a relatively minor burden on Promise Scholars. If any room exists between the two Religion Clauses, it must be here. We need not venture further into this difficult area in order to uphold the Promise Scholarship Program as currently operated by the State of Washington.

The judgment of the Court of Appeals is therefore reversed.

[The dissenting opinion of Justice SCALIA, joined by Justice THOMAS, and the dissenting opinion of Justice THOMAS, are omitted.]

Notes, Comments, and Questions

1. The Court in *Locke* said there is " 'room for play in the joints' " between the Establishment and Free Exercise Clauses. 540 U.S. at 718. What does this mean? Essentially, the phrase is an abstract response to the question neither *Zobrest* nor *Witters* answered: is it possible that the Establishment Clause could permit the government to provide aid that benefits a religious institution while at the same time the Free Exercise Clause does not require the government to provide the aid? The Court in *Locke* provided a concrete answer: the Establishment Clause permits the State of Washington to offer the Scholarship Program to students studying devotional theology but the Free Exercise Clause does not require Washington to do so.

2. Keys to the Court's decision in *Locke* were that Washington's denial of the scholarship was not based on religious animus, that it placed a relatively minor burden on scholarship recipients, and it was based on the compelling government interest in not funding religious studies expressed in Washington's state constitution. Do you think this government interest outweighed the burden that the denial of the scholarship placed on Davey?

3. What are the consequences of *Zobrest* and *Locke* for the provision of IDEA services in religious schools? This question is taken up in Section Three, following Section Two's coverage of the 1997 amendments to the IDEA and subsequent regulations, which describe a school district's obligation to provide IDEA services in private schools.

Section Two The 1997 Amendments to the IDEA and the Subsequent Regulations

Congress amended the IDEA in 1997. Among other changes, Congress added Section 1412(a)(10), which creates obligations for school districts to provide special education and related services to children in private schools and procedures for schools to follow in providing these services. Excerpts from Section 1412(a)(10) and the Department of Education regulations implementing it follow. As you read the excerpts, consider the following questions. Are school districts required to provide IDEA services to students with disabilities in private schools? What services are districts required to provide? Must the services a district provides to students with disabilities in private schools be the same as the services it provides to students with disabilities in public schools? Where are districts required to provide the services? May they provide services at religious schools? Must they? What remedies are available against districts that violate Section 1412(a)(10) and the regulations that implement it?

(10) Children in private schools

(A) Children enrolled in private schools by their parents

(i) In general

To the extent consistent with the number and location of children with disabilities in the State who are enrolled by their parents in private elementary schools and secondary schools in the school district served by a local educational agency, provision is made for the participation of those children in the program assisted or carried out under this subchapter by providing for such children special education and related services in accordance with the following requirements . . . :

(I) Amounts to be expended for the provision of those services (including direct services to parentally placed private school children) by the local educational agency shall be equal to a proportionate amount of Federal funds made available under this subchapter.

(II) In calculating the proportionate amount of Federal funds, the local educational agency . . . shall conduct a thorough and complete child find process to determine the number of parentally placed children with disabilities attending private schools located in the local educational agency.

(III) Such services to parentally placed private school children with disabilities may be provided to the children on the premises of private, including religious, schools, to the extent consistent with law.

. . . .

(ii) Child find requirement

(I) In general

The requirements of paragraph (3) (relating to child find) shall apply with respect to children with disabilities in the State who are enrolled in private, including religious, elementary schools and secondary schools.

(II) Equitable participation

The child find process shall be designed to ensure the equitable participation of parentally placed private school children with disabilities and an accurate count of such children.

(III) Activities

In carrying out this clause, the local educational agency, or where applicable, the State educational agency, shall undertake activities similar to those activities undertaken for the agency's public school children.

. . . .

(iii) Consultation

To ensure timely and meaningful consultation, a local educational agency, or where appropriate, a State educational agency, shall consult with private school representatives and representatives of parents of parentally placed private school children with disabilities during the design and development of special education and related services for the children, including regarding—

(I) the child find process and how parentally placed private school children suspected of having a disability can participate equitably, including how parents, teachers, and private school officials will be informed of the process;

(II) the determination of the proportionate amount of Federal funds available to serve parentally placed private school children with disabilities under this subparagraph, including the determination of how the amount was calculated;

(III) the consultation process among the local educational agency, private school officials, and representatives of parents of parentally placed private school children with disabilities, including how such process will operate throughout the school year to ensure that parentally placed private school children with disabilities identified through the child find process can meaningfully participate in special education and related services;

(IV) how, where, and by whom special education and related services will be provided for parentally placed private school children with disabilities, including a discussion of types of services, including direct services and alternate service delivery mechanisms, how such services will be apportioned if funds are insufficient to serve all children, and how and when these decisions will be made; and

(V) how, if the local educational agency disagrees with the views of the private school officials on the provision of services or the types of services, whether provided directly or through a contract, the local educational agency shall provide to the private school officials a written explanation of the reasons why the local educational agency chose not to provide services directly or through a contract.

. . . .

(v) **Compliance**

(I) **In general**

A private school official shall have the right to submit a complaint to the State educational agency that the local educational agency did not engage in consultation that was meaningful and timely, or did not give due consideration to the views of the private school official.

(II) **Procedure**

If the private school official wishes to submit a complaint, the official shall provide the basis of the noncompliance with this subparagraph by the local educational agency to the State educational agency, and the local educational agency shall forward the appropriate documentation to the State educational agency. If the private school official is dissatisfied with the decision of the State educational agency, such official may submit a complaint to the Secretary by providing the basis of the noncompliance with this subparagraph by the local educational agency to the Secretary, and the State educational agency shall forward the appropriate documentation to the Secretary.

(vi) Provision of equitable services

. . . .

(II) Secular, neutral, nonideological

Special education and related services provided to parentally placed private school children with disabilities, including materials and equipment, shall be secular, neutral, and nonideological.

. . . .

34 C.F.R. Part 300 (excerpts)

§ 300.130 Definition of parentally-placed private school children with disabilities.

Parentally-placed private school children with disabilities means children with disabilities enrolled by their parents in private, including religious, schools or facilities that meet the definition of elementary school in § 300.13 or secondary school in § 300.36 other than children with disabilities covered under §§ 300.145 through 300.147 [which cover students placed in private schools].

§ 300.132 Provision of services for parentally-placed private school children with disabilities—basic requirement.

. . . .

(b) *Services plan for parentally-placed private school children with disabilities.* In accordance with paragraph (a) of this section . . . , a services plan must be developed and implemented for each private school child with a disability who has been designated by the LEA in which the private school is located to receive special education and related services under this part.

. . . .

§ 300.133 Expenditures.

(a) *Formula.* To meet the requirement of . . . [this section], each LEA must spend the following on providing special education and related services . . . to parentally-placed private school children with disabilities:

(1) For children aged 3 through 21, an amount that is the same proportion of the LEA's total subgrant under section 611(f) of the Act as the number of private school children with disabilities aged 3 through 21 who are enrolled by their parents in private, including religious, elementary schools and secondary schools located in the school district served by the LEA, is to the total number of children with disabilities in its jurisdiction aged 3 through 21.

. . . .

(C) *Annual count of the number of parentally-placed private school children with disabilities.* (1) Each LEA must—

(i) After timely and meaningful consultation with representatives of parentally-placed private school children with disabilities . . . , determine the number of parentally-placed private school children with disabilities attending private schools located in the LEA; and

(ii) Ensure that the count is conducted on any date between October 1 and December 1, inclusive, of each year.

(2) The count must be used to determine the amount that the LEA must spend on providing special education and related services to parentally-placed private school children with disabilities in the next subsequent fiscal year.

(d) *Supplement, not supplant.* State and local funds may supplement and in no case supplant the proportionate amount of Federal funds required to be expended for parentally-placed private school children with disabilities under this part.

§ 300.137 Equitable services determined.

(a) *No individual right to special education and related services.* No parentally-placed private school child with a disability has an individual right to receive some or all of the special education and related services that the child would receive if enrolled in a public school.

(b) *Decisions.* (1) Decisions about the services that will be provided to parentally-placed private school children with disabilities . . . must be made in accordance with paragraph (c) of this section and § 300.134(d).

(2) The LEA must make the final decisions with respect to the services to be provided to eligible parentally-placed private school children with disabilities.

(c) *Services plan for each child served under §§ 300.130 through 300.144.* If a child with a disability is enrolled in a religious or other private school by the child's parents and will receive special education or related services from an LEA, the LEA must—

(1) Initiate and conduct meetings to develop, review, and revise a services plan for the child, in accordance with § 300.138(b); and

(2) Ensure that a representative of the religious or other private school attends each meeting. If the representative cannot attend, the LEA shall use other methods to ensure participation by the religious or other private school, including individual or conference telephone calls.

§ 300.138 Equitable services provided.

(a) *General* (1) The services provided to parentally-placed private school children with disabilities must be provided by personnel meeting the same standards as personnel providing services in the public schools . . . .

(2) Parentally-placed private school children with disabilities may receive a different amount of services than children with disabilities in public schools.

(b) *Services provided in accordance with a services plan.* (1) Each parentally-placed private school child with a disability who has been designated to receive services under § 300.132 must have a services plan that describes the specific special education and related services that the LEA will provide to the child in light of the services that the LEA has determined . . . it will make available to parentally-placed private school children with disabilities.

. . . .

(c) *Provision of equitable services.*

. . . .

(2) Special education and related services provided to parentally-placed private school children with disabilities, including materials and equipment, must be secular, neutral, and nonideological.

§ 300.139 Location of services and transportation.

(a) *Services on private school premises.* Services to parentally-placed private school children with disabilities may be provided on the premises of private, including religious, schools, to the extent consistent with law.

(b) *Transportation*—(1) *General.* (i) If necessary for the child to benefit from or participate in the services provided under this part, a parentally-placed private school child with a disability must be provided transportation—

(A) From the child's school or the child's home to a site other than the private school; and

(B) From the service site to the private school, or to the child's home, depending on the timing of the services.

(ii) LEAs are not required to provide transportation from the child's home to the private school.

. . . .

§ 300.140 Due process complaints and State complaints.

(a) *Due process not applicable, except for child find.* (1) Except as provided in paragraph (b) of this section, the procedures in §§ 300.504 through 300.519 [describing the rights of aggrieved parties to an impartial hearing to challenge decisions regarding the evaluation, placement, or services provided to a child under the IDEA] do not apply to complaints that an LEA has failed to meet the requirements of §§ 300.132 through 300.139, including the provision of services indicated on the child's services plan.

(b) *Child find complaints—to be filed with the LEA in which the private school is located.* (1) The procedures in §§ 300.504 through 300.519 apply to complaints that an LEA has failed to meet the child find requirements in § 300.131 . . . .

. . . .

(c) *State complaints.* (1) Any complaint that an SEA or LEA has failed to meet the requirements in §§ 300.132 through 300.135 and 300.137 through 300.144 must be filed in accordance with the procedures described in §§ 300.151 through 300.153 [describing the complaint review process that states must make available pursuant to the IDEA].

. . . .

§ 300.141 Requirement that funds not benefit a private school.

(a) An LEA may not use funds provided under section 611 or 619 of the Act to finance the existing level of instruction in a private school or to otherwise benefit the private school.

(b) The LEA must use funds provided under Part B of the Act to meet the special education and related services needs of parentally-placed private school children with disabilities, but not for meeting—

(1) The needs of a private school; or

(2) The general needs of the students enrolled in the private school.

§ 300.142 Use of personnel.

(a) *Use of public school personnel.* An LEA may use funds available under sections 611 and 619 of the Act to make public school personnel available in other than public facilities—

(1) To the extent necessary to provide services under §§ 300.130 through 300.144 for parentally-placed private school children with disabilities; and

(2) If those services are not normally provided by the private school.

(b) *Use of private school personnel.* An LEA may use funds available under sections 611 and 619 of the Act to pay for the services of an employee of a private school to provide services under §§ 300.130 through 300.144 if—

(1) The employee performs the services outside of his or her regular hours of duty; and

(2) The employee performs the services under public supervision and control.

Notes, Comments, and Questions

1. The 1997 amendments to the IDEA limit the services school districts are required to provide to children with disabilities in private schools when a FAPE is available in the public school. The amendments do not require school districts to provide such children with a FAPE, ensure they are educated in the least restrictive environment, or provide services at the child's private school. Instead, the amendments require a school district to expend only a proportionate share of its federal funds on children with disabilities in private school and to prepare a services plan for students to whom it will provide services. *See* K.R. v. Anderson Cmty. Sch. Corp., 125 F.3d 1017, 1019 (7th Cir. 1997), *cert. denied*, 523 U.S. 1046 (1988) ("[T]he Amendments unambiguously show that participating states and localities have no obligation to spend their money to ensure that disabled children who have chosen to enroll in private schools will receive publicly funded special education services generally '"comparable"' to those provided to public-school children."); Nieuwenhuis v. Delavan-Darien Sch. Dist. Bd. of Educ., 996 F. Supp. 855, 865 (E.D. Wisc. 1998) ("Taken as a whole, the regulatory scheme reflects the fact that under the IDEA, when the parent of an eligible child opts out of a public school where a FAPE could be provided, that parent

is opting for a lesser entitlement."). Why do you think Congress required school districts to provide special education services to children with disabilities at private schools even though a FAPE was available at the child's public school? Having done so, why did Congress create only a limited set of rights for such children? Why not require school districts to provide children with disabilities in private schools the same level of IDEA services they provide to children in public schools? What would be the contours of comparable special education services for children in private schools?

2. Overall, the funding Congress provides to school districts to educate students with disabilities covers only a small portion of the cost. *See* Russman v. Bd. of Educ. of the Enlarged City Sch. Dist. of Watervliet, 150 F.3d 219, 221 (2d Cir. 1998) ("Because the federal funds received by a state under the IDEA are only a fraction of the cost of educating a state's disabled children, children choosing to attend private schools would, under the district's view, be entitled as a group to only a proportionate amount of that fraction."); Cefalu v. East Baton Rouge Parish Sch. Bd., 117 F.3d 231, 232 (5th Cir. 1997) ("[O]nly a small percentage of the cost of the special education services was derived from the federal grants under IDEA and . . . the remainder of the costs were paid through the use of local and state funds."). As a result, students with disabilities in private schools are entitled to only a small part of the overall funding for special education. The consequences of this limited funding are described in *Board of Educ. of the Appoquinimink Sch. Dist. v. Johnson*, 543 F. Supp. 2d 351 (D. Del. 2008):

> In this case, the District has presented evidence that the proportional share of federal . . . funds allocated to it for private school services amounted to $3,639.00. The cost for the student's full time interpreter exceeds $37,000 per year, more than ten times the amount available for all parentally-placed [students in] private schools in the district falling within the provisions of the IDEA. This fact alone demonstrates the inequity that would arise with respect to other parentally-placed private school students if the District were required to fund a one-to-one ASL interpreter for the student.

Id. at 358.

3. Neither Section 1412(a)(10) nor the federal regulations establish substantive standards for districts to use when deciding which services to provide to which students and where to provide them. The Second Circuit raised this issue in *Russman v. Bd. of Educ. of the Enlarged City. Sch. Dist. of Watervliet*, 150 F.3d 219, 221 n.1 (2d Cir. 1998):

> There is nothing in the record indicating how much federal money New York receives under the IDEA, what is the proportionate amount to which disabled children in the state are entitled, or how much it would cost to pay the consultant teacher's and the aide's salaries. . . . Thus, the question of where Colleen's services are to be provided may turn out to be of secondary importance. Unless Colleen is entitled under the program to sufficient federal funds to pay the salaries of the consultant teacher and teacher's aide provided

> for in her IEP, the question of whether the services are delivered to her on-site or off-site never arises.

The Tenth Circuit expressed a similar sentiment:

> The Act does not make clear, however, whether an equal share of the Federal funds must be allocated for *each* disabled child enrolled in a private school, or whether the proportionate amount must be allocated for disabled private school students *collectively*. In the latter case, any particular disabled private school student might receive an amount different from his or her individual proportionate share, and, conceivably, could receive nothing. Moreover, it is not clear whether the local educational agency must spend a proportionate share of Federal funds on *all* special education and related services needed by private school disabled students, or whether it has discretion to determine *which services* it will provide to which students. While we hope that the Department of Education's final regulations will provide some guidance, in the interim we leave it to the district court to initially determine the parameters of the District's obligation to Michael. . . . In any event, the calculation of Michael's share of the "proportionate share" of the Federal funds made available to the District requires further factual findings necessitating a remand to the district court.

Fowler v. Unified Sch. Dist. No. 259, 128 F.3d 1431, 1437–38 (10th Cir. 1997) (emphasis in original). *Russman* and *Fowler* were decided after Congress passed the 1997 amendments but before the Department of Education issued its regulations implementing Section 1412(a)(10). Do the regulations answer the courts' questions?

4. One of the rights parents and students do not have under the 1997 amendments is the right to an impartial hearing if the school district does not fulfill its obligations to students with disabilities in private school, with the exception that a parent or school can request a hearing to allege that a school district failed to follow its child-find obligations. *See* 34 C.F.R §§ 300.140(a), 300.507(a) (2015); Gary S. v. Manchester Sch. Dist., 241 F. Supp. 2d 111, 115 (D.N.H. 2003) ("Because a disabled student in private school does not have an individually enforceable right to receive special education and related services, the IDEA does not give the child's parents a corresponding right to an impartial due process hearing."). Instead, parents must file complaints about a school district's obligations to provide special education and related services to children with disabilities in private school pursuant to the state complaint review procedures described in 34 C.F.R. §§ 300.151-153. *See* 34 C.F.R. § 300.140(a); Board of Educ. of Appoquinimink Sch. Dist. v. Johnson, 543 F. Supp. 2d 351. 359 n.5 (D. Del. 2008) ("Complaints regarding the provision of services to parentally-placed private school students are not subject to due process procedures. Rather, complaints concerning the services received by a disabled student in private school must be brought through the state administrative complaint system.").

5. Although parents have the right to educate their children at home, home-schooled children are entitled to special education and related services under the IDEA only if the home-school qualifies as an "elementary" or "secondary" school under state law. 34 C.F.R. §§ 300.13, 300.36, and 300.130 (2015). *See* Hooks v. Clark Cnty. Sch. Dist., 228 F.3d 1036, 1037 (9th Cir. 2000), *cert. denied*, 534 U.S. 971 (2001) (holding that under the IDEA, states have discretion to determine whether a home-school qualifies for IDEA funds); Jones v. Dist. of Columbia, 646 F. Supp. 2d 62, 64 (D.D.C. 2009) (stating that a home-schooled child is not entitled to IDEA services if the home-school does not meet the state's definition of an elementary or secondary school).

Section Three
Legal Issues Involving the 1997 IDEA Amendments

Two significant legal issues arose in connection with the 1997 amendments: 1) whether a school district has an obligation to provide special education and related services at the child's private school; and 2) whether the reduced level of services for children in private religious schools violates the Free Exercise Clause of the First Amendment.

A. The Location of IDEA Services

Foley v. Special Sch. Dist. of St. Louis Cnty.

153 F.3d 863 (8th Cir. 1998)

Loken, Circuit Judge.

This is an appeal from the denial of equitable relief compelling the Special School District of St. Louis County (SSD) to provide special education and related services to a child at the private religious school where she was voluntarily placed by her parents, rather than at a public school one mile away. We conclude the child has no individual right to such services under the 1997 amendments to the Individuals with Disabilities Education Act . . . (IDEA). Accordingly, we affirm.

Clare Foley is an eleven year-old girl who is mildly mentally retarded. Her parents . . . placed Clare in St. Peter's Catholic School but requested special education services from SSD. An evaluation team determined that Clare should have one hour of occupational therapy, one-half hour of physical therapy, and one hour of language services per week. The Foleys demanded those services in Clare's classroom at St. Peter's but SSD refused, construing state law as precluding public school educators from providing special education services on the premises of parochial schools. SSD offered the Foleys a dual enrollment alternative under which Clare would travel from St. Peter's to a nearby public school to receive the special education services. The Foleys accepted this arrangement under protest and requested an IDEA due process hearing. Prior to the hearing, the SSD and the Foleys stipulated that the Foleys voluntarily placed Clare at St. Peter's after SSD offered Clare a free appropriate public education at Keysor public elementary school. Thus, the issue is whether Clare has a right to special education services at her private school.

....

One month after the Foleys commenced this appeal, Congress enacted the Individuals with Disabilities Education Act Amendments of 1997. Courts previously construed IDEA as granting children with disabilities who voluntarily attend private school a right to special education and related services. This led to litigation, such as this case, over where such services must be provided. The 1997 Amendments addressed this problem in detail by amending 20 U.S.C. § 1412(a)—the section setting forth conditions States must meet to be eligible for federal education assistance—to include a new subsection (10), which provides in relevant part:

> **(A) Children enrolled in private school by their parents**
>
> **(i) In general.** To the extent consistent with the number and location of children with disabilities in the State who are enrolled by their parents in private elementary and secondary schools, provision is made for the participation of those children in the program assisted or carried out under this subchapter by providing for such children special education and related services in accordance with the following requirements . . . :
>
> (I) Amounts expended for the provision of those services by a local educational agency shall be equal to a proportionate amount of Federal funds made available under this subchapter.
>
> (II) Such services may be provided to children with disabilities on the premises of private, including parochial, schools, to the extent consistent with law.
>
> ....
>
> **(C) Payment for education of children enrolled in private schools without consent of or referral by the public agency**
>
> **(i) In general.** Subject to subparagraph (A), this subchapter does not require a local educational agency to pay for the cost of education, including special education and related services, of a child with a disability at a private school or facility if that agency made a free appropriate public education available to the child and the parents elected to place the child in such private school or facility.

....

The Foleys argue that new § 1412(a)(10)(A) gives Clare a right to special education services at St. Peter's because that location is more beneficial educationally and no more costly than providing the services at a public school. Relying on § 1412(a)(10)(C)(i), SSD argues that the Foleys' claim must be rejected because SSD is not "required . . .

to pay for the cost of . . . special education . . . at [Clare's] private school." The Fifth and Seventh Circuits agree with SSD's interpretation of the 1997 Amendments. *See K.R. v. Anderson Community. Sch. Corp.*, 125 F.3d 1017, 1019 (7th Cir. 1997) . . . ; *Cefalu v. East Baton Rouge Parish Sch. Bd.*, 117 F.3d 231, 233 (5th Cir. 1997).

The 1997 Amendments expressly provide that public school agencies are not required to pay the costs of special education services for a particular child; States are required only to spend proportionate amounts on special education services for this class of students as a whole. 20 U.S.C. §§ 1412(a)(10)(A)(i)(I), 1412(a)(10)(C)(i). Thus, whatever their rights under prior law, Clare and her parents now have no individual right under IDEA to the special education and related services in question, so they have no right to a federal court decree mandating that those services be provided at a particular location. This change in prior law compels us to conclude that the Foleys have no statutory right to the relief they seek.

Alternatively, even if we construed the 1997 Amendments as granting private school children a right to some level of special education services, we cannot read § 1412(a)(10)(A)(i)(II)—which provides that such services "*may* be provided" on the premises of private schools "to the extent consistent with law"—as *mandating* that such services be provided on private school premises when that is *in*consistent with Missouri law. Missouri's refusal to allow public school educators on private school premises may not be mandated by the First Amendment, *see* Agostini v. Felton, 521 U.S. 203 . . . (1997), and it may even be unfortunate education policy. But we find nothing in the 1997 Amendments authorizing federal courts to override such a state policy. . . .

For the foregoing reasons, the judgment of the district court is affirmed.

Notes, Comments, and Questions

1. The court in *Foley* issued two significant rulings: 1) children with disabilities in private schools do not have an individual right to IDEA services; and 2) the IDEA does not require a school district to provide services to a child at the child's private school. The Courts of Appeals that have considered one or both of these issues agree. *See* KDM v. Reedsport Sch. Dist., 196 F.3d 1046, 1049–50 (9th Cir. 1999), *cert. denied*, 531 U.S. 1010 (2000) (ruling that the 1997 amendments do not require school districts to provide services at the child's private school); Russman v. Bd. of Educ. of the City Sch. Dist. of Watervliet, 150 F.3d 219, 221–22 (2d Cir. 1998) (ruling that the IDEA requires school districts to provide to children voluntarily enrolled in private schools only those services that the districts can purchase with a proportionate amount of the federal funds they receive and that districts are not required to provide the services at the private school); Fowler v. Unified Sch. Dist. No. 259, 128 F.3d 1431, 1436–37 (10th Cir. 1997) (ruling that a local school district's only obligation to students voluntarily placed in private schools is to spend on such students for special education and related services a proportionate share of federal funds); K.R. v. Anderson Cmty. Sch. Corp., 125 F.3d 1017, 1018 (7th Cir. 1997), *cert.*

denied, 523 U.S. 1046 (1998) (holding that the IDEA does not require school districts to provide comparable special education services to children with a disability voluntarily enrolled in private schools); Cefalu v. East Baton Rouge Parish Sch. Bd., 117 F.3d 231, 232–33 (5th Cir. 1997) (ruling that a school district is required to pay only a proportionate share of its federal funds to provide special education and related services to children voluntarily enrolled in private schools, and is not required to pay for these services from its own funds or to provide services on-site at the child's private school); *see also* Bristol Warren Reg. Sch. Comm. v. Barboza, 253 F. Supp. 2d 236, 242 (D.R.I. 2003) (holding that relevant statutes and regulations "clearly give the . . . [school district] the power to provide on-site resources services at all of the parochial schools in its district, some of them, or none at all.")

2. The fact that courts have ruled that the IDEA does not require school districts to provide IDEA services at private school does not necessarily leave private school students without any rights to receive services at their schools. The IDEA establishes a floor of rights for students with disabilities and states can provide more protection to children with disabilities than the IDEA requires. Bay Shore Union Free Sch. Dist. v. Kain, 485 F.3d 730, 733 (2d Cir. 2007) ("[S]tates may exceed the federal floor and enact their own laws and regulations to guarantee a higher level of entitlement to disabled students."). For example, in *Bay Shore Union Free Sch. Dist. v. Thomas K.*, 14 N.Y. 3d 289, 293–94 (2010), the New York State Court of Appeals ruled that N.Y. Ed. L. §3602-c required the school district to provide an aide at the child's religious school because the on-site aide was required to meet the educational needs of the child.

B. Free Exercise Challenges to the 1997 Amendments

The next two cases continue the discussion started in Section One with *Zobrest* and *Locke* regarding the interplay of the Establishment and Free Exercise Clauses as they relate to the provision of services to children in religious schools; this discussion now takes place in the context of the 1997 amendments. The principle that emerged from *Zobrest* and *Locke* is that although the Establishment Clause does not prohibit certain types of public aid to students in religious schools, the Free Exercise Clause does not always require the provision of such aid to students in religious schools. As you read the next two cases, consider the various sorts of rules school districts can establish involving provision of special education and related services to students with disabilities in religious schools.

Gary S. v. Manchester Sch. Dist.

374 F.3d 15 (1st Cir. 2004) *cert. denied*, 543 U.S. 998 (2004)

LEVIN H. CAMPBELL, *Senior Circuit Judge.*

Appealing from an adverse judgment of the district court, the parents of Andrew S., a disabled child who is attending a Catholic elementary school, assert that the Individuals with Disabilities Education Act (IDEA) . . . is unconstitutional as applied to their son. While he, like other disabled children who go to private schools, receives some educational services under federal and state law, he is not entitled by law to the panoply of services available to disabled public school students under the rubric of . . . FAPE . . . , nor to the due process hearing provided to public school students alone. Appellants argue that the difference in treatment of their disabled son, who is attending a religious school, from other disabled students, who are attending public schools, violates the Free Exercise Clause of the First Amendment to the federal constitution . . . .

The district court considered these contentions upon cross motions for summary judgment. Rejecting appellants' claims, it granted the appellee Manchester School District's motion for summary judgment and denied summary judgment to appellants.

On appeal, appellants reiterate their contentions. After carefully considering them, we find ourselves in agreement with the district court. . . .

I.

Appellants' lead argument on appeal is that the district court erred in determining that the federal law did not violate Andrew's and his parents' free exercise rights under the First Amendment. They reject the district court's assertion that the Supreme Court's decision in *Employment Div. Dep't of Human Res. of Oregon v. Smith*, 494 U.S. 872 . . . (1990), is controlling. *Smith*, according to the district court, exempted most "neutral laws of general applicability" from the compelling interest test. In the district court's view,

> [A] law ordinarily need not be justified by a compelling interest if it is "neutral" in that it is not targeted at religiously motivated conduct and "generally applicable" in that it does not selectively burden religious conduct.

IDEA and its regulations, the district court says, do not target religiously motivated conduct and is "generally applicable" in that it does not selectively burden religious conduct. For these reasons, . . . the district court found no violation of free exercise rights. We do not disagree.

Appellants reject the district court's analysis. They ask us to read *Smith* as limited to instances of socially harmful or criminal conduct. They point out that *Smith* did not purport to overrule the Supreme Court's holdings in the cases of *Hobbie v. Unemployment Appeals Comm'n*, 480 U.S. 136 . . . (1987), *Thomas v. Review Bd. of the Indian Employment Sec. Div.*, 450 U.S. 707 . . . (1981), and *Sherbert v. Verner*, 374 U.S. 398 (1963). In *Hobbie* and *Sherbert*, the complainants were denied unemployment benefits following discharge because of their religiously-based refusal to work on Saturday, complainant's religion's Sabbath. In *Thomas*, the complainant was denied unemployment benefits after discharge based on his religiously-based refusal to help produce armaments. Holding that the denial of a public benefit in these circumstances burdened plaintiff's religion, the Court ruled that, in order to justify an action having such an effect under the free-exercise clause, the government had to demonstrate that the withholding of the benefit served a compelling governmental interest and was the least restrictive means to that end. Appellants have likened the denial of educational disability benefits here to those situations, asking us similarly to apply strict scrutiny. If we do, appellants contend, we will find that Andrew's attendance at a Catholic school is mandated by his parents' sincerely-held religious beliefs. No compelling governmental interest is served, they say, by withholding from him the identical benefits granted to his peers at public schools.

It is not always easy to predict what analytical framework the Supreme Court will apply to the various, factually dissimilar free exercise cases that arise. *Smith* rejected a free exercise claim involving the religiously-based use of peyote, an illegal substance. Writing for five of the Justices, Justice Scalia endorsed the constitutionality of neutral, generally applicable laws even when they impinged incidentally upon individual religious practices.... The *Smith* majority expressly limited *Hobbie, Thomas* and *Sherbert* to the unemployment compensation field. While, as appellants point out, Justice Scalia in *Smith* also distinguished *Hobbie, Thomas* and *Sherbert* on the narrower ground that the use of peyote was illegal, the majority's overall message is unmistakably contrary to appellants' present argument that *Hobbie, Thomas* and *Sherbert*—and, in particular, the "compelling interest" test—are broadly applicable here....

....

While we could perhaps leave the free exercise analysis there, an even more fundamental reason causes us to reject appellants' First Amendment arguments. We cannot accept appellants' contention that providing to all disabled attendees at private schools, both sectarian and secular, fewer benefits than those granted to public school attendees is truly analogous to denying unemployment benefits to persons fired because of their religiously-inspired insistence upon celebrating the Sabbath or not producing weapons.

The state unemployment benefits denied in *Hobbie, Thomas,* and *Sherbert* were public benefits, available to all. Plaintiffs would have received them had their religiously-motivated refusal to work on a certain day or at a certain job not been erroneously viewed by local authorities as misconduct. While appellants say their son's attendance at a Catholic school is likewise a religiously-motivated act, there is a basic difference. He and they are not being deprived of a *generally available* public benefit. Rather, the benefits to which appellants lay claim under the First Amendment are benefits the federal government has earmarked solely for students enrolled in the nation's public schools—benefits still available for Andrew were he sent to a public school, though not otherwise. Since the early days of public education in this country, public financial aid has commonly been limited to public rather than independent schools. While the parents of private school attendees pay the same taxes as public school parents, the former's tax money normally supports their own children's education only if they transfer them to a public school. To be sure, parents have a protected right to send their children to private schools if they so desire. *Pierce v. Soc'y of Sisters*, 268 U.S. 510, 534–35 ... (1925) (state law compelling public school attendance "unreasonably interferes with the liberty of parents and guardians to direct the upbringing and education of children under their control"). But as the very term "private" denotes, it is not ordinarily expected that such schools will be publicly funded, and there is no precedent requiring such funding.

Given the traditional pattern that has so far prevailed of financing public education via the public schools, it would be unreasonable and inconsistent to premise a free exercise violation upon Congress's mere failure to provide to disabled children attending private religious schools the identical financial and other benefits it confers upon those attending public schools. Unlike unemployment benefits that are equally available to all, private school parents can have no legitimate expectancy that they or their children's schools will receive the same federal or state financial benefits provided to public schools. Thus, the non-receipt of equal funding and programmatic benefits cannot be said to impose any cognizable "burden" upon the religion of those choosing to attend such schools. Persons opting to attend private schools, religious or otherwise, must accept the disadvantages as well as any benefits offered by those schools. They cannot insist, as a matter of constitutional right, that the disadvantages be cured by the provision of public funding. It follows that denying the benefits here, to which appellants have no cognizable entitlement, do not burden their free exercise rights.

Indeed, if we were to find a burden here on appellants' right of free exercise, it would follow logically that we should find free exercise violations whenever a state, city or town refuses to fund programs of other types at religious schools, at least insofar as the absence of funding adversely affects students with parents who believe their faith requires attendance at a religious school. Yet, as noted *supra*, it is clear there is no federal constitutional requirement that private schools be permitted to share with public schools in state largesse on an equal basis. . . .

Accordingly, we see no basis for holding that the federal government violates appellants' free exercise rights under the First Amendment by favoring disabled public school attendees in respect to IDEA's programs and benefits. In so doing, the federal government does no more than state and local governments do everyday by funding public school programs while providing lesser or, more likely, no funding to private schools, religious and otherwise. This methodology leaves all parents with ultimate recourse to the public schools whenever the balance of services associated with attendance at a private school appears to them to be unsatisfactory; but the option thus available can necessitate their having to choose, as here, between alternatives each of which may seem imperfect. In any event, we cannot say that the federal government's structuring of benefits here violates appellants' free exercise rights.

. . . .

We AFFIRM the decision of the district court.

KDM v. Reedsport Sch. Dist.

196 F.3d 1046 (9th Cir. 1999) *cert. denied*, 531 U.S. 1510 (2000)

SCHWARZER, Senior District Judge:

WJM's son, KDM, is a minor who is legally blind and has cerebral palsy. As such, KDM is a "child with disabilities" entitled to special education and related services under the Individuals with Disabilities Act . . . (IDEA). Oregon provides such services to children enrolled in public schools. The Oregon administrative regulation leaves it to the discretion of individual school districts whether to provide such services to children enrolled in private school but specifically provides that "such special education and related services shall be provided in a religiously-neutral setting." Defendant Reedsport School District ("District") is willing to provide such services to KDM, but not at KDM's parochial school. We must decide whether the District's refusal to provide services at the school violates the IDEA or KDM's rights under the Free Exercise [or] Establishment . . . Clauses of the Constitution.

I. FACTUAL AND PROCEDURAL BACKGROUND

While attending public school, KDM received from the District the services of a vision specialist, physical therapy and special equipment at his school. Motivated by sincerely-held religious beliefs, KDM's parents transferred him to Harbor Baptist Church School ("Harbor Baptist"), a sectarian school. After the transfer, the District continued to supply him with special equipment (braillers, computers and other special equipment) at his new school. However, viewing the Harbor School setting as not religiously-neutral, it no longer supplied the vision specialist at the school. Instead, it provided that service at a fire hall down the street from Harbor Baptist. The adequacy of the service is not in dispute nor is it disputed that it is safe for KDM to travel to and from the fire hall, transportation being provided by the District. The service is provided for approximately ninety minutes twice a week. If this service were provided at Harbor Baptist, it would be provided in a room separate from the classroom because providing it in class could be disruptive to the instruction both of KDM and the other students in the classroom.

KDM brought this action through his father, WJM, against the District and Norma Paulus, Oregon's Superintendent for Public Instruction, for declaratory and injunctive relief requiring the defendants to place a vision specialist at Harbor Baptist. Plaintiff, in substance, made three claims: First, that defendants' refusal to provide a vision specialist at School violates the IDEA; second, that it violates the Free Exercise and Establishment clauses of the First Amendment; and, third, that it denies plaintiff the equal protection of the laws. Following a bench trial on stipulated facts, the district court entered judgment holding that the IDEA did not require the district to provide services at a private school, but that the Oregon regulation which permits services to be offered private school students only in a religiously-neutral setting violated the Free Exercise, Establishment and Equal Protection Clauses and enjoined its enforcement.[2] . . . .

. . . .

[The court held that the IDEA does not require the school district to provide the services at KDM's school.]

III. THE OREGON REGULATION AS APPLIED DOES NOT VIOLATE THE FEDERAL CONSTITUTION

A. The Free Exercise Clause

The narrow question before us is whether the free exercise rights of KDM and his parents were impermissibly burdened by the application of Oregon's regulation, which precludes the District from providing special education services to KDM at the sectarian school he attended. In deciding that question we are guided by the distinction the Supreme Court has recognized in the Establishment Clause context between a statute's invalidity on its face and its invalidity in particular applications. Whatever the impact of the regulation might be in other factually distinct situations, this is not a case in which the regulation impinges on plaintiffs' free exercise rights. The parties stipulated that the service provided to KDM at the fire hall down the street from the school twice a week for ninety minutes is in compliance with KDM's statutory individualized education plan, the adequacy of which is not in dispute, and that he could safely travel there—indeed, the vision specialist comes to KDM's school, picks him up and then returns him to his school. Moreover, plaintiffs have stipulated that the vision specialist's services would not be provided in-class at Harbor Baptist but in a separate room. Thus, there is no support for the district court's finding that the regulation forces KDM and his parents to choose between enrolling at Harbor Baptist and receiving special education at the fire hall or enrolling at a nonreligious school and receiving in-class services. In sum, there is no showing that application of the regulation to KDM's case burdens KDM's or his parents' free exercise of their religion.

While the Oregon regulation is not "neutral" because it restricts the provision of services to "religiously-neutral settings," as applied here it does not have "the object or purpose . . . [of] suppression of religion or religious conduct." *Church of the Lukumi Babalu Aye, Inc. v. City of Hialeah*, 508 U.S. 520, 533 . . . (1993). KDM is not subjected to "official action that targets religious conduct for distinctive treatment." His case is wholly unlike *Brown v. Borough of Mahaffey*, 35 F.3d 846 (3d Cir. 1994), involving the deliberate installation by the city of a gate impeding access to a particular revival meeting, or *Hartmann v. Stone*, 68 F.3d 973 (6th Cir. 1995), involving an Army regulation banning all religious practice by day care providers on the base. Nor is *Peter v. Wedl* analogous because under the facts of that case, as noted, plaintiff indeed was

2. The record does not disclose whether Reedsport or other school districts provide services at nonsectarian private schools, but the regulation does not preclude them from doing so.

forced to choose between enrolling in the sectarian school or receiving services essential to his ability to attend school.

That the regulation, standing alone, "discriminates" against students in religious schools, i.e., treats them differently by denying them state services on the school grounds, does not result in a burden on the free exercise of religion by someone in the position of KDM or his parents. We agree with the court in *Strout v. Albanese*, 178 F.3d 57 (1st Cir. 1999) . . . , upholding, against a Free Exercise challenge, a Maine statute funding grants to private schools for students in communities without public education facilities, provided the schools are nonsectarian. The court distinguished *Lukumi* because there was no evidence of "a substantial animus . . . that motivated the law in question." Here, the District's solicitousness in accommodating KDM could hardly be said to reflect a purpose to "suppress[] religion or religious conduct." The mere fact that the District makes its service to KDM available in the fire hall down the street from his school does not amount to suppression of religion or religious conduct.

We conclude that Oregon's regulation as applied to KDM and his parents does not impose an impermissible burden on their free exercise of religion.

B. The Establishment Clause

. . . .

[Citing *Zobrest* and *Agostini*, the court found that the program did not violate the Establishment Clause.]

. . . .

Notes, Comments, and Questions

1. *Gary S.* upheld the IDEA insofar as it distinguished between the level of services school districts must provide to children in public schools and private schools and in particular between public schools and private religious schools. *KDM* upheld a restriction against providing IDEA services in religious schools. Compare these decisions with *Peter v. Wedl*, 155 F.3d 992 (8th Cir. 1998). In *Wedl*, the school district asserted that it consistently applied a policy of not providing special education services on-site to children with disabilities in private schools, regardless of whether the schools were religious or secular. *Id.* at 995. However, the court found that despite this policy, the school district provided IDEA services at non-religious private schools and home schools while refusing to do so at religious schools. *Id.* at 995. In vacating an award of summary judgment against the parents, the court stated:

> ISD No. 273's invocation of a "long-standing policy" rings hollow in light of its actual practice of providing services to disabled children at private nonreligious preschools and at home schools. Indeed, ISD No. 273's alleged policy has not been used to deny students at private nonreligious schools paraprofessional services, and appears to manifest itself only when disabled children at private religious schools request these services. While ISD No. 273 has alleged that it created its policy to ensure the quality and integration of

> services and to contain costs, this appears to be a mere ad hoc rationalization of an irrational practice. ISD has not attempted to explain how the goals of its alleged policy are served by denying services to students at private religious schools but allowing these services to students at home schools or at private nonreligious preschools, and there is no evidence that any of these goals are furthered by denying Aaron a paraprofessional at Calvin Christian School. . . .
>
> Viewed in its entirety, the evidence in this case strongly suggests that ISD No. 273's policy is merely a pretext for religious discrimination. . . .

Id. at 997. Can you distinguish *Wedl* from *Gary S.* and *KDM*? Does the Supreme Court's decision in *Locke* shed any light on this question?

2. The Supreme Court decided *Locke* before *Gary S.* and after *KDM* and *Wedl*. Are these cases consistent with *Locke*?

Chapter 8

Change in Educational Placement for Disciplinary Reasons

Introduction

This chapter covers issues relating to the rights of children with disabilities whose local school districts seek to change their educational placement for disciplinary reasons. Section One highlights *Goss v. Lopez*, which established that public school students are entitled to due process protections when their school district seeks to remove them from school for disciplinary reasons. *Goss* helped set the stage for *Honig v. Doe*, the subject of Section Two, in which the Supreme Court recognized that the IDEA prohibits a public school from removing a child with a disability from school for disciplinary reasons without following IDEA's procedural protections. Several years after *Honig*, Congress amended the IDEA to create a process for changing the educational placement of a child with a disability for disciplinary reasons. Section Three provides excerpts from the amendments and describes the process for changing the educational placement of a child for disciplinary reasons. Section Four describes the relationship between the procedures that are available to challenge disciplinary removals and IDEA's other procedural protections.

As you are reading the cases and other materials in this chapter, consider whether Congress and the courts have struck a proper balance between the competing interests school districts have in providing a safe school environment and the interests of students with disabilities in receiving an education. What are the strengths and weaknesses of the system? How would you improve it?

Problem

W.R. is a tenth grader at South Shore High School. He is diagnosed with Attention Deficit Hyperactivity Disorder, Generalized Anxiety Disorder, and Obsessive Compulsive Disorder. He receives special education and related services pursuant to an IEP in the form of resource room, group and individual counseling, and integrated co-teaching classes in which special education and general education teachers share teaching responsibilities. W.R.'s IEP states:

> W.R. often exercises bad judgment, especially in trying to make and keep friends. He is susceptible to suggestion and fails to foresee the consequences of his actions. The school psychologist will meet with W.R. in weekly

> half-hour sessions, primarily focused on discussing good and bad influences among W.R.'s friends. The psychologist will focus on methods to avoid peer pressure and ways to seek good role models.

W.R. was home alone one Saturday night. A group of his friends who were cruising around town stopped at his house and urged him to join them. W.R., both excited about the opportunity yet aware that this might not be a good idea, tried to employ the avoidance techniques the psychologist taught him. Eventually, however, W.R. joined them. While they were driving, one of the guys asked W.R. for a suggestion about what to do. They laughed when W.R. suggested they go see "Justice Team Seven," the latest superhero action movie. They wanted something more exciting. W.R. suggested they go to the high school and break into the athletic department storage shed. (W.R. had just been cut from the baseball team.) When they got there, W.R. broke in and found several bags of soil, fertilizer, and grass seed. One of the group members suggested that they pour the bags onto the field and write an impolite message to the principal. They did so, with W.R. joining in.

Later that night, one of the friends had a bad allergic reaction to the fertilizer. He went to the hospital for treatment and confessed what he had done. The doctor urged him to admit this to the school principal, and he did. The principal investigated the incident. Following a brief hearing at which she allowed W.R. to explain his side of the story, the principal suspended W.R. for ten days and recommended a further suspension of twenty additional days. She notified W.R.'s parents of their right to appeal the ten-day suspension and the additional twenty-day suspension to the Board of Education. She also informed them that, pursuant to the IDEA, they could appeal her decision to an impartial hearing officer. Finally, she indicated that a manifestation determination review was scheduled in seven days and they were free to participate and provide any relevant material or evidence.

The principal removed W.R. from the regular classroom to the in-school suspension room to serve his suspension. There, W.R. works on his assignments under the supervision of a school aide. He receives occasional visits from the resource room teacher to help with his work. He can leave the room for physical education class, counseling sessions, bathroom breaks, and lunch, but otherwise he is not permitted to leave.

W.R.'s parents appealed the suspension to the Board of Education, which denied the appeal. His parents have now come to you for advice and you have agreed to represent them and W.R. Three days have passed since W.R.'s suspension began. The manifestation determination review meeting is scheduled in four days. What are W.R.'s procedural and educational rights? How will you proceed? What evidence will you submit at the manifestation determination review? What arguments can you make that W.R.'s behavior was a manifestation of his disability? What arguments might the district make in opposition? Do you have other procedural options besides participating in the review?

Section One
The Right to Due Process Prior to Suspension from Public School

Goss v. Lopez

419 U.S. 565 (1975)

Mr. Justice White delivered the opinion of the Court.

This appeal by various administrators of the Columbus, Ohio, Public School System (CPSS) challenges the judgment of a three-judge federal court, declaring that appellees—various high school students in the CPSS—were denied due process of law contrary to the command of the Fourteenth Amendment in that they were temporarily suspended from their high schools without a hearing either prior to suspension or within a reasonable time thereafter ....

I

Ohio law, Rev.Code Ann. § 3313.64 (1972), provides for free education to all children between the ages of six and 21. Section 3313.66 of the Code empowers the principal of an Ohio public school to suspend a pupil for misconduct for up to 10 days or to expel him. In either case, he must notify the student's parents within 24 hours and state the reasons for his action. A pupil who is expelled, or his parents, may appeal the decision to the Board of Education and in connection therewith shall be permitted to be heard at the board meeting. ... No similar procedure is provided ... for a suspended student. ...

The nine named appellees, each of whom alleged that he or she had been suspended from public high school in Columbus for up to 10 days without a hearing pursuant to § 3313.66, filed an action under 42 U.S.C. § 1983 against the Columbus Board of Education and various administrators of the CPSS. The complaint sought a declaration that § 3313.66 was unconstitutional in that it permitted public school administrators to deprive plaintiffs of their rights to an education without a hearing of any kind, in violation of the procedural due process component of the Fourteenth Amendment. ...

....

II

At the outset, appellants contend that because there is no constitutional right to an education at public expense, the Due Process Clause does not protect against expulsions from the public school system. This position misconceives the nature of the issue and is refuted by prior decisions. The Fourteenth Amendment forbids the State to deprive any person of life, liberty, or property without due process of law. Protected interests in property are normally "not created by the Constitution. Rather, they are created and their dimensions are defined" by an independent source such as state statutes or rules entitling the citizen to certain benefits.

....

Here, on the basis of state law, appellees plainly had legitimate claims of entitlement to a public education. Ohio Rev.Code Ann. §§ 3313.48 and 3313.64 (1972 and Supp. 1973) direct local authorities to provide a free education to all residents between five and 21 years of age .... It is true that § 3313.66 of the Code permits school principals to suspend students for up to 10 days; but suspensions may not be imposed without any grounds whatsoever. All of the schools had their own rules specifying the grounds for expulsion or suspension. Having chosen to extend the right to an education to people of appellees' class generally, Ohio may not withdraw that right on grounds of misconduct, absent fundamentally fair procedures to determine whether the misconduct has occurred.

Although Ohio may not be constitutionally obligated to establish and maintain a public school system, it has nevertheless done so and has required its children to attend. Those young people do not "shed their constitutional rights" at the schoolhouse door. The authority possessed by the State to prescribe and enforce standards of conduct in its schools, although concededly very broad, must be exercised consistently with constitutional safeguards. Among other things, the State is constrained to recognize a student's legitimate entitlement to a public education as a property interest which is protected by the Due Process Clause and which may not be taken away for misconduct without adherence to the minimum procedures required by that Clause.

The Due Process Clause also forbids arbitrary deprivations of liberty.... School authorities here suspended appellees from school for periods of up to 10 days based on charges of misconduct. If sustained and recorded, those charges could seriously damage the students' standing with their fellow pupils and their teachers as well as interfere with later opportunities for higher education and employment. It is apparent that the claimed right of the State to determine unilaterally and without process whether that misconduct has occurred immediately collides with the requirements of the Constitution.

....

III

"Once it is determined that due process applies, the question remains what process is due." We turn to that question, fully realizing as our cases regularly do that the interpretation and application of the Due Process Clause are intensely practical matters and that "[the] very nature of due process negates any concept of inflexible procedures universally applicable to every imaginable situation." ....

There are certain bench marks to guide us .... *Mullane* v. *Central Hanover Trust Co.*, 339 U.S. 306 ... (1950), a case often invoked by later opinions, said that "[many] controversies have raged about the cryptic and abstract words of the Due Process Clause but there can be no doubt that at a minimum they require that deprivation of life, liberty or property by adjudication be preceded by notice and opportunity for hearing appropriate to the nature of the case." *Id.*, at 313 . . . . At the very minimum, therefore, students facing suspension and the consequent interference with a protected property interest must be given *some* kind of notice and afforded *some* kind of hearing. . . .

It also appears from our cases that the timing and content of the notice and the nature of the hearing will depend on appropriate accommodation of the competing interests involved. The student's interest is to avoid unfair or mistaken exclusion from the educational process, with all of its unfortunate consequences. The Due Process Clause will not shield him from suspensions properly imposed, but it disserves both his interest and the interest of the State if his suspension is in fact unwarranted. The concern would be mostly academic, if the disciplinary process were a totally accurate, unerring process, never mistaken and never unfair. Unfortunately, that is not the case, and no one suggests that it is. Disciplinarians, although proceeding in utmost good faith, frequently act on the reports and advice of others; and the controlling facts and the nature of the conduct under challenge are often disputed. The risk of error is not at all trivial, and it should be guarded against if that may be done without prohibitive cost or interference with the educational process.

The difficulty is that our schools are vast and complex. Some modicum of discipline and order is essential if the educational function is to be performed. Events calling for discipline are frequent occurrences and sometimes require immediate, effective action. Suspension is considered not only to be a necessary tool to maintain order but a valuable educational device. The prospect of imposing elaborate hearing requirements in every suspension case is viewed with great concern, and many school authorities may well prefer the untrammeled power to act unilaterally, unhampered by rules about notice and hearing. But it would be a strange disciplinary system in an educational institution if no communication was sought by the disciplinarian with the student in an effort to inform him of his dereliction and to let him tell his side of the story in order to make sure that an injustice is not done. . . .

We do not believe that school authorities must be totally free from notice and hearing requirements if their schools are to operate with acceptable efficiency. Students facing temporary suspension have interests qualifying for protection of the Due Process Clause, and due process requires, in connection with a suspension of 10 days or less, that the student be given oral or written notice of the charges against him and, if he denies them, an explanation of the evidence the authorities have and an opportunity to present his side of the story. The Clause requires at least these rudimentary precautions against unfair or mistaken findings of misconduct and arbitrary exclusion from school.

There need be no delay between the time "notice" is given and the time of the hearing. In the great majority of cases the disciplinarian may informally discuss the alleged misconduct with the student minutes after it has occurred. We hold only that, in being given an opportunity to explain his version of the facts at this discussion, the student first be told what he is accused of doing and what the basis of the accusation is. . . . Since the hearing may occur almost immediately following the misconduct, it follows that as a general rule notice and hearing should precede removal of the student from school. We agree with the District Court, however, that there are recurring situations in which prior notice and hearing cannot be insisted upon. Students whose presence poses a continuing danger to persons or property or an ongoing threat of disrupting the academic process may be immediately removed from school. In such cases, the necessary notice and rudimentary hearing should follow as soon as practicable . . . .

. . . .

We stop short of construing the Due Process Clause to require, countrywide, that hearings in connection with short suspensions must afford the student the opportunity to secure counsel, to confront and cross-examine witnesses supporting the charge, or to call his own witnesses to verify his version of the incident. Brief disciplinary suspensions are almost countless. To impose in each such case even truncated trial-type procedures might well overwhelm administrative facilities in many places and, by diverting resources, cost more than it would save in educational effectiveness. . . .

On the other hand, requiring effective notice and informal hearing permitting the student to give his version of the events will provide a meaningful hedge against erroneous action. At least the disciplinarian will be alerted to the existence of disputes about facts and arguments about cause and effect. He may then determine himself to summon the accuser, permit cross-examination, and allow the student to present his own witnesses. In more difficult cases, he may permit counsel. In any event, his discretion will be more informed and we think the risk of error substantially reduced.

. . . .

We should also make it clear that we have addressed ourselves solely to the short suspension, not exceeding 10 days. Longer suspensions or expulsions for the remainder of the school term, or permanently, may require more formal procedures. . . .

IV

The District Court found each of the suspensions involved here to have occurred without a hearing, either before or after the suspension, and that each suspension was therefore invalid and the statute unconstitutional insofar as it permits such suspensions without notice or hearing. Accordingly, the judgment is

Affirmed.

[The dissenting opinion of Justice Powell, joined by Chief Justice Burger and Justices Blackmun and Rehnquist, is omitted.]

Notes, Comments, and Questions

1. What was the Court's holding in *Goss*? What rules did the court establish for school districts to follow when suspending a child? What is the rule if a child poses an immediate threat to persons, property, or the academic process?

2. The Court in *Goss* used the following syllogism to find that a child in Ohio has the right to an education: state law is the source of property rights; Ohio State law creates a right to a public education for individuals between the ages of six and twenty-one; therefore, individuals in Ohio between the ages of six and twenty-one have a right to a public education. After stating this syllogism, the Court pointed out that Ohio law also allows a principal to suspend a child for up to ten days without a hearing. Why didn't the Court treat this as a limit on Ohio's right to a public education? Should the Court have ruled that Ohio law gives an individual the right to a public education except when the principal unilaterally suspends the individual for up to ten days? The Court in *Goss* implicitly rejected this argument by stating that a principal cannot suspend a student for no reason, and stated that each school in the case had published grounds for suspension. What if the school districts had not published grounds for suspension? Did the right to due process in *Goss* depend ultimately on the fortuity that the school districts chose to promulgate rules stating grounds for suspension? Does due process require publishing such rules?

3. What if Ohio responded to *Goss* by repealing the law creating the right to a public education? Do you think such an action could be challenged successfully on federal constitutional grounds?

4. Did *Goss* strike the appropriate balance between the rights of students and the need for order in schools?

5. The Court in *Goss* left open the issue of the proper procedures to follow for suspensions longer than ten days. What do you think the procedures should be?

Section Two
The IDEA'S Protections Against Disciplinary Changes in Educational Placement for Children with Disabilities

Honig v. Doe

484 U.S. 305 (1988)

Justice Brennan delivered the opinion of the Court.

As a condition of federal financial assistance, the Education of the Handicapped Act requires states to ensure a "free appropriate public education" for all disabled children within their jurisdictions. In aid of this goal, the Act establishes a comprehensive system of procedural safeguards designed to ensure parental participation in decisions concerning the education of their disabled children and to provide administrative and judicial review of any decisions with which those parents disagree. Among these safeguards is the so-called "stay-put" provision, which directs that a disabled child "shall remain in [his or her] then current placement" pending completion of any review proceedings, unless the parents and state or local educational agencies otherwise agree. 20 U.S.C. § 1415(e)(3). [The "stay-put" provision is currently Section 1415(j).] Today we must decide whether, in the face of this statutory prescription, state or local authorities may nevertheless unilaterally exclude disabled children from the classroom for dangerous or disruptive conduct growing out of their disabilities. . . .

I

. . . .

The present dispute grows out of the effort of certain officials of the San Francisco Unified School District (SFUSD) to expel two emotionally disturbed children from school indefinitely for violent and disruptive conduct related to their disabilities. In November 1980, respondent John Doe assaulted another student at the Louise Lombard School, a developmental center for disabled children. Doe's April 1980 IEP identified him as a socially and physically awkward 17-year old who experienced considerable difficulty controlling his impulses and anger. Among the goals set out in his IEP was "[i]mprovement in [his] ability to relate to [his] peers [and to] cope with frustrating situations without resorting to aggressive acts." Frustrating situations, however, were an unfortunately prominent feature of Doe's school career: physical abnormalities, speech difficulties, and poor grooming habits had made him the target of teasing and ridicule as early as the first grade; his 1980 IEP reflected his continuing difficulties with peers, noting that his social skills had deteriorated and that he could tolerate only minor frustration before exploding.

On November 6, 1980, Doe responded to the taunts of a fellow student in precisely the explosive manner anticipated by his IEP: he choked the student with sufficient force to leave abrasions on the child's neck, and kicked out a school window while being escorted to the principal's office afterwards. Doe admitted his misconduct and the school subsequently suspended him for five days. Thereafter, his principal referred the matter to the SFUSD Student Placement Committee (SPC or Committee) with the recommendation that Doe be expelled. On the day the suspension was to end, the SPC notified Doe's mother that it was proposing to exclude her child permanently from SFUSD and was therefore extending his suspension until such time as the expulsion proceedings were completed. . . .

After unsuccessfully protesting these actions by letter, Doe brought this suit against a host of local school officials and the State Superintendent of Public Instruction. . . .

Respondent Jack Smith was identified as an emotionally disturbed child by the time he entered the second grade in 1976. School records prepared that year indicated that he was unable "to control verbal or physical outburst[s]" and exhibited a "[s]evere disturbance in relationships with peers and adults." Further evaluations subsequently revealed that he had been physically and emotionally abused as an infant and young child and that, despite above average intelligence, he experienced academic and social difficulties as a result of extreme hyperactivity and low self-esteem. Of particular concern was Smith's propensity for verbal hostility; one evaluator noted that the child reacted to stress by "attempt[ing] to cover his feelings of low self worth through aggressive behavior[,] . . . primarily verbal provocations."

Based on these evaluations, SFUSD placed Smith in a learning center for emotionally disturbed children. His grandparents, however, believed that his needs would be better served in the public school setting and, in September 1979, the school district acceded to their requests and enrolled him at A.P. Giannini Middle School. His February 1980 IEP recommended placement in a Learning Disability Group, stressing the need for close supervision and a highly structured environment. Like earlier evaluations, the February 1980 IEP noted that Smith was easily distracted, impulsive, and anxious; it therefore proposed a half-day schedule and suggested that the placement be undertaken on a trial basis.

At the beginning of the next school year, Smith was assigned to a full-day program; almost immediately thereafter he began misbehaving. School officials met twice with his grandparents in October 1980 to discuss returning him to a half-day program; although his grandparents agreed to the reduction, they apparently were never apprised of their right to challenge the decision through EHA procedures. The school officials also warned them that if the child continued his disruptive behavior—which included stealing, extorting money from fellow students, and making sexual comments to female classmates—they would seek to expel him. On November 14, they made good on this threat, suspending Smith for five days after he made further lewd comments. His principal referred the matter to the SPC, which recommended exclusion from SFUSD. As it did in John Doe's case, the Committee scheduled a hearing and extended the suspension indefinitely pending a final disposition in the matter. On November 28, Smith's counsel protested these actions on grounds essentially identical to those raised by Doe, and the SPC agreed to cancel the hearing and return Smith to a half-day program at A.P. Giannini or to provide home tutoring. Smith's grandparents chose the latter option . . . .

. . . .

III

The language of § 1415(e)(3) is unequivocal. It states plainly that during the pendency of any proceedings initiated under the Act, unless the state or local agency and the parents or guardian of a disabled child otherwise agree, "the child *shall* remain in the then current educational placement." § 1415(e)(3) (emphasis added). Faced with this clear directive, petitioner asks us to read a "dangerousness" exception into the stay-put provision on the basis of either of two essentially inconsistent assumptions: first, that Congress thought the residual authority of school officials to exclude dangerous students from the classroom too obvious for comment; or second, that

Congress inadvertently failed to provide such authority and this Court must therefore remedy the oversight. Because we cannot accept either premise, we decline petitioner's invitation to rewrite the statute.

Petitioner's arguments proceed, he suggests, from a simple, common sense proposition: Congress could not have intended the stay-put provision to be read literally, for such a construction leads to the clearly unintended, and untenable, result that school districts must return violent or dangerous students to school while the often lengthy EHA proceedings run their course. We think it clear, however, that Congress very much meant to strip schools of the *unilateral* authority they had traditionally employed to exclude disabled students, particularly emotionally disturbed students, from school. In so doing, Congress did not leave school administrators powerless to deal with dangerous students; it did, however, deny school officials their former right to "self-help," and directed that in the future the removal of disabled students could be accomplished only with the permission of the parents or, as a last resort, the courts.

As noted above, Congress passed the EHA after finding that school systems across the country had excluded one out of every eight disabled children from classes. In drafting the law, Congress was largely guided by the recent decisions in *Mills v. Board of Education of District of Columbia*, 348 F.Supp. 866 (1972), and *PARC*, 343 F.Supp. 279 (1972), both of which involved the exclusion of hard-to-handle disabled students. *Mills* in particular demonstrated the extent to which schools used disciplinary measures to bar children from the classroom. There, school officials had labeled four of the seven minor plaintiffs "behavioral problems," and had excluded them from classes without providing any alternative education to them or any notice to their parents. After finding that this practice was not limited to the named plaintiffs but affected in one way or another an estimated class of 12,000 to 18,000 disabled students, the District Court enjoined future exclusions, suspensions, or expulsions on "grounds of discipline."

Congress attacked such exclusionary practices in a variety of ways. It required participating States to educate *all* disabled children, regardless of the severity of their disabilities, and included within the definition of "handicapped" those children with serious emotional disturbances. It further provided for meaningful parental participation in all aspects of a child's educational placement, and barred schools, through the stay-put provision, from changing that placement over the parent's objection until all review proceedings were completed. Recognizing that those proceedings might prove long and tedious, the Act's drafters did not intend § 1415(e)(3) [the stay-put provision] to operate inflexibly, and they therefore allowed for interim placements where parents and school officials are able to agree on one. Conspicuously absent from § 1415(e)(3), however, is any emergency exception for dangerous students. This absence is all the more telling in light of the injunctive decree issued in *PARC*, which permitted school officials unilaterally to remove students in "'extraordinary circumstances,'" 343 F.Supp., at 301. Given the lack of any similar exception in *Mills*, and the close attention Congress devoted to these "landmark" decisions, we can only include that the omission was intentional; we are therefore not at liberty to engraft onto the statute an exception Congress chose not to create.

Our conclusion that § 1415(e)(3) means what it says does not leave educators hamstrung. The Department of Education has observed that, "[w]hile the [child's] placement may not be changed [during any complaint proceeding], this does not preclude the agency from using its normal procedures for dealing with children who are endangering themselves or others." Such procedures may include the use of study carrels, timeouts, detention, or the restriction of privileges. More drastically, where a student poses an immediate threat to the safety of others, officials may temporarily suspend him or her for up to 10 schooldays. This authority, which respondent in no way disputes, not only ensures that school administrators can protect the safety of others by promptly removing the most dangerous of students, it also provides a "cooling down" period during which officials can initiate IEP review and seek to persuade the child's parents to agree to an interim placement. And in those cases in which the parents of a truly dangerous child adamantly refuse to permit any change in placement, the 10-day respite gives school officials an opportunity to invoke the aid of the courts under § 1415(e)(2) [now § 1415(i)], which empowers courts to grant any appropriate relief.

Petitioner contends, however, that the availability of judicial relief is more illusory than real, because a party seeking review under § 1415(e)(2) must exhaust time-consuming administrative remedies, and because under the Court of Appeals' construction of § 1415(e)(3), courts are as bound by the stay-put provision's "automatic injunction," as are schools. It is true that judicial review is normally not available under § 1415(e)(2) until all administrative proceedings are completed, but as we have previously noted, parents may bypass the administrative process where exhaustion would be futile or inadequate. While many of the EHA's procedural safeguards protect the rights of parents and children, schools can and do seek redress through the administrative review process, and we have no reason to believe that Congress meant to require schools alone to exhaust in all cases, no matter how exigent the circumstances. The burden in such cases, of course, rests with the school to demonstrate the futility or inadequacy of administrative review, but nothing in § 1415(e)(2) suggests that schools are completely barred from attempting to make such a showing. Nor do we think that § 1415(e)(3) operates to limit the equitable powers of district courts such that they cannot, in appropriate cases, temporarily enjoin a dangerous disabled child from attending school. As the EHA's legislative history makes clear, one of the evils Congress sought to remedy was the unilateral exclusion of disabled children by *schools*, not courts, and one of the purposes of § 1415(e)(3), therefore, was "to prevent *school* officials from removing a child from the regular public school classroom over the parents' objection pending completion of the review proceedings." *Burlington Sch. Committee. v. Massachusetts Dep't of Educ.*, 471 U.S., at 373 . . . (emphasis added). The stay-put provision in no way purports to limit or pre-empt the authority conferred on courts by § 1415(e)(2); indeed it says nothing whatever about judicial power.

In short, then, we believe that school officials are entitled to seek injunctive relief under § 1415(e)(2) in appropriate cases. In any such action, § 1415(e)(3) effectively creates a presumption in favor of the child's current educational placement which school officials can overcome only by showing that maintaining the child in his or her current placement is substantially likely to result in injury either to himself or herself, or to others. In the present case, we are satisfied that the District court, in enjoining the state and local defendants from indefinitely suspending respondent or otherwise unilaterally altering his then current placement, properly balanced respondent's interest in receiving a free appropriate public education in accordance with the procedures and requirements of the EHA against the interests of the state and local school officials in maintaining a safe learning environment for all their students.

....

[The concurring opinion of Chief Justice Rehnquist and the dissenting opinion of Justice Scalia, joined by Justice O'Connor, are omitted.]

Notes, Comments, and Questions

1. The school district in *Honig* argued that Congress could not have intended the "stay-put" provision in Section 1415(e)(3) to prevent a school district from removing a dangerous child from school until all due process proceedings were completed. The Court disagreed. Do the 1997 amendments to the IDEA, described in Section Three, address this question?

2. Do you agree with Justice Brennan that the district court properly balanced Doe's and Smith's interest in receiving a free appropriate public education with the school district's interest in ensuring a safe environment for all students? According to Justice Brennan, the school district claimed its "arguments proceed . . . from a simple, commensense proposition: Congress could not have intended the stay-put provision to be read literally, for such a construction leads to the clearly unintended, and untenable, result that school districts must return violent or dangerous students to school while the often lengthy EHA proceedings run their course." 484 U.S. at 323. Justice Brennan answered, "We think it clear, however, that Congress very much meant to strip schools of the *unilateral* authority they had traditionally employed to exclude disabled students, particularly emotionally disturbed students, from school." *Id.* Justice Brennan concluded that although school districts are without power to remove students unilaterally for more than ten days, Congress did not eliminate the authority of courts to remove dangerous students from schools quickly, without requiring school districts to exhaust administrative remedies. Thus, school districts could seek judicial relief to remove from school students with disabilities they deem dangerous. What should a school district be required to prove in such a case?

Section Three
1997 Amendments to the IDEA

A. Selections from Section 1415(k)

In 1997, Congress responded to *Honig* by adding 20 U.S.C. § 1415(k) to the IDEA, which provides procedures for districts to follow when seeking to change the educational placement of a child with a disability for disciplinary reasons. Excerpts from the current version of Section 1415(k) follow. As you read them, consider what, if anything, survives from *Honig*. Compare the procedures in Section 1415(k) with the procedures in *Honig*. Which are more clear? Which more effectively balance the rights of a student with a disability to receive an education with the interest of school officials in ensuring a safe school environment? Consider the impact, if any, that *Goss* had on Section 1415(k). What are the strengths and weaknesses of Section 1415(k)? What, if anything, would you change?

(k) Placement in alternative educational setting

(1) Authority of school personnel

. . . .

(B) Authority

School personnel under this subsection may remove a child with a disability who violates a code of student conduct from their current placement to an appropriate interim alternative educational setting, another setting, or suspension, for not more than 10 school days (to the extent such alternatives are applied to children without disabilities).

(C) Additional authority

If school personnel seek to order a change in placement that would exceed 10 school days and the behavior that gave rise to the violation of the school code is determined not to be a manifestation of the child's disability pursuant to subparagraph (E), the relevant disciplinary procedures applicable to children without disabilities may be applied to the child in the same manner and for the same duration in which the procedures would be applied to children without disabilities . . . although it may be provided in an interim alternative educational setting.

(D) Services

A child with a disability who is removed from the child's current placement under subparagraph (G)(irrespective of whether the behavior is determined to be a manifestation of the child's disability) or subparagraph (C) shall—

(i) continue to receive educational services . . . so as to enable the child to continue to participate in the general education curriculum, although in another setting, and to progress toward meeting the goals set out in the child's IEP; and

(ii) receive, as appropriate, a functional behavioral assessment, behavioral intervention services and modifications, that are designed to address the behavior violation so that it does not recur.

(E) Manifestation determination

(i) In general

Except as provided in subparagraph (B), within 10 school days of any decision to change the placement of a child with a disability because of a violation of a code of student conduct, the local educational agency, the parent, and relevant members of the IEP Team (as determined by the parent and the local educational agency) shall review all relevant information in the student's file, including the child's IEP, any teacher observations, and any relevant information provided by the parents to determine—

(I) if the conduct in question was caused by, or had a direct and substantial relationship to, the child's disability; or

(II) if the conduct in question was the direct result of the local educational agency's failure to implement the IEP.

(ii) Manifestation

If the local educational agency, the parent, and relevant members of the IEP Team determine that either subclause (I) or (II) of clause (i) is applicable for the child, the conduct shall be determined to be a manifestation of the child's disability.

(F) Determination that behavior was a manifestation

If the local educational agency, the parent, and relevant members of the IEP Team make the determination that the conduct was a manifestation of the child's disability, the IEP Team shall—

(i) conduct a functional behavioral assessment, and implement a behavioral intervention plan for such child, provided that the local educational agency had not conducted such assessment prior to such determination before the behavior that resulted in a change in placement described in subparagraph (C) or (G);

(ii) in the situation where a behavioral intervention plan has been developed, review the behavioral intervention plan if the child already has such a behavioral intervention plan, and modify it, as necessary, to address the behavior; and

(iii) except as provided in subparagraph (G), return the child to the placement from which the child was removed, unless the parent and the local educational agency agree to a change of placement as part of the modification of the behavioral intervention plan.

(G) Special circumstances

School personnel may remove a student to an interim alternative educational setting for not more than 45 school days without regard to whether the behavior is determined to be a manifestation of the child's disability, in cases where a child—

(i) carries or possesses a weapon to or at school, on school premises, or to or at a school function under the jurisdiction of a State or local educational agency;

(ii) knowingly possesses or uses illegal drugs, or sells or solicits the sale of a controlled substance, while at school, on school premises, or at a school function under the jurisdiction of a State or local educational agency; or

(iii) has inflicted serious bodily injury upon another person while at school, on school premises, or at a school function under the jurisdiction of a State or local educational agency.

(H) Notification

No later than the date on which the decision to take disciplinary action is made, the local educational agency shall notify the parents of that decision, and of all procedural safeguards accorded under this section.

(2) Determination of setting

The interim alternative educational setting in subparagraph (C) and (G) of paragraph 1 shall be determined by the IEP team.

(3) Appeal

(A) In general

The parent of a child with a disability who disagrees with any decision regarding the placement, or the manifestation determination under this subsection, or a local educational agency that believes that maintaining the current placement of the child is substantially likely to result in injury to the child or to others, may request a hearing.

(B) Authority of the hearing officer

(i) In general

A hearing officer shall hear, and make a determination regarding, an appeal requested under subparagraph (A).

(ii) Change of placement order

In making the determination under clause (i), the hearing officer may order a change in placement of a child with a disability. In such situations, the hearing officer may—

(I) return the child with a disability to the placement from which the child was removed; or

(II) order a change in placement of a child with a disability to an appropriate interim alternative educational setting for not more than 45 school days if the hearing officer determines that maintaining the current placement of such child is substantially likely to result in injury to the child or to others.

(4) Placement during appeals

When an appeal under paragraph (3) has been requested by either the parent or the local educational agency—

(A) the child shall remain in the interim alternative educational setting pending the decision of the hearing officer or until the expiration of the time period provided for in paragraph (1)(C), whichever occurs first, unless the parent and the State or local educational agency agree otherwise; and

(B) the State or local educational agency shall arrange for an expedited hearing, which shall occur within 20 school days of the date the hearing is requested and shall result in a determination within 10 school days after the hearing.

....

B. Substantive and Procedural Rights Under Section 1415(k)

Three key questions arise when considering the rights of a child with a disability who is facing removal or has been removed from school for disciplinary reasons. Does the removal constitute a change in placement? What procedural rights apply to the removal? What educational rights does the child have during the removal?

Change in educational placement: Section 1415(k) creates a ten-day dividing line to determine whether a removal is a change in placement. Determining where the dividing line falls, however, is not necessarily as straightforward as counting to ten, as the following three rules demonstrate:

Single removal of not more than ten school days: A single removal of a child for disciplinary purposes from his or her educational placement "for not more than ten school days" is not a change in placement. 20 U.S.C. § 1415(k)(1)(B) (2012).

Multiple removals in the same school year that total more than ten days: "[A] series of removals . . . that total more than ten days in a school year is a change in placement" when the removals "constitute a pattern" because the behavior that prompted each removals is similar, and other factors such as "the length of each removal, the total amount of time the child has been removed, and the proximity of the removals to one another." 20 C.F.R. § 300.536(a)(2) (2015).

Single removal of more than ten straight school days: A single removal of more than ten straight school days is a change in placement. 20 U.S.C. § 1415(k)(1)(c); 34 C.F.R. § 300.536(a)(1).

Procedural Rights: Notice and appeal rights are identical for students with disabilities whose removal is a change in placement and whose removal is not a change in placement. A school district must notify the parents of a decision to take disciplinary action on the day it makes the decision, along with a description of all procedural rights. 20 U.S.C. § 1415(k)(1)(H). A parent who disagrees with a decision regarding placement or a manifestation determination can request a hearing. *Id.* at § (k)(3). The hearing must occur within twenty school days of the parents' request and the decision must be issued within ten school days of the hearing. *Id.* at § (k)(4)(B). The hearing officer may order a change in placement of the child, including returning the child to the original placement. *Id.* at § (3)(b)(ii)(I).

Procedural rights when the removal is not a change in placement: Section 1415(k) does not specify any additional procedural rights of a student with a disability whose removal does not constitute a change in placement. At the very least, the student should be entitled to the procedural rights described in *Goss*, including oral or written notice of the charges against him and the opportunity to explain his side of the story. Are these rights sufficient to protect a student with a disability? Would a student with a speech and language disorder be able to defend himself? What arguments can you make that the procedures in *Goss* do not protect the due process rights of a child with a disability?

Procedural rights when the removal is a change in placement: If the removal is a change in placement, the school district must determine whether the conduct underlying the discipline was "a manifestation of the child's disability." *Id.* at § 1415(k)(1)(E). To make this determination, a team composed of the school district, a parent, and relevant members of the IEP team as determined by the parent and the school district conducts a manifestation determination review (MDR). *Id.* at § (E)(i). The MDR team must "review all relevant information in the student's file, including the child's IEP, any teacher observations, and any relevant information provided by the student's parents." *Id.* The MDR team must complete the MDR within ten days of the decision to change the placement of a child with a disability. *Id.* If the MDR team determines that the student's disability caused "or had a substantial relationship to" the conduct in question or that the conduct was a "direct result" of the school district's "failure to implement the IEP," the MDR team shall determine that the conduct was "a manifestation of the child's disability." *Id.* at § (E)(i) and (ii).

<u>Educational Rights</u>:

Removal that is not a change in placement: A district has three options when removing a child with a disability from his or her classroom for less than ten days. The district can remove a child to "an appropriate interim educational setting, another setting," or a suspension .... *Id.* at § 1415(k)(1)(B). The district must apply these alternatives to the same extent it applies them to children who do not have disabilities. *Id.*

Removal that is a change in placement:

1) <u>Behavior was not a manifestation of the child's disability</u>: If the behavior that resulted in the discipline was not a manifestation of the child's disability, the district can remove the child for the same amount of time it would remove a child without a disability, but may do so in an interim alternative educational setting. *Id.*

at § 1415(k)(1)(C). The district also must continue to provide the child with educational services necessary to allow "the child to continue to participate in the general education curriculum, although in another setting, and to progress toward meeting the goals set forth in the child's IEP . . . ." *Id.* at § 1415(k)(1)(D)(i). The district must also conduct, as appropriate, a functional behavioral assessment, and provide behavioral intervention services so the behavior does not recur. *Id.* at § (ii). The district must provide all these services even if the district expels the student. *See* Shelton v. Maya Angelou Pub. Charter Sch., 578 F. Supp. 2d 83, 100 (D.D.C. 2008) (finding that hearing officer was correct in concluding that school denied FAPE by failing to conduct a functional behavior analysis and create a behavior intervention plan after it suspended and expelled the child).

2) Behavior was a manifestation of the child's disability: If the behavior "was a manifestation of the child's disability," the district must "return the child to the placement from which" it removed the child. *Id.* at § 1415(k)(1)(F)(iii). The district must also "conduct a functional behavioral assessment and implement a behavioral intervention plan" if it had not already done so or review an existing behavioral intervention plan and make any necessary modifications. *Id.* at § (k)(1)(F)(i) and (ii).

3) Removal for dangerous behavior: Regardless of whether the behavior is a manifestation of a child's disability, a school district may remove the child "to an interim alternative educational setting for not more than 45 school days" for offenses at school or school functions involving weapons, controlled substances, or serious bodily injury. *Id.* at § 1415(k)(1)(G).

4) Appeals: During an appeal, a "child shall remain in the interim alternative setting pending the decision of the hearing officer or the expiration of the time period provided for in the removal . . . , whichever occurs first." *Id.* at § 1415(k)(4)(A).

Note

In creating a ten-day benchmark to trigger a change in educational placement, Congress adopted *Goss*' distinction between a short- and long-term suspension. The Supreme Court has not addressed the issue of what process is due to a student who faces a suspension of more than ten days. Doe v. Todd Cnty. Sch. Dist., 625 F.3d 459, 462 (8th Cir. 2010), *cert. denied*, __ U.S. __, 132 S.Ct. 367 (2011) ("Though the Court has not since addressed what additional process may be required for longer suspensions, ten days has become the statutory benchmark for distinguishing short- and long-term suspensions."). How do you think the Court would rule on a due process challenge to Section 1415(k)'s procedures for removing a child with a disability from his or her educational placement for disciplinary reasons for more than ten days?

C. Legal Issues Involving the Manifestation Determination Review

The manifestation determination review ("MDR") provisions of Sections 1415(k)(1)(E) and (F) raise several policy issues. Why, for example, should the right to a manifestation determination be available only if the removal constitutes a change in educational placement? Is the conduct that prompted the removal any less of a manifestation because the removal was less than ten days? Should the MDR take place prior to the change in placement? Why does the IDEA allow the MDR to take place within ten days of the decision to remove the child rather than immediately? In addition to these policy questions, several legal issues arise in connection with implementing the MDR process.

What if the MDR team does not complete the review within ten days of the decision to remove the child? In *Farrin v. Me. Sch. Admin. Dist. No. 59*, 165 F. Supp. 2d 37 (D. Me. 2001), the court considered a challenge to a manifestation determination on the ground, among others, that the MDR team conducted the review twelve days after the decision to change the child's placement. The court denied the claim, finding that the delay did not prejudice the parents' procedural rights or the child's educational rights:

> The hearing officer found that the preponderance of the evidence in this case failed to demonstrate any harm flowing to the Plaintiffs as a result of the late . . . [manifestation determination]. The Court agrees. Despite the delay, both parents attended the manifestation review meeting, and had an opportunity to participate in it (although they chose not to). There is no evidence that holding the meeting two days late affected its outcome, or the method by which the . . . [MDR team] addressed the issues. Finally, it does not appear that Jacob suffered any ill effects from the tardiness of the meeting, considering that his parents and teacher arranged for him to receive remedial reading instruction to make up for lost time.

Id. at 51.

Who must be on the MDR team? The MDR team is composed of the school district, the parents, and "relevant members of the IEP Team as determined by the parent and the district." 20 U.S.C. § 1415(k)(1)(E)(i). In *Fitzgerald v. Fairfax Cnty. Sch. Bd.*, 556 F. Supp. 2d 543 (E.D. Va. 2008), the parents claimed that the category of individuals included as "relevant members of the IEP team" is limited to individuals who know "the child personally and . . . previously served on one of the child's IEP teams." *Id.* at 555. The court rejected this argument. It stated:

> The IDEA does not so require. First, the IDEA's categories of individuals who must attend a child's IEP meeting demonstrates Congress's intent to include *both* individuals who know the child personally and individuals who have certain professional expertise, but need not know the child personally. . . . Accordingly, the § 1415(k) language stating that only relevant members of the IEP team need attend an MDR hearing does not support the proposition that each MDR committee member must know the student personally; rather, each committee member must serve some purpose pertinent to the MDR.
>
> . . . .

> Nor is there any support for plaintiffs' proposition that all individuals involved in the MDR must have served on one of the child's previous IEP teams. Plaintiffs do not cite to a single case in support of this proposition, nor has any been found. This is hardly surprising because requiring every MDR committee member to have served on the child's IEP teams and to have had personal interactions with the student would pose many practical problems, especially considering that MDR hearings must be held within ten days of the decision to suspend the child for more than ten days. Such practical difficulties were considered by the drafters of the 2004 IDEA amendments, which were designed in part to streamline IEP and MDR processes. A requirement that [a school district] must convene, within ten days of a decision to discipline a disabled child, an MDR committee comprised only of persons who know the child personally and who have served on one of his previous IEP teams is inconsistent with the streamlining purpose of the IDEA's amendments.

Id. at 556.

Who determines the composition of the MDR team? In *Fitzgerald,* the parents also claimed that they had the right to consent to the members of the MDR team. They based their argument on Section 1415(k)(1)(E)(i), which states that the MDR team is to be composed of various categories of individuals "as determined by the parent and" the school district. The court rejected this argument. It reasoned that the MDR team is a subset of the IEP team, and because the parent does not have veto power over the composition of the child's IEP team, the parent does not have veto power over the composition of the MDR team. *Id.* at 552–53. The court stated that under Section 1415(k)(1)(E)(i), the school district decides which school district personnel will serve on the team and the parents may invite other members. *Id.* at 554.

What materials must the MDR team review and when must it review them? In *Fitzgerald*, the court considered the parents' claim that the members of Kevin's MDR team had to review all the material in his file before the MDR hearing. In rejecting the parents' claim, the court ruled:

> As an initial matter, plaintiffs cite no authority for the proposition that all MDR committee members must review every piece of information in the student's file before an MDR hearing. Rather, the statute requires that the MDR committee "shall review all relevant information in the student's file, including the child's IEP, any teacher observations, and any relevant information provided by the parents" to make its manifestation determination. This language does not require each member to read before the meeting every piece of information in the student's file. All the statute requires is that, before reaching a manifestation determination, the team must review the information pertinent to that decision, including the child's IEP, his teacher's comments, and any information provided by the parents. And this review clearly may occur before or during the course of an MDR hearing.

Id. at 559.

Must the decision of the MDR team be unanimous? In *Fitzgerald*, the parents claimed that the school district did not give "them an 'equal right' to determine whether Kevin's conduct was a manifestation of his disability." *Id.* at 557. Construing this as a claim that parents either have a "right to vote at an MDR hearing or that the manifestation determination . . . [must] be unanimous, the court rejected both:

> More importantly, as already noted, the IDEA's emphasis on parental involvement does not give parents the right to veto or otherwise block the . . . [school district's] ability to . . . discipline a student. Parents have a right to participate and be heard in the MDR hearing, but these proceedings may become adversarial, as parents may well disagree with the school's decision to discipline their child. If parents were required to consent to the . . . [school district's] determination, or if parents were allowed to "stack the deck" against the . . . [school district] by inviting several individuals who would vote consistently with the parents' views, the . . . [school district] would effectively be hamstrung, a result not contemplated by the IDEA. Accordingly, the IDEA does not require the . . . [school district] and the parents to reach a consensus regarding the education or discipline of a disabled child. Instead, if a consensus cannot be reached, the . . . [school district] must make a determination, and the parents' only recourse is to appeal that determination.

Id. at 557–58.

In addition to addressing several procedural issues described above, *Fitzgerald* is a good example of a challenge to the merits of a manifestation determination.

Fitzgerald v. Fairfax Cnty. Sch. Bd.

556 F. Supp. 2d 543 (E.D. Va. 2008)

T.S. Ellis, III, United States District Judge.

[P]laintiff Kevin Fitzgerald . . . and his parents challenge the . . . finding of the manifestation determination review ("MDR") held by Fairfax County School Board ("FCSB") that allowed Kevin to be suspended from his school for his involvement in a paintball shooting incident at the school. Specifically, plaintiffs . . . claim that Kevin's conduct was caused by, or had a direct relationship to, Kevin's disability and hence his suspension from school was an impermissible punishment under the IDEA. . . .

I.

In the eighth grade, Kevin, now a senior at Annandale High School, began exhibiting elevated anxiety symptoms, including crying, panic attacks, sweating, tics, and chronic headaches. Because these symptoms interfered with his school attendance and performance, Kevin underwent an evaluation, as a result of which he was categorized as a student with an emotional disability eligible to receive special education services under the IDEA.[3] . . . .

After successfully completing the eighth grade, Kevin began attending Falls Church High School ("FCHS"), where, pursuant to his IEP, he continued receiving special education services. His tenth grade IEP, prepared in April 2005, noted that Kevin had "been drawn into inappropriate behaviors in some of his classes and has been known to be negative and sarcastic toward teachers." As a result, included among the 2005 IEP's objectives for Kevin were to "refrain from conversation with peers that is not on topic of class lesson" and to "distance himself from peers who are behaving inappropriately in class." His eleventh grade IEP, which issued in March 2006 and was in effect at the time of the paintball shooting incident, expressed similar concerns and included a similar objective. . . .

During his eleventh grade year, Kevin engaged in the conduct that is central to this dispute. On December 16, 2006, Kevin and some friends met at a restaurant. At Kevin's suggestion, the boys decided to drive by FCHS and shoot at the school building with paintball guns.[5] Kevin had a paintball gun in his car and offered to drive the four other boys to the school. On the way to the school, Kevin made a detour to another boy's vehicle to retrieve two more paintball guns. The five boys then proceeded to FCHS in Kevin's car where they shot paintballs at the windows of the school building and at various vehicles parked on school property, including school buses. At some point during this first visit to the school, one of the paintball guns malfunctioned, so Kevin drove the boys to retrieve supplies, including CO[2] and more paintballs, from a vehicle belonging to one of the boys. Kevin and the boys then made a second trip to the school and this time Kevin, who was driving, shot at the school while one of the boys held the wheel of Kevin's car. After this second trip, two of the boys decided to leave and asked Kevin to drive them to another location. Kevin did so, and then he and the remaining two boys returned to FCHS to shoot paintballs at the school a third time. As a result of the three attacks on the school, thirty school windows, two school buses, and one school delivery truck had been hit with paintballs. On their way home from the school, Kevin, still driving, failed to obey a stop sign and was stopped by a police officer. The officer noticed the paintball guns and questioned the boys, who denied any wrongdoing. The officer then allowed Kevin and the boys to proceed on their way. Later, when the officer heard reports of paintball vandalism at FCHS, he advised the administration and school police officer, Officer George Davis, that he believed Kevin and his friends had been involved. Officer Davis then questioned Kevin, who, after Officer Davis assured him that the school

3. Kevin has also been diagnosed with Tourette's Syndrome, Attention Deficit Hyperactivity Disorder (ADHD), Generalized Anxiety Disorder (GAD), and Obsessive Compulsive Disorder (OCD).

5. Plaintiffs deny that Kevin was the mastermind of the paintball incident, but three of the four other boys involved in the incident told the school police officer who investigated the incident that it was Kevin's idea to shoot at the school with paintball guns. This is amply supported by the administrative record.

was not planning to pursue criminal charges against the boys, admitted his involvement in the affair.

Virginia law requires the school board to "expel from school attendance for a period of not less than one year any student whom such school board has determined . . . to have possessed . . . a pneumatic gun . . . on school property." Because a paintball gun is statutorily defined as a type of pneumatic gun, the school principal suspended Kevin with a recommendation of expulsion. This recommendation triggered the provisions of the IDEA, which prohibits disciplining a disabled student for more than ten days if the "conduct in question was caused by, or had a direct and substantial relationship to, the child's disability." 20 U.S.C. § 1415(k)(1)(E)(i)(II). Accordingly, school officials scheduled an MDR hearing for January 5, 2007, to determine whether Kevin's conduct in the paintball gun affair was a manifestation of his emotional disability. In accordance with FCSB policies, which required the attendance of certain categories of school personnel at an MDR hearing, the school designated the following people to participate in the MDR hearing: (i) Karen Allison, the special education department chair, (ii) Daniel Eberling, the assistant principal who handled the investigation of the paintball gun incident, (iii) Pamela Wallace, Kevin's special education teacher, (iv) Emily Trudeau, Kevin's eleventh-grade History teacher, and (v) Sonja Hamilton, a school psychologist.

. . . .

The MDR hearing was held on January 5, 2007, and was attended by the five FCSB members, Kevin, and his parents. . . . [T]he MDR hearing included a presentation by Ms. Hamilton of the history of Kevin's disability, his qualification for special education services under the IDEA, and his educational and cognitive test results. The record also reflects that the MDR committee members reviewed evidence regarding Kevin's disciplinary history and inspected reports from Kevin's teachers describing his behavior in class. Finally, the team discussed Kevin's involvement in the paintball incident.

Although Kevin and his parents contended at the MDR hearing that Kevin's conduct in the paintball gun incident was a manifestation of his disability, they did not argue that Kevin had somehow been induced or inveigled by his classmates to participate in the paintball shooting incident. At the conclusion of the MDR hearing, the FCSB members determined, contrary to plaintiffs' view, that Kevin's behavior was not a manifestation of his disability. This MDR finding that Kevin's behavior was not a manifestation of his emotional disability allowed the school to discipline Kevin as it would any other student. 20 U.S.C. § 1415(k)(1)(C). Accordingly, the school principal's recommendation for expulsion was sent to a disciplinary hearing officer for the FCSB superintendent, who reviews all expulsion recommendations before they are sent to the school board. This hearing officer decided that the appropriate sanction was not expulsion, but rather suspension of Kevin for the remainder of his eleventh-grade year. Kevin's parents did not appeal this disciplinary decision.

. . . .

On July 25, 2007, Kevin's parents invoked their right under the due process procedures of the IDEA to a review of the MDR determination that Kevin's behavior was not a manifestation of his disability. . . .

Following the hearing, the IHO . . . . concluded that Kevin's conduct was not a manifestation of his disability. . . .

. . . .

IV.

[T]he only remaining question is whether the IHO's affirmance of the MDR committee's manifestation determination was correct. . . .

First, as the IHO correctly noted, Kevin's anxiety was the "primary basis for his disability classification," rather than the occasional "juvenile outburst[s]" of acting inappropriately in class with friends. The evaluations setting forth Kevin's eligibility under the IDEA described his headaches and school absences, but noted no social problems; indeed, Kevin was described as "academically capable and socially popular." The only evidence of any behavioral problems demonstrated that Kevin sometimes made minor poor choices to impress his friends. For instance, Kevin's 2005 and 2006 IEPs, both of which noted that Kevin had "been drawn into inappropriate behaviors in some of his classes and has been known to be negative and sarcastic toward teachers," suggested that Kevin "refrain from conversation with peers that is not on topic of class lesson" and "distance himself from peers who are behaving inappropriately in class." In addition, at the due process hearing, two of Kevin's teachers testified that Kevin was often persuaded by other students to engage in inappropriate behavior, such as laughing, talking out of turn, or otherwise causing classroom distractions. Such in-class juvenile outbursts to impress friends is not atypical of teenage boys in general.

Even assuming Kevin's disability did cause him to be drawn into inappropriate behaviors at times, the record makes pellucidly clear that far from being drawn into the paintball shooting incident, Kevin played a predominant role in planning and executing it. . . . The entire incident lasted over several hours. Nothing in these facts supports plaintiffs' conclusion that Kevin was impulsively drawn into the paintball incident by his friends as a result of his disability. Indeed, as the IHO pointed out, neither Kevin nor his parents ever suggested at the MDR hearing that Kevin had been drawn into his misconduct by his friends. Kevin simply made a bad decision; he must now live with the consequences.

Finally, the IHO's determination that the live testimony of Ms. Hamilton was more credible than the written reports and letters submitted by Kevin's parents is entitled to due weight. Plaintiffs submitted reports and letters from several individuals, none of whom testified at the due process hearing or was subject to cross-examination.[24] These reports were all solicited by Kevin's parents after the MDR hearing for the purpose of undermining the MDR's result and were based entirely on plaintiffs' versions of the facts; these reports are thus less likely to be objective. Moreover, as Ms. Hamilton pointed out during her testimony, Dr. Waaland's report was based on a factual version of the paintball shooting incident that was inconsistent with the version set forth by Mr. Eberling and Officer Davis. Thus, even if these reports about Kevin's tendency to be drawn into inappropriate behavior are credited, they are, as the IHO correctly concluded, unpersuasive as the facts of the paintball shooting incident convincingly demonstrate Kevin was not drawn into the misconduct by his friends, but was instead an instigator and leader of the event. Accordingly, the IHO's determination that the MDR committee correctly found Kevin's conduct not to be a manifestation of his disability is supported by a preponderance of the evidence, and plaintiffs' claim must fail.

Notes, Comments, and Questions

1. According to Section 1415(k)(1)(E)(i)(I) and (II), the behavior that resulted in the discipline is a manifestation of the disability if it 1) "was caused by, or had a direct and substantial relationship to, the child's disability," or 2) "was the direct result of the . . . school district's failure to implement the IEP." *Id.* Kevin's diagnosis was complex, including an emotional disability, ADHD, Tourette's Syndrome, Generalized Anxiety Disorder, and Obsessive Compulsive Disorder. As the evidence listed in footnote twenty-four of the opinion indicates, whether Kevin's behavior was caused by or substantially related to his disability was a complex question subject to dispute by experts. Is such a decision appropriate for an MDR team? Should the law require the MDR team to seek additional testing, expert evidence, or testimony as necessary prior to making its determination? Did the MDR team apply the correct standard in deciding that Kevin's behavior was not a manifestation of his disability? Can you make an argument that Kevin's behavior was a manifestation of his disability?

2. What were Kevin's educational rights under Section 1415(k) before the MDR began? While the MDR was underway? After the MDR concluded?

---

24. These reports included a report from Dr. Pamela Waaland, who evaluated Kevin two months after his MDR hearing and found that Kevin's "two most prominent personality characteristics are submissiveness and conformity"; given this, she "unequivocally view[ed] Kevin's infraction . . . as related to his disability." Dr. Jeanine R. Carlson, a clinical psychologist who had conducted family counseling sessions with plaintiffs in 2004, wrote a one-page letter stating that "Kevin in no way displayed issues of character or delinquency during my therapeutic work with him." A letter from Dr. James McMurrer, who has been treating Kevin since September 2003, noted that Kevin had "clear symptoms" of ADHD and expressed Dr. McMurrer's view that the paintball incident "seemed related to Kevin's social immaturity and low self-confidence where he was easily led by a group of teens he was trying to befriend." Additionally, a letter from Dr. William McClintock said that Kevin's anxiety, depression, and "impulsivity and obsessiveness related to his Tourette [sic] syndrome have led to Kevin participating in some activities that on closer reflection he probably would not have."

3. In *District of Columbia v. Doe*, 611 F.3d 888 (D.C. Cir. 2010), the child subject to discipline had been diagnosed with attention deficit/hyperactivity disorder. While he was in sixth grade, he was involved in a disciplinary incident with a substitute teacher. Specifically, the child:

> taunted [the substitute] by coming into the classroom with a sucker and getting two (2) more after being told to remove the first one, not giving his name when asked, taking off his hat when asked, but going to the closet to get another hat and then put it on his head, taking an umbrella out of the closet that he thought belonged to the substitute and threatening not to give it back until the end of the school day.

Id. at 892 n. 6. Because Doe had been involved in two prior fighting incidents, the principal removed Doe from school for fifty-four days and placed him in another facility. *Id.* The MDR team determined that Doe's behavior was not a manifestation of his disability. *Id.* Can you make an argument that Doe's behavior was a manifestation of his disability?

4. Why do you think the initial punishment in *Doe* was so severe? The hearing officer reduced the punishment to eleven days on the grounds that Doe's infraction was "nothing more than being a "'nuisance.'" *Doe*, 611 F.3d at 893. The hearing officer also ordered that if Doe had not already served the entire suspension, the district should offer alternatives such as those included in the local law, including:

> (a) Reprimands; (b) Detention; (c) Additional work; (d) Restitution; (e) Mediation; (f) In-school disciplinary centers; (g) Alternative educational programs and placements; (h) Rehabilitative programs; (i) Crime awareness/prevention programs; (j) Probation; (k) Exclusion from extracurricular activities; (l) Peer court; and (m) Transfer.

Id. at 894 n. 8. Why didn't the school offer these alternatives at first? Do you think these alternatives would have been effective?

5. In *Farrin v. Me. Sch. Admin. Dist. No. 59*, 165 F. Supp. 2d 37 (D. Me. 2001), the school disciplined Jacob Farrin for dealing marijuana at school. The dealing took place over a number of hours. Jacob had been diagnosed with a language disability and a tendency "to act impulsively and to become frustrated when confronting his disability." *Id.* at 44. Both the MDR team and the hearing officer found that the behavior was not a manifestation of his disability. The plaintiffs challenged the decision, and the court rejected their argument:

> Plaintiffs have failed to demonstrate by a preponderance of the evidence that an "impulsivity" problem such as the one they describe would manifest itself in a decision to sell marijuana. Plaintiffs apparently assume that drug selling and "impulsivity" are related. However, they have failed to support their assumption with any concrete evidence beyond suggesting that the decision to sell drugs is such a poor one that only a behavioral disability could prompt Jacob to make it.

> Defendant, on the other hand, has presented strong evidence that the tendency to make impulsive decisions and the resolve to peddle narcotics at school are not at all synonymous. In particular, Defendant showed that Jacob understood school rules and that his actions involving the marijuana took place over several hours, involving not a single decision, but many individual ones. These facts are completely antithetical to Plaintiffs' impulsivity theory. Therefore, the preponderance of the evidence supports the conclusion that *even if* the school had treated Jacob as having a behavioral disorder characterized by impulsive decision-making, the . . . [MDR team] would not have decided differently. Therefore, the hearing officer's finding affirming the manifestation review was correct.

Id. at 52. Did the court apply the correct standard? Was plaintiff required to show that the tendency to make impulsive decisions was "synonymous" with the resolve to sell narcotics at school? Did the court consider whether dealing drugs was substantially related to his disability? Was the court correct to view the entire transaction and each decision Jacob made cumulatively over the course of several hours? What if Jacob's original decision to sell drugs had been impulsive and he had been caught immediately? Would Jacob have been able to show that his behavior was caused by or substantially related to his disability?

Section Four
The Relationship Between Disciplinary Removals and the IDEA's Other Procedural Protections

In passing Section 1415(k), Congress did not clearly state how Section 1415(k) relates to the rest of the IDEA. This section considers this issue, including the relationship between: 1) a school district's responsibility to provide a FAPE and its disciplinary authority; 2) the right to an impartial hearing pursuant to Section 1415(f) and to an appeal of a disciplinary decision under 1415(k)(3); 3) and the IDEA's "stay-put" provision (Section 1415(j)) and Section 1415(k)(4)'s "stay-put" provision.

FAPE and a school district's disciplinary authority: In *School Bd. of Norfolk v. Brown*, 769 F. Supp. 2d 928 (E.D. Va. 2010), the court considered whether a district's failure to follow the proper procedures for an MDR denied a FAPE.

> [A] school board's failure to satisfy the procedural requirements of the IDEA can constitute a denial of FAPE. However, "[w]hen such a procedural defect exists, [courts] are obliged to assess whether it resulted in the loss of an educational opportunity for the disabled child, or whether, on the other hand, it was a mere technical contravention of the IDEA." In this case, the Hearing Officer cited five procedural errors which gave rise to her conclusion that the second MDR was procedurally flawed and that the MDR team failed to comply with the VDOE's corrective action plan: (1) the MDR team

> "fragmented" the manifestation determination inquiry by addressing only one question; (2) different individuals were present at the second MDR than were present at the first; (3) Student's parent was denied parental participation; (4) the MDR team conducted only a record review of the evidence; and (5) the MDR team failed to review the Student's psychiatric report which had not been available during the first MDR. It was the compounding of these procedural violations that led the Hearing Officer to conclude that Student was denied FAPE. The Court finds that this determination was supported by substantial evidence.
>
> . . . In this case, the Court finds that the Hearing Officer reasonably concluded that the July 9 MDR was so procedurally faulty as to deny Student FAPE. Both the IDEA and the VDOE's "corrective action plan" required the MDR team to determine "whether [Student's] behavior was a manifestation of his disability." When the MDR team failed to properly conduct this inquiry at the first MDR, it was obligated to reconvene to make this determination during the second MDR. In making the manifestation determination, the MDR team was required to consider each prong of the inquiry as set forth in 20 U.S.C. § 1415(k)(1)(E)(i). Failing to do so not only deprived Student of the full and complete consideration required under the IDEA before removal, but also deprived his parents of participation in the MDR process. The denial of parental participation, as found by the Hearing Officer, is a substantial and serious violation of the IDEA. Further, as the Hearing Officer noted, the most egregious procedural violation was the failure to consider the psychiatric report which was generated as a result of Student's admission to the Virginia Psychiatric Center, which was a direct consequence of the behavioral incident at issue at the MDR. The IDEA requires the MDR team to consider "*all* relevant information" and certainly a psychiatric evaluation based upon the subject disciplinary incident would be relevant to the determination of whether the conduct leading to that disciplinary incident was a manifestation of Student's disability.

Id. at 946–47.

The relationship between Section 1415(f) and Section 1415(k)(3): Section 1415(f) states: "Whenever a complaint has been received under subsection . . . (k), the parents . . . shall have an opportunity for an impartial due process hearing . . . ." 20 U.S.C. § 1415(f)(1)(A)(2012). Section 1415(f) lists several procedural requirements for impartial hearings, including a resolution session, a forty-five day limit for completing the hearing, and rules for disclosing evidence prior to the hearing. *Id.* at §§ (f)(1)(B) and (2); 34 C.F.R. § 300.515 (2015). In addition, pursuant to Section 1415(f)(3)(E)(i), a hearing officer has the authority to decide whether a child received a free appropriate public education. In contrast, Section 1415(k)—which is the IDEA's section involving discipline—requires hearings to be completed within thirty days. 20 U.S.C. § 1415(k)(4)(b). It limits the authority of the hearing officer to ordering a change in the placement, returning the student to the placement from which he or she was removed, or ordering a change in placement of the student "to an appropriate interim alternative educational setting for not more than 45 school days if the hearing officer determines that maintaining the current placement of such child is substantially likely to result in injury to the child or to others." *Id.* at § 1415(k)(3)(B)(ii)(I) and (II). Which rules apply when a parent challenges a disciplinary change in educational placement? Courts have not addressed this issue other than with broad statements. *See* Fitzgerald v. Fairfax Cnty. Sch. Bd., 556 F. Supp. 2d 543, 549 (E.D. Va. 2008) (stating that "parents invoked their right under the due process procedures of the IDEA to a review of the MDR determination"); Farrin v. Me. Sch. Admin. Dist. No. 59, 165 F. Supp. 2d 37, 43 (D. Me. 2001) ("In particular, the parents have a right to request a 'due process hearing' to challenge the adequacy of their child's IEP, the result of a manifestation hearing, or the school's decision to take disciplinary action."). How would you advise a parent who wants to challenge a disciplinary change in educational placement to proceed?

Pendency rights: Congress passed Section 1415(k) in response to *Honig's* construction of IDEA's pendency provision, Section 1415(j). Section 1415(k)(4)(A) contains its own pendency provision. When a child appeals a disciplinary placement or manifestation determination under Section 1415(k)(3)(A), pending the appeal, "the child shall remain in the interim alternative educational setting pending the decision of the hearing officer or until the expiration of . . . [a removal of more than ten days], whichever occurs first . . . ." Section 1415(j) offers more protection, as it provides that during the pendency of any proceedings pursuant to Section 1415, the child "shall remain in the then-current educational placement . . . ." Section 1415(j), however, provides that Section 1415(k)(4)(A) is an exception to its provisions. Thus, a child challenging a disciplinary decision under Section 1415(k) would appear not to benefit from the protection of 1415(j). However, Section 14(j) applies to a child with a disability who has not been classified who is subject to discipline if the district knew of the child's disability before the conduct that was subject to the discipline occurred. *See* § 1415(k)(5)(A); *see also* S.W. v. Holbrook Pub. Sch. 221 F. Supp. 2d 222, 225, 226 (D. Mass. 2002) ("If the school authorities had knowledge that S.W. had a learning disability at the time she was disciplined, then she had a right to stay put . . . while the defendants determined whether her punishable conduct was a manifestation of that disability.")

Part IV

Procedural Rights

Chapter 9

Identification and Evaluation of Children with Disabilities

Introduction

The IDEA requires states that receive federal funds to educate children with disabilities to ensure that:

> All children with disabilities residing in the State, including children with disabilities who are homeless children or are wards of the state and children with disabilities attending private schools, regardless of the severity of their disabilities, and who are in need of special education and related services, are identified, located, and evaluated and a practical method is developed and implemented to determine which children with disabilities are currently receiving needed special education and related services.

20 U.S.C. § 1412(a)(3)(A) (2012); *see also* 34 C.F.R. § 300.111(a)(1)(i) (2015). Identifying children with disabilities and evaluating them to determine whether they need special education and related services—also known as "child-find"—is the cornerstone of the IDEA process. "The core of the statute . . . is the cooperative process that it establishes between parents and schools." Schaffer v. Weast, 546 U.S. 49, 53 (2005); *see* 20 U.S.C. § 1415(b)(1) (stating that the IDEA protects the rights of parents "to participate in meetings with respect to the identification, evaluation, and educational placement of the child, and the provision of a free appropriate education to such child, and to obtain an independent educational evaluation of the child.").

Section One covers identification of children with disabilities, including the circumstances that trigger a school district's child-find obligations, the standard for determining whether a school district has satisfied its child-find obligations, whether a child's positive response to educational interventions short of special education is a defense to a school district's failure to identify the child as a child with disabilities, the time within which a school district must identify a child with disabilities, and the consequences of a child-find violation. Section Two covers the requirements for evaluating children whom the district has identified. It covers the right to obtain an independent educational evaluation (IEE) at public expense, eligibility for obtaining an IEE, the right to a district evaluation, the standards for conducting evaluations, and the evaluation process.

Problem

S.R. is an eight-year old boy in third grade. S.R. progressed normally in kindergarten, first grade, and second grade. Starting in third grade, S.R.'s progress—academic, social, and behavioral—began to deteriorate. He fell behind in reading, fought verbally and physically with other children, and frequently disobeyed his teachers. His various behavioral problems resulted in several classroom "timeouts," exclusions from the classroom, and visits to the principal's office.

S.R.'s teacher was concerned about S.R. academic performance and behavior so she scheduled a conference with his parents in October of S.R.'s third grade year. S.R.'s parents expressed concern about his behavior and progress, but his teacher assured them that S.R.'s academic performance was in a "normal range," especially for an eight year old boy, but they should work together to create an incentive plan to improve his behavior and academic performance. According to the plan, the teacher would send a note home each day describing S.R.'s behavior and progress, and if the note included a star or a smiling face, S.R.'s parents would reward him.

The plan worked for about two weeks. After that, S.R.'s poor behavior and limited progress re-emerged. S.R.'s teacher and parents met again. This time, they agreed to add a punitive aspect to the plan involving deprivation of after-school recreational activities. S.R.'s teacher also recommended that his parents take him to his doctor for a check-up.

S.R.'s parents took him to his pediatrician. They described to the doctor the behavioral and academic issues S.R. was having and the steps they were taking to address the problems. They also mentioned that S.R.'s teacher recommended the exam. The doctor completed a standard physical examination and found no physical problems. She did, however, write a letter to S.R.'s parents suggesting that S.R.'s behavior could be symptomatic of ADHD and autism and that they should consider bringing S.R. to a specialist. S.R.'s parents sent a copy of this letter to S.R.'s teacher and school principal. The principal wrote back, asking S.R.'s parents to keep him apprised of the results of the specialist's examination.

S.R.'s teacher and parents continued with S.R.'s behavior plan through third grade. By the end of third grade, S.R.'s behavior had improved and although he continued to have issues, the frequency of the disciplinary measures against him had decreased. He had not yet attained grade level in math or reading, but he was close by the end of the year, and he was promoted to fourth grade. S.R.'s parents wrote a letter to the principal stating that they were unhappy with S.R.'s performance in third grade and that the school should take more steps to modify his behavior and ensure that he attain grade level in fourth grade.

During the summer between third and fourth grade, S.R.'s parents brought him to see a developmental pediatrician recommended by S.R.'s pediatrician. The doctor issued a report ruling out autism but indicating that S.R. likely had ADHD. S.R.'s parents mailed this report to the school principal during the first week of fourth grade. The principal shared the letter with S.R.'s fourth grade teacher and urged her to develop programs and procedures to ensure that S.R. learned appropriately. S.R.'s fourth grade teacher was more proactive with him than his third grade teacher had been. As a result, S.R.'s behavior improved and his academic performance improved slightly.

In early October of S.R.'s fourth grade year, S.R.'s parents received a letter from the principal stating that the school was seeking their consent to evaluate S.R. for "a disability or disabilities that might be interfering with his ability to learn." S.R.'s parents wrote back, "We consent to the testing on condition that you inform us ahead of time when and where the testing will take place, who will do the testing, and the contents of the test." The school responded that these conditions were not acceptable and that unless the parents dropped these conditions the district would not conduct the evaluation. S.R.'s parents did not drop the conditions and the school district did not conduct the evaluation.

There were no significant changes during the rest of fourth grade. However, soon after the beginning of fifth grade, S.R. refused to attend school. He told his parents that the work was too difficult and that he could not do it. S.R.'s parents requested an impartial hearing. They claimed that the school's delay in identifying and evaluating S.R. deprived him of a FAPE and they also sought reimbursement for the pediatric examination and developmental pediatrician's evaluation. Upon receiving the impartial hearing request, the school notified S.R.'s parents once again that they wanted to evaluate S.R., and that they agreed to the parents' conditions. Following the evaluation, the district found that S.R. was eligible for special education and related services. The district developed an IEP and instituted it by February of S.R.'s fifth grade year, prior to the impartial hearing.

Will the parents prevail in the impartial hearing?

Section One
Identifying Children with Disabilities

D.K. v. Abington Sch. Dist.

696 F.3d 233 (3d Cir. 2012)

Hardiman, Circuit Judge.

This case requires us to decide whether a public school district's failure to designate a struggling student as disabled violated the Individuals with Disabilities Act (IDEA), 20 U.S.C. §§ 1400-1419 . . . .

I

A

In the fall of 2003, D.K. began attending kindergarten in a half-day program at Copper Beech Elementary in the Abington, Pennsylvania, School District (the School District). During that year, he struggled with reading and misbehaved regularly.

According to the School District's psychologist, Dr. Suzanne Grim, and the Copper Beech principal, Dr. Jan Kline, D.K. failed to progress in several areas, including: following oral directions, listening to and acknowledging the contributions of others, exhibiting self-control, following rules, producing neat and legible work, completing class work in the time allotted, and using non-instructional time appropriately. At the same time, Dr. Grim stated that while some preschool and kindergarten students have difficulty following directions, it does not necessarily indicate a disorder. A conference form completed by D.K.'s kindergarten teacher indicated that D.K. exhibited "much growth." D.K. received "proficient," "basic," and "below basic" marks in various reading skills, and received one-on-one reading services from a specialist. At the conclusion of the year, the School District recommended that D.K. repeat kindergarten.

Although D.K.'s second year of kindergarten was a more intensive full-day program, he showed little maturation. In conference forms, D.K.'s teacher noted D.K.'s proficiency in reading and advanced scores in math, but she expressed concern about his behavior, his tendency to rush through classwork and turn in incomplete assignments, and his difficulty controlling himself, especially when he became upset. Indeed, D.K. threw temper tantrums and was "defiant" and "extremely argumentative." His teachers documented forty-three tantrums between March 14 and May 24, 2005.

In response, D.K.'s teachers implemented "behavior plans," including a sticker chart and a system using popsicle sticks, but they did not conduct a functional behavioral assessment. D.K.'s parents were optimistic about, and cooperative in, these behavioral improvement plans. In the meantime, D.K. was "doing very well academically," and, for the most part, "play[ing] well with others." Nevertheless, at the end of the year, having witnessed little behavioral progress, D.K.'s parents and teachers shared a "major concern" about "how well [he] [would] handle a first grade classroom."

Within the first two months of D.K.'s first-grade year, his teacher convened a parent-teacher conference to discuss D.K.'s "listening/following directions and organizational weaknesses." D.K. had been copying another student's work, was unable to recall instructions, exhibited poor organizational and planning skills, misplaced his work, stuttered, and often lost his train of thought. To resolve these problems, the teacher recommended, among other things, measures D.K.'s parents could implement at home. The possibility of a formal evaluation was not discussed at that time.

At a second conference held the following month, D.K.'s parents learned that he continued to struggle in the classroom and was making obscene gestures towards his classmates. At a third conference following the issuance of D.K.'s first report card in December 2005, his teacher noted continuing behavioral challenges, explained that she was "providing as many supports as [she could] to aid" D.K., and opined that while "it was too soon to discuss testing (because he [was] not failing), that might be an option down the road." The teacher's notes reflect that D.K.'s parents saw "no significant problem" and attributed his behavior to "[D.K.] being [D.K.]".

In January 2006, D.K.'s poor social skills led the School District to place him in a special social skills group run by Dr. Grim. According to Dr. Grim, D.K. was "on par with" other students in the group.

That same month, D.K.'s parents requested an evaluation of D.K., and on April 24, 2006, the School District administered a cognitive ability test, which measures "innate ability," and a visual-motor integration test. Dr. Grim also administered a Wechsler Intelligence Scale for Children—Fourth Edition and a Wechsler Individual Achievement Test—Second Edition, and observed D.K. in the classroom setting. She prepared an Evaluation Report using the Behavior Assessment System for Children (BASC), specifically assessing whether D.K. suffered from Attention Deficit/Hyperactivity Disorder (ADHD). She concluded that D.K.'s various scores placed him in average and low-average ranges, and that D.K. was not in need of special education services. Based on the BASC ratings, which are completed by a student's parents and teachers, D.K. was not in an "at risk" or "clinically significant" range. His math and reading tests showed he was proficient in both. D.K.'s parents signed a Notice of Recommended Education Placement form approving the April 2006 evaluation results, and D.K. was promoted to second grade beginning in the fall of 2006.

Plaintiffs claim that despite extra help in math and reading—which consisted of 30 minutes and 180 minutes per week, respectively—D.K. continued to struggle academically during second grade. The School District, on the other hand, contends that D.K. made "considerable progress." The record shows his grades improved compared with first grade, but he fought with other children on the playground and on the bus.

Around January 2007, D.K. began seeing private therapist Dr. Linn Cohen. At the end of March 2007, Dr. Cohen informed D.K.'s teachers and the School District that she was "[e]xtremely convinced" D.K. needed special placement. D.K.'s teachers discussed the results of the April 2006 testing with Dr. Cohen, who mentioned the possibility of re-testing D.K. At the end of the school year, D.K.'s father notified the school that outside testing had diagnosed D.K. with "auditory processing" and "sensory stimulation" problems.

Before D.K. began third grade, in July 2007, his parents formally requested a second, more comprehensive evaluation. Additionally, despite improvement in D.K.'s behavior and academic performance at the beginning of his third-grade year, in September 2007 D.K.'s parents obtained a private pediatric neurological evaluation from Dr. Peter R. Kollros. Dr. Kollros diagnosed D.K. with ADHD and opined that D.K.'s "learning would be enhanced if he were to have the usual kinds of school accommodations for children with ADHD, including if needed preferential seating, taking tests in an environment without unnecessary distractions, organization support, and possibly extra time for tests." Two months later, the School District's own second round of testing determined that D.K. was eligible for special education services as a student with "other health impairment," and he was offered an Individualized Education Program (IEP) on November 30, 2007.

B

On January 8, 2008, in the midst of finalizing D.K.'s IEP, his parents requested a due process hearing pursuant to the IDEA and requested an award of compensatory education for September 2004 through March 12, 2008, after D.K.'s IEP was finalized and implemented. After four hearings, the state agency hearing officer denied Plaintiffs' claims. The appeals panel found no abuse of discretion and affirmed the hearing officer's findings. Having exhausted their administrative remedies, Plaintiffs sought review of those decisions in the District Court.

The District Court affirmed the state agency ....

....

III

[S]chools must: (1) identify children in need of special education services (Child Find); and (2) provide a FAPE to disabled students. Plaintiffs contend that the School District neglected both duties by failing to identify D.K. as a disabled student based on his subpar behavioral and academic performances in kindergarten through third grade ... and by offering inadequate support to D.K. before November 2007.

....

"School districts have a continuing obligation under the IDEA ..."—called "Child Find"—"to identify and evaluate all students who are *reasonably suspected* of having a disability under the statutes." *P.P.*, 585 F.3d at 738 (emphasis added); *accord* 20 U.S.C. § 1412(a)(3); 34 C.F.R. § 300.111. A school's failure to comply with Child Find may constitute a procedural violation of the IDEA.

Child Find extends to children "who are suspected of [having] ... a disability ... and in need of special education, even though they are advancing from grade to grade." 34 C.F.R. § 300.111(c)(1). As several courts have recognized, however, Child Find does not demand that schools conduct a formal evaluation of every struggling student. A school's failure to diagnose a disability at the earliest possible moment is not *per se* actionable, in part because some disabilities "are notoriously difficult to diagnose and even experts disagree about whether [some] should be considered a disability at all." *A.P. ex rel. Powers v. Woodstock Bd. of Educ.*, 572 F. Supp. 2d 221, 226 (D. Conn. 2008).

Plaintiffs claim that the School District violated its Child Find duties in three ways: (1) by failing to evaluate D.K. within a reasonable time after it should reasonably have suspected a disability ... and (3) by failing to suspect disability when D.K.'s struggles continued after April 2006.

We have "'infer[red] a requirement that [schools identify disabled children] within a reasonable time after school officials are on notice of behavior that is likely to indicate a disability.'" *M.R.*, 680 F.3d at 271. This requirement "is implicit in the 'child find' duty." *W.B.*, 67 F.3d at 501 (holding that a jury could reasonably find a violation of Child Find when a school failed to conduct an evaluation within six months after the personal observations of teachers and the receipt of information from parents provided notice of the student's likely disability). Accordingly, such a delay can constitute a procedural Child Find violation.

. . . .

We agree with the decisions below that Plaintiffs have failed to establish an unwarranted delay . . . or evidence showing the School District should reasonably have suspected D.K. was disabled and in need of special education services after April 2006. The School District was not required to jump to the conclusion that D.K.'s misbehavior denoted a disability or disorder because hyperactivity, difficulty following instructions, and tantrums are not atypical during early primary school years. Moreover, D.K.'s report cards and conference forms indicated intermittent progress and even academic success in several areas. . . .

. . . .

We are also unpersuaded that the School District violated its Child Find obligations by failing to suspect D.K. of a disability after the April 2006 evaluation based on further misconduct and additional opinions by his parents and private therapist. Plaintiffs' argument in this respect is belied by the record and inconsistent with the findings of the state agency below. D.K. exhibited improvement after his April 2006 evaluation, and his continuing misbehavior was typical of boys his age. D.K.'s parents consistently approved and cooperated with the behavioral plans devised by his teachers. Moreover, when Dr. Cohen opined in May 2007 that D.K. required special education, teachers discussed with her the results of the April 2006 evaluation. The record does not disclose that she further pressed for formal accommodations.

Finally, the measures the School District did take to assist D.K. in the classroom militate against finding a Child Find violation. His teachers did not neglect his difficulties. Far from it, they and other Copper Beech faculty took proactive steps to afford him extra assistance and worked closely with his parents to maximize his potential for improvement. It would be wrong to conclude that the School District failed to identify D.K. as a challenged student when it offered him substantial accommodations, special instructions, additional time to complete assignments, and one-on-one and specialist attention en route to eventually finding a disability.

In sum, schools need not rush to judgment or immediately evaluate every student exhibiting below-average capabilities, especially at a time when young children are developing at different speeds and acclimating to the school environment. . . . The School District did not breach its Child Find duty by failing to test D.K. until April 2006, during his first-grade year, or by declining to label him disabled under the IDEA until his second-grade year.

. . . .

Notes, Comments, and Questions

1. The standard the court in *D.K.* adopted for triggering a district's child-find obligation is that the district must have "reasonably suspected" that a child has a

disability. *D.K.*, 696 F.3d at 249. Other courts have adopted similar standards. *See* CG v. Pa. Dep't of Educ., 888 F. Supp. 2d 534, 569 (M.D. Pa. 2012), *aff'd*, 734 F.3d 229 (3d Cir. 2013) ("Even children who are only suspected of having a disability, although they are progressing from grade to grade, are protected by the child find requirement."); J.S. v. Scarsdale Union Free Sch. Dist., 826 F. Supp. 2d 635, 661–64 (S.D.N.Y. 2011) (citing various standards, including "sufficient reason to believe the child had a disability"); El Paso Indep. Sch. Dist. v. Richard R., 567 F. Supp. 2d 918, 950 (W.D. Tex. 2008) (holding that district court must "examine whether the local educational agency had reason to suspect that a student had a disability, and whether that agency had reason to suspect that special education services might be needed to address that disability."). The IDEA regulations have a similar standard, stating that a school district's child-find obligations include "Children who are suspected of being a child with a disability . . . and in need of special education, even though they are advancing from grade to grade . . . ." 34 C.F.R. § 300.111(c)(1) (2015). Several courts have adopted this regulatory standard. *See* A.P. v. Woodstock Bd. of Educ., 572 F. Supp. 2d 221, 224–25 (D. Conn. 2008), *aff'd*, 377 F. App'x 202 (2d Cir. 2008) (citing the regulations, holding that child-find applies to "'[c]hildren suspected of having a disability and in need of special education . . . .'"); N.G. v. District of Columbia, 556 F. Supp. 2d 11, 25 (D.D.C. 2008) (citing the regulation, the court stated that the "Child-Find obligation extends to all children *suspected* of having a disability, not merely to those students who are ultimately determined to be disabled.") (emphasis in original).

In *Board of Educ. of Fayette Cnty. v. L.M.*, 478 F.3d 307 (6th Cir. 2007), *cert. denied*, 552 U.S. 1042 (2007), the court adopted a different standard. It ruled that in order to show that a school district violated its child-find obligations, the plaintiff "'must show that school officials overlooked clear signs of disability and were negligent in failing to order testing, or that there was no rational justification for not deciding to evaluate.'" *Id.* at 313 (quoting Clay T. v. Walton Cnty. Sch. Dist., 952 F. Supp. 817, 823 (D. Ga. 1997)). Other courts have adopted a similar standard. *See* Hupp v. Switzerland of Ohio Local Sch. Dist., 912 F. Supp. 2d 572, 590 (S.D. Ohio 2012) (adopting the *L.M.* standard); School Bd. of Norfolk v. Brown, 769 F. Supp. 2d 928, 943 (E.D. Va. 2010) (adopting the *L.M.* standard). Which of these standards places a higher burden on a school district to identify and evaluate a child with a disability? Which standard best implements the goals of child-find?

2. How have courts implemented the standards for determining whether a school district should have identified and evaluated a child with a disability? Courts have accepted the youth of a child as well as lack of evidence that the child was struggling as reasons for failing to identify a child with a disability. In *Board of Educ. of Fayette Cnty. v. L.M.*, 478 F.3d 307 (6th Cir. 2007), the Court ruled that the relative youth of a child could excuse a district from identifying the child:

> [V]irtually all of the witnesses who testified at the due process hearing, including T.D.'s own expert, stated that T.D.'s difficulties would not necessarily indicate a disability or a need for special education, and that it would

> be inappropriate to rush to identify a child that young as disabled. School personnel similarly testified that T.D.'s behavioral and learning problems were not aytipical of immature young boys.

Id. at 314; *see also* Taylor v. Altoona Area Sch. Dist., 737 F. Supp. 2d 474, 486 (W.D. Pa. 2010) (finding no obligation to identify a child who was "not struggling academically such that the school should have been alerted to the possible need for an IEP."); A.P. v. Woodstock Bd. of Educ., 572 F. Supp. 2d 221, 225–27 (D. Conn. 2008), *aff'd*, 370 F. App'x 272 (2d Cir. 2008) (holding that district did not violate child-find when child was performing well academically and there was no evidence of a disability).

In contrast, courts have found that school districts failed to satisfy their child-find obligations when they missed clear warning signs or when children struggled behaviorally or academically. In *School Bd. of Norfolk v. Brown*, 769 F. Supp. 2d 928 (E.D. Va. 2010), the court found that the school district violated its child-find obligations when it failed over a period of several years to evaluate a child for psychiatric issues that could have been the cause of his behavioral problems. The court ruled:

> [T]he court finds that the Hearing Officer's conclusions regarding the school Board's duties under the "child find" provisions are supported by substantial evidence. As early as June 2005, the school's Eligibility Committee reported that Student's psychiatric issues, possibly related to his seizures, could be the basis for Student's behavioral issues. The Hearing Officer also found that the school guidance counselor documented several behavioral incidents involving Student during the 2007–2008 and 2008–2009 academic school years, including making threats against, becoming physical with, and harassing other classmates. Student was also suspended on three other occasions prior to the disciplinary incident of February 2009. Furthermore, the hearing revealed that in October 2008, Student was removed from school and referred to a behavioral program, the Alternatives to Violent Behavior Program ("AVBP"), based on his making verbal threats to other students. AVBP provided several suggestions to school officials concerning Student's unsatisfactory behavior, including recommending that Student receive behavior consequences, appropriate support and immediate feedback in order to achieve behavioral modification, and providing Student with a Positive Behavior Support Plan to address his needs. However, the school failed to implement the plan. Considering the above factual findings of the Hearing Officer, the Court finds that there was substantial evidence to support the Hearing Officer's conclusion that the School Board "overlooked clear signs of disability" and thus failed to fully evaluate Student's suspected disabilities which adversely impacted his academic performance during the 2007–2008 and 2008–2009 academic years. This constituted a procedural violation of the "child find" provisions of the IDEA.

Id. at 943; *see also* El Paso Indep. Sch. Dist. v. Richard R., 567 F. Supp. 2d 918, 951 (W.D. Tex. 2008) (holding that district should have identified and evaluated child in light of three years of continued academic struggle even with academic intervention);

N.G. v. District of Columbia, 556 F. Supp. 2d 11, 26–27 (D.D.C. 2008) (holding that district should have identified and evaluated child who showed "pervasive depression and inappropriate types of behavior" that clearly adversely affected her academic performance); New Paltz Cent. Sch. Dist. v. St. Pierre, 307 F. Supp. 2d 394, 401 (N.D.N.Y. 2003) (holding that district should have referred child for evaluation when the parent informed the superintendent that the child was having emotional problems and the school psychologist suggested an out-of-district placement); Hawaii Dep't of Educ. v. Cari Rae S., 158 F. Supp. 2d 1190, 1195–97 (D. Haw. 2001) (holding that district had "numerous incidents or 'warning signs' of an emotional impairment.").

3. The court in *D.K.* stated that the steps the school district took to assist D.K. supported the district's argument that it did not violate its child-find obligations:

> His teachers did not neglect his difficulties. Far from it, they and other Copper Beech faculty took proactive steps to afford him extra assistance and worked closely with his parents to maximize his potential for improvement. It would be wrong to conclude that the School District failed to identify D.K. as a challenged student when it offered him substantial accommodations, special instructions, additional time to complete assignments, and one-on-one and specialist attention en route to eventually finding a disability. . . .

696 F.3d at 252; *see also* Board of Educ. of Fayette Cnty. v. L.M., 478 F.3d 307, 314 (6th Cir. 2007) ("The School District provided additional services to aid T.D. in catching up to his peers in kindergarten and first grade, even though at that point he was not identified as being disabled within the meaning of the IDEA."); Salley v. St. Tammany Parish Sch. Bd., 57 F.3d 458, 461, 465 (5th Cir. 1995) (noting that child "received adequate educational benefit" under an informal educational plan); Hupp v. Switzerland of Ohio Local Sch. Dist., 912 F. Supp. 2d 572, 591 (S.D. Ohio 2012) ("The fact that Mrs. Stoehr successfully utilized interventions with Timothy during the second semester of the 2004–2005 school year obviates a finding that the School District ignored signs of Timothy's disability, or had no rational justification for not referring him for an evaluation immediately upon suspicion of disability.").

Several courts disagree that providing non-IDEA services excuses a school district from its IDEA obligations. In *Hawaii Dep't of Educ. v. Cari Rae S.*, 158 F. Supp. 2d 1190 (D. Haw. 2001), the school district defended its failure to identify the student as eligible for special education on the grounds, in part, that it provided her with special services and she graduated from high school. The court rejected this argument:

> The state misses the point. It puts the proverbial cart before the horse. . . . While *Rowley* only obligates states or LEAs to provide a "basic floor of opportunity" and "confer some educational benefit," it also requires a program "individually designed to provide [such] benefit." In this case, however, the "some educational benefit" standard under *Rowley* is not dispositive, especially if instruction is not provided under an appropriate IEP. No IEP; no FAPE under the *Rowley* standard.

Id. at 1196. In *N.G. v. District of Columbia*, 556 F. Supp. 2d 11 (D.D.C. 2008), the court ruled:

> Finally, DCPS also makes the unusual argument that because Dr. Robbins also recommended "educational accommodations" under Section 504 of the Rehabilitation Act, it had no obligation under the IDEA to conduct its own evaluation of N.G.'s needs. This argument is absurd and completely undermines the purpose of Child Find. Under Defendants' interpretation, a school district could excuse itself from the obligation to evaluate students merely because parents or therapists had suggested additional, alternative ways to accommodate the child. This is clearly not what Congress intended by imposing an affirmative obligation upon school districts to identify, evaluate, and place potentially disabled students ....

Id. at 29.

4. The court in *D.K.* found that the fact that D.K. was improving in response to the school district's assistance was an additional reason for excusing the district from identifying him as a child with a disability. Should a child's improved performance in response to educational interventions be a defense to a district's failure to identify the child? Consider the court's treatment of the evidence that the child was responding to additional services in *A.P. v. Woodstock Bd. of Educ.*, 572 F. Supp. 2d 221 (D. Conn. 2008), *aff'd*, 370 F. App'x 202 (2d Cir. 2008):

> Here, all evidence suggests that in the fourth grade, A.P. did not need special education services. As Mrs. Fulco testified, A.P. responded well to the assistance she provided. He was performing at grade level and made progress throughout the year. The Parents argue that the ADD screening showed A.P. was "at risk" for ADD and that fact alone should have alerted the school to A.P.'s need for a referral to special education. However, as stated above, the Parents are correct only if A.P. was in need of special education and related services. The record indicates that he was not. Furthermore, A.P. was not merely "advancing from grade to grade," he was making progress. This is decidedly not a case in which a school turned a blind eye to a child in need. To the contrary, Mrs. Fulco acted conscientiously, communicating regularly with Mrs. Powers and utilizing special strategies to help A.P. succeed. In fact, Mrs. Powers admitted in her testimony that she was pleased with A.P.'s progress in the fourth grade. Just because Mrs. Fulco decided that A.P. did not need to be referred to special education does not mean that the Board violated its "Child Find" obligation.

Id. at 225–26. Do you agree with the court's analysis?

5. The IDEA does not include a time limit for identifying a child with a disability. In *D.K.*, the court stated that the Third Circuit had "'infer[red] a requirement that [schools identify disabled children] within a reasonable time after school officials are on notice of behavior that is likely to indicate a disability.'" *D.K.*, 696 F.3d at 250;

see also Ridley Sch. Dist. v. M.R., 680 F.3d 260, 271 (3d Cir. 2012). The court in *Ridley* further elaborated on this "reasonable time" standard:

> In adopting the "reasonable time" standard, we noted the budgetary constraints and staffing pressures facing school officials, and emphasized that we were not establishing any "bright-line rule" as to what constitutes a reasonable time. Rather, we employ a case-by-case approach and assess whether the school district's response was reasonable "in light of the information and resources possessed" by the district at a given point in time.

Id. at 272. In applying this standard, the court found that the district did not violate its child-find obligations when it waited approximately six months before re-evaluating a child for a disability:

> In light of the fact that E.R.'s kindergarten evaluations were appropriate, and she did not qualify as a student in need of special education services in June 2007 (the end of kindergarten), we cannot agree with the Hearing Officer that Ridley violated the IDEA and denied E.R. a FAPE by failing to immediately reevaluate her in September 2007. When a school district has conducted a comprehensive evaluation and concluded that a student does not qualify as disabled under the IDEA, the school district must be afforded a reasonable time to monitor the student's progress before exploring whether further evaluation is required. We assess whether a school district identified and evaluated a student suspected of having a qualifying disability within a reasonable time "in light of the information and resources possessed" by the district. Here, although E.R. struggled during the beginning of first grade, all prior evaluations showed that she did not require special education services. Moreover, as Cenname testified, first grade was the "first time that the children ever ha[d] a chance to be in a test taking situation" and "[t]here were other children that also had difficulty . . . taking a test." It was reasonable for Cenname to assess E.R.'s progress throughout the first marking period of first grade before recommending that E.R. again be evaluated to determine if she had a learning disability. The IDEA does not require a reevaluation every time a student posts a poor grade. Accordingly, we hold that Ridley complied with its "child find" obligations, and E.R. was not denied a FAPE at the beginning of first grade.

Id. at 273; *see also* P.P. v. West Chester Area Sch. Dist., 585 F.3d 727, 732, 738 (3d Cir. 2009) (finding no child-find violation when district took seventy-two days from date of notice to evaluate child); Salley v. St. Tammany Parish Sch. Bd., 57 F.3d 458, 463–64 (5th Cir. 1995) (holding that district's failure to evaluate child for over a year did not violate child-find obligations because child moved into district with only fourteen days left in the year, prior district did not timely forward records, child then enrolled in private school, and district had no reason to think she needed evaluation); Hupp v. Switzerland of Ohio Local Sch. Dist., 912 F. Supp. 2d 572, 591–92 (S.D. Ohio 2012) (holding that roughly six months to evaluate child, during which the district was implementing interventions that were working, did not violate child-find). In contrast, one court found that a school district denied FAPE when it delayed evaluating a child for nearly three years after it identified the child as a candidate for special education when it referred him for a psycho-educational evaluation. Long v. District of Columbia, 780 F. Supp. 2d 49, 57 (D.D.C. 2011); *see also* El Paso Indep. Sch. Dist. v. Richard R., 567 F. Supp. 2d 918, 951 (W.D. Tex. 2008) (holding that thirteen month delay between request for evaluation and evaluation offer violated child-find requirements); O.F. v. Chester Upland Sch. Dist., 246 F. Supp. 2d 409, 415, 417–418 (E.D. Pa. 2002) (holding that delay of nearly twelve months in completing evaluation and creating IEP was not reasonable and violated the IDEA).

6. Child-find obligations are considered "procedural" requirements of the IDEA, in contrast to a district's "substantive" obligation to provide a FAPE to a child with a disability. Procedural violations do not always create a right to relief. Instead, in order to prompt a remedy, the procedural violation must harm the child's education or interfere with the parents' right to participate in the IDEA process. *D.K.*, 696 F.3d at 249. *See, e.g.*, Hupp v. Switzerland of Ohio Local Sch. Dist., 912 F. Supp. 2d 572, 589 (S.D. Ohio) ("Procedural violations that deprive an eligible student of an IEP or result in the loss of an educational opportunity will also constitute a denial of FAPE."). Accordingly, a court in a child-find case must first determine whether the district violated child-find, and if so, whether the child suffered an educational harm as a result. In *N.G. v. District of Columbia*, 556 F. Supp. 2d 11, 15, 37, 40 (D.D.C. 2008), the court ordered the school district to reimburse parents for tuition they paid following the district's failure to identify and evaluate their child.

7. The IDEA regulations require school districts to adopt "policies and procedures" to identify children with disabilities. 34 C.F.R. § 300.111(a)(1) (2015). What should such policies include? One school district "routinely posts child find notices in the local paper, makes the information available on its website, and sends residents the information in their tax bills. Targeted posters and pamphlets are placed in private schools." P.P. v. West Chester Area Sch. Dist., 585 F.3d 727, 738 (3d Cir. 2009). Another district posts information about special education in the parent handbook, invites parents to obtain a copy of their rights notice, and publishes an annual newspaper notice about its special education programs. Taylor v. Altoona Area Sch. Dist., 737 F. Supp. 2d 474, 484 n. 8 (W.D. Pa. 2010). In finding no evidence of a systematic failure to engage in child-find, the court in *C.G. v. Pa. Dep't of Educ.*, 888 F. Supp. 2d 534 (M.D. Pa. 2012), *aff'd*, 734 F.3d 229 (3d Cir. 2013) stated:

> Contrary to Plaintiffs' bald speculation, Defendants have presented ample evidence to support a finding that the . . . districts are compliant with the child find requirement. For example, the uncontested testimony . . . established that the York City School District has in place practices designed to inform parents of students as well as the general public regarding services offered through the IDEA, the process for early identification of students, and the rights of parents under the IDEA. [The special education director] also outlined procedures for identifying eligible students within the school

> as possibly being eligible for special education. Each of the other special education supervisors who testified similarly outlined extensive efforts their districts undertook to identify and evaluate special needs students.

Id. at 570.

Section Two
Evaluating Children for Disabilities

The IDEA requires a school district to "conduct a full and individual initial evaluation . . . before the initial provision of special education and related services to a child with a disability under this subchapter." 20 U.S.C. § 1414(a)(1)(A) (2012). This section begins with *Phillip C. v. Jefferson County Board of Education*, a case in which the Eleventh Circuit considered a challenge from a local school board to the Department of Education's regulation requiring school districts to pay for an independent educational evaluation (IEE) that parents can obtain if they disagree with the evaluation the district conducted. Following *Phillip C.* is *T.G. v. Midland School District. 7*, in which the parents sought reimbursement for several IEEs on the grounds that the school district's evaluations were inappropriate. Finally, this section presents a step-by-step description of the evaluation process.

A. The Right to an Independent Educational Evaluation at Public Expense

Phillip C. v. Jefferson Cnty. Bd. of Educ.

701 F.3d 691 (11th Cir. 2012),
cert. denied, __ U.S. __, 134 S. Ct. 64 (2013)

Barkett, Circuit Judge:

The Jefferson County Board of Education (the "Board") . . . challenges the district court's determination affirming the validity of a Department of Education regulation that requires state and local agencies to reimburse parents and guardians for an independent educational evaluation of their children with disabilities. *See* 34 C.F.R. § 300.502(b)(1) (1999) (stating that a parent "has the right to an independent educational evaluation at public expense if the parent disagrees with an evaluation obtained by the public agency"). We affirm the district court's order holding that 34 C.F.R. § 300.502 is a valid regulation requiring the Board to reimburse Philip and Angie C. for the independent educational evaluation of their child, A.C.

Background

. . . .

The IDEA established at its "core" a "cooperative process . . . between parents and schools" to jointly design the IEP. *Schaffer ex rel. Schaffer v. Weast*, 546 U.S. 49, 53 . . .

(2005). Congress "protect[ed] the informed involvement of parents in the development of an education for their child" by requiring states to provide parents numerous procedural safeguards. *Winkelman*, 550 U.S. at 524. In particular, the IDEA requires that state and local agencies:

> shall establish and maintain procedures . . . to ensure that children with disabilities and their parents are guaranteed procedural safeguards . . . . [that] shall include . . . [a]n opportunity for the parents of a child with a disability . . . to obtain an independent educational evaluation ["IEE"] of the child.

20 U.S.C. § 1415(a)-(b) (2005). Since the inception of the IDEA in 1975, the Secretary of Education has promulgated the regulations at issue in this case specifying that an IEE obtained by a parent . . . will be "at public expense." 34 C.F.R. § 300.502(b)(1) . . . .

In 2002, the Board initially evaluated A.C. and determined that he was eligible for special education services and in 2005, the Board re-evaluated A.C. to assess his current level of functioning in order to plan his educational program. Philip and Angie C. disagreed with the Board's assessments and obtained an IEE of A.C. from Mitchell's Place, a private facility. Notwithstanding the federal and Alabama regulations requiring reimbursement, the Board refused to reimburse the parents for the IEE. . . .

. . . .

DISCUSSION

The Board's primary argument is that 34 C.F.R. § 300.502 must be invalidated as exceeding the Congressional authority granted to the Secretary of Education because the IDEA does not *expressly* state that parents are to be reimbursed for the cost of an IEE, *see* 20 U.S.C. § 1415(b)(1), and because, by requiring state and local agencies to "establish and maintain procedures . . . to ensure . . . procedural safeguards," Congress implicitly delegated to the states the right to decide whether to reimburse parents for the cost of an IEE, *see id.* § 1415(a). Based on the language and structure of the statute, we find no merit to these contentions.

The regulation at issue here is valid so long as public financing of a parent's IEE is consistent with the intent of Congress in enacting the IDEA. To assess Congressional intent, we first look to the language of the statute. If we, "ascertain[] that Congress had an intention on the precise question at issue, that intention is the law and must be given effect." *Chevron, U.S.A., Inc. v. Natural Res. Def. Council, Inc.*, 467 U.S. 837, 843 n.9 (1984).

As the Board notes, 20 U.S.C. § 1415(b) does not expressly state that agencies must pay for a parent's IEE. *See* 20 U.S.C. § 1415(b) (stating only that a parent must "have an opportunity . . . to obtain an [IEE] of the child"). However, another section of the IDEA, 20 U.S.C. § 1406(b)(2), expressly requires the Secretary of Education to preserve any IDEA regulation that existed as of July 20, 1983 and provided protection for children . . . . One of the regulations in effect on July 20, 1983 expressly provided to parents "the right to an independent educational evaluation at public expense if the parent disagrees with an evaluation obtained by the public agency."

By enacting 20 U.S.C. § 1406(b), Congress sought to "reaffirm support for the program and its existing regulations," which included a parent's right to an IEE at public expense. 129 Cong. Rec. 33,316 (1983) (statement of Rep. Biaggi); *see also* H.R. Rep. No. 98-410, at 21 (Oct. 6, 1983) ("[T]he current regulations which govern programs under [the IDEA] have received the strong support of Congress."). Significantly, this reaffirmation was in response to proposed regulations that, in part, would have significantly curtailed a parent's right to a publicly financed IEE by requiring public reimbursement "*only* where a hearing or reviewing officer determines that such an evaluation is necessary to resolve the issues in dispute in a hearing or review." Assistance to States for Education of Handicapped Children, 47 Fed. Reg. 33836-01, 33841 (proposed Aug. 4, 1982) (emphasis added). Congress "remain[ed] strongly opposed to any attempts to alter current regulatory requirements which would result in diminished rights and protections for handicapped children under the [IDEA]." H.R. Rep. No. 98-410, at 21. It is clear that Congress enacted 20 U.S.C. § 1406(b) to ensure that the "Secretary cannot propose any regulations which . . . have the direct or indirect effect of weakening the protections for handicapped children under existing law and regulation." 129 Cong. Rec. 33,316 (1983) (statement of Rep. Biaggi).

Moreover, subsequent to 1983, Congress reauthorized the IDEA in 1990, 1997, and 2004 without altering a parent's right to a publicly financed IEE. Under the reenactment doctrine, "Congress is presumed to be aware of an administrative or judicial interpretation of a statute and to adopt that interpretation when it re-enacts a statute without change." *Lorillard v. Pons*, 434 U.S. 575, 580 . . . (1978). This doctrine is particularly applicable here, where a parent's right to a publicly financed IEE has endured since the Department of Education first implemented the IDEA. . . . Accordingly, Congress has clearly evinced its intent that parents have the right to obtain an IEE at public expense. *See* 34 C.F.R. § 300.502.

Even if 20 U.S.C. § 1406(b)(2) had not been passed, we find clear Congressional intent for reimbursement based on the statutory scheme of the IDEA. Parents already have the right, separate from the IDEA, to spend their own funds to obtain an IEE of their children. *See G.J. v. Muscogee Cnty. Sch. Dist.*, 668 F.3d 1258, 1266 (11th Cir. 2012) ("Obviously, the IDEA does not govern the right of parents to take their child to any privately paid evaluator at any time they wish."). We cannot conclude that Congress extended to parents the "opportunity . . . to obtain an independent educational evaluation" at their own expense merely to secure for parents what they already could obtain without the statute. *See* 20 U.S.C. § 1415(b)(1) . . . . A practical interpretation of 20 U.S.C. § 1415(b)(1) is that Congress intended for state and local agencies to provide to parents the actual benefit of paying for an IEE under appropriate circumstances.

Indeed, the Supreme Court has recognized that states must reimburse parents for the cost of an IEE in order to ensure that parents can exercise their right to an independent expert opinion, which is an essential procedural safeguard.

> School districts have a natural advantage in information and expertise, but Congress addressed this when it obliged schools to safeguard the procedural rights of parents and to share information with them. . . . [Parents] have the right to an independent educational evaluation of the[ir] child. The regulations clarify this entitlement by providing that a parent has the right to an independent educational evaluation at public expense if the parent disagrees with an evaluation obtained by the public agency. IDEA thus ensures parents access to an expert who can evaluate all the materials that the school must make available, and who can give an independent opinion. They are not left to challenge the government without a realistic opportunity to access the necessary evidence, or without an expert with the firepower to match the opposition.

Schaffer, 546 U.S. at 60–61 (addressing the burden of proof in an administrative hearing challenging an IEP).

The right to a publicly financed IEE guarantees meaningful participation throughout the development of the IEP. Without public financing of an IEE, a class of parents would be unable to afford an IEE and their children would not receive, as the IDEA intended, "a free and appropriate public education" as the result of a cooperative process that protects the rights of parents. There is "nothing in the statute to indicate that when Congress required States to provide adequate instruction to a child 'at no cost to parents,' it intended that only some parents would be able to enforce that mandate." *Winkelman*, 550 U.S. at 533.

. . . .

In short, the Secretary of Education did not exceed its authority in promulgating 34 C.F.R. § 300.502, providing parents the right to a publicly financed independent educational evaluation, and the district court did not err in requiring the Board to reimburse Philip and Angie C. for the IEE that they obtained for their child.

T.G. v. Midland Sch. Dist. 7

848 F. Supp. 2d 902 (C.D. Ill. 2012),
aff'd, 524 F. App'x 523 (7th Cir. 2103)

Joe Billy McDade, Senior District Judge

. . . .

C. IHO's finding that Defendant was not required to reimburse Plaintiffs for the private evaluations they obtained

. . . .

A school district must conduct evaluations of a student in order to assist with the IEP process. A school district need not pay for parents' private evaluations of their child unless the parents disagree with the school district's evaluation and request a private evaluation in writing. 34 C.F.R. 300.502(b). In addition, if a district files a due process complaint requesting a hearing, and shows "that its evaluation is appropriate," it is not required to reimburse the parents for a private evaluation. 34 C.F.R. 300.502(b)(2)(i). Defendant evaluated T.G. for speech and language, occupational therapy, and assistive technology. Plaintiffs obtained competing private evaluations with Ms. Ontiveros, Ms. Marshall-Kramer, [and] Don Dalton, . . . , and sought reimbursement from the IHO. Defendant filed a due process complaint, and argued before the IHO that its evaluations were proper; the IHO found in Defendant's favor.

In support of their argument for reimbursement for the evaluations by Ms. Ontiveros, Ms. Marshall-Kramer, and Mr. Dalton, Plaintiffs argue that the IHO "ignored substantial evidence" that Defendant's evaluations were in fact inappropriate. . . .

1. Speech and Language Evaluation

Ms. Grandsart, Defendant's Speech Language Pathologist, administered T.G.'s speech and language evaluation in November 2006. The IHO found that Ms. Grandsart's evaluation was appropriate, as it was "comprehensive and reasonably chosen to identify T.G.'s speech and language needs," and "provided objective insight into T.G.'s skill levels in the areas of oral/motor and articulation, receptive and expressive language, as well as auditory perception, reasoning, and processing." She further found that Ms. Ontiveros' evaluation "was no more thorough," as Ms. Ontiveros' testimony revealed Ms. Grandsart's evaluation to have been "more in depth" than hers, and that their results were mostly consistent. The primary distinction between Defendant's results and Ms. Ontiveros' related to T.G.'s expressive and receptive language: they administered different tests and came to different results, but Ms. Ontiveros was not familiar with the test administered by Ms. Grandsart. The only flaw with Defendant's evaluation identified by the IHO was that Ms. Grandsart did not include written recommendations, but this was not a problem because Ms. Grandsart shared her recommendations with the team orally. About Ms. Ontiveros' report as a whole, the IHO determined that the credibility of her report was undermined by her analysis of areas that were outside of her expertise, including the "appropriateness of various academic goals, social work services and occupational therapy."

. . . .

2. Occupational Therapy Evaluation

The IHO also found that Ms. Armstrong's occupational therapy evaluation of T.G. on behalf of Defendant was appropriate. The evaluation "measured T.G.'s skills in the areas of visual-motor integration, visual perception and motor coordination," and "included a comprehensive functional assessment that measured the degree to which T.G. could perform tasks encountered in the classroom setting." She noted that Ms. Marshall-Kramer's private evaluation concluded, as did Ms. Armstrong's evaluation, "that T.G. has severe deficits in visual perception and fine motor concentration," but Ms. Marshall-Kramer's recommendation of direct occupational therapy was undermined by the fact that she "did not observe T.G. at school and did not base her recommendation on T.G.'s ability to function in the classroom setting," so she could not dispute Ms. Armstrong's conclusion that "T.G.'s skills in the classroom were functional."

. . . .

The only flaw Plaintiffs identify with Ms. Armstrong's evaluation method was that one of the tests was designed for students up to 12 years old, while T.G. took it when she was 14. The IHO noted Ms. Armstrong's testimony that she believed that the test would still be helpful; it was not unreasonable for the IHO to rely on this, and Plaintiffs have put on no evidence that the test's results were actually erroneous. It was also not unreasonable for the IHO to find that Ms. Armstrong's evaluation and recommendations as a whole were appropriate, as she observed T.G. in school, and as Ms. McCartney (Defendant's certified occupational therapy assistant), who had worked with T.G. since second grade, agreed that T.G. was able to function in school. The IHO reasonably chose to prioritize T.G.'s school-related physical abilities, which is an educational policy judgment the Court will not disturb. The fact that Ms. Marshall-Kramer found other deficiencies and recommended more services does not render this judgment unreasonable, as the IHO gave considered reasons for finding otherwise. The Court finds that the IHO's determination that Ms. Armstrong's evaluation was appropriate is reasonable and supported by the record.

3. Assistive Technology Evaluation

Ms. Conklin . . . performed an assistive technology evaluation of T.G. for Defendant, and the IHO concluded that it was appropriate, given that she consulted with the IEP team, observed T.G. in the classroom, and had T.G. attempt using several assistive technology products. Mr. Dalton, Plaintiffs' consultant, recommended a different product than the ones Ms. Conklin recommended, but did not indicate that the product she recommended was inappropriate; the IHO found that though Defendant ultimately chose the product recommended by Mr. Dalton, this fact alone did not render Ms. Conklin's evaluation inappropriate. Plaintiffs make no specific arguments against the IHO's determination that the assistive technology evaluation was appropriate. The Court has reviewed the IHO's decision on this point, and has determined that it was reasonable and supported by the evidence.

. . . .

Notes, Comments, and Questions

1. As the court in *T.G.* made clear, a parent is entitled to an IEE at public expense if "the parent disagrees with" the school district's evaluation. *See* 34 C.F.R. § 300.502(b)(1) (2015). Courts apply this requirement strictly. In *Michael P. v. West Chester Area Sch. Dist.*, 585 F.3d 727, 740 (3d Cir. 2009), the court denied reimbursement for an IEE the parents obtained because they did not obtain the evaluation to challenge the district's evaluation; *see also* G.J. v. Muscogee Cnty. Sch. Dist., 668 F.3d 1258, 1266 (11th Cir. 2012) (ruling that because the district did not re-evaluate the child the parents did not have the right to an IEE at public expense because the right does not

vest "until there is a re-evaluation with which the parents disagree."); R.L. v. Plainville Bd. of Educ., 363 F. Supp. 2d 222, 234 (D. Conn. 2005) (denying reimbursement request because parents obtained IEE for additional information about their child's program and "not because they disagreed with" the school district's evaluation); Krista P. v. Manhattan Sch. Dist., 255 F. Supp. 2d 873, 889 (N.D. Ill. 2003) (ruling that "Parents were not entitled to an IEE" at public expense "because the school district did not conduct an evaluation.").

2. A parent may ask a school district to arrange for an IEE at public expense. *See* 34 C.F.R. § 300.502(b)(1) and (2). However, a parent is not required to notify the school district that it disagrees with the school district's evaluation prior to obtaining an IEE. *See* P.R. v. Woodmore Local Sch. Dist., 256 F. App'x 751, 755 (6th Cir. 2007) (stating that argument that parents must notify school district before obtaining IEE in order to qualify for reimbursement "has been rejected by several Circuit Courts of Appeal."); Warren G. v. Cumberland Cnty. Sch. Dist., 190 F.3d 80, 87 (3d Cir. 1999) (holding that the parents' failure to disagree "with the District's evaluations prior to obtaining their own [evaluation] does not foreclose their right to reimbursement."); Board of Educ. of Murphysboro Cmty. Unit Sch. Dist. No. 186 v. Ill. Bd. of Educ., 41 F.3d 1162, 1169 (7th Cir. 1994) ("[P]arents can initiate an evaluation before notifying a school district that they disagree with the district's evaluation."); Hudson v. Wilson, 828 F.2d 1059, 1065 (4th Cir. 1987) (holding that "The plain thrust of the regulation is that the school can *later* challenge the private testing . . . ."). The court in *T.G.*, as just seen, disagrees. 848 F. Supp. 2d at 929 (stating that under 34 C.F.R. § 300.502(b) a parent must request an IEE in writing in order to be eligible for reimbursement).

3. If a school district refuses to pay for an IEE, it can request an impartial hearing to show that the evaluation it completed was appropriate and thus it is not required to arrange for an IEE at public expense. 34 C.F.R. § (b)(2)(i); *see also P.R.*, 256 F. App'x at 755; *Murphysboro*, 41 F.3d at 1169; *Hudson*, 828 F.2d at 1065. If the school district loses at the hearing, the parent is entitled to an IEE at public expense. *See, e.g.*, Seattle Sch. Dist. No. 1 v. B.S., 82 F.3d 1493, 1500 (9th Cir. 1996) ("Because A.S.'s parent disagreed with the School District's evaluation and the District was unable to establish the appropriateness of its evaluation, A.S. was entitled to an independent evaluation at public expense."). If the school district prevails at the hearing, the district is not required to pay for the evaluation. *See* Council Rock Sch. Dist. v. Bolick, 462 F. App'x 212, 215 (3d Cir. 2012) ("[I]n cases like this one, where there was an administrative hearing, the School District need not reimburse the parent if it can show that its examination was " 'appropriate.' "); Evanston Cmty. Consol. Sch. Dist. No. 65 v. Michael M., 356 F.3d 798, 803–04 (7th Cir. 2004) (rejecting the parents' allegation that the school district's evaluation was inappropriate).

4. Parents also have the right to obtain an IEE at their own expense. 20 U.S.C. § 1415(b)(1); 34 C.F.R. § 300.502 (b)(3). *See* Schaffer v. Weast, 546 U.S. 49, 53 (2005) (stating that parents have the right to obtain an IEE of their child). If a parent obtains an IEE, whether at public or private expense, the school district must consider the

IEE, provided it meets the district's criteria, in its decisions about the provision of special education and related services to the child, and any party may present the IEE at an impartial hearing. 34 C.F.R. § 300.502(c)(1) and (2).

5. A parent has a right to just one IEE "at public expense" each time the school district "conducts an evaluation with which the parent disagrees." 34 C.F.R. § 300.502(b)(5). *See* G.J. v. Muscogee Cnty. Sch. Dist., 668 F.3d 1258, 1266 (11th Cir. 2012) (citing the regulation); Board of Educ. of Murphysboro Cmty. Unit Sch. Dist. No. 186 v. Ill. Bd. of Educ., 41 F.3d 1162, 1169 (7th Cir. 1994) (remanding for determination of whether the parents disagreed with an evaluation); Hudson v. Wilson, 828 F.2d 1059, 1065–66 (4th Cir. 1987) (ruling that parents are entitled to reimbursement for only one evaluation).

B. School District Evaluations

1. The Right to a District Evaluation

N.B. v. Hellgate Elementary Sch. Dist.

541 F.3d 1202 (9th Cir. 2008)

Alarcon, Circuit Judge:

I

Appellants, minor C.B. and his parents . . . allege that Hellgate Elementary School District . . . violated the Individuals with Disabilities Education Act ("IDEA"), 20 U.S.C. § 1400, by failing to provide minor C.B. with a free appropriate public education ("FAPE"). Appellants assert that Hellgate failed to meet its procedural obligation under the IDEA to evaluate C.B. to determine whether he was autistic. . . . We conclude that Hellgate did not fulfill its procedural requirements under the IDEA to evaluate C.B. . . .

II

. . . .

A

Prior to moving to Missoula, Montana, in August 2003, C.B. and his parents resided in Sparta Township, New Jersey. On January 3, 2003, when C.B. was two years and ten months old, he was examined by Dr. Arnold Gold. Dr. Gold concluded that an "autistic component appears to be complicating [C.B.]'s performance" and that speech therapy was mandatory.

The Sparta School District ("Sparta") designed an Individualized Education Program ("IEP") for C.B. on June 4, 2003, to be implemented from the period of July 1 to September 3, 2003, and the following school year. The IEP provided for twelve and a half-hours of special instruction, including speech/language therapy two times per week for thirty minutes, plus individual speech/language therapy two times per week for thirty minutes.

B

After Appellants moved to Missoula, Montana, in the summer of 2003, C.B. enrolled in Hellgate Elementary School. In August 2003, C.B.'s parents hand-delivered a copy of C.B.'s medical and educational records to Hellgate's special education director, Sally Woodruff. At this meeting, C.B.'s parents discussed Dr. Gold's evaluation with Ms. Woodruff.

Hellgate adopted the IEP designed by Sparta in August 2003. When Hellgate personnel observed that the plan was not benefitting C.B., it reduced speech therapy for a two and a half-week period from August to September 2003. Jamie Frost, the Hellgate speech pathologist, disagreed with the need for two hours of weekly speech/language therapy provided for in the Sparta IEP. She stated that it caused C.B. to "shut down" and "refuse to talk" in the classroom.

. . . .

On September 22, 2003, Hellgate convened a meeting to develop a new IEP for C.B. C.B.'s parents were present. At the meeting, Hellgate personnel stated that they lacked sufficient information about C.B.'s educational needs to develop specific IEP goals and objectives for him. Before this meeting, the Hellgate members of the IEP team had read Dr. Gold's evaluation, but did not discuss it at the meeting. The IEP team determined that C.B. should be evaluated by conducting classroom observations for approximately six weeks to assess his speech, language, behavioral, social, and preschool readiness skills. The IEP team's plan was set forth in a document entitled a "diagnostic IEP." The diagnostic IEP reduced educational and related services from thirteen and a half hours to approximately five hours per week. It also reduced speech therapy from two hours per week to one-half hour per week. C.B.'s mother signed the diagnostic IEP.

On November 18, 2003, Hellgate conducted a meeting to create an IEP to replace the diagnostic IEP. During this meeting, C.B.'s parents suggested to Hellgate IEP team members that C.B. might be autistic. The Hellgate IEP team referred the parents to Missoula Child Development Center ("CDC"), where free autism testing could be performed with parental consent. On March 3, 2004, the CDC reported that C.B. exhibited behavior consistent with autism spectrum disorder, including significant ongoing speech and language deficits, motor skill deficits, mild cognitive deficits, and atypical behaviors. In response to the CDC's diagnosis, the IEP team reconvened on March 22, 2004. It revised the IEP, incrementally increasing preschool instruction time from approximately five hours per week to twelve and a half hours per week by May 24, 2004.

C

The IEP team reconvened on May 7, 2004, to develop C.B.'s IEP for the 2004–05 school year . . . . C.B.'s parents were present. . . . The parents did not sign the plan and did not enroll C.B. in Hellgate in September 2004.

. . . .

IV

. . . .

B

. . . .

. . . In determining whether Hellgate denied Plaintiff a FAPE, the court must engage in a two-step inquiry. First, the court must examine "whether 'the State complied with the procedures set forth in the Act' and, second, whether 'the individualized educational program developed through the Act's procedures [was] reasonably calculated to enable the child to receive educational benefits.'" *Amanda J. ex rel. Annette J. v. Clark County Sch. Dist.*, 267 F.3d 877, 890 (9th Cir. 2001) (alteration in original) (quoting *Rowley*, 458 U.S. at 206–07). However, the court need not reach the question of substantive compliance if the court finds "'procedural inadequacies that result in the loss of educational opportunity, or seriously infringe the parents' opportunity to participate in the IEP formulation process, or that caused a deprivation of educational benefits.'" *Ms. S. ex rel. G. v. Vashon Island Sch. Dist.*, 337 F.3d 1115, 1129 (9th Cir. 2003) (quoting *Amanda J.*, 267 F.3d at 892). . . .

C

Compliance with the IDEA procedures is "essential to ensuring that every eligible child receives a FAPE, and those procedures which provide for meaningful parent participation are particularly important." *Amanda J.*, 267 F.3d at 891. "When the elaborate and highly specific procedural safeguards embodied in [the IDEA] are contrasted with the general and somewhat imprecise substantive admonitions contained in the Act, we think that the importance Congress attached to these procedural safeguards cannot be gainsaid." *Rowley*, 458 U.S. at 205. . . .

. . . .

Appellants contend that C.B.'s IEPs were not developed in compliance with the IDEA procedural requirements because . . . Hellgate failed to meet its obligation to evaluate C.B. in all areas of suspected disability. As explained below, we are persuaded that the district court erred in determining that Hellgate complied with the procedural requirements of the IDEA. We conclude that Hellgate's failure to meet its obligation to evaluate C.B. in all areas of suspected disability, including whether he is autistic, was a procedural error that denied C.B. a FAPE. . . .

D

Appellants assert that Hellgate failed to meet its obligation under the IDEA to evaluate C.B. when it referred C.B.'s parents to the CDC, for an autism evaluation, rather than arranging for an evaluation after being apprised of Dr. Gold's diagnosis. Appellants do not object to the fact that the CDC conducted the evaluation; it is undisputed that Hellgate did not have personnel qualified to conduct an autism evaluation. Rather, Appellants maintain that Hellgate's failure to *obtain* the evaluation and to give C.B.'s parents notice that it would pay the cost of an evaluation, if any, violated the IDEA. Appellants contend that the hearing officer and the district court erroneously concluded that C.B.'s parents had the burden of obtaining the evaluation from the CDC. They also argue that Hellgate's failure to obtain a timely autism evaluation was fatal to the development and delivery of a FAPE during the 2003–4 school year.

A child must be tested in all areas of suspected disability. The evaluation includes gathering information "that may assist in determining . . . the content of the child's individualized education program, including information related to enabling the child to be involved in and progress in the general curriculum, or, for preschool children, to participate in appropriate activities." 20 U.S.C. § 1414(b)(2)(A) (1998). The "local educational agency shall administer such tests and other evaluation materials as may be needed to produce the data identified by the IEP Team" in order to determine the needs of the child. *Id.* § 1414(c)(2). "Each local educational agency shall ensure that—(B) any standardized tests that are given to the child— . . . (ii) are administered by trained and knowledgeable personnel." *Id.* § 1414(b)(3)(B)(ii) (1998). In conducting or obtaining an evaluation, the school district "shall ensure that the child is assessed in all areas of suspected disability." *Id.* § 1414(b)(3)(C0) (1997); 34 C.F.R. § 300.532(g) (1999).

As of September 2003, Hellgate's IEP team members were on notice that C.B. likely suffered from some form of autism. The record indicates that C.B.'s parents discussed Dr. Gold's evaluation with Hellgate's special education director in August 2003. Further, it is undisputed that by the time of the September 2003 IEP meeting, Hellgate personnel had reviewed Dr. Gold's evaluation. This evaluation was enclosed in C.B.'s file indicating that there was an "autistic component" to C.B.'s poor performance.

Hellgate suggested to C.B.'s parents that they obtain a general evaluation of C.B. at the September 22, 2003, IEP meeting. It referred C.B.'s parents to the CDC for general testing. Hellgate contends that, despite this recommendation, C.B.'s parents failed to procure an evaluation from the CDC after the September 2003 IEP meeting. The fact that Hellgate referred the parents to the CDC shows that Hellgate was mindful that an evaluation was necessary. Thus, Hellgate's assertion that it did not suspect C.B. had autism prior to the November 2003 IEP meeting, because C.B.'s parents had not raised it at a prior IEP meeting, is not supported by the record. Hellgate failed to meet its obligation to evaluate C.B. in all areas of suspected disabilities after becoming aware of Dr. Gold's diagnosis.

Hellgate did not fulfill its statutory obligations by simply referring C.B.'s parents to the CDC. Such an action does not "ensure that the child is assessed," as required by 20 U.S.C. § 1414(b)(3)(C); *see also Union Sch. Dist. v. Smith,* 15 F.3d 1519, 1523 (9th Cir. 1994) (holding that a parent's failure to secure an evaluation, even if the parents agreed to obtain it, does not excuse the school district's obligation under the IDEA to secure such an evaluation). . . .

. . . .

The failure to obtain critical medical information about whether a child has autism "render[s] the accomplishment of the IDEA's goals—and the achievement of a FAPE—impossible." *Amanda J.*, 267 F.3d at 894. In *Amanda J.*, the school district withheld from Amanda's parents reports indicating possible autism. This court stated:

> We hold that, by failing to disclose Amanda's full records to her parents once they were requested . . . the District denied Amanda a FAPE. The IEP team could not create an IEP that addressed Amanda's special needs as an autistic child without knowing that Amanda was autistic. Even worse, Amanda's parents were not informed of the possibility that their daughter suffered from autism—a disease that benefits from early intensive intervention—despite the fact that the district's records contained test results indicating as much. Not only were Amanda's parents prevented from participating fully, effectively, and in an informed manner in the development of Amanda's IEP, they were not even aware that an independent psychiatric evaluation was recommended, an evaluation that Amanda's mother testified she would have had performed immediately. These procedural violations, which prevented Amanda's parents from learning critical medical information about their child, rendered the accomplishment of the IDEA's goals—and the achievement of a FAPE—impossible.

Id. Similar to the circumstances in *Amanda J.*, without evaluative information that C.B. has autism spectrum disorder, it was not possible for the IEP team to develop a plan reasonably calculated to provide C.B. with a meaningful educational benefit throughout the 2003–04 school year. Because of this procedural error, Appellants are entitled to the costs of the services that they incurred during the 2003–04 school year and associated legal fees.

. . . .

2. The Evaluation Process

Initiating the Evaluation Process: A parent or a school district may request an initial evaluation. 20 U.S.C. § 1414(a)(1)(B) (2012); 34 C.F.R. § 300.301(b) (2015). The IDEA does not require a parent to request an evaluation in order to trigger a school district's obligation to conduct one. Scott v. District of Columbia, 2006 U.S. Dist. WESTLAW 1102839 at *8 (D.D.C. Mar. 31, 2006) ("The Circuit's holdings require DCPS to identify and evaluate students in need of special education services and related services, whether or not parents have made any request, written or oral."). If a school district proposes to conduct an evaluation, it must provide notice to the child's parents that describes the evaluation procedures the district will utilize. 20 U.S.C. § 1414(b)(1).

Informed Parental Consent to Initial Evaluation: A school district must secure informed parental consent prior to commencing the initial evaluation. 20 U.S.C. § 1414 (a)(1)(D)(i)(I); 34 C.F.R. § 300.300(a)(1). In *G.J. v. Muscogee Cnty. Sch. Dist.*, 668 F.3d 1258 (11th Cir. 2012), the parents alleged that the district did not give them an opportunity to consent to a re-evaluation because it did not tell them the names of the tests it planned to use, but instead asked them to sign blank forms. The parental consent form stated:

> [I]f you have any questions about why we feel your child needs testing or want to know more details about the evaluation, please call your child's school. If you agree to have this evaluation done, you can request to know the exact time and place that it will occur. You will have the chance to discuss the results following the evaluation. You will also be invited to a meeting to discuss the findings. No changes will be made in your child's educational program until we hold the meeting. The individual evaluation may include tests in the following areas: vision, hearing, motor skills, social/emotional, achievement, speech/language or others. An explanation of these areas is included. Your parental rights are included, which shows that you have certain rights regarding consent and evaluation procedures.

Id. at 1264. The court ruled that because the scope of the proposed testing was discussed at a previous IEP meeting and the consent form included examples of the tests that would be used, the district provided sufficient information to the parents. *Id.* In *C.H. v. Northwest Indep. Sch. Dist.*, 815 F. Supp. 2d 977 (E.D. Tex. 2011), the court held that although the district failed to receive prior consent to the testing, this did not deny the child a FAPE or interfere with the parents' participation in the decision-making process because the district informed the child's parents orally of the proposed testing before it conducted the tests and the parent signed the consent form after the district conducted the test. *Id.* at 987–88.

Refusal to Consent to Initial Evaluation: If a parent fails to consent to an initial evaluation and the school district nevertheless desires to conduct the evaluation, it must request an impartial hearing to receive approval to do so. 20 U.S.C. § 1414(a)(1)(D)(ii). *See* Schaffer v. Weast, 546 U.S. 49, 53 (2005) (stating that a school district can request an administrative hearing if the parents refuse to consent to an evaluation). However, even if a district receives approval to conduct an evaluation over the parent's objection, it cannot conduct the evaluation if the parents educate their child privately and waive their IDEA rights. Fitzgerald v. Camdenton R-III Sch. Dist., 439 F.3d 773, 777 (8th Cir. 2006) ("Where a home-schooled child's parents refuse consent, privately educate the child, and expressly waive all benefits under the IDEA, an evaluation would have no purpose.").

Timeframe for Completing the Initial Evaluation: The school district must conduct the evaluation "within 60 days of receiving parental consent . . . ." 20 U.S.C. § 1414 (a)(1)(C)(i)(1); 34 C.F.R. § 300.301(c)(1)(i). If a district fails to conduct an evaluation within sixty days, a child is entitled to relief if the delay denied the child a free appropriate public education. D.K. v. Abington Sch. Dist., 696 F.3d 233, 251 n. 6, 252 (3d Cir. 2012) (ruling that failure to conduct an evaluation within sixty days did not result in a substantive violation of the IDEA because the district provided a FAPE during that time). The sixty-day time limit does not apply if the child's parent does not make the child available for evaluation. 20 U.S.C. § 1414(a)(1)(C)(ii)(II); 34 C.F.R. § 300.301(d)(1). *See* Eschenasy v. N.Y.C. Dep't of Educ., 604 F. Supp. 2d 639, 652–53 (S.D.N.Y. 2009) (excusing school from complying with sixty-day time limit because shortly after request for evaluation, child left the country for a vacation, enrolled in an out-of-state school, and did not return for the evaluation). In contrast, in *Integrated Design and Electronics Academic Pub. Charter Sch. v. McKinley*, 570 F. Supp. 2d 28, 35–36 (D.D.C. 2008), the court ruled that the child's parent and advocate were attempting to cooperate with the district and that missed meetings and missed communications did not excuse the district from conducting the evaluation in a timely manner.

Requirements for Conducting an Initial Evaluation: A school district must "conduct a full and individual initial evaluation . . . before the initial provision of special education and related services to a child with a disability . . . ." 20 U.S.C. § 1414(a)(1)(A); 34 C.F.R. § 300.301(a). The IDEA imposes several requirements on districts for conducting initial evaluations. A district must:

a. "use a variety of assessment tools and strategies to gather relevant functional, developmental, and academic information, including information provided by the parent that may assist in determining whether the child is a child with a disability . . . ." 20 U.S.C. § 1414(b)(2)(A)(i); 34 C.F.R. 300.304(b)(1)(i);

b. not use a single criterion or test as the only basis to determine whether a child has a disability. 20 U.S.C. § 1414(b)(2)(B); 34 C.F.R. § 300.304(b)(2);

c. "use technically sound instruments that may assess the relative contribution of cognitive and behavioral factors, in addition to physical or developmental factors." 20 U.S.C. § 1414(b)(2)(C); 34 C.F.R. § 300.304(b)(3). In *M.Z. v. Bethlehem Area Sch. Dist.*, 521 F. App'x 74 (3d Cir. 2013), *cert. denied*, __ U.S.__, 134 S.Ct. 479 (2013), the court upheld a challenge to an evaluation on the grounds that the evaluation did not include relevant information to assist in making a determination:

> The record makes clear that the evaluation's chosen tools and strategies were not "sufficiently comprehensive" and did not satisfy the requirement to "provide relevant information that directly assists persons in determining the educational needs of the child are provided." 34 C.F.R. § 300.304. The Hearing Officer found that the most important factor in determining M.Z.'s progress in acquiring pragmatic language skills was how well he was able to apply those skills in peer settings on a daily basis. The Hearing Officer also found that the data collected on this factor was "anecdotal" and "not specifically directed toward reporting on Student's IEP goals"—evidence that the methods used were inadequate to properly assess M.Z.'s progress. Furthermore, as the Hearing Officer determined, the assessment tools used did not provide relevant information needed to make a prospective determination of future eligibility for services in light of M.Z.'s transition to a new setting, given that M.Z.'s ability to apply pragmatic language skills had been shown to vary based on differences in the classroom environment.

Id. at 76–77;

d. "ensure that assessments and other evaluation materials are . . . not . . . discriminatory on a racial or cultural basis" and "are . . . in the language and form most likely to yield accurate information" about a child. 20 U.S.C. § 1414(b)(3)(A)(i)–(ii); 34 C.F.R. § 300.304(c)(1)(i)-(ii);

e. ensure that assessment and evaluation materials "are used for purposes for which they are valid and reliable" and "administered by trained and knowledgeable personnel . . . ." 20 U.S.C..§ 1414(b)(3)(A)(iii)-(iv); 34 C.F.R. § 300.304(c)(1)(iii)-(iv);

f. assess the child "in all areas of suspected disability . . . ." 20 U.S.C. § 1414(b)(3)(B); 34 C.F.R. § 300.304(c)(4). In *M.M. v. District of Columbia*, 607 F. Supp. 2d 168, 173–74 (D.D.C. 2009), the plaintiffs argued that the district violated this provision by failing to conduct a psychiatric evaluation to determine whether the child had ADHD. The court upheld the district's decision because the child's "psycho-social evaluation did not recommend an immediate evaluation." Instead the district recommended "that a decision about a psychiatric evaluation wait to see if behavioral interventions worked."; *see also* J.W. v. Fresno Unified Sch. Dist., 626 F.3d 431, 443 (9th Cir. 2010) (rejecting plaintiff's claim that district failed to assess student's auditory skills and finding the district's assessments were appropriate); Grant v. Cumberland Cnty. Sch. Dist., 190 F.3d 80, 87 (3d Cir. 1999) (ruling that the school district's evaluations were inappropriate because they failed to identify the children's learning disabilities);

g. use "assessment tools and strategies that provide relevant information that directly assists persons in determining the educational needs of the child . . . ." 20 U.S.C. § 1414(b)(3)(C); 34 C.F.R. § 300.304(c)(7); and

h. "review existing evaluation data on the child, including—evaluations; information provided by the parents of the child; classroom-based, local, or state assessments and classroom-based observations; and observations by teachers and related services providers . . . ." 20 U.S.C § 1414(c)(1)(A)(i)-(iii); 34 C.F.R. § 300.305(a)(1). *See* Babb v. Knox Cnty. Sch. Sys., 965 F.2d 104, 108 (6th Cir. 1992), *cert. denied*, 506 U.S. 941 (1992) (ruling that district did not satisfy its obligation to evaluate the child because the school psychologist "failed to examine . . . [the child's] complete academic, psychological and behavioral history . . . .").

Eligibility Determination: When it completes the initial evaluation, the school district must determine whether the child has a disability. 20 U.S.C. § 1414(b)(4)(A). A school district is prohibited from identifying a child as having a disability if the determining factor was insufficient reading or math instruction or limited English ability. *Id.* at § (b)(5). In deciding whether a child "has a specific learning disability," a school district is not "required to take into consideration whether a child has a severe discrepancy between achievement and intellectual ability in oral expression, listening comprehension, written expression, basic reading skill, reading comprehension, mathematical calculation, or mathematical reasoning." *Id.* at § (b)(6)(A).

Re-evaluation: A school district must re-evaluate a student with a disability if the district determines that a re-evaluation is necessary, if the parents or teacher requests one, and every three years unless the parents and the school district agree it is not necessary. 20 U.S.C. § 1414(a)(2)(A) and (B)(ii); 34 C.F.R. § 300.303(a) and (b)(2). A school district cannot conduct a re-evaluation more than once a year unless the school district and parents agree. 20 U.S.C. § 1414(a)(2)(B)(i); 34 C.F.R. § 300.303(b)(1). A hearing officer or court can order a parent to consent to a re-evaluation in less than one year. *See* M.L. v. El Paso Indep. Sch. Dist., 610 F. Supp. 2d 582, 598 (W.D. Tex. 2009), *aff'd*, 369 F. App'x (rejecting parent's claim that the hearing officer was not authorized to allow district to conduct a re-evaluation in less than one year even though she refused to consent). Failure to conduct a re-evaluation within a three-year period violates the IDEA if the child suffered an educational deprivation as a result. *See* Evans v. Dist. No. 17 of Douglas Cnty., 841 F.2d 824, 830–31 (8th Cir. 1988) (holding that delay in conducting re-evaluation did not violate the IDEA because the school district could not have implemented any changes to child's IEP any sooner and the re-evaluation was nearly the same as the evaluation from three years earlier).

Informed Parental Consent to Re-evaluation: A parent must provide informed consent before a school district may re-evaluate the child. 20 U.S.C. § 1414(c)(3); 34 C.F.R. § 300.300(c)(1). *See* G.J. v. Muscogee Cnty. Sch. Dist., 668 F.3d 1258, 1264 (11th Cir. 2012) (holding that parents did not consent to re-evaluation when they placed several restrictive conditions on their consent, including who would conduct the evaluation, their presence during the evaluation, and when they would receive the results). Parents must consent to a re-evaluation if they want the school district to continue providing special education and related services to their child. Andress v. Cleveland Indep. Sch. Dist., 64 F.3d 176, 178 (5th Cir. 1995) ("If a student's parents want him to receive special education under the IDEA, they must allow the school itself to reevaluate the student and they cannot force the school to rely solely on an independent evaluation."); Gregory K. v. Longview Sch. Dist., 811 F.2d 1307, 1315 (9th Cir. 1987) (stating that parents must allow triennial reassessment of child for child to be eligible for special education); M.L. v. El Paso Indep. Sch. Dist., 610 F. Supp. 2d 582, 599 (W.D. Tex. 2009) (stating that unless parents consent to a re-evaluation their child will no longer be eligible for special education). A school district is not required to obtain consent "if it made reasonable efforts to obtain consent" and the parents did not respond. 20 U.S.C. § 1414(c)(3); 34 C.F.R. § 300.00(c)(2). If a parent refuses to agree to a re-evaluation, the school district may request an impartial hearing seeking an order permitting it to conduct the re-evaluation. 34 C.F.R. § 300.300(c)(1)(ii); *see also M.L.*, 610 F. Supp. 2d at 598 (ruling that the IDEA regulations give a hearing officer "the authority to override lack of parental consent for a reevaluation."). In addition, a hearing officer can order an evaluation in connection with an impartial hearing if necessary to assist the hearing officer to reach a decision. B.J.S. v. State Educ. Dep't, 815 F. Supp. 2d 601, 615 (W.D.N.Y. 2011) (upholding remand for re-evaluation and additional hearing). A district cannot compel a re-evaluation if the parents plan to educate their child privately. Gregory K. v. Longview Sch. Dist., 811 F.2d 1307, 1315 (9th Cir. 1987).

Conducting a Re-evaluation: In conducting a re-evaluation, the school district must follow the same procedural and notice requirements applicable to initial evaluations. 34 C.F.R. § 300.303(a). A school district has the right to have its own educational experts conduct a re-evaluation. M.T.V. v. Dekalb Cnty. Sch. Dist, 446 F.3d 1153, 1160 (11th Cir. 2006) (upholding district court's decision that the school district had the right to re-evaluate the child with its own expert); Johnson v. Duneland Sch. Corp., 92 F.3d 554, 558 (7th Cir. 1996) (holding that "because the school is required to provide the child with an education, it ought to have the right to conduct its own evaluation of the student and the school cannot be forced to rely solely on an independent evaluation conducted at the parents' behest . . . ."); Andress v. Cleveland Indep. Sch. Dist., 64 F.3d 176, 178 (5th Cir. 1995), *cert. denied*, 519 U.S. 812 (1996) (holding that district is entitled to conduct its own re-evaluation and not rely exclusively on an IEE).

Declassifying a Child: Before deciding that a child no longer has a disability, a school district must evaluate a child following the rules for an initial evaluation. 20 U.S.C. § 1414(c)(5).

Functional Behavioral Assessment: In *D.K. v. Abington Sch. Dist.*, 696 F.3d 233 (3d Cir. 2012), the court considered a claim that the school district failed to satisfy its obligation to evaluate the child because, among other reasons, it did not conduct a functional behavioral assessment. The court ruled:

> Plaintiffs contend, among other things, that the School District's failure to use a functional behavioral assessment rendered the testing legally inadequate. But the IDEA and its implementing regulations do not require that a school use a functional behavioral assessment when initially testing students for suspected disabilities. The four tests the School District did employ covered discrepant skill sets and probed for indicia of varying disabilities. The mere fact that a subsequent evaluation of D.K. yielded a different result—*i.e.* he was found disabled with an "other health impairment" in November 2007 but did not qualify in April 2006—does not necessarily render the earlier testing inadequate. Therefore, we will not second-guess the findings of the state agency or the District Court on this question.

Id. at 251.

Chapter 10

The Individualized Education Program

Introduction

The individualized education program (IEP) is a "written statement for each child with a disability. . . ." 20 U.S.C. § 1401(14) (2012). The IEP is drafted by a team that includes representatives of the child's school district and the child's parents. It contains extensive information about the child, including the child's disability, the special education and related services the child will receive, annual goals, and the child's placement. *Id.* § 1414(d)(1)(A).

The Supreme Court has characterized the IEP as "the centerpiece of the . . . education delivery system for disabled children. . . ." Honig v. Doe, 484 U.S. 305, 311 (1988). A school district must provide special education and related services "in conformity with" the child's IEP. 20 U.S.C. § 1401(9)(D); *see also* 34 C.F.R. § 304.323(c)(2) (2015) (requiring school districts to provide special education and related services "in accordance with" the child's IEP). The IEP plays such an important role in providing special education and related services to a child that a school district's failure to adopt an IEP for a child denies the child a FAPE. *See* Baltimore City Bd. of Sch. Comm'r v. Taylorch, 395 F. Supp. 2d 246, 248–49 (D. Md. 2005).

Section One considers the rule prohibiting a school district from "predetermining" a child's educational placement or special education and related services before it completes the IEP. Section Two considers the role of parents and other members of the IEP team in drafting an IEP. Section Three covers the contents of an IEP and Section Four covers issues relating to implementing an IEP.

As you read the cases and materials in this chapter, consider the following excerpts from two district court decisions in cases raising claims that a school district's various violations of the procedural requirements for preparing an IEP denied the child a FAPE. They are paradigmatic of two different approaches courts take in evaluating such claims. In the first case, the school district committed several procedural violations and the court ruled that in doing so, the district violated the IDEA:

> The Court notes that the hearing officer rejected multiple arguments made by the parents that the violation of various procedural safeguards constituted a denial of FAPE. Nevertheless, she ultimately concluded that the 2004, 2005, and 2006 IEPs *all* failed to provide D.S. with a meaningful educational

> benefit and thus denied FAPE. She found that the District failed to do any of the testing that it intended and received parents' consent to perform. Despite D.S.'s new diagnosis of autism in 2004, the only category of disability addressed was cerebral palsy. She found that no regular education teacher was present at the 2004 IEP meeting, and neither the school principal, a Teacher Consultant, or an Administrative Facilitator attended, "thus no District Representative qualified to provide or supervise the provision of specially designed instruction to meet the unique needs of this disabled child . . . was present." The hearing officer went on to find that the April 2005 IEP failed for many of the same reasons. Testing was abandoned and a functional behavior assessment was promised, then forgotten. No testing instruments to determine the educational needs of autistic students were administered. The 2005 IEP meeting took place on a date which the parents were unavailable, and the District declined to change the date. Further, the 2005 IEP lacked a plan for dealing with D.S.'s persistent behaviors that interfered with his learning. Similarly, the hearing officer found that the January 2006 IEP suffered many of the same procedural and substantive flaws as the two previous IEPs. Specifically, it failed to assess D.S.'s needs and contained vague Goals and Objectives without baselines or methods to objectively measure progress.

Anchorage Sch. Dist. v. D.S., 688 F.Supp. 2d 883, 888–89 (D. Alaska 2009). In the second case, the parents alleged a similar list of procedural violations but the court denied their claims, stating:

> We do not minimize the importance which the Courts have attached to the procedural preconditions of an acceptable IEP, but we underscore that an IEP need not have the paradigmatic precision of a military "close order drill" in order to pass muster. . . .
>
> . . . .
>
> As a consequence, a challenge to the validity of an IEP, based upon a "laundry listing" which details a "myriad of technical" deficiencies, may well be insufficient to discredit the appropriateness of the education that was shouldered by that IEP. . . .
>
> . . . .
>
> Moreover, unlike a chemical formula, which will produce the same reaction so long as the laws of science endure, an IEP will not produce a perfect, predictable result with the same inevitability.

Independent Sch. Dist. No. 283 v. S.D., 948 F. Supp. 860, 878, 882–83 (D. Minn. 1995), *aff'd*, 88 F.3d 556 (8th Cir. 1996). As you read through this chapter, consider which of these two approaches to evaluating claims that a school district violated the procedural rules for adopting an IEP is more consistent with the language and purpose of the IDEA.

Problem

L.M. is a second grade student at Harriet Tubman Elementary School. L.M. was diagnosed with autism in first grade. The district prepared an IEP for L.M. for second grade that included ten hours per week of Applied Behavior Analysis (ABA) therapy at school. L.M. was placed in a regular education class the rest of the time.

L.M.'s school district began to plan for L.M.'s IEP for third grade in April of her second-grade year. The district's special education director, Dr. Bell, collected assessment reports and evaluations from L.M.'s general education teacher and ABA therapist. According to the reports, L.M. was not making progress on her IEP goals. The reports also indicated that L.M. was having difficulty paying attention and staying on task and often acted out.

The district set the IEP meeting for April 24. Prior to that meeting, on April 17, Dr. Bell held a meeting with L.M.'s teacher and ABA therapist, a special education teacher, and the school psychologist to discuss L.M.'s placement for third grade. They agreed that, based on L.M.'s lack of progress and behavioral problems, they would suggest at the upcoming IEP meeting that L.M. be assigned full-time to a self-contained class exclusively for children with autism. The classroom would have one teacher, one aide, and six students with autism from various grades. L.M. would continue to receive the same amount of ABA therapy.

In attendance at the IEP meeting on April 24 were Dr. Bell, a special education teacher, L.M.'s ABA therapist, the school psychologist, and L.M.'s parents. Dr. Bell indicated that L.M. was not meeting her goals and that her behavior was an obstacle to her progress. Dr. Bell presented the district's recommendation that L.M. be assigned to a self-contained class. L.M.'s parents were surprised. They said they had noticed marked improvement in L.M.'s language and ability to complete simple self-care tasks. For example, they said that she used approximately twenty-five words, up from ten the year before. They also indicated that L.M. recognized ten letters and could count from one to ten. Dr. Bell responded that given L.M.'s aptitude, she should have made more progress than this.

L.M.'s parents stated that they had not received any indication from L.M.'s teacher that things were not working for L.M. in the general education classroom. They asked why L.M.'s teacher was not at the IEP meeting because they had questions for her. Dr. Bell answered, "She has another obligation and we didn't think L.M. was under consideration for general education next year." L.M.'s parents agreed that L.M. had behavioral issues and stated that she was having similar issues at home. They stated that they had developed some strategies to deal with L.M.'s behavior that were partially successful, including rewards and changing tasks, and asked if L.M.'s teacher had been trying similar strategies. Dr. Bell indicated he would find out and report back. L.M.'s parents also indicated that L.M.'s ABA therapy seemed to have a positive effect, and that they worked with L.M.'s therapist to follow-through with L.M.'s ABA training at home. They stated that they thought additional ABA therapy at home would help, and asked if the district could pay for it because they could not afford to pay for it. Dr. Bell said that the district did not think that extra ABA therapy would be helpful. The district's experience had been that there were diminishing returns on more than ten hours of ABA therapy each week and that the district utilized other strategies to meet the educational needs of children with autism. Finally, L.M.'s parents stated that they had been working with an educational consultant specializing in autism at the Daystrom Center. The consultant had worked with L.M. and had many good ideas for teaching her. L.M.'s parents asked if the consultant could observe L.M. in her classroom to see if she could propose alternatives to the self-contained classroom. Dr. Bell indicated that he would get back to her on this request.

At the end of the meeting, Dr. Bell indicated it would be necessary to convene a second IEP meeting. He scheduled the meeting for May 10. He said he would invite L.M.'s regular education teacher to the meeting. On May 9, L.M.'s mother called Dr. Bell to indicate that an emergency had arisen and neither she nor L.M.'s father could attend the IEP meeting the next day. Dr. Bell suggested several additional dates, but L.M.'s parents were not available on any of them. Dr. Bell indicated that due to impending deadlines and the lack of availability of IEP team members later in the school year, he could not adjourn the meeting. At the May 10 meeting, the team heard from L.M.'s general education teacher about L.M.'s behavioral issues and lack of progress. The teacher indicated that she had attempted to deal with L.M.'s behavioral issues by denying her rewards but this had not worked. They did not make any decisions about L.M.'s IEP. The district held a third IEP meeting on May 17. L.M.'s general education teacher was not at this meeting, but another general education teacher from L.M.'s school, who had been briefed on L.M.'s situation, was there. L.M.'s parents were at the meeting and they pressed Dr. Bell on allowing the Daystrom Center consultant to observe L.M. during class. Dr. Bell agreed. They agreed to re-convene the IEP meeting on May 24.

On May 20, the consultant observed L.M. in her classroom. She prepared a written report and shared it with the IEP team prior to the May 24 meeting. She also summarized the report orally at the meeting. The report confirmed L.M.'s parents' assertion that L.M. had been making progress under the current IEP. The report suggested several alternatives to a self-contained classroom, including a one-to-one aide for L.M. for at least part of the day or assignment to an integrated co-teaching classroom, in which a special education and general education teacher would instruct a class that included general education students and students with IEPs. The consultant's report also documented the positive effect ABA therapy had on L.M. and presented her recommendation that the district provide ten additional hours of ABA therapy per week at L.M.'s home and train L.M.'s parents in ABA techniques. Finally, the consultant recommended that the district conduct a functional behavioral analysis of L.M. and determine appropriate strategies to deal with her behavior issues, and in the meantime that the district adopt the behavioral management techniques that L.M.'s parent utilized. The IEP team listened while the consultant spoke and did not ask any questions. When the consultant finished, Dr. Bell thanked her. He said he considered everything she said but was not persuaded that the proposal would provide L.M. with a FAPE. Dr. Bell stated that the district would prepare an IEP for L.M. that placed her in a self-contained classroom. He did agree, however, to provide L.M.'s parents with ABA training and to utilize different behavioral strategies. L.M.'s parents registered their disagreement and disappointment and the meeting ended.

Four weeks later, L.M.'s parents received L.M.'s IEP in the mail. It indicated that L.M. would be in a self-contained class for children with autism at a different school. L.M.'s parents were surprised and angry; they did not know the self-contained class was in a different elementary school. They felt the school was too far away and felt that it would be very difficult for L.M. to adjust to a new school.

L.M.'s parents have retained you to file a request for an impartial hearing to challenge the IEP. What grounds do they have for challenging the IEP? How would you assess the strengths and weaknesses of the claims?

Section One
Predetermination of the Terms of a Child's IEP

If a school district decides on a child's special education, related services, or educational placement before it finishes drafting the child's IEP, the district has violated the IDEA. As the Fourth Circuit stated:

> Under the EHA, the general rule is that placement should be based on the IEP. The appendix interpreting the EHA regulations states that "IEP objectives must be written before placement." The decision to place Jonathan at Randolph before developing an IEP on which to base that placement violates this regulation .... It also violates the spirit and intent of the EHA, which emphasizes parental involvement. After the fact involvement is not enough.

Spielberg v. Henrico Cnty. Pub. Sch., 853 F.2d 256, 259 (4th Cir. 1988); *see also* 20 U.S.C. § 1401(9)(D) (2012) (requiring school districts to provide special education and related services "in conformity with" the child's IEP); 34 C.F.R. § 300.323(c)(2) (2015) (requiring school districts to provide special education and related services "in accordance with the child's IEP"); Evans v. Bd. of Educ. of Rhinebeck Cent. Sch. Dist., 930 F. Supp. 83, 95 (S.D.N.Y. 1996) (holding that district's placement of the child at school before the IEP was in effect violated the IDEA). The following two cases consider such predetermination claims and reach different results.

Deal v. Hamilton Cnty. Bd. of Educ.

392 F.3d 840 (6th Cir. 2004)

Marbley, District Judge.

... Plaintiffs-Appellants assert that the School System failed to provide Zachary with a ... FAPE ... and that they therefore are entitled to reimbursement from the School System for the education that they provided Zachary at their own expense. ...

....

III. DISCUSSION

C. VIOLATIONS OF THE IDEA

1. Standards Under the IDEA

As part of providing a FAPE, school districts receiving funds under the IDEA are required to establish an IEP for each child with a disability. The IEP must "contain a specific statement of the child's current performance levels, the child's short-term and long-term goals, the educational and other services to be provided, and criteria for evaluating the child's progress."

There are two parts to a court's inquiry in suits brought pursuant to the IDEA. First, the court must determine whether the school system has complied with the procedures set forth in the IDEA. Second, the court must assess whether the IEP developed through those procedures was reasonably calculated to enable the child to receive educational benefits. . . .

With regard to procedural matters, a court should "strictly review an IEP for procedural compliance," although technical deviations will not render an IEP invalid. A finding of procedural violations does not necessarily entitle appellants to relief. Only if a procedural violation has resulted in substantive harm, and thus constitutes a denial of a FAPE, may relief be granted. The Supreme Court has emphasized the importance Congress attached to the IDEA's procedural safeguards:

> [T]he congressional emphasis upon full participation of concerned parties throughout the development of the IEP, as well as the requirements that state and local plans be submitted to the Secretary for approval, demonstrates the legislative conviction that adequate compliance with the procedures prescribed would in most cases assure much if not all of what Congress wished in the way of substantive content in an IEP.

Rowley, 458 U.S. at 206 . . . .

. . . .

2. Procedural Violations

a. Predetermination

The ALJ found that the School System "clearly" had an unofficial policy of refusing to consider Lovaas style ABA for autistic children and that School System personnel consistently attended IEP meetings having "pre-selected" the extant School System program regardless of Zachary's demonstrated individual needs. The ALJ's conclusion of predetermination was based on the following findings of fact:

> 24. Ms. Jane Dixon, an HCDE Special Education Supervisor, met with Mrs. Deal on May 19, 1997 and at the meeting she discussed programs available for autistic children without mentioning the Lovaas style ABA as a methodology for the parents to explore.
>
> . . . .

56. At the May 11, 1998 IEP meeting, Sandra Jerardi told the Deals that there were certain things she would like to give (Zachary) but that she could not because she could not give the same service to everybody.

. . . .

63. The HCDE has consistently rejected providing Lovaas style ABA services to Zachary or any other student in their system . . . .

. . . .

85. HCDE rejects the validity of the Lovaas study and its results and embraces the position of the professionals in the field who have published articles critical of the Lovaas style ABA approach to treating children with autism.

. . . .

105. Jane Dixon told the Deals that they could not ask questions during the March 3, 1999 IEP meeting.

. . . .

111. Ms. Dixon investigated Zachary's parents' dispute with the IEP and interviewed various teachers and providers without interviewing any of the ABA providers even though Lovaas style ABA formed the bulk of Zachary's educational program at that time.

112. HCDE denied the Deal's request for Lovaas style ABA for Zachary in part because HCDE believes it is more expensive than HCDE's current approach.

. . . .

126. *Prior* to the Deals requesting funding for Zachary's ABA program from the HCDE, Ms. Sandra Jerardi authored an internal memo in which she described Zachary's program under IDEA as a "sensitive case with regards to school program and/or Lovaas."

127. Based on other testimony in the record supporting the proposition that the HCDE rejects meaningful consideration of the Lovaas style ABA intervention at least in large part because of its perceived cost, the court finds that Ms. Jerardi was flagging Zachary Deal's education program as sensitive because of its probable cost and adverse impact on the HCDE policy of rejecting any and all requests for Lovaas style ABA for young autistic children.

128. At the May 11, 1998 IEP meeting, the Deals outlined the impressive results Zachary had achieved with the Lovaas style ABA methodology and asked the HCDE to fund a continuation of the program over the summer.

129. HCDE personnel informed the Deals that the "powers that be" were not implementing ABA programs.

> 130. Ms. Jerardi, an HCDE representative and IEP team member in the May 11, 1998 IEP team meeting told the Deals that she wished people would pay their taxes so that HCDE could provide ABA for Zachary.
>
> ....
>
> 157. HCDE has a policy of not considering Lovaas style ABA for autistic children. Sandra Jerardi admits to being impressed by Zachary's present levels of performance yet steadfastly refuses to give any credit to Zachary's intensive Lovaas style ABA program for these achievements. Ms. Jerardi refuses to concede that any progress is attributable to the ABA program even when the progress was obtained over the course of a summer in which the school system provided no services.
>
> ....
>
> 174. HCDE refused the Deal's offer to help train HCDE personnel on Zachary's ABA program and protocols.
>
> ....[12]

... The evidence reveals that the School System, and its representatives, had predecided not to offer Zachary intensive ABA services regardless of any evidence concerning Zachary's individual needs and the effectiveness of his private program. This predetermination amounted to a procedural violation of the IDEA. Because it effectively deprived Zachary's parents of meaningful participation in the IEP process, the predetermination caused substantive harm and therefore deprived Zachary of a FAPE.

The leading case on predetermination is *Spielberg ex rel. Spielberg v. Henrico County Public Schools*, 853 F.2d 256 (4th Cir. 1988). There, the district court had concluded, based on a series of letters written before the IEP meeting that focused on a change in placement, that the school district had decided to change the disabled student's placement before developing an IEP to support the change. The Fourth Circuit affirmed the district court's determination that a procedural violation had occurred that deprived the student of a FAPE:

> Under the EHA ... the general rule is that placement should be based on the IEP. The appendix interpreting the EHA regulations states that "IEP objectives must be written before placement." 34 C.F.R. Part 300, App. C., Question 42. The decision to place Jonathan at Randolph before developing an IEP on which to base that placement violates this regulation as interpreted by

12. The Deals point to two additional pieces of evidence that they claim support a finding of predetermination. First, Donna Palmer, a School System Psychologist, testified at the administrative hearing regarding her familiarity with a publication entitled, "How to Avoid Parents' Demands for Lovass." Second, a letter from the School System's counsel regarding ... the representation in the Deals' administrative hearing stated, "I previously briefed the Board in executive session regarding this litigation and its importance to the system and received its backing in our proposal to defend this litigation vigorously." ...

> the Secretary of Education. It also violates the spirit and intent of the EHA, which emphasizes parental involvement. After the fact involvement is not enough.

Id. at 259. The relevant regulation provides that, in determining the educational placement of a disabled child, the public agency must ensure that the placement "is based on the child's IEP." 34 C.F.R. § 300.552.

W.G. v. Board of Trustees of Target Range School District No. 23, 960 F.2d 1479 (9th Cir. 1992), was a similar case. There, the Ninth Circuit agreed with the district court that the school district had independently developed a proposed IEP that would place the student in a pre-existing, predetermined program. At the IEP meeting, no alternatives to that program were considered. The court held that in order to fulfill the goal of parental participation in the IEP process, the school district was required to conduct, not just an IEP meeting, but a *meaningful* IEP meeting.

Courts often have declined to find predetermination; however, such cases are distinguishable from the case sub judice. *See, e.g.*, *Knox County Sch.*, 315 F.3d at 694–95 (finding no predetermination where parent was not involved in initial, ex parte determination of eligibility but was active participant in final determination); *Fuhrmann ex rel. Fuhrmann v. E. Hanover Bd. of Educ.*, 993 F.2d 1031, 1036 (3d Cir. 1993) (finding parents had opportunity to participate in IEP formulation in meaningful way); *Hanson ex rel. Hanson v. Smith*, 212 F. Supp. 2d 474, 486 (D. Md. 2002) (noting credible evidence that the school board came to IEP meetings with open mind, and that several options were discussed and considered before final recommendation was made); *Doyle v. Arlington Cnty. Sch. Bd.*, 806 F.Supp. 1253, 1262 (E.D. Va. 1992) (holding that school system had merely proposed a placement before IEP was completed and had not "fully made up its mind before the parents ever [got] involved," thereby denying the parents "the opportunity for meaningful input"), *aff'd*, 39 F.3d 1176 (4th Cir. 1994). In *Knox County Schools*, this Court emphasized that school officials are permitted to form opinions and compile reports prior to IEP meetings. The Court cautioned, however, that such conduct is only harmless as long as school officials are "willing to listen to the parents." (noting that school system representatives should "come to the meeting with suggestions and open minds, not a required course of action").

The facts of this case strongly suggest that the School System had an unofficial policy of refusing to provide one-on-one ABA programs and that School System personnel thus did not have open minds and were not willing to consider the provision of such a program. This conclusion is bolstered by evidence that the School System steadfastly refused even to discuss the possibility of providing an ABA program, even in the face of impressive results. Indeed, School System personnel openly admired and were impressed with Zachary's performance (presumably attained through the ABA program), until the Deals asked the School System to pay for the ABA program. Several comments made by School System personnel suggested that they would like to provide Zachary with ABA services, *i.e.*, they recognized the efficacy of such a program, but they were prevented from doing so, *i.e.*, by the School System policy. The clear implication is that no matter how strong the evidence presented by the Deals, the School System still would have refused to provide the services. This is predetermination.

The district court erred in assuming that merely because the Deals were present and spoke at the various IEP meetings, they were afforded adequate opportunity to participate. Participation must be more than a mere form; it must be *meaningful.* Despite the protestations of the Deals, the School System never even treated a one-on-one ABA program as a viable option. Where there was no way that anything the Deals said, or any data the Deals produced, could have changed the School System's determination of appropriate services, their participation was no more than after the fact involvement.

. . . .

The School System seemed to suggest, at oral argument, that it is entitled to invest in a program such as TEACCH and then capitalize on that investment by using the TEACCH program exclusively. But this is precisely what it is not permitted to do, at least without fully considering the individual needs of each child. A school district unquestionably may consider cost in determining appropriate services for a child. The school district is required, however, to base its placement decision on the child's IEP, rather than on the mere fact of a pre-existing investment. In other words, the school district may not, as it appears happened here, decide that because it has spent a lot of money on a program, that program is always going to be appropriate for educating children with a specific disability, *regardless of any evidence to the contrary of the individualized needs of a particular child*. A placement decision may only be considered to have been based on the child's IEP when the child's individual characteristics, including demonstrated response to particular types of educational programs, are taken into account. A "one size fits all" approach to special education will not be countenanced by the IDEA.

A procedural violation can cause substantive harm when it seriously infringes upon the parents' opportunity to participate in the IEP process. Because the School System deprived the Deals of a meaningful opportunity to participate, the predetermination amounts to denial of a FAPE for Zachary. . . .

. . . .

S.P. v. Mamaroneck Union Free Sch. Dist.

554 F.3d 247 (2d Cir. 2008)

PER CURIAM:

. . . .

BACKGROUND

S.P. is an autistic child who attends school in Mamaroneck . . . .

In 2003–2004, S.P. attended a regular-education preschool for 10 hours per week, where he was accompanied by a personal aide. At home, S.P. received 30–35 hours of applied behavioral analysis ("ABA") therapy per week, 5 hours of ABA "supervision," and speech and occupational therapy. ABA is a set of educational principles used to increase or decrease behaviors. Mamaroneck funded these services pursuant to a settlement agreement after S.P.'s parents disagreed with Mamaroneck's proposed IEP.

In January 2004, Mamaroneck's Committee on Special Education (the "Committee"), which included S.P.'s parents, began considering S.P.'s transition into the school district for kindergarten. The Committee discussed reevaluating S.P. to aid it in making recommendations for his IEP, and agreed to observe him at his preschool and then reconvene to discuss transition options. A behavioral consultant retained by Mamaroneck, Susan Young, visited S.P.'s pre-school and administered tests in May 2004. Young also interviewed S.P.'s mother, teacher, and speech therapist. In her report, Young recommended that S.P. attend a special-education kindergarten class. Young noted that S.P. did not require the intensive instructional services of the autistic population, for example ABA, though she recommended that speech and occupational therapy continue.

In June 2004, the Committee met to discuss S.P.'s IEP for 2004–2005. The Committee's recommendations included placement in a 12-student special-education class with a teacher and two assistants, speech therapy three times per week in a group and once individually, and individual occupational therapy two times per week.

After the June meeting, the McCarton Center for Developmental Pediatrics, which had been retained by S.P.'s parents, issued a report containing recommendations contrary to those in Young's report. The McCarton Center recommended that S.P. attend a special-education class where he was to be accompanied by a full-time personal aide. It also recommended that S.P. continue receiving ABA at home, including 25 hours per week of ABA therapy, as well as private speech and occupational therapy five times each per week.

At the parents' request, the Committee reconvened in July 2004 to review the McCarton report and to continue discussing S.P.'s IEP. Though Mamaroneck's consultant, Young, was invited to the meeting and went to the location that morning, she did not attend. Instead, in the hour before the meeting, she reviewed the McCarton report in the Committee chairperson's office. Young's notes of her review include a two-column chart comparing McCarton's recommendations with her own, which she labeled "School Respon." Where McCarton recommended 25 hours of at-home ABA, Young recommended 10 hours of in-school ABA; where McCarton recommended that a full-time personal aide be provided to S.P. at school, Young recommended a part-time personal aide to provide the in-school ABA; and where McCarton recommended five sessions each of private speech and occupational therapy per week, Young recommended, respectively, four and two.

During the meeting, S.P.'s parents expressed concern about his transition to a full-day kindergarten program, and requested that Mamaroneck continue providing at-home ABA. The parents also requested that Mamaroneck provide S.P. with a full-time personal aide during school, that Mamaroneck staff observe S.P. over the summer and meet with his home providers, and that his home providers be allowed to attend school at the beginning of the year to assist with his transition and train Mamaroneck staff. The Committee agreed to have Young observe S.P. and communicate with the home providers over the summer, and to provide training to Mamaroneck staff. However, Young would provide the training and not S.P.'s home providers. The Committee denied the parents' request for at-home ABA and a full-time personal aide, and instead recommended, consistent with Young's premeeting notes and in addition to the programs recommended at the June meeting, 10 hours of in-school ABA to be provided by a part-time personal aide. The Committee's recommendations were adopted in the IEP . . . .

The parents objected to the IEP on the ground that it was insufficient to provide a free appropriate public education to S.P. They therefore supplemented the IEP with at-home services, including 25 hours of ABA therapy and five hours of individual speech therapy per week, and requested an administrative hearing to obtain reimbursement from Mamaroneck for the cost of these services.

. . . .

An IHO held a hearing on the parents' request for reimbursement . . . . The parents challenged Mamaroneck's IEP on numerous grounds, including that Mamaroneck (1) improperly predetermined S.P.'s IEP by (a) agreeing upon educational placements before the July Committee meeting . . . .

During the hearing, witnesses testified inconsistently about the extent to which the Committee discussed goals and objectives for S.P. during the June meeting. . . . Young testified that she was unable to attend the July Committee meeting because of a scheduling mistake. She noted that "School Respon." in her premeeting notes meant "school responsibility." Young did not recall discussing her recommendations with the Committee chairperson before the meeting, and testified that the chairperson was on the phone and attending to other business when Young was reviewing the McCarton report in the chairperson's office. The chairperson testified that she obtained Young's "input into what some of the new recommendations could be" before the meeting. However, both Young and the chairperson testified that there was no premeeting agreement to adopt Young's recommendations.

. . . .

DISCUSSION

. . . .

I. *Procedural Compliance*

The initial procedural inquiry in an IDEA case "is no mere formality," as " 'adequate compliance with the procedures prescribed would in most cases assure much if not all of what Congress wished in the way of substantive content in an IEP.' " *Walczak v. Fla. Union Free Sch. Dist.*, 142 F.3d 119, 129 (2d Cir. 1998) (quoting *Rowley*, 458 U.S. at 206). In considering whether Mamaroneck satisfied the procedural requirements of the IDEA, "we focus on whether the [parents] had an adequate opportunity to participate in the development of [the] IEP." *Cerra*, 427 F.3d at 192.

Here, the parents argue that Mamaroneck predetermined educational programs for S.P. in violation of the procedural requirements of the IDEA by: (1) adopting programs for S.P.'s IEP before the July Committee meeting . . . . These arguments fail.

First, Mamaroneck's consideration of educational programs for S.P. before the July Committee meeting did not violate the procedural requirements of the IDEA. The parents contend that the Committee chairperson repeated Young's premeeting recommendations at the meeting and therefore must have discussed them with Young before the meeting. Even if there was such discussion, this does not mean the parents were denied meaningful participation at the meeting. IDEA regulations allow school districts to engage in "preparatory activities . . . to develop a proposal or response to a parent proposal that will be discussed at a later meeting" without affording the parents an opportunity to participate. *See* 34 C.F.R. §§ 300.501 (b)(1) & (b)(3). Mamaroneck's conduct was consistent with these regulations.

The parents argue, however, that Young's notes delineated the limits of the services Mamaroneck was willing to provide, and therefore under *Deal ex rel. Deal v. Hamilton County Board of Education*, 392 F.3d 840 (6th Cir. 2004), Mamaroneck denied them meaningful participation in the IEP process by improperly predetermining S.P.'s educational program. Though not bound by *Deal*, we find it distinguishable. In *Deal*, the school district had consistently rejected parent requests for intensive ABA and told the parents that "the powers that be" were not implementing such programs. Because the school district did not have an open mind as to whether intensive ABA programs might be appropriate in some cases, the court found that the parents were denied meaningful participation in the IEP process.

S.P.'s parents have failed to show that Mamaroneck did not have an open mind as to the content of S.P.'s IEP. Both Young and the Committee chairperson testified that there was no premeeting agreement to adopt Young's recommendations. There is also evidence that the parents meaningfully participated in the July meeting, for example the Committee's adoption in the IEP of the parents' recommendations that Mamaroneck staff observe S.P. over the summer and meet with his home providers, and that Mamaroneck staff receive training on how to educate S.P. We find that the parents meaningfully participated in the development of S.P.'s IEP, and Mamaroneck's premeeting consideration of programs for S.P. did not violate the procedural requirements of the IDEA.

. . . .

Notes, Comments, and Questions

1. Based on *Deal* and *S.P.*, what must a parent show to prove that a school district predetermined the terms of her child's IEP? Consider the following excerpt from *M.H. v. N.Y.C. Dep't of Educ.*, 685 F.3d 217 (2d Cir. 2012):

> Here, the only evidence indicating that such a policy [not to offer 1:1 placements] was in place was Browser's testimony that as far as she knew, only 6:1:1 programs were provided by the district. This testimony is a far cry from the evidence that troubled the court in *Deal*. In light of the district's broad discretion to adopt programs that, in its educational judgment, are most pedagogically effective, we cannot simply assume that the decision to rely heavily on a single method or style of instruction is necessarily inappropriate. Browser's testimony does not tend to establish that the district would not consider a 1:1 placement in an appropriate case. Absent such evidence, the only issue here is whether the district's proposed placement was insufficient to provide a FAPE to D.S.

Id. at 257.

2. In both *Deal* and *S.P.*, the courts linked the issue of predetermination to parental participation in the IEP process. In *Deal*, the court stated that because the school district "effectively deprived Zachary's parents of meaningful participation in the IEP process, the predetermination caused substantive harm and therefore deprived Zachary of a FAPE." 392 F.3d at 857. In *S.P.*, the court found, in contrast, "There is also evidence that the parents meaningfully participated in the July meeting, for example the Committee's adoption in the IEP of the parents' recommendations that Mamaroneck staff observe S.P. over the summer and meet with his home providers, and that Mamaroneck staff receive training on how to educate S.P." 554 F.3d at 253. The common issue in both cases was whether parental participation was "meaningful." How should a court determine whether parental participation is meaningful?

3. Does parental disagreement with the final IEP mean that the district predetermined the IEP? In *Nack v. Orange City Sch. Dist.*, 454 F.3d 604 (6th Cir. 2006), the court found that it did not, especially because the parent had several opportunities to make her position known:

> However, this evidence, while signaling Mrs. Nack's disagreement with Orange's ultimate decision, does little to prove Nack's claim that Orange had predetermined David's educational path. In fact, three separate IEP meetings were held concerning David's seventh-grade IEP and Mrs. Nack actively participated in each of these meetings. Prior to and during these meetings, Mrs. Nack repeatedly made school officials aware of her "disapproval of David's participation" in the MPASS program and her desire for him to remain in the "regular education" setting. Mrs. Nack was always able to be a significant part of the discussions concerning the 2002–2003 IEP.... Here, Mrs. Nack was given many opportunities to comment on the IEP and, by every indication, Orange took her suggestions seriously. In the end, there is insufficient evidence in the record to prove a procedural violation of the IDEA through predetermination.

Id. at 610–11. Similarly, in *P.K. v. Bedford Cent. Sch. Dist.*, 569 F. Supp. 2d 371 (S.D.N.Y. 2008), the court ruled:

> The fact that the District staff ultimately disagreed with the opinions of plaintiffs and their outside professionals does not mean that plaintiffs were denied the opportunity to participate in the development of the IEPs, or that the outcomes of the CSE meetings were "predetermined." A professional disagreement is not an IDEA violation.

Id. at 383; *see also* A.E. v. Westport Bd. of Educ., 251 F. App'x 685, 687 (2d Cir. 2007) (holding that consensus is not required for an IEP to be valid); Blackmon v. Springfield R-XII Sch. Dist., 198 F.3d 648, 658 (8th Cir. 1999) (holding that district did not violate the IDEA "simply because it did not grant Grace's parents' request."); Tammy S. v. Reedsburg Sch. Dist., 302 F. Supp. 2d 959, 976 (W.D. Wis. 2003) (holding that the IDEA does not require parents to agree with the IEP).

4. The courts in *Deal* and *S.P.* referred to federal regulations relating to predetermination. The regulation reads in pertinent part:

> **§ 300.116 Placements.**
>
> In determining the educational placement of a child with a disability . . . , each public agency must ensure that—
>
> (a) The placement decision—
>
> (1) Is made by a group of persons, including the parents, and other persons knowledgeable about the child, the meaning of the evaluation data, and the placement options; and
>
> (2) Is made in conformity with the LRE provisions of this subpart . . . ;
>
> (b) The child's placement—
>
> (1) Is determined at least annually;
>
> (2) Is based on the child's IEP; and
>
> (3) Is as close as possible to the child's home;
>
> . . . .

34 C.F.R. § 300.116 (2015).

5. Courts have strictly construed the requirement that a child's placement be based on the IEP. For example, in *Spielberg v. Henrico Cnty. Pub. Sch.*, 853 F.2d 256 (4th Cir. 1988), *cert. denied*, 489 U.S. 1066 (1989), the school district decided to change the child's placement prior to the IEP meeting. The court held:

> The defendants violated EHA procedures when they resolved to educate Jonathan Spielberg at Randolph, and then developed an IEP to carry out their decision. This failure to follow EHA procedures is sufficient to hold that the defendants failed to provide Jonathan with a FAPE.

Id. at 259.

6. In *S.P.*, the court stated, "IDEA regulations allow school districts to engage in "'preparatory activities . . . to develop a proposal or response to a parent that will be

discussed at a later meeting'" without affording the parents an opportunity to participate." 554 F.3d at 253. This regulation reads in pertinent part:

> (b) Parent participation in meetings.
>
> (1) The parents of a child with a disability must be afforded an opportunity to participate in meetings with respect to—
>
> (i) The identification, evaluation, and educational placement of the child; and
>
> (ii) The provision of FAPE to the child.
>
> . . . .
>
> (3) A meeting does not include informal or unscheduled conversations involving public agency personnel and conversations on issues such as teaching methodology, lesson plans, or coordination of service provision. A meeting also does not include preparatory activities that public agency personnel engage in to develop a proposal or response to a parent proposal that will be discussed at a later meeting.

34 C.F.R. § 300.501(b) (2015).

7. Several courts agree with *S.P.*'s holding that pre-planning does not constitute predetermination as long as the school district maintains an open mind. In *Doyle v. Arlington Cnty. Sch. Bd.*, 806 F. Supp. 1253 (E.D. Va. 1992), *aff'd*, 39 F.3d 1176 (4th Cir. 1994), the court distinguished between an open and a closed mind:

> The EHA's procedural requirements are designed to insure that parents participate meaningfully in the decision-making process for their handicapped child. Thus, if the school system has already fully made up its mind before the parents ever get involved, it has denied them the opportunity for any meaningful input.
>
> *Spielberg* was a case like that. In *Spielberg*, the school division unilaterally decided to change drastically a student's placement which it had funded for eight years. This decision was made over eight months before the IEP conference with the student's parents. The Fourth Circuit found that the school system's unilateral decision had deprived that student's parents of any opportunity to participate, and held that this action alone invalidated consideration of the school system's proposed program.
>
> Thus, *Spielberg* makes clear that school officials must come to the IEP with an open mind. But this does not mean they should come to the IEP table with a blank mind. . . . Thus, while a school system must not finalize its placement decision before an IEP meeting, it can, and should, have given some thought to that placement. . . .

Id. at 1262; *see also* Nack v. Orange City Sch. Dist., 454 F.3d 604, 611 (6th Cir. 2006) (ruling that preparing "parts . . . of an IEP prior to a meeting did not constitute predetermination because the district was taking the parent's suggestions seriously."); N.L. v. Knox Cnty. Sch., 315 F.3d 688, 694–95 (6th Cir. 2003) (holding that district did not predetermine IEP "when school-appointed experts and school officials conferr[ed] *ex parte* so to coordinate drafting an assessment report because" they maintained open minds and the parents had an opportunity to participate in the IEP meeting); E.G. v. City Sch. Dist. of New Rochelle, 606 F. Supp. 2d 384, 389 (S.D.N.Y. 2009) (holding that discussion about the child's classroom placement prior to the IEP meeting did not violate FAPE when the school district did not make final placement recommendation until after the IEP meeting); M.M. v. N.Y.C. Dep't of Educ., 583 F. Supp. 2d 498, 506 (S.D.N.Y. 2008) (stating that as long as "they do not deprive parents of the opportunity to meaningfully participate in the IEP development process . . . , draft IEPs are not impermissible under the IDEA."); A.E. v. Westport Bd. of Educ., 463 F. Supp. 2d 208, 217 (D. Conn. 2006), *aff'd*, 251 F. App'x 685 (2d Cir. 2007) (holding that the school district "had properly given thought" to the child's placement prior to the IEP meeting, but there was no evidence that the district had predetermined the placement prior to the meeting); W.S. v. Rye City Sch. Dist., 454 F. Supp. 2d 134, 147–48 (S.D.N.Y. 2006) (rejecting argument that a school district should "not suggest an outcome in a first draft IEP").

8. In *Deal*, the court noted, "Courts have often declined to find predetermination . . . ." 392 F.3d at 857. This continues to be true. *See* M.H. v. N.Y.C. Dep't of Educ., 685 F.3d 217, 257 (2d Cir. 2012) (ruling that district did not predetermine placement because the evidence did not establish that "the district would not consider a 1:1 placement in an appropriate case."); S.P. v. Mamaroneck Union Free Sch. Dist. 554 F.3d 247, 253 (2d Cir. 2009) (ruling that district did not predetermine placement because the parents "failed to show that Mamaroneck did not have an open mind as to the content of S.P.'s IEP."); Nack v. Orange City Sch. Dist., 454 F.3d 604, 610–11 (6th Cir. 2006) (finding no predetermination in light of parent's opportunity to participate in the IEP process); Ms. S. v. Vashon Island Sch. Dist., 337 F.3d 1115, 1132–33 (9th Cir. 2003) (rejecting predetermination claim because parent had meaningful opportunity to participate); M.W. v. N.Y.C. Dep't of Educ., 869 F. Supp. 2d 320, 333 (E.D.N.Y. 2012), *aff'd*, 725 F.3d 131 (2d Cir. 2013) (rejecting predetermination claim because all members of the IEP team, including child's mother, participated actively in the development of "the IEP and they considered a number of potentially appropriate program options."); J.G. v. Kiryas Joel Union Free Sch. Dist., 777 F. Supp. 2d 606, 649 (S.D.N.Y. 2011) (holding that the school district did not predetermine the child's IEP because the district was willing to place children in regular education settings); M.R. v. Scarsdale Union Free Sch. Dist., 615 F. Supp. 2d 283, 294 (S.D.N.Y. 2009), *aff'd*, 366 F. App'x, 239 (2d Cir. 2010) (holding that plaintiffs "failed to show that placements and programs were finalized before goals and objectives"); E.G. v. City Sch. Dist. of New Rochelle, 606 F. Supp. 2d 384, 389 (S.D.N.Y. 2009) (rejecting claim that district's policy was not to offer at-home behavioral therapy because the district offered ten hours of it at the IEP meeting); A.M. v. N.Y. City Dep't of Educ., 583 F. Supp. 2d 498, 505–506 (S.D.N.Y. 2008) (denying predetermination claim because the school district did not finalize the

IEP and placement until after the IEP meetings; "the student's mother participated at the IEP meetings . . . , visited these proposed placements, and contributed to the student's . . . IEP;" and the school district responded positively to the mother's suggestions); P.K. v. Bedford Cent. Sch. Dist., 569 F. Supp. 2d 371, 383 (S.D.N.Y. 2008) (finding no predetermination when school district considered input from the child's parents and from their outside experts); A.E. v. Westport Bd. of Educ., 463 F. Supp. 2d 208, 217 (D. Conn. 2006), *aff'd*, 251 F. App'x 685 (2d Cir. 2007) (holding that the school district "had properly given thought" to the child's placement prior to the IEP meeting, but there was no evidence that the district had predetermined the placement prior to the meeting); W.S. v. Rye City Sch. Dist., 454 F. Supp. 2d 134, 147–48 (S.D.N.Y. 2006) (finding no predetermination when parents obtained testing and reports prior to the time the district finalized the IEP and the district changed its recommendations). *But see* D.B. v. Glouscester Twp. Sch. Dist., 489 F. App'x 564, 566–67 (3d Cir. 2012) (finding predetermination when the district made final decision about the child's placement without input from the parents, did not take any of the parents' suggestions, did not discuss possible placements with the parents, and did not listen to their concerns); B.H. v. West Clermont Bd. of Educ., 788 F. Supp. 2d 682, 695 (S.D. Ohio 2011) (holding that "the district ignored the documentation of B.'s need for special services which supports the IHO's conclusion that the District predetermined that B. did not need speech services.").

Why do you think it is so difficult to prove predetermination? Have courts construed the holding in *Deal* too strictly by limiting the holding to the facts of the case, that predetermination occurs only when a school district has a clear policy to deny requested services regardless of the individualized needs of the child?

Section Two
Preparing the IEP

The IDEA and its implementing regulations require a school district to appoint a team of experts and people familiar with the child to draft the IEP. The team must include:

(i) the parents of a child with a disability;

(ii) not less than 1 regular education teacher of such child (if the child is, or may be, participating in the regular education environment);

(iii) not less than 1 special education teacher, or where appropriate, not less than 1 special education provider of such child;

(iv) a representative of the local educational agency who—

(I) is qualified to provide, or supervise the provision of, specially designed instruction to meet the unique needs of children with disabilities;

(II) is knowledgeable about the general education curriculum; and

(III) is knowledgeable about the availability of resources of the local educational agency;

(v) an individual who can interpret the instructional implications of evaluation results, who may be a member of the team described in clauses (ii) through (vi);

(vi) at the discretion of the parent or the agency, other individuals who have knowledge or special expertise regarding the child, including related service personnel as appropriate; and

(vii) whenever appropriate, the child with a disability.

20 U.S.C. § 1414(d)(1)(B)(i)-(vii) (2012); *see also* 34 C.F.R. § 300.321(a)(1)-(7) (2015).

The Supreme Court has recognized that parents play an important role in developing the IEP for a child with a disability:

> The core of the statute . . . is the cooperative process that it establishes between parents and schools. The central vehicle for this collaboration is the IEP process. State educational authorities must identify and evaluate disabled children, §§ 1414(a)-(c), develop an IEP for each one, § 1414(d)(2), and review every IEP at least once a year, § 1414(d)(4). Each IEP must include an assessment of the child's current educational performance, must articulate measurable educational goals, and must specify the nature of the special services that the school will provide. § 1414(d)(1)(A).
>
> Parents and guardians play a significant role in the IEP process. They must be informed about and consent to evaluations of their child under the Act. § 1414(c)(3). Parents are included as members of "IEP teams." § 1414(d)(1)(B). They have the right to examine any records relating to their child, and to obtain an "independent educational evaluation of the[ir] child." § 1415(b)(1). They must be given written prior notice of any changes in an IEP, § 1415(b)(3), and be notified in writing of the procedural safeguards available to them under the Act, § 1415(d)(1). If parents believe that an IEP is not appropriate, they may seek an administrative "due process hearing." § 1415(f). . . .

Schaffer v. Weast, 546 U.S. 49, 53 (2005). Similarly, in *Winkelman v. Parma City Sch. Dist.*, 550 U.S. 516 (2007), the Court recognized the important role for parents in developing the child's IEP:

> Parents serve as members of the team that develops the IEP. § 1414(d)(1)(B). The "concerns" parents have "for enhancing the education of their child" must be considered by the team. § 1414(d)(3)(A)(ii). IDEA accords parents additional protections that apply throughout the IEP process. *See, e.g.*, § 1414(d)(4)(A) (requiring IEP Team to revise the IEP when appropriate to address certain information provided by the parents); § 1414(e) (requiring States to "ensure that the parents of [a child with a disability] are members of any group that makes decisions on the educational placement of their child").

Id. at 524; *see also* Honig v. Doe, 484 U.S. 305, 311 (1988) ("Congress repeatedly emphasized throughout the Act the importance and indeed the necessity of parental participation in both the development of the IEP and any subsequent assessments of its effectiveness.").

This section will focus on the role of parents in drafting the IEP, and will also consider the role of the other members of the IEP team, including general and special education teachers. As you read the materials in this chapter, consider whether or not courts have implemented the Supreme Court's vision for the role of parents in the IEP process.

Shapiro v. Paradise Valley Unified Sch. Dist. No. 69

317 F.3d 1072 (9th Cir. 2003)

Paez, Circuit Judge:

. . . Paradise Valley Unified School District No. 69 ("PVUSD") appeals the district court's ruling that it did not provide . . . Isadora Shapiro ("Dorie"), a profoundly deaf seven year old child with a cochlear implant, a free appropriate education ("FAPE"). The district court determined that the PVUSD violated several procedural mandates required by the Individuals with Disabilities Education Act ("IDEA") in creating Dorie's individualized education program ("IEP") and that Dorie's parents were therefore entitled to reimbursement for the costs of sending her to a private . . . school. By failing to include a teacher from Dorie's private educational placement and her parents in her June 8, 1994 IEP meeting, the PVUSD denied Dorie a FAPE. We therefore agree with the district court that Dorie's parents are entitled to reimbursement for the costs of sending her to a private out-of-district school for the 1994–1995 school year. . . .

BACKGROUND

As part of a study on children with cochlear implants, Dorie attended a private, out-of-state school called the Central Institute for the Deaf ("CID") . . . . In the fall of 1993, as the study's three-year grant period was ending, Dorie's parents approached the PVUSD to seek authorization for her continued placement at CID for the 1994–1995 school year because the PVUSD did not have a program for Dorie in its district.

In March 1994, however, the PVUSD obtained permission to create an oral self-contained program for children with hearing impairments at Sonoran Sky Elementary, a PVUSD school located about a mile from the Shapiros' home. The PVUSD notified Dorie's parents about this new program, and on April 13, 1994, representatives from the school district met with Dorie's parents to discuss the appropriateness of the program for Dorie. Dorie's parents expressed concern that the program was not yet "up and running" and that it may not continue past the 1994–1995 school year. Moreover, Dorie was the only child with a cochlear implant identified for the program.

The parties agreed to meet again on May 4, 1994, to continue to discuss the proposed program at Sonoran Sky Elementary. During the May 4 meeting, the district psychologist began drafting an IEP for Dorie. At the conclusion of the meeting, Dorie's parents expressed concern that the PVUSD had not yet hired a classroom teacher, that in the draft IEP the district had not specified related services to which Dorie would have access, and that Dorie would be a "guinea pig" in the PVUSD's new program. They again requested a placement at CID, which the PVUSD rejected, stating that the program at Sonoran Sky would be appropriate for Dorie.

The district's refusal to place Dorie at CID prompted Dorie's parents to initiate a due process hearing to determine Dorie's school placement for the 1994–1995 school year. Prior to the hearing, the PVUSD notified Dorie's parents that it planned to convene a meeting on June 8, 1994, to develop an IEP for Dorie. In response, Dorie's mother informed the district that she and her husband would be unavailable to meet on June 8 and requested a postponement. The PVUSD claimed it could not postpone the meeting because at least two of its IEP team members would be unavailable to meet after June 10.

The PVUSD convened a meeting on June 8, 1994, without Dorie's parents or a representative from CID. At the meeting, the district representatives drafted an IEP relying solely on information they had gathered from prior meetings with Dorie's parents. The PVUSD did not independently evaluate Dorie.

....

DISCUSSION

I.

We agree with the district court that the PVUSD violated the IDEA's procedural mandates in its development of Dorie's June 8 IEP, and thereby denied Dorie a FAPE, by not including a representative from CID or Dorie's parents at the June 8 meeting. We address each procedural error in turn.

A. Teacher Participation

The IDEA requires that "the teacher" participate in the formation of a child's IEP. 20 U.S.C. § 1401(a)(20). Dorie's parents and the PVUSD disagree about which teacher should have attended the June 8 IEP meeting. Dorie's parents argue that the school district violated the IDEA by not including a representative from CID at the meeting. In contrast, the PVUSD contends that it was not necessary to include a representative from CID at the meeting, and that it complied with IDEA by including the speech pathologist and the hearing impaired instructor from its newly-created program at Sonoran Sky Elementary. We agree that the PVUSD violated the IDEA by not including a representative from CID at the June 8 IEP meeting.

We have held that a school district's failure to include a representative from a private school that a child is currently attending violates the procedural mandates of the IDEA. *See W.G. v. Bd. of Trustees*, 960 F.2d 1479, 1484 (9th Cir. 1992) (holding that the formation of the child's IEP was procedurally flawed because the district "was required to ensure participation by the private school [in which the child was enrolled] in the formulation of the IEP"). IDEA requires the persons most knowledgeable about the child to attend the IEP meeting. *Id.*; *see also* 34 C.F.R. § 300.533. The PVUSD made no attempt to include a representative from CID at the June 8 IEP meeting. As a result, the teachers most knowledgeable about Dorie's special education levels and needs did not attend the meeting, in violation of the IDEA.

The PVUSD argues that the IDEA, 20 U.S.C. § 1401(a)(20), requires "a teacher" to participate in the development of an IEP and that by including "two qualified and credentialed teachers of the hearing impaired" at the June 8 IEP meeting, it was in compliance with the Act. According to § 1401(a)(20), "*the* teacher," not "a teacher," must be included in the development of the IEP. The PVUSD's interpretation of this statutory provision conveys too broad a meaning to the word "teacher," a meaning inconsistent with the statute.

The implementing regulation for § 1401(a)(20) helps clarify what is meant by "the teacher":

> In deciding which teacher will participate in meetings on a child's IEP, the agency may wish to consider the following possibilities: (a) For a child with a disability who is receiving special education, the teacher could be the child's special education teacher. If the child's disability is a speech impairment, the teacher could be the speech-language pathologist; (b) For a child with a disability who is being considered for placement in special education, the teacher could be the child's regular teacher, or a teacher qualified to provide education in the type of program in which the child may be placed, or both. . . .

34 C.F.R. § 300.344, Note 1. Because Dorie had been receiving special education services at CID at the time of the June 8 IEP, subdivision (a) applies here. Under subdivision (a), either Dorie's special education teacher or her speech-language pathologist should have been present at the IEP meeting. Dorie received special education at CID, not in the PVUSD, so, contrary to the PVUSD's assertion, the only teachers who met the subdivision (a) criteria were her CID instructors.

. . . .

B. Parental Participation

As noted, the district court held that the PVUSD's failure to include Dorie's parents at the June 8 IEP meeting was a violation of the IDEA. We agree.

The importance of parental participation in the IEP process is evident. *See* 20 U.S.C. § 1401(a)(20) (inclusion of parents in IEP team); 34 C.F.R. § 300.344(a)(3) (same); *Amanda J.*, 267 F.3d at 892 ("Procedural violations that interfere with parental participation in the IEP formulation process undermine the very essence of the IDEA."). As the Supreme Court made clear in *Board of Education v. Rowley*:

> It seems to us no exaggeration to say that Congress placed every bit as much emphasis upon compliance with procedures giving parents and guardians a large measure of participation at every stage of the administrative process . . . as it did upon the measurement of the resulting IEP against a substantive standard.

The PVUSD argues that despite the IDEA's emphasis on parental participation in the IEP formulation process, the IDEA does not require parents to attend every IEP meeting. It relies on 34 C.F.R. § 300.345(d) for this proposition. This regulation states that "[a] meeting may be conducted without a parent in attendance if the public agency is unable to convince the parents that they should attend." According to the PVUSD, because Dorie's mother chose not to attend the June 8 IEP meeting but had a sufficient opportunity to do so, it was acceptable to hold the meeting without her. The PVUSD misinterprets § 300.345.

Under the regulation, before it can hold an IEP meeting without a child's parents, the school district must document phone calls, correspondence, and visits to the parents demonstrating attempts to reach a mutually agreed upon place and time for the meeting. 34 C.F.R. § 300.345(d)(1)-(3). Here, the Shapiros asked to reschedule the June 8 IEP meeting; they did not refuse to attend. The PVUSD's reliance on § 300.345 therefore misses the mark. The school district simply prioritized its representatives' schedules over that of Dorie's parents.

The PVUSD also contends that Dorie's parents contributed adequately to the June 8 IEP because the PVUSD mailed the IEP to them for their approval and they participated in prior IEP meetings. We disagree. The IDEA "imposes upon the school district the duty to conduct a meaningful meeting *with* the appropriate parties." *W.G.*, 960 F.2d at 1485 (emphasis added). We have made clear that those individuals, like Dorie's parents, "who have first-hand knowledge of the child's needs and who are most concerned about the child must be involved in the IEP *creation* process." *Amanda J.*, 267 F.3d at 891 (emphasis added). After-the-fact parental involvement is not enough. Nor does the PVUSD's inclusion of the Shapiros in certain parts of the process excuse the district's failure to include the Shapiros in the June 8 IEP meeting; involvement in the "creation process" requires the PVUSD to include the Shapiros unless they affirmatively refused to attend. By proceeding with the June 8 IEP meeting without Dorie's parents, the PVUSD violated the IDEA.

II.

We engage in a two-part inquiry to determine whether the PVUSD afforded Dorie a FAPE. First, we must determine whether the PVUSD complied with the procedures set forth in the IDEA. Second, we must determine whether the IEP developed through the IDEA's procedures was reasonably calculated to confer educational benefit upon Dorie.

We agree with the district court's ruling that the PVUSD's violations of the IDEA's procedural mandates resulted in lost educational opportunity for Dorie. We have held that:

> Procedural flaws do not automatically require a finding of a denial of a FAPE. However, procedural inadequacies that result in the loss of educational opportunity, or seriously infringe the parents' opportunity to participate in the IEP formulation process, clearly result in the denial of a FAPE.

The PVUSD's failure to include the persons most knowledgeable about Dorie's educational levels and needs—namely, a representative from CID and Dorie's parents—at the June 8 IEP meeting and its concomitant creation of a defective IEP resulted in lost educational opportunity for Dorie.

Because we conclude that the PVUSD's procedural violations of the IDEA resulted in a loss of educational opportunity for Dorie, it is unnecessary for us to address the second prong of the FAPE analysis. On the basis of the first prong of the FAPE two-part inquiry, which is a procedural analysis, we conclude that the PVUSD denied Dorie a FAPE.

III.

. . . .

The district court affirmed the ALJ's decision that Dorie's program at CID for the 1994–1995 school year was "reasonably calculated to provide [Dorie] with educational benefit" and therefore provided her with an "appropriate education during the 1994–1995 school year." Because CID was an educationally appropriate placement for Dorie and the June 8 IEP denied her a FAPE, the Shapiros are entitled to reimbursement for the costs of educating Dorie at CID for the 1994–1995 school year. . . .

. . . .

Notes, Comments, and Questions

1. The Ninth Circuit reinforced *Shapiro* in *Doug C. v. Haw. Dep't of Educ.*, 720 F.3d 1038 (9th Cir. 2013). The parent, Doug C., could not attend the IEP meeting and the school district eventually held the meeting without him because the deadline for holding the meeting was only a few days away. *Id.* at 1042. The court rejected this justification for holding the meeting without Doug C. It found that Doug C. did not actually refuse to attend the meeting but only sought a different date and that the imminent deadline was not a reasonable justification for holding the meeting in his absence. *Id.* at 1044, 1046. The Court also stated that it is not appropriate for a school district to blame parents for procedural violations:

> The fact that it may have been frustrating to schedule meetings with or difficult to work with Doug C. (as the district repeatedly suggests) does not excuse the Department's failure to include him in Spencer's IEP meeting when he expressed a willingness to participate. We have consistently held that an agency cannot eschew its affirmative duties under the IDEA by blaming the parents.

Id. at 1045. The court then ruled that the district's exclusion of Doug C. from the meeting denied his opportunity to participate in the drafting of the IEP and denied his son a FAPE by limiting the discussion of the merits of remaining in his current placement. *Id.* at 1047.

2. The IDEA regulations contain several provisions requiring school districts to ensure that parents are able to participate in IEP meetings. The district must notify the parents of the meeting with sufficient time to enable them to attend and schedule

the meeting at an agreed on date and place. 34 C.F.R. § 300.322(a)(1) and (2) (2015). If the parents cannot attend the meeting in person, the school district must employ other means to allow parent participation, including a telephone or video conference. 20 U.S.C. § 1414(f) (2012); 34 C.F.R § 300.322(c). If the school district is not able to persuade the parents to attend the meeting, the district may hold the meeting without the parents and must keep a record of its attempts to schedule a meeting the parents could attend. 34 C.F.R. § 300.322(d).

3. Despite the importance the Supreme Court places on parental participation in drafting the IEP, the clarity of *Shapiro*, *Doug C.*, and the IDEA regulations, courts frequently reject claims that school districts violated the IDEA by holding IEP meetings without parents. One frequent reason for rejecting such claims is that the district made efforts to have the parents attend. *See* K.D. v. Dep't of Educ. of Haw., 665 F.3d 1110, 1124–25 (9th Cir. 2011) (holding that parents failed to attend meeting despite district's efforts to have them attend); A.M. v. Monrovia Unified Sch. Dist., 627 F.3d 773, 780 (9th Cir. 2010) (finding that parents cancelled an IEP meeting that district tried to reschedule but parents would not attend and refused to participate by telephone); James M. v. Haw. Dep't of Educ., 803 F. Supp. 2d 1150, 1159–60 (D. Haw. 2011) (holding that district attempted to accommodate parents by requesting consent to extend IEP deadline and holding three additional IEP meetings following the meeting the parents did not attend). Courts have found other reasons for excusing a district's holding an IEP meeting without the child's parents. One court excused a district because of the urgent need to meet. *See* G.R. v. Dallas Sch. Dist. No. 2, 823 F. Supp. 2d 1120, 1135–36 (D. Or. 2011) (holding that district did not violate the IDEA by holding IEP meeting without parents for various reasons, including that child was soon to return to school). Another court excused the district because the parents made it difficult for the district to hold timely meetings. *See* J.J. v. Dist. of Columbia, 768 F. Supp. 2d 214, 219–20 (D.D.C. 2011) (holding that even though district belatedly scheduled IEP meetings, it did not violate the IDEA because parents interfered with attempts to hold the meetings). Even if a district holds an IEP meeting in the absence of the parents without justification, a court might deny a challenge because their absence was not prejudicial. *See* Kings Local Sch. Dist. v. Zelazny, 325 F.3d 724, 731 (6th Cir. 2003) (holding that missing one IEP meeting was not prejudicial because the mother met with the child's teachers, discussed the child's program, recommended a consulting firm, and attended consulting firm meetings).

Courts tend to uphold parental challenges to IEP meetings the district held in their absence only when the school district blatantly violated the IDEA. In *Drobnicki v. Poway Unified Sch. Dist.*, 358 F. App'x 788, 789–90 (9th Cir. 2009), the court found that the district denied the parents meaningful participation in the IEP process by scheduling a date for the IEP meeting without consulting them, holding the meeting without them, and not taking any steps to attempt to reschedule. Citing *Shapiro*, 317 F.3d at 1078, the court stated that a "school district must include the parents of a child with a disability in an IEP meeting 'unless they affirmatively refuse[] to attend.' Daniel's parents did not affirmatively refuse to attend the October 10 meeting." *Id.* at 790. The court also ruled that the district's efforts to allow the parents "to participate in the IEP meeting by speaker phone is of no consequence, as the use of such methods to ensure parent participation is available only '[i]f neither parent can attend an IEP meeting . . . .' 34 C.F.R. § 300.322(c)." *Id.*; *see also* Anchorage Sch. Dist. v. D.S., 688 F. Supp. 2d 883, 888–89 (D. Ala. 2009) (holding that a variety of procedural violations over the course of various IEPs denied FAPE); J.N. v. Dist. of Columbia, 677 F. Supp. 2d 314, 321–22 (D.D.C. 2010) (holding that district denied parental participation because the parties did not agree on the IEP meeting date, there was no evidence that the district could not convince the parent to attend the meeting, and the district did not respond to parent's timely request to reschedule).

4. Recall the discussion in Section One of 34 C.F.R. § 300.501(b)(3), which excludes from the definition of "meetings" preparation sessions to develop proposals to discuss at subsequent IEP meetings. Parents frequently allege that school districts denied their participation in drafting the IEP by holding meetings at which district personnel discussed the child's IEP or even drafted it and did not invite the parents. Generally, courts have ruled that exclusion from such meetings does not improperly deny parental participation. In rejecting such a claim, the court in *R.P. v. Alamo Heights Indep. Sch. Dist.*, 703 F.3d 801 (5th Cir. 2012), stated:

> [R.P.] asserts that AHISD personnel made decisions about her IEP prior to the ARD meetings, and thus her parents' input was not meaningfully considered. Under Federal regulations, not every conversation about a child is a statutorily-defined meeting in which parents must participate. *See* 34 C.F.R. § 300.501(b)(3) ("A meeting also does not include preparatory activities that public agency personnel engage in to develop a proposal or response to a parent proposal that will be discussed at a later meeting.") . . . .
>
> . . . The record shows that AHISD held numerous ARD meetings for R.P., all of which included R.L.P., who had numerous opportunities to voice his thoughts about R.P.'s IEPs. Changes R.P.'s parents proposed were incorporated into R.P.'s IEPs. . . .

Id. at 811. Although the court in *R.P.* cited § 300.501(b)(3), not all courts rely on this regulation. In the typical case, parents identify one or more meetings to which the school district did not invite them during which district personnel discussed the child's disability or services or drafted a significant document, the district identifies one or more other meetings at which parents participated, and the court concludes that this participation was sufficient. A good example of this is *Burilovich v. Bd. of Educ of Lincoln Cons. Sch.*, 208 F.3d 560 (6th Cir. 2000), *cert. denied*, 531 U.S. 957 (2000). There, the parents argued "that they were denied meaningful parental participation in the IEPC process because they were not invited to two meetings in April 1996." *Id.* at 568. The court stated:

> Defendants counter that the meetings on April 16 and April 26 were staff meetings that plaintiffs were not entitled to attend. The . . . plaintiffs do little to suggest that the meetings were in fact IEP meetings. Plaintiffs have not

> indicated how they were prevented from participating in the development of the IEP. The parents attended a December 1996 IEPC, strongly expressed their views at the March 1996 IEPC, had the opportunity to participate in the May 1996 IEPC, and also expressed their views through letters and telephone conversations with district staff. Furthermore, plaintiffs have cited no support for their implicit assertion that schools may never discuss a child's IEP, goals, objectives, or educational methodology out of the presence of parents. For these reasons, plaintiffs have failed to demonstrate that they were denied participation in the IEPC process.

Id. Do you agree that the parents implicitly suggested that schools may never discuss a child's IEP in their absence? Were the meetings from which they were excluded merely discussions or did more occur? Once a school district incorporates its findings and recommendations into an IEP, do you think it would be easy for parents to effectuate significant changes to the draft, regardless of the number of other meetings they attend?

For other examples in which courts rejected parents' claims that the district prevented them from adequately participating in drafting the IEP by excluding them from meetings, *see, e.g.*, N.L. v. Knox Cnty. Sch., 315 F.3d 688, 694 (6th Cir. 2003) ("when a parent fully participates in the IEP Team Meeting and is an active participant in the final determination of the child's eligibility, there is no substantive harm caused when the school-appointed experts and school officials confer ex parte so as to coordinate the drafting of the assessment report"); Blackmon v. Springfield R-XII Sch. Dist., 198 F.3d 648, 657 (8th Cir. 1999) (holding that drafting an unfinished IEP prior to the IEP meeting, including the "present levels of performance" and "goals and objectives" sections, and subsequently explaining them to parents and asking if they agreed did not deny meaningful participation); B.P. v. N.Y.C. Dep't of Educ., 841 F. Supp. 2d 605, 613 (S.D.N.Y. 2012) (stating that parents conceded that law does not require district to draft an IEP at a meeting of the CSE); K.O. v. Cold Spring Harbor Cent. Sch. Dist., 807 F. Supp. 2d 130, 136 (S.D.N.Y. 2011) (holding that although the school district met without parents to discuss the child's placement, it did not make a final decision at the meeting); E.G. v. City Sch. Dist. of New Rochelle, 606 F. Supp. 2d 384, 388–89 (S.D.N.Y. 2009) (holding that drafting goals in absence of parents did not violate the IDEA and pointing out that the parents had an opportunity to comment on the goals after the district drafted them); Tracy v. Beaufort Cnty. Bd. of Educ., 335 F. Supp. 2d 675, 686–87 (D.S.C. 2004) (holding that drafting the IEP in the absence of the parents did not violate the IDEA when the parents consented to drafting in their absence and had significant input into the development of the IEP).

5. In several cases, parents alleged that the school district denied them meaningful participation in drafting the IEP by denying them the opportunity to provide input about the location at which the school district would provide their child's services. In *T.Y. v N.Y.C. Dep't of Educ.*, 584 F.3d 412 (2d Cir. 2009), *cert. denied*, 563 U.S. 904 (2011), the parents claimed that the district's policy not to identify the child's school in the IEP denied their participation rights. *Id.* at 419. In support of their

argument, the parents cited the IDEA's definition of an IEP as a written statement that includes, among other things, "'the anticipated frequency, *location*, and duration of . . . [the child's] services.' (citing 20 U.S.C. § 1414(d)(1)(A)(i)(VII)) (emphasis added)." *Id.* They also argued that the IDEA regulations, which state that "'the parents of a child with a disability must be afforded an opportunity to participate in meetings with respect to . . . [t]he identification, evaluation, and educational *placement* of the child,' 34 C.F.R. § 300.501(b)(1)(i) (emphasis in added)," supported their argument. *Id.* The court rejected the parents' claim. It ruled that the term "educational placement" refers only to the child's educational program, not the location at which the district will provide the services, and that the statutory requirement that the IEP specify the "location" at which the school district will provide the services does not require the district to identify the specific school. *Id.* at 419–20. The court also noted that the parents did have input into the school selection, although apparently after the District prepared the IEP, and that the parents rejected two proposed schools before they enrolled their child in a private school. *Id.* at 420. Other decisions follow a pattern similar to *T.Y.*: courts denied parents' claims because parents do not have a right to participate in site selection and noted that parents nevertheless had input into the site selection. *See* White v. Ascension Parish Sch. Bd., 343 F.3d 373, 380 (5th Cir. 2003) (holding that educational placement means educational program and that parents were part of the IEP team that discussed location); A.L. v. N.Y.C. Dep't of Educ., 812 F. Supp. 2d 492, 504–05 (S.D.N.Y. 2011) (holding that parents do not have the right to participate in school selection but pointing out that the mother had the opportunity to visit the proposed school twice); M.N. v. N.Y.C. Dep't of Educ., 700 F. Supp. 2d 356, 365 (S.D.N.Y. 2010) (ruling that district's failure to identify particular school at IEP meeting did not deny parents the right to participate in preparing the IEP and pointing out that district placed child in parents' choice of school); A.H. v. Dist. of Columbia, 524 F. Supp. 2d 43, 47 (D.D.C. 2007) (without reaching the merits, stating that the parent participated in the meeting at which the IEP team determined the child's placement); *see also* R.E. v. N.Y.C. Dep't of Educ., 694 F.3d 167, 191 (2d Cir. 2012), *cert. denied*, ___U.S.___, 132 S.Ct. 2802 (2013) (rejecting parental claim that not stating the school at which the district will provide services in the IEP violates the IDEA); Greg I. v. Dep't of Educ. of Haw., 869 F. Supp. 2d 1225, 1239 (D. Haw. 2012) (holding that the IDEA does not require a meeting to determine the location of the child's education); Hanson v. Smith, 212 F. Supp. 2d 474, 487 (D. Md. 2002) (holding that the IDEA does not require a school board to allow parents to visit the particular proposed placement); K.L. v. N.Y.C. Dep't of Educ., 2012 U.S. Dist. LEXIS 124460 at *34 (S.D.N.Y. 2012 Aug. 23, 2012), *aff'd*, 520 F. App'x 31 (2d. Cir. 2013) (holding that parents do not have a right to participate in the placement decision). Why do you think the courts have construed "educational placement" to mean "educational program"? Under what theory of statutory interpretation does "placement" mean "program"?

One court of appeals, however, ruled that the IEP at issue violated the IDEA because it did not identify the particular school the child would attend. In *A.K. v.*

Alexandria City Sch. Bd., 484 F.3d 672 (4th Cir. 2007), the court ruled that the IEP violated FAPE because it did not identify the school the child would attend. *Id.* at 769. The Court stated:

> Indeed, this case presents an excellent example of the circumstances under which inclusion of a particular school in an IEP can be determinative of whether a FAPE has been offered. The parents agree that an *appropriate* private day school could provide a FAPE; they favor keeping A.K. at Riverview only because they have not found a private day school in their area that could meet A.K.'s specialized education needs. Yet, the IEP development process concluded without any significant discussion of whether such a school existed, or if it did, how it would be a satisfactory match for A.K.

Id. at 681. The Court, however, did not extend its ruling to all IEPs:

> We emphasize that we do not hold today that a school district could never offer a FAPE without identifying a particular location at which the special education services are expected to be provided. There is no reason for us to frame the issue so broadly. But, certainly in a case in which the parents express doubt concerning the existence of a particular school that can satisfactorily provide the level of services that the IEP describes, the IEP must identify such a school to offer a FAPE.

Id. at 682; *see also* Glendale Unified Sch. Dist. v. Almasi, 122 F. Supp. 2d 1093, 1108 (C.D. Cal. 2000) (holding that district's failure to offer specific placement violated FAPE).

6. A necessary condition for adequate parental participation in the process of drafting the IEP is the right to examine the child's educational records. In *Amanda J. v. Clark Cnty. Sch. Dist.*, 267 F.3d 877 (9th Cir. 2001), the school district failed to provide the parents with copies of the "psychologist's and speech pathologist's reports finding mixed results on the autism tests, his recommendation to consider further psychiatric evaluation, or the speech and language assessment indicating 'extreme autism. . . .'" *Id.* at 892–93. The court found that the district's failure to turn over the documents violated FAPE:

> The IEP team could not create an IEP that addressed Amanda's special needs as an autistic child without knowing that Amanda was autistic. Even worse, Amanda's parents were not informed of the possibility that their daughter suffered from autism—a disease that benefits from early intensive intervention—despite the fact that the district's records contained test results indicating as much. Not only were Amanda's parents prevented from participating fully, effectively, and in an informed manner in the development of Amanda's IEP, they were not even aware that an independent psychiatric evaluation was recommended, an evaluation that Amanda's mother testified she would have performed immediately. These procedural violations, which prevented Amanda's parents from learning critical medical

> information about their child, rendered the accomplishment of the IDEA's goals—and the achievement of a FAPE—impossible.

Id. at 894.

7. Even if parents can convince a court that a school district committed a procedural violation in connection with preparing the IEP, a procedural violation denies a FAPE only when it interferes with the child's receipt of a FAPE, significantly interferes with the parents' opportunity to participate in the IEP process, or deprives the child of educational benefits. 20 U.S.C. § 1415(f)(3)(E)(ii)(I)-(III) (2012). *See* R.P. v Alamo Heights Indep. Sch. Dist., 703 F.3d 801, 811 (5th Cir. 2012) (holding that even if prior violations occurred, "they did not rise to the level of denying R.P. a lost educational opportunity"); R.E. v. N.Y.C. Dep't of Educ., 694 F.3d 167, 190 (2d Cir. 2012) (repeating statutory requirements and noting that the cumulative impact of minor violations could also result in the denial of a FAPE).

The decision in *D.S. v. Bayonne Bd. of Educ.*, 602 F.3d 553 (3d Cir. 2010), is a good example of a harmless error analysis. The school district failed to respond timely to four letters the child's parents sent to the district requesting a meeting to discuss creating a ninth grade IEP for D.S. that incorporated the recommendations of his outside evaluators. *Id.* at 560, 565. The court agreed that the district's failure to respond to these letters violated New Jersey's IDEA regulations, which requires a response to such letters within twenty days. *Id.* at 565. However, the court stated:

> A procedural violation is actionable under the IDEA only if it results in a loss of educational opportunity for the student, seriously deprives parents of their participation rights, or causes a deprivation of educational benefits. Thus, though it is important that a school district comply with the IDEA's procedural requirements, rather than being a goal in itself, such compliance primarily is significant because of the requirements' impact on students' and parents' substantive rights. Here although Bayonne's initial unresponsiveness in the face of Appellants' concerns was unfortunate and undoubtedly frustrating to them, they ultimately had an opportunity to participate meaningfully in the creation of an IEP for D.S. that was in effect for most of his ninth grade year. Appellants and one of their outside experts ... were present at the November 2006 IEP meeting at which they made suggestions, some of which were incorporated in the IEP. Moreover, the revised IEP was presented to Appellants for their approval.
>
> ... Though appellants contend that D.S. was deprived of educational benefits, this alleged deprivation cannot reasonably be traced to Bayonne's delay in responding to Appellant's letters. In these circumstances we find that Bayonne substantially satisfied the IDEA's procedural requirements and that any deficiency in its compliance with the requirements is not a basis for granting relief to Appellants.

Id. at 565–66. The Third Circuit in *D.S.* articulated the statutory standard for prejudice: lost educational opportunity; deprivation of parental participation rights; or lost educational benefits. Do you agree that the district's failure to respond timely to the parents' letters or to implement an IEP for all of ninth grade were not such deprivations? Is it at least possible that the child would have received an educational benefit had the parents and their expert been involved in drafting the IEP several months sooner or if his IEP had been in place for all of ninth grade?

The analysis in *D.S.* is typical of harmless error analysis in IEP cases relating to parental participation. For other examples, *see* L.M. v. Capistrano Unified Sch. Dist., 556 F.3d 900, 907, 910–11 (9th Cir. 2009) (holding that although district's limiting parents to twenty minutes to observe their child in the classroom violated California law, it did not violate the IDEA because the limit did not have a significant impact on their participation); Hjortness v. Neenah Joint Sch. Dist., 507 F.3d 1060, 1065–66 (7th Cir. 2007), *cert. denied*, 554 U.S. 930 (2008) (holding that a district's failure to hold a second IEP meeting did not prejudice parents because they refused to discuss goals at previous IEP meetings); Kings Local Sch. Dist. Bd. of Educ. v. Zelazny, 325 F.3d 724, 732 (6th Cir. 2003) (holding that exclusion of parents from third meeting did not violate FAPE because mother met with child's teachers, recommended a consulting firm that the district hired, and attended consulting firm meetings); N. L. v. Knox Cnty. Sch., 315 F.3d 688, 694–95 (6th Cir. 2003) (holding that creation of assessment report and *ex parte* contacts between school's experts and school officials did not create substantive harm); Independent Sch. Dist. No. 283 v. S.D., 88 F.3d 556, 562 (8th Cir. 1996) (holding that procedural deficiencies did not deny FAPE); Hupp v. Switz. of Ohio Local Sch. Dist., 912 F. Supp. 2d 572, 594 (S.D. Ohio 2012) (holding that adding two pages to the child's IEP without parental knowledge did not cause substantive harm).

8. The Court in *Shapiro* also addressed the composition of the IEP team and ruled that the district's failure to include a regular education teacher at the IEP meeting violated the IDEA. At least two other courts have reached the same conclusion. In *Deal v. Hamilton Cnty. Bd. of Educ.*, 392 F.3d 840 (6th Cir. 2004), a regular education teacher left one IEP meeting before the IEP team discussed the child's goals and placement and did not attend a second IEP meeting. In finding that this violated the IDEA, the court stated:

> The rationale for requiring the attendance of a regular education teacher is closely tied to Congress's "least restrictive environment" mandate. The input provided by a regular education teacher is vitally important in considering the extent to which a disabled student may be integrated into a regular education classroom and how the student's individual needs might be met within that classroom. One of the Deals' main objections to the 1999–2000 IEP developed for Zachary is that it did not provide for sufficient integration. The absence of the unique perspective that could have been provided by a regular education teacher therefore had a real impact on the decision-making process.

Id. at 860–61; *see also* C.R. v. Wappingers Cent. Sch. Dist., 772 F. Supp. 2d 500, 509 (S.D.N.Y. 2010), *aff'd*, 431 F. App'x 12 (2d Cir. 2011) (ruling that in the absence of a regular or special education teacher at the IEP meeting parents could not explore the "possible modifications and alternative services that would help C.R. during that year.").

9. Despite *Deal* and *C.R.*, most courts that have considered the absence of a general education teacher from an IEP meeting have ruled that it did not violate the IDEA. In one line of cases, the courts ruled that a general education teacher was not necessary because the child was not in a general education classroom and there was no reason for the district to think the child should be in one. *See* J.G. v. Kiryas Joel Union Free Sch. Dist., 777 F. Supp. 2d 606, 644–45 (S.D.N.Y. 2011) (ruling that the child was not in regular education and there was no reason for the district to believe he should be); J.T. v. Bd. of Educ. of the Sch. Dist. of N.Y.C., 716 F. Supp. 2d 270, 288 (S.D.N.Y. 2010) (ruling that child was neither in nor being considered for general education); M.N. v. N.Y.C. Dep't of Educ., 700 F. Supp. 2d 356, 365–66 (S.D.N.Y. 2010) (ruling that parents placed child at a school that did not have a general education setting); A.M. v. N.Y.C. Dep't of Educ., 583 F. Supp. 2d 498, 505–06 (S.D.N.Y. 2008) (ruling that child was not in or being considered for regular education); Johnson v. Olathe Dist. Sch. Unified Sch. Dist. No. 233, 316 F. Supp. 2d 960, 969 (D. Kan. 2003) (holding that child was not going to participate in general education); *see also* 20 U.S.C. § 1414(d)(1)(B)(ii) (2012) (the IEP team must be composed of "not less than 1 regular education teacher of such child (if the child is, or may be, participating in the regular education environment")). In a second line of cases, the courts found that the absence of a general education teacher from an IEP meeting was harmless error. *See* J.W. v. Fresno Unified Sch. Dist., 626 F.3d 431, 459 (9th Cir 2010) (holding that the absence of a general education teacher from the second of three IEP meetings was harmless error because the focus of the meeting was not general education, the issues relating to general education had been discussed at a previous meeting that the general education teacher attended, and the parents had already eliminated general education as an option); Anderson v. District of Columbia, 606 F. Supp. 2d 86, 91 (D.D.C. 2009) (holding that absence of general education and special education teachers from IEP meeting did not cause substantive harm because district had sufficient information to prepare IEP); L.R. v. Manheim Twnshp. Sch. Dist., 540 F. Supp. 2d 603, 616 (E.D. Pa. 2008) (holding that there was no showing of prejudice from absence of general education teacher at IEP meeting).

10. Parents have successfully argued that the absence of a special education teacher from the IEP team violated the IDEA. Werner v. Clarkstown Cent. Sch. Dist., 363 F. Supp. 2d 656, 659 (S.D.N.Y. 2005) (holding that absence of teacher from the proposed out of district placement denied FAPE because parents could not inquire about the placement); Brimmer v. Traverse City Area Pub. Sch., 872 F. Supp. 447, 452 (W.D. Mich. 1994) (holding that absence of teachers from child's school for the deaf from IEP meeting violated the IDEA). In contrast, several courts found that the absence of a special education teacher was harmless error. In *A.H. v. Dep't of Educ. of the City of N.Y.*, 394 F. App'x 718 (2d Cir. 2010), the child's special education teacher

allegedly did not attend the IEP meeting, but another special education teacher from the district attended. In finding that this did not prejudice the child, the court stated:

> Even if J.H.'s special education teacher did not participate in formulating the challenged IEP, a certified special education teacher who taught and served as an IEP coordinator at J.H.'s high school did so. Like the SRO, we conclude that nothing in the record indicates that this teacher "in any way lacked knowledge regarding the special education program options for the student."

Id. at 720; *see also* M.T. v. Croton-Harmon Union Free Sch. Dist., 812 F. Supp. 2d 420, 431 (S.D.N.Y. 2011) (holding that absence of special education teacher from student's private school from IEP meeting did not violate IDEA because psychologist and learning lab teacher who would have served child if he returned to the district were present); J.G. v. Kiryas Joel Union Free Sch. Dist., 777 F. Supp. 2d 606, 646 (S.D.N.Y. 2011) (holding that absence of a special education teacher or provider of special education services to the child was not prejudicial because several IEP team members had relevant experience in special education); Johnson v. Olathe Dist. Sch. Unified Sch. Dist. No. 233, 316 F. Supp. 2d 960, 969 (D. Kan. 2003) (excusing absence of special education teacher from IEP meeting because staff who would be working with child in the role a special education teacher would have played was present).

Section Three
Contents of the IEP

The IDEA and its implementing regulations require the IEP to describe: 1) the child's "present levels of academic achievement"; 2) "measurable annual goals"; 3) how the district will measure "the child's progress toward meeting the annual goals"; 4) "the special education and related services" the school district will provide to the child; 5) "the extent, if any, to which the child will not participate" in the general education environment; 6) "the projected date for the beginning of the services . . . and the anticipated frequency, location, and duration of those services"; and 7) "in the first IEP to be in effect when the child is 16, . . . appropriate measurable postsecondary goals . . . and transition services . . . ." 20 U.S.C. § 1414(d)(1)(A)(i)(I)-(VIII) (2012); *see also* 34 C.F.R. § 300.320(a)-(b) (2015).

The following case involves a dispute over reimbursement for private school tuition. One of the issues in the case was whether the IEP that the school district prepared for the student was sufficient. Although Congress has since amended the IDEA, including the provisions relating to the contents of the IEP in this case, many of the current provisions are similar and the decision is a good example of a judicial analysis of whether an IEP contains all the information the IDEA requires in the form the IDEA requires.

Bd. of Educ. of Avon Lake City Sch. Dist. v. Patrick M.

9 F. Supp. 2d 811 (N.D. Ohio 1998),
remanded as moot, 215 F.3d 1325 (6th Cir. 2000)

Gwin, District Judge.

....

As previously noted, IDEA requires that a school district's individualized educational program be reasonably calculated to afford students with disabilities some educational benefit. In determining whether an individualized education program is reasonably calculated to afford some educational benefit, courts must subject the IEP at issue to strict review....

The first element of § 1401(19) requires a school district's individualized education program to include "a statement of the present levels of educational performance of the child." The individual educational program proposed for Patrick's ninth grade year meets this requirement. Specifically, the individual educational program details Patrick's academic performance, his educational evaluations, his social and emotional skills, and his cognitive reasoning abilities. The individualized education program also describes Patrick's trouble areas including weakness in the areas of written assignments, reading and math. The IEP also addresses Patrick's need to improve his organizational skills and to control his impulsive behavior. The individualized education program further proposed methods of intervention and modification to help Patrick overcome his deficiencies....

IDEA next requires an individualized education program to include "a statement of annual goals, including short-term instructional objectives." This requirement is also met. The District's proposed 1995–96 individual educational program outlines numerous long-term goals to be accomplished. These goals are supplemented by meeting certain short-term objectives. Patrick's goals focus on improving his class attendance, increasing his performance on tests and quizzes, improving his self-esteem, controlling his temper and behavior, and learning to express his feelings in an appropriate manner. Both the long-term and short-term goals provide methods and criteria for evaluation....

The third requirement says that the individual educational program must include a "statement of the specific educational services to be provided to each such student, and the extent to which such child will be able to participate in regular educational programs." The District's proposed 1995–96 individual educational program indicates that Patrick's academic and non-academic programs required his participation in science, math, art, industrial art, physical education and lunch. Although the individual educational program does not identify specific course times, the extent of his participation and his projected ability to perform in these areas is discussed at length in the individual educational program. The Court concludes that any minor or technical omission relating to the individual educational program's failure to identify course times or class periods is excusable.

The fourth requirement under § 1401(19) requires that the individual educational program include "the projected date for initiation and anticipated duration of such services." The District's proposed 1995–96 individual educational program shows that Petitioner Avon Lake was to provide services starting on August 28, 1995, and continuing through June 7, 1996. . . . The final requirement under the Act requires an individual educational program to include "appropriate objective criteria and evaluation procedures and schedules for determining, on at least an annual basis, whether instructional objectives are being achieved." Again, the District's proposed 1995–96 individual educational program for Patrick meets this requirement. In addition to outlining long-term goals which are in-turn supported by short-term objectives, each goal on the proposed 1995–96 individual educational program is broken down into methods of achieving the goal or objective, the service providers involved in the process (teachers, students, or through special instruction), and the criteria to be used when monitoring Patrick's progress. The individual educational program shows that Patrick's progress was to be monitored by daily and weekly attendance records, weekly grades, and quarterly progress reports. Some of Patrick's short-term objectives were monitored with task sheets and staff/teacher observation. The individual educational program also shows that Patrick was to undergo an annual review.

Having reviewed the contents of Petitioner Avon Lake's proposed individual educational program for Patrick's ninth grade year . . . , the Court finds that the District developed and provided an individualized educational program for Patrick that, at a minimum, offered a "basic floor of opportunity" for Patrick to have access to some specialized instruction and related services.

. . . .

Notes, Comments, and Questions

1. Courts have considered several issues relating to the contents of an IEP. Their rulings are summarized below.

Statement of level of academic achievement and impact of the child's disability on the child's education: The IDEA requires the IEP to state the child's "present levels of academic achievement" and "how the child's disability affects the child's involvement and progress in the general curriculum . . . ." 20 U.S.C. § 1414(d)(1)(A)(i)(I)(aa) (2012). *See* Lathrop R-II Sch. Dist. v. Gray, 611 F.3d 419, 424 (8th Cir. 2010), *cert. denied*, 562 U.S. 1188 (2011) (upholding IEP that discussed how child's "disability affected his ability to access the general curriculum"); O'Dell v. Special Sch. Dist. of St. Louis Cnty., 503 F. Supp. 2d 1206, 1216 (E.D. Mo. 2007) (upholding IEP that was based on a "Present Level of Educational Performance" form that included the child's "areas of developmental delay" and "areas of concern"); A.I. v. District of Columbia, 402 F. Supp. 2d 152, 164 (D.D.C. 2005) (upholding IEP that included the child's "strengths in math and reading, the impact of her disability in both areas, and test scores in both areas"); Robert B. v. West Chester Area Sch. Dist., 2005

U.S. Dist. LEXIS 21558, at *20 (E.D. Pa. 2005) (upholding IEP that described the skills the child had and had not yet mastered).

In *O'Toole v. Olathe Dist. Sch. Unified Sch. Dist. No. 233*, 144 F.3d 692 (10th Cir. 1998), the court found that although the district did not adequately identify the child's present level of academic performance, it did not violate the IDEA:

> We agree with the reviewing officer that the IEP does not clearly convey Molly's present levels of educational performance in a way that relates those present levels to her disability . . . . However, it does refer to the specialists' reports, which presumably contain more detail and which the O'Toole's do not argue were unavailable for reference. Moreover, there is no doubt that Molly's parents and her teachers were fully aware of Molly's present levels of educational performance and discussed them in detail in formulating her IEPs. Given that one of the primary goals of the procedural requirements of the IDEA is to ensure parental participation in the formulation of a child's IEP, and to ensure that the program developed actually reflects, and is based upon, the child's present levels of performance, we conclude that the statement of present levels of academic performance in the IEPs did not violate the procedural requirements of the IDEA . . . .

Id. at 703–04. Do you agree that parental and teacher participation in drafting the IEP should excuse the district from including a description of how the child's disability relates to her performance levels? Should parental participation shield the district from preparing an adequate IEP?

In contrast, in *Marc M. v. Dep't of Educ. of Haw.*, 762 F. Supp. 2d 1235 (D. Haw. 2011), the school district failed to consider the child's progress report and student profile in preparing his IEP. *Id.* at 1238. The court ruled that as a result the child's IEP did not include "an accurate statement of his current academic performance level. *Id.* at 1245; *see also* Evans v. Bd. of Educ. of the Rhinebeck Cent. Sch. Dist., 930 F. Supp. 83, 95–96 (S.D.N.Y. 1996) (ruling that IEP that did not indicate academic deficits and that was based on test scores that were at least ten months old violated the IDEA); *but see* Anello v. Indian River Sch. Dist., 355 F. App'x 594, 599 (3d Cir. 2009) (holding that statement in IEP that present performance level is "'1.8 grade level'" was a procedural violation but was harmless error).

<u>Measurable annual goals</u>: In *Patrick M.*, the court did not provide much description of the metrics for determining whether Patrick was meeting his goals. Generally, courts have approved IEPs as long as they contain objective goals; the level of specificity varies. *See, e.g.*, R.P. v. Prescott v. Unified Sch. Dist., 631 F.3d 1117, 1122–23 (9th Cir. 2011) (approving IEP that included goals such as "'improve communication skills'" and "'increase self help skills'" and that gave "concrete descriptions" of how the district would measure the child's progress); Nack v. Orange City Sch. Dist., 454 F.3d 604, 612–13 (6th Cir. 2006) (ruling that absence of baseline data was harmless error in light of measurable short-term goals); O'Toole v. Olathe Dist. Sch. Unified Sch. Dist No. 233, 144 F.3d 692, 706 (10th Cir. 1998) (approving an IEP that

contained a mix of "general" and "articulable" goals); Kuszewski v. Chippewa Valley Sch. Dist., 56 F. App'x 655, 659 (6th Cir. 2003) (upholding IEP that included goals such as "recall four story events in sequence, ... use appropriate punctuation, capitalization in sentences, and ... make change up to $1.00."); Red Clay Consol. Sch. Dist. v. T.S., 893 F. Supp. 2d 643, 651–52 (D. Del. 2012) (upholding IEP that included goals such as number of words on a list the child identifies and number of times out of ten attempts the child is able to form the sound of the first letter of a word); M.D. v. Haw. Dep't of Educ., 864 F. Supp. 2d 993, 1010 (D. Haw. 2012) (upholding IEP that contained "more than 30 pages of benchmarks and short-term objectives"); Z.V. v. Arlington Cent. Sch. Dist., 414 F. Supp. 2d 366, 380 (S.D.N.Y. 2006) (approving goals that "listed specific percentages of mastery desired and described the method of evaluation, which included ... standardized test scores."); W.S. v. Rye City Sch. Dist., 454 F. Supp. 2d. 134, 147 (S.D.N.Y. 2006) (finding that IEP's objectives regarding what and when the child should be able to do were specific); A.I. v. District of Columbia, 402 F. Supp. 2d 152, 164 (D.D.C. 2005) (upholding IEP that included six pages of twenty-six "'short-term objectives' ... and six annual goals."); K. L. v. N.Y.C. Dep't of Educ., 2012 U.S. Dist. LEXIS 124460, at *31 (S.D.N.Y. 2012) (approving IEP that stated the teacher "would monitor ... progress using data collection and tracking tools.").

In contrast, other courts have rejected IEPs that contain similar goals and objectives. In *Cleveland Heights-Univ. Heights City Sch. Dist. v. Boss*, 144 F.3d 391, 394 (6th Cir. 1998), the parents claimed that the IEP did not include objective criteria for measuring their child's progress. According to the court:

> The IEP stated that Sommer's progress would be measured in terms of her ability to do things such as "identify" a "list of sight words ... with 80% accuracy" and "improve her reading fluency when reading a passage aloud 8/10 times." Beyond such vague and general statements, the IEP offered no basis for measuring Sommer's progress.

Id. at 394 n.1. The court rejected the district's claim that the absence of more specific criteria was merely a technical violation: "[T]he violation was far from technical, and its absence was not harmless. The omission went to the heart of the substance of the plan ... ." *Id.* at 399; *see also* M.H. v. N.Y.C. Dep't of Educ., 685 F.3d 217, 247–49 (2d Cir. 2012) (rejecting goals on various grounds, including lack of specificity, absence of objective evaluative criteria, and failure to tailor to the needs of the child); Evans v. Bd. of Educ. of the Rhinebeck Cent. Sch. Dist., 930 F. Supp. 83, 97–98 (S.D.N.Y. 1996) (rejecting an IEP that included only "broad, generic objectives and vague, subjective methods" for monitoring progress such as "'teacher observation'" and "'80 percent accuracy.'").

One issue that courts have considered is whether the IDEA requires an IEP to include "baseline" data from which to measure a child's progress. *See* Lathrop R-II Sch. Dist. v. Gray, 611 F.3d 419 (8th Cir. 2010), *cert. denied*, 562 U.S. 1188 (2011). In rejecting this claim, the court also described measurable goals that it apparently approved:

> The panel . . . concluded that IEPs must incorporate "baseline data" to establish a starting point for each objective. Gray has not cited any case in which any court has read such an implied requirement into the law.
>
> Moreover, the challenged IEPs did contain "baseline data" for many of the goals, as the panel acknowledged. For example, the present level section in the 2002 IEP noted that D.G. could give the correct coinage for a purchase with 60% accuracy, but he could not fill out a blank check. Two of D.G.'s goals for the 2002–2003 school year were for him to improve his ability to give the correct amount of money for a purchase between $5.00 and $10.00 from 50% to 80% accuracy and to fill out a blank check from 0% to 100% accuracy. As D.G.'s special education teacher Nance explained, if District staff "had not attempted [an] objective" the starting point would be zero. The 2003 IEP's present level section similarly noted that D.G. had learned to fill out a blank check with 100% accuracy and give the correct amount of money for a purchase between $5.00 and $10.00 with 80% accuracy. His 2003 IEP therefore included the goal of improving his ability to give the amount of money for a $20.00-$30.00 purchase from 0% to 80% accuracy.
>
> Neither the panel nor Gray in his appellate brief specified which goals lacked "baseline data." In any event, we will not compel a school district to put more in its IEPs than is required by law. Gray has not met his burden of showing a procedural deficiency in this regard.

Id. at 424–45.

Transition plan and services: The IDEA does not require an IEP to contain a transition plan. Lessard v. Wilton-Lyndeborough Coop. Sch. Dist., 518 F.3d 18, 25 (1st Cir. 2008) (ruling that the IDEA does not require an IEP to include a transition plan). The IDEA, does, however, require that an IEP contain:

> (VIII) beginning not later than the first IEP to be in effect when the child is 16, and updated annually thereafter—
>
>> (aa) appropriate measurable post-secondary goals based upon age appropriate transition assessments related to training, education, and employment, and, where appropriate, independent living skills;
>>
>> (bb) the transition services . . . needed to assist the child in reaching these goals. . . .

20 U.S.C. § 1414(d)(1)(A)(VIII)(aa)-(bb) (2012); *see also* 34 C.F.R. § 300.320(b)(1)-(2) (2015); *see also* Sebastian M. v. King Philip Reg'l Sch. Dist., 774 F. Supp. 2d 393, 406–07 (D. Mass. 2011), *aff'd*, 685 F.3d 79 (1st Cir. 2012) (upholding IEP because it mentioned transition services and district provided transition services to the child). In two cases, the courts rejected IEPs because they did not contain an appropriate list of transition services. *See* Greg I. v. Dep't of Educ. of Haw., 869 F. Supp. 2d 1225, 1244–45 (D. Haw. 2012) (holding that the school district's failure to include a list of transition services designed to assist the child reach measurable post-secondary goals

in the IEP, among other violations, denied a FAPE); Dracut Sch. Comm. v. Mass. Dep't of Elementary and Secondary Educ., 737 F. Supp. 2d 35, 51 (D. Mass. 2010) (holding that the district failed to provide transition goals that were measurable and based on "timely transition assessments").

2. The IDEA also requires the IEP team to consider several factors about the child in drafting the IEP. These include:

(i) the strengths of the child;

(ii) the concerns of the parents for enhancing the education of their child;

(iii) the results of the initial evaluation or most recent evaluation of the child; and

(iv) the academic, developmental, and functional needs of the child.

20 U.S.C. § 1414(d)(3)(A)(i)-(iv) (2012); *see also* 34 C.F.R § 300.324(a)(1)(i)-(iv) (2015).

3. Finally, the IDEA requires the IEP team to consider the needs of children with behavioral issues that interfere with their learning; who have limited English proficiency or visual or hearing impairments; or who need assistive technology. 20 U.S.C. § 1414(d)(3)(B)(i)-(iv); *see also* 34 C.F.R. § 300.324(a)(2)(i)-(v). Judicial treatment of claims regarding behavioral issues and assistive technology are summarized below.

Behavioral issues: In connection with "a child whose behavior impedes the child's learning or that of others," the IDEA requires the IEP team to "consider the use of positive behavioral interventions and supports, and other strategies, to address that behavior. . . ." 20 U.S.C. § 1414(d)(3)(B)(i) (2012); *see also* 34 C.F.R. § 300.324(a)(2)(i) (2015). Nevertheless, the IDEA does not require a school district to include a behavior intervention plan ("BIP") in the IEP. *See* Lathrop R-H Sch. Dist. v. Gray, 611 F.3d 419, 426 (8th Cir. 2010), *cert. denied*, 562 U.S. 1188 (2011) (noting that the IEPs indicated improvement in child's behavior). The IDEA and its regulations do, however, require the IEP team to consider adopting a BIP if the child has behavioral issues that interfere with her ability to learn. *See* Lessard v. Wilton-Lyndeborough Coop. Sch. Dist., 518 F.3d 18, 26 (1st Cir. 2008) (ruling that the IEP team considered but did not adopt a BIP because it was not necessary to enable the district to provide the child a FAPE); E.Z.-L. v. N.Y.C. Dep't of Educ., 763 F. Supp. 2d 584, 597 (S.D.N.Y. 2011), *aff'd*, 694 F.3d 167 (2d Cir. 2012), *cert. denied*, __U.S.__, 133 S.Ct. 2800 (2013) (ruling that BIP was not necessary because child's behavior did not interfere with her learning). Even though the IDEA does not require an IEP to include a BIP, if a child needs services to improve his or her behavior, the team must include these services in the IEP. In *M.C. v. Byram Hills Sch. Dist.*, 906 F. Supp. 2d 256 (S.D.N.Y. 2012), the court ruled that failure to adopt a BIP "does not render an IEP procedurally inadequate where the child's behavior can be adequately addressed by other means." *Id.* at 269. The court stated:

> Plaintiffs allege that M.C.'s IEP was deficient because it lacked a BIP. However, the SRO determined that the IEP contained modifications to address M.C.'s behavior and that a BIP was not necessary. Modifications including

> verbal cues, manipulative chips to track student questions/comments, a silent signal by teachers, and sticky notes for students to write down their questions were provided to prevent M.C.'s calling out. Additional modifications to address M.C.'s impulsivity and other behavioral issues included behavioral contracts, breaks, choices/options regarding instructional activities, a token system, cues, having material broken down, and communication with parents. . . .

Id. at 270; *see also* T.Y. v. N.Y.C. Dep't of Educ., 584 F.3d 412, 419 (2d Cir. 2009) (excusing district from including BIP in IEP because individual aide helped improve student behavior); T.M. v. Cornwall Cent. Sch. Dist., 900 F. Supp. 2d 344, 354 (S.D.N.Y. 2012) (holding that the absence of a functional behavioral analysis in the student's IEP did not deny a FAPE because the IEP included behavioral interventions); A.L. v. N.Y.C. Dep't of Educ., 812 F. Supp. 2d 492, 503–04 (S.D.N.Y. 2011) (holding that failure to conduct a functional behavioral analysis did not violate the IDEA because the IEP team had sufficient information to develop an IEP that addressed behavioral issues); M.T. v. Croton-Harmon Union Free Sch. Dist., 812 F. Supp. 2d 420, 431 (S.D.N.Y. 2011) (ruling that the IEP included several strategies to manage behavior); Robert B. v. The West Chester Area Sch. Dist., 2005 U.S. Dist. Lexis 21558, at *20–21 (E.D. Pa. 2005) (holding that an IEP that included instructional strategies to address child's inattentiveness satisfied the IDEA).

In contrast to the cases that ruled that school districts treated the child's behavioral issues adequately in the IEP, in *Coventry Pub. Sch. v. Rachel J.*, 893 F. Supp. 2d 322 (D.R.I. 2012), the court ruled that the school district denied a FAPE to the child by failing to include behavioral goals or modifications in the child's IEP. The court found:

> After a thorough and exhaustive review of the entire record, the Court finds that it is undisputed that Billy's behavioral disability hampers his academic advancement and prevents any educational benefit. This reality has been obvious since his early childhood, routinely recognized by his teachers, and diagnosed by some of our state's leading mental health experts. His teachers have stated that his "behaviors continually get in the way of his academic work" and "because of his behaviors *he has missed some essential skills*, which have *set him back*." Although Billy's teachers found that he was academically capable, his behavior consistently got in the way of making academic progress. . . .
>
> . . . Billy's December 2007 IEP contained goals and objectives for his academic deficits, i.e., reading, writing and math. However, despite the resounding chorus of agreement that Billy's obvious and predominate behavioral disability was impeding his academic progress, his sixth grade IEP did not contain "clearly delineated behavioral goals" or "behavioral modification methods." The IEP was not, as required by law, "reasonably calculated to enable [Billy] to receive educational benefits." . . . .

> Moreover, the IDEA mandates that "in the case of a child whose behavior impedes the child's learning" the IEP team must also consider "the use of positive behavioral interventions and supports, and other strategies to address that behavior." Not having clear and defined behavioral goals and modifications in the IEP is tantamount to denying him any education at all. The record is abundantly clear that Billy's behavioral disabilities act like a boulder that blocks his way from making academic and educational advancements. The Coventry IEP's failure to recognize this and to provide for this is clear and convincing evidence that Coventry violated the IDEA.

Id. at 334–35; *see also* Greg I. v. Dep't of Educ. of Haw., 869 F. Supp. 2d 1225, 1241–42, 1246–48 (D. Haw. 2012) (ruling that the absence of a BIP to address admitted behavioral issues violated the IDEA); Lamoine Sch. Comm. v. N.S., 353 F. Supp. 2d 18, 34 (D. Me. 2005) (holding that an IEP that did not address the child's continuing absences and lateness denied a FAPE).

Assistive technology: In *Blake C. v. Dept't of Educ. of Haw.*, 593 F. Supp. 2d 1199 (D. Haw. 2009), the court ruled that the district denied a FAPE for, among other reasons, failing to consider whether the child needed assistive technology. The court stated:

> Here, the record establishes that Blake C.'s mother raised potential assistive technology devices (a "word processor unit" to assist in forming letters and writing without having to focus on fine motor skills) with his home school. There is no evidence, however, that the DOE ever considered, in any manner, any type of AT device. The evidence is that no evaluation was done because "it was not a concern brought up" (either before or after the December 2016 meeting). There certainly are indications in the record that Blake C. should have at least been at some point considered or evaluated for AT.

Id. at 1212.

4. Courts apply the IDEA's harmless error doctrine to violations relating to the contents of the IEP. In *Greg I. v. Dep't of Educ. of Haw.*, 869 F. Supp. 2d 1225 (D. Haw. 2012), the court found that the procedural errors relating to the IEP, including the lack of transition services, were not harmless:

> The court has found several procedural violations of the IDEA—the failure of the IEP team to consider potential harmful effects of the LRE, the failure to consider behavioral issues (no BSP), the failure to comply with transition services requirements, and the failure to invite a DVR representative to the IEP meetings. The court must next address whether the violations were harmless. . . .
>
> . . . .
>
> The procedural violations here were blatant. The DOE admitted it did not consider the potential harmful effects of the LRE. As to transition services, the DOE appears not to have recognized a change in law that occurred seven

> years ago. The offering of transition services was essentially nonexistent .... Although it remains speculative what would have occurred if the DOE had invited a DVR representative ..., the *opportunity* to have a representative during preparation of the ... IEP was certainly lost.
>
> It is also undisputed that no assessments were conducted as required under 34 C.F.R. § 300.320(b)(1) in considering transition services. The lack of assessments alone is enough to constitute a lost educational opportunity....
>
> Moreover, even if there were no "lost educational opportunity," the procedural violations—failing to consider potential harmful effects of an LRE, and to offer transition services—were also not harmless under the second prong of the test: Greg I.'s "parents' opportunity to participate in the IEP formulation process" was certainly "seriously infringed." With no discussion about potential harmful effects of the LRE, with no discussion about transition services, and with no assessments upon which to base those transition services, Carrie I. was denied *any* opportunity to participate in those processes in determining the LRE and its placement.

Id. at 1246–47.

More often, however, courts that conduct a harmless error analysis in connection with a district's failure to comply with the IDEA's requirements for the contents of an IEP generally find harmless error. The decision in *A.I. v. District of Columbia*, 402 F. Supp. 2d 152 (D.D.C.) is a good example:

Plaintiffs allege roughly six deficiencies in A.I.'s IEP .... The alleged deficiencies are:

> 1. The IEP did not include a description of A.I.'s present level of performance in the classroom.
>
> 2. The IEP did not identify goals and objectives appropriate for A.I.'s skill level.
>
> 3. The IEP failed to include those goals from A.I.'s *previous* IEP that she had failed to master.
>
> 4. The IEP failed to include an implementation strategy to insure A.I. met the goals and objectives set forth.
>
> 5. The IEP did not address A.I.'s fine or gross motor skills.
>
> 6. The IEP did not provide A.I. with any classroom modifications.
>
> ....
>
> Upon an analysis of the six alleged procedural deficiencies in the IEP developed at Janney for A.I., the Court concludes that the deficiencies constitute "technical" violations of the IDEA and—by themselves—are not sufficient to have rendered the IEP inappropriate and ensured the denial of a FAPE....

. . . .

> Ultimately, given the fact that (1) Plaintiffs overstate the scope of the alleged procedural deficiencies in the IEP, (2) the remaining deficiencies were essentially "technical" and known to the parties during the evaluation and determination process, (3) Defendants clearly ensured adequate parental involvement, and (4) no "procedural bad faith" took place, the Court concludes that to the extent that the IEP provided by Janney to A.I. failed to meet all of the laundry list of procedural requirements outlined in the IDEA, such deficiencies are insufficient to invalidate the IEP and compel a conclusion that A.I. was denied a FAPE. . . .

Id. at 163–65; *see also* Anello v. Indian River Sch. Dist., 355 F. App'x 594, 599 (3d Cir. 2009) (finding that district's failure to include a statement of how the child's disability affected her ability to learn was harmless error); Watson v. Kingston City Sch. Dist., 142 F. App'x 9, 11 (2d Cir. 2005) (holding that failure to update objectives and goals in IEP was a minor violation that did not warrant relief); Nack v. Orange City Sch. Dist., 454 F.3d 604, 612–13 (6th Cir. 2006) (holding that failure to include baseline data was harmless error because child was deriving educational benefit); O'Toole v. Olathe Dist. Sch. Unified Sch. Dist. No. 233, 144 F.3d 692, 707 (10th Cir. 1998) (holding that the district's failure to specify the related services adequately was harmless error because the district did not deny any related services the parents requested); R.R. v. Scarsdale Union Free Sch. Dist., 615 F. Supp. 2d 283, 295 (S.D.N.Y. 2009), *aff'd*, 366 F. App'x 239 (2d Cir. 2010) (holding that failing to include expected performance level was harmless error).

Section Four
Implementing the IEP

Van Duyn v. Baker Sch. Dist. 5J

502 F.3d 811 (9th Cir. 2007)

Fisher, Circuit Judge:

. . . .

This case arises from the difficult transition of Christopher J. Van Duyn ("Van Duyn"), a severely autistic child, from elementary to middle school. Van Duyn alleges that Baker School District 5J ("District") failed to implement key portions of his individualized educational program (" IEP") during the 2001–02 school year, his first year at Baker Middle School, thereby depriving him of the free appropriate public education guaranteed by the federal Individuals with Disabilities Education Act ("IDEA").

. . . [W]e must decide how much leeway a school district has in implementing an IEP as it translates the plan's provisions into action at school and in the classroom. We hold that when a school district does not perform exactly as called for by the IEP, the district does not violate the IDEA unless it is shown to have materially failed to implement the child's IEP. A material failure occurs when there is more than a minor discrepancy between the services provided to a disabled child and those required by the IEP.

Applying this standard to the various implementation failures Van Duyn alleges, we conclude that none of them was material . . . , and that the District therefore did not violate the IDEA. . . .

I. Factual and Procedural Background

A. Factual History

. . . .

Van Duyn's 2001–02 IEP called for him to work on "language arts—reading and written work" for 6–7 hours per week, "math computation/math computer drills" for 8–10 hours per week and "adaptive P.E.—gymnastics and swimming" for 3–4 hours per week. . . .

Van Duyn's IEP also included a behavior management plan that was to be implemented full-time. . . . [T]he middle school employed a daily behavior card, a visual schedule, social stories and a quiet room. However, his behavior was not accurately recorded on the card, he did not set up his daily schedule before starting each school day, social stories were not properly used and he was not ordered to go to the quiet room after all incidents of misbehavior.

The IEP further called for all material to be presented at Van Duyn's level and for him to be placed in a "self-contained" special education room. During class, he typically received one-on-one instruction from his personal aide . . . , as well as some personal instruction from his two main teachers . . . . It is unclear whether he generally proceeded at his own pace or instead received instruction about whatever subject the class was studying that day. His classes varied in size from 7 to 15 students and were composed entirely of special education students.

. . . .

There is evidence that Van Duyn's reading skills deteriorated during the 2001–02 school year, though it is unclear whether the regression amounted to three years or less than one. However, the school's therapist and psychologist both testified that his behavior improved in 2001–02 and that he was more engaged with his surroundings as the year progressed. Ms. Walker also testified that Van Duyn's math skills showed progress in 2001–02. Finally, his report cards indicated improvement in the vast majority of categories from October 2001 to June 2002.

. . . .

III. Discussion

. . . .

B. Violations of the IDEA's Procedural Requirements

. . . .

Van Duyn's first contention is that by failing to implement portions of the IEP, the District "changed" the IEP without notifying his parents in advance—a violation of the IDEA's procedural requirements for the formulation and revision of IEPs. In his view, this procedural defect impeded his parents' right to participate in decisions regarding the IEP and hence violated the statute . . . .

. . . .

Van Duyn's procedural argument . . . boils down to the novel proposition that failures to *implement* an IEP are equivalent to *changes* to an IEP. If accepted, this proposition would convert all IEP implementation failures into procedural violations of the IDEA, but there is no indication that a conflation of this sort is intended or permitted by the statute. . . .

. . . .

C. Failures to Implement the IEP

. . . .

3. The Materiality Standard

The core of Van Duyn's case is his allegation that the District failed to implement his IEP. . . . [O]ur court has not yet articulated the standard for assessing an IEP's implementation. To determine this standard, we look to both the statutory text and decisions of other courts.

The IDEA defines a free appropriate public education as "special education and related services that . . . are provided in conformity with the [child's] individualized education program." The statute also allows a party to challenge an IEP because of procedural flaws in the IEP's formulation as well as "on substantive grounds based on a determination of whether the child received a free appropriate public education." This language surely indicates that a failure to implement an IEP may deny a child a free appropriate public education and thereby give rise to a claim under the statute. The language also counsels against making minor implementation failures actionable given that "special education and related services" need only be provided "*in conformity with*" the IEP. There is no statutory requirement of perfect adherence to the IEP, nor any reason rooted in the statutory text to view minor implementation failures as denials of a free appropriate public education.

. . . [T]he Supreme Court in *Rowley* was faced with a challenge to an IEP's content. Nevertheless, the Court's approach is instructive in the IEP implementation context as well. In particular, it is significant that, according to the Court, procedural flaws in an IEP's formulation do not automatically violate the IDEA, but rather do so only when the resulting IEP is not "reasonably calculated to enable the child to receive educational benefits." 458 U.S. at 207 . . . . This suggests that minor failures in implementing an IEP, just like minor failures in following the IDEA's procedural requirements, should not automatically be treated as violations of the statute. The Court's description of the IDEA's purpose as providing a "basic floor of opportunity" to disabled students rather than a "potential-maximizing education" also supports granting some flexibility to school districts charged with implementing IEPs. *Id.* at 197 n. 21, 201 . . . .

The two circuits to have explicitly addressed IEP implementation failures both did so in a manner consistent with our reading of the statutory text and *Rowley.* In *Bobby R.*, the Fifth Circuit considered a disabled child whose IEP had not been perfectly implemented and whose academic performance had improved in some areas and declined in others. The court held that "to prevail on a claim under the IDEA, a party challenging the implementation of an IEP must show more than a *de minimis* failure to implement all elements of that IEP, and, instead, must demonstrate that the school board or other authorities failed to implement substantial or significant provisions of the IEP." Employing this standard, the court concluded that conceded implementation failures did not violate the IDEA because "the significant provisions of [the child's] IEP were followed, and, as a result, he received an educational benefit."

Similarly, the Eighth Circuit held in *Clark* that the IDEA is violated "if there is evidence that the school actually failed to implement an essential element of the IEP that was necessary for the child to receive an educational benefit." To determine if the "fact that no cohesive plan was in place to meet [the child's] behavioral needs" gave rise to a statutory violation, the court considered both the shortfall in services provided and evidence regarding the child's progress in several areas. The court concluded that the IDEA was indeed violated because the actions taken by the school "did not appropriately address [the child's] behavior problem," and "any slight benefit obtained was lost due to behavior problems that went unchecked and interfered with [the child's] ability to obtain a benefit from his education."

In accordance with the IDEA itself, the Court's decision in *Rowley* and the decisions of our sister circuits, we hold that a *material* failure to implement an IEP violates the IDEA. A material failure occurs when there is more than a minor discrepancy between the services a school provides to a disabled child and the services required by the child's IEP. Because the parties debate whether Van Duyn's skills and behavior improved or deteriorated during the 2001–02 school year, we clarify that the materiality standard does not require that the child suffer demonstrable educational harm in order to prevail. However, the child's educational progress, or lack of it, may be probative of whether there has been more than a minor shortfall in the services provided. For instance, if the child is not provided the reading instruction called for and there is a shortfall in the child's reading achievement, that would certainly tend to show that the failure to implement the IEP was material. On the other hand, if the child performed at or above the anticipated level, that would tend to show that the shortfall in instruction was not material. We also emphasize that nothing in this opinion weakens schools' obligation to provide services "in conformity with" children's IEPs. IEPs are clearly binding under the IDEA, and the proper course for a school that wishes to make material changes to an IEP is to reconvene the IEP team pursuant to the statute—not to decide on its own no longer to implement part or all of the IEP.

4. Implementation of the IEP

Applying the standard for evaluating alleged IEP implementation failures here, we turn to the various areas in which Van Duyn asserts that the District failed to implement his IEP. . . .

First, Van Duyn's IEP required 8–10 hours of math instruction per week. The ALJ found that he was not being provided with sufficient instruction and therefore ordered that he receive the "five hours per week of instruction in math that he has not been receiving." We agree that the initial five-hour shortfall was a material implementation failure. Van Duyn now claims that only 100 minutes of math instruction per week were added in response to the ALJ's order and that the District was thus still not in compliance with the IEP. However, he makes no effort to rebut the testimony to the contrary by Ms. Walker, who taught three of Van Duyn's eight classes, and Ms. Irby, his other main teacher. Ms. Walker testified that Van Duyn . . . received the requisite math instruction. Similarly, Ms. Irby testified that Van Duyn used math computer programs in her classes for roughly 100 minutes per week. We therefore hold that after the District's corrective actions, there was no material failure to provide Van Duyn with the required amount of weekly math instruction.

Second, Van Duyn is correct that several elements of his behavior management plan were not implemented in the same way at the middle school as at the elementary school. The daily behavior card was not used as strictly as it was before. Social stories were never employed in Ms. Walker's three classes and were improperly used by Ms. Baxter and Ms. Irby. And Van Duyn was not told to go to the "quiet room" after all incidents of misbehavior, nor was the room adequately equipped until just before the administrative hearing.

Although we do not condone these failures to implement the behavior management plan, we conclude that they were not material for several reasons. First, the IEP did not clearly describe how the daily behavior card, social stories and quiet room were used at the elementary school, nor did it require that they be used in the same way at the middle school. It is undisputed that the behavior management plan was not implemented identically at the two schools, but the IEP did not say that it had to be. Second, the middle school did employ many of the techniques outlined in the behavior management plan, even if not quite as Van Duyn envisioned. Third, there is evidence that the elementary school behavior management plan was inappropriate for the middle school context. Van Duyn's former aide testified that "[i]t looks to me like the system that we used at South Baker doesn't work at the middle school, and so it's not being used the same." Finally, Van Duyn's behavior appears to have improved in 2001–02. The school speech therapist stated that while "in the previous [reports] it's mentioned that Chris doesn't notice others in his environment," "[t]he following year we see that Chris does notice others in his environment and is engaging more." The school psychologist added that Van Duyn was being sent to the quiet room only about once per month at the middle school, a much lower rate than at the elementary school.

Next, there is some ambiguity in the record about whether, as required by the IEP, work was presented at Van Duyn's level. On the one hand, Ms. Baxter testified that what Van Duyn would learn about on any given day depended on what the class was taught that day. On the other hand, his two main teachers, Ms. Walker and Ms. Irby, testified that he was never subjected to lecture-style teaching and generally received one-on-one instruction. Ms. Walker described "filter[ing] around to the students" while Ms. Irby stated that Van Duyn's instruction was largely one-on-one with her or the assistant. On this conflicting record, we cannot conclude that the District materially failed to present work at Van Duyn's level. We also note that there is no evidence that his educational progress was hindered as a result of exposure to materials that were too advanced for him.

Finally, the parties dispute the meaning of "self-contained sp[ecial] ed[ucation] room" and whether Van Duyn was provided with such placement. He contends that his IEP required a learning environment like the one he enjoyed at the elementary school, with a single classroom where highly disabled students receive instruction individually or in small groups and there is complete flexibility as to the timing and content of instruction. The District, however, asserts that a self-contained classroom is a "service" rather than a "placement," and exists whenever a student spends more than 60 percent of his time in a special education classroom.

Even under Van Duyn's definition, which appears nowhere in the IEP and is at odds with Oregon practice as well as the testimony of one of his own witnesses, we hold that the District did not materially fail to provide him with a self-contained classroom. His class sizes varied from 7 to 15 students . . . , and there were always one teacher and one aide present . . . .

Furthermore, there was substantial flexibility in the instruction that Van Duyn received at the middle school. While he was on a block schedule with set times for classes, he could take breaks whenever they were necessary, he received constant attention from Ms. Baxter and frequent one-on-one instruction from Ms. Walker and Ms. Irby and the projects he worked on were typically unrelated to his classes' nominal subject matter. This may not have been quite as beneficial a learning environment as the elementary school, but we cannot conclude that it constituted a material failure to provide Van Duyn with a self-contained classroom.

We therefore hold that the District did not materially fail to implement any provisions in Van Duyn's IEP . . . .

. . . .

Notes, Comments, and Questions

1. The court in *Van Duyn* referred to two circuit court decisions that considered IEP implementation issues and came to different results. In *Houston Indep. Sch. Dist. v. Bobby R.*, 200 F.3d 341 (5th Cir. 2000), the district failed to implement services the IEP required, including speech therapy, an alphabet phonics programs, and highlighted and taped texts. *Id.* at 345. In considering the child's claim that the district's failure to implement these services deprived him of a FAPE, the court articulated a standard for considering failure to implement IEP claims:

> [W]e conclude that to prevail on a claim under the IDEA, a party challenging the implementation of an IEP must show more than a *de minimis* failure to implement all elements of that IEP, and, instead, must demonstrate that the school board or other authorities failed to implement substantial or significant provisions of the IEP. This approach affords local agencies some flexibility in implementing IEPs, but it still holds those agencies accountable for material failures and for providing the disabled child a meaningful educational benefit.

Id. at 349. Applying this standard to the facts, the court ruled that the "child received an educational benefit from the IEP, as demonstrated by the objective evidence of increased scores and grade levels." *Id.* at 350. In contrast, in *Neosho R-V Sch. Dist. v. Clark*, 315 F.3d 1022 (8th Cir. 2003), the court ruled that by failing to develop and implement the behavior management plans the child's IEP required, the district failed to provide him with an educational benefit. *Id.* at 1030. The court cited evidence that each time the child approached the fifth grade level, increased stress associated with the more difficult work resulted in behavior problems that forced his teacher to return to a fourth-grade level or lower. *Id.* at 1029. Can you reconcile the different results in these cases?

2. In a footnote, the court in *Bobby R.* discussed how to determine whether a portion of an IEP is significant. The court stated:

> [The] determination of what are "'significant'" provisions of an IEP cannot be made from an exclusively *ex ante* perspective. Thus, one factor to consider under an *ex post* analysis would be whether the IEP services that were provided actually conferred an educational benefit.

200 F.3d at 349 n. 2. One court criticized *Bobby R.*'s attempt to define a "significant" provision of an IEP:

> [T]he Fifth Circuit's language easily could be misread as contemplating an abstract inquiry into the significance of various "provisions" . . . of the IEP, rather than a contextual inquiry into the materiality (in terms of the impact on the child's education) of the failures to meet the IEP's requirements. This is a subtle distinction, but, in this court's view, an important one. Very few, if any, "'provisions'" of an IEP will be insignificant or insubstantial, and the *Bobby R.* standard should not be read to allow educators to distinguish in the abstract between important and unimportant IEP requirements. To the

> contrary, all the requirements of the IEP are significant, and educators should strive to satisfy them. It is in the contextual, *ex post* analysis—i.e whether the requirements are feasible and in the best interest of the child as she progresses—that questions of substantiality and significance arise.

E.C. v. District of Columbia, 478 F. Supp. 2d 73, 76 (D.D.C. 2007). Do you agree that every requirement of an IEP is significant? If so, should a court ever excuse a district's failure to comply with an IEP's requirements? The courts in both *Bobby R.* and *E.C.* accepted the proposition that in determining a failure to implement claim the court could examine the services the child actually received and determine whether they provided the child with an educational benefit. Do you agree with this approach?

3. In adopting its standard, the court in *Van Duyn* also relied on the IDEA's definition of a FAPE as "'special education and related services that . . . are provided in conformity with the child's individualized education program.'" 502 F.3d at 821; *see also* 34 C.F.R. § 300.323(c)(2) (2015) (requiring school districts to provide "special education and related services . . . in accordance with the child's IEP."). The court in *Van Duyn* interpreted "in conformity with" as allowing "minor implementation failures" and not requiring "perfect adherence to the IEP. . . ." 502 F.3d at 821; *see also* M.D. v. Haw. Dep't of Educ., 864 F. Supp. 2d 993, 1010 (D. Haw. 2012) ("The IDEA does not require perfect adherence to an IEP, and minor discrepancies between the services called for and those actually delivered do not give rise to an IDEA violation."). Do you agree with this interpretation of "in conformity with"? One court did not:

> A FAPE by definition requires that the instruction and services "comport with the child's IEP." *See Bd. of Educ. v. Rowley*, 458 U.S. 176, 188–89 . . . (1982). As the court in *B.B. v. Perry Township School Corporation* reasoned, if Plaintiff's argument was accepted, "a school district could draft a detailed and elegant IEP, choose to ignore parts of it, and resist any remedy unless the child and his parents could show that the failures were in fact causing serious educational harm to the child."

Board of Educ. of Chicago v. Ramie P., 741 F. Supp. 2d 920, 924–25 (N.D. Ill. 2010).

4. Several other courts, in addition to *Van Duyn* and *Clark*, have adopted or utilize the *Bobby R.* standard. *See* Melissa S. v. Sch. Dist. of Pittsburgh, 183 F. App'x 184, 187 (3d Cir. 2006) (citing the *Bobby R.* standard); R.M. v. Haddon Heights Bd. of Educ., 822 F. Supp. 2d 439, 455 (D.N.J. 2011) (ruling that district's failure to provide special education teacher for two months did not result in loss of educational benefit); E.C. v. District of Columbia, 478 F. Supp. 2d 73, 76 (D.D.C. 2007) (adopting *Bobby R.* standard); Schoenbach v. District of Columbia, 309 F. Supp. 2d 71, 83 n. 10 (D.D.C. 2004) (stating that "failure to implement all services outlined in an IEP does not constitute a *per se* violation of the IDEA."); Manalansan v. Bd. of Educ. of Balt. City, 2001 U.S. Dist. LEXIS 12608, at **33, 46–47 (D. Md. 2001) (holding that district's failure to provide the child with an aide was a material breach).

5. What do you think of the standard for evaluating an IEP implementation claim that the courts in *Van Duyn*, *Bobby R.*, and *Clark* articulated? Should a school district be allowed to provide fewer educational services than it committed to in the IEP? Does the standard undermine the important role of the IEP the Supreme Court has described? Does it undermine the importance of adherence to procedures? One court thinks it does. In rejecting a school district's defense that it should be excused from providing all the services the IEP required, the court stated:

> It would make the agreement reached by the IEP team and the commitment of services agreed upon and spelled out in the IEP . . . mean little in terms of a guarantee of services for children with special needs.

Manasalan v. Bd. of Educ. of Balt. City, U.S. Dist. LEXIS 12608 at *47 (D. Md. 2001).

6. In *Van Duyn*, the court rejected the parents' claim that the district's failure to provide all the services the IEP required constituted a change in the IEP for which the district did not follow proper procedures. Do you think this holding was correct? If a reduction in services is not a change in the IEP, what is it? Does this decision allow districts to promise to provide services in the IEP while knowing they will not be required to provide them? Might a parent have challenged an IEP in which the district committed to provide only the services the district actually provided?

7. The IDEA and its regulations contain several provisions that establish deadlines for creating and implementing an IEP. They are described below, as construed by relevant case law.

*The IEP team must meet within thirty days of a school district's determination that a child has a disability and "needs special education and related services." 34 C.F.R. § 300.323(c)(1) (2015). *But see* Bd. of Educ. of Montgomery Cnty. v. Brett Y., 1998 U.S. App. LEXIS 13702, at *23 (4th Cir. 1998) (excusing school district from holding timely meeting because the school district "was attempting to obtain a psychological evaluation and thus was moving forward to schedule the . . . meeting.").

*A school district must implement an IEP "as soon as possible" after the IEP team develops it. 34 C.F.R. § 300.323(c)(2). This regulation does not impose a specific deadline for adopting an IEP. D.D. v. N.Y.C. Bd. of Educ., 465 F.3d 503 (2d Cir. 2006). In *D.D.*, the court rejected plaintiffs' claim that the IDEA requires districts to implement IEPs "immediately, or at least within thirty days, after their IEPs are developed." *Id.* at 512. Instead, the court ruled that the regulation "means what it says":

> States must implement a student's IEP "as soon as possible" after it has been developed. In other words, Plaintiffs' right to a free appropriate public education requires that their IEPs be implemented as soon as possible. "As soon as possible" is, by design, a flexible requirement. It permits some delay between when the IEP is developed and when the IEP is implemented. It does not impose a rigid, outside time frame for implementation. Moreover, the requirement necessitates a specific inquiry into the causes of the delay. Factors

> to be considered include, but are not limited to: (1) the length of the delay; (2) the reasons for the delay, including the availability of the mandated educational services; and (3) the steps taken to overcome whatever obstacles have delayed prompt implementation of the IEP. Nonethelesss, just because the as-soon-as-possible-requirement is flexible does not mean it lacks a breaking point. "It is no doubt true that administrative delays, in certain circumstances, can violate the IDEA by depriving a student of his right to a 'free appropriate public education.'"

Id. at 514. Although courts have not set a deadline, one court ruled that a district that took seven months to implement an IEP violated the IDEA. Bd. of Educ. of Chicago v. Ramie P., 741 F. Supp. 2d 920, 925 (N.D. Ill. 2010) (holding that district's failure to adopt IEP for seven months deprived child of compensatory services).

*The school district must review the child's IEP at least annually to determine whether the child is meeting her annual goals and make revisions accordingly. 20 U.S.C. § 1414(d)(4)(A)(i) (2012); 34 C.F.R. § 300.324(b)(1)(i). *See* Cordrey v. Euckert, 917 F.2d 1460, 1467 (6th Cir. 1990), *cert. denied*, 499 U.S. 938 (1991) (stating that the IDEA requires a school district to hold a meeting at least annually to review the IEP and revise it as necessary); Briere v. Fair Haven Grade Sch. Dist. 948 F. Supp. 1242, 1254 (D. Vt. 1996) (holding that this annual review requirement applies even if the parents and district are in litigation about the IEP).

*A school district must have the IEP in place for a child with a disability "at the beginning of each school year." 20 U.S.C. § 1414(d)(2)(A); 34 C.F.R. § 300.323(a). Several courts have ruled that a district's failure to have an IEP in place at the beginning of the school year violated the IDEA. For example, in *Davis v. Wappingers Cent. Sch. Dist.*, 431 F. App'x 12, 14 (2d Cir. 2011), the court ruled that the district's failure to have an IEP for the child at the beginning of the school year, among other violations, deprived him of a FAPE and the parents of the opportunity to participate in the IEP's development. In *Gerstmyer v. Howard Cnty. Pub. Sch.*, 850 F. Supp. 361 (D. Md. 1994), the school district did not have an IEP in place for the child at the beginning of the school year. As a result:

> Alex's first grade year began in a state of complete disarray without special preplanning by . . . [the school]. His first days, weeks and months were disastrous. He became convinced that he was stupid, he had temper tantrums and he developed a hatred for school. . . .
>
> . . . .
>
> . . . The ultimate fact is that Alex's critical first grade year began without an IEP being in place or ready to be in place and, as a result, he was denied the free appropriate public education to which he was entitled.

Id. at 365–66; *see also* Knable v. Bexley City Sch. Dist., 238 F.3d 755, 766 (6th Cir. 2001) (ruling that school district's failure to have any IEP in place during the school year caused child "to lose educational opportunity."); Department of Educ. of Haw. v. M.F., 840 F. Supp. 2d 1214, 1230 (D. Haw. 2011) (refusing to excuse failure to have

IEP ready at beginning of school year because district did not properly confirm child's withdrawal from the district); Evans v. Bd. of Educ. of the Rhinebeck Cent. Sch. Dist., 930 F. Supp. 83, 95 (S.D.N.Y. 1996) (holding that school district's decision to place the child at a school "at the start of the 1994–95 school year, before it had an IEP in effect on which to base that placement, constitutes a procedural violation of the Act.").

Other courts have applied a harmless error analysis to a school district's failure to have an IEP in place at the beginning of the school year and ruled that the delay did not deprive the child of an educational benefit. *See* J.W. v. Fresno Unified Sch. Dist., 626 F.3d 431, 460–61 (9th Cir. 2010) (holding that child did not show how a delay of three days in implementing the IEP deprived him of an educational benefit); C.H. v. Cape Henlopen Sch. Dist., 606 F.3d 59, 69 (3d Cir. 2010) (declining "to hold as a matter of law that any specific period of time without an IEP is a denial of a FAPE in the absence of specific evidence of an educational deprivation."); MM v. Sch. Dist. of Greenville Cnty., 303 F.3d 523, 535 (4th Cir. 2002) (holding that school district's failure to have an IEP in place at the beginning of the school year did not deprive the child of an educational opportunity because there was no evidence that the parents would have agreed to the IEP the district proposed); Myles S. v. Montgomery Cnty. Bd. of Educ., 824 F. Supp. 1549, 1555 (M.D. Ala. 1993) (holding that district's two-week delay in implementing IEP was harmless because the child received an educational benefit during that time).

Courts have also identified lack of parental cooperation as justification for the school district's failure to have an IEP in place when the school year started. *See* C.H., 606 F.3d at 69 (finding that "parents delayed the continuation of . . . [the IEP] meeting until after the start of classes and ultimately terminated the process by filing a due process request."); Lessard v. Wilton-Lyndeborough Coop. Sch. Dist., 518 F.3d 18, 27 (1st Cir. 2008) (holding that delays in implementing the child's IEP were the result of "her mother's own intransigence"); A.S. v. Five Town Cmty. Sch. Dist., 513 F.3d 279, 288 (1st Cir. 2008) (holding that parents were responsible for breakdown in IEP process); Horen v. Bd. of Educ. of the Toldeo Pub. Sch. Dist., 948 F. Supp. 2d 793, 805–06 (N.D. Ohio 2013), *aff'd*, 2014 U.S. App. LEXIS 24976 (6th Cir. 2014) (holding that school district scheduled IEP meetings and parents prevented the meetings from occurring); Doe v. Hampden-Wilbraham Reg'l Sch. Dist., 715 F. Supp. 2d 185, 193–94 (D. Mass. 2010) (finding that by failing to attend and cancelling IEP meetings parents were responsible for district's failure to have IEP in place when school started); Maynard v. District of Columbia, 701 F. Supp. 2d 116, 124–25 (D.D.C. 2010) (holding that parent did not give district sufficient notice that child would be attending a district school); Sanger v. Montgomery Cnty. Bd. of Educ., 916 F. Supp. 518, 527 (D. Md. 1996) (holding parents responsible for delay in implementing IEP because they cancelled two meetings, withdrew their son from school, and then re-entered him in school).

Chapter 11

Impartial Hearings and Appeals

Introduction

Chapter Eleven considers the various rights, obligations, rules, and procedures relating to impartial hearings and appeals in IDEA cases. Section One examines the burden of proof in impartial hearings. Section Two examines the provisions of the IDEA that create the impartial hearing and appeals process. Section Three covers impartial hearings and appeals, focusing on hearing officer impartiality and time limits for holding hearings and issuing decisions.

Problem

L.B. is a tenth grade boy with a high IQ who was diagnosed with learning disabilities and an emotional disturbance. Pursuant to his IEP, L.B. was placed in a residential facility. There, he received counseling, medication, and instruction in a highly structured setting with a 4:1 student-teacher ratio. L.B.'s parents received a prior written notice stating that the district decided to return L.B. to a district school in a class specially designed for children with high IQs but whose academic achievement was hampered due to learning disabilities and emotional disturbance. The notice stated that the district based its decision on psychological testing, an IQ test, L.B.'s record of successful achievement at the residential facility, and the statements of L.B.'s therapist. On June 10, L.B.'s parents timely served a due process complaint notice on the school district. The notice included L.B.'s name, address, and school; a statement that the school district's decision to change L.B.'s placement was wrong because he could not progress without the highly structured setting of his residential school; and that the district should allow L.B. to remain in his current placement. The school district did not reply to the complaint. The district did, however, send a procedural safeguard notice to L.B.'s parents. The notice indicated that the parents were entitled to obtain an independent educational evaluation of L.B. and access to L.B.'s educational records, and that L.B. was entitled to remain in his current placement pending resolution of the dispute.

After the district received the due process complaint, it scheduled a resolution session for July 7. The parties were unable to resolve the case at the session. The district appointed an IHO to conduct the impartial hearing. The IHO is the director of special education at a neighboring school district. He has presided over more than one hundred impartial hearings. He ruled in favor of the school district in ninety percent of these hearings. In comparison, in all impartial hearings, the school district prevailed sixty percent of the time.

At the hearing, L.B.'s parents were not represented by counsel. They were, however, represented by a friend who is a special education teacher in another school district. The parents told the IHO they had never been to a hearing and asked how to proceed. The IHO indicated that they should begin by presenting their case. The parents asked the IHO if the special education teacher could question the district's representative. The IHO asked the teacher whether she had ever examined witnesses or had any training. She said she had not, and the IHO refused to allow her to ask questions and told the parents to proceed. L.B.'s mother then asked the district representative to explain the reasons the district wanted to remove L.B. from his placement. The IHO told her that she had to prove her own case with her own evidence and could not question the district representative until after the district representative testified in favor of the school district's position. The IHO then asked L.B.'s mother to present any documentation she had in support of her complaint. She said she did not have any. The school district had not provided L.B.'s parents with any of the tests or evaluations of L.B. it relied on to make its decision. The IHO then asked L.B.'s mother if she had any witnesses. She did not have any. The IHO asked her if she rested her case, and then L.B.'s mother read a prepared statement that basically restated the allegations in her complaint: L.B. needs a highly structured setting in which to learn and there was no evidence he would succeed in the school district classroom. After L.B.'s mother was finished, the school district representative presented the district's case. She introduced the evaluation and IQ test the district relied on in making its decision. In addition, the teacher of L.B.'s proposed district classroom testified in support of the proposed placement.

The IHO ruled in favor of the school district. During the proceedings, L.B. remained in his private school. L.B.'s parents appealed to the SRO, who is employed full-time by the state education department. The SRO issued her decision affirming the IHO's decision sixty-seven days after the appeal was filed.

L.B.'s parents want to appeal the SRO's decision in federal court. How would you advise them? Did L.B.'s school district violate the IDEA? Did any individual violate the IDEA?

Section One
The Burden of Proof in Impartial Hearings

Schaffer v. Weast

546 U.S. 49 (2005)

Justice O'CONNOR delivered the opinion of the Court.

The Individuals with Disabilities Education Act (IDEA or Act) is a Spending Clause statute that seeks to ensure that "all children with disabilities have available to them a free appropriate public education," § 1400(d)(1)(A). Under IDEA, school districts must create an "individualized education program" (IEP) for each disabled child, 1414(d). If parents believe their child's IEP is inappropriate, they may request an "impartial due process hearing." § 1415(f). The Act is silent, however, as to which party bears the burden of persuasion at such a hearing. We hold that the burden lies, as it typically does, on the party seeking relief.

I

A

Congress first passed IDEA as part of the Education of the Handicapped Act in 1970 and amended it substantially in the Education for All Handicapped Children Act of 1975. At the time the majority of disabled children in America were "either totally excluded from schools or sitting idly in regular classrooms awaiting the time when they were old enough to 'drop out,'" H. R. Rep. No. 94-332, p. 2 (1975). IDEA was intended to reverse this history of neglect. As of 2003, the Act governed the provision of special education services to nearly 7 million children across the country....

....

The core of the statute ... is the cooperative process that it establishes between parents and schools. The central vehicle for the collaboration is the IEP process. State educational authorities must identify and evaluate disabled children, §§ 1414(a)-(c), develop an IEP for each one, § 1414(d)(2), and review every IEP at least once a year, § 1414(d)(4). Each IEP must include an assessment of the child's current educational performance, must articulate measurable educational goals, and must specify the nature of the special services that the school will provide. § 1414(d)(1)(A).

Parents and guardians play a significant role in the IEP process. They must be informed about and consent to evaluations of their child under the Act. § 1414(c)(3). Parents are included as members of "IEP teams." § 1414(d)(1)(B). They have the right to examine any records relating to their child, and to obtain an "independent educational evaluation of the[ir] child." § 1415(b)(1). They must be given written prior notice of any changes in an IEP, § 1415(b)(3), and be notified in writing of the procedural safeguards available to them under the Act, § 1415(d)(1). If parents believe that an IEP is not appropriate, they may seek an administrative "impartial due process hearing." § 1415(f)....

Although state authorities have limited discretion to determine who conducts the hearings, § 1415(f)(1), and responsibility generally for establishing fair hearing procedures, § 1415(a), Congress has chosen to legislate the central components of due process hearings. It has imposed minimal pleading standards, requiring parties to file complaints setting forth "a description of the nature of the problem," § 1415(b)(7)(B)(ii), and "a proposed resolution of the problem to the extent known and available . . . at the time," § 1415(b)(7)(B)(iii). At the hearing, all parties may be accompanied by counsel, and may "present evidence and confront, cross-examine, and compel the attendance of witnesses." §§ 1415(h)(1)–(2). After the hearing, any aggrieved party may bring a civil action in state or federal court. § 1415(i)(2). Prevailing parents may also recover attorney's fees. § 1415(i)(3)(B). Congress has never explicitly stated, however, which party should bear the burden of proof at IDEA hearings.

B

This case concerns the educational services that were due, under IDEA, to petitioner Brian Schaffer. Brian suffers from learning disabilities and speech-language impairments. From prekindergarten through seventh grade he attended a private school and struggled academically. In 1997, school officials informed Brian's mother that he needed a school that could better accommodate his needs. Brian's parents contacted respondent Montgomery County Public Schools System (MCPS) seeking a placement for him for the following school year.

MCPS evaluated Brian and convened an IEP team. The committee generated an initial IEP offering Brian a place in either of two MCPS middle schools. Brian's parents were not satisfied with the arrangement, believing that Brian needed smaller classes and more intensive services. The Schaffers thus enrolled Brian in another private school, and initiated a due process hearing challenging the IEP and seeking compensation for the cost of Brian's subsequent private education.

In Maryland, IEP hearings are conducted by administrative law judges (ALJs). After a 3-day hearing, the ALJ deemed the evidence closed, held that the parents bore the burden of persuasion, and ruled in favor of the school district. The parents brought a civil action challenging the result. The United States District Court for the District of Maryland reversed and remanded, after concluding that the burden of persuasion is on the school district. Around the same time, MCPS offered Brian a placement in a high school with a special learning center. Brian's parents accepted, and Brian was educated in that program until he graduated from high school. The suit remained alive, however, because the parents sought compensation for the private school tuition and related expenses.

Respondents appealed to the United States Court of Appeals for the Fourth Circuit. While the appeal was pending, the ALJ reconsidered the case, deemed the evidence truly in "equipoise," and ruled in favor of the parents. The Fourth Circuit vacated and remanded the appeal so that it could consider the burden of proof issue along with the merits on a later appeal. The District Court reaffirmed its ruling that the school district has the burden of proof. On appeal, a divided panel of the Fourth Circuit reversed. Judge Michael, writing for the majority, concluded that petitioners offered no persuasive reason to "depart from the normal rule of allocating the burden to the party seeking relief." We granted certiorari to resolve the following question: At an administrative hearing assessing the appropriateness of an IEP, which party bears the burden of persuasion?

II

A

The term "burden of proof" is one of the "slipperiest member[s] of the family of legal terms." 2 J. Strong, McCormick on Evidence § 342, p. 433 (5th ed. 1999) (hereinafter McCormick). Part of the confusion surrounding the term arises from the fact that historically, the concept encompassed two distinct burdens: the "burden of persuasion," *i.e.*, which party loses if the evidence is closely balanced, and the "burden of production," *i.e.*, which party bears the obligation to come forward with the evidence at different points in the proceeding. We note at the outset that this case concerns only the burden of persuasion ... and when we speak of burden of proof in this opinion, it is this to which we refer.

When we are determining the burden of proof under a statutory cause of action, the touchstone of our inquiry is, of course, the statute. The plain text of IDEA is silent on the allocation of the burden of persuasion. We therefore begin with the ordinary default rule that plaintiffs bear the risk of failing to prove their claims.

....

The ordinary default rule, of course, admits of exceptions. For example, the burden of persuasion as to certain elements of a plaintiff's claim may be shifted to defendants, when such elements can fairly be characterized as affirmative defenses or exemptions. Under some circumstances this Court has even placed the burden of persuasion over an entire claim on the defendant. But while the normal default rule does not solve all cases, it certainly solves most of them. Decisions that place the *entire* burden of persuasion on the opposing party at the *outset* of a proceeding—as petitioners urge us to do here—are extremely rare. Absent some reason to believe that Congress intended otherwise, therefore, we will conclude that the burden of persuasion lies where it usually falls, upon the party seeking relief.

B

Petitioners contend first that a close reading of IDEA's text compels a conclusion in their favor. They urge that we should interpret the statutory words "due process" in light of their constitutional meaning, and apply the balancing test established by *Mathews v. Eldridge,* 424 U.S. 319 ... (1976). Even assuming that the Act incorporates constitutional due process doctrine, *Eldridge* is no help to petitioners because "[o]utside the criminal law area, where special concerns attend, the locus of the burden of persuasion is normally not an issue of federal constitutional moment."

Petitioners next contend that we should take instruction from the lower court opinions of *Mills v. Board of Education*, 348 F. Supp. 866 (DC 1972), and *Pennsylvania*

Association for Retarded Children v. Pennsylvania, 334 F. Supp. 1257 (ED Pa. 1971) (hereinafter *PARC*). IDEA's drafters were admittedly guided "to a significant extent" by these two landmark cases. . . . As the court below noted, however, the fact that Congress "took a number of the procedural safeguards from *PARC* and *Mills* and wrote them directly into the Act" does not allow us to "conclude . . . that Congress intended to adopt the ideas that it failed to write into the text of the statute."

Petitioners also urge that putting the burden of persuasion on school districts will further IDEA's purposes because it will help ensure that children receive a free appropriate public education. In truth, however, very few cases will be in evidentiary equipoise. Assigning the burden of persuasion to school districts might encourage schools to put more resources into preparing IEPs and presenting their evidence. But IDEA is silent about whether marginal dollars should be allocated to litigation and administrative expenditures or to educational services. Moreover, there is reason to believe that a great deal is already spent on the administration of the Act. Litigating a due process complaint is an expensive affair, costing schools approximately $8,000 to $12,000 per hearing. Congress has also repeatedly amended the Act in order to reduce its administrative and litigation-related costs. For example, in 1997 Congress mandated that States offer mediation for IDEA disputes . . . 20 U.S.C. § 1415(e). In 2004, Congress added a mandatory "resolution session" prior to any due process hearing. . . . 20 U.S.C.A. § 1415(f)(1)(B) (Supp. 2005). It also made new findings that "[p]arents and schools should be given expanded opportunities to resolve their disagreements in positive and constructive ways," and that "[t]eachers, schools, local educational agencies, and States should be relieved of irrelevant and unnecessary paperwork burdens that do not lead to improved educational outcomes." §§ 1400(c)(8)-(9).

Petitioners in effect ask this Court to assume that every IEP is invalid until the school district demonstrates that it is not. The Act does not support this conclusion. IDEA relies heavily upon the expertise of school districts to meet its goals. It also includes a so-called "stay-put" provision, which requires a child to remain in his or her "then-current educational placement" during the pendency of an IDEA hearing. § 1415(j). Congress could have required that a child be given the educational placement that a parent requested during a dispute, but it did no such thing. Congress appears to have presumed instead that, if the Act's procedural requirements are respected, parents will prevail when they have legitimate grievances.

Petitioners' most plausible argument is that "[t]he ordinary rule, based on considerations of fairness, does not place the burden upon a litigant of establishing facts peculiarly within the knowledge of his adversary." But this "rule is far from being universal, and has many qualifications upon its application." School districts have a "natural advantage" in information and expertise, but Congress addressed this when it obliged schools to safeguard the procedural rights of parents and to share information with them. As noted above, parents have the right to review all records that the school possesses in relation to their child. § 1415(b)(1). They also have the right to an "independent educational evaluation of the[ir] child." *Ibid.* The regulations clarify this entitlement by providing that a "parent has the right to an independent educational evaluation at public expense if the parent disagrees with an evaluation obtained by the public agency." 34 CFR § 300.502(b)(1) (2005). IDEA thus ensures parents access to an expert who can evaluate all the materials that the school must make available, and who can give an independent opinion. They are not left to challenge the government without a realistic opportunity to access the necessary evidence, or without an expert with the firepower to match the opposition.

Additionally, in 2004, Congress added provisions requiring school districts to answer the subject matter of a complaint in writing, and to provide parents with the reasoning behind the disputed action, details about the other options considered and rejected by the IEP team, and a description of all evaluations, reports, and other factors that the school used in coming to its decision. . . . 20 U.S.C. § 1415(c)(2)(B)(i)(I) . . . . Prior to a hearing, the parties must disclose evaluations and recommendations that they intend to rely upon. 20 U.S.C. § 1415(f)(2). IDEA hearings are deliberately informal and intended to give ALJs the flexibility that they need to ensure that each side can fairly present its evidence. IDEA, in fact, requires state authorities to organize hearings in a way that guarantees parents and children the procedural protections of the Act. See § 1415(a). Finally, and perhaps most importantly, parents may recover attorney's fees if they prevail. § 1415(i)(3)(B). These protections ensure that the school bears no unique informational advantage.

III

Finally, respondents and several States urge us to decide that States may, if they wish, override the default rule and put the burden always on the school district. Several States have laws or regulations purporting to do so, at least under some circumstances. See, *e.g.*, Minn. Stat. § 125A.091, subd. 16 (2004); Ala. Admin. Code Rule 290-8-9-.08(8)(c)(6) (Supp. 2004); Alaska Admin. Code, tit. 4, § 52.550(e)(9) (2003); Del. Code Ann., Tit. 14, § 3140 (1999). Because no such law or regulation exists in Maryland, we need not decide this issue today. . . .

We hold no more than we must to resolve the case at hand: The burden of proof in an administrative hearing challenging an IEP is properly placed upon the party seeking relief. . . .

[The concurring opinion by Justice Stevens is omitted.]

Justice Ginsburg, dissenting.

When the legislature is silent on the burden of proof, courts ordinarily allocate the burden to the party initiating the proceeding and seeking relief. As the Fourth Circuit [in its decision below] recognized, however, "other factors," prime among them "policy considerations, convenience, and fairness," may warrant a different allocation. The Court has followed the same counsel. I am persuaded that "policy considerations, convenience, and fairness" call for assigning the burden of proof to the school district in this case.

The Individuals with Disabilities Education Act (IDEA) was designed to overcome the pattern of disregard and neglect disabled children historically encountered in seeking access to public education. Under typical civil rights and social welfare legislation, the complaining party must allege and prove discrimination or qualification for statutory benefits. The IDEA is atypical in this respect: It casts an affirmative, beneficiary-specific obligation on providers of public education. School districts are charged with responsibility to offer to each disabled child an individualized education program (IEP) suitable to the child's special needs. The proponent of the IEP, it seems to me, is properly called upon to demonstrate its adequacy.

Familiar with the full range of education facilities in the area, and informed by "their experiences with other, similarly-disabled children," . . . "the school district is . . . in a far better position to demonstrate that it has fulfilled [its statutory] obligation than the disabled student's parents are in to show that the school district has failed to do so."

Understandably, school districts striving to balance their budgets, if "[l]eft to [their] own devices," will favor educational options that enable them to conserve resources. Saddled with a proof burden in administrative "due process" hearings, parents are likely to find a district-proposed IEP "resistant to challenge." Placing the burden on the district to show that its plan measures up to the statutorily mandated "free appropriate public education," 20 U.S.C. § 1400(d)(1)(A), will strengthen school officials' resolve to choose a course genuinely tailored to the child's individual needs.

The Court acknowledges that "[a]ssigning the burden of persuasion to school districts might encourage schools to put more resources into preparing IEPs." Curiously, the Court next suggests that resources spent on developing IEPs rank as "administrative expenditures" not as expenditures for "educational services." Costs entailed in the preparation of suitable IEPs, however, are the very expenditures necessary to ensure each child covered by the IDEA access to a free appropriate education. These outlays surely relate to "educational services." Indeed, a carefully designed IEP may ward off disputes productive of large administrative or litigation expenses.

This case is illustrative. Not until the District Court ruled that the school district had the burden of persuasion did the school design an IEP that met Brian Schaffer's special educational needs. Had the school district, in the first instance, offered Brian a public or private school placement equivalent to the one the district ultimately provided, this entire litigation and its attendant costs could have been avoided.

One can demur to the Fourth Circuit's observation that courts "do not automatically assign the burden of proof to the side with the bigger guns," for no such reflexive action is at issue here. It bears emphasis that "the vast majority of parents whose children require the benefits and protections provided in the IDEA" lack "knowledg[e] about the educational resources available to their [child]" and the "sophisticat[ion]" to mount an effective case against a district-proposed IEP. In this setting, "the party with the 'bigger guns' also has better access to information, greater expertise, and an affirmative obligation to provide the contested services." Policy considerations, convenience, and fairness, I think it plain, point in the same direction. Their collective weight warrants a rule requiring a school district, in "due process" hearings, to explain persuasively why its proposed IEP satisfies IDEA's standards. I would therefore reverse the judgment of the Fourth Circuit.

[The dissenting opinion by Justice Breyer is omitted.]

Notes, Comments, and Questions

1. The Court in *Schaeffer* made clear that its decision involved only the burden of persuasion and not the burden of production. What is the practical consequence of this? What impact will the decision have on the ability of an IHO to determine the order of presentation of evidence in an impartial hearing that a parent instituted to challenge an IEP?

2. The majority in *Schaeffer* stated that the costs a school district incurs in creating an IEP is an administrative expense. The dissent disagreed, stating that such costs are necessary to ensure a child receives a FAPE. With which position do you agree?

3. The Supreme Court rejected the plaintiff's argument that because the relevant facts are particularly within a school district's knowledge the burden of persuasion should be on the school district. The Court stated that parental rights and district obligations "ensure that the school bears no unique informational advantage." *Schaeffer*, 546 U.S. at 61. In support of its conclusion, the Court cited several rights of parents, including obtaining an independent educational evaluation at district expense and the right to a relatively informal due process hearing. The Court also cited several district obligations, including disclosing relevant reports and evaluations to parents and stating in writing the reason and justification for its decision. Do you agree that these rights and obligations ensure that a school district does not have an informational advantage over parents? Do these rights and obligations help children whose parents are not in a position to play an active role in their education?

4. The Supreme Court stated, "Finally, and perhaps most importantly, parents may recover attorneys fees if they prevail." *Schaeffer*, 546 U.S. at 63. Do you agree that the availability of attorneys fees to prevailing parents helps equalize the information balance between parents and school districts?

Section Two
Impartial Hearings and Appeals

Section 1415 of the IDEA creates an extensive procedural structure for impartial hearings and appeals. Section 1415 creates procedural rights for parents, substantive obligations for states and local school districts, and an extensive set of procedural rules. Consider the following summary of the rights, obligations, and rules relating to impartial hearings and appeals that Section 1415 creates. As you read this section, consider whether Section 1415, both as written and as construed by the courts, has the equalizing effect the Court in *Schaffer* envisioned.

Prior Written Notice: A school district must provide prior written notice to parents of a child with a disability when the district "A) proposes to initiate or change; or (B) refuses to initiate or change, the identification, evaluation, or educational placement of the child, or the provision of a free appropriate public education to the child." 20 U.S.C. § 1415(b)(3)(2012); *see also* 34 C.F.R. § 300.503(a)(2015).

Contents of the Prior Written Notice: The prior written notice must contain:

(A) a description of the action proposed or refused by the agency;

(B) an explanation of why the agency proposes or refuses to take the action and a description of each evaluation procedure, assessment, record, or report the agency used as a basis for the proposed or refused action;

(C) a statement that the parents of a child with a disability have protection under the procedural safeguards of this subchapter . . . ;

(D) sources for parents to contact to obtain assistance in understanding the provisions of this part;

(E) a description of other options considered by the IEP Team and the reason why those options were rejected; and

(F) a description of the factors that are relevant to the agency's proposal or refusal.

20 U.S.C. § 1415(c)(1); *see also* 34 C.F.R. § 300.503(b).

Complaint: Any party may submit a complaint "with respect to any matter relating to the identification, evaluation, or educational placement of the child, or the provision of a free appropriate public education to such child. . . ." 20 U.S.C. § 1415(b)(6)(A); *see also* 34 C.F.R. § 300.507(a).

Statute of Limitations: A party must file a complaint "not more than 2 years before the date the parent or public agency knew or should have known about the alleged action that forms the basis of the complaint . . . ." 20 U.S.C. § 1415(b)(6)(B); *see also* 34 C.F.R. § 300.507(a)(2). Alternatively, a party must comply with a state's explicit statute of limitations. 20 U.S.C. § 1415(b)(6)(B); *see also* 34 C.F.R. § 300.507(a)(2). Applying the "knew or should have known" standard, the court in *D.C. v. Klein Indep. Sch. Dist.*, 711 F. Supp. 2d 739, 745–46 (S.D. Tex. 2010), ruled that the one-year Texas statute of limitations banned the parents from challenging an IEP because they filed their complaint more than one year after they began to complain about the IEP.

The IDEA provides two exceptions to the statute of limitations: 1) the district misrepresented that the issue was resolved; or 2) the district withheld required information. 20 U.S.C. § 1415(f)(3)(D)(i) and (ii). A misrepresentation must be knowing or intentional. D.K. v. Abington Sch. Dist., 696 F.3d 233, 254 (3d Cir. 2012) (holding that the IDEA requires "either intentional or knowing misrepresentation"); I.H. v.

Cumberland Valley Sch. Dist., 842 F. Supp. 2d 762, 775 (M.D. Pa. 2012) (requiring intentional misrepresentation). Courts have generally been unwilling to find that an exception to the statute of limitations applies. *See D.K.*, 696 F.3d at 251 (refusing to apply exceptions); *I.H.*, 842 F. Supp. 2d at 775 (dismissing certain claims on statute of limitations grounds); J.L. v. Ambridge Area Sch. Dist., 622 F. Supp. 2d 257, 268 (W.D. Pa. 2008) (ruling that plaintiffs did not allege sufficient facts to show exception); *but see* D.G. v. Somerset Hills Sch. Dist., 559 F. Supp. 2d 484, 492 (D.N.J. 2008) (applying exception because district did not provide parents with written notice).

In addition, plaintiffs have also attempted to avoid dismissal on statute of limitations grounds by raising common law equitable tolling rules. Such rules, for example, stay the statute of limitations if the violation is ongoing, the plaintiff has not reached the age of majority, or there is excusable neglect. Several courts have ruled, however, that common law tolling rules do not apply to the IDEA. *See* P.P. v. West Chester Sch., 585 F.3d 727, 736 (3d Cir. 2009) ("In addition, tolling principles that affect the application of the state statutes of limitations would presumably not affect the IDEA statute of limitations, with its express exceptions to the limitations period."); *D.C.*, 711 F. Supp. 2d at 746–47 (stating that equitable tolling does not apply to the IDEA's statute of limitations); *J.L.*, 622 F. Supp. 2d at 269 (stating that, "the two exceptions specifically set forth in the statute are the exclusive exceptions to the statute of limitations"). What is the practical consequence if an IDEA complaint is dismissed for violating the statute of limitations? What substantive rights do the parent and child lose? Do any rights remain?

Complaint: A party must send the complaint to the other party. The complaint must list the child's name, address, and school; describe the child's problem; identify relevant facts; and propose a resolution. 20 U.S.C. § 1415(b)(7)(A)(ii); *see also* 34 C.F.R. § 300.508(b).

Response to Complaint: If the school district did not send a prior written notice to the parent about the subject of the parent's complaint, the district must send a response that explains the reasons for the district's decision; describes the other options the district considered and the reasons it rejected them; and describes "each evaluation procedure, assessment, record, or report the agency used as the basis for" its decision; and other relevant factors. 20 U.S.C. § 1415(c)(2)(B); *see also* 34 C.F.R. § 300.508(e)(1).

What is the appropriate remedy for a school district's failure to submit a sufficient response to a complaint? In *Sykes v. District of Columbia*, 518 F. Supp. 2d 261 (D.D.C. 2007), the child's grandmother requested a default judgment against the District because it did not include all the required information in its response to her complaint. The court disapproved of the District's practice of submitting a form response to complaints that read, "'[I]t is this attorney-advisor's position that a DCPS response is not required in all IDEA Due Process hearings. Accordingly, DCPS objects to such an expansive reading and practice.'" *Id.* at 266–67. The court stated, "This court rejects DCPS' position that it may make a response of its choosing despite clear statutory language and the explicit precedent to the contrary." *Id.* at 267. Nevertheless, the court rejected a default judgment as the appropriate remedy. Stating that the "purpose of the response requirement is to guarantee meaningful parental participation in the student placement process," the court found that the parents were involved in the process and this would not have happened if a default judgment had been issued." *Id.* The court stated, "[T]he hearing officer sought a full hearing to examine the available documents and to hear testimony of the parties. A default judgment would have subverted the administrative process and assigned D.B. a placement without a full examination of the record or his needs." *Id.* The court held that procedural violations deny FAPE only if they deny educational rights, and the District's failure to submit a sufficient response did not do this. *Id.* Do you agree? Did the parents have other means to obtain the information that should have been in the District's response? Is *Sykes* consistent with *Schaeffer's* view of the equal availability of information to parents?

In *Jalloh v. District of Columbia*, 535 F. Supp. 2d 13 (D.D.C. 2008), the court similarly found that the District's response was inadequate but that the response did not constitute a substantive violation, and suggested that the plaintiff's failure to submit sufficient evidence in support of her claim at the administrative hearing was the result of her attorney's failure to obtain the necessary information and not the district's inadequate response:

> Her presentation at the hearing was limited by her inability to offer records on R.H.'s education and progress or lack thereof and her inability to present testimony from R.H.'s teachers—both caused by the failure of Ms. Jalloh's counsel to follow the correct procedures to obtain records and compel testimony, as discussed below, and not caused by . . . [the District's] meager Response.

Id. at 20. Is *Jalloh* consistent with *Schaffer's* view about the informality of a hearing and the ability of the hearing officer to ensure that all relevant evidence is heard and considered? Could the information the district is required to provide under Section 1415(c)(2)(B) have helped plaintiff? Should a district be excused from providing the information simply because a plaintiff's attorney could have obtained it through other means? What is the purpose of requiring a district to provide information if it can be excused from doing so because the plaintiff could have obtained it in another way?

The courts in both *Sykes* and *Jalloh* were unwilling to issue default judgments against the District of Columbia on the grounds that it failed to provide a sufficient response to the complaint. Are there other remedies beside a default judgment that the courts could have ordered? *Sykes* referred to *Massey v. District of Columbia*, 400 F. Supp. 2d 66 (D.D.C. 2005). There, the District of Columbia provided an insufficient response to a due process complaint, and the court ruled that this failure, combined with other procedural violations, excused the plaintiffs from exhausting administrative remedies prior to bringing their lawsuit in federal court. *Id.* at 72–74.

Procedural Safeguards Notice: When a parent files a complaint, the school district must provide the parent with a notice that explains the IDEA's procedural safeguards, including:

(A) independent education evaluation;

(B) prior written notice;

(C) parental consent;

(D) access to educational records;

. . . .

(F) the child's placement during the pendency of due process proceedings . . . .

. . . .

20 U.S.C. § 1415(d)(2)(A)-(E); *see also* 34 C.F.R. § 300.504(c).

Impartial Hearing: A party that files a complaint has a right to an impartial due process hearing. The state has the option of establishing either: 1) a two-step process, in which the local school district appoints a hearing officer and holds the impartial due process hearing and the state offers appellate review; or 2) a one-step hearing process, in which the state holds the hearing. 20 U.S.C. § 1415(f)(1)(A) and (g); *see also* 34 C.F.R. § 300.511(a)–(b). What are the relevant costs and benefits of a two-step compared with a one-step hearing process?

Resolution Session: Once a school district receives a due process complaint it has fifteen days to hold a resolution meeting with the parents at which they can discuss the case and attempt to resolve it. 20 U.S.C. § 1415(f)(1)(B)(i)(I); 34 C.F.R. § 300.510(a).

Information Disclosure: "Not less than 5 business days prior to" the impartial due process hearing, "each party must disclose to all other parties all evaluations completed by that date, and recommendations based on the offering party's evaluations, that the party intends to use at the hearing." 20 U.S.C. § 1415(f)(2); *see also* 34 C.F.R. § 300.512(b)(i). Should the parties be required to submit all evaluations conducted, whether or not the party intends to use them?

Qualifications and Impartiality of the IHO: The IDEA places limited restrictions on who may conduct a hearing;

(3) Limitations on hearing

(A) Person conducting hearing

A hearing officer conducting a hearing . . . shall, at a minimum—

(i) not be—

(I) an employee of the State educational agency or the local educational agency involved in the education . . . of the child; or

(II) a person having a personal or professional interest that conflicts with the person's objectivity at the hearing;

(ii) possess knowledge of, and the ability to understand, the provisions of . . . [the IDEA] and legal interpretations of . . . [the IDEA] by Federal and State Courts;

(iii) possess the knowledge and ability to conduct hearings in accordance with appropriate, standard legal practice; and

> (iv) possess the knowledge and ability to render and write decisions in accordance with appropriate, standard legal practice.

20 U.S.C. § 1415(f)(3)(A); *see also* 34 C.F.R. § 300.511(c).

Impartial Hearing Rights: Any party to an impartial hearing has:

> (1) the right to be accompanied and advised by counsel and by individuals with special knowledge or training with respect to the problems of children with disabilities;
>
> (2) the right to present evidence and confront, cross-examine, and compel the attendance of witnesses;
>
> (3) the right to a written, or, at the option of the parents, electronic verbatim record of such hearing . . . ;
>
> . . . .

20 U.S.C. § 1415(h)(1)–(2); *see also* 34 C.F.R. § 300.512(a)(1)–(2). Admission of hearsay evidence at an administrative hearing does not violate the right to confront witnesses. Jalloh v. District of Columbia, 535 F. Supp. 2d 13, 22 (D.D.C. 2008) ("[H]earsay rules do not apply to administrative proceedings in IDEIA cases"); Sykes v. District of Columbia, 518 F. Supp. 2d 261, 268 (D.D.C. 2007) (recognizing that it is appropriate to use hearsay evidence in administrative hearings).

Appeal to State Agency: If a school district conducts the impartial due process hearing, an aggrieved party may appeal the decision to the state education department. 20 U.S.C. § 1415(g)(1)–(2); *see also* 34 C.F.R. § 300.514(b)(1). The state education department must review the decision impartially and issue an independent decision. 20 U.S.C. § 1415(g)(2); *see also* § 34 C.F.R. 300.514(b)(2).

Time Limits for Issuing Decisions: A school district is responsible for ensuring that the IHO issue a decision within forty-five days of the end of the resolution period. 34 C.F.R. § 300.515(a). The state education department must issue a decision on appeal within thirty days of receiving the appeal. *Id.* § (b). A hearing or review officer may grant extensions of these time limits upon request by a party. *Id.* § (c). *See* L.C. v. Utah State Bd. of Educ., 125 F. App'x 252, 261 (10th Cir. 2005) (denying claim that the hearing officer violated the IDEA by granting a lengthy extension); I.D. v. N.H. Dep't of Educ., 878 F. Supp. 318, 322 (D.N.H. 1994) (holding that the court reasonably denied extension request in the educational interests of the child).

Maintenance of Educational Placement: While an IDEA proceeding is pending, unless the school district and parents agree, the child remains in his or her current educational placement. 20 U.S.C. § 1415(j); *see also* 34 C.F.R. § 300.518(a).

Section Three
Conducting Impartial Hearings: IHO Impartiality and Time Limits

A. IHO Impartiality

K.B. v. Nebo Sch. Dist.

379 F.3d 966 (10th Cir. 2004)

Murphy, Circuit Judge.

I. INTRODUCTION

. . . .

Hearing officers preside over due process hearings. At the relevant time, persons interested in becoming due process hearing officers could present their candidacy by signing up for training. Utah's hearing officer selection process is designed to avoid appointing hearing officers who might be or appear to be biased. The Utah State Board of Education's ("USBE") list of eligible hearing officers consists of private attorneys, county attorneys, an attorney from the Administrative Office of the Courts, retired university professors, retired school district employees, as well as current school district employees and attorneys. The record shows that from 1998 until K.B.'s hearing in 2000, Utah parents and disability-advocates had expressed concerns that USBE's list of hearing officers appeared to favor school districts, and that certain hearing officers were more often chosen to preside over hearings than others.

At the time relevant to this appeal, the hearing officers underwent training before they were allowed to preside over due process hearings. The trainers were attorneys who represented both school districts and parents, although most trainers represented school districts. Hearing officers were trained to be impartial. When initially assigned a case, the hearing officers were specifically asked if they could be impartial in that particular case and were not selected if they could not be impartial.

The hearing officer who presided over K.B.'s due process hearing was Dr. Steven Hirase. Hirase is an assistant superintendent in the Murray School District. Hirase does not work for the Utah State Office of Education ("USOE"). At the relevant time, Hirase was married to a woman who worked in the Jordan School District, which is the same school district that employed Nebo's autism expert witness, Melisa Genaux. Despite this connection, there is no evidence that Hirase's wife and Genaux had ever worked together. In fact, Appellants do not even allege that the women knew each other.

Appellants moved to disqualify Hirase. Hirase denied the motion and presided over K.B.'s due process hearing. Hirase concluded that the 1998–1999 and the 1999–2000 IEP provided K.B. with a free and appropriate public education ("FAPE") in a least restrictive environment (sometimes referred to as "LRE").

Appellants then filed a complaint in the United States District Court for the District of Utah, seeking review of Hirase's decision and alleging, *inter alia* . . . . that K.B.

was denied an impartial hearing because Hirase was biased. Appellants also argued that they could not secure an impartial hearing officer because the USBE's list of hearing officers was "aligned with the interests of school districts." . . . .

The parties filed cross-motions for summary judgment. The district court affirmed Hirase's decision and granted summary judgment to Nebo. . . . The district court . . . concluded that Hirase was not biased against K.B. in violation of the IDEA's procedural safeguards. . . .

. . . .

III. DISCUSSION

. . . .

On appeal, Appellants argue that Nebo . . . violated the IDEA's procedural mandates because Hirase was not impartial and because of other procedural improprieties . . . .

For the reasons stated below, this court concludes that Hirase was an impartial hearing officer within the meaning of the IDEA. Therefore, K.B. was not denied an impartial hearing in violation of the IDEA's procedural safeguards. . . .

1. *Alleged Procedural Violations of the IDEA*

Appellants' argument that K.B. was denied an impartial hearing in violation of the IDEA is unavailing. Hirase was an impartial hearing officer within the meaning of the IDEA. Under its procedural safeguards, the IDEA sets out a minimum standard of impartiality which prohibits "an employee of the State educational agency or the local educational agency involved in the education . . . of the child" from conducting the due process hearing. 20 U.S.C. § 1415(f)(3). Hirase was neither an employee of USOE nor of the Nebo School District. Hirase's employment at the Murray School District, which is a separate district from Nebo, does not constitute employment at the "local educational agency." Hirase therefore meets the minimum standard of impartiality set out in the statute. *Id.*

Likewise, Hirase did not have a personal or professional interest that would conflict with his objectivity. The IDEA has been interpreted as prohibiting "any person having a personal or professional interest that would conflict with his or her objectivity in the hearing" from conducting a due process hearing. 34 C.F.R. § 300.508(a)(2). Hirase's wife's mere employment in the same school district as Genaux does not constitute a conflicting interest, particularly because there is no evidence that the women even knew each other. Therefore, K.B. was not denied an impartial hearing within the meaning of the IDEA.

[Because of this finding, the court did not address appellants' argument that they could not secure an impartial hearing officer because the list of hearing officers was biased towards school districts.]

. . . .

Thomas v. District of Columbia

407 F. Supp. 2d 102 (D.D.C. 2005)

KOLLAR-KOTELLY, District Judge.

Plaintiff Lisa Ann Thomas, on behalf of her minor son, A.T., brought this action under the Individuals with Disabilities Education Act ("IDEA"), 20 U.S.C. §§ 1400 *et seq.*, against Defendant, the District of Columbia [Public Schools "DCPS"]. . . . This case comes to the Court on appeal from the June 30, 2003 Hearing Officer Determination ("H.O.D.") and related proceedings.

. . . .

I: BACKGROUND

. . . .

In the June 30, 2003 H.O.D. . . . the Hearing Officer found that DCPS was only responsible for failing to comply with the November 30, 2001 H.O.D., and awarded compensatory education only for the period from that date until September 2002 when A.T. was properly placed. . . . Plaintiff filed a Motion for Reconsideration on July 20, 2003, which the Hearing Officer denied on August 1, 2003, two (2) days after the initial deadline for filing an appeal on the H.O.D. had passed. . . . Due to a typographical error, the June 30, 2003 H.O.D. awarded A.T. compensatory education for an eleven (11) year period as opposed to the intended ten (10) month period; this error was corrected subsequently on August 4, 2003. This new ruling reset the thirty (30) day time limit for appeals of the Hearing Officer's decision to this Court, and Plaintiff filed her Complaint in this action on August 26, 2003—safely within the period of appeals. Defendant does not dispute the timeliness of Plaintiff's current action before this Court.

. . . .

IV: DISCUSSION

Plaintiff moves for summary judgment on the grounds that: (1) The Hearing Officer was biased in favor of DCPS; (2) the Hearing Officer engaged in *ex parte* communication with DCPS; [and] (3) DCPS's arrangement with the Hearing Officer ensured that the Hearing Officer was a DCPS "employee" . . . .

. . . .

A. Plaintiff Fails to Establish that the Hearing Officer Was Biased

Plaintiff contends that the Hearing Officer was biased, necessitating the reversal of his June 30, 2003 H.O.D., because (1) bias can be inferred from the Hearing Officer's delayed ruling on her Motion for Reconsideration, which could have prejudiced Plaintiff's attempts at appeal; (2) the Hearing Officer allegedly conducted *ex parte* communications with the DCPS's counsel; and (3) he was apparently an employee of DCPS and was therefore unable to act as a truly neutral arbiter. The Tenth Circuit has held that a Hearing Officer "enjoys a presumption of honesty and integrity, which is only rebutted by a showing of some substantial countervailing reason to conclude that a decisionmaker is actually biased with respect to factual issues being adjudicated." *Harline v. Drug Enforcement Admin.*, 148 F.3d 1100, 1204 (10th Cir. 1998) . . . ; *see also Schweiker v. McClure*, 456 U.S. 188, 195 . . . (1982) ("We must start . . . from the presumption that the hearing officers who decide Part B claims are unbiased. This presumption can be rebutted by a showing of conflict of interest or some other specific reason for disqualification.") . . . ; *Bunnell v. Barnhart*, 336 F.3d 1112, 1114 (9th Cir. 2003) ("appearance of impropriety" standard does not apply to administrative law judges) . . . .

1. The Hearing Officer's Order on Motion for Reconsideration Does Not Establish Bias

Plaintiff alleges that the August 1, 2003 Hearing Officer's Order on Motion for Reconsideration ("Reconsideration Order"), "should speak for itself as to the Hearing Officer's bias."[6] Plaintiff contends that bias is evident from this ruling in two ways. *First*, Plaintiff asserts that a finding of bias may be adduced from the fact that the Hearing Officer did not issue the Reconsideration Order until August 1, 2003—two (2) days after the thirty (30) day period for appealing the June 30, 2003 H.O.D. had expired. Two problems exist with this claim. First, Plaintiff herself sat on her rights for some period of time. Importantly, Plaintiff did not file the Motion for Reconsideration until July 20, 2003, which, despite being "well prior to the 30 days deadline for appealing the H.O.D." was also twenty (20) days after the initial ruling. Given the busy schedule of Hearing Officers in general and the detail and length of the Reconsideration Order itself, the issuance of a ruling within twelve (12) days of a motion is not unreasonable, nor is it the kind of clear sign of bias that Plaintiff contends. Second, the filing of a Motion for Reconsideration is not a prerequisite for successful appeal. Indeed, Motions for Reconsideration are not routine filings, and should only be entered if the motion itself meets the narrow grounds specified in the established standard of review for such a motion. Here, if Plaintiff wanted to avoid the danger that the Hearing Officer might take too long to issue his Reconsideration Order because of scheduling difficulties or the time it takes to draft an opinion, she could simply have appealed directly to this Court and avoided the reconsideration stage. Nevertheless, Plaintiff was not prejudiced in the end, as the Hearing Officer revisited his June 30, 2003 H.O.D. in his August 5, 2003 Typographical Error Order; because of this new Order, the previous June 30, 2003 H.O.D. could not be considered a "final" ruling and the thirty (30) day appeals period was reset. Within this new time window, Plaintiff successfully filed her Complaint with this Court such that her claims were not procedurally barred from consideration on the merits.

---

6. The . . . Reconsideration Order [states]:

The hearing officer notes that counsel filed this Motion, which contains no coherent arguments supporting a reconsideration of the H.O.D., on the day before the deadline for filing an appeal. If counsel seriously believes that the hearing officer's ruling is erroneous, the hearing officer trusts that counsel fulfilled his obligation to preserve his client's right to appeal a decision counsel believes to be factually and legally flawed.

Second, Plaintiff complains that the ruling itself evinces bias. Upon a review, it is clear that the Hearing Officer's Reconsideration Order rejected Plaintiff's Motion for Reconsideration for four reasons: (1) his belief that the IDEA makes no provision for motions for reconsideration; (2) Plaintiff's failure to present new facts; (3) Plaintiff's failure to explain how he impermissibly shifted Plaintiff's burden at the hearing; and (4) the fact that, despite Plaintiff's allegations, Hearing Officers are independent contractors, and are not employees of the DCPS. Defendant now admits that the Hearing Officer "erroneously stated that '[t]he regulations governing due process hearings under IDEA make no provision for motions for reconsideration.'" Jumping on this error of law, Plaintiff asserts, "Here the hearing officer made such a monumental mistake on such a simple litigation point of law that the District had to summarily concede the issue. This justifies an inference [of bias]."

Despite Plaintiff's dramatic conclusions, the mere fact that a Hearing Officer, administrative law judge, or court is ultimately incorrect as to a point of law does not lead to an inference that the adjudicator was biased. As the Seventh Circuit recently noted,

> Rulings that on their face are justifiable therefore tell us little about whether compensatory bias was at work in the judge's decision-making. Likewise, a judge may abuse his discretion, may even commit a "veritable avalanche of errors," without there being reason to suspect that bias was at work. Judges make mistakes, period. Bias, when it is at work, will not necessarily announce itself in either the judge's ruling or his rationale.

Bracy v. Schomig, 286 F.3d 406, 434 (7th Cir. 2002) . . . . Moreover, the Hearing Officer did not rest his Reconsideration Order entirely on his (erroneous) finding that the IDEA makes no provision for motions for reconsideration; rather, the Hearing Officer also considered the merits of Plaintiff s arguments, and found all three (3) of Plaintiff's other central assertions to be without merit. Given these facts, the Court concludes that bias cannot be inferred from the Hearing Officer's Reconsideration Order.

2. The Alleged Ex Parte *Communication Resulting in the Hearing Officer's Typographical Error Order Does Not Establish Bias*

Plaintiff also alleges that language in the Hearing Officer's August 5, 2003 Typographical Error Order establishes Hearing Officer bias. The Typographical Error Order states that "the hearing officer was advised that Petitioner's counsel had made a demand for 1200 hours of compensatory relief from DCPS on the basis [of the typographical error]." Plaintiff has two corresponding complaints regarding this Order. First, Plaintiff asserts that the Hearing Officer must have engaged in *ex parte* communication for him to have been "advised" of the error. Second, Plaintiff contends that the Typographical Error Order incorrectly states that Plaintiff had attempted to wrongfully use the typographical error as the basis for an inflated compensatory relief demand from the DCPS. Plaintiff rejects this finding, and claims that "[b]y its very falsity, [the statement] showed the extent of the hearing officer's bias."

Upon a careful review, it is evident that both of these allegations lack merit. First, Plaintiff fails to introduce any evidence that an *ex parte* communication between the Hearing Officer and the DCPS actually took place. Even assuming *arguendo* that counsel for DCPS did contact the Hearing Officer, Plaintiff fails to show that any prohibited matters were discussed or that DCPS made an improper attempt to influence the trier of the case. Indeed, to the extent that a clerical error in a decision is detected by a party, the party has an affirmative obligation to inform the decision-maker such that the resulting Opinion reflects what was intended and actually decided. Finally, Plaintiff admits that her Motion for Reconsideration itself pointed out "the [H]earing [O]fficer's apparent error in using the year 1991 instead of the year 2001 as a starting point,"—i.e., the very subject of the Hearing Officer's Typographical Error Order. As such, it is entirely possible that upon a re-review of Plaintiff's Motion for Reconsideration after his initial Reconsideration Order, the Hearing Officer discovered the error. Given these factors, the Court cannot conclude that an *ex parte* communication did occur, or that—if such a conversation did take place—that it reflected the bias of the Hearing Officer.

Second, even assuming that Plaintiff is correct in asserting that she never attempted to rely on the typographical error as the basis for the compensatory relief demands made to the DCPS, the apparent error or mistake by the Hearing Officer is simply insufficient to establish that he had bias or personal animus against Plaintiff. Simply because a Hearing Officer misunderstands the oft-confusing and conflicting facts before him does not entail an inference or finding or bias. Once again, the Court is unwilling to infer bias based on a mere mistake or error.

3. Plaintiff has not shown that the Hearing Officer was an employee of DCPS

Plaintiff also alleges that the Hearing Officer was a DCPS employee in violation of the Code of Federal Regulations, which states that a hearing officer cannot be "an employee of the State agency . . . that is involved in the education or care of the child." 34 C.F.R. § 300.508(a)(1). Plaintiff's assertion is based solely on the alleged testimony of "Dr. Wendy Ghee [sic]," Director of the DCPS Office of Management Services . . . . Plaintiff contends that Dr. Gee testified that all hearing officers were full-time DCPS employees. Plaintiff asks that the Court take judicial notice of the remarks or order DCPS to produce the tape. The tape has not been produced by either party.

Upon a review of the record, all available evidence undermines Plaintiff's unsubstantiated recollection of the June 25, 2003 hearing and her argument that Dr. Gee testified that Hearing Officers were DCPS employees. Hearing Officer Banks has consistently notified Plaintiff that he "is not an employee of DCPS, but serves pursuant to a contract with DCPS executed on January 30, 2003, in which the hearing officer was appointed as an independent contractor." Indeed, the District of Columbia has enacted numerous regulations to prevent Hearing Officers from being hired as D.C. employees. *See* D.C. Mun. Regs., tit. 5, § 2406.2 ("All hearing officers shall be contracted for by the D.C. Public Schools on a full-time or part-time basis to serve in that capacity. . . . Hearing officers in cases involving special education issues shall not be employees of public agencies which are involved in the education or care of the child for whom the hearing is being held."); D.C. Mun. Regs., tit. 5 §§ 2407.3, 2407.1, 2407.2 (while DCPS's Student Hearing Office coordinates the hiring and scheduling of Hearing Officers, those Hearing Officers function independently and the Student Hearing Office may not interfere with their decisions). Moreover, Mr. John M. Cashmon, Director of Compliance for DCPS, in an August 18, 2004 memorandum entitled "Request for Information regarding [A.T.] Affidavit," stated:

> I was present at that hearing with Dr. Gee and heard her testimony regarding the hearing officers. She explained to the committee members present the changes that DCPS made in the use of hearing officers and how the system had moved from a payment per hearing system to contracting with individual hearing officers for periods of time where they would be available to hear cases. Dr. Gee further explained that the hearing officers were not employees of DCPS because of the requirements both in the Individuals With Disabilities Education Act (IDEA) and the federal regulations that the hearing officers be independent of DCPS. At no time during this hearing did Dr. Gee state that the hearing officers were employees of DCPS. On the contrary, Dr. Gee had worked to establish a system of contracts for the hearing officers that would keep them as an independent contractor.

Finally, DCPS's own Special Education Student Hearing Office Manual, posted on its web page, outlines the qualifications of hearing officers . . . and specifies that Hearing Officers are not—and cannot be—employees of DCPS.

Given this veritable deluge of evidence, it is evident that Plaintiff's unsupported, unsubstantiated accusation that Hearing Officers are employees of the DCPS is simply without merit. Plaintiff has adduced no evidence whatsoever to support her claim. Such a failure entails that summary judgment in favor of Defendant as to this point is appropriate.

. . . .

Notes, Comments, and Questions

1. The status of hearing officers in Utah as described in *L.B.* is not unusual. Hearing officers are not employees of the school district in which they hold hearings and often hold other jobs. Inevitably, people with experience in public school education are drawn to seek positions as hearing officers. Thus, hearing officers might hold positions with school districts or might be attorneys specializing in representing school districts or parents. The court in *L.B.* was tolerant of what can be called "issue" conflicts between the issues that are important to the hearing officer's clients or employers and the issues the hearing officer is called on to decide in cases before her. But the court in *L.B.* indicated that as long as a hearing officer herself does not have a personal or professional interest in the case that would conflict with her objectivity, courts will tolerate "issue" conflicts. Is this appropriate? Are hearing officers with issue conflicts truly impartial? And even if they are, do they appear to be impartial

to the parties involved? In *Thomas*, the court referred to a case that held that the "appearance of impropriety standard," which applies to judges and may require recusal in cases over which judges are presiding even if it only appears there may be a conflict, does not apply to hearing officers. Should it? Should hearing officers with issue conflicts be precluded from serving as hearing officers?

2. In *L.B.*, the court declined to rule on whether Utah's roster of impartial hearing officer was biased in favor of school districts. If the court had considered this issue, what decision should it have made? What other facts, if any, would have been necessary for a decision?

3. As described in *Thomas*, the District of Columbia moved from a system of hiring and paying hearing officers on a case-by-case basis to a system in which it signs contracts with hearing officers to serve full- or part-time for a specific period of time. The court agreed that this arrangement does not render the hearing officers employees of the District because they are independent from the District even though they are under contract with the District. Do you agree? When is the line between independence and employment crossed? What factors should a court consider?

4. Should Congress amend the IDEA to require impartial hearing officers to serve as full-time administrative law judges? What are the strengths and weaknesses of such a system?

5. As the court in *Thomas* stated, hearing officers enjoy a presumption of honesty and integrity; *see also* L.C. v. Utah State Bd. of Educ., 125 F. App'x 252, 261 (10th Cir. 2005) (holding that a hearing officer "'enjoys a presumption of honesty and integrity, which is only rebutted by a showing of some substantial countervailing reason to conclude that [he] is actually biased with respect to factual issues being adjudicated.'"); H.H. v. Ind. Bd. of Special Educ. Appeals, 501 F. Supp. 2d 1188, 1200 (N.D. Ind. 2007) ("[T]hose serving as adjudicators are presumed to act in good faith, honesty, and with integrity."). This presumption has made it difficult for plaintiffs to prevail in claims that IHOs were biased, as district courts often do no more than review the administrative record to conclude that there was no evidence of bias by the hearing officer. In *D.R. v. Dep't of Educ. of Haw.*, 827 F. Supp. 2d 1161, 1166–67 (D. Haw. 2011), the plaintiff alleged that the hearing officer was biased because the state education department previously employed him, he previously worked with the attorney for the district, and ruled in favor of the department in his previous six cases. The court found that there was not a rule against former state education department attorneys serving as hearing officers, there was no evidence of bias, and "the officer was objective." *Id.* at 1167; *see also* B.J.S. v. State Educ. Dep't. of N.Y., 815 F. Supp. 2d 601, 613 (W.D.N.Y. 2011) (rejecting allegations that the state review officer disliked the plaintiff and was biased in favor of school districts because there was no evidence suggesting partiality); E.S. v. Katonah-Lewisboro Sch. Dist., 742 F. Supp. 2d 417, 434 (S.D.N.Y. 2010), *aff'd*, 487 F. App'x 619 (2d Cir. 2012) (rejecting bias claim based on a review of the record); L.G. v. Sch. Bd. of Palm Beach

Cnty, 512 F. Supp. 2d 1240, 1245 (S.D. Fla. 2007), *aff'd*, 255 F. App'x 360 (11th Cir. 2007) (rejecting claim that ALJ was biased against parents on the grounds that she had not ruled in favor of any since 2000 and ignored evidence favorable to the child because there was no evidence suggesting bias).

6. Consider the impact the presumption of impartiality had on how the courts ruled on bias allegations in the following cases involving state education department and local school district employment, statistical evidence of bias, and alleged personal and professional conflicts of interest.

Employment by the local school district or state educational agency: Although an employee of the local school district or state educational agency cannot conduct an impartial due process hearing, the IDEA does not define what constitutes employment with a local or state educational agency. In *Thomas*, the court ruled that neither selection as a hearing officer nor payment for service by a local district creates an employment relationship; *see also* H.H. v. Ind. Bd. of Special Educ. Appeals, 501 F. Supp. 2d 1188, 1197 (N.D. Ind. 2007) (ruling that state educational agency's appointment of hearing officers and state level review panelists does not make them state employees); Jacky W. v. N.Y.C. Bd. of Educ., 848 F. Supp. 358, 362 (E.D.N.Y. 1994) (holding that IDEA does not prohibit local school districts from selecting or paying impartial hearing officers); Ahern v. Keene, 593 F. Supp. 902, 910 (D. Del. 1984) (holding that district superintendent did not violate IDEA by appointing the hearing officer and state review officer).

One issue that has arisen in connection with impartiality is whether a state employee can conduct the state-level review of district-level impartial due process hearings. Although the IDEA does not explicitly prohibit state educational agency employees from conducting state level reviews of impartial due process hearings, most courts prohibit them from doing so. In *Holmes v. Sobel*, 690 F. Supp. 154 (W.D.N.Y. 1988), the court explained the reasoning behind this:

> The federal statute and the regulations do not expressly prohibit officers assigned to conduct "impartial reviews" from being employees of the state educational agency. However, in light of the mandate that they be "impartial" and render an "independent" decision, and considering the objectives of the review process, the similarity of the responsibilities of hearing officers and reviewing officers, and the legislative history of the EHA, the vast majority of courts that have addressed the issue have held that employees of a state educational agency may *not* be appointed to conduct an impartial review.

Id. at 161. The court found that the New York State Commissioner of Education was an employee of the state education department and thus prohibited from hearing appeals from district-level impartial hearings. *Id.*; *see also* Grymes v. Madden, 672 F.2d 321, 323 (3d Cir. 1982) (holding that the IDEA bars state education department employee from serving as a state level review officer); Louis M. v. Ambach, 714 F. Supp. 1276, 1282 (N.D.N.Y. 1989) (holding that IDEA prohibits state education commissioner or his designate from reviewing impartial hearing officer decisions); Vogel v. Sch. Bd. of Montrose R-14, Sch. Dist., 491 F. Supp. 989, 995–96 (W.D. Mo. 1980) (holding that state education department deputy commissioner was state employee and not eligible to conduct state level review); *but see* Brandon E. v. Wis. Dep't of Pub. Inst., 595 F. Supp. 740, 746 (E.D. Wis. 1984) (rejecting claim that state superintendent of public instruction is prohibited from hearing appeals of impartial hearings because he is not a state employee but a constitutional officer).

Statistical evidence of bias: Plaintiffs have found it difficult to prove bias even when they present statistical evidence that an SRO found in favor of school districts in a very high percentage of cases; the courts cited the absence of evidence of actual bias to dismiss such claims. In *R.E. v. N.Y.C. Dep't of Educ.*, 785 F. Supp. 2d 28 (S.D.N.Y. 2011), *rev'd on other grounds*, 644 F.3d 167 (2d Cir. 2012), *cert. denied*, ___ U.S. ___, 133 S.Ct. 2802 (2013), the plaintiff sought to prove bias by showing that in 187 decisions, the SRO ruled in favor of school districts more than seventy-five percent of the time. *Id.* at 39. The court ruled, "Even if Plaintiffs' characterization of these 187 cases is correct, this statistical 'analysis' does not support a finding of judicial bias that would compel the Court to review the SRO's decision with anything other than its usual deference . . . ." *Id.* In an earlier case, the plaintiff offered evidence showing that in two years, the SRO "ruled in favor of school districts eighty-six percent of the time." W.T. v. Bd. of Educ. of Sch. Dist. of N.Y.C., 716 F.Supp. 2d 270, 283 (S.D.N.Y. 2010). The plaintiff also offered evidence that in cases in which parents sought tuition reimbursement in which the SRO reversed the IHO, the SRO "ruled in favor of the school district ninety-eight percent of the time" and in reimbursement cases in which the SRO upheld the IHO, he found "in favor of the school district seventy-six percent of the time." *Id.* at 283. Although the court referred to these statistics as "remarkable," if accurate, *id.*, it nevertheless ruled that the statistics "do not warrant a finding that . . . [the SRO] should have recused himself in this case." *Id.* at 286. The court explained:

> It seems evident that statistics alone, no matter how computed, cannot establish extrajudicial bias. There is no authority for, and no logic in, assuming that either party to a litigation is entitled to a certain percentage of favorable decisions. The inquiry to be at all meaningful would necessarily require this court to examine each and every ruling to determine whether it was, initially, legally valid. If we determined that some adverse rulings were correctly made, obviously they could not be tainted by bias. Even if they were determined to be incorrect, it of course does not follow that they were motivated by personal bias.

Id.

In *J.N. v. Pitt. City Sch. Dist.*, 536 F. Supp. 2d 564, 579 (W.D. Pa. 2008), the court considered similar statistical evidence. According to the plaintiffs, the appellate officer in the case had ruled in favor of school districts in all of the approximately thirty-eight decisions he wrote in a two-year period. The court rejected these statistics as proof of bias. "Plaintiff's allegations of bias are not supported by evidence. He has not pointed to evidence of bias by . . . [the appeals officer] or the Appeals Review Panel in this case. Whatever may have occurred in other cases is not before the Court in this matter." *Id.*

Based on these decisions, can plaintiffs ever prove bias using statistics? What would the remedy be if a court finds that an IHO or SRO is biased?

Personal and professional interests: Courts have placed a heavy burden on plaintiffs challenging the impartiality of hearing officers based on their professional relationships and activities, generally requiring a showing of actual bias. In *Leon v. Mich. Bd. of Educ.*, 807 F. Supp. 1278 (E.D. Mich. 1992), the plaintiff alleged bias on the grounds that the hearing officer was an attorney who "almost exclusively represents school districts in special education matters . . . ." *Id.* at 1281. Pointing out that plaintiffs offered "no proof of actual bias," the court stated, "Even if . . . [the hearing officer] represents school districts significantly more than parents in special education matters, this does not mean he automatically sympathizes with the school district's viewpoint. The Michigan Rules of Professional Conduct recognize that an advocate can remain independent." *Id.* at 1281–82.

In addition to the statistics plaintiffs cited about the New York SRO in *R.E.* and *W.T.*, plaintiffs submitted a newspaper article that alleged that the SRO previously lived with a senior attorney in the New York State Education Department who had "some involvement with special education matters, including training of IHOs . . . ." *W.T.*, 716 F. Supp. 2d at 283–84; *see also R.E.*, 785 F. Supp. 2d at 40. The courts ruled that this additional allegation was not sufficient to show bias. The courts noted the absence of evidence of personal, professional, or economic interest in the case that would require recusal. *R.E.*, 785 F. Supp. 2d at 40; *W.T.*, 716 F. Supp. 2d at 285. The court in *W.T.* explained:

> In sum, even though . . . [the SRO] apparently lives with an SED attorney, his situation does not differ from that of a judge whose spouse is an attorney in private practice who regularly advances arguments germane to a case before the judge. While that understandably may be a cause for concern, it does not mandate disqualification unless the spouse (or the spouse's firm) represents one of the parties before the judge, has an interest that could be substantially affected by the outcome of the proceeding, or is likely to be a material witness. . . . None of these showings has been made in this case.

Id. at 286.

The plaintiff survived a motion to dismiss a bias claim in *H.H. v. Ind. Bd. of Special Educ. Appeals*, 501 F. Supp. 2d 1188 (N.D. Ind. 2007). Plaintiffs alleged that the hearing officer was not impartial because "he was paid to conduct a workshop for school administrators at Ball State University." *Id.* at 1200. Citing the presumption of honesty and integrity of hearing officers and the absence of allegations of pecuniary interest in the case or that the officer acted with bias, the court stated:

> [If] the Court were ruling on the merits of the Plaintiffs' claim in this Opinion and Order, it would deny the claim. However, because the Plaintiffs can still prove facts that would overcome the presumption and that are not inconsistent with this complaint's allegations, the claim survives . . . a motion to dismiss. . . . While it is not reasonable to assume that the IHO actively sympathizes with the school's point of view because he teaches a seminar for administrators, the plaintiffs could establish facts that prove the IHO was actually biased. . . .

Id.

B. Time Limits for Holding Hearings and Issuing Decisions

Blackman v. District of Columbia

277 F. Supp. 2d 71 (D.D.C. 2003)

Paul L. Friedman, United States District Judge.

This matter is before the Court for consideration of five reports filed by the Special Master in which she recommends that the Court grant the motions for preliminary injunction filed on behalf of eleven members of the class. . . . Underlying each motion for a preliminary injunction is a claim that the plaintiffs are being irreparably harmed by defendants' failure to schedule timely due process hearings in violation of Section 1415(f) of the Individuals with Disabilities Education Act, 20 U.S.C. §§ 1400 *et seq.*, ("IDEA") . . . .

I. BACKGROUND

A. *The Special Master's Findings and Recommended Relief*

In her reports, the Special Master made the following findings of fact with respect to these eleven plaintiffs.

1. Claims of Afra Abdullah, *et al.*

With respect to the claims of Afra Abdullah, Charles "Tucker" Battle III, Elvin Charles, Zachary Devillier and James Tanney-Palmeter, the Special Master determined that in each case: (1) the District of Columbia Public Schools ("DCPS") either failed to find the student eligible for special education and/or related services under the IDEA or issued an individualized education program ("IEP") with which the parents disagreed; (2) the parents placed their child in a private school that provided the special education and related services they believed their child required; (3) the parents concurrently or shortly thereafter filed a request for a due process hearing challenging DCPS's determination, indicating, pursuant to DCPS instructions, three dates on which plaintiffs and plaintiffs' counsel were available for a hearing during the ensuing 35 days; (4) with the exception of Afra Abdullah, DCPS sent a notice of a due process hearing to plaintiffs' counsel scheduled on none of the dates requested and at times at which either plaintiffs or plaintiffs' counsel were unavailable; DCPS made no additional efforts to schedule a hearing; (5) DCPS failed to hold a timely due process hearing pursuant to Section 1415(f) of the IDEA . . . ; (6) plaintiffs' counsel filed a motion for summary determination with the DCPS student hearing office that was not acted upon; (7) plaintiffs filed a motion for a preliminary injunction with this Court; and (8) DCPS sent plaintiffs a hearing notice months after the close of the period within which DCPS was statutorily required to hold the due process hearing and issue a determination, purporting to schedule a hearing two days before the already-scheduled meeting with the Special Master.

[The findings of the Special Master relating to the other plaintiffs were similar to these findings.]

. . . .

B. *The Special Master's Conclusions of Law and Recommendations for Relief*

The Special Master concluded that each plaintiff has met the requirements for emergency injunctive relief. First, the Special Master found that the plaintiffs already had prevailed on the merits of their underlying claims when the Court entered a judgment for plaintiffs in this action on the issue of liability . . . . Second, the Special Master determined that plaintiffs have demonstrated irreparable harm because DCPS's failure to provide timely due process hearings "forced" the parents to unilaterally place and pay for the education of their children in an appropriate setting when in fact DCPS has the statutory obligation to provide an appropriate special education at government expense. Furthermore, she concluded that DCPS's failure to provide timely due process hearings constitutes irreparable harm in and of itself by denying plaintiffs a fundamental right afforded by the IDEA. . . .

. . . .

II. DISCUSSION

. . . .

B. *Denial of Timely Due Process Hearings and Resulting Irreparable Harm*

The crux of the disagreement among the parties lies in the second prong of the preliminary injunction standard: irreparable harm. The Special Master concluded that DCPS's failure to provide timely due process hearings constitutes irreparable harm to plaintiffs because the right to a hearing "is absolute, and the failure to provide a timely hearing has consequences that are absolute—that is, there is no substitute available to the student and his or her family. It is the absolute lack of any alternative to the student that causes 'irreparable harm' at the hands of DCPS." Defendants counter that because the timely provision of due process hearings is a procedural protection provided in the IDEA, plaintiffs must demonstrate that actual harm or prejudice resulted from the denial of a hearing in order to merit injunctive relief. In the absence of such harm, the failure to provide a hearing may be remedied by directing that such a hearing promptly be held.

Defendants' failure to provide a *timely* due process hearing to plaintiffs is not an unimportant or technical violation of the procedural safeguards provided for in the IDEA. Rather, it is the denial of a fundamental component of the due process protections afforded by the statute. As the Supreme Court noted in ... *Rowley* ..., the procedural due process protections included by Congress in the IDEA are of critical importance to effectuating the goals of the statute ....

In light of the primacy the due process hearing has in ensuring plaintiffs' substantive rights under the statute, the Court concludes that DCPS's failure to provide timely due process hearings and determinations can itself constitute the denial of a free appropriate education. While a slight delay in the provision of a hearing after a request has been made or a slight delay in rendering a decision may be an excusable procedural infirmity in some cases, the failure to offer the parents and their children a timely hearing for months after the expiration of the 45-day period, as was the case here, crosses the line from process to substance.

As this Court previously has held, the failure to provide an IEP, the failure to hold a due process hearing, or the failure to provide a written determination in a timely manner after requests for an IEP meeting or a hearing have been made constitutes the denial of a free appropriate public education as required by the IDEA. Where there is a denial of a free appropriate education because no hearing has been held and no determination has been issued, and a proper placement therefore has not been made, there results a *per se* harm to the student and the irreparable injury requirement for a preliminary injunction has been satisfied. Indeed, each day a child is denied a free appropriate education by such procedural dereliction of a school system he or she is harmed yet again. As the Court previously noted in this very case:

> [T]he failure of the District to comply with its statutory obligations and provide appropriate educational placements can have a devastating impact on a child's well-being. "Any agency whose appointed mission is to provide for the education and welfare of children fails that mission when it loses sight of the fact that, to a young, growing person, time is critical. While a month in the life of an adult may be insignificant, at the rate at which a child develops and changes, especially one at the onset of biological adolescence with or without special needs like those of our plaintiff, a few months can make a world of difference in the life of that child."

Blackman v. District of Columbia, 185 F.R.D. 4, 7–8 (D.D.C. 1999) ....

The conclusion that a *per se* harm results from the denial of a free appropriate education stemming from the failure to provide a timely due process hearing relieves plaintiffs from any burden to articulate an additional, particularized harm. When a plaintiff's rights to the due process hearing are circumscribed in significant ways, a plaintiff need not show prejudice in order to demonstrate injury. It follows that where DCPS has outright denied a child a timely due process hearing, DCPS cannot claim that the denial of a free appropriate education has not occurred. It has.

The Court also rejects defendants' argument that these students have not been denied a free appropriate education because, with the exception of Shanice Brooks, they currently attend private schools at which they have been placed by their parents. The issue here is not the parents' financial ability to fund their children at private schools pending the outcome of a due process hearing. The harm is the denial by DCPS of a *free appropriate education*, and this harm is not dependent on the financial resources of an individual plaintiff's family. Put simply, the children cannot be denied their substantive right to a free appropriate education under the IDEA because they are fortunate enough to have parents who can afford to fund their education in private schools while waiting for DCPS to provide the hearings required by law that will determine whether the child's private placement or some other placement is the appropriate one. Any other conclusion would require parents to deny their children an education altogether in order to protect their rights under the statute. The Court will not endorse such a perverse incentive.

. . . .

D. *Adequacy of Recommended Remedy*

The Special Master recommended three remedies for ten of the eleven students: (1) maintenance of those students' placements through the end of the 2002–2003 school year; (2) the provision of due process hearings by DCPS within one month from the date of any Court order; and (3) reimbursement of monies paid by the parents for the private schools currently attended by the students for the 2002–2003 school year. The Special Master's first recommendation—that DCPS be ordered to maintain placements at the private schools through the end of the 2002–2003 school year—is moot because the school year has ended. The children are still without due process hearings, however. The Court therefore directs that DCPS shall issue notices of placement for the children at the private provider of the parents' choice for the upcoming 2003–2004 school year and that such placements shall remain in effect until such due process hearings are conducted and decisions are issued. If the due process hearing officer determines on an individual basis that a child's placement should be elsewhere, DCPS can issue a new notice of placement at that time. As the new school year fast approaches, the Court recognizes the necessity for these students to have appropriate placements as soon as possible. The Court therefore will adopt the Special Master's second recommendation that DCPS conduct the due process hearings requested by these plaintiffs immediately, but no later than 10 business days from the date of this Opinion. . . .

Notes, Comments, and Questions

1. The facts in *Blackman* were particularly egregious and the procedural posture of the case was somewhat unusual in that the District had not held impartial hearings for the plaintiffs despite earlier court orders to do so. The court pointed out that slight delays in providing a hearing would generally not constitute a substantive violation. At what point should a slight delay become a substantive violation? *See* Burr

v. Ambach, 863 F.2d 1071, 1075 (2d Cir. 1988) (holding that delay of four months in holding impartial hearing and one year in issuing the decision violated the IDEA).

2. What should the remedy be for a late decision? In *Walker v. District of Columbia*, 151 F. Supp. 2d 11, 31–32, 35 (D.D.C. 2001), the court ruled that compensatory education is the appropriate remedy for a late hearing and decision. Another court ordered the district to start making tuition reimbursement payments on the date a decision was due and forward after that. Murphy v. Arlington Cent. Sch. Dist. Bd. of Educ., 86 F. Supp. 2d 354, 367 (S.D.N.Y. 2000), *aff'd*, 297 F.3d 195 (2d Cir. 2002) (ordering district to begin making tuition reimbursement payments on date that the SRO decision that was three months late had been due). Finally, a third court ordered the state to issue a decision in ten days, and if it did not do so, the court would excuse the plaintiff from exhausting her administrative remedies. Engwiller v. Pine Plains Cent. Sch. Dist., 110 F. Supp. 2d 236, 245–46, 251 (S.D.N.Y. 2000). In contrast to these cases, other courts that found that districts violated the IDEA's deadlines for issuing decisions did not order remedies. Several courts found that although the decision was not timely, the delay did not substantively harm the child's educational interests, and thus did not violate the child's right to a free appropriate public education. *See* O.O. v. District of Columbia, 573 F. Supp. 2d 41, 50 (D.D.C. 2008) (holding that delay did not harm child's education); Wilkins v. District of Columbia, 571 F. Supp. 2d 163, 172–73 (D.D.C. 2008) (finding that delay in issuing decision did not cause harm because the district's program met the child's needs). Finally, other courts have denied relief because they found the delay was not intentional or was reasonable. *See* J.D.G. v. Colonial Sch. Dist., 748 F. Supp. 2d 362, 376 (D. Del. 2010) ("There is nothing in the record that reflects, or even suggests, an intentional delay of the due process hearing."); Ahern v. Keene, 593 F. Supp. 902, 910 (D. Del. 1984) (finding no evidence that delays were the result of bad faith). Does the IDEA include a good faith exception for failing to meeting its deadlines?

Chapter 12

Stay-Put: Maintenance of Educational Placement Pending Resolution of IDEA Proceedings

Introduction

The Supreme Court addressed the IDEA's "stay-put" provision in *Honig v. Doe*, 484 U.S. 305 (1988). (*Honig v. Doe* is excerpted more fully in Chapter Eight. This is a good time to re-read it.) In *Honig*, school district officials sought "to expel two emotionally disturbed children from school indefinitely for violent and disruptive conduct relating to their disabilities." *Id.* at 598. Quoting the then-current citation for the stay-put provision, the Court stated:

> The language of § 1415(e)(3) is unequivocal. It states plainly that during the pendency of any proceedings initiated under the Act . . . "the child *shall* remain in the then current educational placement." Faced with this clear directive, petitioner asks us to read a "dangerousness" exception into the stay-put provision . . . .

Id. at 604. Rejecting this request, the Court stated:

> We think it clear, however, that Congress very much meant to strip schools of the unilateral authority they had traditionally employed to exclude disabled students, particularly emotionally disturbed students, from school. In so doing, Congress did not leave school administrators powerless to deal with dangerous students; it did, however, deny school officials their former right to "self-help," and directed that in the future the removal of disabled students could be accomplished only with the permission of the parents or, as a last resort, the courts.

Id. Although *Honig* prompted Congress to amend the IDEA to allow school administrators to unilaterally remove allegedly dangerous children with disabilities from school for up to forty-five days, the stay-put provision at issue in *Honig* otherwise remains intact.

The IDEA's stay-put provision reads as follows:

> [D]uring the pendency of any proceedings conducted pursuant to this section, unless the State or local educational agency and the parents otherwise agree, the child shall remain in the then-current educational placement of

> the child, or, if applying for initial admission to a public school, shall, with the consent of the parents, be placed in the public school program until all such proceedings have been completed.

20 U.S.C. § 1415(j) (2012). The stay-put provision is an essential part of the IDEA. It creates a presumption in favor of a child with a disability that her current placement is appropriate, and if her parents disagree with a change in that placement and seek an impartial hearing to challenge it, the stay-put provision requires the school district to allow the child to remain in the placement until the dispute is over. Describing the importance of the stay-put provision, the court in *Susquenita Sch. Dist. v. Raelee S.*, 96 F.3d 78 (3d Cir. 1996), stated:

> The pendent placement provision impacts to some degree virtually every case involving an administrative challenge under the IDEA. A child's placement during the course of administrative and judicial proceedings typically has great significance for all concerned. "Where as in the present case review of a contested IEP takes years to run its course—years critical to the child's development—important practical questions arise concerning interim placement of the child and financial responsibility for that placement." *Sch. Comm. of The Town of Burlington v. Dep't of Educ.*, 471 U.S. 359, 361 . . . (1985). The pendent placement provision was included in the IDEA to protect handicapped children and their parents during the review process. . . .
>
> . . . .
>
> Given the protective purpose underlying the pendent placement provision, it is often invoked by a child's parents in order to maintain a placement where the parents disagree with a change proposed by the school district; the provision is used to block school districts from effectuating unilateral change in a child's educational program. . . .

Id. at 82–83. Pendency rights apply only to a child's current educational placement. If the parents oppose the child's current educational placement, challenge the placement in an impartial due process hearing, and change the child's placement while the due process proceedings are pending, the new placement is not the pendency placement unless the school district agrees or the parents receive a favorable ruling that the new placement is appropriate.

Chapter Twelve is divided into three sections. Section One covers the definition of the "then-current educational placement" from which a school district cannot remove a child pending the outcome of proceedings under Section 1415. Section Two considers what constitutes a change in the then-current educational placement. Section Three covers several implementation issues relating to the stay-put provision, including when the stay-put provision is triggered and its duration, changing the stay-put placement, responsibility for paying tuition for a stay-put placement in a private school, and enforcing the stay-put provision.

Problem

Y.H. is an eighth grade student at Green Lake Middle School (Green Lake). Y.H. has learning disabilities and has an IEP that includes resource room, extra time for homework and exams, and integrated co-teaching (ICT) for math, science, English, and social studies. Y.H. attends classes with approximately twenty-five children, including children with learning disabilities and children in the general education curriculum. The classes are co-taught by a general education subject-matter specialist as well as a special education teacher. Y.H. was doing well in all of the ICT classes, scoring all As and Bs.

Representatives of Green Lake met with Y.H.'s mother to discuss Y.H.'s IEP for ninth grade. They stated that Y.H. would continue to receive resource room and extra time for homework and tests, and that she would be in ICT English and social studies classes. However, they stated that Y.H. would not receive ICT for earth science and algebra. Instead, she would be in special classes for science and math. The special classes would contain twelve students each, all of whom have learning disabilities, and would be taught by a subject matter specialist who also has special education training. Y.H.'s mother objected. She said that math and science are Y.H.'s favorite subjects and that she always received As in math and science in middle school. Green Lake's special education coordinator stated that earth science and algebra were much more difficult than middle school math and science, and that although Y.H. did well in math and science in middle school, her aptitude tests indicated she was not ready for algebra and earth science in ninth grade.

Y.H.'s mother received Y.H.'s IEP in August. As expected, it included special classes in science and math for Y.H. Ms. H. retained counsel who filed a request for an impartial hearing challenging the IEP and asked for an immediate stay-put order requiring the school district to place Y.H. in ICT earth science and algebra classes in ninth grade. The IHO assigned to the case bifurcated the pendency request from the challenge to the IEP on the merits. She issued an order denying the stay-put request on the grounds that the high school IEP did not constitute a change in placement. The IHO reserved judgment on the challenge to the IEP on the merits pending a hearing. Was the IHO's decision on pendency correct? What was Y.H.'s then-current educational placement when Ms. H. filed the impartal hearing request challenging the ninth grade IEP? Does the high school IEP constitute a change in placement?

Immediately following the IHO's pendency decision, Ms. H.'s attorney filed a complaint in federal court seeking a preliminary injunction requiring Green Lake to place Y.H. in ICT classes for earth science and algebra in ninth grade. What factors should the district court consider when ruling on the request for a preliminary injunction?

Ms. H. ultimately decided not to send Y.H. to Green Lake High School and instead sent her to a private school where Y.H. was in ICT classes for earth science and algebra. In the middle of ninth grade, the IHO issued a decision denying Ms. H's challenge to the ninth grade IEP. Ms. H. appealed to the SRO, who upheld the IHO's decision.

Ms. H. appealed this decision to the district court and she prevailed at the beginning of tenth grade. The district court judge ruled that Green Lake's ninth grade IEP did not provide Y.H. with a FAPE and that the private school did. At the end of Y.H.'s eleventh grade year, the court of appeals ruled in favor of Green Lake. The court ruled that the ninth grade IEP was appropriate. Y.H. remained enrolled in the private school through eleventh grade. What was Y.H.'s stay-put placement in ninth grade? Tenth grade? Eleventh grade? Who is ultimately responsible for the tuition for each of these three school years?

Section One
The "Then-Current" Educational Placement

The IDEA does not define "then-current educational placement." Consider how the court defined the term in the following case.

John M. v. Bd. of Educ. of Evanston Twnshp. High Sch. Dist. 202

502 F.3d 708 (7th Cir. 2007)

Ripple, *Circuit Judge.*

John M. . . . filed this action seeking relief under the Individuals with Disabilities Education Act ("IDEA") . . . . He alleged that Evanston Township High School District 202 . . . denied [him] a free, appropriate public education ("FAPE") . . . . In response to John's motion for enforcement of the statute's "stay-put" provision, which requires generally that a child remain in the same educational placement pending any proceedings . . . , the district court entered a preliminary injunction.

For the reasons set forth in this opinion, we have concluded that the injunction cannot stand in its present form because it addresses matters beyond the stay-put provision and does not apply the correct standards when it does address the stay-put provision. Accordingly, we reverse the judgment of the district court and remand the case for further proceedings consistent with this opinion.

I

BACKGROUND

A.

John is a 16 year-old sophomore in high school who has Down's Syndrome. He is enrolled in the School District as a student at Evanston Township High School ("ETHS") . . . . Before beginning his high school career at ETHS, John had attended Haven Middle School ("Haven"). Students from Haven normally transition to ETHS to continue their education.

While John was a student at Haven, he pursued his middle school education under the terms of an Individualized Education Program ("IEP"). This plan, often referred to in this opinion as the "May 2004 IEP," had been formulated in May 2004. While at Haven, John had received a service that the parties refer to as "co-teaching." The phrase "co-teaching" did not appear in the May 2004 IEP.

In Spring 2005, John's parents and representatives of ETHS met to formulate an IEP for John's coming freshman year at ETHS. . . . During this process, ETHS stated that it would not be able to provide the same sort of co-teaching services that Haven had provided to John during his middle school education. Instead, ETHS proposed to afford John 215 minutes per week of special education services. The proposed ETHS IEP also provided that John's special education teacher would *observe* him in his general education classes . . . for 43 to 86 additional minutes per week. . . .

Because John's parents did not believe that the proposed IEP fulfilled the School District's statutory responsibility to their son, they requested an administrative hearing. The hearing officer determined that the IEP complied with statutory requirements. He also concluded that ETHS had complied fully with the requirements of the stay-put placement.

John then filed an action in the district court seeking review of the hearing officer's determination. While this action was pending, John filed a motion for a preliminary injunction to enforce the stay-put placement and a motion to supplement the administrative record and present additional evidence.

B.

In his motion for a preliminary injunction, John sought to maintain the status quo, the May 2004 middle school IEP, while the litigation over the proposed high school IEP was under consideration by the district court.

. . . .

II

DISCUSSION

. . . .

B.

We now must examine whether the district court erred when it held that co-teaching was required as part of John's stay-put placement.

In enacting the stay-put provision, Congress intended "to strip schools of the *unilateral* authority they had traditionally employed to exclude disabled students . . . from school." *Honig v. Doe*, 484 U.S. 305, 323 . . . (1988) (emphasis in original). The statute's stay-put provision requires that a child remain in "the same educational placement pending the outcome of any proceedings brought pursuant to section 1415, unless the parents and the school district otherwise agree." *Bd. of Educ. of Cmty. High Sch. Dist. No. 218 v. Illinois State Bd. of Educ.*, 103 F.3d 545, 548 (7th Cir. 1996). The term " 'educational placement' is not statutorily defined, so that identifying a change in this placement is something of an inexact science." *Id.* Indeed, we have admitted to a hesitancy to establish in any definitive and rigid way the meaning of "educational placement." Rather, we have seen wisdom in, and therefore have adopted, the fact-driven approach employed by our sister circuits. *Id.* at 549. In *Board of Education of Community High School District No. 218 v. Illinois State Board of Education*, 103 F.3d 545 (7th Cir. 1996), we recognized that within the term there must be "enough room to encompass [the child's] experience." *Id.* We recognized that the educational status quo for a "growing, learning" young person often makes rigid adherence to particular educational methodologies "an impossibility." *Id.* Under these circumstances, respect for the *purpose* of the stay-put provision requires that the former IEP be read at a level of generality that focuses on the child's "educational needs and goals." *Id.*

As we pointed out in *High School District No. 218*, our colleagues in the Second Circuit have interpreted "educational placement" along the same lines. They have described it to refer to "the general educational program in which a child who is correctly identified as handicapped is enrolled, rather than mere variations in the program itself." Concerned Parents & Citizens for the Continuing Educ. at Malcolm X (PS 79) v. New York City Bd. of Educ., 629 F.2d 751, 754 (2d Cir. 1980). In a similar vein, the court noted that, the regulations implementing the IDEA also interpret the term "placement" to mean "only the general program of education." *Id.* By contrast, the judges likened a change in "educational placement" to involve moving a child from a "special class in a regular school to a special school." *Id.* A more rigid interpretation of "educational placement," the court pointed out, would impede the school board's ability to make "even minor discretionary changes within the educational programs provided for its students." *Id.* at 755.

This perspective is shared as well by our colleagues in the Ninth Circuit. They have stated, in *Johnson ex rel. Johnson v. Special Education Hearing Office*, 287 F.3d 1176 (9th Cir. 2002), that all "educational placement" requires is "comparable placement." *Id.* at 1182. In *Ms. S ex rel. G. v. Vashon Island School District*, 337 F.3d 1115 (9th Cir. 2003) (superseded by statute on other grounds), the court spoke directly to the situation before us—the progression of a child from one level of education to another. When a child progresses from preschool to elementary school, from elementary school to middle school or from middle school to high school, the "status quo no longer exists." *Id.* at 1133. Under these circumstances, the obligation of the new district is to provide educational services that approximate the student's old IEP as closely as possible. *Id.* at 1134.

We believe that these cases recognize the need for *some* degree of flexibility in interpreting the last agreed-upon IEP in a stay-put situation. In complying with the stay-put provision, we must interpret "educational placement" to incorporate enough flexibility to "encompass [the child's] experience." *High Sch. Dist. No. 218*, 103 F.3d at 549. A child's interim educational regime must produce as closely as possible the overall educational experience enjoyed by the child under his previous IEP. To achieve that result, we must recognize that educational methodologies, appropriate and even necessary in one educational environment, are not always effective in another time and place in serving a child's continuing educational needs and goals.

Nevertheless, when asked to approve an alteration in educational methodology in a stay-put order, we must give careful attention to the purpose of the stay-put provision. The recognized and defined special needs of the child and the educational goals originally set by the parents and by professional educators must be respected. Protestations that educational methodologies proven to be helpful to the child in the past are now impossible must be evaluated with a critical eye to ensure that motivations other than those compatible with the statute, such as bureaucratic inertia, are not driving the decision. Suggestions for methodological change that would dilute the statute's policy of "mainstreaming" disabled children to the "maximum extent appropriate," 20 U.S.C. § 1412(a)(5)(A), deserve particular scrutiny....

C.

On remand, the district court must revisit the request for interim injunctive relief under the stay-put provision. Its starting point must be the May 2004 IEP that governed John's middle school education. This document, as the last educational plan agreed upon by the parents and the professional educators, is the appropriate basis for stay-put relief. Generally, the terms of this IEP should be enforced, without exception, as the stay-put relief.

In examining the May 2004 IEP, the district court must note with particular care the precise requirements of the IEP. Even if a school has provided a particular service in the past, it need not be provided in a stay-put situation if it was not within the governing IEP. If the parties dispute what the IEP requires, as they do here with respect to co-teaching, the court must evaluate the IEP as a whole and determine whether such a methodology is required under the terms of the IEP. Under usual circumstances, the court should find it unnecessary to go beyond the four corners of the document in order to make that determination. However, vagueness in the instrument with respect to how its goals are to be achieved may require that the court turn to extrinsic evidence to determine the intent of those who formulated the plan. A methodology not mentioned in the plan may well indicate that those who formulated the plan did not consider that particular methodology a necessary component to the plan—although they well may have intended that some comparable methodology be implemented. Here, the term "co-teaching" is not mentioned in the May 2004 IEP itself. Therefore, the district court ought to determine, after evaluating the entire May 2004 IEP as a totality, whether the parties regarded this methodology as an essential part of the plan or as simply one of several ways by which the plan could be implemented. As we noted earlier, in answering this question, the court will need to explore *precisely* how the plan was implemented at Haven. The exact method of implementation is not apparent on this record and the accounts of the parties are not compatible.

Knowledge of precisely how this feature of the plan was implemented at Haven is important for another reason. In examining the manner in which the plan was implemented in the middle school environment, the district court will be able to gauge far more accurately the School District's claim that implementation of that methodology in the institutional setting of a high school is not possible. As we have said earlier, *if* the district court finds that the methodology employed in the middle school is actually part of the May 2004 IEP, the court must require very compelling evidence from the School District before permitting a deviation from the course already set. However, the court might determine nevertheless that the high school setting makes the use of such an approach counterproductive in terms of the goals of the IEP or impossible to implement. The court then may allow the parties to propose an alternative. This alternative should be as close as possible to the approach used in the middle school but nevertheless compatible with the goals of the IEP and the institutional demands of the high school setting. On the other hand, if the court determines that the methodology is not part of the IEP but simply a methodology chosen by the middle school educational professionals, that particular methodology need not be included in the stay-put order. The district court should then permit the high school authorities to choose the approach that they believe will be most effective in the implementation of the IEP.

. . . .

Notes, Comments, and Questions

1. As the court in *John M.* recognized, the IDEA does not contain a definition of the "educational placement." 502 F.3d at 714. The court stated that the "IEP that governed John's middle school education . . ." as the "last educational plan agreed upon by the parents and professional educators, is the appropriate basis for stay-put relief." *Id.* at 715. Other courts have adopted similar formulations. *See* K.D. v. Dep't of Educ. of Haw., 665 F.3d 1110, 1118 (9th Cir. 2011) (defining "'current educational placement' to mean 'the placement set forth in the child's last implemented IEP.'"); L.M. v. Capistrano Unified Sch. Dist., 556 F.3d 900, 902–03 (9th Cir. 2009) (defining the current educational placement as "the placement set forth in the child's last implemented IEP."); Mackey v. Bd. of Educ. for Arlington Cent. Sch. Dist., 386 F.3d 158, 163 (2d Cir. 2004) (citing various formulations, including "'the placement described in the child's most recently implemented IEP'"); Cordrey v. Euckert, 917 F.2d 1460, 1468 (6th Cir. 1990) (holding that an extended school year was not in the most recent IEP and is thus not part of the current educational placement); George A. v. Wallingford Swarthmore Sch. Dist., 655 F. Supp. 2d 546, 549–50 (E.D. Pa. 2009) (stating that the IEP placement is the stay-put placement). Other courts have adopted different but similar formulations. *See* Drinker v. Colonial Sch. Dist., 78 F.3d 859, 867 (3d Cir. 1996) (defining current educational placement as "'the operative placement actually functioning at the time the dispute first arises.'"); Hunger v. Leininger, 15 F.3d 664, 667 (7th Cir. 1994), *cert. denied*, 531 U.S. 839 (1994) (holding that stay-put plan is "The plan that was frozen in place when the proceedings were initiated. . . .").

2. Even though the court in *John M.* ruled that the IEP is the "basis for stay-put relief," the court also ruled that a court can go beyond the four corners of the IEP if there is a dispute about what it requires:

> Here, the term "co-teaching" is not mentioned in the May 2004 IEP itself. Therefore, the district court ought to determine, after evaluating the entire

> May 2014 IEP as a totality, whether the parties regarded this methodology as an essential part of the plan or as simply one of several ways by which the plan could be implemented. As we noted earlier, in answering this question, the court will need to explore *precisely* how the plan was implemented at Haven. The exact method of implementation is not apparent on this record and the accounts of the parties are not compatible.

502 F.3d at 716.

3. *John M.* involved an issue that often arises: defining the "then-current educational placement" of a child with a disability who is in transition from one program to another. Consider how the courts defined the "then-current educational placement" in the following transitions:

Initial enrollment in public school: When a child seeks admission to a public school, the child's stay-put placement is the program the district initially offers. *See* 20 U.S.C. § 1415(j) (2012); 34 C.F.R. § 300.518(b) (2015) (stating that "the child, with the consent of the parents, must be placed in the public school until the completion of all the proceedings."); L.M. v. Capistrano Unified Sch. Dist., 556 F.3d 900, 903 (9th Cir. 2009) (citing § 1415(j)); A.S. v. Madison Metro. Sch. Dist., 477 F. Supp. 2d 969, 977 (W.D. Wisc. 2007) (holding that the stay-put placement for a child applying for admission to a public school is the placement the school offered).

General education to special education: In *Thomas v. Cincinnati Bd. of Educ.*, 918 F.2d 618, 626 (6th Cir. 1990), the school district had not yet prepared an IEP for the child "but was providing her one hour of home assistance per day." *Id.* at 625. The court stated that when there is no IEP, a child's stay-put placement is "the operative placement under which the child is actually receiving instruction at the time the dispute arises." *Id.* at 626. As a result, the court required the school district to continue providing the child "five hours of home instruction per week until the dispute was resolved." *Id.* at 625–26. On the other hand, in *Gregory K. v. Longview Sch. Dist.*, 811 F.2d 1307, 1314 (9th Cir. 1987), the court held that tutoring for a child who was not in a special education program was not part of his current educational placement. The court stated, "The 'status quo' provision of the Act applies only to special education received pursuant to an IEP." *Id.* With which decision do you agree?

Part C of the IDEA to Part B: Part C of the IDEA requires counties to provide services to children with disabilities from birth to age three. Under Part C, children have an Individualized Family Service Plan (IFSP). Part B of the IDEA requires school districts to provide services to children pursuant to an IEP once they turn three. If the parents of a child with an IFSP disagree with the proposed IEP, they can challenge it. What should the then-current educational placement be when a child moves from Part C to Part B? The courts disagree.

In *Pardini v. Allegheny Intermediate Unit*, 420 F.3d 181, 192 (3d Cir. 2005), *cert. denied*, 547 U.S. 1050 (2006), the court ruled that the stay-put provision requires a school district to pay for the services the child was receiving pursuant to her IFSP pending resolution of a dispute over her IEP. In reaching its decision, the court rejected the school district's argument that Parts B and C were fundamentally different and the stay-put provision does not apply in the transition from Part C to Part B:

> In addition, 20 U.S.C. § 1415(j) must be read in context with the rest of the IDEA statute. . . . Instead of noting the differences between the Part B and Part C programs, we must remember that Congress sought to ensure continuity in the education of each child under the IDEA. Yet, the AIU's attempt to chisel distinct barriers between services provided under Parts C and B based upon its theory of childhood development would require us to ignore the programmatic and fiscal overlap between Part C and Part B as well as the congressional mandate of a smooth transition between the two. Congress stressed that the amendments it added were "designed to promote a *seamless* system of services for children with disabilities, aged birth to five, inclusive." H.R. Rep. No. 198, 102nd Cong., 1st Sess. 1991 . . . .
>
> Congress has clearly recognized that needs of disabled children do not fit neatly into the age-defined stages suggested by the AIU. Although Georgia was technically transitioning within the administrative and fiscal structure of IDEA's statutory scheme, her needs did not magically change on her third birthday. She still needed substantially the same services she was receiving in the days preceding her birthday. Indeed, 20 U.S.C. § 1412(a)(9) describes the transition to the preschool programs and notes that either an IEP or an IFSP may be used and implemented for the child. The Act expressly states that an IFSP may be used if it is "consistent with State policy," and "agreed to by the agency and the child's parents." Thus, the IDEA both anticipates and condones the possible interchangeability of an IFSP and IEP during transition to pre-school.
>
> Furthermore, even if we could accept the AIU's theory of "development" vs. "education," we would still be convinced that by the analysis in the cases we have discussed, that the conductive education in Georgia's IFSP was part of the status quo that should have been maintained pending resolution of the dispute over her IEP.

Id. at 191; *see also* Johnson v. Special Ed. Hearing Office, 287 F.3d 1176, 1180–81 (9th Cir. 2002) (holding that IFSP was child's then-current "educational placement for 'stay-put' purposes").

In contrast, in *D.P. v. Sch. Bd. of Broward Co.*, 483 F.3d 725, 726 (11th Cir. 2007), *cert. denied*, 552 U.S. 1142 (2008), the Eleventh Circuit ruled that the IFSP was not the child's stay-put placement. The court reasoned:

> In the orders granting the motions to dismiss, the district court relied on the plain language of the pendency, or "stay-put," provision of the IDEA to hold that the statute does not require the Board to provide the services that had previously been provided under the IFSPs. . . .
>
> The "stay put" provision . . . says:
>
> . . . .

> [D]uring the pendency of any proceedings conducted pursuant to this section, unless the State or local educational agency and the parents otherwise agree, the child shall remain in the then-current educational placement of the child, or, if applying for initial admission to a public school, shall, with the consent of the parents, be placed in the public school program until all such proceedings have been completed.

20 U.S.C. § 1415(j).

Appellants contend that, through use of the disjunctive "or," the statutory provision provides alternative placements for the triplets. According to Appellants, while their due process requests were pending, the triplets could have been placed in the public school program or they could have remained in their then-current educational placement. . . .

We find Appellants' argument unpersuasive in light of the unambiguous language of the statute. The disjunctive "or" does indeed provide alternatives; but, contrary to Appellants' contention, the alternatives separated by the "or" are mutually exclusive. As the district court stated, if the educational agency (here, the Board) and parents do not agree to a placement for the child, which of the other two alternatives applies depends on one fact only—whether the child is applying for initial admission to a public school. If the child is not applying for initial admission, he shall remain in his existing educational placement. *Or*, if the child is applying for initial admission, he shall be placed in the public school program. We reach this conclusion based upon the placement of the disjunctive coordinating conjunction—between the two alternatives, but before the imperative, "if applying for initial admission to a public school [the student] shall . . . be placed in the public school program."

In this case, Appellants do not contest the fact that the triplets have never been admitted to a public school program. Therefore, the triplets are "applying for initial admission to a public school." And, in the absence of an agreement otherwise between the Board and the triplets' parents, the only placement available to the triplets is the public school program. The district court properly held that the fact that the parents withheld consent to placement in the program offered by the public school (pursuant to the temporary IEPs) does not create another option for the triplets. Without the parents' consent, the triplets cannot be placed in the public school program; but, they are not entitled to an alternative placement pursuant to the statute. In other words, the IDEA does not entitle the triplets to continue receiving services pursuant to their IFSPs until such time as valid IEPs are put in place for them.

We acknowledge that our decision is at odds with the Third Circuit's holding in *Pardini*. We think that case was incorrectly decided. As stated above, we base our conclusions on the plain language of the "stay-put" provision. We do note, however, that our interpretation of the statute is consistent with that of the Department of Education. The implementing regulation in effect at the time Appellants filed their due process requests stated:

> If the [due process] complaint involves an application for initial admission to public school, the child, with the consent of the parents, must be placed in the public school until the completion of all the proceedings.

34 C.F.R. § 300.514(b).

Id. at 729–30.

Which decision do you find more persuasive? Which embodies the purposes of the stay-put provision? Do you think Congress intended the rule regarding application for initial admission into a public school to apply to a child with an IFSP seeking an IEP from the school district in which she lives? If not, to which students should the rule apply?

Kindergarten to first grade: In *Van Scoy v. San Luis Coastal Unified Sch. Dist.*, 353 F. Supp. 2d 1083 (C.D. Cal. 2005), the child's kindergarten IEP provided for a one-to-one aide for the whole school day and two additional hours after school. The school district asserted that the child would not need the additional two hours in first grade because the day was longer. The court held:

> While the ultimate decision regarding the appropriate placement for Matthew is not currently before the Court, for the purpose of the stay-put provision, the Court believes that the placement that as closely as possible replicates that which Matthew was receiving at the time the dispute arose includes 120 minutes daily with a BHS aide outside of the classroom.

Id. at 1086.

Elementary to middle school: In *Beth B. v. Van Clay*, 126 F. Supp. 2d 532 (N.D. Ill. 2000), the child's placement "was in a regular classroom with special services, during kindergarten, first grade, and second grade." *Id.* at 533. For her transition to middle school, the district proposed, and a hearing officer upheld, placement in a self-contained special education classroom. The parents appealed, and they argued that the child's stay-put placement should be a regular education classroom in the district's middle school. The court agreed:

> We do not believe that the change to junior high school means that there is no longer a current educational placement, or that junior high is unquestionably an inappropriate placement. Junior high school is the normal matriculation progression. Beth will remain with her peers. We think that progression adheres to the status quo, keeping her in her regular public school classroom pending completion of the review proceeding. We recognize that a change to a multi-classroom setting adds complexities, but that is not enough to lead to denial of a statutory right.
>
> We grant plaintiffs' motion for a statutory injunction and rule that Beth's stay-put placement is in Lake Bluff Middle School for now. We leave to the parties the supports, aides and related services necessary to provide a free appropriate public education. . . .

Id. at 534–35.

One school district to another school district in the same state: In *Ms. S. v. Vashon Island Sch. Dist.*, 337 F.3d 1115 (9th Cir. 2003), *cert. denied*, 544 U.S. 928 (2005), the court ruled:

> We hold that when a dispute arises under the IDEA involving a transfer student, and there is disagreement between the parent and student's new school district about the most appropriate educational placement, the new district will satisfy the IDEA if it implements the student's last agreed-upon IEP; but if it is not possible for the new district to implement in full the student's last agreed-upon IEP, the new district must adopt a plan that approximates the student's old IEP as closely as possible. The plan thus adopted will serve the student until the dispute between the parent and school district is resolved by agreement or by administrative hearing with due process.

Id. at 1134. In *Casey K. v. St. Anne Cmty. High Sch. Dist No. 302*, 400 F.3d 508 (7th Cir. 2005), the court issued a similar decision in an unusual fact scenario. A high school district three blocks away from an elementary school district argued that the stay-put provision did not apply to the child's elementary school IEP placement in a private school because the high school district was a different school district and was not required to recognize the elementary school IEP. *Id.* at 510, 513. The court ruled:

> From the Act's standpoint the state is an indivisible unit. It must not be allowed to crawl out from under the Act's requirements—while retaining the federal money that it gets in exchange for submitting itself to those requirements—by multiplying the number of its school districts. It would make no sense if, simply by dividing all its school districts in half and thus doubling their number, a state could reduce the expense to it of compliance with the conditions in IDEA without surrendering a penny of IDEA funds.

Id. at 512.

A school district in one state to a school district in another state: In *Michael C. v. Radnor Twnshp. Sch. Dist.*, 202 F.3d 642, 651 (3d Cir. 2000), *cert. denied*, 531 U.S. 813 (2000), the court ruled, "We hold that the IDEA's overall scheme . . . leads inexorably to the conclusion that when a student moves from State A to State B, any prior IEP in effect in State A need not be treated by State B as continuing automatically in effect." The court based its decision primarily on the federalist structure of the IDEA:

> The IDEA is silent on how its pendency provision is to be applied to students who transfer interstate versus students who transfer intrastate, and the plain language of the pendency provision is at best ambiguous with respect to this issue. On its face, it is not clear that Congress intended the requirement that a student remain in his or her "then-current educational placement" to apply to students who relocate from one state to another. For

example, a student's prior placement no longer seems "current" after he or she withdraws from that placement and moves away. Moreover, it is impossible for the student's new school district in Pennsylvania to keep the student in his or her previous school as required by the "stay put" provision where that school is in another state. Therefore, we must look beyond the isolated text of section 1415(j) for guidance on how to apply this provision in this case.

[The United States Department of Education's Office of Special Education Programs ("OSEP")] is the agency charged with principal responsibility for administering the IDEA. The portion of OSEP Policy Memorandum 96-5 relevant to this case . . . clarifies that the IDEA's pendency provision does not apply to situations where a student moves from one state to another.

The district court deferred to OSEP Policy Memorandum 96-5 . . . .

. . . .

There are strong reasons for that deference and the result reached by the district court. The IDEA recognizes that education is traditionally a state function. Accordingly, it leaves the responsibility of providing a free appropriate public education, or "FAPE," to students with disabilities to state and local educational authorities. Provision of a FAPE requires that special education and related services must "meet the standards of the State educational agency," and must "include an appropriate preschool, elementary, or secondary school education in the State involved." 20 U.S.C. § 1401(8) (1998); 20 U.S.C. § 1401(18) (1996). Under current section 1412, States are eligible for federal financial assistance only when the state demonstrates that it "has in effect policies and procedures to ensure that it meets" the conditions imposed, including that it makes available a FAPE to children with disabilities residing in that state. A local educational authority is eligible to receive these federal funds only if it "has in effect policies, procedures, and programs that are consistent with the State policies and procedures established under section 1412." 20 U.S.C. § 1413 (1998).

Because Congress left primary responsibility for providing a FAPE and for implementing the IDEA to the states, we believe it unlikely that Congress intended the stay-put provision, which dates back to 1975 and the IDEA's predecessor statute, to impose a requirement on states that they must implement an IEP established in another state without considering how consistent that IEP is with the policies and mandates of the student's new residential state.

. . . .

Id. at 649–51. Do a child's needs change when he moves from one state to another? Do the services required to meet those needs change by state? Should the same rule the court in *Ms. S.* adopted for when a student transfers from one school district to another in the same state—that the new district must approximate the former district's IEP as closely as possible—apply when a child moves from a school in one state to a school in a different state?

Section Two
Change in Placement

R.B. v. Mastery Charter Sch.

762 F. Supp. 2d 745 (E.D. Pa. 2010),
aff'd, 532 F. App'x 136 (3rd Cir. 2013),
cert. denied, __U.S.__, 134 S.Ct. 1280 (2014)

Rufe, District Judge.

. . . Plaintiff R.B., acting through her mother ("Parent"), brought this action against Mastery Charter School . . . and The School District of Pennsylvania . . . , appealing the decision of a Due Process Hearing Officer who refused to return R.B. to Mastery during the pendency of due process hearings conducted pursuant to the Individuals with Disabilities Education Act ("IDEA"). Presently before the Court is Plaintiff's Motion for a Mandatory Stay-Put Injunction . . . .

I. BACKGROUND

A. Factual Background

R.B. is a 19-year-old female diagnosed with Trisomy 21 (Down's Syndrome) . . . . She qualifies for special education services under the IDEA because the results of educational, cognitive, and functional assessments identify her as a student with mild to moderate retardation. According to her most recent individualized education program ("IEP")—which is outdated by two years—R.B.'s academic level of functioning ranges between a second to third grade instructional level. In addition to her cognitive disabilities, R.B. also has . . . sleep apnea.

. . . .

The record also shows that Mastery accommodated R.B.'s health needs by modifying its strict attendance policy requirements. Parent testified that R.B.'s sleep apnea, in combination with her heart condition, made it impossible for her to consistently wake up by the beginning of school, and caused her to miss school frequently. Because of the variability of R.B.'s attendance and her medical needs, until April 2009, Mastery did not record attendance for R.B., nor did they pursue standard truancy protocols in response to R.B.'s frequent absences.

In March 2009, a conflict developed between Mastery and Parent after Parent brought R.B. to school earlier than usual, and had difficulty locating R.B.'s classroom.

Ms. Seaton, the principal of Mastery, testified that when Parent entered the building, she refused to sign in and then disrupted an ongoing class and a faculty meeting. After the incident, on March 6, 2009, Ms. Seaton sent Parent a letter limiting Parent's entry into Mastery, informing her that she was "no longer welcome to enter our building unless [she had] a scheduled appointment with an administrator." Parent interpreted the letter as a no-trespass notice, which made it impossible for her to transport R.B. to school and situate her in the classroom, and thus prevented R.B. from attending school. Soon after receiving the letter, Parent stopped bringing R.B. to school.

Emails between Mastery personnel indicate that on April 28, 2009, Mastery—for the first time—began to mark R.B. absent. Although it is unclear what prompted the change in Mastery attendance procedures for R.B., a May 12 email about how to "code" R.B's attendance noted concerns that Parent's "decision to keep [R.B.] out of school due to legal action [was] hurting our attendance figures." On June 19, 2009, after sending three written communications to the parent, and pursuant to Pennsylvania State Law, Mastery unilaterally dropped R.B. from enrollment. There is no evidence that Mastery provided Parent with a copy of the Procedural Safeguards for special education students, attempted to convene a meeting of R.B.'s IEP team, or considered whether or not R.B.'s absences were a manifestation of her disability prior to dropping R.B. from the rolls. . . .

R.B. has not been in school—nor has she received any special education services—since this dispute arose in March 2009. She is now nineteen years old, and will only qualify for special education services until age twenty-one.

B. Procedural History

. . . .

On October 5, 2010, Parent filed a Complaint for Due Process in the Pennsylvania Office for Dispute Resolution against Mastery and the District. After both Defendants moved to dismiss the complaints, the Hearing Officer asked Parent to respond and asked the parties to brief the issue of where R.B. belonged (or should "stay-put") during the pendency of the administrative proceedings. Parent and the District argued that Mastery was the appropriate stay-put placement for R.B. On November 1, 2010, the Hearing Officer declined to determine R.B's stay-put placement until the underlying Due Process complaint was resolved, finding that "there was no operative placement actually functioning at the time this dispute first arose," and that the "legitimacy of the Student's disenrollment is a mixed question of fact and law that cannot be resolved before the hearing."

On November 17, 2010, Parent, on behalf of R.B., appealed the Hearing Officer's refusal to issue a stay-put order during the pendency of these proceedings by filing this Complaint and pending Motion for a Stay-Put Injunction in this Court. . . .

. . . .

III. DISCUSSION

. . . .

C. The Stay-Put Provision

1. *Legal Standard*

The stay-put provision represents Congress's "policy choice" that "the danger of excluding a handicapped child entitled to an educational placement from that placement was much greater than the harm of allowing a child not entitled to an educational placement to remain in that placement during the pendency of judicial proceedings." Accordingly, the stay-put provision "protect[s] handicapped children and their parents during the review process," by "block[ing] school districts from effecting unilateral change in a child's educational program." The stay-put provision functions, "in essence, as an automatic preliminary injunction" by directing that "during the pendency of any proceedings conducted pursuant to this section . . . the child *shall* remain in the then-current educational placement of the child."

Although Plaintiff need not meet the traditional preliminary injunction standard, an injunction under the stay-put provision is only available where the LEA proposes or effects a change in a student's "educational placement." Therefore, the threshold question is whether Mastery's decision to disenroll R.B. constitutes a change in educational placement. If R.B.'s disenrollment is not a change in educational placement within the meaning of the IDEA, then Mastery was free to disenroll R.B. If, however, R.B.'s disenrollment was a change-in-placement, Mastery is obligated to permit R.B. to remain in her "then-current educational placement." Therefore, if Parent shows that a change in placement has occurred, this Court's narrow inquiry is limited to identifying the proper stay-put placement.

2. *Change in Educational Placement*

Although neither the text nor legislative history of IDEA defines the phrase "change in educational placement," the Third Circuit "gives the term . . . an 'expansive reading.'" Because the "touchstone" inquiry is "whether the decision is likely to affect in some significant way the child's learning experience," Plaintiff must "identify, at a minimum, a fundamental change in, or elimination of a basic element of the education program." Under this approach, "'identifying a change in . . . placement is something of an inexact science,'" and "is, necessarily, fact specific."

Although there are no reported judicial decisions considering whether a public school's unilateral disenrollment of special education students is a change in placement, there is a substantial body of case law analyzing whether the modification or termination of an educational program constitutes a "fundamental change" or "elimination." Those cases distinguish between inconsequential modifications in a student's program and those which "significantly affect the child's learning experience." Unlike program modifications, which change an aspect of a child's special education program, eliminations result in the complete cessation of the delivery of special education services. Courts have found indefinite expulsions, graduation, and transfers from a school outside the district to those within the district all implicate the stay-put rule.

Here, Plaintiff argues that Mastery twice changed R.B.'s placement. First, Parent asserts that when Mastery "banned" her from coming to its campus, she was no longer able to act as a one-to-one aide for R.B. In Parent's view, that change eliminated a crucial related service necessary for R.B. to function in the classroom and constituted a "fundamental change." Second, Parent argues more compellingly that Mastery terminated R.B.'s educational placement by unilaterally disenrolling her on June 19, 2009.

In response, Mastery argues that "there has been no change in this student' [sic] program or placement," and claims that the true issue here "is not program or placement under the IDEA, but truancy." Citing Pennsylvania Law, Mastery claims that it was obligated to disenroll R.B.—regardless of either her Special Education status or the dispute between the Parties—because R.B. had been absent for ten consecutive days. Mastery shifts the blame for R.B.'s disenrollment from itself to Parent, and claims that "[i]t was not Mastery that precluded the student's attendance, it was the parent." In addition, Mastery argues that R.B.'s disenrollment was only a "change in location" and not a change in educational placement.

Because this Court now holds that Mastery's unilateral disenrollment of R.B. was a change in placement, it need not decide herein the highly controverted issue of whether R.B.'s Parent was a "fundamental part" of R.B.'s program—or whether Mastery actually barred Parent from its campus. . . .

The decision to disenroll R.B., however, is a different matter. Although the question of whether a disenrollment constitutes a change in placement is a matter of first impression, principles drawn from the body of law governing disciplinary-based exclusions and graduations provide a useful analytical framework. In both graduation and disciplinary exclusion cases, any change in a special education child's placement must comply with the procedural safeguards—regardless of what outcome state or local laws might dictate for a special education student's non-disabled peers.

For instance, the disciplinary removal of a student with a disability is construed as a change in placement, and may require a school to evaluate the student, conduct a team meeting, propose an alternate special education plan, and provide special education services pending an agreed upon placement. Similarly, courts have held that graduation is a "change in placement" which triggers the protections of the stay-put provision. In *Cronin v. Board of Education*, the court analogized graduation to long-term suspensions and expulsions because both "result[ed] in total exclusion of a child from his or her educational placement." Noting that "[n]o change in placement seems quite so serious nor as worthy of parental involvement and procedural protections as the termination of placement in special education," the Court found that a student's removal from his high school program by graduation during the pendency of proceedings violated the stay-put provision. Like a graduation, indefinite suspension, or expulsion, the unilateral disenrollment of a special education student, which results in the absolute termination of a child's special education program, and purportedly the termination of a LEA's responsibility to deliver FAPE, is a change in placement.

Although R.B.'s disenrollment was not necessarily a disciplinary action, it was precipitated by R.B.'s chronic absenteeism. The record . . . provides ample documentation that R.B.'s disability and medical condition frequently caused her to miss school, and that Mastery modified R.B.'s schedule to accommodate her individual needs. As the agency responsible for administering R.B's educational program, Mastery arguably had an affirmative duty to respond to the absences—potentially caused by R.B.'s disability—through educational intervention. If R.B.'s absences were caused by Mastery's policy choice to require Parent to make an appointment in order to visit the school, Mastery was obligated to provide alternate arrangements so that R.B. could consistently get to school and to her classroom. If every school was able to rid itself of a problematic special education student or her parent by treating them exactly the same as a non-disabled student, as Mastery has done here, the protections of IDEA would be eviscerated.

Finally, Mastery's argument that this was merely a "change in location" is not compelling. It is true, as Mastery claims, that "the stay-put provision of the IDEA is not construed so narrowly as to mandate the student remain in the exact physical location where he or she was schooled at the time the dispute arose." The LEA may, in its discretion, make changes in the physical location of a child's program, if it does not significantly affect the student's program. But although LEAs may exercise discretion over how and where they implement a student's IEP, their primary obligation to implement the IEP remains. At the time Mastery improperly disenrolled R.B., it was—pursuant to its charter and state law—responsible for providing a FAPE to R.B.; and as the party that effected the allegedly unlawful change in placement during the pendency of judicial proceedings, that responsibility continues. Mastery's argument, that when it disenrolled R.B. the responsibility to provide a FAPE to R.B. shifted automatically to the School District of Philadelphia, has no support in fact or in law. Case law does not present a single ruling where an LEA's responsibility for delivering FAPE to an individual student was vitiated simply by closing its doors to that student. Even where a child's then-current educational placement is simply no longer available, the LEA retains responsibility for providing the student with placement in a similar program during the pendency of proceedings.

The line of cases relied on by Mastery are inapposite, because most "program not placement" cases involve proposed changes of schools or classrooms (over which the LEA retains responsibility). Without exception, each case in which the court stresses the importance of program over placement arises where a LEA proposes an interdistrict transfer between classes or schools. There is no case where an LEA has successfully cited "program over placement," to justify its refusal to fulfill its responsibilities under FAPE where no alternative location has been provided by the school district for IEP program implementation. Here, Mastery claims that because the District has similar programming options available for R.B., the District then assumes responsibility for R.B.'s educational placement.

Mastery's attempt to evade its obligations under the IDEA by passing the buck—in this case, a special-needs student's education—to the District is troubling. As a Charter School, Mastery is bound by all the obligations of IDEA. Children with disabilities who attend public charter schools and their parents retain all rights under IDEA and its regulations—a body of laws which were enacted to "strip schools of the *unilateral* authority they had traditionally employed to exclude disabled students, from school." Indeed, the sole purpose of the stay-put provision is to "prevent[] local educational authorities from unilaterally changing a student's existing educational program."

Mastery is correct in asserting that state law provides that a student must be disenrolled after ten consecutive absences. But that law does not exist in a vacuum; because R.B. is a student eligible for special education, Pennsylvania Education Code and the IDEA are also applicable. And to the extent that IDEA might conflict with that state law, it prevails under the Supremacy Clause of the Constitution. Ultimately, Mastery's legal position is untenable. If Mastery seeks to remove her, it must follow the IDEA—it cannot unilaterally expel her from her educational placement during the pendency of proceedings. We therefore conclude that R.B.'s removal from Mastery in June 2009 violated the stay-put provision of the IDEA because proceedings were initiated by the Parent in April 2009 and remained pending at that time and the disenrollment constituted a change in placement.

3. *R.B's Current Educational Placement*

Mastery implausibly argues that it was not R.B.'s then-current educational placement at the time she was disenrolled. "Because the term [stay-put] connotes preservation of the status quo, it refers to the operative placement actually functioning at the time the dispute first arises." If an IEP has been implemented then that program's placement will be the one subject to the stay-put provision.

As this Court has noted, Mastery's argument that location is not synonymous with program is unpersuasive; as R.B.'s LEA, Mastery bears ultimate responsibility for ensuring that R.B.'s program is implemented. Mastery's argument that location is not a component of "educational placement" is not compelling. While "as a general matter, the location of the services is not conclusive in determining what constitutes the educational placement of the student," the physical location of services "cannot be entirely divorced from the inquiry." Instead, "'[t]he meaning of 'educational placement' falls somewhere between the physical school attended by a child and the abstract goals of a child's IEP.'" In *George A.*, the District Court rejected Defendant's argument that the location of services was irrelevant, and acknowledged student's "extensive history" at a particular school as relevant to the determination of his current educational placement. Similarly, in *M.K. & R.K v. Roselle Bd. of Education*, factors including the distance between classrooms, available facilities, and physical location were relevant to the determination of then-current educational placement.

Here, we find that Mastery's location is relevant to R.B.'s educational placement. As Parent testified, Mastery's proximity to R.B.'s home (essentially across the street) mitigated R.B.'s difficulty getting to school, and provided needed access to R.B.'s doctor's office in the case of medical emergency. In addition, Mastery is a small school, which R.B. is able to navigate because of her familiarity with the location. Finally, Mastery provided R.B. with instruction in very small classes, where she was given "lot[s] of individual attention."

Since R.B. was attending Mastery at the time the dispute arose, and because Mastery's learning support program is R.B.'s identified placement in the most recent IEP . . . , R.B.'s current educational placement is Mastery Charter School . . . .

CONCLUSION

For all the reasons detailed above, Mastery must immediately reinstate R.B.'s enrollment during the pendency of the state proceedings, unless Mastery officials and Parent agree on a satisfactory alternative arrangement.

. . . .

Notes, Comments, and Questions

1. The court in *R.B.* used a fact-specific approach to determine whether there was a change in placement, focusing on whether there was a fundamental change in the child's education program that would have a significant effect on the child's learning experience. In adopting this approach, the court cited decisions from the Third Circuit and the District of Columbia Circuit. In the Third Circuit case, the court ruled that changes in the child's school transportation plan did not constitute a change in placement:

> The question of what constitutes a change in educational placement is, necessarily, fact specific. . . . Thus, in determining whether a given modification in a child's school day should be considered a "change in placement," we should focus on the importance of the particular modification involved.
>
> . . . .
>
> . . . We believe that, given the remedial purposes of the Act, the term "change in educational placement" should be given an expansive reading . . . .
>
> . . . The touchstone in interpreting section 1415 has to be whether the decision is likely to affect in some significant way the child's learning experience. In some areas, it may be possible to draw bright lines: for instance, replacing one teacher or aide with another should not require a hearing before the change is made. On the other hand, there are areas where such bright lines will be impossible to draw.
>
> We believe that transportation is such an area. Under some circumstances, transportation may have a significant effect on a child's learning experience. Minor changes in the daily transportation routine, however, will not

> generally have such an impact on the child's learning experience.... In this case, transportation by a parent was replaced with transportation by a stranger, and transportation alone was replaced with transportation as part of a group of children. There was also a slight increase, of approximately ten minutes, in the length of time to be spent in transit, but only on the way home from school.

DeLeon v. Susquehanna Cmty. Sch. Dist., 747 F.2d 149, 153–54 (3d Cir. 1984). Was the Third Circuit's decision that the change in the driver, duration, and number of students did not constitute a change in placement consistent with its "expansive" approach to defining a change in placement?

The District of Columbia Circuit Court of Appeals ruled that the child "must identify, at a minimum, a fundamental change in, or elimination of a basic element of the education program in order for the change to qualify as a change in educational placement." Lunceford v. D. C. Bd. of Educ., 745 F.2d 1577, 1582 (D.C. Cir. 1984) (holding that change in feeding regime for a child with serious disabilities were not changes in placement). Other circuit court formulations of the definition of a change in placement include:

Second Circuit: "[T]he pendency provision does not guarantee a disabled child the right to remain in the exact same school with the exact same service providers while his administrative and judicial proceedings are pending. Instead, it guarantees only the same general level and type of services that the disabled child was receiving." T.M. v. Cornwall Cent. Sch. Dist., 752 F.3d 142, 171 (2d Cir. 2015) (holding that change in service providers but not in services did not constitute a change in placement).

Fifth Circuit: "An educational placement . . . is not changed unless a fundamental change in, or elimination of, a basic element of the educational program has occurred." Sherri A.D. v. W.N. Kirby, 975 F.2d 193, 197, 206 (5th Cir. 1992) (ruling that removing child from her school while continuing to provide appropriate services was not a change in placement).

Eighth Circuit: "The district court properly construed the statute, correctly identifying the change-in-placement issue as fact intensive. The court then made specific findings as to the impact of this change on Jeffrey's education that are not clearly erroneous." Hale v. Poplar Bluff R-I Sch. Dist., 280 F.3d 831, 833, 834 (8th Cir. 2002) (holding that change in location of services from home to school was not a change in placement).

Ninth Circuit: "[A] change in educational placement relates to whether the student is moved from one type of program—i.e., regular class—to another type—i.e., home instruction. A change in the educational placement can also result when there is a significant change in the student's program even if the student remains in the same setting." N.D. v. Haw. Dep't of Educ., 600 F.3d 1104, 1116 (9th Cir. 2010) (holding that teacher furloughs and shutdown of public school did not constitute a change in placement).

Tenth Circuit: "An educational placement is changed when a fundamental change in, or elimination of, a basic element of the educational program has occurred." Erickson v. Albuquerque Pub. Sch., 199 F.3d 1116, 1122 (10th Cir. 1999) (holding that a change in the type of occupational therapy did not violate stay-put provision).

2. Can you discern a consistent principle for defining a change in educational placement from these formulations? How would you apply the principle to the question the court in *R.B.* left open: whether prohibiting the child's mother from acting as an aide constituted a change in educational placement?

3. The court in *R.B.* rejected Mastery's argument that once it disenrolled R.B. the state was responsible for educating the child. The court stated that Mastery could not simply forego its obligation to educate R.B. To what degree was this ruling based on Pennsylvania law, pursuant to which a charter school is its own school district? Would the court have issued the same ruling if Mastery were one school in a larger school district rather than its own district?

4. The court in *R.B.* considered an issue that often arises in stay-put disputes: whether moving a child from one location to another constitutes a change in placement. The court rejected Mastery's argument that it did not violate the IDEA by disenrolling R.B. because in doing so it changed only the location of her services and not her program. The court ruled that although the stay-put provision does not require that a student remain in the same physical location in which she is receiving services, the location where the child is receiving services is related to the implementation of the IEP, and if a change in location creates a significant change in the child's program, it is prohibited. 762 F. Supp. 2d at 760, 763; *see also* Hale v. Poplar Bluff R-I Sch. Dist., 280 F.3d 831, 833 (8th Cir. 2002) (ruling that change in location of services from home to school was a change in placement).

Despite the rulings in *R.B.* and *Hale*, courts have been generally unwilling to find that a change in the location of a child's services constitutes a change in placement. In *A.W. v. Fairfax Cnty. Sch. Bd.*, 372 F.3d 674 (4th Cir. 2004), the court articulated a standard for determining whether a change in location was a change in placement. The court stated:

> Consideration of the structure and the goals of the IDEA as a whole, in addition to its implementing regulations, reinforces our conclusion that the touchstone of the term "educational placement" is not the location to which the student is assigned but rather the environment in which educational services are provided. To the extent that a new setting replicates the educational program contemplated by the student's original assignment and is consistent with the principles of "mainstreaming" and affording access to a FAPE, the goal of protecting the student's "educational placement" served by the "stay-put" provision appears to be met. Likewise, where a change in location results in a dilution of the quality of a student's education or a departure from the student's LRE-compliant setting, a change in "educational placement" occurs.

Id. at 682. Applying this standard, the court found that the transfer of a student to a different elementary school with a "materially" identical program was not a change in placement. *Id.* at 683; *see also* Sherri A.D. v. Kirby, 975 F.2d 193, 206 (5th Cir. 1992) (holding that change in location of services from School for the Blind to a community placement with no accompanying changes to the IEP was not a change in placement); Lunceford v. D.C. Bd. of Educ., 745 F.2d 1577, 1582–83 (D.C. Cir. 1984) (holding that change from in-patient to out-patient treatment was not a change in placement because feeding program was not changed, only providers were changed); Middlebrook v. Sch. Dist. of Cnty. of Knox, 805 F. Supp. 534, 541 (E.D. Tenn. 1991) (ruling that transfer of students with disabilities to different schools pursuant to a desegregation plan was not a change in placement because the students would continue to receive personal review of their educational programs).

5. One court made an exception to the general rule that if a change in location constitutes a change in services it violates the stay-put provision. In *Tilton v. Jefferson Cnty. Bd. of Educ.*, 705 F.2d 800 (6th Cir. 1983), *cert. denied*, 456 U.S. 1056 (1984), the court considered a claim that Kentucky's decision to close the only full-year day treatment program for children with serious emotional handicaps in Jefferson County violated the stay-put provision. The court ruled that the transfer of the students from the school to other schools constituted a change in placement because the other schools did not provide year-round programs. *Id.* at 804. Nevertheless, the court ruled that the stay-put provision does not apply to schools that were closed for purely budgetary reasons. *Id.* at 805. The court reasoned:

> [N]othing in the legislative history or the language of the Act implies a legislative intent to permit interested parties to utilize the automatic injunctive procedure of § 1415(e)(3) to frustrate the fiscal policy of participating states.
>
> It is well-settled that "[b]y and large, public education in our Nation is committed to the control of state and local authorities." These authorities do not, by electing to receive funds under the EHCA, abdicate their control of the fiscal decisions of their school systems. Stated in the alternative, Congress did not compel, as the price for federal participation in education for the handicapped, a wholesale transfer of authority over the allocation of educational resources from the duly elected or appointed state and local boards to the parents of individual handicapped children.
>
> Clearly, however, applying the statutory injunction of § 1415(e)(3) to changes in placement occasioned solely by economic decisions would effect a transfer of power. The appellants could forestall implementation of a fiscal policy decision while pursuing complaints through the procedural framework of § 1415. The exhaustion of administrative remedies coupled with available judicial review contemplated by § 1415 could conceivably entail several years of protracted litigation. During this period, were the Court to accept appellants' position, the state would be obliged to finance a program

> it had determined to be unaffordable simply because concerned parents or guardians alleged deficiencies in substitute programs. Congress certainly never intended such a result.
>
> ....
>
> Finally, our conclusion that § 1415(e)(3) cannot be invoked to foreclose a change in placement arising solely as a result of economic considerations does not necessarily leave appellants without an adequate remedy to contest the sufficiency of the new placements. Appellants may initiate complaints "with respect to any matter relating to the . . . educational placement" of the children pursuant to § 1415(b)(1)(E) and they are insured due process regarding any complaints by virtue of § 1415(b)(2).

Id. at 804–05. Do you agree with the court that the appellants had an adequate remedy in the absence of stay-put protection? The court recognized that, "Because of its belief that erroneous classifications were widespread, Congress determined that the interests of the handicapped child would best be served by imposing the status quo upon placement pending the resolution of any parental complaints prompted by a proposed change in placement." *Id.* at 804. Why did the court decide that this policy should yield to state fiscal policy? The court stated that, "nothing in the legislative history or the language of the Act implies a legislative intent to permit interested parties to utilize the automatic injunctive procedure of § 1415(e)(3) to frustrate the fiscal policy of participating states." *Id.* Should the court also have examined whether there was any support in the legislative history for the proposition that states could not unilaterally change the education it provided to children with disabilities for economic reasons without following the IDEA's procedures? The Court expressed concern that a decision in the children's favor would have transferred power from school boards to parents of children with disabilities. In trying to avoid this, did the court grant too much power to school boards?

The Ninth Circuit distinguished *Tilton's* ruling that the termination of the year-round program was a change of placement in finding that a statewide teacher furlough that resulted in the elimination of seventeen Fridays for all school children did not create a change of placement. The court stated:

> When Congress enacted the IDEA, Congress did not intend it to apply to system-wide administrative decisions. Hawaii's furloughs affect all public schools and all students, disabled and non-disabled alike. An across the board reduction of school days such as the one here does not conflict with Congress' intent of protecting disabled children from being singled out. In comparison to cases in which a child is singled out in relation to her peers, the furlough days do not remove the plaintiffs from the regular classroom setting anymore than they do the other children. Disabled children are not singled out for furlough days. To the extent possible under the new school calendar, the disabled children are still "mainstreamed" with "regular" children at school. To allow the stay-put provisions to apply in this instance

> would be essentially to give the parents of disabled children veto power over a state's decisions regarding the management of its schools. The IDEA did not intend to strip administrative powers away from local school boards and give them to parents of individual children, and we do not read it as doing so.
>
> In *Tilton*, disabled children were transferred from a year-round school to 180-day programs. The court ruled that such a change constituted a change in educational placement. This case is different, as the Sixth Circuit recognized, because year-round school versus the 180-day school reflects two completely different educational programs. The two programs were not comparable. Here, however, the cut in the number of days does not change the model of education, and the educational setting and program pre and post-furlough are comparable.

N.D. v. Haw. Dep't of Educ., 600 F.3d 1104, 116–17 (9th Cir. 2010). Was the Ninth Circuit correct that the Congressional purpose in passing the IDEA was to protect children from being singled out? If so, was this the only purpose or the main purpose? Were there other Congressional purposes for the stay-put provision that are relevant to this case? Upon what authority did the court rely when it said Congress did not intend the IDEA to apply to system-wide administrative decisions? Is the court correct that if the parent prevailed it would allow the stay-put provision to act as a veto power over state administrative decisions?

Section Three
Implementation Issues

A. The Duration of a Stay-Put Order

1. Administrative Hearings and Subsequent Litigation

Courts agree that the phrase in the stay-put provision—"during the pendency of any proceedings"—means that stay-put protection begins when the parent files a due process complaint. K.D. v. Dep't of Educ. of Haw., 665 F.3d 1110, 1117 (9th Cir. 2011). There is controversy, however, over when a stay-put placement ends. One line of cases, commencing with *Andersen v. District of Columbia*, 877 F.2d 1018 (D.C. Cir. 1989), holds that the stay-put placement ends when a parent loses in district court, even if the parent appeals. The court reasoned:

> Subsection 1415(e)(3) states that a stay-put injunction shall be granted during "the pendency of any proceedings conducted pursuant to this section." The "section," 1415, speaks of only three types of proceedings: due process hearings, state administrative review where available, and civil actions for review brought "in any State court of competent jurisdiction or in a district court of the United States." The only other reference in the section to court proceedings (other than the stay-put provision itself) is the last

> sentence of § 1415(e)(2), authorizing "the court" to hear additional evidence; this obviously contemplates only the trial court. Thus, although an appeal is part of a "civil action," Congress' focus appears to have been on the trial stage of proceedings.
>
> ....
>
> Assuming plaintiffs' contention could be shoehorned into the literal language of § 1415(e)(3), it would run counter to the section's purpose. In *Honig v. Doe*, the Supreme Court considered a contention that school districts should be entitled to change a child's placement, despite § 1415(e)(3), when the child's presence posed a danger to others; the Court made clear that the section was intended to protect children from *unilateral* displacement *by school authorities*:
>
> ....
>
> Once a district court has rendered its decision approving a change in placement, that change is no longer the consequence of a unilateral decision by school authorities; the issuance of an automatic injunction perpetuating the prior placement would not serve the section's purpose.

Id. at 1023–24. *See also* Kari H. v. Franklin Special Sch. Dist., 125 F.3d 855 (6th Cir. 1997) (holding that stay-put protection does not apply beyond federal district court); J.E. v. Boyertown Area Sch. Dist., 807 F. Supp. 2d 236, 239–40 (E.D. Pa. 2011) (holding that a stay-put placement does not remain in effect during a parental appeal from a district court decision).

A second line of cases, represented in *Joshua A. v. Rocklin Unified Sch. Dist.*, 559 F.3d 1036, 1040 (9th Cir. 2009), holds that stay-put protection continues until all litigation is over. In rejecting the school district's claim that "the plain language of the stay-put provision" prevents a stay-put placement from continuing on appeal from a district court, the court stated:

> This is an unnecessarily narrow reading of § 1415(j). Civil actions under the IDEA may be brought in federal district courts. Circuit courts have jurisdiction to hear appeals from final judgments of district courts pursuant to 28 U.S.C. § 1291. By giving Joshua the right to appeal the ALJ's decision to the district court, § 1415 also made it possible for Joshua to appeal the dispute to this circuit court. We presume that Congress was aware of this fact when it enacted § 1415(j). We therefore reject the District's position that the plain language of the stay put provision excludes appeals from final judgments of the district courts from civil actions. The Department of Education, in implementing § 1415(j), reaches the same result, requiring maintenance of a child's educational placement "during the pendency of *any* . . . judicial proceeding." *See* 34 C.F.R. § 300.518(a) (2006).

Id. at 1038; *see also* Rome Sch. Comm. v. Mrs. B., 247 F.3d 29, 33 (1st Cir. 2001) (ruling that a stay-put placement ends with circuit court's opinion); Ringwood Bd. of

Educ. v. K.H.J., 469 F. Supp. 2d 267, 270–71 (D.N.J. 2006) (pursuant to IDEA's stay-put provision, granting stay of court's order approving district IEP pending appeal).

2. The Age of the Child

What should happen to a child's stay-put placement if the proceedings do not end by the time the child turns twenty-one, when the child's eligibility for services under the IDEA ends? In *Bd. of Educ. of Oak Park & River Forest High Sch. Dist. 200 v. Ill. State Bd. of Educ.*, 79 F.3d 654, 659–60 (7th Cir. 1996), the Seventh Circuit answered:

> We think that the stay-put provision does indeed cease to operate when a child reaches the age of 21. Except for the judge-created remedial exception for claims for compensatory education, the entitlements created by the Individuals with Disabilities Act expire when the disabled individual turns 21. The purpose of the stay-put provision is to give the child's parents the choice of keeping the child in his existing program until their dispute with the school authorities is resolved. Once the child reaches the age at which he no longer is entitled to the protections of the Act, the stay-put provision, which is intended to prevent the child from losing benefits to which he is entitled, loses its rationale. Its continued application would confer benefits beyond the limit set by Congress.
>
> The exception is where a claim for compensatory education is made. Compensatory education is a benefit that can extend beyond the age of 21. But to allow the stay-put provision, which operates automatically, to operate beyond the age of 21 would enable parents to obtain adult benefits for their child to which they had no entitlement by the simple expedient of filing a claim for compensatory education on the eve of their child's turning 21—exactly what happened here.

Id. at 659–60.

B. Changing the Stay-Put Placement

There are two ways a stay-put placement can be changed: 1) by agreement of the parents and the school district or state, 20 U.S.C. § 1415(j) (2012); and 2) by a state administrative order that agrees that a change in placement is appropriate.

1. Agreement of the Parents and the School District

Although the IDEA provides that the parents and school district can agree to a stay-put placement that is different from the then-current placement, the parties do not always agree that they agreed. *See* J.E. v. Boyertown Area Sch. Dist., 807 F. Supp. 2d 236, 241 (E.D. Pa. 2011) (ruling against parents that the placement in an agreed-upon transition plan was the stay-put placement). In *Millay v. Surry Sch. Dep't*, 584 F. Supp. 2d 219 (D. Me. 2008), for example, the school district argued that the private school placement to which it agreed was not the current placement because the placement was never implemented. In rejecting this argument, the court ruled, "For stay-put purposes, it is sufficient that the MDOE agreed with Ms. Millay that the Perkins IEP should be implemented at Surry, regardless as to whether it actually was implemented." *Id.* at 233; *see also* Evans v. Bd. of Educ. of the Rhinebeck Cent. Sch. Dist., 921 F. Supp. 1184, 1187–88 (S.D.N.Y. 1996) (ruling that agreed-upon private school placement was stay-put placement despite district's claim that the placement was only temporary).

One frequent subject of dispute is whether an agreed-upon placement is temporary and thus not a stay-put placement. The answer depends on whether there were limiting conditions on the duration of the agreement. In *K.D. v. Dep't of Educ. of Haw.*, 665 F.3d 1110 (9th Cir. 2011), the school district agreed to settle an IDEA complaint by paying the child's private school tuition for the 2006–2007 school year. The parent and the school district could not agree on a placement for the child during either the 2007–2008 or 2008–2009 school years, and the parent filed an administrative complaint and argued that the child's private school placement was the stay-put placement because of the agreement for the 2006–2007 school year. In rejecting the parent's argument, the district court ruled, "[W]e hold that Loveland Academy is not K.D.'s stay–put placement because the DOE only agreed to pay tuition for the limited 2006–2007 school year, and never affirmatively agreed to place K.D. at Loveland." *Id.* at 1121; *see also* Verhoeven v. Brunswick Sch. Comm., 207 F.3d 1, 10 (1st Cir. 1999) (ruling that placement at private school was not the stay-put placement because it was temporary); Zvi D. v. Ambach, 694 F.2d 904, 908 (2d Cir. 1982) (holding that district's agreement to pay for private school placement for one year and hearing officer order for it to pay for a second year for failure to provide a physician at an IEP meeting did not render the private school placement the stay-put placement). In contrast, in *Gabel v. Bd. of Educ. of the Hyde Park Cent. Sch. Dist.*, 368 F. Supp. 2d 313, 325 (S.D.N.Y. 2005), the district court ruled that a settlement agreement that required the school district to pay for one year of tuition at a private school was the stay-put placement because there was no durational limit on the placement. Similarly, in *Doe v. Indep. Sch. Dist. No. 9 of Tulsa City*, 938 F. Supp. 758 (N.D. Okla. 1996), the court ruled that the private school to which the district agreed to pay tuition for the child for two years was the stay-put placement after the two years ended:

> Because Union failed to state affirmatively in the agreement that Janice's placement at Private School would be re-evaluated at the end of the 1994–95 school year with a view toward placing her in an appropriate public program for the 1995–96 school year, the parents were entitled to assume that Union would continue to fund Janice's Private School education until such time as another placement was either agreed to by the parties or dictated by administrative and judicial proceedings.

Id. at 761.

2. Decision by the State Level Review Officer

In *School Comm. of the Twn. of Burlington v. Dep't of Educ. of Mass.*, 471 U.S. 359 (1985), the Supreme Court ruled that a decision by a state hearing panel that a parental placement was appropriate constituted an implicit consent by the state to the placement. "The BSEA's decision in favor of the Panicos and the Carroll School placement would seem to constitute agreement by the State to the change of placement." *Id.* at 371; *see also* K.D. v. Dep't of Educ. of Haw., 665 F.3d 1110, 1118 (9th Cir. 2011) ("[A] post-placement administrative or judicial determination can operate to define the 'current educational placement' of a child."); Mackey v. Bd. of Educ. for the Arlington Cent. Sch. Dist., 386 F.3d 158, 163 (2d Cir. 2004) ("[O]nce the SRO rendered a decision in November 2001, there was an agreement changing T.M.'s pendency placement from the public school to the private school."); Board of Educ. v. Schutz, 290 F.3d 476, 484 (2d Cir. 2002), *cert. denied*, 537 U.S. 1227 (2003) (holding that the hearing officer's decision awarding private school tuition reimbursement, affirmed by the state review officer, created the pendency placement); St. Tammany Parish Sch. Bd. v. Slocum, 142 F.3d 776, 781 (5th Cir. 1998), *cert. denied*, 552 U.S. 1076 (1998) (holding that district court did not abuse its discretion by concluding that decision by state review panel constituted an agreement that private school was pendency placement); Susquenita Sch. Dist. v. Raelee S., 96 F.3d 78, 84 (3d Cir. 1996) ("[F]rom the point of the [state appeals] panel decision forward . . . Raelee's pendent placement, by agreement of the state, is the private school . . . ."); Sudbury Pub. Sch. v. Mass. Dep't of Elementary and Secondary Educ., 762 F. Supp. 2d 254, 269 (D. Mass. 2010) (holding that hearing officer's decision "constituted an agreement between the state and Parent regarding student's" stay-put placement); County Sch. Bd. of Henrico Cnty. v. R.T., 433 F. Supp. 2d 692, 710 (E.D. Va. 2006) (holding that "once the State hearing officer decides that the proper placement is in a private school, the school board must bear the cost of that placement, including whether the school board is appealing the State Hearing Officer's decision."); Murphy v. Arlington Cent. Sch. Dist. Bd. of Educ., 86 F. Supp. 2d 354, 358 (S.D.N.Y. 2000), *aff'd*, 297 F.3d 195 (2d Cir. 2002) (holding that once the SRO determined that the private school offered an appropriate placement, there was an agreement between the parents and the school district that changed the child's pendency placement to the private school).

Can other authoritative decisions constitute state consent? One court ruled that judicial decisions in favor of parents create state consent. *K.D.*, 665 F.3d at 1118 (holding that when "a parent unilaterally changes the placement of a child, but a subsequent administrative or judicial decision confirms that the parental placement is appropriate, the decision 'constitutes [a]n agreement by the State to the change of placement'"). Do local hearing officer decisions create state consent? In *T.H. v. Bd. of Educ. of Palatine Cmty. Consol. Sch. Dist.*, 55 F. Supp. 2d 830, 845–46 (N.D. Ill. 1999), the court ruled that a change in the stay-put placement begins on the date the local hearing officer issues its decision in the parents' favor.

Two courts made an exception to the general rule that a decision by an SRO in favor of the parents creates a stay-put placement, ruling that a placement based on a ruling that the school district had committed a procedural violation does not constitute a stay-put placement. *See* L.M. v. Capistrano Unified Sch. Dist., 556 F.3d 900, 903–04 (9th Cir. 2009), *cert. denied*, 558 U.S. 819 (2009) (making an exception for a placement based on a procedural violation); Leonard v. McKenzie, 869 F.2d 1558, 1563–64 (D.C. Cir.1989) (holding that hearing officer's decision allowing child to finish year at current placement was based on procedural violations and that the placement would not continue past the current school year).

C. Obligation to Pay Private School Tuition

Several issues arise regarding who must pay tuition when a child with a disability is in a private school during the pendency of IDEA proceedings under Section 1415. The issue arises in at least three different scenarios: 1) the private school placement is the then-current educational placement; 2) the parents transferred the child from the then-current placement in a public school to a private school; 3) the then-current placement is a private school but the final determination in the case is that the private school placement was not an appropriate placement.

1. The Current Placement is a Private School

If the child's current placement is in a private school, the school district must pay the tuition during the pendency of the case. Ashland Sch. Dist. v. Parents of Student E.H., 587 F.3d 1175, 1186 (9th Cir. 2009) ("Once a state hearing officer concludes that a residential placement is necessary to provide a child with FAPE, the child's school district must pay for the cost of the placement for the pendency of any subsequent appeal."); Susquenita Sch. Dist. v. Raelee S., 96 F.3d 78, 85 (3d Cir. 1996) (holding that the school district is required to pay for pendent school placement in a private school); Drinker v. Colonial Sch. Dist., 78 F.3d 859, 867 (3d Cir. 1996) (ruling that school district was requried to pay for a stay-put placement at a private school); Clovis Unified Sch. Dist. v. California Office of Admin. Hearings., 903 F.2d 635, 640 (9th Cir. 1990) (holding that school district is responsible for paying the costs of stay-put placement at private school "regardless of which party prevails in this appeal.").

2. The Parents Transferred their Child to a Private School

Who is obliged to pay tuition when the parents transfer their child from a current public school placement to a private school prior to the resolution of a case and an SRO ultimately rules that the private school is the appropriate placement? The courts' starting point in deciding this question has been *Sch. Comm. of the Twn. of Burlington v. Dep't of Educ. of Mass.*, 471 U.S. 359 (1985). There, the Supreme Court stated:

> This is not to say that . . . [the stay-put] provision has no effect on parents. While we doubt that this provision would authorize a court to order parents to leave their child in a particular placement, we think it operates in such a

> way that parents who unilaterally change their child's placement during the pendency of review proceedings, without the consent of state or local school officials, do so at their own financial risk. If the courts ultimately determine that the IEP proposed by the school officials was appropriate, the parents would be barred from obtaining reimbursement for any interim period in which their child's placement violated . . . [the stay-put provision].

Id. at 373–74. Courts have construed this to mean that parents who transfer their child out of the then-current placement during the pendency of proceedings are not entitled to reimbursement under the stay-put provision until the state issues a decision that the private school placement is the appropriate placement. In *Mackey v. Bd. of Educ. for the Arlington Cent. Sch. Dist. Bd. of Educ.*, 386 F.3d 158, 164–166 (2d Cir. 2004), the Second Circuit agreed that the SRO's decision in favor of the parents created a change in placement and ruled that the effective date of the stay-put placement was the date the state review officer should have issued the decision based on time limits specified in the IDEA regulations. As a result, the parents were entitled to tuition reimbursement; *see also* Murphy v. Arlington Cent. Sch. Dist. Bd. of Educ., 86 F. Supp. 2d 354, 367 (S.D.N.Y. 2000), *aff'd*, 297 F.3d 195 (2d Cir. 2002) (holding that the school district's financial responsibility for the stay-put placement began on the date the SRO should have issued a ruling).

3. A Private School Stay-Put Placement is not the Ultimate FAPE Placement

Who is required to pay for a stay-put placement in a private school if the parents ultimately lose the case and a hearing officer or court rules that a public school placement is appropriate? Courts have offered various opinions. Two courts ruled that the district would not be reimbursed. In *Clovis Unified Sch. Dist. v. Cal. Office of Amin. Hearings*, 903 F.2d 635 (9th Cir. 1990), the court held:

> The Shoreys . . . argue persuasively that the school district and the state are responsible for the costs of Michelle's placement during the court review proceedings regardless of which party prevails in the appeal. They argue that the purpose and the language of the Act support a holding that Clovis, under the stay put provisions, was responsible for keeping Michelle in the King's View placement after the administrative decision that the placement was appropriate, and until a court directed otherwise.

Id. at 641; *see also* Henry v. Sch. Admin. Unit No. 29, 70 F. Supp. 2d 52, 59 (D.N.H. 1999) (stating that "school district must pay for the [stay-put] placement from the date of the agency decision without right to reimbursement," even if the district ultimately prevails).

Two courts identified the question as open but opined that the school district should not be reimbursed. In *Casey K. v. St. Anne Cmty. High Sch. Dist. No. 302*, 400 F.3d 508 (7th Cir. 2005), *cert. denied*, 596 U.S. 821 (2005), the court stated:

> It is an open question whether, even if the parents lose their challenge, they must reimburse the public entity for the expense of the private-school placement to which the child, it turns out, was not entitled. The Act doesn't say; doubtless the draftsmen had in mind that the stay-put provision would be invoked to keep the child in his current public school . . . rather than in a private school, although there is no doubt that the state must pay for the private school if the state's own schools don't have a program to which the Act entitles a disabled child, and a private school does. The argument for giving the parents a free ride is that otherwise they might be timid about trying to enforce their statutory right to a free private education in an appropriate case. The educational services required by the Individuals with Disabilities Education Act are often very costly–and when provided by a public school, far beyond the means of the average public school parent. The risk of an adverse decision by a hearing officer that would require reimbursement of the private school's charges would deter many parents from enrolling their child in a private school unless they were certain of their right to do so.

Id. at 510–11. The court in *Murphy v. Arlington Cent. Sch. Dist. Bd. of Educ.*, 86 F. Supp. 2d 354 (S.D.N.Y. 2000), *aff'd*, 297 F.3d 195 (2d Cir. 2002), also identified the question as open, and expressed a similar opinion regarding reimbursement:

> I do not decide whether the District may recoup payments made to maintain the current educational placement should it ultimately prevail on the merits. That question is not presently before me. However, the District's claim for recoupment in that circumstance may be problematical. . . . Only when parents unilaterally change the child's placement do they do so at their own financial risk. Once there is an "agreement" regarding the private school placement, the parents are again entitled to all the protections of the IDEA. Parents should not be held accountable for the cost of a placement to which the state or school district has "agreed." Otherwise, the stay-put provision is rendered meaningless.

Id. at 367, n.9.

Finally, two courts identified the question as open and did not offer an opinion. *See* St. Tammany Parish Sch. Bd., 142 F.3d 776, 789 (5th Cir. 1998) ("[W]e do not now address whether, should the State defendants prevail, the Department can recover some, if not all, of the stay-put costs."); Susquenita Sch. Dist. v. Raelee S., 96 F.3d 78, 87, n.10 (3d Cir. 1996) ("We do not address the issue of the school district's ability to recover tuition payments from Raelee's parents should the school district ultimately prevail.").

D. Enforcing the Stay-Put Provision

The stay-put provision is mandatory and self-activating upon the commencement of any proceedings pursuant to Section 1415. Nevertheless, as described above, parents and school districts often disagree about what constitutes a child's then-current educational placement, whether the district is implementing the placement, and whether the district has changed it. The IDEA does not contain specific language about how to resolve disputes over the stay-put placement. Enforcing a stay-put placement has some urgency, and thus parents will often seek a rapid resolution of a stay-put dispute in federal court by seeking a preliminary injunction ordering the district to implement the stay-put placement the parents seek. Ordinarily, a party seeking a preliminary injunction in federal court must prove several factors, including likelihood of success on the merits, irreparable harm in the absence of immediate injunctive relief, and a balance of equities in the moving party's favor. Courts, however, often describe the stay-put provision "as an 'automatic' preliminary injunction, meaning the moving party need not show the traditionally required factors (e.g. irreparable harm) in order to obtain preliminary relief." Joshua A. v. Rocklin Unified Sch. Dist., 559 F.3d 1036, 1037 (9th Cir. 2009). The Second Circuit agrees. In *Zvi D. v. Ambach*, 694 F.2d 904 (2d Cir. 1982), the court stated:

> This [the stay-put] provision is, in effect, an automatic preliminary injunction. The statute substitutes an absolute rule in favor of the status quo for the court's discretionary consideration of the factors of irreparable harm and either a likelihood of success on the merits or a fair ground for litigation and a balance of hardships.

Id. at 906.

Several courts agree and have not required parents to prevail on the discretionary factors for granting a preliminary injunction in order to obtain a stay-put remedy. *See, e.g.*, Board of Educ. of Cmty. High Sch. Dist. No. 218 v. Ill. State Bd. of Educ., 103 F.3d 545, 550 (7th Cir. 1996) ("The equitable balancing required for preliminary injunction has no place in this context."); R.B. v. Mastery Charter Sch., 762 F. Supp. 2d 745, 756–57 (E.D. Pa. 2010) (stating that "Plaintiff need not meet the traditional preliminary injunction standard"); Ringwood Bd. of Educ. v. K.H.J., 469 F. Supp. 2d 267, 271 (D.N.J. 2006) (stating that the usual preliminary injunction analysis does not apply to stay-put relief); Laster v. District of Columbia, 439 F. Supp. 2d 93, 98–99 (D.D.C. 2006) (holding that stay-put provision is an automatic preliminary injunction to which the traditional preliminary injunction factors do not apply); Beth B. v. Van Clay, 126 F. Supp. 2d 532, 533 (N.D. Ill. 2000) ("[W]e do not engage in the equitable balancing customary in determining whether or not a preliminary injunction should issue.").

In contrast, two courts ruled that the traditional preliminary injunction analysis applies to requests for a stay-put remedy. *See* Van Scoy v. San Luis Coastal Unified Sch. Dist., 353 F. Supp. 2d 1083, 1084–85 (C.D. Cal. 2005) (requiring plaintiff to show discretionary factors); Henry v. Sch. Admin. Unit No. 29, 70 F. Supp. 2d 52, 58 (D.N.H. 1999) ("[T]he stay-put provision entitles the parents of a disabled child to a preliminary injunction preserving the child's current placement during the pendency of an IDEA dispute unless the School District can demonstrate that the application of the traditional preliminary injunction criteria warrant a different result."). With which position do you agree? Does the application of traditional preliminary injunction standards to a stay-put request weaken stay-put protection?

Courts have also employed the traditional preliminary injunction analysis in two distinct scenarios. First, courts have applied it to parental requests to change the stay-put placement pending completion of due process proceedings. *See* Johnson v. Special Educ. Hearing Office, 287 F.3d 1176, 1180 (9th Cir. 2002) (holding that the district court appropriately considered preliminary injunction factors because the parents were seeking to enjoin an existing stay-put order); Doe v. Brookline Sch. Comm., 722 F.2d 910, 917 (1st Cir. 1983) (holding that preliminary injunction analysis applies to change the current placement); Millay v. Surry Sch. Dep't, 584 F. Supp. 2d 219, 234 (D. Me. 2008) (holding that traditional preliminary injunction analysis applies when parent is seeking to change the stay-put placement). Second, courts have applied the traditional preliminary injunction analysis in litigation that relates to whether stay-put protection applies in a particular circumstance. *See* N.D. v. Haw. Dep't of Educ., 600 F.3d 1104, 1112 (9th Cir. 2010) (holding that in challenge to a statewide reduction in the number of school days, the traditional preliminary injunction analysis applies because the underlying issue is whether the stay-put provision applies); Aliah K. v. Haw. Dep't of Educ., 788 F. Supp. 2d 1176, 1187 (D. Haw. 2011) (holding that automatic injunction standard applies when the court considers a direct invocation of the stay-put provision; preliminary injunction analysis applies to a motion that affects a stay-put invocation but is not itself the invocation).

Part V

Enforcing the IDEA

Chapter 13

Enforcing the IDEA in Federal Court: Constitutional Requirements

Introduction

Federal courts are courts of limited jurisdiction, meaning that they do not have unlimited authority to hear cases. Instead, they have only the power to hear cases that the Constitution authorizes them to hear. Two constitutional provisions are relevant in IDEA cases. First, Article III, Section 2 of the United States Constitution, which vests the federal courts with their jurisdiction to hear cases, limits federal court jurisdiction to "cases" and "controversies"arising under federal law:

> The judicial power [of the United States] shall extend to all cases, in law and equity, arising under this constitution, the laws of the United States, and treaties made, or which shall be made, under their authority; to all cases affecting ambassadors, other public ministers and consuls; to all cases of admiralty and maritime jurisdiction; to controversies to which the United States shall be a party; to controversies between two or more States . . . , between citizens of different States, between citizens of the same state claiming lands under grants of different States, and between a state, or the citizens thereof, and foreign states, citizens, or subjects.

U.S. Const. art. III, § 2. As a result of the "case or controversy" requirement of Article III, federal courts have developed the "standing" and "mootness" doctrines to ensure that the cases they hear are real, live controversies between at least two opposing parties.

Second, the Eleventh Amendment to the Constitution states:

> The Judicial power of the United States shall not be construed to extend to any suit in law or equity, commenced or prosecuted against one of the United States by Citizens of another State, or by Citizens or Subjects of any Foreign State.

U.S. Const. amend. XI. The Supreme Court has construed the Eleventh Amendment to give immunity to states against lawsuits in federal court, which is known as "sovereign immunity."

This chapter will cover the three constitutional limits on enforcing the IDEA in federal court: standing (Section One); mootness (Section Two); and sovereign immunity (Section Three).

The law relating to federal court enforcement of the IDEA is complex and at times seemingly contradictory. Courts often reach different decisions in similar cases that are often difficult to reconcile. As you work through the issues raised by federal court enforcement of the IDEA, you may feel frustrated, but take heart. Federal court enforcement of the IDEA vexes even federal court judges, one of whom was prompted to observe:

> The Individuals with Disabilities Act is not a well-drafted law. Its goal of providing a free and meaningful education to every disabled child in America is undoubtedly a noble one. By all accounts it has done much to achieve that goal. Yet, as this case illustrates, after thirty years and much congressional tinkering, the text of the IDEA still leaves courts at a loss to answer many basic questions about how it is to be enforced, such as who may sue whom, for what, and in what court.

S.C. v. Deptford Twp. Bd. of Educ., 213 F. Supp. 2d 452, 454 (D.N.J. 2002). As you read this and subsequent chapters on federal court enforcement of the IDEA, remember the judge's plaint and consider whether you agree.

Problem

Jean is an attorney who specializes in representing parents and children in special education cases. She has recently noticed an increase in the number of parents who have come to see her complaining that the local school district suspended their children for more than ten days without convening a manifestation determination review team (MDRT). Yesterday, Jean met with a group that included parents, an organization that advocates for people with disabilities, and a local company that provides tutoring services, about this issue. They each described their experiences. The basic story the parents provided was the same. Each of their children is in high school. Each is classified with one or more disabilities, including emotional disturbance, learning disability, and speech and language impairment. The high school principal sent a letter to each parent that their child had been suspended, each for more than ten days. None of the parents, children, or organizations have filed an IDEA complaint.

In addition to these general common facts, each participant in the meeting presented unique facts as follows:

- Parents B.G. and C.G. are divorced. Parent B.G. has custody of child D.G. as well as complete control over decisions regarding her education. B.G. is not interested in pursuing a remedy, but C.G. is. C.G. wants to hire Jean to represent her and D.G.
- Parent E.K. is the non-custodial parent of child F.K. E.K. attended the meeting because G.K., the custodial parent, could not attend.

* Child H.W. dropped out of school, in large part because he got so far behind due to several suspensions—all of which occurred without convening an MDRT—that he was discouraged from continuing school and dropped out. He is nineteen years old, working, and is not sure whether he will return to school.

* Y.D.'s record of suspensions is similar to H.W.'s, but Y.D., also nineteen, graduated from high school.

* Advocates for People with Disabilities (APD) is a disability rights organization. Its activities include assisting parents of children with disabilities navigate all aspects of the special education process, including dealing with disciplinary proceedings. APD has worked with several parents relating to the issues described above, including writing letters to the school district's superintendent complaining about the district's failure to convene appropriate MDRTs and sending a letter to the state commissioner of education about the same issue.

* Learning Made E-Z (LME-Z) is a for-profit company that provides tutoring services to high school students. LME-Z has a contract with the district pursuant to which it receives a flat fee for the entire school year for providing tutoring services to children with disabilities who are suspended. LME-Z claims that because the district does not convene MDRTs the number of suspended students with disabilities is fifty percent higher than anticipated and that it is losing money on its contract.

Jean is considering whether to take these cases. She is considering several questions. Please help her think through them:

(1) Who among the group can file a request for an impartial hearing?

(2) What claims could they each raise?

(3) Which complainants would have standing in federal court to challenge an unfavorable impartial hearing decision?

(4) Who can be named as a respondent in the impartial hearing requests?

(5) Could those respondents subsequently be sued as defendants in federal court?

(6) What additional information, if any, does Jean need to answer these questions?

Section One
Standing

Broadly speaking, the rules of standing govern who can bring a claim in federal court. Standing doctrine "encompasses both constitutional and prudential requirements." Weber v. Cranston Sch. Comm., 212 F.3d 41, 50, 51 (1st Cir. 2000) (ruling that plaintiff had standing to pursue retaliation claim under the IDEA). The constitutional requirements are based on Article III of the Constitution, which allows federal courts to hear only cases or controversies. The federal courts have interpreted this to mean that a plaintiff must suffer an actual injury traceable to the defendant that can be redressed by a positive judicial decision. *Id.* at 50. The prudential requirements are that the plaintiff must assert her own rights rather than the rights of others, the harm must be particular to her and not a general grievance, and the plaintiff's claims must be within the "zone of interests" the relevant statute protects. *Id.* at 50–51.

Standing in IDEA cases is made complicated by the IDEA's requirement that a plaintiff must exhaust administrative remedies before filing a case in federal court. Because of the exhaustion requirement, there are two paths to bringing an IDEA case in federal court. First, any party aggrieved at the administrative level can file a case in federal court:

> Any party aggrieved by the findings and decisions made under subsection (f) [an impartial hearing] or (k) [a hearing relating to a disciplinary change in placement] who does not have the right to an appeal under subsection (g) [an appeal to a state level official], and any party aggrieved by the findings and decision made under this subsection, shall have the right to bring a civil action with respect to the complaint presented pursuant to this section, which action may be brought in any State court of competent jurisdiction or in a district court of the United States, without regard to the amount in controversy.

20 U.S.C. § 1415(i)(2)(A)(2012). In cases filed in federal court pursuant to Section 1415(i)(2)(A), the issues regarding standing are thus whether the plaintiff is: 1) a party; and 2) aggrieved by the administrative proceeding.

The courts also allow a plaintiff to bypass the IDEA's administrative procedures and bring a case directly in federal court in certain circumstances that are described more fully in Chapter Fourteen. When a plaintiff has bypassed the IDEA's administrative procedures, she cannot invoke Section 1415(i)(2)(A) in support of her claim for standing. Instead, the courts apply the constitutional and prudential requirements for standing in such cases. As you read the cases in this section, consider whether plaintiffs pursued administrative remedies or bypassed them and how that made a difference in the court's standing analysis.

This section considers whether several categories of plaintiffs have standing to bring claims under the IDEA. These include parents, third-party plaintiffs, and organizations.

A. Parents

As mentioned, Section 1415(i)(A)(2) states that any "party" to an impartial hearing aggrieved by an administrative decision can challenge the decision in federal court. However, Section 1415(i)(A)(2) does not define "party." Is the parent of a child with a disability who was aggrieved at the administrative level a party under Section 1415(i)(A)(2) with standing to bring a claim in federal court on her own behalf? In *Winkleman v. Parma City Sch. Dist.*, the Supreme Court considered whether parents have their own rights under the IDEA and can thus be a "party" under the IDEA with standing to bring a case in federal court if aggrieved at the administrative level.

Winkleman v. Parma City Sch. Dist.

550 U.S. 516 (2007)

Justice Kennedy delivered the opinion of the Court.

. . . .

Jacob has autism spectrum disorder . . . . His parents worked with the school district to develop an individualized education program (IEP) . . . . All concede that Jacob's parents had the statutory right to contribute to this process and, when agreement could not be reached, to participate in . . . an "impartial due process hearing."

The disagreement at the center of the current dispute concerns the procedures to be followed when parents and their child, dissatisfied with the outcome of the due process hearing, seek further review in a United States District Court. The question is whether parents, either on their own behalf or as representatives of the child, may proceed in court unrepresented by counsel though they are not trained or licensed as attorneys. Resolution of this issue requires us to examine and explain the provisions of IDEA to determine if it accords to parents rights of their own that can be vindicated in court proceedings, or alternatively, whether the Act allows them, in their status as parents, to represent their child in court proceedings.

I

. . . .

The school district proposed an IEP for the 2003–2004 school year that would have placed Jacob at a public elementary school. Regarding this IEP as deficient under IDEA, Jacob's nonlawyer parents availed themselves of the administrative review provided by IDEA. They filed a complaint alleging respondent had failed to provide Jacob with a free appropriate public education; they appealed the hearing officer's rejection of the claims . . . to a state-level review officer; and after losing that appeal they filed, on their own behalf and on behalf of Jacob, a complaint in the United States District Court for the Northern District of Ohio. In reliance upon 20 U.S.C. § 1415(i)(2) . . . , they challenged the administrative decision, alleging, among other matters: that Jacob had not been provided with a free appropriate public education; that his IEP was inadequate; and that the school district had failed to follow procedures mandated by IDEA. . . .

The District Court granted respondent's motion for judgment on the pleadings, finding it had provided Jacob with a free appropriate public education. Petitioners, proceeding without counsel, filed an appeal with the Court of Appeals for the Sixth

Circuit. . . . [T]he Court of Appeals entered an order dismissing the Winkelmans' appeal unless they obtained counsel to represent Jacob. . . .

Petitioners sought review in this Court. In light of the disagreement among the Courts of Appeals as to whether a nonlawyer parent of a child with a disability may prosecute IDEA actions *pro se* in federal court, we granted certiorari. . . .

II

Our resolution of this case turns upon the significance of IDEA's interlocking statutory provisions. Petitioners' primary theory is that the Act makes parents real parties in interest to IDEA actions, not "mer[e] guardians of their children's rights." If correct, this allows Mr. and Mrs. Winkleman back into court, for there is no question that a party may represent his or her own interests in federal court without the aid of counsel. Petitioners cannot cite a specific provision in IDEA mandating in direct and explicit terms that parents have the status of real parties in interest. They instead base their argument on a comprehensive reading of IDEA. Taken as a whole, they contend, the Act leads to the necessary conclusion that parents have independent, enforceable rights. Respondent, accusing petitioners of "knit[ting] together various provisions pulled from the crevices of the statute" to support these claims, reads the text of IDEA to mean that any redressable rights under the Act belong only to children.

We agree that the text of IDEA resolves the question presented. We recognize, in addition, that a proper interpretation of the Act requires a consideration of the entire statutory scheme. Turning to the current version of IDEA, which the parties agree governs this case, we begin with an overview of the relevant statutory provisions.

A

The goals of IDEA include "ensur[ing] that all children with disabilities have available to them a free appropriate public education" and "ensur[ing] that the rights of children with disabilities and parents of such children are protected." 20 U.S.C. §§ 1400(d)(1)(A)-(B). . . . To this end, the Act includes provisions governing four areas of particular relevance to the Winkelmans' claim: procedures to be followed when developing a child's IEP; criteria governing the sufficiency of an education provided to a child; mechanisms for review that must be made available when there are objections to the IEP or to other aspects of IDEA proceedings; and the requirement in certain circumstances that States reimburse parents for various expenses. *See generally* §§ 1412(a)(10), 1414, 1415. . . .

IDEA requires school districts to develop an IEP for each child with a disability, see §§ 1412(a)(4), 1414(d), with parents playing "a significant role" in this process, *Schaffer v. Weast*, 546 U.S. 49 (2005). . . . Parents serve as members of the team that develops the IEP. § 1414(d)(1)(B). The "concerns" parents have "for enhancing the education of their child" must be considered by the team. § 1414(d)(3)(A)(ii). IDEA accords parents additional protections that apply throughout the IEP process. See, *e.g.*, § 1414(d)(4)(A) (requiring the IEP Team to revise the IEP when appropriate to address certain information provided by the parents); § 1414(e) (requiring States to "ensure that the parents of [a child with a disability] are members of any group that makes decisions on the educational placement of their child"). The statute also sets up general procedural safeguards that protect the informed involvement of parents in the development of an education for their child. See, *e.g.*, § 1415(a) (requiring States to "establish and maintain procedures . . . to ensure that children with disabilities and their parents are guaranteed procedural safeguards with respect to the provision of a free appropriate public education"); § 1415(b)(1) (mandating that States provide an opportunity for parents to examine all relevant records). See generally §§ 1414, 1415. A central purpose of the parental protections is to facilitate the provision of a "'free appropriate public education,'" § 1401(9), which must be made available to the child "in conformity with the [IEP]," § 1401(9)(D).

The Act defines a "free appropriate public education" pursuant to an IEP to be an educational instruction "specially designed . . . to meet the unique needs of a child with a disability," § 1401(29), coupled with any additional "'related services'" that are "required to assist a child with a disability to benefit from [that instruction]," § 1401(26)(A). The education must, among other things, be provided "under public supervision and direction," "meet the standards of the State educational agency," and "include an appropriate preschool, elementary school, or secondary school education in the State involved." The instruction must, in addition, be provided at "no cost to parents." § 1401(29).

When a party objects to the adequacy of the education provided, the construction of the IEP, or some related matter, IDEA provides procedural recourse: It requires that a State provide "[a]n opportunity for any party to present a complaint . . . with respect to any matter relating to the identification, evaluation, or educational placement of the child, or the provision of a free appropriate public education to such child." § 1415(b)(6). By presenting a complaint a party is able to pursue a process of review that, as relevant, begins with a preliminary meeting "where the parents of the child discuss their complaint" and the local educational agency "is provided the opportunity to [reach a resolution]." § 1415(f)(1)(B)(i)(IV). If the agency "has not resolved the complaint to the satisfaction of the parents within 30 days," § 1415(f)(1)(B)(ii), the parents may request an "impartial due process hearing," § 1415(f)(1)(A), which must be conducted either by the local educational agency or by the state educational agency . . . and where a hearing officer will resolve issues raised in the complaint, § 1415(f)(3).

. . . .

IDEA . . . provides for at least two means of cost recovery that inform our analysis. First, in certain circumstances it allows a court or hearing officer to require a state agency "to reimburse the parents [of a child with a disability] for the cost of [private-school] enrollment if the court or hearing officer finds that the agency had not made a free appropriate public education available to the child." § 1412(a)(10)(C)(ii). Second, it sets forth rules governing when and to what extent a court may award attorney's fees. See § 1415(i)(3)(B). Included in this section is a provision allowing an award "to a prevailing party who is the parent of a child with a disability." § 1415(i)(3)(B)(i)(I).

B

Petitioners construe these various provisions to accord parents independent, enforceable rights under IDEA. We agree. The parents enjoy enforceable rights at the administrative stage, and it would be inconsistent with the statutory scheme to bar them from continuing to assert these rights in federal court.

The statute sets forth procedures for resolving disputes in a manner that, in the Act's express terms, contemplates parents will be the parties bringing the administrative complaints. In addition to the provisions we have cited, we refer also to § 1415(b)(8) (requiring a state educational agency to "develop a model form to assist parents in filing a complaint"); § 1415(c)(2) (addressing the response an agency must provide to a "parent's due process complaint notice"); and § 1415(i)(3)(B)(i) (referring to "the parent's complaint"). A wide range of review is available: Administrative complaints may be brought with respect to "any matter relating to . . . the provision of a free appropriate public education." § 1415(b)(6)(A). Claims raised in these complaints are then resolved at impartial due process hearings, where, again, the statute makes clear that parents will be participating as parties. See also § 1415(f)(3) (indicating "[a] parent or agency shall request an impartial due process hearing" within a certain period of time); § 1415(e)(2)(A)(ii) (referring to "a parent's right to a due process hearing"). The statute then grants "[a]ny party aggrieved by the findings and decision made [by the hearing officer] . . . the right to bring a civil action with respect to the complaint." § 1415(i)(2)(A).

Nothing in these interlocking provisions excludes a parent who has exercised his or her own rights from statutory protection the moment the administrative proceedings end. Put another way, the Act does not *sub silentio* or by implication bar parents from seeking to vindicate the rights accorded to them once the time comes to file a civil action. Through its provisions for expansive review and extensive parental involvement, the statute leads to just the opposite result.

Respondent, resisting this line of analysis, asks us to read these provisions as contemplating parental involvement only to the extent parents represent their child's interests. In respondent's view IDEA accords parents nothing more than "collateral tools related to the child's underlying substantive rights—not freestanding or independently enforceable rights."

This interpretation, though, is foreclosed by provisions of the statute. IDEA defines one of its purposes as seeking "to ensure that the rights of children with disabilities and parents of such children are protected." § 1400(d)(1)(B). The word "rights" in the quoted language refers to the rights of parents as well as the rights of the child; otherwise the grammatical structure would make no sense.

Further provisions confirm this view. IDEA mandates that educational agencies establish procedures "to ensure that children with disabilities and their parents are guaranteed procedural safeguards with respect to the provision of a free appropriate public education." § 1415(a). It presumes parents have rights of their own when it defines how States might provide for the transfer of the "rights accorded to parents" by IDEA, § 1415(m)(1)(B), and it prohibits the raising of certain challenges "[n]otwithstanding any other individual right of action that a parent or student may maintain under [the relevant provisions of IDEA]," §§ 1401(10)(E), 1412(a)(14)(E). To adopt respondent's reading of the statute would require an interpretation of these statutory provisions (and others) far too strained to be correct.

Defending its countertextual reading of the statute, respondent cites a decision by a Court of Appeals concluding that the Act's "references to parents are best understood as accommodations to the fact of the child's incapacity." *Doe v. Board of Ed. of Baltimore Cty.*, 165 F.3d 260, 263 (CA4 1998). This, according to respondent, requires us to interpret all references to parents' rights as referring in implicit terms to the child's rights—which, under this view, are the only enforceable rights accorded by IDEA. Even if we were inclined to ignore the plain text of the statute in considering this theory, we disagree that the sole purpose driving IDEA's involvement of parents is to facilitate vindication of a child's rights. It is not a novel proposition to say that parents have a recognized legal interest in the education and upbringing of their child. There is no necessary bar or obstacle in the law, then, to finding an intention by Congress to grant parents a stake in the entitlements created by IDEA. Without question a parent of a child with a disability has a particular and personal interest in fulfilling "our national policy of ensuring equality of opportunity, full participation, independent living, and economic self-sufficiency for individuals with disabilities." § 1400(c)(1).

We therefore find no reason to read into the plain language of the statute an implicit rejection of the notion that Congress would accord parents independent, enforceable rights concerning the education of their children. We instead interpret the statute's references to parents' rights to mean what they say: that IDEA includes provisions conveying rights to parents as well as to children.

A variation on respondent's argument has persuaded some Courts of Appeals. The argument is that while a parent can be a "party aggrieved" for aspects of the hearing officer's findings and decision, he or she cannot be a "party aggrieved" with respect to all IDEA-based challenges. Under this view the causes of action available to a parent might relate, for example, to various procedural mandates and reimbursement demands, see, *e.g.*, § 1412(a)(10)(C)(ii). The argument supporting this conclusion proceeds as follows: Because a "party aggrieved" is, by definition, entitled to a remedy, and parents are, under IDEA, only entitled to certain procedures and reimbursements as remedies, a parent cannot be a "party aggrieved" with regard to any claim not implicating these limited matters.

This argument is contradicted by the statutory provisions we have recited. True, there are provisions in IDEA stating parents are entitled to certain procedural protections and reimbursements; but the statute prevents us from placing too much weight on the implications to be drawn when other entitlements are accorded in less clear language. We find little support for the inference that parents are excluded by implication whenever a child is mentioned, and vice versa. Compare, *e.g.*, § 1411(e)(3)(E) (barring States from using certain funds for costs associated with actions "brought on behalf of a child" but failing to acknowledge that actions might also be brought on behalf of a parent) with § 1415(i)(3)(B)(I) (allowing recovery of attorney's fees to a "prevailing party who is the parent of a child with a disability" but failing to acknowledge that a child might also be a prevailing party). Without more, then, the language in IDEA confirming that parents enjoy particular procedural and reimbursement-related rights does not resolve whether they are also entitled to enforce IDEA's other mandates, including the one most fundamental to the Act: the provision of a free appropriate public education to a child with a disability.

We consider the statutory structure. The IEP proceedings entitle parents to participate not only in the implementation of IDEA's procedures but also in the substantive formulation of their child's educational program. Among other things, IDEA requires the IEP Team, which includes the parents as members, to take into account any "concerns" parents have "for enhancing the education of their child" when it formulates the IEP. § 1414(d)(3)(A)(ii). The IEP, in turn, sets the boundaries of the central entitlement provided by IDEA: It defines a "'free appropriate public education'" for that parent's child. § 1401(9).

The statute also empowers parents to bring challenges based on a broad range of issues. The parent may seek a hearing on "any matter relating to the identification, evaluation, or educational placement of the child, or the provision of a free appropriate public education to such child." § 1415(b)(6)(A). To resolve these challenges a hearing officer must make a decision based on whether the child "received a free appropriate public education." § 1415(f)(3)(E). When this hearing has been conducted by a local educational agency rather than a state educational agency, "any party aggrieved by the findings and decision rendered in such a hearing may appeal such findings and decision" to the state educational agency. § 1415(g)(1). Judicial review follows, authorized by a broadly worded provision phrased in the same terms used to describe the prior stage of review: "Any party aggrieved" may bring "a civil action." § 1415(i)(2)(A).

These provisions confirm that IDEA, through its text and structure, creates in parents an independent stake not only in the procedures and costs implicated by this process but also in the substantive decisions to be made. We therefore conclude that IDEA does not differentiate, through isolated references to various procedures and remedies, between the rights accorded to children and the rights accorded to parents. As a consequence, a parent may be a "party aggrieved" for purposes of § 1415(i)(2) with regard to "any matter" implicating these rights. See § 1415(b)(6)(A). The status of parents as parties is not limited to matters that relate to procedure and cost recovery. To find otherwise would be inconsistent with the collaborative framework and expansive system of review established by the Act.

Our conclusion is confirmed by noting the incongruous results that would follow were we to accept the proposition that parents' IDEA rights are limited to certain nonsubstantive matters. The statute's procedural and reimbursement-related rights are intertwined with the substantive adequacy of the education provided to a child, see, *e.g.*, § 1415(f)(3)(E), see also § 1412(a)(10)(C)(ii), and it is difficult to disentangle the provisions in order to conclude that some rights adhere to both parent and child while others do not. Were we nevertheless to recognize a distinction of this sort it would impose upon parties a confusing and onerous legal regime, one worsened by the absence of any express guidance in IDEA concerning how a court might in practice differentiate between these matters. It is, in addition, out of accord with the statute's design to interpret the Act to require that parents prove the substantive inadequacy of their child's education as a predicate for obtaining, for example, reimbursement under § 1412(a)(10)(C)(ii), yet to prevent them from obtaining a judgment mandating that the school district provide their child with an educational program demonstrated to be an appropriate one. The adequacy of the educational program is, after all, the central issue in the litigation. The provisions of IDEA do not set forth these distinctions, and we decline to infer them.

The bifurcated regime suggested by the courts that have employed it, moreover, leaves some parents without a remedy. The statute requires, in express terms, that States provide a child with a free appropriate public education "at public expense," § 1401(9)(A), including specially designed instruction "at no cost to parents," § 1401(29). Parents may seek to enforce this mandate through the federal courts, we conclude, because among the rights they enjoy is the right to a free appropriate public education for their child. Under the countervailing view, which would make a parent's ability to enforce IDEA dependent on certain procedural and reimbursement-related rights, a parent whose disabled child has not received a free appropriate public education would have recourse in the federal courts only under two circumstances: when the parent happens to have some claim related to the procedures employed; and when he or she is able to incur, and has in fact incurred, expenses creating a right to reimbursement. Otherwise the adequacy of the child's education would not be regarded as relevant to any cause of action the parent might bring; and, as a result, only the child could vindicate the right accorded by IDEA to a free appropriate public education.

The potential for injustice in this result is apparent. What is more, we find nothing in the statute to indicate that when Congress required States to provide adequate instruction to a child "at no cost to parents," it intended that only some parents would be able to enforce that mandate. The statute instead takes pains to "ensure that the rights of children with disabilities and parents of such children are protected." § 1400(d)(1)(B). See, *e.g.*, § 1415(e)(2) (requiring that States implement procedures to ensure parents are guaranteed procedural safeguards with respect to the provision of a free appropriate public education); § 1415(e)(2)(A)(ii) (requiring that mediation procedures not be "used to deny or delay a parent's right to a due process hearing . . . or to deny any other rights afforded under this subchapter"); cf. § 1400(c)(3) (noting IDEA's success in "ensuring children with disabilities and the families of such children access to a free appropriate public education").

We conclude IDEA grants parents independent, enforceable rights. These rights, which are not limited to certain procedural and reimbursement-related matters, encompass the entitlement to a free appropriate public education for the parents' child.

. . . .

III

The Court of Appeals erred when it dismissed the Winkelmans' appeal for lack of counsel. Parents enjoy rights under IDEA; and they are, as a result, entitled to prosecute IDEA claims on their own behalf. . . .

In light of our holding we need not reach petitioners' alternative argument, which concerns whether IDEA entitles parents to litigate their child's claims *pro se.*

The judgment of the Court of Appeals is reversed, and the case is remanded for further proceedings consistent with this opinion.

Justice SCALIA, with whom Justice THOMAS joins, concurring in the judgment in part and dissenting in part.

I would hold that parents have the right to proceed *pro se* under the Individuals with Disabilities Education Act (IDEA) when they seek reimbursement for private school expenses or redress for violations of their own procedural rights, but not when they seek a judicial determination that their child's free appropriate public education (or FAPE) is substantively inadequate.

. . . .

A review of the statutory text makes clear that, as relevant here, the IDEA grants parents only two types of rights. First, under certain circumstances "a court or a hearing officer may require the [school district] to reimburse *the parents*" for private school expenditures "if the court or hearing officer finds that the [school district] had not made a free appropriate public education available to the child." 20 U.S.C. § 1412(a)(10)(C)(ii) . . . (emphasis added). Second, parents are accorded a variety of procedural protections, both during the development of their child's individualized education program (IEP), see, *e.g.*, § 1414(d)(1)(B)(i) (parents are members of their child's IEP team); § 1415(b)(1) (parents must have an opportunity to examine records and participate in IEP meetings), and in any subsequent administrative challenges, see, *e.g.*, §§ 1415(b)(6), (8) (parents may file administrative due process complaints). It is clear that parents may object to procedural violations at the administrative due process hearing, see § 1415(b)(6)(A), and that a hearing officer may provide relief to parents for certain procedural infractions, see § 1415(f)(3)(E)(ii). Because the rights to reimbursement and to the various procedural protections are accorded to parents themselves, they are "parties aggrieved" when those rights are infringed, and may accordingly proceed *pro se* when seeking to vindicate them.

The Court goes further, however, concluding that parents may proceed *pro se* not only when they seek reimbursement or assert procedural violations, but also when they challenge the substantive adequacy of their child's FAPE—so that parents may act without a lawyer *in every IDEA case*. In my view, this sweeps far more broadly than the text allows. Out of this sprawling statute the Court cannot identify even *a single* provision stating that parents have the substantive right to a FAPE. The reason for this is readily understandable: The right to a free appropriate public education obviously inheres in the child, for it is he who receives the education. As the IDEA instructs, participating States must provide a "free appropriate public education . . . to all children with disabilities. . . ." § 1412(a)(1)(A). . . . The statute is replete with references to the fact that a FAPE belongs to the child. See, *e.g.*, § 1400(d)(1)(A) (IDEA designed "to ensure that all children with disabilities have available to them a free appropriate public education"); § 1408(a)(2)(C)(i) (referring to "the right of a child" to "receive a free appropriate public education"); § 1411(e)(3)(F)(i) (same); § 1414(a)(1)(D)(i)(II) (referring to an agency "that is responsible for making a free appropriate public education available to a child"); § 1415(b)(6)(A) (referring to "the provision of a free appropriate public education to [a] child"). The parents of a disabled child no doubt have an *interest* in seeing their child receive a proper education. But there is a difference between an *interest* and a statutory *right*. The text of the IDEA makes clear that parents have no *right* to the education itself.

The Court concedes, as it must, that while the IDEA gives parents the right to reimbursement and procedural protection in explicit terms, it does not do so for the supposed right to the education itself. The obvious inference to be drawn from the statute's clear and explicit conferral of discrete types of rights upon parents and children, respectively, is that it does not by accident confer the parent-designated rights upon children, or the children-designated rights upon parents. The Court believes, however, that "the statute prevents us from placing too much weight on [this] implicatio[n]." That conclusion is in error. Nothing in "the statute" undermines the obvious "implication" of Congress's scheme. What the Court relies upon for its conclusion that parents have a substantive right to a FAPE is not the "statutory structure," but rather the myriad *procedural* guarantees accorded to parents in the administrative process. . . . But allowing parents, by means of these guarantees, to help shape the contours of their child's education is simply not the same as giving *them* the right to that education. Nor can the Court sensibly rely on the provisions governing due process hearings and administrative appeals, the various provisions that refer to the "parent's complaint," see, *e.g.*, 20 U.S.C. § 1415(i)(3)(B)(i)(III), or the fact that the right-to-sue provision, § 1415(i)(2)(A), refers to the administrative complaint, which in turn allows parents to challenge "any matter" relating to the provision of a FAPE, § 1415(b)(6)(A). These provisions prove nothing except what all parties concede: that parents *may* represent their child *pro se* at the administrative level. Parents thus have the power, at the administrative stage, to litigate *all* of the various rights under the statute since at that stage they are acting not only on their *own* behalf, but on behalf of *their child* as well. This tells us nothing whatever about *whose* rights they are. The Court's spraying statutory sections about like buckshot cannot create a substantive parental right to education where none exists.

Harkening back to its earlier discussion of the IDEA's "text and structure" (by which it means the statute's procedural protections), the Court announces the startling proposition that, in fact, the "IDEA does not differentiate . . . between the rights accorded to children and the rights accorded to parents." If that were so, the Court could have spared us its painful effort to craft a distinctive parental right out of scattered procedural provisions. But of course it is not so. The IDEA quite clearly differentiates between the rights accorded to parents and their children. As even petitioners' *amici* agree, "Congress specifically indicated that parents have rights under the Act that are separate from and independent of their children's rights." Does the Court seriously contend that a child has a right to reimbursement, when the statute most definitively provides that if "*the parents* of a child with a disability" enroll that child in private school, "a court . . . may require the [school district] to reimburse *the parents* for the cost of that enrollment"? § 1412(a)(10)(C)(ii) . . . (emphasis added) . . . ("The right of reimbursement runs to the parents"). Does the Court believe that a child has a procedural right under §§ 1414(d)(1)(C)(i)-(iii) . . . which gives *parents* the power to excuse an IEP team member from attending an IEP meeting? The IDEA does not remotely envision communal "family" rights.

The Court believes that because parents must prove the substantive inadequacy of a FAPE before obtaining reimbursement, § 1412(a)(10)(C)(ii) . . . , and because the suitability of a FAPE may also be at issue when procedural violations are alleged, § 1415(f)(3)(E)(ii), it is "out of accord with the statute's design" to "prevent [parents] from obtaining a judgment mandating that the school district provide their child" with a FAPE. That is a total non sequitur. That Congress has required parents to demonstrate the inadequacy of their child's FAPE in order to vindicate their own rights says nothing about whether parents possess an underlying right to education. The Court insists that the right to a FAPE is the right "most fundamental to the Act." Undoubtedly so, but that sheds no light upon whom the right belongs to, and hence upon who can sue in their own right. . . .

. . . .

Finally, the Court charges that the approach taken by the majority of Courts of Appeals would perpetrate an "injustice," since parents who do not seek reimbursement or allege procedural violations would be "without a remedy," . . . . That, of course, is not true. They will have the same remedy as all parents who sue to vindicate their children's rights: the power to bring suit, represented by counsel. But even indulging the Court's perception that it is unfair to allow some but not all IDEA parents to proceed *pro se*, that complaint is properly addressed to Congress, which structured the rights as it has, and limited suit to "party aggrieved." And there are good reasons for it to have done so. *Pro se* cases impose unique burdens on lower courts—and on defendants, in this case the schools and school districts that must hire their own lawyers. Since *pro se* complaints are prosecuted essentially for free, without screening by knowledgeable attorneys, they are much more likely to be unmeritorious. And for courts to figure them out without the assistance of plaintiff's counsel is much more difficult and time consuming. In both categories of *pro se* parental suit permitted under a proper interpretation of the statute, one or the other of these burdens is reduced. Actions seeking reimbursement are less likely to be frivolous, since not many parents will be willing to lay out the money for private education without some solid reason to believe the FAPE was inadequate. And actions alleging procedural violations can ordinarily be disposed of without the intensive record review that characterizes suits challenging the suitability of a FAPE.

Petitioners sought reimbursement, alleged procedural violations, and requested a declaration that their child's FAPE was substantively inadequate. I agree with the Court that they may proceed *pro se* with respect to the first two claims, but I disagree that they may do so with respect to the third.

Notes, Comments, and Questions

1. On remand from the Supreme Court, the Sixth Circuit in a brief decision ruled against the Winklemans. The substantive portion of the court's decision reads:

> The district court had allowed the parents to proceed *pro se*, but when the case reached this court on appeal, we ordered the parents to obtain counsel, lest their appeal be dismissed. Instead, they petitioned the Supreme Court for certiorari, which the Court granted. Ultimately, the court held that parents have rights under the IDEA independent of the rights of their child, the parents' rights encompass the child's right to a FAPE, and the parents may proceed *pro se* on their own independent rights. On remand, we are again presented with the merits question.
>
> The Winklemans first argue that the district court erred by placing the burden of proof on them, rather than on the school district. Next, they argue that the district court erred by finding that the school district had provided the FAPE with regard to music therapy, occupational therapy, and speech therapy. Finally, they contend that the district court erred by approving the hearing officer's decision to disregard the Winklemans' expert-witness testimony as not credible.
>
> After carefully reviewing the record, the law, and the arguments presented in the appellate briefs, we conclude that each of the Winklemans' assignments of error is without merit, and the district court's [original 2005] opinion correctly sets out the applicable law and correctly applies that law to the facts in the record. The issuance of a full written opinion by this court would serve no useful purpose. Accordingly, for the reasons stated in the district court's opionion, we AFFIRM.

Winkleman v. Parma City Sch. Dist., 294 F. App'x 997, 998 (6th Cir. 2008), *cert. denied*, 557 U.S. 946 (2009). How would you characterize the Sixth Circuit's attitude about the Winklemans? Did they get a fair hearing in the Sixth Circuit?

2. The Supreme Court in *Winkleman* did not address whether parents have a right to represent their children *pro se* in IDEA claims in federal court. The dissent in *Winkleman*, as well as the lower courts that had considered the question prior to *Winkleman*, agreed that parents cannot enforce the IDEA rights of their children *pro se*. *See* Mosely v. Bd. of Educ. of Chi., 434 F.3d 527, 532 (7th Cir. 2006) (ruling that mother cannot "proceed *pro se* with an IDEA action on behalf of her child."); Tindall v. Poultney High Sch. Dist., 414 F.3d 281, 284 (2d Cir. 2005) ("It is thus a well-established general rule in this Circuit that a parent not admitted to the bar cannot bring an action *pro se* in federal court on behalf of her child."); Cavanaugh v. Cardinal Local Sch. Dist., 409 F.3d 753, 756 (6th Cir. 2005) (holding that "non-lawyer parents may not represent their child in an action brought under the IDEA."); Navin v. Park Ridge Sch. Dist. 64, 270 F.3d 1147, 1149 (7th Cir. 2001) (holding that non-lawyer could represent himself but not his son); Collinsgru v. Palmyra Bd. of Educ., 161 F.3d 225, 237 (3rd Cir. 1998) (ruling that parents cannot represent child in federal court IDEA case); Wenger v. Canastota Cent. Sch. Dist., 146 F.3d 123, 124 (2d Cir. 1998) (stating that non-attorney parent could not represent child *pro se*); Devine v. Indian River Cty. Sch. Bd., 121 F.3d 576, 581–82 (11th Cir. 1997) (stating that parents cannot represent children in federal court), *cert. denied*, 522 U.S. 1110 (1988). The court in *Devine* explained the reason for the rule: "IDEA allows parents to sue in their children's stead, but does not authorize them to act as counsel in such a lawsuit. We are aware of no authority permitting non-lawyers to represent their children *pro se* in cases brought pursuant to the IDEA." 121 F.3d at 581. Recognizing that parents can introduce witnesses and examine witnesses during administrative proceedings under the IDEA, the court nevertheless precluded non-attorney parents from representing children in court. "[P]arents who are not attorneys may not bring a *pro se* action on their children's behalf—because it helps to ensure that children rightfully entitled to legal relief are not deprived of their day in court by unskilled, if caring, parents." *Id.* at 582. Do you agree with the court's reasoning? A child cannot bring a case on her own behalf *pro se*. If her parents cannot represent her *pro se* in federal court, cannot afford to pay an attorney, and cannot find an attorney to take the case without payment of fees, the child is left without legal recourse to challenge an unfavorable administrative decision in federal court. Is this better for a child than being represented by "unskilled, if caring, parents"?

3. Based on *Winkleman's* holding that parents have their own substantive IDEA rights, including the right to a free appropriate education for their children, is there any practical significance to the general rule that parents cannot represent their children *pro se* in federal court? The dissent, in stating that "parents may act without a lawyer in *every IDEA case*," implies that there is no significance. *Winkleman*, 550 U.S. at 538 (emphasis in original). Do children have substantive rights under the IDEA that parents do not have? One case provides a possible example. In *Loch v. Edwardsville School District No. 7*, 327 F. App'x 647 (7th Cir. 2009), *cert. denied*, 559 U.S. 991 (2010), the court recognized that parents have IDEA rights but found that "under Illinois law those rights are transferred to the student when that

student reaches majority." *Id.* at 650. "Kayla was eighteen when the Lochs filed this action and so she alone can assert claims under the IDEA." *Id.* Should the court have deferred to Illinois law? Generally, the IDEA sets a floor of rights below which individual states cannot go. Did the court allow the Illinois law go below the IDEA's floor?

4. The majority and dissent in *Winkleman* used arguments based on the language and structure of the IDEA, policy considerations, and the purpose of the IDEA to support their positions. Which position do you find most persuasive? Why?

5. In his dissent, Justice Scalia stated that *pro se* cases are much more likely to lack merit than cases with attorneys representing plaintiffs, and it "is more difficult and time-consuming" for courts to figure out *pro se* cases. *Winkleman*, 550 U.S. at 542–43. If Justice Scalia was correct, does this justify prohibiting parents from representing their children *pro se*?

6. How would you draft an amendment to the IDEA that implements the majority decision in *Winkleman*? The dissent's position?

7. Section 1415(i)(2)(A) requires that a party be aggrieved by the findings and decision at an impartial hearing before filing a complaint in federal court. Impartial hearings often include several different issues relating to the child's placement, special education program, and related services. In a case that includes several issues, a parent could prevail on some, partially prevail on others, and lose on others. Parents are aggrieved parties in these mixed-results cases and can challenge in federal court the issues on which they partially prevailed or lost. *See* Board of Educ. of Cnty. of Cabell v. Dienelt, 843 F.2d. 813, 814 (4th Cir. 1988) (holding that parents were aggrieved by order that required the school district to reimburse parents only for part of the child's tuition and failed to order the district to reimburse parents for other expenses); Moubry v. Indep. Sch. Dist. No. 696, 951 F. Supp. 867, 883–87 (D. Minn. 1996) (holding that parent who prevailed on FAPE claim was aggrieved by hearing officer's failure to disqualify a speech therapist from providing services and award compensatory education); Slack v. Del. Dep't of Pub. Instruction, 826 F. Supp. 115, 120 (D. Del. 1993) (ruling that plaintiff who prevailed on the legal issues at the due process hearing but did not get the relief requested was aggrieved); Diamond v. McKenzie, 602 F. Supp. 632, 635 (D.D.C. 1985) (ruling that plaintiffs were aggrieved by hearing officer's decision that school district's proposed placement was inappropriate because she did not award residential placement).

8. An interesting twist on the issue of when a party is aggrieved occurs when a party prevails at an impartial hearing but the school district fails to implement the favorable decision. Is that party aggrieved under Section 1415(i)(2)(A)? Can the party file a complaint in federal court pursuant to Section 1415(i)(A)(2) to enforce the favorable decision? Generally, the courts have ruled that the answer is no. Robinson v. Pinderhughes, 810 F.2d 1270, 1273–74 (4th Cir. 1987) (ruling that IDEA has no provision to enforce impartial hearing orders); James S. v. Sch. Dist. of Phila., 559 F. Supp. 2d 600, 615 (E.D. Pa. 2008) (denying jurisdiction in case to enforce a hearing

officer's order because factual allegations in complaint were insufficient); Brennan v. Reg'l Sch. Dist. No. 1 Bd. of Educ., 531 F. Supp. 2d 245, 261–62 (D. Conn. 2008) (dismissing parents' claim to enforce hearing officer's decision); C.C. v. Granby Bd. of Educ., 453 F. Supp. 2d 569, 577 (D. Conn. 2006) (ruling that IDEA does not allow a prevailing party to enforce a favorable decision in federal court); Moubry v. Indep. Sch. Dist. No. 696, 951 F. Supp. 867, 885–86 (D. Minn. 1996) (ruling that "jurisdiction under the Act is limited to parties who are aggrieved by an administrative decision."); Metropolitan Sch. Dist. of Martinsville v. Buskirk, 950 F. Supp. 899, 903 (S.D. Ind. 1997) (declining to allow federal jurisdiction in action to enforce administrative decision); Reid v. Bd. of Educ., Lincolnshire-Prarie View Sch. Dist. 103, 765 F. Supp. 965, 969 (N.D. Ill. 1991) (dismissing plaintiff's petition to enforce administrative order); Grace B. v. Lexington Sch. Comm., 762 F. Supp. 416, 418 (D. Mass. 1991) (ruling that court did not have jurisdiction under the IDEA to enforce favorable hearing officer order). The First Circuit, however, disagrees, and has ruled that a party who prevails at an impartial hearing may file a complaint in federal court pursuant to the IDEA to enforce the decision. Nieves-Marquez v. Puerto Rico, 353 F.3d 108 (1st Cir. 2003). The court reasoned:

> We conclude that Congress could not have intended to leave plaintiffs without an IDEA statutory remedy when they succeed before the hearing officer and the school system does not appeal the administrative decision but simply fails to fulfill a continuing obligation to provide services. Statutory phrases must be read not in isolation but in light of the statute's overall structure and intent. Congress could not have intended for a school system to be in a *better* position under IDEA when it refuses to comply with a final administrative order and its continuing obligations than when it exercises its statutory right to appeal from the order. Where the school system exercises its right to appeal, the court is empowered by IDEA to issue injunctive relief. It cannot be said that a court is powerless under IDEA to issue injunctive relief when the school system neither appeals from nor complies with a valid administrative order and its continuing obligations. That would open a gaping hole in IDEA's coverage. It would create incentives for school systems to drag out the administrative process, not to appeal administrative orders, not to announce their intention to refuse to comply with those orders, and generally not to comply.

Id. at 115–116. *See also* Dudley v. Lower Merion Sch. Dist., 768 F. Supp. 2d 779, 783–84 (E.D. Pa. 2011) (ruling that a plaintiff may seek enforcement of a hearing officer's decision under the IDEA). Which position do you find more persuasive?

9. Generally, although most courts agree that a party cannot enforce a favorable administrative decision in an IDEA case in federal court pursuant to the IDEA, the courts agree that the party can do so by bringing a case pursuant to 42 U.S.C. § 1983 (2012), which creates a cause of action in federal court for violation of federal rights by state officials. *See* Jeremy H. v. Mount Lebanon Sch. Dist., 95 F.3d 272, 278 (3d

Cir. 1996) (ruling that Section 1983 "provides an adequate vehicle for enforcing an IDEA administrative decision."); Robinson v. Pinderhughes, 810 F.2d 1270, 1274 (4th Cir. 1987) (allowing plaintiffs to pursue their remedy pursuant to Section 1983); Moubry v. Ind. Sch. Dist. No. 696, 951 F. Supp. 867, 886 n.13 (D. Minn. 1996) (stating that a parent can enforce a favorable impartial hearing decision pursuant to Section 1983); Slack v. Del. Dep't of Pub. Instruction, 826 F. Supp. 115, 120 (D. Del. 1993) ("Where a due process panel grants plaintiffs the relief requested, plaintiffs may proceed in federal court under 42 U.S.C. § 1983 only if the panel's order is not followed."); Reid v. Bd. of Educ., Lincolnshire-Prairie View Sch. Dist.103, 765 F. Supp. 965, 969 (N.D. Ill. 1991) (permitting plaintiff to amend complaint to assert a Section 1983 claim); Grace B. v. Lexington Sch. Comm., 762 F. Supp. 416, 418 (D. Mass. 1991) (ruling that court does not have jurisdiction under the IDEA to enforce a hearing decision order but does have jurisdiction under Section 1983).

10. As the Supreme Court made clear in *Winkleman*, parents generally have standing to enforce their children's and their own rights under the IDEA. But not every parent is a parent for IDEA purposes. The next case explores how to determine who is a parent under the IDEA.

Taylor v. Vt. Dep't of Educ.

313 F.3d 768 (2d Cir. 2002)

Sotomayor, Circuit Judge.

We are presented with the question of who is entitled to exercise the rights afforded to a "parent" under the Individuals with Disabilities Education Act ("IDEA") .... Plaintiff-appellant Pam Taylor alleges that the defendants have violated statutory rights she possesses as the natural mother of a child who suffers from a disability. The United States District Court for the District of Vermont granted defendants' motion to dismiss plaintiff's action for failure to state a claim ... holding that plaintiff, whose legal authority over the child had been curtailed by a state divorce decree, lacked standing to pursue an action under ... [the IDEA].

On appeal, Taylor argues that a natural mother is entitled to exercise parental rights under the IDEA ... and that state law cannot abrogate these federal rights. We decline plaintiff's invitation to federalize the law of domestic relations and hold that the IDEA ... leave[s] intact a state's authority to determine who may make educational decisions on behalf of a child, so long as a state does so in a manner consistent with the federal statutes. We therefore affirm the district court's dismissal of the claims related to plaintiff's requests for an Individual Educational Evaluation .... Nevertheless, because plaintiff retains some important rights under the divorce decree—specifically the right to reasonable information regarding her daughter's health and progress in school—we vacate the district court's judgment insofar as it dismissed her IDEA claim that she was denied access to her child's educational records....

BACKGROUND

... Taylor is the natural mother of L.D., who at the time of the complaint was a student at the Weybridge Elementary School in Vermont. Taylor obtained a divorce from L.D.'s father in February 1992 .... The divorce decree ... provides:

> The court allocates all legal rights and physical rights regarding the choice of schooling for the child ... to the father. Such rights shall include the right to choose the school location, and participate in all parent teacher conferences ... with full authority on behalf of the child....
>
> The mother shall have a right to reasonable information regarding the child's progress in school ....
>
> ....

....

L.D. and her father moved to Weybridge, Vermont in the summer of 1998. That September, L.D. commenced fourth grade at the Weybridge Elementary School .... The Weybridge School District formed an Education Support Team to evaluate L.D. for disabilities....

In May 1999, in response to letters Taylor had sent ..., the Weybridge Elementary School finally sent her complete copies of L.D.'s educational records. It was after reviewing these records that Taylor first realized that the school district suspected that L.D. suffered from a disability.

During that same month, Weybridge psychologist Patricia Messerle began her disability evaluation.... Messerle issued her completed report on July 2, 1999, in which she concluded that L.D. qualified for special education due to her emotional-behavioral problems. Taylor received a copy of Messerle's evaluation on July 19, 1999. On August 25, 1999, she wrote to Weybridge with concerns regarding the accuracy of the report and asked for certain factual corrections. Some, but not all, of the requested changes were made.

On July 9, 1999, an Individualized Education Program ("IEP") team ... determined that L.D. suffered from an emotional-behavioral disability.... On August 30, 1999, the IEP team met to create L.D.'s first IEP, and on September 7, they sent L.D. for a neuropsychological evaluation at the Dartmouth Medical School....

On September 3, 1999, Taylor ... asked to be included as a member of L.D.'s IEP team, for access to L.D.'s educational records, and to be allowed input into the content of those records....

On October 1, Weybridge's legal counsel informed Taylor that the school would provide her with information on L.D.'s progress, that it would consider information and input from her that did not contradict input received from L.D.'s father, and that she would be given notice of and allowed to attend future meetings. Taylor did participate in subsequent meetings by phone, although she contends that she did not receive the background information she needed in order to take part in them fully.

On October 31, 1999, Taylor demanded an Independent Educational Evaluation ("IEE") .... The federal regulations permit a "parent" who disagrees with a public agency's evaluation either to initiate a hearing in which the agency must show that its initial evaluation was appropriate or to obtain a second IEE at public expense. This requirement was discussed at a subsequent IDEA meeting in November. As L.D.'s father opposed further evaluation, and the team likewise concluded that further evaluation would impact L.D. negatively, Taylor's request was denied. Taylor then filed a Request for a Due Process Hearing with the Commissioner of the VDOE to compel Weybridge to substantiate its determination that L.D. was "seriously emotionally disturbed." A ... hearing officer dismissed the petition on the ground that, as a result of the ... custody order, plaintiff lacked legal standing to pursue any claim under the IDEA.

In October and December 1999, plaintiff again notified the school that she believed that L.D.'s educational file contained inaccurate information and asked that the file be amended. Specifically, Taylor sought to eliminate any reference to L.D.'s stepmother as the child's "mother" or "parent," among other changes. Weybridge did not respond to Taylor's letters but on February 4, 2000, Taylor received a copy of a letter addressed to L.D.'s father. The letter stated that the school had removed certain letters written by Taylor from L.D.'s files but, pursuant to the father's written request, would not amend the school records further. Taylor's petition for a hearing to challenge the content of L.D.'s records was denied ... on the ground that, as Taylor lacked decision-making authority for L.D., there were "no justiceable [sic] issues to be heard by a Hearing Officer."

Taylor brought suit *pro se* in federal court .... In count one, Taylor sought an order compelling the Weybridge School District to demonstrate the appropriateness of its disability determination ... as well as compensatory and punitive damages for defendants' IDEA violations. In count two, Taylor asked that the Weybridge School District be compelled to ensure that L.D.'s educational records contain accurate information pursuant to the procedures set forth in ... the IDEA, and the implementing regulations; that the Weybridge School District be compelled to supply Taylor with all of L.D.'s educational records; and that the Court award Taylor compensatory and punitive damages for the violations of her rights under ... the IDEA with respect to record access and record content ....

DISCUSSION

....

II. Taylor's Standing to Request an Independent Educational Evaluation

It is uncontested that one of the primary purposes of the IDEA is to "to ensure that the rights of children with disabilities and parents of such children are protected," 20 U.S.C. § 1400(d)(1)(B), including a parent's right to demand an IEE, *see* 20 U.S.C. § 1415(b)(1); 34 C.F.R. § 300.502. Yet the invocation of this general statutory purpose is of little assistance in helping us determine whether Taylor is entitled to exercise parental rights under the statute. Whether Taylor may avail herself of the IDEA's procedural protections in this case depends upon whether Taylor is considered a "parent" within the meaning of the Act. Unfortunately, neither the IDEA nor its federal regulatory scheme are models of clarity.

. . . .

[P]rior to 1997 the IDEA did not contain any definition of the term "parent." The statute was amended by the Individuals with Disabilities Education Act Amendments for 1997, Pub. L. No. 105-17, 111 Stat. 37, to include the following provision:

> The term "parent"—
>
> (A) includes a legal guardian; and
>
> (B) except as used in sections 1415(b)(2) and 1439(a)(5) of this title, includes an individual assigned under either of those sections to be a surrogate parent.

20 U.S.C. § 1401(19). By its terms, this statutory provision is not exhaustive. Clearly, legal guardians and educational surrogates are not the only persons entitled to the IDEA's procedural protections. Even if the use of the expansive term "includes" did not carry with it the strong implication that the statute's definition of parent encompassed more than the two categories specifically referenced, we would find it difficult to credit a reading that excluded natural parents from the list of persons who could exercise parental rights under the statute. Indeed, the legislative history indicates that this definition was added merely so that "most references to 'guardian' [could be] deleted throughout the act when accompanied by the term 'parent.'" S. Rep. 104–275, at 32 (1996). Thus, the statutory language provides us with little assistance.

The Department of Education's current set of regulations implementing the IDEA, effective since 1999, contains a more comprehensive definition of parent:

> (a) General. As used in this part, the term parent means—
>
> (1) A natural or adoptive parent of a child;
>
> (2) A guardian but not the State if the child is a ward of the State;
>
> (3) A person acting in the place of a parent (such as a grandparent or stepparent with whom the child lives, or a person who is legally responsible for the child's welfare); *or*
>
> (4) A surrogate parent who has been appointed in accordance with § 300.515.
>
> (b) Foster parent. Unless State law prohibits a foster parent from acting as a parent, a State may allow a foster parent to act as a parent . . . , if—
>
> (1) The natural parents' authority to make educational decisions on the child's behalf has been extinguished under State law; and

(2) The foster parent—

(i) Has an ongoing, long-term parental relationship with the child;

(ii) Is willing to make the educational decisions required of parents under the Act; and

(iii) Has no interest that would conflict with the interests of the child.

34 C.F.R. § 300.20 (emphasis added).

The regulation does not purport to list all those who are granted rights under the statute. In fact, by using the disjunctive, it indicates exactly the opposite—that the listed persons may or may not be entitled to exercise parental rights under the statute. Hence, the natural reading is that the federal regulation establishes a range of persons who *may be* considered a parent for purposes of the IDEA, but does not require that any and all such persons *must be* granted statutory rights.

Plaintiff nonetheless claims that, under § 300.20, natural parents retain their IDEA rights unless the state brings a proceeding to terminate their parental status. We cannot accept such a reading of the regulation. Section 300.20 does not state, for example, that all the persons listed as possible parents possess standing to bring a claim under the IDEA until their parental rights are permanently revoked. Indeed, such a construction of the regulation would lead to the absurd result that natural parents, guardians, and persons acting in the place of a parent may *all* exercise the same rights under the IDEA simultaneously. The Department of Education could not have intended that there would be a superfluity of parties able to exercise authority over the child under the regulation simultaneously, each of whom may have conflicting ideas with respect to the child's education, with no means of choosing among them.

....

The only way to read the regulation so that it is intelligible is with reference to state law. The regulation does not establish a method for choosing which of the possible parents is entitled to exercise rights under the statute. Given the nature of the statutory scheme, we look to state law to fill this gap and to establish which potential parent has authority to make special education decisions for the child. This conclusion is supported by the fact that the regulation refers to adoptive parents, legal guardians, and other persons "legally responsible for the child's welfare." None of these concepts is given content in federal law; rather, state domestic law assigns these rights. Thus, the regulation explicitly relies upon the state to assign parental rights.

We acknowledge that the federal regulations are inartfully drafted. To the extent that there is ambiguity, we may look to how the federal Department of Education has construed its own regulation.... In a 1987 policy letter, the Department of Education's Office of Special Education Programs ("OSEP") stated:

> The question of which divorced parent should be allowed to perform parental functions under the [IDEA] is not properly a matter for OSEP to decide. Rather, this is a matter for State or local divorce courts. Just as these courts deal with matters of custody, they can appropriately deal with matters related

> to the responsibility for making educational decisions on behalf of the child. OSEP would not seek to create a rule intruding on the jurisdiction of the courts and State family law in this area.

As OSEP's interpretation is perfectly consistent with both the gap left in the regulations and the strong presumption that issues of domestic relations fall within the traditional sphere of state authority, we accord deference to the Department of Education's decision that the allocation of parental rights under the IDEA is best left to local domestic law.

Our conclusion is further reinforced by caselaw. The only other circuit court decision to have addressed this precise issue has likewise held that the extent of a natural parent's rights under the IDEA must be determined with reference to state law. *See Navin v. Park Ridge Sch. Dist. 64*, 270 F.3d 1147, 1149 (7th Cir. 2001). In *Navin*, the natural father of a child with a disability sought to bring a due process challenge to the school district's IEP. In analyzing whether the non-custodial father had standing to bring an action under the IDEA, the Seventh Circuit looked to the rights that the father retained under a state custody decree. *Id.* ("If the divorce decree had given [the mother] not only custody but also *every* instrument of influence over [the child's] education, then [the father would have no claim under the IDEA]. Although the IDEA grants rights to 'parents,' . . . nothing in the IDEA overrides states' allocation of authority as part of a custody determination."). Finding that, although the mother had authority to make final educational decisions, the father nonetheless retained the right under the custody decree to be involved in and to influence his son's education, the *Navin* court remanded for the district court to determine whether the father's wishes were incompatible with the mother's.[9]

Having determined that state law will inform our resolution of the standing issue, we now look to Taylor's parental rights under Vermont law. Vermont's implementing regulations comport with the requirements set forth in the IDEA, and in fact substantially mirror the federal regulations. . . . Vermont looks to its domestic law in deciding when it would be "appropriate" to allow a natural parent to exercise rights granted by the IDEA. Vermont . . . does not allow natural parents whose legal authority to make educational decisions on behalf of a child has been terminated by operation of local domestic law to challenge an IEP determination.

---

9. The plaintiff cites to two district court opinions to support her claim that non-custodial natural parents may participate in the IEP process unless there has been an official termination of their parental rights. *See W.T. v. Andalusia City Schs.*, 977 F. Supp. 1437, 1444 (M.D. Ala. 1997) ("[U]nder its plain language, the IDEA gives to the 'parents or guardian' of a child—regardless as to whether the parent or guardian has actual custody—the right to request a due-process hearing. . . . The fact that the custodial guardian at the time of the administrative proceedings disagreed with [the mother] did not necessarily abrogate [her] standing. . . ."); *Doe v. Anrig*, 651 F. Supp. 424, 429 (D. Mass. 1987) (holding that non-custodial father who had financial responsibility for son's education had right to participate in IEP process), *vacated and remanded* (Apr. 3, 1987). To the extent that these cases hold that natural parents may challenge educational decisions under the IDEA regardless of whether they have legal authority over the child, we find them unpersuasive.

In contrast to the facts of the *Navin* case, here Taylor's parental right to participate in her daughter's education has been revoked by a Vermont family court. Moreover, the father, upon whom Vermont has bestowed this legal authority, has opposed the due process hearing requested by Taylor as against the child's best interests. As Taylor does not have the authority to make educational decisions on behalf of L.D., we agree that she lacks standing to demand a hearing under the IDEA on the appropriateness of defendants' IEP evaluation.

III. Taylor's Records-Access Claim

. . . .

B. Taylor's IDEA Claim

. . . Taylor retains important rights related to her daughter's education under the Vermont custody decree, specifically the right to "reasonable information regarding the child's progress in school and her health and safety." Because the custody decree has not "specifically revoked" her informational access prerogatives, Taylor may pursue her record-access claim under the IDEA.

Notes, Comments, and Questions

1. Are *Winkleman* and *Taylor* consistent? Should a parent's rights under the IDEA be determined by state law?

2. Based on *Taylor*, how would you advise a client who was getting a divorce who has a child with a disability? What are her options regarding her IDEA rights?

3. In *Susan R.M. v. Northeast Indep. Sch. Dist.*, 818 F.2d 455 (5th Cir. 1987), the Fifth Circuit looked to state law to determine parental standing. The court ruled that under Texas law, the child's "conservator, and not her father, has . . . [s]tanding to bring actions on her behalf." *Id.* at 457–58.

B. Third-Party Plaintiffs

Third-party plaintiffs seek to recover damages they suffered because the rights of others were violated. The following case considers whether a third-party plaintiff has standing to assert the rights of others in the IDEA context. It also provides a useful overview of standing rules in general and in IDEA cases in particular.

Family & Children's Ctr., Inc. v. Sch. City of Mishawaka

13 F.3d 1052 (7th Cir. 1994),
cert. denied, 513 U.S. 591 (1994)

Flaum, Circuit Judge.

This case presents the narrow issue of whether Family & Children's Center, Inc. ("FCC"), an Indiana non-profit corporation which operates a licensed, private child care facility, should be accorded third-party standing to advocate the rights of children with disabilities who have been placed in its physical but not legal custody by state or local child welfare departments. FCC seeks an order declaring that the Individuals with Disabilities Education Act ("IDEA"), 20 U.S.C. §§ 1400-85 . . . , obligates School City of Mishawaka ("School City"): (1) to provide classrooms and related facilities for the education of the children with disabilities, and (2) to educate the children with disabilities placed with FCC who are periodically and temporarily cared for at two group homes owned by FCC and located in the City of South Bend. Following oral argument, the District Court granted School City's motion to dismiss . . . on the ground that FCC lacks standing to assert claims under the IDEA. We reverse.

I.

. . . .

. . . Section 1415(b) of the IDEA requires states to provide an impartial administrative process that assures compliance with the federal mandates of a "free appropriate public education" by the relevant state agencies. . . . According to the IDEA, the required process "shall include, but not be limited to" an opportunity for parents, guardians, or surrogates to examine records and file complaints with state or local education authorities. 20 U.S.C. § 1415(b). As the district court noted, the scope of Indiana's regulatory scheme extends beyond the minimum required by § 1415 in that it permits "any individual, group of individuals, agency, or organization" to file a complaint alleging violation of federal or state laws that apply to special education. Finally, the IDEA provides a right of action in federal district court, 20 U.S.C. § 1415(e), but only after a prospective plaintiff has exhausted state administrative remedies. . . .

. . . .

II.

. . . The only issue presented here, whether FCC has standing to assert claims under the IDEA, is a threshold matter because putative plaintiffs lacking standing are not entitled to have their claims litigated in federal courts. . . . The Supreme Court has directed us to resolve questions of standing according to a two-part inquiry that considers "both constitutional limitations of federal-court jurisdiction and prudential limitations in its exercise." *Gladstone Realtors v. Village of Bellwood*, 441 U.S. 91, 99 . . . (1979) . . . . In both dimensions—Article III and prudential—the test for standing "is founded in concern about the proper—and properly limited—role of the courts in a democratic society." *Id.* Ordinarily, "a litigant seeking relief in federal court must satisfy *both* constitutional and prudential limitations in order to have standing to sue."

A.

Under Article III, the federal judicial power extends only to "cases" or "controversies." The constitutional limitation on standing eliminates cases in which a plaintiff can demonstrate no "case or controversy" between himself and the defendant. To satisfy Article III, a plaintiff must allege: (1) an immediate threat of injury; (2) fairly traceable to the defendant's conduct; that (3) a favorable federal court decision likely would redress or remedy. . . .

As this court has noted, the Article III standing requirements are rather "undemanding." The first prong probes for an "actual or imminent" injury that is "concrete and particularized" to the party asserting the claim. In other words, the plaintiff must have an actual stake in the outcome that goes beyond "intellectual or academic curiosity." Provided the plaintiff has thus established his or her *bona fides*, even a minor or non-economic injury will satisfy the strictures of Article III, though purely psychological harm will not. In addition, the plaintiff need not show absolutely that a favorable judgment would redress his injury; a "probabilistic benefit from winning a suit" is adequate.

[B]ecause standing is a jurisdictional matter, we consider the sufficiency of FCC's allegations. FCC contends that School City's refusal to pay rent or expenses associated with the education of the children with disabilities . . . constitutes an injury to it directly traceable to School City's conduct. According to FCC, School City has an obligation under the IDEA either to reimburse FCC for the cost of educating the children or to educate the children themselves. Because School City has done neither, FCC has been deprived of the rental value of its facilities while absorbing the costs of wear and tear on the premises. FCC further submits that a court order requiring School City to comply with IDEA's mandate that the children receive a "free and appropriate public education" by providing classrooms and other facilities and financially supporting the group home concept would redress FCC's injury.

Accepting as true all facts alleged in the well-pleaded complaint and drawing all reasonable inferences in favor of the plaintiff, as we must, we agree that FCC fulfills the Article III standing requirements. . . .

B.

Even if a party satisfies the Article III criteria, there are several judicially self-imposed limits on the exercise of federal jurisdiction that may preclude a litigant's standing, including:

> the general prohibition on a litigant's raising another person's legal rights, the rule barring adjudication of generalized grievances more appropriately addressed in the representative branches, and the requirement that a plaintiff's complaint fall within the zone of interests protected by the law invoked.

Allen v. Wright, 468 U.S. 737, 751 . . . (1984). These prudential limitations on standing eliminate cases "where no individual rights would be vindicated" and restrict "access to federal courts to those litigants best suited to assert a particular claim." Unlike the Article III barriers to suit, however, Congress may override the prudential limits on standing by statute. . . . In fact, Congress frequently has exercised this prerogative, most often in statutes that involve civil rights, consumer issues, or environmental interests. Where a statute grants standing to the full limits of Article III, courts "lack authority to create prudential barriers to standing" in suits brought under that statute.

We now examine the IDEA to determine whether the statutory language grants a cause of action to FCC to seek relief on the basis of the children's rights and interests. This court repeatedly has held that, in cases of statutory interpretation, "[o]ur starting point must be the language of the statute." If the statute is unambiguous, we must enforce the plain meaning of the language enacted by Congress.

As explained above, § 1415 of the IDEA conditions federal assistance upon a state's compliance with the substantive and procedural goals of the Act. Section 1415(b) sets out a number of required procedures, including an opportunity for parents, guardians, or surrogates to examine records and file complaints with state or local education authorities. Significantly, the statutory language expressly states that "the procedures required by this section *shall include, but shall not be limited to*" the mandatory ones summarized above. 20 U.S.C. § 1415(b)(1) (emphasis supplied). Thus, Congress created a procedural minimum below which a state cannot fall if it wishes to retain eligibility for federal assistance. In so doing, Congress gave no indication of forbidding a state from providing greater protection for the rights of the children. By enacting 511 IAC 74, which permits "any individual, group of individuals, agency, or organization" to file a complaint alleging the violation of federal laws that apply to special education, like the IDEA, the Indiana legislature has complied fully with the dictates of § 1415(b). In other words, the Indiana legislature has invited FCC to initiate the state administrative process required by § 1415(b) as a condition of federal assistance for the education of Indiana's children with disabilities. And the IDEA clearly authorized Indiana to do so.

The record shows that FCC exhausted its state remedies as an aggrieved party is required to do by subsection (b) before filing suit. Thus, FCC was entitled to proceed under paragraph (2) of § 1415(e). . . . Again reading the plain language of the statute, it is evident that FCC qualifies as a "party aggrieved by the findings and decision made under subsection (b) of [§ 1415]" by virtue of the enhanced scope of Indiana's process for reviewing complaints about special education programs. Thus, viewing the statute as a whole, we conclude that by clear implication § 1415 grants a right of action to FCC on behalf of the children with disabilities.

By implicitly granting standing to a broad group of plaintiffs, Congress has removed the rationale for invoking our usual prudential restraints on judicial review. As the D.C. Circuit opined in *Center for Auto Safety*,

> It would make no sense to deny standing under a principle designed to prevent courts from encroaching on the legislature's domain where Congress itself has already 'weighed the need for and the value of judicial review of a given category of administrative decisions, and has decided it is warranted.'

793 F.2d at 1337. FCC, therefore, need not run the gauntlet of prudential standing tests; satisfying Article III is enough.

III.

Following the plain language of § 1415, and reading that statute as a whole, we are convinced that Congress has implicitly granted standing under the IDEA to the limits of Article III. In § 1415, Congress created a flexible scheme to protect the educational rights and interests of children with disabilities. With respect to the boundaries of third-party standing under the IDEA, § 1415 establishes the required procedures in subsection (b) as the floor and Article III as the ceiling. Within that range, Congress has deferred to the judgment of the states and localities. Indiana's procedural scheme, enacted in compliance with § 1415, broadly grants third-party standing to raise complaints alleging violations of the IDEA. Having properly invoked and exhausted available state administrative remedies, FCC then was entitled to bring this action in federal court if it could satisfy the requirements of Article III standing. FCC has standing in the Article III sense on the basis of its allegations of injury in fact, fairly traceable to School City, that a favorable decision on the merits might redress. Accordingly, we REVERSE the judgment of the district court and REMAND the case for further proceedings consistent with this opinion.

Notes, Comments, and Questions

1. Absent the Indiana statute that permits "any individual, group of individuals, agency, or organization" the right to file an administrative complaint, do you think that FCC would have had standing? Consider the following decisions denying standing to two educational service providers. In *Piedmont Behavioral Health Cntr. v. Stewart*, 413 F. Supp. 2d 746, 754 (S.D. W. Va. 2006), plaintiffs claimed that defendants were responsible for paying for the care they provided to a child. The court ruled that because the IDEA does not provide an administrative remedy to education service providers, the service provider-plaintiffs did not have standing to sue. *Id.* at 753–54. The Court distinguished *FCC* on the grounds that unlike Indiana, West Virginia had not passed legislation expanding the pool of entities that could file administrative claims. *Id.* at 754 n.2. Similarly, in *Ryan v. Shawnee Mission U.S.D. 512*, 416 F. Supp. 2d 1090 (D. Kan. 2006), the plaintiff, a former physical therapist for the school district, alleged she was fired in retaliation for asserting the school district was not complying with its obligation to teach children with disabilities. She claimed the district violated the IDEA when it terminated her. In dismissing for lack of standing, the court ruled:

> The stated purpose of the IDEA is to ensure that all disabled children have available to them a free appropriate public education and, to that end, to protect the rights of disabled children and their parents. . . . Because plaintiff's complaint does not allege that she is a disabled child or a parent of a disabled child, then, she can prove no set of facts which would entitle her to relief under the IDEA because the IDEA does not provide her with a private right of action.

Id. at 1098.

2. The court in *FCC* stated that the required injury for Article III standing could be minor or non-economic. How far are courts willing to go to find standing for minor or non-economic injuries? In *S.W. v. N.Y.C. Dep't. of Educ.*, 646 F. Supp. 2d 346 (S.D.N.Y. 2009), plaintiff sought payment of her child's private school tuition even though she had not paid the tuition and the court ruled she did not owe tuition to the school. *Id.* at 357. Nevertheless, the court found plaintiff had suffered an injury to her right to a free appropriate public education at public expense under the IDEA because an entity other than the government had paid for it. *Id.* at 359. In contrast, in *Piedmont Behavioral Health Cntr. v. Stewart*, 413 F. Supp. 2d 746 (S.D. W. Va. 2006), the court, facing very similar facts, denied standing to plaintiff because she did not pay for her son's education and the provider did not seek payment. *Id.* at 755. With which decision do you agree?

3. Courts have also addressed standing issues when insurance has paid for the child's educational expenses, and have reached different results. In *Shook v. Gaston Cnty. Bd. of Educ.*, 882 F.2d 119 (4th Cir. 1989), *cert. denied*, 493 U.S. 1093 (1990), the plaintiffs sought recovery from the school district for the amount her insurance company had paid for her treatment, which diminished the amount of benefits available to her. *Id.* at 120. The court found that, based on state law, the plaintiff had a financial interest in the policy amount and had standing. *Id.* at 122. In *Emery v. Roanoke City Sch. Bd.*, 432 F.3d 294 (4th Cir. 2005), the court distinguished *Shook* and denied standing to the plaintiff because the insurance policy had not belonged to him and no longer covered him and thus he did not suffer an injury when it was depleted. *Id.* at 300.

C. Organizational Standing

Recall the legal movement to create and enforce the educational rights of children with disabilities described in Chapter One. In *PARC*, one of the plaintiffs was Parents Associated for Retarded Children, an organization seeking to protect the rights of children with disabilities. Since then, organizations have played an important role in protecting the rights of children with disabilities, including through filing federal court cases to enforce the IDEA. One issue that arises in such cases is whether an organization that brings a federal case as a plaintiff has standing. Organizations, like individual plaintiffs, must satisfy the constitutional and prudential rules of standing, but the rules for organizations are somewhat different. The court in *N.J. Prot. and & Advocacy, Inc. v. N.J. Department of Educ.*, 563 F. Supp. 2d 474 (D.N.J. 2008) ("NJPA"), stated the rule as follows:

> An organization or association may have standing when it (1) has standing "in its own right to seek judicial relief from *injury to itself* and to vindicate whatever rights and immunities the [organization or] association itself may enjoy" or (2) asserts claims on behalf of its constituents or members, and such constituents or members themselves would have standing to bring the claims. The latter is referred to "representational" or "associational" standing.

> Representational standing requires that (1) the organization's members would have standing on their own to bring the action, (2) "the interests the organization seeks to protect are germane to its purpose," and (3) the claims asserted and the relief requested do not require individual participation by its members. . . .

Id. at 482. *See* Peter v. Johnson, 958 F. Supp. 1383, 1391 (D. Minn. 1997) (denying standing to Choice in Education Foundation because it did not allege that its members sought special education assistance, that special education was denied to its members, or that its members lived in the district), *rev'd and remanded on other grounds*, 155 F.3d 992 (8th Cir.1988).

Consider the application of the organizational standing rule in the following two cases involving the standing of "protection and advocacy" organizations, which are federally funded organizations authorized to " 'pursue legal, administrative, and other appropriate remedies or other opportunities to ensure the protection of, and advocacy for, the rights of [disabled] individuals,' 42 U.S.C. § 6042(a)(2)(A)(1) . . . ." Tennessee Prot. and Advocacy v. Bd. of Educ. of Putnam Cnty., 24 F. Supp. 2d 808, 814 (M.D. Tenn. 1998) ("*TPA*"). In *TPA*, the court denied standing to the Tennessee Protection and Advocacy Organization ("TPAO"), which had sued claiming that the school district used unqualified therapists to provide physical and occupational therapy to children with disabilities. *Id.* at 811. The court denied standing because TPAO did not file "on behalf of specific, named injured individuals." *Id.* at 816. The court also ruled that TPAO could not show injury to itself because the only injury it could show was payment of litigation expenses, and litigation expenses alone do not create standing. *Id.* at 817–18. In contrast, in NJPA, the court granted standing to New Jersey Protection & Advocacy ("NPA"), which had brought suit claiming that the defendant was denying children with disabilities the right to an education in the least restrictive environment. 563 F. Supp. 2d at 479. The court found that NJPA had standing because individuals it represents suffered injuries that would give them standing on their own, the interests NJPA was seeking to enforce were related to its purpose, and the case did not require participation of its individual student members. *Id.* at 482–83. Can the court's decisions in *TPA* and *NJPA* be reconciled? Is the key difference that NJPA identified specific children whom the defendant had allegedly harmed while TPAO did not?

D. Application of the Standing Rules

Consider the application of the standing rules in the following cases. Are the decisions consistent? Do they follow the standing rules set forth in the cases in this chapter?

<u>Reid L. v. Ill. State Bd. of Educ., 358 F.3d 511 (7th Cir. 2004)</u>: The court ruled that students did not have standing under the IDEA to challenge new special education teacher certification regulations. The court reasoned:

> The student-plaintiffs claim that the new certification rules violate their right to a "free appropriate public education." The teacher-plaintiffs claim that the new certification rules were adopted in violation of Illinois' rule-making procedures. . . .
>
> The student-plaintiffs argue that they are injured because, under the new certification rules, students with disabilities will be taught by less qualified teachers and will thus be denied their right to a "free appropriate public education." This harm will occur in two different ways, in their view. First, during the transition period, because teachers may be assigned to students with disabilities outside their prior certification, these students may be taught by teachers not yet trained to meet their needs. Second, under the permanent certification standards, teachers on the whole will be less qualified, because they will be required to demonstrate knowledge of many disability areas and therefore will be unable to meet students' specific needs.
>
> All of these claims, however, are entirely speculative, and as such, they do not demonstrate an injury in fact. . . . There is no reason to assume that the student-plaintiffs as a group would not receive an "appropriate" education under a less categorical certification system . . . .

Id. at 515–516.

Heldman v. Sobol, 962 F.2d 148 (2d Cir. 1992): The court ruled that the parent-plaintiff, "as the father of a child with disabling conditions, has standing to challenge the New York procedures for the selection of hearing officers." *Id.* at 158. The court held that the plaintiff alleged an injury in the form of denial of his right to an impartial hearing, that the injury was traceable to the state regulations that allowed a school district to select the hearing officers, and that the relief plaintiff sought—an injunction against the school district selecting hearing officers—would redress his injury. *Id.* at 154–57.

Bitsilly v. Bureau of Indian Affairs, 253 F. Supp. 2d 1257 (D.N.M. 2003): The plaintiffs alleged that the defendants failed to ensure that the tribally-controlled schools complied with the IDEA and as a result they were denied a FAPE. *Id.* at 1260. The defendant moved to dismiss for lack of standing. The court ruled:

> Plaintiffs have alleged that they suffered an injury in fact, that is, the denial of a FAPE and a regression in their academic achievement. The Court is convinced that, by law, this injury is fairly traceable to the inaction of Defendants in their failure to provide a structure for the implementation of IDEA programs at tribally controlled schools, and to assure that the substantive and procedural rights of disabled Indian children are protected, as required by the statutes and regulations. Finally, if the Court awards compensatory education to Plaintiffs, it is clear that such award would be causally connected to their injuries and would personally benefit them. Therefore, Plaintiffs have standing to pursue their claims for past harms, and their claims for compensatory relief will not be dismissed.

Id. at 1268.

Peter v. Johnson, 958 F. Supp. 1383 (D. Minn. 1997), *rev'd and remanded on other grounds*, 155 F.3d 992 (8th Cir. 1988): The court granted standing to plaintiffs who challenged the defendant's refusal to provide special education services to students in private religious schools even though the parents had withdrawn the students from the schools as a result of the district's policies. The Court ruled:

> [B]oth . . . children were enrolled in private religious schools. . . . By a fair reading of the allegations in the complaint and attached exhibits, the parents withdrew their children from the private religious schools as a result of the district's alleged policies . . . . The court concludes that the fact the children are not currently enrolled in private religious school does not make their injuries hypothetical or conjectural. Plaintiffs have alleged, to the satisfaction of the court, that there was injury.

Id. at 1391.

Section Two: Mootness

Honig v. Doe

484 U.S. 305 (1988)

Justice Brennan delivered the opinion of the Court.

. . . .

I

. . . .

The present dispute grows out of the efforts of certain officials of the San Francisco Unified School District (SFUSD) to expel two emotionally disturbed children from school indefinitely for violent and disruptive conduct related to their disabilities. In November 1980, respondent John Doe assaulted another student at the Louise Lombard School, a developmental center for disabled children. . . .

. . . Doe admitted his misconduct and the school subsequently suspended him for five days. Thereafter, his principal referred the matter to the SFUSD Student Placement Committee (SPC or Committee) with the recommendation that Doe be expelled. On the day the suspension was to end, the SPC notified Doe's mother that it was proposing to exclude her child permanently from SFUSD and was therefore extending his suspension until such time as the expulsion proceedings were completed. . . .

After unsuccessfully protesting these actions by letter, Doe brought this suit against a host of local school officials and the State Superintendent of Public Instruction. Alleging that the suspension and proposed expulsion violated the EHA, he sought a temporary restraining order canceling the SPC hearing and requiring school officials to convene an IEP meeting. The District Judge granted the requested injunctive relief and further ordered defendants to provide home tutoring for Doe on an interim basis; shortly thereafter, she issued a preliminary injunction directing defendants to return Doe to his then current educational placement . . . .

Respondent Jack Smith was identified as an emotionally disturbed child by the time he entered the second grade in 1976. . . .

. . . SFUSD placed Smith in a learning center for emotionally disturbed children. His grandparents, however, believed that his needs would be better served in the public school setting and, in September 1979, the school district acceded to their requests and enrolled him at A. P. Giannini Middle School. . . .

At the beginning of the next school year, Smith was assigned to a full-day program; almost immediately thereafter he began misbehaving. School officials met twice with his grandparents in October 1980 to discuss returning him to a half-day program; although the grandparents agreed to the reduction, they apparently were never apprised of their right to challenge the decision through EHA procedures. The school officials also warned them that if the child continued his disruptive behavior . . . they would seek to expel him. On November 14, they made good on this threat, suspending Smith for five days after he made further lewd comments. His principal referred the matter to the SPC, which recommended exclusion from SFUSD. As it did in John Doe's case, the Committee scheduled a hearing and extended the suspension indefinitely pending a final disposition in the matter. On November 28, Smith's counsel protested these actions on grounds essentially identical to those raised by Doe, and the SPC agreed to cancel the hearing and to return Smith to a half-day program at A. P. Giannini or to provide home tutoring. Smith's grandparents chose the latter option and the school began home instruction on December 10 . . . .

After learning of Doe's action, Smith sought and obtained leave to intervene in the suit. The District Court subsequently entered summary judgment in favor of respondents on their EHA claims and issued a permanent injunction. In a series of decisions, the District Judge found that the proposed expulsions and indefinite suspensions of respondents for conduct attributable to their disabilities deprived them of their congressionally mandated right to a free appropriate public education, as well as their right to have that education provided in accordance with the procedures set out in the EHA. The District Judge therefore permanently enjoined the school district from taking any disciplinary action other than a 2- or 5-day suspension against any disabled child for disability-related misconduct, or from effecting any other change in the educational placement of any such child without parental consent pending completion of any EHA proceedings. . . . In addition, the judge barred the State from authorizing unilateral placement changes and directed it to establish an EHA compliance-monitoring system or, alternatively, to enact guidelines governing local school responses to disability-related misconduct. . . .

. . . . .

II

At the outset, we address the suggestion, raised for the first time during oral argument, that this case is moot.[5] Under Article III of the Constitution this Court may only adjudicate actual, ongoing controversies. That the dispute between the parties was very much alive when suit was filed . . . , cannot substitute for the actual case or controversy that an exercise of this Court's jurisdiction requires. In the present case, we have jurisdiction if there is a reasonable likelihood that respondents will again suffer the deprivation of EHA-mandated rights that gave rise to this suit. We believe that, at least with respect to respondent Smith, such a possibility does in fact exist and that the case therefore remains justiciable.

Respondent John Doe is now 24 years old and, accordingly, is no longer entitled to the protections and benefits of the EHA, which limits eligibility to disabled children between the ages of 3 and 21. See 20 U. S. C. § 1412(2)(B). It is clear, therefore, that whatever rights to state educational services he may yet have as a ward of the State . . . , the Act would not govern the State's provision of those services, and thus the case is moot as to him. Respondent Jack Smith, however, is currently 20 and has not yet completed high school. Although at present he is not faced with any proposed expulsion or suspension proceedings, and indeed no longer even resides within the SFUSD, he remains a resident of California and is entitled to a "free appropriate public education" within that State. His claims under the EHA, therefore, are not moot if the conduct he originally complained of is "'capable of repetition, yet evading review.'" Given Smith's continued eligibility for educational services under the EHA[6]

5. We note that both petitioner and respondents believe that this case presents a live controversy. Only the United States, appearing as *amicus curiae*, urges that the case is presently nonjusticiable. . . .

6. Notwithstanding respondent's undisputed right to a free appropriate public education in California, Justice SCALIA argues in dissent that there is no "demonstrated probability" that Smith will actually avail himself of that right because his counsel was unable to state affirmatively during oral argument that her client would seek to reenter the state school system. We believe the dissent overstates the stringency of the "capable of repetition" test. Although Justice SCALIA equates "reasonable expectation" with "demonstrated probability," the very case he cites for this proposition described these standards in the disjunctive, see *Murphy* v. *Hunt*, 455 U.S., at 482 ("[T]here must be a 'reasonable expectation' *or* a 'demonstrated probability' that the same controversy will recur" (emphasis added)), and in numerous cases decided both before and since *Hunt* we have found controversies capable of repetition based on expectations that, while reasonable, were hardly demonstrably probable. Our concern in these cases, as in all others involving potentially moot claims, was whether the controversy was *capable* of repetition and not, as the dissent seems to insist, whether the claimant had demonstrated that a recurrence of the dispute was more probable than not. Regardless, then, of whether respondent has established with mathematical precision the likelihood that he will enroll in public school during the next two years, we think there is at the very least a reasonable expectation that he will exercise his rights under the EHA. In this regard, we believe respondent's actions over the course of the last seven years speak louder than his counsel's momentary equivocation during oral argument. Since 1980, he has sought to vindicate his right to an appropriate public education that is not only free of charge, but also free from the threat that school officials will unilaterally change his placement or exclude him from class altogether. As a disabled young man, he has as at least as great a need of a high school education and diploma as any of his peers, and his counsel advises us that he is awaiting the outcome of this case to decide

the nature of his disability, and petitioner's insistence that all local school districts retain residual authority to exclude disabled children for dangerous conduct, we have little difficulty concluding that there is a "reasonable expectation" that Smith would once again be subjected to a unilateral "change in placement" for conduct growing out of his disabilities were it not for the statewide injunctive relief issued below.

Our cases reveal that, for purposes of assessing the likelihood that state authorities will reinflict a given injury, we generally have been unwilling to assume that the party seeking relief will repeat the type of misconduct that would once again place him or her at risk of that injury. No such reluctance, however, is warranted here. It is respondent Smith's very inability to conform his conduct to socially acceptable norms that renders him "handicapped" within the meaning of the EHA. As noted above, the record is replete with evidence that Smith is unable to govern his aggressive, impulsive behavior—indeed, his notice of suspension acknowledged that "Jack's actions seem beyond his control." In the absence of any suggestion that respondent has overcome his earlier difficulties, it is certainly reasonable to expect, based on his prior history of behavioral problems, that he will again engage in classroom misconduct. Nor is it reasonable to suppose that Smith's future educational placement will so perfectly suit his emotional and academic needs that further disruptions on his part are improbable. Although Justice SCALIA suggests in his dissent that school officials are unlikely to place Smith in a setting where they cannot control his misbehavior, any efforts to ensure such total control must be tempered by the school system's statutory obligations to provide respondent with a free appropriate public education in "the least restrictive environment"; to educate him, "to the maximum extent appropriate," with children who are not disabled; and to consult with his parents or guardians, and presumably with respondent himself, before choosing a placement. Indeed, it is only by ignoring these mandates, as well as Congress' unquestioned desire to wrest from school officials their former unilateral authority to determine the placement of emotionally disturbed children, that the dissent can so readily assume that respondent's future placement will satisfactorily prevent any further dangerous conduct on his part. Overarching these statutory obligations, moreover, is the inescapable fact that the preparation of an IEP, like any other effort at predicting human behavior, is an inexact science at best. Given the unique circumstances and context of this case, therefore, we think it reasonable to expect that respondent will again engage in the type of misconduct that precipitated this suit.

We think it equally probable that, should he do so, respondent will again be subjected to the same unilateral school action for which he initially sought relief. In this regard, it matters not that Smith no longer resides within the SFUSD. While the actions of SFUSD officials first gave rise to this litigation, the District Judge expressly

---

whether to pursue his degree. Under these circumstances, we think it not only counterintuitive but also unreasonable to assume that respondent will forgo the exercise of a right that he has for so long sought to defend.

found that the lack of a state policy governing local school responses to disability-related misconduct had led to, and would continue to result in, EHA violations, and she therefore enjoined the state defendant from authorizing, among other things, unilateral placement changes. She of course also issued injunctions directed at the local defendants, but they did not seek review of those orders in this Court. Only petitioner, the State Superintendent of Public Instruction, has invoked our jurisdiction, and he now urges us to hold that local school districts retain unilateral authority under the EHA to suspend or otherwise remove disabled children for dangerous conduct. Given these representations, we have every reason to believe that were it not for the injunction barring petitioner from authorizing such unilateral action, respondent would be faced with a real and substantial threat of such action in any California school district in which he enrolled. Certainly, if the SFUSD's past practice of unilateral exclusions was at odds with state policy and the practice of local school districts generally, petitioner would not now stand before us seeking to defend the right of all local school districts to engage in such aberrant behavior.[7]

We have previously noted that administrative and judicial review under the EHA is often "ponderous," *Burlington School Committee* v. *Massachusetts Dept. of Education*, 471 U.S. 359, 370 (1985), and this case, which has taken seven years to reach us, amply confirms that observation. For obvious reasons, the misconduct of an emotionally disturbed or otherwise disabled child who has not yet reached adolescence typically will not pose such a serious threat to the well-being of other students that school officials can only ensure classroom safety by excluding the child. Yet, the adolescent student improperly disciplined for misconduct that does pose such a threat will often be finished with school or otherwise ineligible for EHA protections by the time review can be had in this Court. Because we believe that respondent Smith has demonstrated both "a sufficient likelihood that he will again be wronged in a similar way," and that any resulting claim he may have for relief will surely evade our review, we turn to the merits of his case.

. . . .

Justice Scalia, with whom Justice O'Connor joins, dissenting.

Without expressing any views on the merits of this case, I respectfully dissent because in my opinion we have no authority to decide it. I think the controversy is moot.

. . . .

7. Petitioner concedes that the school district "made a number of procedural mistakes in its eagerness to protect other students from Doe and Smith." . . . According to petitioner, however, unilaterally excluding respondents from school was not among them; indeed, petitioner insists that the SFUSD acted properly in removing respondents and urges that the stay-put provision "should not be interpreted to require a school district to maintain such dangerous children with other children." . . .

II

If our established mode of analysis were followed, the conclusion that a live controversy exists in the present case would require a demonstrated probability that *all* of the following events will occur: (1) Smith will return to public school; (2) he will be placed in an educational setting that is unable to tolerate his dangerous behavior; (3) he will again engage in dangerous behavior; and (4) local school officials will again attempt unilaterally to change his placement and the state defendants will fail to prevent such action. The Court spends considerable time establishing that the last two of these events are likely to recur, but relegates to a footnote its discussion of the first event, upon which all others depend, and only briefly alludes to the second. Neither the facts in the record, nor even the extrarecord assurances of counsel, establish a demonstrated probability of either of them.

With respect to whether Smith will return to school, at oral argument Smith's counsel forthrightly conceded that she "cannot represent whether in fact either of these students will ask for further education from the Petitioners." Rather, she observed, respondents would "look to [our decision in this case] to find out what will happen after that." When pressed, the most counsel would say was that, in her view, the 20-year-old Smith *could* seek to return to public school because he has not graduated, he is handicapped, and he has a right to an education. I do not perceive the principle that would enable us to leap from the proposition that Smith could reenter public school to the conclusion that it is a demonstrated probability he will do so.

The Court nevertheless concludes that "there is at the very least a reasonable expectation" that Smith will return to school.... It is worth pointing out, however, how slim are the reeds upon which this conclusion of "reasonable expectation" (whatever that means) rests. The Court bases its determination on three observations from the record and oral argument. First, it notes that Smith has been pressing this lawsuit since 1980. It suffices to observe that the equivalent argument can be made in every case that remains active and pending; we have hitherto avoided equating the existence of a case or controversy with the existence of a lawsuit. Second, the Court observes that Smith has "as great a need of a high school education and diploma as any of his peers." While this is undoubtedly good advice, it hardly establishes that the 20-year-old Smith is likely to return to high school, much less to public high school. Finally, the Court notes that counsel "advises us that [Smith] is awaiting the outcome of this case to decide whether to pursue his degree." Not only do I not think this establishes a current case or controversy, I think it a most conclusive indication that no current case or controversy exists.

Notes, Comments, and Questions

1. Several factors in special education cases combine to make it difficult to complete judicial review of a dispute in a timely manner: a school year is only ten months; a new IEP must be prepared every year; and it takes well over a year for a challenge to a child's special education services to work its way through administrative

proceedings and the courts. *See* Board of Educ. of Hendrick Hudson Cent. Sch. Dist. v. Rowley, 458 U.S. 176, 186 n.9 (1982) ("Judicial review invariably takes more than nine months to complete, not to mention the time consumed during the preceding state administrative hearings."); *see also Honig*, 484 U.S. at 322 ("We have previously noted that administrative and judicial review under the EHA is often '"ponderous,"' and this case, which has taken seven years to reach us, amply confirms that observation."). In addition, children graduate from high school, age out of IDEA eligibility, or move out of the district. *See* Russman v. Bd. of Educ. of Enlarged City Sch. Dist. of Watervliet, 260 F.3d 114, 119 (2d Cir. 2001) ("Mootness is a recurring phenomenon in students' suits to vindicate constitutional rights associated with the conditions of their education: a student's graduation ends his individual interest in the conditions of education at his former school."). These factors raise several mootness issues in special education cases: Is a challenge to the IEP for year X moot in year X+1 when a new IEP is in place? Is a case brought when the plaintiff is twenty years old moot when the plaintiff turns twenty-one? The court in *Honig* addressed these issues by applying an exception to the mootness doctrine for disputes that have ended but are "capable of repetition yet evading review," and found that the claim was not moot because it was capable of repetition. Justice Scalia dissented, arguing that the exception required not just a remote possibility of repetition, but a demonstrated possibility. Do you find the majority or dissent more compelling?

2. The lower courts have considered whether the "capable of repetition yet evading review" exception to the mootness doctrine applies in several cases and have reached different results. As you read the case descriptions below, can you generate a principle of general applicability for finding the "capable of repetition yet evading review" exception to the mootness doctrine in special education cases?

<u>Decisions declining to find that the dispute was capable of repetition yet evading review</u>:

> *The child challenged the school district's proposed placement in a school outside the district. The Second Circuit, distinguishing *Honig*, found the challenge was moot because the child was currently in a district placement, his disability was not likely to lead to his removal from the district, and the school district stated that it did not intend to remove him from the public schools. The court ruled, "repetition of the defendants' challenged conduct—the proposed removal of Lindsey from the Redding public schools—is not reasonably likely but, at best, only a theoretical and speculative possibility." Lillbask v. Conn. Dep't of Educ., 397 F.3d 77, 86–87 (2d Cir. 2005).
>
> *The child received an IEP diploma, was no longer enrolled in school, and her parents did not plan to re-enroll her. They only wanted to keep open the option to re-enroll her. Russman v. Bd. of Educ. of Enlarged City Sch. Dist. of Watervliet, 260 F.3d 114, 119–121 (2d Cir. 2001).

*A child who challenged the school district's failure to provide him a one-to-one aide at his private school graduated from the private school, was enrolled in a public high school, and demonstrated no intent to transfer to a private high school. Thomas R.W. v. Mass. Dep't of Educ., 130 F.3d 477, 479 (1st Cir. 1997).

*The parents alleged that the child's supervised reading assistance was reduced in fifth grade in violation of the IDEA. The child had since graduated from eighth grade and moved to a new district. The parents had agreed to a new IEP for him at the high school in the new district. Board of Educ. of Downers Grove Grade Sch. Dist. No. 58 v. Steven L., 89 F.3d 464, 464–67 (7th Cir. 1996).

*The child's parent sought a declaratory judgment that the IDEA applies to the child's previous school and that the child's discharge from the school violated the IDEA. By the time the Second Circuit heard the case, the child was in an out-of-district placement for which the school district paid. The court found that the repetition of the dispute was very unlikely; it would require the child to leave his current placement, be readmitted to the former school, and be discharged once again without consent. Christopher P. v. Marcus, 915 F.2d 794, 803–04 (2d Cir. 1990), *aff'd*, 498 U.S. 1123 (1991).

*In a case that included a challenge to the child's eligibility for special education, the court ruled, "The issues pertaining to A.G.'s preliminary eligibility for special education have been resolved through testing and preparation of an IEP. Future litigation may arise over A.G.'s education, but the threshold issue of preliminary eligibility is a unique 'legal wrong' that is not subject to repetition. Hence, plaintiff's claim for independent evaluations, an IEP meeting, and an IEP are moot and do not fall within the 'capable of repetition but evading review' exception to mootness." Theodore v. District of Columbia, 655 F. Supp. 2d 136, 145 (D.D.C. 2009).

<u>Decisions finding that the dispute was capable of repetition yet evading review</u>:

*The child challenged a suspension that had occurred six years earlier. The child was no longer attending school in the district. The court found that "the legal issue—an IDEA hearing officer's authority to revise discipline upon finding that an infraction was not a manifestation of a disability—is almost certainly to 'be a recurring one.'" District of Columbia v. Doe, 611 F.3d 888, 895 (D.C. Cir. 2010).

*A dispute over the appropriate placement for a child was resolved by placing the child full-time in a regular-education classroom. However, the court found that the school district and the child's parents:

> have conflicting educational philosophies and perceptions of the District's mainstreaming obligation. The District has consistently taken the view that a child with Rachel's I.Q. is too severely disabled to benefit from full-time placement in a regular class, while the Hollands maintain that Rachel learns both social and academic skills in a regular class and

> would not benefit from being in a special education class. This conflict is a continuing one and will arise frequently.

Sacramento City Unified Sch. Dist. Bd. of Educ. v. Rachel H., 14 F.3d 1398, 1403 (9th Cir. 1994), *cert. denied*, 512 U.S. 1207 (1994); *see also* Daniel R.R. v. State Bd. of Educ., 874 F.2d 1036, 1040–41 (5th Cir. 1989) (ruling that dispute over placement of child in general education classroom likely to recur because of "the parties' irreconcilable views on the issue").

*The plaintiff challenged the procedure for appointing impartial hearing officers to preside over IDEA administrative hearings. The plaintiff's son was nineteen years old and no longer in school, but was still eligible for a FAPE. The court ruled that the case was not moot. Comparing the facts to *Honig*, the court stated:

> First, with regard to the reasonable expectation prong of the analysis, if T.H. were to return to school, there is a likelihood that a dispute would arise concerning his IEP, that Minisink would select a hearing officer pursuant to . . . [the challenged regulation], giving rise to the same alleged violation of T.H.'s IDEA rights. Second, the time required for review under IDEA is likely to prevent review of future claims brought by T.H.

Heldman v. Sobol, 962 F.2d 148, 157 n.9 (2d Cir. 1992).

*In a dispute about the educational services to be provided to a child with an intellectual disability, the parent consented to the IEP that was the subject of an appeal in federal court while the appeal was pending. The school district moved to dismiss on the ground that the appeal was moot. Basing its decision in large part on *Honig*, the court ruled that the case was not moot:

> Abney is almost eighteen years old, which means that he will qualify for EHA benefits for another three years. There is no evidence that his medical problems will disappear . . . . If his ulcers recur, or if he injures himself in some other manner . . . there is a reasonable possibility that he will once again be denied instruction conforming to his IEP during his convalescence, or that the District will again neglect to notify his surrogate parent that his educational instruction has ceased. In the instant case, District officials failed to diagnose Abney's medical problems promptly and they seemed indifferent to his education while awaiting confirmation of the initial diagnosis; these past failures enhance the probability that the violations will recur.

Abney v. District of Columbia, 849 F.2d 1491, 1495 (D.C. Cir. 1988).

*The school district challenged the hearing officer's authority to order the district to provide guidance counseling services. The court found that the dispute was capable of repetition because the school district could be required to provide such services in the future. School Bd. of Norfolk v. Brown, 769 F. Supp. 2d 928, 953 (E.D. Va. 2010).

> *The dispute over the child's 1997–1998 placement was resolved when the district agreed to his placement and agreed to pay his educational costs. However, the child was eligible for a FAPE for two more years, needed a new placement during the current school year, and was having difficulty getting a response from the district about the need for a new placement. The court ruled, "there is, therefore, a 'reasonable expectation' that Ian and his parents will be subject to the same action again." Zearley v. Ackerman, 116 F. Supp. 2d 109, 112 (D.D.C. 2000).

3. In addition to considering whether a dispute is capable of repetition yet evading review, courts examine the nature of the relief the child is seeking to determine whether a case is moot. If a child is seeking relief for past violations in the form of tuition reimbursement or compensatory education, or if the parents are seeking attorneys fees, the court will generally not dismiss the case, even if the dispute over the child's education had been resolved and was not likely to recur. *See, e.g.*, E.D. v. Newburyport Pub. Sch., 654 F.3d 140, 143 (1st Cir. 2011) (ruling that claim for compensatory education and attorneys fees was not moot even though plaintiffs moved from the school district); Garcia v. Bd. of Educ. of Albuquerque Pub. Sch., 520 F.3d 1116, 1123–24 (10th Cir. 2008) (denying mootness claim because plaintiffs alleged "an actual injury traceable to the school district for which ... [the court] *can* issue a remedy.") (emphasis in original); Lesesne v. District of Columbia, 447 F.3d 828, 833 (D.C. Cir. 2006) (denying mootness defense against claim for compensatory education); Maine Sch. Admin. Dist. No. 35 v. Mr. and Mrs. R., 321 F.3d 9, 19 (1st Cir. 2003) (denying mootness claim in light of claim for compensatory education); Capistrano Unified Sch. Dist. v. Wartenberg, 59 F.3d 884, 890 (9th Cir. 1995) (ruling that the case was not moot even though child graduated from high school because of pending claims for tuition reimbursement and attorneys fees); Theodore v. District of Columbia, 655 F. Supp. 2d 136, 145 (D.D.C. 2009) (ruling that claims for compensatory education and attorneys fees and costs were not moot); Hicks v. Purchase Line Sch. Dist., 251 F. Supp. 2d 1250, 1253 n. 1 (W.D. Pa. 2003) (ruling that child's graduation did not moot the case because plaintiffs were seeking compensation for past violations of the IDEA); Max M. v. Thompson, 592 F. Supp. 1450, 1458 (N.D. Ill. 1984) (ruling that claim for compensatory education were not moot even after child was no longer eligible for special education). On the other hand, if the child did not request retroactive relief in the complaint or the request for the hearing, and the controversy is no longer live, the court will dismiss the case as moot. *See, e.g.*, Moseley v. Bd. of Educ. of Albuquerque Pub. Sch., 483 F.3d 689, 692–94 (10th Cir. 2007) (ruling that failure to raise reimbursement or compensatory education claims in complaint rendered case moot in light of child's graduation); Brown v. Bartholomew Consol. Sch. Corp., 442 F.3d 588, 597 (7th Cir. 2006) (ruling that case was moot because plaintiff did not request compensatory education until reply brief); Lillbask v. Conn. Dep't of Educ., 397 F.3d 77, 89–91 (2d Cir. 2005) (dismissing complaint as moot because plaintiff did not request compensatory education in original complaint); T.S. v. Indep. Sch. Dist. No. 54, 265 F.3d 1090, 1092–93 (10th Cir. 2001) (ruling that "inkling" of a claim for compensatory education did not overcome mootness of claim), *cert. denied*, 482 F.3d 689 (2007).

Section Three
Sovereign Immunity

Dellmuth v. Muth

491 U.S. 223 (1989)

Justice KENNEDY delivered the opinion of the Court.

The question before us is whether the Education of the Handicapped Act abrogates the States' Eleventh Amendment immunity from suit in the federal courts.

I

....

Alex Muth ... is ... handicapped within the meaning of the EHA by a language learning disability and associated emotional problems.... In the summer of 1983, respondent requested a statutory administrative hearing to challenge the district's IEP for Alex....

The hearing examiner found that Alex's original IEP was inappropriate and made a number of recommendations. Both respondent and the school district then appealed the decision to the secretary of education, as provided under Pennsylvania law. The secretary remanded the case to the hearing examiner with instructions to the school district to revise Alex's IEP. After the district did so, the hearing examiner issued a decision declaring the revised IEP appropriate, and the secretary affirmed that decision ....

While the administrative proceedings were underway, respondent brought this suit against the school district and the state secretary of education.... As amended, respondent's complaint alleged that the district's IEP for Alex was inappropriate and that the Commonwealth's administrative proceedings had violated the procedural requirements of the EHA ....

The District Court found various procedural infirmities in Pennsylvania's administrative scheme and entered summary judgment on respondent's procedural claims. The court held a hearing to resolve the remaining issues in the case and to determine the proper remedy for the procedural violations. The court concluded that, while the district's proposed IEP for 1983–1984 had been appropriate within the meaning of the EHA, respondent was entitled to reimbursement for Alex's tuition that year because the procedural flaws had delayed the administrative process. The District Court further determined that the school district and the Commonwealth of Pennsylvania were jointly and severally liable, agreeing with respondent that the EHA abrogated Pennsylvania's Eleventh Amendment immunity from suit....

The United States Court of Appeals for the Third Circuit affirmed. Most pertinent for this case, the Court of Appeals agreed with the District Court that the Eleventh Amendment did not bar the reimbursement award against the Commonwealth....

To resolve a conflict among the Circuits, we granted certiorari on the question whether the EHA abrogates the States' sovereign immunity under the Eleventh Amendment. We now reverse.

II

We have recognized that Congress, acting in the exercise of its enforcement authority under § 5 of the Fourteenth Amendment,[1] may abrogate the States' Eleventh Amendment immunity. We have stressed, however, that abrogation of sovereign immunity upsets "the fundamental constitutional balance between the Federal Government and the States," *Atascadero State Hospital v. Scanlon*, 473 U.S. 234, 238 (1985), placing a considerable strain on "'[t]he principles of federalism that inform Eleventh Amendment doctrine,'" *Pennhurst State School and Hospital v. Halderman*, 465 U.S. 89, 100 (1984), quoting *Hutto v. Finney*, 437 U.S. 678, 691 (1978). To temper Congress' acknowledged powers of abrogation with due concern for the Eleventh Amendment's role as an essential component of our constitutional structure, we have applied a simple but stringent test: "Congress may abrogate the States' constitutionally secured immunity from suit in federal court only by making its intention unmistakably clear in the language of the statute." *Atascadero, supra*, at 242.

In concluding that the EHA contains the requisite clear statement of congressional intent, the Court of Appeals rested principally on three textual provisions. The court first cited the Act's preamble, which states Congress' finding that "it is in the national interest that the Federal government assist State and local efforts to provide programs to meet the education needs of handicapped children in order to assure equal protection of the law." 20 U. S. C. § 1400(b)(9). Second . . . was the Act's judicial review provision, which permits parties aggrieved by the administrative process to "bring a civil action . . . in any State court of competent jurisdiction or in a district court of the United States without regard to the amount in controversy." 20 U.S.C. § 1415(e)(2). Finally, the Court of Appeals pointed to a 1986 amendment to the EHA, which states that the Act's provision for a reduction of attorney's fees shall not apply "if the court finds that the State or local educational agency unreasonably protracted the final resolution of the action or proceeding or there was a violation of this section." 20 U.S.C. § 1415(e)(4)(G). . . . In the view of the Court of Appeals, this amendment represented an express statement of Congress' understanding that States can be parties in civil actions brought under the EHA.

Respondent supplements these points with some nontextual arguments. . . .[2]

. . . .

---

1. Petitioner concedes that the EHA was enacted pursuant to Congress' authority under § 5 of the Fourteenth Amendment, and that Congress has the power to abrogate the Eleventh Amendment with respect to the Act. We decide the case on these assumptions.

2. Respondent also offers us another avenue to affirm the result below, which is to overrule the longstanding holding of *Hans v. Louisiana*, 134 U.S. 1 . . . (1890), that an unconsenting State is immune from liability for damages in a suit brought in federal court by one of its own citizens. We decline this most recent invitation to overrule our opinion in *Hans*.

We now turn our attention to the proper focus of an inquiry into congressional abrogation of sovereign immunity, the language of the statute. We cannot agree that the textual provisions on which the Court of Appeals relied, or any other provisions of the EHA, demonstrate with unmistakable clarity that Congress intended to abrogate the States' immunity from suit. The EHA makes no reference whatsoever to either the Eleventh Amendment or the States' sovereign immunity. Nor does any provision cited by the Court of Appeals address abrogation in even oblique terms, much less with the clarity *Atascadero* requires. The general statement of legislative purpose in the Act's preamble simply has nothing to do with the States' sovereign immunity. The 1986 amendment to the EHA deals only with attorney's fees, and does not alter or speak to what parties are subject to suit. . . . . Finally, 20 U.S.C. § 1415(e)(2) . . . provides judicial review for aggrieved parties, but in no way intimates that the States' sovereign immunity is abrogated. As we made plain in *Atascadero:* "A general authorization for suit in federal court is not the kind of unequivocal statutory language sufficient to abrogate the Eleventh Amendment." 473 U.S., at 246.

At its core, respondent's attempt to distinguish this case from *Atascadero* appears to reduce to the proposition that the EHA "is replete with references to the states," whereas in "*Atascadero* . . . the statutory language at issue did not include mention of states." We recognize that the EHA's frequent reference to the States, and its delineation of the States' important role in securing an appropriate education for handicapped children, make the States, along with local agencies, logical defendants in suits alleging violations of the EHA. This statutory structure lends force to the inference that the States were intended to be subject to damages actions for violations of the EHA. But such a permissible inference, whatever its logical force, would remain just that: a permissible inference. It would not be the unequivocal declaration which, we reaffirm today, is necessary before we will determine that Congress intended to exercise its powers of abrogation.

III

We hold that the statutory language of the EHA does not evince an unmistakably clear intention to abrogate the States' constitutionally secured immunity from suit. The Eleventh Amendment bars respondent's attempt to collect tuition reimbursement from the Commonwealth of Pennsylvania. The judgment of the Court of Appeals is reversed, and the case is remanded for proceedings consistent with this opinion.

. . . .

Justice Brennan, with whom Justice Marshall, Justice Blackmun, and Justice Stevens join, dissenting.

I respectfully dissent from the Court's holding that the Commonwealth of Pennsylvania is immune from suit in the federal courts for violations of the Education of the Handicapped Act (EHA). For reasons I have set out elsewhere, I would accept respondent Muth's invitation to overrule *Hans v. Louisiana*, 134 U.S. 1 . . . (1890), as that case has been interpreted in this Court's recent decisions. Even if I did not hold that view, I would nevertheless affirm the decision of the Court of Appeals on the ground that Congress in the EHA abrogated state immunity.

I

Applying the standard method for ascertaining congressional intent, I conclude, with the Court of Appeals, that "[t]he text of EHA and its legislative history leave no doubt that Congress intended to abrogate the 11th amendment immunity of the states."

The EHA imposes substantial obligations on the States, as well as on local education authorities, as might be expected in an Act authorizing federal financial aid "to assist States and localities to provide for the education of all handicapped children." 20 U.S.C. § 1400(c). To be eligible for federal assistance, a State must develop a plan for the education of all handicapped children and establish the procedural safeguards mandated in § 1415. §§ 1412(2), (5). It is the state educational agency that is "responsible for assuring that the requirements of [EHA . . .] are carried out and that all educational programs for handicapped children within the State, including all such programs administered by any other State or local agency, [are] under the general supervision of the persons responsible for educational programs for handicapped children in the State educational agency." § 1412(6).

In accord with this overarching responsibility placed upon the States, the EHA contemplates that in a number of situations where a local education authority cannot or will not provide appropriate educational services to the handicapped, the State will do so directly. See 20 U.S.C. § 1411(c)(4)(A)(ii) (State to assure provision of services where local authority barred from receiving federal funds because it has failed to submit a proper application); § 1414(d) (State "to provide special education and related services directly to handicapped children residing in the area served by [a] local educational agency" that is unable or unwilling to establish or maintain programs, or to be merged with other local agencies to enable it to do so, or that has "handicapped children who can best be served by a regional or State center"). And in any event, where a local education authority would be entitled to less than $7,500 in EHA funding for a fiscal year, the State may not distribute the funds, but must use the funds itself to ensure provision of appropriate services. §§ 1411(c)(4)(A)(i), (c)(4)(B). Moreover, a State may choose to administer up to 25 percent of its federal funding itself, rather than distributing these funds to local education authorities, and use such funds to provide direct services to the handicapped. §§ 1411(c)(1), (c)(2).

"[T]he EHA confers upon disabled students an *enforceable* substantive right to public education in participating States and conditions federal financial assistance upon a State's compliance with the substantive and procedural goals of the Act." *Honig v. Doe*, 484 U.S. 305, 310 . . . (1988) . . . . Thus, § 1415(e)(2) provides that "any party aggrieved by the findings and decision [made in an administrative process] shall have the right to bring a civil action . . . in any State court of competent jurisdiction or in a district court of the United States without regard to the amount in controversy." This provision makes no distinction between civil actions based upon the type of relief sought and hence plainly contemplates tuition-reimbursement actions. See *School Committee of Burlington v. Department of Education of Massachusetts*, 471 U.S. 359 (1985). In light of the States' pervasive role under the EHA, and the clarity with which the statute imposes both procedural and substantive obligations on the States, I have no trouble in inferring from the text of the EHA that "Congress intended that the state should be named as an opposing party, if not the sole party, to [a] proceeding" brought under § 1415(e)(2), whatever remedy is sought, and that Congress thereby abrogated Eleventh Amendment immunity from suit in federal court. Indeed, in those situations where a State has elected to provide educational services to the handicapped directly, or where under the EHA it is required to provide direct services, the State would appear to be the only proper defendant in a federal action to enforce EHA rights.

This solely textually based interpretation of the EHA is supported by the statute's legislative history. Senator Williams, a primary author of the EHA, explained to Congress that, under the Act,

> "it should be clear that a parent or guardian may present a complaint *alleging that a State* or local educational agency has refused to provide services to which a child may be entitled or *alleging that a State* or local educational agency has erroneously classified a child as a handicapped child." 121 Cong. Rec. 37415 (1975) (emphasis added).

In addition, he emphasized that "any party aggrieved by the findings and decision rendered in the due process hearing o[r] the State educational agency review of such hearing shall have the right to bring a civil action *with respect to the original complaint*," *id.*, at 37416 (emphasis added), that is, with respect to the administrative complaint, which of course may allege EHA violations by the State. The text and legislative history of the EHA thus make it unmistakably clear that Congress there intended to abrogate state immunity from suit.

. . . .

Notes, Comments, and Questions

1. The doctrine of sovereign immunity protects a sovereign from lawsuits in its own courts absent its consent. The Eleventh Amendment to the United States Constitution extends sovereign immunity to states against lawsuits by citizens of another state in federal courts:

> The Judicial power of the United States shall not be construed to extend to any suit in law or equity, commenced or prosecuted against one of the United States by Citizens of another State, or by Citizens or Subjects of any Foreign State.

U.S. Const. amend. XI. As mentioned in *Dellumth*, the Supreme Court extended immunity to states from suit in federal court by their own citizens in *Hans v. Louisiana*, 134 U.S. 1 (1890).

2. Congress reacted to *Dellmuth* in 1990 by passing Section 1403 of the IDEA, which is entitled, "Abrogation of state sovereign immunity." Section 1403(a) states:

> A State shall not be immune under the 11th amendment to the Constitution of the United States from suit in Federal court for a violation of this chapter.

20 U.S.C. § 1403(a)(2012). Does this language satisfy *Dellmuth*'s requirement of an unequivocal abrogation of sovereign immunity? Two courts of appeals disagree. In *Bradley v. Ark. Dep't of Educ.*, 189 F.3d 745, 752 (8th Cir. 1999), *vacated on other grounds*, 197 F.3d 958 (8th Cir. 1999), the court ruled that IDEA was not a valid exercise of Congress' authority under Section Five of the Fourteenth Amendment. The court listed the six findings Congress made when it passed the IDEA and stated, "In making these six findings, however, Congress did not find that the disparate treatment of students with disabilities resulted from action by the states or, if it did, that such state action violated the Equal Protection Clause." *Id.* at 752. On the other hand, in *Little Rock Sch. Dist. v. Mauney*, 183 F.3d 816 (8th Cir. 1999), the court ruled that Congress abrogated sovereign immunity. *Id.* at 832.

In contrast to the disagreement among the appellate courts, federal district courts have agreed that Section 1403 did abrogate Eleventh Amendment immunity. *See* J.R. v. Waterbury Bd. of Educ., 272 F. Supp. 2d 174, 177 (D. Conn. 2001) (ruling that "a Section 1983 action is allowed against a state or an agency of the state under the plain language of the IDEA."); Virginia Office of Prot. and Advocacy v. Va. Dep't of Educ., 262 F. Supp. 2d 648, 655 (E.D. Va. 2003) (ruling that Section 1403 abrogated sovereign immunity); S.C. v. Deptford Twp. Bd. of Educ., 248 F. Supp. 2d 368, 383–85 (D.N.J. 2003) (finding that Section 1403 unequivocally abrogated sovereign immunity); Emma C. v. Eastin, 985 F. Supp. 940, 946–47 (N.D. Cal. 1997) (ruling that the IDEA "includes an express, unequivocal abrogation of Eleventh Amendment immunity."); Straube v. Fla. Union Free Sch. Dist., 801 F. Supp. 1164, 1171 (S.D.N.Y. 1992) (ruling that the IDEA abrogates Eleventh Amendment immunity); Joshua B. v. New Trier Twp. High Sch. Dist. 203, 770 F. Supp. 431, 433–34 (N.D. Ill. 1991) (ruling that the IDEA abrogated sovereign immunity). With which rulings do you agree?

3. Where does all this leave a potential plaintiff in an IDEA case who wants to sue a state in federal court for an alleged IDEA violation? Immediately after *Dellmuth*, she could not. But, one year after *Dellmuth*, according to Section 1403, she could. But according to one court of appeals she could not but according to another she could.

4. Even if Section 1403 did not abrogate sovereign immunity, there are at least two other ways a plaintiff can sue a state in federal court pursuant to the IDEA. First, a state can consent to suit in federal court by waiving sovereign immunity by accepting federal funds. Congress has authority under Article I, Section 8, clause 1 of the U.S. Constitution to provide for the general welfare. Congress has used this authority to pass funding statutes, including the IDEA, that make money available to a state on the condition that it comply with the underlying law, including waiving the state's Eleventh Amendment immunity. In order to do so, the funding statute must meet the following guidelines:

> 1) Federal expenditures must benefit the general welfare; 2) The conditions imposed on the states must be unambiguous; 3) The conditions must be reasonably related to the purpose of the expenditure; and 4) No condition may violate any independent constitutional prohibitions. In addition, . . . the condition [may] not be coercive.

Pace v. Bogalusa City Sch. Bd., 403 F.3d 272, 278 (5th Cir. 2005), *cert. denied*, 546 U.S. 933 (2005) (ruling that Louisiana waived sovereign immunity by accepting funds under the IDEA). Courts have consistently held that by accepting funds under the IDEA, states waive their sovereign immunity. *See* M. A. v. State-Operated Sch. Dist. of Newark, 344 F.3d 335, 338 (3d Cir. 2003) (affirming district court decision that state waived sovereign immunity by accepting IDEA funds); A.W. v. Jersey City Pub. Sch., 341 F.3d 234, 238 (3d Cir. 2003) ("Congress unequivocally expressed its intent to condition participation in . . . [the IDEA] on the state's relinquishment of its immunity"); Board of Educ. of Oak Park and River High Sch. Dist. No. 200 v. Kelly E., 207 F.3d 931, 935 (7th Cir. 2000), *cert. denied*, 531 U.S. 824 (2000) ("One string attached to money under the IDEA is submitting to suit in federal court."); Bradley v. Ark. Dep't of Educ., 189 F.3d 745, 753 (8th Cir. 1999) ("Arkansas waived its Eleventh Amendment immunity . . . when it chose to participate . . . in the IDEA.").

Second, a plaintiff may sue a state indirectly in federal court by seeking prospective (injunctive or declaratory) relief against a state official. Eleventh Amendment immunity protects states from damages claims for past violations of law; it does not protect states from claims against state officials for prospective relief against alleged ongoing state violations of federal law. *See M.A.*, 344 F.3d at 345 (stating that a suit against a state official for prospective relief is an exception to Eleventh Amendment immunity); Kerr Ctr. Parents Ass'n v. Charles, 897 F.2d 1463, 1469 (9th Cir. 1990) (upholding against immunity claim a court order to the state to comply prospectively with its special education obligations); Goleta Union Elementary Sch. Dist. v. Ordway, 166 F. Supp. 2d 1287, 1297 (C.D. Cal. 2001) ("The Eleventh Amendment does not bar a federal court from granting prospective relief against an officer of the state who acts outside the bounds of his authority."); Straube v. Fla. Union Free Sch. Dist., 801 F. Supp. 1164, 1172 (S.D.N.Y. 1992) (ruling that "the Eleventh Amendment is not a bar" to prospective relief).

5. Do abrogation, consent/waiver, and prospective relief leave a state without a means to protect itself from suit in federal court? Not necessarily. Even if a state is not able to convince a court to dismiss a claim against it on the basis of sovereign immunity, states often seek to dismiss claims against them on the basis that they are not "proper" defendants because they were not involved in the case, cannot provide the relief plaintiff seeks, or they were not responsible for providing special education to the child. The weight of more recent authority agrees with these defenses. *See* B.J.S. v. State Educ. Dep't, 699 F. Supp. 2d 586, 599–600 (W.D.N.Y. 2010) (holding that school district and not state has the primary responsibility for formulating and implementing FAPE and IEP); Quatroche v. East Lyme Bd. of Educ., 604 F. Supp. 2d

403, 411 (D. Conn. 2009) (dismissing state defendants from appeal of a hearing decision because "there is no basis upon which relief can be granted against the state defendants"); M.K. v. Sergi, 554 F. Supp. 2d 233, 241 (D. Conn. 2008) (ruling that "the proper respondent in a due process hearing is the local school board," not the state); Fritschle v. Andes, 25 F. Supp. 2d 699, 705 (D. Md. 1998) (dismissing claim against state defendants because plaintiff did not allege that they "failed to assure compliance with the IDEA."); Yamen v. Bd. of Educ. of the Arlington Cent. Sch. Dist., 909 F. Supp. 207, 210–11 (S.D.N.Y. 1996) (dismissing claims against state defendants because plaintiffs did not adequately allege how state defendants violated their rights).

6. In addition to states, plaintiffs in IDEA cases also seek to sue state agencies. The Eleventh Amendment, however, has been construed to prohibit damages claims not only against states but against state agencies as well. Belanger v. Madera Unified Sch. Dist., 963 F.2d 248, 250 (9th Cir. 1992), *cert. denied*, 507 U.S. 919 (1993). In *Belanger*, the Ninth Circuit applied a five-part test to conclude that the school district was a state agency. *Id.* at 250–254. Prominent in the court's analysis was that a judgment against the District would be paid out of state funds. The Court stated, "Unlike most states, California school districts have budgets that are controlled and funded by the state government rather than the local districts." *Id.* at 251. In contrast, in New York, where school districts raise funds through local property taxes, school districts are not state agencies and not rendered immune by the Eleventh Amendment. Gerasimou v. Ambach, 636 F. Supp. 1504, 1512–13 (E.D.N.Y. 1986) (ruling that the Eleventh Amendment does not immunize a school district from a damages claim in federal court).

7. In addition to suing states, state agencies, and local school districts, plaintiffs in IDEA cases also sue a wide range of public officials, including state level officials such as education commissioners or special education directors, and local school district officials including superintendents, principals, special education directors, teachers, and school board members. Plaintiffs often sue public officials under the IDEA in their individual and official capacities. When sued in her official capacity, a public official is not personally liable for damages. P.C. v. McLaughlin, 913 F.2d 1033, 1039 (2d Cir. 1990) ("[A] suit brought against a public officer in his official capacity is treated as a suit against the government; damages are available only from the public fisc . . . ."); Jackson v. District of Columbia, 826 F. Supp. 2d 109, 123–24 (D.D.C. 2011), *aff'd*, 2013 WL 500809 (D.C. Cir. 2013) ("Government officials sued in their official capacities are not personally liable for damages."); Carruthers v. Ludlow Taylor Elem. Sch., 432 F.Supp. 2d 75, 76 n.1 (D.D.C. 2006) (ruling that "individual government officials sued in their official capacities are not personally liable for damages.").

8. In contrast to lawsuits against public officials in their official capacities, public officials sued in their individual capacities are subject to claims for monetary damages. They can, however, raise the defense of qualified immunity, which, if granted, insulates them from monetary damages. In order to raise a successful defense of

qualified immunity, a public official sued in his individual capacity must show that either the right that the plaintiff claims he violated was not a clearly established right of which a reasonable person would have known at the time of the defendant's action or that it was objectively reasonable for the defendant to believe his actions did not violate this right. *See* Christopher P. v. Marcus, 915 F.2d 794, 798–99 (2d Cir. 1990) (holding that defendants were entitled to qualified immunity because the plaintiffs' rights under the EAHCA "were not clearly established."); *P.C.*, 913 F. 2d at 1039-1040, 1041.

One court listed IDEA rights that are clearly established:

> The IDEA, besides conferring the right to a FAPE on a child with a disability, also grants parents a number of procedural rights. Among the procedural rights guaranteed to parents by the IDEA are the right to examine all records relating to the child, to participate in meetings dealing with the identification, evaluation, and educational placement of the child, to obtain independent educational evaluations of the child, to participate as a member of the IEP team in designing the child's IEP and, as a member of the team, review existing evaluation data on the child.
>
> A school district's failure to disclose a child's full records to his parents is a violation of the IDEA, as is a district's independent development of an IEP without meaningful parental participation.

C. O. v. Portland Pub. Sch., 406 F. Supp. 2d 1157, 1173 (D. Or. 2005). A child has a clearly established right to an IEP that addresses his specific needs. Butler v. South Glens Falls Cent. Sch. Dist., 106 F. Supp. 2d 414, 421–22 (N.D.N.Y. 2000) (denying qualified immunity). One court found that a public official was entitled to qualified immunity because the parents' procedural rights were not clearly established. Bray v. Hobart City Sch. Corp., 818 F. Supp. 1226, 1237–38 (N.D. Ind. 1993).

9. Several courts ruled that individual defendants, in their official or individual capacities, are not subject to lawsuits under the IDEA. In *B.I. v. Montgomery Cnty. Bd. of Educ.*,750 F. Supp. 2d 1280, 1283 (M.D. Ala. 2010), the court ruled that because Section 1415 applies only to "'[any] State educational agency, State agency, or local educational agency that receives assistance under this subchapter,'" individuals cannot be defendants in IDEA cases. (citing 20 U.S.C. § 1415(a)); *see also* Alston v. District of Columbia, 561 F. Supp. 2d 29, 33 (D.D.C. 2008) (dismissing claims against individual defendants because the IDEA does not provide for individual capacity suits); L.M.P. v. Sch. Bd. of Broward Cnty., 516 F. Supp. 2d 1305, 1312–13 (S.D. Fla. 2007) (dismissing claims against individual defendants). One court ruled that because the IDEA abrogates Eleventh Amendment immunity, there is no reason to permit IDEA claims against individual defendants. S.W. v. Warren, 528 F. Supp. 2d 282, 298 (S.D.N.Y. 2007) (dismissing claims against individual defendants in IDEA case because there is no reason to permit such claims in light of Eleventh Amendment abrogation). Another court dismissed claims for injunctive relief

against individual defendants in their official capacities as duplicative because the plaintiff also sued state agencies and if the court ordered injunctive relief against the state entities the individual defendants would have to help carry it out. N.J. Prot. and Advocacy v. N.J. Dep't of Educ., 563 F. Supp. 2d 474, 491–92 (D.N.J. 2008). Finally, a court ruled that a state level hearing officer, as a judicial officer, was absolutely immune from liability in an IDEA claim. B.J.S. v. State Educ. Dep't of State of New York, 699 F. Supp. 2d 586, 594–95 (W.D.N.Y. 2010).

Chapter 14

Enforcing the IDEA in Federal Court: Statutory Requirements

Introduction

The IDEA allows a party who is aggrieved by the results of an administrative proceeding under Section 1415 to bring a case in federal court challenging the results. This chapter examines two requirements the IDEA imposes on plaintiffs before they can seek to enforce the IDEA in federal court: that they have exhausted the IDEA's administrative remedies and complied with the statute of limitations. Section One examines the exhaustion requirement, Section Two covers exceptions to the exhaustion requirement, and Section Three covers the IDEA's statute of limitations.

Problem

Recall the problem from Chapter Thirteen. After completing her investigation, Jean is considering bringing one or more of the following cases in federal court:

*A class action lawsuit on behalf of all children receiving special education and related services in the school district who are classified with an emotional disturbance or learning disability, whom the district suspended for more than ten days without convening a Multi-Disciplinary Review Team (MDRT), and who have already served the suspension or are still serving the suspension. The complaint would allege that the school district violated the IDEA, Section 504, and the ADA by failing to convene MDRTs when it suspended students with disabilities for more than ten days. The complaint would seek a preliminary and permanent injunction requiring the school district to convene an MDRT within five days of issuing a decision suspending a child for more than ten days and monetary damages for children whom the district suspended for more than ten days without convening an MDRT. None of the known class members whom the district suspended for more than ten days exhausted their administrative remedies.

*Individual claims on behalf of B.G. and C.G. claiming that the district's suspension of B.G. violated the IDEA, Section 504, and the ADA, and seeking monetary damages. C.G. is in tenth grade and continues to attend high school in the district.

*Individual claims on behalf of H.W. and Y.D. claiming that the district's suspension of them violated the IDEA, Section 504, and the ADA, and seeking monetary damages.

*In addition, Jean's colleague, Jackie, just completed an interview of W.A. The school district suspended her daughter, R.A., for 60 days without convening an MDRT team. R.A. is classified with an emotional disturbance, is not in school, and is not receiving special education or related services. She has completed thirty days of her suspension. Her mother fears that she is regressing and may become dangerous to herself. Jackie is considering taking legal action on R.A.'s behalf.

Are the potential plaintiffs required to exhaust administrative remedies for any of these claims? What additional information, if any, does Jean or Jackie need before they can advise them about exhaustion?

Section One
Exhaustion of Administrative Remedies

The IDEA requires a plaintiff to exhaust administrative remedies before seeking to enforce her IDEA rights in federal court. The relevant statutory provision is the same one that relates to standing, but this chapter focuses on exhaustion of administrative remedies:

> Any party aggrieved by the findings and decision made under subsection (f) [impartial due process hearings] or (k) [relating to placement of children in alternative educational settings] who does not have the right to appeal under subsection (g) [state level review of impartial hearing decisions], and any party aggrieved by the findings and decision made under this subsection, shall have the right to bring a civil action with respect to the complaint presented pursuant to this section, which action may be brought in any State court of competent jurisdiction or in a district court of the United States....

20 U.S.C. § 1415(i)(2) (2012). Consider the court's application of the exhaustion requirement in the following case.

Christopher W. v. Portsmouth Sch. Comm.

877 F.2d 1089 (1st Cir. 1989)

Bownes, Circuit Judge.

Plaintiff-appellant Christopher W. appeals an order of the district court which held that he had not exhausted administrative remedies pursuant to the Education for All Handicapped Children Act prior to seeking relief in district court, and that therefore the court lacked jurisdiction to hear the case. We affirm.

I. BACKGROUND

Christopher W. ... entered school in 1975, and began to manifest attendance and behavior problems. In 1978, he was evaluated as being learning disabled and requiring special education services in speech therapy. On October 10, 1979, the school's psychiatrist diagnosed Christopher W. as being school phobic and eligible for major behaviorally disordered support services. The child was placed in the Bradly Hospital Day (School) Program. In the 1981–1982 school year he was placed in the local school system in a self-contained setting at Portsmouth Middle School, where he continued to have tardiness and behavior problems. In the 1984–1985 and 1985–1986 school years, pursuant to an individualized education program (IEP) approved by his mother, Christopher W. was enrolled as a special education student in Portsmouth High School. He missed many classes due to absences and being late, and was frequently placed on suspension by the school authorities. The Portsmouth School Committee's policy is that if a student is absent 25% of the time from a class, the student is removed from the class and receives a failing grade for that course. In accord with this policy, Christopher W. received no academic credit for any of his courses. Christopher W.'s mother testified that she was never informed of her right to challenge the school's disciplinary decisions through an administrative process.

On May 15, 1985, a psychiatric evaluation of Christopher W. confirmed the previous diagnosis of 1979, that he was behaviorally disordered. On May 29, 1985, a multi-disciplinary team (MDT) met and recommended continued placement in a self-contained classroom; it did not determine if there was a relationship between the misbehavior for which he was being disciplined, and his handicapping condition.

On June 7, 1985, Christopher W. filed a complaint with the Rhode Island Department of Education pursuant to the Education Division General Administrative Regulations (EDGAR), 34 C.F.R. §76.790, alleging noncompliance with federal and state regulations regarding procedural safeguards. On November 8, 1985, the Rhode Island Department of Education notified the Superintendent of Portsmouth Schools that the disciplinary actions taken against Christopher W. violated the law because the MDT had not met to determine if there was a causal relationship between the misbehavior for which he was being disciplined and his handicap, and if his educational placement was appropriate. After yet another suspension of Christopher W. by the school on November 29, 1985, a letter was sent by the Rhode Island Commissioner of Education to the Portsmouth School Committee stating:

> [I]t has come to my attention that Christopher W. has again been suspended from school without benefit of evaluation and due process proceedings available to handicapped students. If this is the case, the suspension must be stayed pending the outcome of the special education evaluation process and the subsequent due process review of this evaluation under the Education of the Handicapped Act.

The school made no written response to this letter, but out-of-school suspensions were replaced by in-school detentions.

On December 3, 1985, the Superintendent of Schools responded to the EDGAR complaint that had been filed on June 7, 1985, by forwarding to the Rhode Island Department of Education a November 27, 1985 letter from Mr. William Hilton,

Regional Administrator of Special Education. The letter stated: that the MDT had met on November 18, 1985; that it had determined that Christopher W. was behaviorally disordered, but that "not all of his inappropriate behavior [was] due to his handicapping condition;" and that the MDT had decided upon a course of action for Christopher W., which included placement in another school, tutoring, a psychiatric evaluation, and counseling. . . .

In 1986, Christopher W. continued to experience attendance problems in school. On February 6, 1986, the Rhode Island Department of Education sent a letter to the Portsmouth School Committee stating:

> It appears that Christopher's handicapping condition contributes to his inability to attend school on a regular and timely basis. The fact that he received no credit last year in any subject areas because he missed 25% of those courses appears to be contrary to § 504 of the Rehabilitation Act of 1973. . . . [A] full evaluation of Christopher, to include a vocational assessment, should take place as soon as possible for the purpose of identifying an appropriate educational program.

Several meetings were held between the school and Christopher W. in the spring of 1986, but no IEP was agreed upon. Christopher W. received no academic credit for the 1985–1986 school year, because of his absences. The Portsmouth School Committee refused to implement a behavioral management program which had been developed by Dr. Steven Imber, a psychologist, to alleviate Christopher W.'s attendance and behavior problems. In June 1987, the school committee arranged a residential placement for Christopher W. at Grove School to begin in September, but Christopher W. voluntarily left that school on September 17, 1987. On March 28, 1988, an IEP was agreed upon for Christopher W. to attend Middletown High School, but at the end of April, 1988, Christopher W. left that school also. He has since attempted to re-enroll at Portsmouth High School without success. Christopher W. is currently not attending any school.

Christopher W. filed a complaint on December 6, 1985, in district court, under the Education for All Handicapped Children Act (20 U.S.C. § 1400 *et seq.*), § 504 of the Rehabilitation Act of 1973 (29 U.S.C. § 795), and the Civil Rights Act (42 U.S.C. § 1983). The complaint requested: that injunctive relief be granted prohibiting the Portsmouth School Committee from imposing any further disciplinary sanctions against Christopher W. without the procedural safeguards mandated by the Education for All Handicapped Children Act; that the Portsmouth School Committee's policy of denying academic credit for absences exceeding 25% of class meetings without considering how a student's handicapping condition affects his attendance, not be applied to Christopher W.; that Christopher W. receive the academic credits he had earned and would have received but for this policy; and that any reference to suspensions be expunged from his permanent school record. . . . [E]xcept for the EDGAR complaint that had been filed on June 7, 1985, Christopher W. had not pursued any other administrative remedies.

. . . .

II. JURISDICTION

A. Exhaustion Requirement

The Education for All Handicapped Children's Act (EHA), provides procedural safeguards for a handicapped child and his or her parents with respect to the provision of a free appropriate public education. . . . The statute . . . provides for a civil action by an aggrieved party:

> *Any party aggrieved by the findings and decision* made under subsection (b) of this section who does not have the right to an appeal under subsection (c) of this section, and any party aggrieved by the findings and decision under subsection (c) of this section, *shall have the right to bring a civil action* with respect to the complaint presented pursuant to this section, which action may be brought in any State court of competent jurisdiction or *in a district court* of the United States without regard to the amount in controversy. . . .

20 U.S.C. § 1415(e)(2) (emphasis added). . . .

Thus, the language of § 1415 of the EHA indicates that the administrative procedures outlined in the statute are to be pursued *prior* to recourse to the district courts. . . . This doctrine enables the agency to develop a factual record, to apply its expertise to the problem, to exercise its discretion, and to correct its own mistakes, and is credited with promoting accuracy, efficiency, agency autonomy, and judicial economy. But, where agency proceedings will be futile, such benefits do not accrue.

Specifically in relation to the EHA, the courts have interpreted the statute to mean that ordinarily, plaintiffs must exhaust administrative remedies before initiating court action. In *Smith v. Robinson*, 468 U.S. 992 . . . (1984), the Supreme Court concluded that the EHA was a comprehensive statute in which "Congress intended handicapped children with constitutional claims to a free appropriate education to pursue those claims through the carefully tailored administrative and judicial mechanism set out in the statute," *id.* at 1009, . . . , and that to "allow[] a plaintiff to circumvent the EHA administrative remedies would be inconsistent with Congress' carefully tailored scheme." *Id.* at 1012. . . . *See also David D. v. Dartmouth School Committee*, 775 F.2d 411, 422 (1st Cir. 1985), where we iterated the procedural steps that were to be followed in complaints authorized by the EHA, noting that the "*culmination* of the state administrative appeals process is . . . to take the matter to either state or federal court." (Emphasis added). We went on to emphasize that "a complaint may be brought and *pursued up the reviewing ladder* to a state or federal court per § 1415(e)(2)," *id.* at 418 (emphasis added), and that "for issues to be preserved for judicial review they must first be presented to the administrative hearing officer." *Id.* at 424.

It is clear, however, that under certain circumstances, exhaustion may not be required under the EHA:

> The EHA does set out specific procedural safeguards that must be guaranteed by a State seeking funds under the Act. And although some courts have concluded that the EHA does not authorize injunctive relief to remedy

> procedural deficiencies, other courts have construed the district courts' authority under § 1415(e)(2) to grant "appropriate relief" as including the authority to grant injunctive relief, either after an unsuccessful and allegedly unfair administrative proceeding, or *prior to exhaustion of the state remedies if pursuing those remedies would be futile or inadequate.*

Smith v. Robinson, 468 U.S. at 1014 n.17 . . . (emphasis added). The Court went on to quote the principal author of the EHA, Senator Williams, that "exhaustion of the administrative procedures established under this part should not be required for any individual complainant filing a judicial action in cases where such exhaustion would be *futile either as a legal or practical matter.*" 121 Cong. Rec. 37416 (1975) (emphasis added). The House report for the 1986 EHA amendments also listed permissible exceptions to the exhaustion requirement when:

> (1) it would be *futile* to use the due process procedures . . . ; (2) an agency has adopted *a policy* or pursued a practice of general applicability that is *contrary to the law*; (3) it is *improbable that adequate relief* can be obtained by pursuing administrative remedies (e.g. the hearing officer lacks the authority to grant the relief sought). . . .

H.R. Rep. No. 296, 99th Cong., 1st Sess. 7 (1985) (emphasis added). *See* also *Honig v. Doe*, 484 U.S. 305 . . . (1988) ("It is true that judicial review is normally not available under § 1415(e)(2) until all administrative proceedings are completed, but as we have previously noted, parents may bypass the administrative process where exhaustion would be *futile or inadequate*") (emphasis added). Our holding in *Ezratty*, 648 F.2d at 778, is also on point: Where an action is filed in district court pursuant to the EHA, considerations of agency expertise, accuracy and judicial economy suggest that the plaintiffs should exhaust their administrative remedies prior to pursuing a court action, even where it is the agency's fault that administrative remedies were not exhausted in the first place. We did note, however, that there are instances in which application of the exhaustion doctrine will not serve these interests, e.g. when the issue is "*a pure matter of law*," or when exhaustion "*will work severe harm upon a litigant*," or when "[f]urther agency proceedings may be *futile*, only delaying an ultimate resolution," and that "the legislative history of the Act reflects the understanding that exhaustion is not a rigid requirement." *Id.* at 774. *Accord Mrs. W. v. Tirozzi*, 832 F.2d 748, 759 (2d Cir. 1987) ("courts seldom defer to an administrative agency when the issue involved is *purely a legal question* not involving either administrative experience or expertise," e.g. whether EHA provides a private right of action or whether other remedies under the EHA have been exhausted) (emphasis added).

B. The Case of Christopher W.

[T]he procedural violations that Christopher W. claims were committed by the local educational agency regarding his educational placement fit within the protectional provisions of § 1415 of the EHA. Consequently, Christopher W. would ordinarily have to exhaust the administrative remedies outlined in the EHA before proceeding with any action in the district court.

It is undisputed that Christopher W. did not pursue any administrative remedies, other than the initial EDGAR complaint on June 7, 1985.[4] Christopher W. has never challenged any individualized education program (IEP) that was developed for him. Throughout this protracted dispute, he has never requested a due process hearing, as delineated by the EHA, on any of the complaints he has raised. Therefore, we must determine if this case falls under one of the exceptions to the exhaustion doctrine that has been accepted by the courts.

(1) *Futility*:

In *Association for Retarded Citizens of Alabama v. Teague*, 830 F.2d 158 (11th Cir. 1987), the court held: that in an action alleging violations of the EHA, plaintiffs were ordinarily required to first exhaust state administrative remedies before bringing action in federal court; and that plaintiffs produced no evidence to support their allegations of futility, relying only on conclusory statements that the available administrative remedies denied them due process because they were "a sham" or "incapable of resolving the issues." Likewise, Christopher W. has produced no such evidence and has rested only on conclusory statements. In the many years that have already elapsed since Christopher W. was first subjected to disciplinary measures because of his behavior problems, he has never made a request for a due process hearing under the EHA. No evidence has been presented which suggests that asking for such a due process hearing would have been futile. Indeed, the Rhode Island Department of Education was quite receptive to Christopher W.'s initial complaints .... Far from any evidence of futility, the record indicates a sympathetic ear on the part of the state agency. It is probable that if a due process hearing had actually convened, the question of Christopher W.'s disability-misbehavior relationship could have been expeditiously decided and appropriate action taken in response to that decision, such as receiving credit for certain courses, expunging his record of evidence of his suspensions, receiving a more appropriate educational placement, or any other remedy deemed appropriate. Christopher W. offers no evidence to the contrary. The administrative remedies available certainly seem capable of resolving the issues involved, and any exhaustion exception based on futility is not warranted.

....

(2) *Severe harm to litigant*:

Nor does Christopher W. present any evidence to support a finding of severe or irreparable harm if a federal court does not take some sort of immediate action. Christopher W. is not currently under indefinite suspension or expulsion, which arguably might require immediate attention. At this point, he is basically requesting academic credit for past courses, the expunging from his permanent school record of any references to his suspensions, and injunctive relief prohibiting any future

4. Exhaustion of administrative remedies under EDGAR is different from exhaustion of administrative remedies under the EHA. *See Mrs. W. v. Tirozzi*, 832 F.2d 748, 757–58 (2d Cir. 1987).

disciplinary sanctions against him without the EHA's procedural safeguards. Christopher W. does not explain what immediate harm will befall him if he is required to follow the administrative path, why administrative remedies cannot be pursued, or why immediate court action is required for the relief he seeks. An examination of the cases cited by Christopher W. does not support his contention that he is entitled to an exhaustion exception based on severe or irreparable harm.

. . . .

(3) *Inadequate relief*:

Christopher W. has presented no evidence that the administrative process is not able to grant the relief he seeks. Indeed, the findings required in this case are precisely the types of issues in which administrative expertise and experience are most valuable. The state agency is much better equipped than the federal courts to determine issues such as the relationship between Christopher W.'s misbehavior and his handicap, and the amount of work he performed in classes for which he received no credit. Moreover, the granting of course credit and expunging the suspensions from Christopher W.'s permanent school record is certainly the type of relief within the hearing officer's province.

Christopher W.'s argument that bypassing the administrative procedures was justified because the suspensions would have been over before a due process hearing could have been convened and the hearing officer had no authority to issue prospective relief, is unpersuasive. The hearing officer surely could have found that Christopher W.'s absences were due to his handicap, that disciplining him for such misbehavior was prohibited by the EHA, and that perhaps a more appropriate IEP was required. If the hearing officer so found, the school committee could not legally defy the administrative ruling and repeat the same type of discipline in response to the same type of disability-related misconduct in the future. . . . Thus, any contention of impracticability due to inadequate relief if Christopher W. pursues the administrative route also fails.

(4) *Pure matter of law*:

Nor are the issues raised by Christopher W. ones of pure law. Indeed, the issues are extremely fact-specific and require the development of a factual record before any review can intelligently be made.

III. CONCLUSION

The EHA embodies a clear comprehensive scheme of procedural safeguards which are to be followed for any alleged violations of the statute. Administrative remedies are to be exhausted before recourse to the district courts is permitted. While the courts have recognized certain exceptions to this exhaustion requirement, the case of Christopher W. does not fit into any of them. We conclude that under the facts of this case, the plaintiff has resorted to an end-run of the administrative process established by the EHA without any legally cognizable justification.

We hold that Christopher W. must first exhaust the administrative remedies as described in § 1415 of the EHA, before he can bring an action in the district court. We therefore lack jurisdiction to reach the merits of this case.

. . . .

Notes, Comments, and Questions

1. Is a plaintiff required to raise a claim during an impartial hearing in order to have exhausted it? Courts have generally required plaintiffs to do so. *See* Thomas v. District of Columbia, 773 F. Supp. 2d 15, 18 (D.D.C. 2011) (finding that plaintiff's federal court complaint "did not exceed the scope of the administrative proceeding."); Kristi H. v. Tri-Valley Sch. Dist., 107 F. Supp. 2d 628, 632 (M.D. Pa. 2000) (ruling that plaintiffs failed to exhaust claims relating to three school years because they failed to raise these years in the administrative appeal); Moubry v. Indep. Sch. Dist. 696, 9 F. Supp. 2d 1086, 1100–01 (D. Minn. 1998) (ruling that plaintiff failed to exhaust claim that hearing officer improperly excluded issues from case by failing to appeal it in the administrative appeal); *see also* 20 U.S.C. § 1415(i)(2) (stating aggrieved party has a "right to bring a civil action with respect to the complaint presented pursuant to this section"). Similarly, a plaintiff must participate fully at all administrative levels in order to satisfy the exhaustion requirement. *See* B.J.S. v. State Educ. Dep't, 815 F. Supp. 2d 601, 610–11 (W.D.N.Y. 2011) (holding that plaintiff who refused to participate in remanded hearing before IHO and failed to appeal IHO decision on remand did not exhaust).

2. Does a plaintiff's failure to exhaust administrative remedies deprive a court of subject matter jurisdiction to hear her case? The court in *Christopher W.* dismissed the case for lack of jurisdiction. Not all courts agree. The opinion in *Sagan v. Sumner Cnty. Bd. of Educ.*, 726 F. Supp. 2d 868 (M.D. Tenn. 2010) provides a good summary of how the courts treat failure to exhaust under the IDEA and the practical consequences of the different approaches:

> There is a dispute among the Circuit Courts of Appeals as to whether exhaustion of administrative remedies under the IDEA is a jurisdictional requirement or whether exhaustion is merely a condition precedent for filing an IDEA lawsuit. The Seventh and Eleventh Circuits have held that the failure to exhaust administrative remedies does not deprive a court of subject-matter jurisdiction. *See, e.g., Charlie F. v. Bd. of Educ. of Skokie Sch. Dist. 68*, 98 F.3d 989, 991 (7th Cir.1996); *N.B. by D.G. v. Aluchua County Sch. Bd.*, 84 F.3d 1376, 1379 (11th Cir. 1996). These courts reason that the lack of exhaustion is usually waivable while lack of jurisdiction is not. In these jurisdictions, the failure to exhaust administrative remedies is an unmet condition precedent for filing a lawsuit, and may result in dismissal for failure to state a claim under Rule 12(b)(6) or on a motion for summary judgment.
>
> Other courts have concluded that exhaustion of administrative remedies is a jurisdictional prerequisite. *See, e.g., Polera v. Bd. of Educ.*, 288 F.3d 478,

> 483 (2d Cir. 2002); *MM v. Sch. Dist. of Greenville County*, 303 F.3d 523, 536 (4th Cir. 2002); *Cudjoe v. Indep. Sch. Dist. No. 12*, 297 F.3d 1058, 1063 (10th Cir. 2002); *Witte v. Clark County Sch. Dist.*, 197 F.3d 1271, 1274 (9th Cir. 1999). In these jurisdictions, the failure to exhaust administrative remedies results in dismissal for lack of subject-matter jurisdiction.
>
> While the Sixth Circuit does not appear to have expressly decided this issue, a recent Supreme Court decision has made it clear that exhaustion generally, when statutorily required, is not a jurisdictional bar. Rather, exhaustion is an affirmative defense that must be raised and proved by the defendant. . . . [A]t least one other district court within the Sixth Circuit has concluded that failure to exhaust administrative remedies in the context of a claim brought under the IDEA is an affirmative defense, not a jurisdictional bar. *B.H. v. Portage Pub. Sch. Bd. of Educ.*, No. 1:08-cv-293, 2009 WL 277051, at *3 (W.D. Mich. Feb. 2, 2009) (converting defendant's Rule 12(b)(1) motion into Rule 56 motion). Other district courts within the Sixth Circuit have similarly considered the failure-to-exhaust issue without couching it as jurisdictional. *See, e.g., Doe v. Dublin City Sch. Dist.*, No. 2:09-cv-738, 2010 WL 1434318 (S.D. Ohio April 8, 2010) (dismissing complaint under Fed. R. Civ. P. 12(b)(6) based upon plaintiffs' failure to exhaust remedies).
>
> As the disposition of *Doe v. Dublin City School District* suggests, the distinction is largely academic unless the objection has been waived, as the failure to exhaust may provide a grounds for dismissal, just not on the basis of lack of subject-matter jurisdiction. Further, although construing the exhaustion requirement as an affirmative defense would ordinarily shift the burden of proof to the Board, the Sixth Circuit has clearly held that the "burden . . . rests with the [plaintiff] to demonstrate the futility or inadequacy of administrative review." *Gean v. Hattaway*, 330 F.3d 758, 774 (quoting *Honig v. Doe*, 484 U.S. 305, 327 . . . (1988)). . . .

Id. at 871–872.

Polera, which is one of the cases *Sagan* cites as supporting the position that the exhaustion requirement is jurisdictional, was cast in doubt by *Coleman v. Newburgh Enlarged City Sch. Dist.*, 503 F.3d 198 (2d Cir. 2007). The Second Circuit stated:

> Recently, however, the Supreme Court has admonished lower courts to more carefully distinguish between jurisdictional rules and mandatory claims-processing rules . . . , the latter being subject to waiver and forfeiture. . . . [W]e have been equivocal in our discussion of the IDEA's exhaustion requirement, acknowledging our statement in *Polera* that the failure to "exhaust IDEA administrative remedies deprive[s] [a] court of subject matter jurisdiction" but also referring to the IDEA's exhaustion requirements as the defendants' "non-exhaustion defense," in a case where we contemplated, but did not decide, whether those requirements are subject to waiver.

Id. at 203. The court, however, did not decide the issue because there was no claim that the defendant waived or forfeited the defense; *see also* Piazza v. Florida Union

Free Sch. Dist., 777 F. Supp. 2d 669, 680–81 n.7 (S.D.N.Y. 2011) (noting Second Circuit's doubt about whether exhaustion is jurisdictional). In light of the Second Circuit's ambivalence about whether exhaustion is a jurisdictional requirement, what advice would you give to a school district located in the Second Circuit that is preparing an answer to a federal complaint in which plaintiffs did not exhaust administrative remedies?

Section Two
Exceptions to the Exhaustion Requirement

The Court in *Christopher W.* recognized four exceptions to the exhaustion requirement: futility; severe harm to the plaintiff; the administrative process offers inadequate relief; and pure matter of law. Other courts have recognized similar exceptions. *See, e.g.*, MM v. Sch. Dist. of Greenville Cnty., 303 F.3d 523, 536 (4th Cir. 2002) (ruling that exceptions to the exhaustion requirement include futility, failure to notify parents of their procedural rights, and severe harm to the child); Komninos v. Upper Saddle River Bd. of Educ., 13 F.3d 775, 778 (3d Cir. 1994) (holding that exhaustion exceptions include futility, inadequacy, pure legal question, relief not available, and severe harm); Mrs. W. v. Tirozzi, 832 F.2d 748, 756 (2d Cir. 1987) (ruling that futility, agency action contrary to law, and inadequate relief are exceptions to the exhaustion requirement). Many of the exceptions to exhaustion overlap; futility, inadequacy, and unavailable relief, for example, are different ways of saying that the administrative process does not provide a forum in which the alleged harms can be remedied. Controlling for this overlap, five distinct exceptions to IDEA's exhaustion requirement can be identified:

1. the plaintiff is challenging a statute, practice, or procedure that the plaintiff alleges is contrary to law;

2. the relief plaintiff seeks is not available through the administrative process;

3. the administrative process is inadequate to provide a forum to adjudicate the plaintiff's claims;

4. resort to the administrative process would cause the child severe or irreparable harm; and

5. the school district did not give notice of the availability of administrative procedures.

1. The Plaintiff is Challenging a Statute, Practice, or Procedure that is Contrary to Law

Mrs. M. v. Bridgeport Bd. of Educ.

96 F. Supp. 2d 124 (D. Conn. 2000)

DRONEY, District Judge.

The plaintiffs, Mrs. M., on her own and on behalf of her daughter I., and the Puerto Rican Coalition in Bridgeport ("PRC") bring this action against the Bridgeport Board of Education ("BBE") . . . .

In addition to their individual claims, the plaintiffs have styled their complaint as a class action brought on behalf of the minority children in the Bridgeport school system who allegedly have been misidentified by the BBE as mentally retarded. Pending before the Court is the defendants' partial motion to dismiss the plaintiffs' amended complaint for lack of subject matter jurisdiction on the basis that all of the purported plaintiffs, except for Mrs. M. and I., have failed to exhaust their administrative remedies. . . . For the reasons set forth below, the defendants' motion to dismiss is GRANTED.

I. BACKGROUND

The initial complaint filed in this action was brought . . . as an appeal of an August 11, 1998 decision issued by a special education hearing officer . . . . The initial complaint alleged that the hearing officer had improperly rejected Mrs. M.'s claim that I. had been misidentified by the BBE as mentally retarded and should have been identified as "Language Impaired Learning Disabled." . . . .

The plaintiffs claim that the misidentification and misplacement of I. and others similarly situated violates the IDEA, the Rehabilitation Act, the ADA, and the equal protection clause of the Fourteenth Amendment to the United States Constitution. In support of their claims, the plaintiffs allege that the BBE engages in a pattern and practice of over-identifying minority school children as mentally retarded, at a rate of more than three times the state-wide average for such identification, while simultaneously failing to identify correctly the disabilities of such children and provide them with a proper education. . . .

In support of their motion to dismiss, the defendants argue that, other than Mrs. M. and I., all of the purported class plaintiffs described by the amended complaint have failed to exhaust their administrative remedies before bringing their claims to federal court. . . .

In response, the plaintiffs do not contest that they have not sought relief through the administrative remedies provided by the SDE. Instead, they argue that, because of the nature of their claims, they need not exhaust their administrative remedies.

. . . .

III. DISCUSSION

. . . .

B. Exhaustion

"A basic principle of the IDEA is that a plaintiff must first exhaust the state administrative remedies provided under the Act, including the administrative appeals provisions, before bringing an action in federal court to challenge the evaluation and placement of a child." *Riley v. Ambach*, 668 F.2d 635, 640 (2d Cir. 1980) . . . . In this case, with the exception of Mrs. M. and I., the purported class plaintiffs have failed to exhaust their administrative remedies. Absent an applicable exception to the exhaustion requirement, all of the purported plaintiffs, other than Mrs. M. and I., are not yet entitled to federal judicial relief for their claims.

. . . .

1. Exceptions to the Exhaustion Requirement

The plaintiffs in this case assert that their claims should be excused from the exhaustion requirement because they fall within the second and third exceptions to the exhaustion requirement identified in Mrs. W. . . .

a. "Policy or Practice of General Applicability Contrary to Law"

Under the second exception set forth in *Mrs. W.*, exhaustion is not a prerequisite to filing suit under the IDEA when an agency has adopted a policy or pursued a practice of general applicability that is contrary to law. "The rationale behind this exception is that while the administrative hearing officers have the authority to enforce established regulations, policies and procedures, they generally do not have the authority to set new policies or alter existing ones." *King v. Pine Plains Cent. Sch. Dist.*, 918 F. Supp. 772, 781 (S.D.N.Y. 1996). Exhaustion thus is not required "where the wrongs alleged could not or would not have been corrected by resort to the administrative hearing process," because the hearing officers are powerless to remedy an illegal policy or practice of general applicability. *J.G. v. Board of Educ. of Rochester City Sch. Dist.*, 830 F.2d 444, 447 (2d Cir. 1987).

Mrs. W. was an action brought by parents of handicapped children and CLS against the Connecticut State Board of Education for violations of the IDEA. *See Mrs. W.*, 832 F.2d 748 at 757. The plaintiffs claimed that "the [Bridgeport] school system had violated the IDEA by failing to provide an adequate psychologist staff and to conduct triennial evaluations of handicapped children." *Id.* at 752. They further claimed that "the State Board did not provide them with an opportunity to raise their system-wide complaints [against the Bridgeport School Board] in a due process hearing pursuant to 20 U.S.C. § 1415(b)(2)." *Id.* The district court dismissed the case on the basis, among others, that exhaustion was required. In reversing on the basis that exhaustion was not required, however, the Second Circuit reasoned that the plaintiffs' complaint alleged a "pattern and practice of systematic . . . violations unable to be addressed at the due process hearings provided in Connecticut." *Id.* at 757. Specifically, the Second Circuit reasoned that the plaintiffs' complaint sufficiently alleged that the Bridgeport School Board had adopted a policy contrary to law and that the due process hearing officers provided by Connecticut lacked the authority to effectuate system-wide relief.

Unlike the situation in Mrs. W., however, this case does not involve a situation where the challenged policy or practice of general applicability is incapable of being remedied through the available administrative process. Although the plaintiffs in this case have alleged that the BBE engages in a pattern and practice of illegally over-identifying minority school children as mentally retarded, such a pattern or practice is subject to review by the SDE hearing officers on a case-by-case basis. More importantly, if the hearing officers detect an improper identification method, they can reject it, which would impact favorably on other children.

In light of Congress's intent in enacting the statutory and regulatory scheme of the IDEA, the plaintiffs' claims challenging the identification of certain children as mentally retarded are also the type of claims that should be addressed in a due process hearing before the SDE. Assuming that there are eligibility criteria and methodology employed by the BBE in identifying children as mentally retarded which can be classified as a policy or practice of general applicability, such criteria or methodology "are classic examples of the kind of technical questions of educational policy best resolved with the benefit of agency expertise and a fully developed administrative record." *Hoeft*, 967 F.2d at 1305.

A similar approach was endorsed in *Riley v. Ambach*, 668 F.2d 635 (2d Cir. 1981). In Riley, eighteen learning disabled children and their parents challenged the New York State standard for determining when a child was considered learning disabled and eligible for special education services. After the district court decided that administrative exhaustion was not required and conducted a trial on the merits, it held that the defendants' actions were inconsistent with the IDEA. On appeal, however, the Second Circuit reversed the district court on the ground that the plaintiffs had failed to exhaust their administrative remedies. The Second Circuit reasoned that the issues raised by the plaintiffs were difficult and technical, that the state experts should first have their say, and that "if that say does not resolve the issue, the record created by the application of their expertise to those problems will certainly help the federal court resolve the issue in a more informed manner." *Id.* at 640; see also *Hoeft*, 967 F.2d at 1307 ("A dispute over such eligibility criteria policies concerns, in essence, questions about the identification and evaluation of individual disabled children, precisely the kind of dispute to which the IDEA's administrative scheme is addressed.").

. . . .

The conclusion that exhaustion is not excused under this prong of the Mrs. W. elements does not mean it could never apply. But, as in this case, an examination of whether the BBE is improperly identifying children as mentally retarded would most likely require the Court to undertake an evaluation of each child—or at least a number of children—for which the prior administrative record would be critical. Effective judicial review needs the administrative process to explore fully the technical educational issues and develop a complete factual record for each child. This approach also would promote judicial efficiency by giving the BBE and the SDE the first opportunity to correct shortcomings or errors made by the BBE when identifying a particular child.[10] The situation here is different from *Mrs. W.*, where the alleged systematic violations—inadequate staffing and failure to conduct evaluations—could not be remedied by the due process hearing officers and were of a type that did not require an administrative record for the district court to address the issues in an informed way.

. . . .

c. *Substantive v. Structural Claims*

Finally, as to the Court's conclusion that neither the second or third exception set forth under Mrs. W. excuses administrative exhaustion in this case, the Court determines that the plaintiffs' complaint in essence presents a challenge to the identification decisions made by the BBE with respect to certain children and not to the actual framework under which the identification decisions were made. In other words, their challenge really is to the *substantive determinations* reached by the BBE concerning certain children, not to the *structure* of the system under which the identification was made. The question of whether a child has been properly identified by the BBE is the type of claim which was intended by Congress to be addressed on a case-by-case basis, with the needs of the particular child determined by the child's parents and educators. The plaintiffs, however, challenge multiple identification decisions by bringing one lawsuit despite the unique circumstances and needs of each child and without first attempting to have the identification issues explored by each child's parents, educators, and the SDE hearing officers. In that sense, the plaintiffs' approach would ignore Congress's intent to craft the IDEA in such a way as to promote individual educational programs tailored to a specific child's needs. . . .

. . . .

IV. CONCLUSION

For the foregoing reasons, the defendants' partial motion to dismiss the claims brought by the PRC and the class plaintiffs is GRANTED. Only the claims brought by Mrs. M., on her own and on behalf of her daughter I., shall proceed in this matter.

. . . .

Notes, Comments, and Questions

1. *Mrs. M.* posed a dilemma for the court. On the one hand, the plaintiffs alleged that the defendants were pursuing an illegal policy and supported the allegations with

10. In support of their claim that minority children are over-identified as mentally retarded by the BBE, at a higher rate than other cities and towns in Connecticut, the plaintiffs have presented evidence of special education disability rates in Connecticut for the 1996–97 school year. The evidence sets forth various disability rates for each school district in the state, and indicates that the rate of mental retardation in Bridgeport is approximately three times higher than in other districts.

evidence of disproportionate classification of mental retardation based on race. This would suggest that exhaustion should be waived. On the other hand, it is also possible that the disproportionate classifications were explained not by a policy or practice of discrimination, but by legitimate factors in individual cases. The court ruled that plaintiffs were required to exhaust administrative remedies because a record developed by an educational expert in each individual student's case was necessary to determine if each decision was based on legitimate factors. Do you agree? Should the court have allowed plaintiffs to pursue their claim of race discrimination, in support of which they had submitted *prima facie* evidence of disproportionate impact? If plaintiffs are not able to bypass exhaustion in a class action under these circumstances, how could plaintiffs ever file a class action alleging system-wide race discrimination absent direct evidence of discriminatory intent?

2. The court in *Mrs. M.* stated that "Although the plaintiffs in this case have alleged that the BBE engages in a pattern and practice of illegally over-identifying minority school children as mentally retarded, such a pattern or practice is subject to review by the SDE hearing officers on a case-by-case basis." 96 F. Supp. 2d at 130–31. The court went on to say, "More importantly, if the hearing officers detect an improper identification method they can reject it, which would impact favorably on other children." *Id.* at 131. Do you agree? How can a hearing officer detect evidence of a pattern or practice of discrimination in an individual case? Do the decisions of hearing officers have precedential value? Do hearing officers have the power to bind state officials or override rules or regulations of general applicability?

3. Compare the court's holding in *Mrs. M.* with the holding in *N.J. Prot. & Advocacy, Inc. v. N.J. Dep't of Educ.*, 563 F. Supp. 2d 474 (D.N.J. 2008) (*NJPA*), in which the court ruled that plaintiffs were not required to exhaust their claims that defendants failed to comply with the IDEA's inclusion requirements:

> The Court finds that Plaintiffs were not required to exhaust any administrative remedies under the IDEA because their IDEA claim is not premised on the individual needs of particular students, but instead alleges that Defendants have systematically failed to comply with the statute's inclusion mandates. Plaintiffs do not seek individual remedies necessary to make themselves or their constituents whole. In contrast, they seek "relief that requires restructuring, by judicial order, of the mechanism that the state has in place to meet the needs of students with special educational problems," because such students are currently not receiving educational instruction in the least restrictive environment.
>
> The court must accept as true, for purposes of his motion, Plaintiffs' allegation that Defendants have adopted policies and practices causing systematic and widespread violation of the right of disabled children under the IDEA.... Such allegations implicate the integrity of the IDEA and, if established, could require this Court to order Defendants to restructure New Jersey's education system so that it no longer conflicts with the IDEA's mandate

> that disabled children must be educated with non-disabled children in regular classrooms to the maximum extent appropriate. Accordingly, the Court concludes that although such allegations may be difficult to prove, as the litigation progresses, Plaintiffs have sufficiently pleaded that New Jersey's special education system contains systematic legal deficiencies that violate the IDEA.

Id. at 486–87. Can *Mrs. M.* and *NJPA* be reconciled? Why didn't the court in *Mrs. M.* assume the plaintiff's allegations to be true?

4. The court in *Mrs. M.* referred to the distinction between claims challenging substantive decisions about special education for specific children for which exhaustion is required, and systemic claims challenging the structure of the system under which decisions are made, for which exhaustion is not required. *Mrs. M.*, 96 F. Supp. 2d at 132. The court ruled that the plaintiffs were challenging individual substantive decisions about individual children, and thus they were required to exhaust administrative remedies. Do you agree? Did the court correctly characterize plaintiffs' claim?

5. The court in *Mrs. M* referred to *Doe v. Ariz. Dep't of Educ.*, 111 F.3d 678 (9th Cir. 1997), in support of its conclusion that substantive claims require exhaustion and systemic claims do not. In *Doe*, the court considered a challenge to Arizona's failure to provide special education and related services to children in an adult prison. The plaintiffs did not pursue administrative remedies prior to filing the case. In finding that the plaintiffs were required to exhaust, the court distinguished between systemic challenges, for which exhaustion is not required, and non-systemic challenges, for which exhaustion is required. The court stated that a systemic challenge:

> implicates the integrity or reliability of the IDEA dispute resolution procedures themselves, or requires restructuring the education system itself in order to comply with the dictates of the Act . . . ; [a non-systemic claim] involves only a substantive claim having to do with limited components of a program, and if the administrative process is capable of correcting the problem.

Id. at 682. The court ruled that the plaintiffs' challenge to the state's failure to provide special education services to children in prison was not a systemic challenge because the state did not know the children were there. Once the state learned of the children, it took action to remedy its failure. *Id.* at 682. Do you agree this was not a systemic challenge? Was the state's failure to identify the children the result of the absence of a system to identify children with special education needs in prison? Was it a failure that required restructuring of the special education system to identify children in prisons and evaluate them for special education?

6. The rule that has emerged regarding exhaustion and systemic challenges is that exhaustion is not required when a plaintiff is challenging the framework and procedures for placing children in special education or the structure of the education system itself, but is required when the challenge depends on the individual characteristics of a child. Is this distinction easy to make? *See, e.g.*, Quatroche v. East Lyme

Bd. of Educ., 604 F. Supp. 2d 403, 411–12 (D. Conn. 2009) (stating rules for categorizing claims as systemic or not); Kalliope R. v. N.Y.S. Dep't of Educ., 827 F. Supp. 2d 130, 134, 140 (E.D.N.Y. 2010) (ruling that exhaustion was not required in a challenge to the state's prohibition of 12:2:2 classrooms for children with disabilities); *see also* N.M. Ass'n for Retarded Citizens v. New Mexico, 678 F.2d 847, 849–50, 851 (10th Cir. 1982) (ruling that plaintiffs were not required to exhaust claim that the state's system for providing services to children with disabilities violated Section 504). Consider how the courts applied the systemic exception to the exhaustion requirement in the following examples. Did they apply the exception consistently?

Provision of Services to Incarcerated Children: In contrast to *Doe v. Ariz. Dep't of Educ.*, in *Handberry v. Thompson*, 446 F.3d 335 (2d Cir. 2006), the court waived exhaustion in a case in which the plaintiffs alleged that defendants failed to provide special education services to children incarcerated in New York City jails. The court stated:

> [T]he plaintiffs challenge the . . . [defendants'] actions with respect to providing educational services to all entitled inmates at Rikers Island. . . . [I]ndividual administrative remedies would be insufficient to address the defendants' failure to provide the service required by the IDEA to all relevant inmates. . . . The purposes of exhaustion — to "allow [] for the exercise of discretion and educational expertise by state and local agencies," . . . are unavailing where the alleged issue is the absence of any services whatsoever. . . . As to the plaintiffs' claim, then, exhaustion is futile, and administrative remedies are effectively unavailable. We therefore conclude that the plaintiffs' failure to exhaust administrative remedies . . . does not bar our subject matter jurisdiction over this suit.

Id. at 344–345.

Extended day and year services: In *Association for Community Living v. Romer*, 992 F.2d 1040 (10th Cir. 1993), the plaintiff alleged that Colorado "has denied them appropriately individualized IEPs because its policies arbitrarily predetermine the duration of ESD and ESY service and use a single criterion to determine eligibility for ESY services." *Id.* at 1043. The court ruled that plaintiffs' challenges to the state's policies for providing extended day and extended year services to children with disabilities was not systemic and thus they were required to exhaust their administrative remedies. *Id.* at 1042. The court held that whether the state's policies "have denied children with disabilities appropriately individualized IEPs entails a factually intensive inquiry into the circumstances of each individual child's case." *Id.* at 1044. Similarly, in *Hoeft v. Tucson Unified Sch. Dist.*, 967 F.2d 1298 (9th Cir. 1992), the court required plaintiffs, who claimed that the district's extended year policies deprived children of a FAPE, to exhaust administrative remedies. *Id.* at 1299–1300. The court ruled:

> [E]ven where local school policies appear on their face to violate the IDEA, administrative exhaustion may be necessary to give the state a reasonable

> opportunity to investigate and correct such policies. Challenging an individualized education program by recourse to the IDEA's procedural scheme affords the state such an opportunity. Although hearing officers lack power to adjudicate questions of statutory compliance, they are empowered to order the provision of an appropriate education program for an individual child, as guaranteed by the IDEA.

Id. at 1307.

Service limits: In *Ass'n for Retarded Citizens of Alabama, Inc. v. Teague*, 830 F.2d 158 (11th Cir. 1987), the plaintiffs claimed that the state failed to provide them with a FAPE because of insufficient funding. *Id.* at 159. The court dismissed the case for failure to exhaust administrative remedies. *Id.* at 161. It stated:

> The underlying issue—whether defendants were providing the educational facilities and programs to which the handicapped children were entitled—calls out for resolution initially at the administrative level. An examination of defendant's efforts at educating the handicapped will demand the expertise and discretion for which the state agency is especially qualified. Such a determination also will require extensive factfinding and expert testimony about the present facilities and programs and the needs of handicapped children, and judicial economy would be well-served by having a state hearing officer develop the record on these questions prior to court review.

Id. at 161. In contrast, in *Christopher S. v. Stanislaus Cnty. Office of Educ.*, 384 F.3d 1205 (9th Cir. 2004), the plaintiffs challenged California's policy of offering shorter school days to children with autism. *Id.* at 1207. The court reversed the district court's dismissal for failure to exhaust:

> Here, we conclude that the pursuit of the IDEA due process remedies under the facts of this case will not "further the general purposes of exhaustion and the congressional intent behind the administrative scheme." SCOE's decisions to have a shorter school day for autistic students and to have a minimum day each Tuesday were blanket policies that had nothing to do with the content of individual IEPs—no individualized decisions were made on a case-by-case basis. As the LEAs admit, the school schedule was an across-the-board administrative decision by SCOE, not a decision that resulted from any individual Student's IEP process.

Id. at 1211. Similarly in *S.W. v. Warren*, 528 F. Supp. 2d 282 (S.D.N.Y. 2007), the plaintiffs claimed that the county failed to evaluate properly and provide services to children with autism because of a policy limiting the number of service providers and the number of hours of ABA therapy they could provide. *Id.* at 287. In denying the defendants' motion to dismiss for failure to exhaust administrative remedies, the court ruled:

> The Second Circuit excuses the requirement to exhaust administrative remedies where plaintiffs allege systemic violations. This is because systemic

> violations are often the result of implemented policies and procedures, and administrative hearing officers do not have the ability to alter already existing policies.
>
> . . . .
>
> . . . Because plaintiffs' complaints are caused by the policies of the County, a hearing officer could not offer a remedy, and therefore it would be futile for them to exhaust their administrative remedies. . . .

Id. at 293–95.

7. What impact does requiring exhaustion in cases such as *Mrs. M.* have on the ability of plaintiffs to bring law reform cases? The IDEA was passed in large part in response to successful law reform litigation. Would the courts in *PARC* and *Mills* have dismissed those cases for failure to exhaust administrative remedies if there had been an exhaustion requirement?

8. Courts have had an easier time applying this exception consistently when the plaintiffs are challenging a law, regulation, or policy that they claim on its face violates the IDEA. In these cases, the courts frequently waive exhaustion because administrative hearing officers lack the authority to overturn laws or regulations or do not have jurisdiction over the officials who are carrying out the policy. *See, e.g.*, Petit v. U.S. Dep't of Educ., 578 F. Supp. 2d 145, 152 (D.D.C. 2008) (waiving exhaustion because department regulation prohibited payment for cochlear mapping and denial of relief plaintiffs sought was certain); L.M.P. v. Sch. Bd. of Broward Cnty., 516 F. Supp. 2d 1294, 1305 (S.D. Fla. 2007) (ruling that exhaustion was not required in challenge to district's alleged policy of automatically denying ABA therapy to children with autism spectrum disorder); Andree v. Cnty. of Nassau, 311 F. Supp. 2d 325, 333–34 (E.D.N.Y 2004) (waiving exhaustion in a challenge to the county's alleged policy of imposing Medicaid liens on personal injury awards to children with disabilities to obtain reimbursement for related services payments); Jacky W. v. N.Y.C. Bd. of Educ., 848 F. Supp. 358, 361 (E.D.N.Y. 1994) (waiving exhaustion in a challenge to the Department's regulations for hiring and paying impartial hearing officers); Bray v. Hobart City Sch. Corp., 818 F. Supp. 1226, 1233 (N.D. Ind. 1993) (waiving exhaustion in a challenge to the state's review process). Similarly, courts have ruled that plaintiffs are not required to exhaust administrative remedies when the issue they raised involved a "pure question of law." *See, e.g.*, Connors v. Mills, 34 F. Supp. 2d 795, 800–01 (N.D.N.Y 1998) (excusing exhaustion in a challenge to the state's policy of refusing to pay tuition to private schools that were not on a state-approved list); Doe v. Town of Framingham, 965 F. Supp. 226, 229 (D. Mass. 1997) (ruling that exhaustion was not required prior to bringing claim that exclusion from school violated the IDEA); *but see* Kristi H. v. Tri-Valley Sch. Dist., 107 F. Supp. 2d 628, 633 (M.D. Pa. 2000) (holding that issue of whether a one-year statute of limitations applies to compensatory education claims was not purely legal).

2. Plaintiff Seeks Relief that is Not Available Through the Administrative Process

The rights protected by the IDEA overlap to a significant degree with the rights protected by Section 504 of the Rehabilitation Act, 29 U.S.C. § 794 (2012) ("Section 504"), and the Americans with Disabilities Act, 42 U.S.C. §§ 12132–12133 (2012) (ADA). Section 504 and the ADA allow for monetary damages, while monetary damages for IDEA violations are generally not available. The IDEA imposes an exhaustion requirement for parties seeking relief under the Section 504 or the ADA that is also available under the IDEA:

> Nothing in this Chapter shall be construed to restrict or limit the rights, procedures, and remedies available under the Constitution, the Americans with Disabilities Act of 1990, title V of the Rehabilitation Act of 1973, or other Federal laws protecting the rights of children with disabilities, except that before the filing of a civil action under such laws seeking relief that is also available under this subchapter, the procedures under subsection (f) [impartial hearings] and (g) [state level review of hearing decisions] shall be exhausted to the same extent had the action been brought under this subchapter.

20 U.S.C. § 1415(l). Consider how the Supreme Court applied this rule in *Fry v. Napoleon Community Schools.*

Fry v. Napoleon Cmty. Sch.

137 S. Ct. 743 (2017)

Justice Kagan delivered the opinion of the Court.

The Individuals with Disabilities Education Act ensures that children with disabilities receive needed special education services. One of its provisions, § 1415(l), addresses the Act's relationship with other laws protecting those children. Section 1415(l) makes clear that nothing in the IDEA "restrict[s] or limit[s] the rights [or] remedies" that other federal laws, including antidiscrimination statutes, confer on children with disabilities. At the same time, the section states that if a suit brought under such a law "seek[s] relief that is also available under" the IDEA, the plaintiff must first exhaust the IDEA's administrative procedures. In this case, we consider the scope of that exhaustion requirement. We hold that exhaustion is not necessary when the gravamen of the plaintiff's suit is something other than the denial of the IDEA's core guarantee—what the Act calls a "free appropriate public education." § 1412(a)(1)(A).

I

A

. . . .

Important as the IDEA is for children with disabilities, it is not the only federal statute protecting their interests. Of particular relevance to this case are two antidiscrimination laws—Title II of the Americans with Disabilities Act (ADA), 42 U.S.C. § 12131 *et seq.*, and § 504 of the Rehabilitation Act, 29 U.S.C. § 794—which cover both adults and children with disabilities, in both public schools and other settings. Title II forbids any "public entity" from discriminating based on disability; Section 504 applies the same prohibition to any federally funded "program or activity." 42 U.S.C. §§ 12131–12132; 29 U.S.C. § 794(a).... [B]oth statutes authorize individuals to seek redress for violations of their substantive guarantees by bringing suits for injunctive relief or money damages. See 29 U.S.C. § 794a(a)(2); 42 U.S.C. § 12133.

This Court first considered the interaction between such laws and the IDEA in *Smith v. Robinson,* 468 U.S. 992 .... The plaintiffs there sought "to secure a 'free appropriate public education' for [their] handicapped child." But instead of bringing suit under the IDEA alone, they appended "virtually identical" claims ... under § 504 of the Rehabilitation Act and the Fourteenth Amendment's Equal Protection Clause....

Congress was quick to respond. In the Handicapped Children's Protection Act of 1986, it overturned *Smith* 's preclusion of non-IDEA claims while also adding a carefully defined exhaustion requirement. Now codified at 20 U.S.C. § 1415(l), the relevant provision of that statute reads:

> "Nothing in [the IDEA] shall be construed to restrict or limit the rights, procedures, and remedies available under the Constitution, the [ADA], title V of the Rehabilitation Act [including § 504], or other Federal laws protecting the rights of children with disabilities, except that before the filing of a civil action under such laws seeking relief that is also available under [the IDEA], the [IDEA's administrative procedures] shall be exhausted to the same extent as would be required had the action been brought under [the IDEA]."

The first half of § 1415(l) (up until "except that") "reaffirm[s] the viability" of federal statutes like the ADA or Rehabilitation Act "as separate vehicles," no less integral than the IDEA, "for ensuring the rights of handicapped children." H.R.Rep. No. 99–296, p. 4 (1985). According to that opening phrase, the IDEA does not prevent a plaintiff from asserting claims under such laws even if ... those claims allege the denial of an appropriate public education .... But the second half of § 1415(l) (from "except that" onward) imposes a limit on that "anything goes" regime, in the form of an exhaustion provision. According to that closing phrase, a plaintiff bringing suit under the ADA, the Rehabilitation Act, or similar laws must in certain circumstances—that is, when "seeking relief that is also available under" the IDEA—first exhaust the IDEA's administrative procedures. The reach of that requirement is the issue in this case.

B

Petitioner E.F. is a child with a severe form of cerebral palsy, which "significantly limits her motor skills and mobility." When E.F. was five years old, her parents—petitioners Stacy and Brent Fry—obtained a trained service dog for her, as recommended by her pediatrician. The dog, a goldendoodle named Wonder, "help[s E.F.] to live as independently as possible" by assisting her with various life activities. In particular, Wonder aids E.F. by "retrieving dropped items, helping her balance when she uses her walker, opening and closing doors, turning on and off lights, helping her take off her coat, [and] helping her transfer to and from the toilet."

But when the Frys sought permission for Wonder to join E.F. in kindergarten, officials at Ezra Eby Elementary School refused the request. Under E.F.'s existing IEP, a human aide provided E.F. with one-on-one support throughout the day; that two-legged assistance, the school officials thought, rendered Wonder superfluous. . . .

[T]he Frys filed a complaint with the U.S. Department of Education's Office for Civil Rights (OCR), charging that Ezra Eby's exclusion of E.F.'s service animal violated her rights under Title II of the ADA and § 504 of the Rehabilitation Act. . . . OCR agreed. . . .

In response to OCR's decision, school officials at last agreed that E.F. could come to school with Wonder. But after meeting with Ezra Eby's principal, the Frys became concerned that the school administration "would resent [E.F.] and make her return to school difficult." Accordingly, the Frys found a different public school, in a different district, where administrators and teachers enthusiastically received both E.F. and Wonder.

C

The Frys then filed this suit in federal court against the local and regional school districts in which Ezra Eby is located, along with the school's principal . . . . The complaint alleged that the school districts violated Title II of the ADA and § 504 of the Rehabilitation Act by "denying [E.F.] equal access" to Ezra Eby and its programs, "refus[ing] to reasonably accommodate" E.F.'s use of a service animal, and otherwise "discriminat[ing] against [E.F.] as a person with disabilities." According to the complaint, E.F. suffered harm as a result of that discrimination, including "emotional distress and pain, embarrassment, [and] mental anguish." In their prayer for relief, the Frys sought a declaration that the school districts had violated Title II and § 504, along with money damages to compensate for E.F.'s injuries.

The District Court granted the school districts' motion to dismiss the suit, holding that § 1415(l) required the Frys to first exhaust the IDEA's administrative procedures. A divided panel of the Court of Appeals for the Sixth Circuit affirmed . . . . In that court's view, § 1415(l) applies if "the injuries [alleged in a suit] relate to the specific substantive protections of the IDEA." And that means, the court continued, that exhaustion is necessary whenever "the genesis and the manifestations" of the complained-of harms were "educational" in nature. On that understanding of § 1415(l), the Sixth Circuit held, the Frys' suit could not proceed . . . . Judge Daughtrey dissented, emphasizing that in bringing their Title II and § 504 claims, the Frys "did not allege the denial of a FAPE" or "seek to modify [E.F.'s] IEP in any way."

We granted certiorari to address confusion in the courts of appeals as to the scope of § 1415(l)'s exhaustion requirement. . . . [3] We now vacate the Sixth Circuit's decision.

3. See *Payne v. Peninsula School Dist.*, 653 F.3d 863, 874 (C.A.9 2011) (en banc) (cataloguing different Circuits' understandings of § 1415(l)). In particular, the Ninth Circuit has criticized an

II

Section 1415(l) requires that a plaintiff exhaust the IDEA's procedures before filing an action under the ADA, the Rehabilitation Act, or similar laws when (but only when) her suit "seek[s] relief that is also available" under the IDEA. We first hold that to meet that statutory standard, a suit must seek relief for the denial of a FAPE, because that is the only "relief" the IDEA makes "available." We next conclude that in determining whether a suit indeed "seeks" relief for such a denial, a court should look to the substance, or gravamen, of the plaintiff's complaint.[4]

A

In this Court, the parties have reached substantial agreement about what "relief" the IDEA makes "available" for children with disabilities—and about how the Sixth Circuit went wrong in addressing that question. The Frys maintain that such a child can obtain remedies under the IDEA for decisions that deprive her of a FAPE, but none for those that do not. So in the Frys' view, § 1415(l)'s exhaustion requirement can come into play only when a suit concerns the denial of a FAPE—and not, as the Sixth Circuit held, when it merely has some articulable connection to the education of a child with a disability. The school districts, for their part, also believe that the Sixth Circuit's exhaustion standard "goes too far" because it could mandate exhaustion when a plaintiff is "seeking relief that is *not* in substance available" under the IDEA. And in particular, the school districts acknowledge that the IDEA makes remedies available only in suits that "directly implicate[ ]" a FAPE—so that only in those suits can § 1415(l) apply. For the reasons that follow, we agree with the parties' shared view: The only relief that an IDEA officer can give—hence the thing a plaintiff must seek in order to trigger § 1415(l)'s exhaustion rule—is relief for the denial of a FAPE.

We begin, as always, with the statutory language at issue, which . . . compels exhaustion when a plaintiff seeks "relief" that is "available" under the IDEA. The ordinary meaning of "relief" in the context of a lawsuit is the "redress[ ] or benefit" that attends a favorable judgment. Black's Law Dictionary 1161 (5th ed. 1979). And such relief is "available," as we recently explained, when it is "accessible or may be obtained." So to establish the scope of § 1415(l), we must identify the circumstances in which the IDEA enables a person to obtain redress . . . .

---

approach similar to the Sixth Circuit's for "treat[ing] § 1415(l) as a quasi-preemption provision, requiring administrative exhaustion for any case that falls within the general 'field' of educating disabled students." *Id.*, at 875.

4. In reaching these conclusions, we leave for another day a further question about the meaning of § 1415(l): Is exhaustion required when the plaintiff complains of the denial of a FAPE, but the specific remedy she requests—here, money damages for emotional distress—is not one that an IDEA hearing officer may award? The Frys, along with the Solicitor General, say the answer is no. But resolution of that question might not be needed in this case because the Frys also say that their complaint is not about the denial of a FAPE,—and, as later explained, we must remand that distinct issue to the Sixth Circuit. Only if that court rejects the Frys' view of their lawsuit, using the analysis we set out below, will the question about the effect of their request for money damages arise.

That inquiry immediately reveals the primacy of a FAPE in the statutory scheme. In its first section, the IDEA declares as its first purpose "to ensure that all children with disabilities have available to them a free appropriate public education." § 1400(d)(1)(A). That principal purpose then becomes the Act's principal command: A State receiving federal funding under the IDEA must make such an education "available to all children with disabilities." § 1412(a)(1)(A). The guarantee of a FAPE to those children gives rise to the bulk of the statute's more specific provisions. For example, the IEP—"the centerpiece of the statute's education delivery system"—serves as the "vehicle" or "means" of providing a FAPE. And finally, as all the above suggests, the FAPE requirement provides the yardstick for measuring the adequacy of the education that a school offers to a child with a disability: Under that standard, this Court has held, a child is entitled to "meaningful" access to education based on her individual needs.

The IDEA's administrative procedures test whether a school has met that obligation—and so center on the Act's FAPE requirement. As noted earlier, any decision by a hearing officer on a request for substantive relief "shall" be "based on a determination of whether the child received a free appropriate public education. . . . Suppose that a parent's complaint protests a school's failure to provide some accommodation for a child with a disability. If that accommodation is needed to fulfill the IDEA's FAPE requirement, the hearing officer must order relief. But if it is not, he cannot—even though the dispute is between a child with a disability and the school she attends. . . .

For that reason, § 1415(l)'s exhaustion rule hinges on whether a lawsuit seeks relief for the denial of a free appropriate public education. If a lawsuit charges such a denial, the plaintiff cannot escape § 1415(l) merely by bringing her suit under a statute other than the IDEA—as when, for example, the plaintiffs in *Smith* claimed that a school's failure to provide a FAPE also violated the Rehabilitation Act.[8] Rather, that plaintiff must first submit her case to an IDEA hearing officer . . . . But if, in a suit brought under a different statute, the remedy sought is not for the denial of a FAPE, then exhaustion of the IDEA's procedures is not required. After all, the plaintiff could not get any relief from those procedures . . . . And that is true even when the suit arises directly from a school's treatment of a child with a disability—and so could be said to relate in some way to her education. A school's conduct toward such a child—say, some refusal to make an accommodation—might injure her in ways unrelated to a FAPE, which are addressed in statutes other than the IDEA. A complaint seeking redress for those other harms, independent of any FAPE denial, is not subject to § 1415(l)'s exhaustion rule because, once again, the only "relief" the IDEA makes "available" is relief for the denial of a FAPE.

---

8. Once again, we do not address . . . a case in which plaintiffs, although charging the denial of a FAPE, seek a remedy that an IDEA hearing officer cannot give—for example, as in the Frys' complaint, money damages for resulting emotional injury.

B

Still, an important question remains: How is a court to tell when a plaintiff "seeks" relief for the denial of a FAPE and when she does not? Here, too, the parties have found some common ground: By looking, they both say, to the "substance" of, rather than the labels used in, the plaintiff's complaint. And here, too, we agree with that view: What matters is the crux—or, in legal-speak, the gravamen—of the plaintiff's complaint, setting aside any attempts at artful pleading.

That inquiry makes central the plaintiff's own claims, as § 1415(l) explicitly requires. The statutory language asks whether a lawsuit in fact "seeks" relief available under the IDEA—not, as a stricter exhaustion statute might, whether the suit "could have sought" relief available under the IDEA .... In effect, § 1415(l) treats the plaintiff as "the master of the claim": She identifies its remedial basis—and is subject to exhaustion or not based on that choice. A court deciding whether § 1415(l) applies must therefore examine whether a plaintiff's complaint—the principal instrument by which she describes her case—seeks relief for the denial of an appropriate education.

But that examination should consider substance, not surface. The use (or nonuse) of particular labels and terms is not what matters. The inquiry, for example, does not ride on whether a complaint includes (or, alternatively, omits) the precise words "FAPE" or "IEP." After all, § 1415(l)'s premise is that the plaintiff is suing under a statute *other than* the IDEA, like the Rehabilitation Act; in such a suit, the plaintiff might see no need to use the IDEA's distinctive language—even if she is in essence contesting the adequacy of a special education program. And still more critically, a "magic words" approach would make § 1415(l)'s exhaustion rule too easy to bypass.... Section 1415(l) is not merely a pleading hurdle. It requires exhaustion when the gravamen of a complaint seeks redress for a school's failure to provide a FAPE, even if not phrased or framed in precisely that way.

In addressing whether a complaint fits that description, a court should attend to the diverse means and ends of the statutes covering persons with disabilities—the IDEA on the one hand, the ADA and Rehabilitation Act (most notably) on the other. The IDEA, of course, protects only "children" ... and concerns only their schooling. § 1412(a)(1)(A). And as earlier noted, the statute's goal is to provide each child with meaningful access to education by offering individualized instruction and related services appropriate to her "unique needs." § 1401(29). By contrast, Title II of the ADA and § 504 of the Rehabilitation Act cover people with disabilities of all ages, and do so both inside and outside schools. And those statutes aim to root out disability-based discrimination, enabling each covered person (sometimes by means of reasonable accommodations) to participate equally to all others in public facilities and federally funded programs. In short, the IDEA guarantees individually tailored educational services, while Title II and § 504 promise non-discriminatory access to public institutions. That is not to deny some overlap in coverage: The same conduct might violate all three statutes ....

One clue to whether the gravamen of a complaint against a school concerns the denial of a FAPE, or instead addresses disability-based discrimination, can come from asking a pair of hypothetical questions. First, could the plaintiff have brought essentially the same claim if the alleged conduct had occurred at a public facility that was *not* a school—say, a public theater or library? And second, could an *adult* at the school—say, an employee or visitor—have pressed essentially the same grievance? When the answer to those questions is yes, a complaint that does not expressly allege the denial of a FAPE is also unlikely to be truly about that subject; after all, in those other situations there is no FAPE obligation and yet the same basic suit could go forward. But when the answer is no, then the complaint probably does concern a FAPE, even if it does not explicitly say so; for the FAPE requirement is all that explains why only a child in the school setting (not an adult in that setting or a child in some other) has a viable claim.

Take two contrasting examples. Suppose first that a wheelchair-bound child sues his school for discrimination under Title II (again, without mentioning the denial of a FAPE) because the building lacks access ramps. In some sense, that architectural feature has educational consequences, and a different lawsuit might have alleged that it violates the IDEA: After all, if the child cannot get inside the school, he cannot receive instruction there; and if he must be carried inside, he may not achieve the sense of independence conducive to academic (or later to real-world) success. But is the denial of a FAPE really the gravamen of the plaintiff's Title II complaint? Consider that the child could file the same basic complaint if a municipal library or theater had no ramps. And similarly, an employee or visitor could bring a mostly identical complaint against the school. That the claim can stay the same in those alternative scenarios suggests that its essence is equality of access to public facilities, not adequacy of special education. And so § 1415(l) does not require exhaustion.[9]

But suppose next that a student with a learning disability sues his school under Title II for failing to provide remedial tutoring in mathematics. That suit, too, might be cast as one for disability-based discrimination, grounded on the school's refusal to make a reasonable accommodation; the complaint might make no reference at all to a FAPE or an IEP. But can anyone imagine the student making the same claim against a public theater or library? Or, similarly, imagine an adult visitor or employee

9. The school districts offer another example illustrating the point. They suppose that a teacher, acting out of animus or frustration, strikes a student with a disability, who then sues the school under a statute other than the IDEA. Here too, the suit could be said to relate, in both genesis and effect, to the child's education. But the school districts opine, we think correctly, that the substance of the plaintiff's claim is unlikely to involve the adequacy of special education—and thus is unlikely to require exhaustion. A telling indicator of that conclusion is that a child could file the same kind of suit against an official at another public facility for inflicting such physical abuse—as could an adult subject to similar treatment by a school official. To be sure, the particular circumstances of such a suit (school or theater? student or employee?) might be pertinent in assessing the reasonableness of the challenged conduct. But even if that is so, the plausibility of bringing other variants of the suit indicates that the gravamen of the plaintiff's complaint does not concern the appropriateness of an educational program.

suing the school to obtain a math tutorial? The difficulty of transplanting the complaint to those other contexts suggests that its essence—even though not its wording—is the provision of a FAPE, thus bringing § 1415(l) into play.[10]

A further sign that the gravamen of a suit is the denial of a FAPE can emerge from the history of the proceedings. In particular, a court may consider that a plaintiff has previously invoked the IDEA's formal procedures to handle the dispute—thus starting to exhaust the Act's remedies before switching midstream. . . . A plaintiff's initial choice to pursue that process may suggest that she is indeed seeking relief for the denial of a FAPE—with the shift to judicial proceedings prior to full exhaustion reflecting only strategic calculations about how to maximize the prospects of such a remedy. Whether that is so depends on the facts; a court may conclude, for example, that the move to a courtroom came from a late-acquired awareness that the school had fulfilled its FAPE obligation and that the grievance involves something else entirely. But prior pursuit of the IDEA's administrative remedies will often provide strong evidence that the substance of a plaintiff's claim concerns the denial of a FAPE, even if the complaint never explicitly uses that term.

III

The Court of Appeals did not undertake the analysis we have just set forward. As noted above, it asked whether E.F.'s injuries were, broadly speaking, "educational" in nature. That is not the same as asking whether the gravamen of E.F.'s complaint charges, and seeks relief for, the denial of a FAPE. And that difference in standard may have led to a difference in result in this case. Understood correctly, § 1415(l) might not require exhaustion of the Frys' claim. We lack some important information on that score, however, and so we remand the issue to the court below.

The Frys' complaint alleges only disability-based discrimination, without making any reference to the adequacy of the special education services E.F.'s school provided. The school districts' "refusal to allow Wonder to act as a service dog," the complaint states, "discriminated against [E.F.] as a person with disabilities . . . by denying her equal access" to public facilities. The complaint contains no allegation about the denial of a FAPE or about any deficiency in E.F.'s IEP. More, it does not accuse the school even in general terms of refusing to provide the educational instruction and services that E.F. needs. As the Frys explained in this Court: The school districts "have said all along that because they gave [E.F.] a one-on-one [human] aide, that all of her . . . educational needs were satisfied. And we have not challenged that,

10. According to Justice ALITO, the hypothetical inquiries described above are useful only if the IDEA and other federal laws are mutually exclusive in scope. That is incorrect. The point of the questions is not to show that a plaintiff faced with a particular set of circumstances could *only* have proceeded under Title II or § 504—or, alternatively, could *only* have proceeded under the IDEA. (Depending on the circumstances, she might well have been able to proceed under both.) Rather, these questions help determine whether a plaintiff who has chosen to bring a claim under Title II or § 504 instead of the IDEA—and whose complaint makes no mention of a FAPE—nevertheless raises a claim whose *substance* is the denial of an appropriate education.

and it would be difficult for us to challenge that." The Frys instead maintained . . . that the school districts infringed E.F.'s right to equal access—even if their actions complied in full with the IDEA's requirements.

And nothing in the nature of the Frys' suit suggests any implicit focus on the adequacy of E.F.'s education. Consider, as suggested above, that the Frys could have filed essentially the same complaint if a public library or theater had refused admittance to Wonder. Or similarly, consider that an adult visitor to the school could have leveled much the same charges if prevented from entering with his service dog. In each case, the plaintiff would challenge a public facility's policy of precluding service dogs (just as a blind person might challenge a policy of barring guide dogs) as violating Title II's and § 504's equal access requirements. The suit would have nothing to do with the provision of educational services. From all that we know now, that is exactly the kind of action the Frys have brought.

But we do not foreclose the possibility that the history of these proceedings might suggest something different. As earlier discussed, a plaintiff's initial pursuit of the IDEA's administrative remedies can serve as evidence that the gravamen of her later suit is the denial of a FAPE, even though that does not appear on the face of her complaint. The Frys may or may not have sought those remedies before filing this case: None of the parties here have addressed that issue, and the record is cloudy as to the relevant facts. Accordingly, on remand, the court below should establish whether (or to what extent) the Frys invoked the IDEA's dispute resolution process before bringing this suit. And if the Frys started down that road, the court should decide whether their actions reveal that the gravamen of their complaint is indeed the denial of a FAPE, thus necessitating further exhaustion.

With these instructions and for the reasons stated, we vacate the judgment of the Court of Appeals and remand the case for further proceedings consistent with this opinion.

It is so ordered.

Justice Alito, with whom Justice Thomas joins, concurring in part and concurring in the judgment.

I join all of the opinion of the Court with the exception of its discussion (in the text from the beginning of the first new paragraph on page 15 to the end of the opinion) in which the Court provides several misleading "clue[s]" for the lower courts.

. . . These clues make sense only if there is no overlap between the relief available under . . . the Individuals with Disabilities Education Act (IDEA), and . . . other federal laws (including the Constitution, the Americans with Disabilities Act of 1990(ADA), and the Rehabilitation Act of 1973). The Court does not show or even claim that there is no such overlap—to the contrary, it observes that "[t]he same conduct might violate" the ADA, the Rehabilitation Act and the IDEA. And since these clues work only in the absence of overlap, I would not suggest them.

The Court provides another false clue by suggesting that lower courts take into account whether parents, before filing suit under the ADA or the Rehabilitation Act, began to pursue but then abandoned the IDEA's formal procedures. This clue also seems to me to be ill-advised. It is easy to imagine circumstances under which parents might start down the IDEA road and then change course and file an action under the ADA or the Rehabilitation Act that seeks relief that the IDEA cannot provide. The parents might be advised by their attorney that the relief they were seeking under the IDEA is not available under that law but is available under another. Or the parents might change their minds about the relief that they want, give up on the relief that the IDEA can provide, and turn to another statute.

Although the Court provides these clues for the purpose of assisting the lower courts, I am afraid that they may have the opposite effect. They are likely to confuse and lead courts astray.

Once again, we do not address here . . . a case in which a plaintiff, although charging the denial of a FAPE, seeks a form of remedy that an IDEA officer cannot give—for example, as in the Frys' complaint, money damages for resulting emotional injury.

. . . . .

Notes, Comments, and Questions

1. Do you think it will be easy for courts to determine whether the "gravamen" of a plaintiff's complaint is a denial of FAPE denial? Is this question much different from the standard the Sixth Circuit or other courts utilized for determining whether exhaustion is required?

2. What do you think of the clues the Court suggested for determining the gravamen of a complaint? Do you agree with Justice Alito that they will cause confusion because the IDEA and the ADA/Section 504 are not exclusive remedies and because the early history of a case can be misleading? How should a court handle a situation in which the answer to first two questions is "yes" but the child is also not receiving a FAPE? Do the Court's clues cover all the facts that are relevant to deciding whether exhaustion is necessary? For example, E.F. no longer attends school in the district. Doest that fact alone provide a negative answer to the question whether the relief she seeks is available under the IDEA?

3. Why was the Court reluctant to let the plaintiff choose the relief she seeks? Would allowing the plaintiff to choose be inconsistent with the language of § 1415(l)? Is it possible to construe the statutory phrase "a civil action under such laws seeking relief that is also available under [the IDEA]" to mean only "explicitly" seeking such relief? Or is it necessary, as the Court concludes, to determine whether the complaint also implicitly seeks such relief?

4. Is the Court's reason for remanding the case persuasive? The answer to the first two clues was "yes." Shouldn't that have been sufficient? Even if the case began as an impartial hearing, would this have enough weight to overcome the "yes" answer to the first two questions? Will the court's remand help resolve the split among the circuits regarding when exhaustion is necessary?

5. Why did the Court in *Fry* fail to determine whether exhaustion is required when a plaintiff files a complaint the gravamen of which is a FAPE denial but that seeks monetary damages only? The plaintiffs were seeking monetary damages, which are generally not available under the IDEA. If, on remand, the Sixth Circuit determines that the gravamen of the plaintiffs' complaint is a FAPE denial, and the case returns to the Supreme Court, will the Court be able to avoid answering the question? How do you think the Court will rule?

6. Two lower federal courts that considered claims involving service dogs reached differing conclusions. In *Cave v. East Meadow Union Free Sch. Dist.*, 514 F.3d 240 (2d Cir. 2008), plaintiffs sought damages and an injunction pursuant to the ADA, Section 504, and 42 U.S.C. § 1983 prohibiting the defendants from denying the student's service dog from accompanying him to school. They argued that they were not challenging John Jr.'s IEP, but claiming discrimination. The court ruled that they were required to exhaust their administrative remedies:

> We are not convinced that appellants' claims are materially distinguishable from claims that could fall within the ambit of the IDEA. The high school principal and the school district's director of special education testified before the district court that John, Jr.'s class schedule under his existing IEP would have to be changed to accommodate the concerns of allergic students and teachers and to diminish the distractions that Simba's presence would engender.... These issues implicate John, Jr.'s IEP and would be best dealt with through the administrative process....
>
> We thus agree with the district court here that "at least in part, the plaintiffs are challenging the adequacy of John, Jr.'s IEP because it does not include a service dog." The relief appellants seek, "namely permission to bring the service dog to school, is in substance a modification of John, Jr.'s IEP.... [and] is available under the IDEA." We also concur with the district court's finding that "'[e]ducation,' as used within the IDEA, encompasses more than simply academics." We note in that regard that one of the goals of the IDEA is "to ensure that all children with disabilities have available to them a free appropriate public education that emphasizes special education and related *services designed to* meet their unique needs and *prepare them for* further education, employment, and *independent living*." 20 U.S.C. § 1400(d)(1)(A) (emphasis added). A request for a service dog to be permitted to escort a disabled student at school as an "independent life tool" is hence not entirely beyond the bounds of the IDEA's educational scheme.

Id. at 247–48.

In contrast, in *Sullivan v. Vallejo City Unified Sch. Dist.*, 731 F. Supp. 947 (E.D. Cal. 1990), the plaintiff, a child with cerebral palsy, learning disabilities, and a hearing impairment, sought an injunction pursuant to Section 504 requiring the school district to permit her to bring her service dog to school. *Id.* at 949. The district moved to dismiss on the grounds that the plaintiff had failed to exhaust her administrative remedies under the EHA. The court ruled in favor of the plaintiff:

> Defendants' argument is premised on the erroneous assumption that plaintiff claims she is being deprived of a "free appropriate public education" within the meaning of EHA as a result of defendants' decision to exclude her service dog from the school premises. Plaintiff, however, does not dispute that the IEP created for her pursuant to EHA is adequate from an educational standpoint, nor has she alleged that the service dog is educationally necessary. Properly construed, plaintiff's claim is that whether or not the service dog is educationally necessary, defendants have discriminated against her on the basis of her handicap by arbitrarily refusing her access if she is accompanied by her service dog.

Id. at 951.

7. Prior to *Fry*, Courts that considered arguments that cases alleging disability discrimination should be dismissed for failure to exhaust tended to decide based on whether the claim was based on the child's educational program. *See, e.g.*, S.E. v. Grant Cnty. Bd. of Educ., 544 F.3d 633, 642–43 (6th Cir. 2008) (ruling that the plaintiff was required to exhaust a Section 504 disability discrimination claim relating to discipline because the complaint implicated educational issues); Ellenberg v. N.M. Military Inst., 478 F.3d 1262, 1280–81 (10th Cir. 2007) (ruling that exhaustion was not required in a claim under the ADA and Section 504 alleging disability discrimination in the school's admissions policy); Ashford v. Edmond Pub. Sch. Dist., 822 F. Supp. 2d 1189, 1197–98 (W.D. Okl. 2011) (ruling that exhaustion of ADA, Section 504, and Section 1983 claims was required because they were based on the same facts as the IDEA claim); Ebonie S. v. Pueblo Sch. Dist., 819 F. Supp. 2d 1179, 1192 (D. Col. 2011), *aff'd*, 695 F.3d 1051(10th Cir. 2012), *cert. denied*, ___ U.S. ___, 133 S. Ct. 1583 (2013) (holding that exhaustion was not required in a Section 504 disability discrimination claim alleging discriminatory use of restraints on children with disabilities). How would *Fry* change the analyses in these cases?

8. Does a plaintiff satisfy the exhaustion requirement for ADA, Section 504, and Section 1983 claims simply by following the IDEA's procedures, or must the plaintiff raise these claims in the administrative hearing, even if they relate only to issues not covered by or relief not available pursuant to the IDEA? In *Loch v. Bd. of Educ. of Edwardsville Cmty. Sch. Dist. No. 7*, 573 F. Supp. 2d 1072 (S.D. Ill. 2008), *aff'd*, 327 F.App'x 647, *cert. denied*, 559 U.S. 991 (2010), the plaintiffs argued that they exhausted their administrative remedies by requesting an impartial hearing even though they did not raise their discrimination and retaliation claims before the hearing officer. The court rejected this argument:

> [T]he Lochs were required to properly raise their claims at the due process hearing and to give the District the opportunity to provide a remedy before repairing to the courts. The Loch's contention that merely requesting and

> attending an IDEA due process hearing is sufficient to exhaust claims under § 504, the ADA and § 1983 must fail.

Id. at 1081. Can you explain the logic behind the court's ruling?

9. Courts have waived exhaustion on the grounds of unavailability of relief when the school district failed to implement an IDEA; the justification is that, in that instance, there is no relief that a hearing could provide. For example, in *Derrick F. v. Red Lion Area Sch. Dist.*, 586 F. Supp. 2d 282 (M.D. Pa. 2008), plaintiff prevailed at an administrative hearing and the district prepared a new IEP. The plaintiff, alleging that the district failed to implement the new IEP, sued in federal court without exhausting administrative remedies. In response to defendant's motion to dismiss, the plaintiff argued, "the futility exception to exhaustion applies because Plaintiff is challenging the implementation of his IEP, and not the substance of the IEP itself." *Id.* at 294. The court agreed:

> Exhaustion is generally futile where a plaintiff challenges a district's failure to implement an IEP because administrative procedures do not provide an adequate remedy. . . .
>
> Here, exhaustion of administrative remedies would be futile because Plaintiff does not challenge the substance of his IEP, but rather its implementation by Defendants. The parties have already exhausted administrative remedies with respect to Derrick's placement, and Plaintiff received the administrative remedy he was seeking. . . . Now plaintiff seeks to enforce those remedies in this court. The administrative process can provide no further relief to Plaintiff. Accordingly, Plaintiff's failure to implement claim falls within the futility exception to the IDEA exhaustion requirement.

Id. at 294–95; *but see Piazza v. Florida Union Free Sch. Dist.*, 777 F. Supp. 2d 669, 682–85 (S.D.N.Y. 2011) (refusing to waive exhaustion because challenge was to the substance of the IEP rather than its implementation).

10. Relief is not available if the hearing officer does not have the authority to order the officials the plaintiffs are suing to change their conduct. In *D.B. v. S.D. Bd. of Regents*, 655 F.3d 787 (8th Cir. 2011), plaintiffs challenged South Dakota's decision to close the state's school for children with deafness. The state "conceded that an administrative law judge could not order the Board to reestablish educational programs at the school's Sioux Fall Campus." *Id.* at 792. In ruling that the plaintiffs were not required to exhaust administrative remedies, the court stated, "We conclude that the parents were not required to exhaust because . . . adequate relief likely could not have been obtained through the administrative process." *Id.*

11. The Supreme Court in *Fry* left open the question of whether a plaintiff must exhaust administrative remedies if the gravamen of the complaint is the IDEA but she seeks only monetary damages, which are ordinarily not available in IDEA cases. The courts of appeals have not squarely answered this question either, instead determining whether exhaustion is required based essentially on their own versions of the

question the court in *Fry* asked: is the relief plaintiff seeks available under the IDEA? Consider the following example.

McCormick v. Waukegan Sch. Dist. No. 60

374 F.3d 564 (7th Cir. 2004)

Kanne, Circuit Judge.

Eron McCormick suffers from a rare form of muscular dystrophy known as McArdle's Disease. This disease, characterized by deficient levels of glycogen phosphorylase and a concomitant inability to process glycogen in the muscles, severely constrains Eron's physical capabilities. As a result, Eron and his parents developed an "individualized education program" ("IEP") with Waukegan School District #60 officials pursuant to the Individuals with Disabilities Act ("IDEA"), 20 U.S.C. § 1400 et seq., that limited Eron's participation in physical education class. After the relevant IEP was developed, Eron allegedly suffered muscle and kidney damage caused by overexertion in physical education class. His parents brought suit against the school district and several individual defendants under 42 U.S.C. § 1983 and various Illinois tort-law theories. The district court, ruling on a Federal Rule of Civil Procedure 12(b)(6) motion, dismissed the complaint without prejudice because Eron failed to exhaust the administrative remedies available under IDEA. . . . For the reasons stated herein, we reverse.

I. History

. . . .

In August of 1999, Eron began attending the Waukegan School District Freshman Center, a school serving only students in the ninth grade. The Freshman Center received notice of Eron's physical limitations and the dangers of exceeding those limitations from correspondence signed by Dr. Teepu Siddique . . . . An October 27, 1999, letter, for example, explained:

> [Eron] is a patient in our Muscular Dystrophy Clinic and has been under our care since 1992. Eron has a condition known as McArdle's Disease. This is a genetic metabolic disorder of the muscles that typically begins in childhood and progresses through adulthood.
>
> The characteristics of this disease are muscle fatigue, especially during physical activities, muscle pain and cramps, muscle stiffness with exercise and muscle wasting (loss of muscle mass). These patients will often develop dark burgundy colored urine from the abnormal presence of myoglobin (a muscle protein) which is released by the muscles following physical activities that exceed their limitations. Kidney and permanent muscle damage can occur as a result of this and vigorous exercise is to be avoided.

The Freshman Center provided Eron with elevator access and a bathroom pass to accommodate his needs throughout the school year.

Eron was scheduled to participate in physical education during his second (and final) semester at the Freshman Center. . . . [N]ear the beginning of the semester, Eron and his parents met with school officials for a reevaluation of his IEP. The IEP approved "adaptive physical education," with limited exertion. The McCormicks submitted several recommendations from doctors that advised Eron to be cautious when exercising and to stop anytime he was winded or felt muscle pain. The doctors suggested non-strenuous activities like walking, throwing lightweight objects, and social games. Jan Neterer, the physical education instructor, called Eron's parents after reviewing the IEP; during the conversation, she claimed to understand the limitations set forth in the IEP and agreed to follow it.

. . . [J]ust prior to the end of the semester (and Eron's stint at the Freshman Center), Neterer instructed Eron to run laps and perform push-ups. Neterer advised Eron that if he could not complete the tasks she assigned, he would receive a failing grade in physical education and would have to repeat the ninth grade. Despite Eron's protestations and references to his IEP, Neterer continued to threaten Eron with failure and berate him until he consented to the exercises. Eron informed Neterer that his muscles were cramping and hurting during the exercise; she nevertheless insisted that he should continue, again ignoring the IEP.

The day after these alleged events . . . , Eron was taken to the emergency room because of painful and cramping muscles, severe exhaustion, and bloody urine, a sign of kidney damage . . . . Eron missed the last few days of the school year, but graduated from the Freshman Center and moved on to his sophomore year at the high school. Eron has experienced increased muscle weakness and pain . . . . Moreover, permanent damage occurred to his kidneys, evidenced by the abnormal color of his urine following the overexertion. This damage may well have hastened the need for a kidney dialysis regimen and has increased the possibility of other kidney complications.

. . . Pamela McCormick, Eron's mother, filed a complaint in federal court on behalf of Eron. Count I, brought under 42 U.S.C. § 1983, alleged that the Defendants, acting under color of state law, violated Eron's constitutional rights to equal protection, to personal privacy, and to be free from cruel and unusual punishment. . . .

The district court, relying on *Charlie F. v. Board of Educ. of Skokie Sch. Dist. 68*, 98 F.3d 989 (7th Cir. 1996), dismissed the complaint without prejudice on the grounds that Eron had failed to exhaust the administrative remedies available to him under IDEA. This appeal ensued.

II. Analysis

Even though Eron did not invoke IDEA in his complaint, the district court properly considered whether he was required to exhaust under IDEA. The relevant section of IDEA is as follows:

> Nothing in this chapter shall be construed to restrict or limit the rights, procedures, and remedies available under the Constitution, the Americans

> with Disabilities Act of 1990, title V of the Rehabilitation Act of 1973, or other Federal laws protecting the rights of children with disabilities, except that *before the filing of a civil action under such laws seeking relief that is also available under this subchapter*, the procedures under subsections (f) and (g) of this section shall be exhausted to the same extent as would be required had the action been brought under this subchapter.

20 U.S.C. § 1415(l) (emphasis added). It is uncontested that Eron did not exhaust the administrative remedies available under IDEA. The sole issue on appeal is whether Eron is required to exhaust before filing a complaint in federal court.

In *Charlie F.*, we answered the same question in the affirmative. In that case, a teacher invited her pupils to air their grievances against Charlie, a student whose disabilities (attention deficit disorder and panic attacks) apparently disrupted the class. Charlie's ensuing humiliation caused a loss of confidence and self-esteem; this, allegedly, led to fistfights and disruptions of Charlie's educational progress.

Like Eron, Charlie filed a federal lawsuit with both federal and state-law theories of recovery, seeking only money damages (which IDEA administrative process does not provide). *Charlie F.* rejected outright the argument that a plaintiff could avoid IDEA administrative process by requesting only money damages: "[t]he statute speaks of available relief, and what relief is 'available' does not necessarily depend on what the aggrieved party wants." *Id.* at 991. Instead, courts should look to the "theory behind the grievance" to see if IDEA's process was activated: in Charlie's case, "the complaint [] filed on his behalf deals with acts that have both an educational source and an adverse educational consequence." *Id.* at 991–92. Thus, the damage done to Charlie, if proven, could in fact be remedied (in part at least) by services available under IDEA, such as psychological counseling or educational assistance. *Id.*

The Defendants insist that *Charlie F.* compels dismissal of the instant case for failure to exhaust IDEA administrative processes. Waukegan emphasizes that "developmental, corrective, and other supportive services (including . . . psychological services, physical and occupational therapy . . . , counseling services, and medical services, except that such medical services shall be for diagnostic and evaluation purposes only) as may be required to assist a child with a disability . . ." are available under IDEA. 20 U.S.C. § 1401(a)(17). . . . Like *Charlie F.*, reasons Waukegan, we should find that IDEA could remedy at least some of Eron's damages through in-kind services, such as psychological counseling, rather than money damages.

Conversely, the McCormicks assert that Eron's case is distinguishable from *Charlie F.* For one, Eron's case is premised on physical injury. IDEA does not provide medical services to disabled individuals (beyond diagnostic and evaluative services). The heart of Eron's claim is the permanent damage to his body from overexertion caused by Defendants' conduct. Second, Eron has not alleged any need for prospective educational assistance, whereas in *Charlie F.*, the court deduced that a significant amount of the damages requested would be premised on the harm to Charlie's education caused by his teacher's actions. The McCormicks were fully satisfied with

Eron's high school experience after his graduation from the Freshman Center and did not claim that the physical education incident interfered in Eron's academic development. Finally, with regard to the state emotional distress claim, Eron insists that he is suing only for the negative emotional experience on June 9, 2000, and that day's immediate aftermath (his hospitalization), not for an ongoing emotional condition, which might be addressed by prospective psychological counseling.

"Parents may bypass the [IDEA] administrative process where exhaustion would be futile . . . ." *Honig v. Doe*, 484 U.S. 305, 327 . . . (1988). Eron contends that the particular circumstances of his case, as set out in the complaint, necessitate a finding that pursuing administrative remedies under IDEA would be futile. . . .

. . . .

In Eron's case, his complaint asserts that he suffered permanent physical injuries that will reduce the quality of his life—and perhaps even shorten it. The nature of his claim is not educational; no change to his IEP could remedy, even in part, the damage done to Eron's body. By adding an intentional infliction of emotional distress claim to his complaint, Eron only seeks to recover for the arguably outrageous actions of Neterer, the physical education instructor. He does not allege any ongoing emotional difficulties that might be addressed through IDEA. After closely examining the "theory behind the grievance" in Eron's complaint, we are convinced that it would be futile for Eron to exhaust the administrative process under the circumstances of this case because IDEA does not provide a remedy for his alleged injuries, which are non-educational in nature.

III. CONCLUSION

For the foregoing reasons, we REVERSE the district court's dismissal of Eron's lawsuit and REMAND for further proceedings consistent with this opinion.

Notes, Comments, and Questions

1. Are the rulings in *McCormick* and *Charlie F.* consistent? Should the court in *McCormick* have required Eron to exhaust his administrative remedies to determine whether he was eligible under the IDEA for occupational or physical therapy for his condition in the same way the court in *Charlie F.* ruled that Charlie was required to exhaust administrative remedies to determine whether he could benefit from counseling? Or should the court in *Charlie F.* have waived exhaustion for the same reason the court in *McCormick* waived exhaustion? How would these cases have been decided under *Fry*?

2. How would you apply *Fry* to the following sample decisions from various courts of appeal? How do you think the courts ruled? (The answers are provided at the end of this note.) Would the rulings have been different under *Fry*? Do the clues in *Fry* cover all the factors that courts should consider in determining whether exhaustion applies?

*The school district sent the plaintiff, a child with a hearing impairment, by bus to a school for children with hearing impairments. The child claimed that this segregated her from students with hearing and that the bus trip caused her to miss a significant part of her school day. She sued the school district, alleging IDEA violations and seeking damages under Section 1983. She no longer attended school in the state in which the case arose. N.B. v. Alachua Co. Sch. Bd., 84 F.3d 1376 (11th Cir. 1996), *cert. denied*, 519 U.S. 1092 (1997).

*Plaintiff sought damages for her son under various federal statutes and constitutional provisions, including Section1983, the ADA, and Section 504. The child suffered from Epstein-Barr virus, an illness that causes debilitating fatigue. He did not attend school from fifth through eleventh grade but instead received homebound services. He had never been identified as eligible for services under the IDEA. His mother claimed the school replaced her son's teacher with a teacher who was "educationally incompatible" with her son, that the school was late to provide teaching materials, and that the school created intimidating annual review meetings. Cudjoe v. Indep. Sch. Dist. No. 12, 297 F.3d 1058, 1068 (10th Cir. 2002).

*The plaintiff alleged that during a five-year period the defendants failed to provide her with services required in her IEP, including "behavioral programming, augmentative communication, and tube-feeding services. . . ." She also claimed that defendants repeatedly locked her in a closet and restrained her in a stroller and that during one of these incidents she fell and fractured her skull. At the time she filed the case, she had moved to another district. She sued under both the ADA and Section 1983 for IDEA violations. Padilla v. Sch. Dist. No. 1 in the City and Cnty. of Denver, 233 F.3d 1268, 1271 (10th Cir. 2000).

*Plaintiffs sued under Section 1983 seeking damages for violation of federal constitutional rights and state law based on abusive disciplinary practices, including placing them in a three- by four-foot room for time-out periods and in-school suspensions. Hayes v. Unified Sch. Dist. No. 377, 877 F.2d 809 (10th Cir. 1989).

*Plaintiffs alleged that the defendant used a small room to punish D.P., a child with autism. They sued the defendants under 42 U.S.C. § 1983, seeking damages for alleged violations of D.P.'s constitutional and IDEA rights. At the time of the lawsuit, the parents had removed the child from the school and were home-schooling him. Payne v. Peninsula Sch. Dist., 653 F.3d 863 (9th Cir. 2011), *cert. denied*, __ U.S. __, 132 S.Ct. 1540 (2012).

*The plaintiff, who suffered from multiple emotional and mental disabilities, filed a claim under Section 1983 for damages for violating the child's constitutional rights and for intentional infliction of emotional distress and false imprisonment. The complaint alleged that, on several occasions, the district locked the plaintiff in a small time-out room for several hours at a time. The child had graduated from the school in which the events allegedly took place. Covington v. Knox Cnty. Sch. Sys., 205 F.3d 912 (6th Cir. 2000).

(Answers: Exhaustion required—*N.B.*, *Cudjoe*, *Hayes*; Exhaustion not required—*Padilla*, *Payne*, *Covington*).

3. What do you think of the following summary of the exhaustion rule in cases in which plaintiffs are seeking damages under Section 1983, the ADA, and Section 504? How does it compare with the ruling in *Fry*?

> In sum, although Plaintiffs proceed under the auspices of the ADA, the Rehabilitation Act, and § 1983, the IDEA nonetheless requires them to first exhaust its administrative procedures and remedies prior to commencing a suit under the ADA or other statutory schemes if they are "seeking relief that is also available under" the IDEA . . . .
>
> "'[A]vailable' relief" means "'relief for the events, condition, or consequences of which the person complains, not necessarily relief of the kind the person prefers,' or specifically seeks." *Padilla*, 233 F.3d at 1274 (quoting *Charlie F. v. Bd. of Educ.*, 98 F.3d 989, 992 (7th Cir.1996)). Thus, the question facing this Court in determining whether a plaintiff must utilize the IDEA's administrative procedures "relates to the source and nature of the alleged injuries for which he or she seeks a remedy, not the specific remedy itself." *Id.* (citing *Hayes v. Unified Sch. Dist. No. 377*, 877 F.2d 809, 812 (10th Cir. 1989)). In other words, the Court must ask whether the Plaintiffs' alleged injuries could be redressed to any degree by the IDEA's administrative procedures and remedies. If so, exhaustion of those remedies is required. If not, the claim necessarily falls outside the IDEA's scope, and exhaustion is unnecessary. Where the IDEA's ability to remedy a particular injury is unclear, exhaustion should be required in order to give educational agencies an initial opportunity to ascertain and alleviate the alleged problem.

Sagan v. Sumner Cnty. Bd. of Educ., 726 F. Supp. 2d 868, 880 (M.D. Tenn. 2010).

3. The Administrative Process is Inadequate to Adjudicate Plaintiff's Claims

Massey v. District of Columbia

400 F. Supp. 2d 66 (D.D.C. 2005)

LAMBERTH, District Judge.

. . . .

I. BACKGROUND

This case centers on the education of a troubled teenager. Tiffany . . . has been diagnosed with learning disabilities and emotional disturbances. . . . Over approximately the past two months . . . , Tiffany's parents claim that DCPS has failed to appropriately place her, leaving her without any school to attend.

For approximately the past year, Tiffany resided in Riverside Hospital, a residential treatment facility. As a resident of the hospital, she attended the adjacent school, Riverside Academy, which DCPS had authorized as a placement for her. On September 8, 2005, Tiffany was discharged from the hospital. Since Riverside Academy is only available for children who are current residents of the hospital, she was no longer eligible to attend. Tiffany therefore was in need of a new school placement.

Tiffany's parents . . . notified DCPS of Tiffany's impending release three weeks in advance. Upon her release, the Masseys had not received any indication that DCPS had taken any action on her case. The Masseys had already begun their own research into appropriate school placements for Tiffany, and four days after Tiffany's release, she and her parents interviewed with one promising possibility: Leary School, a private institution in Maryland for children with disabilities. Tiffany was accepted, but Leary School notified the Masseys that it would not enroll her without DCPS authorization. Accordingly, on September 16, 2005, Mr. and Mrs. Massey requested that DCPS place Tiffany at Leary School.

Five days later, on September 21, 2005, the Masseys participated in an Individual Educational Plan ("IEP") meeting convened by DCPS to begin the process of determining an appropriate placement. DCPS advised the Masseys that it could not authorize Leary School, or propose any placement for Tiffany, until it received a signed medical release. Mrs. Massey signed the release at the meeting. DCPS requested a copy of the Leary School admission letter, and indicated that DCPS would provide a proposed placement no later than September 26, 2005.

September 26 came and went with no word from DCPS. The Masseys, through their attorneys, forwarded the Leary School acceptance letter and renewed their request for a placement there on September 29, 2005. Nearly two weeks later, on October 11, 2005, the Masseys made a request for a due process hearing, a remedy provided under the administrative scheme of the IDEA. The next day, October 12, 2005, DCPS spoke to the Masseys' counsel and offered two possible placements, MM Washington Center and the DCALA Center. The Masseys did not respond to DCPS' suggestions, but rather filed the instant complaint in District of Columbia Superior Court on October 13, 2005, requesting that DCPS be required by temporary restraining order and preliminary injunction to place Tiffany at Leary School. . . .

DCPS then issued an official placement for Tiffany on October 14, 2005, placing her at MM Washington Center. This was communicated to the Masseys via facsimile to their attorney three days later, on October 17. The Masseys did not respond to the placement, but argued to this Court that neither placement was appropriate for Tiffany. . . .

In addition to failing to place Tiffany in an appropriate school, plaintiffs claim that DCPS further violated the IDEA by failing to abide by the statutory deadlines. When the Masseys filed their request for a due process hearing on October 11, 2005, the school district was required to respond within ten days. Plaintiffs claim that DCPS made no reply. The next deadline was to hold a resolution conference within 15 days of the filing. Again, plaintiffs allege, DCPS made no attempt to schedule the conference until this legal action was well underway, nine days after the statutory deadline.

DCPS argues that it did, in fact, meet the first deadline to respond to the due process hearing. It issued the Prior Notice placing Tiffany at MM Washington Center on October 14, and transmitted it to plaintiffs on October 17, 2005, six days after their request for the due process hearing. The October 14 Prior Notice, DCPS contends, satisfies the IDEA's requirement that DCPS respond. As to the next deadline, DCPS asserts that the only reason it failed to hold the resolution conference is because the Masseys did not return its telephone calls. In an effort to schedule a mutually convenient time for the meeting, the DCPS Resolution Session Scheduling Coordinator allegedly called Mr. Massey on four separate occasions within the ten days following receipt of the due process hearing request. There was no answer, and she received no response to her messages. Finally, on October 25, 2005, she scheduled the hearing for November 4, 2005 and notified the Masseys thereof.

On the basis of the foregoing, plaintiffs conclude that DCPS has acted in bad faith. Plaintiffs argue that they should not be required to continue through DCPS' administrative process, which has been revealed as inadequate. . . .

DCPS counters that it is the Masseys who have impeded the administrative process, and that DCPS, for its part, has satisfied its obligations under the IDEA; thus, it contends, there is no basis for a finding that its administrative resolution procedures are inadequate. The Masseys, DCPS argues, must give the administrative process a chance to work before asking this Court to inject itself into the dispute.

II. DISCUSSION

A. Subject Matter Jurisdiction

1. Legal Standard

Before parents may challenge a school district's action under the IDEA, they must first exhaust their administrative remedies available under the statute. § 1415(l). . . . Exhaustion is not required, however, when it is demonstrated that continuing through the administrative process would be futile or inadequate. . . .

. . . Plaintiffs argue that the administrative process would be inadequate because DCPS already failed to meet three of its obligations under the IDEA. First, DCPS has failed to provide Tiffany with an appropriate placement. Second, DCPS failed to hold the resolution session in a timely manner. Third, DCPS failed to respond to the hearing request in the substance required by the statute. DCPS' failures on these three points, plaintiffs contend, illustrate that it is unable to provide an adequate administrative process. As such, it would be pointless to continue pursuing an administrative remedy before seeking redress in this Court.

2. DCPS' Failure to Place Tiffany

DCPS left Tiffany without any placement for several weeks after her discharge from Riverside Hospital and termination from Riverside Academy. DCPS offers no explanation for why, when it was on notice that she would require a new placement, it failed even to begin the process of finding an appropriate placement until two weeks after her discharge (more than a month after DCPS had been notified). At that point, when DCPS held Tiffany's IEP meeting, it promised that a proposed placement would be forthcoming within five days. DCPS also indicated at that meeting that it would consider Leary School, the parents' preferred placement. DCPS failed to contact the parents about Leary School, or *any* placement, for Tiffany within the promised time frame. The Masseys contacted DCPS three days after the deadline passed, reiterating their request, and again DCPS failed to respond. In fact, DCPS took no action—and did not even communicate that it was considering Tiffany's case at all—until after plaintiffs filed their request for a due process hearing and indicated that they were considering litigation.

Finally, threatened with legal action, DCPS quickly made the two proposed placements. It did not explain how either placement was appropriate for Tiffany, given her IEP, nor did it explain why it declined to place Tiffany at Leary School. Without response from the Masseys, DCPS placed Tiffany at one of the schools it had proposed, MM Washington Center. One week later, at the hearing on the temporary restraining order, DCPS was unable to explain how either proposed placement was appropriate for Tiffany.... This is simply one example of what was revealed to be a pattern by DCPS of paying lip service to its responsibilities under the IDEA and related local laws while making no apparent effort to actually comply with them.

3. DCPS' Failure to Hold Resolution Conference

DCPS' next failure was close behind. Once the Masseys initiated a complaint with DCPS, it was obligated to follow the statutory deadlines in the IDEA. Doing so might have provided the Masseys and this Court with some reassurance that pursuing administrative remedies would not be futile or inadequate. DCPS claims that it failed to schedule the resolution session in a timely manner because it could not reach the Masseys by telephone....

The Masseys concede that they did receive one message and further acknowledge that they do not frequently check to see if they have any messages. For purposes of compliance with the IDEA's requirement to hold a resolution session within 15 days of receipt of a due process hearing request, this Court finds that it is immaterial how many times DCPS called the Masseys. It was appropriate for DCPS to attempt to consult with the Masseys in order to schedule the conference, but it should not have used their lack of response as an excuse for allowing the statutory deadline to pass unheeded.....

4. DCPS' Failure to Respond in Writing

Finally, the inadequacy of DCPS' administrative remedy is illustrated by its blatant disregard for the statutory requirement of a written response to the Masseys' request for a due process hearing. Under the statute, if DCPS had not previously issued a Prior Notice for Tiffany, it was required to respond in writing to the request for a due process hearing. § 1415(c)(2)(B) (i)(I). Furthermore, DCPS may not determine the form of its response: the required content of the written response is precisely detailed in the IDEA. § 1415(c)(2)(B)(i)(I)(aa)-(dd). Since DCPS had not issued a Prior Notice for Tiffany at the time of receiving the due process hearing request, it was obligated to respond in writing within ten days.

....

5. DCPS' Administrative Process is Inadequate

Because of DCPS' repeated failures to follow unambiguous terms of the law and to acknowledge and correct its mistakes, this Court cannot find that DCPS' process for administrative relief would be adequate. DCPS has provided this Court no basis on which to infer it is taking seriously the Masseys' claims, nor to trust that it will be able to follow the IDEA in addressing those claims. Tiffany was idle at home, awaiting an appropriate placement, for more than five weeks before DCPS issued a placement. Since then, she has remained out of school because her parents are legitimately concerned, based on firsthand experience and expert advice, that MM Washington Center is not appropriate for her. They have received no assurance from DCPS that the placement was based on Tiffany's IEP. Leaving Tiffany without schooling until the administrative process has been exhausted will certainly mean that she will remain with no appropriate school placement for the remainder of this calendar year, as the due process hearing is not scheduled to occur until December. Without any assurance that DCPS will observe the statute as it proceeds through administrative review, this Court is not confident that the Masseys will be afforded a meaningful remedy.

... In this Court's opinion, the litany of DCPS failures reveals that it is apparently unable to follow statutory procedures in the first place. Worse yet, DCPS appears to be incompetent to address, in the manner required by the IDEA, a parent's complaints about those failures. Therefore, this Court finds that plaintiffs have demonstrated that pursuing their claim through the administrative process would be inadequate, and the Masseys are not required to exhaust their administrative remedies....

....

Notes, Comments, and Questions

1. Do you agree with the court's rationale in *Massey*? Should the exception for inadequacy of the administrative procedures relate to all IDEA procedural requirements, as the court in *Massey* implied, or just those relating to impartial hearings? *See also* Christopher T. v. S.F. Unif. Sch. Dist., 553 F. Supp. 1107, 1115–16 (N.D. Cal. 1982) (waiving exhaustion because the district, "over a period of many months consistently refused to comply with its obligation under the EHA to extend advice or assistance regarding the Act to the families of children who might be eligible for funding under its provisions."). How far-reaching do you think the *Massey* decision is? Could plaintiffs in other cases in federal court in the District of Columbia use *Massey* to support a claim that the District's IDEA procedures are fundamentally flawed, thus excusing exhaustion for all IDEA plaintiffs?

2. Courts evaluate whether an impartial hearing can offer relief when deciding whether the exception for administrative inadequacy applies. For example, in *Padilla v. Sch. Dist. No. 1*, 35 F. Supp. 2d 1260 (D. Colo. 1999), *aff'd in relevant part and rev'd on other grounds*, 233 F.3d 1268 (10th Cir. 2000), the IHO dismissed the hearing request in part because he did not "'see any relief a Hearing Officer [could] grant a student presently residing and attending school in another county and in another school district.'" *Id.* at 1265. The court ruled that plaintiff did not have to exhaust further administrative remedies:

> [F]urther administrative appeal would have been futile. Here plaintiff was never granted a due process hearing, but instead was denied one on the grounds that the hearing officer did not have authority to grant "any relief.". . . . It is simply illogical for DPS to try and argue that Plaintiff must have exhausted her administrative remedies in one breath, when at the same time it was argued that plaintiff has no right to such a hearing.

Id. at 1265; *see also* Taylor v. Vt. Dep't of Educ., 313 F.3d 768, 789 (2d Cir. 2002) (holding that administrative remedies were inadequate because hearing officer had ruled that the impartial hearing was not the proper forum to determine parental IDEA rights).

3. Failure of the hearing officer to issue a decision within the period required by law is also grounds for applying this exception. *See* McAdams v. Bd. of Educ. of the Rocky Point Union Free Sch. Dist., 216 F. Supp. 2d 86, 95 (E.D.N.Y. 2002) (waiving exhaustion when the administrative process had already taken nearly two years); Engwiller v. Pine Plains Cent. Sch. Dist., 110 F. Supp. 2d 236, 245–46 (S.D.N.Y. 2000) (ordering late decision to be rendered within ten days, after which court would rule that pursuing the administrative process would be futile); Sabatini v. Corning-Painted Post Area Sch. Dist., 78 F. Supp. 2d 138, 141 (W.D.N.Y. 1999) (waiving exhaustion because state review officer failed to issue decision within mandatory time limit); Meehan v. Patchogue-Medford Sch. Dist., 29 F. Supp. 2d 129, 133–34 (E.D.N.Y. 1998) (waiving exhaustion because district did not schedule a hearing following plaintiff's request); *but see* Williams v. Overturf, 580 F. Supp. 1365, 1370 (W.D. Wis. 1984) (holding that remedy for a late decision is mandamus, not waiver of exhaustion).

4. Courts have also waived the exhaustion requirement when the plaintiffs challenged the legality of the hearing process itself. For example, in *Heldman v. Sobol*, 962 F.2d 148 (2d Cir. 1992), the court waived exhaustion in plaintiffs' challenge to the process for selecting and paying IHOs. The court stated:

> Resort to the New York state administrative process in this case would be futile. Heldman claims that the NYSED regulation specifying the hearing officer selection procedure violates the mandate of IDEA. Because the regulation implements a New York statute, neither the Commissioner nor the assigned hearing officer has the authority to alter the procedure; therefore, it would be an exercise in futility to require Heldman to exhaust the state administrative remedies. To require a systematic challenge, such as

> Heldman's, to pursue administrative remedies would not further the purposes of IDEA and would only serve to insulate state procedures from review—an outcome that would undermine the system Congress selected for the protection of the rights of children with disabilities.

Id. at 159; *see also* Jose P. v. Ambach, 669 F.2d 865, 868–70 (2d Cir. 1982) (refusing to require plaintiffs to exhaust when the adequacy of the administrative proceedings was the very thing they were challenging). One court, however, did not waive exhaustion when the plaintiff claimed the SRO was biased. TC v. Valley Cent. Sch. Dist., 777 F. Supp. 2d 577, 601 (S.D.N.Y. 2011).

4. Resort to the Administrative Process Would Cause the Child Severe or Irreparable Harm

Komninos v. Upper Saddle River Bd. of Educ.

13 F.3d 775 (3d Cir. 1994)

Weis, *Circuit Judge*.

In this appeal, we determine that a district court may entertain a motion for a preliminary injunction before administrative remedies have been exhausted if a School Board's interim placement decision under the Individuals with Disabilities Education Act will cause irreparable harm to a child. . . .

Stephen Komninos is a severely retarded eight-year-old boy who has cerebral palsy as well as associated communicative and behavioral disorders. . . .

In April 1993, Stephen's parents . . . requested that he be placed in a residential facility . . . . After the Board refused to comply with the wishes of the parents, they sought administrative relief pursuant to the Individuals with Disabilities Education Act . . . .

Unwilling to await the completion of the administrative proceedings, the parents moved Stephen in May 1993 to Heartspring, a residential school located in Wichita, Kansas. . . .

In July 1993, plaintiffs moved for emergency relief before the ALJ assigned to the case. They asked for an administrative order directing the Board to pay Stephen's expenses at Heartspring for the new school year beginning August 23, 1993 during the pendency of the administrative proceedings. Noting that material facts were in dispute and that plaintiffs had failed to demonstrate "irreparability of harm or irretrievable interruption of [the] educational program," the ALJ denied the motion. . . .

The parents filed a second motion in September 1993 asserting that Stephen would be forced to change schools because their funds would be exhausted before the completion of the administrative proceedings. The ALJ found that plaintiffs' claim was essentially "dollar driven," and therefore, not irreparable. The ALJ concluded that Stephen's danger to himself was no "more predictably acute everywhere except at Heartspring," and . . . denied the renewed motion . . . .

In the interim, on September 3, 1993, plaintiffs submitted a verified complaint to the district court "by way of appeal" from the ruling of the ALJ and asked for a preliminary injunction. The parents requested that the Board be directed to place Stephen and fund his schooling at Heartspring or another similar residential facility while the administrative hearings were proceeding.

The complaint asserted that, absent the socialization and specialized care offered at Heartspring or a similar institution, Stephen would be "physically, permanently and irreparably educationally harmed." Plaintiffs alleged that because the Board had refused to provide interim funds, the child was "suffering immediate, substantial and irreparable harm."

Before the Board filed responsive pleadings, the district court dismissed the complaint. The order stated that 20 U.S.C. §§ 1400–1484a vests a district court "with jurisdiction only when a plaintiff has first followed the procedures set forth in the Act and exhausted the administrative remedies under the Act." Accordingly, "plaintiffs not having yet exhausted the procedures required by the Act," the district court dismissed the complaint "for lack of jurisdiction."

I.

The Individuals with Disabilities Education Act provides for a "free appropriate public education" for all handicapped children and establishes an elaborate procedural mechanism to protect the rights of those individuals. One procedural safeguard is the right to a due process hearing before an administrative official. Parties aggrieved by the findings and decision made in the administrative proceedings provided by the Act have the right to bring a civil action in either federal or state court. . . .

. . . [I]t is clear from the language of the Act that Congress intended plaintiffs to complete the administrative process before resorting to federal court. . . .

Even though the policy of requiring exhaustion of remedies in the Disabilities Education Act is a strong one, some exceptions have been recognized. . . .

At least one Court of Appeals has recognized another exception—when exhaustion would work "severe or irreparable harm" upon a litigant. *Christopher W. v. Portsmouth Sch. Comm.*, 877 F.2d 1089, 1097 (1st Cir. 1989) . . . . This last exception finds support in the legislative history of the . . . Act which states that exhaustion would not be necessary when "an emergency situation exists (e.g., the failure to take immediate action will adversely affect a child's mental or physical health)." H.R. Rep. No. 296, 99th Cong., 1st Sess. 7 (1985). In accordance with the position taken by the Court of Appeals for the First Circuit and legislative history, we also adopt an emergency situation exception to the exhaustion requirement of the Individuals with Disabilities Education Act. Having recognized such a category, however, we caution that it is to be sparingly invoked.

. . . .

. . . [M]ere allegations by plaintiffs of irreversible harm will not be enough to excuse the completion of administrative proceedings. Plaintiffs must provide a sufficient preliminary showing that the child will suffer serious and irreversible mental or physical damage (e.g., irremediable intellectual regression) before the administrative process may be circumvented.

In order to meet that threshold, plaintiffs must provide affidavits from competent professionals along with other hard evidence that the child faces irreversible damage if the relief is not granted. If plaintiffs meet that burden but the defendant in connection with a 12(b)(1) motion to dismiss presents convincing evidence that such harm will not occur, the court should not proceed, but rather must require plaintiffs to exhaust their administrative remedies. We leave the means to determine whether the threshold requirements have been met to the discretion of the district court.

If plaintiffs satisfy the preliminary inquiry, the district court should then proceed with the traditional preliminary injunction procedures. . . .

II.

We turn then to the facts at hand. The Komninos family has not yet exhausted its administrative remedies. The due process hearings on the child's proper permanent placement are continuing, but the parents asked the district court to direct that the Board provide immediate funding, a step it had refused to take in the due process hearings. Exhibits to the verified complaint in the district court include reports by a neuropsychiatrist, by the Director of Psychological Services at Heartspring, by Stephen's parents and by others who have observed Stephen's behavior. These reports describe Stephen's continued, unpredictable, aggressive and assaultive actions, his favorable progress in toilet training at Heartspring, and his very limited attention span in classroom efforts. Dr. Williams, the neuropsychiatrist, opined that a twenty-four-hour residential program is necessary, that Stephen is a danger to himself and to others around him, and that moving him from Heartspring to a non-residential school would cause the child to "suffer serious regression."

Because of the procedural posture of the case, however, the district court record does not contain any materials or reports obtained by the Board. At oral argument in this Court, however, we were advised that in the continuing hearings before the ALJ, the Board had produced evidence challenging some of the plaintiffs' contentions about Stephen's possible regression. The fact that the pending administrative hearings are delving into many of the same factual issues presented to the district court graphically illustrates the disadvantages of concurrent activity in the two forums.

We do not presume to issue a definitive ruling in the absence of a more complete record, but we doubt that "regression" per se constitutes such irreparable harm as to justify an exception to the exhaustion requirement. It is our understanding that, in general, the skills lost in regression may be recouped, but that the disabled take longer than the non-handicapped to regain their previous achievements.

The decisional law discussing the regression problem in reviewing final placement decisions is helpful, but the cited cases differ from the one here where the critical question is whether there is such immediacy of harm as to preclude delay until the administrative process is completed. When awaiting the outcome of agency proceedings does not jeopardize the child's future progress to any substantial degree, courts should be wary of foregoing the benefits to be derived from a thorough development of the issues in the administrative proceeding. If a court does insist on exhaustion of the administrative process and ultimately the Board is found to have erred in failing to provide a proper placement, a remedy is available. The delay in obtaining the expected benefit may be redressed by compensable extensions of eligibility for educational aid.

A showing at the time the suit is filed in the district court, however, that the regression will be irreversible would demonstrate irreparable harm and would relieve plaintiffs from the obligation to finish the administrative process before seeking judicial relief.

. . . .

Because the district court was under the misapprehension that it lacked authority to exempt parties from exhaustion of remedies in proper circumstances in Disabilities Education Act cases, we must return this case for further consideration. We do so with full understanding of the difficulty with litigation of this nature. We recognize that the intense and commendable concern of the parents for the welfare of their child, as well as society's concern for protecting these children, must be weighed against the duty of school boards to carefully allocate their limited resources in fairness to all, as best as can be done. We intimate no views on the appropriate disposition of the case by the district court.

. . . .

Notes, Comments, and Questions

1. The court in *Komninos* stated that it doubted that "'regression' per se constitutes such irreparable harm as to justify an exception to the exhaustion requirement." 13 F.3d at 780. Was regression the only grounds plaintiffs raised for irreparable injury? The plaintiffs also claimed, based on an affidavit from a neuropsychiatrist, that Stephen was a threat to himself and others. Did the court consider this evidence? Is the claim that Stephen was a danger to himself and others, and the evidence to support it, sufficient to justify the application of an exception to the exhaustion requirement?

2. As suggested in *Komninos*, courts that have considered waiving the exhaustion requirement based on the threat of irreparable harm to the child generally examine the nature of the potential harm. In *Coleman v. Newburgh Enlarged City School District*, 503 F.3d 198 (2d Cir. 2007), the court declined to waive exhaustion for a child who claimed his suspension violated the IDEA and would cause him to miss his graduation. The court stated, "there was no showing that the delay that would have occurred in exhausting administrative remedies, which may have entailed his missing his graduation . . . and participation in certain school activities, would have affected Coleman's mental or physical health . . . ." *Id.* at 206; *see also* TC v. Valley Cent. Sch. Dist., 777 F. Supp. 2d 577, 600 (S.D.N.Y. 2011) (refusing to waive

exhaustion in challenge to disciplinary action on grounds that plaintiff would graduate prior to resolution of case because plaintiffs could have filed case sooner but chose to wait until they could find an attorney). In contrast, in *N.M. Ass'n for Retarded Citizens v. New Mexico*, 678 F.2d 847, 851 (10th Cir. 1982), the court waived exhaustion:

> Six school years have already been irretrievably lost while this litigation has run its course. To subject this sizeable class of handicapped children to further delay in obtaining adequate services would jeopardize its receipt of appropriate education at the precollege level.

Id. at 851; *see also* Parks v. Pavkovic, 536 F. Supp. 296, 302 (N.D. Ill. 1982) (waiving exhaustion because of threat that child's school would discharge him during pendency of administrative hearing because state had not paid for placement).

3. Courts have ruled that plaintiffs are not required to exhaust administrative remedies when they are challenging a district's alleged violation of the IDEA's stay-put provision, 20 U.S.C. § 1415(j) (2012). The justification is similar to the reason for waiving exhaustion if the child would face irreparable harm. In *N.D. v. Haw. Dep't of Educ.*, 600 F.3d 1104 (9th Cir. 2010), the court waived exhaustion of plaintiffs' claim that Hawaii's decision to close schools on seventeen Fridays during the school year violated Section 1415(j). The court reasoned:

> The claimed right is the right to maintain the disabled student's current educational placement while the judicial proceeding is ongoing to determine if the new placement is appropriate. The relief requested in the preliminary injunction is essentially the same relief provided by the stay-put provision. Exhausting the administrative process would be inadequate because the stay-put provision (and therefore the preliminary injunction) is designed precisely to prevent harm while the proceeding is ongoing. The stay-put provision recognizes the need for the child to keep her current educational placement as the administrative process tries to sort out alternatives. If the child is moved from the current placement during the process, then the deprivation of the right has occurred. The completion of the administrative process cannot remedy the harm. Access to the preliminary injunction is essential to vindicate this particular IDEA right.

Id. at 1111; *see also* Murphy v. Arlington Cent. Sch. Dist. Bd. of Educ., 297 F.3d 195, 199–200 (2d Cir. 2002) ("A belated administrative decision upholding a student's stay-put rights provides no remedy for the disruption already suffered by the student. Hence, as a practical matter, access to immediate interim relief is essential for the vindication of this particular IDEA right."); R.B. v. Mastery Charter Sch., 762 F. Supp. 2d 745, 755 (E.D. Pa. 2010), *aff'd*, 532 F. App'x 136 (3d Cir. 2013), *cert. denied*, __ U.S. __, 134 S.Ct. 1280 (2014) ("[T]he exhaustion requirement does not apply to stay-put injunctions because the purpose of the stay-put is to prevent disruption during proceedings to exhaust.").

4. The irreparable injury exception to the exhaustion requirement applies to school districts as well. In *Honig v. Doe*, 484 U.S. 305 (1988), the Court referred to

exhaustion in the context of school disciplinary proceedings. The Court held that the suspension of a child with a disability for more than ten days constituted a change in placement and could not be imposed without resort to the IDEA's administrative procedures. In response to the argument that requiring school districts to resort to administrative procedures would delay removal of dangerous children, the Court indicated that schools could bypass administrative remedies and seek a court order removing a dangerous child from school:

> It is true that judicial review is normally not available . . . until all administrative proceedings are completed, but as we have previously noted, parents may bypass the administrative process where exhaustion would be futile or inadequate. While many of the EHA's procedural safeguards protect the rights of parents and children, schools can and do seek redress through the administrative review process, and we have no reason to believe that Congress meant to require schools alone to exhaust in all cases, no matter how exigent the circumstances.

Id. at 326–27.

5. The School District Did Not Give Notice of the Availability of Administrative Procedures

Courts will generally excuse failure to exhaust administrative remedies if the school district failed to give notice to the plaintiffs of their administrative rights and as a result they were deprived of the opportunity to pursue them. *See* Weixel v. Bd. of Educ. of City of N.Y., 287 F.3d 138, 149 (2d Cir. 2002) (waiving exhaustion because school district did not give parents notice of their administrative remedies); Briere v. Fair Haven Grade Sch. Dist., 948 F. Supp. 1242, 1253 (D. Vt. 1996) (ruling that school district's failure to notify parent of her right to request a supplemental evaluation excused her failure to exhaust); Mason v. Schenectady City Sch. Dist., 879 F. Supp. 215, 218–19 (N.D.N.Y. 1993) (waiving exhaustion because school district failed to inform parent of her procedural rights); Gordon M. v. Alvin Indep. Sch. Dist., 532 F. Supp. 460, 463 (S.D. Tex. 1982) (waiving exhaustion when school district did not inform parents of their procedural rights).

This exception to the exhaustion requirement is not without qualification. The court in *Frith v. Galeton Area Sch. Dist.*, 900 F. Supp. 706 (M.D. Pa. 1995), stated that, "technical non-compliance with the notice provisions is not a violation of the Act if the parents had actual notice and were not deprived of any substantive right." *Id.* at 713. In *Ruecker v. Sommer*, 567 F. Supp. 2d 1276 (D. Or. 2008), the court elaborated on this:

> Ruecker argues he is excused from completing the administrative process because the District failed to provide him with appropriate process and notice under the IDEA . . . .
>
> . . . .

> [W]here a school district violates its statutory duty to provide notice to the plaintiff of his rights under the IDEA, which causes the plaintiff not to exhaust the IDEA administrative remedies, it cannot hide behind the exhaustion requirement as a defense to a lawsuit brought by the plaintiff. Ruecker does not fall within this exception. Even assuming defendants were obligated and failed to provide appropriate notice, Ruecker . . . actually exercised his procedural rights under § 504 and the IDEA by filing a complaint requesting a due process hearing.
>
> Furthermore, Ruecker's failure to exhaust his administrative remedies had nothing to do with any lack of notice by the District. This is not a case where the school district failed to notify the plaintiff of his rights and then seeks to penalize him for failing to exercise them. Rather, Ruecker was aware of his rights to administrative review, actually initiated administrative proceedings, and then voluntarily withdrew his complaint for reasons not relevant to this exception. Additionally, the fact that Ruecker initially was represented by counsel weighs against applying this exception.

Id. at 1298.

Section Three
The IDEA's Statute of Limitations

Originally, the IDEA did not contain a statute of limitations for seeking judicial review of an administrative decision. The lack of a statute of limitations generated a significant amount of litigation, as federal courts were left to create one by borrowing the statute of limitations from the state law that was most analogous to the IDEA. Most of these decisions are no longer relevant; in 2004 Congress amended the IDEA to impose a ninety day statute of limitations for bringing a federal or state court action seeking review of a state administrative decision or within the state's statute of limitations if it has one. The provision reads:

> The party bringing the action shall have 90 days from the date of the decision of the hearing officer to bring such an action, or, if the State has an explicit time limitation for bringing such action under this part, in such time as the State law allows.

20 U.S.C. § 1415(i)(2)(B) (2012). By its terms, this statute of limitations applies only to exhausted IDEA claims. The IDEA does not have a statute of limitations for bringing claims that are not required to be exhausted. This section is divided into two sections; the first covers exhausted claims and the second involves claims that are not required to be exhausted.

A. Exhausted IDEA Claims

This section will analyze four issues regarding the statute of limitations in exhausted claims: whether compliance with the IDEA's statute of limitations is a jurisdictional requirement; when the statute of limitations begins to run; the grounds for tolling the statute of limitations; and the applicability of the statute of limitations.

1. Whether the IDEA's Statute of Limitations is Jurisdictional

If compliance with the statute of limitations is jurisdictional, failure to meet the statute of limitations deprives the court of jurisdiction, and this can be brought up at any time, including by the court, as a basis for dismissing the claim. If compliance with the statute of limitations is not a jurisdictional requirement, then the defendant must plead the failure "as an affirmative defense that is subject to exceptions, such as equitable tolling." Maynard v. District of Columbia, 579 F. Supp. 2d 137, 140 (D.D.C. 2008) (refusing to take a position because even if not jurisdictional, the complaint was late and court would refuse to apply equitable tolling). If a defendant fails to plead the plaintiff's failure to satisfy the statute of limitations as an affirmative defense, the defendant waives the defense. The Seventh Circuit has stated in *dicta* that the statute of limitations is not jurisdictional. *See* Farzana K. v. Ind. Dep't of Educ., 473 F.3d 703, 705 (7th Cir. 2007) ("Federal courts have been authorized to resolve disputes under the IDEA, so procedural hurdles—whether these concern timely filing or verification—are not 'jurisdictional.'"). One federal district court agreed. *See* Wall Twp. Bd. of Educ. v. C.M., 534 F. Supp. 2d 487, 493 (D.N.J. 2008) ("[B]y permitting the individual states to set forth the time limitation for an aggrieved party to appeal a decision made following an IDEA due process hearing, Congress intended for Section 1415(i)(2)(B) to be treated as a statute of limitations subject to waiver, estoppel, and equitable tolling."). Other district courts that have addressed the issue suggested an absence of definitive guidance and ultimately did not resolve the question. *See Maynard*, 579 F. Supp. 2d at 140 ("The issue has generated disparate appellate opinions and has not yet been fully resolved."); Smith v. District of Columbia, 496 F. Supp. 2d 125, 128 (D.D.C. 2007) (stating that "waters have been muddled" as to whether the IDEA's statute of limitations is jurisdictional).

2. When the Statute of Limitations Begins to Run

According to Section 1415(i)(2)(B), the ninety-day limitations period begins to run "from the date of the decision of the hearing officer . . . ." Courts have been clear that the ninety days begins to run on the date the decision is issued, not on the date on which it is mailed or served. *See* R.P. v. District of Columbia, 276 F. App'x 1, 2 (D.C. Cir. 2008) (ruling that the IDEA's plain language states that the statute of limitations begins on "the date of the hearing officer's decision, rather than from the date of service or notice."); J.S. v. District of Columbia, 533 F. Supp. 2d 160, 162 (D.D.C. 2008) (rejecting argument that three days should be added to the date of the mailing based on Fed. R. Civ. P. 6(e)); Smith v. District of Columbia, 496 F. Supp. 2d 125, 128 (D.D.C. 2007) ("[T]he IDEA starts the running of the limitations period from the date of the . . . [hearing officer decision], not from the date of service of the . . . [hearing officer decision] upon the party.").

3. Grounds for Tolling the Statute of Limitations

The running of the IDEA's statute of limitations can be tolled in certain circumstances. For example, courts generally agree that the hearing officer's failure to notify the parties' of the time to file a case in court tolls the statute of limitations. *See* Spiegler v. District of Columbia, 866 F.2d 461, 469 (D.C. Cir. 1989) (ruling that school district's failure to give notice of the thirty day statute of limitations barred it from raising the statute of limitations as a defense); Hebert v. Manchester N.H. Sch. Dist., 833 F. Supp. 80, 84–85 (D.N.H. 1993) (tolling the statute of limitations because of the hearing officer's failure to notify them of the statute of limitations). Courts differ over whether a motion for reconsideration of an administrative decision tolls the statute of limitations. Two district courts in the District of Columbia tolled the statute while motions to reconsider pursuant to District rules were pending. Theodore v. District of Columbia, 655 F. Supp. 2d 136, 143 (D.D.C. 2009) (holding that a timely reconsideration motion tolled the statute of limitations under District of Columbia law); Stanton v. District of Columbia, 639 F. Supp. 2d 1, 3 (D.D.C. 2009) (same).

4. The Applicability of the Statute of Limitations

The Fifth Circuit ruled that the statute of limitations for filing a complaint does not apply to a mandatory counterclaim. Jonathan H. v. Souderton Area Sch. Dist., 562 F.3d 527, 530 (3d Cir. 2009) (ruling that the IDEA's plain language permits a claimant to file a compulsory counterclaim after the statutory period). The court reasoned that a counterclaim was not an action, and thus not covered by the statute of limitations, which sets a time limit only for bringing an action. *Id.* Although the court did not adopt a statute of limitations for filing a mandatory counterclaim, the reasoning in the decision implies that a timely counterclaim under the Federal Rules of Civil Procedure is sufficient; *see also* Bd. of Educ. of Chi. v. Wolinsky, 842 F. Supp. 1080, 1082–84 (N.D. Ill. 1994) (declining to apply the statute of limitations to a counterclaim).

B. IDEA Claims that Are Not Required to be Exhausted

1. Selecting a Statute of Limitations

In determining the appropriate statute of limitations in unexhausted IDEA claims, courts borrow the statute of limitations from the state law that is most analogous to the IDEA. *See* Piazza v. Florida Union Free Sch. Dist., 777 F. Supp. 2d 669, 688, 690 (S.D.N.Y. 2011) (applying New York's three-year statute of limitations); Jeffrey Y. v. St. Mary's Area Sch. Dist., 967 F. Supp. 852, 855 (W.D. Pa. 1997), *aff'd*, 698 F.2d 685 (9th Cir. 1982), *cert. denied*, 460 U.S. 1052 (1983) (stating that Pennsylvania's two-year statute of limitations applies to IDEA cases). Courts in the Second Circuit have adopted a three-year statute of limitations for unexhausted IDEA claims and a district court in the Fourth Circuit adopted a one-year statute of limitations. *See Piazza*, 777 F. Supp. 2d at 690 (applying three-year statute of limitations); Mason v. Schenectady City Sch. Dist., 879 F. Supp. 215, 220 (N.D.N.Y. 1993) (applying three-year statute of limitations); Richards v. Fairfax Cnty. Sch. Bd., 798 F. Supp. 338, 340 (E.D. Va. 1992), *aff'd*, 798 F.2d 338 (4th Cir. 1093) (applying one-year statute of limitations).

2. When the Statute of Limitations Begins to Run

Despite the use of a state statute of limitations in unexhausted IDEA claims, the date on which an unexhausted IDEA claim accrues for purposes of the statute of limitations is based on federal law. *See* Nieves-Marquez v. Puerto Rico, 353 F.3d 108, 119 (1st Cir. 2003) (ruling that federal law governs the date on which the time at which an IDEA claim accrues); Richards v. Fairfax Cnty. Sch. Dist., 798 F. Supp. 338, 340 (E.D. Va 1992) (ruling that federal law governs date on which federal claim accrues, even when state statute of limitations governs). Under federal law, a claim accrues when the plaintiff " 'knew or should have known about the alleged action that forms the basis of the complaint.' " Somoza v. N.Y.C. Dep't. of Educ., 538 F.3d 106, 114 (2d Cir. 2008) (quoting 20 U.S.C § 1415(b)(6)(B)); *see also Nieves-Marquez*, 353 F.3d at 120 (using similar standard); *Richards*, 798 F. Supp. at 340-341 (stating that claim accrues when the plaintiff knows of the event or injury that created the claim). Courts have ruled, for example, that an unexhausted claim accrues when the plaintiff noticed her daughter was progressing rapidly under a different program and the program director opined that she had previously been denied a FAPE, *Somoza*, 538 F.3d at 114; when the plaintiff had reason to conclude that the school district would not comply with the administrative decision, *Nieves-Marquez*, 353 F.3d at 119–120; and when the school district told the parents that they would no longer provide special education to their daughter. *Richards*, 798 F. Supp. 2d at 341.

3. Grounds for Tolling the Statute of Limitations

In unexhausted IDEA claims for which there is no statute of limitations, courts must not only adopt the statute of limitations from the state law that is most analogous to the IDEA, but use the state's tolling rules as well, unless the rules are inconsistent with the IDEA. Piazza v. Florida Union Free Sch. Dist., 777 F. Supp. 2d 669, 689–692 (S.D.N.Y. 2011). In *Piazza*, the court adopted the state's statute of limitations, but did not adopt the state's minority tolling rule, finding that tolling the statute of limitations until a child reached majority age was inconsistent with the IDEA's goal of resolving disputes quickly. *Id.* at 692; *but see* Mason v. Schenectady City Sch. Dist., 879 F. Supp. 215, 220 n. 4 (N.D.N.Y. 1993) (applying state minority tolling provision without further discussion of the issue).

Chapter 15

Enforcing the IDEA in Federal Court: Litigating IDEA Cases

Introduction

This chapter examines the law relating to litigating IDEA cases in federal court, focusing on challenges to administrative decisions in IDEA cases. The IDEA grants federal district courts jurisdiction to hear complaints by parties aggrieved by an impartial hearing decision or a state level appeal decision. 20 U.S.C. § 1415(i)(2)(A) (2012). The IDEA further provides:

> In any action brought under this paragraph, the court—
>
> (i) shall receive the records of the administrative proceedings;
>
> (ii) shall hear additional evidence at the request of a party; and
>
> (iii) basing its decision on the preponderance of the evidence, shall grant such relief as the court determines is appropriate.

Id. at § (2)(C). This provision raises many questions about the procedures and standards a federal district court should follow when an aggrieved party asks the court to review a state administrative decision. As the Eleventh Circuit observed:

> [T]he IDEA provision for judicial review has been described as "puzzling" and "somewhat confusing," because it differs from the norm in a way that produces three distinct issues: (1) How much deference, if any, should be given to the administrative decision if additional evidence may be taken and the standard to be applied is the preponderance of the evidence? (2) What standard should be applied in deciding what "additional" evidence, if any, should be admitted in the district court proceeding? And (3) What is the appropriate procedural mechanism to be implemented in the district court in bringing the case before the court for a final decision?

Walker Cnty. Sch. Dist. v. Bennett, 203 F.3d 1293, 1297 (11th Cir. 2000), *cert. denied*, 531 U.S. 1059 (2000). This chapter presents material that will help answer these questions. Corresponding to the order in which the Eleventh Circuit raised these questions, Section One examines the standard of review federal courts employ in reviewing state administrative decisions in IDEA cases, Section Two considers the circumstances in which courts will receive additional evidence when reviewing administrative decisions, and Section Three considers the procedural mechanism for deciding IDEA cases. Finally, Section Four considers several miscellaneous topics that arise in connection with litigating IDEA cases, including the burden of proof, governing law, and the circumstances in which federal courts will remand a case to the hearing officer for further proceedings.

Problem

M.O. is a tenth grade student living in the Madison Park School District (the "District). M.O. progressed normally academically and socially through fifth grade. Starting at the beginning of sixth grade, M.O. began to have difficulty in school. He fell behind academically, failed several classes, cut class, received several detentions, and withdrew socially. Concerned about this, M.O.'s parents consulted with his pediatrician in early October. She referred M.O. for a psychological evaluation. In November, the psychologist found that M.O. had a low-average IQ and now that he is in middle school and the work is more difficult, his performance has declined. The psychologist suggested that M.O. was frustrated with his poor performance, leading to his behavioral problems and withdrawal. M.O.'s parents tried to work with him on his homework and hired a tutor. However, M.O.'s performance and behavior did not improve and in March, M.O.'s parents brought the psychological evaluation to the attention of the principal of Madison Park Middle School. His parents asked the principal to evaluate M.O. for special education services but the principal declined. The principal said that there were several children in the School with a similar diagnosis, that the School does not provide them with special education, but that the School provides "building level" services for them, including meeting with a reading specialist twice a week, a weekly group counseling session, and speech and language therapy. M.O.'s parents agreed to allow M.O. to participate in this program.

In seventh grade, M.O.'s performance did not improve; in fact it deteriorated, and he failed math and science in the fall. His parents brought M.O. to the psychologist once again, and this time the psychologist diagnosed M.O. as having an intellectual disability. M.O.'s parents brought this report to the principal in the spring, and the principal agreed to refer M.O. to the District to evaluate him for special education. The District concluded that M.O. was eligible for special education and classified him as having an intellectual disability and an emotional disturbance. The District convened an IEP team to prepare an IEP for M.O. for eighth grade. The IEP included group and individual counseling, speech and language therapy, and placement in the middle school's self-contained classroom for children with intellectual disabilities and emotional disturbances. M.O.'s parents disagreed with the placement, feeling that M.O. could learn in a general education classroom provided he had adequate academic and behavioral supports. Nevertheless, they decided not to challenge the IEP, hoping that M.O. would be able to return to a general education classroom in ninth grade.

In eighth grade, M.O.'s performance stabilized, but remained unsatisfactory. He barely passed his courses and he received several reprimands. M.O.'s parents felt he should have been doing better, and threatened to remove him to a private school.

The principal convinced them to leave M.O. in the program, at least for the remainder of eighth grade.

In the spring of M.O.'s eighth grade year, the District prepared his ninth grade IEP. It was basically unchanged. This time, M.O.'s parents notified the district that the IEP did not provide M.O. with a free appropriate public education in the least restrictive environment, and that if the District did not modify the IEP accordingly, they would place him in a private school that would provide an appropriate education to M.O. and seek tuition reimbursement. M.O.'s parents found a private school for M.O., placed him there, and sought tuition reimbursement. The district refused, and M.O.'s parents requested an impartial hearing in September of M.O.'s ninth grade year.

The IHO refused to allow the psychologist who evaluated M.O. in sixth and seventh grade to testify. The hearing officer ruled that all evidence of events prior to September of M.O.'s eighth grade year were irrelevant because they occurred prior to the commencement of the state's one-year statute of limitations. Nevertheless, the IHO ruled in favor of M.O. She ruled that the District did not provide M.O. with a FAPE in the least restrictive environment in ninth grade and that the private school placement did. In issuing her ruling, the IHO placed particular reliance on the testimony of M.O.'s eighth grade teacher, which she found to be credible. He testified that the academic program in the self-contained class was too easy for M.O., that it was impossible to differentiate instruction for M.O. because of the demands on the teacher's time, and that M.O. did not receive an educational benefit from being in the self-contained classroom.

The District appealed the IHO's decision to the SRO. The SRO reversed, rejecting the testimony of M.O.'s teacher and instead adopting the uncorroborated testimony of the District's special education coordinator, who testified that based on her observations, M.O. benefitted from his eighth grade instruction.

(1) M.O.'s parents want to appeal the SRO's decision in federal court. What is the proper procedural mechanism for doing so? What standard of review will the court utilize in reviewing the SRO's decision? How much weight should the court give to the IHO's findings?

(2) After they filed the case in federal court, M.O.'s parents asked the federal court judge to admit the testimony of the psychologist that the hearing officer refused to admit. How should the judge rule?

(3) By the time the case reached federal court, M.O. was in tenth grade and had returned to the District. The District had adopted an IEP that placed M.O. in an integrated co-teaching classroom for all academic classes in tenth grade, meaning that each class was taught by a general education subject matter specialist and a special education teacher. M.O. was not performing well in that setting, either academically or socially. The District asked the judge to admit evidence of his poor performance in tenth grade. How should the judge rule?

(4) The federal court ruled in favor of the parents. The District appealed. What standard of review of the district court's decision will the court of appeals utilize to decide the case?

Section One
Standard of Review

A. The "Due Weight" Standard

Although the IDEA requires a federal court to consider the administrative record and additional evidence at the request of a party and to base its decision on a preponderance of the evidence, the IDEA is silent about the amount of deference the court should give to the administrative decision. For this, we turn to our old friend, *Board of the Hendrick Hudson Central School District v. Rowley.*

Board of Educ. of Hendrick Hudson Cent. Sch. Dist. v. Rowley

458 U.S. 176 (1982)

. . . .

IV

A

. . . [T]he . . . [IDEA] permits "[any] party aggrieved by the findings and decision" of the state administrative hearings "to bring a civil action" in "any State court of competent jurisdiction or in a district court of the United States without regard to the amount in controversy." § 1415(e)(2). The complaint, and therefore the civil action, may concern "any matter relating to the identification, evaluation, or educational placement of the child, or the provision of a free appropriate public education to such child." § 1415(b)(1)(E). In reviewing the complaint, the Act provides that a court "shall receive the record of the [state] administrative proceedings, shall hear additional evidence at the request of a party, and, basing its decision on the preponderance of the evidence, shall grant such relief as the court determines is appropriate." § 1415(e)(2).

The parties disagree sharply over the meaning of these provisions, petitioners contending that courts are given only limited authority to review for state compliance with the Act's procedural requirements and no power to review the substance of the state program, and respondents contending that the Act requires courts to exercise *de novo* review over state educational decisions and policies. We find petitioners' contention unpersuasive, for Congress expressly rejected provisions that would have so severely restricted the role of reviewing courts. In substituting the current language of the statute for language that would have made state administrative findings conclusive if supported by substantial evidence, the Conference Committee explained that courts were to make "independent [decisions] based on a preponderance of the evidence." S. Conf. Rep. No. 94-455, p. 50 (1975), U.S. Code Cong. and Admin. News 1975, p. 1503. See also 121 Cong. Rec. 37416 (1975 (remarks of Sen. Williams).

But although we find that this grant of authority is broader than claimed by petitioners, we think the fact that it is found in § 1415, which is entitled "Procedural safeguards," is not without significance. When the elaborate and highly specific procedural safeguards embodied in § 1415 are contrasted with the general and somewhat imprecise substantive admonitions contained in the Act, we think that the importance Congress attached to these procedural safeguards cannot be gainsaid. It seems to us no exaggeration to say that Congress placed every bit as much emphasis upon compliance with procedures giving parents and guardians a large measure of participation at every stage of the administrative process as it did upon the measurement of the resulting IEP against a substantive standard. We think that the congressional emphasis upon full participation of concerned parties throughout the development of the IEP, as well as the requirements that state and local plans be submitted to the Secretary for approval, demonstrates the legislative conviction that adequate compliance with the procedures prescribed would in most cases assure much if not all of what Congress wished in the way of substantive content in an IEP.

Thus the provision that a reviewing court base its decision on the "preponderance of the evidence" is by no means an invitation to the courts to substitute their own notions of sound educational policy for those of the school authorities which they review. The very importance which Congress has attached to compliance with certain procedures in the preparation of an IEP would be frustrated if a court were permitted simply to set state decisions at nought. The fact that § 1415(e) requires that the reviewing court "receive the records of the [state] administrative proceedings" carries with it the implied requirement that due weight shall be given to these proceedings. And we find nothing in the Act to suggest that merely because Congress was rather sketchy in establishing substantive requirements, as opposed to procedural requirements for the preparation of an IEP, it intended that reviewing courts should have a free hand to impose substantive standards of review which cannot be derived from the Act itself. In short, the statutory authorization to grant "such relief as the court determines is appropriate" cannot be read without reference to the obligations, largely procedural in nature, which are imposed upon recipient States by Congress.

Therefore, a court's inquiry in suits brought under § 1415(e)(2) is twofold. First, has the State complied with the procedures set forth in the Act? And second, is the individualized educational program developed through the Act's procedures reasonably calculated to enable the child to receive educational benefits? If these requirements are met, the State has complied with the obligations imposed by Congress and the courts can require no more.

B

In assuring that the requirements of the Act have been met, courts must be careful to avoid imposing their view of preferable educational methods upon the States.

The primary responsibility for formulating the education to be accorded a handicapped child, and for choosing the educational method most suitable to the child's needs, was left by the Act to state and local educational agencies in cooperation with the parents or guardian of the child. The Act expressly charges States with the responsibility of "acquiring and disseminating to teachers and administrators of programs for handicapped children significant information derived from educational research, demonstration, and similar projects, and [of] adopting, where appropriate, promising educational practices and materials." § 1413(a)(3). In the face of such a clear statutory directive, it seems highly unlikely that Congress intended courts to overturn a State's choice of appropriate educational theories in a proceeding conducted pursuant to § 1415(e)(2).

....

VI

Applying these principles to the facts of this case, we conclude that the Court of Appeals erred in affirming the decision of the District Court. Neither the District Court nor the Court of Appeals found that petitioners had failed to comply with the procedures of the Act, and the findings of neither court would support a conclusion that Amy's educational program failed to comply with the substantive requirements of the Act. On the contrary, the District Court found that the "evidence firmly establishes that Amy is receiving an 'adequate' education, since she performs better than the average child in her class and is advancing easily from grade to grade." In light of this finding, and of the fact that Amy was receiving personalized instruction and related services calculated by the Furnace Woods school administrators to meet her educational needs, the lower courts should not have concluded that the Act requires the provision of a sign-language interpreter. Accordingly, the decision of the Court of Appeals is reversed, and the case is remanded for further proceedings consistent with this opinion.

Notes, Comments, and Questions

1. The Court in *Rowley* found itself in between two fairly extreme positions about the appropriate standard of review of administrative decisions. The Board of Education argued that the courts have limited authority to review the decisions of state authorities. The Court rejected this position on the grounds that Congress rejected such a limited review. The Court also rejected Rowley's argument that courts should apply the "*de novo*" standard of review to the decisions of state authorities in special education cases. The *de novo* standard is perhaps the least deferential standard of review, as it permits the reviewing court virtually complete authority to reconsider the entire case and make its own findings, regardless of the findings of the administrative agency. The court rejected this standard of review because courts are not educational experts and should defer to the educational decisions of experts. Why do you think that the parties took such extreme positions, especially in light of the legislative history and statutory language that do not support either position?

2. It appears that three factors played a significant role in *Rowley's* determination that courts should give "due weight" to state administrative decisions. First, the court found that implicit in the statutory requirement that the court receive the administrative record is that the court give due weight to administrative proceedings. *Rowley*, 458 U.S. at 206. Do you agree that the "due weight" standard is implicit in this requirement? Could the requirement be read as implying other standards? Second, the court found that local state authorities, and not federal courts, have the educational expertise necessary to educate children with disabilities, and courts should generally defer to their judgment. *Id.* at 207–08. Finally, the Court cited the importance the IDEA places on procedures in developing an educational program for children with disabilities and the significant role the IDEA reserves for parents in that process, reasoning that as long as the state followed the procedures and gave parents a voice, the courts should defer to the results. *Id.* at 208–09. Is parental involvement a sufficient substitute for a stricter standard of review of administrative decisions? Are all parents able to play an active, assertive, and informed role in their chid's education?

3. Imagine you are the law clerk for the federal district court judge who is the first judge who will apply the *Rowley* standard for reviewing a state administrative decision. Draft a paragraph that states the standard. Review your answer as you read the next section.

B. Determining the Weight that is Due

In stating that the IDEA's requirement "that the reviewing court 'receive the records of the [state] administrative proceedings' carries with it the implied requirement that due weight shall be given to these proceedings," *Board of Educ. of Hendrick Hudson Cent. Sch. Dist. v. Rowley*, 458 U.S. 176, 206 (1982), the Supreme Court in *Rowley* left open the definition of "due weight." It also left open many other questions about the standard federal courts should use in reviewing administrative decisions in IDEA cases:

> *Rowley* left many issues unresolved, including: How much weight is "due" to the administrative rulings? Is there a difference between administrative rulings that appear grounded in findings of fact and those based on conclusions of law? Is there a different level of deference owed to questions of procedural compliance as opposed to substantive compliance? And how should courts treat a question of appropriate educational methodology that is bound up with a determination of whether the requirements of the Act have been met?

M.H. v. N.Y.C. Dep't of Educ., 685 F.3d 217, 242 (2d Cir. 2012). Lower courts have struggled to answer these questions. This section will present several of the issues they have faced. To begin, the following case is representative of how courts go about determining how much weight is due.

Burilovich v. Bd. of Educ. of Lincoln Consol. Sch.

208 F.3d 560 (6th Cir. 2000),
cert. denied, 531 U.S. 957 (2000)

Alan E. Norris, Circuit Judge.

Plaintiffs Edwin Burilovich and Dr. Linda Burilovich ("plaintiffs"), acting on behalf of their autistic son Bradley ("B.J."), sued the Board of Education of the Lincoln Consolidated Schools and its special education director ("defendants") under the Individuals with Disabilities Education Act ("IDEA"). Plaintiffs challenge the district court's grant of summary judgment for defendants, maintaining that a proposal to place B.J. in a mainstream kindergarten violated procedural and substantive provisions of the IDEA. For the following reasons, we affirm the judgment of the district court.

I.

B.J. was born on November 15, 1990. At an early age, his parents noticed that his language skills were significantly delayed. When he was three, plaintiffs sought assistance from their local school district, Lincoln Consolidated Schools. B.J. was evaluated by a Multidisciplinary Evaluation Team ("MET") at Willow Run Community Schools, which was providing Preprimary Impaired ("PPI") services for Lincoln. The MET generated an Individualized Education Program ("IEP") providing B.J. with nonclassroom PPI services, along with speech and language therapy.

On February 24, 1994, B.J. was evaluated by Dr. Luke Tsai at the University of Michigan Adult/Child Psychiatric Hospitals. Suzanne Boyer, B.J.'s teacher, was present for the last part of the appointment. Dr. Tsai diagnosed B.J. as autistic; Dr. Burilovich later hand-delivered a copy of Dr. Tsai's evaluation to Ms. Boyer. This evaluation was not placed in B.J.'s school file.

Plaintiffs began researching educational approaches to treating autism. They learned of an approach developed by Dr. Ivar Lovaas, called discrete trial training ("DTT"). DTT emphasizes heavy parental involvement, early intervention, and treatment in the home and elsewhere in the community, rather than in professional settings. Plaintiffs started a home-based DTT program for B.J.

In June 1994, Dr. Burilovich wrote to Willow Run's Superintendent, Dr. Yomtoob, expressing her concerns about the downsizing of the Willow Run infant-toddler program and B.J.'s being given only three hours of instruction a week. That letter also indicated that B.J. was autistic.

In September 1994, Lincoln notified B.J.'s parents that it was transferring B.J. from the Willow Run program to the Lincoln PPI program. On October 1, 1994, the parents consulted with Dr. Patricia Meinhold, a psychology professor at Western Michigan University, who concluded that B.J. was an appropriate candidate for DTT and suggested the parents request assistance from their school district. An IEP Committee meeting ("IEPC") was held with the school. The resulting IEP placed B.J. in the district's PPI program 2.5 hours a day, four days a week, with 40–80 minutes per week of speech and language therapy. The parents requested that part of B.J.'s school time be used for DTT, but the district did not include DTT in the IEP. B.J.'s teacher Betsy McMillin offered to, and did, provide DTT therapy for a half hour before the school day began.

B.J.'s home program continued to develop. By Thanksgiving he was receiving at least 20 hours per week of DTT. The parents decided to reduce B.J.'s school participation to two days a week following Christmas vacation; his time spent on DTT increased to 20–25 hours a week. According to plaintiffs, in the first half of 1995, B.J. made progress with his language and imitative skills, but was not involved in classroom activities. By the last half of 1995, B.J. was averaging 25–30 hours of home-based DTT. On November 28, 1995, Mr. Burilovich visited B.J.'s classroom and made a videotape. The parents maintain that the behavior on the videotape confirmed Dr. Burilovich's concerns that B.J.'s behavior in school was more regressed than at home.

On July 1, 1995, defendant Ronald Greiner became the Director of Special Education for the Lincoln Consolidated Schools. He began working with the Burilovich family in the fall of 1995 and an IEPC for B.J. was held on December 1, 1995. On December 7, 1995, Mr. Greiner sent a letter to plaintiffs memorializing conversations he had with them and setting out the district's perspective on an appropriate program for B.J. The letter also indicated that the parents had mentioned they were having some medical evaluations completed addressing autism, and asked for access to that information. In response, plaintiffs requested an independent educational evaluation ("IEE") by Dr. Meinhold. Plaintiffs later provided Mr. Greiner with a copy of Dr. Tsai's March 1994 evaluation. In January 1996, Mr. Greiner initiated an evaluation of B.J. for autism. The evaluation included some home observation by the school psychologist, school social worker, and Mr. Greiner.

Another IEPC was scheduled for March 18, 1996. Before that meeting, Dr. Meinhold submitted a report that included a formal written program proposal for B.J. At the meeting, Mr. Greiner proposed a program predominantly consisting of DTT, accepting the goals and objectives developed by Dr. Meinhold, and providing for staff training by Dr. Meinhold. According to Mr. Greiner, he proposed the plan involving DTT because he wanted to avoid conflict and a due process hearing. The staff, however, did not support the proposal. While most of the meeting was taped, the proposal was not written in a formal IEP. The parties disagree over the reason why there was no written document. Nonetheless, the participants left with the understanding that Dr. Meinhold would begin training the staff the next week. That training session was later canceled, according to Mr. Greiner, because of recent snow days.

After the meeting, Mr. Greiner realized that the staff did not think DTT was a good program for B.J. Mr. Greiner met privately with his staff on April 16 and 26, 1996 to discuss DTT and develop a new proposal. A proposal was drafted and sent to the parents, with goals similar to those proposed by Dr. Meinhold, but without any DTT. Instead, the proposal placed B.J. in a mainstream kindergarten class with one-to-one support from a trained paraprofessional.

An IEPC was scheduled for May 17, 1996, to which Dr. Meinhold was not invited. At the May IEPC, plaintiffs had serious concerns about placing B.J. in a mainstream kindergarten program without any DTT and discussed why the proposal differed from the March proposal for B.J. According to defendants, Mr. Greiner tried to explain the rationale for the proposal, but the parents were not interested in hearing details. Plaintiffs signed the IEPC, noting their disagreement, on May 23, 1996.

Pursuant to the IDEA, the parents requested an impartial due process hearing before a local hearing officer ("LHO"). The LHO decided in favor of B.J.'s parents, finding that the March 1996 oral proposal was an IEP that should be implemented, and directing the district to reimburse the parents for the expenses of providing DTT at home. Both parties appealed aspects of the decision. The state hearing review officer ("SHO") reversed the LHO, finding that no IEP had been created in March and the May IEP was valid. The SHO determined that the May IEP was developed without procedural or substantive violations and provided a free appropriate public education ("FAPE") designed to maximize B.J.'s potential, in accordance with federal and state law. The SHO also denied reimbursement to the parents.

Plaintiffs filed a complaint in district court appealing the SHO's determination and alleging violations of the IDEA .... Defendants filed a motion for summary judgment addressing all counts of the complaint; plaintiffs filed a motion for partial summary judgment addressing their IDEA claim. The district court granted defendants' motion and denied plaintiffs' motions for partial summary judgment and for reconsideration. The court determined that the parents had the burden of proof.....

The district court apparently believed that the parties had submitted the case for review of the administrative decision on the record. Because plaintiffs dispute that the case was submitted in that manner, we will treat the cause as having been submitted on summary judgment.

II.

A. Standard of Review

... There are two parts to a court's inquiry in suits brought under 20 U.S.C. § 1415(i)(2). First, the court determines whether the state has complied with the procedures set forth in the IDEA. Second, the court assesses whether the IEP developed through the act's procedures is reasonably calculated to enable the child to receive educational benefits. Michigan has added to this standard by requiring that an IEP be designed to develop the "maximum potential" of a child.

This court reviews both the procedural and substantive matters under a standard of "modified de novo review." *Renner*, 185 F.3d at 641. This standard of review stems from the Supreme Court's holding that courts must give "due weight" to the state administrative proceedings. *Rowley*, 458 U.S. at 206 ....

....

This court has not elaborated on the meaning of "due weight."[1] We have held that a court cannot simply adopt the state administrative findings without an independent re-examination of the evidence. We have also indicated that the weight due will vary, depending on whether the court is reviewing procedural or substantive matters and whether educational expertise is essential to the administrative findings.

With regard to procedural matters, a court should "strictly review an IEP for procedural compliance," although technical deviations will not render an IEP invalid. *Dong v. Board of Educ.*, 197 F.3d 793, 800 (6th Cir. 1999); *see also Doe v. Defendant I*, 898 F.2d 1186, 1190–91 (6th Cir. 1990).... Furthermore, "[i]f the procedural requirements of the IDEA are met, greater deference is to be afforded to the district's placement decision." *Dong*, 197 F.3d at 800.

As for substantive issues, "the 'preponderance of the evidence' language in the [IDEA] 'is by no means an invitation to the courts to substitute their own notions of sound educational policy for those of the school authorities which they review.'" *See Thomas v. Cincinnati Bd. of Educ.*, 918 F.2d 618, 624 (6th Cir. 1990) (*quoting Rowley*, 458 U.S. at 206 ...). The Supreme Court has pointed out that:

> In assuring that the requirements of the Act have been met, courts must be careful to avoid imposing their view of preferable educational methods upon the States. The primary responsibility for formulating the education to be accorded a handicapped child, and for choosing the educational method most suitable to the child's needs, was left by the Act to state and local educational agencies in cooperation with the parents or guardian of the child.

Rowley, 458 U.S. at 207. Indeed, federal courts are generalists with no expertise in the educational needs of handicapped children and will benefit from the factfinding of a state agency, which is presumed to have expertise in the field....

Therefore, when reviewing an IEP we must keep in mind that the state and local educational agencies are deemed to possess expertise in education policy and practice. The focus of the Supreme Court and this court upon the presumed educational expertise of state and local agencies leads to the conclusion that the amount of weight

---

1. Other circuits have adopted a variety of interpretations of "due weight." *See, e.g., Adams v. Oregon*, 195 F.3d 1141, 1145 (9th Cir. 1999) (courts, in recognition of the expertise of the administrative agency, must consider the findings carefully and endeavor to respond to the hearing officer's resolution of each material issue; after such consideration the court is free to accept or reject the findings in part or in whole, bestowing increased deference upon the hearing officer where her findings are thorough and complete); *Fort Zumwalt Sch. Dist. v. Clynes*, 119 F.3d 607, 610 (8th Cir. 1997) ... (the level of deference is less than required under the substantial evidence test, but consideration should be given to the state hearing panel's opportunity to observe the demeanor of the witnesses); *Teague Independent Sch. Dist. v. Todd L.*, 999 F.2d 127, 131 (5th Cir. 1993) (court's review is "virtually de novo"); *Doyle v. Arlington County Sch. Bd.*, 953 F.2d 100, 105 (4th Cir. 1992) (findings of fact are entitled to be considered *prima facie* correct; the court must explain its reasons if it will not follow the findings); *Doe v. Alabama State Dep't of Educ.*, 915 F.2d 651, 657 n.3 (11th Cir. 1990) (the extent of deference to be given the administrative findings of fact is an issue left to the discretion of the district court; the court must consider the administrative findings of fact, but is free to accept or reject them).

due depends upon whether such expertise is relevant to the decision-making process. As a result, less weight is due to an agency's determinations on matters for which educational expertise is not relevant, so that a federal court would be just as well suited to evaluate the situation. More weight is due to an agency's determinations on matters for which educational expertise would be relevant. Furthermore, while the court may not substitute its own view for that of the state and local educational agencies, the deference due to the administrative findings is less than that generally accorded to administrative decisions, whereby the court will uphold a decision if it is supported by "substantial evidence."

This court recently described the substantial evidence test as one in which an agency's findings would be set aside only when the record clearly precludes the administrative decision from being justified by a fair estimate of the worth of the testimony of witnesses, the agency's informed judgment on matters within its special competence, or both. Because administrative findings in IDEA cases should be afforded less deference than that given to agencies under the substantial evidence test, and in view of the IDEA's preponderance of the evidence standard, we hold that administrative findings in an IDEA case may be set aside only if the evidence before the court is more likely than not to preclude the administrative decision from being justified based on the agency's presumed educational expertise, a fair estimate of the worth of the testimony, or both. A court should defer to the administrative findings only when educational expertise is relevant to those findings and the decision is reasonable. By so deferring, "due weight" will have been given to the state administrative proceedings. We also reiterate that, when there is a conflict between the holdings of the local and state hearing officers, the court must defer to the state hearing officer's decision in reviewing the record on appeal.

In a case involving a motion for summary judgment, the court should still apply modified de novo review, but must ensure that there are no genuine issues regarding the facts essential to the hearing officer's decision. In rendering its decision, the court may still rely upon the hearing officer's presumed educational expertise, as long as the material facts underlying the officer's determination are not in dispute.

B. Discussion

Plaintiffs raised numerous issues in their brief. With regard to procedural matters, plaintiffs argue that an IEP was finalized in March, not May, of 1996; two meetings in April 1996 were IEPC meetings from which the parents were excluded; the school district failed to consult with knowledgeable professionals regarding B.J.'s placement; he was not properly evaluated; and he was not timely recertified as autistic. Plaintiffs contend that even if the procedural requirements of the IDEA were met, the IEP was substantively invalid because it failed to address B.J.'s unique needs and was not designed to allow him to attain his maximum potential. Each issue will be addressed in turn.

1. Existence of March 1996 IEP

Plaintiffs argue that the district court erred in determining that there never was a March 1996 IEP. They maintain that despite the absence of a written document the evidence shows that Mr. Greiner did not intend his proposal to be tentative and planned to implement the IEP. Federal law and Michigan regulation, however, both indicate that an IEP is a written document. Therefore, plaintiffs cannot prevail on their claim that an IEP existed in March when there was no written document until May. . . .

2. April 16 & 26 Meetings

Next, plaintiffs argue that they were denied meaningful parental participation in the IEPC process because they were not invited to two meetings in April 1996. Defendants counter that the meetings on April 16 and 26 were staff meetings that plaintiffs were not entitled to attend. The SHO and district court agreed with defendants' characterization of the meetings and plaintiffs do little to suggest that the meetings were in fact IEP meetings. Plaintiffs have not indicated how they were prevented from participating in the development of the IEP. The parents attended a December 1996 IEPC, strongly expressed their views at the March 1996 IEPC, had the opportunity to participate in the May 1996 IEPC, and also expressed their views through letters and telephone conversations with district staff. For these reasons, plaintiffs have failed to demonstrate that they were denied participation in the IEPC process.

3. Qualifications of District Staff

Plaintiffs also argue that the district failed to consult with knowledgeable professionals regarding B.J.'s placement as required by IDEA regulations. Plaintiffs maintain that because they preferred Lovaas-style DTT therapy, at least one decision-maker should have been well-versed in that treatment. More specifically, plaintiffs argue that the district should have, but did not, consult Dr. Meinhold.

This court has rejected "the contention that [a school district] must include an expert in the particular teaching method preferred by the parents in order to satisfy the requirement that the IEPC include persons knowledgeable about 'placement options.'" Furthermore, the record indicates that Marianne Miller, a teacher consultant for the district, had experience using DTT. The district also had Dr. Meinhold's report and was able to consider it at the IEPC.

Plaintiffs also point out that the district court used the wrong standard when it found they had failed to prove "by a preponderance of the evidence" that the district's staff members were unqualified. The district court reviewed the qualifications of the district's staff and concluded that there was "no evidence" they were unqualified. This holding indicates that plaintiffs did not meet their summary judgment burden of coming forward with evidence to create a genuine issue as to qualifications. Plaintiffs have failed to suggest on appeal how they would demonstrate a genuine issue. Therefore, while the district court cited the wrong standard, the holding was correct.

. . . .

4. Evaluation of B.J. Before IEP

Plaintiffs argue that the district did not conduct a required comprehensive evaluation of B.J. before making a significant change in his placement. Assuming that there was a proposed significant change in placement, we must address whether the evaluation in February 1996 was adequate. Plaintiffs maintain it was inadequate because B.J. was evaluated solely for the purpose of recertification and placement options were not considered. Both the LHO and the SHO determined that the evaluation was adequate. Plaintiffs have not made a persuasive argument otherwise, especially considering the district had before it previous evaluations of B.J. and Dr. Meinhold's report. Nor have plaintiffs shown how there is a genuine issue of material fact as to whether B.J. needed a new evaluation before developing his May 1996 IEP. As the district court pointed out, B.J. was evaluated in early 1996 and "neither plaintiffs nor defendants argue that a new evaluation would have yielded different results."

5. Timely Recertification of B.J.

Plaintiffs also maintain that defendants failed to timely recertify B.J. by waiting until 1996 to certify him as autistic, even though defendants knew he was diagnosed as autistic in 1994. Defendants dispute the date they learned of B.J.'s autism diagnosis.

... Yet plaintiffs do not suggest how the delay could have caused a substantive problem with B.J.'s IEP, since by the time the March and May IEPCs occurred, B.J. had been certified as autistic. For these reasons, plaintiffs have failed to explain the relevance of the failure to recertify B.J. sooner, even if a time limitation was applicable.

6. B.J.'s Unique Needs

Plaintiffs suggest that the IEP failed to take B.J.'s unique needs into consideration, asserting that the district proposed the IEP because its personnel had insufficient experience for any other program. To support this allegation, plaintiffs point to the testimony of Amy Stamps, the school psychologist, who indicated that the school personnel was not trained sufficiently to provide B.J. with DTT. Ms. Stamps' testimony does not support plaintiffs' assertion, however, because the record indicates that she still had concerns about DTT even when she assumed that personnel could be properly trained.

The district court and the SHO correctly determined that defendants' program took B.J.'s unique needs into consideration. As the district court pointed out, defendants' program set goals for B.J. and created a detailed daily schedule to address each of the goals with a program including both group instruction and one-on-one therapy. In contrast, the court noted that it did not see how the parents' proposed "standard" 40 hours of DTT therapy "was tailored to B.J.'s needs." The court later stated that the "school's proposal is the only one which took into consideration B.J.'s goals and abilities, and developed a plan specifically to accommodate him." After reviewing the record, and giving due weight to the SHO's opinion, we agree with the district court that the IEP did take into account B.J.'s unique needs.

. . . .

Plaintiffs further maintain that the district court improperly resolved a material question of fact by deferring to the SHO's decision perceived by the court as discrediting plaintiffs' expert, Dr. Meinhold. Review of the SHO's opinion reveals that, while the SHO said that he discounted (not "discredited") Dr. Meinhold's testimony, the SHO actually did consider her proposed DTT package when assessing whether B.J.'s unique needs were met. There is no issue of material fact because the SHO's findings did take into account Dr. Meinhold's views. After independent review of the record, and giving due weight to the SHO's decision, we agree with the SHO's conclusion.

7. Whether the IEP was Designed to Allow B.J. to Attain his Maximum Potential

Plaintiffs maintain that there was conflicting testimony addressing the question of whether the IEP would allow B.J. to attain his "maximum potential." Plaintiffs suggest that the only expert opinion based upon a professional, individual assessment of B.J. showed that he needs an intensive program of individualized, one-to-one instruction. Plaintiffs note that defendants' expert, Dr. Gary Mesibov, had never met B.J., while plaintiffs' experts, Drs. Meinhold and Holmes, had met and observed B.J. Plaintiffs also indicate that other defense witnesses included school district staff, some of whom had never met B.J. or who had only met him once. Plaintiffs reiterate their assertion that the IEP was based on the availability of resources and experience of school personnel, not B.J.'s needs. Plaintiffs also cite several cases approving of DTT. Finally, plaintiffs maintain that the IDEA's goal that a student be in the least restrictive environment did not weigh in favor of the district's IEP because B.J. was not ready for the fully mainstreamed class suggested by the IEP.

Independent review of the record confirms that the parties had widely differing views of the best method of education for B.J. Dr. Burilovich felt that when B.J. had less DTT, he tended to be less social, to engage in less speech, and to increase his self-stimulation. She felt he was very different in school, and that he would be totally overwhelmed in a mainstream class. Dr. Meinhold testified that B.J. would not benefit from mainstream kindergarten, even with a one-to-one paraprofessional. Dr. Holmes also indicated that DTT would be better than kindergarten for B.J., noting that B.J. would not benefit from being with peers until he developed better communication skills.

The district's witnesses, on the other hand, saw problems with DTT. Dr. Mesibov indicated that the DTT proposal emphasized B.J.'s deficits, not his strengths, and that isolating B.J. would only make his social relationships worse. Mr. Greiner stated that the staff never wanted the DTT proposal because they thought it would be bad for B.J. Some of the concerns expressed over the proposal were that DTT, unlike the school program, did not account for a natural environment, peer reinforcement, or independence. Staff members also had problems with DTT because it appeared to be a package deal, without individualization for B.J. Even Dr. Meinhold acknowledged that B.J. would learn in kindergarten, just not in his area of weakness.

The district court reviewed the testimony and concluded that the school's proposal was the only one tailored to B.J.'s needs, holding that the SHO's findings were well supported by the evidence. Given the differing opinions on both sides as to the best program for B.J. and the reasonable bases in the record for the opinions, we emphasize that courts should not "substitute their own notions of sound educational policy for those of the school authorities which they review." *Rowley*, 458 U.S. at 206. . . . Giving due weight to the SHO's decision, we conclude that the IEP was designed to allow B.J. to achieve his maximum potential.

Notes, Comments, and Questions

1. The Sixth Circuit in *Burilovich* described the standard of review it adopted as "modified *de novo*." In elaborating on this standard, the court stated that "a court cannot simply adopt the state administrative findings without an independent re-examination of the evidence." 208 F.3d at 565–66. The extent of the review "will vary, depending on whether the court is reviewing procedural matters or substantive matters and whether educational expertise is essential to the administrative findings." *Id.* Courts should review procedural questions strictly and when reviewing substantive issues should not substitute their judgment for that of educational experts. *Id.* at 566. How did the court in *Burilovich* apply these standards to the facts before it? Which issues were procedural? Which were substantive? Which involved educational judgments? Did the court apply the due weight standard appropriately? To which issues? How did the court resolve disputed issues of fact? Did the court abide by the preponderance of the evidence standard?

2. In describing modified *de novo* review, the court in *Burilovich* stated that it is less deferential than the "substantial evidence" standard of review that courts traditionally apply to agency decisions. The substantial evidence test is "one in which an agency's findings would be set aside only when the record clearly precludes the administrative decision from being justified by a fair estimate of the worth of the testimony of witnesses, the agency's informed judgment on matters within its special competence, or both." 208 F.3d at 567. The modified *de novo* standard, however, substitutes "more likely than not to preclude" for "clearly precludes":

> Because administrative findings in IDEA cases should be afforded less deference than that given to agencies under the substantial evidence test, and in view of the IDEA's preponderance of the evidence standard, we hold that administrative findings in an IDEA case may be set aside only if the evidence before the court is more likely than not to preclude the administrative decision from being justified based on the agency's presumed educational expertise, a fair estimate of the worth of the testimony, or both. A court should defer to the administrative findings only when educational expertise is relevant to those findings and the decision is reasonable. By so deferring "due weight" will have been given to the state administrative proceedings.

Id. at 567.

3. In footnote one of its decision, the *Burilovich* court listed several examples of definitions of "due weight" from other courts of appeal. Here is another example:

> [W]hen the district judge does not take fresh evidence but instead bases his review of the hearing officer's decision on the record compiled in the administrative proceedings, he is required to give "due deference" to that decision.

> That is, the fact that he disagrees with the officer is not enough to justify setting aside the latter's order; he must be strongly convinced that the order is erroneous.

Dale M. v. Bd. of Educ. of Bradley-Bourbonnais High Sch. Dist. No. 307, 237 F.3d 813, 815 (7th Cir. 2001). Recognizing the various standards, one court stated, "Each of these interpretations of the due weight standard is sensible, and they are not mutually exclusive." Doe v. Metro. Nashville Pub. Sch., 133 F.3d 384, 387 (6th Cir. 1998), *cert. denied*, 525 U.S. 813 (1998). Do you agree?

4. Determining how much weight is due to an administrative decision in an IDEA case depends on several factors, including whether the administrative decision was based on credibility determinations, the degree to which the district court received additional evidence, the quality and thoroughness of the administrative record and decision, and whether the agency made legal determinations in the decision. The following examples show how courts have applied these factors in determining the due weight standard.

Credibility determinations: The Third Circuit has suggested that facts that state agencies have found are *prima facie* correct, especially if based on credibility determinations:

> Under this standard, "[f]actual findings from the administrative proceedings are presumed to be considered prima facie correct," and "[i]f a reviewing court fails to adhere to them, it is obliged to explain why." In addition, if a state administrative agency has heard live testimony and has found the testimony of one witness to be more worthy of belief than the contradictory testimony of another witness, that determination is due special weight. Specifically, this means that a District Court must accept the state agency's credibility determinations "unless the non-testimonial, extrinsic evidence in the record would *justify* a contrary conclusion."

Shore Reg'l High Sch. Bd. of Educ. v. P.S., 381 F.3d 194, 199 (3d Cir. 2004) (emphasis in the original); *see also* D.S. v. Bayonne Bd. of Educ., 602 F.3d 553, 568 (3d Cir. 2010) ("The ALJ chose to credit Appellants' witnesses, and under the established standard of review, the District Court was not at liberty to credit the witnesses who expressed a contrary opinion without a showing that there was good reason to do so ...."); School Bd. of Henrico Cnty. v. Z.P., 399 F.3d 298, 305 (4th Cir. 2005) (citing ruling in previous case that "state administrative appeals officer ... violated the accepted norms of the factfinding process by rejecting, on review of a cold record, the testimony of a witness that the hearing officer had found credible, simply because the reviewing officer believed that the witness was acting as an advocate"). On the other hand, if credibility determinations are based not on observation, but on substantive legal conclusions, a court may be less deferential. In *K.S. v. Fremont Unified Sch. Dist.*, 545 F. Supp. 2d 995, 1004 (N.D. Cal. 2008), the court overturned many of the hearing officer's credibility determinations on the grounds that they were based on erroneous legal conclusions. The court disagreed with the hearing officer's findings, based on legal conclusions, that the plaintiff's witnesses were not credible because they disagreed with the school district's witnesses' interpretation of records they created, "that the lack of extensive personal contact between parents' witnesses and the plaintiff made them less credible," and the plaintiff's father was not a credible witness because he acted as her advocate. *Id.* at 1004–05.

Additional Evidence: The Seventh Circuit suggested that the level of deference owed to the state administrative agency decision is lower when the district court receives additional evidence:

> [A] reviewing court that has before it evidence not considered at the administrative level will naturally defer less to the administrative decision, as it has an information advantage over the administrator that it lacks when judicial review is limited to the record that was before him. Judicial review is more searching the greater the amount (weighted by significance) of the evidence that the court has but the agency did not have . . . .

School Dist. of Wis. Dells v. Z.S., 295 F.3d 671, 675 (7th Cir. 2002); *see also* Alex R. v. Forrestville Valley Cmty. Sch. Dist. No. 221, 375 F.3d 603, 612 (7th Cir. 2004), *cert. denied*, 543 U.S. 1009 (2004) ("The more that the district court relies on new evidence, however, the less it should defer to the administrative decision . . . .").

Quality of the decision: Courts also are not willing to give deference to administrative decisions that are not thorough and well-reasoned. Capistrano Unified Sch. Dist. v. Wartenberg, 59 F.3d 884, 891 (9th Cir. 1995) (stating that the amount of deference given to the hearing officer's decision increases when it is thorough and careful). In Marc M. v. Dep't of Educ. of Haw., 762 F. Supp. 2d 1235 (D. Haw. 2011), the court ruled:

> Having read the transcript and considered the record, the Court is concerned with the Hearing Office's decision. While there is little question that the Hearings Officer meticulously reviewed the facts and participated in the questioning of witnesses at the hearing, the conclusions of law are sparse and cursory in nature. For instance, the Hearings Officer concluded in one sentence that Defendant conducted an evaluation . . . without citing to the record. Indeed, nearly all of the Hearings Officer's conclusions of law are conclusory in nature and the Officer rarely cited to facts on the record to support his conclusions . . . . Similarly here, the court cannot determine which facts the Hearing Officer relied on in making his conclusions of law. The Court will therefore grant the decision little deference.

Id. at 1242; *see also* Reid v. District of Columbia, 401 F.3d 516, 521 (D.C. Cir. 2005) (ruling that the district court could not rely on the discretion of the hearing officer who awarded 810 hours of compensatory education without any reasoning or factual findings to support the award).

In contrast, courts give deference to well-crafted decisions by hearing officers:

> [T]he court finds that the ALJ's decision is entitled to considerable deference. The ALJ heard a great deal of evidence, holding a hearing that took place over eight days during a span of two and a half weeks. In total, thirteen witnesses

> testified at the hearing, producing a voluminous hearing transcript of almost 2000 pages and over 500 pages of exhibits. After carefully considering the evidence, the ALJ produced a 40-page order detailing the factual and legal bases for his decision. In the Court's view, both the diligence with which the ALJ approached this task, and the administrative expertise that the ALJ represents, weigh heavily in favor of considerable deference to the ALJ's findings.

K.S. v. Fremont Unified Sch. Dist., 545 F. Supp. 2d 995, 1000 (N.D. Cal. 2008).

Legal conclusions: The courts are clear that state administrative decisions are entitled to no deference on their findings of law. Alex R. v. Forrestville Valley Cmty. Sch. Dist. No. 221, 375 F.3d 603, 611 (7th Cir. 2004), *cert. denied*, 543 U.S. 1009 (2004) ("On issues of law, the hearing officer is entitled to no deference."); Harris v. District of Columbia, 561 F. Supp. 2d 63, 67 (D.D.C. 2008) (reviewing claim *de novo* because hearing officer's decision was "purely a matter of statutory interpretation" for "which he provided no support"). Courts have ruled, for example, that a hearing officer's decision that a child did not have a disability under the IDEA was a legal decision not entitled to deference:

> Resolution of this issue involves interpretation of the IDEA and the definition of "emotional disturbance" under the applicable federal and New York State regulations. In this matter of statutory interpretation, the district court was as well-positioned as the state administrative officials to determine Treena's eligibility. As the underlying facts of this case as to Treena's behavior and performance were not in dispute, but only the legal conclusions to be drawn from those facts, the state administrative officials were in no better position than the district court to make conclusions with respect to Treena's statutory eligibility based on the record.

Muller v. Comm. on Special Educ. of the East Islip Union Free Sch. Dist., 145 F.3d 95, 102 (2d Cir. 1998). Do you agree with this? Can you think of reasons that state administrative officials are in a better position than a district court judge to draw conclusions about a child's eligibility for special education based on undisputed facts? *See* W.G. v. N.Y.C. Dep't of Educ., 801 F. Supp. 2d 142, 167 (S.D.N.Y. 2011) (quoting *Muller*); K.S. v. Fremont Unified Sch. Dist., 545 F. Supp. 2d 995, 1000 (N.D. Cal. 2008) (stating that "certain of the ALJ's findings are entitled to little or no deference where the ALJ committed legal error.").

5. A federal district judge in Maine provided a good summary of the task of the court in reviewing a state administrative decision in an IDEA claim:

> The district court's standard of review is synthesized as follows:
>
> > First, the court carefully reviews the record of the due process hearing. Second, appropriate deference is given the Hearing Officer and his expertise, particularly with regard to factual determinations. Finally, the Court makes an independent decision whether the hearing officer's determination is supported by a preponderance of the evidence.

Mr. & Mrs. K., 949 F.Supp. at 938. When questions of law are also presented, the court makes an independent determination whether the requirements of the IDEA have been met. The party challenging the hearing officer's decision "must carry the burden of proving that the educational agency erred in its substantive judgment."

Lamoine Sch. Comm. v. Ms. Z., 353 F. Supp. 2d 18, 29–30 (D. Me. 2005). The Second Circuit, after observing that the basic principles of the standard of review "are more easily stated by appellate courts, even if at some length, than they are applied by district courts . . . ," M.H. v. N. Y.C. Dep't of Educ., 685 F.3d 217 (2d Cir. 2012), offered its own guidance:

> In many determinations made by administrative officers, the district court's analysis will hinge on the kinds of considerations that normally determine whether any particular judgment is persuasive, for example whether the decision being reviewed is well-reasoned, and whether it was based on substantially greater familiarity with the evidence and the witnesses than the reviewing court. But the district court's determination of the persuasiveness of an administrative finding must also be colored by an acute awareness of institutional competence and role. As the Supreme Court made clear in *Rowley*, the purpose of the IDEA is to provide funding to states so that *they* can provide a decent education for disabled students consistent with their traditional role in educating their residents. In policing the states' adjudication of IDEA matters, the courts are required to remain conscious of these considerations in determining the weight due any particular administrative finding.
>
> By way of illustration, determinations regarding the substantive adequacy of an IEP should be afforded more weight than determinations concerning whether the IEP was developed according to the proper procedures. Decisions involving a dispute over an appropriate educational methodology should be afforded more deference than determinations concerning whether there have been objective indications of progress. Determinations grounded in thorough and logical reasoning should be provided more deference than decisions that are not. And the district court should apply more deference when its review is based entirely on the same evidence as that before the SRO than when the district court has before it additional evidence that was not considered by the state agency.

Id. at 241, 244–45.

C. Application of the Due Weight Standard in a Multi-Layered Administrative System

Many states have two levels of administrative review of IDEA claims. The first level of review is conducted at the school district level by an IHO; the second is conducted at the state level by an SRO or a panel. What happens when the SRO reverses the IHO?

Should the court defer to the SRO? The IHO? Should the court's degree of deference to the SRO be lower than if the SRO had agreed with the IHO? Consider how the following opinions from two courts of appeal resolved these questions.

Amanda J. v. Clark Cnty. Sch. Dist.

267 F.3d 877 (9th Cir. 2001)

WARDLAW, Circuit Judge:

Amanda J. . . . appeals from the district court's decision to affirm the State Review Officer's ("SRO") conclusion that she received a free appropriate public education ("FAPE") under the Individuals with Disabilities Education Act, 20 U.S.C. §§ 1400–1487 ("IDEA" or "the Act"). As part of Nevada's two-tiered administrative review process, the SRO reversed the State Hearing Officer's ("HO") determination that the Clark County School District (the "District") denied Amanda a FAPE. The HO's determination would have provided Amanda reimbursement for the cost of the 1996 assessments indicating autism and the cost of an in-home program funded by her parents from April 1, 1996–July 1, 1996 . . . .

We must initially decide a question of first impression for our court: what level of deference do we give to the state agencies involved in a two-tiered review process when each reaches a different result predicated on a credibility determination? In other words, to which administrative body do we accord the "due weight" standard of review for IDEA cases . . . ? . . . . We . . . hold that the district court erred by according greater deference to the credibility determinations of the State Review Officer than to those of the Hearing Officer in applying the due weight standard. We . . . reverse.

. . . .

III. Amanda J.

. . . .

Amanda's parents requested a due process hearing . . . to resolve whether Amanda had been correctly identified and whether she had received a FAPE. . . . The Hearing Officer concluded that Amanda had been misidentified as developmentally delayed and had therefore been denied a FAPE. . . . [T]he State Review Officer reversed, overturning the credibility determinations of the HO, concluding that Amanda's parents had been informed of the tests suggesting a diagnosis of autism. . . . Amanda's family challenged the SRO's decisions in federal court. Construing this case as an appeal from an adverse administrative decision, the district court deferred to the factual and legal conclusions of the SRO and found that Amanda had neither been misdiagnosed nor denied a FAPE. . . .

IV. Standard of Review

This case requires us to conduct a multi-layered review of decisions of the district court, the Nevada State Review Officer, and the District's Due Process Hearing

Officer. We review the district court's findings of fact for clear error even when they are based on the written record of administrative proceedings. A finding of fact is clearly erroneous when the evidence in the record supports the finding but "the reviewing court is left with a definite and firm conviction that a mistake has been committed." Questions of law and mixed questions of fact and law are reviewed *de novo*, unless the mixed question is primarily factual. We review *de novo* the question of whether a school district's proposed individualized education program provided a free appropriate public education.

. . . .

Here we are confronted with a question the Supreme Court did not address when it articulated the "due weight" standard of review in *Rowley*. At the Due Process Hearing, the Hearing Officer concluded that: (1) the District failed to properly identify Amanda as an autistic child; (2) Amanda "gained very minimal educational benefits" from the program she attended; and (3) Amanda's parents should be compensated for past educational costs and awarded compensatory education. The State Review Officer disagreed and reversed the HO's decision, in part because the SRO disagreed with the credibility determinations of the HO. Thus we must decide to which state administrative body's decision we accord due weight when the decisions are at odds due to conflicting credibility determinations.

Because we have not previously addressed this question, we turn to our sister circuits for guidance. We find ourselves in agreement with the conclusions of the Second, Sixth, and Seventh Circuits that, in most situations, due weight must be given to the final decision of the state authorities, which in a two-tiered system is that of the SRO. *See Karl v. Bd. of Educ. of Geneseo Cent. Sch. Dist.*, 736 F.2d 873, 877 (2d Cir. 1984) ("We believe *Rowley* requires that federal courts defer to the final decision of the state authorities, and that deference may not be eschewed merely because a decision is not unanimous or the reviewing authority disagrees with the hearing officer."); *Thomas*, 918 F.2d at 624 ("Federal courts are required to defer to the final decision of the state authorities . . . ."); *Heather S. v. Wisconsin*, 125 F.3d 1045, 1052 (7th Cir. 1997) (relying on *Thomas* and *Karl* in holding that due weight must be given to the final state determination in a two-tiered review process).

We also agree with our colleagues in the Second, Third, Fourth, and Tenth Circuits that when an SRO overturns the credibility determinations of an HO, due weight to the decision of the SRO is not warranted. The Fourth Circuit has held, for example, that in situations where two state administrative decisions differ only with respect to the credibility of a witness, the HO is "entitled to be considered *prima facie* correct." *Doyle v. Arlington County Sch. Bd.*, 953 F.2d 100, 105 (4th Cir. 1992). In *Doyle*, the SRO reversed the HO's decision on the grounds that a particular witness's testimony was not credible even though the SRO had neither seen nor heard the witness testify. Because reviewing the credibility determination of a fact-finder was "so far from the accepted norm of a fact-finding process designed to discover truth," the court accorded due weight to the HO on the credibility determination.

Id. The court, however, was careful to limit its holding to cases in which "a state administrative appeals authority has departed from the fact-finding norm to such an extent as here." *Id.* at 105. *See, e.g., Springer v. Fairfax County Sch. Bd.*, 134 F.3d 659, 663 n.* (4th Cir. 1998) (rejecting Springer's contention that, under *Doyle*, the decision of the HO must be given deference over that of the SRO because (1) the HO had "no special claim to deference" as it did in *Doyle*; (2) the HO's decision did not turn on witness credibility as it did in *Doyle*; and (3) the SRO provided specific reasons for departing from the HO's decision which the SRO in *Doyle* did not).

The Fourth Circuit is not alone in recognizing this exception to the general rule that deference should be accorded to the final decision of state authorities. According to the Second Circuit,

> [t]here is no principle of administrative law which, absent a disagreement between a hearing officer and reviewing agency over demeanor evidence, obviates the need for deference to an agency's final decision where such deference is otherwise appropriate.

Karl, 736 F.2d at 877. Similarly, the Third Circuit has held that the:

> credibility-based findings [of the HO] deserve deference unless non-testimonial, extrinsic evidence in the record would justify a contrary conclusion or unless the record read in its entirety would compel a contrary conclusion. But beyond this rather narrow class of record-supported, credibility-based factual findings, we think that, to give the statute's language about 'independent' decisions effect, the appeals panel must have much more leeway in reviewing other non-credibility based findings of the hearing officer. We will therefore defer to the appeals panel rather than the hearing officer in most circumstances.

See Carlisle Area Sch. Dist. v. Scott P., 62 F.3d 520, 528–29 (3d Cir. 1995).[10] The Tenth Circuit is also in accord:

> [W]e will give "due weight" to the reviewing officer's decision on the issues with which he disagreed with the hearing officer, unless the hearing officer's decisions involved credibility determinations and assuming, of course, that the record supports the reviewing officer's decision.

O'Toole v. Olathe Dist. Sch. Unified Sch. Dist. No. 233, 144 F.3d 692, 699 (10th Cir. 1998).

We join our colleagues in holding that in a two-tiered state administrative system due weight should be accorded to the final state determination—that of the

10. The *Carlisle* court stated that "[t]he circuits have split on the question whether federal district courts acting pursuant to *Rowley* should accord due weight to the trial level hearing officer or to the appeals panel where the two bodies differ and where the appeals panel may not have properly deferred to the hearing officer's findings." *Carlisle Area Sch. Dist.*, 62 F.3d at 527. We do not believe a circuit split exists on this question. The cases are consistent when read in light of *Doyle's* limiting principle.

SRO—unless the SRO's decision deviates from the credibility determination of a witness whom only the HO observed testify. Traditional notions of the deference owed to the fact finder compel this conclusion. The State Review Officer is in no better position than the district court or an appellate court to weigh the competing credibility of witnesses observed only by the Hearing Officer. This standard comports with general principles of administrative law which give deference to the unique knowledge and experience of state agencies while recognizing that a HO who receives live testimony is in the best position to determine issues of credibility.

V. Free Appropriate Public Education

. . . .

Our inquiry in determining whether Amanda received a free appropriate public education is twofold. We must determine first whether "the State complied with the procedures set forth in the Act" and, second, whether "the individualized educational program developed through the Act's procedures [was] reasonably calculated to enable the child to receive educational benefits." *Rowley*, 458 U.S. at 206–07. "If these requirements are met, the State has complied with the obligations imposed by Congress and the courts can require no more." *Id.* at 207 . . . .

A. Procedural Compliance

. . . .

Procedural violations that interfere with parental participation in the IEP formulation process undermine the very essence of the IDEA. An IEP which addresses the unique needs of the child cannot be developed if those people who are most familiar with the child's needs are not involved or fully informed. . . .

Here, the HO found that the District did not give Amanda's parents copies of the psychologist's and speech pathologist's reports finding mixed results on the autism tests, his recommendation to consider further psychiatric evaluation, or the speech and language assessment indicating "extreme autism," all of which should have been disclosed under the IDEA. Although Amanda's parents did receive the "Summary of Present Levels of Performance" pursuant to their request after the initial IEP meeting, this document was merely a paraphrase of [District representative] Kenney's report which omitted all reference to autism and to the recommendation to have a medical evaluation by a psychiatrist.

The first time Amanda's parents saw the reports indicating possible autism was in April 1996 during an IEP review in Woodland, California, after the files had been transferred from the District in December 1995. At the due process hearing before the HO, Kenney testified that, according to his "usual practices," he had considered [speech and language pathologist] Zuckerman's report before writing his own. He also testified that he told Amanda's mother the results over the phone, including the possibility that Amanda was autistic. The HO did not believe him, and found that "apparently Mr. Kenney had no knowledge of the results of Ms. Zuckerman's speech and language evaluation," as his report made no mention of them. This lessened his credibility in her opinion, as did the fact that another relevant report—that of the Special Children's Clinic—was not prepared in time to be included in his evaluation. Also damaging to Kenney's credibility was the fact that he testified, incorrectly, that Amanda did not meet the criteria for autism. On the other hand, the HO found Amanda's mother to be a credible witness. The HO believed that she never received reports recommending psychiatric evaluation, for if she had, she would have followed up immediately. Because we must accord the credibility determinations of the HO due weight, we conclude that Amanda's parents were not given copies of the reports indicating the possibility of autism or the need for further psychiatric evaluation after requesting them. The hearing officer based her credibility determination on the live testimony of Mrs. J., Kenney, and several other people involved in the evaluation process. Hence, they deserve due weight so long as they are supported by the record. Because they are so supported, we accept the finding that Amanda's parents were not given copies of the reports indicating the possibility of autism or the need for further psychiatric evaluation after requesting them.

. . . .

We hold that, by failing to disclose Amanda's full records to her parents once they were requested, the District denied Amanda a FAPE. The IEP team could not create an IEP that addressed Amanda's special needs as an autistic child without knowing that Amanda was autistic. Even worse, Amanda's parents were not informed of the possibility that their daughter suffered from autism—a disease that benefits from early intensive intervention—despite the fact that the district's records contained test results indicating as much. Not only were Amanda's parents prevented from participating fully, effectively, and in an informed manner in the development of Amanda's IEP, they were not even aware that an independent psychiatric evaluation was recommended, an evaluation that Amanda's mother testified she would have had performed immediately. These procedural violations, which prevented Amanda's parents from learning critical medical information about their child, rendered the accomplishment of the IDEA's goals—and the achievement of a FAPE—impossible.

. . . .

Carlisle Area Sch. v. Scott P.

62 F.3d 520 (3d Cir. 1995),
cert. denied, 517 U.S. 1135 (1996)

BECKER, Circuit Judge.

This case arises under the Individuals with Disabilities Education Act, (IDEA), 20 U.S.C. §§ 1400–1485 (1990). The underlying administrative proceeding against the Carlisle Area School District was commenced by Scott P., a disabled twenty year old, through his parents, Richard P. and Bess P., on the grounds that the school district had not fulfilled its statutory obligations to Scott under IDEA. The hearing officer at the local educational level granted the relief requested, i.e., residential placement, and six months' compensatory education (to extend beyond Scott's 21st birthday.)

An appeals panel at the state education agency level reversed the residential placement order but affirmed the award of compensatory education. The school district appealed this decision to the District Court for the Middle District of Pennsylvania, and the parents cross-appealed. The district court affirmed the decision of the appeals panel. The parents appeal the denial of residential placement. The school district appeals the award of compensatory education.

....

... [T]he appeal requires us to decide the proper scope of review to be used by a state appeals panel reviewing a local hearing officer's decision, and the proper scope of review by the district court in reviewing a ruling of a state appeals panel. We conclude that the appeals panel's review is plenary except that it is required to defer to the hearing officer's credibility determinations unless non-testimonial, extrinsic evidence in the record would justify a contrary conclusion or unless the record read in its entirety would compel a contrary conclusion. The district court may reach an independent decision, except that it must accord the decision of the state agency "due weight" in its consideration....

....

III. STANDARD OF REVIEW

A. Introduction

A good deal of the briefing and argument in this appeal has focused on the standard of review. This attention results from the fact that three applicable levels of review are at issue—our review of the district court's order; the district court's review of the state appeals panel's decision; and the appeals panel's review of the hearing officer's decision. We, of course, exercise plenary review over the district court's conclusions of law and review its findings of fact for clear error. Because the parents here allege that the district court failed to observe its own proper scope of review, we must determine whether the district court erred in its interpretation or application of the law governing the administrative review process, a question over which we exercise plenary review.

The parents' burden of proof and finality arguments also hinge on legal interpretations, and are thus subject to plenary review. We review the district court's determination of the 1992–93 IEP's appropriateness, a factual question, under a clearly erroneous standard, while we exercise plenary review over the legal standard relied upon to evaluate the IEP and to approve the award of compensatory education.

B. Discussion

The parents' threshold argument is that the district court erred when, despite the fact that the state appeals panel did not properly defer to the findings and recommendations of the hearing officer, it affirmed the panel's order. As we have noted, the administrative regime at issue here creates two questions pertaining to the appropriate standard of review. First, we must determine what degree of deference the appeals panel owes the hearing officer. Second, we must decide the degree of deference owed by a district court reviewing an appeals panel's reversal of the hearing officer, and we must determine whether the appeals panel deserves less deference when it contravenes the hearing officer's factual findings.

1. The Statutory Framework.

....

... [T]he Supreme Court has required that federal district courts afford "due weight" to state administrative proceedings in evaluating claims under IDEA....

The ramifications of *Rowley*'s injunction to give "due weight" are unclear where a state creates a two-tiered administrative regime and each tier arrives at a different conclusion. The circuits have split on the question whether federal district courts acting pursuant to *Rowley* should accord due weight to the trial level hearing officer or to the appeals panel where the two bodies differ and where the appeals panel may not have properly deferred to the hearing officer's findings. In *Thomas v. Cincinnati Board of Education*, the Court of Appeals for the Sixth Circuit held that the "only logical position" was to defer to the appeals panel, the final decision-maker of the state agency, over the hearing officer. 918 F.2d 618, 624 (6th Cir. 1990). *See also Karl v. Board of Education of Geneseo County School Dist.*, 736 F.2d 873, 877 (2d Cir. 1984) ("We believe *Rowley* requires that federal courts defer to the final decision of the state authorities, and that deference may not be eschewed merely because a decision is not unanimous or the reviewing authority disagrees with the hearing officer."). In contrast, the Fourth Circuit has held that the district court erred in deferring to a reviewing officer who, reversing the hearing officer, discredited a witness he had not seen or heard testify. *See Doyle*, 953 F.2d at 100.

At the threshold, we must decide whether the appeals panel failed to defer to the hearing officer, for if we find that the appeals panel adequately deferred to the hearing officer, then the district court plainly complied with *Rowley* in according "considerable deference" to the appeals panel's decision. Because the provisions of IDEA that accommodate the two-tier due process system do not specify the proper standard, we must first decide what that standard is.

a. *Appeals Panel Review of the Hearing Officer's Decision*

Section 1415(c) describes the state agency's review as follows: "If the [initial impartial] hearing ... is conducted by a local educational agency ..., any party aggrieved by the findings and decision rendered in such a hearing may appeal to the State Education Agency which shall conduct an impartial review of such hearing. The officer conducting such review shall make an *independent decision* upon completion of such review." 20 U.S.C. § 1415(c) (emphasis added). The regulation interpreting this provision further provides that the reviewing officer *may "seek additional evidence if necessary,"* and may "[a]fford the parties an opportunity for oral or written argument, or both, at the discretion of the reviewing official." 34 C.F.R. § 300.510(b)(3)–(4) (1993) (emphasis added). Although this language does not explicitly define the appeals panel's scope of review, it suggests a non-deferential standard. The fact that the statute contemplates that the appeals body will make an "independent decision" suggests not that the appellate body should defer but that it should reach a decision based on its own evaluation of the evidence, "independent" of the findings of the hearing officer. The language of the regulation, *see* 34 C.F.R. § 300.510(b)(3) (1993), bolsters this interpretation, since the receipt of additional evidence necessarily entails the weighing of the new evidence against the evidence presented in the first (administrative) hearing.

As a matter of general appellate principle, however, appeals panels ordinarily defer to the trial presider's factual findings based on credibility judgments about the witnesses presented at the trial or hearing. For example, Rule 52(a) of the Federal Rules of Civil Procedure states: "Findings of fact, whether based on oral or documentary evidence, shall not be set aside unless clearly erroneous, and due regard shall be given to the opportunity of the trial court to judge the credibility of the witnesses." Fed. R. Civ. P. 52(a). *See also Anderson v. Bessemer City*, 470 U.S. 564, 575 . . . (1985) (requiring even greater deference to the trial court's findings regarding the credibility of witnesses than to the court's other fact findings). But deference to a factfinder's particular credibility judgment does not necessarily result in deference to all of the findings of fact based on that judgment.

. . . .

We thus embrace the Fourth Circuit's approach in *Doyle v. Arlington County School Board*, 953 F.2d at 105, to the extent that that decision was premised on this specific principle, that credibility-based findings deserve deference unless non-testimonial, extrinsic evidence in the record would justify a contrary conclusion or unless the record read in its entirety would compel a contrary conclusion. But beyond this rather narrow class of record-supported, credibility-based factual findings, we think that, to give the statute's language about "independent" decisions effect, the appeals panel must have much more leeway in reviewing other non-credibility based findings of the hearing officer. We will therefore defer to the appeals panel rather than the hearing officer in most circumstances, bringing us closer to the approach taken by the Second and Sixth Circuits in *Karl v. Board of Education of Geneseo* and *Thomas v. Cincinnati Board of Education*, respectively.

. . . .

We thus hold that appeals panels reviewing the fact findings of hearing officers in two-tier schemes (such as Pennsylvania's) exercise plenary review, except that they should defer to the hearing officer's findings based on credibility judgments unless the non-testimonial, extrinsic evidence in the record would justify a contrary conclusion or unless the record read in its entirety would compel a contrary conclusion.

b. *District Court Review of the Appeals Panel*

. . . IDEA empowers the district court to hear additional evidence, and directs the court to base its decision on the preponderance of the evidence. We have interpreted *Rowley*'s mandate to accord "due weight" to the administrative proceedings as a requirement to consider—although not necessarily to accept—the administrative fact findings. The precise question here is whether the district court owes less consideration to the administrative fact findings when the second tier reversed the first tier. Clearly, the district court's review should be unaffected where the appeals panel owes no deference to the hearing officer. Thus, the issue is whether the district court's review should be any less deferential where the appeals panel disregarded a record-supported, credibility-based factual determination of the hearing officer.

Given our decision about the appeals panel's scope of review, we conclude that a district court should still give "due weight" to the appeals panel's decision when it reverses the hearing officer's conclusions of law, inferences from proven facts, and factual findings based on credibility judgments where non-testimonial, extrinsic evidence justified the appeals panel's contrary decision.[4] In this case, because the appeals panel found that the extrinsic evidence in the record supported conclusions contrary to those of the hearing officer, the district court correctly gave the panel's decision "due weight" notwithstanding the panel's differences with the hearing officer.

2. The Nature of the Disputed Rulings.

We turn to the nature of the disputed rulings, for application of the standard of review turns thereon. While this discussion will propel us to some degree into a discussion of the merits, treated *infra*, that cannot be avoided. Although Scott's parents understandably want this court to view the contested portions of the hearing officer's ruling as record-supported credibility judgments that would be shielded from appeals panel review, they are in reality credibility findings that are contradicted by not insubstantial record evidence. With respect to the appeals panel's finding that the 1992–93 IEP was appropriate, the parents claim that the appeals panel "effectively overturned the critical finding by the Hearing Officer that 'for the last few years [Scott's] academic achievement, as determined by his teacher, has been (only) maintained and when measured by standardized tests has continued to be at the fourth to fifth grade level.'" The record, however, contained ample evidence that Scott had made progress. When measured by teacher-constructed exams, Scott's academic achievement had improved. The record also notes that Scott had made progress in reading and writing braille. *Id.*

In any event, appropriateness is judged prospectively so that any lack of progress under a particular IEP, assuming *arguendo* that there was no progress, does not render that IEP inappropriate. However, even if the observation about progress under the 1991–92 IEP did reflect on the legal appropriateness of the 1992–93 IEP, it could

4. We assume without deciding that, under IDEA, a district court should accord somewhat less consideration to an appeals panel ruling that disregards a hearing officer's credibility judgments where this standard is not met. We base this assumption on the standards applicable in other statutory regimes that also involve a two-level administrative proceeding.... Because the disputed portions of the hearing officer's opinion did not find support in the non-testimonial, extrinsic evidence in the record, however, they were not entitled to deference by the appeals panel, and we need not decide this issue.

not, standing alone, support the hearing officer's conclusions about the 1992–93 IEP: additional inferences and conclusions would have to be drawn. For example, one would have to assume that Scott's needs had remained completely unchanged between the years, and that one could attribute Scott's lack of progress during 1992–93, for example, to the failure of the 1992–93 program to provide a service for a need that had manifested itself during the 1991–92 year (prior to the development of the relevant IEP).

Consequently, the appeals panel would not have needed to set aside . . . [the IHO's] "findings" about the credibility of the teacher and the mobility specialist who testified that they had seen no progress in recent years to find that the 1992–93 IEP was appropriate. Rather, the appeals panel could have credited their statements and nevertheless found that the 1992–93 plan passed muster because of the additions to the 1992–93 program or because of changes in Scott's needs. Alternatively, the appeals panel could have concluded that the non-testimonial, extrinsic evidence in the record evidence did not support the findings.

While either of these approaches could independently justify the appeals panel in making a finding different from the hearing officer, the appeals panel invoked both bases in this case. The panel carefully distinguished the content of the 1992–93 IEP from that of the 1991–92 IEP . . . thus breaking the link between progress made under prior IEPs and the appropriateness of the 1992–93 IEP. The panel also evidenced its searching review of all the record evidence when it stated that "there was sufficient evidence in the record so as to allow the officer to find that the District had attempted to provide Scott with an [appropriate] IEP . . . ."

At all events, the core issue in this case pertains to the state appeals panel's reversal of the hearing officer's award of residential education at the MSB. The parents contend that the appeals panel "simply rejected . . . [the IHO's] critical factual findings that 'in addition to regular therapy, Scott needs help from peers with similar problems . . . . He needs programming beyond typical school hours to have sufficient intensity to make additional gains.'" But here too, the appeals panel did not simply reject the testimony relied on by the hearing officer so much as find that the record did not support the officer's conclusion. In particular, the hearing officer relied on testimony that Scott needed his school instruction to be reinforced by other activities to find that these reinforcing activities needed to occur "during other hours of his day," a phrase he took to require residential placement. The appeals panel believed, however, "that there was insufficient evidence in the record" to support the conclusion that those reinforcing activities had to occur "during other hours of his day."

The appeals panel's rejection of the residential placement also resulted from its doubts about the attribution of Scott's failure to accept his blindness (and its effects on his progress) to the deficiency of peer contact afforded by the school district's IEP. . . . ("The record seems to indicate that this inability or unwillingness by Scott to accept his handicap may account for his apparent lack of progress as anticipated by his teachers and parents. The issue, however, is whether more contact with blind peers is the remedy or whether increased skills will help Scott accept his handicap.").

Had the appeals panel found that Scott did not need any peer contact and/or that he did not require *any* additional programming, the appeals panel would have been rejecting well-supported testimony credited by the hearing officer. But the record evidence did not unequivocally support the hearing officer's findings with respect to progress under prior IEP's, off-hour programming, or the need for more peer contact. Because the record evidence did not support the findings, this is simply not a case where the panel encroached on the credibility judgments of the hearing officer, for we agree with the appeals panel that "the reasons why Scott has not made the anticipated progress in his educational placement remain unclear." More specifically, it appears that Scott was not attending school for the full day and missed certain extended periods due to various illnesses.

Both the appeals panel and the hearing officer felt that full implementation of the school district's IEP was impeded by those factors. ("The panel agreed with the Hearing Officer that a significant difficulty in evaluating the appropriateness of the proposed '92 IEP was Scott's failure to attend his school program for a full day. The officer speculated, if Scott did not go home at 1 p.m., he could have training in daily living skills provided at the school."). As a consequence, the testimony that Scott needed more programming, even if credited, does not compel residential placement, especially in light of the 1992–93 IEP's proposal to provide "full day" programming.

Neither does Scott's need for peer contact necessarily require residential placement, since the appeals panel found that:

> there was sufficient evidence in the record so as to allow the officer to find that the District had attempted to provide Scott with an IEP that would permit him an opportunity to interact with peers. While the opportunity to interact, as provided by the District, may not be [sic] have been ideal or optimal, nevertheless, the panel concluded that the District had acted in a manner that would have allowed Scott to reasonably benefit from his placement, in this context of interaction with peers.

Aside from the fact that evidence supporting the need for more peer contact was contradicted, to give such testimony dispositive effect would run afoul of at least two legal propositions under IDEA (discussed below): that the district need not provide the *optimal* IEP, and that the program be provided in the least restrictive educational environment appropriate to the needs of the child. . . .

The panel correctly stated the law when it wrote: "The Hearing Officer's conclusion that Scott must then be entitled to a residential placement is incorrect. The standard to be applied in determining the least restrictive alternative is not to find an optimum placement for Scott but rather to decide whether an appropriate educational placement can be achieved in a non-restrictive setting." Under the appropriate legal framework, therefore, even uncontroverted testimony that *many* more hours of programming or that contact with *many* peers would benefit Scott would not support the adoption of a more restrictive residential placement. Moreover, even if the appeals panel had reversed findings based on uncontradicted testimony, it would not necessarily change the result in this case. . . . [A]fter considering the administrative findings of fact, the district court was free to reach a different conclusion from its independent review of the record.

Thus, the district court could effectively affirm the panel by independently finding its own facts contrary to those found by the hearing officer. Because we are confident that the district court did independently consider the record, we believe that it could affirm the appeals panel decision even if the appeals panel had acted improperly in reversing the hearing officer's findings. The same arguments refute the parents' contention that the district court erred when it affirmed an appeals panel ruling it conceded to be "somewhat confusing." The district court could effectively affirm the panel, despite its inability to precisely discern the panel's ratio decidendi, by making rulings based on its independent review of the record and the preponderance of evidence.

3. Conclusion

Because the contested "findings" of . . . [the IHO] (i.e., those over which the appeals panel and . . . [the IHO] disagree) do not find unmixed record support, we conclude that the district court correctly accorded the appeals panel "substantial consideration," notwithstanding the fact that the panel did not adopt the hearing officer's credibility-based recommendations. Moreover, to the extent that the hearing officer's recommendations offended other provisions of IDEA, they rested on an error of law over which the appeals panel exercised plenary review. Thus, we need not address the question whether the "consideration" the district court afforded the appeals panel would have been appropriate if the panel had in fact encroached on the limited terrain of credibility judgments falling within the primary purview of the hearing officer.

. . . .

VII. CONCLUSION

For the foregoing reasons, we will affirm the order of the district court insofar as it upheld the denial of the residential placement. . . .

Notes, Comments, and Questions

1. The multi-layered review of IDEA claims can get quite complicated. In *Amanda J.*, the local hearing officer found that the school district had denied Amanda a FAPE, the state review officer reversed, the district court affirmed the state review officer, and the court of appeals reversed the district court, thus reinstating the hearing officer's original decision. In *Scott P.*, the local hearing officer awarded a private residential placement and compensatory education to Scott, the state appeals panel affirmed the compensatory education award but reversed the residential placement, the district court affirmed the state appeals panel's decision, and the court of appeals upheld that portion of the district court's order denying the residential placement but reversed the grant of compensatory education.

2. Recall the discussion in Section One about the amount of weight that is due to state administrative decisions and the factors courts take into account in determining the amount of weight that is due. What level of deference did the courts in *Amanda J.* and *Scott P.* apply? What factors were important in their determinations of the amount of weight that was due?

3. The decisions in both *Amanda J.* and *Scott P.* reviewed the testimony and other evidence in great detail. These cases serve as good examples of the importance of details when deciding the appropriate education for a child with a disability. In *Amanda J.*, whether Amanda's parents received information about her in a timely manner was dispositive, because, as the court said, parental awareness of a child's disability is crucial both to the process and to ensuring the child receives an appropriate education. In *Scott P.*, nearly every detail of Scott's school performance was important to the court's decision.

4. According to *Scott P.*, "The circuits have split on the question whether federal district courts acting pursuant to *Rowley* should accord due weight to the trial level hearing officer or to the appeals panel where the two bodies differ and where the appeals panel may not have properly deferred to the hearing officer's findings." *Scott P.*, 62 F.3d at 527. In footnote ten of the *Amanda J.* decision, the court stated that there was not a circuit split. *Amanda J.*, 267 F.3d at 889 n. 10. Can you resolve this seeming inconsistency?

5. What is the standard of review that a court of appeals uses when considering a decision of the district court in an IDEA case? Like the standard of review of administrative decisions by federal district courts, the standard of appellate review of district court decisions in IDEA cases is stated in many different ways. Consider an early statement of the level of review that links it to the *Rowley* standard of review of administrative decisions:

> Where, as here, both the standard of review employed by the district court and its decision on the merits are challenged, we think *Rowley* conditions our standard of review as well as the district court's. In analyzing whether the district court applied the correct standard, we determine whether it independently reviewed the record and heard any requested additional evidence as required by the statute. We then determine whether the district court evaluated that evidence in terms of the substantive standards embodied in *Rowley's* twofold inquiry, i.e., did the district court ask and answer the *Rowley* questions? If the district court answered the *Rowley* questions based on a preponderance of the evidence, then it employed the correct standard.
>
> Our standard of review of the district court's decision on the merits, i.e., did the district court answer the *Rowley* questions correctly, is likewise colored by *Rowley*. We exercise plenary review over the district court's conclusions of law, and employ a clearly erroneous standard of review over the court's findings of historical fact. The inquiries directed by *Rowley* are mixed questions of fact and law. In deciding whether the district court has

> correctly answered those questions, the issue of whether the district court has properly applied *Rowley's* substantive rules is subject to our plenary review. However, our review, while plenary, must be conducted within the general framework of deference to state decision-makers dictated by the EAHCA and *Rowley* itself.

Wexler v. Westfield Bd. of Educ., 784 F.2d 176, 181 (3d Cir. 1986), *cert. denied*, 479 U.S. 825 (1986). More recent statements of the standard of appellate review of district court decisions include the First Circuit's:

> In IDEA cases, as elsewhere, we review the district court's answers to questions of law de novo and its findings of fact for clear error. Clear-error review demands substantial deference to the trier; under that standard, we may reverse only if the record, read as a whole, gives rise to a "strong, unyielding belief that a mistake has been made." Whether an IEP is adequate and appropriate is a mixed question of law and fact. Thus, appellate review involves a degree-of-deference continuum, which takes into account whether particular aspects of that determination are fact-dominated or law-dominated.

C.G. v. Five Town Cmty. Sch. Dist., 513 F.3d 279, 284 (1st Cir. 2008). The Fourth Circuit has suggested a somewhat less deferential standard of review of district court findings of fact that accounts for the more limited role the district court has in an IDEA case than in an ordinary civil action:

> Whether a district court has accorded the proper "due weight" to the administrative proceedings is a question of law—or at least a mixed question of law and fact—to be reviewed de novo by an appellate court. In our review, we need not defer to factual recitations made by a district court from the administrative record, because that court stands in no better position than do we in reviewing the record. In conducting our review in an IDEA proceeding, we therefore must examine the entire record, and we must afford "due weight" to the administrative determinations, applying the standard of review utilized by the district court. However, where a district court has heard and considered additional evidence . . . we review its findings of fact for clear error.

MM v. Sch. Dist. of Greenville Cnty., 303 F.3d 523, 531 (4th Cir. 2002). Which of these standards do you think best reflects the structure of the IDEA's judicial review process?

6. Imagine you are a clerk for a court of appeals judge who has asked you to draft a one paragraph statement of the standard of appellate review of district court decisions in IDEA cases. Draft the paragraph. Consider the following additional cases for guidance: District of Columbia v. Doe, 611 F.3d 888, 897 (D.C. Cir. 2010) (reviewing district court's summary judgment grant *de novo*, utilizing the same standard of review the district court used to review the IHO's decision because the district court based its review exclusively on the administrative record); Reid v. District of Columbia, 401 F.3d 516, 521–22 (D.C. Cir. 2005) (applying *de novo* review); Shore Regional

High Sch. Bd. of Educ. v. P.S., 381 F.3d 194, 197, 199 (3d Cir. 2004) (applying full review of district court's application of the law and reviewing its findings of fact for clear error); Muller v. Comm. on Special Educ. of the East Islip Union Free Sch. Dist., 145 F.3d 95, 102 (2d Cir. 1998) (reviewing the district court's rulings on "mixed question of law and fact" de novo).

Section Two
Additional Evidence

A. The Definition of Additional Evidence

The IDEA provides, "In any action brought under this paragraph, the court . . . (ii) shall hear additional evidence at the request of a party . . . ." 20 U.S.C. § 1415(i)(2)(C)(ii) (2012). The statute does not define additional evidence. Does additional simply mean "more" evidence? Does it mean evidence not introduced at the administrative hearing? What if the evidence could have been admitted at the hearing but was not? To what degree should "additional evidence" be defined in the context of a federal district court's obligation to give due weight to the state's administrative decision?

As the courts have grappled with these questions, three approaches to defining additional evidence have emerged. The first, which is the majority view, is based on the First Circuit's decision in *Town of Burlington v. Dep't of Educ. of Mass.*, 736 F.2d 773 (1st Cir. 1984), *aff'd*, 471 U.S. 359 (1985). According to the First Circuit:

> We construe "additional" in the ordinary sense of the word, to mean supplemental. Thus construed, this clause does not authorize witnesses at trial to repeat or embellish their prior administrative hearing testimony; this would be entirely inconsistent with the usual meaning of "additional." We are fortified in this interpretation because it structurally assists in giving due weight to the administrative proceeding, as *Rowley* requires.
>
> A trial court must make an independent ruling based on the preponderance of the evidence, but the Act contemplates that the source of the evidence generally will be the administrative hearing record, with some supplementation at trial. The reasons for supplementation will vary; they might include gaps in the administrative transcript owing to mechanical failure, unavailability of a witness, an improper exclusion of evidence by the administrative agency, and evidence concerning relevant events occurring subsequent to the administrative proceeding.
>
> We decline to adopt the rule urged by defendants that the appropriate construction is to disallow testimony from all who did, or could have, testified before the administrative hearing. We believe that, although an appropriate limit in many cases, a rigid rule to this effect would unduly limit a court's

> discretion and constrict its ability to form the independent judgment Congress expressly directed. A salient effect of defendants' proposed rule would be to limit expert testimony to the administrative hearing. Our review of the cases involving the Act reveals that in many instances the district court found expert testimony helpful in illuminating the nature of the controversy and relied on it in its decisional process. There could be some valid reasons for not presenting some or all expert testimony before the state agency. Experts are expensive—the parties at the state level may feel that their cases can be adequately made with less backup, especially since the administrative hearing in Massachusetts is conducted by an expert. We also recognize that in many instances experts who have testified at the administrative hearing will be bringing the court up to date on the child's progress from the time of the hearing to the trial. It would be difficult to draw a sharp line between what had or could have been testified to at the administrative hearing and the trial testimony.
>
> The determination of what is "additional" evidence must be left to the discretion of the trial court which must be careful not to allow such evidence to change the character of the hearing from one of review to a trial *de novo*. A practicable approach, we believe, is that an administrative hearing witness is rebuttably presumed to be foreclosed from testifying at trial. A motion may then be made to allow such a witness to testify within specified limits stating the justification for the testimony. In ruling on motions for witnesses to testify, a court should weigh heavily the important concerns of not allowing a party to undercut the statutory role of administrative expertise, the unfairness involved in one party's reserving its best evidence for trial, the reason the witness did not testify at the administrative hearing, and the conservation of judicial resources. The court should look with a critical eye on a claim, such as made here, that the credibility of a witness is a central issue. The claim of credibility should not be an "open sesame" for additional evidence. Such an approach followed by a pretrial order that identifies who may testify and limits the scope of the testimony will enable the court to avoid a trial *de novo*.

Id. at 790–91. Other circuits that have explicitly adopted or otherwise adhere to the *Burlington* definition that additional evidence means supplemental include the Tenth Circuit, Miller v. Bd. of Educ. of Albuquerque Pub. Sch., 565 F.3d 1232, 1241 (10th Cir. 2009) (stating that the district court's discretion to accept additional evidence is limited to supplemental evidence); Eleventh Circuit, Walker Cnty. Sch. Dist. v. Bennett, 203 F.3d 1293, 1299 (11th Cir. 2000) (adopting the "well-reasoned" resolution of the issue by the *Burlington* court); the Fourth Circuit, Springer v. Fairfax Cnty. Sch. Bd., 134 F.3d 659, 666–67 (4th Cir. 1998) (adopting *Burlington*); the Seventh Circuit, Monticello Sch. Dist. No. 25 v. George L., 102 F.3d 895, 901–02 (7th Cir. 1996) (agreeing with *Burlington*); and the Ninth Circuit, Ojai Unified Sch. Dist. v. Jackson, 4 F.3d 1467, 1472–73 (9th Cir. 1993) (adopting the *Burlington* standard).

The second approach, articulated by the Sixth Circuit, is a more expansive definition of additional:

> Insofar as . . . [*Burlington*] suggests that additional evidence is admissible only in limited circumstances, such as to supplement or fill in the gaps in the evidence previously introduced, we decline to adopt the position taken by the First Circuit. "Additional," in its ordinary usage, implies something that is added, or something that exists by way of addition. To "add" means to join or unite; the limitation on what can be joined inherent in the term "supplement" is not present in the term "add."

Nashville and Davidson Cnty. v. Cook, 915 F.2d 232, 234 (6th Cir. 1990).

Finally, the Third Circuit, in explicitly not adopting a definition of additional evidence, forged a middle ground between *Burlington* and *Cook*, ruling that in determining whether to admit additional evidence, a district court should make a particularized evaluation of the proffered evidence in light of the purposes of the IDEA to provide individually tailored education to meet the changing needs of children with disabilities. The court stated:

> Although we make no explicit interpretation of section 1415(e)(2)'s "additional evidence" clause, even under *Burlington*'s restrictive approach a district court first must evaluate a party's proffered evidence before deciding to exclude it. Moreover, while the purpose of the *Burlington* construction is to "structurally assist[] in giving due weight to the administrative proceeding, as *Rowley* requires," the court of appeals did not say that a district court arbitrarily or summarily could exclude additional evidence submitted by a party in pursuit of that deference. On the contrary, the examples that *Burlington* provided of additional evidence that should *not* be admitted were all types of evidence that courts might decide to exclude in a conventional civil proceeding. For instance, the court stated that the additional evidence clause "does not authorize witnesses at trial to repeat or embellish their prior administrative hearing testimony; this would be entirely inconsistent with the usual meaning of 'additional.'" Even while making this statement, though, the court stressed that it would not be wise to devise a hard-and-fast rule . . . .
>
> Thus, the *Burlington* court stated that certain evidence may be excluded under IDEA judicial review out of deference to the administrative proceedings. The court, however, declined to devise a bright-line rule, choosing instead to leave "the question of the weight due the administrative findings of fact" to the discretion of the trial court. Other courts, including ours, likewise have condoned the exclusion of additional evidence submitted by the parties to an IDEA proceeding when, for a particular reason, the court properly could exclude the evidence.
>
> It is regularly held that the question of what additional evidence to admit in an IDEA judicial review proceeding, as well as the question of the weight due

> the administrative findings of fact, should be left to the discretion of the trial court. As appellants note, Congress' central goal in enacting the IDEA was to ensure "that each child with disabilities has access to a program that is tailored to his or her changing needs and designed to achieve educational progress." Children are not static beings; neither their academic progress nor their disabilities wait for the resolution of legal conflicts. While a district court appropriately may exclude additional evidence, a court must exercise particularized discretion in its rulings so that it will consider evidence relevant, non-cumulative and useful in determining whether Congress' goal has been reached for the child involved. Consequently, on the remand the district court should use this standard in determining whether to admit the proferred additional evidence, *i.e.*, would the evidence assist the court in ascertaining whether Congress' goal has been and is being reached for the child involved.

Susan N. v. Wilson Sch. Dist., 70 F.3d 751, 759–60 (3d Cir. 1995).

Notes, Comments, and Questions

1. *Burlington*, *Cook*, and *Susan N.* each took a different approach to defining "additional" evidence. For the court in *Burlington*, the important consideration was maintaining the due weight that *Rowley* requires be given to IDEA administrative proceedings. Thus, the court defined additional evidence as "supplemental," ensuring a limited review of the administrative proceedings by district courts. In *Cook*, the court relied on the "ordinary usage" of additional to disagree with *Burlington* and define additional evidence as more evidence. Finally, in *Susan N.*, the court applied a different principle for defining additional evidence. Relying on Congress' goal of ensuring that each child with a disability receive an individualized education designed to achieve educational progress, the court ruled that the standard a court should use in determining whether to admit additional evidence is whether the evidence would assist the court in determining whether the child is receiving such an education.

2. Imagine you are a clerk for a federal district court judge who is presiding over an appeal from an IDEA administrative ruling. One of the parties has made a motion to submit additional evidence. The judge asks you to recommend a standard for making the decision and wants you to explain your reasons. How would you answer the judge's questions? In determining your answer, consider the following: Which standard better captures the purpose of allowing courts to consider additional evidence? Which standard is a better reflection of the IDEA's multi-layered review process? Which standard better reflects the IDEA's educational goals?

B. Application of the Standards for Admitting Additional Evidence

District courts in Texas and Pennsylvania, considering whether to admit additional evidence and reaching different results, provide good examples of the application of the standards for admitting additional evidence.

Marc V. v. North East Indep. Sch. Dist.

455 F. Supp. 2d 577 (W.D. Tex. 2006),
aff'd, 242 F. App'x 271 (5th Cir. 2007)

Rodriguez, District Judge.

. . . .

The "additional evidence" Plaintiffs seek to admit comes in the form of eight fact witnesses, one expert witness, and six exhibits. Plaintiffs' designated fact witnesses who did not testify in the administrative hearing are (1) Richard Middleton, NEISD Superintendent; (2) Sandy Hughey, NEISD Board Member; (3) Katie Coleman, NEISD Assessment Representative, Oak Grove; (4) Jan Longfellow, Campus/Program Coordinator, Oak Grove; (5) Peggy Hannon, Campus/Program Coordinator, Oak Grove; (6) Cheryl Moore, Music Therapist, Oak Grove; (7) Jennifer Ozuna, Intake Evaluator for Marc; and (8) Gloria Kutach, Marc's Pre-K teacher in 2003. Plaintiffs also designated an expert witness who did not testify in the administrative hearing, Dr. Bruce D. Perry, M.D., Ph.D. Defendants move to limit any additional evidence and to strike Plaintiffs' expert reports and testimony. . . .

. . . .

The Court refuses to admit Plaintiffs' additional evidence because that evidence is (1) cumulative; (2) or irrelevant; (3) or bolstering of existing evidence, (4) or untimely proffered. The Court refuses to admit the testimony of Plaintiffs' eight additional fact witnesses because their identity was known by Plaintiffs prior to the hearing and Plaintiffs could have called them to testify. Each of the nine additional witnesses was known to Plaintiffs prior to the hearing; indeed, eight of the witnesses were specifically listed as potential witnesses in Plaintiffs' pre-hearing disclosures. The eight exhibits that Plaintiffs seek to introduce as additional evidence were also in existence prior to the administrative hearing and could have been presented in the administrative hearing through the exercise of diligence. The Court believes that Plaintiffs' additional evidence is cumulative or bolstering of existing evidence. In absence of special circumstances, the Court will ordinarily exercise its discretion in favor of excluding belatedly offered evidence.

In both their response to Defendants' motion to limit additional evidence and their response to Defendants' motion to strike Plaintiffs' expert reports and testimony, Plaintiffs have failed to provide "solid justification" for supplementing the existing record. The Court notes that the hearing officer admitted over 140 exhibits and heard testimony from 18 live witnesses, in addition to considering other evidence presented by Plaintiffs that included deposition testimony of two witnesses and transcribed recorded statements or affidavits of seven other witnesses. The administrative record consists of five volumes totaling more than 1,427 pages. The Court simply does not need to admit additional evidence in order to determine whether Marc's IEP was reasonably calculated to afford him some educational benefit.

Plaintiffs did give three plausible justifications for admission of additional evidence in their responses: (1) the hearing officer imposed certain limits on the amount of evidence admitted at the hearing; (2) Dr. Perry was unavailable to attend the hearing because he was attending a conference in Canada; and (3) Ms. Kutach could not be located at the time of the due process hearing. The Court finds that the limitations imposed by the hearing officer were minimal and provided Plaintiffs with ample opportunity to develop their case. Plaintiffs have failed to state what additional evidence any of their designated witnesses, including Dr. Perry and Ms. Kutach, would provide to the Court that is not irrelevant, cumulative, or bolstering of existing evidence. Dr. Perry's opinion letter only appears bolstering of Dr. Harkin's testimony, and Dr. Perry only appears to have evaluated Dr. Harkin's diagnosis, not Marc himself. Consequently, the Court finds that their additional testimony is unnecessary.

. . . .

Antoine M. v. Chester Upland Sch. Dist.

420 F. Supp. 2d 396 (E.D. Pa. 2006)

Robreno, District Judge.

Plaintiffs, Antoine M. and his parent Samuel M., are appealing the determination of a special education hearing officer that Antoine M. is ineligible for remedies under the Individuals with Disabilities Education Act ("IDEA"). . . . Before the Court today are the parties' pretrial submissions on the issue of whether the parties should be permitted to offer evidence to supplement the administrative record for the Court's review of the hearing officer's decision. For the reasons below, the Court will permit the additional evidence proffered by plaintiffs to be offered at the hearing.

. . . .

II. DISCUSSION

A. *The Introduction of Evidence in Addition to the Administrative Record*

1. *Proposed Witnesses*

Plaintiffs propose to present the testimony of four witnesses in addition to the witnesses they presented at the administrative hearing:

(1) **Karen J. Stillis**, Antoine's learning support teacher from November 19, 1999 to June 2000;

(2) **Nancy Brown**, Antoine's learning support teacher from September 2000 to January 30, 2001;

(3) **Judy Kay Maxwell**, the District's school psychologist who evaluated Antoine in 1999; and

(4) **Dr. Barbara Domingos**, a certified school psychologist, who will be called as an expert witness.

Plaintiffs argue that they did not present the testimony of Stillis, Brown, or Maxwell earlier because the professional involvement of these witnesses took place outside of the limitations period imposed by the hearing officer. The testimony of Dr. Domingos was not introduced at the administrative hearing, state plaintiffs, because plaintiffs did not have the burden of proof at the hearing.

Defendant opposes the introduction of any additional evidence beyond the administrative record, asserting that Antoine's entire record was part of the due process hearing, and that all of plaintiffs' proposed witnesses were available at the time of the due process hearing.

2. *Legal Standard*

. . . .

b. The admission of additional evidence

Whether evidence which was not proffered at the earlier hearing may be admitted in an IDEA judicial review proceeding, and if so, what type, is left to the discretion of the trial court. *Susan N.*, 70 F.3d at 760. In exercising this discretion, the court is charged with determining whether the proffered evidence is "relevant, non-cumulative, and useful in determining whether Congress' goal has been reached for the child involved." *Id.* In doing so, the court should ensure that the admission of the additional evidence will be consistent with the " 'general framework of deference to state decision-makers that is dictated by the IDEA.' " *Id.* at 758.

i. *Relevancy, cumulativeness, usefulness*

In determining whether the proffered evidence is "relevant, non-cumulative, and useful in determining whether Congress' goal has been reached for the child involved," *Susan N.*, 70 F.3d at 760, a court must look at the evidence or testimony proffered in the context of the case. Each analysis should be individualized to the particular circumstances before the court. *See, e.g., Robert B. v. W. Chester Area Sch. Dist.*, 2005 WL 2396968, at *9–10 (E.D.Pa. 2005) (proffered testimony would repeat earlier testimony and would offer no additional insight into the "reasonableness of the school district's original decision") (quoting *Susan N.*, 70 F.3d at 762); *Alex K. v. Wissahickon Sch. Dist.*, 2004 WL 286871, at *7 (E.D. Pa. 2004) (two witnesses excluded because they would repeat administrative hearing testimony, three new witnesses excluded because testimony would not assist court in determining whether school district met its legal obligations).

ii. *Deference to state proceedings*

Although a court may not summarily exclude a party's proffered evidence before evaluating its content, *Susan N.*, 70 F.3d at 78, neither may a court grant carte blanche to a party to introduce evidence that was not offered at the administrative hearing, and thus render the administrative proceedings a mere formality. *See, e.g ., Susan N.*, 70 F.3d at 762 (a court has the authority to exclude certain evidence that could have been available at the administrative hearing); *Town of Burlington v. Department of Educ.*, 736 F.2d 773, 790 (1st Cir. 1984) ("A trial court must make an independent ruling based on the preponderance of the evidence, but the [IDEA] contemplates that the source of the evidence generally will be the administrative hearing record, with some supplementation at trial.") Rendering the administrative proceeding a mere formality would thwart the notion of cooperative federalism enshrined by the IDEA.

To negotiate this statutorily prescribed deference, a court must determine whether the party introducing the additional evidence has presented a sufficient justification for not proffering the evidence at the administrative hearing. *Susan N.*, 70 F.3d at 790 (quoting *Burlington*, 736 F.2d at 790–91). The following is a non-exhaustive list of factors that a court may take into account when making this determination:

> (A) The existence of a procedural bar which prevented the introduction of the proffered evidence below, such as a limitations period or a restriction on the number of witnesses;
>
> (B) Whether the evidence was deliberately withheld at the administrative level for strategic reasons;
>
> (C) Whether the introduction of the additional evidence at the district court level would be prejudicial to the other party, i.e. if the additional evidence would interfere with the adverse party's ability to rebut it; and
>
> (D) The potential impact on the administration of justice, i.e. does the party seek to introduce a new theory under which it will be entitled to relief.... In that regard, a party should not be permitted to introduce evidence unrelated to a legal theory presented at the prior hearing.

In sum, a court's discretion in admitting additional evidence in an IDEA judicial review proceeding is bounded by the need to respect the statute's cooperative federalism on one hand, and the need to consider evidence that is relevant... and useful on the other hand. To negotiate these principles, a court should make an individualized assessment of the offered evidence, and determine whether the party offering the evidence has a valid reason for not introducing it below.

Ultimately, in assessing the party's justification for failing to submit the evidence at the administrative hearing, the court should ensure that the party is not attempting to "leapfrog the agency proceedings." *Roland M.*, 910 F.2d at 998.

3. *Application*

Plaintiffs here seek to introduce the testimony of four witnesses, none of whom testified at the administrative level. Defendants argue, however, that plaintiffs could have presented this testimony at the administrative level but chose not to, and that this evidence will be cumulative of evidence already put before the administrative process because several of the witnesses' reports were already submitted.

Plaintiffs offer two justifications for the non-introduction of their proffered witnesses at the administrative hearing level: (1) the hearing officer imposed a time limitation on the proceedings below by adopting a one-year limitations period on claims for compensatory education; and (2) because the burden of proof was on the school district to show the appropriateness of its decision, the plaintiffs chose not to present expert testimony below.

a. *Limitations period*

Following *Montour School District v. S.T.*, 805 A.2d 29 (Pa. Commw. 2002), which established a one year statute of limitations on a request for a due process hearing, Hearing Officer Valentini found that plaintiffs could not seek compensatory education before December 9, 2003. For this reason, the Findings of Fact contained in the decision were largely limited to the relevant period, December 9, 2003 to April 20, 2005. The Appeals Panel affirmed Officer Valentini's decision.

Although the Court has not yet resolved the limitations issue in this case, it recently overturned the application of a one-year statute of limitations to a claim for compensatory education in a similar case, as has every court in this district that has recently considered the issue. It is probable, therefore, that if the Court finds Antoine to be eligible for special education under the IDEA, the Court will find the limitations period imposed by the hearing officer to have been improper. The Third Circuit has noted that the improper exclusion of evidence by the administrative agency may be a ground for admitting additional evidence during judicial review. *Susan N.*, 70 F.3d at 759 (quoting *Burlington v. Department of Educ.*, 736 F.2d 773, 791 (1st Cir. 1984)).

Officer Valentini's decision contained a footnote indicating that she allowed some testimony to go beyond the limitations period in order to create a complete record for future proceedings. Plaintiffs assert, however, that introducing such testimony would have been impracticable and inefficient. For this reason, plaintiffs did not introduce the testimony of Stillis or Brown, Antoine's learning support teachers from November 1999 through January 2001, or the testimony of Maxwell, the District's psychologist, who evaluated Antoine in 1999. Because of the likelihood that the Court will not apply a limitations period to Antoine's claim for compensatory education, plaintiffs seek to introduce this testimony here.

b. *Burden of proof*

Plaintiffs assert they did not offer the expert testimony of Dr. Domingos because they were not the party with the burden of proof at the administrative hearing. Prior to the United States Supreme Court's decision in *Schaffer v. Weast* . . . , the burden of demonstrating compliance with the IDEA in this jurisdiction was with the school district. In *Schaffer*, however, the Supreme Court held that the "burden of proof in an administrative hearing challenging an IEP is properly placed upon the party seeking relief." 127 S.Ct. at 537. This rule is properly applied to cases pending when *Schaffer* was decided, as was the instant case.

In this case, Antoine M. is not challenging the appropriateness of an IEP, but rather the failure of the school district to find him eligible for one. Nevertheless, the overarching logic of *Schaffer*—that, in the context of the IDEA, the party bringing the challenge bears the burden of proof—can be applied to the situation before the Court today. A student's challenge to a district's determination that he or she is not eligible for an IEP should not be treated any differently than a challenge to the adequacy of an IEP. For this reason, the burden of proof is now on Antoine and his guardian, whereas the burden was on the District at the administrative level. Plaintiffs' decision to present expert opinion now, whereas they chose not to at the administrative hearing, may very well be related to this shift in the burden of proof.

The Court is therefore satisfied that plaintiffs have presented sufficient justifications for introducing this evidence at the district court level. Although the witnesses were available for the administrative hearing, plaintiffs have set forth adequate reasons for their failure to present the testimony earlier. There is not evidence here that the testimony was withheld for strategic reasons, nor that the District will be prejudiced by its admission.

The Court is also satisfied that the evidence is non-cumulative, relevant, and useful for determining whether the goal of the IDEA has been reached. The testimony of these witnesses has not been introduced before. The testimony of Antoine's special education teachers, as well as that of a school psychologist who evaluated him will surely assist the Court in understanding the extent and nature of Antoine's alleged disability. In regards to the expert testimony, plaintiffs contend that her testimony will establish that Antoine was wrongly exited from the special education program in 2001, and is currently a student with a learning disability. It is likely that the Court will find such testimony "helpful in illuminating the nature of the controversy." *Susan N.*, 70 F.3d at 760 (quoting *Town of Burlington v. Department of Educ.*, 736 F.2d 773, 791 (1st Cir. 1984)).

In summary, the Court finds plaintiffs have presented sufficient justifications to introduce the proffered testimony that was not presented below, and that the proffered testimony is non-cumulative, relevant, and will assist the Court in its determination of whether the District has properly assessed Antoine's eligibility under the IDEA.

. . . .

Notes, Comments, and Questions

1. Did the courts in *Marc V.* and *Antoine M.* utilize any of the standards for admitting additional evidence set forth in *Burlington*, *Cook*, or *Susan N.*? Did they apply the same standard for admitting additional evidence? Are the holdings consistent?

2. On appeal, a district court's decision whether to admit additional evidence is evaluated for abuse of discretion. Miller v. Bd. of Educ. of the Albuquerque Pub. Sch., 565 F.3d 1232, 1240, 1241 (10th Cir. 2009). In *Miller*, the court applied the abuse of discretion standard to uphold the district court's refusal to admit evidence about the district's provision of books on tape to children with disabilities in the district on the grounds that it was not relevant.

C. Common Issues Relating to the Admission of Additional Evidence

Several common issues have arisen in connection with the admission of additional evidence in IDEA court proceedings. These include whether the evidence is cumulative, repetitive, or irrelevant; whether the evidence was available at the time of the hearing but strategically withheld; and whether evidence of subsequent developments after the adoption of the relevant IEP or the conclusion of the administrative hearing should be admitted. Courts have handled these issues in various ways.

Cumulative, Repetitive, and Irrelevant Evidence: In *Walker Cnty. Sch. Dist. v. Bennett*, 203 F.3d 1293 (11th Cir. 2000), *cert. denied*, 531 U.S. 1059 (2000), the court of appeals upheld the district court's refusal to admit evidence offered by the school district. It stated:

> In the district court the School District moved for an evidentiary hearing to present "additional evidence." The court required a proffer of the evidence the School District wished to present. The School District responded by listing the names of nineteen witnesses . . . plus three categories of tangible or documentary evidence. . . . The court found that five of the witnesses had already testified to the same general subject matter at the administrative hearing, and that the proposed testimony of several of the remaining witnesses was already in the record in the form of their written reports or the testimony of the other witnesses who had described their findings, so that, in either case, the proposed testimony before the district court would be cumulative. In two instances the court found the proffered testimony to be irrelevant. The court also found that all of the proffered witnesses who had not already testified were available at the time of the administrative hearing; that no explanation was given for not calling them at that time; and that permitting them to be called in the district court would raise the dual concerns of unfairly permitting the parties to reserve their best evidence for trial while essentially converting an administrative review proceeding into a trial *de novo*. Thus, with two minor exceptions, the district court concluded that the admission of any of the additional evidence in the judicial review proceedings would not only be cumulative but would undercut or unduly minimize the statutory role of the administrative process thereby resulting in an unnecessary expenditure of judicial resources.

Id. at 1296–97.

Strategic Withholding of Evidence: In *Springer v. Fairfax Cnty. Sch. Bd.*, 134 F.3d 659 (4th Cir. 1998), the court of appeals upheld the district court's decision to refuse to permit plaintiffs' expert, Dr. Joseph Novello, to testify. The court stated:

> The Springers do not contend that Dr. Novello's testimony was not available during the administrative review process. In fact, Dr. Novello examined Edward months before Fairfax County's initial eligibility committee meeting and had not seen him again after that time. Therefore, Dr. Novello's evaluation of Edward—and anything he might have added to the letter that is contained in the record—was available well before the administrative process began. Neither does it appear that Dr. Novello himself was unavailable well before the administrative process began. Neither does it

> appear that Dr. Novello himself was unavailable to testify during any phase of the administrative process. Although the Springers adverted to scheduling difficulties, we see no error in the district court's finding that, despite these difficulties, Dr. Novello "doesn't fall within the category of being unavailable."
>
> Instead, what seems to have happened here is that the Springers made the tactical decision to reserve the expense—and the impact—of live testimony by Dr. Novello until trial in federal court. We shall assume that their decision was made in good faith. However, were we to allow these litigants to escape the consequences of a litigation strategy gone awry, we would invite future litigants to engage in strategic behavior that might not be so innocent.

Id. at 167.

The court in *Springer* did not allow plaintiffs to base their decision on when to offer evidence on strategic concerns. Similarly, in *Roland M. v. Concord Sch. Comm.*, 910 F.2d 983 (1st Cir. 1990), *cert. denied*, 499 U.S. 912 (1991), referred to in *Springer*, the parents' attorneys refused to call as witnesses at the administrative proceedings three doctors who were treating the child at the time. The district court refused to allow the parents to call the doctors as witnesses before the district court. In upholding the district court's decision, the court of appeals stated:

> Appellants' lawyer indicated that he would squirrel the witnesses away until the court trial. The hearing officer implored counsel to adduce the witnesses' testimony and warned him against undermining the administrative process. Despite this request and warning, appellants steadfastly refused to produce the experts, citing an avowed distrust of the . . . [administrative] proceedings. . . .
>
> When the case went before the district court, appellants wanted to have this trio of witnesses testify. Defendants objected. The judge granted their motion *in limine*. Appellants claim that the preclusion was unwarranted.
>
> . . . . A court's customary discretion in evidentiary matters is channeled by the special goals and procedures of the Act. As a means of assuring that the administrative process is accorded its due weight and that judicial review does not become a trial *de novo*, thereby rendering the administrative hearing nugatory, a party seeking to introduce additional evidence at the district court level must provide some solid justification for doing so.
>
> Here, the parents were given every opportunity to present the desired testimony at the administrative level. They flatly refused. The unfairness of appellants' gambit is patent—as is the potentially insidious effect of rewarding such a maneuver. In its wisdom, Congress prescribed a two-tier model for these cases. To allow litigants to husband their witnesses, arbitrarily withholding them from the administrative process, would effectively sabotage the statutory scheme.

> The hearing officer, echoing these concerns, found categorically that there was no good reason why the witnesses were not brought forward; appellants' strategy was based on an "intent to withhold relevant evidence from the administrative hearing, to demean the statutory role of administrative expertise, and to bypass the due process framework generated by federal and state provisions" in order to reserve the evidence for a judicial trial. Before us, and below, the parents conceded that the core element of this finding was true: they deliberately withheld the witnesses from the second round of ... [the administrative process], preferring to use them in court. And they have come forward with no convincing explanation why their game of cat-and-mouse should have been countenanced or the evidence admitted in the district court.
>
> We refuse to reduce the proceedings before the state agency to a mere dress rehearsal by allowing appellants to transform the Act's judicial review mechanism into an unrestricted trial *de novo*. Where parties could have, but purposely chose not to, call certain witnesses at the administrative hearing, the district court has discretion to exclude the testimony on judicial review. In the absence of special circumstances, courts should ordinarily exercise that discretion in favor of excluding the belatedly offered evidence.

Id. at 996–97.

Evidence of Subsequent Developments After the Adoption of the IEP or the Administrative Hearing: By the time an IDEA claim reaches district court, much time will have passed since the initial challenge to the child's special education. Children can develop or regress quickly, so it is likely that additional evidence about the child's development and the impact of the IEP on the child's education will become available. Courts have dealt with whether to admit this as additional evidence in various ways. The Sixth Circuit, which has adopted a more expansive standard for admitting additional evidence, considered this issue in *Deal v. Hamilton Cnty. Bd. of Educ.*, 392 F.3d 840 (6th Cir. 2004), *cert. denied*, 546 U.S. 936 (2005). In upholding the district court's decision allowing additional evidence relating to the child's subsequent development, the court stated:

> Here, Plaintiffs-Appellants have not given this Court any basis for concluding that the district court abused its discretion in permitting (1) the testimony of four additional expert witnesses who addressed the Lovaas study and accepted principles for educating autistic students; (2) the testimony of two additional fact witnesses who had worked with Zachary in the 2001–2002 school year, limited in scope to the extent to which their observations were relevant to the challenged decisions for the 1999–2000 school year; or (3) the introduction of new documentary evidence, consisting of the *curricula vitae* of the expert witnesses who testified, records regarding Zachary's educational progress, and the results of psychological evaluations conducted by certain experts. There is no evidence, for example, that the district court

> used the additional evidence to go beyond the scope of the matters before the ALJ; indeed, the district court took great care to limit testimony to matters relevant to the 1999–2000 IEP.

Id. at 850–51. In an earlier decision in a different case, the Sixth Circuit reached a different conclusion because the judge considered additional evidence to rule on issues that were beyond those presented to the ALJ. In ruling that the judge inappropriately considered additional evidence, the court stated:

> The Guests argue that the district court only had subject matter jurisdiction to review evidence relating to the 1995–1996 school year and the recommended IEP for the 1996–1997 school year. The district court, however, heard evidence and decided issues concerning the 1996–1997 and 1997–1998 school years. The Guests contend, therefore, that the district court exceeded its jurisdiction when it considered evidence beyond the administrative record developed for the September 1996 administrative hearing and decided issues arising after the administrative hearing.
>
> . . . .
>
> . . . Evidence arising from events occurring during the 1996–1997 school years was properly admitted by the district court, but only for the purpose of deciding whether the proposed IEP for the 1996–1997 school year was reasonably calculated to lead to educational benefits. . . . The court holds, therefore, that the district court exceeded its jurisdiction to the extent it used additional evidence to rule upon issues beyond those presented to the ALJ.
>
> The district court lacked authority to evaluate the appropriateness of later proposed IEPs because the Guests did not first seek a due process review of those hearings. The district court committed error, therefore, to the extent it admitted evidence for the purpose of evaluating the later proposed IEPs. The district court exceeded its jurisdiction when it adjudicated the propriety of the Guest's proposal to send Joel to a private, residential facility. Similarly, the district court committed error when it admitted evidence concerning the parents' request for unrestricted observation of Joel at school and when it denied that request in its ruling. Those issues were not before the ALJ in 1996, and the Guests have failed to otherwise exhaust their administrative remedies.

Metropolitan Bd. of Pub. Educ. v. Guest, 193 F.3d 457, 462–63 (6th Cir. 1999).

In *Susan N. v. Wilson Sch. Dist.*, 70 F.3d 751 (3d Cir. 1995), the court also addressed the issue of the admissibility of evidence that was not available at the time of the hearing or the creation of the IEP, including testimony of the child's private school teachers and expert witnesses regarding her disability. According to the court of appeals:

> As the appellants "proposed that they be allowed to supplement the record with additional evidence which was not available in 1992," the district court chose to address the merits of their case without evaluating or admitting that

> evidence because in the eyes of the district court, doing so would be "second guessing the judgment of the administrative panel with evidence that was not before the panel when it made its decision." The court proceeded to "confine its analysis to the evidence that was before the panel in 1992, and . . . give due deference to the [administrative] panel's findings."

Id. at 760–61. The court of appeals, recognizing both the danger of second-guessing and the district court's obligation at least to consider proffers of additional evidence, remanded the case:

> In remanding this case to the district court, then, we hold that it was not within the court's discretion to reject appellants' offer of additional evidence without even evaluating it for its admissibility. However, we also note that, because at least some of appellants' proffered additional evidence was acquired after the school district's decision regarding M.'s need for special education, the district court will need to examine such evidence carefully. Such evidence may be considered only with respect to the *reasonableness* of the district's decision at the time it was made. Of course, this caveat does not mean that the court cannot exclude evidence that could have been available when the school district made its decisions.

Id. at 762.

Notes, Comments, and Questions

1. When deciding whether to admit evidence of subsequent developments in IDEA cases, courts generally admit such evidence only as it relates to the reasonableness of the IEP at the time it was adopted as opposed to using the evidence to help determine whether the IEP at issue actually provided the child with a free appropriate public education. Is this distinction an easy one to make? For examples of courts attempting to determine whether to admit evidence of subsequent developments, *see, e.g.*, Lebron v. North Penn Sch. Dist., 769 F. Supp. 2d 788, 795–96 (E.D. Pa. 2011) (refusing to admit progress report based on child's post-hearing academic performance); A.S. v. Trumbull Bd. of Educ., 414 F. Supp. 2d 152, 170–72 (D. Conn. 2006) (refusing to admit the child's medical and educational records for the school year after the year at issue in the administrative hearing).

2. If you were on the staff of a member of Congress who asked you to write a memo listing the pros and cons of legislation that would ban consideration of evidence of developments subsequent to the adoption of the IEP, what would be on your list?

Section Three
The Procedural Mechanism for Resolving IDEA Cases

Courts often decide cases challenging IDEA administrative decisions on motions for summary judgment while at the same time acknowledging that there is not a perfect fit between the procedural posture of an IDEA case and the standards for deciding a summary judgment motion. *See* M.H. v. N.Y.C. Dep't of Educ., 685 F.3d 217, 225–26 (2d Cir. 2012) (stating that courts typically decide IDEA cases on motions for summary judgment while acknowledging that the court's inquiry goes beyond whether facts are in dispute).

<u>Procedural posture of IDEA cases in federal district court</u>: Challenges to state IDEA administrative decisions under Section 1415(i) of the IDEA in federal court are double-hybrids. First, they are hybrids between original civil actions and appeals from agency decisions. Second, the standard of review federal courts exercise over agency decisions in IDEA cases is a hybrid between *de novo* review and the substantial evidence standard of review. This procedural posture of IDEA cases resulted in the "due weight" standard of review of IDEA administrative decisions set forth in *Rowley*. *See* Jonathan H. v. Souderton Area Sch. Dist., 562 F.3d 527, 529 (3d Cir. 2009) (stating that an IDEA action in federal court is an original civil action); Kirkpatrick v. Lenoir Cnty. Bd. of Educ., 216 F.3d 380, 383–84 (4th Cir. 2000) (ruling that an appeal from an administrative decision in an IDEA case is an original civil action); Capistrano Unified Sch. Dist. v. Wartenberg, 59 F.3d 884, 890 (9th Cir. 1995) (noting the hybrid nature of the court's review of administrative proceedings in which it reviews the administrative record, reviews additional evidence at its discretion, and decides the case based on "the preponderance of the evidence"); Hunger v. Leininger, 15 F.3d 664, 669 (7th Cir. 1994), *cert. denied*, 513 U.S. 839 (1994) (ruling that judicial review under the IDEA is different in that the court reviews the administrative record and additional evidence); Wall v. Mattituck-Cutchogue Sch. Dist., 945 F. Supp. 501, 507 (E.D.N.Y. 1996) ("The courts that have addressed the issue have recognized the paradoxical position of the district court as both an independent fact finder and a judicial body bound to review and give deference to the findings of an administrative agency."); D.F. v. Western Sch. Corp., 921 F.Supp. 559, 564 (S.D. Ind. 1996) ("The standard of review under the IDEA lies somewhere between *de novo* review and the substantial evidence/otherwise according to law standard frequently applied to administrative decisions.").

<u>The standard for granting summary judgment motions</u>: There is an uneasy relationship between the "due weight"standard and the standard for granting summary judgment. According to Rule 56 of the Federal Rules of Civil Procedure:

> A party may move for summary judgment, identifying each claim or defense . . . on which summary judgment is sought. The court should grant summary judgment if the movant shows that there is no genuine dispute as to any material fact and the movant is entitled to judgment as a matter of law. . . .

Fed. R. Civ. P. 56(a) (2015). It is rare that there is no genuine dispute as to material facts in an IDEA case, and a federal court judge's discretion to receive additional evidence potentially further clouds the factual issues. Recognizing this, some courts take the position that summary judgment is appropriate only when the district court does not accept additional evidence.

> Cross-motions for summary judgment are the standard method for presenting a case to a district court for decision on the record compiled by the administrative tribunal that the court is reviewing. The grant of the plaintiffs' motion thus implied that the judge was not considering any evidence not presented in the administrative proceedings.

Dale M. v. Bd. of Educ. of the Bradley-Bourbonnais High Sch. Dist. No. 307, 237 F.3d 813, 816 (7th Cir. 2001). As one court stated, "If 'no additional evidence is introduced [by the parties] in a civil suit seeking review of [an administrative decision], a motion for summary judgment operates as a motion for judgment based on the evidence comprising the record.'" Phillips v. District of Columbia, 736 F. Supp. 2d 240, 246 (D.D.C. 2010) (quoting Thomas v. District of Columbia, 407 F. Supp. 2d 102, 109 (D.D.C. 2005)).

But fitting an IDEA case into summary judgment, even when the court does not receive additional evidence, relies on two potential legal fictions: 1) that there is no genuine dispute as to material facts in the administrative record; and 2) that the judge does not review the record to identify and resolve those disputes as appropriate under the modified *de novo* standard of review and make a decision based on the preponderance of the evidence. Courts recognize these fictions. The Seventh Circuit, for example, stated:

> When no new evidence is presented to the district court in an IDEA suit, as was the case here, "the motion for summary judgment is simply the procedural vehicle for asking the judge to decide the case on the basis of the administrative record." Thus, even though it is termed "summary judgment," the district court's decision is based on the preponderance of the evidence, and we reverse only if the court's findings were clearly erroneous.

Loch v. Edwardsville Sch. Dist. No. 7, 327 F. App'x 647, 650–51 (7th Cir. 2009), *cert. denied*, 559 U.S. 991 (2010); *see also* Walker Cnty. Sch. Dist. v. Bennett, 203 F.3d 1293, 1297 n.11 (11th Cir. 2000) ("[A] motion for summary judgment . . . may not be an appropriate procedural device for triggering a district court decision because the district court in reviewing the administrative record, whether additional evidence is taken or not, must weigh and decide disputed issues of fact, an improper exercise under Rule 56."); Sebastian M. v. King Philip Reg'l Sch. Dist., 774 F. Supp. 2d 393, 406 (D. Mass. 2011), *aff'd*, 685 F.3d 79 (1st Cir. 2012) (stating that it is not clear how a court is to incorporate the due weight standard into the summary judgment standard).

Resolving IDEA cases through summary judgment motions: Nevertheless, summary judgment remains the favored procedural mechanism for resolving IDEA cases. Courts see it is a "pragmatic" way to resolve IDEA cases, while recognizing that the court's task is different from the traditional summary judgment motion. P.K. v. N.Y.C. Dep't of Educ., 819 F. Supp. 2d 90, 103 (E.D.N.Y 2011), *aff'd*, 576 F. App'x 135 (2d Cir. 2013); *see also* Loren F. v. Atlanta Indep. Sch. Sys., 349 F.3d 1309, 1313 (11th Cir. 2003) (stating that summary judgment is appropriate in IDEA cases even when facts are disputed); C.G. v. N.Y.C. Dep't of Educ., 752 F. Supp. 2d 355, 358 (S.D.N.Y. 2010) (stating that while summary judgment is the most pragmatic way to resolve IDEA cases, the court's role is not to determine whether there are disputed fact issues); N.M. v. Sch. Dist. of Phil., 585 F. Supp. 2d 657, 663 (E.D. Pa. 2008), *aff'd*, 395 F. App'x 920 (3d Cir. 2010) (recognizing that many IDEA claims do not fit into the typical summary judgment standard); Wall v. Mattituck-Cutchogue Sch. Dist., 945 F. Supp. 501, 508 (E.D.N.Y. 1996) ("the court is not dealing with summary judgment in its traditional setting."). One court gave a good description of how courts use summary judgment differently in IDEA cases:

> The parties' submissions are structured as motions for summary judgment. However, the procedure, in substance, is an appeal from an administrative determination. Thus, unlike in ordinary summary judgment motion practice, the existence of a disputed issue of material fact will not necessarily defeat a motion for summary judgment in the IDEA context. Rather, the court conducts an independent review of the administrative record, basing its decision on the preponderance of the evidence developed at the administrative hearings and any further evidence presented by the parties. Summary judgment thus serves "as a pragmatic procedural mechanism for reviewing a state's compliance with the procedures set forth in IDEA." *Lillbask*, 397 F.3d at 83 n.3.

W.G. v. N.Y.C. Dep't of Educ., 801 F. Supp. 2d 142, 166 (S.D.N.Y. 2011); *see also* Linda E. v. Bristol Warren Reg'l Sch. Dist., 758 F. Supp. 2d 75, 87 (D.R.I. 2010) (stating that courts use summary judgment to decide IDEA cases on the record developed in the administrative process); Manchester-Essex Reg'l Sch. Dist. v. Bureau of Special Educ. Appeals, 490 F. Supp. 2d 49, 51 (D. Mass. 2007) (stating that IDEA cases are administrative appeals even if the parties refer to them as summary judgment cases); Mr. X. v. N.Y.S. Educ. Dep't, 975 F. Supp. 546, 554 (S.D.N.Y. 1997) ("When a party moves for summary judgment in an IDEA action, the court does not make traditional inquiry into whether there are disputed material issues of fact, but rather, whether the administrative record and any additional evidence shows that there has been compliance with IDEA's procedures, and that the IEP has addressed the child's educational needs."); V.S. v. N.Y.C. Dep't of Educ., 25 F. Supp. 3d 295 (E.D.N.Y. 2014) ("Although styled a motion for summary judgment, the parties in effect are prosecuting an administrative appeal.").

Not every court accepts the legal fictions that allow IDEA cases to be resolved through summary judgment motions. The Sixth Circuit, for example, has rejected summary judgment when there are disputed material facts, even if the parties have not submitted additional evidence. Doe v. Metro. Nashville Pub. Sch., 133 F.3d 384, 387 (6th Cir. 1998), *cert. denied*, 525 U.S. 813 (1998) ("As such, if genuine issues of material fact remained, summary judgment was inappropriate."). Other courts have suggested alternatives to summary judgment. Several courts of appeals have indicated that IDEA cases should more appropriately be resolved as motions for judgment. *See* Cnty. Sch. Bd. of Henrico Cnty. v. Z.P., 399 F.3d 298, 309 n.7 (4th Cir. 2005) ("It therefore would seem that the court is entering judgment after what amounts to a bench trial, whether the district court considered new evidence or simply proceeded on the basis of an unsupplemented administrative record."); Alex R. v. Forestville Valley Cmty. Unit Sch. Dist. No. 221, 375 F.3d 603, 611 (7th Cir. 2004) (stating that summary judgment motions in IDEA cases "might more accurately have been titled 'motion for judgment under the IDEA.'"); Beth B. v. Van Clay, 282 F.3d 493, 496 n.2 (7th Cir. 2002), *cert. denied*, 537 U.S. 948 (2002) (noting that district court's disposition of an IDEA case "is perhaps better described as judgment on the record."); Kirkpatrick v. Lenoir Cnty. Bd. of Educ., 216 F.3d 380, 385 n.4 (4th Cir. 2000) ("Several courts also indicate that the matter is before the court on cross-appeals or cross-motions for summary judgment despite the fact that there are clearly disputed issues of material fact. As we conclude, IDEA actions are original civil actions that should typically be disposed of by motions for judgment."). One district court followed this guidance, allowing the parties to resolve the cases through "a motion for judgment on the administrative record." Fitzgerald v. Fairfax Cnty. Sch. Bd., 556 F. Supp. 2d 543, 550 (E.D. Va. 2008). Another district court noted that the parties moved for different relief; the defendant school district for summary judgment and the plaintiffs for "modified *de novo* review." C.G. v. N.Y.C. Dep't of Educ., 752 F. Supp. 2d 355, 358 n.1 (E.D.N.Y. 2010). A third district court suggested that in cases in which parties do not submit additional evidence, they could move for "judgment on the pleadings" instead of summary judgment. Wall v. Mattituck-Cutchogue Sch. Dist., 945 F. Supp. 501 508 n.6 (E.D.N.Y. 1986).

Section Four
Miscellaneous Federal Court Litigation Issues

A. Burden of Proof

In *Schaffer v. Weast*, 546 U.S. 49, 51 (2005), the Supreme Court ruled that the moving party in an impartial hearing under Section 1415(f) of the IDEA bears the burden of persuasion. Similarly, in federal court challenges to state administrative decisions under Section 1415(i), the courts have ruled that the party challenging the administrative decision has the burden of proving that the decision was incorrect. *See, e.g.*, A.K. v. Alexandria City Sch. Bd., 484 F.3d 672, 679 (4th Cir. 2007), *cert. denied*, 552 U.S. 1170 (2008) (ruling that the party challenging the hearing officer's decision has the "burden . . . of proving that the IEP was substantively deficient."); Alex R. v. Forrestville Valley Cmty. Sch. Dist. No. 221, 375 F.3d 603, 611 (7th Cir. 2004), *cert. denied*, 543 U.S. 1009 (2004) (stating that "the party challenging the outcome of the administrative proceeding bears the burden of proof."); McLaughlin v. Holt Pub. Sch. Bd. of Educ., 320 F.3d 663, 669 (6th Cir. 2003) ("It is clearly established that the McLaughlins bear the burden of proving by a preponderance of the evidence that the IEP developed by Holt Public Schools is inappropriate."). Thus, the burden of proof may switch from one party to another as the case moves from the administrative level to judicial review.

B. Governing Law

The IDEA provides states with federal funds to provide educational services to children with learning disabilities on the condition that the states adhere to the IDEA's requirements. Honig v. Doe, 484 U.S. 305, 310 (1988). Most states have also passed their own laws requiring school districts to provide special education services to children with learning disabilities. In *Board of Educ. of Hendrick Hudson Cent. Sch. Dist. v. Rowley*, 458 U.S. 176 (1982), the Supreme Court established a floor of services that states must provide to children under the IDEA:

> We therefore conclude that the "basic floor of opportunity" provided by the . . . [IDEA] consists of access to specialized instruction and related services which are individually designed to provide educational benefit to the handicapped child.

Id. at 201. Several states have passed laws that require school districts to provide a higher level of services than the "basic floor of opportunity" that the IDEA requires. For example, North Carolina law requires school districts to "provide the child with an equal opportunity to learn if that is reasonably possible, ensuring that the child has an opportunity to reach her full potential commensurate with the opportunity given other children." Burke Cnty. Bd. of Educ. v. Denton, 895 F.2d 973, 983 (4th Cir. 1990). Massachusetts requires the Department of Education "to administer special education programs 'to assure the maximum possible development of a child with special needs.'" David D. v. Dartmouth Sch. Comm., 775 F.2d 411, 423 (1st Cir. 1985), *cert. denied*, 475 U.S. 1140 (1986). A California regulation requires educational programs for children with disabilities to "'provide the equal opportunity for each individual with exceptional needs to achieve his or her full potential commensurate with the opportunity provided to other pupils.'" Pink v. Mt. Diablo Unified Sch. Dist., 738 F. Supp. 345, 346 (N.D. Cal. 1990). Finally, New Jersey law requires "that handicapped pupils be provided a special education program and related services 'according to how the pupil can best achieve success in learning . . . .'" Geis v. Bd. of Educ. of Parsippany-Troy Hills, 774 F.2d 575, 582 (3d Cir. 1985).

What law does a federal district court apply when a state's law requires a higher level of service than the IDEA? The issue has been resolved and does not often arise in federal court litigation. "[A] federal court must determine whether an IEP meets the requirements of state law if the state requires a level of substantive benefit greater than that required under federal law." *Denton*, 895 F.2d at 982–83; *see also* Union Sch. Dist. v. Smith, 15 F.3d 1519, 1527 (9th Cir. 1994) (enforcing state law because it "is not inconsistent with the IDEA"); Antkowiak v. Ambach, 838 F.2d 635, 641 (2d Cir. 1988) ("[S]tate procedures which more stringently protect the rights of the handicapped and their parents are consistent with the EHA and thus enforceable . . . ."); *David D.*, 775 F.2d at 420 (holding that the IDEA "incorporates relevant state substantive law and enforces that law as part of the federal right to a free appropriate public education."); *Geis*, 774 F.2d at 581 (ruling that "federal law incorporates any state standards that go beyond the minimum standards of the . . . [IDEA] and thereby confers on the federal courts authority to enforce state standards . . . ."); *Pink*, 738 F.Supp. at 347 ("Under the EHA, each state is given the power to enunciate its own procedural and substantive protections for its handicapped, provided it meets the federal minimum standard.").

C. Remand to the IHO

Federal district courts have the authority to remand an IDEA case to the hearing officer for further findings. *See* Kingsmore v. District of Columbia, 466 F.3d 118, 120 (D.C. Cir. 2006) (stating that the district court could have remanded the case to the hearing officer); *see also* Taylor v. District of Columbia, 770 F. Supp. 2d 105, 111 (D.D.C. 2011) (remanding to hearing officer for consideration of plaintiff's new evidence). When should a court remand a case as opposed to taking additional evidence? What factors should a court consider? Consider the following analysis in Options Pub. Charter Sch. v. Howe, 512 F.Supp. 2d 55 (D.D.C. 2007):

> In an instance in which another judge of this court, in an action brought pursuant to IDEA, determined that the hearing officer failed to make findings of fact and conclusions of law consistent with the applicable burden of proof at an administrative due process hearing, or misapplied the applicable burden of proof, that judge remanded the action to the hearing officer for further consideration and for findings and conclusions consistent with the applicable burden of proof. In other instances, other judges of this court have remanded IDEA actions to the hearing officer for reformulation of a compensatory education award. In yet another instance, the United States District Judge to whom this action is assigned remanded an IDEA action for findings with respect to reimbursement of the cost of private school education.
>
> Common to all four opinions was a determination that the Hearing Officer's Decision provided an incomplete basis for review by the court in accordance with IDEA, and recognition of "the admonition that reviewing courts not substitute their assessment of the evidence for that of hearing officers[.]" Here, the undersigned—as the other judges who exercised their discretion to remand an IDEA action for further consideration, findings and conclusions—is unable to determine the degree of deference to accord the Hearing Officer's Decision. In this action, the impediment to meaningful review stems largely from the absence from the decision of virtually any findings. For example, the hearing officer refers to "[t]he credible testimony of Paris Adon" and the "compelling[,]" "logical and credible" testimony of "Dr. [Cranford][,]" [sic], but makes no findings with respect to the basis upon which she credited their testimony. Elsewhere in the decision, the hearing officer relies upon speculation, and offers no findings of fact or conclusions of law: "it is **entirely conceivable** . . . that the mother's participation in the IEP meetings should have alerted . . . Options that more comprehensive evaluations were warranted[]"; "it is **most probable** that the

> provision of a FAPE to this Petitioner might have required . . . Options to alert . . . DCPS to file a due process hearing complaint once the mother insisted on a change of special education instruction hours." (emphasis supplied). Even the hearing officer's statement of the issues presented at the hearing is ambiguous. ("Frankly, Respondent Options['] good faith effort to appease the parent backfired and **perhaps** escalated to a claim which now includes an allegation of insufficient evaluations due to respondent's willingness to change the [student's] programming at the whim of the parent."). Finally, the hearing officer did not articulate the burden of proof which she applied, or identify the party on which the burden was rested.
>
> In this circumstance, the undersigned cannot determine what findings and conclusions the hearing officer made, and on what evidence in the record any such findings and conclusions were based. Because the undersigned is precluded from "substitut[ing] [her] assessment of the evidence for that of [the] hearing [officer][,]" a remand for further consideration of the evidence, and for further findings of fact and conclusions of law, is the only vehicle by which review consistent with the applicable statutory scheme can be accomplished.

Id. at 56–58 (emphasis in original).

Another court in remanding a case to the hearing officer was sensitive to the institutional roles the IDEA creates and the need to expedite IDEA cases:

> However, because the Hearing Officer erred by finding that K.T. was only deprived of a FAPE for two weeks and failed to properly consider the evidence produced by plaintiff, the administrative record is "absen[t] of pertinent findings." Additional evidence, such as evaluations of all of K.T.'s IEP goals, may also be useful. "[T]he record in an IDEA case is supposed to be made not in the district court but primarily at the administrative level[.]". . Thus, although the Court is "troubled at the prospect of further delay," it will remand this case to the Hearing Officer for further proceedings that should be conducted as expeditiously as possible. The Officer should supplement the record with the information needed to "best correct" K.T.'s educational "deficits," and to "determine an appropriate award of compensatory education" based on the District's failure to provide K.T. with an FAPE..

Stanton v. District of Columbia, 680 F. Supp. 2d 201, 208 (D.D.C. 2010).

Based on these considerations, courts have remanded cases for several reasons. The most frequent reason is that the hearing was deficient in some manner, including that the transcript of the hearing was defective, or that the hearing officer failed to follow applicable legal standards, failed to develop the record, failed to state the reasons for the decision, or made a factual or legal error. In *Kingsmore v. District of Columbia*, 466 F.3d 118, 119–20 (D.C. Cir. 2006), the court of appeals stated that instead of finding a denial of FAPE based on an inadequate administrative transcript, the district court should have remanded to develop an appropriate record. In *Phillips v. District of Columbia*, 736 F. Supp. 2d 240, 249–50 (D.D.C. 2010), the court remanded to the hearing officer for consideration of a compensatory education award; *see also* Banks v. District of Columbia, 720 F. Supp. 2d 83, 86 (D.D.C. 2010) (remanding to hearing officer hearing to explain why the district's failure to provide all the IEP services was not an IDEA violation); D.S. v. District of Columbia, 699 F. Supp. 2d 229, 231 (D.D.C. 2010) (remanding for hearing officer to consider the merits of the complaint after the officer mistakenly dismissed the case on jurisdictional grounds); Brown v. District of Columbia, 568 F. Supp. 2d 44, 54–55 (D.D.C. 2008) (remanding to determine if district denied child FAPE and for consideration of compensatory education award); K.S. v. Fremont Unified Sch. Dist., 545 F. Supp. 2d 995, 1005–06 (N.D. Cal. 2008) (remanding case for reconsideration of the evidence in light of the court's instructions about credibility determinations); Mary McLeod Bethune Day Acad. Pub. Charter Sch. v. Bland, 534 F. Supp. 2d 109, 118 (D.D.C. 2008) (remanding for "further explanation of compensatory education award."). Another basis for remand is when the district court reverses a hearing officer's finding that the district did not deny the child a FAPE and thus remands for consideration of an award of compensatory education. *Stanton*, 680 F. Supp. 2d at 208. Finally, one court remanded for consideration of new evidence. *Taylor*, 770 F. Supp. 2d at 110–11.

Chapter 16

Relief for IDEA Violations: Monetary Damages, Compensatory Education, and Injunctive Relief

Introduction

This chapter will cover the availability of several forms of relief for IDEA violations, including compensatory monetary damages, compensatory education, and injunctive relief. Section One considers whether courts can award compensatory monetary damages for IDEA violations. Section Two considers whether courts can award compensatory monetary damages for violations of other federal laws that protect the rights of children with disabilities. Section Three covers the availability of compensatory education for IDEA violations. Finally, Section Four examines the availability of injunctive relief in IDEA cases.

Problem

When D.J. was beginning second grade, his mother noticed that he was not able to read. She told D.J.'s teacher, who said it was not unusual for children not to read by second grade. Dissatisfied with this response, D.J.'s mother told the principal, who gave the same response. The principal failed to follow the school district's protocol in such situations, which required the principal to refer such concerns to the special education director. Near the end of third grade, D.J. took standardized reading and math tests. His reading score was in the bottom one percent. As a result of this score, the school district evaluated D.J. and diagnosed him with dyslexia and attention deficit hyperactivity disorder (ADHD). The district prepared an IEP for fourth grade for D.J. that included ten hours per week of special education in a special class and thirty minutes each of speech and language therapy and individual counseling each week. D.J.'s mother disagreed with the IEP and requested twenty hours of special education per week and one hour of speech and language therapy and counseling per week. She did not request an impartial hearing to challenge the IEP. By the end of fourth grade, D.J.'s reading had not significantly improved. By then, his reading was three years below grade level.

D.J.'s mother wants to sue the school district for violating D.J.'s rights. She wants damages from the district for failing to educate D.J. and to compensate her for tutors she hired to help D.J. learn. She also wants an order immediately changing D.J.'s IEP.

In the beginning of D.J.'s fifth grade year, she retained Maria to represent her. In deciding how to proceed, Maria is considering the following questions: Under what statutes does D.J. have a viable claim? Can Maria file claims under these statutes directly in federal court or must she exhaust D.J.'s administrative remedies? If the school district violated any of these statutes, is D.J. entitled to compensatory monetary damages? Under which statutes? Is D.J. entitled to compensatory education? If so, how would such an award be calculated? What evidence would Maria need to introduce to support a compensatory education claim? If Maria requests a preliminary injunction adjusting D.J.'s IEP to add more special education and related services, would it be granted? If Maria seeks a permanent injunction, what would she need to prove to succeed? For purposes of this problem, the applicable statute of limitations for IDEA claims is two years and for all other statutes it is three years. You will need to review previous topics to answer these questions sufficiently, including FAPE, related services, pendency, and exhaustion of administrative remedies.

Section One
Compensatory Monetary Damages Under the IDEA

The IDEA gives federal courts a grant of broad authority to award relief: "In any action brought under this paragraph, the court . . . basing its decision on a preponderance of the evidence, shall grant such relief as the court determines is appropriate." 20 U.S.C. § 1415(i)(2)(C)(iii) (2012). The Supreme Court has ruled that this provision "confers broad discretion on the court. The type of relief is not further specified, except that it must be " 'appropriate.' " School Comm. of the Town of Burlington v. Dep't of Educ. of Mass., 471 U.S. 359, 369 (1985). This section considers whether courts can award compensatory monetary damages as "appropriate relief" for IDEA violations. Recall from Chapter Six that the Supreme Court has ruled that school districts are required to reimburse parents for tuition or other expenses they incurred in unilaterally placing their children in private schools when a school district failed to provide their children with a FAPE. The courts, however, consider compensatory monetary damages to be different from tuition reimbursement, and thus the availability of tuition reimbursement does not mean that compensatory monetary damages are also available. In *Burlington*, the Court stated, "the Town repeatedly characterizes reimbursement as 'damages,' but that simply is not the case. Reimbursement merely requires the Town to belatedly pay expenses that it should have paid all along and would have borne in the first instance had it developed a proper IEP." *Id.* at 370–71; *see also* Hall v. Knott Cnty. Bd. of Educ. 941 F.2d 402, 407 (6th Cir. 1991), *cert. denied*, 502 U.S. 1077 (1992) ("A judgment that simply reimburses a parent for the cost of obtaining educational services that ought to have been provided free does not constitute an award of 'damages,' the Supreme Court has told us . . . ."). In contrast to compensatory monetary damages, equitable remedies, including reimbursement, "involve the payment of money . . . to parents for expenses incurred on private educational services to which their child was later found to have been entitled . . . ." Nieves-Marquez v. Puerto Rico, 353 F.3d 108, 124 (1st Cir. 2003). In contrast, compensatory monetary damages include intangible damages such as "pain and suffering, emotional distress, and other consequential damages caused by the lack of a free appropriate public education." Sellers v. Sch. Bd. of Manassas, Va., 141 F.3d 524, 527, 528 (4th Cir. 1998) (ruling that the IDEA does not support compensatory monetary damages); *see also* Hurry v. Jones, 734 F.2d 879, 883–85 (1st Cir. 1984) (upholding award of $4,600 to parents to reimburse them for driving their son to school but reversing award of $8,796 to child as damages for the time he was not in school due to the district's IDEA violation); D.L. v. Waukee Cmty. Sch. Dist., 578 F. Supp. 2d 1178, 1185 (S.D. Iowa 2008) (". . . Plaintiffs impermissibly attempt to use IDEA as a 'tort-like mechanism' by seeking compensation for the following: past medical expenses, physical and mental pain and suffering, and loss of enjoyment of life."). In the following case, the court considers whether compensatory monetary damages are available for IDEA violations.

Sellers v. Sch. Bd. of Manassas, Va.

141 F.3d 524 (4th Cir.1998)

WILKINSON, Chief Judge:

Kristopher Sellers and his parents sued the School Board of the City of Manassas . . . alleging violations of the Individuals with Disabilities Education Act ("IDEA"), section 504 of the Rehabilitation Act, 42 U.S.C. § 1983, and Virginia law. The Sellers sought compensatory and punitive damages. The district court granted the defendants' motion to dismiss primarily on the grounds that such damages are unavailable under IDEA . . . . We agree that IDEA does not provide for compensatory or punitive damages . . . .

I.

. . . At the time the Sellers filed their complaint, Kristopher was eighteen years old. Although he had recently been diagnosed as learning disabled and emotionally disturbed, his disability apparently had gone undiscovered for many years. Kristopher received no special education services until the 1995–1996 school year. The complaint states, however, that his test scores as early as fourth grade "should have alerted" the defendants of the need to test and evaluate Kristopher for disabilities. . . .

According to the complaint, the parties to the present suit reached a settlement as to all educational issues. After the settlement, a hearing officer held due process hearings and decided that he lacked authority to award compensatory and punitive damages. The Sellers sought review of the decision by a state-level hearing officer. He too, however, concluded that hearing officers lacked authority to award such damages. The Sellers then filed the present suit . . . seeking . . . compensatory and punitive damages for violations of IDEA . . . . The Sellers . . . disputed the hearing officers' refusal to award compensatory and punitive damages. Terming the Sellers' action [as] one for educational malpractice, the district court dismissed the Sellers' lawsuit . . . for failure to state a claim. . . .

II.

. . . .

IDEA provides that a court reviewing the findings and determination of a hearing officer "shall grant such relief as [it] determines is appropriate." 20 U.S.C. § 1415(e)(2). In *Hall by Hall v. Vance County Bd. of Educ.*, 774 F.2d 629 (4th Cir. 1985) ("*Vance*"), this court interpreted the meaning of "appropriate" relief in an earlier version of IDEA. *Vance* held that appropriate relief could include reimbursement for private school tuition where a county board of education had failed to provide a free appropriate public education to a disabled child. *Id.* at 633. It followed an earlier decision of the Supreme Court that had likewise found appropriate relief could include tuition reimbursement. *School Comm. of Burlington v. Department of Educ. of Mass.*, 471 U.S. 359, 370 . . . (1985). However, *Vance* made clear that not all forms of relief are appropriate. While the Act permitted reimbursement, it did "not create a private cause of action for damages for educational malpractice." *Vance*, 774 F.2d at 633 n.3.

Vance bars the Sellers' recovery under IDEA. Their claim is indistinguishable from one of educational malpractice. The Sellers simply allege that the defendants improperly diagnosed Kristopher and that, as a result, either they or Kristopher have suffered some unspecified tort-like injuries. To award compensatory or punitive damages under these circumstances would disregard settled circuit precedent.

Nothing in the years since *Vance* has undermined the soundness of its holding. Tort-like damages are simply inconsistent with IDEA's statutory scheme. The touchstone of a traditional tort-like remedy is redress for a broad range of harms "associated with personal injury, such as pain and suffering, emotional distress, harm to reputation, or other consequential damages." *United States v. Burke*, 504 U.S. 229, 239 . . . (1992) (interpreting Title VII). By contrast, the touchstone of IDEA is the actual provision of a free appropriate public education.

To advance this goal, IDEA provides a panoply of procedural rights to parents to ensure their involvement in decisions about their disabled child's education. For example, parents may examine all relevant records relating to their disabled child's identification, evaluation, placement, and receipt of a free appropriate public education. 20 U.S.C. § 1415(b)(1)(A). They must receive written notice prior to changes in the child's identification, evaluation, placement, or receipt of a free appropriate public education. *Id.* § 1415(b)(1)(C). They also may present complaints with respect to such matters. *Id.* § 1415(b)(1)(E). They can air these complaints in an "impartial due process hearing," *id.* § 1415(b)(2), and, in some cases, can appeal the findings and decision rendered in that hearing. *Id.* § 1415(c). Finally, a party aggrieved by the findings or decision of a hearing officer may seek judicial review. *Id.* § 1415(e)(2).

The purpose of these procedural mechanisms is to preserve the right to a free appropriate public education, not to provide a forum for tort-like claims of educational malpractice. Accordingly, the Supreme Court has noted that "equitable considerations are relevant in fashioning relief." *Burlington*, 471 U.S. at 374 . . . ; *see also Florence County Sch. Dist. Four v. Carter*, 510 U.S. 7, 16 . . . (1993). For example, the Court in *Burlington* concluded that "by empowering the court to grant 'appropriate' relief Congress meant to include retroactive reimbursement to parents as an available remedy in a proper case." 471 U.S. at 370. . . . Tuition reimbursement requires an education agency "to belatedly pay expenses that it should have paid all along." *Burlington*, 471 U.S. at 370–71. . . . Likewise, appropriate relief may include special education services. Such services are part and parcel of the free appropriate public education to which the child is entitled. But the Court has never approved an award of compensatory or punitive damages under IDEA for a violation of its requirements. In fact, it "took pains to emphasize that . . . reimbursement [for appropriate specialized education] should not be characterized as 'damages.'" *Hall v. Knott County Bd. of Educ.*, 941 F.2d 402, 407 (6th Cir. 1991) (citing *Burlington*, 471 U.S. at 370 . . .). Compensatory or punitive damages would transform IDEA into a remedy for pain and suffering, emotional distress, and other consequential damages caused by the lack of a free appropriate public education. Such a result would be inconsistent with the structure of the statute, which so strongly favors the provision of and, where appropriate, the restoration of educational rights.

. . . .

Not only are awards of compensatory and punitive damages inconsistent with IDEA's structure, they present acute problems of measurability. Relief such as retroactive reimbursement is definable and concrete. The actual costs borne by parents for special education and related services provide an ascertainable benchmark for calculating the relief to which they may be entitled. By contrast, IDEA lacks any particular standard by which a court could evaluate what amount of compensatory or punitive damages is appropriate in a particular case. Absent any such standards, the range of possible monetary awards would be vast, particularly in cases seeking recovery for less tangible injuries such as emotional distress or pain and suffering. Such a result is not consistent with a statute designed primarily to provide education to disabled children.

. . . .

Notes, Comments, and Questions

1. It is widely accepted that compensatory monetary damages are not available for lawsuits under the IDEA. With two limited exceptions, all of the courts of appeals that have considered this question agree with *Sellers*:

First Circuit: Diaz-Fonseca v. Puerto Rico, 451 F.3d 13, 28 (1st Cir. 2006) ("It is black letter law that punitive damages—indeed money damages of any sort—are not available in a private suit under the IDEA."); Nieves-Marquez v. Puerto Rico, 353 F.3d 108, 124 (1st Cir. 2003) ("We conclude that tort-like money damages, as opposed to compensatory equitable relief, are not available under [the] IDEA."); Hurry v. Jones, 734 F.2d 879, 885 (1st Cir. 1984) (upholding award of $4,600 to parents to reimburse them for driving their son to school but reversing award of $8,796 to child as damages for the time he was not in school due to the district's IDEA violation).

Second Circuit: Polera v. Bd. of Educ. of the Newburgh Enlarged City Sch. Dist., 288 F.3d 478, 486 (2d Cir. 2002):

> The purpose of the IDEA is to provide educational services, not compensation for personal injury, and a damages remedy—as contrasted with reimbursement of expenses—is fundamentally inconsistent with this goal. The availability of damages also would undercut the IDEA's carefully structured procedure for administrative remedies, a mechanism that encourages parents to seek relief at the time that a deficiency occurs and that allows the educational system to bring its expertise to bear in correcting its own mistakes. We therefore hold that monetary damages are not available under the IDEA.

Fourth Circuit: Sellers v. Sch. Bd. of Manassas, Va., 141 F.3d 524, 528 (4th Cir. 1998) (ruling that the district court properly dismissed plaintiffs' IDEA damages request).

Fifth Circuit: Marvin H. v. Austin Indep. Sch. Dist.,714 F.2d 1348, 1356 (5th Cir. 1983) (denying claim for compensatory and punitive damages); *but see* Salley v. St. Tammany Parish Sch. Bd., 57 F.3d 458 (5th Cir. 1995), in which the court, without discussion of the issue of the availability of compensatory monetary damages in IDEA cases, upheld a "nominal" damages award under IDEA for procedural violations: "St. Tammany's procedural violations therefore can not be said to have harmed Danielle. The district court acted correctly when it awarded only nominal damages to the Salleys." *Id.* at 466.

Sixth Circuit: Gean v. Hattaway, 330 F.3d 758, 774 (6th Cir. 2003) (stating that a district court's "discretion to award monetary damages under this statute extends only to restitution for money that should have been paid by the state for educational services—not to 'general damages.'"); *see also* Crocker v. Tenn. Secondary Sch. Athletic Ass'n, 980 F.2d 382, 386 (6th Cir. 1992) ("[W]e do not find case authority interpreting the Act to allow an award of general damages for emotional injury or injury to a dignitary interest."); Hall v. Knott Cnty. Bd. of Educ., 941 F.2d 402, 407 (6th Cir. 1991), *cert. denied*, 502 U.S. 1077 (1992) (holding that there is no right to recover lost earnings caused by a school district's failure to provide appropriate education to the child).

Seventh Circuit: Charlie F. v. Bd. of Educ. of Skokie Sch. Dist., 98 F.3d 989, 991 (7th Cir. 1996) (holding that the IDEA does not allow damages).

Eighth Circuit: Birmingham v. Omaha Sch. Dist., 220 F.3d 850, 856 (8th Cir. 2000) (holding that relief under the IDEA does not include compensatory or punitive damages); Thompson v. Bd. of Special Sch. Dist. No. 1, 144 F.3d 574, 580 (8th Cir. 1998) (ruling that neither compensatory nor punitive damages are available under the IDEA); Fort Zumwalt Sch. Dist. v. Clynes, 119 F.3d 607, 615 (8th Cir. 1997), *cert. denied*, 523 U.S. 1137 (1998) (ruling that "damages are not available for IDEA violations."); Hoekstra v. Indep. Sch. Dist. No. 283, 103 F.3d 624, 625–26 (8th Cir. 1996) *cert. denied*, 520 U.S. 1244 (1997) (ruling that IDEA does not allow general or punitive damages awards); Miener v. Missouri, 673 F.2d 969, 980 (8th Cir. 1982), *cert. denied*, 459 U.S. 909 (1982) (finding that damages are not available under the IDEA).

<u>Ninth Circuit</u>: Blanchard v. Morton Sch. Dist., 420 F.3d 918, 921 (9th Cir. 2005), *overruled on other grounds*, Payne v. Peninsula Sch. Dist., 635 F.3d 863 (9th Cir. 2011) ("Money damages for retrospective and non-educational injuries are not available under the IDEA."); Witte v. Clark Cnty. Sch. Dist., 197 F.3d 1271, 1275 (9th Cir. 1999) (stating that "ordinarily monetary damages are not ordinarily available under" the IDEA); Mountain View-Los Altos Union High Sch. Dist. v. Sharron B.H., 709 F.2d 28, 30 (9th Cir. 1983) ("Damage remedies for placement before full compliance with EAHCA procedures are not in keeping with the design of the Act.").

<u>Eleventh Circuit</u>: Ortega v. Bibb Cnty. Sch. Dist., 397 F.3d 1321, 1326 (11th Cir. 2005) (holding that "the IDEA does not provide a cause of action for tort-like relief").

2. The Third Circuit Court of Appeals has not settled the issue. District courts in the Third Circuit, however, have concluded that compensatory monetary damages are not available for IDEA violations. *See* J.L. v. Ambridge Area Sch. Dist., 622 F. Supp. 2d 257, 272 (W.D. Pa. 2008) (dismissing "Plaintiffs' claims for monetary damages under the IDEA."); Derrick F. v. Red Lion Area Sch. Dist., 586 F. Supp. 2d 282, 297 (M.D. Pa. 2008) (ruling that compensatory damages are not available under the IDEA); D.G. v. Somerset Hills Sch. Dist., 559 F. Supp. 2d 484, 494 (D.N.J. 2008) (dismissing "plaintiffs' claim for compensatory and punitive damages under the IDEA.").

3. The Tenth Circuit has not settled the issue either. *See* Cudjoe v. Indep. Sch. Dist. No. 12, 297 F.3d 1058, 1067 n. 10 (10th Cir. 2002) (declining to determine whether compensatory monetary damages are available for IDEA violations); Swenson v. Lincoln Cnty. Sch. Dist., 260 F. Supp. 2d 1136, 1148 (D. Wyo. 2003) (recognizing that "the Tenth Circuit has not addressed the issue" but agreeing with the "weight of authority that an award of compensatory or punitive damages" is inconsistent with the IDEA).

4. Do you agree with *Sellers* and the other courts of appeals that the IDEA does not permit an award of compensatory monetary damages? What are the opposing arguments?

5. Do you agree with *Sellers* that it would be difficult to measure damages for violations of the IDEA? As you will see in the next section, plaintiffs are entitled to compensatory monetary damages for violations of other federal laws that protect the rights of students with disabilities. As you read Section Two, consider whether damages are any more quantifiable for violations of those statutes than for IDEA violations.

6. Do you agree that Sellers' claim is essentially one of educational malpractice? Is it appropriate to frame a claim that a school district failed to comply with the IDEA's

statutory obligations to identify, evaluate, and classify a child with a disability as an act of educational malpractice?

Section Two
Compensatory Monetary Damages Under Related Federal Statutes

In addition to the IDEA, several other federal statutes and constitutional provisions protect the rights of children with disabilities. Two statutes prohibit discrimination on the basis of disability. The Americans with Disabilities Act (ADA) provides that "[N]o qualified individual with a disability shall, by reason of such disability, be excluded from participation in or be denied the benefits of the services, programs, or activities of a public entity, or be subjected to discrimination by any such entity." 42 U.S.C. § 12132 (2012). Section 504 of the Rehabilitation Act of 1975 ("Section 504") contains a similar prohibition, but applies only to programs or activities that receive federal financial assistance: "No otherwise qualified individual with a disability . . . shall, solely by reason of her or his disability, be excluded from the participation in, be denied the benefits of, or be subjected to discrimination under any program or activity receiving Federal financial assistance . . . ." 29 U.S.C. § 794(a) (2012).

The Fourteenth Amendment to the Constitution of the United States does not explicitly prohibit discrimination against people with disabilities, but it does guarantee due process and equal protection of laws to all persons. The Fourteenth Amendment states: "[Nor] shall any state deprive any person of life, liberty, or property, without due process of law; nor deny to any person within its jurisdiction the equal protection of the laws." U.S. Const. amend. XIV, § 1.

Finally, the Civil Rights Act of 1871, 42 U.S.C. § 1983 (2012), plays an important role in enforcing the IDEA, ADA, Section 504, and the Fourteenth Amendment. Section 1983, as it is commonly called, does not create additional substantive rights. Rather, it provides a cause of action against state officials who violate federal statutory or constitutional rights, including the statutes that protect the rights of people with disabilities and the Fourteenth Amendment. Section 1983 reads as follows:

> Every person who, under color of any statute, ordinance, regulation, custom, or usage, of any State or Territory or the District of Columbia, subjects, or causes to be subjected, any citizen of the United States or other person within the jurisdiction thereof to the deprivation of any rights, privileges, or immunities secured by the Constitution and laws, shall be liable to the party injured in an action at law, suit in equity, or other proper proceeding for redress . . . .

This section will first examine whether a plaintiff can receive compensatory monetary damages for violation of the ADA, Section 504, or the Fourteenth Amendment.

The Supreme Court addressed this issue in *Smith v. Robinson*, 468 U.S. 992 (1984). *Smith* involved a dispute over the educational placement of Tommy Smith, who suffered from cerebral palsy and emotional and physical difficulties. His parents claimed that defendants denied Tommy a free appropriate public education. They brought claims pursuant to the IDEA, Section 504, Section 1983, and the Due Process and Equal Protection Clauses of the Fourteenth Amendment. The parents prevailed, and by the time the dispute reached the Supreme Court, the issue was whether the parents could recover attorneys fees. The issue for the Court was whether the IDEA is the exclusive remedy to protect the rights covered by the IDEA. If the Court ruled that it was, then the parents could not recover fees, because the IDEA did not at the time provide attorneys fees to a prevailing party. If the court decided that the IDEA was not the exclusive remedy, then the parents could recover fees pursuant to the other statutes, which provided for attorneys fees to prevailing parties.

Smith v. Robinson

468 U.S. 992 (1984)

Justice Blackmun delivered the opinion of the Court.

. . . .

III.

. . . .

B

We have little difficulty concluding that Congress intended the EHA to be the exclusive avenue through which a plaintiff may assert an equal protection claim to a publicly financed special education. The EHA is a comprehensive scheme set up by Congress to aid the States in complying with their constitutional obligations to provide public education for handicapped children. Both the provisions of the statute and its legislative history indicate that Congress intended handicapped children with constitutional claims to a free appropriate public education to pursue those claims through the carefully tailored administrative and judicial mechanism set out in the statute.

In the statement of findings with which the EHA begins, Congress noted that there were more than 8 million handicapped children in the country, the special education needs of most of whom were not being fully met. Congress also recognized that in a series of "landmark court cases," the right to an equal education opportunity for handicapped children had been established. S. Rep. No. 94-168, p. 6 (1975). See also *id.*, at 13 ("It is the intent of the Committee to establish and protect the right to education for all handicapped children and to provide assistance to the States in carrying out their responsibilities under State law and the Constitution of the United States to provide equal protection of the laws"). The EHA was an attempt to relieve the fiscal burden placed on States and localities by their responsibility to provide education for all handicapped children. At the same time, however, Congress made clear that the EHA is not simply a funding statute. The responsibility for providing the required education remains on the States. And the Act establishes an enforceable substantive right to a free appropriate public education. Finally, the Act establishes an elaborate procedural mechanism to protect the rights of handicapped children. The procedures not only ensure that hearings conducted by the State are fair and adequate. They also effect Congress' intent that each child's individual educational needs be worked out through a process that begins on the local level and includes ongoing parental involvement, detailed procedural safeguards, and a right to judicial review.

In light of the comprehensive nature of the procedures and guarantees set out in the EHA and Congress' express efforts to place on local and state educational agencies the primary responsibility for developing a plan to accommodate the needs of each individual handicapped child, we find it difficult to believe that Congress also meant to leave undisturbed the ability of a handicapped child to go directly to court with an equal protection claim to a free appropriate public education. Not only would such a result render superfluous most of the detailed procedural protections outlined in the statute, but, more important, it would also run counter to Congress' view that the needs of handicapped children are best accommodated by having the parents and the local education agency work together to formulate an individualized plan for each handicapped child's education. No federal district court presented with a constitutional claim to a public education can duplicate that process.

We do not lightly conclude that Congress intended to preclude reliance on § 1983 as a remedy for a substantial equal protection claim. Since 1871, when it was passed by Congress, § 1983 has stood as an independent safeguard against deprivations of federal constitutional and statutory rights. Nevertheless, § 1983 is a statutory remedy and Congress retains the authority to repeal it or replace it with an alternative remedy. The crucial consideration is what Congress intended.

In this case, we think Congress' intent is clear. Allowing a plaintiff to circumvent the EHA administrative remedies would be inconsistent with Congress' carefully tailored scheme. The legislative history gives no indication that Congress intended such a result. Rather, it indicates that Congress perceived the EHA as the most effective vehicle for protecting the constitutional right of a handicapped child to a public education. We conclude, therefore, that where the EHA is available to a handicapped child asserting a right to a free appropriate public education, based either on the EHA or on the Equal Protection Clause of the Fourteenth Amendment, the EHA is the exclusive avenue through which the child and his parents or guardian can pursue their claim.

. . . .

IV.

We turn, finally, to petitioners' claim that they were entitled to fees under § 505 of the Rehabilitation Act, because they asserted a substantial claim for relief under § 504 of that Act.

. . . .

Section 504 and the EHA are different substantive statutes. While the EHA guarantees a right to a free appropriate public education, § 504 simply prevents discrimination on the basis of handicap. But while the EHA is limited to handicapped children seeking access to public education, § 504 protects handicapped persons of all ages from discrimination in a variety of programs and activities receiving federal financial assistance.

Because both statutes are built around fundamental notions of equal access to state programs and facilities, their substantive requirements, as applied to the right of a handicapped child to a public education, have been interpreted to be strikingly similar. In regulations promulgated pursuant to § 504, the Secretary of Education has interpreted § 504 as requiring a recipient of federal funds that operates a public elementary or secondary education program to provide a free appropriate public education to each qualified handicapped person in the recipient's jurisdiction. . . . The regulations also require that the recipient implement procedural safeguards, including notice, an opportunity for the parents or guardian to examine relevant records, an impartial hearing with opportunity for participation by the parents or guardian and representation by counsel, and a review procedure.

. . . .

On the other hand, although both statutes begin with an equal protection premise that handicapped children must be given access to public education, it does not follow that the affirmative requirements imposed by the two statutes are the same. The significant difference between the two, as applied to special education claims, is that the substantive and procedural rights assumed to be guaranteed by both statutes are specifically required only by the EHA.

In *Southeastern Community College v. Davis*, 442 U.S. 397 . . . (1979), the Court emphasized that § 504 does not require affirmative action on behalf of handicapped persons, but only the absence of discrimination against those persons. In light of *Davis*, courts construing § 504 as applied to the educational needs of handicapped children have expressed confusion about the extent to which § 504 requires special services necessary to make public education accessible to handicapped children.

In the EHA, on the other hand, Congress specified the affirmative obligations imposed on States to ensure that equal access to a public education is not an empty guarantee, but offers some benefit to a handicapped child. Thus, the statute specifically requires "such . . . supportive services . . . as may be required to assist a handicapped child to benefit from special education," see *Board of Education v.*

Rowley, 458 U.S., at 200 . . . , including, if the public facilities are inadequate for the needs of the child, "instruction in hospitals and institutions." 20 U. S. C. §§ 1401(16) and (17).

We need not decide the extent of the guarantee of a free appropriate public education Congress intended to impose under § 504. We note the uncertainty regarding the reach of § 504 to emphasize that it is only in the EHA that Congress specified the rights and remedies available to a handicapped child seeking access to public education. Even assuming that the reach of § 504 is coextensive with that of the EHA, there is no doubt that the remedies, rights, and procedures Congress set out in the EHA are the ones it intended to apply to a handicapped child's claim to a free appropriate public education. We are satisfied that Congress did not intend a handicapped child to be able to circumvent the requirements or supplement the remedies of the EHA by resort to the general antidiscrimination provision of § 504.

There is no suggestion that § 504 adds anything to petitioners' substantive right to a free appropriate public education. The only elements added by § 504 are the possibility of circumventing EHA administrative procedures and going straight to court with a § 504 claim, the possibility of a damages award in cases where no such award is available under the EHA, and attorney's fees. As discussed above, Congress' intent to place on local and state educational agencies the responsibility for determining the most appropriate educational plan for a handicapped child is clear. To the extent § 504 otherwise would allow a plaintiff to circumvent that state procedure, we are satisfied that the remedy conflicts with Congress' intent in the EHA.

Congress did not explain the absence of a provision for a damages remedy and attorney's fees in the EHA. Several references in the statute itself and in its legislative history, however, indicate that the omissions were in response to Congress' awareness of the financial burden already imposed on States by the responsibility of providing education for handicapped children. As noted above, one of the stated purposes of the statute was to relieve this financial burden. Discussions of the EHA by its proponents reflect Congress' intent to "make every resource, or as much as possible, available to the direct activities and the direct programs that are going to benefit the handicapped." 121 Cong. Rec. 19501 (1975) (remarks of Sen. Dole). The Act appears to represent Congress' judgment that the best way to ensure a free appropriate public education for handicapped children is to clarify and make enforceable the rights of those children while at the same time endeavoring to relieve the financial burden imposed on the agencies responsible to guarantee those rights. Where § 504 adds nothing to the substantive rights of a handicapped child, we cannot believe that Congress intended to have the careful balance struck in the EHA upset by reliance on § 504 for otherwise unavailable damages or for an award of attorney's fees.

We emphasize the narrowness of our holding. We do not address a situation where the EHA is not available or where § 504 guarantees substantive rights greater than those available under the EHA. We hold only that where, as here, whatever remedy might be provided under § 504 is provided with more clarity and precision under the EHA, a plaintiff may not circumvent or enlarge on the remedies available under the EHA by resort to § 504.

. . . .

Justice Brennan, with whom Justice Marshall and Justice Stevens join, dissenting.

In this case we are called upon to analyze the interaction among five statutory provisions: § 1 of the Civil Rights Act of 1871, as amended, 42 U.S.C. § 1983; § 2 of the Civil Rights Attorney's Fees Awards Act of 1976, 42 U.S.C. § 1988; § 504 of the Rehabilitation Act of 1973, as amended, 29 U.S.C. § 794; § 505(b) of the Rehabilitation Act, 29 U.S.C. § 794a(b); and § 615(e)(2) of the Education of the Handicapped Act (EHA or Act), as added, 89 Stat. 789, 20 U.S.C. § 1415(e)(2).

. . . .

. . . § 1988 provides that the prevailing party in an action prosecuted under § 1983 may be awarded reasonable attorney's fees. Similarly, §§ 504 and 505(b) of the Rehabilitation Act provide a cause of action and attorney's fees, respectively, to an individual who, "solely by reason of his handicap," has been "excluded from the participation in, . . . denied the benefits of, . . . [or] subjected to discrimination under any program or activity receiving Federal financial assistance." Finally, § 615(e)(2) of the EHA authorizes judicial review of the States' provision of "free appropriate public education" to handicapped children. Unlike 42 U.S.C. § 1983 and § 504 of the Rehabilitation Act, however, § 615(e)(2) has no counterpart in the EHA authorizing the award of attorney's fees to prevailing parties.

Petitioners challenge Rhode Island's discriminatory failure to afford Thomas F. Smith III access to certain educational programs made available to other handicapped children. As the Court recognizes, this challenge states a meritorious claim under the EHA and a substantial claim under the Equal Protection Clause of the Fourteenth Amendment. In addition, petitioners' claim appears to fall squarely within the terms of § 504 of the Rehabilitation Act. Consequently, if §§ 504 and 1983 are available as bases for petitioners' action, petitioners are entitled to recover reasonable attorney's fees under § 1988 and, at a minimum, to be given an opportunity to establish the meritoriousness of their § 504 claim.

To determine whether § 504 or § 1983 is available, each provision must be read together with the EHA.[2] As the Court demonstrates, in enacting the EHA, Congress surely intended that individuals with claims covered by that Act would pursue relief through the administrative channels that the Act established before seeking redress in court. It would make little sense for Congress to have established such a detailed and comprehensive administrative system and yet allow individuals to bypass the

2. Some claims covered by the EHA are also grounded in the Constitution and hence could be pursued under § 1983. Others are nonconstitutional claims cognizable under § 504. Still others are nonconstitutional claims cognizable only under the EHA. This case is concerned only with claims that have as a substantive basis both the EHA and either the Constitution or § 504.

system, at their option, by bringing suits directly to the courts under either § 504 or § 1983. To that extent, therefore, the statutes before us are in conflict with one another. Accordingly, our guide must be the familiar principle of statutory construction that conflicting statutes should be interpreted so as to give effect to each but to allow a later enacted, more specific statute to amend an earlier, more general statute only to the extent of the repugnancy between the two statutes. We must, therefore, construe the statutory provisions at issue here so as to promote the congressional intent underlying the EHA, which was enacted after §§ 504 and 1983 and which is addressed specifically to the problems facing handicapped schoolchildren. At the same time, however, we must preserve those aspects of §§ 504 and 1983 that are not in irreconcilable conflict with the EHA.

The natural resolution of the conflict between the EHA, on the one hand, and §§ 504 and 1983, on the other, is to require a plaintiff with a claim covered by the EHA to pursue relief through the administrative channels established by that Act before seeking redress in the courts under § 504 or § 1983. Under this resolution, the integrity of the EHA is preserved entirely, and yet §§ 504 and 1983 are also preserved to the extent that they do not undermine the EHA. Although the primary function of §§ 504 and 1983 is to provide direct access to the courts for certain types of claims, these provisions also operate, as this case demonstrates, to identify those types of causes of action for which Congress has authorized the award of attorney's fees to prevailing parties. Significantly, this function does not in any way conflict with the goals or operation of the EHA. There is no basis, therefore, for concluding that either § 504 or § 1983 is unavailable for this limited purpose.

The Court, however, has responded to the conflict among these statutes by restricting the applicability of §§ 504 and 1983 far more than is necessary to resolve their inconsistency. Indeed, the Court holds that both §§ 504 and 1983 are wholly unavailable to individuals seeking to secure their rights to a free appropriate public education, despite the fact that the terms and intent of Congress in enacting each of these provisions unquestionably extend to many of those claims. As a result, the Court finds that attorney's fees, which would otherwise be available to those individuals under §§ 505(b) and 1988, are now unavailable. Yet the Court recognizes that there is absolutely no indication in the language of the EHA or in the Act's legislative history that Congress meant to effect such a repeal, let alone any indication that Congress specifically intended to bar the recovery of attorney's fees for parties that prevail in this type of action. The Court's rationale for effectively repealing §§ 504, 505(b), 1983, and 1988 to the extent that they cover petitioners' claim is that the comprehensiveness and detail with which the EHA addresses the problem of providing schooling to handicapped children implies that Congress intended to repeal all other remedies that overlap with the EHA, even if they do not conflict with the EHA.

....

In sum, the Court's conclusion that the EHA repealed the availability of §§ 504 and 1983 to individuals seeking a free appropriate public education runs counter to well-established principles of statutory interpretation. It finds no support in the terms or legislative history of the EHA. And, most importantly, it undermines the intent of Congress in enacting both §§ 505(b) and 1988. . . . [W]ith today's decision coming as it does after Congress has spoken on the subject of attorney's fees, Congress will now have to take the time to revisit the matter. And until it does, the handicapped children of this country whose difficulties are compounded by discrimination and by other deprivations of constitutional rights will have to pay the costs. It is at best ironic that the Court has managed to impose this burden on handicapped children in the course of interpreting a statute wholly intended to promote the educational rights of those children.

Notes, Comments, and Questions

1. As Justice Brennan suggested it might, Congress did "revisit the matter" soon after *Smith*, and in 1986, passed the Handicapped Children's Protection Act of 1986, Pub. L. No. 99-372, 100 Stat. 796 (1986) (HCPA). In addition to permitting prevailing parties to recover attorneys fees in IDEA cases, the statute now reads:

> Nothing in this Chapter be construed to restrict or limit the rights, procedures, and remedies available under the Constitution, the Americans with Disabilities Act of 1990, title V of the Rehabilitation Act of 1973, or other Federal laws protecting the rights of children with disabilities, except that before the filing of a civil action under such laws seeking relief that is also available under this subchapter, the procedures under subsections (f) and (g) shall be exhausted to the same extent as would be required had the action been brought under this subchapter.

20 U.S.C. § 1415(l) (2012). Congress thus made clear that the IDEA does not preclude claims on behalf of children with disabilities pursuant to the Constitution, Section 504, the ADA, or other laws protecting the rights of children with disabilities.

2. Following the passage of the HCPA, courts have agreed that a child with a disability can pursue claims under Section 504 and the ADA, even if relief is available under the IDEA, as long as the plaintiff exhausts IDEA's administrative remedies. *See, e.g.*, Mark H. v. Lemahieu, 513 F.3d 922, 935 (9th Cir. 2007) (ruling that "availability of relief under the IDEA does not limit the availability of a damages remedy under § 504 . . . ."); J.L. v. Ambridge Area Sch. Dist., 622 F. Supp. 2d 257, 272, 273 (W.D. Pa. 2008) (allowing plaintiffs to pursue ADA and 504 claims even though they did not explicitly raise them in the impartial hearing); D.L. v. Waukee Cmty. Sch. Dist., 578 F. Supp. 2d 1178, 1189 (S.D. Iowa 2008) (stating that plaintiffs cannot proceed with Section 504 claims until they exhaust their IDEA administrative remedies).

3. Section 1415(l) does not list Section 1983 as one of the statutes not restricted by the IDEA. This omission has resulted in disagreement among the courts over whether plaintiffs can use Section 1983 to enforce violations of the IDEA. If plaintiffs can use Section 1983 to enforce the IDEA, they can recover compensatory monetary damages because, as opposed to the IDEA, compensatory monetary damages are available to

successful Section 1983 claimants. Three cases follow. The first finds that Section 1983 cannot be used to enforce the IDEA, the second finds that it can, and the third overrules an earlier case that had ruled that Section 1983 could be used to enforce the IDEA.

Sellers v. Sch. Bd. of Manassas, Va.

141 F.3d 524 (6th Cir. 1988)

[The facts of the case are described in the *Sellers* excerpt at the beginning of Section One.]

....

IV.

The Sellers next contend that they still may recover compensatory and punitive damages under 42 U.S.C. § 1983. They argue that other courts have recognized both that Section 1983 actions may be premised on IDEA violations, and that plaintiffs may recover monetary damages pursuant to such actions. We disagree. Because IDEA provides a comprehensive remedial scheme for violations of its own requirements, we hold that parties may not sue under section 1983 for an IDEA violation.

A.

....

The Sellers argue ... that the 1986 amendments to EHA, enacted in response to the *Smith* decision, demonstrate a clear congressional intent that plaintiffs once again be permitted to sue under section 1983 for IDEA violations. We disagree. A closer reading of the 1986 provision relied upon by the Sellers—20 U.S.C. § 1415(f) [currently § 1415(l)]—reveals no intent that parties be able to bypass the remedies provided in IDEA by suing instead under section 1983 for an IDEA violation.

... Concededly, section 1415(f) overrules much of *Smith*'s holding. The amendment specifically rejects the *Smith* Court's interpretation of EHA as precluding claims under the Constitution or the Rehabilitation Act that are virtually identical to EHA claims. But while section 1415(f) explicitly preserves remedies under the Constitution, the Rehabilitation Act, and specified "other" statutes, it simply fails to mention section 1983. The reference to "other" statutes protecting the rights of disabled children cannot naturally be read to include 42 U.S.C. § 1983, a statute which speaks generally and mentions neither disability nor youth. By preserving rights and remedies "under the Constitution," section 1415(f) does permit plaintiffs to resort to section 1983 for *constitutional* violations, notwithstanding the similarity of such claims to those stated directly under IDEA. But section 1415(f) does not permit plaintiffs to sue under section 1983 for an IDEA violation, which is *statutory* in nature. Nothing in section 1415(f) overrules the Court's decision in *Smith* to the extent it held that Congress intended IDEA to provide the sole remedies for violations of that same statute. If Congress meant to overrule *Smith* on this significant point, it certainly chose an oblique and essentially implausible means of doing so.

The different standards of liability applicable to constitutional equal protection claims and to statutory IDEA claims confirm our interpretation of section 1415(f). Under IDEA, the simple failure to provide a child with a free appropriate public education constitutes a violation of the statute. By contrast, plaintiffs must meet a higher standard of liability to prevail on a constitutional claim. The Supreme Court's decision in *Washington v. Davis*, 426 U.S. 229, 239 . . . (1976), requires that an equal protection claim be supported by evidence of purposeful discrimination. In the context of education of disabled children, *Washington*'s purpose requirement is similar to that recognized under section 504 of the Rehabilitation Act. And even if a plaintiff can prove a school board intended to treat children differently because of their disabilities, another hurdle would remain. Because the Supreme Court has yet to classify disabled persons as a suspect class, *see City of Cleburne v. Cleburne Living Ctr., Inc.*, 473 U.S. 432, 445–46 . . . (1985), and because the Court also has not identified education as a fundamental right, *San Antonio Indep. Sch. Dist. v. Rodriguez*, 411 U.S. 1, 33–37 . . . (1973), a plaintiff in this context would have to prove that a school board's decision was without any rational basis. Naturally school boards will be subject to liability for statutory IDEA violations much more frequently than for similarly pled constitutional claims. It is easy therefore to understand why Congress intended to subject school boards to the more expansive remedies available under section 1983 for their more culpable constitutional failures, yet not for breaches of IDEA. Section 1415(f) sensibly retains IDEA's comprehensive scheme as the remedy for violations of that Act.

The Sellers nevertheless attempt to supplement, and thereby evade, the limited textual command of section 1415(f) by relying on the legislative history of the 1986 amendments. Even if the text were not the sole authoritative source of section 1415(f)'s meaning, the legislative history would still fail to support the proposition that Congress intended that plaintiffs be able to sue under section 1983 for IDEA violations. The Sellers first rely on the following excerpt from the House Committee Report:

> In sum, since 1978, it has been Congress' intent to permit parents or guardians to pursue the rights of handicapped children through EHA, section 504, and section 1983. . . . Congressional intent was ignored by the U.S. Supreme Court when, on July 5, 1984, it handed down its decision in *Smith v. Robinson*.

H.R. Rep. No. 99-296, at 4 (1985). The Sellers also support their argument with a brief excerpt from the House Conference Report, which states: "It is the conferees' intent that actions brought under 42 U.S.C. 1983 are governed by this provision." H.R. Conf. Rep. No. 9-687, at 7 (1986), *reprinted in* 1986 U.S.C.C.A.N. 1807, 1809.

Nothing in these portions of the legislative history contradicts our construction, grounded in the text of section 1415(f). The House Reports indicate a legislative intent that disabled children be able to protect their rights through IDEA, the Rehabilitation Act, other statutes protecting the rights of disabled children, and the Constitution itself. The Reports naturally refer to section 1983, as it supplies disabled children and their parents or guardians with a private right of action for constitutional violations. Again, however, even when read in the light most favorable to the Sellers' claims, these portions of the House Reports fail to indicate any legislative intent with respect to section 1983 claims premised on IDEA violations. When construed in their most natural form, the excerpts demonstrate the unremarkable proposition that Congress intended section 1415(f) to restore the ability of disabled children and their parents or guardians to utilize section 1983 to protect constitutional rights.

. . . .

. . . In light of the Court's holding in *Smith*, [and] section 1415(f)'s effect on that decision . . . , we hold that the Sellers cannot sue under section 1983 for alleged IDEA violations. As a result, we reject their attempt to recover compensatory and punitive damages unavailable in an action directly under IDEA. . . .

. . . .

Mrs. W. v. Tirozzi

832 F.2d 748 (2d Cir. 1987)

Cardamone, Circuit Judge:

. . . .

BACKGROUND

I *The Statutory Framework*

. . . .

Prior to 1986 no express private right of action was found in the EHA. In response to the Supreme Court's decision in *Smith*, Congress in 1986 added § 1415(f) [currently § 1415(l)] . . . . The new § 1415(f) states that the provisions of the EHA do not provide the exclusive avenue for redress available to handicapped children, and that § 504 of the Rehabilitation Act of 1973, and 42 U.S.C. § 1983, and other constitutional or statutory provisions may be used as remedies to enforce EHA educational rights, subject to the Act's existing exhaustion requirements.

. . . .

II *Facts*

. . . Mrs. W. and Mrs. B., parents of handicapped children, and Connecticut Legal Services . . . , commenced this civil rights action pursuant to 42 U.S.C. § 1983 (1982), on their own behalf and on behalf of others similarly situated, against the Connecticut State Board of Education, Gerald N. Tirozzi, the Connecticut Commissioner of Education, and the members of the Connecticut State Board of Education . . . . Plaintiffs' complaint alleges that the defendants' failure to make bona fide attempts to resolve their complaints against the Bridgeport Board of Education . . . violates the . . . [IDEA], § 504 of the Rehabilitation Act of 1973, 29 U.S.C. § 794 (1982), and the Due Process and Equal Protection clauses of the Fourteenth Amendment. . . .

. . . .

III *The Proceedings Below*

As a result of what they perceived as inadequacies in Connecticut's treatment of their complaints, plaintiffs instituted this § 1983 action . . . requesting declaratory and injunctive relief. The complaint does not seek judicial review of the State Board's substantive decisions, but requests instead an injunction requiring defendants to formulate and implement adequate complaint resolution procedures.

Defendants moved for a judgment on the pleadings claiming that plaintiffs have no private right of action under § 1983. . . . The district court ruled that since the EHA is a comprehensive remedial statute, no private right of action lies against defendants . . . and dismissed plaintiffs' complaint. This appeal followed. We reverse and remand for further proceedings on the merits.

DISCUSSION

I *Private Right of Action*

Plaintiffs brought their § 1983 action based on alleged violations of the Act, of § 504 of the Rehabilitation Act of 1973, and of the Due Process and Equal Protection clauses. . . . It is well settled that § 1983 does not create any new substantive rights, but merely provides a federal cause of action for violations of certain federal rights. . . .

The availability of § 1983 federal jurisdiction to enforce federal statutory violations is limited by two exceptions. No such action is available when Congress has foreclosed enforcement of the statute in the statute itself, or when a statutory remedial scheme is so comprehensive that there is an implication that it provides the exclusive remedy foreclosing all other remedies. Of course, even the existence of a comprehensive remedial scheme will not bar resort to § 1983, if Congress states that it did not want its enactment construed to restrict or limit the remedies otherwise available.

Applying these rules to the EHA's extensive remedial scheme, the Supreme Court concluded in 1984 that the Act was the exclusive avenue through which a plaintiff may assert an EHA, a § 504, or an equal protection claim to a publicly financed special education. *Smith*, 468 U.S. at 1013, 1019. Accordingly, it held that a plaintiff is precluded from resorting to [a] § 1983 cause of action or obtaining attorneys' fees pursuant to 42 U.S.C. § 1988 based on such claims. *Id.* at 1009–13. The Court reasoned that the comprehensiveness and detail with which the Act addressed the provision of special education for handicapped children indicated that Congress wanted to limit remedies to those explicitly provided for. Understandably, the district court adopted this position in the instant case and held that the EHA's comprehensive nature precluded present plaintiffs from instituting a private right of action under § 1983.

But, as noted, Congress amended the EHA in 1986 and enacted the Handicapped Children's Protection Act of 1986. In section 3 of that Act, Congress added . . . [Section 1415(l)] . . . . By enacting this nonexclusivity provision Congress expressly overruled *Smith*.

Congress stated that § 1415(f) was designed to "reestablish statutory rights repealed by the U.S. Supreme Court in *Smith v. Robinson*" and to "*reaffirm*, in light of this decision, the viability of section 504, 42 U.S.C. 1983, and other statutes as separate vehicles for ensuring the rights of handicapped children." H.R. Rep. No. 296, 99th Cong., 1st Sess. 4 (1985) (hereinafter 1985 House Report); *see also id.* at 3 (need for legislation), 6 (effect on *Smith*); S. Rep. No. 112, 99th Cong., 2d Sess. 2–3, *reprinted in* 1986 U.S. Code Cong. & Admin. News 1798, 1799–1800 (discussing *Smith*) (1986 Senate Report).

Congress stressed that its original aim had been to allow resort to other judicial remedies for claims based on the EHA. *See* 1985 House Report, *supra*, at 7; 1986 Senate Report, *supra*, at 15; *see also Handicapped Children's Protection Act of 1985: Hearings on S.415 Before the Subcomm. on the Handicapped of the Senate Comm. on Labor and Human Resources*, 99th Cong., 1st Sess. 2 (1985) (opening statement of Senator Weicker) (Section 1415(f) "is intended to be a simple restoration and clarification of congressional intent.") Moreover, Congress specifically identified § 1983, § 504 of the Rehabilitation Act of 1973, and the Constitution as other sources of rights and remedies in special education cases. *See* 20 U.S.C. § 1415(f); H.R. Conf. Rep. No. 687, 99th Cong., 2d Sess. 7, *reprinted in* 1986 U.S. Code Cong. & Admin. News 1807, 1809. ("It is the conferees' intent that actions brought under 42 U.S.C. 1983 are governed by this provision."); 1985 House Report, *supra*, at 3 ("Section 1983 prohibits, among other things, an agency acting under color of state law from abridging a handicapped person's rights under the Constitution.")

. . . .

In light of this clear legislative history, we hold that parents are entitled to bring a § 1983 action based on alleged violations of the EHA or the Due Process and Equal Protection clauses of the federal Constitution. Thus, the district court erred when it dismissed plaintiffs' complaint on the ground that no private right of action could be maintained other than by way of an EHA suit. Plaintiffs may therefore pursue their § 1983 action.

. . . .

A.W. v. Jersey City Pub. Sch.

486 F.3d 791 (3d Cir. 2007)

RENDELL, Circuit Judge.

In this appeal, we reexamine our holding in *W.B. v. Matula*, 67 F.3d 484 (3d Cir. 1995), that an action can be maintained against school officials under 42 U.S.C. § 1983 for violations of the Individuals with Disabilities Education Act ("IDEA"). We do so in light of the Supreme Court's reasoning in *City of Rancho Palos Verdes v. Abrams*, 544 U.S. 113 . . . (2005), regarding the availability of § 1983 to redress violations of federal statutory rights and the opinions of our sister courts of appeals that have questioned *Matula*.

The District Court, relying on *Matula*, held that the alleged violations of plaintiff's rights were actionable under § 1983 and denied defendants' motion for summary judgment on the ground of qualified immunity, concluding that plaintiff's cause of action could be maintained and there was sufficient evidence for a jury to find that defendants violated clearly established federal law. We will reverse.

....

III. DISCUSSION

....

... In light of the recent, clear guidance provided by the Supreme Court in *City of Rancho Palos Verdes* ... regarding the availability of § 1983 to remedy statutory violations, and the well-reasoned opinions of the Courts of Appeals for the Fourth and Tenth Circuits in *Sellers v. School Board of Manassas, Virginia*, 141 F.3d 524 (4th Cir. 1998), and *Padilla v. School District No. 1*, 233 F.3d 1268, 1273 (10th Cir. 2000), rejecting our holding in *Matula*, we now conclude that we should not continue to adhere to the principle we established in *Matula*.

B. *W.B. v. Matula*

Matula involved the precise issue before us: can school officials be sued pursuant to § 1983 based on alleged violations of a child's rights secured by the IDEA. In addressing this question, we strove to determine Congress' intent, noting the distinction regarding the use of § 1983 to redress statutory, rather than constitutional, violations:

> When the rights at issue are statutory, however, a § 1983 action is impermissible when "Congress intended to foreclose such private enforcement." *Wright v. Roanoke Redevelopment & Housing Authority*, 479 U.S. 418, 423 ... (1987). Such an intent is generally found either in the express language of a statute or where a statutory remedial scheme is so comprehensive that an intent to prohibit enforcement other than by the statute's own means may be inferred. *Id.*

Matula, 67 F.3d at 493.

In *Matula*, we concerned ourselves with the jurisprudential and legislative directives regarding the availability of relief for IDEA violations. We noted that in *Smith v. Robinson* the Supreme Court held that the IDEA provided the exclusive means by which parents and children could remedy violations of the rights guaranteed therein, and that no constitutional claim would be therefore allowed.... However, in response to this decision, Congress enacted § 1415(*l*) of the IDEA, to countermand *Smith* and make clear that actions *can* be maintained under the Constitution or under federal laws protecting the rights of children with disabilities notwithstanding the fact that the IDEA also protects these rights....

In an attempt to ascertain the significance of Congress' addition of this provision, we reviewed its legislative history in some detail:

> The Senate Report [on § 1415(*l*)] discussed *Smith* at length, including quoting favorably from the *Smith* dissent, *see* S.Rep. No. 99–112, 99th Cong., 2d Sess. (1986), *reprinted in* 1986 U.S.C.C.A.N. 1798, 1799 ("Senate Report"). The House Conference Report stated "[i]t is the conferees' intent that actions

> brought under 42 U.S.C. 1983 are governed by [§ 1415(*l*)]." H.R.Conf.Rep. No. 99–687, 99th Cong., 2d Sess. (1986); 1986 U.S.C.C.A.N. 1807, 1809. In addition, the House Report made explicit that "since 1978, it has been Congress' intent to permit parents or guardians to pursue the rights of handicapped children through EHA, section 504, *and section 1983*. . . . Congressional intent was ignored by the U.S. Supreme Court when . . . it handed down its decision in *Smith v. Robinson.* " H.R.Rep. No. 99–296, 99th Cong., 1st Sess. 4 (1985) ("House Report") (first emphasis added). Section 1415[(*l*)] was thus enacted to "reaffirm, in light of [*Smith*], the viability of section 504, 42 U.S.C 1983, and other statutes as separate vehicles for ensuring the rights of handicapped children." *Id.*

Id. at 494. In *Matula*, we concluded that "[f]ar from inferring a congressional intent to *prevent* § 1983 actions predicated on IDEA then, we conclude that Congress explicitly *approved* such actions." *Id.*

. . . .

However, following *Matula*, reasonable minds have differed as to the correctness of our interpretation of the congressional reaction to *Smith v. Robinson* embodied in § 1415(*l*). In addition, over the past decade, the Supreme Court has further refined its guidance as to how we should decide whether § 1983 relief is available for violations of statutory rights, most recently in *City of Rancho Palos Verdes v. Abrams*, 544 U.S. 113, 120 . . . (2005). All of these developments since *Matula* have informed our analysis in a way that requires us to reconsider our view.

. . . .

C. *Rancho Palos Verdes*

. . . .

[In Rancho Palos Verdes], [t]he Court reiterated that to sustain a § 1983 action for the violation of a statutory right, a plaintiff must demonstrate that the federal statute creates an individually enforceable right in the class of beneficiaries to which he belongs. This demonstration creates a rebuttable presumption that the right is enforceable under § 1983. However, the "defendant may defeat this presumption by demonstrating that Congress did not intend that remedy for a newly created right." *Rancho Palos Verdes*, 544 U.S. at 120. "[E]vidence of such congressional intent may be found directly in the statute creating the right, or inferred from the statute's creation of a 'comprehensive enforcement scheme that is incompatible with individual enforcement under § 1983.'" *Id.*

In discussing its prior decisions on the availability of § 1983 as a remedy for violations of statutory rights, the Court noted that in *all* of the cases in which it found § 1983 available to provide a remedy for a violation of statutory rights, the statute at issue did not contain a private judicial remedy (or, in most of the cases, even a private administrative remedy). . . .

The Court noted the significance of Congress' inclusion of private remedial provisions in the statute: it is ordinarily an indication that Congress did not intend "to leave open a more expansive remedy under § 1983." *Id.* However, the "ordinary inference that the remedy provided in the statute is exclusive" can be overcome by "textual indication, express or implicit, that the remedy is to complement, rather than supplant, § 1983." *Id.* at 122. In framing the issue in this way, the Court seems to have upended the *Blessing* "presumption," with the inclusion of a private remedy being the pivotal factor. The inclusion of a private remedy gives rise to a presumption that this remedy is to be exclusive. This presumption may be defeated by a "textual" showing that the remedy was not intended to be comprehensive.

. . . .

1. The IDEA

Guided by the method of analysis outlined in *Rancho Palos Verdes*, we now look to the IDEA to determine whether Congress intended to allow rights granted by the IDEA to be remedied through a § 1983 action. For purposes of this appeal, the parties do not dispute that the IDEA creates individually enforceable rights in the class of beneficiaries to which A.W. belongs. Therefore, we presume that Congress intended § 1983 to be an available remedy for violations of the IDEA. Defendants, however, can rebut this presumption by showing that Congress did not so intend. Accordingly, we look to whether there is an express, private means of redress in the IDEA itself, which, absent some textual indication to the contrary, would indicate that Congress did not intend to leave open a more expansive remedy under § 1983.

Under the IDEA, any aggrieved party may "present a complaint . . . with respect to any matter relating to the identification, evaluation, or educational placement of the child, or the provision of a free appropriate public education to such child." 20 U.S.C. § 1415(b)(6). The party may elect to have the complaint investigated by the state educational agency, *see* 34 C.F.R. § 300.661, or avail itself of an "impartial due process hearing," 20 U.S.C. § 1415(f). Any party aggrieved by the outcome of the due process hearing "shall have the right to bring a civil action with respect to the complaint presented . . . in a district court of the United States, without regard to the amount in controversy." 20 U.S.C. § 1415(i)(2)(A). This action must be initiated within 90 days from the date of the hearing officer's decision. § 1415(i)(2)(B). The district court is authorized to grant "such relief as the court determines is appropriate," including attorneys' fees, reimbursement for a private educational placement, and compensatory education. We conclude that these provisions of the IDEA create an express, private means of redress. This, then, means that a § 1983 action is not available to remedy violations of IDEA-created rights, absent some "textual indication, express or implicit, that the [statutory] remedy is to complement, rather than supplant, § 1983." *Rancho Palos Verdes*, 544 U.S. at 122.

. . . .

We agree with the reasoning of the Courts of Appeals for the Fourth and Tenth Circuits, to say nothing of that of the Supreme Court in *Smith*, regarding the comprehensive nature of the IDEA's remedial scheme. The holding in *Smith*, although superseded in part by the passage of § 1415(*l*) of the IDEA, was not overruled to the extent that the Court found that the IDEA provides a comprehensive remedial scheme. Indeed, since *Smith*, the Court has continued to refer to the IDEA as an example of a statutory enforcement scheme that precludes a § 1983 remedy. *See Rancho Palos Verdes*, 544 U.S. at 121; *Blessing v. Freestone*, 520 U.S. 329, 347–48 ... (1997); *Wright v. Roanoke Redev. & Hous. Auth.*, 479 U.S. 418, 423–24, 427 ... (1987). The IDEA includes a judicial remedy for violations of any right "relating to the identification, evaluation, or educational placement of [a] child, or the provision of a free appropriate public education to such child." § 1415(b)(6). Given this comprehensive scheme, Congress did not intend § 1983 to be available to remedy violations of the IDEA such as those alleged by A.W.

....

Notes, Comments, and Questions

1. Four courts of appeals have ruled that Section 1983 is not available to enforce the IDEA, four courts of appeals have issued conflicting rulings, and one court of appeals has ruled that Section 1983 can be used to enforce Section 1983. How would you rule?

The First, Third, Fourth, and Tenth Circuit Courts of Appeals have ruled that Section 1983 is not available to enforce the IDEA:

First Circuit: Diaz-Fonseca v. Puerto Rico, 451 F.3d 13, 28 (1st Cir. 2006) (holding that "§ 1983 cannot be used to escape the strictures on damages under the IDEA").

Third Circuit: A.W. v. Jersey City Pub. Sch., 486 F.3d 791, 803 (3d Cir. 2007) (ruling that "Congress did not intend § 1983 to be available to remedy violations of the IDEA").

Fourth Circuit: J.S. v. Isle of Wight Cnty. Sch. Bd., 402 F.3d 468, 480 (4th Cir. 2005) ("Having obtained exactly what he was entitled to receive under the IDEA, J.S. cannot reasonably maintain that a deficiency in the statute's remedial scheme justifies an enforcement action under § 1983."); Sellers v. Sch. Bd. of Manassas, 141 F.3d 524, 525 (4th Cir. 1998) (ruling that plaintiffs "cannot sue under Section 1983 for IDEA violations.").

Tenth Circuit: Padilla v. Sch. Dist. No. 1, 233 F.3d 1268, 1274 (10th Cir. 2000) (ruling that *Smith* is "alive and well insofar as it asserts that § 1983 may not be used to remedy IDEA violations.").

The Second, Sixth, Seventh, Eighth, and Eleventh Circuit Courts of Appeals have issued conflicting rulings:

Second Circuit: Subsequent to *Mrs. W.*, two cases ruled that Section 1983 is available to enforce the IDEA. *See* Taylor v. Vt. Dep't of Educ., 313 F.3d 768, 786 n. 14 (2d Cir. 2002) ("Although monetary damages are not available under the IDEA itself, a plaintiff may recover monetary damages for a violation of the IDEA pursuant to § 1983."); Weixel v. Bd. of Educ. of the City of N.Y., 287 F.3d 138, 151 (2d

Cir. 2002) ("Because . . . plaintiffs have stated causes of action under Section 504/ ADA and the IDEA, the district court erred in dismissing their claims for damages under Section 1983."). On the other hand, two other cases stated that the use of Section 1983 to enforce the IDEA is limited to violations of procedural rights. *See* Polera v. Bd. of Educ. of Newburgh Enlarged City Sch. Dist., 288 F.3d 478, 483 n. 5 (2d Cir. 2002) ("We have held that monetary damages are available in claims brought pursuant to 42 U.S.C. § 1983 for denial of access to administrative remedies under the IDEA's predecessor statute, the EHA.") (citing Quackenbush v. Johnson City Sch. Dist., 716 F.2d 141, 148 (2d Cir. 1983), *cert. denied*, 465 U.S. 1071 (1974) (pre-*Smith* case ruling that Section 1983 could be used to enforce IDEA procedural rights).

Sixth Circuit: The Sixth Circuit has ruled that Section 1983 can be used to enforce the IDEA but not to recover damages. *See* Gean v. Hattaway, 330 F.3d 758, 773 (6th Cir. 2003) (allowing plaintiffs to bring a Section 1983 claim based on the IDEA to recover restitution of Social Security benefits defendants used to pay for their child's education); Crocker v. Tenn. Secondary Sch. Ass'n, 980 F.2d 382, 387 (6th Cir. 1992) (allowing plaintiff to bring a Section 1983 action to enforce the IDEA but not to recover general damages).

Seventh Circuit: In *Marie O. v. Edgar*, 131 F.3d 610 (7th Cir. 1997), the court considered whether Section 1983 could be used to enforce Part H (currently Part C) of the IDEA relating to children from birth to age three. In answering in the affirmative, the court stated that Section 1983 is available to enforce the IDEA. *Id.* at 622. On the other hand, in *Anderson v. Thompson*, 658 F.2d 1205, 1217 (7th Cir. 1981), the court ruled, in a pre-*Smith* case, that the IDEA was an exclusive remedy that could not be enforced through Section 1983.

Eighth Circuit: Several Eighth Circuit cases have ruled that Section 1983 cannot be used to enforce the IDEA; one earlier case disagrees. *See* Bradley v. Ark. Dep't of Educ., 301 F.3d 952, 957 (8th Cir. 2002) (ruling that plaintiffs cannot recover damages under a Section 1983 claim for IDEA violations); Heidemann v. Rother, 84 F.3d 1021, 1033 (8th Cir. 1996) (ruling that plaintiff may not pursue alleged IDEA violations in a Section 1983 action because general and punitive damages for the type of injury plaintiff alleges are not available under the IDEA); Hoekstra v. Indep. Sch. Dist. No. 238, 103 F.3d 624, 625–26 (8th Cir. 1996), *cert. denied*, 520 U.S. 1024 (1997) (ruling that plaintiffs could not pursue Section 1983 action to enforce the IDEA); Digre v. Roseville Sch. Indep. Dist. No, 623, 841 F.2d 245, 249 (8th Cir. 1988) (ruling that Section 1983 is available to remedy violations of the EHA).

Eleventh Circuit: The Eleventh Circuit ruled that Section 1983 is the appropriate vehicle for enforcing IDEA procedural rights. Manecke v. Sch. Bd. of Pinellas Cnty., 762 F.2d 912, 918 (11th Cir. 1985), *cert. denied*, 474 U.S. 1062 (1986) ("[W]here, as here, a party is denied due process by effectively being denied access 'to the carefully tailored administrative and judicial mechanism' found in the EHA, that party may seek relief under § 1983.").

Except for *A.W.*, the cases described in this note were decided before *Ranchos Palos Verdes*. Do you think they would have been decided differently had they been decided after *Rancho Palos Verdes*?

2. The plain language of Section 1415(l) does not include Section 1983, but as described in *Tirozzi*, the legislative history does include Section 1983 as a statute that could be utilized to protect the rights of children with disabilities. How did the court in *Sellers* explain this difference? When the language of a statute and its legislative history differ, which should prevail?

3. Should the courts allow plaintiffs to use Section 1983 to challenge a state's failure to implement the IDEA's administrative procedures but preclude the use of Section 1983 to challenge violations of substantive IDEA rights? If so, does this resolve the apparent conflict between *Sellers*, in which the plaintiffs alleged substantive violations, and *Mrs. W.*, in which the plaintiffs alleged failure to adopt appropriate administrative proceedings? As we have seen, the basis for ruling that Section 1983 is not available to remedy IDEA violations is that the IDEA contains a comprehensive remedial scheme sufficient to supplant Section 1983. In *Blessing v. Freestone*, 520 U.S. 329 (1997), the Court stated:

> Only twice have we found a remedial scheme sufficiently comprehensive to supplant § 1983: in *Sea Clammers*, *supra*, and *Smith* .... [I]n *Smith*, the review scheme in the Education of the Handicapped Act permitted aggrieved individuals to invoke "carefully tailored" local administrative procedures followed by federal judicial review. We reasoned that Congress could not possibly have wanted parents to skip these procedures and go straight to court by way of § 1983, since that would have "render[ed] superfluous most of the detailed procedural protections outlined in the statute." *Id.* at 1011....

Id. at 347. But if a state has not implemented all or part of the administrative scheme, should it be protected from Section 1983 claims to enforce the IDEA? Consider the Second Circuit's perspective on this:

> After examining both ... [the IDEA and Section 1983] as well as the circumstances of this case, we believe and conclude that the better solution is to permit § 1983 to supply the right of action to a plaintiff who has been denied procedural safeguards under § 1415 and who, as a result thereof, has not received the findings and decision following the impartial due process hearing contemplated by § 1415.... By limiting relief under § 1415(e)(2) only to parties aggrieved by the findings and decision of the administrative agency, Congress rather clearly disclosed its intention that that section not be used to provide relief for procedural deprivations whose effect was to prevent a handicapped child from ever reaching the stage of a final administrative determination. Because of the availability of § 1983 to remedy the deprivations of the procedural rights granted by the statute, it was unnecessary for Congress to provide a separate scheme of judicial relief for plaintiffs who never reach the stage of "findings and decision" due to defendants' misconduct.

> In short, the district court did not err in refusing to dismiss, because, as we have interpreted the complaint, it sets forth a cause of action against the school district under § 1983 for compensatory damages based upon its alleged policy to avoid providing expensive special education services by preventing handicapped children from gaining access to the procedural safeguards guaranteed by the statute.

Quackenbush v. Johnson City Sch. Dist., 716 F.2d 141, 148 (2d Cir. 1983).

Section Three
Compensatory Education

As we saw in Chapter Six, parents have the right to recover tuition they paid to a private school to provide their child with a FAPE when the school district failed to do so. This right extends to parents who have not paid, but are obligated to pay, private school tuition to provide their child with a FAPE. Where does this leave the children of parents who are without means to front the costs of private school tuition or are unable to make a deal with a private school to delay paying tuition pending the outcome of a court challenge? This section investigates the right of such children to receive compensatory education for periods during which their school district did not provide them with a FAPE. Topics include the right to compensatory education, eligibility for compensatory education, and calculating an award of compensatory education.

A. The Right to Compensatory Education

Miener v. Missouri

800 F.2d 749 (8th Cir. 1986)

Arnold, Circuit Judge.

Terri Ann Miener . . . brought this action . . . charging that several state and local government entities denied educational services due her as a handicapped child. She now appeals from two District Court orders that . . . dismiss her complaint for failure to state a claim. In part, she challenges the decision of this Court in an earlier appeal that the compensatory educational services she seeks are "damages," and therefore are not recoverable under the . . . EHA . . . ; she argues that our conclusion is inconsistent with the Supreme Court's recent decision in *Burlington* . . . . We agree with Miener that relief is available under the EHA . . . .

I.

Terri Ann Miener suffers serious learning disabilities and behavioral disorders caused by a recurrent brain tumor and attendant surgery. . . . [I]n September 1976, Terri Ann, who was then 14 years old, was released from the hospital after cranial surgery. Her father, Clyde Miener, took her to the Special School District of St. Louis

County, Missouri (SSD) for evaluation, requesting special educational services for his daughter. The SSD's evaluation clinic reported in February 1977 that Terri Ann suffered serious educational, emotional, and behavioral disorders, but no educational services were provided for her. Instead, in June 1977, Terri Ann's father found it necessary, for lack of any other financially viable alternative, to have her admitted as a full-time resident in the Youth Center of the St. Louis State Hospital, a facility operated by the Missouri Department of Mental Health. At Clyde Miener's request, the SSD reevaluated Terri Ann in 1978, but again, the educational services he sought were not provided.

. . . .

II.

. . . .

The defendants maintain that the compensatory educational services the plaintiff seeks to recover do not fit within the purview of *Burlington* because they do not constitute "retroactive reimbursement" for expenditures made on Terri Ann's education during the contested period, the period of her Youth Center placement. Unlike *Burlington*, the remedy sought here is not, for the most part, reimbursement for the expenses Terri Ann's father bore in order to provide his daughter a proper placement during the contested period. Instead, Clyde Miener contends that he did not have the money to pay these expenses himself, and, receiving no support from the defendants, had to place his daughter in the Youth Center rather than in what he considered a proper placement; the plaintiff seeks to recover the educational services she claims she should have received during this three-year period, services that her father could not provide, and that the defendants were unwilling to provide.

We cannot agree with the defendants that they should escape liability for these services simply because Clyde Miener was unable to provide them in the first instance; we believe that such a result would be consistent neither with *Burlington* nor with congressional intent. Like the retroactive reimbursement in *Burlington*, imposing liability for compensatory educational services on the defendants "merely requires [them] to belatedly pay expenses that [they] should have paid all along." Here, as in *Burlington*, recovery is necessary to secure the child's right to a free appropriate public education. We are confident that Congress did not intend the child's entitlement to a *free* education to turn upon her parent's ability to "front" its costs.

We find further support for this view in the Supreme Court's discussion in *Smith* of the reasons for Congress's decision not to establish a general damages remedy in the EHA. . . . Congress's apparent goal, *Smith* explains, was to relieve the providers of education for handicapped children of such burdens in order to "'make every resource, or as much as possible, available to the direct activities and the direct programs that are going to benefit the handicapped.'" 468 U.S. at 1020 . . . , quoting 121 Cong. Rec. 19501 (1975) (remarks of Sen. Dole). The relief Miener requests is entirely consistent with this goal, since she wishes to recover compensatory educational services to remedy denial of the benefits Congress sought to protect through denying a damages remedy, a free appropriate education. She does not request educational services as compensation for, *e.g.*, the physical injuries she suffered while at the Youth Center. Indeed, this case may present an even more compelling claim for relief than did *Burlington*, since in *Burlington* the child had already received educational services without resort to the governmental resources devoted to that purpose, resources whose effectiveness Congress desired to promote through safeguarding them against damage claims.

Accordingly, we hold that the plaintiff is entitled to recover compensatory educational services if she prevails on her claim that the defendants denied her a free appropriate education in violation of the EHA.

. . . .

Notes, Comments, and Questions

1. Several courts of appeals have agreed with the Eighth Circuit that the IDEA authorizes courts and hearing officers to award compensatory education as a remedy for failure to provide a FAPE. *See, e.g.*, Ferren C. v. Sch. Dist. of Phila., 612 F.3d 712, 717–18 (3d Cir. 2010) (upholding compensatory education award); P. v. Newington Bd. of Educ., 546 F.3d 111, 123 (2d Cir. 2008) (upholding compensatory education award in the form of an inclusion consultant for one year); Draper v. Atlanta Indep. Sch. Sys., 518 F.3d 1275, 1279–80, 1290 (11th Cir. 2008) (upholding award of placement in a private school as compensation for IDEA violations); Bd. of Educ. of Fayette Cnty. v. L.M., 478 F.3d 307, 316 (6th Cir. 2007), *cert. denied*, 522 U.S. 1042 (2007) ("An award of compensatory education is an equitable remedy that a court can grant as it finds appropriate."); Park v. Anaheim Union High Sch. Dist., 464 F.3d 1025, 1033–34 (9th Cir. 2006) (upholding training for student's teachers as compensatory education); Reid v. District of Columbia, 401 F.3d 516, 522–23 (D.C. Cir. 2005) ("[W]ere it possible to obtain an award of the instruction itself, children's access to appropriate education could depend on their parents' capacity to front its costs—a result manifestly incompatible with IDEA's purpose"); G. v. Fort Bragg Dependent Sch., 343 F.3d 295, 309 (4th Cir. 2003) (reversing denial of compensatory education award); Pihl v. Mass. Dep't of Educ., 9 F.3d 184, 188 (1st Cir. 1993) (upholding availability of compensatory education as a remedy for FAPE violation).

2. To what extent does compensatory education level the playing field between children whose parents can afford to send them to private school and children of parents who cannot afford to do so? Does compensatory education make up for lost time? Are there other means for securing an appropriate education for children of less affluent parents? In *Draper v. Atlanta Indep. Sch. Sys.*, 518 F.3d 1275 (11th Cir. 2008), the court upheld an award of prospective private school tuition as a form of compensatory education. The court stated:

> We do not read the Act as requiring compensatory awards of prospective education to be inferior to awards of reimbursement. The Act does not relegate families who lack the resources to place their children unilaterally in private schools to shouldering the burden of proving that the public school

> cannot adequately educate their child before those parents can obtain a placement in a private school. The Act instead empowers the district court to use broad discretion to fashion appropriate equitable relief.

Id. at 1286; *see also* Brantley v. Indep. Sch. Dist. No. 625, 936 F. Supp. 649, 655 (D. Minn. 1996) ("[C]ompensatory education in the form of placement in a private school at public expense is appropriate relief where it is demonstrated that FAPE is not possible in public schools."); Sabatini v. Corning-Painted Post Area Sch. Dist., 78 F. Supp. 2d 138, 147 (W.D.N.Y. 1999) (granting preliminary injunction requiring school district to place child in a private school).

3. Are compensatory education, retroactive tuition payment, and prospective tuition payment sufficient remedies for children who have been deprived of a FAPE? As you read Section Three regarding injunctive relief, consider the role of preliminary and permanent injunctive relief in guaranteeing a FAPE to children with disabilities.

4. Courts have awarded many forms of compensatory education. These include:

> *retaining an inclusion consultant for one year, P. v. Newington Bd. of Educ., 546 F.3d 111, 123 (2d Cir. 2008);
>
> *prospective placement at a private school or college, Draper v. Atlanta Indep. Sch. Sys., 518 F.3d 1275, 1279–80 (11th Cir. 2008);
>
> *teacher training, Park v. Anaheim Union High Sch. Dist., 464 F.3d 1025, 1033–34 (9th Cir. 2006);
>
> *occupational therapy, Evanston Cmty. Consolidated Sch. Dist. No. 65 v. Michael M., 356 F.3d 798, 803 (7th Cir. 2004);
>
> *speech and language and occupational therapy, B.H. v. West Clermont Bd. of Educ., 788 F. Supp. 2d 682, 701–02 (S.D. Ohio 2011);
>
> *Applied Behavioral Analysis, Diatta v. District of Columbia, 319 F. Supp. 2d 57, 68 (D.D.C. 2004); and
>
> *paraprofessional services, Westendorp v. Indep. Sch. Dist. No. 273, 35 F. Supp. 2d 1134, 1138 (D. Minn. 1998).

5. The IDEA requires states to provide a student with a FAPE until she graduates from high school or turns twenty-one. Nevertheless, courts have ruled that compensatory education is available to a student after she graduates from high school or turns twenty-one if it is necessary to compensate her for an IDEA violation. *See, e.g.*, Pihl v. Mass. Dep't of Educ., 9 F.3d 184 (1st Cir. 1993). In establishing the right to compensatory education past the age of twenty-one in the First Circuit, the court explained:

> Common sense commands such a conclusion. In order to give meaning to a disabled student's right to an education between the ages of three and twenty-one, compensatory education must be available beyond a student's twenty-first birthday. Otherwise, school districts simply could

> stop providing required services to older teenagers, relying on the Act's time-consuming review process to protect them from further obligations. Although students able to front the costs of an appropriate education later could claim reimbursement . . . , absent a compensatory education award, courts would be powerless to aid intended beneficiaries who were over twenty-one but who had not sought out an alternative educational program. We cannot believe that Congress, in establishing a disabled student's right to public education, would allow a school district to suspend the educational rights of such disabled eighteen- or nineteen-year olds without a remedy.

Id. at 189–90; *see also* Frazier v. Fairhaven Sch. Comm., 276 F.3d 52, 63 (1st Cir. 2002) (ruling that compensatory education is available after graduation). Was the court in *Pihl* correct that eighteen- and nineteen-year old students do not have a remedy without the availability of compensatory education? Recall the pendency rights described in Chapter Nine. Is pendency an adequate remedy?

In addition to the First Circuit, the Second, Third, Seventh, and Eleventh Circuits have confirmed the availability of compensatory education past graduation or the age of twenty-one, as have district courts in the District of Columbia and the Fifth and Sixth Circuits. *See, e.g.*, Ferren C. v. Sch. Dist. of Phila., 612 F.3d 712, 717–18 (3d Cir. 2010) (affirming order to provide annual IEPs to student after the age of twenty-one); Board of Educ. of Oak Park & River Forest High Sch. Dist. 200 v. Ill. State Bd. of Educ., 79 F.3d 654, 656 (7th Cir. 1996) (stating that the IDEA "empowers a court to order adult compensatory education to cure a violation"); Jefferson Cnty. Bd. of Educ. v. Breen, 853 F.2d 853, 857–58 (11th Cir. 1988) (affirming award of two years of compensatory education past the student's twenty-first birthday); Brooks v. District of Columbia, 841 F. Supp. 2d 253, 254 (D.D.C. 2012) (awarding compensatory education after high school graduation); Wayne Cnty. Regional Educ. Serv. Agency v. Pappas, 56 F. Supp. 2d 807, 813–14 (E.D. Mich. 1999) (upholding award of 250 days of compensatory education after the student passed the age of eligibility); Campbell v. Talladega Cnty. Bd. of Educ., 518 F. Supp. 47, 56 (N.D. Ala. 1981) (ordering school district to provide student with a FAPE for two years after he turns twenty-one).

6. Denial of a FAPE does not always result in compensatory education. In *G.R. v. Dal. Sch. Dist. No. 2*, 823 F. Supp. 2d 1120, 1144 (D. Ore. 2011), the court ruled that even though the district denied the child a FAPE, he was not entitled to compensatory education because he graduated from high school with a standard diploma. The court explained:

> G.R. graduated from high school and earned a standard diploma rather than a modified diploma. He accomplished this without any additional educational services to make up for the District's denial of a FAPE . . . . Plaintiffs have not suggested any educational services which would assist G.R. as he begins his community college education. . . . There is no proof of any areas

> in which G.R. is lacking because of the past denial of a FAPE. The opposite appears to be true. G.R.'s father listed numerous awards G.R. earned at high school . . . .

Id at 1144. Do you agree with the court? Did the court properly implement the *Rowley* standard?; *see also* Parents of Student W. v. Puyallup Sch. Dist. No. 3, 31 F.3d 1489, 1497 (9th Cir. 1994) ("Student W. was able to graduate from high school, before reaching age 21, without more services than provided for in his annual IEP. The IDEA promises him no more.").

7. Procedural violations of the IDEA that do not result in denial of FAPE do not entitle a child to compensatory education. P.P. v. West Chester Area Sch. Dist., 585 F.3d 727, 738 (3d Cir. 2009) (holding that delay in evaluation and providing an IEP did not entitle the child to compensatory education because the child received a FAPE); Maine Sch. Admin. Dist. No. 35 v. Mr. R., 321 F.3d 9, 25–26 (1st Cir. 2003) (recognizing that compensatory education is not available for procedural violations); Erickson v. Albuquerque Pub. Sch., 199 F.3d 1116, 1123 (10th Cir. 1999) ("The award of compensatory education is not an appropriate remedy for a failure to provide an individualized determination when the school district provided the student with a FAPE."); Shawsheen Valley Reg'l Vocational Technical Sch. Dist. Sch. Comm. v. Mass. Bureau of Special Ed. Appeals, 367 F. Supp. 2d 44, 57 (D. Mass. 2005) (holding that the child was not entitled to compensatory education for procedural violations without substantive impact).

8. Courts have accounted for equitable factors in denying compensatory education to children. In *Parents of Student W. v. Puyallup Sch. Dist., No. 3*, 31 F.3d 1489 (9th Cir. 1994), the court denied compensatory education, in part due to the behavior of the child's parents:

> The behavior of Student W.'s parents is also relevant in fashioning equitable relief. His mother declined special education for her son in 1989, and when transferring him back into the District, never again asked for special services. More importantly, after Student W. was reassessed and found to be disabled, his parents twice declined to take advantage of summer school which might have helped Student W. regain his grade level in math.

Id. at 1497; *see also* C.G. v. Five Town Cmty. Sch. Dist., 513 F.3d 279, 289–90 (1st Cir. 2008) (denying relief, including compensatory education, because the parents abandoned the IEP process); J.G. v. Kiryas Joel Union Free Sch. Dist., 777 F. Supp. 2d 606, 643 (S.D.N.Y. 2011) (denying compensatory education in part because parents failed to respond adequately to the district's offer of services). On the other hand, in *Keystone Cent. Sch. Dist. v. E.E.*, 438 F. Supp. 2d 519, 524–25 (M.D. Pa. 2006), the court agreed with the state-level ruling reversing the hearing officer's decision to cut the compensatory education award in half because the child's mother delayed obtaining a psychiatric evaluation. The court found that the delay did not harm the child's education.

B. The Standard for Awarding Compensatory Education

J.C. v. Cent. Reg'l Sch. Dist.

81 F.3d 389 (3d Cir. 1996),
cert. denied, 519 U.S. 866 (1996)

BECKER, Circuit Judge.

... J.C., a severely mentally retarded sixteen-year-old male, has attended the Ocean County Day Training Center ("OCDTC") since 1987. In 1992, concerned about the appropriateness of their son's instruction, J.C.'s father and stepmother, M.C. and G.C. ("plaintiffs"), began proceedings to secure ... compensatory education beyond his twenty-first year to make up for what they believed to be long-standing deficiencies in his program. In 1995, the district court ... refused to award compensatory education because it found that the defendant, Central Regional School District ... had, in good faith, provided J.C. with some educational program. ... [P]laintiffs cross-appeal the determination regarding compensatory education.

... The cross-appeal requires us to ... decide the proper standard for an award of compensatory education. A school district that knows or should know that a child has an inappropriate ... IEP ... or is not receiving more than a *de minimis* educational benefit must, of course, correct the situation. We hold that, if it fails to do so, a disabled child is entitled to compensatory education for a period equal to the period of deprivation, excluding only the time reasonably required for the school district to rectify the problem. Because the district court applied an incorrect "good faith" standard, we will reverse on the cross-appeal and remand for further proceedings consistent with this opinion.

I. Factual Background/Procedural History

A. *Factual Background*

J.C.'s IEP stresses personal and self-help goals such as toileting and eating as well as more general communication, domestic, recreation, vocation, and community training skills. His preschool records reflect that he progressed well during his initial years of education. Following J.C.'s placement at OCDTC in 1987, his development slowed. Since 1989, J.C. has made little consistent improvement and in some aspects has even regressed.

For example, in 1988 and 1989, J.C.'s teachers, Juanita Jones and Susan Trainor, reported that J.C. could remove his shirt independently. In 1990, Trainor indicated that J.C. could remove his shirt only after it was started for him. By 1992, J.C.'s school records did not reflect any independent disrobing efforts. Trainor related only that J.C. was "cooperative" and would "extend [his] arm/leg for dressing."

Likewise, pulling his pants up and down in preparation for toileting has been a self-help goal in J.C.'s IEP since 1989. By February 1991, J.C. was reportedly pulling his pants down with "moderate" physical assistance on two out of five days. In May 1991, J.C. continued to lower his pants with "moderate" assistance. In May 1992,

J.C. had regressed to where he was able to pull his pants down on two out of five days only with "maximum" physical assistance. Similar reversion occurred in J.C.'s ability to spear food, to drink from a cup, to communicate, and to pay attention.

Not only did J.C. perform poorly on stated IEP goals, but his IEP also failed to include several important objectives. For example, Central Regional's records indicate that J.C.'s self-stimulatory behavior, like chewing his shirt, was a serious problem impairing his educational progress. Despite this fact, J.C.'s IEP contained no strategies to reduce the incidence of this behavior.

Another gap in J.C.'s IEP was parent training. According to Trainor, in order for J.C. to make steady progress, his program needed to be consistently implemented both inside and outside of the classroom throughout all his waking hours. Nevertheless, the IEP did not include parent training. . . . [T]he plaintiffs requested someone from the school to come to their home to help with toileting and independent feeding. They were never told that parent training was a related service that could be provided under J.C.'s IEP.

B. *Procedural History*

[J.C.'s parents challenged J.C.'s IEP in an impartial hearing. The ALJ ruled against J.C. and they appealed to federal district court. The district court ruled that the limited progress J.C. made violated the IDEA and ordered a residential placement but denied the plaintiff's request for compensatory education. The defendants appealed the residential placement order and the plaintiffs appealed the denial of compensatory education.]

. . . .

III. Compensatory Education

. . . .

B. *Formulating a Standard*

In the case at bar, the [district] court devoted only one paragraph of its opinion to compensatory education . . . . [T]he district court applied a "good faith" standard in determining whether to award compensatory education. We review this approach de novo.

In order to define the correct standard for granting compensatory education, we must delineate the threshold of deficiency in the school board's stewardship necessary to trigger an award. . . .

. . . .

If the compensatory education standard is to spring from the Act, it must focus from the outset upon the IEP—the road map for a disabled child's education. When an IEP fails to confer some (i.e., more than *de minimis*) educational benefit to a student, that student has been deprived of the appropriate education guaranteed by IDEA. It seems clear, therefore, that the right to compensatory education should accrue from the point that the school district knows or should know of the IEP's failure.

The school district, however, may not be able to act immediately to correct an inappropriate IEP; it may require some time to respond to a complex problem. Thus, our holding can be summarized as follows: a school district that knows or should know that a child has an inappropriate IEP or is not receiving more than a *de minimis* educational benefit must correct the situation. If it fails to do so, a disabled child is entitled to compensatory education for a period equal to the period of deprivation, but excluding the time reasonably required for the school district to rectify the problem. We believe that this formula harmonizes the interests of the child, who is entitled to a free appropriate education under IDEA, with those of the school district, to whom special education and compensatory education is quite costly.

Obviously the case against the school district will be stronger if the district actually knew of the educational deficiency or the parents had complained. But a child's entitlement to special education should not depend upon the vigilance of the parents (who may not be sufficiently sophisticated to comprehend the problem) nor be abridged because the district's behavior did not rise to the level of slothfulness or bad faith. Rather, it is the responsibility of the child's teachers, therapists, and administrators—and of the multi-disciplinary team that annually evaluates the student's progress—to ascertain the child's educational needs, respond to deficiencies, and place him or her accordingly.

. . . .

Since the district court applied an incorrect standard, its order denying compensatory education must be reversed. The court found that J.C.'s IEP was inappropriate. It determined that the majority of the skills that J.C. possessed . . . were gained *before* J.C. was placed at OCDTC in 1987, that the same rate of progress did not continue after he was placed at OCDTC, and that J.C. plateaued in 1989. Thus, J.C.'s educational deprivation appears to have lasted a long time. On remand, the district court should determine when the Central Regional knew or should have known that J.C.'s IEP was inappropriate or that he was not receiving more than *de minimis* educational benefit; it should also define the reasonable time within which the district should have done something about it. Compensatory education should accrue from that point forward.

The order of the district court will therefore be . . . reversed in part and the case remanded for further proceedings consistent with this opinion.

Notes, Comments, and Questions

1. In determining whether a district knew or should have known that a child was not receiving an appropriate education, courts have generally employed a fact-driven approach. For example, in *Heather D. v. Northampton Area Sch. Dist.*, 511 F. Supp. 2d 549 (E.D. Pa. 2007), the court listed several facts that should have alerted the district that the child should have been evaluated for special education. The child was "hospitalized for . . . thirteen weeks for self-abusive behavior," she "had problems with urinating in her clothing at school . . . ," and "had problems paying attention in

class." *Id.* at 556; *see also* Diatta v. District of Columbia, 319 F. Supp. 2d 57, 67–68 (D.D.C. 2004) (holding that the school was on notice when doctor diagnosed child as having autism); Mr. R. v. Me. Sch. Admin. Dist. No. 35, 295 F. Supp. 2d 113, 118 (D. Me. 2003) (holding that the district was on notice because the school held ten team meetings about the student in one school year, the district subsequently developed a significantly different IEP for him, and the child had behavioral difficulties).

2. On the other hand, in *Gregory R. v. Penn Delco Sch. Dist.*, 262 F. Supp. 2d 488 (E.D. Pa. 2003), the court ruled that the district did not have notice under the following circumstances:

> The parents' unilateral transfer of the child without a stated reason or any expression of dissatisfaction in any form does not put the District on reasonably adequate notice that it knew or should have known that Gregory was not receiving an appropriate education. Thus, even if Gregory was not receiving an appropriate education, the record does not indicate that the District knew or should have known of that fact.

Id. at 493. Did the court place the burden to make the district aware of the child's inappropriate education solely on the child's parents? Is this consistent with the IDEA's procedural protections? Is it consistent with *J.C.*? In contrast, in *Me. Sch. Admin Dist. No. 35 v. Mr. R.*, 321 F.3d 9, 18 (1st Cir. 2003), the First Circuit ruled that a claim for compensatory education "begins to accrue when his or her IEP is so inappropriate that the child is receiving no real educational benefit." Which standard is stricter on the district?

C. Calculating an Award of Compensatory Education

Reid v. District of Columbia

401 F.3d 516 (D.C. Cir. 2005)

TATEL, Circuit Judge.

When a school district deprives a disabled child of free appropriate public education in violation of the Individuals with Disabilities Education Act, a court fashioning "appropriate" relief, as the statute allows, may order compensatory education, i.e., replacement of educational services the child should have received in the first place. This commonsense proposition — conceded by the school district here and supported by the Supreme Court's decision compelling reimbursement for such services in . . . *Burlington* . . . , led a hearing officer to award appellant, a sixteen-year-old with severe learning disabilities, 810 hours of compensatory education, one hour for each day in the four-and-a-half years during which the school system denied the student appropriate instruction. Pointing out that neither reasoning nor evidence supported this hour-per-day calculation and insisting that hour-per-hour relief was instead the child's due, the child and his mother argue that the hearing officer abused his authority. . . . Because we agree that the hearing officer's mechanical calculation merits no deference . . . , we reverse the district court's grant of summary judgment to the school district. We reject, however, appellants' equally mechanical hour-per-hour calculation and instead adopt a qualitative standard: compensatory awards should aim to place disabled children in the same position they would have occupied but for the school district's violations of IDEA.

I.

. . . .

In this case . . . , the District of Columbia Public Schools ("DCPS") failed to meet its IDEA obligations with respect to appellant Mathew Reid. A sixteen-year-old District of Columbia resident, Mathew suffers from documented learning disabilities, including dyslexia and attention deficit hyperactivity disorder, that affect his short-term auditory memory, formation of grammatical sentences, and articulation of word sounds. Though Mathew's mother had noticed by the fall of her son's second-grade year that he had difficulty reading, when she contacted a school district counselor, the counselor refused to provide the necessary form for requesting a disability evaluation. The following spring, during a meeting with Mathew's teacher and school principal, the teacher recommended that Mathew be retained in second grade due to behavioral and academic problems. . . .

Mathew spent the next year in California and then returned to D.C. By that time, test scores placed him in the bottom one percent of his age group for reading comprehension and the bottom five percent for reading overall. Nonetheless, without performing any disability evaluation, the school district placed Mathew in a regular fourth-grade class. Only after a full school year of unsatisfactory grades did DCPS recognize Mathew's disability and develop an IEP.

Under this IEP, Mathew was retained in fourth grade and attended ten hours per week of special education instruction plus twice-weekly half-hour language therapy sessions and one half hour per week of counseling. In accordance with IDEA's preference for avoiding separate instruction "[t]o the maximum extent possible," *see* 20 U.S.C. § 1412(a)(5), Mathew spent the remainder of the school day mainstreamed in regular classes, but received accommodations such as preferential seating and extended time for assignments. Two years later, DCPS revised Mathew's IEP to provide seventeen-and-a-half hours of special education services per week. Despite these services, testing in November of Mathew's sixth-grade year revealed him reading at a second-grade level, even though six months earlier he had been reading at a third-grade level. Mathew's overall intellectual ability placed him in the ninth percentile for his age.

Despite further testing confirming these results, Mathew's IEP team made no change in his program until April of that school year. At that point, presumably because Mathew's math skills had risen from low fourth-grade level to low sixth-grade level (though at the time Mathew was entering seventh grade and was old enough to be entering eighth), the team eliminated 250 minutes per week of math tutoring while adding 200 minutes per week of reading instruction and fifteen extra minutes per week of counseling.

Objecting to this new IEP, Mathew's mother exercised her statutory right to demand an "impartial due process hearing[.]" She argued that "the IEP is inappropriate because Mathew requires a full-time special education program and the IEP calls for a part time special education program." The hearing officer agreed. Based on "the student's serious and extensive needs and the glaring inappropriateness of the IEP in terms of placing Mathew in a part-time program when he requires a full-time program," the officer ordered the school district to place Mathew in "a full-time special education program with a low student teacher ratio and intensive work in reading with the other related services," designating one such program, the Accotink Academy, as Mathew's placement "at least on an interim basis." . . . .

To make up for deficiencies in Mathew's prior education, Ms. Reid also sought extra instruction beyond his Accotink Academy IEP—in other words, "compensatory education." In separate proceedings related to that claim, a second hearing officer heard expert testimony indicating, among other things, that in struggling to read, Mathew had "learned compensatory strategies that are counterproductive," that "there was a gap in between what [Mathew] was capable of, and actually what he was performing," and that because of academic and interpersonal difficulties, Mathew had grown "significantly depressed." Three experts—a psychologist, a speech language pathologist/audiologist, and an educational consultant—all testified that the school district should have known Mathew was disabled in second grade or earlier. Based on this evidence, and building on the earlier hearing, the hearing officer concluded that DCPS had denied Mathew FAPE for roughly four-and-a-half years, from midway through second grade until the Accotink placement at the end of sixth grade (skipping Mathew's year in California and counting both fourth-grade years).

As a remedy, the officer ordered 810 hours of compensatory education, a figure he derived by awarding "1 hour for each day of special education services not provided." [The officer did not indicate] . . . why he chose this formula nor what specific services should be provided . . . .

. . . Seeking . . . review in the U.S. District Court for the District of Columbia, Mathew and his mother challenged . . . the number of hours awarded as compensatory instruction . . . . On cross-motions for summary judgment, the district court . . . affirmed the administrative award. The Reids now appeal.

II.

. . . .

Compensatory Award

Under the theory of "compensatory education," courts and hearing officers may award "educational services . . . to be provided prospectively to compensate for a past deficient program." *See G. ex. rel. RG v. Fort Bragg Dependent Schs.*, 343 F.3rd 295, 308 (4th Cir. 2003). Embraced in some form by several circuits, this theory builds on the Supreme Court's holding in *Burlington* that "appropriate" IDEA relief may include reimbursement for parents who place children in private school rather than accept a deficient public school IEP. If IDEA permits reimbursement for educational services, courts have reasoned, then it must also allow awards of the services themselves. Based on such logic, courts have upheld awards requiring . . . special programs to make up for prior deficiencies, and instruction beyond age twenty-one . . . .

. . . .

. . . [W]e part company with the Reids regarding how such awards are calculated. They urge us to adopt a presumption that each hour without FAPE entitles the student to one hour of compensatory instruction, a standard apparently embraced by several courts. *See, e.g.*, *M.C. v. Cent. Reg'l Sch. Dist.*, 81 F.3d 389, 391–92, 396–97 (3d Cir. 1996) (holding that when "a school district . . . knows or should know" that a disabled child's educational program is deficient yet fails to correct the problem, the child "is entitled to compensatory education for a period equal to the period of deprivation, but excluding the time reasonably required for the school district to rectify the problem"); *Westendorp*, 35 F. Supp. 2d at 1137 (holding that "where [plaintiff] was denied his IDEA rights for six academic years, the court will presume that he is entitled to six academic years of compensatory relief"). In our view, this cookie-cutter approach runs counter to both the "broad discretion" afforded by IDEA's remedial provision and the substantive FAPE standard that provision is meant to enforce.

As to the remedial provision, the Supreme Court has emphasized that IDEA relief depends on "equitable considerations." *See Carter*, 510 U.S. at 15–16 . . . ; *Burlington*, 471 U.S. at 374. . . . Accordingly, "compensatory education is not a contractual remedy, but an equitable remedy, part of the court's resources in crafting 'appropriate relief.'" *Parents of Student W.*, 31 F.3d at 1497. More specifically, as the Fourth Circuit has explained, "[c]ompensatory education involves discretionary, prospective, injunctive relief crafted by a court to remedy what might be termed an educational deficit created by an educational agency's failure over a given period of time to provide a FAPE to a student." *G. ex rel. RG*, 343 F.3d at 309. Overlooking this equitable focus, the Reids' hour-for-hour formula in effect treats compensatory education as a form of damages—a charge on school districts equal to expenditures they should have made previously. Yet "[t]he essence of equity jurisdiction" is "to do equity and to mould each decree to the necessities of the particular case. Flexibility rather than rigidity has distinguished it." *Hecht Co. v. Bowles*, 321 U.S. 321, 329 . . . (1944). In keeping with that principle of case-specific flexibility, we agree with the Ninth Circuit that "[t]here is no obligation to provide a day-for-day compensation for time missed. Appropriate relief is relief designed to ensure that the student is appropriately educated within the meaning of the IDEA." *Parents of Student W.*, 31 F.3d at 1497.

Reinforcing this conclusion, the substantive FAPE standard—the rule of law the Reids seek to enforce—also carries a qualitative rather than quantitative focus. As IDEA itself states, the statute's aim is to guarantee disabled students "specialized education and related services *designed to meet their unique needs*." *See* 20 U.S.C.

§ 1400(d)(1)(A) (emphasis added). Hence, as the Supreme Court explained in *Rowley*, "the basic floor of opportunity provided by the Act consists of access to specialized instruction and related services which are *individually designed* to provide educational benefit to the handicapped child." *See* 458 U.S. at 201 . . . (emphasis added). We think it would be highly incongruous if this qualitative focus on individual needs gave way to mechanical hour-counting when past rather than current violations of the FAPE standard were at issue. Accordingly, just as IEPs focus on disabled students' individual needs, so must awards compensating past violations rely on individualized assessments.

Unlike the Reids' one-for-one standard, this flexible approach will produce different results in different cases depending on the child's needs. Some students may require only short, intensive compensatory programs targeted at specific problems or deficiencies. Others may need extended programs, perhaps even exceeding hour-for-hour replacement of time spent without FAPE. In addition, courts have recognized that in setting the award, equity may sometimes require consideration of the parties' conduct, such as when the school system reasonably "require[s] some time to respond to a complex problem," *M.C.*, 81 F.3d at 397, or when parents' refusal to accept special education delays the child's receipt of appropriate services, *Parents of Student W.*, 31 F.3d at 1497. In every case, however, the inquiry must be fact-specific and, to accomplish IDEA's purposes, the ultimate award must be reasonably calculated to provide the educational benefits that likely would have accrued from special education services the school district should have supplied in the first place.

Given this standard, neither party in this case is entitled to summary judgment. As to the Reids, because we reject the one-for-one formula they advocate, the amount of compensatory education appropriate in Mathew's case cannot be determined as a matter of law. Rather, designing Mathew's remedy will require a fact-specific exercise of discretion by either the district court or a hearing officer. As to the school district, although 810 hours certainly seems like a significant award, without grounds for deference to the hearing officer we may conclude at summary judgment that this remedy was correct as a matter of law only if our review of the record reveals that any greater remedy would amount to an abuse of discretion. We cannot reach that conclusion because, drawing all inferences in Mathew's favor, as we must at summary judgment, we have no basis for concluding that 810 hours—barely more than half of a single academic year—would suffice to make up for Mathew's four-and-a-half years without FAPE, especially considering that during that period he developed "counterproductive" reading habits.

The district court appears to have granted summary judgment to the school district simply because it assumed that compensatory awards need only provide "some benefit" going forward, as in an ordinary non-compensatory IEP under *Rowley*. Applying this standard and assuming that it could defer to the hearing officer, the district court faulted Mathew for "fail[ing] to offer proof regarding why the hearing officer's award is 'inappropriate' to achieve what is required by the Act, *i.e.*, a basic floor of opportunity and 'access to specialized instruction and related services which are individually designed to provide educational benefit to [Mathew].'" In particular, based on the additional assumption that the Accotink Academy IEP already compensated Mathew to some degree, the court faulted the Reids for "failing to provide the Court with a copy of Mathew's current IEP," a lapse the court believed left it "unable to assess whether the services [Mathew] is already receiving are inadequate to compensate for the prior denial of FAPE, which might justify a larger compensatory education award."

As we have explained, however, whereas ordinary IEPs need only provide "some benefit," compensatory awards must do more—they must *compensate*. Accordingly, the district court should not have assumed that the Accotink Academy placement, based as it was only on *Rowley*, provided compensation. If anything, at summary judgment the court should have assumed the opposite, requiring DCPS to offer proof that the placement compensated for prior FAPE denials in addition to providing some benefit going forward. Nor should the district court have assumed the adequacy of the 810-hour award, for that award, as we have also explained, deserved "little deference," *Kerkan II*, 931 F.2d at 87. To be sure, as the "party challenging the administrative determination," the Reids "must at least take on the burden of persuading the court that the hearing officer was wrong," but given the minimal deference owed to the hearing award in this case, they could satisfy that burden simply by pointing to the award's evident arbitrariness. Thus, with the district court's incorrect assumptions stripped away, the Reids' failure to present evidence beyond the administrative record provides no justification for awarding summary judgment to the school district.

....

Accordingly, we will affirm the district court's denial of the Reids' motion but reverse its grant of summary judgment to the school district. On remand, the district court may solicit additional evidence from the parties and fashion an appropriate compensatory education award based on the principles outlined in this opinion. Alternatively, in light of the absence of pertinent findings in the administrative record and given that both parties previously filed cross-motions for summary judgment rather than exercising their right to "request" consideration of additional evidence, the district court may determine that the "appropriate" relief is a remand to the hearing officer for further proceedings. Whichever path the court chooses, the parties must have some opportunity to present evidence regarding Mathew's specific educational deficits resulting from his loss of FAPE and the specific compensatory measures needed to best correct those deficits.

....

III.

Neglected by the school system charged with affording him free appropriate education, Mathew Reid is entitled to compensatory instruction. He is not entitled, however, to an amount of such instruction predetermined by a cookie-cutter formula, but rather to an informed and reasonable exercise of discretion regarding what services he needs to elevate him to the position he would have occupied absent the school district's failures. Accordingly, the district court's award of summary judgment to the school district is reversed and the matter remanded for further proceedings consistent with this opinion. . . .

Notes, Comments, and Questions

1. The court in *Reid* rejected the "mechanical hour-per-hour calculation" the parents sought to use to calculate the compensatory award and instead adopted a "qualitative standard." According to the court, compensatory awards should aim to place children with disabilities in the same position they would have occupied but for the school district's violations of IDEA. Several other courts have followed *Reid. See, e.g.*, Board of Educ. of Fayette Cnty. v. L.M., 478 F.3d 307, 316, 18 (6th Cir. 2007), *cert. denied*, 522 U.S. 1042 (2007) (reversing compensatory education award of two years and remanding for consideration in light of *Reid*); Park v. Anaheim Union High Sch. Dist., 464 F.3d 1025, 1034 (9th Cir. 2006) (upholding compensatory education award in the form of training student's teachers because it "was designed to compensate Joseph for the District's violations by better training his teachers to meet Joseph's particular needs."); Banks v. District of Columbia, 720 F. Supp. 2d 83, 90–91 (D.D.C. 2010) (adopting the *Reid* standard for calculating an award of compensatory education); S.S. v. Howard Rd. Acad., 585 F. Supp. 2d 56, 71–72 (D.D.C. 2008) (citing *Reid* for the standard for setting an award of compensatory education); Friendship Edison Pub.Charter Sch. v. Nesbitt, 583 F. Supp. 2d 169, 172 (D.D.C. 2008) ("To comply with the *Reid* standard, Nesbitt must propose a well-articulated plan that reflects his current educational needs and is supported by the record."); Thomas v. District of Columbia, 407 F. Supp. 2d 102, 115 (D.D.C. 2005) (adopting the *Reid* method for calculating an award of compensatory education).

2. Despite the popularity of the *Reid* method, the courts are not uniform in their approach to calculating an award of compensatory education. Some courts, for example, have taken a hybrid approach, combining an hourly calculation with an individualized analysis. In *Mary McLeod Bethune Day Acad. Pub. Charter Sch. v. Bland*, 555 F. Supp. 2d 130, 136 (D.D.C. 2008), the court ruled that a compensatory education award based on a formula, combined with an individualized assessment of the child's needs, was acceptable. The court thus upheld an award of 375 hours of compensatory education that was based on the number of hours of specialized education the child missed, on the grounds that "the Hearing Officer conducted a fact-specific inquiry and tailored the award to T.B.'s individual needs by taking into account the results of the QRI-IV and the recommendations of the Sylvan Learning Center." *Id.* at 136–37. The court in *Brown v. District of Columbia*, 568 F. Supp. 2d 44 (D.D.C. 2008), took a similar approach.

> If E.M. had been placed in a full-time special education program at an earlier date, Dr. Booker testified, E.M. would have made at least six months growth instead of showing regression as he did for the past two years. To put E.M. in the position he would have been in but for the District's denial of services,

> Dr. Booker testified that E.M. required a full-time specialized instruction program and 633 hours of compensatory education in the form of tutorial services or a reading program. To reach the figure of 633 hours, Dr. Booker suggested that three hours of compensatory education were needed for each day that the District denied E.M. appropriate education services.
>
> Looking at Dr. Booker's final calculation in an isolated fashion, the hearing officer concluded that her "formulation specifically violates the 'hour-for-hour' approach criticized in Reid." However, this Court agrees with other opinions from this district, which have concluded that "[a] compensatory award constructed with the aid of a formula is not *per se* invalid." *Friendship Edison Pub. Charter Sch. Collegiate Campus v. Nesbitt*, 532 F. Supp. 2d 121, 123 (D.D.C. 2008). A formula-based award may in some circumstances be acceptable if it represents an individually-tailored approach to meet a student's unique prospective needs, as opposed to a backwards-looking calculation of education units denied to a student." *Id.*
>
> . . . .
>
> Here, although Dr. Booker did rely in part on a calculation, she similarly offered an individually-tailored assessment of E.M. and his compensatory education needs. Dr. Booker testified about the District's shortcomings with regard to educating E.M. She explained how much progress E.M. would have been expected to make if the District had provided him with appropriate special education services, and she testified about what would be required to place E.M. in the position he would have been in had he not been denied appropriate services.

Id. at 53–54; *see also* Breanne C. v. Southern York Cnty. Sch. Dist., 732 F. Supp. 2d 474, 487 (M.D. Pa. 2010) (upholding award of one hour for each day FAPE denied based on circumstances of child).

3. One court considered equitable factors when calculating an award:

> Considering all of the circumstances in this case, the Court finds that an award of eight weeks of summer-level education is an appropriate equitable compensation for the Student's loss of a FAPE during the 2005–2006 school year. The award takes into account the behavior of the parties, the evidence that the Student regresses when not in an academic environment, and Defendant's efforts, since the 2006–2007 school year, to make up the deficit for which it was largely responsible.

Hogan v. Fairfax Cnty. Sch. Bd., 645 F. Supp. 2d 554, 575 (E.D. Va. 2009).

4. The court in *Reid* identified two decisions that adopted an hour-for-hour approach to calculating an award of compensatory education. In *M.C. v. Cent. Reg'l Sch. Dist.*, 81 F.3d 389, 395-97 (3d Cir. 1996), *cert. denied*, 519 U.S. 866 (1996), the Third Circuit held that when a school district deprives a child of a FAPE, the child "is entitled to compensatory education for a period equal to the period of deprivation, but excluding the time reasonably required for the school district to rectify the

problem." *Id.* at 397. In *Westendorp v. Indep. Sch. Dist. No. 273*, 35 F. Supp. 2d 1134 (D. Minn. 1998), the court ruled that "where . . . [plaintiff] was denied his IDEA rights for six academic years, the court will presume that he is entitled to six academic years of compensatory relief". *Id.* at 1137. Additionally, in *Heather D. v. Northampton Area Sch. Dist.*, 511 F. Supp. 2d 549 (E.D. Pa. 2007), the court rejected the *Reid* approach in favor of the *M.C.* approach. The court stated:

> Based on . . . [the ruling in *M.C.*], the Court concludes that Defendant's approach, which ties an award of compensatory education to services denied in the past, rather than a corrective approach designed to help the student perform in accordance with some speculated potential, is more in line with the standard elucidated by the Third Circuit.

Id. at 557. The court awarded the child 2,428 hours of compensatory education based on its calculation of the number of hours of special education she should have received. *Id.* at 557–59, 563; *see also* Lester H. v. Gilhool, 916 F.2d 865, 873–74 (3d Cir. 1990), *cert. denied*, 499 U.S. 923 (1991) (awarding thirty months of compensatory education for thirty months of inappropriate placement); G. "J" D. v. Wissahickon Sch. Dist., 832 F. Supp. 2d 455 (E.D. Pa. 2011) (upholding an "award of two hours of compensatory education for every day . . . the child was denied a FAPE."); Keystone Cent. Sch. Dist. v. E.E., 438 F. Supp. 2d 519, 524–26 (M.D. Pa. 2006) (upholding an award of 630 hours of compensatory education based on the number of hours in the school years during which FAPE was denied).

5. Which of the various approaches to calculating awards of compensatory education do you think is most consistent with the purposes of the IDEA? The "equitable" approach of *Reid*, the hybrid approach that permits a formula but requires individualization of the award, or the hour-by-hour approach of *M.C.*?

6. What should a court do when the compensatory education award is not properly calculated? In *Reid*, the court remanded the case to the district court and indicated that the district court could either take additional evidence to develop a compensatory education award or remand the case to do so. Remand is a common remedy for an inappropriate compensatory award calculation or the court's or IHO's failure to calculate an award at all. *See, e.g.*, Board of Educ. of Fayette Cnty. v. L.M., 478 F.3d 307, 318 (6th Cir. 2007), *cert. denied*, 522 U.S. 1042 (2007) (reversing compensatory education award to reconsider based on *Reid*); Branham v. District of Columbia, 427 F.3d 7, 11 (D.C. Cir. 2005) (reversing compensatory education award of four years of tutoring and remanding for consideration in light of *Reid*); G. v. Fort Bragg Dependent Sch., 343 F.3d 295, 309 (4th Cir. 2003) (remanding for consideration of whether compensatory education award was merited based on correct legal standard); Stanton v. District of Columbia, 680 F. Supp. 2d 201, 208 (D.D.C. 2010) (remanding for district court to consider an appropriate compensatory education award); S.S. v. Howard Rd. Acad., 585 F. Supp. 2d 56, 72 (D.D.C. 2008) (remanding for consideration of an appropriate compensatory education award based on *Reid*);

Brown v. District of Columbia, 568 F. Supp. 2d 44, 55 (D.D.C. 2008) (remanding for consideration of whether district denied FAPE and if so, for determination of appropriate compensatory education award); Thomas v. District of Columbia, 407 F. Supp. 2d 102, 116 (D.D.C. 2005) (remanding for determination of compensatory education award to put student in position he would have been in had the school district not denied FAPE).

Section Four
Injunctive Relief

This section covers preliminary injunctive relief and permanent injunctive relief. A court can grant a preliminary injunction requiring a defendant to take or refrain from taking an action pending final resolution of a case if it finds that the plaintiff will likely prevail on the merits of the underlying claims and will likely suffer irreparable injury in the absence of relief, and the balance of equities is in the plaintiff's favor. A court can order permanent injunctive relief requiring a defendant to take or refrain from taking an action if the court finds that the plaintiff will suffer irreparable injury in the absence of an injunction and succeeds on the merits of the claim.

A. Preliminary Injunctive Relief

Honig v. Doe

484 U.S. 305 (1988)

[Review *Honig v. Doe*, excerpted in Chapter Six, and the Notes, Comments, and Questions following the excerpt. Also review Section Three, Part A of Chapter Six, relating to the 1997 amendments to the IDEA.]

Notes, Comments, and Questions

1. Do the 1997 amendments to the IDEA make preliminary injunctive relief to remove a dangerous child unnecessary? Do they strike an appropriate balance between the interests of a school district in protecting the safety of its students and the interests of children with disabilities in remaining in school?

2. As *Honig* made clear, a federal court's authority to issue a preliminary injunction can override a stay-put order. Courts can issue injunctive relief overriding a stay-put order even in the absence of a disciplinary problem. *See* Doe v. Brookline Sch. Comm., 722 F.2d 910, 917, 919 (1st Cir. 1983) ("[A] party that seeks to modify an existing educational placement, program, or services must proceed by a motion for preliminary injunction.").

3. Courts in IDEA cases have granted requests for preliminary injunctive relief in many different contexts. For example, they have ordered districts to:

*provide services a hearing officer had previously ordered, Nieves-Marquez v. Puerto Rico, 353 F. 3d 108, 112, 122 (1st Cir. 2003) (sign-language interpreter);

*place a student in a particular school and pay for her education, Massey v. District of Columbia, 400 F. Supp. 2d 66, 76 (D.D.C. 2005); Sabatini v. Corning-Painted Post Area Sch. Dist., 78 F. Supp. 2d 138, 147 (W.D.N.Y. 1999); Grace B. v. Lexington Sch. Comm., 762 F. Supp. 416, 421 (D. Mass. 1991);

*make timely payments for educational services to service providers, Petties v. District of Columbia, 238 F. Supp. 2d 88, 98–99 (D.D.C. 2002); and

*"convene . . . [an IEP] meeting within thirty days to prepare an IEP . . . , based on . . . [the student's] unique needs" that includes instruction in daily living skills, J.B. v. Killingly Bd. of Educ., 990 F. Supp. 57, 80 (D. Conn. 1997).

4. Courts have also considered requests for preliminary injunctive relief in cases seeking to remedy systemic violations of the IDEA. The following case is a good example.

Blackman v. District of Columbia

277 F. Supp. 2d 71 (D.D.C. 2003)

Paul L. Friedman, District Judge.

This matter is before the Court for consideration of five reports filed by the Special Master in which she recommends that the Court grant the motions for preliminary injunction filed on behalf of eleven members of the class. . . . Underlying each motion for a preliminary injunction is a claim that the plaintiffs are being irreparably harmed by defendants' failure to schedule timely due process hearings in violation Section 1415(f) of the Individuals with Disabilities Education Act, 20 U.S.C. §§ 1450, *et seq.* ("IDEA"). . . .

I. BACKGROUND

A. *The Special Master's Findings and Recommended Relief*

In her reports, the Special Master made the following findings of fact with respect to these eleven plaintiffs.

1. Claims of Afra Abdullah, *et al.*

With respect to the claims of Afra Abdullah, Charles "Tucker" Battle III, Elvin Charles, Zachary Devillier and James Tanney-Palmeter, the Special Master determined that in each case: (1) the District of Columbia Public Schools ("DCPS") either failed to find the student eligible for special education and/or related services under the IDEA or issued an individualized education program ("IEP") with which the parents disagreed; (2) the parents placed their child in a private school that provided the special education and related services they believed their child required; (3) the parents concurrently or shortly thereafter filed a request for a due process hearing challenging DCPS's determination, indicating, pursuant to DCPS instructions, three dates on which plaintiffs and plaintiffs' counsel were available for a hearing during the ensuing 35 days; (4) with the exception of Afra Abdullah, DCPS sent a notice of a due process hearing to plaintiffs' counsel scheduled on none of the dates requested and at times at which either plaintiffs or plaintiffs' counsel were unavailable . . . ; (5) DCPS failed to hold a timely due process hearing . . . ; (6) plaintiffs' counsel filed a motion for summary determination with the DCPS student hearing office that was not acted upon; (7) plaintiffs filed a motion for a preliminary injunction with this Court; and (8) DCPS sent plaintiffs a hearing notice months after the close of the period within which DCPS was statutorily required to hold the due process hearing and issue a determination, purporting to schedule a hearing two days before the already-scheduled meeting with the Special Master.

. . . .

[The special master made similar findings about the remaining plaintiffs.]

. . . .

II. DISCUSSION

A. *Standard of Review for Emergency Injunctive Relief*

Under the familiar standard for deciding whether to grant emergency injunctive relief, the Court must consider (1) whether there is a substantial likelihood that plaintiffs will succeed on the merits of their claims, (2) whether plaintiffs will suffer irreparable injury absent an injunction, (3) the harm to defendants or other interested parties (balance of harms), and (4) whether an injunction would be in the public interest or at least not be adverse to the public interest.

Plaintiffs are not required to prevail on each of these factors. Rather, the factors must be viewed as a continuum, with more of one factor compensating for less of another. "If the arguments for one factor are particularly strong, an injunction may issue even if the arguments in other areas are rather weak." *CityFed Fin. Corp. v. Office of Thrift Supervision*, 58 F.3d 738, 747 (D.C. Cir. 1995). An injunction may be justified "where there is a particularly strong likelihood of success on the merits even if there is a relatively slight showing of irreparable injury." *Id.* Conversely, when the other three factors strongly favor interim relief, a court may grant injunctive relief when the moving party has merely made out a "substantial" case on the merits. The necessary level or degree of likelihood of success that must be shown will vary according to the Court's assessment of the other factors. In sum, an injunction may be issued "with either a high probability of success and some injury, or vice versa." *Cuomo v. United States Nuclear Regulatory Comm'n.*, 772 F.2d 972, 974 (D.C. Cir. 1985).

B. *Denial of Timely Due Process Hearings and Resulting Irreparable Harm*

The crux of the disagreement among the parties lies in the second prong of the preliminary injunction standard: irreparable harm. The Special Master concluded that DCPS's failure to provide timely due process hearings constitutes irreparable harm to plaintiffs because the right to a hearing "is absolute, and the failure to provide a timely hearing has consequences that are absolute—that is, there is no substitute available to the student and his or her family. It is the absolute lack of any alternative to the student that causes 'irreparable harm' at the hands of DCPS." Defendants counter that because the timely provision of due process hearings is a procedural protection provided in the IDEA, plaintiffs must demonstrate that actual harm or prejudice resulted from the denial of a hearing in order to merit injunctive relief. In the absence of such harm, the failure to provide a hearing may be remedied by directing that such a hearing promptly be held.

Defendants' failure to provide a *timely* due process hearing to plaintiffs is not an unimportant or technical violation of the procedural safeguards provided for in the IDEA. Rather, it is the denial of a fundamental component of the due process protections afforded by the statute. As the Supreme Court noted in *Board of Education of the Hendrick Hudson Central School District v. Rowley*, 458 U.S. 176 . . . (1982), the procedural due process protections included by Congress in the IDEA are of critical importance to effectuating the goals of the statute . . . . "The Act . . . was intended to ensure prompt resolution of disputes regarding appropriate education for handicapped children." *Spiegler v. District of Columbia*, 866 F.2d 461, 467 (D.C. Cir. 1989). Of all the procedural rights provided by Congress in the IDEA, "[t]he due process hearing is the Act's primary procedural protection" in effectuating this purpose. *Kroot v. District of Columbia*, 800 F. Supp. 976, 982 (D.D.C. 1992).

In light of the primacy the due process hearing has in ensuring plaintiffs' substantive rights under the statute, the Court concludes that DCPS's failure to provide timely due process hearings and determinations can itself constitute the denial of a free appropriate education. While a slight delay in the provision of a hearing after a request has been made or a slight delay in rendering a decision may be an excusable procedural infirmity in some cases, the failure to offer the parents and their children a timely hearing for months after the expiration of the 45-day period, as was the case here, crosses the line from process to substance.

As this Court previously has held, the failure to provide an IEP, the failure to hold a due process hearing, or the failure to provide a written determination in a timely manner after requests for an IEP meeting or a hearing have been made constitutes the denial of a free appropriate public education as required by the IDEA. Where there is a denial of a free appropriate education because no hearing has been held and no determination has been issued, and a proper placement therefore has not been made, there results a *per se* harm to the student and the irreparable injury requirement for a preliminary injunction has been satisfied. Indeed, each day a child is denied a free appropriate education by such procedural dereliction of a school system, he or she is harmed yet again. . . .

. . . .

The conclusion that a *per se* harm results from the denial of a free appropriate education stemming from the failure to provide a timely due process hearing relieves plaintiffs from any burden to articulate an additional, particularized harm. When a plaintiff's rights to the due process hearing are circumscribed in significant ways, a plaintiff need not show prejudice in order to demonstrate injury. It follows that where DCPS has outright denied a child a timely due process hearing, DCPS cannot claim that the denial of a free appropriate education has not occurred. It has.

The Court also rejects defendants' argument that these students have not been denied a free appropriate education because, with the exception of . . . [one student], they currently attend private schools at which they have been placed by their parents. The issue here is not the parents' financial ability to fund their children at private schools pending the outcome of a due process hearing. The harm is the denial by DCPS of a *free appropriate education*, and this harm is not dependent on the financial resources of an individual plaintiff's family. Put simply, the children cannot be denied their substantive right to a free appropriate education under the IDEA because they are fortunate enough to have parents who can afford to fund their education in private schools while waiting for DCPS to provide the hearings required by law that will determine whether the child's private placement or some other placement is the appropriate one. Any other conclusion would require parents to deny their children an education altogether in order to protect their rights under the statute. The Court will not endorse such a perverse incentive.

. . . .

C. *The Remaining Prongs of the Injunctive Relief Standard*

The Court adopts the Special Master's conclusions with respect to the remaining prongs of the standard for emergency injunctive relief. Success on the merits of the underlying claim is assured in light of the Court's previous finding of liability in this matter. The Special Master also is correct that the provision of injunctive relief to these eleven plaintiffs does not disturb the ongoing rights of defendants because the defendants remain able to change any placement ordered by the Court, provided the change is made in a manner that complies with the IDEA. Finally, the Special Master properly acknowledged the significant public interest in the proper implementation of the IDEA.

D. *Adequacy of Recommended Remedy*

The Special Master recommended three remedies for ten of the eleven students: (1) maintenance of those students' placements through the end of the 2002–2003 school year; (2) the provision of due process hearings by DCPS within one month from the date of any Court order; and (3) reimbursement of monies paid by the parents for the private schools currently attended by the students for the 2002–2003 school year. The Special Master's first recommendation—that DCPS be ordered to maintain placements at the private schools through the end of the 2002–2003 school year—is moot because the school year has ended. The children are still without due process hearings, however. The Court therefore directs that DCPS shall issue notices of placement for the children at the private provider of the parents' choice for the upcoming 2003–2004 school year and that such placements shall remain in effect until such due process hearings are conducted and decisions are issued. If the due process hearing officer determines on an individual basis that a child's placement should be elsewhere, DCPS can issue a new notice of placement at that time. As the new school year fast approaches, the Court recognizes the necessity for these students to have appropriate placements as soon as possible. The Court therefore will adopt the Special Master's second recommendation that DCPS conduct the due process hearings requested by these plaintiffs immediately, but no later than 10 business days from the date of this Opinion.

Finally, the Court adopts the Special Master's third recommendation, with one caveat. The Special Master recommended that the parents be reimbursed for the money they have paid and may continue to pay to private providers until DCPS complies with the IDEA. Reimbursement for payments made to private providers by parents who unilaterally place their child in a private placement after the child has been denied a free appropriate education by his or her public school system is not a novel remedy. In fact, the IDEA itself expressly provides for the reimbursement of monies paid by parents who unilaterally place their children with private providers under certain circumstances....

Nor does reimbursement for payments to private providers to parents whose children have been denied a free appropriate education unduly or unfairly burden defendants. As the Supreme Court has announced, "public educational authorities who want to avoid reimbursing parents for the private education of a disabled child can do one of two things: give the child a free appropriate public education in a public setting, or place the child in an appropriate private setting of the State's choice." *Florence County School District Four v. Carter*, 510 U.S. 7, 15 ... (1993)....

As the Court already has determined, DCPS denied plaintiffs a free appropriate education when the 45-day period within which DCPS was required to conduct due process hearings and issue determinations expired without any hearings having taken place. It is appropriate therefore that the plaintiff parents be reimbursed for those months in which their children were denied due process hearings following the expiration of the 45-day period.

....

ORDER

For the reasons set forth in a separate Opinion issued this same day, it is hereby ORDERED that the motion for preliminary injunction filed by Idriys and Melva Abdullah, parents and next friends of Afra Abdullah is GRANTED; it is

FURTHER ORDERED that

1. the District of Columbia Public Schools ("DCPS") shall issue immediately a notice of a placement for Afra Abdullah at Kingsbury Day School and shall fund this placement prospectively until such time as DCPS issues a notice of change in placement that is in accordance with the procedural protections provided for by the Individuals with Disabilities Education Act[ ] . . . ;

2. DCPS shall fund this placement retroactively to October 27, 2002, 45 days after plaintiffs Idriys and Melva Abdullah filed their administrative due process hearing request on September 12, 2002;

3. DCPS shall conduct a due process hearing to determine the need for special education services for Afra Abdullah and the appropriateness of the Kingsbury Day School placement 10 business days from the date of this Order. . . .

[The court issued similar orders for each plaintiff.]

B. Permanent Injunctive Relief

United States v. Arkansas

794 F. Supp. 2d 935 (E.D. Ark. 2011)

J. Leon Holmes, District Judge.

. . . .

I.

FINDINGS OF FACT

A. *INTRODUCTORY FINDINGS OF FACT*

. . . .

1. The Residents of Conway Human Development Center

. . . .

Conway Human Development Center is the only human development center operated by the State of Arkansas that provides services to children. In July of 2009, fifty-two of the residents at the Center were school-aged children, and at the time of trial, forty-eight of the residents were under the age of twenty-one. Many of these children came to Conway Human Development Center as a result of maladaptive behaviors. They previously lived at home, in foster care, in group homes, or in other such settings and may have attended public schools. Unfortunately, their maladaptive behaviors proved to be more than their caregivers and school officials could manage, so their parents or guardians sought to have them admitted to Conway Human Development Center. Some of the children are in the custody of the Division of Child and Family Services due to neglect, physical maltreatment, or sexual maltreatment.

. . . .

D. *ALLEGATIONS THAT CONWAY HUMAN DEVELOPMENT CENTER VIOLATES THE INDIVIDUALS WITH DISABILITIES EDUCATION ACT*

The plaintiff's third claim for relief is for alleged violations of the Individuals with Disabilities Education Act, which requires certain institutions to provide a free appropriate public education in the least restrictive setting appropriate to school-aged children with disabilities. At the time of trial, Conway Human Development Center had forty-eight school-aged residents and a total of fifty-three children in its special education classes.

The parties presented conflicting expert testimony on the issue of whether Conway Human Development Center complies with the Individuals with Disabilities Education Act. The plaintiff called as an expert witness Susan Thibadeau, Ph.D., while the defendants called Derek Nye, Ph.D., and Bruce Gale, Ph.D. All three were qualified as experts and all three testified credibly.

Dr. Thibadeau's ultimate conclusion was that Conway Human Development Center did not meet its obligation under the Individuals with Disabilities Education Act to provide each child with a free appropriate public education. She testified that many of the children were receiving only ninety minutes per day of special education services, or 450 minutes per week, which she believed was inadequate. Although the students, according to Dr. Thibadeau, nominally spent more than six hours per day in special education services, much of that time was actually spent in habilitation classes that were neither taught nor supervised by special education teachers. Furthermore, Dr. Thibadeau did not believe that the special education teachers at Conway Human Development Center received adequate supervision or sufficient ongoing training.

Dr. Thibadeau also testified that Conway Human Development Center did not educate children in the least restrictive environment, as required by the Individuals with Disabilities Education Act. She testified that several of the children had mild cognitive disabilities and came to Conway Human Development Center because of behavioral problems, but with the improvement of the behavioral problems at the Center, she believed that those children could transition to a less restrictive environment.

In addition, Dr. Thibadeau criticized the assessment test used at Conway Human Development Center and the quality of the individualized education plans, including the transition plans. As a part of her criticism of the transition plans, Dr. Thibadeau testified that there was no indication that adult service agencies participated in transition planning. Dr. Thibadeau also "had concerns" about the "integration of different therapies," saying that the psychological examiners did not spend enough time in the classrooms. She also "had some concerns" about the students' "quality of life," referring specifically to the fact that nineteen of the forty-five children whose records she reviewed were not toilet trained and several were eating chopped or pureed food instead of being taught to eat more slowly.

Needless to say, the experts for the defendants disagreed with Dr. Thibadeau's conclusions. Their ultimate conclusion was that Conway Human Development Center complied with the Individuals with Disabilities Education Act and specifically that it provided a free appropriate public education. Contrary to Dr. Thibadeau, they testified that the amount of time spent in special education classes each day was adequate to comply with the requirements of the Individuals with Disabilities Education Act. They disagreed that the assessment tool used by the Center was inappropriate. Dr. Nye testified that Conway Human Development Center is the least restrictive environment for the children there.

The Arkansas Department of Education is charged with monitoring schools in Arkansas and enforcing compliance with the Individuals with Disabilities Education Act. In January of 2010—after Dr. Thibadeau had completed her report—the Arkansas Department of Education officially investigated Conway Human Development Center for compliance with that Act. The Arkansas Department of Education issued its official report on June 16, 2010, in the form of a letter to Calvin Price, Superintendent of the Center. The report found that Conway Human Development Center was in substantial compliance with the least restrictive environment requirements of the Individuals with Disabilities Education Act, as well as some of the other significant requirements of the Act, but that there were fifteen areas of noncompliance.

Several of the areas of noncompliance involved procedural or technical requirements that readily can be remedied. For example, Conway Human Development Center was found not to be in compliance with the requirement that evaluation procedures be completed and a written report submitted to the Arkansas Department of Education within sixty days from receiving formal consent from a parent or guardian. Another area of noncompliance related to the fact that in its evaluations the Center used categories applicable to the Medicaid program rather than categories applicable to the Individuals with Disabilities Education Act. An example of this type of noncompliance given at trial was that the Center would classify a child as having cerebral palsy, whereas the proper category for special education purposes would be "health impaired" or "multiply disabled."

Not all of the criticisms by the Arkansas Department of Education are merely technical. First, the Arkansas Department of Education found that the individualized education plans at Conway Human Development Center did not sufficiently take into account special factors that impede a child's learning, such as maladaptive behaviors, lack of English proficiency, impaired vision or hearing, and the like; did not adequately address the unique needs of each child; and did not adequately plan for children's transition after secondary school. In regard to transition planning, it appeared that representatives of other agencies were not invited to meetings to discuss post-secondary goals and transition services. Second, the Arkansas Department of Education found that Conway Human Development Center failed to provide a free appropriate public education because it failed to meet the required ratio of teachers to pupils. For students whose primary program is special education, the teacher to pupil ratio should be one to fifteen, one to ten, or one to six, depending on how much time, attention, and related services each child needs. Although the record is not as explicit on this point as the Court would like, it appears that for most of the children at Conway Human Development Center the requirement is no more than six pupils to every one teacher; the Center had more than six pupils per teacher. Third, the Arkansas Department of Education found that Conway Human Development Center was not providing a free appropriate public education because children did not spend sufficient time in school receiving special education services. The Arkansas Department of Education seemed to agree with Dr. Thibadeau that many of the children at Conway Human Development Center were receiving only ninety minutes per day of special education. Fourth, the Arkansas Department of Education found that Conway Human Development Center failed to provide a free appropriate public education because it failed to adopt "promising educational practices proven effective through research and demonstration for the provision of special education instruction." As explained at trial, this finding means that teachers at Conway Human Development Center were not acquainted with some of the more current types of strategies, interventions, and programs that can be effective with children like those served at the Center, and no system was in place to keep teachers current.

In short, the Arkansas Department of Education found that Conway Human Development Center did not adequately plan special education for each child, did not provide the children with adequate time in special education classes, did not provide an adequate number of teachers, and did not provide for continuing education adequate to enable the teachers to do their job well.

As noted above, the monitoring by the Arkansas Department of Education was conducted after Dr. Thibadeau had submitted her report, and the persons who conducted the monitoring reviewed Dr. Thibadeau's report. It is apparent that the monitors from the Arkansas Department of Education examined the program at Conway Human Development Center with a view toward determining whether the criticisms made by Dr. Thibadeau were accurate or not, and they did so using a process that was systematic and impartial. They confirmed many but not all of Dr. Thibadeau's criticisms. After considering all of the evidence, the Court is persuaded that the findings of the Arkansas Department of Education are true. The finding that Conway Human Development Center educates children in the least restrictive environment is supported not only by the testimony of Dr. Nye but also by the determination of each child's individual education plan team—a team that consists of the persons who are best situated to make that decision regarding that child. The findings that Conway Human Development Center has failed to provide adequate plans and has failed to include other agencies in transition planning is supported by the testimony of Dr. Thibadeau. The finding that children spend too little time in special education classes is supported by the testimony of Dr. Thibadeau. The finding that teachers are not given appropriate continuing education is supported by the testimony of Dr. Thibadeau. Finally, as to the finding that the teacher to pupil ratio was inadequate, it is within the province of the Arkansas Department of Education to set a standard for the teacher to pupil ratio inasmuch as one element of the definition of "free appropriate public education" is compliance with standards of the state educational agency. 20 U.S.C. § 1401(9). The greater weight of the evidence supports the findings of the Arkansas Department of Education, as described above, so those findings are adopted as the findings of this Court.

In response to the letter of noncompliance, Conway Human Development Center was required to submit a corrective action plan. The process of submitting the corrective action plan had begun before trial, but was continuing at the time of trial. At the time of trial, the Center had added special education instruction times and developed new pupil schedules. Additional special education teachers had been hired. Conway Human Development Center was in the process of hiring additional staff. The Center was also changing its professional development policies to bring them into compliance.

When the trial concluded and the record closed, the Arkansas Department of Education had not yet determined whether the corrective action taken by Conway Human Development Center would be sufficient to bring the Center's special education program into compliance with the Individuals with Disabilities Education Act. The process was ongoing and was not scheduled to be completed until sometime after trial. Nonetheless, the evidence was sufficient to show that the Arkansas Department of Education will ensure that the appropriate corrective action is taken to bring the Center's special education program into compliance with the Individuals with Disabilities Education Act. Although the monitors from the Arkansas Department of Education did not review the file of every child at Conway Human Development Center, in the corrective action process, the Center will be required to review the programs for all similarly situated children and correct them. As Marcia Harding testified, "[W]e set out corrective actions, and we go in and assure that it gets corrected." The Court believes her.

II.

CONCLUSIONS OF LAW

. . . .

D. *CONCLUSIONS OF LAW REGARDING THE INDIVIDUALS WITH DISABILITIES EDUCATION ACT*

. . . .

Having concluded that Conway Human Development Center has failed to comply fully with the Individuals with Disabilities Education Act, the issue is whether to enter an injunction. An injunction is an equitable remedy that does not issue as a matter of course. An injunction should issue only when legal remedies are inadequate and irreparable injury will occur without the injunction. A court should be especially cautious when contemplating relief that implicates public interests. In determining whether to exercise the Court's equitable discretion to enter an injunction in a case such as this one, where Congress has provided a regulatory scheme, the Court should consider the regulatory scheme at issue and the enforcement mechanisms provided therein. . . .

The Individuals with Disabilities Education Act imposes a duty for monitoring and supervising compliance with the Individuals with Disabilities Education Act on a state educational agency to be selected by the state:

> . . . .
>
> The State educational agency is responsible for ensuring that—
>
> (i) the requirements of this subchapter are met;
>
> (ii) all educational programs for children with disabilities in the State, including all such programs administered by any other State agency or local agency—
>
> (I) are under the general supervision of individuals in the State who are responsible for educational programs for children with disabilities; and
>
> (II) meet the educational standards of the State educational agency[.]

20 U.S.C. § 1412(a)(11)(A).

As section 1412(a)(11)(A) makes clear, the state agency's responsibility to supervise special education programs includes not only a duty to monitor but also to enforce. Section 1416(a)(1)(C) provides that the Secretary of Education must "require States to—(i) monitor implementation of this subchapter by local educational agencies; and (ii) enforce this subchapter . . . ." In Arkansas, the state educational agency responsible for monitoring and ensuring compliance with the Individuals with Disabilities Education Act is the Arkansas Department of Education.

As stated above, the Arkansas Department of Education has required Conway Human Development Center to submit a corrective action plan for bringing its special education program into compliance with the Individuals with Disabilities Education Act. The Arkansas Department of Education will evaluate and determine whether the corrective action plan is appropriate and will ensure that the special education program at Conway Human Development Center complies with the Individuals with Disabilities Education Act. Therefore, it is not necessary for this Court to enter an injunction in order to secure the rights guaranteed by the Individuals with Disabilities Education Act to students at Conway Human Development Center.

CONCLUSION

The Court finds and concludes that Conway Human Development Center . . . [has not complied] with . . . all of the requirements of the Individuals with Disabilities Education Act. Because Congress has provided for a state educational agency to enforce compliance with that Act, and because the evidence established that the state educational agency here is enforcing and will enforce compliance, no injunction is necessary or appropriate.

A judgment dismissing this action with prejudice will be entered separately.

Notes, Comments, and Questions

1. Affirmative litigation and institutional reform litigation have played a crucial role in protecting the rights of children with disabilities. The *PARC* and *Mills* cases described in Chapter One were catalysts for the legislation to protect the educational rights of children with disabilities. Are there any parallels between the relief the courts ordered in those cases and the relief the plaintiffs sought but the court refused to order in *United States v. Arkansas*? If Pennsylvania and the District of Columbia had committed to fix the problems raised in *PARC* and *Mills*, would that have been sufficient to preclude the injunctions that the courts in those cases ordered? What arguments could be made in favor of granting the injunction? Should the court have taken account of the apparent failure of the Arkansas Department of Education to enforce the IDEA at the Conway Human Development Center in determining whether it could trust the Department to enforce the IDEA without an injunction? Why do you think the court dismissed the case with prejudice? Should the court have dismissed the case without prejudice? What is the difference? Instead of dismissing the case, should the court have given a compliance deadline to the Arkansas Department of Education?

2. The court in *Schmelzer v. New York*, 363 F. Supp. 2d 453, 461 (E.D.N.Y. 2003), issued a permanent injunction requiring the SRO to issue decisions on appeals from IHO decisions within thirty days. The court ruled as follows:

> The standard to be applied in determining whether a permanent injunction should issue is, whether in the absence of injunctive relief, the party will suffer irreparable harm and whether the party will actually succeed on the merits.
>
> Plaintiffs have asserted that the irreparable injury in this case is harm to the disabled children as a result of the SRO delays.... Pending an SRO decision, a student could be in an improper educational setting notwithstanding the stay-put provisions of the IDEA. The Plaintiffs have not put forth a substantial amount of evidence of irreparable injury because, in this Court's opinion, such injury is obvious.... Inordinate delays in the decision making process deprive those students of the rights provided to them under the IDEA and cause those students to suffer irreparable harm.... Accordingly, this Court finds that Plaintiffs sufficiently proved that they will suffer irreparable harm absent some form of injunctive relief.
>
> The second element necessary to issue a permanent injunction is actual success on the merits. Plaintiffs argue that they have succeeded on the merits of their case because they have shown that Defendants continuously

> violated 34 C.F.R. § 300.511 . . . by failing to comply with the timeliness requirements. Defendants argue that an injunction does not merely issue upon a showing of a violation, but rather it only issues in the discretion of the judge. Defendants request a reasonable opportunity to get into compliance. However, this Court notes that the case was filed in 2001, and Defendants have had more than two years to comply.

Id. at 459–60. Should the court have given the state more time to comply? Can you distinguish *Schmelzer* from *U.S. v. Arkansas*? *See* Bitsilly v. Bureau of Indian Affairs, 253 F. Supp. 2d 1257, 1269 (D.N.M. 2003) (denying injunction because there was no showing that the children's former schools would not follow the IDEA if the children returned to school).

Chapter 17

Attorneys Fees, Costs, and Expenses

Introduction

This chapter will cover the availability of attorneys fees, costs, and expenses to prevailing parties in IDEA cases. Section One covers attorneys fees and Section Two covers costs and expenses.

Problem

Gary filed an IDEA complaint notice on behalf of his client W.G., currently a fifth grader, claiming that W.G.'s school district had failed to identify W.G. as a child with a disability in need of special education by the end of second grade, when her behavioral issues and difficulties with learning put the district on notice that she might have a disability. The complaint stated that the district evaluated W.G. at the end of her third grade year and determined that she suffered from attention deficit hyperactivity disorder and dyslexia. The district prepared an IEP for W.G. for fourth grade. The IEP stated that W.G. was approximately six months behind in reading and math. The IEP's goals included closing this gap by the end of fifth grade. The IEP prescribed individual and group counseling, speech and language therapy, reading instruction in the Wilson method, and extra time on tests. By the end of fourth grade, the complaint asserts, W.G. had not made adequate progress. The complaint asserted that W.G.'s fifth grade IEP did not address this lack of progress, and simply provided the same special education and related services as the fourth grade IEP. The complaint requested the following relief: 1) compensatory education for the district's failure to provide an IEP for W.G. in third grade in the form of forty hours of reading instruction in the Wilson method and forty hours of speech and language therapy; 2) the same amount of compensatory education for the district's failure to provide adequate special education and related services in fourth grade; 3) an increase in speech and language therapy from once a week for thirty minutes per session to three times a week for thirty minutes per session; 4) after-school instruction in the Wilson method; 5) summer instruction between fifth and sixth grade; and 6) reimbursement for the costs of hiring a private tutor and therapist for W.G. during fourth grade in the amount of $25,000.

Two weeks before the impartial hearing, the District made the following settlement offer to Gary: 1) twenty hours of reading instruction and twenty hours of speech and language therapy as compensatory education; 2) two sessions of speech and language therapy per week for thirty minutes per session; 3) five hours per week of after-school instruction in the Wilson method; and 4) reimbursement of $12,500 for tutoring and therapists during fourth grade. Gary rejected the settlement offer.

Following the hearing, the IHO ruled in favor of W.G. The IHO ruled that the district should have identified W.G. as a child with a disability in need of special education by the end of third grade and that the District denied W.G. a FAPE in the third and fourth grades. The IHO awarded W.G. the following relief: 1) thirty hours of reading instruction in the Wilson method as compensatory education; 2) an additional half-hour session per week of speech and language therapy; 3) five hours per week of after-school instruction in the Wilson method; 4) four weeks of summer instruction between fifth and sixth grade; and 5) reimbursement of $10,000 for tutoring and therapists during fourth grade.

After the time for appealing the IHO's decision to the SRO expired, Gary submitted a request for attorneys fees and expenses to the district. The district rejected the request. Gary then filed a lawsuit in federal district court seeking attorneys fees and costs. Gary filed the lawsuit one year and thirty days after the IHO issued her decision. The state in which Gary filed suit does not have a statute of limitations for filing attorneys fees claims but does have a one-year statute of limitations for claims based on statutes and two years for claims for which there is no statute of limitations.

Gary requested fees for his legal work in the amount of $12,000. This represented forty hours of work at a rate of $300 per hour. Gary did not charge W.G.'s parents a fee for representing them in the case, and in return the parents agreed to assign their attorneys fee claim to Gary if they prevailed in the case. Gary submitted an affidavit that stated his normal rate for administrative and federal court litigation was $300 per hour and he also submitted affidavits from three attorneys in the community that stated they charged $350 per hour for representing clients in IDEA administrative and federal court litigation.

Also included in the fee request was $3,000 for ten hours of legal work by W.G.'s mother, who is an experienced federal court litigator. Her work consisted of drafting the complaint in the federal court case, attending a pre-motion conference, and assisting in drafting the brief in support of the attorneys fees request.

Finally, the request included $3,000 in expenses. These included $1,500 for an expert in learning disabilities to review the post-hearing brief from the impartial hearing, $1,000 for paralegal and law student fees, and the rest in various costs, including Lexis research, copying, Federal Express and mailing, and travel.

The District asserted the following objections to Gary's request for attorneys fees, costs, and expenses: 1) the request should be denied because it was filed after the applicable statute of limitations; 2) the request should be denied because W.G. was not a prevailing party; 2) the request should be denied because the final relief W.G. obtained was not more favorable than the settlement offer; 4) the fee should be reduced by at least fifty percent because W.G. prevailed only partially; 5) Gary is not entitled to fees because he did not charge the parents fees for the case; 6) Gary's rate should be reduced because the rate for administrative litigation is lower than for federal court litigation; 7) the fee should be reduced because the number of hours was excessive; and 8) the court should not award fees to W.G.'s mother or to the learning disabilities expert.

Section One
Attorneys Fees

The IDEA allows a court, "in its discretion," to award "reasonable attorneys fees" to parents of a child with a disability who prevail in an action or proceeding under the IDEA. 20 U.S.C. § 1415(i)(3)(B)(i)(I) (2012). The IDEA also allows a court to award fees to a prevailing school district in limited circumstances, including bad faith or frivolous litigation by parents or their attorneys. *Id.* at § (B)(i)(II) and (III). The hourly rate for the fee is to be based on the rate prevailing in the community in which the case arose "for the kind and quality of services provided." *Id.* at § (C). A court can reduce the amount of fees if it finds that the parent or parent's attorney unreasonably delayed, the amount requested unreasonably exceeds the prevailing hourly rate, or the time spent on the case was excessive. *Id.* at § (F)(i)–(iii). Finally, the IDEA bars fees in several circumstances, including when a party rejects a settlement offer that was more favorable than the ultimate relief the party obtained. *Id.* at § (D)(i)(I)–(III).

This section considers several issues that arise in connection with attorneys fees applications. These include: 1) the definition of prevailing party; 2) determining whether a party prevailed; 3) categorical eligibility to receive attorneys fees; 4) the method for calculating attorneys fees; 5) discretionary reductions in attorneys fees based on a limited degree of success; and 6) mandatory reductions in or denials of attorneys fees.

A. The Definition of Prevailing Party

The IDEA states:

(B) Award of attorneys fees

(i) In general

In any action or proceeding brought under this section, the court, in its discretion, may award reasonable attorneys' fees as part of the costs—

(I) to a prevailing party who is the parent of a child with a disability;

(II) to a prevailing party who is a State educational agency or local educational agency against the attorney of a parent who files a complaint or subsequent cause of action that is frivolous, unreasonable, or without foundation, or against the attorney of a parent who continued to

> litigate after the litigation clearly became frivolous, unreasonable, or without foundation; or
>
> (III) to a prevailing State educational agency or local educational agency against the attorney of a parent, or against the parent, if the parent's complaint or subsequent cause of action was presented for any improper purpose, such as to harass, to cause unnecessary delay, or to needlessly increase the cost of litigation.

20 U.S.C. § 1415(i)(3)(B)(i)(I)–(III) (2012).

The IDEA does not define "prevailing party." Instead, federal courts have considered whether the Supreme Court's definition of "prevailing party" in *Buckhannon Bd. & Care Home, Inc. v. W. Va. Dep't of Health and Human Res.*, 532 U.S. 598 (2001)—a case involving attorneys fees under the federal Fair Housing Act and Americans with Disabilities Act—should apply to the IDEA. A representative case that considers this question follows.

Doe v. Boston Pub. Sch.

358 F.3d 20 (1st Cir. 2004)

STAHL, Senior Circuit Judge.

Plaintiff-appellant Jane Doe sued defendant-appellee City of Boston Public Schools ("Boston") pursuant to the Individuals with Disabilities Education Act ("IDEA"), 20 U.S.C. § 1415, *et seq.*, seeking placement in a private therapeutic day school. After negotiations, Boston offered Doe the placement she sought. When Doe requested attorneys' fees, the district court dismissed her complaint on the ground that she was not a "prevailing party" within the meaning of *Buckhannon Bd. & Care Home, Inc. v. W. Va. Dep't of Health and Human Res.*, 532 U.S. 598 . . . (2001). We affirm the district court's dismissal.

. . . .

II. DISCUSSION

The central question we must decide is whether *Buckhannon* applies to the IDEA's definition of "prevailing party," thus precluding recovery of attorneys' fees following a private settlement. This is a question of first impression in our circuit. . . .

A. *The IDEA and HCPA*

The IDEA was enacted in 1975 to ensure that disabled children could receive an appropriate education free of cost. It authorizes students and their parents to enforce this substantive right by filing suit against school departments. In *Smith v. Robinson*, 468 U.S. 992, 1014 . . . (1984), the Supreme Court held that Congress had not intended to permit prevailing parties to recover attorneys' fees in IDEA cases. This decision brought a quick response from Congress, with bills filed almost immediately seeking to amend the statute to add an express fee-shifting provision.

In 1986, Congress passed the Handicapped Children's Protection Act (HCPA). HCPA was the result of a series of legislative compromises; what began as a simple fee-shifting clause mimicking other federal civil rights statutes evolved into a more complex provision, with multiple restrictions on who could recover fees, when they could be recovered, and the amount of recovery.

....

B. *The Buckhannon decision and its application to other fee-shifting statutes*

In 2001, fifteen years after HCPA initially was enacted, the Supreme Court decided *Buckhannon*. There, the plaintiffs sought attorneys fees pursuant to the Fair Housing Amendments Act of 1988 (FHAA) and the Americans with Disabilities Act of 1990 (ADA). The plaintiffs cited the "catalyst theory" of recovery: because their lawsuit had brought about a voluntary change in the conduct of the defendant, they were "prevailing parties" and thus entitled to recover fees.

The Supreme Court rejected the catalyst theory as a basis for the fee award. It held that the term "prevailing party," as used in the FHAA, ADA and "numerous" other federal statutes, meant a party who has received a judgment on the merits or a court-ordered consent decree. The Court listed several statutes, in addition to the FHAA and ADA, that employed the term "prevailing party," and noted that the term appears in numerous other federal statutes as well. It did not specifically reference the IDEA.

At the core of the Court's reasoning was the concept of "judicial imprimatur"; in order to prevail, a party must achieve a "court-ordered" change in the legal relationship of the parties. Absent this imprimatur, a federal court may be unable to retain jurisdiction so it can oversee execution of the settlement. "Our precedents thus counsel against holding that the term 'prevailing party' authorizes an award of attorney's fees *without* a corresponding alteration in the legal relationship of the parties."

Buckhannon's prohibition on catalyst theory-based fee-shifting applies expansively. . . . [T]he principles underlying *Buckhannon*'s holding are broadly stated and are not statute-specific. The *Buckhannon* court used "prevailing party" as a legal term of art (meaning "a party in whose favor a judgment is rendered") to be interpreted consistently across fee-shifting statutes. It also relied on the general baseline "American Rule" that each party pays its own fees. Moreover, the Court expressed a preference for avoiding a "second major litigation" that would frequently ensue from an application of the catalyst theory, which would involve "analysis of the defendant's subjective motivations in changing its conduct." *Id.* at 609.

Doe urges that we follow the minority interpretation of *Buckhannon* set forth in *Barrios v. Calif. Interscholastic Fed'n*, 277 F.3d 1128, 1134 n.5 (9th Cir.) . . . . There, the Ninth Circuit held that *Buckhannon* permitted the award of attorneys' fees to an ADA plaintiff who settled privately. It stated that *Buckhannon* barred recovery of fees only by a plaintiff who was the catalyst for legislative change, and that the Supreme Court's limitation of prevailing party status to plaintiffs who win judgments or enter consent decrees was merely dicta.

The *Barrios* court's reading of *Buckhannon* seems to contravene the Supreme Court's unambiguous rejection of private settlement as sufficient grounds for "prevailing party" status:

> Private settlements do not entail the judicial approval and oversight involved in consent decrees. And federal jurisdiction to enforce a private contractual settlement will often be lacking unless the terms of the agreement are incorporated into the order of dismissal.

532 U.S. at 604 n.7. Accordingly, we decline to adopt the Ninth Circuit's narrow interpretation. Other circuits considering the issue have applied *Buckhannon* as precluding fee awards in private settlement situations, explicitly or impliedly rejecting *Barrios'* interpretation. *See, e.g., T.D. v. La Grange Sch. Dist. No. 102*, 349 F.3d 469, 476 (7th Cir. 2003); *John T. v. Del. County Intermediate Unit*, 318 F.3d 545, 560–61 (3rd Cir. 2003) . . . .

C. *Buckhannon's application to the IDEA*

To date, each of the three circuit courts that have considered the application of *Buckhannon* to the IDEA have held that IDEA plaintiffs who achieve their desired result via private settlement may not be considered "prevailing parties," and thus cannot recover attorneys fees under 20 U.S.C. § 1415(i). *T.D.*, 349 F.3d at 476–78; *John T.*, 318 F.3d at 557; *J.C. v. Reg'l Sch. Dist. 10*, 278 F.3d 119, 124 (2d Cir. 2002).

Consistent with our "American Rule," in which parties bear their own fees in the absence of explicit statutory authority, we hold that *Buckhannon* is presumed to apply generally to all fee-shifting statutes that use the "prevailing party" terminology, including the IDEA. "Because this provision employs the phrase 'prevailing party'—a term of art—it must be interpreted and applied in the same manner as other federal fee-shifting statutes that use the same phraseology." *Me. Sch. Admin. Dist.*, 321 F.3d at 14. That presumption may be rebutted, however, if the statutory text, structure, or legislative history indicate that Congress intended to permit prevailing parties to recover fees where the desired result was achieved through settlement. *T.D.*, 349 F.3d at 475 . . . . We consider each of these possibilities in turn.

1. *Legislative text and structure*

Doe contends that the text and structure of § 1415(i) suggest that Congress intended "prevailing party" to include settlement-based fee awards. She maintains that most other fee- shifting statutes are simply constructed, and that *Buckhannon*'s holding does not extend to complex provisions such as § 1415(i). Doe also points out that § 1415(i)(3)(D)(i) explicitly links settlement to attorneys' fees by providing that under certain specified circumstances such fees may not be awarded "for services performed subsequent to the time of a written offer of settlement to a parent."

We disagree that these features place the IDEA beyond the ambit of *Buckhannon*. First, the structural complexity of the IDEA's fee-shifting provision does not, by itself, change the meaning of "prevailing party." Although the fee-shifting provisions in the FHAA and ADA are simple, *Buckhannon* additionally referenced the complex fee-shifting provision in the Equal Access to Justice Act . . . . The Court thus did not appear to intend to limit its holding to simple fee-shifting provisions. While we recognize that the IDEA's fee-shifting provision is more complex than most, nothing inherent in its structure indicates legislative support for preserving the catalyst theory in the IDEA context.

Second, the limiting exceptions enumerated in section 1415(i)(3) do not indicate that the term "prevailing party" was intended to have a broader scope than in other fee-shifting statutes. "These provisions do not inform anything about the meaning of the term 'prevailing party' in the IDEA because they are relevant only after a plaintiff has been deemed a 'prevailing party.'" *T.D.*, 349 F.3d at 476. The reference in section 1415(i)(3)(D)(i) to attorneys fees speaks only to settlement offers, not actual settlements. It does not specify whether the settlement offer is followed by additional litigation and judgment or by the successful acceptance of the offer. Thus, nothing in this text plainly indicates an intent to reimburse fees for work resulting in private settlements.

2. *Legislative history*

The legislative history of HCPA presents closer questions as to whether Congress intended to define "prevailing party" to include private settlements. The most germane legislative history available suggests simply that the IDEA's fee provisions are to be interpreted consistently with Supreme Court law and with other fee-shifting statutes. Two weeks before HCPA was passed, Representative Williams read into the record a letter by Senator Hatch: "The right to reimbursement of reasonable attorneys fees provided for in the conference report is exactly the same right that Congress has extended to other persons protected by fees statutes—no more and no less." 132 Cong. Rec. 4841 (1986). The letter went on to state that fees may be awarded to parents "consistent with applicable Supreme Court decisions interpreting 42 U.S.C. § 1988; including interpretations of such concepts as . . . 'prevailing' parent . . . .

. . . .

Several members of Congress filed an amicus curiae brief in this case . . . . They present a detailed and nuanced argument for reading the legislative history as supporting a definition of "prevailing party" to include those who settle privately. After careful review, however, we conclude that the history is ambiguous as to this question. While a reading of this history that supports providing attorneys' fees could be teased out, it is just as susceptible to other interpretations. . . . In short, the legislative history cannot supply the clear-cut intent necessary to overcome Buckhannon's presumption against settlement-based fee awards. . . .

. . . .

Doe also cites a statement made in reference to the House version of HCPA. "[I]f a parent brings an attorney to the initial complaint resolution meeting, and the school officials and the parents reach a settlement, then according to H.R. 1523 the school system is liable for the parents' attorneys fees." The bill that emerged from conference, however, was far more complex than either the House or Senate version. This statement, then, carries little weight in guiding our understanding of what Congress intended in the version of HCPA that ultimately was enacted.

Another piece of legislative history is a statement made by Senator Jeffords during the proceedings for renewing the IDEA: "If they had a good deal and didn't accept it, they don't get attorneys fees." 143 Cong. Rec. S435,402 (1997). This statement was uttered some ten years after HCPA's enactment, and seems to be nothing more than a casual restatement of § 1415(i)(3)(D)(i). As we have said, this provision reasonably could be interpreted as pertaining to settlement offers made before an order of judgment, not situations such as this. In sum, Doe has not pointed to any convincing indicia of Congressional intent to define "prevailing party" to include those who prevail via private settlements.

Doe protests that at the time the HCPA was enacted in 1986, the catalyst theory was widely considered a permissible basis for recovery of attorneys fees. Fifteen years before *Buckhannon*, she contends, Congress would have had to have been prescient to include in the statutory text or history a clear statement that attorneys fees are intended to be recoverable following settlement.

While perhaps that may be so, the same argument would extend to any statute adopted prior to *Buckhannon*, including the statutes at issue in that case itself. To rely on that argument is to disregard the Supreme Court's own conclusion in *Buckhannon*, which we cannot properly do. Should Congress wish to expressly ensure that fees are available following private settlements, it may amend the IDEA accordingly.

3. *Policy arguments*

Finally, Doe makes two cursory policy-based arguments for permitting fee awards in IDEA private settlement situations....

... [W]hen considered on their merits, neither policy argument lifts Doe over the presumption created by *Buckhannon*. First, Doe contends that we must interpret HCPA so as to effectuate one of the underlying purposes of the IDEA: the "prompt resolution of disputes regarding appropriate education for handicapped children." *Spiegler v. Dist. of Columbia*, 866 F.2d 461, 467 (D.C. Cir. 1989). This goal, although undeniably laudable, does not affect our interpretation of the term "prevailing party." As the Seventh Circuit explained in *T.D.*:

> We recognize the importance and benefit of quick resolution to any litigation; particularly, litigation that involves the educational placement of a child. But many of the same factors that make quick resolution through settlement beneficial under the IDEA apply to the statutes that were at issue in *Buckhannon* as well. For instance, there are surely strong policy reasons for quickly resolving a disabled person's claims under the ADA. Nonetheless, *Buckhannon* held that ADA plaintiffs may receive attorney's fees only upon receipt of some judicially sanctioned victory. In other words, *Buckhannon* simply has closed the door on this argument.

349 F.3d at 477.

Doe cites another purpose of the IDEA: to provide a "free appropriate public education." 20 U.S.C. § 1400(d)(1)(A). If parents cannot recover attorneys' fees after settling a dispute with a school district, she argues, then the appropriate public education is not truly "free." Although this is admittedly a practical limitation on the right protected by the statute, this is no less true of other statutes creating or protecting rights that are unquestionably subject to *Buckhannon*, and so does not change the result in this case. The IDEA guarantees the right to a free education, but "it does not explicitly guarantee the right to attorney's fees incurred in pursuit of that education . . . it is not clear that it would be against the purpose of the IDEA to require plaintiffs who do not achieve judicial imprimatur on their victory to bear their own attorney's fees." *T.D.*, 349 F.3d at 477. Again, the concern is for Congress to address.

III. CONCLUSION

Consistent with each of the circuit courts that have considered the application of *Buckhannon* to the IDEA, we hold that IDEA plaintiffs who achieve their desired result via private settlement may not, in the absence of judicial imprimatur, be considered "prevailing parties." Hence, Doe cannot recover attorneys' fees under 20 U.S.C. § 1415(i).

Notes, Comments, and Questions

1. The Second, Third, Fourth, Fifth, Seventh, Eighth, Ninth, and District of Columbia Circuit Courts of Appeals agree with the First Circuit that *Buckhannon* controls the definition of a "prevailing party" under the IDEA's fee-shifting provision. *See* J.C. v. Reg'l Sch. Dist. 10, 278 F.3d 119, 124–25 (2d Cir. 2002) (rejecting arguments that *Buckhannon* does not apply to the IDEA because the IDEA requires a two-tiered administrative process and is structured to encourage quick settlements); John T. v. Del. Cnty. Intermediate Unit, 318 F.3d 545, 556 (3d Cir. 2003) (adopting the reasoning of *J.C.*); J.D. v. Kanawha Cnty. Bd. of Educ., 571 F.3d 381, 386–87 (4th Cir. 2009) (applying *Buckhannon* to attorneys fee dispute); El Paso Indep. Sch. Dist. v. Richard R., 591 F.3d 417, 422 (5th Cir. 2009) (joining other circuits in applying *Buckhannon* to the IDEA); T.D. v. LaGrange Sch. Dist. No. 102, 349 F.3d 469, 475–78 (7th Cir. 2003) (rejecting plaintiff's arguments that *Buckhannon* does not apply because the IDEA contains provisions requiring denial or reduction of fees in certain circumstances, that the IDEA encourages quick settlements, and that denying attorneys fees would deny FAPE); Christina A. v. Bloomberg, 315 F.3d 990, 991 n.2 (8th Cir. 2003) (agreeing with other circuits that *Buckhannon* applies to statutes similar to the IDEA); Shapiro v. Paradise Valley Unified Sch. Dist. No. 69, 374 F.3d 857, 865 (9th Cir. 2004) ("[A]ll of the other circuits to confront the issue have held that *Buckhannon* applies to the attorney's fees provision of the IDEA."); Alegria v. District of Columbia, 391 F.3d 262, 266–69 (D.C. Cir. 2004) (rejecting attorneys fees claim in a case that the parties settled privately). District courts in the Sixth and Eleventh Circuits have also ruled that *Buckhannon* applies to the IDEA. *See* A.T. v. Troy Sch. Dist., 407 F. Supp. 2d 827, 830 (E.D. Mich. 2005) (applying *Buckhannon* to define prevailing party under the IDEA); Gross v. Perrysburg Exempted Village Sch. Dist., 306 F. Supp. 2d 726, 731

(N.D. Ohio 2004) (citing *Buckhannon* in support of the proposition that the court must determine whether the plaintiff was the prevailing party); Matthew v. DeKalb Cnty. Sch. Sys., 244 F. Supp. 2d 1331, 1342 (N.D. Ga. 2003) (ruling that "*Buckhannon* applies to the IDEA's fee-shifting provision").

2. The court in *Doe* rejected Doe's argument that the IDEA's legislative text, structure, history, and underlying policy precluded application of *Buckhannon's* definition of prevailing party to the IDEA. Based on what you have learned about the IDEA, do you agree? Can you develop an alternative argument that *Buckhannon* should not apply to the IDEA and that parents who prevail through non-judicial settlements should be able to receive attorneys fees? Is it relevant that the IDEA envisions a cooperative ongoing relationship between parents and the school district and that all parties are encouraged to resolve disputes quickly and cooperatively? Is requiring parents to obtain an enforceable judicial order to recover attorneys fees conducive to a cooperative relationship? Or are the policies underlying IDEA's structure served better by allowing attorneys to recover fees for assisting parents to resolve their disputes without need for judicial intervention? Is it relevant to the question of the applicability of *Buckhannon* to the IDEA that the Supreme Court failed to mention the IDEA in its list of statutes that contain the phrase "prevailing party"?

3. The court in *Doe* recognized that the IDEA's fee-shifting statute is relatively complex, but ruled that complexity does not "by itself" change the definition of prevailing party. The court was referring to the provisions of the IDEA that allow courts to reduce fees for prevailing parties that engage in unreasonable delay and that preclude fees for participation in IEP meetings and resolution sessions and for unreasonably rejecting a settlement offer that was more favorable than the ultimate relief. What do these provisions suggest about the applicability of *Buckhannon* to the IDEA?

4. As the court in *Doe* described, Congress acted swiftly to overturn the result in *Smith* and allow for attorneys fees to prevailing parties in IDEA cases. As we have seen, Congress is not reluctant to overturn the Supreme Court's IDEA decisions with which it disagrees, including not only *Smith* but also *Honig v. Doe* and *Dellmuth v. Muth*. Does Congress' failure to act in response to the prevailing view that *Buckhannon* applies to the IDEA suggest that Congress agrees?

5. The IDEA provides for payment of attorneys fees to school districts when they are prevailing parties in limited circumstances. A court can award fees to a prevailing district against:

> (II) . . . the attorney of a parent who files a complaint or subsequent cause of action that is frivolous, unreasonable, or without foundation, or . . . who continued to litigate after the litigation clearly became frivolous, unreasonable, or without foundation; or
>
> (III) . . . the attorney of a parent, or against the parent, if the parent's complaint or subsequent cause of action was presented for any improper purpose, such as to harass, to cause unnecessary delay, or to needlessly increase the cost of litigation.

20 U.S.C. § 1415(i)(3)(B)(i)(II) and (III) (2012). There are only a few reported cases in which school districts sought attorneys fees against parents or their attorneys, and even fewer in which the court awarded fees to a district. *See, e.g.*, El Paso Indep. Sch. Dist. v. Richard R., 591 F.3d 417, 430 (5th Cir. 2009), *cert. denied*, 561 U.S. 1006 (2010) (denying school district's request for attorneys fees because the district did not prevail); District of Columbia v. Barrie, 741 F. Supp. 2d 250, 261–66 (ruling that defendant's litigation "was not frivolous, unreasonable, or without foundation."); School for Arts in Learning Pub. Charter Sch. v. Barrie, 724 F. Supp. 2d 86, 89–90 (D.D.C. 2010) (ruling that the school was not a prevailing party because the parent's attorney withdrew her complaint orally); District of Columbia v. West, 699 F. Supp. 2d 273, 280 (D.D.C. 2010) (declining to award fees to prevailing district because the litigation was not "'frivolous, unreasonable, or without foundation. . . .'"); District of Columbia v. Nahass, 699 F. Supp. 2d 175, 183 (D.D.C. 2010) (denying district's request for attorneys fees); Hiller v. Bd. of Educ. of Brunswick Cent. Sch. Dist., 743 F. Supp. 958, 976 (N.D.N.Y. 1990) (denying fees to district that prevailed on parent's counterclaims because there was no evidence that parents acted in bad faith); Hawkins v. Berkeley Unified Sch. Dist., 250 F.R.D. 459, 468 (N.D. Cal. 2008) (denying attorneys fees because issues on which District prevailed were related to issues on which parents partially prevailed).

6. Section 1415(i)(3)(B)(i) gives "the court" in an action or proceeding the authority to award attorneys fees. There is no similar provision allowing hearing officers to award fees. Does this mean that a party who prevailed in an administrative proceeding under the IDEA cannot recover attorneys fees if there is no subsequent court case on the merits? The courts have ruled that a party who prevails in an administrative proceeding with no subsequent court case can start a new case under Section 1415(i)(3)(B) seeking attorneys fees for the successful administrative proceeding. *See* T.N. v. Seattle Sch. Dist. No. 1, 474 F.3d 1165, 1169 (9th Cir. 2007) (holding that "the IDEA authorizes an action solely to recover attorneys fees); A.R. v. N.Y.C. Dep't of Educ., 407 F.3d 65, 75 (2d Cir. 2005) (ruling that a party who prevails in an impartial hearing is eligible for an award of attorneys fees"); T.D. v. LaGrange Sch. Dist. No. 102, 349 F.3d 469, 479 (7th Cir. 2003) (stating that the IDEA allows courts to award fees to prevailing parties in impartial hearings); Johnson v. Bismarck Pub. Sch. Dist., 949 F.2d 1000, 1003 (8th Cir. 1991) ("Many circuits have held, and we agree, that this statute permits a parent to recover attorneys' fees after prevailing at the state administrative level by filing a separate suit in federal court solely for that purpose."); Moore v. District of Columbia, 907 F.2d 165, 166–67, 176–77 (D.C. Cir. 1990), *cert. denied*, 498 U.S. 998 (1990) (ruling that a parent who prevailed in an impartial hearing can recover fees for the hearing in a separate federal court action); Mitten v. Muscogee Cnty. Sch. Dist., 877 F.2d 932, 935 (11th Cir. 1989), *cert. denied*, 490 U.S. 998 (1990) (ruling that prevailing parties in impartial hearing can recover attorneys fees); Duane M. v. Orleans Parish Sch. Bd., 861 F.2d 115, 116 (5th Cir. 1988) (ruling that the IDEA authorizes successful parent in administrative proceeding to file a separate suit to recover attorneys fees); Eggers v. Bullitt Cnty. Sch. Dist.,

854 F.2d 892, 894 (6th Cir. 1988) (ruling that the IDEA allows attorneys fees to plaintiffs who prevailed in administrative proceedings).

7. The IDEA does not include a statute of limitations for prevailing parties to seek attorneys fees. In the absence of a statute of limitations in the IDEA, federal courts have several options. Judge Posner's description of this situation is apt:

> The process by which judges pick a statute of limitations for a federal statute that lacks one is at best uncertain and at worst arbitrary. Should a state statute of limitations be "borrowed" to do service? If so, which statute of limitations? Or should a federal statute of limitations be borrowed? If so, which one? Or should no statute of limitations be applied . . . , but instead the doctrine of laches—which allows the plaintiff to wait as long as he wants, provided his delay does not hamper the defendant's ability to defend against the suit, or otherwise harm the defendant? Or should he be allowed a "reasonable" time within which to sue, period? Or should there be no time limitation at all?
>
> With reference specifically to the federal rights of disabled schoolchildren, "federal courts have borrowed from no fewer than four types of state statutes, giving parents anywhere from 30 days to six years in which to file their . . . claims [for attorneys fees]."

McCartney C. v. Herrin Cmty. Sch. Dist. No. 4, 21 F.3d 173, 174–75 (7th Cir. 1994).

Traditionally, federal courts in IDEA attorneys fees cases have attempted to select the statute of limitations in the state in which the case arose from the cause of action that is most analagous to the IDEA. *See, e.g.*, Dickerson v. Brodgen, 80 F. Supp. 2d 1319, 1320 (S.D. Ala. 1999) ("[T]he Supreme Court has held that where Congress has failed to provide a statute of limitations for a federal cause of action, courts should 'adopt' the 'local time limitation' most analagous to the case at hand, unless that limitations period is inconsistent with the policies of the federal statute."). As Judge Posner indicated, however, the courts have split over the most analogous state statute, often choosing among a "catch-all" statute for claims with no statute of limitations, the statute of limitations for appealing decisions of state administrative agencies, and the time period for filing claims based on statutory rights. The choice is significant, as the statute of limitations for appealing from a state administrative decision is generally much shorter than other statutes of limitations. And as Judge Posner stated, these choices have resulted in deadlines to file attorneys fees claims ranging from thirty days to six years.

The Sixth and Seventh Circuits have applied shorter statutes of limitations, as have district courts in the First and Fourth Circuits. *See, e.g.*, King v. Floyd Cnty. Bd. of Educ., 228 F.3d 622, 627 (6th Cir. 2000) (selecting thirty-day statute of limitations for appealing state administrative decisions); Powers v. Ind. Dep't of Educ., 61 F.3d 552, 556–58 (7th Cir. 1995) (selecting thirty-day statute of limitations for appealing state administrative decisions); Reed v. Mokena Sch. Dist. No. 159, 41 F.3d 1153, 1154 (7th Cir. 1994) (selecting 120-day statute of limitations for review of decisions by school authorities); Mayo v. Booker, 56 F. Supp. 2d 597, 598 (D. Md. 1999) (selecting

180-day statute of limitations for appealing an impartial hearing decision); Bow Sch. Dist. v. Quentin W., 750 F. Supp. 546, 549 (D.N.H. 1990) (selecting thirty-day statute of limitations for administrative appeals).

In contrast, the Eleventh Circuit and district courts in the District of Columbia and the First, Second, Third, Eighth, and Eleventh Circuits have applied longer statutes, ranging from two to six years. *See e.g.*, Zipperer v. Sch. Bd. of Seminole Cnty., 111 F.3d 847, 851–52 (11th Cir. 1997) (selecting four-year statute of limitations for claims based on statutory liability); Davidson v. District of Columbia, 736 F. Supp. 2d 115, 123 n.8, 124 (D.D.C. 2010) (selecting three-year statute of limitations for actions for which there is not a statute of limitations); Murphy v. Girard Sch. Dist., 134 F. Supp. 2d 431, 436 (W.D. Pa. 1999) (concluding that the statute of limitations is at least two years); Dickerson v. Brodgen, 80 F. Supp. 2d 1319, 1321 (S.D. Ala. 1999) (selecting two-year statute of limitations for personal injury claims or rights violations); Shanahan v. Bd. of Educ. of the Jamesville-DeWitt Sch. Dist., 953 F. Supp. 440, 443 (N.D.N.Y. 1997) (selecting three-year statute of limitations for actions seeking to recover for actions based on statutes); J.B. v. Essex-Caledonia Supervisory Union, 943 F. Supp. 387, 391–392 (D. Vt. 1996) (selecting six-year "'catch-all'" statute of limitations); Curtis K. v. Sioux City Cmty. Sch. Dist., 895 F. Supp. 1197, 1220 (N.D. Iowa 1995) (selecting five-year statute of limitations for claims that do not have a statute of limitations); James v. Nashua Sch. Dist., 720 F. Supp. 1053, 1058 (D.N.H. 1989) (selecting three-year state statute of limitations for personal actions for which a limitations period is not provided); Robert D. v. Sobel, 688 F. Supp. 861, 864 (S.D.N.Y. 1988) (selecting three-year statute of limitations for claim based on a statute); Michael M. v. Bd. of Educ. of the N.Y.C. Sch. Dist., 686 F. Supp. 995, 1002 (E.D.N.Y. 1988) (selecting three-year statute of limitations for a liability created by statute).

In choosing a statute of limitations, courts generally contrast the policy in favor of resolving disputes rapidly with the policy of encouraging parental involvement. *See, e.g.*, B.K. v. Toms River Bd. of Educ., 998 F. Supp. 462, 473 (D.N.J. 1998). The court in *B.K.* ruled that the policy of resolving disputes quickly applies to cases involving the educational interests of the child, which were not present in attorneys fees claims because by then, the educational issues had been resolved. *Id.* at 471. In contrast, allowing for a longer statute of limitations to file attorneys fees claims allowed parties time to try to settle. *Id.* The court in *B.K.* did not adopt a particular statute of limitations, instead relying on "a balancing of the equities and consideration of the reasons for the delay in the institution of suit . . . ." *Id.* at 473. The court allowed a claim for attorneys fees, filed two years after the administrative hearing was dismissed, to proceed. The court ruled:

> [P]reventing plaintiff from seeking reimbursement for counsel fees paid to her former attorney would only serve to discourage parents from advocating for the rights of their children. Such a result is incongruent with the statutory mandate, as IDEA contemplates parental involvement in determining the appropriateness of the child's educational placement.

Id.

B. Determining Whether a Party Prevailed

In order to be a prevailing party under *Buckhannon*, the party must show that there was a material change in the legal relationship and the change was judicially sanctioned. *See* Kress v. District of Columbia, 448 F. Supp. 2d 203, 205 (D. D.C. 2006). The next two sub-sections focus on how courts determine whether there was a change in the legal relationship and whether the change was judicially sanctioned.

1. Change in the Legal Relationship

A party need not prevail on every issue or even on the most important issue to be considered a prevailing party. In order to achieve a change in the legal relationship, a party must obtain more than *de minimis* relief and the relief must constitute a change in the legal relationship with the opposing party. Several courts have ruled that parties who achieved some relief, even though not the central relief they were seeking, were nevertheless prevailing parties. *See, e.g.*, J.D. v. Kanawah Cnty. Bd. of Educ., 571 F.3d 381, 386–87 (4th Cir. 2009) (ruling that parents did not prevail on their claim that the IEP was inappropriate but prevailed on claims for additional evaluations, an additional IEP meeting, and speech and language therapy and thus were prevailing parties); Park v. Anaheim Union High Sch. Dist., 464 F.3d 1025, 1034–35, 1037 (9th Cir. 2006) (ruling that although parents did not prevail on all claims, they were prevailing parties because they received a decision that the district denied FAPE to their child and an order requiring the district to provide compensatory education, create self-help IEP goals, undertake a new functional behavior assessment, and provide a behavioral intervention plan); Gross v. Perrysburg Exempted Village Sch. Dist., 306 F. Supp. 2d 726, 731–33 (N.D. Ohio 2004) (ruling that parents prevailed because the IHO found that the district denied their child a FAPE and that the IEP was inappropriate, and ordered additional services, even though the IHO denied parents' request to transfer their child to another school).

It is difficult to draw general principles from the cases about what level of relief is sufficient to change the legal relationship. Some examples of relief that courts found sufficient to change the legal relationship include:

*change in disability classification, Weissburg v. Lancaster Sch. Dist., 591 F.3d 1255, 1260 (9th Cir. 2010);

*increased math instruction, Van Duyn v. Baker Sch. Dist. 5J, 502 F.3d 811, 825–26 (9th Cir. 2007);

*eligibility for special education as a child with a disability, A.O. v. Los Gatos-Saratoga Joint Union High Sch. Dist., 484 F.3d 1230, 1234 (9th Cir. 2007);

*award of special education services, P.N. v. Seattle Sch. Dist. No. 1, 474 F.3d 1165, 1173–74 (9th Cir. 2007);

*additional speech and language therapy and occupational therapy, Krichinsky v. Knox Cnty. Sch., 963 F.2d 847, 850 (6th Cir. 1992);

*move "to a new school with full-day, year-round educational and therapeutic services," Ryan M. v. Bd. of Educ. of Chi., Dist. 299, 731 F. Supp. 2d 776, 788 (N.D. Ill. 2010);

*order to prepare "a new IEP that provides greater benefits than the initial IEP," B.W. v. N.Y.C. Dep't of Educ., 716 F. Supp. 2d 336, 348 (S.D.N.Y. 2010);

*order to convene MDT meetings and to provide or consider providing compensatory education, Dickens v. Friendship Edison P.C.S., 639 F. Supp. 2d 51, 58 (D.D.C. 2009); and

*order to provide related services "with sufficient intensity," tutoring, and a new IEP "including reading instruction using the Wilson method," John M. v. Bd. of Educ. of Chi., 612 F. Supp. 2d 981, 991 (N.D. Ill 2009).

Courts do not often find that parents who obtained some relief under the IDEA were not prevailing parties under *Buckhannon*, but there are several reported decisions. Again, it is difficult to develop general principles about the level of relief that is not sufficient to create prevailing party status. Examples include:

*conditional, unrealized grant of two years of extended services in core academic subjects, Drennan v. Pulaski Cnty. Special Sch. Dist., 458 F. 3d 755, 757 (8th Cir. 2006);

*order that IEP team reconvene to add specificity to the teacher training requirement and identify more mainstreaming opportunities ruled to be *de minimis* in the context of the parents' loss of their placement claim, Linda T. v. Rice Lake Area Sch. Dist. 417 F.3d 704, 707–10 (7th Cir. 2005);

*understanding that the IEP team would meet earlier than planned was *de minimis* relief in light of the denial of all eight forms of relief the parents requested, Student W. v. Puyallup Sch. Dist., 31 F.3d 1489, 1498 (9th Cir. 1994);

*district's voluntary agreement to hold an MDT meeting combined with the court's order to provide the student with compensatory education only if the student was found eligible for special education was *de minimis* relief, Dickens v. Friendship-Edison P.C.S., 639 F. Supp. 2d 51, 59–60 (D.D.C. 2005);

*administrative order that the district list the services and add an FM system to the IEP did not make plaintiffs prevailing party because the child was already receiving the services and the district had expressed its intention to provide the FM system, R.L. v. Plainville Bd. of Educ., 363 F. Supp. 2d 222, 238 (D. Conn. 2005); and

*enforceable order to hold a meeting to evaluate the child for transition services and to graduate the child once certain conditions were met were *de minimis* relief, Petrovich v. Consol. High Sch. Dist. No. 230, 959 F. Supp. 884, 890 (N.D. Ill. 1997).

Several courts have ruled that relief that is not on the merits or is not permanent does not change the legal relationship between the parties and does not confer prevailing party status. Thus, a party that prevailed on the ground that the case was moot was not a prevailing party for purposes of attorneys fees because the dismissal of the case as moot did not change the legal relationship between the parties. *See, e.g.*, District of Columbia v. Straus, 590 F.3d 898, 902 (D.C. Cir. 2010) (denying attorneys fees because district's agreement to provide evaluation the parents requested rendered the case moot); Moseley v. Bd. of Educ. of Albuquerque Pub. Sch., 483 F.3d 689, 692, 694 (10th Cir. 2007) (denying attorneys fees because graduation rendered the case moot). Similarly, courts have ruled that a party that achieved only preliminary or temporary relief or relief not on the merits did not obtain a change in the legal relationship between the parties and thus is not a prevailing party for purposes of attorneys fees. *See, e.g.,* Paul T. v. Del. Cnty. Intermediate Unit, 318 F.3d 545, 548 (3d Cir. 2003) (ruling that plaintiff who obtained a preliminary injunction and contempt order prior to reaching a settlement and voluntarily dismissing the case was not a prevailing party); C.O. v. Orange Twp. Bd. of Educ., 287 F.3d 267, 272–74 (3d Cir. 2002) (ruling that temporary relief in the form of reinstatement to school and a functional behavioral assessment did not entitle parents to attorneys fees because the decision was not based on the underlying merits); Board of Educ. of Oak Park v. Nathan R., 199 F.3d 377, 382 (7th Cir. 2000), *cert. denied*, 531 U.S. 822 (2000) (holding that a "stay-put" order is temporary and did not change the legal relationship between the parties and thus does not entitle moving party to attorneys fees); Hunger v. Leininger, 15 F.3d 664, 670–71 (7th Cir. 1994), *cert. denied*, 513 U.S. 839 (1994) (ruling that attorneys fees are not available for an award of interim relief in the form of transitional services pending the child's return to school when she did not return to school); Christopher P. v. Marcus, 915 F.2d 794, 805 (2d Cir. 1990), *cert. denied*, 498 U.S. 1123 (1991) (ruling that receiving a temporary restraining order that did not address the merits but preserved the *status quo* by readmitting child to the school did not make plaintiff a prevailing party); J.C. v. Mendham Twp. Bd. of Educ., 29 F. Supp. 2d 214, 221 (D.N.J. 1998) (ruling that success in enforcing stay-put provision did not render parents prevailing party). Can you develop an argument that these cases are analagous to the cases in which the parties obtained partial relief and thus the parents were prevailing parties?

2. *Judicial Imprimatur*

In addition to changing the legal relationship, a party is entitled to attorneys fees only if the change in the relationship is judicially sanctioned; this judicial sanction is often referred to as a "judicial imprimatur." A decision at the administrative level qualifies as a judicially sanctioned change in legal relationship. In *A.R. v. N.Y.C. Dep't of Educ.*, 407 F. 3d 65, 76–77 (2d Cir. 2005), the Second Circuit explained the reasoning behind this:

> But an IHO's decision on the merits in an IDEA proceeding does constitute "*administrative imprimatur.*" Although not "judicial," such an order changes the legal relationship between the parties: Its terms are enforceable, if not by the IHO itself, then by a court, including through an action under 42 U.S.C.

> § 1983. In order to give effect to the IDEA's intent to permit awards to winning parties in administrative proceedings even where there has been no judicial involvement, as the parties agree that we must, we conclude that the combination of administrative *imprimatur*, the change in the legal relationship of the parties arising from it, and subsequent judicial enforceability, render such a winning party a "prevailing party" under *Buckhannon*'s principles.

Id. at 76.

Courts have generally ruled that a private settlement agreement without any judicial sanction lacks the judicial imprimatur necessary to entitle the plaintiff to attorneys fees, even if the settlement changed the legal relationship. P.N. v. Seattle Sch. Dist. No. 1, 474 F.3d 1165, 1172–73 (9th Cir. 2007) (denying attorneys fees because the settlement agreement did not receive a judicial imprimatur); *A.R.*, 407 F.3d at 77 (ruling that plaintiff who settled an impartial hearing was not a prevailing party); Alegria v. District of Columbia, 391 F.3d 262, 263 (D.C. Cir. 2004) (denying attorneys fees for private settlements reached prior to impartial hearings); Doe v. Boston Pub. Sch., 358 F.3d 20, 22, 30 (1st Cir. 2004) (denying attorneys fees to plaintiffs who reached private settlement agreement before the impartial hearing began); T.D. v. LaGrange Sch. Dist. No. 102, 349 F.3d 469, 479–80 (7th Cir. 2003) (denying attorneys fees because private settlement agreement lacked indicia of a consent decree, including an order or judgment, judge's signature, or enforcement provision); Christina A. v. Bloomberg, 315 F.3d 990, 992–93 (8th Cir. 2003) (ruling that a private settlement agreement in which the court retained jurisdiction but did not have a greater role did not render plaintiff a prevailing party); J.C. v. Reg'l Sch. Dist. 10, Bd. of Educ., 278 F.3d 119, 122, 125 (2d Cir. 2002) (denying attorneys fees because private agreement was not placed on the record).

In contrast to private settlement agreements, courts have also ruled that settlement agreements reached at administrative hearings that are placed on the record or that are incorporated in hearing officer orders have a judicial imprimatur because such agreements are enforceable. *See A.R.*, 407 F.3d at 77–78 (IHO-endorsed settlement agreements are administrative consent decrees rendering plaintiffs prevailing parties); S.G. v. District of Columbia, 533 F. Supp. 2d 105, 106–07 (D.D.C. 2008) (ruling that a settlement agreement incorporated into a hearing officer decision entitles the plaintiffs to an award of attorneys fees); James T. v. Troy Sch. Dist., 407 F. Supp. 2d 827, 831 (E.D. Mich. 2005) (ruling that plaintiffs were prevailing parties because their administrative settlement was incorporated into the order of dismissal).

C. Categorical Eligibility for Attorneys Fees

Courts have considered arguments that prevailing parties are ineligible for attorneys fees despite their prevailing party status. In considering these arguments, the courts have created several exceptions to the IDEA's fee-shifting provisions that preclude or reduce payment of attorneys fees to prevailing parties in certain circumstances.

1. Parents of a Child Who Does Not Have a Disability

The IDEA allows a prevailing party who is the parent of a child with a disability to recover attorneys fees. Consequently, parents who prevail in an IDEA case whose child is not a "child with a disability" as defined in the IDEA cannot recover attorneys fees even if they prevail on the merits of their claim. *See* T.B. v. Bryan Indep. Sch. Dist., 628 F.3d 240, 242, 245 (5th Cir. 2010) (vacating an award of attorneys fees to the parents because although they prevailed on their claim that their child had a disability, he did not need special education and thus did not fall within the IDEA's definition of a child with a disability); D.S. v. Neptune Twp. Bd. of Educ., 264 F. App'x 186, 189 (3d Cir. 2008) (ruling that parents were not eligible for attorneys fees because there was never a finding that the child needed special education); Durkee v. Livonia Cent. Sch. Dist., 487 F. Supp. 2d 318, 320 (W.D.N.Y. 2007) (refusing to award attorneys fees to parents who prevailed in their request for a declaration that they were not required to submit their child for an evaluation to determine if he was eligible for special education and related services).

2. Parents Who Are Attorneys

Parents who are attorneys often represent their children in IDEA cases. The courts have ruled that attorney-parents who represent their children successfully in IDEA cases are not entitled to recover attorneys fees. *See* Van Duyn v. Baker Sch. Dist. 5J, 502 F.3d 811, 826 (9th Cir. 2007) (awarding attorneys fees to plaintiff except for his mother's legal work); S.N. v. Pittsford Cent. Sch. Dist., 448 F.3d 601, 602 (2d Cir. 2006) (ruling that attorney-parent is not eligible to receive attorneys fees); Woodside v. Sch. Dist. of Phila. Bd. of Educ., 248 F.3d 129, 131 (3d Cir. 2001) (holding that "an attorney-parent cannot receive attorney fees for work representing his minor child in proceedings under the IDEA"); Doe v. Bd. of Educ. of Balt. Cnty., 165 F.3d 260, 261 (4th Cir. 1998), *cert. denied*, 524 U.S. 1159 (1999) (denying attorneys fees to attorney who represented his child in IDEA proceedings); *but see* Craig V. v. Dekalb Cnty. Sch. Sys., 244 F. Supp. 2d 1331, 1337–38 (N.D. Ga. 2003) (citing the IDEA's legislative history, protections offered to clients by the rules of professional responsibility, and the economics of law practice in declining to follow the rule, but declining to award fees on other grounds).

The primary rationale for the rule is that the fee-shifting provision of the IDEA is intended to provide independent and emotionally detached legal advice to children with disabilities, and parents who are attorneys are too heavily invested in their children's well-being and education to provide such advice. *See* Ford v. Long Beach Unified Sch. Dist., 461 F.3d 1087, 1091 (9th Cir. 2006) ("Like an attorney appearing *pro se*, a disabled child represented by his or her parent does not benefit from the judgment of an independent third party."); *S.N.*, 448 F.3d at 603 ("The danger that a parent-attorney would lack sufficient emotional detachment to provide effective representation is undeniably present in disputes arising under the IDEA."); *Woodside*, 248 F.3d at 131 ("[T]he better rule is one which encourages parents to seek independent, emotionally detached counsel for their children's IDEA actions"); *Doe*, 165

F.3d at 263 ("Like attorneys appearing pro se, attorney-parents are generally incapable of exercising sufficient judgment on behalf of their children to ensure that " 'reason, rather than emotion,' " will dictate the conduct of the litigation."). The court in *Doe* was also concerned that attorney-parents who are not experienced in special education law will unduly delay cases. *Id.* (stating that although parent-attorney obtained "excellent" result, his procedural errors delayed and increased the costs of obtaining ultimate relief). Finally the court was concerned that allowing attorney-parents to recover fees could deter them from seeking independent advice. *Id.* at 264.

Courts support this rule even while recognizing that attorney-parents did or could provide adequate legal representation. *See Ford*, 461 F.3d at 1091 (stating that based on the positive results, the attorney-parent provided competent representation); *Doe*, 165 F.3d at 263 (recognizing that the parent obtained "an excellent result" for his son).

Do you agree with this rule? Is the basis for the rule undermined by the fact that it applies only in situations in which parent-attorneys prevailed? Do you agree with the courts' generalizations about parents who represent their children in IDEA cases? Is the rule likely to deter attorney-parents from representing their children in IDEA cases? Should the rule apply if the parents could not find an independent attorney to take the case?

At least one court has declined to extend the rule against paying fees to attorney-parents to attorney-grandparents. Weissburg v. Lancaster Sch. Dist., 591 F.3d 1255 (9th Cir. 2010). The Ninth Circuit reasoned: "Unlike parents, who have a special role under the IDEA as enforcers of their children's education rights, other relatives are not so uniquely invested in IDEA proceedings." *Id.* at 1260. Do you agree that because attorney-grandparents do not have a special role in the IDEA process that they are not as invested in IDEA proceedings as attorney-parents? Are grandparents known for being detached and unemotional about their grandchildren's education? Should this exception extend to attorney-grandparents who are the guardians of their grandchildren? To attorney-siblings? Attorney-step-parents?

3. Lay Advocates, Out of State Counsel, Paralegals, and Students

The IDEA permits lay advocates to represent parents in IDEA administrative proceedings: "Any party to a hearing . . . shall be accorded . . . the right to be accompanied and advised by . . . individuals with special knowledge and training . . . ." 20 U.S.C. § 1415(h)(1) (2012). However, prevailing parties are not permitted to recover fees for lay advocates if state law prohibits payment of fees to lay advocates for work done in administrative proceedings. *See* Arons v. N.J. State Bd. of Educ., 842 F.2d 58, 63 (3d Cir. 1988), *cert. denied*, 488 U.S. 942 (1988) (ruling that the IDEA does not "supersede the state's authority to regulate the legal profession"); Bowman v. District of Columbia, 496 F. Supp. 2d 160, 166 (D.D.C. 2007) (holding that court-appointed education advocate was not eligible to collect attorneys fees); Connors v. Mills, 34 F. Supp. 2d 795, 807–08 (N.D.N.Y. 1998) (ruling that fees for lay advocate are not available "[i]n the absence of affirmative state action in promulgating regulations that govern training and conduct of lay advocates."). This rule extends to an attorney who is not admitted to practice in the state in which he represented the parent in administrative proceedings. *See* Z.A. v. San Bruno Park Sch. Dist., 165 F.3d 1273, 1276 (9th Cir. 1999) (ruling that the attorney could not collect fees because he did not have a license to practice in administrative proceedings in the state); Agapito v. District of Columbia, 477 F. Supp. 2d 103, 106 (D.D.C. 2007) (ruling that attorney who did not have a license to practice in the District of Columbia could not collect attorneys fees); *see also* Shapiro v. Paradise Valley Unified Sch. Dist. No. 9, 374 F.3d 857, 862 (9th Cir. 2004) (holding that attorney was eligible to recover fees only for the time after his *pro hac vice* admission to Arizona bar). In contast, the court in *Dickens v. Friendship-Edison P.C.S.*, 724 F. Supp. 2d 113 (D.D.C. 2010), awarded attorneys not licensed in the District of Columbia fees at the paralegal rate. *Id.* at 119–20.

Prevailing parties are not precluded from recovering fees for non-attorneys who did legal work. Plaintiffs can recover fees for law students working under the supervision of attorneys. *See, e.g.*, Burr v. Sobol, 748 F. Supp. 97, 102 (S.D.N.Y. 1990) (awarding fifty dollars per hour for work of law student interns). They can also recover fees for paralegal services. *See, e.g.*, Mass. Dep't of Pub. Health v. Sch. Comm. of Tewksbury, 841 F. Supp. 449, 458 (D. Mass. 1993) (awarding fifty dollars per hour for paralegal work).

4. Pro Bono *Attorneys*

Prevailing parties can recover attorneys fees even if their attorneys worked *pro bono*. *See* Dudley v. Lower Merion Sch. Dist., 768 F. Supp. 2d 779, 782 (E.D. Pa. 2011); L.V. v. N.Y.C. Dep't of Educ., 700 F. Supp. 2d 510, 518–19 (S.D.N.Y. 2010) (awarding fees to a firm that represented the plaintiffs *pro bono* at a slightly reduced rate). Parties can also recover attorneys fees for attorneys who are publicly funded. *See* Yankton Sch. Dist. v. Schramm, 93 F.3d 1369, 1377 (8th Cir. 1996) ("The fact that . . . [the parents] were represented by publicly funded counsel does not affect their right to fees.").

D. The Method for Calculating Attorneys Fees

In calculating the amount of attorneys fees to award to prevailing parties, courts in IDEA cases generally follow a two-step method, often referred to as the "lodestar" method. First, they determine the hourly rate, and then they multiply the rate by the hours reasonably expended. The next two sub-sections examine each of these steps in turn.

1. Determining the Prevailing Hourly Rate

According to the IDEA, "Fees awarded under this paragraph shall be based on rates prevailing in the community in which the action or proceeding arose for the kind and quality of services furnished. No bonus or multiplier may be used in calculating the fees awarded under this subsection." 20 U.S.C. § 1415(i)(3)(C) (2012). This clause contains two key components for determining the hourly rate. First, the court must define the community in which the case arose. Second, the court must determine the prevailing hourly rate in that community for the kind and quality of services provided. The following case is representative of how courts make these determinations.

A.R. v. N.Y.C. Dep't of Educ.

407 F.3d 65 (2d Cir. 2005)

SACK, Circuit Judge:

....

The plaintiffs-appellees ... instituted four separate New York State administrative proceedings challenging, under the Individuals with Disabilities Education Act ("IDEA"), 20 U.S.C. § 1400 *et seq.*, the special educational programs that the ... New York City Department of Education (the "DOE") had provided for the Parents' disabled children. In two of the four proceedings, impartial hearing officers ("IHOs") entered decisions for the plaintiffs on the merits. In the two others, IHOs issued "Statements of Agreement and Order" that recorded the terms of settlement agreements between the parties....

The IDEA grants courts the discretionary power to "award reasonable attorneys' fees ... [to] the prevailing party" "[i]n any action or proceeding brought under" the IDEA. 20 U.S.C. § 1415(i)(3)(B). Each parent sought, under that provision, to recover the legal fees he or she incurred in pursuing administrative proceedings against the DOE. When their non-judicial efforts proved unsuccessful, the parties brought suit in separate but similar actions in the United States District Court for the Southern District of New York.... The district judges awarded the Parents, as "prevailing parties" under the IDEA, the attorneys' fees that they sought.

....

BACKGROUND

....

Retention of Counsel

Before instituting these administrative proceedings, the Parents all retained counsel to represent them. Two lawyers, Todd Silverblatt and Michael Hampden, associated with Legal Services for Children ("LSC"), a not-for-profit legal services organization that specializes in, *inter alia*, education law, represented A.R., M.S., and M.L. (the "LSC plaintiffs") in their administrative hearings. LSC did not charge the LSC plaintiffs legal fees. Instead, the LSC plaintiffs assigned to LSC their rights to recover from the DOE under the fee-shifting provisions of the IDEA. That is "how [LSC] obtains a good portion of its funding." Gary Mayerson represented S.W. and M.M. in their IDEA hearing ... for which representation he charged them legal fees.

Request for Attorneys' Fees and District Court Proceedings

Following the completion of the administrative hearings, LSC, and Mayerson on behalf of S.W. and M.M., requested attorneys' fees from the DOE. For the representation of M.S., LSC sought from the DOE a total of $3,225, reflecting 20.5 hours of legal services rendered by Hampden and Silverblatt. Hampden and Silverblatt billed at an hourly rate of $250 per hour for 12.9 hours and offered to provide 7.6 hours of services without charge. For the representation of M.L., LSC sought from the DOE $2,370, which reflected 7.0 hours of legal services, primarily provided by Hampden at a rate of $350 per hour. For the representation of A.R., LSC sought from the DOE $3,458.50, which reflected primarily 9.25 hours of legal services rendered by Hampden at a rate of $350 per hour. For his representation of S.W. and M.M., Mayerson, on behalf of his clients, sought from the DOE $14,747, which reflected 40.4 hours of legal services rendered by Mayerson at a rate of $365 per hour. The DOE refused to pay any of the fee requests on the grounds that the hourly rates of $250 to $365 per hour were unreasonable.

Thereafter, the Parents filed complaints in the United States District Court for the Southern District of New York claiming that they had been denied attorneys' fees to which they were entitled under the IDEA. . . . [A]fter the LSC plaintiffs' cases were consolidated, they moved for summary judgment, seeking a total award of $18,706, of which $13,003.50 represented legal services rendered in the course of the administrative representation of the LSC plaintiffs and $5,702.50 reflected lawyers fees for the district court litigation for attorneys' fees itself. Together with their summary judgment motion, the LSC plaintiffs included affidavits supporting their assertion that $350 per hour was the hourly "rate[] prevailing in the community in which the action or proceeding arose for the kind and quality of services furnished." 20 U.S.C. § 1415(i)(3)(C). In response, the DOE argued, *inter alia*, that the appropriate rate should be between $125 and $175 per hour and submitted affidavits supporting that contention. . . . Judge Motley granted the LSC plaintiffs' motion for summary judgment, awarding them $18,706 in fees.

[I]n a separate proceeding before Judge Scheindlin, S.W. and M.M. filed a motion for attorneys' fees, requesting fees for Mayerson's services at a rate of $350 to $375 per hour. . . . The DOE asserted . . . that the fees sought were not reasonable, and that a rate of $125 to $190 per hour was proper for the services provided.

[T]he district court granted S.W. and M.M. $10,644.73 in attorneys' fees and related expenses for their administrative hearings. Relying in part on the award of attorneys' fees to the LSC plaintiffs in their action, the court found that $350 per hour was a reasonable rate for Mayerson's legal representation during the administrative proceedings. The court also found that Mayerson "spent a total of 30.2 hours in connection with the administrative proceedings" but reduced this figure slightly because it found that some of the relevant time records were vague or incomplete. The court also determined that Mayerson spent 6.8 hours on the fee application process in the district court and that, because Mayerson's expertise had increased since he represented S.W. and M.M. in their administrative proceedings in 1999, the reasonable rate for these services was $375 per hour. The court awarded the plaintiffs $3,998.15 in attorneys' fees and related costs in connection with the fee application.

The DOE appeals from both district court decisions. Because of the similarities of the appeals, we heard argument in them together and now decide them together.

DISCUSSION

I. The IDEA

. . . .

[T]he IDEA provides that "[i]n any action or proceeding brought under [the IDEA], [a] court, in its discretion, may award reasonable attorneys' fees as part of the costs to the parents of a child with a disability who is the prevailing party." 20 U.S.C. § 1415(i)(3)(B). Such fees "shall be based on rates prevailing in the community in which the action or proceeding arose for the kind and quality of services furnished." *Id.* § 1415(i)(3)(C).

II. The DOE's Position on Appeal

. . . [T]he DOE argues that the "community" for determining the appropriate hourly rate for attorneys' fees should be the community of practitioners who appear before the DOE for IDEA hearings, rather than the community of practitioners in the federal district in which the fee application was commenced. . . . [T]he DOE [also] argues that the district court abused its discretion in determining that rates of $350 to $375 per hour were reasonable for the Parents' counsel's representation with respect to administrative hearings, because such representation "is simply of a different 'kind and quality' than the more sophisticated legal services required to vindicate statutory or constitutional rights in a federal forum." . . .

III. Standard of Review

Generally, we review a district court's grant of attorneys' fees under the IDEA for abuse of discretion. "We review de novo the District Court's interpretation of the relevant fee statute itself[,] . . . interpret[ing] the IDEA fee provisions in consonance with those of other civil rights fee-shifting statutes."

. . . .

V. Calculation of Attorneys' Fees

The IDEA provides that the fees that district courts award must be "reasonable" and "based on rates prevailing in the community in which the action or proceeding arose for the kind and quality of services furnished." 20 U.S.C. § 1415(i)(3)(B)-(C). To calculate such attorneys' fees, courts apply the "lodestar" method, "whereby an attorney fee award is derived 'by multiplying the number of hours reasonably expended on the litigation [by] a reasonable hourly rate.'" . . . "'There is . . . a strong presumption that the lodestar figure represents a reasonable fee.'" *Id.*

A. Community in Which the Action or Proceeding Arose

The DOE complains that the district judges wrongly looked to the legal "community" of the Southern District of New York, where they sit, rather than to the community of all practitioners appearing before the DOE in IDEA administrative actions, to measure the level of legal fees to be awarded to the Parents' counsel.

The "community" to which the IDEA's fee calculation provision refers is typically measured by the geographic area in which "the action was commenced and litigated."

Where the legal dispute has been pursued through an action in federal court, "[n]ormally a district court, awarding attorney's fees under [a fee-shifting statute], will consider the prevailing rates in the district in which the court sits."

The disputes in the cases before us were pursued through IDEA administrative proceedings, not the district court. The DOE exercises jurisdiction over public schooling in the five boroughs of the City of New York, three of which lie within the jurisdiction of one United States District Court and two of which are in another. The students involved in these proceedings attended schools in Bronx and New York Counties, both in the Southern District of New York; administrative hearings were held there as well as in Kings County, which is in the Eastern District. The Parents' lawyers have their offices in New York County, in the Southern District. Our case law does not provide us with a litmus test for determining, in these circumstances, the "community" in which the proceedings for which the Parents were awarded legal fees "arose."

The Parents urge us to affirm the district court's fee awards because the awards comply with the "typical" rule. They suggest that the cases arose entirely or principally in the Southern District of New York and contend that the district court therefore properly treated the rates prevailing in the Southern District as the fee structure against which the attorneys' fees here should be measured. The DOE contends to the contrary that the relevant community must be co-extensive with the group of lawyers who bring IDEA actions against the DOE: in other words, that the district court must refer to rates across the five boroughs of the City of New York in determining a reasonable rate for representation in IDEA hearings.

The text of section 1415(i)(3)(C) does not appear to compel either conclusion. The requirement that the relevant community be that "in which the action or proceeding arose" does not tell us whether a proceeding "arises" where it is held (in this case, the Southern *and* Eastern Districts) or where the events that gave rise to the hearings occurred (here, the Southern District). Nor can we conclude from the fact that the proceedings undeniably arose in the City of New York as a whole that they cannot also be said to have arisen in the Southern District of New York or that the community of lawyers throughout the City of New York, i.e., those lawyers appearing before the DOE, is necessarily the only group whose fees provide the yardstick by which to measure the fee award.

The DOE expresses a concern that, under what it sees as the district court's district-specific approach, the same lawyer may be paid at different hourly rates for services rendered in similar proceedings against the same defendant depending upon the happenstance of where in New York City, and therefore in which federal district, "the action or proceeding [against the DOE] arose." But such distinctions are inherent in any approach that distinguishes between the level of legal payments in different districts when setting the rate at which legal fees are to be awarded: The same lawyer may be paid at different rates with respect to otherwise identical legal services provided in cases heard in the Southern District of New York (New York County

(Manhattan), Bronx County, and points north) from those at which he or she is paid with respect to legal services provided in cases heard in the Eastern District of New York (Richmond County (Staten Island), Kings County (Brooklyn), Queens County, and points east). So long as the law provides for or permits fee awards based on geographic markets for services, a lawyer may be paid at different rates for otherwise indistinguishable services....

We acknowledge, on the other side of the ledger, that there is good reason for a district court not to be wed to the rates in its own community. If they are lower than those in another district, skilled lawyers from such other district will be dissuaded from taking meritorious cases in the district with lower rates. If lawyers are paid for their participation in IDEA proceedings that clearly arise in Queens at a rate considerably lower than what they are paid for representation in proceedings that clearly arise in Manhattan, experienced, Manhattan-based lawyers like Mr. Hampden, Mr. Silverblatt, and Mr. Mayerson may decide to devote their time and expertise to IDEA cases that arise in Manhattan rather than those cases in which parents are equally needful of their services, but that arise in Queens.

But we need not arrive at a crisp rule that a district court must employ to make this determination. We have held in somewhat comparable circumstances that the district court has discretion—to be sure, discretion that may not be abused—to determine the relevant community for calculating attorneys' fees where the case was not commenced and litigated in a single federal district.

Similarly here, there is more than one community that the district court might reasonably have considered in determining fees. But the contacts between the administrative proceedings and the Southern District, which is the place where the clients reside, where the facts giving rise to their successful claims occurred, and where the lawyers who represented them hang their shingles, appear clearly to predominate. By comparison, the fact that the DOE held hearings on the other side of an intracity bridge provides minimal support for treating the place where the proceedings were held as that in which they "arose" on the facts of these cases. Although none of this means that the district court was required to reach the result that it did, it does confirm that the court did not abuse its discretion in treating the Southern District as "the community in which the ... proceeding arose," and therefore in relying primarily on the level of legal fees charged by comparable lawyers in comparable circumstances in the Southern District of New York in setting legal fees for the plaintiffs under the IDEA.

B. Reasonableness of the Rate

1. *Fees in M.S.'s, M.L.'s, and A.R.'s cases.* As we have noted, the district court credited the affidavits submitted on behalf of M.S., M.L., and A.R. in which special education lawyers represented that they charged fees of \$300 to \$350 per hour in the Southern District. The district court also observed that in 1998, the Southern District awarded attorneys' fees at an hourly rate of \$375 for representation at an IDEA hearing and subsequent litigation in federal court. It was not an abuse of discretion

for the district court to credit evidence submitted by the plaintiffs instead of countervailing evidence submitted by the defendant.

The district court found unpersuasive the affidavits and arguments submitted by the DOE indicating that the prevailing rate should be $125 to $175 per hour. Similarly, the district court found irrelevant the two lawyers' declarations supporting the DOE's assertion that a lower hourly rate was appropriate. The court also found unpersuasive the DOE's records of the amounts that it previously paid to lawyers for representation at IDEA administrative hearings. The court noted that these figures did not accurately represent market figures because many of these payments involved settlements for amounts substantially less than the requested attorneys' fees. We conclude that the district court did not abuse its discretion when it determined, based on the evidence before it, that a range of $300 to $350 was reasonable for representation at the administrative hearings.

Nor did the district court abuse its discretion in awarding the LSC lawyers fees at the top end of this range based on their experience.[18] Even though much of the lawyers' careers was spent practicing in areas other than education law, their overall legal experience merited a higher hourly rate because "most important legal skills are transferrable." Indeed, we have observed that Mr. Hampden, who is one of the lawyers in the instant case, possesses considerable experience in education law despite having spent much of his career focusing on different kinds of law.

2. *Fees in S.W. and M.M.'s case.* In S.W. and M.M.'s case, the district court awarded fees for representation during the administrative hearing at the rate of $350 per hour. S.W. and M.M.'s child, N.W., attended school in Manhattan. Their administrative proceedings appear to have taken place in Brooklyn. In awarding them fees at an hourly rate of $350 for the administrative hearings, the district judge relied upon the decisions in *M.S.* and *Mr. X.* that such a rate was reasonable for services of this type in the Southern District. The district court also relied on its decision in *R.E.*, in which it concluded that $350 per hour in 1998 and $365 per hour in 1999 were reasonable hourly rates for Mayerson for representation in IDEA administrative hearings. For the reasons stated above, the district judge in S.W. and M.M.'s case had the discretion to consider the Southern District as the relevant community in setting fees. Because we affirm the court's decision in M.S., we also find here that awarding fees at a rate of $350 was not an abuse of discretion.

. . . .

---

18. Plaintiffs' attorneys in this case are likewise the beneficiaries of many years of experience (thirty-five years in Mr. Hampden's case; twenty-four in Mr. Silverblatt's) in areas outside the IDEA. Furthermore, their prior experience, while not focused exclusively on the IDEA, was in related areas of law: Mr. Hampden has spent much of his career at legal services organizations (Legal Aid Society of New York City; Bronx Legal Services; Westchester/Putnam Legal Services), representing clients in administrative hearings and litigation related thereto; Mr. Silverblatt was an attorney in the Juvenile Rights Division of the Legal Aid Society for twenty years prior to joining LSC, in which capacity he served as law guardian to countless children, representing them in numerous administrative proceedings before defendant Board.

C. *For the Kind and Quality of Services Furnished*

The DOE argues that because section 1415(i)(3)(C) limits rates for calculating attorneys fees to those for "the kind and quality of services furnished," the relevant market for determining reasonable rates for representation in administrative proceedings is the market for representation at the administrative level. The DOE asserts that administrative proceedings are "not legally complex," and that, as a matter of law, they involve legal assistance of a different "kind and quality" than is involved in representation in court proceedings. The DOE asserts that the district judges therefore erred in determining the reasonable hourly rates for administrative representation by relying on hourly rates for proceedings commenced in federal courts.

While any comparison of degrees of difficulty of administrative and judicial hearings may itself raise considerable difficulties, we conclude that we need not address that issue here. The district court, in determining attorneys' fees for the administrative proceedings, relied substantially on hourly rates for representation in administrative proceedings. Two of the affidavits that were submitted by the LSC plaintiffs in support of their motions for attorneys' fees describe lawyers' hourly rates in the Southern District of New York for administrative representation. As we have noted, both district judges relied on the court's previous decision in *Mr. X*, which involved attorneys' fees for IDEA administrative hearings. And in *S.W.*, the district court also relied on *M.S.*, which, of course, also deals with fees in administrative hearings. Whether or not it would have been an abuse of discretion for either judge to rely solely on the level of attorneys' fees prevailing in judicially litigated matters, they did not do so here.

. . . .

For the foregoing reasons, we affirm the judgment of the district court . . . .

Notes, Comments, and Questions

1. How should a court determine what the prevailing rate is? Should it use data? Which data? How much? The district court in *A.R.* relied on affidavits from attorneys and awards in other cases. Was this sufficient? One court ruled:

> The market rate for similar services in the community must be established "through affidavits reciting the precise fees that counsel with similar qualifications have received in comparable cases; information concerning recent fee awards by courts in comparable cases; and specific evidence of counsel's actual billing practice or other evidence of the actual rates which counsel can command in the market."

JP v. Cnty. Sch. Bd. of Hanover Cnty., 641 F. Supp. 2d 499, 513 (E.D. Va. 2009) (quoting Spell v. McDaniel, 824 F.2d 1380, 1402 (4th Cir. 1987)).

In *Bailey v. District of Columbia*, 839 F.Supp. 888 (D.D.C. 1993), the court included a chart that contained the names of seven attorneys practicing special education law in the jurisdiction, their years of experience, and their hourly billing rates. The court ruled:

> Concededly, there is not much data here upon which to base a prevailing market rate. The field of special education lawyers—the sub-market in which plaintiffs' counsel places himself—is small. Nevertheless, it is clear from the data available that the prevailing market rate for special education lawyers in the District of Columbia with Mr. Drake's many years of experience is $175 to $230 per hour. . . . Mr. Drake's requested rate—$200 per hour—is well within the prevailing market rates for similar legal work performed in the community.

Id. at 891.

Courts in the District of Columbia often use the "Laffey Matrix," which shows hourly rates for attorneys involved in federal civil litigation based on years of experience, to determine attorneys fees awards in IDEA cases. *See, e.g.*, Cox v. District of Columbia, 754 F. Supp. 2d 66, 75–76 (D.D.C. 2010) (upholding use of the Laffey Matrix against the District's argument that the court should use the District's chart of fees in IDEA administrative proceedings).

2. The court in *A.R.* was confronted with the claim that administrative proceedings are easier than court proceedings so the hourly rate should be lower for administrative proceedings. The court did not decide this claim. If you had been the judge's law clerk and she asked you for your opinion, what would you have said? How would you compare an IDEA administrative proceeding and federal court civil litigation? One court, answering the District of Columbia's argument that its chart of fees for IDEA administrative proceedings, and not the Laffey Matrix for federal civil litigation, should apply to IDEA administrative proceedings because they are less difficult than civil litigation, ruled:

> Furthermore, the court is not persuaded that IDEA administrative proceedings, which typically require testimony from education experts regarding whether a student has been denied a free and appropriate education and the need for any compensatory educational services, are categorically less complex than other forms of litigation.

Jackson v. District of Columbia, 696 F. Supp. 2d 97, 102 (D.D.C. 2010). Another court agreed:

> The basic legal precepts on which an IDEA case is based are not themselves complex. However, as shown by the record, the factual issues which animate the legal principles are quite complex. In particular, it is necessary for a lawyer to work his way through quite complex and often confusing public educational records and assess the conclusions of public educators in perspective of experts in the education of autistic children. Then all of that must be sorted and presented by effective use of the records, effective cross-examination of witnesses, and mustering an effective presentation of expert

> witnesses. This case called for the exercise of considerable skill on the part of Mr. Strother, and his experience in handling special education cases in other contexts was apparent in the skillful and effective way in which the factual record here was developed and in which expert evidence in support of JP's case was assembled and presented.

JP v. Cnty. Sch. Bd. of Hanover Cnty., 641 F. Supp. 2d 499, 514 (E.D. Va. 2009). The court in Cox v. District of Columbia, 754 F. Supp. 2d 66 (D.D.C. 2010), also rejecting an argument that it should not use the Laffey Matrix, described the level of difficulty in the administrative proceedings that were the subject of the attorneys fees petition in the case:

> Moreover, Defendant's claim that B.S. and E.J.'s hearings were "uncomplicated" is absurd, as any reading of the comprehensive decisions by the two Hearing Officers in these cases demonstrates. In B.S.'s case, it took nearly two years—which included a suspension from school and a two-week stay in a psychiatric hospital—and a hearing with sixty-five documentary exhibits, four witnesses, and written closing statements to obtain an order forcing DCPS to provide desperately needed treatment and educational assistance. As for E.J., it took more than seven months and a hearing with fifty documentary exhibits, four witnesses, and written closing statements to obtain a ruling that would, hopefully, provide the help that E.J.'s MDT made clear was needed.

Id. .at 76.

3. Of what relevance is the rate that the attorney actually charged the client in determining the prevailing rate? In *JP v. Cnty. Sch. Bd. of Hanover Cnty.*, 641 F. Supp. 2d 499 (E.D. Va. 2009), the court addressed this question. The attorney's retainer agreement set reduced rates, but stated that if the plaintiffs prevailed, the attorney would request fees at the prevailing rate. *Id.* at 513. The attorney's explanation for the disparity was that without this discount, most parents would not bring IDEA cases. The defendants objected to paying a rate higher than the attorney charged. The court rejected this argument. It stated:

> There is no doubt that the fee actually charged is relevant in determining a reasonable hourly rate. . . . That, however, does not mean that the rate normally charged and paid is the prevailing rate in the community or that such datum is the only factor to be considered in determining the prevailing community rate.
>
> In fact, if Congress had wanted IDEA attorneys fees for prevailing plaintiffs to be the hourly rate normally received by plaintiff's counsel, it could have said precisely that. It did not. Instead, Congress used different words, and courts are obligated to give the words of Congress effect. . . .
>
> Rather clearly, by specifying the prevailing rate in the community, Congress looked beyond the rate which the plaintiff's lawyer usually charges and

> receives. Congress chose that measure to provide incentives to lawyers to take IDEA cases. Here, the record shows that the prevailing rate in the community is $350 per hour for the lead partner.

Id. at 515–16.

4. What are the competing interests in setting attorneys fee awards? Should these interests matter in determining the fee amount in particular cases? Fee-shifting provisions create a market for legal services when there might otherwise not have been one, allowing people without sufficient means to retain an attorney to pursue their legal claims. However, although fees are available in IDEA cases, they are available only to prevailing parties, so attorneys have an interest in taking only those cases they think might be successful and also are sufficiently complex to justify their time and create a significant return on their investment. Does this system create benefits for students other than those who are represented by counsel in successful IDEA cases? Does the threat to a district of having to pay large attorneys fee awards create an incentive for the district to comply with the IDEA? Or do large fee awards diminish the funds available for educating all students with disabilities? Consider how the court in J.P. v. Cnty. Sch. Bd. of Hanover Cnty., 641 F. Supp. 2d 499 (E.D. Va. 2009), resolved these competing interests:

> HCPS makes the related argument that an [attorneys fee] award of this amount [$307,150.20] might have a negative effect on HCPS itself. This argument is based on a comment at oral argument on appeal in which one of the judges said:
>
> > But on the other side, we also have School Boards who are strapped for money, that can barely get enough every year from a legislature, from whatever source they can get the money. And if we have every one of the special education students going through and spending a quarter of a million dollars individually on litigation, we're going to bankrupt the educational system. And I don't think that was the purpose either as a matter of policy.
>
> The Supreme Court has considered the financial burden placed on school districts by the IDEA. *See Florence County Sch. Dist. v. Carter,* 510 U.S. 7, 15–16 . . . (1993). In *Carter,* the school district claimed that allowing reimbursement for public school placements would place an unreasonable burden on schools' finances. In response to this argument, the Supreme Court observed:
>
> > There is no doubt that Congress has imposed a significant financial burden on States and school districts that participate in IDEA. Yet public educational authorities who also want to avoid reimbursing parents for the private education of a disabled child can do one of two things: give the child a free appropriate public education in a public setting, or place the child in an appropriate private setting of the State's choice. This is IDEA's mandate, and school officials who conform to it need not worry about reimbursement claims.
>
> *Id.*
>
> . . . .

In sum, it is clear that the Supreme Court has provided a clear answer to HCPS' contention that the burden placed on it by attorneys' fees indicates that an award of those fees is inappropriate: school districts assume the risk of substantial-but-reasonable awards when they violate the IDEA. HCPS' argument is further undercut by its own vigorous defense throughout the course of this litigation. In a very real sense, therefore, the size of the attorneys' fees award in this case is attributable, in significant part, to the conduct of HCPS in violating the IDEA and then engaging in an aggressive defense. Hence, reducing the size of the attorneys fee award because of the financial burden placed on HCPS certainly is not appropriate on the facts of this case if, indeed, it ever would be appropriate to do so.

Finally, it is the office of Congress, not the Courts, to establish policy. The Court certainly is neither unaware of, nor insensitive to, the burden that IDEA places on the resources of school systems. But, the consequence of accepting federal funds under IDEA is compliance with the duties imposed by the statute and the attendant fiscal responsibility for failing to comply, one of which is the payment of fees to a prevailing plaintiff. If Congress should conclude that compensating prevailing plaintiffs by using the statutory mode specified by IDEA presents an undue burden on school systems, then Congress can change the mode for determining attorneys fees. The Court cannot.

Id. at 524–25. The court makes the assertion that HCPS deserved the high fee award against it because it violated the IDEA and then engaged in an aggressive defense. Do you agree? What should a school district's approach to defending IDEA claims be?

2. Determining the Number of Hours Reasonably Expended

The following case is representative of how courts determine the number of hours reasonably expended on a case.

Ryan M. v. Bd. of Educ. of Chic., Dist. 299

731 F. Supp. 2d 776 (N.D. Ill. 2010)

Virginia M. Kendall, District Judge.

Plaintiffs . . . filed suit against Defendant Board of Education of the City of Chicago, District 299 ("the Board") pursuant to 20 U.S.C. § 1415(i)(3), seeking attorneys fees and costs incurred by Plaintiffs in prevailing in a due process hearing against the Board. Plaintiffs and the Board have filed cross-motions for summary judgment. . . .

. . . .

. . . Plaintiffs request $95,173.02 in attorneys' fees. The Board admits that $53,577.00 of this request is appropriate for the work related to Ryan M.'s due process hearing, but contests the remaining $41,596.02 based on eight specific objections to the petition. . . .

. . . .

B. Reasonableness of the Fee Award

After finding that a plaintiff qualifies as a prevailing party under the IDEA, the Court considers the reasonableness of a prevailing party's request for an award. In determining a fee's reasonableness, the degree of the plaintiff's success is the most significant factor for the Court's consideration. The Court begins with the lodestar figure, which represents "the number of hours reasonably expended on the litigation multiplied by a reasonable hourly rate." *See Enoch v. Tienor*, 570 F.3d 821, 823 (7th Cir. 2009) (quoting *Hensley*, 461 U.S. at 433). . . . The Court may then adjust that figure based on the factors set forth in *Hensley*, such as the time and labor required, the novelty or difficulty of the case, the degree of success achieved, the experience and ability of the attorneys, the adequacy of the documentation of the hours, and whether appropriate billing judgment was used. The party requesting the fee has the burden of proving its reasonableness, including the hourly rate and appropriate hours expended. Finally, federal district courts have considerable discretion in granting an award of attorney's fees.

. . . .

The Board outlines eight general objections to the hours billed by Plaintiff's counsel in their fee petition, arguing that the lodestar should be reduced based on these objections. Specifically, the Board asserts that Plaintiffs should not be able to recover fees relating to unsuccessful motions, mediation, or duplicate entries, and that certain charges for drafting and researching several documents, preparing witnesses, nonlegal research, and travel were excessive and therefore unreasonable. The Board also contends that because the Plaintiffs did not achieve full relief, they should not be entitled to the full fee. Based on these objections, the Board asks that the Court reduce the Plaintiff's fee to $53,577.00. The Court considers each of these arguments in turn.

1. Unsuccessful Motion for Reconsideration

The Board first objects to Plaintiffs' bill of 10.0 hours preparing an unsuccessful motion for reconsideration and reply brief following the hearing officer's denial of expert classroom observation by Lane. It asserts that time related to an unsuccessful motion is not recoverable and asks the Court to reduce the lodestar amount accordingly. A plaintiff may not recover fees for unsuccessful claims that were unrelated to those claims that are successful. The Court in *Hensley* explained that if two claims could have been brought in separate cases, an attorney should not be able to recover for work relating to the losing issue simply because it was filed with other successful claims. . . .

Here, Plaintiffs' motion for reconsideration was far from a distinct "claim" as described in *Hensley*—instead, it was an intermediate, procedural request aimed at gaining evidence to achieve the ultimate goal of amending Ryan M.'s IEP. The motion is, therefore, more analogous to a non-dispositive discovery or pretrial motion than a separate, unrelated claim based on a different legal theory. The time related to briefing of the motion for reconsideration is therefore reasonable and recoverable by Plaintiffs' counsel.

2. Drafting, Researching, and Reviewing Documents

The Board next requests the Court to reduce Plaintiffs' fee award based on excessive time billed for drafting, researching, and reviewing various documents. Specifically, the Board contends that 14.0 hours drafting a Due Process Complaint; 6.5 hours drafting a response to the Board's notice of insufficiency; 2.3 hours drafting a motion for a hearing date; 0.50 hours emailing clients and experts; 3.0 hours drafting a dissent to the IEP; 3.0 hours drafting stipulations of fact; 0.50 hours drafting a letter to the Board's counsel; 10.5 hours of attorney time and 11.5 hours of non-attorney time preparing a trial binder; 4.0 hours writing an opening statement; and 66.4 hours preparing a post-hearing brief are all excessive charges and should be reduced by fifty percent. The Board's objections amount to a total of $17,036.25 in requested reductions.

Using its discretion, the Court may reduce an attorneys' fee award when the hours billed are excessive in light of the attorneys' experience and the work produced. Although "[a]n attorney's hours are subject to the scrutiny of the court and unreasonable hours should not be compensated," however, the court will not "eyeball the fee request and cut it down by an arbitrary percentage because it seem[s] excessive." . . . Instead, the party opposing the fee must make some showing as to why the time billed should be reduced by a certain amount.

Plaintiffs argue that the time billed on each of these documents was reasonable, in many cases directing the Court to the actual documents in question. Plaintiffs also claim, and the undisputed facts show, that this case "involved fact intensive, complex matters touching on child development problems including language, behavior, psychology and autism," and that these complex issues justified the time expended on the documents to which the Board objects. The Board, in response, has failed to present any legal support for its proposed reductions, relying only on conclusory assertions that the time billed is excessive and should be reduced by fifty percent based on the general level of experience of Plaintiffs' counsel.

After careful review of the documents in question, the Court determines that the hours requested by Plaintiffs' counsel are reasonable. For example, the Due Process Complaint consists of a 12 page document making detailed factual allegations. Unlike in *M.*, where the defendants submitted evidence from the Illinois Administrative Code and other complaints to support their assertions that the time billed for drafting the Due Process Complaint was unreasonable, the Board's request to reduce the time billed on the Due Process Complaint would require the Court to "eyeball the fee request and cut it down by an arbitrary percentage." Likewise, Plaintiffs' motion requesting scheduling of a hearing date is a 7 page document outlining the procedural history of the complaint and Plaintiffs' Response to the Notice of Insufficiency is a 6 page document defending against the District's allegations of insufficiency of notice. The 2.3 hours and 6.5 hours respectively billed for the preparation and drafting of these documents is reasonable given their length, detail, and import to the litigation as a whole. Similarly, the 3.0 hours billed drafting a 4 page single spaced letter dissenting to the IEP, 3.0 hours billed drafting 4 pages of stipulations of fact, and 4.0 hours billed preparing a 7 page opening statement are reasonable considering the length of these documents and complexity of the issues in this case as shown in the undisputed facts. The 10.5 hours of attorney time and 11.5 hours of non-attorney time preparing the hearing book is also justified in light of the 509 page book that was produced and the 4 to 5 day duration of the due process hearing. Finally, the 66.4 hours spent preparing a post-hearing brief is justifiable in light of the 45 page detailed memorandum of law that Plaintiffs' attorneys submitted. Because Plaintiffs have sufficiently justified the time spent on these and all other documents that the Board contests, and the Board has provided nothing but conclusory assertions in its objections, the Court awards the full fee amount relating to the preparation and drafting of these documents.

3. Preparing Witnesses and Direct Examinations

The Board claims that the Plaintiffs' time spent preparing witnesses is excessive and should be reduced by fifty percent. Specifically, the Board objects to 8.0 hours working with Dr. Daniels; 15.0 hours preparing and writing the direct examination for Lane; 7.0 hours working with Cutler; 21.0 hours preparing the Plaintiffs' direct examination; and 12.0 hours preparing the direct examinations of other Board witnesses such as Chicago Public Schools case managers and administrators. Plaintiffs assert that this time was reasonable based on the complexity of Ryan M.'s case, education history, medical diagnoses, and behavioral symptoms.

Just as with objections for excessive drafting time, the Court may reduce an award of attorneys' fees for any time that it believes is excessive in light of the work performed, but will not arbitrarily make reductions to the billed amounts. In its objections, the Board again provides conclusory statements suggesting that Plaintiffs' counsel's preparation time is excessive with no legal authority to support its position. Plaintiffs' counsel, however, points to specific facts about the complexity of the case in arguing that the time spent was reasonable, such as the emotional state of Geysy M. during her preparation, as well as the intensive nature of the hearing that spanned several days throughout a three month period. Given the extensive medical and educational history reflected in the undisputed facts, it is also reasonable that Plaintiffs' counsel expended several hours working with each of the witnesses from CPS. Moreover, given the seriousness of Ryan M.'s behavior and other problems alleged with his IEP, it also appears reasonable that Plaintiffs counsel would have spent 8 hours writing and practicing the direct examination for Dr. Daniels, as well as 15 hours for Lane and 7 hours for Cutler. After reviewing the hours asserted for the various witnesses, the Court concludes that the witness preparation time is reasonable and recoverable.

4. Non-legal Research

With respect to billing for non-legal research, the Board objects to 3.0 hours of billed attorney time related to researching preschool programs, asserting that this time is unreasonable because it should have been performed by a paralegal at the $75 per hour rate rather than the $300 per hour attorney rate. The Board requests a reduction of $675 from the lodestar amount to reflect the appropriate fee for this task. Plaintiffs contend that this attorney time is reasonable and therefore should be reflected in the lodestar amount because it was more cost efficient for the attorney to perform the research herself rather than train a legal assistant to perform the task.

When non-legal work has been billed at an attorney's hourly rate, the Court may reduce the fee to reflect the proper hourly rate of a legal assistant who could have performed the work. Here, the task of researching preschools is clearly non-legal in nature, and while it would require background knowledge of the requirements for a preschool program for Ryan M., Plaintiffs have asserted only that the research involved viewing numerous websites and that training a legal assistant would have taken more time than the research itself. Plaintiffs have provided no information about the complexity of the considerations involved or any details about the time it would have required to train a legal assistant. Therefore, Plaintiffs have failed to meet their burden of justifying the reasonableness of this time billed at an attorney's rate, and the Court reduces the lodestar amount by $675 to reflect the appropriate $75 per hour paralegal rate for the 3.0 hours of research.

5. Travel Time

The Board next argues that the 1.0 hour billed for travel time to and from Otis Elementary on February 13, 2009, February 25, 2009, and March 24, 2009 is excessive and should be reduced by fifty percent to correspond with the 0.5 hours of travel time billed for the same trip on January 23, 2009. The Board also contends that the 2.0 hours billed on January 14, 2009 for counsel to meet with Dr. Daniels was excessive and should be reduced. Plaintiffs make the unsubstantiated assertion that the one hour travel times were affected by severe weather, and that the two hour travel on January 14 was the result of "severe inclement weather." Plaintiffs have not put forth any evidence to support these driving times, however, so as to meet their burden of establishing reasonableness. Plaintiffs could have submitted various kinds of information supporting their assertion that the times of the trips were reasonable, such as weather reports from the days in question, the distance and route of the trip, or affidavits regarding the average and maximum travel times of the route, but failed to do so. Without evidence to demonstrate the reasonableness of the asserted travel times, the Court reduces Plaintiffs' fees to 0.5 hours (the amount billed on January 23, 2009) for each trip to and from Otis Elementary on February 13, 2009, February 25, 2009, and March 24, 2009, and 1.0 hours to meet with Dr. Daniels on January 14, 2009. Thus, the Court reduces the total amount of billed travel time by 4.0 hours multiplied by the $300 hourly attorney billing rate, for a $1,200 reduction in the lodestar amount.

6. Time Related to Mediation

Turning to the time billed related to mediation, the Board objects to 1.6 hours of time for which it believes the fees are unrecoverable. Plaintiffs' counsel billed 1.5 hours for a post-mediation meeting with clients . . . regarding the status of the litigation, as well as 0.10 hours to draft an email to the hearing officer to notify him that the mediation had failed and that the hearing must proceed. The Board asserts that because the time was related to mediation, it may not be considered in an award of attorneys' fees.

Under the IDEA, fees relating to resolution meetings or mediation are specifically excluded from attorneys' fees that may be awarded. *See* 20 U.S.C. § 1415(i)(3)(D)(iii) (preliminary resolution meetings shall not be considered meetings, administrative hearings or judicial action for which attorneys' fees may be recovered). Plaintiffs contend that the 1.5 hours counsel billed for the post-mediation client meeting was not related to mediation, but instead was to conference with Plaintiffs regarding the next steps in the proceedings. Additionally, Plaintiffs argue that the email to the hearing officer simply advised the officer that the hearing must proceed because mediation had failed. A review of the undisputed facts makes clear that both the meeting and email were procedural steps that were necessary to continue with litigation. Just because the events were the result of mediation does not mean that they were related to mediation. Indeed, if all events that occurred because mediation failed qualified as proceedings related to mediation, the entirety of the litigation post-mediation could be considered as such. Because there is no evidence in the record to suggest that the meeting and email at issue constituted part of a preliminary resolution meeting, *see* 20 U.S.C. § 1415(i)(3)(D)(iii), the Court finds these hours to be recoverable under the IDEA.

7. Duplicative Entries

The Board next objects to 4.9 hours of work that it claims is duplicative, unnecessary, and therefore unrecoverable. It asserts that it was improper for both attorneys to bill for a 0.3 hour status call, a 1.0 hour pre-hearing conference, a 0.5 hour telephone conference with Plaintiffs, and 4.0 hours preparing potential witness Mara Lane. From an award of attorneys' fees, the Court may deduct time that it believes is unnecessary, duplicative, or redundant.

First, with respect to the 4.0 hours of witness preparation for Lane billed by both counsel, Plaintiffs have put forth no evidence to show why both of them were required to participate in Lane's preparation but not in the preparation of any of the other witnesses. Although they contend that her preparation "cut across areas of respective responsibility," they do not substantiate this assertion or explain why and how Lane's substantive testimony differed from that of the other witnesses. Similarly, Plaintiffs offer no rationale as to why both attorneys needed to participate in the 0.5 hour telephone conference with Plaintiffs or the 0.3 hour status call other than the fact that "both parties participated in most telephone conferences." Because Plaintiffs have not met their burden of showing reasonableness for these billings, the Court deducts these hours as redundant.

With respect to the 1.0 hour pre-hearing conference, on the other hand, Plaintiffs contend that it was "of sufficient importance to engage both co-counsel." Because it seems appropriate for both attorneys who will be involved in conducting the hearing to be present at a pre-hearing conference with the hearings officer, Plaintiffs have met their burden of establishing that this time billed is reasonable. Thus, the Court deducts a total of $1,440 (4.8 hours multiplied by the $300 billing rate) from the lodestar amount for duplicative entries.

. . . .

. . . In sum, the Court reduces Plaintiffs' fee petition of $95,173.02 by $675 for non-legal research, $1,200 for travel time, $1,440 for duplicative entries, and then by fifteen percent to account for Plaintiffs' degree of success. That brings the total attorneys' fee award to $78,079.32, plus prejudgment interest.

Note

The court in *Ryan M.* referred to the "*Hensley*" factors to use when evaluating attorneys fees requests. There are twelve *Hensley* factors, and courts in IDEA cases often refer to them in making fee determinations. *See, e.g.*, M.K. v. Sergi, 554 F. Supp. 2d 233, 246 n. 5 (D. Conn. 2008) (listing the twelve *Hensley* factors); M.L. v. Fed. Way Sch. Dist., 401 F. Supp. 2d 1158, 1168–69 (W.D. Wash. 2005) (stating that courts in the Ninth Circuit are required to consider these factors in making an award of attorneys fees); Doucet v. Chilton Cnty. Bd. of Educ., 65 F. Supp. 2d 1249, 1259–60 (M.D. Ala. 1999) (utilizing the twelve *Hensley* factors). The factors, which originated in *Johnson v. Ga. Highway Express, Inc.*, 488 F.2d 714 (5th Cir. 1974), and cited approvingly in *Hensley* v. *Eckerhart*, 461 U.S. 424, 434, n. 9 (1983), are:

> (1) *The time and labor required.* . . . (2) *The novelty and difficulty of the questions.* . . . (3) *The skill required to perform the legal service properly.* . . . (4) *The preclusion of other employment by the attorney due to the acceptance of the case.* . . . (5) *The customary fee.* . . . (6) *Whether the fee is fixed or contingent.* . . . (7) *Time limitations imposed by the client or circumstances.* . . . (8) *The amount involved and the results obtained.* . . . (9) *The experience, reputation, and ability of the attorneys.* . . . (10) *The "undesirability" of the case.* . . . (11) *The nature and length of the professional relationship with the client.* . . . (12) *Awards in similar cases.*

Johnson, 488 F.2d at 717–19 (emphasis in original).

E. Discretionary Reductions of Attorneys Fees Based on a Limited Degree of Success

Courts have often used their discretionary authority to award attorneys fees to reduce fee awards to a prevailing party based on a limited degree of success. *See, e.g.*, J.D. v. Kanawaha Cnty. Bd. of Educ., 571 F.3d 381, 387 (4th Cir. 2009) (reducing fee from $112,292 to $34,072 because, although the parents prevailed on several claims, they lost their most important claim challenging the IEP); Jason D.W. v. Hous. Indep. Sch. Dist., 158 F.3d 205, 208, 211 (5th Cir. 1998) (reducing fee from $32,943.97 to $8,340.49 because plaintiff prevailed on three of nineteen issues and spent more than half of the hearing on an issue that he lost); Mrs. M. v. Tri-Valley Cent. Sch. Dist., 363 F. Supp. 2d 566, 573 (S.D.N.Y. 2002) (reducing fee by fifty percent, from $16,000 to $8,300, to reflect limited degree of success in the form of a new 1:1 aide); Chagnon v. Town of Shrewsbury, 901 F. Supp. 32, 36 (D. Mass. 1995) (reducing fee by fifty percent because the parents did not secure the placement they wanted for their child).

Determining the degree of a party's success is not an exact science. Comparing the relief a party sought to the relief it received and translating this into a percentage reduction is inherently arbitrary. One court recognized this:

> In the present case, the facts all centered around the treatment of John by Defendant. The legal issues focused on whether Defendant's actions denied a FAPE to John over a period of more than two years. The claims were legally and factually related, making segregation of time spent on unsuccessful claims difficult. . . .
>
> Plaintiffs suggest an inherent difficulty in placing a pecuniary value on the relief they originally requested, urging that the issues on which they prevailed are intertwined and inseparable from issues on which they did not prevail. For example, the Court notes the IHO denied Plaintiffs' request for reimbursement for an independent speech/language evaluation, but relied upon Plaintiffs' private speech pathologist in finding John's direct speech/language services should be increased from thirty to sixty minutes per week.
>
> While a valuation may be difficult, some type of valuation of success is necessary. However, such a valuation is a qualitative inquiry, and the overall success of Plaintiffs in the litigation is therefore critical.
>
> To be sure, Plaintiffs did not prevail on several forms of requested relief, including therapeutic day school placement and payment for independent evaluations. . . . Plaintiffs sought a substantial improvement in educational resources available to John, and proposed a therapeutic day school placement remedy by which to remove inadequacies in John's educational program. Plaintiffs' failure to earn this placement is not fatal to their claim for attorney's fees. Instead, this Court finds the full scope of relief the IHO awarded accomplished Plaintiffs' aims.
>
> . . . .
>
> . . . In light of the issues on which Plaintiffs did not prevail, as well as the difficulty in segregating the time spent on those issues, the Court finds Plaintiffs' proposed reduction in the amount of 15 percent is reasonable . . . .

John M. v. Bd. of Educ. of Chic., Dist. 299, 612 F. Supp. 2d 981, 998–99 (N.D. Ill. 2009).

Courts have applied different percentage reductions, ranging from fifteen percent to one hundred percent, depending on whether plaintiff obtained anywhere from "substantial relief" to "*de minimis*" relief. There are no clear guidelines for making these reductions. In *Ryan M. v. Bd. of Educ. of Chic., Dist. 299*, 731 F. Supp. 2d 776 (N.D. Ill. 2010), the court suggested that "fifteen percent is a common reduction when a plaintiff achieved substantial, but not complete, relief." *Id.* at 796. The court reduced the lodestar amount of $93,298 by fifteen percent, to $79,303 (including additional small miscellaneous deductions), to reflect the plaintiff's substantial, but not complete, degree of success. *Id.* at 795. The plaintiff had sought "individual, one-on-one speech, language, and occupational therapy and direct social work," and the court found that the hearing officer did not order this relief. *Id.* at 794; *see also John M.*, 612 F. Supp. 2d at 999 (reducing fee request by fifteen percent). In another case, the court reduced the fee by fifteen percent when the IHO affirmed the child's unilateral placement and granted compensatory speech services but denied additional compensatory speech services, reimbursement for educational evaluations, compensatory occupational therapy, and tutoring. Benito M. v. Bd. of Educ. of Chic., Dist. 299, 544 F. Supp. 2d 713, 721 (N.D. Ill. 2008). The court stated, "Reducing fees devoted to these denied services would be impossible because there is no precise method to parse the time devoted to them. Accordingly, counsel's overall request is reduced by a percentage to account for the degree of success his clients obtained." *Id.*

In other cases in which courts found lower levels of success, they have reduced fees by higher percentages. In *Max M. v. Ill. State Bd .of Educ.*, 684 F. Supp. 514 (N.D. Ill. 1988), the court reduced the fee by fifty percent:

> Although a number of important decisions concerning the rights of parents and handicapped children under the EACHA resulted from this action, this court cannot overlook the fact that the Ms only succeeded in obtaining a fraction of the relief they originally sought. Though the Ms obtained reimbursement for Max' psychotherapy, they failed to secure revocation of Max' diploma, compensatory education, and reimbursement for funds expended in connection with Max' placement in a residential educational facility. This relief was clearly the most important sought by the Ms. Moreover, the Ms' request for monetary damages was denied when the Ms' non-EAHCA claims were dismissed in *Max M. I.* Even considering the benefits accruing to other handicapped children as a result of this action, the level of success achieved in this case can only support a limited award of attorneys fees. In the view of this court, a fifty percent reduction in the lodestar will produce a fee which is reasonable in light of the results obtained.

Id. at 531; *see also* Chagnon v. Town of Shrewsbury, 901 F. Supp. 32, 36 (D. Mass. 1995) (reducing fee by fifty percent due to failure to obtain desired placement). One court reduced the fee by fifty percent because the parents won on one significant claim and lost on the other claim. K.C. v. Me. Sch. Admin. Dist. No. 6, 582 F. Supp. 2d 65, 67–68 (D. Me. 2008); *see also* Dickens v. Friendship-Edison P.C.S., 724 F. Supp. 2d 113, 122 (D.D.C. 2010) (reducing fee by fifty percent due to limited degree of success compared with the large number of claims, including inadequate IEP).

In *Fenneman v. Gorham Sch. Dep't*, 802 F. Supp. 542 (D. Me. 1992), the court weighed the relative importance of plaintiffs' claims and their degree of success and reduced the fee request by eighty percent:

> I find that the plaintiffs' claim concerning private residential placement was the predominant reason they sought an administrative hearing. Rather than representing equal importance, the claim for residential placement accounted for 60% of the plaintiffs' efforts at the hearing; the claim seeking a declaration that the IEP was inadequate accounted for 40% of the plaintiffs' efforts at the hearing. However, I find that the relief granted the plaintiffs on the IEP claims represents 50% of the relief they were seeking on that claim. Thus, the plaintiffs are entitled to recover 20% of the fees and costs expended at the administrative hearing.

Id. at 548; *see also* J.D. v. Kanawha Cnty. Bd. of Educ., 571 F.3d 381, 387 (4th Cir. 2009) (confirming district court decision reducing fee award from $112,292 to $34,072 to reflect the fact that plaintiff's parents received some relief in the form of additional evaluations, another IEP meeting with an independent facilitator, and additional speech and language therapy, but failed on their primary claim challenging the adequacy of the IEP); V.S. v. Colts Neck Bd. of Educ., 190 F. App'x 140, 143 (3d Cir. 2006) (reducing attorneys fees request by eighty percent due to limited success on only one issue); Koswenda v. Flossmoor Sch. Dist. No. 161, 227 F. Supp. 2d 979, 992, 996–97 (N.D. Ill. 2002) (reducing fees and costs request from $101,319.20 to $18,000 to reflect fact that plaintiffs lost their FAPE claim and prevailed on less than half their claims).

Finally, the Seventh Circuit refused to upset a district court's denial of fees to a prevailing party on the grounds that the party received only *de minimis* relief:

> This Court agrees with the Parents that they are "prevailing parties" for purposes of the attorneys' fees provision of the IDEA, given the changes to the IEP-1 ordered by the level I hearing officer. However . . . , we still must determine whether the district court abused its discretion in finding that the Parents' successes in this case were technical or *de minimis* because they did not prevail on their assertion that Brehm was the LRE for Brock, although they did secure reimbursement for Brock's attendance at Brehm on an interim basis. . . . The Parents did achieve a better program for Brock in the School District, with more personal attention to be paid to his specific needs. Nevertheless, although this is a close case, we cannot say the district court abused its discretion in finding such achievement *de minimis* in the context of the Parents' broader goals in this case [to approve Brock's placement in a private school].

Monticello Sch. Dist. No. 25 v. George L., 102 F.3d 895, 908 (7th Cir. 1996).

F. Mandatory Reductions in or Denials of Attorneys Fees

Even if a party prevails, there are circumstances in which the IDEA mandates attorneys fee reductions or denials. The next three sub-sections consider these circumstances.

1. Unreasonable Delay

The court can reduce a parent's request for attorneys fees if, "the parent, or the parent's attorney, during the course of the action or proceeding, unreasonably protracted the final resolution of the controversy . . . ." 20 U.S.C. § 1415(i)(3)(F)(i) (2012). Discernible standards regarding what constitutes an unreasonable delay do not emerge from the few reported cases that have considered claims for reductions on this ground. In *Howey v. Tippecanoe Sch. Corp.*, 734 F. Supp. 1485 (N.D. Ind. 1990), the court reduced the fee request for a hearing that covered forty-seven hours over six days, the longest in Indiana's history, on the grounds that the parents and their attorneys had unreasonably delayed the litigation. *Id.* at 1490, 1492. The court suggested at least three interrelated reasons for the finding: the plaintiffs litigated too extensively; the litigation was unnecessary in light of the relief the plaintiffs had already obtained; and their motive was malicious. The court stated:

> This court is of the very strong opinion that litigation continued in this case in an extensive and expansive fashion after these plaintiffs had achieved most, if not all, of the substantial results with regard to an appropriate public education for this child. It is for that reason as discussed below, that this court has reduced the claimed attorney fees in the administrative proceedings for this case. It is all too apparent in the record of this case that these plaintiffs and their counsel have engaged in a large scale attempt to punish these defendants for the latters' past perceived sins. To the extent that such has happened, and it has, these defendants are not obligated to pay counsel fees for the same, if these defendants took appropriate and timely corrective actions to provide this child with a free appropriate public education. Here, these defendants have done just that.

Id. at 1490; *see also* Jason D.W. v. Hous. Indep. Sch. Dist., 158 F.3d 205, 209, 211–12 (5th Cir. 1998) (reducing fee from $32,943.97 to $8,340.49 award on the grounds, among others, that the plaintiffs unreasonably protracted the case by refusing to settle for $10,000); J.T. v. Medford Bd. of Educ., 118 F. App'x 605, 607 (3d Cir. 2004) (upholding the district court's denial of fees to prevailing parents on the grounds they unreasonably delayed the litigation). In contrast, another court declined to reduce fees for the parents' failure to attend any meetings following the resolution session, despite its finding that such failure was inconsistent with the IDEA's goal of parents and schools working together to resolve disputes, on the grounds that such meetings are not required and there was no evidence that such meetings would have resolved the dispute. Ector Cnty. Indep. Sch. Dist. v. VB, 420 F. App'x 338, 347–348 (5th Cir. 2011).

2. IEP Meetings and Resolution Sessions

Courts may not award attorneys fees relating to IEP meetings or resolution sessions. 20 U.S.C. § 1415(i)(3)(D)(ii) and (iii) (2012). Courts have readily applied these prohibitions. *See, e.g.*, El Paso Indep. Sch. Dist. v. Richard R., 591 F.3d 417, 429 (5th Cir. 2009), *cert. denied*, 516 U.S. 1006 (2010) (denying fees for resolution session);

Kletzelman v. Capistrano Unified Sch. Dist., 91 F.3d 68, 70–71 (9th 1996) (ruling that attorney was not entitled to fees for IEP meetings); Shanahan v. Bd. of Educ. of Jamesville-DeWitt Sch. Dist., 953 F. Supp. 440, 444 (N.D.N.Y. 1997) (stating that attorneys fees are not available for IEP meetings); Fenneman v. Gorham, 802 F. Supp. 542, 545–546 (D. Me. 1992) (denying fees for participation in IEP meeting). In *Ryan M. v. Bd. of Educ. of Chic., Dist. 299*, 731 F.Supp. 2d 776 (N.D. Ill. 2010), however, the court construed the phrase, "relating to," to allow fees for time spent on a client meeting to discuss the next steps after a failed mediation and an email to the hearing officer informing him that the mediation had failed and litigation would be necessary. *Id.* at 793.

3. *Rejection of a More Favorable Settlement Offer*

The IDEA prohibits a court from awarding attorneys fees to a prevailing parent for services performed after the parent received a settlement offer if the relief the parent finally received is not more favorable than the settlement offer, provided the settlement offer was made in conformity with certain procedural requirements, unless the parent was substantially justified in rejecting the offer. The IDEA states:

> **(D) Prohibition of attorneys fees and related costs for certain services**
>
> **(i) In general**
>
> Attorneys fees may not be awarded and related costs may not be reimbursed in any action or proceeding under this section for services performed subsequent to the time of a written offer of settlement to a parent if—
>
> (I) the offer is made within the time prescribed by Rule 68 of the Federal Rules of Civil Procedure or, in the case of an administrative proceeding, at any time more than 10 days before the proceeding begins;
>
> (II) the offer is not accepted within 10 days; and
>
> (III) the court or administrative hearing officer finds that the relief finally obtained by the parents is not more favorable to the parents than the offer of settlement.
>
> ....
>
> **(E) Exception to prohibition on attorneys fees and related costs.**
>
> Notwithstanding subparagraph (D), an award of attorneys fees and related costs may be made to a parent who is the prevailing party and who was substantially justified in rejecting the settlement offer.

20 U.S.C. § 1415(i)(3)(D) and (E) (2012).

i. Determining Whether the Relief Obtained is More Favorable

Final resolutions of IDEA cases—either through settlements or an administrative or judicial order—often contain non-monetary provisions, including changes to the IEP, additional related services, compensatory education, additional evaluations, or a change in placement, all of which are difficult to value. It thus can be difficult to compare the terms of a settlement offer with the terms of the final relief to determine which is more favorable. Perhaps as a result, there are not many reported cases denying attorneys fees to prevailing parents in IDEA cases on the basis that the final relief is not more favorable than the settlement offer. A good example of a case that shows the difficulties of comparing a settlement offer with final relief is *John M. v. Bd. of Educ. of Chic.*, 612 F. Supp. 2d 981, (N.D. Ill. 2009):

> Here, Plaintiffs achieved some degree of success at the administrative level. For example, the IHO materially altered the legal relationship between the parties when she ordered CPS to: (1) provide related services with sufficient intensity with respect to speech and language and AT; (2) offer John compensatory services, including after school tutoring for one hour per week for the 2008–2009 school year and reading instruction during the summers of 2008 and 2009; (3) craft a new IEP in order to provide sufficient time for John to receive reading instruction using the Wilson method at least one hour a day, at least four days per week; and (4) provide proof of compliance with her orders within one month of the date of her decision.
>
> . . . .
>
> CPS' . . . settlement offer included one hour per week of after school tutoring by a certified special education provider or qualified tutor for one school year (i.e. forty weeks); sixty minutes per week of direct speech and language services; payment of the independent speech and language evaluation . . . ; and an IEP meeting to consider the results of the independent evaluation and to implement the previous terms of the settlement. There are substantive differences between this offer and the relief obtained. For example, the IHO granted a number of items of relief Defendant did not offer, including a total of sixty hours of reading instruction using the Wilson method in the summers of 2008 and 2009; AT instruction for a minimum of forty minutes per week; training in the use of AT for both teacher and student; additional training in Wilson method instruction for the teacher; and one hour per day of reading instruction, four days per week, using the Wilson method. Thus, due to Defendant's failure in certain respects to provide John with FAPE, the IHO awarded compensatory services to Plaintiffs, a number of which were not included in Defendant's settlement offer.
>
> Thus, the settlement offer was not more favorable than the relief finally obtained.

Id. at 991–92. Another court compared a settlement offer of a two-year placement at an undisclosed day school, transportation, and an assistive technology evaluation with ultimate relief in the form of a one-year placement at a specific school and weekly thirty-minute compensatory speech/language services for one year. Benito M. v. Bd. of Educ. of Chic., Dist. 299, 544 F. Supp. 2d 713, 719 (N.D. Ill. 2008). The court ruled that the ultimate relief was more favorable than the settlement offer. The court's ruling shows the inherent difficulty in comparing settlement offers with final awards:

> The Board of Education proffers evidence that the cost of private placement and transportation for the 2007–2008 school year far exceeds the cost of weekly 30–minute compensatory speech/language services for the 2007–2008 school year. However, this fact does not demonstrate that the offer was more favorable than the relief obtained. Indeed, the settlement offer was not more favorable than the relief finally obtained.
>
> For one, the offer failed to specify where Benito would be placed. This is significant because the hearing officer's decision affirmed Benito's *specific* placement at the Hyde Park Day School. . . . [T]here is no basis to conclude that a two-year private placement offer at an *unidentified* school was more favorable than Benito's *specific* placement at the Hyde Park Day School. Furthermore, it is unclear whether plaintiffs even sought private placement for more than one year.
>
> Additionally, the settlement offer was not more favorable because it did not provide compensatory services. . . . The hearing officer awarded compensatory speech services to plaintiffs due to the Board of Education's failure to provide Benito a free and appropriate public education. Thus, the settlement offer was not more favorable than the relief finally obtained.

Id. at 719–20.

It is not always difficult for the court to compare non-quantifiable terms:

> This Court is of the opinion that the letter of July 5 was not only a "serious" settlement offer—it came close to a capitulation. It provided for placement of Lori in a class with other four-year-olds with access to continual speech and vision therapy. More importantly, it is evident that the relief offered in this letter does not differ materially from that eventually obtained through the hearing.

Hyden v. Bd. of Educ. of Wilson Cnty., 714 F. Supp. 290, 292–293 (M.D. Tenn. 1989); *see also* El Paso Indep. Sch. Dist. v. Richard R., 591 F.3d 417, 428 (5th Cir. 2009), *cert. denied*, 561 U.S. 1006 (2010) (denying fees because parents rejected an offer that provided all the relief they requested).

Several courts have parsed the difference between a settlement offer and the final relief very carefully, and found that, although barely, the final award was superior to the settlement offer, and thus awarded fees. In *Mrs. M. v. Tri-Valley Cent. Sch. Dist.*, 363 F. Supp. 2d 566 (S.D.N.Y. 2002), the court found that, "Although just barely, the final settlement afforded plaintiff slightly more relief than she was offered in the . . . settlement letter." *Id.* at 572. The final settlement included a minor change in the

IEP instead of a conference to discuss changes to the IEP, a future change in the child's aide, and a reduction in counseling (the parents wanted no counseling). *Id.* at 569–72; *see also* M.L. v. Fed. Way Sch. Dist., 401 F. Supp. 2d 1158, 1165–66 (W.D. Wash. 2005) (ruling that a final monetary award for essentially the same amount of money as the settlement offer and an order to convene an IDEA-compliant team was superior to an offer of a specific amount of ABA services); Gross v. Perrysburg Exempted Village Sch. Dist., 306 F. Supp. 2d 726, 735 (N.D. Ohio 2004) (stating that "[T]he outcome achieved by the plaintiff at the due process hearing was more favorable to Lucas than the settlement offer because it included directives and orders intended specifically to ensure that Lucas would receive the services plaintiff sought for him.").

Although infrequently, courts have denied attorneys fees to prevailing parents. In *Dell v. Bd. of Educ., Twp. High Sch. Dist. 113*, 918 F. Supp. 212 (N.D. Ill. 1995), both the settlement and final relief involved a monetary payment only:

> Although the Dells are prevailing parties within the meaning of the Act, the *relief* they won consists only of reimbursement of $2,000.00 for the reasonable and customary expense of an independent evaluation of their son's needs. Because the sum is not more favorable than the $3,000.00 payment offered by Defendant School District before the administrative hearing, the Dells are barred from recovery of fees for services rendered at that hearing or in these proceedings. Defendant's motion for summary judgment is granted.

Id. at 217.

In a case involving a combination of a monetary award and other services, the court did not award fees. In *Matthew L. v. Woonsocket Educ. Dep't*, 793 F. Supp. 41, 44–45 (D.R.I. 1992), the school district offered $5,000 and the reviewing officer (RO) awarded $1,987.50; the district offered the same amount of resource room instruction as the RO ordered; the district offered similar home tutoring and counseling as the RO ordered; the district offered weekly progress reports which the RO did not require; and the RO ordered a deadline for a new evaluation and IEP, which the school district did not offer. The RO also ordered a re-evaluation and a new IEP. The court stated it was not clear if this would have offered greater relief than the settlement offer. "While the relief finally obtained by plaintiffs may have been somewhat different than the offer of settlement, I am unwilling to rule categorically that the former was *more favorable* than the latter." *Id.* at 45.

In one case involving services only, the court denied fees because the services offered and received were identical:

> The extended year services ordered by Hearing Officer Gordon in her . . . Order are identical to those offered by the District in its written settlement. Both the settlement offer and the Interim Order provided that Joshua would

> be placed in the District's summer school program and that the District would incorporate modifications consistent with Josuah's IEP, at no cost to Plaintiffs. Plaintiffs gained nothing with respect to extended school year services at the due process hearing. The District's pre-hearing settlement offer of "summer school" was as favorable as the extended school year relief received by Plaintiffs at the hearing. Moreover, in her Clarification of Decision and Order, Hearing Officer Gordon clarified that "the terms 'summer school' and 'extended year school' are interchangeable for purposes of understanding the Decision and Order." Because the court finds that the District made an offer of settlement more than 10 days prior to the due process hearing, that Plaintiffs rejected the District's offer and that the relief granted to Plaintiffs as a result of the due process hearing was not more favorable than the offer of settlement, Plaintiffs are statutorily barred from recovering attorney's fees in this matter.

Joshua H. v. Lansing Pub. Sch., Dist. No. 158, 161 F. Supp. 2d 888, 894 (N.D. Ill. 2001).

What do you think of the "all or nothing" character of the rule barring fees in the case of final relief that is not more favorable than a settlement offer? Should a "tie" go to the parents? How would you design an amendment to the IDEA to allow a court to reduce fees rather than deny them?

ii. Substantial Justification for Rejecting a Settlement Offer

Even if a parent obtained relief that was not more favorable than a settlement offer, a court can award fees if the parent "was substantially justified in rejecting the settlement offer." 20 U.S.C. § 1415(i)(3)(E) (2012). In *J.P. v. Cnty. Sch. Bd. of Hanover Cnty.*, 641 F. Supp. 2d 499 (E.D. Va. 2009), the court stated, "While there is a paucity of precedent interpreting the phrase 'substantially justified,' most courts addressing the issue have found substantial justification when the Plaintiffs had a good faith, reasonable belief that their eventual recovery would be higher than the offer." *Id.* at 508. The court ruled that the plaintiffs were justified in rejecting the settlement "offer because a court decision with an impact on the amount of the award was still pending, and they had a reasonable, good faith belief that their eventual award would be more favorable than the offer." *Id.* at 509. In contrast, in *El Paso Indep. Sch. Dist. v. Richard R.*, 591 F.3d 417 (5th Cir. 2009), *cert. denied*, 561 U.S. 1006 (2010), the parents argued that they were substantially justified in rejecting a pre-hearing settlement offer that gave them all the relief they requested because they wanted an enforceable order. The court rejected this argument, ruling that because settlement agreements reached at resolution meetings are enforceable in federal court, the parents were not substantially justified in rejecting the settlement offer. *Id.* at 428. What is the consequence of this ruling for attorneys fees claims?

Section Two
Costs and Expenses

Arlington Cent. Sch. Dist. Bd. of Educ. v. Murphy

548 U.S. 291 (2006)

Justice ALITO delivered the opinion of the Court.

The Individuals with Disabilities Education Act (IDEA or Act) provides that a court "may award reasonable attorneys' fees as part of the costs" to parents who prevail in an action brought under the Act. We granted certiorari to decide whether this fee-shifting provision authorizes prevailing parents to recover fees for services rendered by experts in IDEA actions. We hold that it does not.

I

Respondents Pearl and Theodore Murphy filed an action under the IDEA on behalf of their son, Joseph Murphy, seeking to require petitioner Arlington Central School District Board of Education to pay for their son's private school tuition for specified school years. Respondents prevailed in the District Court and the Court of Appeals for the Second Circuit affirmed.

As prevailing parents, respondents then sought $29,350 in fees for the services of an educational consultant, Marilyn Arons, who assisted respondents throughout the IDEA proceedings. The District Court granted respondents' request in part. . . .

The Court of Appeals for the Second Circuit affirmed. . . .

. . . .

We granted certiorari to resolve the conflict among the Circuits with respect to whether Congress authorized the compensation of expert fees to prevailing parents in IDEA actions. We now reverse.

II

Our resolution of the question presented in this case is guided by the fact that Congress enacted the IDEA pursuant to the Spending Clause. U.S. Const., Art. I, § 8, cl. 1. Like its statutory predecessor, the IDEA provides federal funds to assist state and local agencies in educating children with disabilities "and conditions such funding upon a State's compliance with extensive goals and procedures." *Board of Ed. of Hendrick Hudson Central School Dist., Westchester Cty. v. Rowley*, 458 U.S. 176, 179 . . . (1982).

Congress has broad power to set the terms on which it disburses federal money to the States, but when Congress attaches conditions to a State's acceptance of federal funds, the conditions must be set out "unambiguously," see *Pennhurst State School and Hospital v. Halderman*, 451 U.S. 1, 17 . . . (1981); *Rowley, supra*, at 204, n. 26 . . . . "[L]egislation enacted pursuant to the spending power is much in the nature of a contract," and therefore, to be bound by "federally imposed conditions," recipients of federal funds must accept them "voluntarily and knowingly." *Pennhurst*, 451 U.S., at 17 . . . . States cannot knowingly accept conditions of which they are "unaware" or which they are "unable to ascertain." *Ibid.* Thus, in the present case, we must view the IDEA from the perspective of a state official who is engaged in the process of deciding whether the State should accept IDEA funds and the obligations that go with those funds. We must ask whether such a state official would clearly understand that one of the obligations of the Act is the obligation to compensate prevailing parents for expert fees. In other words, we must ask whether the IDEA furnishes clear notice regarding the liability at issue in this case.

III

A

In considering whether the IDEA provides clear notice, we begin with the text. We have "stated time and again that courts must presume that a legislature says in a statute what it means and means in a statute what it says there." *Connecticut Nat. Bank v. Germain*, 503 U.S. 249, 253–254 . . . (1992). When the statutory "language is plain, the sole function of the courts—at least where the disposition required by the text is not absurd—is to enforce it according to its terms." *Hartford Underwriters Ins. Co. v. Union Planters Bank, N.A.*, 530 U.S. 1, 6 . . . (2000) (quoting *United States v. Ron Pair Enterprises, Inc.*, 489 U.S. 235, 241 . . . (1989), in turn quoting *Caminetti v. United States*, 242 U.S. 470, 485 . . . (1917); internal quotation marks omitted).

The governing provision of the IDEA, 20 U.S.C. § 1415(i)(3)(B), provides that "[i]n any action or proceeding brought under this section, the court, in its discretion, may award reasonable attorneys' fees as part of the costs" to the parents of "a child with a disability" who is the "prevailing party." While this provision provides for an award of "reasonable attorneys' fees," this provision does not even hint that acceptance of IDEA funds makes a State responsible for reimbursing prevailing parents for services rendered by experts.

Respondents contend that we should interpret the term "costs" in accordance with its meaning in ordinary usage and that § 1415(i)(3)(B) should therefore be read to "authorize reimbursement of all costs parents incur in IDEA proceedings, including expert costs."

This argument has multiple flaws. For one thing, as the Court of Appeals in this case acknowledged, "'costs' is a term of art that generally does not include expert fees." The use of this term of art, rather than a term such as "expenses," strongly suggests that § 1415(i)(3)(B) was not meant to be an open-ended provision that makes participating States liable for all expenses incurred by prevailing parents in connection with an IDEA case—for example, travel and lodging expenses or lost wages due to time taken off from work. Moreover, contrary to respondents' suggestion, § 1415(i)(3)(B) does not say that a court may award "costs" to prevailing parents; rather, it says that a court may award reasonable attorney's fees "as part of the costs" to prevailing parents. This language simply adds reasonable attorney's fees incurred by prevailing parents to the list of costs that prevailing parents are otherwise entitled to recover. This list of otherwise recoverable costs is obviously the list set out in 28 U.S.C. § 1920, the general statute governing the taxation of costs in federal court, and the recovery of witness fees under § 1920 is strictly limited by § 1821, which authorizes travel reimbursement and a $40 per diem. Thus, the text of 20 U.S.C. § 1415(i)(3)(B) does not authorize an award of any additional expert fees, and it certainly fails to provide the clear notice that is required under the Spending Clause.

Other provisions of the IDEA point strongly in the same direction. While authorizing the award of reasonable attorney's fees, the Act contains detailed provisions that are designed to ensure that such awards are indeed reasonable. See §§ 1415(i)(3)(C)–(G). The absence of any comparable provisions relating to expert fees strongly suggests that recovery of expert fees is not authorized. Moreover, the lack of any reference to expert fees in § 1415(d)(2) gives rise to a similar inference. This provision, which generally requires that parents receive "a full explanation of the procedural safeguards" available under § 1415 and refers expressly to "attorneys' fees," makes no mention of expert fees.

. . . .

V

Respondents make several arguments that are not based on the text of the IDEA, but these arguments do not show that the IDEA provides clear notice regarding the award of expert fees.

Respondents argue that their interpretation of the IDEA furthers the Act's overarching goal of "ensur[ing] that all children with disabilities have available to them a free appropriate public education," 20 U.S.C. § 1400(d)(1)(A), as well as the goal of "safeguard[ing] the rights of parents to challenge school decisions that adversely affect their child." These goals, however, are too general to provide much support for respondents' reading of the terms of the IDEA. The IDEA obviously does not seek to promote these goals at the expense of all other considerations, including fiscal considerations. Because the IDEA is not intended in all instances to further the broad goals identified by respondents at the expense of fiscal considerations, the goals cited by respondents do little to bolster their argument on the narrow question presented here.

Finally, respondents vigorously argue that Congress clearly intended for prevailing parents to be compensated for expert fees. They rely on the legislative history of § 1415 and in particular on the following statement in the Conference Committee Report, discussed above: "The conferees intend that the term 'attorneys' fees as part of the costs' include reasonable expenses and fees of expert witnesses and the reasonable costs of any test or evaluation which is found to be necessary for the preparation of the . . . case." H.R. Conf. Rep. No. 99-687, at 5. . . .

Whatever weight this legislative history would merit in another context, it is not sufficient here. Putting the legislative history aside, we see virtually no support for respondents' position. Under these circumstances, where everything other than the legislative history overwhelmingly suggests that expert fees may not be recovered, the legislative history is simply not enough. In a Spending Clause case, the key is not what a majority of the Members of both Houses intend but what the States are clearly told regarding the conditions that go along with the acceptance of those funds. Here, in the face of the unambiguous text of the IDEA . . . , we cannot say that the legislative history on which respondents rely is sufficient to provide the requisite fair notice.

We reverse the judgment of the Court of Appeals for the Second Circuit and remand the case for further proceedings consistent with this opinion.

Justice GINSBURG, concurring in part and concurring in the judgment.

. . . .

The Court's repeated references to a Spending Clause derived "clear notice" requirement are questionable . . . . For one thing, IDEA was enacted not only pursuant to Congress' Spending Clause authority, but also pursuant to § 5 of the Fourteenth Amendment. See *Smith v. Robinson*, 468 U.S. 992, 1009 . . . (1984) (IDEA's predecessor, the Education of the Handicapped Act, was "set up by Congress to aid the States in complying with their constitutional obligations to provide public education for handicapped children.").

. . . .

Justice BREYER, with whom Justice STEVENS and Justice SOUTER join, dissenting.

. . . Unlike the Court, I believe that the word "costs" includes, and authorizes payment of, the costs of experts. The word "costs" does not define its own scope. Neither does the phrase "attorneys' fees as part of costs." But Members of Congress did make clear their intent by, among other things, approving a Conference Report that specified that "the term 'attorneys' fees as part of the costs' include[s] reasonable expenses and fees of expert witnesses and the reasonable costs of any test or evaluation which is found to be necessary for the preparation of the parent or guardian's case in the action or proceeding." H.R. Conf. Rep. No. 99-687, p 5 (1986) . . . . No Senator or Representative voiced *any* opposition to this statement in the discussion preceding the vote on the Conference Report—the last vote on the bill before it was sent to the President. I can find no good reason for this Court to interpret the language of this statute as meaning the precise opposite of what Congress told us it intended.

I

There are two strong reasons for interpreting the statutory phrase to include the award of expert fees. First, that is what Congress said it intended by the phrase. Second, that interpretation furthers the IDEA's statutorily defined purposes.

. . . .

B

The Act's basic purpose further supports interpreting the provision's language to include expert costs. The IDEA guarantees a "free" and "appropriate" public education for "all" children with disabilities. 20 U.S.C. § 1400(d)(1)(A) (2000 ed., Supp. V); see also § 1401(9)(A) (defining "free appropriate public education" as one "provided at public expense," "without charge"); § 1401(29) (defining "special education" as "specially designed instruction, at *no cost* to parents, to meet the unique needs of a child with a disability" (emphasis added)).

Parents have every right to become involved in the Act's efforts to provide that education; indeed, the Act encourages their participation. § 1400(c)(5)(B) (IDEA "ensur[es] that families of [disabled] children have meaningful opportunities to participate in the education of their children at school"). It assures parents that they may question a school district's decisions about what is "appropriate" for their child. And in doing so, they may secure the help of experts. § 1415(h)(1) (parents have "the right to be accompanied and advised by counsel and by individuals with special knowledge or training with respect to the problems of children with disabilities").

The practical significance of the Act's participatory rights and procedural protections may be seriously diminished if parents are unable to obtain reimbursement for the costs of their experts. In IDEA cases, experts are necessary. See Kuriloff & Goldberg, Is Mediation a Fair ... Way to Resolve Special Education Disputes? First Empirical Findings, 2 Harv. Negotiation L. Rev. 35, 40 (1997) (detailing findings of study showing high correlation between use of experts and success of parents in challenging school district's plan); *cf. Schaffer, supra*, at 67 ... (Ginsburg, J., dissenting) ("[T]he vast majority of parents whose children require the benefits and protections provided in the IDEA lack knowledge about the educational resources available to their child and the sophistication to mount an effective case against a district-proposed," individualized education program (IEP) (internal quotation marks and brackets omitted)).

Experts are also expensive. See Brief for Respondents 28, n 17 (collecting District Court decisions awarding expert costs ranging from $200 to $7,600, and noting three reported cases in which expert awards exceeded $10,000). The costs of experts may not make much of a dent in a school district's budget, as many of the experts they use in IDEA proceedings are already on the staff. But to parents, the award of costs may matter enormously. Without potential reimbursement, parents may well lack the services of experts entirely. See Dept. of Education, M. Wagner et al., The Individual and Household Characteristics of Youth With Disabilities: A Report from the National Longitudinal Transition Study-2 ..., online at http://www.nlts2.org/reports/2003_08/nlts2_report_2003_08_complete.pdf ... (finding that 25% of disabled children live in poverty and 65% live in households with incomes less than $50,000); see Dept. of Education, M. Wagner, C. Marder, J. Blackorby & D. Cardoso, The Children We Serve: The Demographic Characteristics of Elementary and Middle School Students with Disabilities and Their Households 28 (Sept. 2002) ..., online at http://www.seels.net/designdocs/SEELS_Children_We_Serve_Report.pdf (finding that 36% of disabled children live in households with incomes of $25,000 or less).

In a word, the Act's statutory right to a "free" and "appropriate" education may mean little to those who must pay hundreds of dollars to obtain it. That is why this Court has previously avoided interpretations that would bring about this kind of result. See *School Comm. of Burlington v. Department of Ed. of Mass.*, 471 U.S. 359 ... (1985) (construing IDEA provision granting equitable authority to courts to include the power to order reimbursement for parents who switch their child to private schools if that decision later proves correct); *id.*, at 370 ... (without cost reimbursement for prevailing parents, "the child's right to a *free* appropriate public education, the parents' right to participate fully in developing a proper IEP, and all of the procedural safeguards would be less than complete"); *Florence County School Dist. Four v. Carter*, 510 U.S. 7, 13 . . . (1993) (holding that prevailing parents are not barred from reimbursement for switching their child to a private school that does not meet the IDEA's definition of a free and appropriate education). In *Carter*, we explained: "IDEA was intended to ensure that children with disabilities receive an education that is both appropriate and free. To read the provisions of § 1401(a)(18) to bar reimbursement in the circumstances of this case would defeat this statutory purpose." *Id.*, at 13–14 . . . (citation omitted).

To read the word "costs" as requiring successful parents to bear their own expenses for experts suffers from the same problem. Today's result will leave many parents and guardians "without an expert with the firepower to match the opposition," *Schaffer*, 546 U.S., at 61, . . . , a far cry from the level playing field that Congress envisioned.

II

The majority makes essentially three arguments against this interpretation. It says that the statute's purpose and "legislative history is simply not enough" to overcome: (1) the fact that this is a Spending Clause case; (2) the text of the statute; and (3) our prior cases which hold that the term "costs" does not include expert costs. . . .

A

. . . .

I agree that the statute on its face does not *clearly* tell the States that they must pay expert fees to prevailing parents. But I do not agree that the majority has posed the right question. For one thing, we have repeatedly examined the nature and extent of the financial burdens that the IDEA imposes without reference to the Spending Clause or any "clear-statement rule." See, *e.g., Burlington, supra*, at 369 . . . (private school fees); *Carter* . . . (same); *Smith* . . . (attorney's fees); *Garret F.* . . . (1999) (continuous nursing service) . . . . Those cases did not ask whether the statute "furnishes clear notice" to the affirmative obligation or liability at issue.

For another thing, neither *Pennhurst* nor any other case suggests that *every spending detail* of a Spending Clause statute must be spelled out with unusual clarity. . . . We have added that *Pennhurst* does not require Congress "specifically" to "identify" and "proscribe *each* condition in [Spending Clause] legislation." *Jackson v. Birmingham Bd. of Ed.*, 544 U.S. 167, 183 . . . (2006), ... And we have denied any implication that "suits under Spending Clause legislation are suits in contract, or that contract-law principles apply to *all* issues that they raise."

These statements and holdings are not surprising. After all, the basic objective of *Pennhurst*'s clear-statement requirement does not demand textual clarity in respect to every detail. That is because ambiguity about the precise nature of a statutory program's details—particularly where they are of a kind that States might have anticipated—is rarely relevant to the basic question: Would the States have accepted the Federal Government's funds *had they only known* the nature of the accompanying conditions? Often, the later filling-in of details through judicial interpretation will not lead one to wonder whether funding recipients would have agreed to enter the basic program at all. Given the nature of such details, it is clear that the States would have entered the program regardless. At the same time, to view each statutory detail of a highly complex federal/state program (involving, say, transportation, schools, the environment) simply through the lens of linguistic clarity, rather than to assess its meanings in terms of basic legislative purpose, is to risk a set of judicial interpretations that can prevent the program, overall, from achieving its basic objectives or that might well reduce a program in its details to incoherence.

This case is about just such a detail. Permitting parents to recover expert fees will not lead to awards of "indeterminate magnitude, untethered to compensable harm" and consequently will not "pose a concern that recipients of federal funding could not reasonably have anticipated." Unlike, say, punitive damages, an award of costs to expert parties is neither "unorthodox" nor "indeterminate," and thus does not throw into doubt whether the States would have entered into the program. If determinations as to whether the IDEA requires States to provide continuing nursing services, *Cedar Rapids, supra*, or reimbursement for private school tuition, *Burlington*, 471 U.S. 359 . . . , do not call for linguistic clarity, then the precise content of recoverable "costs" does not call for such clarity here *a fortiori*.

B

If the Court believes that the statute's language is unambiguous, I must disagree. The provision at issue says that a court "may award reasonable attorneys' fees as part of the costs" to parents who prevail in an action brought under the Act. 20 U.S.C. § 1415(i)(3)(B). The statute neither defines the word "costs" nor points to any other source of law for a definition. And the word "costs," alone, says nothing at all about which costs fall within its scope.

Neither does the statutory phrase—"as part of the costs to the parents of a child with a disability who is the prevailing party"—taken in its entirety unambiguously foreclose an award of expert fees. I agree that, read literally, that provision does not clearly grant authority to award any costs at all. . . . But such a reading is not inevitable. . . . And one can, consistent with the language, read the provision as both embodying a general authority to award costs while also specifying the inclusion of "reasonable attorneys' fees" as part of those costs . . . .

III

For the reasons I have set forth, I cannot agree with the majority's conclusion. Even less can I agree with its failure to consider fully the statute's legislative history. That history makes Congress' purpose clear. And our ultimate judicial goal is to interpret language in light of the statute's purpose. Only by seeking that purpose can we avoid the substitution of judicial for legislative will. Only by reading language in its light can we maintain the democratic link between voters, legislators, statutes, and ultimate implementation, upon which the legitimacy of our constitutional system rests.

In my view, to keep faith with that interpretive goal, we must retain all traditional interpretive tools—text, structure, history, and purpose. And, because faithful interpretation is art as well as science, we cannot, through rule or canon, rule out the use of any of these tools, automatically and in advance.

Nothing in the Constitution forbids us to give significant weight to legislative history. By disregarding a clear statement in a legislative Report adopted without opposition in both Houses of Congress, the majority has reached a result no Member of Congress expected or overtly desired. It has adopted an interpretation that undercuts, rather than furthers, the statute's purpose, a "free" and "appropriate" public education for "all" children with disabilities. And it has adopted an approach that, I fear, divorces law from life.

For these reasons, I respectfully dissent.

Notes, Comments, and Questions

1. Justice Breyer's dissent raises several significant jurisprudential questions. How do you explain the Court's sudden invocation of Spending Clause restrictions in cases involving expenses when it failed to do so in cases involving tuition reimbursement and medical services? What role should the purpose of a law play in interpreting its provisions? What role should the legislative history play?

2. The Supreme Court decided in *Arlington* that expert witness fees are not part of the "costs" that federal courts can award to prevailing parties in IDEA cases. What costs can a court award to a prevailing party? A non-exhaustive list of costs that courts have awarded in IDEA cases include costs for photocopying, facsimiles, postage, parking, travel, service and court filing fees, service of deposition subpoenas, Federal Express, court reporters, UPS, telephone, Lexis/Nexis research, statutory witness attendance fees, and translations. *See, e.g.*, JP v. Cnty. Sch. Bd. of Hanover Cty., 641 F. Supp. 2d 499, 525 (E.D. Va. 2009) (awarding plaintiffs $8,369.69 in costs); M.K. v. Sergi, 578 F. Supp. 2d 425, 433–35 (D. Conn. 2008) (awarding $7,955.68 in costs); C.C. v. Granby Bd. of Educ., 453 F. Supp. 2d 569, 576 (D. Conn. 2006) (awarding $156.72 in fees); Eirschele v. Craven Cnty. Bd. of Educ., 7 F. Supp. 2d 655, 660 (E.D.N.C. 1998) (rejecting expert witness fee but approving $40.00 statutory fee for expert witness). Not all courts agree that all of these costs are available; local court rules often govern which costs are included. *See, e.g.*, Zayas v. Puerto Rico, 451 F. Supp. 2d 310, 319 (D.P.R. 2006) (rejecting costs for messenger service, faxes, telephone, parking, postage, and Westlaw). Finally, costs must be reasonable, Bailey v. District of Columbia, 839 F. Supp. 888, 892 (D.D.C. 1993) (holding that the "costs requested are quite modest"), and sufficiently documented. Grinsted v. Houston Cnty. Sch. Bd., 826 F. Supp. 482, 487 (M.D. Ga. 1993) (requiring documentation of "the number of copies made and the cost per page," the "exact mileage incurred," and "specificity in describing expenses such as witness fees, subpoena costs, federal express, postage, and long distance phone charges").

Appendix A

The Individuals with Disabilities Education Act 20 U.S.C. §§ 1400–1482 (2012) (Selected provisions)

§ 1400. Short title; findings; purposes

(a) Short title

This chapter may be cited as the "Individuals with Disabilities Education Act."

. . . .

(c) Findings

Congress finds the following:

(1) Disability is a natural part of the human experience and in no way diminishes the right of individuals to participate in or contribute to society. Improving educational results for children with disabilities is an essential element of our national policy of ensuring equality of opportunity, full participation, independent living, and economic self-sufficiency for individuals with disabilities.

(2) Before the date of enactment of the Education for All Handicapped Children Act of 1975 . . . the educational needs of millions of children with disabilities were not being fully met because—

(A) the children did not receive appropriate educational services;

(B) the children were excluded entirely from the public school system and from being educated with their peers;

(C) undiagnosed disabilities prevented the children from having a successful educational experience; or

(D) a lack of adequate resources within the public school system forced families to find services outside the public school system.

. . . .

(d) Purposes

The purposes of this title are—

(1) (A) to ensure that all children with disabilities have available to them a free appropriate public education that emphasizes special education and related services designed to meet their unique needs and prepare them for further education, employment, and independent living;

. . . .

§ 1401. Definitions

. . . .

(3) Child with a disability

(A) In general

The term "child with a disability" means a child—

(I) with intellectual disabilities, hearing impairments (including deafness), speech or language impairments, visual impairments (including blindness), serious emotional disturbance . . . , orthopedic impairments, autism, traumatic brain injury, other health impairments, or specific learning disabilities; and

(ii) who, by reason thereof, needs special education and related services.

. . . .

(9) Free appropriate public education

The term "free appropriate public education" means special education and related services that—

(A) have been provided at public expense, under public supervision and direction, and without charge;

(B) meet the standards of the State educational agency;

(C) include an appropriate preschool, elementary school, or secondary school education in the State involved; and

(D) are provided in conformity with the individualized education program required under section 1414(d).

. . . .

(14) Individualized education program; IEP

The term "individualized education program" or "IEP" means a written statement for each child with a disability that is developed, reviewed, and revised in accordance with section 1414(d) of this title.

. . . .

(26) Related services

(A) In general

The term "related services" means transportation, and such developmental, corrective, and other supportive services (including speech-language pathology and audiology services, interpreting services, psychological services, physical and occupational therapy, recreation, including therapeutic recreation, social work services, school nurse services designed to enable a child with a disability to receive a free appropriate public education as described in the individualized education program of the child, counseling services, including rehabilitation counseling, orientation and mobility services, and medical services, except that such medical services shall be for diagnostic and evaluation purposes only) as may be required to assist a child with a disability to benefit from special education, and includes the early identification and assessment of disabling conditions in children.

. . . .

(29) Special education

The term "special education" means specially designed instruction, at no cost to parents, to meet the unique needs of a child with a disability, including—

(A) instruction conducted in the classroom, in the home, in hospitals and institutions, and in other settings; and

(B) instruction in physical education.

. . . .

§ 1403. Abrogation of State sovereign immunity

(a) In general

A State shall not be immune under the 11th amendment to the Constitution of the United States from suit in Federal court for a violation of this chapter.

. . . .

§ 1411. Authorization; allotment; use of funds; authorization of appropriations

(a) Grants to States

(1) Purpose of grants

The Secretary shall make grants to States . . . to assist them to provide special education and related services to children with disabilities in accordance with this subchapter.

. . . .

§ 1412. State eligibility

(a) In general

A State is eligible for assistance under this part for a fiscal year if the State submits a plan that provides assurances to the Secretary that the State has in effect policies and procedures to ensure that the State meets each of the following conditions:

(1) Free appropriate public education

(A) In general

A free appropriate public education is available to all children with disabilities residing in the State between the ages of 3 and 21, inclusive ....

....

(3) Child find

(A) In general

All children with disabilities residing in the State, including children with disabilities who are homeless children or are wards of the State and children with disabilities attending private schools, regardless of the severity of their disabilities, and who are in need of special education and related services, are identified, located, and evaluated ....

....

(4) Individualized education program

An individualized education program ... is developed, reviewed, and revised for each child with a disability ....

(5) Least restrictive environment

(A) In general

To the maximum extent appropriate, children with disabilities ... are educated with children who are not disabled, and special classes, separate schooling, or other removal of children with disabilities from the regular educational environment occurs only when the nature or severity of the disability of a child is such that education in regular classes with the use of supplementary aids and services cannot be achieved satisfactorily.

....

(6) Procedural safeguards

(A) In general

Children with disabilities and their parents are afforded the procedural safeguards required by section 1415 of this title.

....

(7) Evaluation

Children with disabilities are evaluated in accordance with subsections (a) through (c) of section 1414 of this title.

....

(10) Children in private schools

(A) Children enrolled in private schools by their parents

(i) In general

To the extent consistent with the number and location of children with disabilities in the Sate who are enrolled by their parents in private elementary schools and secondary schools in the district served by a local educational agency, provision is made for the participation of those children in the program assisted or carried out under this subchapter by providing for such children special education and related services in accordance with the following requirements . . . :

(I) Amounts to be expended for the provision of those services (including direct services to parentally placed private school children) by the local educational agency shall be equal to a proportionate amount of Federal funds made available under this subchapter.

(II) In calculating the proportionate amount of Federal funds, the local educational agency, after timely and meaningful consultation with representatives of private schools as described in clause (iii), shall conduct a thorough and complete child find process to determine the number of parentally placed children with disabilities attending private schools located in the local educational agency.

(III) Such services to parentally placed private school children with disabilities may be provided to the children on the premises of private, including religious, schools, to the extent consistent with the law.

. . . .

(ii) Child find requirement

(I) In general

The requirement of paragraph (3) (relating to child find) shall apply with respect to children with disabilities in the State who are enrolled in private, including religious, elementary schools and secondary schools.

(II) Equitable participation

The child find process shall be designed to ensure the equitable participation of parentally placed private school children with disabilities and an accurate count of such children.

(III) Activities

In carrying out this clause, the local educational agency, or where applicable, the State educational agency, shall undertake activities similar to those activities undertaken for the agency's public school children.

. . . .

(B) Children placed in, or referred to, private schools by public agencies

(I) In general

Children with disabilities in private schools and facilities are provided special education and related services, in accordance with an individualized educational program, at no cost to their parents, if such children are placed in, or referred to, such schools or facilities by the State or appropriate local educational agency as the means of carrying out the requirements of this subchapter or any other applicable law requiring the provision of special education and related services to all children with disabilities in such state.

(ii) Standards

In all cases described in clause (I), the State educational agency shall determine whether such schools and facilities meet standards that apply to State educational agencies and local educational agencies and that children so served have all the rights the children would have if served by such agencies.

(C) Payment for education of children enrolled in private schools without consent of or referral by the public agency

(I) In general

Subject to subparagraph (A), this subchapter does not require a local educational agency to pay for the cost of education, including special education and related services, of a child with a disability at a private school or facility if that agency made a free appropriate public education available to the child and the parents elected to place the child in such private school or facility.

(ii) Reimbursement for private school placement

If the parents of a child with a disability, who previously received special education and related services under the authority of a public agency, enroll the child in a private elementary school or secondary school without the consent of or referral by the public agency, a court or hearing officer may require the agency to reimburse the parents for the cost of that enrollment if the court or hearing officer finds that the agency had not made a free appropriate public education available to the child in a timely manner prior to the enrollment.

(iii) Limitation on reimbursement

The cost of reimbursement described in clause (ii) may be reduced or denied—

(I) if—

(aa) at the most recent IEP meeting that the parents attended prior to removal of the child from the public school, the parents did not inform the IEP Team that they were rejecting the placement proposed by the public agency to provide a free appropriate public education to their child, including stating their concerns and their intent to enroll their child in a public school at public expense; or

(bb) 10 business days (including any holidays that occur on a business day) prior to the removal of the child from the public school, the parents did not give written notice to the public agency of the information described in item (aa);

(II) if, prior to the parents' removal of the child from the public school, the public agency informed the parents, through the notice requirements described in section 1415(b)(3) of this title, of its intent to evaluate the child (including a statement of the purpose of the evaluation that was appropriate and reasonable), but the parents did not make the child available for such evaluation; or

(III) upon a judicial finding of unreasonableness with respect to actions taken by the parents.

(iv) Exception

Notwithstanding the notice requirement in clause (iii)(I), the cost of reimbursement—

(I) shall not be reduced or denied for failure to provide such notice if—

(aa) the school prevented the parent from providing such notice;

(bb) the parents had not received notice, pursuant to section 1415 of this title, of the notice requirement in clause (iii)(I); or

(cc) compliance with clause (iii)(I) would likely result in physical harm to the child; and

(II) may, in the discretion of a court or a hearing officer, not be reduced or denied for failure to provide such notice if—

(aa) the parent is illiterate or cannot write in English; or

(bb) compliance with clause (iii)(I) would likely result in serious emotional harm to the child.

. . . .

§ 1414. Evaluations, eligibility determinations, individualized education programs, and educational placements

(a) Evaluations, parental consent, and reevaluations

(1) Initial evaluations

(A) In general

A State educational agency, other State agency, or local educational agency shall conduct a full and individual initial evaluation in accordance with this paragraph and subsection (b), before the initial provision of special education and related services to a child with a disability under this subchapter.

(B) Request for initial evaluation

[E]ither a parent of a child, or a State educational agency, other State agency, or local educational agency may initiate a request for an initial evaluation to determine if the child is a child with a disability.

(C) Procedures

(I) In general

Such initial evaluation shall consist of procedures—

(I) to determine whether a child is a child with a disability . . . within 60 days of receiving parental consent for the evaluation, or if the State establishes a timeframe within which the evaluation must be conducted, within such timeframe; and

(II) to determine the educational needs of such child.

. . . .

(D) Parental consent

(I) In general

(I) Consent for initial evaluation

The agency proposing to conduct an initial evaluation to determine if the child qualifies as a child with a disability . . . shall obtain informed consent from the parent of such child before conducting the evaluation. Parental consent for evaluation shall not be construed as consent for placement or receipt of special education and related services.

(II) Consent for services

An agency that is responsible for making a free appropriate education available to a child with a disability under this subchapter shall seek to obtain informed consent from the parent of such child before providing special education and related services to the child.

(ii) Absence of consent

(I) For initial evaluation

If the parent of such child does not provide consent for an initial evaluation under clause (i)(I), or the parent fails to respond to a request to provide the consent, the local educational agency may pursue the initial evaluation of the child by utilizing the procedures described in section 1415 of this title, except to the extent inconsistent with State law relating to such parental consent.

(II) For services

If the parent of such child refuses to consent to services under clause (i)(II), the local educational agency shall not provide special education and related services to the child by utilizing the procedures described in section 1415 of this title.

(III) Effect on agency obligations

If the parent of such child refuses to consent to the receipt of special education and related services, or the parent fails to respond to a request to provide such consent—

(aa) the local educational agency shall not be considered to be in violation of the requirement to make a free appropriate public education to the child with the special education and related services for which the local educational agency requests such consent; and

(bb) the local educational agency shall not be required to convene an IEP meeting or develop an IEP under this section for the child for the special education and related services for which the local educational agency requests such consent.

. . . .

(2) Reevaluations

(A) In general

A local educational agency shall ensure that a reevaluation of each child with a disability is conducted in accordance with subsections (b) and (c)—

(i) if the local educational agency determines that the educational or related services needs, including improved academic achievement and functional performance, of the child warrant a reevaluation; or

(ii) if the child's parents or teacher requests a reevaluation.

(B) Limitation

A reevaluation conducted under subparagraph (A) shall occur—

(i) not more frequently than once a year, unless the parent and the local educational agency agree otherwise; and

(ii) at least once every 3 years, unless the parent and the local educational agency agree that a reevaluation is unnecessary.

(b) Evaluation procedures

(1) Notice

The local educational agency shall provide notice to the parents of a child with a disability, in accordance with subsections (b)(3), (b)(4), and (c) of section 1415 of this title, that describes any evaluation procedures such agency proposes to conduct.

(2) Conduct of evaluation

In conducting the evaluation, the local educational agency shall—

(A) use a variety of assessment tools and strategies to gather relevant functional, developmental, and academic information, including information provided by the parent, that may assist in determining—

(i) whether the child is a child with a disability; and

(ii) the content of the child's individualized education program, including information related to enabling the child to be involved in and progress in the general education curriculum . . . ;

(B) not use any single measure of assessment as the sole criterion for determining whether a child is a child with a disability or determining an appropriate educational program for the child; and

(C) use technically sound instruments that may assess the relative contribution of cognitive and behavioral factors, in addition to physical or developmental factors.

(3) Additional requirements

Each local educational agency shall ensure that—

(A) assessments and other evaluation materials used to assess a child under this section—

(i) are selected and administered so as not to be discriminatory on a racial or cultural basis;

(ii) are provided and administered in the language and form most likely to yield accurate information on what the child knows and can do academically, developmentally, and functionally, unless it is not feasible to so provide or administer;

(iii) are used for purposes for which the assessments or measures are valid and reliable;

(iv) are administered by trained and knowledgeable personnel; and

(v) are administered in accordance with any instructions provided by the producer of such assessments;

(B) the child is assessed in all areas of suspected disability;

(C) assessment tools and strategies that provide relevant information that directly assists persons in determining the educational needs of the child are provided; and

. . . .

(4) Determination of eligibility and educational need

Upon completion of the administration of assessments and other evaluation measures—

(A) the determination of whether the child is a child with a disability as defined in section 1401(3) and the educational needs of the child shall be made by a team of qualified professionals and the parent of the child . . . ; and

. . . .

(5) Special rule for eligibility determination

In making a determination of eligibility under paragraph (4)(A), a child shall not be determined to be a child with a disability if the determining factor is—

(A) lack of appropriate instruction in reading, including in the essential components of reading instruction . . . ;

(B) lack of instruction in math; or

(C) limited English proficiency.

(6) Specific learning disabilities

(A) In general

[W]hen determining whether a child has a specific learning disability . . . , a local educational agency shall not be required to take into consideration whether a child has a severe discrepancy between achievement and intellectual ability in oral expression, listening comprehension, written expression, basic reading skill, reading comprehension, mathematical calculation, or mathematical reasoning.

(B) Additional authority

In determining whether a child has a specific learning disability, a local educational agency may use a process that determines if the child responds to scientific, research-based intervention as part of the evaluation procedures described in paragraphs (2) and (3).

(c) Additional requirements for evaluation and reevaluations

(1) Review of existing evaluation data

As part of an initial evaluation (if appropriate) and as part of any reevaluation under this section, the IEP Team and other qualified professionals, as appropriate, shall—

(A) review existing evaluation data on the child, including—

(i) evaluations and information provided by the parents of the child;

(ii) current classroom-based, local, or State assessments, and classroom-based observations; and

(iii) observations by teachers and related service providers; and

(B) on the basis of that review, and input from the child's parents, identify what additional data, if any, are needed to determine—

(i) whether the child is a child with a disability . . . , and the educational needs of the child, or, in the case of a reevaluation of a child, whether the child continues to have such a disability and such educational needs;

(ii) the present levels of academic achievement and related developmental needs of the child;

(iii) whether the child needs special education and related services, or in the case of a reevaluation of a child, whether the child continues to need special education and related services; and

(iv) whether any additions or modifications to the special education and related services are needed to enable the child to meet the measurable annual goals set out in the individualized education program of the child and to participate, as appropriate, in the general education curriculum.

(2) Source of data

The local educational agency shall administer such assessments and other evaluation measures as may be needed to produce the data identified by the IEP Team under paragraph (1)(B).

(3) Parental consent

Each local educational agency shall obtain informed parental consent, in accordance with subsection (a)(1)(D), prior to conducting any reevaluation of a child with a disability, except that such informed parental consent need not be obtained if the local educational agency can demonstrate that it had taken reasonable measures to obtain such consent and the child's parent has failed to respond.

. . . .

(5) Evaluations before change in eligibility

(A) In general

Except as provided in subparagraph (B), a local educational agency shall evaluate a child with a disability in accordance with this section before determining in accordance with this section that the child is no longer a child with a disability.

. . . .

(d) Individualized education programs

(1) Definitions

In this chapter:

(A) Individualized education program

(i) In general

The term "individualized education program" or "IEP" means a written statement for each child with a disability that is developed, reviewed, and revised in accordance with this section and that includes—

(I) a statement of the child's present levels of academic achievement and functional performance, including—

(aa) how the child's disability affects the child's involvement and progress in the general education curriculum;

....

(II) a statement of measurable annual goals, including academic and functional goals, designed to—

(aa) meet the child's needs that result from the child's disability to enable the child to be involved in and make progress in the general education curriculum; and

(bb) meet each of the child's other educational needs that result from the child's disability;

(III) a description of how the child's progress toward meeting the annual goals described in subclause (II) will be measured and when periodic reports on the progress the child is making toward meeting the annual goals . . . will be provided;

(IV) a statement of the special education and related services . . . to be provided to the child . . . and a statement of the program modifications or supports for school personnel that will be provided for the child—

(aa) to advance appropriately toward attaining the annual goals;

(bb) to be involved in and make progress in the general education curriculum . . . and to participate in extracurricular and other nonacademic activities; and

(cc) to be educated and participate with other children with disabilities and nondisabled children in the activities described in this section;

(V) an explanation of the extent, if any, to which the child will not participate with nondisabled children in the regular class . . . ;

....

(VII) the projected date for the beginning of the services and modifications described in subclause (IV), and the anticipated frequency, location, and duration of those services and modifications; and

(VIII) beginning not later than the first IEP to be in effect when the child is 16, and updated annually thereafter—

(aa) appropriate measurable postsecondary goals based upon age appropriate transition goals related to training, education, employment, and, where appropriate, independent living skills;

(bb) the transition services (including courses of study) needed to assist the child in reaching those goals; and

. . . .

(B) Individualized education program team

The term "individualized education program team" or "IEP Team" means a group of individuals composed of—

(i) the parents of a child with a disability;

(ii) not less than 1 regular education teacher of such child (if the child is, or may be, participating in the regular education environment);

(iii) not less than 1 special education teacher, or where appropriate, not less than 1 special education provider of such child;

(iv) a representative of the local educational agency who—

(I) is qualified to provide, or supervise the provision of, specially designed instruction to meet the unique needs of children with disabilities;

(II) is knowledgeable about the general education curriculum; and

(III) is knowledgeable about the availability of resources of the local educational agency;

(v) an individual who can interpret the instructional implications of evaluation results . . . ;

(vi) at the discretion of the parent or the agency, other individuals who have knowledge or special expertise regarding the child, including related services personnel as appropriate; and

(vii) whenever appropriate, the child with a disability.

(C) IEP Team Attendance

(i) Attendance not necessary

A member of the IEP Team shall not be required to attend an IEP meeting, in whole or in part, if the parent of a child with a disability and the local educational agency agree that the attendance of such member is not necessary because the member's area of the curriculum or related services is not being modified or discussed in the meeting.

(ii) Excusal

A member of the IEP Team may be excused from attending an IEP meeting, in whole or in part, when the meeting involves a modification to or discussion of the member's area of the curriculum or related services, if—

(I) the parent and the local educational agency consent to the excusal; and

(II) the member submits, in writing to the parent and the IEP Team, input into the development of the IEP prior to the meeting.

(iii) Written agreement and consent required

A parent's agreement under clause (i) and consent under clause (ii) shall be in writing.

. . . .

(2) Requirement that program be in effect

(A) In general

At the beginning of each school year, each local education agency, State educational agency, or other State agency, as the case may be, shall have in effect, for each child with a disability in the agency's jurisdiction, an individualized education program . . . .

. . . .

(3) Development of IEP

(A) In general

In developing each child's IEP, the IEP Team, subject to subparagraph (C), shall consider—

(i) the strengths of the child;

(ii) the concerns of the parents for enhancing the education of their child;

(iii) the results of the initial evaluation or most recent evaluation of the child; and

(iv) the academic, developmental, and functional needs of the child.

(B) Consideration of special factors

The IEP Team shall—

(i) in the case of a child whose behavior impedes the child's learning or that of others, consider the use of positive behavioral interventions and supports, and other strategies, to address that behavior;

(ii) in the case of a child with limited English proficiency, consider the language needs of the child as such needs relate to the child's IEP;

. . . .

(v) consider whether the child needs assistive technology devices and services.

(C) Requirement with respect to regular education teacher

A regular education teacher of the child, as a member of the IEP Team, shall, to the extent appropriate, participate in the development of the IEP of the child, including the determination of appropriate positive behavioral interventions and supports, and other strategies, and the determination of supplementary aids and services, program modifications, and support for school personnel. . . .

. . . .

(4) Review and revision of IEP

(A) In general

The local educational agency shall ensure that, subject to subparagraph (B), the IEP Team—

(i) reviews the child's IEP periodically, but not less frequently than annually, to determine whether the annual goals for the child are being achieved; and

(ii) revises the IEP as appropriate to address—

(I) any lack of expected progress toward the annual goals and in the general education curriculum, where appropriate;

(II) the results of any reevaluation conducted under this section;

(III) information about the child provided to, or by, the parents . . . ;

(IV) the child's anticipated needs; or

(V) other matters.

(B) Requirement with respect to regular education teacher

A regular education teacher of the child, as a member of the IEP Team, shall . . . participate in the review and revision of the IEP of the child.

. . . .

§ 1415. Procedural safeguards

(a) Establishment of procedures

Any State educational agency, State agency, or local educational agency that receives assistance under this subchapter shall establish and maintain procedures in accordance with this section to ensure that children with disabilities and their parents are guaranteed procedural safeguards with respect to the provision of a free appropriate public education by such agencies.

(b) Types of procedures

The procedures required by this section shall include the following:

(1) An opportunity for the parents of a child with a disability to examine all records relating to such child and to participate in meetings with respect to the identification, evaluation, and educational placement of the child, and

the provision of a free appropriate public education to such child, and to obtain an independent educational evaluation of the child;

. . . .

(3) Written prior notice to the parents of the child, in accordance with subsection (c)(1), whenever the local educational agency—

(A) proposes to initiate or change; or

(B) refuses to initiate or change, the identification, evaluation, or educational placement of the child, or the provision of a free appropriate public education to the child.

. . . .

(6) An opportunity for any party to present a complaint—

(A) with respect to any matter relating to the identification, evaluation, or educational placement of the child, or the provision of a free appropriate public education to such child; and

(B) which sets forth an alleged violation that occurred not more than 2 years before the date the parent or public agency knew or should have known about the alleged action that forms the basis of the complaint, or, if the State has an explicit time limitation for presenting such a complaint under this part, in such time as the State law allows . . . .

(7)(A) Procedures that require either party . . . to provide due process complaint notice in accordance with subsection (c)(2) (which shall remain confidential)—

(i) to the other party . . . ; and

(ii) that shall include—

(I) the name of the child, the address of the residence of the child . . . and the name of the school the child is attending;

. . . .

(III) a description of the nature of the problem of the child relating to such proposed initiation or change, including facts relating to such problem; and

(IV) a proposed resolution of the problem . . . .

. . . .

(c) Notification requirements

(1) Content of prior written notice

The notice required by subsection (b)(3) shall include—

(A) a description of the action proposed or refused by the agency;

(B) an explanation of why the agency proposes or refuses to take the action and a description of each evaluation procedure, assessment, record, or report the agency used as a basis for the proposed or refused action;

(C) a statement that the parents of a child with a disability have protection under the procedural safeguards of this subchapter . . . ;

. . . .

(d) Procedural safeguards notice

(1) In general

(A) Copy to parents

A copy of the procedural safeguards available to the parents of a child with a disability shall be given to the parents only one time a year, except that a copy also shall be given to the parents—

(i) upon initial referral or parental request for evaluation;

(ii) upon the first occurrence of the filing of a complaint under subsection (b)(6); and

(iii) upon request by a parent.

. . . .

(2) Contents

The procedural safeguards notice shall include a full explanation of the procedural safeguards, written in the native language of the parents (unless it clearly is not feasible to do so) and written in an easily understandable manner, available under this section and under regulations promulgated by the Secretary relating to—

(A) independent educational evaluation;

(B) prior written notice;

(C) parental consent;

(D) access to educational records;

(E) the opportunity to present and resolve complaints, including—

(i) the time period in which to make a complaint;

(ii) the opportunity for the agency to resolve the complaint; and

(iii) the availability of mediation;

(F) the child's placement during pendency of the due process proceedings;

(G) procedures for students who are subject to placement in an interim educational setting;

(H) requirements for unilateral placement by parents of children in private schools at public expense;

(I) due process hearings, including requirements for disclosure of evaluation results and recommendations;

(J) state-level appeals (if applicable in that State);

(K) civil actions, including the time period in which to file such actions; and

(L) attorneys' fees.

(e) Mediation

(1) In general

Any State educational agency or local educational agency that receives assistance under this part shall ensure that procedures are established and implemented to allow parties to disputes involving any matter, including matters arising prior to the filing of a complaint pursuant to subsection (b)(6), to resolve such disputes through a mediation process.

. . . .

(f) Impartial due process hearing

(1) In general

(A) Hearing

Whenever a complaint has been received under subsection (b)(6) or (k), the parents or the local educational agency involved in such complaint shall have an opportunity for an impartial due process hearing, which shall be conducted by the State educational agency or by the local educational agency, as determined by State law or by the State educational agency.

(B) Resolution session

(i) Preliminary meeting

Prior to the opportunity for an impartial due process hearing under subparagraph (A), the local educational agency shall convene a meeting with the parents and the relevant member or members of the IEP Team who have specific knowledge of the facts identified in the complaint—

(I) within 15 days of receiving notice of the parents' complaint;

. . . .

(IV) where the parents of the child discuss their complaint, and the facts that form the basis of the complaint, and the local educational agency is provided the opportunity to resolve the complaint,

unless the parents and the local educational agency agree in writing to waive such meeting, or agree to use the mediation process described in subsection (e).

(ii) Hearing

If the local educational agency has not resolved the complaint to the satisfaction of the parents within 30 days of the receipt of the complaint, the due process hearing may occur, and all of the applicable timelines for a due process hearing under this part shall commence.

. . . .

(2) Disclosure of evaluations and recommendations

(A) In general

Not less than 5 business days prior to a hearing conducted pursuant to paragraph (1), each party shall disclose to all other parties all evaluations completed by that date, and recommendations based on the offering party's evaluations, that the party intends to use at the hearing.

(B) Failure to disclose

A hearing officer may bar any party that fails to comply with subparagraph (A) from introducing the relevant evaluation or recommendation at the hearing without the consent of the other party.

(3) Limitations on hearing

(A) Person conducting hearing

A hearing officer conducting a hearing pursuant to paragraph (1)(A) shall, at a minimum—

(i) not be—

(I) an employee of the State educational agency or the local educational agency involved in the education or care of the child; or

(II) a person having a personal or professional interest that conflicts with the person's objectivity in the hearing;

(ii) possess knowledge of, and the ability to understand, the provisions of this chapter, Federal and State regulations pertaining to this chapter, and legal interpretations of this chapter by Federal and State courts;

(iii) possess the knowledge and ability to conduct hearings in accordance with appropriate, standard legal practice; and

(iv) possess the knowledge and ability to render and write decisions in accordance with appropriate, standard legal practice.

. . . .

(C) Timeline for requesting hearing

A parent or agency shall request an impartial due process hearing within two years of the date the parent or agency knew or should have known about the alleged action that forms the basis of the complaint, or, if the State has an explicit time limitation for requesting such a hearing under this part, in such time as the State law allows.

. . . .

(E) Decision of hearing officer

(i) In general

Subject to clause (ii), a decision made by a hearing officer shall be made on substantive grounds based on a determination of whether the child received a free appropriate public education.

(ii) Procedural issues

In matters alleging a procedural violation, a hearing officer may find that a child did not receive a free appropriate public education only if the procedural inadequacies—

(I) impeded the child's right to a free appropriate public education;

(II) significantly impeded the parents' opportunity to participate in the decisionmaking process regarding the provision of a free appropriate public education to the parents' child; or

(III) caused a deprivation of educational benefits.

. . . .

(g) Appeal

(1) In general

If the hearing required by subsection (f) is conducted by a local educational agency, any party aggrieved by the findings and decision rendered in such a hearing may appeal such findings and decision to the State educational agency.

(2) Impartial review and independent decision

The State educational agency shall conduct an impartial review of the findings and decision appealed under paragraph (1). The officer conducting such review shall make an independent decision upon completion of such review.

(h) Safeguards

Any party to a hearing conducted pursuant to subsection (f) or (k), or an appeal conducted pursuant to subsection (g), shall be accorded—

(1) the right to be accompanied and advised by counsel and by individuals with special knowledge or training with respect to the problems of children with disabilities;

(2) the right to present evidence and confront, cross-examine, and compel the attendance of witnesses;

(3) the right to a written, or, at the option of the parents, electronic verbatim record of such hearing; and

(4) the right to written, or, at the option of the parents, electronic findings of fact and decisions—

(i) Administrative procedures

(1) In general

(A) Decision made in hearing

A decision made in a hearing conducted pursuant to subsection (f) or (k) shall be final, except that any party involved in such hearing may appeal such decision under the provisions of subsection (g) and paragraph (2).

(B) Decision made at appeal

A decision made under subsection (g) shall be final, except that any party may bring an action under paragraph (2).

(2) Right to bring civil action

(A) In general

Any party aggrieved by the findings and decision made under subsection (f) or (k) who does not have the right to an appeal under subsection (g), and any party aggrieved by the findings and decision made under this subsection, shall have the right to bring a civil action with respect to the complaint presented pursuant to this section, which action may be brought in any State court of competent jurisdiction or in a district court of the United States, without regard to the amount in controversy.

(B) Limitation

The party bringing the action shall have 90 days from the date of the decision of the hearing officer to bring such an action, or, if the State has an explicit time limitation for bringing such action under this part, in such time as the State law allows.

(C) Additional requirements

In any action brought under this paragraph, the court—

(i) shall receive the records of the administrative proceedings;

(ii) shall hear additional evidence at the request of a party; and

(iii) basing its decision on the preponderance of the evidence, shall grant such relief as the court determines is appropriate.

(3) Jurisdiction of district courts; attorneys' fees

(A) In general

The district courts of the United States shall have jurisdiction of actions brought under this section without regard to the amount in controversy.

(B) Award of attorneys' fees

(i) In general

In any action or proceeding brought under this section, the court, in its discretion, may award reasonable attorneys' fees as part of the costs—

(I) to a prevailing party who is the parent of a child with a disability;

(II) to a prevailing party who is a State educational agency or local educational agency against the attorney of a parent who files a complaint or subsequent cause of action that is frivolous, unreasonable, or without foundation, or against the attorney of a parent who continued to litigate after the litigation clearly became frivolous, unreasonable, or without foundation; or

(III) to a prevailing State educational agency or local educational agency against the attorney of a parent, or against the parent, if the parent's complaint or subsequent cause of action was presented for any improper purpose, such as to harass, to cause unnecessary delay, or to needlessly increase the cost of litigation.

. . . .

(C) Determination of amount of attorneys' fees

Fees awarded under this paragraph shall be based on rates prevailing in the community in which the action or proceeding arose for the kind and quality of services furnished. No bonus or multiplier may be used in calculating the fees awarded under this subsection.

(D) Prohibition of attorneys fees and related costs for certain services

(i) In general

Attorneys fees may not be awarded and related costs may not be reimbursed in any action or proceeding under this section for services performed subsequent to the time of a written offer of settlement to a parent if—

(I) the offer is made within the time prescribed by Rule 68 of the Federal Rules of Civil Procedure or, in the case of an administrative proceeding, at any time more than 10 days before the proceeding begins;

(II) the offer is not accepted within 10 days; and

(III) the court or administrative hearing officer finds that the relief finally obtained by the parents is not more favorable to the parents than the offer of settlement.

(ii) IEP Team Meetings

Attorneys fees may not be awarded relating to any meeting of the IEP Team unless such meeting is convened as a result of an administrative proceeding or judicial action, or, at the discretion of the State, for a mediation described in subsection (e).

. . . .

(E) Exception to prohibition on attorneys' fees and related costs

Notwithstanding subparagraph (D), an award of attorneys fees and related costs may be made to a parent who is the prevailing party and who was substantially justified in rejecting the settlement offer.

(F) Reduction in amount of attorneys' fees

Except as provided in subparagraph (G), whenever the court finds that—

(i) the parent, or the parent's attorney, during the course of the action or proceeding unreasonably protracted the final resolution of the controversy;

(ii) the amount of the attorneys' fees otherwise authorized to be awarded unreasonably exceeds the hourly rate prevailing in the community for similar services by attorneys of reasonably comparable skill, reputation, and experience;

(iii) the time spent and legal services furnished were excessive considering the nature of the action or proceeding; or

(iv) the attorney representing the parent did not provide to the local educational agency the appropriate information in the notice of the complaint described in subsection (b)(7)(A),

the court shall reduce, accordingly, the amount of the attorneys fees awarded under this section.

(G) Exception to reduction in amount of attorneys fees

The provisions of subparagraph (F) shall not apply in any action or proceeding if the court finds that the State or local educational agency unreasonably protracted the final resolution of the action or proceeding or there was a violation of this section.

(j) Maintenance of current educational placement

Except as provided in subsection (k)(4), during the pendency of any proceedings conducted pursuant to this section, unless the State or local educational agency and the parents otherwise agree, the child shall remain in the then-current educational placement of the child, or, if applying for initial admission to a public school, shall, with the consent of the parents, be placed in the public school program until all such proceedings have been completed.

(k) Placement in alternative educational setting

(1) Authority of school personnel

. . . .

(B) Authority

School personnel under this subsection may remove a child with a disability who violates a code of student conduct from their current placement to an appropriate interim alternative educational setting, another setting, or suspension, for not more than ten school days . . . .

(C) Additional authority

If school personnel seek to order a change in placement that would exceed 10 school days and the behavior that gave rise to the violation of the school code is determined not to be a manifestation of the child's disability . . . the relevant disciplinary procedures applicable to children without disabilities may be applied to the child in the same manner and for the same duration in which the procedures would be applied to children without disabilities . . . .

(D) Services

A child with a disability who is removed from the child's current placement under subparagraph (G) (irrespective of whether the behavior is determined to be a manifestation of the child's disability) or subparagraph (C) shall—

(i) continue to receive educational services . . . so as to enable the child to continue to participate in the general education curriculum, although in another setting, and to progress toward meeting the goals set out in the child's IEP; and

(ii) receive, as appropriate, a functional behavioral assessment, behavioral intervention services and modifications, that are designed to address the behavior violation so that it does not recur.

(E) Manifestation determination

(i) In general

Except as provided in subparagraph (B), within ten school days of any decision to change the placement of a child with a disability because of a violation of a code of student conduct, the local educational agency, the parent, and relevant members of the IEP Team (as determined by the parent and the local educational agency) shall review all relevant information in the student's file . . . to determine—

(I) if the conduct in question was caused by, or had a direct and substantial relationship to, the child's disability; or

(II) if the conduct in question was the direct result of the local educational agency's failure to implement the IEP.

(ii) Manifestation

If the local educational agency, the parent, and relevant members of the IEP Team determine that either subclause (I) or (II) of clause (i) is applicable for the child, the conduct shall be determined to be a manifestation of the child's disability.

(F) Determination that behavior was a manifestation

If the local educational agency, the parent, and relevant members of the IEP Team make the determination that the conduct was a manifestation of the child's disability, the IEP Team shall—

(i) conduct a functional behavioral assessment, and implement a behavioral intervention plan for such child . . . ;

(ii) in the situation where a behavioral intervention plan has been developed, review the behavioral intervention plan if the child already has such a behavioral intervention plan, and modify it, as necessary, to address the behavior; and

(iii) except as provided in subparagraph (G), return the child to the placement from which the child was removed, unless the parent and the local educational agency agree to a change of placement as part of the modification of the behavioral intervention plan.

(G) Special circumstances

School personnel may remove a student to an interim alternative educational setting for not more than 45 school days without regard to whether the behavior is determined to be a manifestation of the child's disability, in cases where a child—

(i) carries or possesses a weapon to or at school, on school premises, or to or at a school function under the jurisdiction of a State or local educational agency;

(ii) knowingly possesses or uses illegal drugs, or sells or solicits the sale of a controlled substance, while at school, on school premises, or at a school function under the jurisdiction of a State or local educational agency; or

(iii) has inflicted serious bodily injury upon another person while at school, on school premises, or at a school function under the jurisdiction of a State or local educational agency.

(H) Notification

Not later than the date on which the decision to take disciplinary action is made, the local educational agency shall notify the parents of that decision, and of all procedural safeguards accorded under this section.

(2) Determination of setting

The interim alternative educational setting in subparagraphs (C) and (G) of paragraph (1) shall be determined by the IEP Team.

(3) Appeal

(A) In general

The parent of a child with a disability who disagrees with any decision regarding placement, or the manifestation determination under this section, or a local educational agency that believes that maintaining the current placement of the child is substantially likely to result in injury to the child or to others, may request a hearing.

(B) Authority of hearing officer

(i) In general

A hearing officer shall hear, and make a determination regarding, an appeal requested under subparagraph (A).

(ii) Change of placement order

In making the determination under clause (i), the hearing officer may order a change in placement of a child with a disability. In such situations, the hearing officer may—

(I) return a child with a disability to the placement from which the child was removed; or

(II) order a change in placement of a child with a disability to an appropriate interim alternative educational setting for not more than 45 school days if the hearing officer determines that maintaining the current placement of such child is substantially likely to result in injury to the child or to others.

(4) Placement during appeals

When an appeal under paragraph (3) has been requested by either the parent or the local educational agency—

(A) the child shall remain in the interim alternative educational setting pending the decision of the hearing officer or until the expiration of the time period provided for in paragraph (1)(C), whichever occurs first, unless the parent and the State or local educational agency shall arrange for an expedited hearing, which shall occur within 20 school days of the date the hearing is requested and shall result in a determination within 10 school days.

. . . .

(l) Rule of construction

Nothing in this chapter shall be construed to restrict or limit the rights, procedures, and remedies available under the Constitution, the Americans with Disabilities Act of 1990, title V of the Rehabilitation Act of 1973, or other Federal laws protecting the rights of children with disabilities, except that before the filing of a civil action under such laws seeking relief that is also available under this subchapter, the procedures under subsections (f) and (g) shall be exhausted to the same extent as would be required had the action been brought under this subchapter.

Appendix B

Common Acronyms in IDEA Cases

ABA	Applied behavioral therapy
ADA	Americans with Disabilities Act
BIP	Behavior Improvement Plan
CSE	Committee on Special Education
DOE	The United States Department of Education
EAHCA	Education for All Handicapped Children Act (1975)
EHA	Education of the Handicapped Act (1970)
FAPE	Free Appropriate Public Education
IDEA	Individuals with Disabilities Education Act (1990)
IEP	Individualized Education Program
IHO	Impartial Hearing Officer
LEA	Local educational agency (a local school district)
LRE	Least restrictive environment
MDRT	Multi-disciplinary review team
SEA	State educational agency
Section 504	Section 504 of the Rehabilitation Act
SRO	State Review Officer

Index